January 15–19, 2015
Stanford, California, USA

Association for
Computing Machinery

Advancing Computing as a Science & Profession

TEI 2015

Proceedings of the Ninth International Conference on
Tangible, Embedded, and Embodied Interaction

Sponsored by:

ACM SIGCHI

Supported by:

Intel, Sparkfun Electronics, Citi Ventures, SeeedStudio, Google & Microsoft Research

Association for
Computing Machinery

Advancing Computing as a Science & Profession

The Association for Computing Machinery
2 Penn Plaza, Suite 701
New York, New York 10121-0701

ISBN: 978-1-4503-3305-4 (Digital)

ISBN: 978-1-4503-3507-2 (Print)

Additional copies may be ordered prepaid from:

ACM Order Department
PO Box 30777
New York, NY 10087-0777, USA

Phone: 1-800-342-6626 (USA and Canada)
+1-212-626-0500 (Global)
Fax: +1-212-944-1318
E-mail: acmhelp@acm.org
Hours of Operation: 8:30 am – 4:30 pm ET

Printed in the USA

TEI 2015 Chairs' Welcome

Welcome to ACM TEI 2015, the 9th International Conference on Tangible, Embedded and Embodied Interaction, hosted at Stanford University in California, USA from January 15th to January 19th, 2015!

This year's conference continues TEI's tradition of being the premiere forum for research and design on tangible and physical interaction. While we are starting to see consumer electronics for the home, wearable computers for the body, and the internet embedded into the everyday things that surround us, TEI as a community is still digging deeper, planting the seeds for the technologies, methods, and interactions to come. We are especially focused on design as a theme this year, as the conference reception is jointly hosted by Stanford's d.school, Center for Design Research, and Design Program.

The conference starts out with **Studios and Workshops** that embody the cornerstones of TEI—community building through hands-on making and thoughtful reflection. The main program starts off with the renowned author **Dr. Frank R. Wilson's** opening keynote, which contemplates our high hopes for the prosthetic technologies we are creating, questioning the "perverse idea that our biology is our undoing, and that only technology can save us." The **Demos and Posters** provide an interactive venue for attendees to engage with and try out novel designs, interaction technologies, and material experiences. The **Art Exhibition** explores sensory connections among people and the world around them through interactive artworks. We end with **Wendy Mackay's** "whirlwind tour" of tangible computing with interactive paper—a view of where we've come from as a community, and a look out towards where we are headed next.

And then there are of course also **Papers**. In the practice-oriented style of TEI, they are presented as either **Talks** or **Demos** or both. Authors could choose their own contribution-matching-paper length ratio, with all submissions subsequently equally subjected to a blind peer review process of at least 3 reviewers. Accepted papers are published in the ACM Digital Library. In total, we received a staggering 222 submissions to the papers category. We accepted 63 papers, making for an acceptance rate of 28%. And finally, in the **Work-in-Progress** category, we had 72 submissions and accepted 40, making for an acceptance rate of 55%.

We would like to thank everyone who contributed to this conference: the authors who submitted their quality work to the conference, the organizing committee chairs who each managed their part of the conference, the programme committee and external reviewers who ensured a high-quality conference, the local organizing committee, the supporters and partners, and the TEI steering committee. Without the commitment of all these people, organizing this conference would not have been possible.

Wendy Ju
TEI'15 General Chair
Stanford University, USA

Bill Verplank
TEI'15 General Chair
Stanford University, USA

Alissa Antle
TEI'15 Program Chair
Simon Fraser University, Canada

Ali Mazalek
TEI'15 Program Chair
Ryerson University, Canada & Georgia Tech, USA

Florian 'Floyd' Mueller
TEI'15 Program Chair
RMIT University, Australia

Table of Contents

Paper Session 3: Techie: How it Works

Session Chair: Floyd Mueller *(RMIT University)*

Paper Session 4: Making Connections

Session Chair: Katrin Wolf *(Universität Stuttgart)*

Paper Session 5: Toolkits: How to Make It

Session Chair: Brygg Ullmer *(Louisiana State University)*

Paper Session 6: Cool New Stuff

Session Chair: Peter Bennett *(University of Bristol)*

Art Exhibition

Session Chairs: Elizabeth Goodman *(University of California, Berkeley)*
Younghui Kim *(Hongik University)*

Graduate Student Consortium

Session Chair: Kimiko Ryokai *(University of California, Berkeley)*
Brygg Ullmer *(Louisiana State University)*

Workshops, Workshop-Studios, & Studios

Session Chairs: Jason Alexander *(Lancaster University)*
Daniela Busse *(Citi Ventures)*

Work-in-Progress: Poster Presentations

Work-in-Progress: Poster/Demo Presentations

Work-in-Progress: Demonstration Presentations

TEI 2015 Conference Organization

Conference Co-Chairs:	Bill Verplank *(Stanford University, USA)* Wendy Ju *(Stanford University, USA)*
Program Co-Chairs:	Alissa Antle *(Simon Fraser University, Canada)* Ali Mazalek *(Georgia Institute of Technology, USA)* Florian "Floyd" Mueller *(RMIT, Australia)*
Publication Chair:	Haakon Faste *(California College of the Arts, USA)*
Venue Co-Chairs:	Larry Leifer *(Stanford University, USA)* Charlotte Burgess Auburn *(Stanford University, USA)*
Studios & Workshops Co-Chairs:	Daniela Busse *(Citi Ventures, USA)* Jason Alexander *(Lancaster University, UK)*
Demonstration Co-Chairs:	Jonathan Edelman *(Stanford University, USA)* Yasuto Nakanishi *(Keio University, Japan)* Michael Shiloh *(California College of the Arts, USA)*
Arts Exhibition Co-Chairs:	Elizabeth Goodman *(UC Berkeley, USA)* Younghui Kim *(Hongik University, South Korea)*
Sponsorship Chair:	Alicia Gibb *(Open Source Hardware Association, USA)*
Graduate Student Consortium:	Kimiko Ryokai *(UC Berkeley, USA)* Brygg Ullmer *(Louisiana State University, USA)*
Student Volunteer Co-Chairs:	Andy Wu *(GE Global Research, USA)* Nik Martelaro *(Stanford University, USA)*
Student Design Challenge:	Tom Igoe *(New York University, USA)*
Steering Committee:	Albrecht Schmidt *(Universität Stuttgart, Germany)* Ali Mazalek *(Georgia Tech (USA) & Ryerson University, Canada)* Andreas Butz *(LMU, Germany)* Audrey Girouard *(Carleton University, Canada)* Brygg Ullmer *(Louisiana State University, USA)* Caroline Hummels *(TU/e, the Netherlands)* Elise van den Hoven *(UTS, Australia, & TU/e, the Netherlands)* Ellen Yi-Luen Do *(Georgia Institute of Technology, USA)* Eva Hornecker *(Bauhaus-Universität Weimar, Germany)* Hiroshi Ishii *(MIT Media Lab, USA)* Lian Loke *(University of Sydney, Australia)* Martin Kaltenbrunner *(UFG, Austria)*

Steering Committee (continued):

Nicolas Villar *(Microsoft Research, UK)*
Rob Jacob *(Tufts University, USA)*
Ron Wakkary *(Simon Fraser University, Canada)*
Saskia Bakker *(TU/e, the Netherlands)*
Sergi Jorda *(UPF, Spain)*
Ylva Fernaeus *(KTH, Sweden)*

Past Steering Committee Members:

Hans Gellersen *(Lancaster University, UK)*
Jamie Zigelbaum *(Zigelbaum + Coelho, USA)*
Mike Fraser *(Unversity of Bristol, UK)*
Shahram Izadi *(Microsoft Research, UK)*

Program Committee:

Dzmitry Aliakseyeu
Saskia Bakker
Peter Bennett
Bert Bongers
Martin Brynskov
Alvaro Cassinelli
Audrey Desjardins
Ellen Do
Tanja Doering
Florian Echtler
Augusto Esteves
Frank Feltham
Ylva Fernaeus
Eelke Folmer
Marcus Foth
Mike Fraser
Christian Geiger
Luc Geurts
Jonna Hakkila
Juan David Hincapié-Ramos
Mike Horn
Jorn Hurtienne
Giulio Jacucci
Sergi Jorda
Martin Kaltenbrunner
Rohit Ashok Khot
Matthias Kranz
Hyosun Kwon
Geehyuk Lee
Hyun Jean Lee
Lian Loke
Valérie Maquil
Nicolai Marquardt
Paul Marshall
Sebastian Mealla
Tom Moher
Ian Oakley
Claudia Rebola
Michael Rohs
Enrico Rukzio
Orit Shaer
Ehud Sharlin
Renata Sheppard
Beat Signer
Erin Solovey
Dag Svanaes
Jakob Tholander
Jelle van Dijk
Daniel Wessolek
Alexander Wiethoff
Raphael Wimmer
Peta Wyeth

TEI 2015 Paper Committee Members & Additional Reviewers

Committee Member

Dzmitry Aliakseyeu, *Philips Research Europe*
Saskia Bakker, *Eindhoven University of Technology*
Peter Bennett, *University of Bristol*
Bert Bongers, *University of Technology Sydney*
Martin Brynskov, *Aarhus University*
Alvaro Cassinelli, *University of Tokyo*
Audrey Desjardins, *Simon Fraser University*
Ellen Do, *Georgia Institute of Technology*
Tanja Doering, *University of Bremen*
Florian Echtler, *Siemens Corporate Technology*
Augusto Esteves, *University of Madeira, UMa*
Frank Feltham, *RMIT University*
Ylva Fernaeus, *KTH*
Eelke Folmer, *University of Nevada, Reno*
Marcus Foth, *Queensland University of Technology*
Mike Fraser, *University of Bristol*
Christian Geiger, *Duesseldorf University of Applied Sciences*
Luc Geurts, *KU Leuven*
Jonna Hakkila, *University of Oulu*
Juan David Hincapié-Ramos, *University of Manitoba*
Mike Horn, *Northwestern University*
Jorn Hurtienne, *University of Cambridge*
Giulio Jacucci, *Helsinki Institute for Information Technology*
Sergi Jorda, *Universitat Pompeu Fabra*
Martin Kaltenbrunner, *University of Art and Design Linz*
Rohit Ashok Khot, *RMIT University*
Matthias Kranz, *Department of Informatics and Mathematics*
Hyosun Kwon, *University of Nottingham*
Geehyuk Lee, *KAIST*
Hyun Jean Lee, *Georgia Institute of Technology*
Lian Loke, *University of Sydney*
Valérie Maquil, *Public Research Center Henri Tudor*
Nicolai Marquardt, *University College London*
Paul Marshall, *University College London*
Sebastian Mealla, *Universitat Pompeu Fabra*
Tom Moher, *University of Illinois at Chicago*
Ian Oakley, *Ulsan National Institute of Science and Technology*
Claudia Rebola, *Rhode Island School of Design*
Michael Rohs, *University of Hannover*
Enrico Rukzio, *University of Duisburg-Essen*
Orit Shaer, *Wellesley College*
Ehud Sharlin, *University of Calgary*
Renata Sheppard, *Free Lance Artist*
Beat Signer, *Vrije Universiteit Brussel*
Erin Solovey, *Drexel*
Dag Svanaes, *NTNU - Norway*
Jakob Tholander, *MobileLife@Stockholm University*
Jelle van Dijk, *University of Southern Denmark*
Daniel Wessolek, *Bauhaus-University Weimar*
Alexander Wiethoff, *University of Munich*
Raphael Wimmer, *University of Munich*
Peta Wyeth, *University of Queensland, Brisbane*

Reviewers

Imtiaj Ahmed, *University of Helsinki*
Jason Alexander, *Lancaster University*
Zerroug Alexis, *Exvision*
Sarah Alsulaiman, *Northwestern University*
Florian Alt, *LMU München*
Dimitra Anastasiou, *University of Bremen*
Margarita Anastassova, *CEA LIST*
Fraser Anderson, *University of Alberta*
Salvatore Andolina, *University of Helsinki*
Chang Angela, *MIT Media Lab*
Lisa Anthony, *University of Florida*
Ahmed Sabbir Arif, *Ryerson University*
Daniel Ashbrook, *Samsung Research America*
Ilhan Aslan, *ICT&S Center, University of Salzburg*
Chris Baber, *University of Birmingham*
Naveen Bagalkot, *IT-University of Copenhagen*
Jakob Bak, *Copenhagen Institute of Interaction Design*
Martina Balestra, *New York University*
Malcolm Ballantine, *University College London*
Amartya Banerjee, *Northwestern University*
Eric Baumer, *Cornell University*
Alexander Bazo, *Universität Regensburg*
Elham Beheshti, *Northwestern University*
Andrea Bellucci, *Universidad Carlos III de Madrid*
Florent Berthaut, *University of Bristol*
Nadia Berthouze, *University College London*
Luca Bertuccelli, *United Techonologies Research Center*
Alberto Betella, *SPECS - Universitat Pompeu Fabra*
Chris Bevan, *University of Bath*
Andrea Bianchi, *KAIST*
Alan Blackwell, *University of Cambridge*
Paulo Blikstein, *Stanford University*
Florian Block, *Lancaster*
Laurens Boer, *University of Southern Denmark*

Dirk Börner, *Open University of the Netherlands*
Mathieu Bosi, *Universitat Pompeu Fabra*
Leonardo Botega, *UFSCar*
Oliver Bown, *Design Lab, University of Sydney*
stephen brewster, *University of Glasgow*
Andrew Brown, *Griffith University*
Miguel Bruns Alonso, *TU/e*
Erin Buehler, *University of Maryland, Baltimore County*
Jesse Burstyn, *Queen's University*
Daniel Buschek, *University of Munich (LMU)*
Diogo Cabral, *University of Helsinki*
Baptiste Caramiaux, *Goldsmiths, University of London*
Stefan Carmien, *Tecnalia*
Miguel Carvalhais, *University of Porto*
Daniel Cernea, *University of Kaiserslautern*
Liwei Chan, *National Taiwan University*
Sonny Chan, *University of Calgary*
Xiang Chen, *University of Calgary*
Cynthia Ching, *University of California, Davis*
Jean Chu, *Georgia Tech*
Laurence Claeys, *VUB*
Paul Clifton, *Georgia Institute of Technology*
Rebecca Cober
Ashley Colley, *University of Oulu*
Enrico Costanza, *University of Southhampton*
Andrew Crossan, *University of Glasgow*
R. Jordan Crouser, *MIT Lincoln Laboratory*
Saakes Daniel, *TU Delft & MIT Media*
Jessica Dawson, *Unviersity of British Columbia*
Eva Deckers, *Philips*
Laura Devendorf, *University of California, Berkeley*
Vyas Dhaval, *QUT*
Stefan Diewald, *Technische Universität München*
Tilman Dingler, *University of Stuttgart*
Andreas Dippon, *Technische Universität München*
Jared Donovan, *Queensland University of Technology*
Ralf Dörner, *RheinMain University of Applied Sciences*
Jakub Dostal, *University of St Andrews*
John Downs, *The University of Melbourne*
Daniel Drochtert, *University of Applied Sciences Duesseldorf*
Jon Drummond, *University of Technology*
Carlos Duarte, *University of Lisbon*
Jonathan Duckworth, *RMIT University*
Bruno Dumas, *University of Namur*
Michael Eisenberg, *University of Colorado, Boulder*
Yasmine Elglaly, *Port Said University*
Morten Esbensen, *IT University of Copenhagen*
Georg Essl, *University of Michigan*
Jens Alexander Ewald, *Muthesius Academy of Fine Arts and Design*
Daniel Fallman, *Interactive Institute Umea*
William Farr, *Sussex community NHS Trust*
Sarah Fdili Alaoui, *SIAT, SFU*
Jamie Ferguson, *Bauhaus University Weimar*
Morten Fjeld, *Chalmers University of Technology*
Rowanne Fleck, *University College London*
Steven Fokkinga, *Delft University of Technology*
John Foley, *SUNY Cortland*
Sean Follmer, *Massachusetts Institute of Technology*
Florian Fortmann, *OFFIS - Institute for Information Technology*
Derek Foster, *University of Lincoln*
Simon Fothergill, *University of Cambridge*
Joep W. Frens, *Carnegie Mellon University*
Krzysztof Gajos, *Harvard University*
Jens Geelhaar, *Bauhaus-University Weimar*
Sven Gehring, *German Research Center for Artificial Intelligence*
Toby Gifford, *Griffith University*
Audrey Girouard, *Carleton University*
Kristian Gohlke, *Bauhaus-Universität Weimar*
Antonio Gomes, *Human Media Lab, Queen's University*
Ruben Gouveia, *Madeira-ITI*
Tom Grill, *UXfocus*
Mark Grimshaw, *Aalborg Universitet*
Laurent Grisoni, *University Lille 1*
Shad Gross, *Indiana University*
Jens Grubert, *Graz University of Technology*
Karin Guminski, *Ludwig-Maximilians-University*
Cheng Guo, *University of Calgary*
Joshua Hall, *QUT*
James Hallam, *Georgia Institute of Technology*
Mark Hancock, *University of Waterloo*
Chris Harrison, *Carnegie Mellon University*
Daniel Harrison, *University College London*
Shoichi Hasegawa, *Tokyo Institute of Technolgy*
Adrian Hazzard, *University of Nottingham*
Fabian Hemmert, *Deutsche Telekom Laboratories*
Niels Henze, *University of Stuttgart*
Seongkook Heo, *Korea Advanced Institute of Science and Technology*
Luke Hespanhol, *University of Sydney*
Wilko Heuten, *OFFIS - Institute for Information Technology*
Guy Hoffman, *Media Innovation Lab, IDC Herzliya*
Trevor Hogan, *Cork Institute of Technology*
Michael Hohl, *Anhalt University of Applied Sciences*
David Holman, *Queen's University*
Christian Holz, *Hasso Plattner Institute*
Eva Hornecker, *Bauhaus-Universität Weimar*
Steven Houben, *IT University of Copenhagen*

Chih-Pin Hsiao, *Georgia Institute of Technology*
Yingdan Huang, *University of Colorado at Boulder*
Alina Huldtgren, *Duesseldorf University of Applied Sciences*
Caroline Hummels, *Eindhoven University of Technology*
Amy Hurst, *University of Maryland, Baltimore County*
Pourang Irani, *U of M*
Johann Habakuk Israel, *BTK*
Ali Israr, *Disney Research*
Robert J. K. Jacob, *Tufts University*
Jennifer Jacobs, *Massachusetts Institute of Technology*
Mattias Jacobsson, *SICS*
Nils Jäger, *University of Nottingham*
Yvonne Jansen, *University of Copenhagen*
Tom Jenkins, *Georgia Institute of Technology*
Nova Jiang, *N/A*
Kazuhiro Jo, *IAMAS*
Daniel Johnson, *Queensland University of Technology*
Martin Jonsson, *Södertörn University*
Carles F. Julià, *Universitat Pompeu Fabra*
Antti Jylhä, *Department of Computer Science*
Yasuaki Kakehi, *Keio University*
Denis Kalkofen, *Graz University of Technology*
Thorsten Karrer, *RWTH Aachen University*
Frederic Kerber, *German Research Center for Artificial Intelligence (DFKI)*
Maryam Khademi, *University of California, Irvine*
George Khut, *UNSW Australia, Art and Design*
Johan Kildal, *Nokia Research Center*
Hwan Kim, *KAIST (Korea Advanced Institute of Science and Technology)*
Hyungsin Kim, *Georgia Institute of Technology*
Hyunjung Kim, *KAIST*
Ju-Whan Kim,
Sunjun Kim, *Korea Advanced Institute of Science and Techonology*
Younghui Kim, *Hongik University*
David Kirk, *University of Nottingham*
Anja Knöfel, *TU Dresden*
Nicholas Knouf, *Wellesley College*
Marion Koelle, *University of Passau, Embedded Interactive Systems Laboratory*
Henrik Korsgaard, *Aarhus University*
Sven Kratz, *FX Palo Alto Laboratory*
Rolf Kruse, *Erfurt University of Applied Sciences*
Christoffel Kuenen, *Umeå Institute of Design, Sweden*
Andreas Kunz, *Swiss Federal Institute of Technology Zurich*
Pei-Yi Kuo, *Northwestern University*
Stacey Kuznetsov, *Carnegie Mellon University*
Jarmo Laaksolahti, *Mobile Life @ SICS*
Pascal Landry, *UPF*
Astrid Larssen, *Ashesi University College*
Tomas Laurenzo, *City University of Hong Kong*
Lucian Leahu, *Mobile Life*
David Ledo, *University of Calgary*
Jung-Joo Lee, *National University of Singapore*
Woohun Lee, *KAIST*
Daniel Leithinger, *Massachusetts Institute of Technology*
Catherine Letondal, *ENAC*
Pierre Levy, *Eindhoven University of Technology*
Jiannan Li, *University of Calgary*
Nico Li, *University of Calgary*
Rong-Hao Liang, *National Taiwan University*
Stefan Lie, *University of Technology Sydney*
Youn-kyung Lim, *KAIST*
Henry Lin, *Simon Fraser University*
Patrick Lindemann, *University of Passau*
Silvia Lindtner, *University of Michigan*
Xin Liu, *Rhode Island School of Design*
Diana Löffler, *University of Würzburg*
Pedro Lopes, *INESC-ID*
Jacquie Lorber-kasunic, *University of Technology, Sydney*
Andrés Lucero, *University of Southern Denmark*
Pereira Luisa, *New York University*
Anders Lundström, *KTH*
Kris Luyten, *Hasselt University*
Vangelis Lympouridis, *USC School of Cinematic Arts*
Leilah Lyons, *University of Illinois at Chicago*
Andrew Manches, *University of Nottingham*
Brade Marius, *Technische Universität Dresden*
Mark Marshall, *Sheffield Hallam University*
Diego Martinez, *University of Bristol*
Aaron May, *Simon Fraser University*
Mitchell McEwan, *Queensland University of Technology*
Jodie McNeilly, *Australian Catholic University*
Erica Mealy, *Queensland University of Technology*
Richard Medland, *Queensland University of Technology*
Bernt Meerbeek, *Philips Research*
Bruce Mehler, *Massachusetts Institute of Technology*
David Mellis, *MIT Media Lab*
Emma Mercier, *University of Illinois at Urbana Champaign*
Timothy Merritt, *Aarhus School of Architecture*
Amon Millner, *MIT Media Lab*
Robb Mitchell, *University of Southern Denmark*
Scott Mitchell, *RMIT University*
Andreas Möller, *Technische Universität München*
Simone Mora, *Norwegian University of Science and Technology*
Joan Mora Guiard, *Universitat Pompeu Fabra*
Tony Morelli, *Central Michigan University*

Cecily Morrison, *University of Cambridge*
Ahmed Mostafa, *University of Calgary*
Camille Moussette, *Umeå Institute of Design*
Stefanie Mueller, *Hasso Plattner Institute*
Tara Mullaney, *Umeå Institute of Design*
Martin Murer, *ICT&S Center, University of Salzburg*
Alexandra Murray-Leslie, *University of Technology Sydney*
Miguel Nacenta, *University of St Andrews*
Tek-Jin Nam, *KAIST*
Elena Nazzi, *IT-University of Copenhagen*
Kachornnamsong Nedine, *Linneaus University*
Hiroki Nishino, *NGS - NUS Graduate School for Integrative Sciences & Engineering*
Valentina Nisi, *CMU Portugal*
Aditya Nittala, *University of Calgary*
Maria Normark, *School of Communication Media and IT*
Diana Nowacka, *Newcastle University*
Claudia Núñez-Pacheco, *University of Sydney*
Stina Nylander, *Mobile Life@SICS*
Yoichi Ochiai, *The University of Tokyo*
Hyunjoo Oh, *Carnegie Mellon University*
Johanna Okerlund, *Wellesley College*
Sile O'Modhrain, *Queen's University Belfast*
Valeria Orso, *University of Padova*
Jifei Ou, *MIT Media Lab*
Minna Pakanen, *University of Oulu*
Henri Palleis, *University of Munich (LMU)*
Carolyn Pang, *Simon Fraser University*
Nadia Pantidi, *University of Nottingham*
Anastasia Evangelia Papadopoulou, *Delft University of Technology*
Young-Woo Park, *NASA Ames*
Jaime Parra-Damborenea, *Universitat Pompeu Fabra*
Gaurav Patekar, *National Institute of Design, India*
Esben W. Pedersen, *University of Copenhagen*
Huaishu Peng, *Carnegie Mellon University*
Stephane Perrin, *University of Electro-Communications*
Anthony Perritano, *University of Illinois at Chicago*
Mariane Graves Petersen, *Aarhus University*
Max Pfeiffer, *FG Mensch-Computer-Interaktion*
Ken Pfeuffer, *Lancaster University*
Bastian Pfleging, *University of Stuttgart*
Laura Pina, *University of California, San Diego*
Antonio Pizzo, *Università degli Studi di Torino*
Bernd Ploderer, *The University of Melbourne*
Patrick Pogscheba, *University of Applied Sciences Mainz*
Henning Pohl, *Leibniz University Hannover*
Ingrid Maria Pohl, *Graz University of Technology*
Deb Polson, *Queensland University of Technology*
Taciana Pontual Falcao, *University of London*
Michael Poor, *Baylor University*
Sara Price, *Institute of Education, London*
Andrew Pringle, *University of Surrey*
Kathrin Probst, *University of Applied Sciences Upper Austria*
Jie Qi, *MIT Media Lab*
Chris Quintana, *University of Michigan*
Roman Rädle, *University of Konstanz*
Nimesha Ranasinghe, *New York University*
Daniel Rea, *The University of Manitoba*
Holger Reckter, *University of Applied Sciences Mainz*
Kyle Rector, *University of Washington*
Harald Reiterer, *University of Konstanz*
Andreas Riener, *Johannes Kepler University*
Markus Rittenbruch, *Queensland University of Technology*
Carsten Röcker, *RWTH Aachen University*
Andres Rodriguez, *Universidad Nacional de La Plata*
Paul Roe, *Queensland University of Technology*
Asta Roseway, *Microsoft Research*
Daniela Rosner, *School of Information*
Thijs Roumen, *Hasso Plattner Institute*
Paulami Roy Choudhury, *Srishti School of Art, Design and Technology*
Sonja Rümelin, *BMW Forschung und Technik GmbH*
Javad Sadeghi, *University of Calgary*
Zoe Sadokierski, *University of Technology, Sydney*
Daisuke Sakamoto, *Japan Science and Technology Agency*
Bahador Saket, *University of Arizona*
Jelle Saldien, *Ghent University*
Alvaro Sarasua, *Universitat Pompeu Fabra*
Greg Saul, *JST ERATO Design UI Group*
Ronald Schroeter, *Queensland University of Technology*
Eric Schweikardt, *Cornell University*
Sue Ann Seah, *University of Bristol*
Jennifer Seevinck, *Queensland University of Technology*
Ben Shapiro, *Tufts University*
Vygandas Simbelis, *KTH*
Tanya Singh, *Indiana University*
David Sirkin, *Stanford University*
Synne Skjulstad, *Westerdals School of Communication*
Stuart Smith, *University of Tasmania*
Fabrizzio Soares, *Universidade Federal de Goiás*
Tomas Sokoler, *IT University of Copenhagen*
Sowmya Somanath, *University of Calgary*
Andrew Sorensen, *Queensland University of Technology*
Alessandro Soro, *Queensland University of Technology*
Michiel Sovijärvi-spapé, *Helsinki Institute for Information Technology*
Jocelyn Spence, *University of Surrey*
Anna Ståhl, *Swedish Institute of Computer Science*
Danae Stanton Fraser, *University of Bath*
Jürgen Steimle, *MIT Media Lab*

Jelle Stienstra, *Eindhoven University of Technology*
Tobias Stockinger, *University of Passau*
Jörg Stöcklein, *University of Paderborn*
Paul Strohmeier, *University College Maastricht*
Simon Stusak, *University of Munich (LMU)*
Ozge SUBASI, *Vienna University of Technology*
Nicole Sultanum, *University of Calgary*
Cristina Sylla, *engageLab, University of Minho*
Axel Sylvester, *None*
Aurelien Tabard, *IT University of Copenhagen*
Yuichiro Takeuchi, *Sony Computer Science Laboratories Inc.*
Joshua Tanenbaum, *Simon Fraser University*
Karen Tanenbaum, *University of California, Santa Cruz*
Aneesh Tarun, *Queen's University*
Sarah Tausch, *University of Munich (LMU)*
Anja Thieme, *Newcastle University*
Michael Tissenbaum, *University of Toronto*
Eric Tobias, *Public Research Centre Henri Tudor*
Martin Tomitsch, *The University of Sydney*
Cornelius Toole, *Louisiana State University*
Christoph Trappe, *OFFIS*
Vasiliki Tsaknaki, *Mobile Life Centre*
Edward Tse, *SMART Technologies*
Brygg Ullmer, *Louisiana State University*
Anna Vallgårda, *IT University of Copenhagen*
Aadjan van der Helm, *Delft University of Technology*
Janet van der Linden, *The Open University*
Vero Vanden Abeele, *KU Leuven, e-Media Lab*
Katia Vega, *PUC-Rio*
Chi Vi, *University of Bristol*
Vasilis Vlachokyriakos,
Fangzhou Wang, *Google Research*
Peter Wardrip, *University of Pittsburgh*
Christian Weichel, *Lancaster University*
Richard Wetzel, *University of Nottingham*
Mikael Wiberg, *UmeŒ University*
John Williamson, *University of Glasgow*
Julie Williamson, *University of Glasgow*
Jan Wojdziak, *Technische Universität Dresden*
Katrin Wolf, *T-Labs (Quality & Usability Lab)*
Gavin Wood,
Pawel Wozniak, *Chalmers University of Technology*
Michael Wright, *University of Bath*
Andy Wu, *Georgia Institute of Technology*
Gordon Wyeth, *Queensland University of Technology*
Anna Xambó, *The Open University*
Robert Xiao, *Carnegie Mellon University*
Xiao Xiao Xiao, *Massachusetts Institute of Technology*
Xing-Dong Yang, *University of Alberta*
Lining Yao, *MIT Media Lab*
Ji-Dong Yim, *Simon Fraser University*
Sang Ho Yoon, *Purdue University*
Jim Young, *University of Manitoba*
Xiao Zhang, *Simon Fraser University*
Yanqing Zhang, *Mobile Life Center*
Andreas Zingerle, *University of Art and Design*
Oren Zuckerman, *IDC Herzliya*

TEI 2015 Sponsor & Supporters

Sponsor:

Platinum Supporter:

Gold Supporter:

Silver Supporters:

Helping Hands: Wonders and Woes of Prosthetics Technologies

Frank R Wilson, MD
Lemelson Center at the Smithsonian

Abstract

The human hand is not merely useful. It is arguably the most openly and inexhaustibly programmable biological machine in the universe. The partnership it forged with the brain and the rest of the human body over the span of many thousands of years not only made human life possible but reappears in every healthy new human baby as a legacy of wide-open prospects for adventure and discovery.

For most large organisms, survival of the species has been won through the tactic of genetic and behavioral conservatism – settling into a niche where skills are suited to needs, and where environmental change comes slowly compared to the pace of generational renewal. Humans, too, are genetically conservative, but our evolutionary path liberated us from repertoires of fixed and safe routines and turned us into behavioral improvisers. Possibly this happened because the childhood and adolescence of our species was spent crossing unfamiliar landscapes and chancing life in unpredictable environments. This migratory strategy didn't just save us, it transformed us. Over time we became "modern Homo sapiens" – highly resourceful tool-makers and users who had learned to live together and to share labor, knowledge, and ideas. Eventually, having no real competitors, we put ourselves in charge of the shallow global compartment of oxygen-rich terrain where our ancestors had started hanging out millions of years ago.

The downside of our survival strategy has been that what makes us so successful also makes us a danger to ourselves, as Greek mythology and Shakespeare so eloquently remind us. The latest irony and most recent danger is the perverse idea that our biology is our undoing, and that only technology can save us. It is this idea, or part of this idea, that I want to talk about here. Specifically, I want to consider our high hopes for "prosthetics technologies," by which I mean not only those devices and machines that are created to repair and replace broken or missing parts of ourselves but also the devices and machines we design and build to outdo ourselves.

ACM Classification

H.5.2 User Interfaces

Author Keywords: Hand, Neurology, Tangible, Culture, Prosthetics, Universal Design

TEI 2015, January 15–19, 2015, Stanford, California, USA.
ACM 978-1-4503-3305-4/15/01
http://dx.doi.org/10.1145/2677199.2683577

Short Bio

Frank Wilson made the care of performing artists, and other professionals whose work depends on what they do with their hands, the focus of his research and neurological practice for over 25 years. Through his many collaborations, publications, and presentations he has been influential in bringing researchers, practitioners, and educators in a broad range of disciplines into closer theoretical and practical contact. He has served as Visiting Professor of Neurology at the University of Düsseldorf; Medical Director of the Health Program for Performing Artists at the University of California, San Francisco; and Clinical Professor of Neurology at Stanford University School of Medicine. He is the author of The Hand: How Its Use Shapes the Brain, Language, and Human Culture, published by Pantheon Books in 1998; he was awarded an Honorary Doctorate in Fine Arts by the Massachusetts College of Art and Design in Boston in 2012; and was a Goldman Sachs Senior Research Fellow at the Smithsonian Institute's Lemelson Center for the Study of Invention and Innovation in 2013.

Interactive Paper: A Whirlwind Tour of Tangible Computing from the Digital Desk to Music Composition

Wendy E. Mackay
Research Director, In Situ lab, Inria
LRI, Université Paris-Sud, France
http://insitu.lri.fr/~mackay

Abstract

Interactive paper is a form of tangible computing that allows people to take full advantage of their existing cognitive and physical skills, and encourages us, as designers, to explore novel strategies for supporting creativity. This talk traces my own history with interactive paper, based on participatory design projects with creative professionals who successfully combine paper and computers. I begin with Pierre Wellner's ground-breaking Digital Desk in the 1990's and continue through to Phillippe LeRoux's Quid Sit Musicus in 2014, which used interactive paper both during composition and as an integral part of the live performance. The insights we gained from these projects has led to a new way of thinking about interaction design. Our concept of co-adaptive instruments is based on instrumental Interaction, which treats interaction as a first class object and co-adaptation, which helps users both learn (adapt to) and appropriate (adapt) interactive systems. By taking cues from how people interact in the physical world, we can create less brittle systems that are easier to learn and appropriate, and support a wide variety of creative activities.

ACM Classification: H.5.m

TEI 2015, January 15–19, 2015, Stanford, California, USA.
ACM 978-1-4503-3305-4/15/01
http://dx.doi.org/10.1145/2677199.2683578

Short Bio

Wendy Mackay is a Research Director, Classe Exceptionnelle, at Inria, France, where she heads the In|Situ| research group in Human-Computer Interaction at the Université Paris-Sud. After receiving her Ph.D. from MIT, she managed research groups at Digital Equipment and Xerox EuroPARC, which were among the first to explore interactive video and tangible computing. She has been a visiting professor at University of Aarhus and Stanford University and recently served as Vice President for Research at the University of Paris-Sud. Wendy is a member of the ACM CHI academy, is a past chair of ACM/SIGCHI, chaired CHI'13 and recently received the ACM/SIGCHI Lifetime Acheivement Service Award. She also received the prestigious ERC Advanced Grant for her research on co-adaptive instruments. She has published over 150 peer-reviewed research articles in the area of Human-computer Interaction. Her current research interests include participatory design, creativity, co-adaptive instruments, mixed reality and interactive paper, and multidisciplinary research methods.

What do Objects Mean?
Early Tangibility in and around Interval Research

Meg Withgott
Panafold
San Francisco, CA
meg@panafold.com

ABSTRACT
How can designers benefit from the physical and symbol-using practices that define people? Projects in and around Interval Research Corporation explored tangibles in audio, video and physical token-based computation. Four endeavors clarify what happens offscreen when participants play and collaborate. Understanding deeper issues of on- and offscreen distinctiveness, representation and embodiment is of interest, we maintain, because our current understanding of tangible design has undersold one core virtue of TUIs: tangible computing enables hardware/software systems that are non-isolating. When people are not isolated from the physical world, or from other people, they can rely on a supportive environment to help them manage confusingly large sets of objects and referents, and to share the knowledge with large sets of others. This very human part of computer interaction, we submit, gives rise to language-like structure, games, sorting, stealing, and more. If we let it, it could fundamentally change our relationship to the computer as we design new interfaces for the increasing number of computerized objects around us.

Author Keywords
Tangible Interaction; Embodied Interaction; Natural language; Video; Collaboration; Social Interaction; Play.

ACM Classification Keywords
H.5.1 Multimedia Information Systems, H.5.2. Information interfaces and presentation, H.5.3 Collaborative computing.

TEI '15, January 15 - 19 2015, Stanford, CA, USA

ACM 978-1-4503-3305-4/15/01$15.00

INTRODUCTION: OFFICE PRODUCTS AND SYMBOLS TWENTY YEARS AGO
The story of tangible computing has been told in interesting and wide-ranging ways, notably by [17, 4]. Adding to the account, the tangible computing projects in the Bay Area in the mid-nineties explored tangibility alongside audio and video. Two companies redefined computer play settings where children no longer used remote controllers. All of these efforts were aimed at changing our relationship to computing via the tangible, signal-rich world.

We hope it becomes plain that despite the seeming diversity of systems emerging today, the same questions and patterns seen then recur now. The second thing we wish to accomplish concerns meaning: stepping back and examining the texture of tangibility in a systematic way lets us profit from thought in philosophy, computer science and linguistics. This will be needed as tangible user interaction/interfaces (TUIs) and objects multiply, and as multiple platforms compete in the home or public spaces.

We can start with how effortlessly people instantiate symbols, making meaning physical. The writer Peter Hessler describes the habit of clarifying speech in China:

> ...a conversation will sometimes pause as the speaker writes a word in order to clarify the meaning... They write them in the air, on the palm of their hand, in tea water on a table; and to watch a Chinese person do this is to realize how unique the written language is, and how its words are truly shapes-not just sounds, or collections of letters, but tangible things that are handled and touched....[7] p. 223.

It's possible to reify symbolic thought. Unpacking this remarkable but everyday phenomenon reminds us of the genesis of tangible computing as we saw it. Although there's now a large literature and taxonomies related to TUIs, some basic observations about symbol-assignment and multi-user engagement appear elusive.

Taking stock of seemingly innate and effortless physical symbol manipulation led researchers in and around Interval

Research to design for children learning and playing with computers, and to help people collaborating on computational tasks in a physical setting. We turn to the questions that were unearthed then and that remain now.

The Context: Computer Science Looks at the Physical World in the 1990's

Along with hardware advances in the early nineties, there was excitement around machine perception and robotics as researchers developed methods for effectively dealing with the complexity of the real world. Computers could finally store and perform operations on large amounts of data that included video and audio. At the same time, thoughtful researchers were asking what computer science was, and saying it was not about computers *per se*, just as astronomy was not about telescopes.[1] TUIs forced us, nonetheless, to reflect on how computer science is rooted in matter where the physical meets the representational in whatever form that might take, including ubiquitous devices, DNA, distributed networks, and actual embodiment in the physical world. Being physical, computers also enable complex actions to occur non-locally in space or in time.[2] The physical coupled with the representational would be taken to new levels with TUIs in this decade.

In this period as well, inventors created new products for the office and new ways to control them. At Xerox Palo Alto Research Center and EuroPARC, we explored how the office environment could become alive to computation. Most notably, Pierre Wellner and colleagues developed the DigitalDesk that used a video camera to register symbolic content projected onto paper documents [19]. This was the environment in 1992 when Interval Research was founded.

At the new company, Tom Ngo, Marc Davis, Subutai Ahmad and Michele Covell demonstrated that objects in video could be directly manipulated. Margaret Minsky insisted that the future include haptic feedback. Durrell Bishop from the Royal Academy of Art moved in for a while and influenced us with his marble answering machine prototype [2]. Coupled with the PARC outlook, such ideas sparked creative system building that led to the work we will now describe.

One research question spurred us on from the beginning: what is the relationship between tangibility and audio and video—and us? When we observed solitary children in front of enormous 1990's workstations, we felt we had no choice but to design the physical world back into computing. The impetus was not about office products, or productivity, or communication, but closer to Jeremijenko's intriguing art demonstration down the road[3]—we wished to change how we might relate to other people and our environment in the presence of computers.

In the context of tangible interfaces, "physicality" is not a precise concept. To focus our analysis across a broad sweep of systems, we exclude some systems where tangibility was not "baked-in," that is, essential for the task. We think that physicality includes interpreting light that reflects off of objects—thus systems that use image sensors and software such as the DigitalDesk are analyzed as TUIs, as are sensor-based systems where the relationship between participant and computer is upended (Freeblenux, Me2Cam, below). Likewise systems that include computationally interpreted or signal-emitting tokens in conjunction with audio (Marble Answering Machine or Toontown, below) make the cut, as do systems employing objects + sensors/transducers. In contrast, video game systems that were sold with action figures that trigger the imagination but not the software are excluded. In addition, *contra* Rose who defines 'tangible' as where "the interaction between human being and object does not require a screen (p. 50 [14])," we think that screens, like faces, are an especially expressive element in a toolkit for tangible systems.

What else should be excluded from the inventory? Systems designed to track and even interpret audio, video and location signals in order to replace conference call technology and existing input systems (think keyboard,

[1] Variously attributed to E. Dijkstra or M.R. Fellows. Also, H. Abelson: "...the reason that we think computer science is about computers is pretty much the same reason that the Egyptians thought geometry was about surveying instruments: when some field is just getting started … it's very easy to confuse the essence of what you're doing with the tools that you use. [1]

[2] Brian C. Smith: "If a system—creature, network router, robot, mind—cannot "reach out and touch" some situation in which it is interested, another strategy, deucedly clever, is available: it can instead exploit meaningful or representational structures in place of the situation itself, so as to allow it to behave appropriately with respect to that distal, currently inaccessible, state of affairs." p 35 [Smith18].

[3] At PARC, Natalie Jeremijenko was creating an ambient art piece called Live Wire. Assembled from an actuator and dangling LED cables, it displayed ethernet traffic haptically, acoustically, and visually.

mouse, glove or joystick) did not seem to us to fundamentally change the role of the computer like TUIs did. Even audio experiments using multiple live mics (such as Interval's Somewire [15]) in the end, could be viewed as direct translations of existing computational or even electronic capabilities. Table I lists many Bay Area systems that exhibit enough of these properties to count as tangible interfaces. Looking back, they went beyond action figures, walkie-talkies and telephones; via bits, they connected people to their physical environments and to each in new ways that proved non-isolating (cf. Dourish [4]).

Making this clearer, we'll first reanalyze objects + video in Logjam, a collaborative system for video logging (annotating footage), then objects + audio in ToonTown, used for controlling interaction in a shared audio space [3, 15]. We'll next turn to Zowie and ePlanet, two companies that spun off from Interval and that made products encouraging children's movement in the physical world.

TWO EXPERIMENTS IN TANGIBLE REPRESENTATION: LOGJAM AND TOONTOWN, 1994

In 1994, Interval video ethnographers accompanied the summer Lollapalooza concert tour, accumulating a hundred hours of videotape and a mammoth video logging problem. Logjam enabled loggers to use physical tokens to better perform the demanding task of logging video [3]. It used a custom-built game-board that sensed the location and identities of the video-logging play pieces (tokens or "containers" [17]). No commercial or experimental logging software available then supported group-logging.

When we built the electronic game-board we were faced with an interface design problem. What kind of interface could support a group of impatient, talkative loggers? The goal was to support, not replace the loggers' practice, and to transform wooden blocks into tools that let loggers more easily attach meaning to raw footage.

A logger would drop a hardwood block onto the board and it would snap into place with a click and a tone, automatically labeling video events as footage was screened. What were these new blocks? The Logjam blocks were not buttons—their job was not to make a fixed event happen (though they did send messages to a program). The blocks were not icons—in general, the loggers did not try to make blocks look like their referents in the video. The blocks were not indexes (the usual Peircean example is a thermometer as an index of the weather). The Logjam blocks served as units of meaning in a system of perceptual contrasts and agreed-upon referents.[4]

Interaction> Relies on:	Virtual character <> Person (+ data)	Person <> Virtual environment (+ others)	
TOUCH to perceive			
to create			
VISION to perceive	*Freeblenux*	*DigitalDesk, Me2Cam, Live Wire*	*logjam (cf.video editor)*
to create			
AUDIO to perceive			
to create			
WHOLE BODY	*Freeblenux*	*Me2Cam*	
SCREEN DISPLAY			
AUGMENTED OBJECTS	*Ellie's Enchanted Garden*	*Redbeard, Live Wire, Marble Ansr. Mchine, DigitalDesk*	*Logjam, ToonTown*

Table I. Tangible Systems in the 1990's Bay Area. (For comparison: a Video Editor.)

Symbols exhibit an agreed-upon meaning, often arbitrarily agreed upon through time by a community. Our physical tokens could signify human beings or another object in the video, but also abstract events, a category of objects, or even a time interval. Absence of a block event was significant as well, usually indicating the completion of an action. Such symbol-using behavior seemed to work. Loggers said time passed quickly because the sessions with

[4] See Mingers *et al.* [13] on computation and meaning, although they disregard the early structuralists and perceptual space.

other loggers were more fun. Group assignment of meaning to tokens or toys is, after all, a kind of imaginative play.

The facility with which multiple participants devised and shared a complicated meaning-assignment task leads us to wonder: how exactly do TUIs exploit the richness of symbolic usage seen in other human activity, notably language?

Complexity Gives Rise to Symbol Systems

Loggers created and reassigned new categories as they identified new events, locations, or behaviors in the video. Remembering Peirce, an object we endow with computational properties in a TUI is 'something that stands for something, to someone in some respect'—and all those somethings and someones are modifiable. An object can acquire a new meaning if and only if it appears different from other objects. This we observed, and it is language-like behavior. By the end of the experiment, loggers defined more than eighty categories, with around twenty proving especially popular. The number of tangible tokens mattered then, and set size in TUIs continues to matter now.

The sheer number of labels elicited interesting behaviors around shared meaning.[5] As it happened, we stumbled upon sophisticated symbolic behavior. One behavior in particular demands an account. When loggers defined a new category, they attached a sticky label to the block to differentiate it. What kind of system did our loggers come up with?

Perceptually Distinct Symbol Systems

At first the labels were handwritten, then printed out. Eventually, even labels with printed text were augmented with minimally distinctive images and color-coding. Such marks emphasized related, abstract categories in a large semantic inventory.

This idea could be employed today with very large sets of shared computational objects. The idea of marks augmented by category information is familiar. We all recognize *pictograms* such as "wheelchair access." *Logographic* systems can augment pictograms with other information and escape having to make a symbol for each word in a language (an impossible task). For instance, Chinese characters that fuse sound and meaning help keep down the size of the inventory of ideograms. We observed that multiple cues and colors—designed entirely by the loggers—helped them retrieve and use the blocks as well as manage the size of the set.

What emerged in a social context was a system of re-bindable physical tokens that were endowed with contrasts that triggered meaning. No block being dropped, a zero-sign, meant something, too. This kind of multidimensional system of distinctions was what the structuralists were fond of describing.

Figure 1. Hybrid symbolic content characterized the participant-designed blocks.

Thinking now of the Prague school of linguistics (for an overview, see [10]), it's telling that loggers constructed an inventory of categories that consisted of an efficient series of contrasts using perceptual distinctions. The environment and location of the blocks mattered, and not only when they were on the board. Just as in language, objects in a certain position in a given environment assumed different meanings. The blocks meant different things to the participants depending on if the blocks were on or off the board, and how a logger arranged them in his or her workspace. The multidimensional space was efficient: As Cohen *et al.* [3] note, unlike in a GUI, loggers could select one item from 80 without having to scroll or pop up a menu.

Tokens and Referents in Tangible Computing

When lots of perceptually distinctive features are available to lots of people, the design space for communication is big enough to be useful. This is easy to understand: At one extreme, one wouldn't label all blocks in Logjam with the same label—that would wash out meaning. At the other extreme, it would be hard if the blocks were all different along one dimension, say numbered 1-80, because of human memory constraints. The solution is to make some things more similar than others and, to be efficacious, to hang shared meaning on those similarities. What counts as "the same" is a perceptual issue when determining the look of the token, and is a semantic issue as regards its reference.

Finally, the ability to both label and physically group and otherwise move the Logjam blocks gave rise to behaviors not seen in systems where each block is pre-labeled, fixed

[5] Just for comparison: Existing languages each use under 100 distinctive sounds (as can be seen in looking at International Phonetic Alphabet (IPA) lists); The "Deutsch limit" (a seat-of-the-pants guess of 50 primitives as the upper bound in visual programming languages) is knocked back to around 20 displayed icons on most pocket-sized phones. [18]

in place, or otherwise intended to serve fewer functions. A good contrast is a modern video editing keyboard.

Less Abstract Representation Arises, too

At this point, it is appropriate to consider the following objection: Most of what we and other animals do in the physical world doesn't involve language-like symbols at all. Physical interaction and nonlinguistic perception are key to our existence, so how do they fit in TUIs?

Logjam participants also used blocks in ways that went beyond their function as distinctive, representational tokens. The aspect of being in the physical world is betrayed in the behaviors such as snatching a block to log it ahead of someone else, or sweeping the board [3, 17]. These large gestures conveyed meaning even if they were not tied to any particular symbol.

Before testing Logjam, we didn't anticipate actions such as categorizing using distinctive features or offscreen sweeping and snatching—the loggers improvised them. Cohen *et al.* observe that, "...All the ways people make use of the physical world do not have to be mirrored in the computational one—just as the logjam system did not need to 'know' how the category blocks were arranged when they were not on the board, though that was important to the loggers. In a TUI system, this kind of capability comes without extra programming."

Representations of other People

By now, we trust that the shape of this analysis is becoming evident: TUIs mirror the ways human beings deal with symbols and physical instantiations of symbols, and creatively employ representation and meaning. But the significance is only evident when there is a sufficient quantity of tokens in the TUI system, and when users are not isolated from others. A GUI on a small screen suffices for one user and a limited set of objects.

Logjam's method of binding a physical container to virtual content was to echo a method used in another incarnation of the same game-board, ToonTown [15]. Toontown tackled live audio and asked a set of questions about representation. In ToonTown, a participant could interact with physical representations of other participants to control an acoustic space using haptic direct manipulation [8]. Tokens stood for real people. A participant did not represent himself or herself with a token—they were already speaking into the microphone. So others represented them.

Representational issues led the team to a phenomenological research perspective: The researchers suspended any formal overlay understanding the system, and noticed challenges involving physicality and identity. They let the system under investigation teach them in unexpected ways:

> Such a representation of people has social implications. For the ToonTown interface, each user selects his representations for the other users...social implications can result from using physical objects to represent people. How will users feel about picking up people by their heads? Would they 'flick' people off the board when they don't want to listen to them? What kinds of interactions would become acceptable practice? (p.109) [15].

We can add, how can tangible representations serve as loci of meaning, and even power, in different contexts? With the ability to make the remote person present, or silent, in audio, a ToonTown participant could step back and examine and then influence the flow of audio from different vantage points. Yet participants also experienced themselves as vulnerable subjects who might be "flicked" or silenced in the TuneTown world. Someone's TUI that includes self-definition, authenticity and affordances for resistance and complicity with authority will be enlightening in the years to come.

THE "NATURAL" PHYSICAL WORLD, COMPUTATION AND PLAY: EPLANET AND ZOWIE

Children are perceptive, and skilled at handling objects, and at learning. Could we exercise these natural abilities and let them play with computers? Tangibility was central: Could kids understand and blend the physical world with the symbolic, offscreen and onscreen?

One early Interval experiment involved embodied tangible spaces for games controlled by a toy glockenspiel plus realtime digital bluescreening. We were led to ask, what if kids could put themselves in games onscreen, not in a studio but in their own homes, with no bluescreen or special cameras? By 1997 we spun off ePlanet Interactive to create such products. At the same time, we investigated physical toys controlling onscreen action, and created Zowie.

Figure 2. Automatic compositing without a bluescreen.

At ePlanet we developed technology for tracking bodies, head location, and arms at over 30 frames per second using a standard USB webcam and home PCs. We achieved the

"Virtual Blue Screen" for inserting people into scenes in real time in a normal home setting. That was hard because we could not control the light conditions or extraneous movement such as curtains blowing or the family dog wandering by. Kids understood what to do and how to play instantly, and prized seeing themselves on the screen.

Our IntelPlay Me2Cam™ was produced and distributed by Mattel and Intel.[6] In the following decade, the first Xbox Kinect™ (Project Natal) was demoed at E3 2009, tracking multiple players. Children now played in ordinary rooms, no longer tethered to the mouse or to remote controllers.

A separate ePlanet product did not come to market but nonetheless challenged our relationship to the computer. Using the same image recognition technology, Greg Johnson, Mark Voorsanger and team created a 3D onscreen character, Freeblenux, "the world's first virtual alien with the gift with sight." Instead of bringing the player into the computer, the character in the computer looked out at the players and their world and remarked on what they were doing in their physical world.

Along with ePlanet, Zowie created a real world play setting. Toys were embedded with antennae that allowed children to direct action onscreen as they played. For example, Redbeard's Pirate Quest™ was sold with a plastic pirate ship that connected to a serial port. Sensing movement on the ship, the tracking technology triggered animation of the toy characters onscreen. And when the child adjusted the ship's toy telescope, the scenery onscreen changed. In Ellie's Enchanted Garden™, two toys that were moved together began to converse onscreen. It was okay that the world in the screen did not exactly match the world next to their knees and elbows—kids could abstract away from the loose coupling between their physical environment and the virtual onscreen one, and moreover, could understand that from the perspective of the computer, only certain objects were tightly coupled to the program. (Fitzmaurice et al., define tightly coupled systems as those that keep their "physical and virtual representations perfectly synchronized [6].) Again more generally, Zowie's products showed that even young children understood the complex relation between real world objects, interaction, and symbolic display on a screen. [7]

Figure 3. Freeblenux, the alien "with the gift of sight."

EPlanet and Zowie both pushed at the boundary between the world and symbolic content on a computer in service of intuitive, ordinary play.[8] The loose coupling did not lead to confusion.

The real and the virtual intermix differently in an embodied tangible space than in a head-mounted display. At ePlanet we also discarded the use of hand-held objects to make tracking easier—we guessed it would interfere with the sense of play. The Nintendo Wii™, while very successful, later encountered an issue with people letting loose of their hand-held controllers when caught up in throwing a virtual object[9]. With controller-free TUIs, physical objects can play a variety of roles in the embodied tangible space.

It's a good design challenge to let the real world help, not hurt, the play experience. Given a sufficiently large system

[6] The product won the Bologna 2000 New Media Prize for the Most Innovative Children's Software Product. The judges were interested in the physical aspect, "...It is one of the few software products out there which get children up off their seats and using their muscles." [13]

[7] Zowie was acquired by the Lego Company.

[8] Hurtienne et al. [10] usefully define intuitive,"A technical system is intuitively usable if the users' unconscious application of pre-existing knowledge leads to effective interaction." p. 128.

[9] Don Norman uses the Wii's hand-held controller to critique "natural" interfaces. Chaos ensued when a player would swing an arm as if bowling a bowling ball, holding the controller, "Releasing the pressure on the switch was analogous to releasing the ball from the hand and it was readily learned and employed. Alas, in the heat of the game ...the controller ...would fly thorough the air, sometimes with enough force to hit and break the television screen."[12]

where participants can associate and assign symbolic content to tokens in tandem with a computer program, the real world helps participants, both on- and offscreen. Esteves *et al.* [5] argue convincingly that "inherent support for offline activities—activities that are not sensed by the system—is one of strongest benefits of tangible interaction over more traditional interface paradigms."

Figure 4. Redbeard's Ship, Computer History Museum.

CONCLUSION

The offscreen—that is to say real—world is filled with sound and light as well as objects. People create symbolic systems on the fly in and with the environment around them. And this brings us to the heart of the matter: TUIs are non-isolating and can bring in the benefits of the world around us, and make use of our perceptual and linguistic abilities, and more generally, our social and cognitive abilities as well as vulnerabilities.

The three basic concepts of distinctiveness and representation (Jakobson) and embodiment (Peirce) help us to understand how meaning is assigned and reassigned. In the next few years, when your future smart environment is realized, and computational objects abound, we can hope that all the inhabitants have access to a common understanding of the tokens, referents, syntax and semantics of the system. In 2015, we're squarely in an age of connected objects, and multiple objects will eventually sense each other even across proprietary platforms. As designers, we will surely grapple with how to design for larger spaces and how to address ever more computational objects.

Some early TUI intuitions were about beauty and function. The hunches behind the work described here were about how properties of symbolic systems are readily available for TUIs, including the assignment of new symbols to tokens, and the loose coupling between symbol and referent. Most consequential, participants could remain rooted in the real world: Light and sound as well as touch enabled people to interact with their world and with each other.

Given a new world of objects in socially-organized settings, Hornecker and Burr [8] demand that designers architect not only the digital but also the material, plus their interrelations. In the home, we now have computer-aware objects but still observe old practices. We "solved" the problem of multiple people accessing a television by imposing an access bottleneck (one remote control). Objects are growing smarter, and the loci of control is becoming distributed, but current app-driven devices pay scent heed to better human interaction design. Continuing the system controller paradigm, new systems use touchscreen GUI displays for each participant via their cellphones, or even via that remote control again. System controller interfaces can result in, for instance, you trying to change your t.v. channel on a sleek Logitech Harmony remote and with a slip of the thumb, turning the cook green in the kitchen with the Philips hue lightbulb. We look forward to a designer following Hornecker and Burr's advice to make action publicly available. We'd also like to see a manufacturer let people collaboratively construct their own experience using richer tools than a 2D GUI display.

What happens offscreen forms an integral part of TUIs and so these systems are not limited to the onscreen semantics of GUIs. We saw participants engage in behaviors that involve physics, and enable human activities such as games, gathering, sorting, stealing, and more. We are also faced with socio-representational issues. How do representations in TUIs serve as loci of meaning, and even power, in different contexts? This question remains live today.

People can write characters in the air, or in tea water on a table. Symbols can be handled and touched, sorted, categorized, and played with. This retrospective look demonstrated it's not the gesture technology, the speech, the gaze or the brainwaves we design with that really matter—it's how the design shapes the way people interact with each other, and play. Logjam and ToonTown showed the value of meaning-rich, collaboratively constructed, multi-person interfaces, and ePlanet and Zowie demonstrated how readily even young children take to a blend of the physical, tangible world and the computational. A foundational theory of TUIs that embraces symbol-assignment behavior and multi-participant engagement is still needed, one that can serve a variety of applications and concerns such as learning, living with other people, and working together.

Figure 5: A Video Editing Keyboard. The keys are fixed in place, labeled, and not meant to be shared, let alone swept away. (Photo courtesy of Reel Monkey © Mehul Patel / Reel Monkey Productions).

ACKNOWLEDGMENTS

We are perhaps 30 co-authors on this paper. On the theory side, as well as system building, might have been Jonathan Cohen, Subutai Ahmad, Philippe Piernot, Durrell Bishop, Debbie Hindus, Lee Felsenstein and Bill Verplank. Brygg Ullmer was the student in the 1990's who turned this work into a field. Thanks to the readers, especially Per-Kristian Halvorsen, Guillaume Arnaud and the anonymous reviewers. Thank you to David Liddle and Paul Allen who supported much of the work, as well as to Kit Halvorsen and Emily McCabe. This paper was written remembering the considerable contributions of Bonnie Johnson, Andrew Singer and Mark Weiser—skeptics, gadflies, and helpful galvanizers for us all.

REFERENCES

1. Abelson, H. Video lectures, *The Structure and Interpretation of Computer Programs*. MIT. (1986). http://groups.csail.mit.edu/mac/classes/6.001/abelson-sussman-lectures/
2. Bishop, D. http://ccdc11.wordpress.com/2011/02/15/durrell-bishops-marble-answering-machine/
3. Cohen, J. , Withgott, M. and Piernot, P. Logjam: a Tangible Multi-Person Interface for Video Logging. In *Proc. of CHI '99*, ACM Press (1999) 128-135.
4. Dourish, P. *Where the Action is. The Foundations of Embodied Interaction*. MIT Press (2001).
5. Esteves, A., Scott, M. and Oakley, I. Supporting offline activities on interactive surfaces. *Proc. of TEI '13*, ACM Press (2013) 147-154.
6. Fitzmaurice, G., Ishii H., Buxton W. Bricks: Laying the Foundations for Graspable User Interfaces. In *Proc. CHI* 2 1995, ACM Press (1995), 442-449.
7. Hessler, P. *River Town: Two Years on the Yangtze*. Harper Collins. (2001).
8. Hornecker, E. and Buur., J. 'Getting a Grip on Tangible Interaction: A Framework on Physical Space and Social Interaction. In *Proc. CHI 2006*, ACM Press (2006) 437-446.
9. Hurtienne, J. and Israel, J.H. Image Schemas and Their Metaphorical Extensions – Intuitive Patterns for Tangible Interaction. In *Proc. TEI '07*, ACM Press (2007) 15-17.
10. Jakobson, R., and Halle, M. *Fundamentals of language*, Mouton (1956).
11. Mingers, J and Willcocks, L. An integrative semiotic framework for information systems: The social, personal and material worlds. (2014) *Information and Organization*, 24 (1). 48-70.
12. Norman, D. A. Natural User Interfaces Are Not Natural.(2010). Interactions, 17, No. 3 (May - June). http://interactions.acm.org/content/?p=1355
13. Press release. "Announcing the 2000 New Media Prize awards." Available at: http://www.subutai.com/Bologna/BolognaPrize.html
14. Rose, D. *Enchanted Objects*. Scribner. (2014).
15. Singer, A., Hindus, D., Stifleman, L., and White, S. Tangible Progress: Less is More in Somewire Audio Spaces. In *Proc. CHI 1999*, ACM (1999), 104-111.
16. Smith, B.C. *The Age of Significance*. (2001). http://www.ageofsignificance.org/aos/aos-v1c0.xhtml
17. Ullmer, B. Tangible Interfaces for Manipulating Aggregates of Digital Information. PhD thesis. MIT Media Lab (2002).
18. Ullmer B. and Ishii H. Emerging frameworks for tangible user interfaces. IBM Systems Journal 39(3-4) (2000), 915-931.
19. Wellner, P., Mackay, W., Gold, R. Communications of the ACM. *Computer Augmented Environments: Back to the Real World.* (July 1993) Vol. 36, 7, 24-26.

The ATB Framework: Quantifying and Classifying Epistemic Strategies in Tangible Problem-Solving Tasks

Augusto Esteves[1], Saskia Bakker[2], Alissa N. Antle[3], Aaron May[3], Jillian Warren[3], Ian Oakley[4]
[1]Exact Sciences and Engineering Center, University of Madeira, Funchal, Portugal
[2]Department of Industrial Design, Eindhoven University of Technology, Eindhoven, the Netherlands
[3]School of Interactive Arts and Technology, Simon Fraser University, Surrey, B.C., Canada
[4]Department of Human and Systems Engineering, UNIST, Ulsan, Republic of Korea
augustoeae@gmail.com, s.bakker@tue.nl, {aantle, amay, jlw29}@sfu.ca, ian.r.oakley@gmail.com

ABSTRACT
In task performance, pragmatic actions refer to behaviors that make direct progress, while epistemic actions involve altering the world so that cognitive processes are faster, more reliable or less taxing. Epistemic actions are frequently presented as a beneficial consequence of interacting with tangible systems. However, we currently lack tools to measure epistemic behaviors, making substantiating such claims highly challenging. This paper addresses this problem by presenting ATB, a video-coding framework that enables the identification and measurement of different epistemic actions during problem-solving tasks. The framework was developed through a systematic literature review of 78 papers, and analyzed through a study involving a jigsaw puzzle – a classical spatial problem – involving 60 participants. In order to assess the framework's value as a metric, we analyze the study with respect to its reliability, validity and predictive power. The broadly supportive results lead us to conclude that the ATB framework enables the use of observed epistemic behaviors as a performance metric for tangible systems. We believe that the development of metrics focused explicitly on the properties of tangible interaction are currently required to gain insight into the genuine and unique benefits of tangible interaction. The ATB framework is a step towards this goal.

Author Keywords
Epistemic actions; tangible interaction; video-coding.

ACM Classification Keywords
H5.2. User Interfaces: Theory & Methods.

INTRODUCTION AND RELATED WORK
Tangible interaction [24], an interface paradigm based on manipulating physical artifacts that both represent and control digital information, provides a compelling directness and physicality that has long made it a topic of study in research labs. As the field matures, successful products in areas such as musical performance (e.g. Reactable [14]) or play (e.g. Siftables [23]) illustrate how notions of users literally grasping information with their hands can be converted into rich, expressive and viable commercial systems. However, while users and designers continue to be drawn by the allure of physically handling digital data, it remains challenging to understand and quantify the genuine benefits of tangible interaction [30]. Indeed, we argue there is currently no systemic account of the underlying properties or qualities of tangible systems that can explain or justify their enduring appeal. There is no comprehensive way to answer questions regarding the true value provided by tangible systems to their users.

However, steps are being taken to develop such answers and explanations. One fertile source is the cognitive science literature that focuses on embodied (or situated) cognition. Work on this topic typically contends that the body and its interactions with the world play a central role in human thought and experience [25, 29]. More concretely, numerous authors assert that the worldly, physical representations of a problem, situation or task radically impact the strategies people employ to tackle it, their reasoning abilities and ultimately their overall performance [18, 21]. One aspect of this literature that is highly relevant to tangible interaction deals with how objects and their inherent properties (e.g., their ability to be stacked, ordered, annotated) can be leveraged by people to simplify or aid performance of information processing tasks [1].

Work has elaborated on this claim in a number of ways. For example, authors have described how users can manipulate objects to not only conduct pragmatic, goal-driven actions, but also to employ complementary actions [3] that involve exploring, testing, annotating or re-structuring a system state. In the field of Human-Computer Interaction (HCI), these kinds of activities are comprehensively documented in, for example, work analysis of air-traffic control – an activity in which operators rely heavily on physical paper strips to mediate their complex and safety-critical work tasks [22]. Other authors have depicted how users leverage external (non-mental) structures as tools to simplify

TEI '15, January 15–19, 2015, Stanford, California, USA..

ACM 978-1-4503-3305-4/15/01...$15.00.
http://dx.doi.org/10.1145/2677199.2680546

cognitive work [19]. For example, experienced jigsaw puzzle-solvers often cluster physical pieces together (e.g. by color) to simplify subsequent processes of visual search and recognition [2]. These kinds of account are important as they provide a basis for explaining the appeal and value of tangible systems – they cast light on the ways in which problem-centric tangible systems, such as the Senseboard [13] or Urp [27], really provide benefits to their users, potentially steering future design and development efforts.

However, applying principles from cognitive science to the design of tangible systems remains a challenging and intricate task. Although work on this topic remains embryonic, several distinct approaches exist. One key thread, instantiated as illustrative design frameworks [e.g. 10, 12, 21], aims to provide high level guidance and recommendations for how tangible systems can best be created. A second strand, more directly related to the literature on embodied cognition, seeks to expand our repertoire of metrics for understanding and assessing performance with tangible systems. Basically, it argues that theoretically grounded techniques that enable us to rigorously and empirically examine the mechanisms by which users rely on physical objects to aid their cognitive work will help us assess (and ultimately learn how best to design) such systems.

This latter approach has been explicitly explored in the context of Kirsh et al.'s [20] categorization of behaviors into either *pragmatic* or *epistemic* actions – a contrast between activities that users conduct to directly move towards a desired goal state versus those that are intended to alter the world to make the cognitive processes faster, more reliable or less taxing. While Kirsh originally explored this idea in the context of a purely virtual computer game (Tetris), Antle et al. [2] were arguably the first to apply it to a tangible system. Their work compares tangible and touch interfaces to a classic problem-solving task – a jigsaw puzzle – and they use video-coding analysis to classify user behaviors as either pragmatic or epistemic. Their results suggest that the tangible representation afforded more natural and efficient epistemic strategies such as clustering pieces to improve subsequent visual search, or relying on the elevated edges of the table to help structure the puzzle. In broadly similar work, Esteves et al. [6] report on user performance when playing a modified game of Four-in-a-row with three different interfaces (tangible, touch and mouse). Using video coding, specific epistemic actions relating to gesturing and receiving feedback on the game-board were measured and the results suggested that while epistemic activity was a significant component of all interfaces, users were more efficient in performing them with the tangible system.

While this work provides evidence for the conjecture that tangible interaction aids performance of epistemic actions, one major weakness is in terms of the granularity with which the activities are recorded. Basically, work that defines and discusses epistemic activity is typically highly specific and contextual – particular epistemic behaviors are described as being used to achieve particular ends in particular situations. However, the evaluation frameworks in HCI are broad and general [e.g. 2], often reducing the diversity of epistemic activity to a single categorical label. This paper aims to address this issue by expanding an existing video-coding framework [1, 2] that categorizes hand actions to include a detailed classification scheme for epistemic activity – the ATB (Artifact, Tool and Body) framework. This paper argues that this framework will contribute to our understanding of how epistemic actions are used in human problem-solving tasks, providing researchers with a tool to more systematically assess this complex type of behavior in tangible interaction.

In terms of HCI, this tool has two objectives. Firstly, it is intended as a mechanism to evaluate tangible systems in terms of the type, diversity and appropriateness of the epistemic actions they support, and in terms of the impact these actions can have on more traditional metrics such as performance time or errors. Secondly, in the long term, we argue that a series of such evaluations will result in a corpus of knowledge describing the use of epistemic actions in real tasks. This data can be used as the basis for grounded, practical design knowledge on how to create novel systems that truly support epistemic actions, and thus, improve our ability to design tangible interaction that is natural and meets the real needs of the user.

As such, this paper makes two contributions. Firstly, we describe a detailed framework of epistemic activity based on a systematic literature review of 78 papers (an early version of the framework was previously introduced in [5]). Although loosely related prior classifications exist [e.g. 18, 20], the framework presented in this paper is the first to be based on a systematic review, the first to aim for a focused, fine-grained description of epistemic behavior, and the first to be specifically directed towards the development of an actionable empirical tool for capturing and expressing observed epistemic actions. Secondly, this paper presents an initial experiment to explore the framework's reliability, validity and predictive power. This substantial lab study involved 60 participants across three countries completing a physical problem-solving task – a jigsaw puzzle. Three raters analyzed the data to support commentary on reliability. Validity is explored by contrasting the video-coding results among our purposely diverse participant group with other measures such as spatial ability tests and task completion rates and times. The outcomes of this study provide insights into epistemic activity and demonstrate the usefulness of the framework as an analytic tool that other researchers can apply in their own design and evaluation activities in the field of tangible interaction.

THE ATB VIDEO-CODING FRAMEWORK

The work in this paper builds on the action classification framework presented by Antle et al. [1, 2]. In their work, an action can be classified as either a *direct placement* (DP), an *indirect placement* (IP), or as *exploratory* (EXP). In the puzzle task they studied, a *DP* action corresponded to those situations where users already know where to place a piece before picking it up, leading to a fast and direct transition between acquiring a piece, moving to the final destination and correctly placing it. *IP* represented similar outcomes but described situations in which users are not initially certain of where to position the pieces they pick up. As such, they translated or rotated the piece while searching for its correct destination. Finally, *EXP* represented those actions where pieces do not end in their final and correct position. As with IP, if these intermediary actions make the task easier for the user they are considered epistemic (e.g., if a user organizes pieces into different piles for subsequent identification and retrieval).

Antle's framework [1, 2] provides basic features that enables the study of epistemic actions. It allows researchers to measure epistemic activity levels within a task, reporting on the frequency, duration, and moments at which epistemic actions occur. While valuable, we argue that this classification is too broad to fully articulate and explain the role of epistemic action in problem solving. For example, different types of epistemic action may be used in different tasks [6], and recording such variations in detail will better characterize the role and importance of epistemic activity. This paper argues that only by considering epistemic actions at a fine-grained level of detail will we be able to understand not just how many epistemic actions are performed during a task, but also which epistemic actions are chosen and to which purpose. In terms of tangible interfaces, a detailed classification scheme will support investigations of what interface elements facilitate what epistemic actions, quantifying the differences between novel systems, and allowing designers to tailor interaction that better supports users' natural, epistemic behaviors.

ATB Framework Development and Use

To develop the ATB framework we conducted an extensive literature review with the goal of capturing a wide range of epistemic activity descriptions [5]. A set of keywords was used to conduct a literature search on both Google Scholar and Science Direct. The search terms were 'epistemic action(s)', 'complementary action(s)' and 'complementary strategies'. The first 60 results from each of these searches were kept for further inspection. Additionally, papers referencing seminal work in the area (specifically [16] and [20]) and including the keywords defined above were also retained. Ultimately, 78 papers were obtained through this process – a typical number for meta-analysis papers in the area of HCI [e.g. 9]. Each paper was then inspected for any mention of actions that could be interpreted as epistemic, or were directly treated as epistemic, and quotes such as: "(...) *preparing the workplace, for example, by partially sorting nuts and bolts before beginning an assembly task in order to reduce later search* (...)" [26, p. 515] were extracted. These represented concrete examples of epistemic actions from research literature in a range of fields (such as mathematics, cognitive science, HCI and design) from the last three decades. A complete list of references for all 78 publications can be found at http://www.mysecondplace.org/ATB/ full-reference-list.txt.

In total, 335 quotes were compiled. Two of the authors then worked collaboratively to create an affinity diagram that identified different clusters of epistemic actions. Quotes judged to depict actions with unclear epistemic value were discarded. This process led to the identification of 20 types of epistemic action based on a subset of 225 of the original quotes. These were then grouped by actions performed with 1) task artifacts (e.g. objects marked with fiducials), 2) tools (e.g. a pencil that can be used for annotations) or 3) the users own bodies (summarized in Table 1). A full scheme

#	Epistemic actions
A1	**Manipulation of an artifact**
A2	Spatial arrangement of artifacts in relation to one another, the task environment, or the users
2.1	Cluster or group artifacts together
2.2	Divide workspace into several stations in which only a subset of actions are afforded
2.3	Place an artifact in a contrasting environment
2.4	Rearrange a representation
2.5	Clear and clean clutter
A3	Parallel use of two artifacts, two representations, or an artifact and a representation
A4	Artifact trial-and-error positioning
A5	Shuffle artifacts
A6	Compare an artifact with a possible destination or other artifacts
A7	Mark an artifact
A8	Test the state or response of a system, model or other user
	Manipulation of a tool
T9	Tag or annotate an artifact
T10	General notes and annotations
T11	Use of a tool to physically constraint the user or the use of other artifacts and tools
T12	Build a model or external representation
	Bodily action
B13	Use the body to externalize an internal process
B14	Talk or gesture to guide and direct attention
B15	Move the body, problem space, or representation

Table 1. A list of all the 20 types of epistemic actions present in the ATB video-coding framework, which groups actions by those performed with an artifact (an epistemic action in itself), a tool, or the user's body. Five types of epistemic action are grouped under A2, a broad type of action.

describing these 20 types of epistemic action can be found at http://www.mysecondplace.org/ATB/atb-framework.pdf.

These categories are then used as the basis for classifying behaviors through video-analysis, according to the following procedure. Firstly, raters should categorize actions as being either DP, IP, or EXP, as in Antle et al's framework [1, 2]. After this process is completed, raters should review each action that can contain epistemic activity (i.e. those coded as either IP or EXP) and match these to one (or more) of the 20 types of epistemic actions identified. For a graphical workflow of how to video-code with using the ATB framework, please consult http://www.mysecondplace.org/ATB/coding-flowchart.pdf. A coding scheme file was created to facilitate the process of video coding with Anvil, a free and popular video-coding tool. This file can be downloaded from http://www.mysecondplace.org/ATB/atb.xml.

APPLYING THE ATB FRAMEWORK: AN INITIAL STUDY

To determine the usefulness of the ATB framework in capturing and distinguishing among different epistemic actions, and the fundamental value and worth of this kind of information, we conducted an observational study of users performing a classical problem-solving task – a jigsaw puzzle. This task was selected as there is a large body of work on epistemic actions using puzzles in both HCI [e.g. 1, 2], and cognitive science [e.g. 15, 16, 17]. Furthermore, puzzle metaphors are commonplace in the design of tangible systems [e.g. 8]. The goal of this initial study was to explore the reliability and sensitivity of the framework, and to assess its internal and external validity, and predictive power. To meet these classic methodological objectives, a diverse participant pool was recruited (from Korea, Canada and the Netherlands) and a range of spatial and subjective workload tests were performed to establish the main results in a theoretical context.

Experimental Design and Participants

All participants in this study completed a single condition. In total, there were 60 participants, 20 of whom were Korean, 20 Dutch, and 20 Canadian – 10 male and 10 female participants from each nationality. The study also took place at three sites, one in each of these countries, with all participants residing in their respective countries of origin. Participant ages ranged from 20 to 76 (M = 27.33, SD = 10.72) and occupied a wide range of professions, from undergraduate to postgraduate students, to sailors, game designers, artists, drivers, and writers. Before the study, all participants filled in a brief online questionnaire to exclude puzzle hobbyists. To motivate participants to perform to the best of their capabilities, a prize of $25 (or equivalent) was awarded to the fastest participant to solve the puzzle in each of the three countries. In addition to this prize, Korean and Canadian participants received a $10 compensation for participating. Dutch participation was not compensated due to different funding policies in the three research groups.

Procedure

Each session involved a single participant solving two puzzles, and performing an additional test at the beginning and end of the study. All tasks were performed in small and otherwise empty offices, and all sessions followed the same structure. Sessions commenced with a brief introduction to the first task, a paper folding spatial ability test [4]. Participants were then introduced to the first jigsaw puzzle, an unmeasured practice task, which they were asked to solve in a maximum time of 10 minutes. This was followed by the main task of the study, a second jigsaw puzzle which participants were asked to solve in a maximum time of 15 minutes. Though the two puzzles presented different images, each consisted of 70 pieces and was 38x26cm in size. The order in which the puzzles were presented was the same for each participant. Before starting the main puzzle, participants were reminded of the monetary prize. During both puzzle tasks participants were left alone to ensure that their epistemic actions were unmediated and private. Both tasks were recorded on video for later analysis. At the end of the main puzzle, participants completed a subjective test to measure the perceived workload of the main task.

Measures

In addition to recording the time that it took participants to finish the puzzles, the following metrics were used:

Spatial ability (paper folding test): Upon starting the study, participants were required to solve two sets of spatial tests [4], each in under three minutes.

Video-coding framework: Several metrics were derived from the data obtained through the video-coding framework being examined. These include the mean number of pragmatic (coded as DP) and epistemic actions (coded as either IP or EXP) performed; and, the individual mean frequency of each of the 20 types of epistemic action in the framework. These frequency metrics include both aggregate and running means, on a minute-by-minute basis.

Subjective Workload: Each participant completed the NASA TLX [7] after the main puzzle task.

Participant group		Spatial ability	Overall Workload	Overall time to finish
Puzzle completion	Finished	15.11 (4.14)	8.74 (2.31)	9:38.10
	Incomplete	11.67 (6.27)	11.36 (2.75)	-
Gender	Male	15.61 (3.59)	9.36 (2.69)	10:49.22
	Female	13.13 (5.62)	9.19 (2.48)	10:46.26
Cultural background	Korean	17.48 (2.76)	8.79 (2.47)	12:44.00
	Dutch	15.06 (3.50)	10.29 (1.57)	08:58.54
	Canadian	10.56 (5.19)	9.00 (3.24)	10:40.48
Rater	Rater 1	15.15 (4.70)	9.18 (2.56)	10:52.03
	Rater 2	13.94 (5.07)	9.96 (2.27)	11:34.39
	Rater 3	14.01 (4.89)	8.67 (2.76)	09:57.00

Table 2. Mean scores for the spatial ability paper folding test (higher is better), the NASA TLX (lower is better), and the overall time to finish the task (mm:ss.ms). Std. dev in brackets.

RESULTS AND DISCUSSION

The study presented in this paper has two goals. Firstly, to assess the usefulness and correctness of the ATB framework. Secondly, to introduce epistemic actions as a comprehensive new performance metric for systems incorporating tangible interaction. To facilitate this discussion, the results of the study are divided into four sections: *spatial ability*; *framework reliability*; *framework validity*; and, *framework predictive power*. Workload test results are described when relevant throughout this section.

Spatial Ability

The paper folding test [4] was performed to provide meaningful data on participant's inherent spatial ability, as it could have a significant impact in how they perform during a jigsaw puzzle task (and how they might ultimately rely on epistemic actions). As expected, participants that were able to finish the main task in less than 15 minutes obtained higher scores than those who did not (see Table 2). An independent-samples t-test revealed that this difference was not statistically significant ($p = 0.062$), which may be attributable to the disparity between the two group sizes – of 60 participants, only 13 failed to complete the task. Additionally, each group of twenty participants coded by the three individual raters exhibited statistically similar spatial scores (one-way ANOVA, $p = 0.744$), demonstrating the equivalence of these groupings. These results will be further discussed in the following sections.

Framework Reliability

The first step when introducing a new measurement instrument, such as a video-coding framework, is to establish its reliability. To do this, three independent raters applied the video-coding framework proposed in this paper to the videos of the 60 participants performing the main puzzle task. Each rater coded 20 videos: 10 male and 10 female participants, with either six or seven of these from each of the three cultural backgrounds sampled. Events were classified with a timestamp, Antle's classification (DP, IP or EXP), and one or more types of epistemic action (if epistemic activity was observed). Additionally, two of these raters acted as second-coders for eight of the 60 videos, providing a selection of double-coded content. These two raters obtained a substantial agreement in terms of Antle et al.'s three categories of action (85.6%), and in the main three categories of the ATB framework – artifact, tool, and body (75.7%). These high level results illustrate how the ATB framework can inform how future tangible systems are designed and implemented. Basically, these results demonstrate that the framework enables researchers to reliably identify the most common source of epistemic activity during interaction with a system, be it through artifact, tool or body. Understanding where the focus of epistemic activity lies will help direct research and design efforts in the most appropriate directions. For instance, if users depend on task artifacts (as we observed in our task, see e.g., Figure 2), attention can be directed to improving these. Alternatively, if users look at tools to alleviate cognitive burdens, these should serve as inspiration for new artifacts or systems that effortlessly accommodate tool use. Finally, if a task is most suited for bodily actions, designers can focus on how best to sense and enable these.

Beyond this point, the strength of the ATB framework is in the granularity of the epistemic actions recorded. In regards to its 20 different types of action, coders reached a moderate level of agreement of 60.9%. A confusion matrix (not shown) revealed that 87.86% of misclassified actions belonged to two groups: actions in which one rater observes

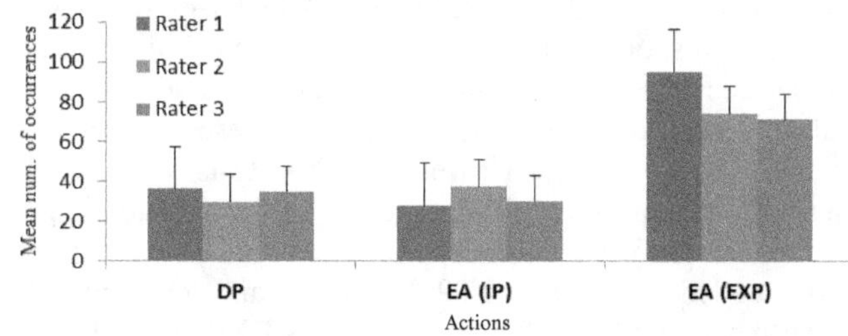

Figure 1. Mean number of pragmatic (DP) and epistemic actions (EA, grouped by actions classified as IP or EXP). Overall data grouped by rater, standard deviation in bars.

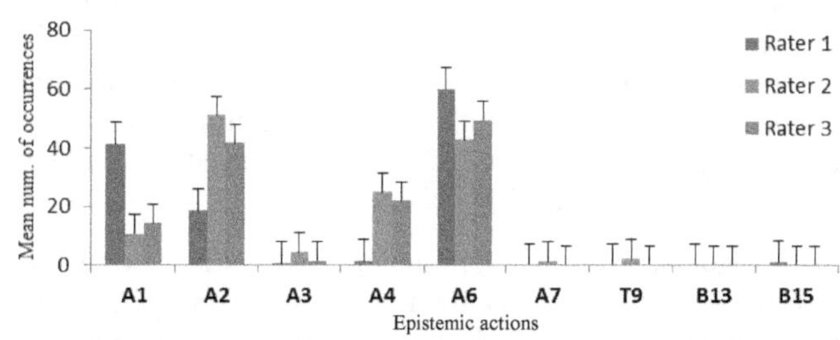

Figure 2. Mean number of individual types of epistemic action, with A2 grouping actions classified from 2.1 to 2.5. Data clustered by rater, standard deviation in bars.

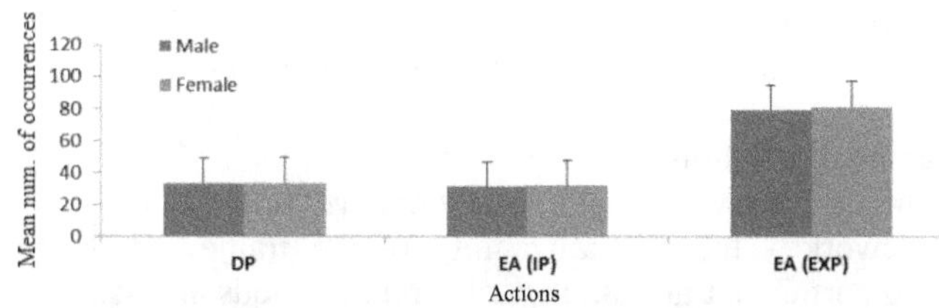

Figure 3. Mean number of pragmatic (DP) and epistemic actions (EA, grouped by actions classified as IP or EXP). Overall data grouped by gender, standard deviation in bars.

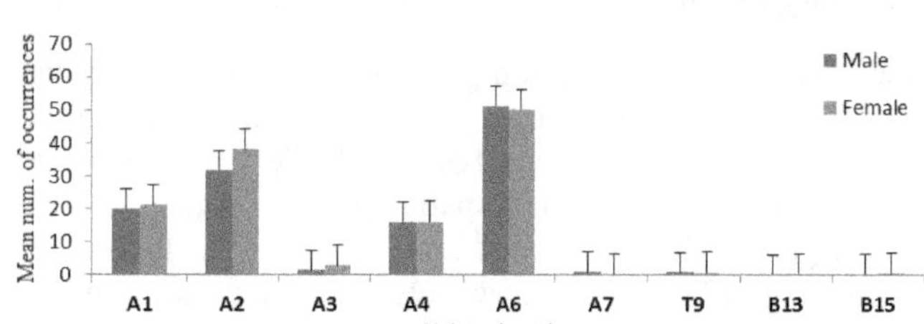

Figure 4. Mean number of individual types of epistemic action, with A2 grouping actions classified from 2.1 to 2.5. Data clustered by gender, standard deviation in bars.

some epistemic activity, but the other does not (61.15% of all misclassifications) and 'vertical' misclassifications, where both raters use nested epistemic actions to classify a particular event (e.g. between IP: A2 and IP: A2.2, 26.7% of all misclassifications). The most common of these misclassifications occurred with action A1, under which all epistemic actions performed with an artifact fit.

Given the limited number of videos double-coded by two raters, additional statistical tests were performed on data from all the 60 sessions to further explore and qualify agreement levels between the three individual raters (subsequently termed *R1*, *R2*, and *R3*) in terms of mean categorical response rates across all rated data. This data is summarized in Figures 1 and 2. A one-way ANOVA was used to study the differences between these datasets – Welsch's F and Games-Howell post-hoc tests were used when the assumption of homogeneity was violated. All three raters reported similar mean numbers of epistemic actions coded as **IP** ($p = 0.090$), and R2 and R3 reported similar mean numbers of actions coded as **EXP** ($p = 0.952$), **A1** ($p = 0.343$), **A2** ($p = 0.573$), **A4** ($p = 0.699$), and **A6** ($p = 0.448$) – the four most common epistemic actions coded by these raters. While these four epistemic actions were also the most commonly reported by R1, most of their occurrence rates significantly varied from the other two raters ($p < 0.015$). Close examination of this pattern suggests it can be explained by the confusion matrix described earlier – R1 tended to classify events with the broad A1 action (Figure 2).

Taken together, these are promising results that vouch for the reliability of the ATB framework as an instrument to record epistemic work. Substantial to moderate agreement levels were attained on different levels of the framework and examination of the raw data shows clear parallels between rater performance. Observed misclassifications fall in a limited number of acceptable types. We believe this data effective illustrates the reliability of the framework.

Framework Validity

In this section we assess the *external validity* of the ATB framework – the generalizability of the framework to a broad participant group. Two different methods are used to achieve this: (1) contrasting the obtained results with current theory on gender differences in spatial ability; and (2), comparing the results of participants from different cultural backgrounds.

There is a long tradition of studying of cognitive differences between the genders, with predictably conflicting and controversial results. While men are often regarded as having higher spatial ability, some studies suggest gender differences are small [e.g. 11] and, indeed, diminishing [28]. Our own results show that male participants obtained higher spatial scores than female participants ($p = 0.029$), but both reported a similar perceived workload when performing the task ($p = 0.797$) and finished with statistically similar mean times ($p = 0.893$) – see Table 2. We argue that this can be explained by examining the results obtained with the ATB framework. These show no statistically significant differences between the mean number of actions performed between the genders (see Figure 3 and 4): **DP** ($p = 0.908$), **IP** ($p = 0.728$), and **EXP** ($p = 0.840$); **A1** ($p = 0.801$), **A2** ($p = 0.244$), **A4** ($p = 0.985$), and **A6** ($p = 0.842$). We suggest that by performing the same number of epistemic actions as their male counterparts, female participants were able to make up for any differences in spatial ability, and indeed that adopting appropriate epistemic behaviors may be more important in this task than high spatial ability.

Furthermore, the experimental data also supports the framework's ability to generate coherent results across broad and varied participant groups. Specifically, the spatial tests recorded a lower spatial score from Canadian participants when compared to both Korean and Dutch participants (one-way ANOVA, Games-Howell post-hoc tests: $p < 0.001$ and $p = 0.003$, respectively). As with the gender groups, however, Canadian participants reported similar workload levels as participants from the other two cultural backgrounds (one-way ANOVA, $p = 0.055$) – see Table 2. We again argue this is attributable to the similar mean number of epistemic actions performed by participants from each cultural group: **A1** ($p = 0.145$), **A2** ($p = 0.064$), **A4** ($p = 0.561$), and **A6** ($p = 0.329$). More so, Canadian participants completed the main task in an average of 10 minutes and 40 seconds, two minutes and four seconds quicker than Korean participants (independent samples t-test, $p = 0.037$). The reason for this result may be in the first minute of the task [2, 19], where Canadian participants performed almost twice the number of epistemic actions than Korean participants. This idea will be explored in more detail in the next section.

Framework Predictive Power

This section explores whether the ATB framework records data that meaningfully relates to other performance metrics (extending the discussion of validity), and whether or not it offers novel explanatory insights into participants' epistemic work. It does this by contrasting the results of participants who successfully finished the main puzzle task with those who did not. Specifically, informed by prior suggestions that early performance of epistemic actions is important in successful performance of spatial problems such as puzzle tasks [e.g. 2, 19], we firstly examined the impact of the rate of epistemic action performance in the first moments of interaction (see Figure 7 and 8). A linear regression showed that the aggregate number of epistemic actions performed in the first minute of the task were statistically significant in predicting participant's required time to finish the task (adjusted $R^2 = 0.177$, $F(1, 58) = 12.501$, $p = 0.001$). These results reinforce current suggestions [e.g. 2, 19] that successful use of epistemic

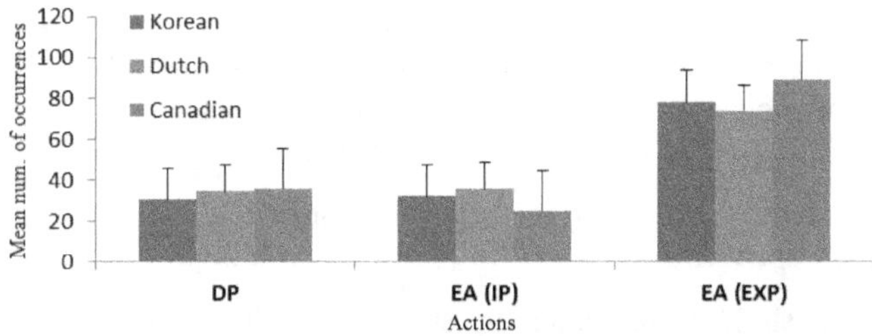

Figure 5. Mean number of pragmatic (DP) and epistemic actions (EA, grouped by actions classified as IP or EXP). Overall data grouped by country, standard deviation in bars.

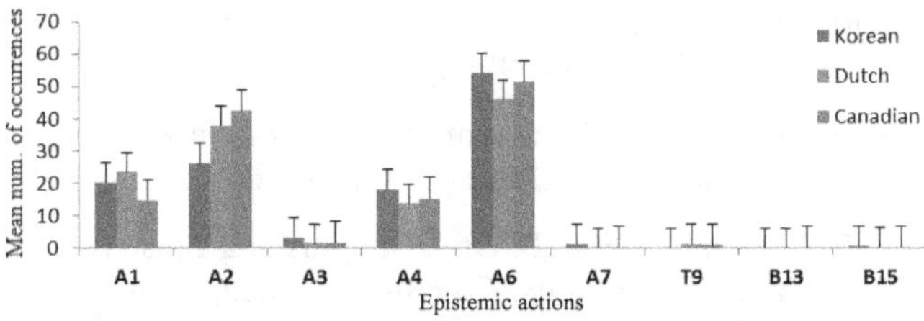

Figure 6. Mean number of individual types of epistemic action (A2 groups actions from 2.1 to 2.5). Data clustered by country, standard deviation in bars.

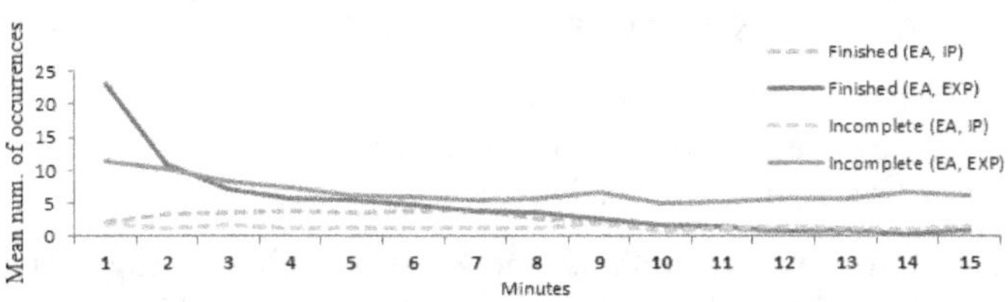

Figure 7. Running mean number of epistemic actions (EA, grouped by actions classified as IP or EXP). Overall data grouped by puzzle completion.

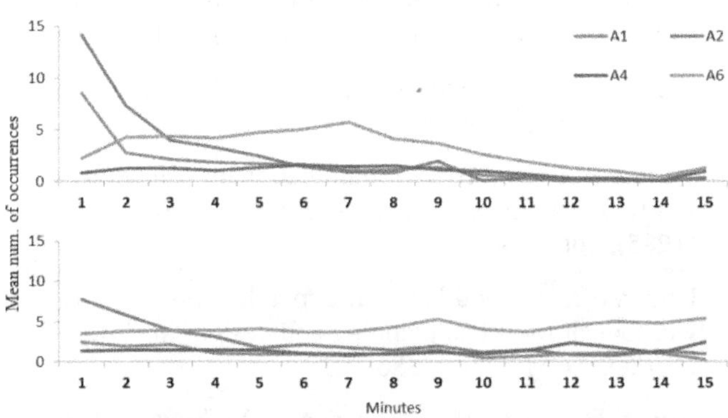

Figure 8. Running mean number of four types of epistemic action (A2 groups actions from 2.1 to 2.5). Data clustered by puzzle completion: finished (top) and incomplete (bottom).

actions relates, not simply to frequency of activity, but in knowing when specifically it is worth performing them.

We then examined this data at the level of individual epistemic action as performed over the entire experimental task. Figure 8 shows this data for the most common epistemic actions performed (Table 1: A1, A2, A4, and A6, accounting for 96.48% of all actions). A multiple regression revealed that the ocurrence of these actions in the first

Variable	*B*	*p*	*Beta*
Intercept	12.663	-	-
A1	-0.077	0.008	-0.378
A2	-0.104	0.001	-0.470
A4	0.139	0.645	0.058
A6	-0.101	0.393	-0.110

Table 3. Regression coefficients and *p* values of a multiple regression that successfully predicts the time it takes participants to finish the main puzzle by measuring how many EA (A1, A2, A4, and A6) occur in the first minute of the task.

minute of the task was a significant predictor of the time it took participants to complete the puzzle (adjusted R^2 = 0.232, F (4, 55) = 4.158, p = 0.005). Interestingly, not all of these variables added statistically significantly to the prediction (see Table 3). As such, we suggest the ATB framework was successful in identifying which epistemic actions are more relevant and helpful for the user in the context of the early stages of a puzzle task (A1 and A2), which were not particularly helpful (A6), and which had (non-significantly) detrimental effects on user performance (A4). These findings provide evidence that ATB framework is a useful tool that can highlight what kinds of epistemic work are suitable for what kinds of problem and, we argue, this kind of knowledge is valuable for the both the design and assessment of tangible systems.

FUTURE WORK AND CONCLUSIONS

This paper provides the basis for studies capturing granular data about epistemic activity. It does so by presenting and validating a novel framework that enables the measurement and detailed categorization of epistemic actions. Not only did the presented study test methodological aspects of the framework, it also took concrete steps towards developing evaluation metrics specifically targeted towards user experience in tangible systems. Limitations of this work include that, while it presents a study that looks at a substantial and diverse group of participants, it focuses on a single spatial task. While the framework was informed by epistemic actions collected from various fields, and thus should be applicable to most problems with physical properties, the most pressing future work lies on applying the framework to additional problem-solving tasks. This work will allow us to reinforce, extend and generalize the findings currently presented. These include understanding the importance of actions A1 (*Manipulation of an artifact*) and A2 (*Spatial arrangement of artifacts in relation to one another, the task environment, or the users*) in other spatial problems and developing knowledge about which epistemic actions are relevant for non-spatial, problem-solving tasks. These understandings will ultimately lead to design guidelines specific to tangible interaction, allowing for the development of new interactive systems that support not only goal-directed, pragmatic actions, but epistemic strategies that enable users to apply natural, real-world knowledge to interaction with digital information.

ACKNOWLEDGEMENTS

This research was supported by: the Portuguese Foundation of Science and Technology (FCT, SFRH/BD70203/2010); the SSHRC and GRAND NCE (Canada); and the Basic Science Research Program through the National Research Foundation of Korea (NRF), funded by the Ministry of Science, ICT and Future Planning (2014R1A1A1002223).

REFERENCES

1. Antle, A. N. Exploring how children use their hands to think: an embodied interactional analysis. *Behaviour & Information Technology* (2012).
2. Antle, A. N. and Wang, S. Comparing motor-cognitive strategies for spatial problem solving with tangible and multi-touch interfaces. In *Procs of TEI'13*, ACM, 65-72.
3. Clark, A. *Being There: Putting Brain, Body, and World Together Again*. MIT Press, 1998.
4. Ekstrom, R. B., French, J. W., Harman, H. H. and Dermen, D. *Manual for Kit of Factor-Referenced Cognitive Tests*. Educational Testing Service, 1976.
5. Esteves, A., Bakker, S., Antle, A. N., May, A., Warren, J. and Oakley, I. Classifying physical strategies in tangible tasks: a video-coding framework for epistemic actions. In *Extended Abs. of CHI'14*, ACM, 1843-1848.
6. Esteves, A., Hoven, E. v. d. and Oakley, I. Physical games or digital games?: comparing support for mental projection in tangible and virtual representations of a problem-solving task. In *Procs of TEI'13*, ACM (2013).
7. Hart, S. G. and Staveland, L. E. Development of NASA-TLX (Task Load Index): Results of Empirical and Theoretical Research. In A. H. Peter and M. Najmedin (eds.) *Advances in Psychology*, *52*, (1988), 139-183.
8. Horn, M. S. and Jacob, R. J. K. Tangible programming in the classroom with tern. In *Extended Abs. of CHI'07*, ACM (2007), 1965-1970.
9. Hornbæk, K. and Law, E. L.-C. Meta-analysis of correlations among usability measures. In *Procs of CHI'07*, ACM (2007), 617-626.
10. Hornecker, E. and Buur, J. Getting a grip on tangible interaction: a framework on physical space and social interaction. In *Procs of CHI'06*, ACM (2006), 437-446.
11. Hyde, J. S. How large are cognitive gender differences? A meta-analysis using !w² and d. *American Psychologist*, *36*, 8 (1981), 892-901.
12. Jacob, R. J. K., Girouard, A., Hirshfield, L. M., Horn, M. S., Shaer, O., Solovey, E. T. and Zigelbaum, J. Reality-based interaction: a framework for post-WIMP interfaces. In *Procs of CHI'08*, ACM (2008), 201-210.
13. Jacob, R. J. K., Ishii, H., Pangaro, G. and Patten, J. A tangible interface for organizing information using a grid. In *Procs of CHI'02*, ACM (2002), 339-346.
14. Jordà, S., Geiger, G., Alonso, M. and Kaltenbrunner, M. The reacTable: exploring the synergy between live music performance and tabletop tangible interfaces. In *Procs of TEI'07*, ACM (2007), 139-146.
15. Kirsh, D. Adapting the Environment Instead of Oneself. *Adaptive Behavior*, *4*, 3/4 (1996), 415-452.
16. Kirsh, D. Complementary strategies: Why we use our hands when we think. In *Procs of CogSci'85*, 212-217.
17. Kirsh, D. Distributed Cognition, Coordination and Environment Design. In *Procs of EuroCog'99*, 1-11.
18. Kirsh, D. The intelligent use of space. *Artificial Intelligence*, *73*, 1-2 (1995), 31-68.
19. Kirsh, D. Interactivity and multimedia interfaces. *Instructional Science*, *25*, 2 (1997), 79-96.
20. Kirsh, D. and Maglio, P. On Distinguishing Epistemic from Pragmatic Actions. *Cognitive Science*, *18*, 4 (1994), 513–549.
21. Klemmer, S. R., Hartmann, B. and Takayama, L. How bodies matter: five themes for interaction design. In *Procs of DIS'06*, ACM (2006), 140-149.
22. MacKay, W. E. Is paper safer? The role of paper flight strips in air traffic control. *ACM Trans. Comput.-Hum. Interact.*, *6*, 4 (1999), 311-340.
23. Merrill, D., Kalanithi, J. and Maes, P. Siftables: towards sensor network user interfaces. In *Procs of TEI'07*, ACM (2007), 75-78.
24. Shaer, O. and Hornecker, E. Tangible User Interfaces: Past, Present, and Future Directions. *Foundations and Trends in Human-Computer Interaction*, *3*, 1-137.
25. Shapiro, L. *Embodied Cognition (New Problems of Philosophy)*. Routledge, 2011.
26. Tarjan, R. E. Amortized Computational Complexity. *SIAM. J. on Algebraic and Discrete Methods*, *6*, 2 (1985), 306-318.
27. Underkoffler, J. and Ishii, H. Urp: a luminous-tangible workbench for urban planning and design. In *Procs of CHI'99*, ACM (1999), 386-393.
28. Voyer, D., Voyer, S. and Bryden, P. M. Magnitude of sex differences in spatial abilities: A meta-analysis and consideration of critical variables. *Psychological Bulletin*, *117*, 2 (1995), 250-270.
29. Wilson, M. Six views of embodied cognition. *Psychonomic Bulletin & Review*, *9*, 4 (2002).
30. Zaman, B., Abeele, V. V., Markopoulos, P. and Marshall, P. Editorial: the evolving field of tangible interaction for children: the challenge of empirical validation. *Personal Ubi. Comput.*, *16*, 4, 367-378.

Seven Principles to Design for Embodied Sensemaking

Caroline Hummels
DQI group, Department of Industrial Design,
Eindhoven University of Technology
P.O.Box 513, 5600 MB Eindhoven, Netherlands
c.c.m.hummels@tue.nl

Jelle van Dijk
Technology and Innovation, Utrecht Univ. of
Appl. Sciences & Dep. of Industrial Design, TU/e
P.O.Box 182, 3500 AD Utrecht, the Netherlands
jelle.vandijk@hu.nl

ABSTRACT
The TEI-community is based a various paradigms. We believe that the community matures by scrutinising these different paradigms and unravelling the consequences for designing for tangible, embedded and embodied interaction. In this paper we explore the consequences and possibilities of phenomenology-inspired embodied theory, and more specifically the concept of embodied sensemaking, i.e. human sensemaking using sensorimotor couplings to support social coordination between people. Based on our theoretical setting, we introduce seven design principles for developing face-to-face embodied sensemaking technology. We show in this paper how we used these principles to develop a mobile design and sensemaking studio for the encounter between two persons to sketch a future at the cross-section of their disciplines. By explaining these principles, we aim to show what embodied theory can bring the TEI-community, and invite others to do the same.

Author Keywords
Sensemaking; embodiment; social coordination; tangible interaction; communication; design process

ACM Classification Keywords
H.5.2. User Interfaces: Theory and methods.

INTRODUCTION
The TEI conference and community originated at the cross-section of different disciplines such as HCI, the arts, design and engineering, with the aim to develop the field by bringing viewpoints together at an equal level and by creating an atmosphere of experiencing, informing, reflecting and inspiring [16]. As we discussed in our paper 'Radical Clashes" [35] these differences in disciplines and viewpoint relate to different paradigms within the TEI community, which result in different designs for interaction. For example, Ishii et al.'s vision of Radical Atoms [20] is a representative of what we loosely call a Cartesian computer science and engineering-based way of thinking, and could not have been the result of a phenomenology-inspired design way of thinking [35]. Since we consider a multiplicity of perspectives to be desirable, we believe that the TEI community requires scrutinising different paradigms and unravelling the consequences for tangible, embedded and embodied interaction, in order to learn from each other and bring the field forward.

TEI '15, January 15 - 19 2015, Stanford, CA, USA

ACM 978-1-4503-3305-4/15/01...$15.00
http://dx.doi.org/10.1145/2677199.2680577

In this paper we describe our design process in which we explore the consequences of phenomenology-inspired embodied theory, and more specifically the concept of embodied sensemaking, for the design of a tangible mobile design and sensemaking studio (D&S studio). We will first explain our theoretical underpinning and the concept of embodied sensemaking. Thereupon, we introduce the context of the design project. In the remaining part of this paper we describe seven design principles for developing face-to-face embodied sensemaking technology, and how we applied these into our own design.

EMBODIED SENSEMAKING
Our work is inspired by phenomenology, embodied cognition and the ecological theory of perception, which all take the body-in-action as a starting point and which do not make the Cartesian mind-body division [9]. Merleau-Ponty considered 'embodiment' and 'skilful coping' to be unique characteristics of man; that is, we are able to engage with the world and develop skills while acting in the world. We perceive the world in terms of what we can do with it, and by physically interacting with it we access and express this meaning. *"The meaning of things ... exist[s] neither 'inside' our minds nor in the world itself, but in the space between us and the world, in the interaction"* [24, p.33]. To cope skilfully in the world from day to day, we do not need a mental representation of the world itself; our body is simply solicited by the situation to find the right balance so as to gain a maximum grip on the situation [7, 25]. When looking at cognition from a body-in-action perspective, it can be described as a coordination achieved through a self-organizing network of elements [1]. This network includes not only our brain, but also our body and the dynamic relationships between our body and the physical- and social environment [1, 4, 10] (figure 1). So, our cognitive system consists of the brain, the body and the environment [36].

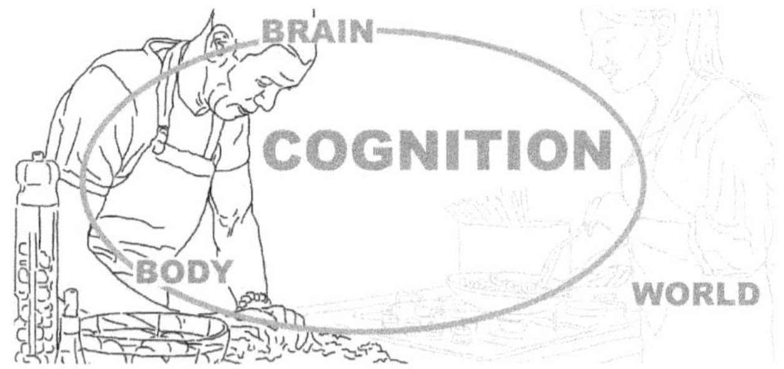

Figure 1: From an embodied cognition perspective, cognition is seen as an emergent property of interactions between brain, body and the physical- and social environment.

We start from an embodied perspective on sensemaking, in which there is an ongoing sensorimotor coupling in a social situation. Embodied sensemaking is closely connected to De Jaegher and Di Paolo's concept of participatory sensemaking [5]. They see participatory sensemaking as a shared process grounded in ongoing embodied and situated interactions in a shared action space, instead of exchanging messages originating in one 'mind' and received and interpreted by another. It relies on a process of social coordination, in line with Suchman's Situated Cognition theory, referring to the way people, embedded in a socio-cultural situation, continuously coordinate their own actions in relation to those of others [29, 36].

Before we describe the implications of embodied sensemaking for tangible/embodied interaction, let us first introduce the context and focus of our design project Engaging Encounters: sketching our future together.

ENGAGING ENCOUNTERS

Over the years we have noticed the difficulty of communication between people from different backgrounds and paradigms, e.g. people from industry, governance or research. Also within the TEI community we sometimes feel this tension, but we also experience the pleasant willingness to communicate, understand and learn from each other. Having the luxurious prospect of a sabbatical, the first author decided to use this time to travel around the world and help bridging communication gaps between her design research world and colleagues and people from other backgrounds, which resulted in the project 'Engaging Encounters: sketching our future together':

The aim of the project is to visit 50 inspirators around the world, including politicians, researchers, people from industry and NGOs, designers and artists, and envision with them what our future can be at the cross-section of their expertise and design (my expertise). By sketching this future together and creating a joined vision, I aim at bridging our worlds in action. Through this encounter, I like to show examples of the phenomenology-inspired work from our DQI group (dep. of Industrial Design, TU Eindhoven) and other design work; I like to inspire the inspirators by revealing what design could bring and vice versa get inspired by them; and I like introduce to them to the ideas and vision of the other inspirators. This way I hope all participants get new insights and can grow, which might even create potential ground for further collaboration. Moreover, I hope that the overall result, documented in a blog, book and a movie, will inspire others in their work and perspective on the world.

Since our work is based on phenomenology-inspired embodied theory, we want to develop a mobile design and sensemaking studio that facilitates these encounters from an embodied sensemaking perspective. In the remaining part of this paper we describe our design process and explain the consequences of starting from this perspective, captured in seven design principles.

IMPLICATIONS FOR TANGIBLE AND EMBODIED INTERACTION

Van Dijk and Mitchell [37] showed the relation between a Cartesian perspective on tangible interaction and a sensemaking perspective, which we updated in Figure 2. The left side of the picture shows the Cartesian perspective where the mind and the body are divided, so where mental processes in the virtual world of information are divided from mechanical movements in physical space. One could say that the field of computer science originally targets at the upper part (supporting cognitive tasks) and the field of industrial design in the lower part of the figure (supporting physical tasks). Tangible interaction was once introduced as the new, mixed discipline, integrating the physical with the digital [15]. But it feels to us that tangible interaction is bridging the two aspects by mapping the digital to the physical, while not really resolving the split [37]. We see for example the approach in which tangible objects are used to access digital information, by representing digital forms [19]. And we see the approach in which tangible objects are digitally 'augmented' for example to learn a physical skill [27]. In both types, however, we feel that the theoretical split between mind and body, mental and physical, remains.

As a consequence, we do not use Ishii's take on TUI: *"the key idea of TUIs is to give physical forms to digital information. The physical forms serve as both representations and controls for their digital counterparts."* [19, p. xvi]. We start the other way around by saying that there is value in interacting with our environment, or as Klemmer et al. state:

"Clearly, the digital world can provide advantages. To temper that, we argue that because there is so much benefit in the physical world, we should take great care before unreflectively replacing it. More precisely, from a design perspective, solutions that carefully integrate the physical and digital worlds — leaving the physical world alone to the extent possible — are likely to be more successful by admitting the improvisations of practice that the physical world offers." [22]

The perspective we use at the right side of the figure, 'opens up' the mind-body split to reveal a new design space

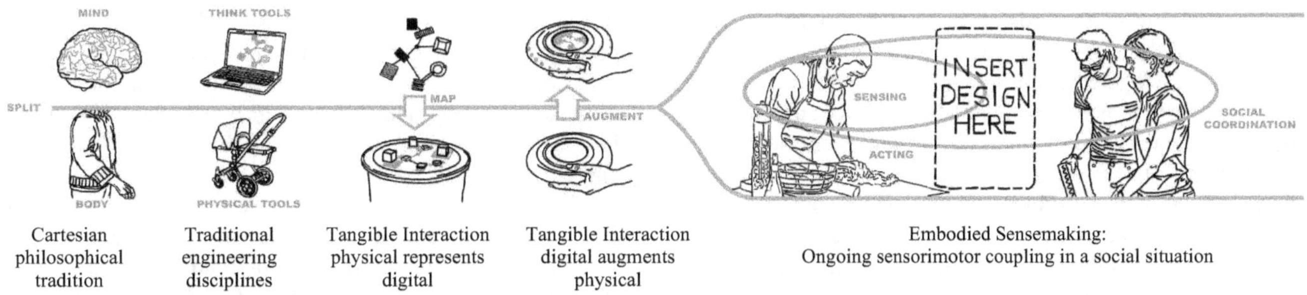

Figure 2. Tangible interaction within the Cartesian tradition (left side of picture) and on the basis of an Embodied perspective (right side of picture). Further details in text.

grounded in our embodied being-in-the-world [37]. To make this practically applicable for design is no easy task. One of the strengths of the information processing perspective has always been that tasks and actions of both human and machine could be represented in a model by breaking up the complexity into component parts and -processes. Consequently, they are often communicated more easily, and transformed into design guidelines in a rather straightforward manner. The blurriness on the right-hand side of our picture is inherent in the way a product will figure in embodied couplings. Couplings contain physical, social, sensory and action aspects, and they all form part of the self-organizing dynamic that creates the coupling. We 'address' this holistic process by introducing our principles as design scaffolds: they may help the designer to keep switching perspective and look at the design from a multitude of angles, precisely in order to deal with the complexity of the challenge without reducing it. In all, each principle is one way of looking at the whole of the socially situated, embodied process of coupling.

The Engaging Encounters project uses interactive technologies to create a new space for embodied sensemaking between the inspirator and the host (the first author) defined by the seven design principles. Based on the concept of social coordination, we therefore situate our new to-be-designed studio/platform in the actual, embodied space, supporting also nonverbal communication and social coordination in action, and focusing less on 'message passing' over a communication channel [36]. Through designing our D&S studio we explore new roles for digital processes as an element in the larger process of meaning generation, sustained by the embodied engagements of a person with her social/ physical environment at large. What can digital computing bring embodied sensemaking [35]?

THE SETTING

The host (1st author) will visit inspirators around the world and sketch with them possible futures, setting the following boundaries for our D&S studio, which should:

- facilitate the social coordination process between the host and inspirator and support them to inspire each other, explore common ground and sketch possible futures.
- support the inspiration and communication process beyond the specific encounters, towards other people.
- adjust to the social situation at hand (e.g. the environment is it used in, the existing conventions within the inspirator's world).
- be transportable, preferably as hand luggage in an aeroplane, and easy to set-up upon arrival.

Based on these criteria we formulated seven design principles for developing face-to-face embodied sensemaking technology as we will discuss in the remaining part of this paper.

SEVEN DESIGN PRINCIPLES FOR FACE-TO-FACE EMBODIED SENSEMAKING TECHNOLOGY

1. *Social situatedness*

From a socially situated practice perspective [29], cognition is seen as an on-going achievement of social coordination in a setting, which includes e.g. social interrelations, roles, norms, culture and politics. Stressing the importance of social situatedness, all encounters take (in principle) place in the environment that is valuable for the inspirator (his/her home, workplace, …), which requires a mobile D&S studio that can be used in situ. However, the D&S studio might stimulate behaviour that is not entirely common for the setting. As the majority of inspirators will be CEOs, senior researchers, ministers and majors (white collar jobs) we developed the D&S studio that is able to seduce the inspirators to doing as well as talking, in a way that fits of the expected environments such as offices, design studios and homes.

In order to blend into the environment, our D&S studio *"should not be "an object that I interact with, but the ground upon which the possibility of interaction is based"* [18], similar to the way a spider uses his web [8]. We take a physical stage as 'our web' in the encounter, which invites participants to sketch their envisioned future together using all kind of materials and objects, including the ones present at the inspirator's environment. The stage can be easily adjusted to the situation at hand. The stage is a wooden suitcase that can be transformed into a standing table with telescopic legs. At first we developed a horizontal stage with screens at the back (see figure 3, top). This set-up turned the attention towards the screens and away from each other and the stage. Thereafter we developed a smaller curved-shaped stage to enable people to sit/stand either on one side or on opposite sides, and through its curved form affords to keep the focus point at the centre of the stage (see figure 3, middle). After experimentation, we fine-tuned this design again and are now building a foldable standing table with a small suitcase as table top, offering a variety of tools. The table stimulates the participants to walk around and use the entire environment (social situation) at hand. Moreover, the stage and the accompanying tools embed sensors that track the behaviour of the participants, which help us afterwards to analyse how the D&S studio was used in the different social situations, thus giving us insights for further refinement of the D&S studio.

Figure 3: Explorations of the stage design. After trying out the first prototypes (top left), the design moved towards a curved-shaped desktop (top right) and a standing table with with a top of veneer (bottom left). We are currently building the final table with storage in the top (inspired by Naoki Hirakoso's storage table (http://dornob.com/100-storage-wooden-table-made-up-of-secret-spaces/)).

2. Scaffolds

Andy Clark [4] introduced the concept of 'cognitive scaffolds', in reference to Vygotsky's theory of *scaffolded* learning [38], by which Clark meant tools and ad hoc recruited props in the environment that enable people to solve problems in ways that would have been much more difficult using purely brain-internal computation [4, 34]. We prefer to take the Socially Situated Practice perspective, in which a scaffold gets meaning in the social context of a situated practice [29]. For example, in creativity sessions where people draw sketches and write down text on sticky notes, these sticky notes are used as scaffolds to enable creative thought and create shared insight between the participants during their conversation. So they mediate collaborative sensemaking between people and function as a guide towards interactive couplings between the various participants and the emerging idea in situ [14, 23, 29, 34].

As can be seen in figure 3, our D&S studio uses a stage for scaffolding, using e.g. prototypes, materials, cards, sketches, keywords, articles, booklets, movies and websites. Moreover, we developed a so-called Ideating in Skills toolset, a set of tangible interactive objects that trigger skill-based interaction. They can be used to explore scenarios in a physical way by acting them out, while being inspired by the interaction possibilities of the objects and their connections (see figure 4 top). Moreover, to stress the physical invitation of scaffolds, we discarded our initial idea to use screens at a fixed place of the stage, but instead introduced separate screens (iPods/iPads) that can be used as scaffolds similar to other scaffolds, see figure 4 bottom.

Figure 4: The Ideating in Skill set stimulates to exploit sensorimotor skills during the design process (top). Digital information is accessed via separate physical scaffolds (iPods/iPads, bottom) instead of fixed screens (middle).

We offer a set of screens in order to access websites and digital content easily. For practical reasons we now use iPods and Ipads and since the number is limited, we have now developed various ways to bring the digital scaffolds to the stage. Firstly, we developed a database to store digital content related to the encounters. This way the participants can bring along digital information to the encounter (e.g. movies and photos of designs) and collected material during the encounter can be stored (e.g. websites or photos/videos made during the encounter), see figure 5.

Next, we make use of small RFID stickers to easily retrieve digital content via physical scaffolds. The stickers can be attached to any object (cards, prototypes, materials, papers etc), thus retracing digital material easily when needed, by scanning the scaffold. Moreover, we make use of a small handheld printer (LG pocket photo printer), so we can print small photos (2x3 inch) of the collected material during the encounter and connect it to any digital material through a RFID sticker if preferred.

We realise that our digital solutions are rather pragmatic, since the D&Sstudio has to up and running before 2015, be fully stable to run for well over a year, and it has to be affordable using off-the-shelf materials. Despite the fact

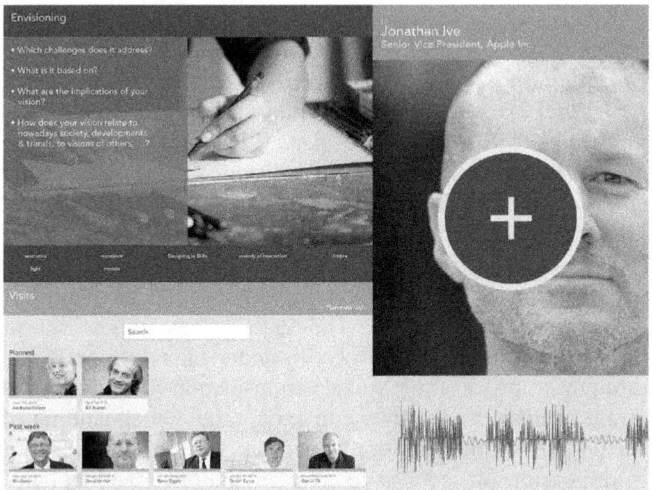

Figure 5: Top left: database of which every digital file can also be displayed full screen. Bottom left: All information is automatically connected to the encounters it is used in. Right: audio recordings are made during every encounter and connected (time stamped) to the RFID-tagged objects.

that the design is based on sensorimotor couplings as well as social coordination, the merger of the digital and the physical world is far from ideal in our current design. Consequently, we will continue developing the D&S studio the upcoming years, to explore the full potential of TEI and build some of our ideas, see Figure 6.

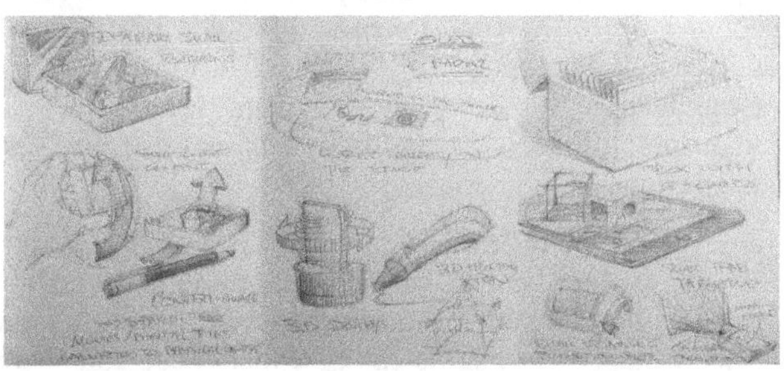

Figure 6: Initial ideas to merge the physical with the digital: Using context-aware small screens to pick of digital context related to the social situation at hand (left), using a stage with a top of OLED or ePaper (middle), experiment with various forms of 3D or augmented displays (middle and right), and using 3D printers and pens to create objects quickly (middle).

3. Traces

As said, objects and notes can be used as scaffolds, for example to enable creative thought and determine shared insight between the participants during the encounter. The selected objects, the photos and scribbles made, and their relative position in space form the traces of the conversation and can come again the 'scaffolding' elements further on in the conversation. We are inspired by the biological phenomenon called stigmergy [30] when referring to traces. "*Stigmergy describes how animals leave physical markers in the environment as a natural consequence of their actions, upon which these same markers come to play a crucial role in the further coordination of the very same behaviors that produce them: ... the trail formed by an animal walking in the forest may at first be purely a by-effect of a goal- directed action (accidently breaking a leaf, flattening the grass in walking) and at the same time later on come to function as a coordinating, 'epistemic' structure for action (animals following the path formed by the broken leaves).*" So, one may say that stigmergic traces create 'physical history', without the need for internal memory of past events [34].

By offering a stage to place scaffolds, we stimulate the process of leaving traces. We realise that our approach to retrieving digital information via physical scaffolds can be seen as a Cartesian solution, where the physical scaffold is a representation of digital information. However it appears that 'scaffolding traces' such as scribbles on sticky notes are not simply external representations of insights stored into the artefact [see also 3, 13, 29], but they guide the way people interact with one another and make sense together. So, it is not so much the content of trace that determines the insight, but the fact that it enables "*a 'sense-making activity', i.e., a conversation between people, which in this case creates a meaningful connection between what one of the team- members had experienced at an earlier moment, and how this may then be understood as relevant for the group as a whole, in the present context. It is in that reflective activity that the shared insight is to be found, as an aspect of the conversation itself*" [34, p.134]. So, although the digital content like movies and websites is important to inspire the other person and stress specific ideas and content, it is at least as important to use the physical scaffold as a trace of the shared insight.

Next to the leaving traces with the scaffolds, we also capture an auditive trace (see figure 5), as we have done before in one of our tools called NOOT [36]. NOOT uses small physical tags with RFID that can be connected to time-points in a continuous audio-recording. The tags can be placed in the spatial setting, e.g. on a sticky-note, and by using a playback device the participants can revisit earlier moments in the conversation, thus stimulating the shared reflection process. In our current D&S studio one can use any RFID-enhanced object to time-stamp the audio-recording e.g. during insightful moments. These audio-recordings can be played back during as well as after the encounter, e.g. when the host summarises the insights and sketched future for others (captured e.g. in a book, movie or blog). Moreover, the time-stamped parts of the audio-recordings can be used during new encounters with other inspirators. Next to the audio-recordings, we have sensors-recordings of the interaction with the table and the objects, e.g. how do people interact with it for how long?

Finally, after every encounter, the inspirator gets a trace of the session, existing of 1) photos of the encounter, 2) a box with cards related to the scaffolds used during the encounter, and 3) an URL to the digital database of the encounter, including the audio recording. This way the inspirators get scaffolds that they can use to show and discuss their envisioned future with their colleagues.

4. Interactive Imagery

According to Suchman [29] people act within the concrete circumstances of their environment and in doing so, their plans evolve in an improvised manner, instead of executing an internally created 'plan for action'. Given the task at hand, i.e. sketching a possible future at the cross-section of disciplines, our D&S studio needs to enhance this improvised exploration of a possible future. Next to using the concept of scaffolds in our platform, we make use of interactive imagery. Goldschmidt [11] introduced this concept in the realm of sketching (with paper and pen), but we consider it to be useful for any type of sketching, also sketching with scaffolds such as the Ideating in Skills set. Interactive imagery indicates that percepts arising from sketches can facilitate and amplify imagery. When interacting with pencil and paper and leaving traces behind on the paper with a beautiful ambiguity, the flow of thoughts can be stimulated. Or as Leonardo da Vinci *pointed out, "confused things rouse the mind to new inventions"* [12] and with these confused things he referred to the ambiguous character of sketches.

Consequently, our D&S studio stimulates ambiguity, openness and confusion in order to trigger imagination, storytelling and inviting people to 'sketch' a future. The ambiguity and openness stimulate people in their sensemaking process. The design of the tool supports this fleeting emergence of insight. We offer this in several ways. Firstly, we value the physicality as is, and do not try to digitally capture everything or refine the content. For example, we offer a box with materials, objects (the Ideating in Skills toolset) and snippets of white paper with pencils, to make scenarios with the objects, and add hand-written cards that give a personal character to the trace. Moreover, the collage of scaffolds, i.e. the traces of the overall encounter, is not a finished story. It is insightful for the participants but these insights cannot be transferred to others by simply showing the traces. Finally, the D&S studio offers different sets of Inspiration and Assessment (IA) cards. Each set consist of hundred small visually attractive cards (slightly smaller than credit cards), divided in different categories, such as people, products, consumables, environments, and abstract images [17], to trigger ones imagination.

5. Dialogical system

The engaging encounter revolve all around communication. Coming from an Embodied Cognition perspective "*communication [. . .] is not the transmission of information but rather the co-ordination of behaviour between living organisms through mutual structural coupling* [2, p. 46]. Coming from the world of linguistics, Steffensen [28] proposes a theory of dialogical systems, i.e. *"systems of co-present human beings engaged in interactivity that bring forth situated behavioural coordination (or a communicative, structural coupling). [...] The participants in the dialogical system act face-to-face: they co-ordinate with each other, they co-adapt to each other, and they co-regulate their co-ordination and co-adaptation."* Also Sennett [26] introduces the concept of dialogic conversations, in which the discussion does not resolve itself by finding common ground or synthesis, but where curiosity sustains the cooperation and exchange of ideas based on empathy. The listener has to get out of his/her own perspective trying to understand the other, and through a process of social coordination become more aware of his/her own view and expand the understanding of each other and the situation. According to Steffensen [28] it is important for people to stay in dialogue and balance dialogical engagement and individual integrity, thus maintaining a multi-stable dialogical system.

Consequently, the platform is designed as a studio in which people can create and discuss in a face-to-face process, instead of only talking or transferring information e.g. via mail or webpages. It aims at triggering Sennett's curiosity actively, tempting people to get out of ones comfort zone without loosing ones individual integrity, by offering a dedicated stage with scaffolds that can act as a trusted and safe environment to explore a potential future. This aspect of trust and safety starts already from the first moment of connection. So, from the first physical invitation for the encounter up to the final token of gratitude (the box with collected scaffolds), all designs and means of communication are designed to breath respect, care and preciousness by showing craftsmanship and eye for details in the designs and materials used (see figure 3).

Moreover, Sennett [26] indicates that sustained cooperation has been reached since ancient times through workshops. Consequently, we developed our D&S platform as a studio and workshop, where skills can be experienced and shared, and ideas can be explored. The D&S studio will consist of tools, such as Ideating in Skills and Engagement Catalysers [33] and the host invites the inspirators to bring along their tools, so they can both actively learn from each other.

6. 1st person perspective

Merleau-Ponty [25] showed that we do not perceive ourselves as one more object in the world; we perceive ourselves as the point of view from which we perceive objects in the world [32]. Consequently, we take a first-person perspective towards designing and towards our D&S studio. Drew and Heritage [6] indicate that specific patterns in social systems influence the dialogical system. Consequently, interactional patterns in the dialogical system differ for example between intimate and more formalized social systems. So, a person will most likely communicate differently in an intimate setting with friends and family than in a formalized setting with colleagues and clients. Although the role of the inspirator is an important reason for meeting the person in the first place, it are his/her actual experience, point of view, skills, unspoken ideas and dreams etc. that brings the encounter and envisioned future beyond convention and obvious results. So, how to create engagement, empathy and maybe even intimacy?

In our previous research we have seen that exploiting bodily skills in a co-design process has a positively influence on engagement and cooperation. Bodily involvement of participants, e.g. by using bodystorms, tinkering sessions or choreographies of interaction during workshops, seem to elicit a direct engagement and a (pro)active, empathic and responsible attitude propelled by personal experiences. Bodily engagement seems to push participants away from the abstract towards concrete ideas. Moreover, bodily encounters seem to lower the threshold to merge the perspectives from people with different backgrounds [21, 31].

Consequently, the D&S studio facilitates physical encounters based on bodily skills, e.g. though scaffolds on the physical and socially situated stage, and through workshops by exploring each other's tools and techniques.

7. Catalysing engagement

Exploiting bodily skills in a co-design process positively influence engagement and cooperation, which again is a reason for stressing the validity of taking a body-in-action perspective for TEI. This stimulated us a few years ago, to design tools to boost engagement at the beginning of multi-stakeholder design processes. These so-called Engagement Catalysers (ECs) are open tools without a predefined goal that serve as a means to physically connect strangers, and thus enhance engagement, empathy and respect.

We used our ECs in several workshops, in which the tools helped hundreds of participants from very different cultural and professional background, to get familiar and connected in a short period of time, and to inspire the design process [33]. The Catalysers have effect on the physical / emotional connection between people while drawing upon aspects such as surprise, fascination, amusement and admiration.

Consequently, the D&S studio consists of an EC especially developed for this setting with two persons. In order to get the host and the inspirator as quickly as possible engaged and working at an empathic level, every encounter starts with a brief introduction session using a variation of the EC "We feel like talking", see figure 7. The participants physically interact through a sheet, while discussing which values drives them in their work and life.

CONCLUSION

In this paper, we have shown the design of a mobile design and sensemaking studio, through which we explore the consequences of phenomenology-inspired embodied theory. When designing face-to-face embodied sensemaking technology, we see seven design principles that can help the TEI community to apply phenomenology-inspired embodied theory into practice: social situatedness, scaffolds, traces, interactive imagery, dialogical system, 1st person perspective and catalysing engagement. All the principles are based on eliciting sensorimotor couplings in order to support social coordination between participants. We are currently finalizing the development and first tests of our D&S studio, which has incorporated all seven design principles. As of January 2015, the first author will travel around the world with this studio, to envision and sketch a possible future at the cross-section of the disciplines of the host and the inspirator. That is also the moment that the proof of the pudding will be really in the eating, starting with several encounters at the TEI'15 conference. We hope that these encounters will help to explore the existing paradigms in the TEI community, and explore together the future of tangible, embedded and embodied interaction.

Figure 7: "We feel like talking' makes use of little magnets connected to the fingers, through which two people can feel each other, but not see each other due to a aluminum sheet in between (top, designed by Master students Chris Gruijters, Janne van Kollenburg and Kevin Andersen).

REFERENCES

1. Beer, R.D. (2008). Dynamical systems and embedded cognition. In: K. Frankish and W. Ramsey (Eds.), *The Cambridge Handbook of Artificial Intelligence*. Cambridge: University Press.
2. Capra, F. (2002). *The Hidden Connections. A Science for Sustainable Living.* Harper Collins, London.
3. Clancey, W. J. (1997). *Situated cognition : On human knowledge and computer representation.* Cambridge, MA: Cambridge University Press.
4. Clark, A. (1997). *Being there: Putting brain, body and world together again*. Cambridge, MA: MIT Press
5. De Jaegher, H. and Di Paolo, E. (2007). Participatory sense-making: An enactive approach to social cognition. *Phenomenology and the Cognitive Sciences*, 6(4), 485-507.
6. Drew, P. and Heritage, J. (1992). *Talk at Work: Interaction in Institutional Settings*. Cambridge University Press, Cambridge.
7. Dreyfus, H. (1996). The Current Relevance of Merleau-Ponty's Phenomenology of Embodiment. In Haber and Weiss (eds), *Perspectives on Embodiment*. London: Routledge.

8. Dreyfus, H.L. (2002). Intelligence without representation: Merleau-ponty's critique of mental representation. *Phenomenology and the Cognitive Sciences*, 1, 367-83

9. Dreyfus, H. Wrathall, M., Kelly, S., Carman, T., Haugeland, J., Thomson, I., Taylor, C. and Borgmann, A. (2010). *Being in the world.* In a film by Tao Ruspoli. Mangusta Productions.

10. Gibson, J.J. (1979) *The ecological approach to visual perception.* London: Lawrence Erlbaum (reprinted in 1986).

11. Goldschmidt, G. (1991). The dialects of sketching. *Creativity Research Journal*, 4 (2), 123 – 143.

12. Gombrich, E.H. (1966). Leonardo's method for working out compositions. *Norm and form: studies in the art of the Renaissance.* Oxford: Phaidon Press.

13. Goodwin (2000). Action and embodiment within situated human interaction. *Journal of pragmatics*, 32, 1489-1522.

14. Goodwin, C. (2003). The semiotic body in its environment. In: Coupland & Gwyn (Eds.), *Discourses of the Body*, 19-42. New York: Palgrave/Macmillan.

15. Hornecker, E. and Buur, J. (2006). Getting a grip on tangible interaction: a framework on physical space and social interaction. *Proc. of Human Factors in Comput. Sys. '06,* Apr. 22-27, 437-446, New York: ACM.

16. Hornecker, E., Jacob, R., Hummels, C., Ullmer, B., Schmidt, A., Hoven, van den E. and Mazalek, A. (2008). TEI Goes On: Tangible and Embedded Interaction. In: D. Hong (Ed.). *IEEE Pervasive Computing*, 7 (2), 91-96

17. Hummels, C.C.M (2004). Educating interaction, experience and diversity. In: The changing face of design education; *Proceedings of the 2nd IEPDE Conference* (Delft, NL, September 2-3), 247-254.

18. Ingold, T. (2008). When Ant Meets Spider. Social theory for arthropods. In: C. Knappett, L. Malafouris (eds.), *Material Agency*, 209-215.

19. Ishii, H. (2008). Tangible bits: beyond pixels. In *Proceedings of the 2nd int. TEI Conference* (Bonn, Germany, February 18 - 20). New York: ACM, xv-xxv.

20. Ishii, H., Lakatos, D., Bonanni, L. and Labrune, J.B. (2012) Radical Atoms: Beyond tangible bits, toward transformable materials. Interactions 19(1).

21. Jaasma, Ph., Trotto, A. and Hummels, C. (2014). Irresistible brushes or open stickies? Bodystorming vs. Brainstorming. In: *Proceedings of DRS'14* (Umeå, Sweden, June 15-19).

22. Klemmer, S.R., Hartman, B. and Takayama, L. (2008) How bodies matter: five themes for interaction design. *Proceedings of the 2nd int. TEI Conference* (Bonn, Germany, February 18 - 20). ACM, New York.

23. Lave, J., (1988). *Cognition in Practice. Mind, mathematics and culture in everyday life.* Cambridge University Press.

24. Matthews, E. (2006). *Merleau Ponty. A guide for the perplexed,* Continuum: London, UK.

25. Merleau-Ponty, M. (1962) *Phenomenology of Perception*, trans. Colin Smith. New York: Humanities Press.

26. Sennett, R. (2012). *Together. The rituals, pleasures and politics of cooperation.* London: Penguin Group

27. Solomon, C., Banerjee, A., Horn, M. (2014). Ultimate trainer: instructional feedback for ultimate frisbee players. *Proc TEI 2014.* ACM, New York, 137-140.

28. Steffensen, S.V. (2012). Care and conversing in dialogical systems. In: *Language Sciences*, http://dx.doi.org/10.1016/ j.langsci.2012.03.008

29. Suchman, L.A. (2007). *Human-Machine Reconfigurations: Plans and Situated Actions 2nd expanded edition.* New York and Cambridge UK: Cambridge University Press.

30. Theraulaz & Bonabeau (1999). A brief history of stigmergy. *Artificial Life*, 5, 97-116.

31. Trotto (2011). *Rights through Making.* Doctoral dissertation, Eindhoven University of Technology.

32. Trotto, A., Hummels, C. and Levy, P. (2012). Developing a Kansei design approach to cater for ethics. In: *Proceedings of KEER 2012 Conference* (Penghu, Taiwan, May 22 – 25).

33. Trotto, A. & Hummels, C.C.M. (2013). Engage me, do! Engagement Catalysers to ignite a (design) conversation. In: *Proc. of DPPI '13.* (Newcastle, September 3-5), 136-145.

34. Van Dijk, J. (2013). *Creating traces, sharing insight: explorations in embodied cognition design.* Doctoral dissertation. Eindhoven University of Technology.

35. Van Dijk, J., Mousette, C., Kuenen, C.D. & Hummels, C.C.M. (2013). Radical Clashes: What Tangible Interaction is Made of. In *Proceedings of the 7th Int. TEI'13 Conference.* New York, USA: ACM, 323-326.

36. Van Dijk, J., Van der Lugt, R. and Hummels, C. (2014a). Beyond distributed representation: embodied cognition design supporting socio-sensorimotor couplings. In: *Proceedings of the 8th Int. TEI'14 Conference.* New York, USA: ACM, 181-188

37. Van Dijk, J. & Mitchell, R. (2014b) Co-Embodied Technology: A Design space for Human Being. *TEI'14 WIP poster.*Vygotsky, L. S. (1956). *Thought and Language.* Cambridge (Mass): MIT Press

Escaping the Sandbox: Making and its Future

Tom Jenkins
Georgia Institute of Technology
Digital Media Program
Atlanta, GA, 30332, USA
tom.jenkins@gatech.edu

Ian Bogost
Georgia Institute of Technology
Digital Media Program
Atlanta, GA, 30332, USA
ian.bogost@lmc.gatech.edu

ABSTRACT
"Making" has been gaining traction in HCI and related fields both as a community of practice and as a method for creating objects and systems. While making is an important cultural practice, this paper claims that there is a disconnect between the rhetoric of making and "real world" notions of domain relevance and embedded hardware development. In considering how making operates in practice, we offer the metaphor of a sandbox to describe this contradiction. We exemplify the metaphor with a small-scale prototyping platform of our own, and offer visions on how making might progress in the future.

Author Keywords
Making; design; engineering; embedded hardware; prototyping platforms

ACM Classification Keywords
H.5.m. Information interfaces and presentation (e.g., HCI): Miscellaneous.

INTRODUCTION
Within many computing communities, "making" is offered as a means to provide deeper, richer learning experiences with computational materials or to help support initiatives around STEAM education [3,6,8]. Meanwhile, outside the academy, making has been amplified by the technology hype machine. The "maker movement" valorizes making for the sake of making, offering Make magazines, books on Making, and Maker Faires to spread the gospel of personal production to anyone who will listen [2].

The most common critique of the maker movement and its associated culture involves the accusation that it exhibits a cyberlibertarian ideology:

The maker movement is born out of, and contributes to, the individualistic, market-based society that has become dominant in our time. ... new technologies promise to create a class of high-tech entrepreneurs ... while allowing them to ignore or simply design their own way around the established political, economic and legal system [16].

TEI '15, January 15 - 19 2015, Stanford, CA, USA

ACM 978-1-4503-3305-4/15/01...$15.00
http://dx.doi.org/10.1145/2677199.2680558

It is a reasonable critique of maker culture, but also increasingly indistinguishable from a critique one could levy at all of technology culture today. Indeed, the cyber-libertarian ideology critique might cover over a more mundane but possibly more fundamental issue in maker culture, namely that it is *functionally hermetic* before it is *politically hermetic*. That is, even before making implicitly assumes the cyberlibertarian agenda, it isolates itself from the broader application domains from which it draws inspiration—electrical engineering, home automation, and even ordinary software development, for example.

To illustrate how making works, and what it does and doesn't do, this paper offers the metaphor of a sandbox describing the role of making as a part of broader modes of industrial production; it illustrates this metaphor with a project of our own, in progress; and finally, it offers visions of how the rhetoric of "making" might move forward.

MAKING IN HCI RESEARCH
Making, along with hacking and other DIY practices, has been making inroads among the HCI community in recent years. At CHI 2014, events were even held that modeled themselves after common maker culture practices: a workshop that was itself a hackathon [18]. The ambiguity inherent discussions about making was also reflected in a panel that discussed the ambiguity of making [1].

This current interest around making is rooted in previous work. Kuznetsov and Paulos [7] offered a survey of online fora that support different kinds of DIY communities, positioning the "expert amateur" as creating and supporting knowledge transfer and expertise among groups invested in various modes of creative practice. Rosner and Bean have covered IKEA hacking as a way to express individuality [15] and Rosner and Goodman have taken up other DIY practices like gardening and knitting [4], emphasizing in particular material practices that come alongside personal hand-work.

While we criticize making as a cultural construct in this paper, we don't seek to trivialize the work of those who are doing research with making communities. For example, Tanenbaum et al. [17] take making as a broad category of practice, including ad-hoc design and production as a response to natural disaster. Lindtner has been working on a series of projects focusing on hardware manufacturers that identify as makers in Shenzhen, China—particularly the cultural bridges between Western entrepreneurs looking to produce electronics there [10] as well as how these emerging communities understand themselves [9]. Those developing and supporting practices around makers and making are also conducting interesting, worthwhile work. Mellis and Beuchley emphasize the malleability of electronics and its ability to let novices create fully functional, personalized objects as a means of gaining a particular kind of media literacy [11,12,13].

While research in HCI concerned with making is growing, relatively little work attempts to unpack or describe what "making" is or how it operates. Critical making [5,14], deploys making as part of a method to interrogate cultural practices, but it doesn't concern itself with the nature of producing artifacts, but instead the knowledge that the experience of making produces.

It is not easy to discern what "making" might actually *be*. Both scholarly and popular writing on the topic describe such a broad range of activities as to defy being understood as a single practice. Sometimes it seems as if anyone who creates anything whatsoever could be construed as a "maker," and their practices as a kind of "making." It's a deft rhetorical strategy: by construing anything whatsoever as "making," its proponents gain substantial momentum.

The rhetorical cleverness of "making" notwithstanding, in this article we aim to take the concept at face value. We use this definition described in the introduction above to motivate the rest of our discussion.

THE SANDBOX CONFLICT

Think of the community that comprises the maker movement as a sandbox on a lawn. The sandbox is the domain of the makers, distinct from the lawn of "real-world" professional practice. Sand is great in a sandbox, but it only has use and value within the borders of that sandbox. Inside the sandbox, sand is a resource. Outside of it, sand is a nuisance. From the opposite perspective, sand on the lawn doesn't make the lawn a beach; it just kills the grass. Likewise, grass in the sandbox has no function other than as waste.

The Making Sandbox

This metaphor describes how hardware devices like Arduino, Raspberry Pi and other electronics platforms—systems for "making," relate to other kinds of practices. For example, the Raspberry Pi's founders see education as its primary goal. They describe their platform as a "tiny, cheap computer for kids" that was developed to counter a trend among novice computer science students who had little experience with the real material of computing—embedded electronics [19]. Whether or not the Raspberry Pi has been successful at popularizing embedded development, however, is debatable: for much of the device's life (and during the period when the most diverse communities wanted one), actually obtaining the hardware was nearly impossible, becoming a kind of a meta-activity in itself.

The rise of Processing, Wiring, and Arduino came at the same time (and to some extent, were built to service) as the rise of courses and then programs of study in art, design, culture, and computation at NYU, USC, Carnegie Mellon, Georgia Tech, and others. The devices found homes in these programs and then began to spread out into the world after students graduated and took those platforms to other venues in the art, design, and education communities. The primary success of these platforms is not in providing a deep understanding of electronics, but in creating a new ecosystem of tinkering activity—one separate from both electrical engineering and traditional arts practice.

It's no surprise, then, that there are fusions of making and everyday life. The Twine, for example, is a Wi-Fi-operated sensor-based monitoring device [20]. An example application for the Twine shows it placed it in a basement attached to a moisture sensor. It is programmed through a web-based tool, which sends you a text message if your basement floods. At a first glance, the Twine looks like a success for the everyday relevance of making. It is a finished product that has gone on to be sold and used—a proper hybrid of sand and lawn. But further inspection reveals that this isn't quite the case. The Twine is expensive (several hundred dollars with all the sensors), and as such its use as a piece of sensor hardware is at odds with its role as a tinkering platform one can use and reuse through web-based programming—particularly if it is also meant to be put to a permanent, single-purpose use as is suggested. Instead of becoming a disposable ubiquitous computing tool, it is a trinket to let a user to participate in a particular discourse of electronics startups and technological novelty.

Like the Processing programming environment from which it arose, Arduino also becomes a sandbox that creators tend not to leave once they've entered it. The sand can't easily be taken outside into the yard, partly because the tools themselves do not scaffold users to develop more sophisticated expertise with electronics, and partly because the Arduino community itself turns out to be a satisfactory, comfortable universe in which to conduct one's making.

On the one hand, we might praise devices like Twine and Arduino for creating their own ecosystems. But on the other hand, the development of those very ecosystems was always predicated on the promise of "graduating" into other communities—home DIY, or electronics manufacture, or even product development. The sandbox conflict turns these activities into private, rhetorical experiences with very little interest in the world outside the domain of their creation and support.

It's revealing to compare these computational examples of maker culture to other creative communities like knitting or woodworking. In such cases, we tend to find specialty infrastructures that facilitate and support them, like hardware stores and craft stores. They come with a clear understanding that the craft practice operates on the register of avocation and hobby *as well as* on the register of usable output. Here, the sandbox is viewed as a transitional object. It involves working with the actual materials that the broader world uses to accomplish goals, ratcheting up abilities with such materials, and eventually graduating into different levels of skill and professionalism. Of course, one can also knit or woodwork "for its own sake"—not all yarn must be rendered into sweaters, and knitters partake of their own communities for the sake of socialization as much as collaboration and support [7]. But the activity of knitting and woodworking is not *so completely* bound up with the latter type of activity that it entirely replaces the former.

Our Tiny Tinkering Platform

We've not just been thinking about the sandbox problem, but also we've tried to apply the hardware store metaphor to electronics tinkering platforms themselves, developing a small, inexpensive, and ubiquitous prototyping platform that can handle low-level varieties of input and output—creating basic sensing nodes. This "tiny tinkering platform" has a hypothetical target price of $1 per device (a constraint meant to help us avoid the expensive Twine scenario). We are focused on very low-cost, low-complexity hardware components, which have resulted in working prototypes that do things akin to the Twine and other devices but with far less capability out of the box. This approach to these sorts of systems assumes that a minimal, flexible, and very inexpensive platform could overcome obstacles around the price that broad experimentation requires, and might make permanent use in application-specific objects more viable.

In the process, we have been attempting to make design choices that would make our platform behave more like how we imagine a Twine would have to in order to acknowledge both the sand and the lawn sides of its life cycle—that is, not just to be talked about, but also to be used. Not just as a celebratory, "disruptive" lever in discourses about technology practice, but to be used so that it disappears into the background as infrastructure. While our project is a hybrid as well, we feel that tinkering with a platform should be straightforward, and solutions in the world should be simple and semi-permanent. Although we have experience in producing electronics as hobbyists and tinkerers, our inexperience with the architecture we have chosen has helped us to emphasize the difference between taking satisfaction in the creative practice itself (the sand) and taking satisfaction in the end product (the lawn).

MAKING IN PRACTICE

In order to get a sense of how our process has played out, we offer an overview of approximately two years of development of this simple remote sensing platform.

We started using the PIC10F200, a 6-pin microcontroller. In order to get around some of the missing functionality in this baseline part's lack of analog input, we produced a design using a potentiometer attached to its input pin to "tune" the attached analog sensor by adjusting its voltage. This let actuators to trip based on context. This worked but was not reliable across multiple sensors. We moved on to the PIC10F220, which added true analog input. It solved our sensor problem, but still didn't allow us any communication beyond immediately detectable output such as piezoelectric buzzers or LEDs. We did manage to revise the board and reduce the battery size while adding two analog inputs.

In order to try to leverage communications standards, we began to test the low-power PIC12F1552 microcontroller, which includes an SPI interface for peripherals like radio transceivers. As it was newly-released, we needed an updated PICkit programmer to be able to upload software to the chip—a process that, like all of the steps described here, involved ordering and waiting for parts to arrive. Programmer in hand, we implemented SPI for our radio. Although the datasheet for the microcontroller includes enough pins, we didn't have enough to control SPI due to an unforeseen issue: one of the 12LF1552's pins is unable to be addressed in code. It is exclusively a digital reset pin for embedded systems applications. As a result, SPI communication using this device was impossible.

We then shifted to the PIC12LF1840T48A, a version that includes an on-board radio transmitter. Its radio operates at 433 MHz, so we had to build custom hardware to receive signals at that frequency. Because this design is TSSOP (thin-shrink small outline package) rather than DIP, we also needed an adapter to use the chip on a breadboard. This also meant we had to test the radio transceiver we hoped to use with a new base-station design we are working on for this platform. That required the design, writing and testing of a communications protocol compatible with the transmission methods of the P12LF1840T48A. We also needed to build an antenna powerful enough for the transmitter to reach transmission ranges. All of this is ongoing, with setbacks, and while we're sometimes confused and frustrated, we feel as if we're building something using the native materials in which it needs to be made.

This kind of frustrating, sloppy, contingent, iterative production is what the knitting or woodworking equivalent of hardware making looks like. Being embedded in these lower-level electronics making practices reveals that constructing a prototype using an Arduino or its ilk are not really comparable to knitting, woodworking and the like. In most cases, the maker takes a pre-constructed prototyping board, a pack of sensors and uses open-source software libraries to assemble a project. It is a bit like buying a sweater, cutting off the tags, and calling yourself a knitter.

In some ways, the attributes that make platforms like the Arduino so popular—namely frictionless prototyping, relatively low cost of entry, and the availability of nearly ubiquitous sample code—are what prevent the novice from taking an uncomfortable step and moving into command-line code compiling C into machine instructions to be loaded into a microcontroller via a hand-built serial port. Toy projects, novelties, and small personal solutions can be cobbled together quickly and easily. At larger scale, however, the platform becomes wasteful and expensive. Indeed, one of the distinguishing features of the Arduino landscape is that there is no such thing as mass-produced Arduino project: with the exception of the fabricators producing the prototyping boards themselves, Arduino projects are one-offs, art projects, midterms, and hobbies; at their closest, they represent the output of a fledgling group of hobbyists who produce hardware for other hardware hobbyists. As a platform, the Arduino has dramatically increased the population of people interested in producing, sharing and being excited about electronic hardware manufacturing. At the same time, the dearth of "exit strategies" and successes for the platform may mean that Arduino for most people is both the beginning and the end of a hobby creating electronic objects.

THREE ENDGAMES FOR MAKER CULTURE

Given the implications of this sandbox problem in today's maker culture, we observe three possible endgames for it. We phrase these in terms of three configurations of the sandbox conflict—new rhetorical framings to think about the role of making in broader practice.

The first configuration involves no change to the status quo. Those inside the sandboxes continue servicing their own desires, in some cases producing industries around themselves, but not affecting the outside reference activities to which the maker activity aspired or laid claim. Makers remain makers, but nothing more. In this mode, making remains a self-serving meta-hobby that *refers* to a real-world activity but does not interact with it. While this outcome may seem like a failure of the revolutionary rhetoric surrounding making, it is really an honest appraisal of the outcomes of the current modes of production within making culture: making is a creative and expressive practice, but a practice unto itself.

The second outcome denies that the sandbox exists at all. Prior reference activities are abandoned in favor of the sandboxed "maker" activity. Here we find a growing commercial ecosystem to support joining and becoming a part of this "movement," supported by specialist shops like Adafruit Industries, Sparkfun, and Seeed Studios—not to mention "reference" hardware manufacturers like Arduino. Even industrial behemoths are getting into the game, as Intel has released enthusiast-oriented hardware like the Galileo both to position themselves as responsive to the maker community and to stake a claim within it.

Finally, the third end game situates the sandbox as a playground for evolutionary effort that "graduates" to professional practice. Those inside maker activities should recognize that the being a maker risks self-reference unless the sandbox itself is abandoned once it offers enough lessons to inform a broader set of activities. People risk aspiring to be "makers" instead of makers of *things*.

In practice, all of these configurations look very similar. In examining the goals of making, attending to both the sand and lawn is essential. By considering the future of making—supporting people who make these real, useful, things—the third option is the most appealing to us. It might also seem retrograde and even boring. Ultimately, making in this third style really just looks like ordinary craft or traditional engineering. This outcome may even be incompatible with the very concept of "maker culture." The point of a maker culture is to reject the desirability of a return to the reference domain in favor of the spawning of new sandboxes. Put differently, maker culture may be incompatible with anything but its own self-propagation.

ACKNOWLEDGEMENTS

This work was supported by the Intel Science and Technology Center for Social Computing (ISTC-Social). Thanks especially to the reviewers for their feedback.

REFERENCES

1. Ames, M. et al. Making Cultures. *Ext Abstracts of CHI'14*, (2014), 1087–1092.
2. Anderson, C. *Makers: the new industrial revolution*. Crown Business, New York, 2012.
3. Blikstein, P. and Krannich, D. The Maker Movement and FabLabs in Education. *Proc. IDC'13* (2013), 613–616.
4. Goodman, E. and Rosner, D. From garments to gardens. *Proc. CHI'11*, (2011), 2257–2266.
5. Hertz, G. *Critical Making*. Telharmonium Press, 2012.
6. Krannich, D. et al. Digital Fabrication for Educational Contexts. *Proc. IDC'12*, ACM (2012), 375–376.
7. Kuznetsov, S. and Paulos, E. Rise of the expert amateur. *Proc. NordiCHI'10*, (2010), 295–304.
8. Leduc-Mills, B. et al.. Evaluating Accessibility in Fabrication Tools for Children. *IDC'13*, (2013), 617–620.
9. Lindtner, S., Hertz, G., and Dourish, P. Emerging Sites of HCI Innovation. *Proc. CHI'14*, (2014), 439–448.
10. Lindtner, S. and Li, D. Created in China:. *interactions 19*, 6 (2012), 18–22.
11. Mellis, D. and Buechley, L. Collaboration in open-source hardware. *Proc. CSCW'12*, (2012), 1175–1178.
12. Mellis, D. and Buechley, L. Scaffolding creativity with open-source hardware. *Proc. C&C'11*, (2011), 373–374.
13. Mellis, D.A. and Buechley, L. Case studies in the personal fabrication of electronic products. *Proc. DIS'12*, (2012), 268–277.
14. Ratto, Matt. Critical Making. *The Information Society 27*, (2011), 252–260.
15. Rosner, D. and Bean, J. Learning from IKEA Hacking. *Proc. CHI'09*, (2009), 419–422.
16. Sadowski, J. and Manson, P. 3-D print your way to freedom and prosperity. http://alj.am/1kanblT.
17. Tanenbaum, J. et al. Democratizing Technology. *Proc. CHI'13*, (2013), 2603–2612.
18. Tanenbaum, K. et.al. Critical Making Hackathon. *Ext. Abstracts CHI'14*, (2014), 17–20.
19. About us | Raspberry Pi. http://raspberrypi.org/about.
20. Supermechanical : Twine. http://supermechanical.com/

Using a Tangible Versus a Multi-touch Graphical User Interface to Support Data Exploration at a Museum Exhibit

Joyce Ma [1] Lisa Sindorf [1] Isaac Liao [2] Jennifer Frazier [1]
[1] Exploratorium, Pier 15, San Francisco, CA 94111, USA
[2] Visualization & Interface Design Innovation, UC Davis, 2063 Kemper Hall, One Shields Avenue, Davis, CA 94720, USA
{jma, lsindorf}@exploratorium.edu, iliao@ucdavis.edu, jfrazier@exploratorium.edu

ABSTRACT
We describe a study comparing the behavior of museum visitors at an interactive exhibit that used physical versus virtual objects to explore a large scientific dataset. The exhibit visualized the distribution of phytoplankton in the world's oceans on a multi-touch table. In one version, visitors used physical rings to look at the type and proportion of phytoplankton in different areas of the oceans, and in the other version they used virtual rings. The findings suggest that the physical rings better afforded touching and manipulations, which were prerequisites to further exploration, and attracted more groups, thereby providing opportunities for people to talk and share. However, the comparison did not detect any measurable differences in the thoroughness of visitors' interactions, the questions they asked, or on-topic talk with others at the exhibit. These results should help museum professionals and interaction designers better weigh the costs and benefits of tangible user interfaces.

Author Keywords
Tangible; multi-touch; informal learning; tabletop; user interaction; museums; information visualization; TUI.

ACM Classification Keywords
H.5.2. Information interfaces and presentation (e.g., HCI): User Interfaces.

INTRODUCTION
Researchers posit that interactive tabletops with Tangible User Interfaces (TUIs) hold great promise in supporting learning. They theorize that unlike technologies such as purely multi-touch surfaces, large projections, or individual display devices, TUIs enable direct, hands-on interaction with physical objects. This technology can thereby provide novices with familiar physical objects and actions to manipulate and make sense of more abstract and less familiar digital representations [8, 14, 9, 15]. In addition to aiding usability, these physical objects may make interactions appear more playful, thereby promoting use and engagement [24, 17]. Furthermore, with TUIs, multiple users can manipulate an interactive simultaneously and see each other's activities, a valuable means for establishing referential anchors critical to collaborative learning [7, 11, 26].

With these properties, tabletops with TUIs seem particularly well suited to fostering the type of learning that happens in museums, science centers, and other informal learning venues. These environments have a long tradition of engaging visitors with hands-on interactions to promote visitor-driven inquiry [1, 5, 18] in a highly social environment where learning happens with each other and not just individually [5, 4]. With advances in TUI technology, tangible interfaces are becoming an increasingly viable and attractive option in the design of engaging, hands-on, social exhibits to foster learning.

Despite the theoretical promises of TUIs, empirical evidence for using TUIs to support learning has yielded mixed results. For example, in a study by Horn et al. [13] comparing a virtual to a tangible version of a programmable robots exhibit, the version with the tangible interface attracted more visitors and was more effective at fostering child-centered activities. However, the same study failed to find any differences in visitors' engagement, comprehension, or programming skill. In a study on individual learning with physical versus graphical materials, Marshall, Chen and Luckin [20] found no measurable differences in learning. In contrast, Fails et al. [10] found higher interest, engagement, and understanding when children used the tangible version, versus its graphical counterpart, of a game about environmental health hazards. Although physical objects are presumed to afford more natural interactions, Hornecker and Dünser [16] found that physical objects can suggest unanticipated and, therefore, unsupported uses, resulting in learner confusion. Marshall et al. [21] alternatively point out that a tangible interface can make the interaction so effortless as to precipitate short and superficial engagement with the contents of the interaction.

The field is continuing to construct a coherent framework to explain the strengths and weaknesses of using TUIs

TEI '15, January 15–19, 2015, Stanford, California, USA.
Copyright 2015 © ACM 978-1-4503-3305-4/15/01...$15.00.
http://dx.doi.org/10.1145/2677199.2680555

versus multi-touch GUIs and to inform the design and use of TUIs in learning [3, 15, 23]. Part of this larger effort involves studying TUIs, which are still largely custom-built for particular applications, across their many different manifestations and contexts of use. This work also requires conducting more comparative studies on TUIs and multi-touch GUIs. As noted by Zaman et al. [28], without these comparative studies, it is difficult to attribute TUIs with promoting learning interactions, especially social interactions, since many of the design affordances for collaboration are shared by both types of interfaces on interactive tabletops. In more recent years, the few comparative studies that have looked at interactive tabletops with TUIs versus multi-touch GUIs have focused on task efficiency [19, 27] or have been conducted with learners in laboratory settings [2, 26]. Although these studies add to our general understanding of interactive tabletops with TUIs, efficiency studies shed little light on TUIs in the museum setting, where their ability to attract, engage and support learning are more important indicators of their value. Likewise, the highly social, free-choice learning environment of a museum elicits different behaviors than a laboratory. Understanding how an interactive tabletop with a TUI versus a touch-only GUI attracts, engages, and promotes learning would require talking with and observing visitors *in situ*.

PURPOSE

The comparative study described in this paper sought to answer the question: What affordances does an interactive tabletop with a TUI provide in the informal learning environment of a museum? More specifically,

- Do TUIs attract a different demographic of users?
- Are visitors more engaged with TUIs? That is, do they stay at the exhibit longer? Do they use an exhibit with a TUI more thoroughly?
- Are TUIs better at fostering inquiry at an exhibit?
- Do TUIs better afford social interaction?

This work examined these questions by taking a close look at two versions of an interactive tabletop exhibit, one that used physical objects for the main interaction, supplemented by touchscreen interactions, and one that used only interactive graphical elements with touch points. Both versions were implemented on the same platform.

This study contributes to the larger effort underway in Human Computer Interaction (HCI) to more clearly identify the strengths and weaknesses of tangible interfaces for tabletop interactions. Findings also inform researchers and practitioners in the informal learning field about how to use TUIs in tabletop exhibits.

THE PLANKTON POPULATION EXHIBIT

Plankton Population is an exhibit developed at the Exploratorium in collaboration with the Visualization Interface & Design Innovation (ViDi) group at the University of California, Davis and the Darwin Project at the Massachusetts Institute of Technology. The exhibit aims to actively engage visitors, eight years old and older, with emerging research about the ocean's microbes by providing visitors with an interactive visualization that allows them to explore data about ocean microbes and the environment.

The interactive visualization shows the distribution of four different types of phytoplankton in the ocean as they change over the months of a year. See Figure 1 for a screenshot.

Figure 1: Screenshot of the visualization.

The visualization of the swirling patterns of colors, each representing a different phytoplankton type, is dynamic and plays continuously; visitors cannot pause or otherwise control the visualization's timeline. Instead, visitors can investigate different areas of the ocean with any of the three lenses available. The lenses are designed to connote magnifying glasses, a familiar cultural tool used to examine the very small.

When a lens is placed at a location in the ocean for one second or more, the portion of the global map under the lens fades out while icons representing the different phytoplankton types appear as shown in Figure 2.

Figure 2: Close-up of a virtual ring with icons transparent (left) and opaque (right).

These icons convey the morphology of the different plankton as well as relative size. The proportion of different icons that appear in the lens reflects the distribution of the represented types at that location. A tab on the side of the lens allows visitors to access a guide that describes, in text, the four different phytoplankton types including the environmental conditions that favor their survival.

The interactive visualization runs on a Dell OptiPlex 990 with an Intel Core i5-2400 and a GeForce GTX 560, and a MultiTaction™ Cell, capable of detecting both fiducial markers and multiple finger touches on its surface. A custom built table houses the 55-inch MultiTaction™ Cell, positioned horizontally like a tabletop, as shown in Figure 3. The Dell OptiPlex 990 sits in a secured box underneath the Cell.

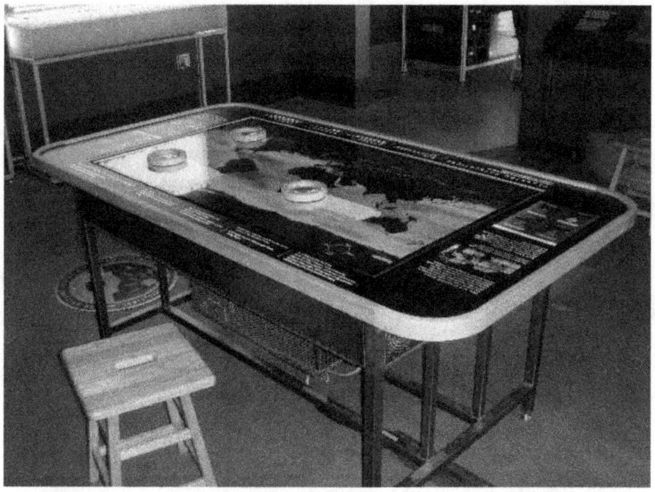

Figure 3: MultiTaction™ Cell and custom-built table.

The exhibit is designed to give visitors access to a real scientific dataset and, more importantly, to allow and encourage them to explore the dataset and to ask and answer their own questions with the data.

The TUI Version – Physical Rings

In the TUI version used in this study, the three lenses were implemented as physical rings shown in Figure 4. An infrared-reflective fiducial marker was embedded in the glass of the ring so that an individual could see through the invisible fiducial and glass; yet, the MultiTaction™ Cell could still detect and distinguish each fiducial marker.

Figure 4: One of the physical rings.

The Multi-touch, GUI Version – Virtual Rings

The comparable version of the exhibit with a multi-touch interface and only graphical elements was similar to the TUI version in every regard except that the three physical rings were replaced with three virtual rings of the same size and shape. The application developer went so far as to mimic the magnification effect of the lens in the virtual rings so that the multi-touch GUI version would also play up the metaphor of a magnifying glass. Like the physical rings, the virtual rings were always present, and users could move them around the table by dragging them with their fingers. See Figure 2 for a screenshot of a virtual ring.

Heeding Zaman et al.'s call to guard ecological validity [28], we sought to design a multi-touch GUI version that would be an exhibit in its own right and not just a 'damaged' counterpart. Toward this end, the exhibit with the virtual rings was reviewed and approved by exhibit developers and the gallery's curator who decided that the multi-touch GUI version could be a part of the museum collection, regardless of the research study, and would be used when the physical rings were not available.

METHOD

We used a mixed method design to understand the strengths and weaknesses of a TUI versus a multi-touch GUI. For each version of the exhibit, we collected two sets of data. First, we collected observation data of the naturalistic behavior of visitors who self-selected to approach and use Plankton Population. Second, we recruited dyads to use the exhibit and speak with us about their experience. For the dyads, we used a think aloud protocol to capture visitors' thinking as they used Plankton Population.

Observation Data

Using overhead cameras, wireless microphones attached to the rim of the exhibit table, and a screen capture application, we recorded 24 hours of observation data over the course of four weekdays and two weekend days in August, 2013. Following the procedure outlined by Gutwill [12], we cordoned off the area around Plankton Population and posted signs informing visitors that they would be audio and videotaped in that area. This procedure allowed us to secure informed consent for recording visitors' naturalistic behavior. We switched between the two versions of the exhibit once each day so that the twelve hours we collected for the physical rings were matched in time and type of day with the twelve hours captured for the virtual rings.

The two video recordings, one from the overhead camera and one from the screen capture of the interactive visualization, were synchronized in post-processing, with each other and with the audio, to produce a composite picture-in-picture video. See Figure 5.

Using this set of videos, we systematically sampled every sixth visitor who approached and stopped at the exhibit for more than five seconds. At the end of this process, our observation data corpus consisted of recordings of the behavior of 253 visitors, 128 using the physical ring and 125 using the virtual ring version of the exhibit.

Figure 5: Screenshot of composite picture-in-picture.

Think Aloud Data from Recruited Dyads

To recruit dyads for the think aloud protocol, we approached every third visitor who appeared 8 years or older (our target demographic), who was with one other person, and who crossed a predetermined imaginary line near Plankton Population; we asked this person if s/he and one other person in her/his group would be willing to participate in our study. We intentionally selected dyads since most people come to the museum with others and because we believed that visitors would have an easier time articulating and sharing their thoughts with a person they came with.

Once both visitors consented, we turned on the microphones and asked the dyad to think aloud, articulating their thoughts with each other as they used the exhibit. Each dyad saw only one version of the exhibit. We alternated between the physical and the virtual rings with each pair recruited.

In total, we collected think aloud data from 75 dyads, 36 for the physical rings and 39 for the virtual rings. (Three of the recordings for the physical ring version were either lost due to technical issues during recording or inaudible and dropped from the corpus.) These participants' demographic breakdown is shown in Table 1 and Table 2.

Ring Version	Female & Female	Male & Male	Female & Male
Physical $n = 36$	12	9	15
Virtual $n = 39$	7	5	27
Total $N = 75$	19	14	42

Table 1: Gender of think aloud participants.

Ring Version	Child & Child	Child & Teen	Child & Adult	Teen & Adult	Adult & Adult
Physical $n = 36$	2	4	7	7	16
Virtual $n = 39$	6	0	8	4	21
Total $N = 75$	8	4	15	11	37

Table 2: Age group of think aloud participants.

RESULTS

Did TUIs attract a different demographic of users?

To answer this question, we looked at the observation data and coded each observed visitor by gender and age group (under 8 years old, child between eight and twelve, teenager, and adult). The results are shown in Table 3 and Table 4.

Ring Version	Female	Male
Physical $n = 128$	67 (52%)	61 (48%)
Virtual $n = 125$	52 (42%)	73 (58%)
Total $N = 253$	119 (47%)	134 (53%)

Table 3: Gender of visitors observed at the exhibit for physical and virtual rings. The percentage of the total number of observed visitors for each version is in parentheses.

Ring Version	Under 8	Child	Teen	Adult
Physical $n = 128$	18 (14%)	8 (6%)	41 (32%)	61 (48%)
Virtual $n = 125$	21 (17%)	15 (12%)	32 (26%)	57 (46%)
Total $N = 253$	39 (15%)	23 (9%)	73 (29%)	118 (47%)

Table 4: Age group of visitors observed at the exhibit for physical and virtual rings. The percentage of the total number of observed visitors for each version is in parentheses.

A chi-square test found no significant difference in the gender of the visitors the physical versus the virtual rings attracted; $\chi^2(1, N = 253) = 2.51, p > 0.05$. Similarly, the analysis detected no statistically significant difference in the age group of the visitors who stopped at the exhibit for the two versions. $\chi^2(3, N = 253) = 3.57, p > 0.05$.

Were visitors more engaged with TUIs?

Did they stay at the exhibit longer?

Holding time, the amount of time a visitor spends at an exhibit, is a commonly accepted metric for engagement or interest in museum research [25]. Its validity derives from the fact that museums and science centers are free-choice learning environments, where visitors themselves choose what to attend to and for how long, based on their personal interests, rather than a set curriculum that characterizes formal education settings. A comparison of the holding times between the physical and virtual rings, therefore, is one way of assessing if one interface is more engaging than the other. We used the observation data of visitors' naturalist behavior to measure holding time at the exhibit.

The holding time data were subject to a log transformation to normalize the distribution before statistical analysis. A Welch's t-test on the log-transformed data showed that visitors who stopped at the exhibit with the physical rings stayed longer (M = 92.4, SD = 82.0) than the visitors who stopped at Plankton Population with the virtual rings (M = 73.0, SD = 65.3); $t(250) = 2.21$, $p = 0.028$.

We took a closer look at the video to determine the nature of visitors' engagement with the rings, and found a higher percentage of visitors touched the physical (113 out of 128, 88%) versus the virtual rings (97 out of 125, 78%); $\chi^2(1, N = 253) = 4.39$, $p = 0.036$. (We checked to see if a ring was available at some point during each observed visitor's exhibit visit and found that in all cases, a visitor could use a ring at some point during her/his visit if s/he chose to.)

When the visitors who did not touch any ring were eliminated from the sample, we found no statistically significant difference between the log- transformed holding times for visitors who touched and used a physical (M = 98.2, SD = 84.3) versus a virtual ring (M = 85.4, SD = 67.5), $t(207) = 0.77$, p >0.05. In other words, the physical rings better afforded touching and manipulation, the first step to further explorations at the exhibit.

Did visitors use the exhibit more thoroughly?

To understand the nature of their explorations with the rings, we looked at two types of data: observation data from self-selected visitors and think aloud data from recruited dyads.

Results from the observation data.

The synchronized video recordings, from the screen capture and the overhead exhibit camera, were analyzed to derive the number of times a visitor moved a ring and stopped on a location on the visualized map. A pause counted as a stop if it lasted one second or more, enough time for the map under the lens to fade out and for the icons of the phytoplankton to appear within the physical or virtual lens (Figure 2). The analysis distinguished between a stop on land, where a "No plankton on land" label would appear inside the ring, and a stop in the ocean, where icons of phytoplankton would appear.

Considering only those visitors who touched a ring, we compared the log(x+1) transform of the number of stops visitors made with the physical rings (M = 6.28, SD = 6.56) versus the virtual rings (M = 6.68, SD = 6.20) and found no significant difference, $t(206) = -0.79$, $p > 0.05$. Nor was there a statistical difference in the number of stops visitors made on land with the physical (M = 0.95, SD = 1.65) versus the virtual rings (M = 0.61, SD = 1.17); $t(208) = 1.63$, p >0.05. This suggests that visitors with the physical rings explored the oceans no more or less than the visitors with the virtual rings.

We then plotted the distribution of stops to determine the coverage afforded by the physical versus the virtual rings. The resulting plots, Figure 6 and Figure 7, indicate that the stops visitors made with the virtual rings were more tightly clustered. This is borne out in a comparison between the log-transformed median search radius for each visitor's stops; visitors used the physical rings (M = 325, SD = 178) in a larger area on the interactive map than the virtual rings (M = 256, SD = 150); $t(171) = 2.93$, $p = 0.0038$. That is, the TUI better enabled broader exploration of the data in the map visualization.

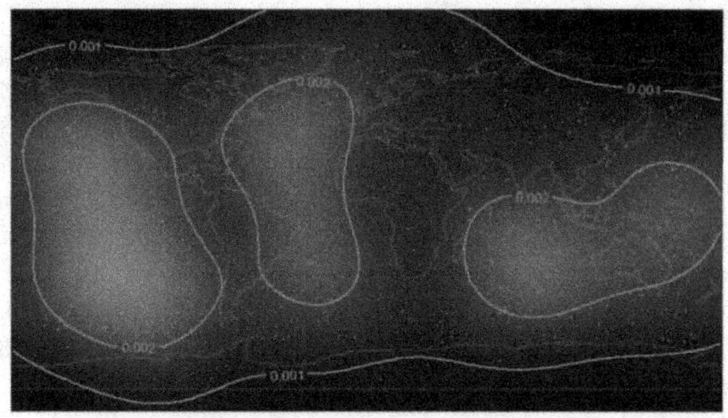

Figure 6. Density map of stops visitors made with the physical rings. Brightness denotes stops per pixel.

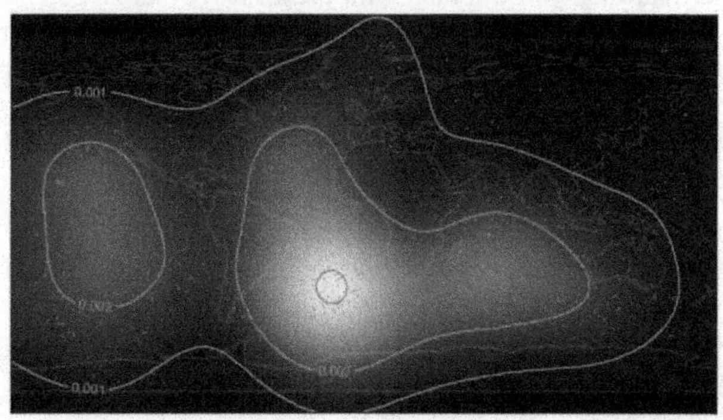

Figure 7. Density map of stops visitors made with the virtual rings. Brightness denotes stops per pixel.

Results from the think aloud data.

The think aloud data gave us an opportunity to learn about what visitors were thinking while they were using the rings to explore the data. To analyze these data, two data coders listened to the audiotaped think alouds and independently coded for absence or presence of each of five data variables visualized at the exhibit (listed in Table 5) in each dyad's talk. Sixteen randomly selected think alouds were coded by both coders to assess inter-rater reliability with the Cohen's Kappa statistic. A comparison between physical and virtual rings detected no difference for any of these data variables. The statistics for these tests are summarized in Table 5.

Data Variable	$\chi^2(1, N=75)$	Kappa
Prochlorococcus	1.51	0.85^{+++}
Synechococcus	0.21	0.86^{+++}
Diatom	1	0.50^{+}
Dinoflagellate	0	0.85^{+++}
Time	0.04	0.71^{++}

* $p < 0.05$
\+ moderate agreement
++ substantial agreement
+++ almost perfect agreement

Table 5: Chi-square test statistics comparing the number of dyads who noted a data variable with the physical versus the virtual rings. The Cohen's Kappa inter-rater score provides the reliability of each code.

Were TUIs better at fostering inquiry at the exhibit?

Looking at the think aloud data, two independent coders listened for instances of visitors posing questions that were answerable with the data visualized and for instances of visitors answering their own questions. The inter-rater reliability for 16 randomly selected dyads, coded by both raters independently, was ICC(A,1) = 0.78 for questions answerable with the data visualized and was ICC(A,1) = 0.70 for visitors answering questions using the data in front of them. These inter-rater statistics are considered excellent and good, respectively [6].

We found that dyads using the physical rings (M = 2.39, SD = 2.45) did not generate more or less questions about the data than those dyads who used the virtual rings (M = 3.05, SD = 2.95); $t(72.3) = 1.06$, $p > 0.05$. Furthermore, the visitors who did pose questions were no better at answering their questions between the physical (M = 2.21, SD = 1.70) and virtual (M = 2.33, SD = 1.81) versions; $t(48.8) = -0.24$, $p > 0.05$.

Did TUIs better afford social interaction?

We considered three behaviors in the observation data: Were visitors at the exhibit with other visitors? Were their conversations on-task? Were there instances of sharing rings?

We found that a large majority of the visitors were at the table with other visitors, 126 out of 128 visitors (98%) for the physical rings and 113 out of 125 visitors (90%) for the virtual rings. Statistically, visitors were more often at the exhibit with other people in the physical versus the virtual version; $\chi^2(1, N = 253) = 6.35$, $p = 0.012$.

Assuming that a visitor could participate in conversation as either a listener or speaker, we listened for any talk about the data visualized from anyone at the table during the time an observed visitor was at the exhibit. Looking only at those visitors who were at the exhibit with others, we found no significant difference in the number of visitors who participated in on-task talk between the two ring versions, $\chi^2(1, N = 239) = 1.67$, $p > 0.05$.

We further looked through the observation videotapes and coded instances of ring sharing (when multiple visitors have their hands on the same ring). In both versions, about a quarter of the visitors, who were at the table with others and who touched a ring, shared a ring: 29 out of 112 (26%) for the physical rings and 22 out of 91 (24%) for the virtual rings. A comparison found no difference in the number of visitors sharing; $\chi^2(1, N = 203) = 0.014$, $p > 0.05$.

DISCUSSION

In this study, we found that the TUI did not attract a different demographic of visitors to stop at the exhibit, compared to its GUI only counterpart. That is, we found no difference in the proportion of females to males or the distribution of children (under or above 8 years), teenagers, and adults who stopped at the exhibit with the physical versus the virtual rings. This was a little surprising since prior studies emphasized the appeal of tangibles to children [24, 13]. A possible explanation for this null finding may lie in the physical construction of the table. Sitting 80cm high, the MultiTaction™ Cell and the physical rings were difficult for small children to see unless they were already at the table and standing on a stool. In fact, this design better serves the exhibit's target age group, visitors 8-years and older. This null result points to the importance of the overall design of an exhibit, in which a TUI is used, in attracting the target demographic.

However, when we looked at the visitors who did stop, we found that the physical rings better afforded touch and manipulation compared to the virtual rings. Touching a ring was a critical precursor to continued engagement with the exhibit; we found that those people who touched a ring stayed longer at the exhibit, regardless of whether the ring was a physical or a virtual ring. In other words, the physical rings were better at encouraging the initial interaction necessary for continued engagement. This difference may be because the physical rings appeared to be a graspable object. Manipulable objects like the physical rings are common and even expected within the context of a hands-on museum.

Hornecker and Buur have also suggested that because TUIs can be directly manipulated, they may invite users to interact with the interface in specific ways [15]. In our case, the physical rings easily moved from one end of the tabletop to the other because they could be grasped and picked up. In contrast, the virtual rings had to be dragged across the table to explore different parts of the visualized map. The physical rings, therefore, afforded the exploration of a larger area of the map, an advantage for this particular exhibit, which sought to engage visitors with the exploration of a large scientific dataset.

O'Malley and Fraser have posited that a strong metaphorical mapping between a TUI object and its real-world counterpart may cue learners to the device's intended use [23]. In this case, the physical rings' similarity to a familiar object—a magnifying glass—may have helped visitors see them as a portal to the visualized representation of the microscopic world of phytoplankton. However, the graphical design of the virtual rings also strongly connoted magnifying lenses. This may partially explain why we found no measurable differences in how visitors engaged with the contents of the exhibit once they touched a ring, including the thoroughness of their data exploration, the number of questions they asked that were answerable with the data, and the number of those questions they tried to answer by exploring the exhibit.

O'Malley and Fraser have further suggested that in cases where learners are expected to make inferences from the representation, 'direct manipulation' may draw focus on the physical object (the physical rings) rather than the symbolic one (the distribution of plankton and the environmental factors related to that distribution) [23]. Although we did not find any quantitative evidence that the physical rings detracted from the content represented, we note that a few visitors were interested particularly in the technology behind the physical rings. On the videotapes, we noticed these visitors picking up the ring, peering through the glass and talking about possible enabling technologies. Likewise, a few participants in the think aloud study asked the interviewer afterwards for more information about the rings' underlying technology. As TUIs become more prevalent, their novelty may diminish along with their initial attractiveness for some individuals.

Findings from prior studies suggest that tangible technologies may support increased social interaction [e.g. 15, 23]. Our look into the social affordances of the TUI and multi-touch GUI detected only one difference: the TUI attracted more groups. One possible explanation for this finding may lie in the fact that the virtual rings were hard to see unless a visitor was already on top of the exhibit. In contrast, the physical rings were more noticeable from further away, especially when there was already another visitor at the table holding a ring. The physical rings themselves may have also appeared more novel than a touchscreen. We postulate that the combination of visibility and novelty attracted additional visitors to join visitors already at the exhibit. However, we note that the multi-touch GUI version was also highly popular with groups, suggesting that large multi-touch surfaces also provide opportunities for social interaction. Although a significantly higher proportion of visitors used the TUI with others, the physical rings did not elicit more on-topic talk about the exhibit's content (i.e., plankton distributions) or encourage more sharing of the tools (i.e., the rings) with which to explore that content.

CONCLUSIONS AND NEXT STEPS

The results of this study suggest that there is an advantage to using TUIs in interactive exhibits. Practitioners looking to develop tabletop exhibits may consider using TUIs to foster manipulation or encourage group use. As we work to improve the robustness of the technology, the maintenance cost should diminish making the choice of TUIs, as compared to multi-touch GUIs, a more attractive option in informal learning contexts.

However, several findings from this study merit further investigation. Hornecker and Buur have suggested that tangible objects may help focus conversation and reflection [15]. This study took a narrow look at the discussions engendered by the physical and virtual rings, focusing on visitor inquiry. Future studies might look for qualitative and quantitative differences in broader categories of talk. For example, a comparison of talk about the tool (i.e., ring) versus the content visualized might better characterize the discussions that occur and the differences in those conversations at the TUI versus the multi-touch GUI versions of this exhibit.

Similarly, the nature of collaboration at the TUI version can be better elucidated. For example, Marshall has argued that tangible interfaces may give access to views of others' activity, which may assist learning [22]. Alternately, Price et al. have suggested that shared surfaces may engender conflict, which in turn may lead to collaboration [24]. In this study, visitors did not differ in the ways they shared the rings, but future studies might investigate other ways visitors share investigations, and whether a physical or virtual object affects the nature of that collaboration. Understanding more about the quality of users' experiences with tangible interfaces will help to inform future decisions about whether they are the appropriate choice to support learning in museum settings. This study is a part in a series of steps to that better understanding.

ACKNOWLEDGMENTS

The authors wish to thank Mick Follows, Stephanie Dutkiewicz, and Oliver Jahn for sharing the Darwin Project dataset and for their time and expertise. We would also like to thank Eric Socolofsky for his insights on exhibit design, and Adam Klinger, Claudia Schidlow, Sarah Kimmerle, Anna Rosenbluth, Alyssa Freedman, Mandy Ice, Quinci Lee, and Beatriz Florez for their evaluation assistance. This material is based upon work supported by the Gordon and Betty Moore Foundation. Any opinions, findings, and conclusions or recommendations expressed in this material are those of the authors and do not necessarily reflect the views of the Gordon and Betty Moore Foundation.

REFERENCES

1. Allen, S. and Gutwill, J. Creating a program to deepen family inquiry at interactive science exhibits. *Curator 52*, 3 (2009), 289–306.
2. Antle, A.N. and Wang, S. Comparing motor-cognitive strategies for spatial problem solving with tangible and multi-touch interfaces. In *Proc. TEI 2013*, ACM Press (2013), 65-72.
3. Antle, A.N. and Wise, A. Getting down to details: Using theories of cognition and learning to inform tangible user interface design. *Interacting with Computers 25*, 1 (2013), 1–20.

4. Bell, P., Lewenstein, B., Shouse, W.A., and Feder, M.A. *Learning Science in Informal Environments-People, Places and Pursuits*. National Academies Press, Washington D.C., 2009.
5. Borun, M., Chambers, M.B., Dritsas, J., and Johnson, J.I. Enhancing family learning through exhibits. *Curator 40*, 4 (1997), 279–295.
6. Cicchetti, D. V. Guidelines, criteria, and rules of thumb for evaluating normed and standardized assessment instruments in psychology. *Psychological Assessment 6*, 4 (1994), 284–290.
7. Clark, H. and Brennan, S. Grounding in communication. In L.B. Resnick, J.M. Levine and S.D. Teasley, eds., *Perspectives on socially shared cognition*. American Psychological Association, Washington D.C., 1991.
8. Dillenbourg, P. and Evans, M. Interactive tabletops in education. *International Journal of Computer-Supported Collaborative Learning 6*, 4 (2011), 491–514.
9. Dourish, P. *Where the action is: the foundations of embodied interaction*. The MIT Press, Cambridge, Massachusetts, 2001.
10. Fails, J.A., Druin, A., Guha, M.L., Chipman, G., Simms, S., and Churaman, W. Child's play: a comparison of desktop and physical interactive environments. In *Proc. IDC 2005*, ACM Press (2005), 48–55.
11. Fernaeus, Y. and Tholander, J. Finding design qualities in a tangible programming space. In *Proc. CHI 2006*, ACM Press (2006), 447–456.
12. Gutwill, J. Gaining visitor consent for research II: Improving the posted sign method. *Curator 46*, 2 (2003), 228–235.
13. Horn, M.S., Solovey, E.T., Crouser, R.J., and Jacob, R.J.K. Comparing the use of tangible and graphical programming languages for informal science education. In *Proc. CHI 2009*, ACM Press (2009), 975–984.
14. Horn, M.S. The role of cultural forms in tangible interaction design. In *Proc. TEI 2013*, ACM Press (2013), 117-124.
15. Hornecker, E. and Buur, J. Getting a grip on tangible interaction: a framework on physical space and social interaction. In *Proc. CHI 2006*, ACM (2006), 437–446.
16. Hornecker, E. and Dünser, A. Of pages and paddles: Children's expectations and mistaken interactions with physical–digital tools. *Interacting with Computers 21*, 1-2 (2009), 95–107.
17. Hornecker, E., Marshall, P., and Rogers, Y. From entry to access: how shareability comes about. In *Proc. DPPI 2007*, ACM Press (2007), 328–342.
18. Humphrey, T. and Gutwill, J., eds. *Fostering active prolonged engagement: The art of creating APE exhibits*. Left Coast Press, San Francisco, CA, 2005.
19. Lucchi, A. and Jermann, P. An empirical evaluation of touch and tangible interfaces for tabletop displays. In *Proc. TEI 2010*, ACM Press (2010), 177–184.
20. Marshall, P., Cheng, P., and Luckin, R. Tangibles in the balance: A discovery learning task with physical or graphical materials. In *Proc. TEI 2010*, ACM Press (2010), 153–160.
21. Marshall, P., Fleck, R., Harris, A., et al. Fighting for control: children's embodied interactions when using physical and digital representations. In *Proc. CHI 2009*, ACM Press (2009), 2149-2152.
22. Marshall, P. Do tangible interfaces enhance learning? In *Proc. TEI 2007*, ACM Press (2007), 163–170.
23. O'Malley, C. and Stanton Fraser, D. *Literature Review in Learning with Tangible Technologies*. 2004.
24. Price, S., Rogers, Y., Scaife, M., Stanton, D., and Neale, H. Using 'tangibles' to promote novel forms of playful learning. *Interacting with Computers 15*, 2 (2003), 169–185.
25. Serrell, B. and Adams, R. *Paying attention: Visitors and museum exhibitions*. American Association of Museums, 1998.
26. Speelpenning, T., Antle, A.N., Doering, T., and van den Hoven, E. Exploring how tangible tools enable collaboration in a multi-touch tabletop game. In *Proc. INTERACT 2011*, Springer-Verlag (2011), 605–621.
27. Tuddenham, P., Kirk, D., and Izadi, S. Graspables revisited: multi-touch vs. tangible input for tabletop displays in acquisition and manipulation tasks. In *Proc. CHI 2010*, ACM Press (2010), 2223–2232.
28. Zaman, B., Vanden Abeele, V., Markopoulos, P., and Marshall, P. Editorial: the evolving field of tangible interaction for children: the challenge of empirical validation. *Personal and Ubiquitous Computing 16*, 4 (2011), 367–378.

Designing the Unexpected: Endlessly Fascinating Interaction for Interactive Installations

Lindsay MacDonald[1], John Brosz[1], Miguel A. Nacenta[2] and Sheelagh Carpendale[1]
[1]University of Calgary, Canada
{macdonla, jdlbrosz, sheelagh}@ucalgary.ca
University of St. Andrews, Scotland
mans@st-andrews.ac.uk

ABSTRACT
We present *A Delicate Agreement*, an interactive art installation designed to intrigue viewers by offering them an unfolding story that is endlessly fascinating. To achieve this, we set our story in the liminal space of an elevator, and populated this elevator with a set of unique characters. Viewers watch the story unfold through peepholes in the elevator's doors, where in turn their gaze can trigger changes in the storyline. This storyline's interactive response was created via a complex adaptive system using simple rules based on Goffman's performance theory.

Author Keywords
Interaction design; interactive installation; interactive art; complex adaptive systems.

ACM Classification Keywords
H.5.m. Information interfaces and presentation (e.g., HCI): Miscellaneous.

General Terms
Human Factors; Design.

INTRODUCTION
When creating an interactive installation many challenges are apparent including such factors as attracting attention, engaging interest and sustaining interest. In this paper, we focus on the latter—sustaining interest—with the over-arching goal of creating endlessly fascinating interaction (EFI). Our focus on EFI frames our goal to provide observable actions that: (1) are interesting at any time; (2) are not repetitive; and (3) offer unfolding actions in which story lines are emergent. Also, we explore passive interaction, which offers the possibility of providing continual variation without requiring people to take actions beyond what they would normally do when viewing an installation. Our aim is to provide viewers with a dynamic experience that unfolds as they watch and is different for every viewer and for each time a viewer encounters the work. To establish stories of interest that resonate with a large part of possible viewers we set our piece in the context of the liminal space of an uncomfortable elevator ride. To create a varying story line with the possibility of emergent sequences we borrowed ideas from complex adaptive systems (CAS). The characters within our story lines were designed employing art and social theory from Bang and Goffman. Together, these concepts allowed us to explore the possibility of passive interaction with endlessly fascinating unfolding stories.

Our installation, *A Delicate Agreement*, offers the viewers a rich interactive narrative made up of encounters between the characters within the installation and, occasionally, with the viewer. Externally, it appears as a false elevator with a peephole in each door, allowing viewers to peer inside and observe the characters riding the elevator together and interacting with each other (see Figure 1). The combination of these elements constitutes our gaze-triggered interactive art installation that explores the concept of EFI.

The next section briefly covers related background from interaction design and interactive art installations and presents some well-known examples of complex adaptive systems. We go on to describe the conceptual basis of our work: its *liminal setting*; our *passive interaction* strategy; our interactive narrative structure and related social theory from Goffman; and our interaction challenges. Next, we discuss the physicality of our installation, and how we generate EFI using a CAS to offer continually varying interaction. We then discuss the exhibition of the piece and conclude the paper by noting our main contributions.

BACKGROUND
We draw from research on interactive technology in public spaces, interactive art and CAS to establish a background for this work.

Figure 1. ***A Delicate Agreement*** **placed next to real elevators.**

TEI '15, January 16 - 19 2015, Stanford, CA, USA

ACM 978-1-4503-3305-4/15/01...$15.00
http://dx.doi.org/10.1145/2677199.2680603

Interactive Technology in Public Spaces

Encouraging passersby in public spaces to engage with technology is a relevant issue that has been much discussed in the area of human-computer interaction (HCI) for public spaces. Müller et al.'s Looking Glass [18] attracts viewers' attention by showing their reflections interacting with objects on large displays. In Proxemic Peddler, Wang et al. [27] make use of animations that change as the viewer's proximity and physical orientation to a large display change in order to attract their attention. Brignull and Rogers [4] discuss the honey pot effect as a phenomenon of how even one person's attention would attract other people to a large display. Hinrichs et al. [13] noted that different configurations of a large display, such as the degree to which interactions are visible, has an impact on the honey pot effect and can be another powerful way to attract people's attention. Similarly, we engage passersby in public spaces by placing peepholes in the doors of the elevators, through which light and movement inside the elevator can be seen. Viewers looking through these peepholes did indeed trigger the honey pot effect.

Interactive Art Installations

Krueger's *Videoplace* [16] sets up an active playful dynamic for viewers to explore how the piece will respond. Our work relies on less explicit interaction, requiring little beyond what the viewer is already doing to explore the installation.

Hill's *Tall Ships* engages people by enabling the exchange of gaze with projected videos of ghosts activated by pressure sensors [12]. This creates an uncomfortable social situation due to proximity of the life-sized projections to the interacting viewer. The ghosts are only capable of approaching the viewer, staring and walking away [12]. Based on similar experiences with other people, viewers get a sense that the ghosts are conveying a sense of longing through their gaze. In contrast, *A Delicate Agreement* does not force the viewer to exchange a prolonged gaze with the characters to directly control the characters' movement. Instead, the viewer's gaze is just one of the factors that influence the next action. However, a similarity with *Tall Ships* is the expectation that the viewer will reflect upon the presented situation and relate to the characters that live in the world of the piece by using their own experiences, and that the gaze will function as a vehicle to achieve this.

Gonsalves' *Chameleon* [10] is a large scale installation that examines social relationships, trust and intimacy within the context of interactive technology, using neuroscience research and face-sensing technology. The piece consists of video portraits arranged around a gallery of individual actors performing various emotions, ranging from anger to sadness, tiredness to happiness. Gonsalves worked with an interdisciplinary collaborative team that included experts from neuroscience, HCI and affective computing to get the video characters in the piece to mimic empathy and emotional contagion [11]. Face-reading technology estimates the emotional state of the viewer and incorporates that into software that controls the emotional reaction of the portraits. *Chameleon* is closely related to *A Delicate Agreement* in that both pieces only require passive interaction and feature a cast of characters that have software-constructed personalities. We take a different approach in our piece by using these ideas to structure emotional landscapes for our characters, going beyond establishing empathy to develop an interactive narrative.

Complex Adaptive Systems

Complex adaptive systems (CASs) are neither fully constrained as in linear systems nor fully chaotic. They are often said to be on the chaotic fringe in that they incorporate considerable freedoms yet do have rules which are followed [26]. One way in which these systems can operate is to have entities or agents that are merely locally aware. That is, these agents only know how they respond to a given set of situations. There is no overview or central control of the whole system, thus, sequences and storylines are flexible. Waldrop uses the example of an economy as a CAS, and describes individuals or households as being the agents [26:145]. We use this understanding of the term agent in our work – our agents are the characters in the elevator. Gell-Mann [8] describes how a CAS can create complex and diverse phenomena such as eco-systems, the operation of the immune system, and the behavior of investors in financial markets. Miller and Page [17] demonstrate the use of an agent-based CAS to model varied and interesting social systems including bees, theatre audiences, city formation, and many others.

Many systems exist where CASs have been used to create complex, interesting, and unpredictable outcomes. Conway's Game of Life [7] employs three simple rules governing whether cells in a grid live, reproduce or die based on their local neighborhood and is able to produce extremely complex behaviors up to and including an operational Turing machine [1]. Boids [22] use three simple rules for separation, alignment, and cohesion to reproduce the realistic group movements of flocks and herds; this technique is widely used in the animation industry [21] and has been expanded upon to create interactive art [3]. Turk [25] used the reaction-diffusion process, noted as a CAS [15] to produce widely varied biological patterns matching those of zebras, giraffes, leopards, and many others.

We use a CAS to support interactions between our characters (or agents), the viewers' gaze and the elevator in motion to produce complex, responsive, and emergent behaviors.

CONCEPT

To provide the appropriate context for our CAS we first describe liminality, and the exchange of expression and impression from Goffman's performance theory.

Using a Liminal Setting

The term *liminal* refers to a transformational or transitory space [24]. Johnston defines these as "spaces … lying between otherwise defined areas without belonging to either of them" [14:209]. Common examples of liminal spaces are doorways and hallways where one has left one room but not yet entered the next. We set the interaction of our piece in the liminal space of an elevator to be able to leverage the social awkwardness inherent in such places.

The liminal space of the elevator is an appropriate setting to examine the effects of gaze on interaction. Elevators offer a protracted moment of liminality when two strangers ride together, awkwardly waiting for the machinery to complete the transition from one floor to the next, moving towards their desired destinations. There are unspoken rules about what behavior is acceptable. If these rules are broken, the elevator ride can become uncomfortable. If a stranger casts their gaze in any direction other than towards the doors, this can threaten the delicate agreement that tacitly exists between the occupants of the elevator. The context of the elevator sensitizes the viewer, making small behavioral changes more noticeable while shedding light on the viewers' awareness of the unspoken rules.

Short narratives that can unfold along these lines are, for example, a moment of mutual attraction and flirtation between two characters or, conversely, unwanted attention. Discord can occur when one character behaves inappropriately, such as writing graffiti on the wall or brandishing a weapon. Depending on each character's personality, different responses can occur to these events, creating spontaneous and varied narratives that can engage and intrigue the viewer.

Using Passive Gaze Interaction

A theme in our work is the interplay between passive and active viewer interaction. Active interaction is the normal approach where people must do specific activities such as clicking with a mouse or typing on a keyboard. In contrast, passive interaction occurs when people viewing the piece are not required to do anything outside of what they would normally be doing [19]. We use the idea of incidental interaction [6], meaning that by the act of looking in through the peepholes in the elevator doors with the expectation to observe the interior of the elevator, viewers affect the course of the unfolding narrative happening in the elevator by means of the direction of their gaze. This interaction can become active if the viewer realizes that their gaze is affecting the behavior of the characters.

Interactive Narrative and Social Theory

To create our interactive narrative, we drew from Bang's [2] discussion of open text. Here, he stipulates that open text, or interactive narratives, can have many plot climaxes compared to linear narratives, which have just one. Participants in interactive narratives are drawn into a state of contemplation when experiencing the work, reflecting on his or her own life experience in order to inform decisions

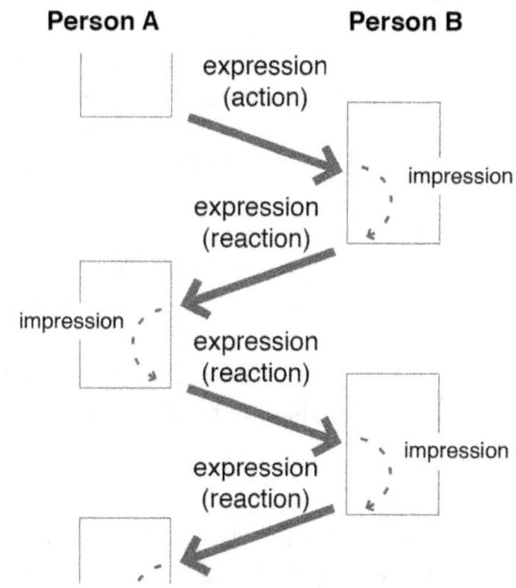

Figure 2. An illustration showing Goffman's theory of expression and impression, reflected in our software implementation.

made while interacting. Similarly, Goffman [9] indicates that one draws upon one's experiences when interacting with other people in order to decide how to react or present oneself. In this way, *expression* can be bisected into that which is given, which can be controlled by the person expressing, and that which is given off, which is how the expression exists after leaving the character and how it is received by the other person. *Impression*, on the other hand, is the effect left by the expression on the other person. Goffman's expression and impression exchange, illustrated in Figure 2, is used in the design of our characters' interactions. Our goal was to model the behavior of the characters and their reaction to viewers on this existing sociological theory in order to make encounters in the space of the elevator more believable. Thus, this model of human interaction and behavior is applied to the exchange between a person and a character–or between two characters–in *A Delicate Agreement*.

Our artistic vision was to create mini action sequences that fit with a given character and could be combined with other characters' sequences to create narratives. To produce the exponential number of spontaneous narratives possible in *A Delicate Agreement*, we harness combinations of characters, their behaviors, and the direction of the viewers' gaze. Due to the fact that the elevator is traveling up and down the building and the characters do not remain on board for an extended period of time, the story can be divided into subplots or micro-stories as people enter and leave. Based on previous similar real life experiences, viewers choose where to look, triggering any number of new and different plot climaxes within a single viewing and interaction session and creating a unique experience each time the piece is revisited.

Interaction Challenges

Art installations using interactive technologies are becoming increasingly prevalent both in galleries and in public spaces. People encountering these installations must discover how to interact with them to subsequently reveal the installation's reaction. The reaction of the installation can serve to sustain the viewer's attention, encouraging deeper exploration and appreciation of the content. However, in some cases, the viewer's interaction with the installation can yield repetitive results. Our goal for *A Delicate Agreement* is to extend possibilities for viewer interaction to make the experience endlessly fascinating. In summary our interaction challenges are that:

- the observed reactions of the piece are both understandable and intriguing;
- the viewer is not required to discover difficult or obscure actions to trigger a response;
- the viewer does not need to be aware of the effect of their own interaction; and
- the story that unfolds is non-repetitive, and endlessly fascinating.

We address the first challenge through our choice of setting–the *liminal setting* of elevators that is familiar to all of us and yet remains socially awkward. The next two challenges are addressed together through the use of *passive gaze interaction.* The last challenge—developing EFI—is addressed primarily through the creation of our CAS (see the next section). However, other factors in its creation include a combination of *interactive narrative* and ideas from *social theory* described in a later subsection.

REALIZING *A DELICATE AGREEMENT*

In this section, we first discuss the physical aspect of our installation and its gaze tracking interaction; then we present the design and implementation of our CAS.

Physical Form

A Delicate Agreement is an interactive installation that explores the liminal time and space of an elevator ride. Viewers are presented with a false set of elevator doors (Figure 1 shows the exterior) augmented with a pair of peepholes that allow them to look into the interior of the elevator (Figure 3). Two LCD monitors are set inside the elevator behind the peepholes. The monitors display a composite stop motion animation of a cast of sixteen characters riding the elevator (Figure 4 shows six of these characters). From either peephole the viewer can see the interior of the elevator, up to two characters at a time as passengers, and an elevator display that indicates the floor the elevator is currently on (Figure 5). Each character has a set of pre-recorded photo sequences shot on a theatrical set in a photography studio that provides the appearance of the interior of the elevator. The photo sets for each character illustrate the range of possible behaviors that each character can perform. A character's set of photos ranges from several hundred to several thousand still frames that are played in sequence as a stop-motion animation. Each elevator

Figure 3. Two viewers looking into the interior of the elevator.

Figure 4. Six of the sixteen characters (L to R, Top to Bottom): Max, Nicole, Bert, Terry, Danny and Kathy.

Figure 5. Example of the interior of the elevator with floor indicator.

passenger, or character, has a programmed personality that enables them to act and react to the other characters' behavior and the viewers' gaze (see next subsection).

Immediately behind each peephole is a custom-made eye-tracker. The eye-tracker was designed to: a) be invisible to the viewer so that interaction could be, at least initially, implicit; b) not require calibration; c) be reliable and able to run long periods of time; d) be inexpensive, so that the piece could be left unattended in public spaces. Each of the two eye-trackers consisted of a hot mirror (a mirror that only reflects infrared light), a low-resolution Logitech webcam, modified with a filter to be sensitive only to infra-red light (with its internal infrared-blocking filter removed), two sources of infrared light (LEDs) to generate corneal reflections, and a customized version of the ITU Gaze Tracker software [23] to perform the analysis, which was fed to the CAS software described below and run in the same machine (a Windows PC). The hot mirror, located at 45° from the line of sight, allowed us to place the camera and infrared light sources very close and perpendicular to the eye and therefore obtain a very large image of the pupil without making any of the machinery visible. Although this eye-tracker is not comparable in sample-rate or performance to commercial ones, it was able to satisfy our requirements which were comparatively simple. We merely needed to know which character a viewer was looking at and whether they were looking at the character's head or torso.

The Character Engine (a Complex Adaptive System)

The underlying CAS that powers our piece is based on the idea that a few simple rules governing individual agents (characters) can produce a wide variety of emergent behavior. Neither the characters nor the overarching system need to know the full complexity possible. Each character merely needs to know its own rules for actions and reactions. By creating a CAS based on simple mechanisms we enable the generation of emergent narratives between the characters in the installation.

Our intention was to make it possible for interactive responses to emerge from the system. That is, we avoided specifying defined sequences of character actions, such as where if action A happens, then response B will follow. This type of sequential response would lead to a repetitive and predictable viewing experience. We chose to create a CAS in which characters know their own set of behaviors and know how they respond to simple changes in their environment. To do this we have defined the characters, their environment, and the events that will cause them to react.

The characters in the elevator

The elevator currently contains sixteen different characters (see six of them in Figure 4). Some of the characters are Nicole and Max, young university students; Kevin and Rose, teenagers; Alice, a little girl; Toby, a bike messenger; and Leo, a dangerous-looking man with a gun.

Each character has his or her own list of possible behaviors. A behavior is a sequence of photos that together provides a stop motion animation expressing an emotion or reaction. For example, Max—a generally friendly and happy character—cheerfully acknowledges other characters entering the elevator that glance over at him.

The characters' interaction environment

In our system, the characters' interactions are determined by their emotions. Their emotions, in turn, trigger their behaviors. To model their emotional space, we use a coordinate system. This coordinate system encompasses each character's personality, with enclosed regions marking behaviors (Figure 6). This was inspired by Zeeman's relational graphic of a dog's response to cusp catastrophe that is based on catastrophe theory research [28]. Zeeman's graphic displays a coordinate space with rage as the *X*-axis and fear as the *Y*-axis where nine drawings of the profile a dog's face are laid out in this grid pattern. The dog's facial expression changes according to where his emotional response lies within this coordinate space. This coordinate space of changing emotions inspired our emotional coordinate space for each character. The axis of the space, however, need not be rage and fear; Nass [20] asserts that personality can be defined by two meaningful dimensions: extraversion and agreeableness.

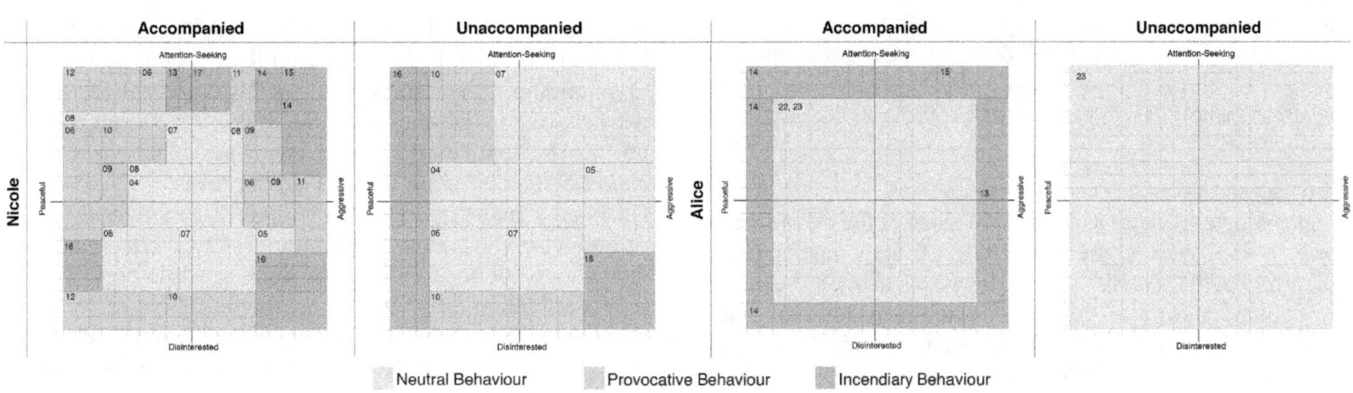

Figure 6. Personality grids for a complex character, Nicole, and a simple character, Alice. Some of the behaviors mapped above include: neutral/calm (4), bored (5), glance at other person (8), disbelief (11), disgust (13), and aggressive anger (14).

Our characters' emotional behavior is represented as a 2D grid of states (personality grid) but based on Nass' two dimensions. At a given moment a character's emotional state (mood) is represented by a 2D coordinate in the grid. One dimension of the grid represents agreeableness (from peaceful to aggressive) while the other one represents extraversion (from disinterested to attention-seeking). The grid is divided in areas of emotional state that result in behaviors; for a given range of extraversion and agreeableness the character will display a certain visual behaviour corresponding to a particular sequence of pictures. For example, when the character Nicole has an agreeableness value of 8 and an extraversion value of 1, she will express the behavior "disbelief" (Figure 6 leftmost).

Behaviors are not, however, limited to the selection of visual output. Behaviors also affect the emotional state of other characters in different ways. For example, the aggressive *anger* behavior of Leo causes other characters to become more aggressive (the exact calculation is described in the next subsection). This is the basic mechanism of interaction between characters: Leo's *anger* behavior is his *expression* and triggers the other character's *impression.* Therefore, the personality grids are a representation of the visual output of the character, and also hold their current state and describe the dynamics of how characters can influence one another.

There are a total of 26 different behaviors, and each character possesses a subset of these, although different characters have behaviors associated to different areas of their personality grid. Examples include: neutral, attracted, angry, frightened, bored, and shocked. Each character has two personality grids: one for when they are alone in the elevator and one for when they are accompanied. Nicole's emotional space (Figure 6, left) is representative of a more complex character as she has a large number of possible behaviors. In contrast, Alice has only five behaviors (Figure 6, right). The getting on/off the elevator or recognizing the viewer behaviors are not represented on the characters' emotional spaces as these are triggered by the elevator's state rather than by interaction with other characters.

Events & behavior changes

Characters experience a variety of different events. First the elevator has its own actions; it goes up and down, characters get on and off. Characters will only get on or off at specific floors. The elevator's actions keep the story moving. If the elevator is empty it will pick up the character at the next floor in sequence.

Stepping through the character interactions, we start with a simple situation where a character is alone in the elevator and there is no viewer present. Under these situations the character will slowly move towards neutral behavior (emotional coordinate $(0,0)$) because there are no other characters present that can alter their mood. If another character enters the elevator, expression/impression exchange begins, where one character's behavior will influence the other's mood and vice versa. In our CAS, we build on small simple reactions that only required knowledge of the immediate context making it possible to design the interacting factors independently.

To implement this, every behavior for each character has an expression vector e. This relates how their current behavior changes the behavior of the other person in the elevator by nudging them in a particular direction along both the x- and y- axes. Each character also possesses an impression filter i that scales their responses to other character's expressions, allowing different characters to be more or less reactive. A character with $i=(2,2)$ will be very reactive while a character with $i=(0.5,0.5)$ will be less influenced by others' expressions. Lastly, each character has a constant impression vector c that is added to all changes making some characters consistently move towards particular parts of their personality grids. This serves to allow for slight variations in behavior when characters are riding the elevator alone.

Given a character with a particular emotional coordinate s_i, the character's next coordinate is calculated by:

$$s_{i+1} = s + i\, e_o + c$$

where e_o is the other character's (if present) expression vector matching their current behavior.

To illustrate this, consider a scenario in which the characters Kevin and Rose are in the elevator together. Kevin's current behavior, "obnoxious antagonism" has $e=(10,2)$; i.e., this behavior expresses a great deal of aggressiveness (10) as well as a smaller amount of attention seeking (2). Similarly, let us say that Rose's behavior is currently "Neutral" due to her emotional coordinate being at $(0,0)$. Rose's character has $i=(.5,3)$ and $c=(1,4)$. If Rose's neutral behavior finishes its animation, her emotional state will be recalculated with:

$$s_{i+1} = s + i\, e_o + c = (0,0) + (.5,3)\,(10,2) + (1,4) = (6,10).$$

This change of emotional coordinate to $(6,10)$ will place Rose in her "openly angry" behavior.

Visually, this plays out as Kevin turning up the speakers on his iPod and dancing around (his particular obnoxious antagonism stop-motion animation), which in turn causes Rose to get frustrated or angry at this obnoxious display.

When he reaches the end of his image sequence for his behavior, Kevin will collect e from Rose's updated behavior to determine which behavior to perform next. At the end of her behavior image sequence, Rose will use e from Kevin's new behavior to determine her next behavior. This expression/impression exchange process, based on Goffman's theory and shown in Figure 2, continues until one or both characters exit the elevator. The characters maintain their mood for a certain length of time while they stay on their destination floor in the building. If they re-enter the elevator within a certain period of time, they will likely perform the same behavior, affecting whomever they happen to be riding with.

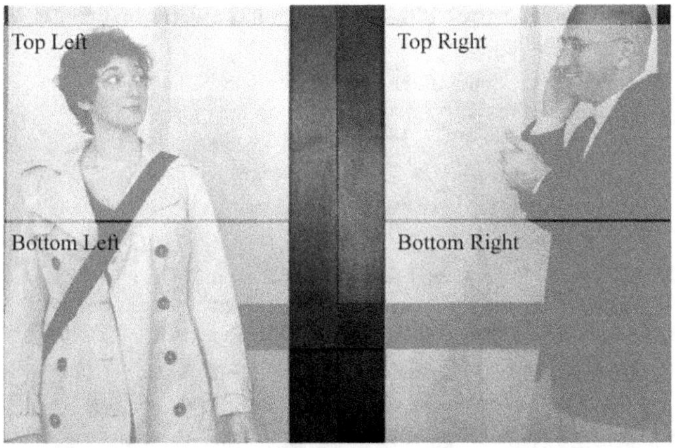

Figure 7. The four regions of the image that trigger response to the gaze of the viewer.

The viewer's gaze also affects characters' emotional coordinates and resulting behavior. The systems' gaze detection is coarse, only indicating whether each of the two possible viewers is looking at one of five regions: four correspond to the top or bottom half of either character (Figure 7); the fifth is anywhere else. Each character also has two viewing vectors that change his or her emotional state when either viewer is looking through a peephole. v_{st} for the top of the character, v_{sb} for the bottom of the character as well as v_{ot} and v_{ob} that are triggered when viewers look at the top and bottom respectively of the other character in the elevator. The emotional state update formula then becomes:

$$s_{i+1} = s + i\,e_o + c + v_1 + v_2$$

where v_1 is either v_{st}, v_{sb}, v_{ot}, v_{ob}, if the viewer in the first peephole is looking at one of the aforementioned character regions or *(0,0)* if looking elsewhere or not present. Similarly v_2 is the appropriate vector for the viewer, if any, looking through the second peephole.

In the event that the viewer is looking at the top of a character at the instance that the character is changing behaviors, the character will perform his or her acknowledgment of the viewer behavior (Figure 5). This special behaviour trigger is designed to bring awareness to the viewer that their presence is affecting the piece's state.

DISCUSSION

The biggest point for discussion is: did we achieve EFI? Of course, that is an impossible notion to gauge. However, we can say that in the three times that *A Delicate Agreement* has been exhibited, people have not been able to trigger repeat performances. So while our unfolding story is undoubtedly not endless, it definitely has considerable variation. On the other hand, we have experienced emergent behavior. As an example, we intentionally included mild flirting sequences that could be triggered when the character was in a safe, relatively happy space in their emotional landscape. These sequences did add amusement and highlights to the story. However, it became apparent that all characters in our elevator had bisexual tendencies. During the creation time and times between exhibitions, the piece was operational for long periods of time in our lab, a large research group of approximately 40 to 50 people. There are still amusing anecdotes from this piece that people tell each other.

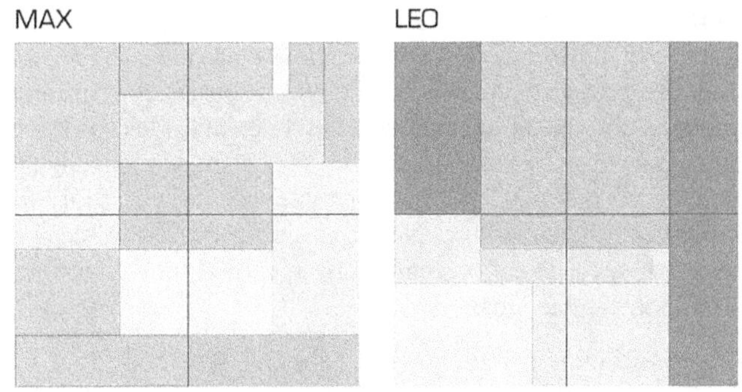

Figure 8. Choropleth behavior visualization for Max and Leo. Aggressive behavior regions are red, provocative purple, and neutral blue. The more opaque the color, the more time the character has spent exhibiting that behavior.

While to a large extent our custom made passive gaze tracker served as intended, it did have trouble with people wearing glasses. People commented simultaneously that although they felt that there was no response to them as viewers, they noted that some of the elevator characters had waved at them. This specific sequence requires gaze interaction to occur. This combined response does speak to the piece's ability to walk the line between passive and active interaction.

As creators, this piece challenges our notion of authorship, and intrigued us sufficiently that we explored possible ways of influencing the unfolding story. One simple method was to add new characters, as we did at one gallery's request. A more complex approach was to work with each character's emotional landscape. To enable this we wanted to have some idea of where, in emotional coordinates, characters frequently spent time. This led to an intensity visualization of their behavior over time. We visualized each character's behavior through a simulation with a choropleth map (Figure 8). These maps allow us to see if a character was spending too much, or not enough, time in a given space. For example, from the maps it was apparent that Leo's was frightening the other characters too much, and we were able to modify his expression vector to reduce his expressed aggression.

CONCLUSION

In this paper we have presented *A Delicate Agreement*, which we designed to provide endlessly fascinating interaction (EFI). We have shown how:

- complex adaptive systems (CASs) can be used to provide a non-repetitive storyline;
- how Goffman's theory of expression/impression can be used to create rules in a CAS that offer convincing approximations of behaviors; and
- the liminal setting of continued awkwardness in elevator rides can provide a story line intensifier.

While other CASs have been built on spatial grids such as SELES, a landscape scale simulation environment [5], we used the grid concept but spatialized a series of common emotions and used Goffman's theory to create rules for travel throughout this emotional grid. We also visualized the spatialized behavior frequencies to use as a tool for influencing the story line. Note that in our endlessly varying story line specific actions cannot be specified; however, their likelihood can be enhanced.

The possibilities for future work abound. We hope that we have opened the door for a new approach to designing interactive experiences.

ACKNOWLEDGMENTS

This research was supported in part by SSHRC, NSERC, SMART Technologies, AITF, SurfNet and GRAND.

REFERENCES

1. Adamatzky, A., ed. *Collision-Based Computing*. Springer, Berlin, 2002.
2. Bang, J. The meaning of plot and narrative. In *The computer as medium*. Cambridge University Press, Cambridge, New York, 1993, 209–220.
3. Boyd, J.E., Hushlak, G., and Jacob, C.J. SwarmArt: interactive art from swarm intelligence. *Proc. of the 12th Annual ACM International Conference on Multimedia*, ACM (2004), 628–635.
4. Brignull, H. and Rogers, Y. Enticing people to interact with large public displays in public spaces. *Proc. of INTERACT*, (2003), 17–24.
5. Carpendale, M.S.T., Cowperthwaite, D.J., Tigges, M., Fall, A.J., and Fracchia, F.D. The Tardis: a visual exploration environment for landscape dynamics. *Electronic Imaging '99*, International Society for Optics and Photonics (1999), 110–119.
6. Dix, A. Beyond intention-pushing boundaries with incidental interaction. *Proc. of Building Bridges: Interdisciplinary Context-Sensitive Computing, Glasgow University*, (2002).
7. Gardner, M. Mathematical Games – The fantastic combinations of John Conway's new solitaire game "life." *Scientific American*, 1970, 120–123.
8. Gell-Mann, M. *The Quark and the Jaguar: Adventures in the Simple and the Complex*. Henry Holt and Company, New York, 1994.
9. Goffman, E. *The Presentation of Self in Everyday Life*. Doubleday Anchor Books, New York, 1959.
10. Gonsalves, T., Frith, C., Critchley, H., Picard, R., and El Kaliouby, R. Chameleon. 2008. http://www.tinagonsalves.com/chamselectframe.html (accessed 7/11/2014).
11. Gonsalves, T. Empathy and Interactivity: Creating Emotionally Empathic Circuits between Audiences and Interactive Arts. In R. Ascott, G. Bast, W. Fiel, M. Jahrmann and R. Schnell, eds., *New Realities: Being Syncretic*. Springer, Vienna, 2009, 136–139.
12. Hill, G. Tall Ships. 1992. http://garyhill.com/left/work/tall-ships.html?q=569 (accessed 7/11/2014).
13. Hinrichs, U., Schmidt, H., and Carpendale, S. EMDialog: Bringing information visualization into the museum. *IEEE Transactions on Visualization and Computer Graphics 14*, 6 (2008), 1181–1188.
14. Johnston, S.I. *Restless Dead: Encounters between the Living and the Dead in Ancient Greece*. London, 1999.
15. Kondo, S. and Miura, T. Reaction-diffusion model as a framework for understanding biological pattern formation. *Science 329*, 5999 (2010), 1616–1620.
16. Krueger, M.W. Responsive environments. *Proc. of the June 13-16, 1977, national computer conference*, ACM (1977), 423–433.
17. Miller, J.H. and Page, S.E. *Complex Adaptive Systems: An Introduction to Computational Models of Social Life*. Princeton university press, 2009.
18. Müller, J., Walter, R., Bailly, G., Nischt, M., and Alt, F. Looking glass: a field study on noticing interactivity of a shop window. *Proc. of SIGCHI Conference on Human Factors in Computing Systems*, ACM (2012), 297–306.
19. Nakatsu, R., Rauterberg, M., and Vorderer, P. A New Framework for Entertainment Computing: From Passive to Active Experience. In F. Kishino, Y. Kitamura, H. Kato and N. Nagata, eds., *Entertainment Computing - ICEC 2005*. Springer, Berlin, 2005, 1–12.
20. Nass, C., Moon, Y., Fogg, B.J., Reeves, B., and Dryer, D.C. Can computer personalities be human personalities? *International Journal of Human-Computer Studies 43*, 2 (1995), 223–239.
21. Parent, R. *Computer animation: algorithms and techniques*. Newnes, 2012.
22. Reynolds, C.W. Flocks, herds and schools: A distributed behavioral model. *ACM SIGGRAPH Computer Graphics*, ACM (1987), 25–34.
23. San Agustin, J., Skovsgaard, H., Mollenbach, E., et al. Evaluation of a low-cost open-source gaze tracker. *Proc. of the 2010 Symposium on Eye-Tracking Research & Applications - ETRA '10*, ACM Press (2010), 77.
24. Thomassen, B. The uses and meanings of liminality. *International Political Anthropology 2*, 1 (2009), 5–27.
25. Turk, G. Generating textures on arbitrary surfaces using reaction-diffusion. *Proc. of the 18th Annual Conference on Computer Graphics and Interactive Techniques*, ACM (1991), 289–298.
26. Waldrop, M.M. *Complexity: The emerging science at the edge of order and chaos*. Simon and Schuster, New York, 1992.
27. Wang, M., Boring, S., and Greenberg, S. Proxemic Peddler: A public advertising display that captures and preserves the attention of a passerby. *Proc. of the 2012 International Symposium on Pervasive Displays*, ACM (2012), 3:1–3:6.
28. Zeeman, E.C. Catastrophe Theory. *Scientific American*, 1976, 65–83.

Resonant Bits: Harmonic Interaction with Virtual Pendulums

Peter Bennett
University of Bristol
peter.bennett@bristol.ac.uk

Stuart Nolan
University of Bristol
nolan@hexinduction.com

Ved Uttamchandani
University of Bristol
ved.uttamchandani@gmail.com

Michael Pages
University of Bristol
michael.pages28@em-normandie.fr

Kirsten Cater
University of Bristol
cater@compsci.bristol.ac.uk

Mike Fraser
University of Bristol
Mike.Fraser@bristol.ac.uk

ABSTRACT
This paper presents the concept of *Resonant Bits*, an interaction technique for encouraging engaging, slow and skilful interaction with tangible, mobile and ubiquitous devices. The technique is based on the resonant excitation of harmonic oscillators and allows the exploration of a number of novel types of tangible interaction including: *ideomotor control*, where subliminal micro-movements accumulate over time to produce a visible outcome; *indirect tangible interaction*, where a number of devices can be controlled simultaneously through an intermediary object such as a table; and *slow interaction*, with meditative and repetitive gestures being used for control.

The Resonant Bits concept is tested as an interaction method in a study where participants resonate with virtual pendulums on a mobile device. The Harmonic Tuner, a resonance-based music player, is presented as a simple example of using resonant bits. Overall, our ambition in proposing the *Resonant Bits* concept is to promote skilful, engaging and ultimately rewarding forms of interaction with tangible devices that takes time and patience to learn and master.

Author Keywords
Human-Computer Interaction; Tangible User Interface; Ideomotor Control; Slow Technology; Resonance.

ACM Classification Keywords
H.5.2. User Interfaces: Interaction Styles

INTRODUCTION
Resonant Bits aims to bridge the 'divide between the worlds of bits and atoms' [9] by using resonance as a metaphor that spans both domains. We propose that this technique offers a number of novel methods of interacting with tangible interfaces including ideomotor control, indirect interaction and slow interaction.

The inspiration for developing an interaction technique around resonance arose from our experience investigating the ideomotor response [10] while developing new technology for stage magic. In particular we explored the effect that occurs when a participant holding a pendulum is asked to will it to move purely through the power of the mind. In many cases the pendulum will start to swing and will actually follow the participant's command. Perhaps counter-intuitively, even when the physical nature of the effect is explained (as the resonant amplification of many micro-movements of the fingers holding the string) the feeling of directly controlling the pendulum by thought alone persists. We envisage that an advanced resonance-based system will be able to recreate this effect for use in tangible interaction.

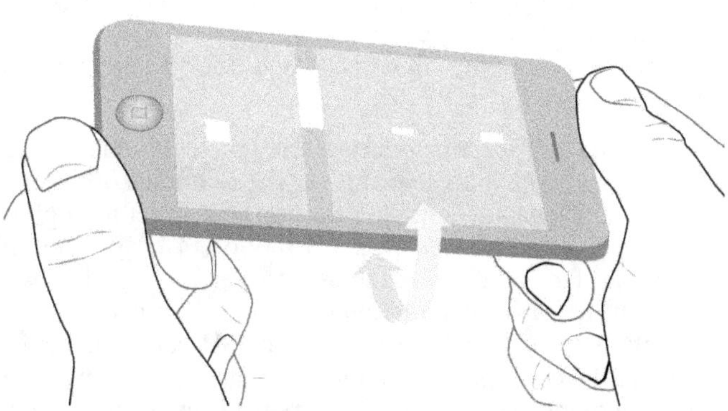

Figure 1. Resonating with virtual pendulums. Rocking the phone at the same frequency as one of the pendulums will gradually increase the pendulum's amplitude.

To test the feasibility of using resonance as an interaction technique we developed a mobile device application based on interaction with virtual pendulums. The procedure of evaluating the Resonant Bits concept is not straight-forward, as the goals are not the typical HCI criteria of efficiency, speed, or reduced mental workload, and the goals we wish to achieve (slowness, engagement, skilful interaction) require longitudinal study which we will conduct in future work. In this paper,

TEI 2015, January 15–19, 2015, Stanford, California, USA.

http://dx.doi.org/10.1145/2677199.2680569

our initial study aims to verify whether the Resonant Bits concept will work as an input technique. In particular, can people after a brief period of familiarisation physically resonate with a digital bit?

RELATED WORK

The Resonant Bits concept has been developed as a method for informing the design of new Tangible User Interfaces [9] in particular with the aim of moving 'from data centred to perceptual-motor centred' tangible interaction [3]. This move promotes the development of rich and tightly coupled interactions with tangibles that encourage the 'challenge and pride that comes with acquiring and possessing motor skills' [2]. In particular, Resonant Bits supports new methods of exploring affordance and 'feedforward' [14] in tangible interaction, by revealing to the user partial outcomes of an action before it is completed.

The Resonant Bits concept is based on the ideomotor response which occurs when a person unconsciously makes micro-movements to achieve a goal. When the point is reached that these micro-movements are near-invisible to both user and observer, then Resonant Bits may be used as a platform for exploring 'magical interaction'. Using magic as a metaphor may later on help to inform future Resonant Bits designs, helping users build mental models of 'rationally impossible' interactions [13].

Resonant Bits explores how slowness can be encouraged during interaction. This form of slow, or 'time-aware', interaction has been likened to playing a musical instrument, in that the device encourages the stretching of the present moment. The difficulty in designing such a device is that it 'should not be technology that is tiresome and time consuming, but technology that stretches time and slows things down' [5]. We propose Resonant Bits as a potential method for achieving slow interaction in tangible interfaces and also a possible method of promoting 'flow' [1] when using a tangible interface.

There are a few existing interfaces and projects which share a similar approach to Resonant Bits. The technique of 'motion-pointing' allows the indirect selection of a target through the matching of the target's elliptical motion [4]. Shoogle [16] is an interface that allows the user to 'read' a mobile device through the active exploration of a physical model that represents data within the device. The ISH series of devices explore the concept of emotional resonance in tangible interfaces, looking at 'the ability of a product to evoke positive images, memories, and emotions, and to encourage a prolonged, subtle, or stimulating effect beyond the initial impact' [7]. It is proposed that this resonance with a device is reinforced by a 'fit between the product and the kind of interaction on the one hand, and a persons (latent) concerns, value system, personality, skills, senses' [6]. The possibility of using resonant agents controlled by sympathetic movement has been proposed as a method for 'continuous uncertain interaction' [15]. This work also includes the technique of dynamically changing the resonant frequency of each agent, thus forcing the user into closely following the changing resonance.

VIRTUAL PENDULUM STUDY

In order to test the basic feasibility of Resonant Bits as interaction technique we conducted a study determining whether novice users could intentionally isolate a single pendulum from multiple on screen. The study was also designed to collect general feedback on the Resonant Bits concept.

Virtual Pendulum Application

The application runs on a phone, presenting the user with a set of pendulums represented by a line of bars (Fig.2). Each pendulum has an individual frequency laid out in order from lowest to highest across the phone.

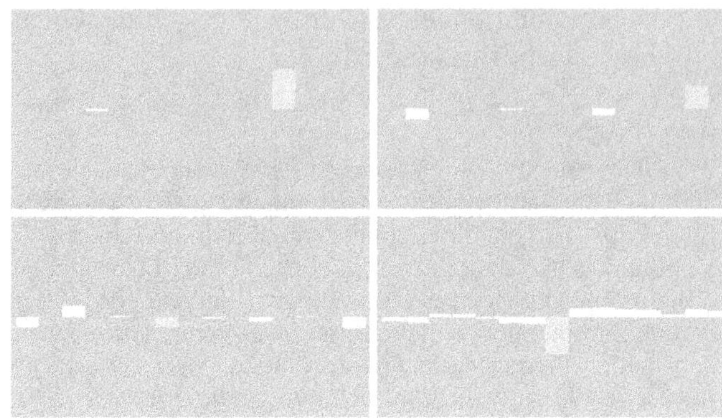

Figure 2. The four tasks from the user study with 2, 4, 8 and 15 pendulums. In each, the pendulum highlighted in blue is the target pendulum.

The physical model for each pendulum is a driven harmonic oscillator with velocity proportional damping. The damping value is chosen to provide an underdamped response so the mass oscillates around the centre point when disturbed. In this discrete model, the next position of the mass x_{n+1} is calculated from the sum of the force F_n, the returning force of the spring Ax_n and damping proportional to the velocity $B(x_{n-1} - x_n)$.

$$x_{n+1} = F_n - Ax_n + B(x_{n-1} - x_n)$$

The force value F is calculated from the differential of the phone's x-axis accelerometer, so that the constant of gravity is cancelled and only movement is registered. Use of the phone's gyroscope was trialled, but found to be less sensitive than the accelerometer. The maximum value of F is capped so that small movements provide the same value as large movements. The force value is scaled by a coefficient chosen to provide a level of influence on the model that can build up a resonant oscillation but without overpowering the returning force of the spring. The spring coefficient A is the primary influence on the dominant frequency of each oscillator and the values are chosen to span the frequency range of 0.5Hz to 4Hz.

Procedure

Twenty participants took part in the study. We asked a number of background questions to gain knowledge of their past experience with mobile devices. Most used touchscreen phones regularly, but most participants didn't use their phones often for games although they did play some form of computer games. Overall the participants gave a neutral response on being asked if they had a good sense of rhythm.

Each participant was introduced to the mechanics of the system with a test application that presented a single pendulum at a time. The participants were then presented with the main task of moving a single highlighted pendulum with multiple pendulums on screen. Four tasks were presented to the participant consisting of 15, 8, 4 and 2 pendulums on screen at a time. In each task, a single target pendulum is highlighted with a blue bar and the user is asked to maximise the 'swing height' of the highlighted pendulum. Each task (of 15, 8, 4, 2 pendulums) was presented to the participant 6 times, totalling 24 trials per participant with each trial lasting 10 seconds. Both the trial order and target pendulum were randomised. After the 24 trials were complete, the participant was asked to fill out a questionnaire and give general feedback.

Selection and Isolation Results

To measure the success of isolating one pendulum's movement, the maximum amplitude reached by each pendulum is observed over the 10 seconds of each trial. If the target pendulum had the largest maximum amplitude then a successful selection of that pendulum is counted. The first column of Table 1 shows the success of achieving maximum amplitude in each of the trial conditions. A second method of measuring the success of isolation is to measure how much energy is put into each pendulum. This can be achieved by integrating the position of the pendulum over each ten second period of the trial. These 'energy' values can then be compared, and if the largest is the target pendulum, this counts as a successful isolation (second column of Table 1). The findings indicate that using the maximum amplitude maximum energy offer very similar possibilities of successfully detecting the target pendulum. It also indicates that without much practice, participants had a better than average chance of picking out the correct pendulum in all of the four tasks.

Pendulums	Amp.	Energy	Amp.Ratio	Energy Ratio
2	77%	77%	3.46	4.91
4	63%	64%	1.63	2.08
8	41%	47%	1.00	1.12
15	29%	30%	0.77	0.77

Table 1. Success rate across all trials of making the target pendulum gain a higher maximum amplitude or energy value than any other pendulum. Ratio of the maximum amplitude and integral values between target pendulum and the highest non-target pendulum.

We then looked at the level of certainty at which maximum values were obtained. This was calculated by dividing the maximum value of the target pendulum by the maximum value found across the other pendulums, resulting in a ratio value (Table 1). A ratio of 1.00 indicates that the target pendulum has the same maximum amplitude as the highest of the non-target pendulums, a ratio of 2.00 indicates that the target pendulum achieved twice the maximum of the next highest pendulum. In this case the energy shows a stronger result than the maximum amplitude.

Oscillator Frequencies

The user study also tested the choice of frequencies for the dynamic models. Ideally each pendulum has the possibility of reaching the same maximum amplitude as the others when handled by a skilled operator. Though relatively flat across the middle frequencies, the lower frequencies (oscillators 1 & 2) reach a higher maximum and there is a peak in the higher frequencies at oscillator 13. The average maximum height across all the trials shows a trend towards higher amplitude at lower frequencies. This correlates with feedback from the survey that the higher frequencies were harder to resonate with and generally were more frustrating. Using the data from the study, a scaling value for each pendulum has been implemented, making each pendulum more equally weighted.

Questionnaire

Results for the participants ability to concentrate on the task was neutral with a lean towards agreement. Half of the participants agreed that they had lost track of time, which we took as an indicator they may have entered a state of flow during the task. The majority of participants responded with 'neutral' to feeling in control of the pendulums. The majority of people were neutral on the task being frustrating, however this question was commonly queried as being difficult to answer, as the participants were only frustrated with some of the tasks. This was elaborated in the comments section where many participants only felt frustrated with the higher frequency pendulums and in a couple of cases the frustration was seen in a positive manner, 'almost like a mini-game'. Six participants disagreed strongly with the statement that it was frustrating. Most people agreed to enjoying the task, with five strongly agreeing.

> *There seems to be a range in which I can control the task. For lower frequencies (say first half of the screen) I felt I was in control. Higher frequencies on the other hand, were really frustrating. I just kept shaking the phone! When in control, you quickly "feel the beat".*

Observations on Types of Interaction

From observing participants during the study and from informal testing, a number of interaction methods have been observed: *Excitation*, where the device is initially given a shake to observe the natural frequencies of the pendulums. *Damping* of a pendulum, where the swing of a pendulum is deliberately slowed. *Guiding* of one person by another to teach how to resonate with a pendulum. *Priming* of the interface, by getting the desired pendulum swinging so it is ready to hit the threshold when the user desires. *Topping Up*, with the user attending to the energy level of multiple oscillators. *Flicking* energy into the system. *Full body* rocking and swaying. These observations indicate some of potentially rich physical interactions that may develop when interacting with Resonant Bits.

HARMONIC TUNER

To explore an application of how Resonant Bits can be used in practice, a simple music player inspired by Bottles [8] was created. In the Bottles project, sounds were *contained* in the bottles and uncorking lets the sound out. In Harmonic Tuner the sounds are contained in the resonant bits and are released by sympathetic excitation. Multiple permutations of the Harmonic Tuner have been explored. The most basic has three music tracks being represented by three resonant bits of different frequencies, with faster music mapped to the faster frequency oscillators. Another version plays musical notes, having a second set of oscillators laid out at right angles to the first set but using the same set of frequencies. This allows the user to select between bits with the same frequency by changing the axis of rocking. Two oscillators can then be played at the same time through a circular tilting motion.

Initial work has been made into incorporating dynamic damping into the Harmonic Tuner, so as the device is moved less the damping coefficient is decreased. This has the effect of penalising large movements and guides the user towards the micro-movements necessary for ideomotor control. Informal testing of this prototype indicates that the 'spooky' feeling of ideomotor control can occasionally be achieved. This experience may be enhanced further by using the strategies of 'misdirecting attention and setting false expectations' [12], in the case of the Harmonic Tuner, perhaps setting a second diversionary task, allowing the resonant gesture to be disguised within a larger movement.

CONCLUSION AND FUTURE WORK

This paper has proposed the concept of Resonant Bits as an interaction technique for tangible interaction, and the study has shown that it is feasible for a simple selection task even with complete novices. Although this first exploration of the Resonant Bits concept has been carried out on phones and tablets, we intend to extend this work by creating new Tangible User Interfaces specifically designed to support resonant interaction. One area in particular for further exploration is how the movement used to control a resonant bit can be transmitted *through* an intermediary object such as shelf, table or floor to allow indirect tangible interaction.

Further work on the Harmonic Tuner will investigate the addition of haptic feedback and also continuous sound feedback, an approach that has been shown to aid the learning of new tangible control mechanisms [11]. Currently the Harmonic Tuner only operates with pre-determined resonant bits with fixed frequencies and content, further work will explore methods to create new resonant bits 'on the fly' through oscillatory input. More complex dynamic models that involve for instance circular motion will also be investigated.

We hope that further work on the Resonant Bits concept will result in a range of physically engaging tangible interfaces that require the development of nuanced motor skills, which in turn may reward the user of such devices with immediate satisfaction and long term enjoyment.

ACKNOWLEDGMENTS

Many thanks to both the study participants and everyone who has had a play with the system. Thanks to the reviewers for insightful feedback and suggestions. The Resonant Bits concept was developed within the Tangible Memories project, AHRC grant AH/L007886/1.

REFERENCES

1. Csikszentmihalyi, M., and Csikzentmihaly, M. *Flow: The psychology of optimal experience*. Harper & Row, 1990.
2. Djajadiningrat, T., Matthews, B., and Stienstra, M. Easy doesn't do it: Skill and expression in tangible aesthetics. *Personal Ubiquitous Comput.* (2007).
3. Djajadiningrat, T., Wensveen, S., Frens, J., and Overbeeke, K. Tangible products: Redressing the balance between appearance and action. *Personal Ubiquitous Comput.* (2004).
4. Fekete, J.-D., Elmqvist, N., and Guiard, Y. Motion-pointing: Target selection using elliptical motions. In *Proc. of CHI* (2009).
5. Hallnäs, L., and Redström, J. Slow technology – designing for reflections. *Personal Ubiquitous Comput. 5* (2001), 201–212.
6. Hummels, C. Searching for salient aspects of resonant interaction. *Knowledge, Technology & Policy 20* (2007), 19–29.
7. Hummels, C., and van der Helm, A. ISH and the search for resonant tangible interaction. *Personal Ubiquitous Comput. 8* (2004), 385–388.
8. Ishii, H. Bottles: A transparent interface as a tribute to Mark Weiser. *IEICE Trans. Inf. & Syst.* (2004).
9. Ishii, H., and Ullmer, B. Tangible bits: Towards seamless interfaces between people, bits and atoms. In *Proc. of CHI* (1997).
10. Knuf, L., Aschersleben, G., and Prinz, W. An analysis of ideomotor action. *Journal of Experimental Psychology: General 130*, 4 (2001), 779.
11. Lemaitre, G., Houix, O., Visell, Y., Franinovi, K., Misdariis, N., and Susini, P. Toward the design and evaluation of continuous sound in tangible interfaces: The spinotron. *International Journal of Human-Computer Studies 67* (2009).
12. Marshall, J., Benford, S., and Pridmore, T. Deception and magic in collaborative interaction. In *Proc. of CHI* (2010).
13. Svanaes, D., and Verplank, W. In search of metaphors for tangible user intefaces. In *Proc. of DARE* (2000).
14. Wensveen, S. A. G., Djajadiningrat, J. P., and Overbeeke, C. J. Interaction frogger: A design framework to couple action and function through feedback and feedforward. In *Proc. of DIS* (2004).
15. Williamson, J. *Continuous Uncertain Interaction*. PhD thesis, University of Glasgow, 2006.
16. Williamson, J., Murray-Smith, R., and Hughes, S. Shoogle: excitatory multimodal interaction on mobile devices. In *Proc. of CHI* (2007).

Material Significance of Tangibles for Young Children

Jinsil Hwaryoung Seo, Janelle Arita, Sharon Lynn Chu, Francis Quek, Stephen Aldriedge
Texas A&M University
College Station, TA 77843
hwaryoung, jarita07, sharilyn, quek, stevo25@tamu.edu

ABSTRACT

The purpose of this paper is to investigate how young children associate materiality and meanings and how it can benefit tangible interaction design. To study this, we developed a research prototype, *Stampies* that allows playful tangible interactions. *Stampies* consists of tangible objects made out of different materials (wood, felt, silicone, and plastic) and an iPad drawing application. We describe results from our empirical study involving 19 children aged 4 to 7. The study indicates that children associate materials with meanings through "material essences", feel, and tactile preference. We conclude with design implications for tangible interaction for children.

Author Keywords

Materiality; Meaning; Children; Touch screens

ACM Classification Keywords

H.5.2. User Interfaces: Interaction Styles.

INTRODUCTION

In 2008, Ishii [5] proposed the idea of the 'tangible bits' and articulated a model for its utility to user interfaces, arguing that TUIs (tangible user interfaces) serve the function of making "digital information directly manipulatable with our hands, and perceptible through our peripheral senses by physically embodying it". Since then, a large number of research projects have looked at exploiting physicality for purposes of education and learning, information visualization, entertainment, social communication, performance, etc. [14], especially for applications targeted at young children (e.g., [2, 6, 12, 19]). Commercial toy products as well, like *Skylanders* [1] and *Invizimals* [15], and educational applications, like *Tiggly* [7] and *Fisher Price Stamp On* [4], have expanded digital experiences into the physical realm.

However, a 'tangible bit' does not present only the affordance of its mere persistence and physicality, but brings with it a range of material properties (e.g., size, shape, texture, temperature, weight) that can be associated with digital representations to convey information [8] and to create personal meanings. TUIs provide immediate tactile feedback to the user, potentially facilitating or reinforcing the uptake of the digital representations.

We investigate how the materiality of objects is perceived by young children, and how it can benefit their digital interactions. This paper first presents an overview of arguments for the association of materiality and meaning, and then describe a study with children aged 4 to 7 to explore the issue using a digital drawing application that is coupled with physical '*stampies*' as our testbed.

MATERIALITY AND MEANING

The significance of materiality to thinking has been advanced by such philosophers as Merleau-Ponty and Gibson, who conceived of perception *as* behavior [13]. Gibson's notion of affordances, through Norman's [10] reframing of the concept, has been used extensively in HCI to guide user actions and understanding. We posit that the influence of materiality is particularly prominent for children.

Studying project work of 37 children aged 8 to 11, Ormerod and Ivanic [11] describe how they made use of physical characteristics of objects in their meaning-making practices, for example embedding broken egg shells and feathers in a project on birds. Vygotsky's [17] studies with toddlers demonstrated the importance of object iconicity in their cognition: the children could not think of a toy model of a bench as a bench if the model was placed upside down, or a bucket had to be drawn as such ∪ for the child to be able to identify its representation (for the child, ∩ cannot be a bucket). In a study on how play objects affect imaginative play in 3½ to 5 year-olds, McLoyd [9] found that high structure objects (objects whose "identity and functions ... most preschoolers are aware of", e.g., dolls, trucks) significantly generated more pretend play themes than low-structure objects (objects that were "less specific and unique", e.g., boxes, pipes).

While these studies investigate the shape and form of artifacts with children, 'graspable media' (using Ishii's term [5]) is multi-dimensional. In a survey of material-centered interaction design research, Wiberg [18] defines four interrelated levels of analysis that have been adopted to understand materiality: at the level of *materials*, attention is paid to the particular material properties (what is it made of?) and character (what can it be used for?) of the object. At the level of *details*, one looks at the aesthetics and quality of the object. At the level of *texture*, one studies how material properties are communicated through the material surface

TEI '15, January 15–19, 2015, Stanford, California, USA.
Copyright 2015 © ACM 978-1-4503-3305-4/15/01...$15.00.
http://dx.doi.org/10.1145/2677199.2680583

and appearance. And at the level of *wholeness*, the overall composition and holistic meaning conveyed come into play.

Thus the study of materiality moves back and forth between the micro and the macro. We are precisely interested to understand the relationship between the two, and whether the association can be extrapolated into digital interactions to benefit a child's learning or creativity with technology. In other words, 1) can the micro-level characteristics (material properties and texture) of an object intrinsically convey meaning to a child?; and 2) does the association of the object (based on its micro-level properties) with particular meanings help the child in digital interactions?

Cognitive load theory [16] may help to explain why exploiting micro-level properties of tangible objects in interaction design may improve performance. Given our limited working memory, minimizing the load on memory may facilitate the extension of thinking at higher levels. Designing tangible objects with specific material properties supports the use of existing schemas that we have of things in our environments (e.g., a desk is made of wood, a plushy toy is soft, etc.) to ease the memory load by facilitating dynamic reassociation. Although there has been significant theoretical work on the issue of materiality and meaning, little work can be found that presents empirical support for its relevance to interaction design.

STUDY TESTBED

To study how children associate different material types (e.g., wood and felt) with meaningful digital content (e.g., graphical representations of familiar objects like clothing and toys) we needed a flexible system that allows for playful interaction by young children, and that features: i) tangible objects whose materiality can be manipulated; ii) a graphical digital application, whose content can be manipulated; and iii) a way to manipulate the association of the graphical content and the tangible objects. Our design took the form of a stamping tool for toddlers that we modeled after the shape of the '*stampies*' objects used in the color-matching prototype developed by Arita et al. [3].

Stampies are objects with a simple standard shape that can be fabricated using different materials (see Figure 2). The bottom of each *stampie* is adorned with a unique pattern of conductive fabric that can be detected as touch patterns by a standard iPad touch screen (see Figure 3). Conductive threads or copper tapes connect this pattern to the upper area of the object, allowing a connection between the screen and the user's hand when it is grasped. The iPad application presents the child with a grid of graphical objects, and allows her to associate a *stampie* with each displayed object by placing the *stampie* over the object in the grid (see Figure 1). Once associations are made, the child is presented with a blank canvas into which she can 'stamp' graphical objects by applying their associated *stampies* to the iPad screen. The child can also 'paint' with the *stampie* by dragging it over the iPad screen, leaving a trail of the concomitant graphical objects.

STUDY MATERIALS AND DESIGN

For the purpose of our study, we created 2 sets of *stampies*, each set with one *stampie* made out of a different type of material (wood, felt, silicone, and plastic). Three types of meaningful digital content were chosen to be tested in the iPad application: colors, colored familiar items, and line-drawn familiar items (Figure 1). Six colors and 16 familiar items (representative of 4 categories with 4 items in each) were used in the study. Table 1 shows the colors, item categories and the representative items used.

For the testing of colors on the iPad, all *stampies* in one set were colored a neutral white to avoid biases. This was done as such: the wood *stampie* was painted with white acrylic paint, needle felted natural wool was used for the felt *stampie*, and white food coloring was added to the cast silicone and plastic *stampies*. The *stampies* from the other set were left with their natural material color (see Figure 2) for the testing of colored and line-drawn familiar items. We thus had a study design of 4 (*Stampie* Material Type) × 6 (Color) and 4 (Material Type) × 4 (categories of familiar items) × 2 (colored and line-drawn). All children underwent a within-subjects study whereby they engaged in all the conditions.

STUDY PARTICIPANTS AND METHODOLOGY

Nineteen children (10 girls and 9 boys), aged 4 to 7, participated in the study. Their parents volunteered their participation through a university mailing list. All of the children had previous experiences with personal touch devices (iPad, Leappad, Kindle, etc.), but none of them had experience with touch screen devices coupled with tangible objects.

Table 1. *Stampie* materials and digital items

Item categories	Items presented on the iPad
Animals	Dog, Cat, Rabbit, Pig
Fruits	Apple, Grape, Orange, Banana
Musical instruments	Piano, Violin, Xylophone, Drum
Clothing	Pants, Skirt, Shirts, Jacket

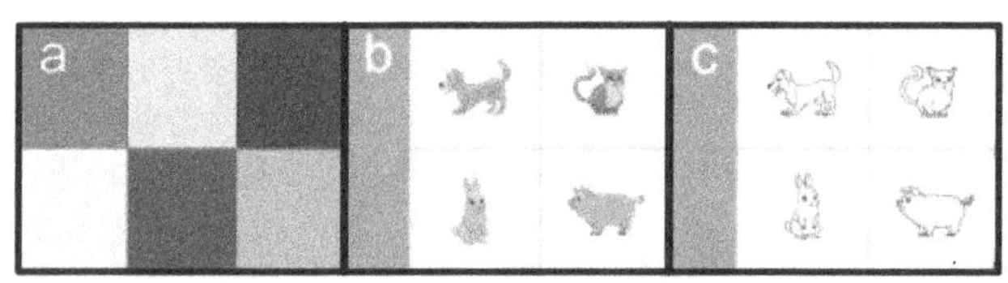

Figure 1. iPad screenshots for the sessions on: (a) colors, (b) colored items, (c) line-drawn items

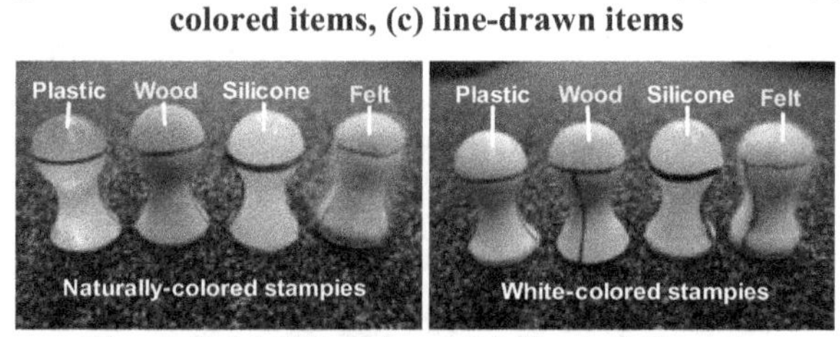

Figure 2. (a) Natural and (b) Neutral *Stampies*

Figure 3. *Stampies* with a unique conductive pattern

At a scheduled time, the child came to a laboratory with a parent(s). The room was set up to be child-friendly with child-sized tables, chairs and toys. After the child was introduced to the researchers and the setting, she was separated from her parent and the study was formally started. The study was made up of 4 stages: i) a familiarization session – the child was introduced by a researcher to a set of *stampies*, and was asked to physically experience them (see, touch, smell, etc.). Any remarks expressing their initial impression of the materials were recorded; ii) a *stampie*-digital item association task – the child was presented with a set of digital items on the iPad, and asked to select one *stampie* for each (Figure 4); iii) a recall task – with only the *stampies* in view, the child was asked whether she could recall what each *stampie* represented; and iv) a creative drawing task – the child was asked to create an artwork using the *stampies* that she had associated with the digital items previously.

The association, recall, and drawing tasks (representing one session) were repeated for the colors, line-drawn items and colored items with the appropriate natural or neutral *stampies*. A session was often repeated multiple times upon the child's request, resulting in a grand total of 94 sessions across all children. The order in which the digital content (colors, line-drawn items, colored items) was presented was counterbalanced such that 9 of the children started with colors first and then familiar items, and 10 of them did the reverse. On average, a child used the system for around 25 minutes in total. While the child took part in the study, her parent was set in an adjacent room, where a second researcher interviewed her about the child's prior experiences with touch devices.

DATA ANALYSIS AND FINDINGS

All sessions were video recorded. A researcher acted as an observer during the study and interview sessions, taking notes of relevant points. Collected data was analyzed using mixed methods (quantitative and qualitative research methods). The independent variable for the study included the colors, colored items, and line-drawn items (grouped into 4 categories – animals, fruits, musical instruments and clothing) chosen by the child to associate with a particular *stampie* type, which was the dependent variable. For the purpose of quantitative analysis, each *stampie* type, color and item category was assigned an ID number. The choices of the children were entered into the SPSS statistical package using the ID numbers (e.g. the choice of a plastic *stampie* for a colored animal was entered as a '3 – plastic' for material type, '1 – natural' for material color, and '1 – animal' for item category.

A chi-square test of association yielded a statistically significant relationship between the colored item category and the *stampie* material type, $X^2(9, N = 119) = 29.00, p < 0.01$. As shown in Figure 5A, wood was more likely to be associated with musical instruments, felt was more likely to be associated with clothes, plastic was more likely to be associated

Figure 4. A child engaging with the *Stampies* and the iPad app.

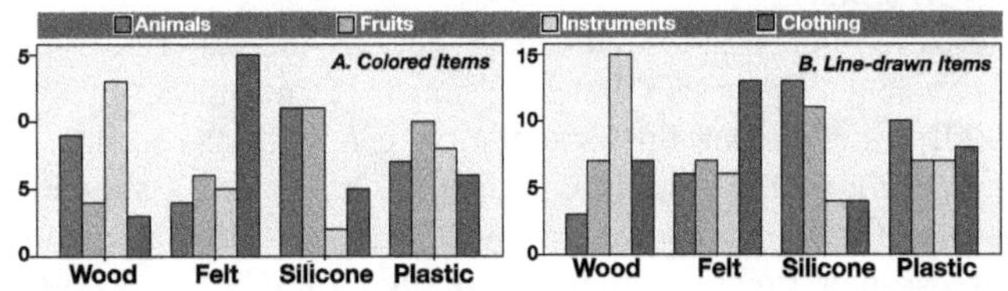

Figure 5. *Material type X Item category* for A. Colored items; B. Line-drawn items

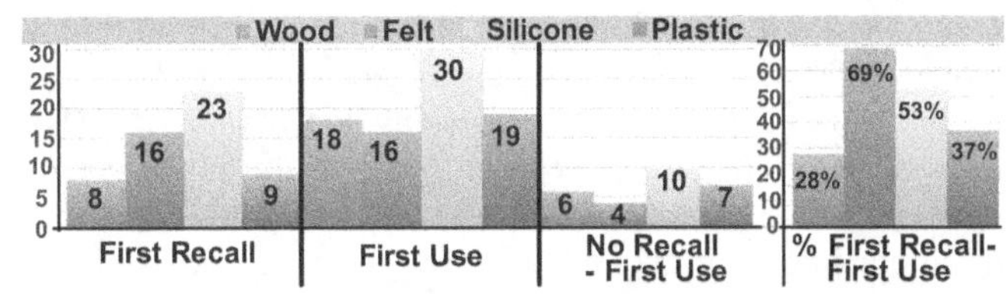

Figure 6 (L) 1. First association recalled; 2. First *stampie* used; 3. First *stampie* used when child could not recall associations; (R) % of first use that were also association first recalled

with fruits, and silicone was as likely to be associated with fruits and animals. A chi-square test of association also found a statistically significant relationship between the line-drawn item category and the *stampie* material type, $\chi^2(9, N = 128) = 22.75, p < 0.01$ (Figure 5B). Wood was more likely to be associated with musical instruments, felt was more likely to be associated with clothes, silicone was more likely to be associated with animals or fruits, and plastic was more likely to be associated with animals. No significant association was found for colors.

From video data, we coded the choices the children made with respect to first recall in the 'Recall' task of the study, and first use of the *stampies* during the 'Drawing' stage. We see that (left to right in Figure 6): 1. The children generally recalled the associations for the silicone and felt *stampies* first more frequently; 2. The children used the silicone *stampie* for drawing first most often; 3. When the children failed to recall any *stampie*-object associations (38/94 times or 40.43%), they drew first with the silicone *stampie* most often, and with felt least. This indicates that absent association bias, there is a preference for silicone as a material and a general bias against felt; and 4. Graph 4 charts the frequency of joint recall-use pairs as a percentage of total incidences of use of each material for drawing. Of the number of times the children chose to use the felt *stampie* for drawing, nearly 70% of this choice is accounted for by their vividness of recall of the felt material's association with its graphical object affiliate. This indicates that semantic drawing purpose rather than material preference accounts more for the use frequency of the felt *stampie*.

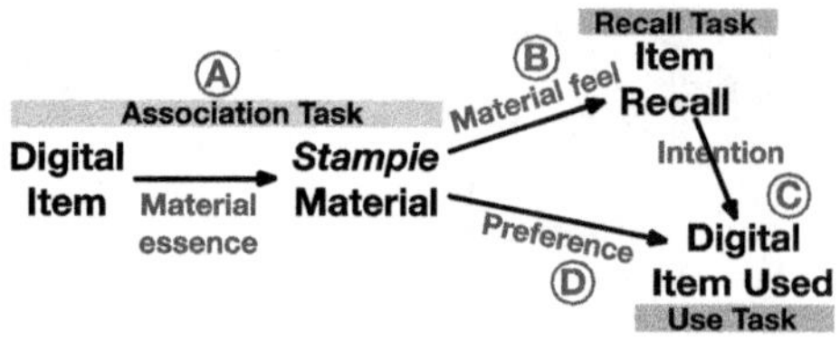

Figure 7. Model of study findings

DISCUSSION

We were interested to investigate whether the materiality of a physical object can have an intrinsic meaning for the child, and whether this association can help the child in interacting with a digital application. Our findings showed that digital items may possess what may be called a 'material essence', making them more likely to be associated with certain types of material than others (A in Figure 7). The associations by the child of wood with musical instruments, and felt with clothing, for instance, were prominent. However, the material feel of the object seems to dominate as the guiding factor for reaccessing the association (B). Silicone and felt were the two 'soft materials' in the set, as opposed to the plastic and wood *stampies*. The unique feel of silicone and felt may explain why their recall of associations for these two *stampies* was the best. Their use of *stampies* for drawing on the iPad appeared to have been led by both the semantic associations and the material feel (C & D). The felt and silicone materials illustrate this best. The children evidently had a tactile preference for the material feel of silicone, and would use it even when they did not have any drawing intention. Although they liked the feel of felt less, they used it for specific drawing content.

There is great potential to enhance the transparency of interfaces and to guide user actions by tapping into the power of materiality in systems for young children. Material essences, feel and liking are all aspects that can guide interaction design for a population that has low access to and understanding of text, language, and culturally-learnt symbols and conventions.

CONCLUSION

We presented empirical research that show how digital items carry meaning that are more readily associated with the intrinsic material essences of tangible interaction objects. Material feel can aid recall, and can be perceptually reaccessed. Specifically, we showed how children make use of material feel and tactile preference during interaction with a digital application. This paper thus contributes to the discourse on tangible interaction by showing the importance of materiality to supporting TUI design through enhanced embodied experience. We extend understanding of TUI design for young children for whom tactile experience is an important aspect of interacting with the world.

REFERENCES

1. Activision Publishing Inc. *Skylanders*. 2014 [cited 7 Aug. 2014]: http://www.skylanders.com/trapteam.
2. Antle, A.N., A.F. Wise, and K. Nielsen. *Towards utopia: designing tangibles for learning*. in *Proc. 10th Int'l Conf. Interaction Design & Children*. 2011. ACM.
3. Arita, J., J.H. Seo, and S. Aldriedge. *Soft tangible interaction design with tablets for young children*. in *ACM SIGGRAPH 2014 Posters*. 2014. ACM.
4. Fisher Price Inc. *Laugh & Learn™ Apptivity™ Creation Center*. 2014 [cited 7 Aug. 2014]: http://www.fisher-price.com/en_US/brands/laughandlearn/products/74898.
5. Ishii, H. *Tangible bits: beyond pixels*. in *TEI*. 2008. ACM.
6. Khaled, R., et al. *Let's clean up this mess: exploring multi-touch collaborative play*. in *CHI'09 Ext. Abs*. 2009. ACM.
7. Kidtellect Inc. *Tiggly: Unlock your imagination!* 2014 [cited 7th Aug. 2014]; http://tiggly.com/.
8. Macaranas, A., A.N. Antle, and B.E. Riecke. *Bridging the gap: Attribute and spatial metaphors for tangible interface design*. in *TEI*. 2012. ACM.
9. McLoyd, V.C., *The effects of the structure of play objects on the pretend play of low-income preschool children*. Child Dev., 1983: p. 626-635.
10. Norman, D., *Affordance, Conventions and Design*, in *Interactions*. 1999, ACM. p. 38-42.
11. Ormerod, F. and R. Ivanič, *Materiality in children's meaning-making practices*. Visual Comm., 2002. **1**(1): p. 65-91.
12. Rick, J., P. Marshall, and N. Yuill. *Beyond one-size-fits-all: How interactive tabletops support collaborative learning*. in *Proc. 10th Int'l Conf. on Interaction Design & Children*. 2011. ACM.
13. Sanders, J.T., *Merleau-Ponty, Gibson, and the materiality of meaning*. Man and World, 1993. **26**(3): p. 287-302.
14. Shaer, O. and E. Hornecker, *Tangible user interfaces: past, present, and future directions*. Foundations and Trends in HCI, 2010. **3**(1–2): p. 1-137.
15. Sony Computer Entertainment Europe. *Invizimals*. 2014 [cited 7 Aug. 2014]: http://invizimals.eu.playstation.com/en_GB/home.
16. Sweller, J., *Cognitive load theory, learning difficulty, and instructional design*. Learning and instruction, 1994. **4**(4): p. 295-312.
17. Vygotsky, L.S., *Mind in Society: The Development of Higher Psychological Processes*. 1978: Harvard U. Pr.
18. Wiberg, M., *Methodology for materiality: interaction design research through a material lens*. Personal and ubiquitous computing, 2014. **18**(3): p. 625-636.
19. Zanchi, C., A.L. Presser, and P. Vahey. *Next generation preschool math demo: tablet games for preschool classrooms*. in *Proc. 12th Int'l Conf Interaction Design & Children*. 2013. ACM.

MugShots: A Mug Display for Front & Back Stage Social Interaction in the Workplace

Hsin-Liu (Cindy) Kao, Chris Schmandt
MIT Media Lab
20 Ames Street, Cambridge, MA USA
{cindykao, geek}@media.mit.edu

ABSTRACT
We explore creating objects for expressive communication in the workspace. As an initial step, we created MugShots, a coffee mug with a wireless OLED display that switches between public and private social interaction modes. Targeted for the workplace, MugShots is an intimate communication device in the personal office space, yet alternates to become a social catalyst to trigger conversation when brought to public areas. We present a prototype of MugShots along with a 21-person study, providing initial discussions and insight on designing objects for communication.

Author Keywords
Social Catalyst; Computer Mediated Communication

ACM Classification Keywords
H.5.3. Group and Organization Interfaces

INTRODUCTION
Humans have always surrounded themselves with objects. Beyond using the objects, people also form emotional attachments to them. In the era of Ubiquitous Computing, electronics are being embedded into existing objects to further enhance their functionality, making them smarter, quicker and more responsive. Going beyond speed and convenience, what if technology could also be used to enhance the social, emotional, and expressive aspects of an object, creating objects that facilitate creativity, self-expression and communication with others?

We look into a familiar, frequently used object in the office space - the coffee mug, and explore how it can become a medium for expressive communication by embedding electronics and a wireless OLED (organic light-emitting diode) display on the mug exterior for visual communication. We find the mug interesting as it is a mobile object carried around by its owner, going into both public areas (e.g., coffee machine spaces) and private office spaces. We see this mobility as a design potential for different modes of communication.

TEI '15, January 16 - 19 2015, Stanford, CA, USA

http://dx.doi.org/10.1145/2677199.2680557

Figure 1. Envisioned panorama appearance of MugShots. (Electronics, including WiFi, are embedded in the bottom of the mug)

Drawing inspiration from Goffman's theory [7] of front and back stages in social interaction, we wanted to enable different modes of social interaction with the mug. Using theatrical metaphors, Goffman defines the "front stage" as where individuals are in front of an "audience" and where the desired self is presented. The "backstage," on the other hand, is a private and hidden space where people can be themselves without maintaining an ideal self-image. We design the mug to be an intimate communication device with close ones in the private "back stage" (personal office space), which would switch to become a catalyst to trigger conversation with colleagues when brought to the "front stage" (public area). Through the switching of stages, we design MugShots to facilitate varying degrees of self-expression in the formal office space.

We envisioned a MugShots as shown in Figure 1. A flexible OLED is wrapped around a mug body, with the ability to show high quality images for visual communication. The transferring of images is done through wireless communication. However, as we will discuss in the paper, the current display technology limits the design of our prototype.

BACKGROUND

Promoting Social Interaction in the Workplace
We target MugShots for use in office environments, as research has shown there are multiple benefits to increasing informal social interaction in the workplace. Research from Allen et al. [1] indicates that informal communications between colleagues may increase productivity and innovation; especially in creativity-driven work places, serendipitous encounters between people from different groups and disciplines may lead to cross-pollination of novel ideas [12]. In a recent study by Pentland et al. [16], exploration, i.e., informal communication people engage in outside their teams, serves as a major factor in the higher performance level of successful

teams. Moreover, exploration beyond the team was especially important for creative teams seeking fresh perspectives.

Social Catalyst

How can we create opportunities for informal communication in the workplace? Social catalysts, the term coined by Karahalios & Donath [13], are objects or events that stimulate mutual involvement to engage people in conversation. For example, when people bring their pets to public places, the pet often becomes a catalyst, inviting conversation from strangers.

This work explores the mug as a social catalyst to encourage interaction due to (1) its mobility, and (2) its known role for signaling personal qualities. The mug is an object we drink from daily and place next to us while we work. Yet, we also take it to public areas (i.e., coffee machine areas) where social interactions occur. This mobility opens opportunity for the mug to serve as a social interaction stimulator.

Moreover, as our clothing and accessories may serve as extensions of self-identity, the mugs we choose also reveal qualities about ourselves. Social signaling theory [14] states that we form an impression for and of others based on the commodities we own. MugShots builds upon this notion, allowing the user to designate, and even alternate the signal they wish to broadcast to the world by selecting and editing the images displayed on the mug. A smiley face may reveal a positive mood, while a rock-climbing photo may reveal one's outdoor interests.

Through these self-expressive signals, we explore how the mug may invite the interests of others to start a conversation. The mug facilitates a communication pull from the audience by seeding a conversation topic though the display.

Intimacy and Evocative Objects

The mug is designed to shift from a front stage social catalyst to an intimate object for communication when it is taken back to the private office space (i.e., "backstage"). We see the mug as having potential for intimate communication due to the vast body of research on the emotional relationship people have with their objects and processions. Belk [2] states that people establish a love and attachment for their things because they become "extensions of self," supporting our self-identity through their existence. On another note, Turkle [15] focuses on the sentimental element of human-object relations, viewing objects as "evocative" and as "companions to our emotional lives, or provocations to thought." Beyond serving as widely used objects of utility in offices, mugs also become objects of intimacy to the owner over time. It is not surprising to hear people having a mug they claim as "their own," or hear of someone looking for their "beloved lost mug." Similar to prior researchers exploring alternative channels to express intimacy, we see this as an opportunity to explore mugs as an intimate communication channel.

Related Technology

Previous work on smart cups technically inspires our work. The Mediacup [6] records data about the mug user and surrounding environment, converting the data into ambient sounds. Mr.Java [8] is a coffee machine that recognizes user coffee preferences through RFID mug tags. Playful Bottle [4] is a pervasive technology to encourage water drinking. Lover's Cup [5] connects remote lovers through LED lights that light up when drinking. The Buddy Cup [3] connects people on Facebook when they toast their cups.

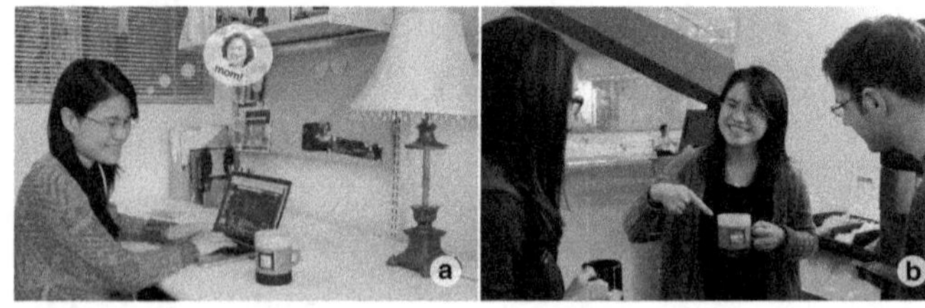

Figure 2. (a) User receiving images from intimate connection(s) in personal office mode. (b) Mug switches to public image when user enters a social space.

MugShots explores how a mug can become a medium for different modes of interaction in the workplace. It differs from Lover's Cup, which targets co-experience for remote lovers, and BuddyCup, which connects co-located people into the digital world. MugShots explores how an object can facilitate front and back stage social interaction in the workspace.

MUGSHOTS

Interaction Design

The interaction design of MugShots is based on two assumptions: (1) The users' workspace consists of at least one public area where informal interaction and beverage/liquid consumption can take place, e.g., water cooler or coffee machine area, (2) the user has her own personal office or desk space.

MugShots is designed to switch between two modes of interaction: the public area mode and personal office mode. The two modes switch automatically based on user location.

- Personal Office Mode (Figure 2(a)): In the personal space, the mug resumes its position as an intimate object and becomes a device for intimate communication. The user selects one or a few "mug buddies;" presumably close family or friends. The mug buddy (-ies) can send an image to the user's mug through a phone or web interface. At the bottom of the image, text indicates the person sending the image. Likewise, the user can also send images to the mug buddies.
- Public Area Mode (Figure 2(b)): From a web/phone interface, the mug owner can select images for public display. When the mug is taken to a public area, the mug switches to the public image, becoming a social catalyst to invite conversation. The user will not receive image updates in the public area; they will be buffered and appear when she returns to her office.

Prototype

The current hardware prototype consist of: 1) an 1.5" OLED 2) CC3000 Wi-Fi module, and 3) Arduino [9] central processor. The Wi-Fi module serves two functions: connecting to the server to pull image updates, and detecting location (public versus private) based on the different Wi-Fi

Figure 3. MugShots current prototype.

Figure 4. Web UI, and UI seen though phone.

footprints. Once the Wi-Fi module receives image updates from the server, the image will display on the OLED. Both OLED and Wi-Fi modules are driven by the central processor, an Arduino Pro Mini, via Serial Peripheral Interface. The mug body was modeled in Rhino [11] and fabricated with the MakerBot [10], taking the size of a typical coffee mug, with 3.3" in height, and 3.2" in diameter. In the near future we will fabricate in ceramic so users can drink from the mug.

The backend server consists of a web UI (Figure 4) with two main functions: 1) Selecting the images to display on the mug for public mode. 2) Selecting an image to send to a remote friend for personal mode. The web UI is compatible with phone interfaces (Figure 4); enabling wireless image updates though phones. The UI hosts a set of pre-selected images, and users also have freedom to add additional personal images.

When the Wi-Fi module in the cup detects the user leaving his/her office and entering the public space based on RSSI, it sends a signal to the Arduino board, and the OLED will switch to the public image. When the mug is taken into the office, the OLED will switch back to the private mode and receive image updates from friends. Note that in the current prototype, both images are stored in the mug for smooth switching. This also preserves privacy; if wireless communication is lost, the mug automatically switches to public mode.

MUGSHOTS STUDY

We recruited 21 participants (11 female, 10 male) to experience the MugShots system. Ages ranged from 22 to 47 (mean: 28.5). We screened for users with a personal office space. Before the interviews, users had the option to provide a self-selected public image that we would pre-load into the mug. All but two participants provided images.

We visited the participants in their workplaces for each study, deploying the MugShots system in their office. The actual study took 40 to 60 minutes, consisting of three parts: (1) Asking questions about the participant's current mug usage, and past histories with mugs. (2) Demoing the MugShots system and handing it over for the participant to experience. The participants could send and receive images (with the author taking the part of the "mug buddy"), select and update images, and move between personal and public spaces (where they would get coffee or beverages) to experience the image switching. When walking around with the mug, users were encouraged to act as if they had their usual mug with them, and to welcome any natural social interactions during the process. (3) Afterwards, a follow up semi-structured interview was conducted eliciting users' reflections.

Study Results

Public/Personal Modes

Many participants (N=15) appreciated the public/private interaction modes. They expressed it made the mug more "functional" as it enabled different interactions in public and private spaces. One participant mentioned that in the personal mode, the mug became "special" since she could receive images from her family, and yet it could also "switch to a formal looking mug with a neutral image" to maintain her professional image when taken around lounge spaces. Participants also expressed how MugShots protected the boundaries between public and private self. One participant expressed interest in receiving images from family while at work, but would feel "less enthusiastic if they sent me something public in a meeting." He appreciated how the system was "considerate" to the need for different levels of self-revelation in the workspace. We are encouraged that users reactions supported Goffman's front and back stage social interaction theory. However, there were a few users who did not enjoy the personal office mode due to privacy concerns (people walking into their offices), and preferred only the public mode.

Social Catalyst

For the public mode, several users (N=7) expressed interest in using the mug as a social catalyst to interact with other people, stating they would like to put up images that would "get people to talk to them." A user also expressed how the mug might alleviate social awkwardness in public areas, since the mug could trigger "a new topic for conversation." For example, one participant put up an image of his dog. During the study, this raised rapport about pets in the coffee machine area. Through the interviews, we are observing the user's attitude towards using the mug as a social catalyst, and not claiming that it works as one, as this would require a long-term study to observe shifts in social interaction.

Image Selection

The MugShots web and phone interface hosted a variety of images. We found it interesting how people from different cultures and demographic had different image preferences.

Several Asian participants (N=4) selected emoticon stickers. Others, who were active photo sharers on social media, selected images from Instagram or Facebook. Still others preferred logos of brands and organizations they identified with. We are intrigued by the how people express self-identity though different types of images.

Image Change Frequency

The system allows users to change images anytime, anywhere. Preference towards change frequency can be separated into two camps: the first preferring to keep the same image for one to six months (N=6). They viewed the mug as an extension of their public image, and were cautious about what they displayed. The other camp (N=8) preferred to change images every few days. They took a more playful attitude, wanting to update the image to anything "cool" they came across. A few users even went as extreme as to switching images every hour, suggesting the mug to automatically loop through a series of self-designated images throughout the day.

Display Placement

Currently, the OLED display is designed to be facing the user when they hold the mug. We have prototyped left and right-handed versions. Participants had mixed comments, some preferring the inward facing design since it felt more personal, while others (N=5) wanted an outward facing display so it would be apparent to others. Still others suggested placing the display in the middle of the afore-mentioned locations, expressing it would be "the best of both worlds."

Display Size

Limited by current technology, the MugShots prototype is implemented with a 1.5" OLED. One camp of participants (N=7), consisting mostly of those who desired an outward facing display, felt the current display size was too small. They were enthusiastic about having a large wrap-around OLED on the mug. Another set of participants preferred the current size, expressing it was visible yet discreet.

LESSONS LEARNED

- Many users found the MugShots appealing as it opened opportunities for self-expression in a formal setting - the workplace. However, since sustaining a professional image is critical, it is important for the system to be privacy preserving and "protective" of the user's personal mode and intimate images. The system needs to switch to public mode robustly whenever the user exits their personal space.
- As an object for expressive communication, users had different preferences towards images and the geometry of the mug. To enable self-expression, it is important for the mug to become an open canvas for various image configurations. This could be achieved with a large flexible wrap-around OLED. For example, the image could be on the left or right side for public/personal modes, and also alternative between different sizes. The unused pixels could either be turned off, or used as abstract decorations or mug motifs.

CONCLUSION AND FUTURE WORK

As a first exploration in creating objects for expressive communication, we created MugShots, a mug display for front and back stage social interaction. Targeted for the workplace, the mug switches between an intimate communication device and a social catalyst in public areas. When we exposed the prototype to potential users, many were enthusiastic and found the idea attractive for enhancing social interaction. During the study, we identified several aspects for future improvements including robust protection of user privacy and a flexible display exterior to enhance freedoms in self-expression.

ACKNOWLEDGMENTS

We thank the Living Mobile group for brainstorming sessions, and our study participants for their time and feedback.

REFERENCES

1. Allen, T. J. and Henn, G. W., *The Organization and Architecture of Innovation: Managing the Flow of Technology*. Butterworth-Heinemann, 2007.
2. Belk, R. W. Possessions and the Extended Self. *Journal of Consumer Research*, (1988)
3. Budweiser Buddy Cup. `http://vimeo.com/6706486`.
4. Chiu, M.-C., et al. Playful bottle: a mobile social persuasion system to motivate healthy water intake. In *Proc. UbiComp 2009*
5. Chung, H., et al. Lover's cups: drinking interfaces as new communication channels. In *Proc. CHI EA 2006*
6. Gellersen, H., et al. The MediaCup: Awareness Technology Embedded in an Everyday Object. In *Proc. HUC 1999*
7. Goffman E. *The Presentation of Self in Everyday Life*. Anchor, 1959.
8. Mr. Java. `http://www.media.mit.edu/ci/projects/mrjava.html`.
9. Arduino. `http://www.arduino.cc/`.
10. MakerBot. `http://www.makerbot.com/`.
11. Rhino. `http://www.rhino3d.com/`.
12. Isaacs, E. A., et al. Piazza: a desktop environment supporting impromptu and planned interactions. In *Proc. CSCW 1996*
13. Karahalios, K. and Donath, J. Telemurals: Linking Remote Spaces with Social Catalysts. In *Proc. CHI 2004*
14. Liu, C., and Donath, J. Urbanhermes: social signaling with electronic fashion In *Proc. CHI 2006*
15. Turkle, S. *Evocative Objects: Things We Think With*. MIT Press, 2007.
16. Pentland, A. The new science of building great teams. *Harvard Business Review 90*, 4 (2012).

MagnID: Tracking Multiple Magnetic Tokens

Andrea Bianchi
Sungkyunkwan University
Suwon, Korea
andrea.whites@gmail.com

Ian Oakley
Department of Human and Systems Engineering
UNIST, Ulsan, Korea
ian.r.oakley@gmail.com

ABSTRACT

Tangible systems present compelling interaction opportunities but are typically enabled by complex, bulky, awkward or expensive sensing infrastructures. This hinders their adoption in many application areas. In order to address this issue, this paper explores the use of simple active magnetic tokens that create carefully controlled patterns of varying magnetic flux as the building blocks of tangible systems. We describe the construction of these tokens and a software system capable of detecting their presence and inferring their location based on data sampled from a single triaxial magnetometer - a standard component of most current mobile devices. The system can recognize token positions from a set of six pre-calibrated locations with an accuracy of 99%. We describe the hardware and software components of this system and five demonstration applications that illustrate its functionality.

Author Keywords

Magnet; Near-Device Interaction; Tangible Interaction.

ACM Classification Keywords

H.5.2 [Information interfaces and presentation]: User Interfaces. – Input devices and strategies.

INTRODUCTION

Tangible interaction is a compelling paradigm in which users manipulate real objects to control digital contents [23, 24]. It promises to bring the benefits of physical affordance, fine-grained manipulation and natural understandings to interaction with virtual contents. However, while potentially powerful, most current tangible systems are also inaccessible to most users as they rely on large and expensive sensing infrastructures, such as tabletop computers [11]. We argue this dependency has hindered the adoption, development and deployment of tangible interfaces in real world applications and to real world users.

Numerous authors have made similar observations and there has been a recent trend to develop tangible systems based on the sensing capabilities of modern mobile devices - low cost and prevalent hardware platforms. One approach

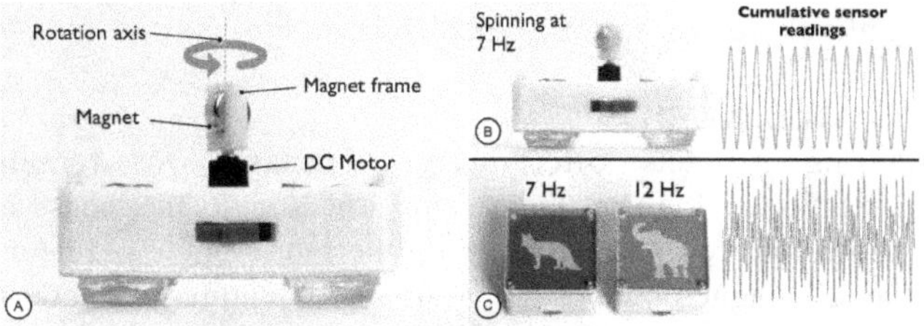

Figure 1. MagnID tokens work by spinning a magnet with a motor (A). A magnetometer senses changes of polarity as a continuous wave with a specific frequency (B, C).

has been to use visual tracking techniques [1], but these require bulky additional physical setups to ensure clear visual fields of view onto tracked objects. Another approach has been to create systems of tokens that can be placed on the touch screen of devices. Through careful design involving conductive materials placed on capacitive screens, these tokens create unique and recognizable patterns of on-screen touches that can be mapped to object tracking [5] or control activity [25]. While this is powerful, such systems suffer from inherent limitations: available screen size is small and the number of objects and touches that devices can recognize is relatively low (typically between two and four independently tracked objects based on a maximum of five to 11 touch points), restricting the expressive potential of such approaches.

Another approach has been to embed magnets in tokens or objects [e.g., 3, 8]. These can be sensed by the on-board magnetometers present in modern mobile devices and confer numerous advantages - magnets require no power, are inexpensive and can be detected both on and around a device. Reflecting these advantages researchers have built a range of systems for tasks such as device customization [10], cursor control [7], or adding physical buttons, sliders and dials to the area around a device [8]. However, a fundamental limitation of such systems is that magnetometers return a single aggregate vector summing the magnetic fields surrounding them. This makes it challenging to create systems based on more than one independently tracked object or token. While some authors have trained recognizers to achieve this objective when the available movements are highly restricted in scope [3, 8], there is no currently available system based on commodity sensors such as magnetometers that can recognize the independent location of a set of tokens based the magnetic fields they generate.

This paper aims to address this issue by designing and developing MagnID, a novel magnetic object tracking

TEI '15, January 15–19, 2015, Stanford, California, USA.

http://dx.doi.org/10.1145/2677199.2680582

system. The main contribution of this paper is the design of the system. It innovates over prior work by supporting tracking multiple magnetic tokens simultaneously, in locations both on and around a device and via data recorded from a single magnetometer. Secondary contributions are a description and characterization of the performance of one possible implementation of the MagnID concept, and the presentation of five demonstration applications that highlight the design space enabled by MagnID.

RELATED WORK

Sensing magnets offer many advantages for mobile interaction. Magnets themselves are small, inexpensive, unpowered components [7]. Furthermore, high precision triaxial magnetometers are a standard feature of modern mobile devices and tablets. Finally, magnetic fields are largely immune to issues of field-of-view - magnetic interaction systems can function seamlessly in the spherical volume surrounding a single sensor. However there are also challenges unique to magnetic tracking. Typical magnetic sensors (e.g. triaxial magnetometers) return a cumulative reading derived from all the magnetic fields affecting the sensor (including those attributable to environmental noise) effectively making accurate disambiguation of multiple independent magnetic sources an under-constrained problem - there are many possible solutions for any given state. Dipole magnetic field strength (such that generated by many common permanent magnets) also varies with the inverse-cube of distance, meaning that small spatial displacements of magnets near the sensor results in greater changes to detected data than relatively large displacements of more distant magnets [22]. Combining the properties and features of this sensing channel, researchers have developed a wide range of interaction techniques and applications based on detecting the position and/or rotation of fixed magnets with respect to a magnetometer or similar sensor.

In one of the earliest systems to exploit magnets, Abracadabra [7] demonstrated how a small permanent magnet could expand the input space of a wristwatch computer. A ring-shaped magnet was worn on a user's finger and tracked by a magnetometer embedded in the watch in order to determine its relative position. This data was used to control a cursor, make selections and issue basic gestures. Other authors have extended this basic concept. For example, Ketabdar et al.'s Magnetic signature [14] and MagiWrite [15] track magnets on fingers to allow smartphone users to write their signature or input numbers by gesturing in the space around a mobile device. Similarly MagiMusic [13] allows users to strum a virtual guitar by swinging a magnetic ring around their mobile.

Researchers have also explored the possibilities of mounting magnetic sensors on fingers. FingerPad [4], for example, uses a grid of hall-effect sensors on the nail of a user's index finger and a magnet on the thumbnail. With this setup subtle and private finger gestures, such as pinching, or writing numbers with the thumb, can be effectively tracked. Chen et al.'s uTrack [6] achieves a similar goal by requiring users to wear a pair of three-axial magnetometers on their fingers and a permanent magnet on their thumb. Software processes the resultant sensor data to provide a measure of continuous relative thumb position that can be used for pointing or gesturing in a 3D space.

Embedding magnets into peripherals or tokens offers the potential to track these items as part of an interactive system. MagPen [9] demonstrates how interaction with a capacitive stylus on a tablet touchscreen can be augmented with an embedded fixed magnet. Using the in-device magnetometer, the system supports sensing the orientation of the pen, the identity (or type) of the pen, pen gestures such as flipping and the pressure exerted against the screen during drawing. GaussSense [19], a magnetic sensor grid based on 512 hall-effect sensors, can also be used to track a fixed magnet within a pen to report stylus tip location, height, pressure and angle. Although complex, the GaussSense sensing system is slim and can be placed behind any screen or surface to create a drawable display.

Magnetic systems can also be used to track other forms of input device. Bianchi and Oakley's Magnetic Appcessories [3], for example, show how a mobile device magnetometer can sense fixed magnets attached to a range of physical objects, such as cubes, sliders or dials, to detect meaningful physical manipulations such as flipping, moving or spinning. A substantial limitation to this work is that only a single physical control can be tracked at any one time. Various techniques have been proposed to sidestep this issue and support simultaneous tracking of multiple objects. MagGetz [8] fixes the locations of a small set of controls around a device (e.g. two sliders and one button) and trains a machine learning classifier to disambiguate simultaneous or overlapping one-dimensional changes to these widget positions. While elegant, this approach cannot track large scale or unconstrained movements and is limited in the number of items it can distinguish. GaussBits [18] and GaussBricks [17], based on the powerful and expressive GaussSense system [19], use the sensor grid to track the position, rotation and orientation of multiple magnetic objects simultaneously. This supports a rich set of interactions based on unconstrained movements of objects over the sensor surface. While large numbers of objects can be tracked, the system relies on complex bespoke hardware and, in contrast to the volumes of sensing space available in other magnetic systems, works only when objects are positioned directly over the top of the sensor surface.

MAGNID SYSTEM OVERVIEW

The MagnID system adopts the novel approach of designing active magnetic tokens with the goal of supporting detection of relatively unconstrained movements of multiple objects in the area around a single standard magnetometer. All models, schematics, part lists and source code are available online at https://github.com/makinteract/MagnID.

MagnID is composed of a set of eight custom tokens, a standard sensor and a software recognition system. Each token spins a magnet around the axis perpendicular to its magnetic flux at a carefully selected unique frequency. By doing so, the tokens systematically flip the polarity of their magnetic fields in sinusoidal temporal patterns (Figure 1). The sensor, a triaxial magnetometer, detects the cumulative magnetic field generated by multiple tokens on each of its three sensor axis. The software system applies a series of bandpass filters to this data to recover signals from the individual tokens. This enables us to determine the presence or absence of the different tokens. Furthermore, by extracting the power within each frequency band, we are also able to infer the distance between each token and the sensor on each axis. Using this distance data, we can determine the spatial position of each token with respect to a set of previously calibrated locations, or linearly interpolate token position between two previously calibrated points to get a more fine-grained measurement. In summary, MagnID innovates over prior work by creating a novel magnetic token system with this set of properties:

Multiple tokens: MagnID supports use of up to eight simultaneous tokens, similar to tangible platforms based on other sensing systems such as Lumino [2] or Siftables [20].

Multiple locations: Movements are relatively unconstrained - each token can be freely placed and detected in a large set of possible locations.

Sensing Area: MagnID tokens can be tracked both over the surface of a mobile device and in the "around-device" interaction space (10-20 cm around a mobile) [16].

Commodity sensor: MagnID tokens are sensed by a single triaxial magnetometer, a common component in most smart mobile devices [8].

Tokens and Sensor Unit

Each MagnID token (see Figure 2) consists of a plastic housing designed in SolidWorks and printed with PLA on an Ultimaker 3D printer. Mounted on top of this unit are a sheet of colored card and a 5mm thick layer of Plexiglas with engraved token icons. Rubber feet insulate the token from the surface it is situated on. The final dimensions are 50mm by 50mm by 40mm high and each token weighs 67 grams when assembled. Each token contains a single Neodymium 7mm diameter x 3mm depth 3T disc-shaped permanent magnet, attached via a 3D printed mount to an upwards facing 3V DC motor. The motor is situated in the center of the token and spins the magnet perpendicularly to its magnetic axis (Figure 1), resulting in rotation invariant tokens. The motor is inexpensive, small, and features low power consumption (50 mA), low noise (48 dB), a small reduction ratio (1/5.14), a low stall current (<200mA) and a maximum speed of 6420 RPM. These features allow it to spin the magnet at frequencies between 5Hz and 100 Hz. The motor is connected to a 100Ω variable resistor that can

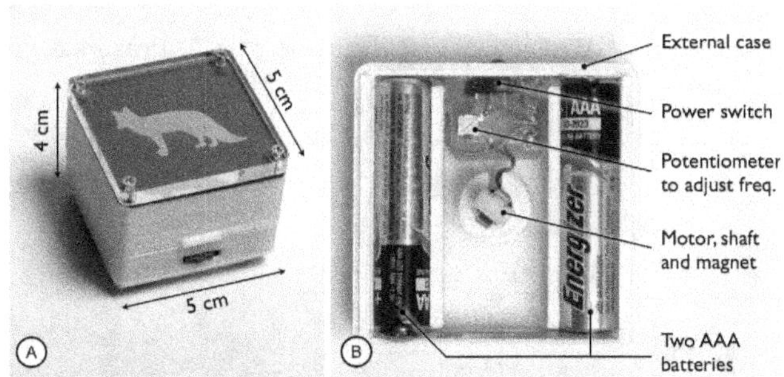

Figure 2. Outside (A) and inside (B) view of token hardware.

adjust the current and therefore the spinning frequency. Using this setup, in the current version of MagnID, eight tokens were created and set to spin at frequencies of 7.5Hz, 12.5Hz, 17.5Hz, 22.5Hz, 27.5Hz, 32.5Hz, 37.5Hz, and 42.5Hz.

MagnID tokens are powered by two AAA batteries connected in series that support up to 24 hours of continuous usage. Early tests showed that tokens with this simple design produced highly consistent (e.g. ±1Hz) rotation frequencies for periods in excess of two hours, more than sufficient for application development and test purposes. Finally, the tokens feature a switch that toggles the unit on and off. All components were mounted on a custom PCB. These design choices offer flexibility in terms of the rotational frequencies we can generate as well as simplicity, reliability and cost-effectiveness. The total price for a single MagnID token is under ten USD: motor (4$), batteries (2$), magnet (0.1$), electronic components (1$) and housing (2$). Furthermore, after materials have been gathered and produced, token assembly is a simple task requiring approximately 30 minutes. These choices enabled production of a large token set for application development.

For development purposes, we also constructed a sensor prototype using an external magnetometer unit connected to a PC. This is because our software system requires libraries and tools that are not currently available for mobile platforms (see limitation section). However, to ensure compatibility with current mobile devices, our sensing system was based on a cheap, commercially available triaxial magnetometer (Honeywell HMC5883L, available for under 2 USD) capable of a sample rate of 100 Hz (and therefore able to detect spinning magnetic fields at frequencies up to 50Hz). We connected this device directly to an Arduino Uno and, via a USB based 115200 baud RS232 link, to the host PC that then executed all signal processing and the location detection algorithm.

Software Implementation

The MagnID software consists of a configuration and calibration interface, a sensing and filtering system, a message broadcasting system. All software was written in Java and runs on a desktop computer.

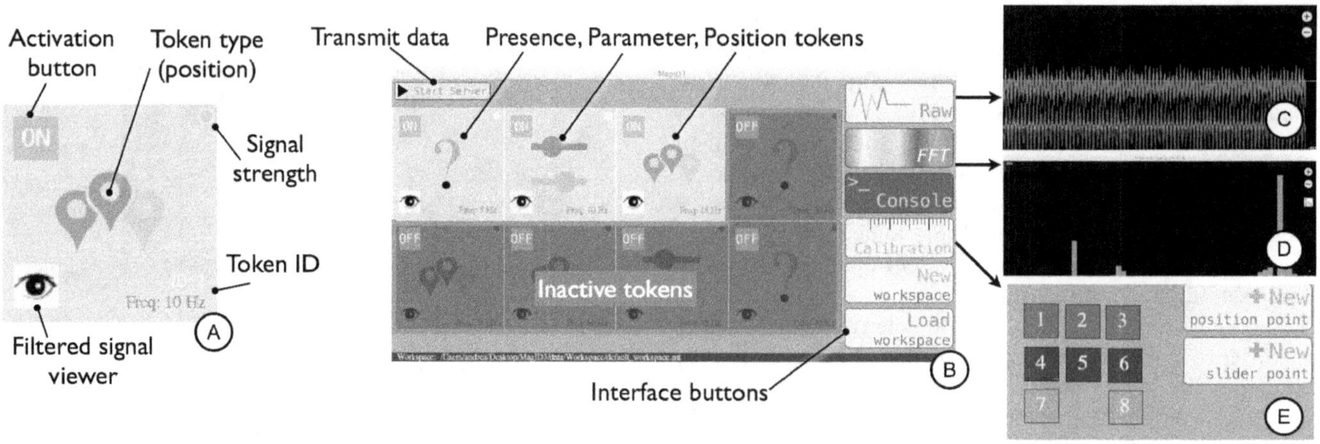

Figure 3. The main software interface (B) is composed by eight identical interface elements representing frequency bands and their parameters (A). Users can customize the token type, and activate/deactivate the frequency band. Tools for displaying the raw three-axial signal (C), the frequency spectrum (D), or for calibrating tokens (E) are also available from the main interface.

Calibration and Configuration: User interface

To use MagnID an application developer must first calibrate and configure the tokens they will use. MagnID provides an interactive application to support these activities. The main interface (Figure 3.B) shows the eight possible MagnID tokens, each with its own unique spinning frequency and ID. The frequencies used match those of the token set (but are labeled at the lower bound of a 5Hz window around the token frequency, e.g. 5Hz for a token frequency of 7.5 Hz, see Figure 3). Users can click to activate/deactivate tokens and select the recognition type from among three possible options: presence, position, or parameter. Setting a token as presence means that its state will be reported by the MagnID system as binary - data will be returned simply indicating whether or not the token is detected. Tokens configured as position return not only presence, but also location information from a set of pre-calibrated options. Finally, parameter tokens return a more fine-grained measure of location derived from a linear interpolation between two or more pre-calibrated locations.

The location calibration process also takes place in this application (Figure 3.E). This is done on a separate screen in which users can add and position calibration points, shown as colored boxes, in a 2D space. Each calibration point represents categorical data, and the spatial arrangement is solely used as a planning or mnemonic technique for users. After a layout is complete, clicking on a calibration point starts a data capture process. This involves physically positioning a MagnID token in a desired real-world location and then logging one second of data from the system magnetometer (100 samples). This data is then associated with the calibration point. This process is repeated for each remaining calibration point and the final data logs are stored in a single calibration file that can be loaded at runtime by a MagnID application. The calibration process can be performed with just one MagnID token (and generalized to the whole set) as the power of the magnetic field generated by each token is identical - only the frequency varies between the tokens.

The configuration system also contains visualization and debug tools (Figure 3.C and D). Users can toggle the server message broadcast and open a console to examine the broadcasted messages. Furthermore, they can view the filtered data for each token, a quick and effective way to see if the tokens are visible to the system and gauge the power of the signal being measured. The interface also supports viewing the raw sensor data and the frequency spectrum of the aggregate signal. This is a useful way to view, debug or fine tune token frequencies.

Sensing and token location detection

The filtering algorithms operate on the raw triaxial magnetic field data sampled by the sensing hardware at 100 Hz. Eight frequency bands are used (one for each MagnID token) each spanning five Hz and centered on the MagnID token frequencies (e.g. 5Hz-10Hz, 10Hz-15Hz, 15Hz-20Hz, etc.). Using the Matlab Filter Design and Analysis toolkit we produced FIR bandpass filters using either the Equiripple method or a Hamming window (order 100) for each of these eight bands. Different token types used the two different filters to optimize performance. Coefficients were stored in files and loaded in our software at run time. The filtered signal captured from each token takes the form of three independent zero-centered sinusoidal bipolar waves (one on each sensor axis) with identical frequencies but different amplitudes. The amplitudes express the distance between the token and the sensor according to the inverse cubic law [22]. Before further processing, we rectify the waves then apply a median filter to reduce noise (of size equal to the wave period). This yields a steady waveform representing the strength of the magnetic field emanating from each token.

We then process the tokens according to their recognition type. Presence tokens are processed to determine whether they are in range of the sensor by comparing the overall power in the frequency band against a user configurable threshold value. For position tokens, the aggregate magnitude (for each axis of sensor data) is matched against the data from the calibration points using a Support Vector Machine (SVM). Finally, data from parameter tokens is analyzed using linear regression to interpolate between two or more pre-calibrated locations in order to infer the tokens relative position with respect to these points.

Broadcasting Token Events

After determining the presence, position or parameters of the tokens around the sensor, the MagnID software system broadcasts this data at a user-configurable rate using the OSC protocol. The application is configured as a server and simply sends packets in real time to an IP broadcast address, a technique that is also used in the popular TUIO toolkit [12]. Each broadcast packet contains the token type (presence, position or parameter), the token ID (or frequency band), the filtered triaxial magnetometer readings and, in the case of position and parameter tokens, the categorical or interpolated token location. To listen in to this data, a client application needs simply to capture packets sent to the broadcast IP address, avoiding the need to integrate computationally intensive signal processing code into end-user applications.

EVALUATION

MagnID tracks tokens based on their distance from the sensor unit. As such, token tracking performance may be influenced by the number of locations considered and the spacing between them. Generally, accuracy can be expected to drop when the number of locations and/or their spatial density goes up. Furthermore, the distance between locations and the sensor can also impact performance - tokens at very short ranges lead to noisy data, while distant tokens are too faint for reliable detection. However, the system should be robust to increasing numbers of simultaneously active tokens and also perform similarly with all tokens (e.g. across all frequency bands regardless of the band that was initially used for training the classifier). To verify system performance, particularly with regard to tracking accuracy, we constructed five typical arrangements of tokens: two in the form of rows, and three in the form of 2D grids (see Table 1). In all cases locations were immediately adjacent to each other (e.g. spaced at five cm intervals, the size of the tokens). The sensor was also always located at the top right of the layout, 10 cm away from the nearest location and rotated 45° to face the grid.

Layout	1D / 2D	Mean Token Distance (cm)	Calibration token 10-15 Hz	Test token 30-35 Hz
●●	1	13	99.5% K=0.99	99.5% K=0.99
●●●	1	14	99.6% K=0.99	99.6% K=0.99
●● ●●	2	15	99.7% K=0.99	99.7% K=0.99
●●● ●●●	2	16	99.8% K=0.99	99.8% K=0.99
●●● ●●● ●●●	2	18	99.8% K=0.99	93.8% K=0.93

Table 1. Table shows accuracy for different layout. Distance is computed between the sensor and the centroid of the layout.

For each arrangement, we trained our software with the corresponding calibration data. We used a calibration token (12.5Hz) and sampled 100 samples of filtered data per location. We then collected 100 samples of test data for each location using both the calibration token and a test token (32.5Hz). Table 1 shows the recognition results. These indicate that for all save one configuration location recognition is achieved with above 99% accuracy. In the final, and most complex configuration of nine locations, accuracy dropped to 93%. A close examination of these cases showed that approximately half of the errors involved misclassification of the top-left location as the central location. This is likely due to either the large mean distance of tokens in the layout and the sensor (18 cm) or the similar radial distance between the sensor and these two specific locations. These data suggest that for optimal accuracy, sample applications should work with two-dimensional layouts with a maximum of six different token locations.

We also recorded recognition time during this process. Tokens were recognized within one second, but localization showed greater variability. Basically, depending on factors such as distance from the sensor, the number of tokens used simultaneously and the proximity of other tokens, the time to localize a token varied by up to one additional second.

EXAMPLE APPLICATIONS

To showcase the capabilities of the MagnID system, we constructed five demonstration applications that highlight a range of interaction types, scenarios and possibilities. All applications were developed in Processing on a Samsung Galaxy Note 8.0 Android tablet and wirelessly connected to the MagnID server application to receive information about the tokens. In each case, the MagnID sensor unit was placed near the tablet (the exact position varied according to the desired token arrangement) during calibration and application use. The applications are described below, organized according to the token features they deploy.

Token Presence: We constructed a playful application that associates content shown on a tablet with the placement and removal of physical tokens around a device (Figure 4). The context was animals appearing and disappearing from a zoo cage. In the application, two cages are shown - one on the tablet screen and one on an adjacent paper game board. By placing a lion, elephant or other animal token on top of the

Figure 4. Token presence application. If there is no token in the physical cage (A), the virtual cage is empty as well. If token are present (B, C), the application detects them.

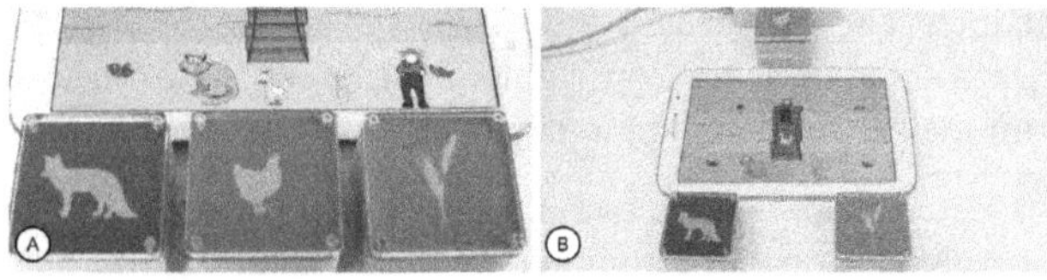

Figure 5. The tokens for a fox, chicken and grain (A) are moved and the system independently tracks their location (B).

paper cage, a virtual icon showing this animal appears on-screen. Removal of the token leads to the disappearance of the animal. Up to five animals can share the cage simultaneously, creating a playful and attractive on-screen scene that directly reflects the tokens that are present on the paper game board.

Token Position: Independently detecting the absolute and/or relative positions of multiple tokens is a fundamental enabling feature of tangible systems [24]. Accordingly, we developed three applications that take advantage of MagnID's ability to independently detect the position of multiple tokens. In the first, shown in Figure 5, we developed a simple game based on the riddle of farmer who needs transport a fox, a chicken and a sack of grain across a river. Only one item can be moved at once and, if left alone, the fox will eat the chicken and the chicken the grain. In the game, each commodity is represented by a token and an on-screen icons, initially clustered on one side of the river (in the case of icons) and tablet (in the case of the tokens). Users can move a token to the other side of the tablet to instruct the on-screen farmer to move the appropriate item across the river. Simple game logic maintains the state of the system and informs users when they win or lose. In this application three tokens are simultaneously and accurately tracked between six valid positions.

The second position related application is based on the scenario of language learning and tracks a larger number of tokens and locations (Figure 6). The tablet screen shows four locations labeled by flags, each representing a different nation and language. Different animal tokens (e.g. elephant, fox) can be placed on each on-screen box and then tapping on the associated flag triggers a audio sample in which a native speaker states the animal's name in the appropriate language. For example, placing the fox token on the Portuguese game board flag, then tapping the on-screen icon will play "raposa", the Portuguese for fox. This application extends the previous position-tracking demo in two ways. Firstly, it showcases a larger number of tokens and locations - any of six animals can be placed on any of four language flags. Secondly, it shows the possibility of

Figure 6. Tracking multiple tokens in multiple locations: tokens representing animals and located on flag-labelled boxes trigger the animal's name in the appropriate language.

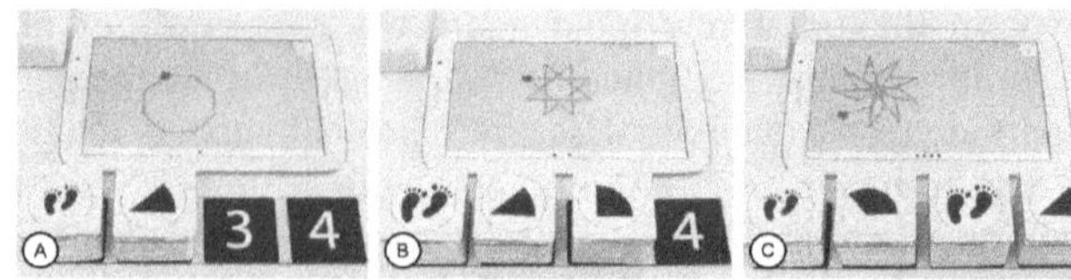

Figure 7. In this LOGO-like application, the system detects different sequences of tokens and uses them to instruct a turtle how to move (draw) on the screen.

using tokens on top of a mobile device and in combination with traditional on-screen activities such as tapping and selecting. This showcases a rich interaction space merging tangible tokens with traditional graphical input.

The final position based application implements a simple LOGO inspired turtle [21]. Eight tokens are used, representing instructions that control the movement and rotation of a turtle icon shown on the tablet screen (Figure 7). Three tokens represent movements of different amounts (small, medium and large) and five tokens represent rotations (between 9 and 155 degrees, selected to allow a rich range of shapes). Up to four of these commands can be arranged in a row adjacent to the tablet at any one time. Then, by tapping the screen, the turtle commences to execute the commands in a loop - the leftmost command first and the rightmost last. By arranging the commands in different sequences a wide range of shapes including squares, circles, triangles, and stars can be produced programmatically. This application moves beyond the prior demonstrations by showing the ability to infer and respond to relative position - eight tokens can be freely arranged in any of four locations and the order in which they are arranged can be determined.

Token Parameter: The final application showcases the ability of MagnID to detect token state beyond categorical positions (Figure 8). It is a stylus based paint application for a tablet with tangible controls in the form of two tokens located to one side of the device. The position of each token controls a different quality of the pen - one its color, the other its brush size. Control is achieved by moving the tokens to the left and right (like a one dimensional slider) and each token supports an analogue interpolation of its position along a predetermined movement range. Furthermore, both tokens can be operated independently and simultaneously. Basically, this setup allows a user to paint with the pen in their dominant hand and make fine-grained adjustments to the color and size of their strokes using the two tokens. This application showcases the

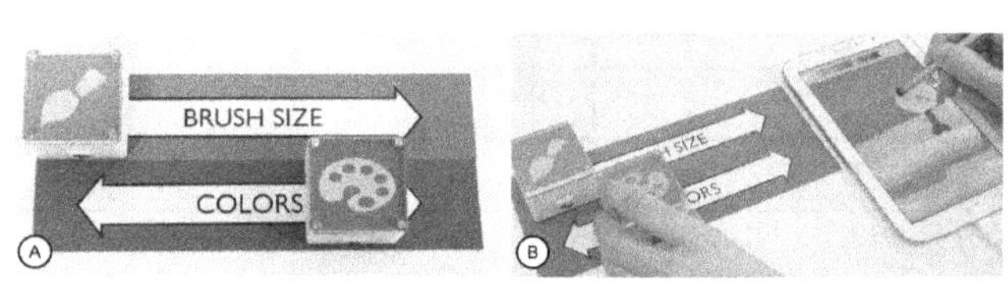

Figure 8. Two tokens are used as sliders to control the brush size and the color (A), in a drawing application (B).

sensitivity of the parameter tokens in MagnID and the ability to reliably interpolate between two positions given pre-calibrated locations.

DISCUSSION

There are a number of limitations to the current MagnID system. Although magnetism is immune to many of the field of view problems that affect optical tracking systems, its range is relatively limited. With the current 7mm magnets and magnetometer, tokens can be reliably recognized in the range of between 3cm and 25cm from the sensor. The use of stronger magnets would boost the maximum range at the cost of increasingly noisy data at close range. One potential solution to this problem may be to base future versions of the system on two magnetometers, each optimally sensitive to magnetic fields of different strengths.

The tracking system used in MagnID, fundamentally based on detecting the distance between tokens and the sensor also imposes some limits in terms of the arrangements of locations that are supported. Basically, while the system is sufficiently accurate to detect tokens arranged in common structures such as rows or simple grids, more complex structures (e.g. Table 1, final row) result in locations that are hard to distinguish from one another. Application designers using the MagnID approach will have to carefully select the token locations used in their systems to optimize their distinguishability.

There are also several issues with the tokens physical design. Firstly, although the current hardware prototypes are equivalently sized to the tokens in many tangible systems (five by five cm, similar to Siftables [20]) the limited sensing range available restricts interaction to approximately 25 unique locations in the area immediately around the sensor. This issue could be partly addressed through miniaturizing the tokens. Secondly, the tokens are based on mechanical movement and thus emit low-level noise and vibrations. Measured in a quiet room (40-45dB ambient), a microphone placed 10 cm away from a MagnID tokens registers between 50 dB for low frequencies and 70 dB for high frequencies, an audible level of noise. One potential solution to this problem is to develop non-mechanical solutions based on electromagnets powered in timer controlled oscillating patterns (PWM). A disadvantage to this purely digital approach would likely be substantially greater power consumption.

The software systems also suffer from a number of limitations. Although this paper makes a case for MagnID as an effective tool to expand the interaction potential of mobile devices through physical tokens, our system prototype does not currently natively run on a mobile platform. Instead, a custom sensor is connected to a desktop computer as this approach simplifies sensing and data processing. However, we argue this issue does not detract from the main objective of this paper - to show the feasibility of the MagnID system independently of the computational platform it is based on. Furthermore, in order to test the feasibility of a fully mobile approach, we ported the sensing system to the mobile device (Samsung Galaxy Note 8.0) used to develop the demonstration applications. We used the on-board magnetometer to capture signals at 100Hz and streamed them over the Android Debug Bridge (ADB) on USB to a PC running the MagnID software. Initial tests show the on-board sensor (a Yamaha MS-3R YAS532) is capable of analogous frequency recognition to our dedicated sensor unit. However, sensitivity was reduced - the effective sensing range around the device was reduced from 25 cm to approximately 10 cm. Future work will rectify this problem by integrating stronger magnets into the system, or seeking a mobile device that features a magnetometer than is configured for high sensitivity applications (such hardware settings are not typically made available to developers on standard Android devices).

CONCLUSIONS

Tangible computing is a compelling and promising interaction paradigm [23, 24] that faces many challenges before it can be adopted in mainstream commercial products. One of these relates to the demanding hardware requirements of both current research systems [e.g. 1, 2] and existing product offerings [e.g. 11]. The work in this paper contributes to a growing body of literature that addresses this problem by exploring how the sensing capabilities of existing mobile computers can be leveraged to create physical, tangible interfaces [3, 5, 25].

Fixed magnets - cheap, small and portable - have been previously proposed in order to achieve this objective. The magnetic interaction system introduced in this paper moves beyond this prior work by constructing simple, active tokens that can be independently detected. This allows us to consider a greater range of interaction scenarios than those based on a single magnet (e.g. the fingertip cursor control in Abracadabra [7], Hwang et al.'s MagPen [9] or the magnetic widgets proposed by Bianchi and Oakley [3]) or the highly constrained movement of two to three magnets [8]. Indeed, the ability to detect the location of multiple independent tokens or objects is a defining aspect of many typical tangible systems [24], and it is this functionality that our system seeks to enable.

Furthermore, unlike prior systems capable of detecting multiple magnets [17, 18], the work in this paper achieves this objective using only a single triaxial magnetometer - a standard piece of equipment in most current mobile devices. This contrasts strongly with the approaches of other magnetic sensing systems capable of tracking multiple objects. For example, the rich interactions that the impressive Gaussbits system can achieve are enabled by a large, expensive array of 768 independent sensors [18]. While the Gaussbits prototype affords many opportunities for exploring interaction scenarios [17], its bulk, cost and complexity make it an unlikely candidate for integration into real mobile device products. Moreover, Gaussbits tokens can only be sensed if positioned on, or immediately over, the screen while MagnID's approach allows application designers to take advantage of the full volume of space around a device.

In conclusion, the goal of this paper is to create and document a magnetic tracking system that supports multiple tokens that can be freely positioned in multiple locations in the area on and around a tablet and requires only commodity sensors already integrated into smart devices. MagnID achieves these objectives and we argue this combination of functionality opens the door for a new class of tangible interfaces designed expressly for current mobile devices. We hope the availability of the MagnID platform will inspire and enable application designers and developers to create a new generation of tangible interfaces targeted towards everyday consumers.

ACKNOWLEDGMENTS

This paper was supported by Samsung Research Fund, Sungkyunkwan University, 2014, and by Basic Science Research Program through the National Research Foundation of Korea (NRF) funded by the Ministry of Science, ICT and Future Planning (2014R1A1A1002223).

REFERENCES

1. Avrahami, D., Wobbrock, J.O., Izadi, S., Portico: tangible interaction on and around a tablet, in UIST'11, 347-356.
2. Baudisch, P., Becker, T., Rudeck, F., Lumino: tangible blocks for tabletop computers based on glass fiber bundles, in CHI'10, 1165-1174.
3. Bianchi, A., Oakley, I., Designing Tangible Magnetic Appcessories, in TEI'13, 255-258.
4. Chan, L., Liang, R.H., Tsai, M.C., Cheng, K.Y., Su, C.H., Chen, M.Y., Cheng, W.H., Chen, B.Y., FingerPad: private and subtle interaction using fingertips, in UIST'13, 255-260.
5. Chan, L., Müller, S., Roudaut, A., Baudisch, P., CapStones and ZebraWidgets, in CHI'12, 2189-2192.
6. Chen, K.Y., Lyons,K., White,S., Patel,S., uTrack: 3D input using two magnetic sensors, in UIST'13, 237-244.
7. Harrison, C., Hudson, S.E., Abracadabra: wireless, high-precision, and unpowered finger input for very small mobile devices, in UIST'09, 121–124.
8. Hwang, S., Ahn, M., Wohn, K, MagGetz: customizable passive tangible controllers on and around conventional mobile devices, in UIST'13, 411-416.
9. Hwang, S., Bianchi, A., Ahn, M., Wohn, K, MagPen: magnetically driven pen interactions on and around conventional smartphones, in MobileHCI'13, 412-415.
10. Jacobsson, M., Fernaeus, Y., Nylander, S., Mobile ActDresses: programming mobile devices by accessorizing, in CHI EA'12, 1071-1074.
11. Jordà, S., Geiger, G.G., Alonso,M., Kaltenbrunner, M., The reacTable: exploring the synergy between live music performance and tabletop tangible interfaces, in TEI'07, 139-146.
12. Kaltenbrunner, M., reacTIVision and TUIO: a tangible tabletop toolkit, in ITS'09, 9-16.
13. Ketabdar, H., Jahanbekam, A., Yuksel, K.A., Hirsch, T., Abolhassani, A.H., MagiMusic: using embedded compass (magnetic) sensor for touch-less gesture based interaction with digital music instruments in mobile devices, in TEI '11, 241-244.
14. Ketabdar, H., Moghadam,P., Naderi,B., Roshandel, M., Magnetic signatures in air for mobile devices, in MobileHCI '12, 185-188.
15. Ketabdar, H., Roshandel, M., Yuksel, K.A., MagiWrite: towards touchless digit entry using 3D space around mobile devices, in MobileHCI'10, 443-446.
16. Kratz, S., Rohs, M., Hoverflow: exploring around-device interaction with IR distance sensors, in MobileHCI'09, Article 42.
17. Liang, R.H., Chan, L., Tseng, H.Y., Kuo, H.C., Huang, D.Y., Yang, D.N., Chen, B.Y., GaussBricks: magnetic building blocks for constructive tangible interactions on portable displays, in CHI'14, 3153-3162.
18. Liang, R.H., Cheng, K.Y., Chan, L., Peng, C.X., Chen, M.Y., Liang, R.H., Yang, D.N., Chen, B.Y., GaussBits: magnetic tangible bits for portable and occlusion-free near-surface interactions, in CHI'13, 1391-1400.
19. Liang, R.H., Cheng, K.Y., Su, C.H., Weng, C.T., Chen, B.Y., Yang, D.N., GaussSense: attachable stylus sensing using magnetic sensor grid, in UIST'12, 319-326.
20. Merrill, D., Kalanithi, J., Maes, P., Siftables: towards sensor network user interfaces, in TEI '07, 75-78.
21. Papert, S., Mindstorms: Children, Computers, and Powerful Ideas. 1980, New York: Basic Books.
22. Raab, F.H., Blood, E.B., Steiner, T.O., Jones, H.R., Magnetic Position and Orientation Tracking System, in IEEE Transactions on Aerospace and Electronic Systems, 1979, vol.AES-15, no.5, 709-718.
23. Shaer, O., Hornecker, E., Tangible User Interfaces: Past, Present, and Future Directions, in Found. Trends Hum.-Comput. Interact. 3, 1–2 (January 2010), 1-137.
24. Ullmer, B., Ishii, H., Emerging frameworks for tangible user interfaces, in IBM Syst. J. 2000, 39, 3-4, 915-931.
25. Yu, N., Chan, L., Lau, S.Y., Tsai, S., Hsiao, I., Tsai, D., Hsiao, F., Cheng, L., Chen, M., Huang, P., Hung, Y., TUIC: enabling tangible interaction on capacitive multi-touch displays, in CHI'11, 2995-3004.

Shimmering Smartwatches: Exploring the Smartwatch Design Space

Cheng Xu, Kent Lyons
Yahoo Labs
701 First Ave.
Sunnyvale CA 94089
{chengxu, klyons}@yahoo-inc.com

ABSTRACT

We examine the nature of smartwatches and explore their associated user interface design space in this paper. Several smartwatches are using small graphical displays and as such are adopting similar forms. However, there are indications that other designs could be feasible. We discuss how smartwatches might use non-graphical displays and still offer "smart" capabilities. To demonstrate feasibility, we present two smartwatch prototypes and show how LED arrays can be used to dynamically support several functions needed by smartwatch applications. Finally, we discuss some tradeoffs associated with this approach and point to additional opportunities for investigating smartwatch designs.

Author Keywords

smartwatch; LEDs; displays; wearable

ACM Classification Keywords

H.5.m. Information Interfaces and Presentation (e.g. HCI): Miscellaneous

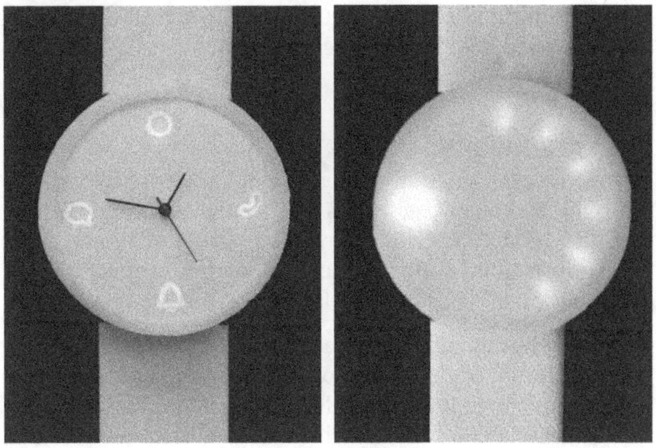

(a) (b)

Figure 1: Our two prototype smartwatches. *Point* (a) has four backlit icons for different apps and an analog watch face. *Circle* (b) uses 12 LEDs to show time and app data.

INTRODUCTION

Smartwatches are one form of wearable computing that is seeing a lot of activity with companies large and small now offering smartwatch products. While there are numerous devices being labeled as smartwatches, we are seeing some diversity in designs with differing capabilities. Many design choices are being driven by technology limitations (such as power use) and other decisions are centered around different user experience goals. While we are seeing some convergence around devices with small capacitive touch screens running a variety of apps, we believe there is a larger design space that encompasses the notion of a smartwatch.

To begin, it is useful to ask the question: What is a smartwatch? For all of the smartwatches on the market, the "watch" part of the device is conceptually rather straightforward. These devices are designed to be worn on the wrist and provide quick access to the time. As such, they have various watch faces controlled by an embedded processor to show the current time. In contrast, the "smart" aspect of these devices is more nuanced.

Superficially, we can examine the functionality of the devices to understand their smart (or not) aspects. Analog watches offer rather limited functionality. For the most part, these watches focus on displaying the time. A digital watch might have additional features and offer a few different modes (time, alarm, timer, stopwatch, etc). At the opposite end of the spectrum are smartwatches with fully capable computing hardware and operating systems. For example, the inWatch Z[1] is an Android device that runs apps on the watch and even has a GSM radio. Other smartwatches seem to be positioned more towards the middle of the spectrum. For example, the Pebble smartwatch can run apps, but these tend to be more limited. It is focused on a very power conscious design with a black and white display and buttons. The Pebble is still a smartwatch, but leverages its hardware to enable "smart" capabilities in a different way. A commonality of smartwatches is that they offer the user the ability to run general purpose apps on the watch.

TEI 2015, January 15–19, 2015, Stanford, California, USA.

ACM 978-1-4503-3305-4/15/01...$15.00.
http://dx.doi.org/10.1145/2677199.2680599

[1]`http://www.inwatchz.com/`

In this paper, we explore the notion of a smartwatch more broadly to understand possible alternative smartwatch designs. We examine the different capabilities of existing smartwatches, several product concepts, and research to show how different smartwatches use different hardware capabilities to create their "smart" functionality. Our first contribution is to articulate the design opportunities for smartwatches that emerge from this analysis. Furthermore, we show that there is a portion of the design space that is currently rather underexplored. In particular, there is an opportunity to create devices that provide smartwatch functionality that do not use the small high resolution graphical displays often associated with smartwatches. To validate this gap in the design space, we present our second contribution as a pair of prototypes that provide general purpose smartwatch application support (Figure 1).

RELATED WORK

In the research literature, there was a lot of early work exploring the technical challenges of creating watches. The work on the IBM Linux watch by Narayanaswami *et al.* details the efforts of creating a device which offered general purpose computing in a watch form-factor [13, 14].

Other research has investigated novel ways to provide input to watch-like devices. For example, Blasko *et al.* researched watch touch input [3] while Ashbrook *et al.* specifically looked at input for round displays [1]. Text entry for small watch sized devices is also explored [16, 17]. Alternative forms of input have also been the subject of research. There has been work looking at capacitive wrist sensing for input [20]. Perrault *et al.* extended the interaction space to a watch band [19] while Oakley *et al.* examined the use of touch on outside edge of round watch-sized device [15]. Other work has moved beyond the body of the watch. For example, GestureWatch used infrared proximity sensors to detect gestures made above and around a watch [9] and Blasko and Feiner examined string-based watch interactions [4].

With all of this work exploring novel input, there has been comparatively less work examining watch output. Some research here includes wrist worn non-visual displays such as electro-tactile [10] and vibro-tactile displays [11, 18]. Moving beyond watches, there have been several concepts proposed that utilize LEDs worn on the wrist often with forms resembling jewelry [6, 12]. One of the first efforts in this area was by Hansson *et al.* They prototyped a notification bracelet connected to a PDA where LEDs would "twinkle" 15 minutes before a meeting. More recently Harrison *et al.* looked at the time it takes to notice and react to an LED notification on the wrist (amongst other onbody locations) [8]. Wrist worn LEDs have also been explored for social purposes in various bracelet forms. Kanis *et al.* showed "logos" on a 5x5 LED array for people that met at a conference, while Williams *et al.* investigated remote messaging using a few LEDs for a display [23]. Although notification and messaging fall into the category of smartwatch apps, these explorations tended to provide only a small set of functionality. Notably, these devices do not offer the diversity of apps one might expect from a smartwatch and most do not have very watch-like forms.

There has also been some work exploring the use of LEDs to encode information. For example, there was a series of research by Campbell, Tarasewich and others investigating how much information could be encoded and understood by users in only a few LEDs [5, 22]. Time varying patterns have also been investigated [7].

SMARTWATCH SURVEY

Moving beyond the research literature, it is useful to examine current products and associated product concepts. Most smartwatches on the market today utilize small high resolution graphical displays, have onboard computation and are tethered to a smartphone using Bluetooth. In general, these watches somewhat resemble a traditional digital watch but have additional "smart" functionality (Figure 2a, 2b). They have the ability to run different apps which tend to be tightly coupled to a smartphone. For example, many smartwatches provide a notification mechanism showing the user information about incoming messages, phone calls, etc. The Kairos is a smartwatch concept[2] that combines a traditional analog watch with a transparent OLED display as an overlay. This is a hybrid design and various renderings indicate that it typically acts as a traditional analog watch. However, by using the transparent OLED display, the watch can switch modes to show graphical information like other smartwatches.

Another take on adding some additional "smart" capabilities to an analog watch is the HotBlack[3]. This device again resembles a traditional analog watch; however, there are several additional small hands that can be controlled by an app. One example provided by HotBlack shows details about an ongoing soccer match by moving the secondary hands to indicate the score. Similarly, the Casio G-Shock GB-6900B[4] is a traditional digital watch with Bluetooth Low Energy. A connection to a phone enables a few "smart" capabilities. Instead of using a user interface on the watch for configuration (set the time, alarm, etc.), a phone app is used. It also has a small graphical display showing one of four notification icons (phone call, email, calendar and social network).

While not specifically smartwatches, several activity monitors are worn on the wrist. Some of these devices have display capabilities to show fitness information and might have a mode to show the time. One example of such a device is the Nike Fuel (Figure 2c). The Fuel uses an LED array embedded in the body of the device that shows through small holes. As a result, when the LEDs are off (the default state) they are not visible. While these type of devices might offer several different modes, in general they would not be considered smartwatches since they do not offer the ability to run general purpose apps. They also echo some of the research explorations investigating wrist worn LEDs [8, 12, 23].

ANALYZING THE DESIGN SPACE

As we can see from current smartwatches and the research literature, the notion of what constitutes a smartwatch is still

[2] `https://kairoswatches.com/`

[3] `https://www.kickstarter.com/projects/1087611122/hotblack-the-premium-watch-with-live-football-scor`

[4] `http://world.g-shock.com/us/en/ble/`

(a) (b) (c)

Figure 2: Smartwatch faces of the Samsung Gear (a), Pebble (b) & the Nike Fuel showing time (c).

and emerging concept with various capabilities being explored. The extreme end of the smartwatch spectrum is rather easy to identify offering most of the capabilities of a smartphone in a scaled down form (such as the inWatch Z). The Samsung Galaxy Gear (Figure 2a) and Android Wear watches are not quite as capable, but still offer a lot of functionality in the watch itself. They have capable processors, capacitive touch input and color graphical displays.

Once we look at smartwatches like the Pebble (Figure 2b) and include other devices like the HotBlack or Casio G-Shock, we see there are several additional points in the design space that could be included in the notion of a smartwatch. All of these devices support general purpose applications on the watch which are supported by being tethered to a smartphone. As we examine these smartwatches in more detail, we see rather large differences in the various watches' computation, input, and output capabilities.

Computation: While smartwatches support general purpose applications, they do so in a few different ways. In particular, there are a few different architectures used to enable smartwatch application experiences. For example, the Samsung Gear runs a full mobile phone OS (originally Android and now Tizen). Applications are deployed and run on the watch hardware. The Android Wear smartwatches use a similar approach. Even the Pebble which is on the opposite end of the compute spectrum with a small embedded processor, runs apps on the watch. However, all of these devices are tethered by Bluetooth to a smartphone. The smartphone might run software supporting the watch app or provide a bridge to web services. The Sony Smartwatch 2 relies on the smartphone even more. For this device, the watch acts as a thin client. It again uses a Bluetooth connection to the phone; however, the watch software is rather minimal. The phone runs all of the application logic and the watch is only responsible for displaying the graphical user interface generated by the apps on the phone. The Casio G-Shock also depends heavily on the phone to support applications. Given that these smartwatches are tethered, it does not matter too much where the processing occurs as both of these architectures support a user interface with "smart" capabilities.

Input: Next, we turn to the different input capabilities of smartwatches. Current products are relatively limited. The more capable watches offer capacitive touch screens. Watches like the Pebble and Casio instead opt for the lower power of a physical button. Many of the watches also have sensing such as an accelerometer that could be used for input. While current products have relatively modest input options, the research literature has explored many more potential solutions as discussed above.

Output: There are comparatively fewer options for smartwatch displays. The smartwatches using touch screens also have full color OLED or LCD displays. These include the Android Wear watches, the Samsung Gear and the inWatch Z. The Kairos relies upon an analog watch to show time; however, the transparent OLED would enable full color graphics. The Pebble uses a different display technology in an effort to conserve power. It uses a bi-stable LCD that takes minimal power to show a static image onscreen. While it does not offer color, it can otherwise display arbitrary 2D graphics. Finally, the HotBlack and Casio push the boundary the farthest on what might be considered a smartwatch. By using the secondary mechanical hands the HotBlack can display a limited set of information to the user. Even though it can only show a few 1D parameters, we include this in our smartwatch analysis since it can be controlled by different apps to represent different types of content. Finally, while not smartwatches, the fitness devices described above and the several research projects uses LEDs to convey different information for some specific functionality.

Smartwatch Opportunities

Given this analysis, we can see where there might be opportunities for novel smartwatch designs. In particular, as long as smartwatches are tethered to smartphones, the amount of processing power on the watch itself is probably not a key differentiator for "smart" capabilities. Furthermore, Moore's Law implies that in the future we will have more processing capabilities in even smaller forms. Likewise, while input options are relatively modest on many smartwatches, the research literature has investigated this area in some depth.

In contrast, many current smartwatches utilize graphical displays but there are hints at a larger smartwatch design space that still use visual displays but in different ways. These devices may not offer as much flexibility as a graphical watch but could be sufficiently capable so as to allow for numerous smartwatch applications. For example, building off the HotBlack, might there be other ways to add richer smartwatch capabilities to traditional analog watches? Likewise, the research literature has proposed a variety of wrist worn devices using LEDs that offer fixed functionality. Is it possible to support a broader range of applications on such devices?

In the rest of this paper, we investigate these questions and we present two smartwatch prototypes we built that explore this part of the smartwatch design space. The key research question we address is not how to show a limited set of information on a relatively simple display. Instead, we want to understand if these types of displays can support basic watch functionality while simultaneously allowing the device to show information from a diversity of applications. As such, our prototypes serve as validation that this portion of the smartwatch design space is viable.

SMARTWATCH PROTOTYPES

Here we present two different smartwatch prototypes that explore the broader smartwatch design space (Figure 1). Our prototypes use LED arrays for a display in two different ways. Our first prototype, *Point*, uses an analog watch face and four LEDs to illuminate icons to dynamically show needed information (Figure 1a). In contrast, *Circle* uses 12 LEDs arranged similar to the hours on a watch face to present data (Figure 1b). Both of these emit light through the face of the watch with time varying patterns. This design aspect inspired the notion of *shimmering* smartwatches.

For these prototypes, we selected eight different applications to represent a breadth of possible apps. We show how our watches support those apps to demonstrate our approach. For our applications we selected a few different types including basic time keeping (time, countdown timer), information from a smartphone (messaging, phone call information, calendar reminders) [21] and other more general applications we are seeing emerge on smartwatches(weather, fitness tracking and sports scores). This list is not intended to be all-inclusive of smartwatch apps, but instead to cover several different types of content.

For each of our applications, there are numerous parameters to convey to the user. For the time, we show the hour, minutes and seconds. The timer shows the length of time until a count down expires. For messaging, we show message notifications, status about unread messages, and information about who sent a message. For phone calls, we again show notifications, missed call counts, voice mail, and the caller. Calendar reminders are shown for upcoming events (e.g. informing the user 15 minutes before a meeting).

As we consider these applications, there are a few different primitive types of information our watches need to support. Some require notifications while others rely upon a more persistent display of content (e.g. time, unread messages). Many also require showing numeric information about one or more quantities. Again the time requires showing three numbers (hours, minutes, seconds), messaging would benefit by showing the number of unread messages, etc. Finally, some applications need to show the source of information (the message sender).

From the opposite perspective, our use of an array of LEDs offers a variety of capabilities. Each LED is individually addressable and therefore we can control which LED is illuminated. We can also control the color and/or brightness. Finally, we can change these aspects over time; for example, showing blinking or breathing patterns. Harrison *et al.* explored time varying patterns of a single LED of one color [7]. We leverage these patterns and use his nomenclature in the following prototype descriptions. Furthermore, we vary position and color to encode additional information needed for our different apps. To reiterate, our contribution is not to create novel LED encodings. Instead, we show how those encodings can be used to represent the different pieces of information needed for a variety of smartwatch applications. The examples we provide are one possible mapping we made as a design decision to demonstrate this concept and other mappings with different affordances are possible.

Hardware and Software

For our prototypes, we used a Bluetooth Low Energy (BLE) module that has a Nordic Semiconducor nRF51822 SoC. This SoC has an embedded BLE radio and a 32-bit Cortex M0 processor running at 16MHz. It also has 16KB of RAM, 256KB of flash, and numerous GPIO pins. Overall, this device compares very favorably to most Arduinos and has the bonus of the built-in radio. We are also using Adafruit NeoPixel RGB LED arrays that have the built-in WS2812 controller. The NeoPixels only require supply voltage, ground, and one control line. These devices have very specific timing requirements and we ported the NeoPixel Arduino library from AVR to ARM assembly. We are using a fully self contained solution with a LiPo battery and a custom breakout board for a Xuntong BLE module.

Our software is split in two parts similar to other smartwatch solutions. We used the ARM CPU on the Nordic SoC to run firmware that reads commands over the BLE connection. That software is responsible for driving the LEDs in the patterns needed and keeping high resolution timing. We connect to our prototypes over BLE from an Android phone. The phone runs a custom app that simulates a variety of smartwatch application functionality. In this work, we did not tie into any specific smartwatch applications and associated data. Instead, our software controls the display sequences to show what applications look like. Likewise, we have not implemented any on-watch input such as buttons or capacitive touch. Such additions should be straightforward engineering exercises.

Finally, we 3D printed different enclosures for our prototypes to hold the electronics. We used a translucent white filament that acts as a diffuser for our LEDs. For our *Point* prototype we dismantled an analog watch and incorporated it into our design. We also attached off the shelf watch bands to our prototypes.

Point

Our first smartwatch builds off a traditional analog watch as a platform to show the time. We added four backlit icons that are under smartphone control to show app data (Figure 1a). This design is a bit reminiscent of the HotBlack watch that uses an analog watch face to show the time. However instead of controlling hands to show data, we use our LEDs. For this design, we placed LEDs underneath the watch face so that they are not visible until they are illuminated (Figure 3a). We use a mask over the LEDs so they show an icon instead of just a glowing point. While our watch is clearly a technology prototype, this design allows for a form more reminiscent of traditional analog watches when just showing the time. For apps, we focus on three categories (messaging, phone, and calendar), while the fourth is a generic indicator for other applications. We selected these applications as they account for many notifications a user interacts with on smartphones [21]. Figure 4 details our encodings for the different applications.

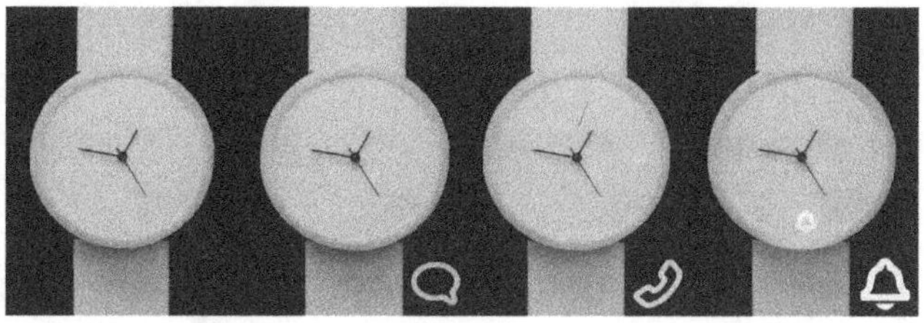

(a) (b) (c) (d)

Figure 3: Our *Point* prototype showing only the time (a), a message (b) and a call (c) from different people, and a calendar event (d). Our icons are also overlayed for clarity.

For messaging, we have an icon that represents various forms of text messages (Figure 3b). Here we use color to show the identity of the message sender. We allow the user to specify a color for up to 5 people. By default, we show the total number of unread messages by encoding the count into the number of pulses. Multiple messages are shown in succession with their appropriate color. Finally, for the notification of a new message, the icon is modulated with a with a heartbeat pattern periodically for 30 seconds, again in the correct color for the associated person. Our second icon shows information about phone calls (Figure 3c). Again we use color to show the identity of the caller. The number of missed calls is displayed by showing that number of pulses. We also show the presence of a voice mail in the same sequence by using a fast in, slow out pattern.

Our next icon is for calendar events (Figure 3d). Starting 15 minutes before an event, this icon is slowly pulsed in a 0.25Hz frequency. In the last minute, we switch to a 1Hz pulse. Finally, at the start of an appointment, we show a blink (square wave) for 30 seconds. We also use this icon to display a countdown timer. The encoding is the same, only driven by setting a timer in the phone app.

Finally, our forth icon is for generic notifications. Given our limited display capability, it is probably not feasible to generate an LED encoding for all possible smartwatch apps without becoming extremely complex. Instead, we reserved this last position for informing the user that information from another source is waiting. Here, we pulse the LED to show the notification count, but otherwise the user needs to turn to their phone for details. In many ways, this is similar a notification LED on a smartphone.

Circle

Our second prototype is *Circle* which has a circular array of 12 LEDs that echos an analog watch but otherwise lacks a watch face or mechanical hands (Figure 1b). In addition to having more LEDs relative to *Point*, *Circle* relies upon changing modes to display different app information instead of simultaneously displaying multiple apps. This design decision allows us to support more applications directly. Figure 5 shows photos of several applications and Figure 6 show our the encodings diagrammatically.

First, we use the LED array to display the time. We use the same circular arrangement as an analog watch. For the hour,

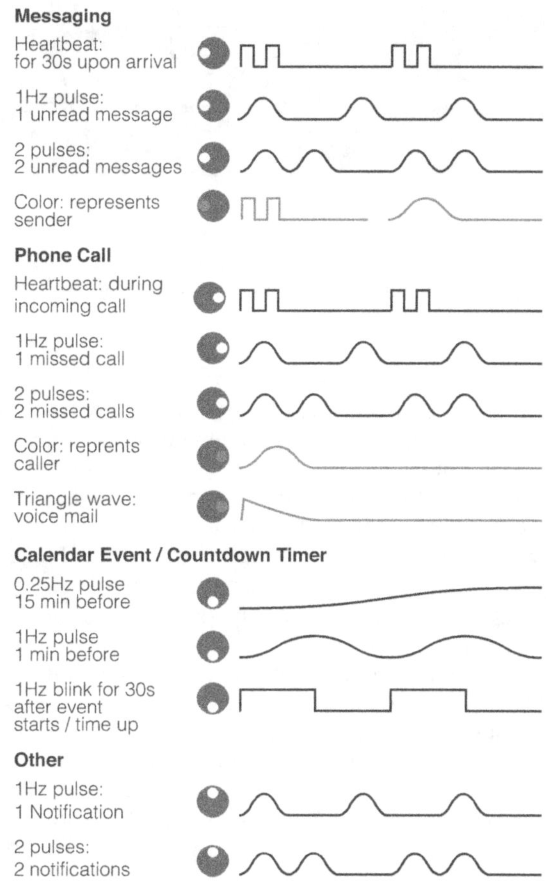

Figure 4: Our *Point* prototype application mappings. The circle depicts the watch face and associated illuminated icon and LED used by our different applications. The sparklines represent illumination intensity over time (similar to [7]).

a single bright pixel is shown at the hour hand position. To show minutes, we display a dimmed arc extending from the 12 o'clock position to the position where the minute hand would be located on an analog watch. This representation provides a 5 minute resolution. Finally, we blink the final minute LED at 0.5Hz to show the passage of seconds.

To show messages, we use a similar encoding as *Point*. When a new message arrives, we shift out of the time mode and flash with a heartbeat for 30 seconds. To show multiple messages we illuminate multiple LEDs (instead of showing a number of pulses over time). Finally, we again use color to denote which person the message is from. Building off of the messaging display, our phone app shows a notification by pulsing all of the LEDs. To show missed calls, we illuminate all of the LEDs at a low intensity echoing the use of all of the LEDs for a phone call. The number of calls is then represented by full illumination on the corresponding number of LEDs. Finally, to distinguish missed calls from a voice mail, we alter the shape of the pulse and use color to denote the individual.

To show a notification of an upcoming calendar event, we display a wave animation from the current minute LED to the

Figure 5: Our *Circle* prototype showing the calendar overview (a), countdown timer (b, c), weather (d) and fitness tracker level (e).

minute LED corresponding to the start of the meeting. This representation thus serves as a countdown in 5 minute increments. We show this animation at a 0.25Hz frequency starting 15 minutes before the event. Starting one minute before the event we show a 1Hz pulse and for the first 30 seconds we show a blink to denote the start of the event. For this prototype, we also support an overview showing free and busy times from the calendar. In this mode, we display which hours are currently scheduled. The start of a meeting is displayed in dark blue and subsequent busy hours are shown in light blue (Figure 5a). Our countdown timer uses a similar encoding as calendar events, only it is not overlayed with the current time. An arc corresponding to the duration of the time in minutes is displayed and animated at 0.25Hz (Figure 5b,5c). With one minute left, we use a 1Hz pulse and it blinks for 30s when time expires.

Given our ability to switch modes, we are also able to directly represent other apps as well. For weather, we use a color coding to show temperature over the next 12 hours (Figure 5d). We map cooler temperatures onto blue and warmer temperatures on to orange. To show the chance of precipitation, we flicker the LED using the transmission pattern for the given hour position. For fitness tracking we have a mode that again uses a color mapping to show information over time (Figure 5e). Here we display fitness tracking going into the past 12 hours (red low activity, yellow moderate, green high). Finally we prototyped a pair of modes to show information about a sports game such as a soccer match. The first mode shows an arc similar to the timer to denote time passed in the game. The second sports mode shows the score. Here, we split the 12 LED segments into left and right halves to represent the two teams. We illuminate the LEDs to match the team's color and the number of segments denotes the current score. We also use the heartbeat notification pattern from our other modes to highlight when a team scores.

DISCUSSION

When embarking on this work, we wanted to explore the breadth of possibilities that might be encompassed by the notion of a smartwatch. Through our examination of the literature, products on the market and product concepts, we can see that the "smart" aspect of these devices is in their ability to move beyond the fixed functionality of a tradition watch and to support a variety of apps. In doing so, these watches rely upon a smartphone as a conduit to external services and in

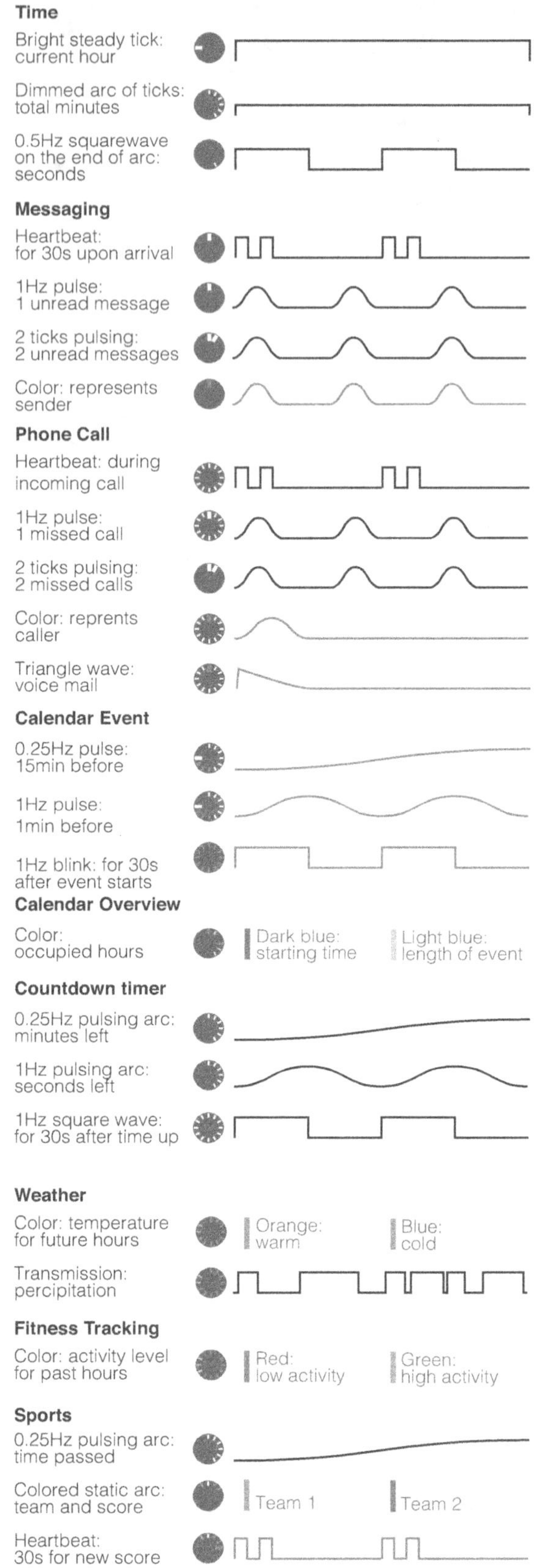

Figure 6: The *Circle* prototype uses a circular array of 12 LEDs. This figure details the applications and associated parameters we display on the LEDs. Similar to *Point*, the circle depicts the watch face and LEDs and the sparklines show variation over time.

many cases the phone runs application logic. With this architecture, we see a larger design space open up — well beyond devices with small 1 inch graphical displays. Our prototypes help demonstrate how one might develop smartwatches in this design space and some of the issues that might be raised.

First, it seems possible to support a subset of smartwatch apps without the use of high-resolution graphical displays. Our *Point* prototype offers the ability to show several different aspects of three different apps in detail in addition to the time and general purpose notifications. In contrast, *Circle* uses modes and therefore is not constrained by the spatial limitations of *Point*. As such, we are able more directly support several additional applications.

Through these prototypes, we can see there are several tradeoffs that can arise. By eliminating a full graphical display, we are also likely reducing the types of applications a watch might support. Presenting different types of notifications, small numerical values, and displaying the category of an item from a small set (e.g. a specific person from a predefined group) is rather straightforward. More complex information, such as the details about an email message, are likely impossible to show without at least a small graphical display. However this issue might not be a huge limitation. In general, smartwatches support quick glancable interactions [2]. And while it might be possible to read the full contents of an email on a Pebble of Android Wear watch, extended uses like these are probably going to be rare. Instead, a user will fall back to a smartphone. By using less capable displays, we still support showing small pieces of information from numerous application sources, but for more details the user will also need to turn to their smartphone.

The need for displaying persistent information also poses some design challenges. For information that only needs to be shown for a short time (like a notification), the device can switch modes. However to show persistent information (like message counts), this mode shift strategy does not work as well. Furthermore, given that this is a watch, ideally the time is always displayed as well. For *Point* the dedicated analog watch makes this easy. For *Circle* it is more of a challenge since the LEDs are used for both the time and app content and could require mappings that allow both to be displayed simultaneously.

A related issue in using these displays is that of encoding information. Our prototypes make use of relatively few patterns and for the most part our designs use those patterns in similar ways across the different applications. *Point* makes further use of iconography to expose semantics about the information we are displaying to a user. We made these design decision so that the information is relatively easy to understand. However, other choices are possible. For example Campbell, Tarasewich, and others showed more complex mappings between LEDs and information sources can be learned [5, 22]. Such patterns might allow even deeper application support.

One of the interesting prospects of using different types of displays is to move away from the design constraints imposed by small capacitive graphical displays. Just as the touch screens of smartphones have driven a lot of variation out of smartphone designs (they have converged to large pieces of glass wrapped in a shell), many smartwatches are adopting similar forms. In contrast, traditional watches have a variety of forms and are as much a piece of the user's fashion identity as they are a piece of technology. This framing will likely extend to smartwatches as well. Other display options like the LEDs from our prototypes or the controllable hands of the HotBlack provide some more flexibility in the watch design.

FUTURE WORK

This research points to several additional areas to explore. First, our prototypes were functional enough to demonstrate several different smartwatch apps. However, it would be interesting to tie into smartphone data sources. This development work would let us start to explore issues that might arise from daily use. Likewise, we decomposed input and output in our analysis of the design space. It might be useful to investigate how various display options might be complemented by input techniques to create novel interactions.

We explored two different designs in this work. One could imagine many more options that provide smartwatch application functionality. For example, we built a version of *Circle* that had an analog watch in the middle similar to *Point*. It is conceptually rather similar to our two designs so we excluded it here. However, there are likely other configurations of analog watches, digital display technologies (LEDs or graphical), and physical forms that might present interesting opportunities. *Point* uses masks to show the icons. Our current implementation uses fixed icons; however, we might be able to increase that number by having a mask that that rotates between different icons. We could also revisit existing devices. How might we alter a digital watch to provide more smart capabilities? The Casio G-Shock uses a small 2D display to show icons. However, even a fixed function LCD might be programmatically controlled to offer additional features much like we did with *Blink*'s icons. Alternatively, one could explore modulating the LCD backlight colors to provide an extra dimension of expressivity. It would also interesting to take devices like the Nike Fuel and add more general purpose application support.

We would also like to further explore the different embodiments that might be enabled by having LEDs illuminate through the surface of a device. We used the translucency of our 3D printed forms in both of our designs. This notion could be extended in several ways. For example, the watch might be covered with fabric and therefore look more like a bracelet when not illuminated. While there has been some work exploring digital jewery, this approach might lead to functional devices that provide different aesthetic options.

CONCLUSION

Smartwatches are still in their formative stages of development and adoption. While there are some commonalities in designs, we believe we have demonstrated that there are a broader set of opportunities to provide "smart" capabilities in watch-like devices. Our two prototypes use LEDs in different ways to enable smartwatch apps. By building off existing work on LED encodings we developed mappings to display the information needed for several different smartwatch apps and their associated parameters. In doing so, our implementations show the feasibility of this approach and more broadly provide evidence that this larger smartwatch design space is viable. As we continue to develop the notion of what constitutes a smartwatch, this work points towards a larger space of possible smartwatch designs.

REFERENCES

1. Ashbrook, D., Lyons, K., and Starner, T. An investigation into round touchscreen wristwatch interaction. In *Proceedings of MobileHCI '08* (2008), 311–314.
2. Ashbrook, D. L., Clawson, J. R., Lyons, K., Starner, T. E., and Patel, N. Quickdraw: The impact of mobility and on-body placement on device access time. In *Proceedings of CHI '08* (2008), 219–222.
3. Blasko, G., and Feiner, S. An interaction system for watch computers using tactile guidance and bidirectional segmented strokes. In *Proceedings of ISWC '04* (2004), 120–123.
4. Blasko, G., Narayanaswami, C., and Feiner, S. Prototyping retractable string-based interaction techniques for dual-display mobile devices. In *Proceedings of CHI '06* (2006), 369–372.
5. Campbell, C., and Tarasewich, P. What can you say with only three pixels? In *Proceedings of MobileHCI '04* (2004), 1–12.
6. Fortmann, J., Müller, H., Boll, S., and Heuten, W. Illumee: Aesthetic light bracelet as a wearable information display for everyday life. In *UbiComp '13 Adjunct Proceedings* (2013), 393–396.
7. Harrison, C., Horstman, J., Hsieh, G., and Hudson, S. Unlocking the expressivity of point lights. In *Proceedings of CHI '12* (2012), 1683–1692.
8. Harrison, C., Lim, B. Y., Shick, A., and Hudson, S. E. Where to locate wearable displays?: Reaction time performance of visual alerts from tip to toe. In *Proceedings of CHI '09* (2009), 941–944.
9. Kim, J., He, J., Lyons, K., and Starner, T. The gesture watch: A wireless contact-free gesture based wrist interface. In *Proceedings ISWC '07* (2007), 1–8.
10. Lee, S. C., and Starner, T. Stop burdening your eyes: A wearable electro-tactile display. In *Proceedings of ISWC '08* (2008), 115–116.
11. Lee, S. C., and Starner, T. Buzzwear: Alert perception in wearable tactile displays on the wrist. In *Proceedings of the CHI '10* (2010), 433–442.
12. Miner, C. S., Chan, D. M., and Campbell, C. Digital jewelry: Wearable technology for everyday life. In *Extended Abstracts of CHI '01* (2001), 45–46.
13. Narayanaswami, C., Kamijoh, N., Raghunath, M., Inoue, T., Cipolla, T., Sanford, J., Schlig, E., Venkiteswaran, S., Guniguntala, D., Kulkarni, V., et al. Ibm's linux watch, the challenge of miniaturization. *IEEE Computer 35*, 1 (2002), 33–41.
14. Narayanaswami, C., and Raghunath, M. T. Application design for a smart watch with a high resolution display. In *Proceedings of ISWC '00* (2000), 7–14.
15. Oakley, I., and Lee, D. Interaction on the edge: Offset sensing for small devices. In *Proceedings of CHI '14* (2014), 169–178.
16. Oney, S., Harrison, C., Ogan, A., and Wiese, J. Zoomboard: A diminutive qwerty soft keyboard using iterative zooming for ultra-small devices. In *Proc. of CHI '13*, ACM (2013), 2799–2802.
17. Partridge, K., Chatterjee, S., Sazawal, V., Borriello, G., and Want, R. Tilttype: Accelerometer-supported text entry for very small devices. In *Proceedings of UIST '02* (2002), 201–204.
18. Pasquero, J., Stobbe, S. J., and Stonehouse, N. A haptic wristwatch for eyes-free interactions. In *Proceedings CHI '11* (2011), 3257–3266.
19. Perrault, S. T., Lecolinet, E., Eagan, J., and Guiard, Y. s. Watchit: Simple gestures and eyes-free interaction for wristwatches and bracelets. In *Proceedings CHI '13* (2013), 1451–1460.
20. Rekimoto, J. Gesturewrist and gesturepad: Unobtrusive wearable interaction devices. In *Proceedings of ISWC '01* (2001), 21–27.
21. Sahami Shirazi, A., Henze, N., Dingler, T., Pielot, M., Weber, D., and Schmidt, A. Large-scale assessment of mobile notifications. In *Proceedings of CHI '14* (2014), 3055–3064.
22. Tarasewich, P., Campbell, C. S., Xia, T., and Dideles, M. Evaluation of visual notification cues for ubiquitous computing. In *Proceedings of UbiComp '03* (2003), 349–366.
23. Williams, A., Farnham, S., and Counts, S. Exploring wearable ambient displays for social awareness. In *Ext. Abs. of CHI '06* (2006), 1529–1534.

Sticky Actuator: Free-Form Planar Actuators for Animated Objects

Ryuma Niiyama[1], Xu Sun[2], Lining Yao[3], Hiroshi Ishii[3], Daniela Rus[4], Sangbae Kim[2]

[1] University of Tokyo
Tokyo, Japan
niiyama@isi.imi.i.u-tokyo.ac.jp

[2] MIT Mechanical Engineering
Cambridge, MA, USA
{xusun, sangbae}@mit.edu

[3] MIT Media Lab
Cambridge, MA, USA
{lining, ishii}@media.mit.edu

[4] MIT CSAIL
Cambridge, MA, USA
rus@csail.mit.edu

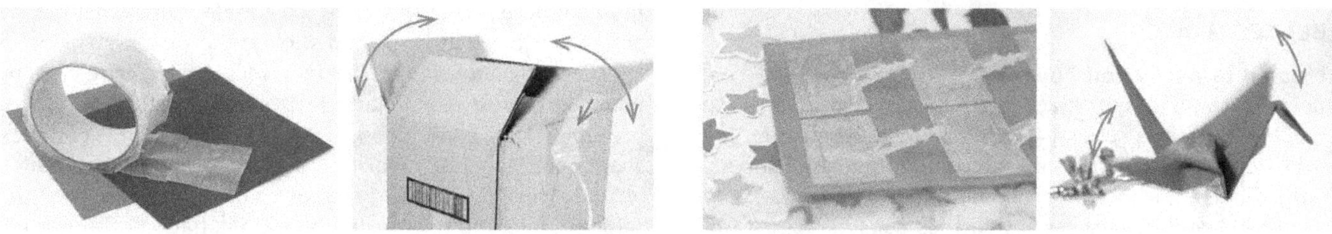

Figure 1. The tape actuator and an active box (left). The sticker actuator and an actuated origami crane (right)

ABSTRACT
We propose soft planar actuators enhanced by free-form fabrication that are suitable for making everyday objects move. The actuator consists of one or more inflatable pouches with an adhesive back. We have developed a machine for the fabrication of free-from pouches; squares, circles and ribbons are all possible. The deformation of the pouches can provide linear, rotational, and more complicated motion corresponding to the pouch's geometry. We also provide a both manual and programmable control system. In a user study, we organized a hands-on workshop of actuated origami for children. The results show that the combination of the actuator and classic materials can enhance rapid prototyping of animated objects.

Author Keywords
Tangible Media; Soft Robotics; Soft Actuator; Robot Toy; Origami; Shape-Changing Interface; Pneumatic;

ACM Classification Keywords
H.5.2. Information interfaces and presentation (e.g., HCI): User Interfaces---Haptic I/O.

TEI 2015, January 16 - 19 2015, Stanford, CA, USA

ACM 978-1-4503-3305-4/15/01…$15.00
http://dx.doi.org/10.1145/2677199.2680600

INTRODUCTION
Programmable and interactive features of computation can be extended into physical interactions, such as a shape-changing interface [1] that allows users to change physical parameters of the objects. Altering material properties through computation is a potential new frontier in human-computer interaction. In order to go beyond the simple changing of RGB values of pixels and delve into changing the shape, volume, and physical texture of three-dimensional objects, the system requires smart actuators embedded into its materials. There are only a few practical actuation techniques [2][3] due to limitations in technology. As such, shape-changing materials require costly delicate hardware that is not flexible. The goal of this research is to provide accessible smart actuators with a flexible fabrication method.

Another important aspect of the shape-changing user interface is the compatibility with classic materials. The programmable matter approach assumes that the shape-changing objects are made from programmable materials. This approach conflict with classic materials and does not support existing objects. Robotic construction toys and modular robots also have compatibility issues with other pieces of hardware. Classic materials such as paper, fabric, and clay have good flexibility and support tangible interactions. On the other hand, they do not have active motion or programmable features. Thus, we focus on an additive approach: adding free-form actuators on existing materials and objects.

As such, we propose planar soft actuators called "sticky actuators" (Fig.1). The actuator consists of inflatable bladders with an adhesive back. We have developed a fabrication method for making free-form bladders from inexpensive plastic sheets. We also provide a simple, portable teaching-playback control system for programming actions of multiple actuators. Users can simply attach and detach the actuators by peeling and sticking. Potential applications include adding motion to a specific object to attract attention in a crowded environment, animating static artworks such as paper crafts or picture books, and motorizing everyday products by simply sticking on an actuator. This simple approach is suitable for people who have limited knowledge of robotics, and the proposed system allows users to make robotic system from passive objects.

RELATED WORK

Actuated Construction Toys

One of the most popular actuated construction toys is the LEGO Mindstorms series [4], which contains software and hardware to create customizable, programmable robots. Those robots can be either motor driven or pneumatically driven, and are equipped with various sensors. The form factor is constructed from existing units. Topobo[5] and Kinematics[6] are constructive toys that include both active and passive units. Instead of software interfaces, their movements can be recorded and replayed by manipulating the tangible parts. These toys have limited compatibility with other hardware. Pinoky[7] is the project based on the additive approach that utilizes ring actuators that can be attached to plush toys to turn the toys into soft robots.

Cuttable Electronics

Cuttable electronics have been explored for ad-hoc customization of inkjet printed circuits [8][9]. Different topological layouts of conductive circuitry have been compared to achieve a cuttable capacitive sensing unit. There are also circuit stickers [10] that contain both passive and positive electronic components. These components are manufactured on a flexible substrate, and can be peeled off and attached to other substrates to make a circuit. These cuttable electronics enable fast prototyping and flexible customization of function and form. However, it is hard to apply such techniques to mechanical systems.

Shape-Changing Interface

Shape-changing interfaces with pneumatic actuation have been explored in the HCI field, including PneUI[2], dynamic changeable buttons[11], inflatable multitouch displays [12] and the inflatable mouse[13]. Compared to other actuation methods, pneumatic actuation provides a large force per weight ratio, softness, and controllability. Beyond HCI, pneumatic actuations have been adapted in the soft robotics field [14][15]. Complex and organic motion can be achieved with pneumatic bladders.

The PneUI paper provided a guide to replacing classic materials with shape-changing composites. In contrast, this paper focuses on applying new actuation techniques to classic materials. We believe that the additive approach would provide more practical applications than less popular shape-changing composites. Furthermore, while the PneUI paper broadly discussed various structures and materials for pneumatic actuation, this paper explores in depth planar actuators with non-elastic materials. We explore new forms such as tape and stickers with a computer-controlled platform for complex pouch fabrication. We also provide quantitative measurement of the physical properties and analysis of the usability through a user study.

FREE-FORM PLANAR SOFT ACTUATOR

Overview

Our free-form actuators are enhanced by a custom-built fabrication machine (Fig.2). Two simple shapes that can be easily fabricated are tape and sticker: the ribbon-shape with a series of pouches and the individual square/circle-shape pouches. These elementary shapes can generate inflation, bending, and contraction. Pouches with more complex shapes can generate a variety of motions and texture which we call corrugation. All types of actuators are based on the same principle of pneumatic inflation/deflation of the pouch.

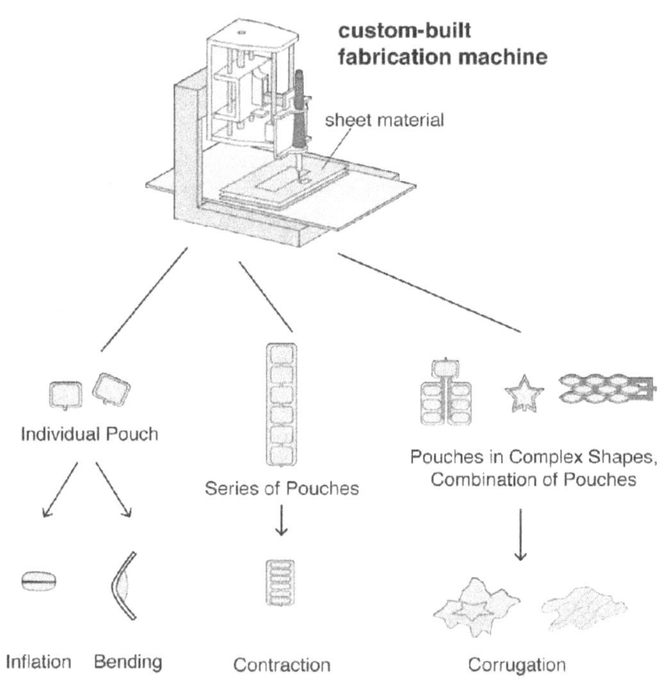

Figure 2. Overview of the sticky actuator family.

Tape Actuator

Like a muscle, the tape actuator provides linear motion. If the tape actuator is adhered to the two wings of a hinge joint, the inflation can result in a rotational motion.

In this prototype model (Fig.3), the tape actuator is 50mm wide, and each pouch unit 24mm long, manufactured from 0.004" (4mil) thick Polyethylene (PE) sheets. To make a tape actuator, a user simply tears off the tape at any desired length, plugs in the connector at one end, and seals the back of the tape actuator with a piece of sticky tape.

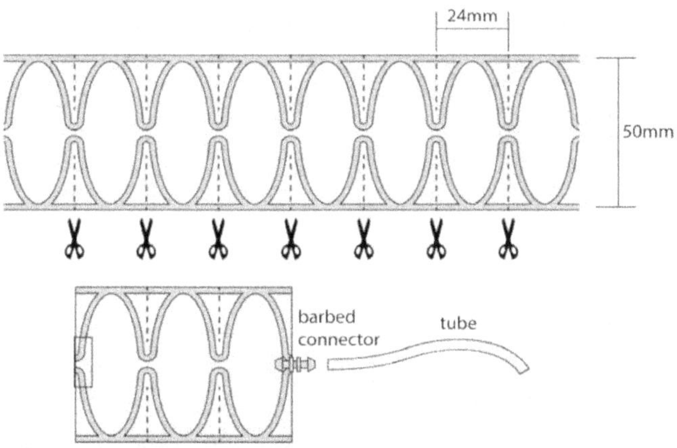

Figure 3. Design of the tape actuator (top), and an sample of three pouches tape actuator with connector (bottom).

Sticker Actuator

The sticker actuator provides rotational motion when adhered to a hinge joint or equivalent flexible substrate. Users can also utilize a 'push' effect through inflation.

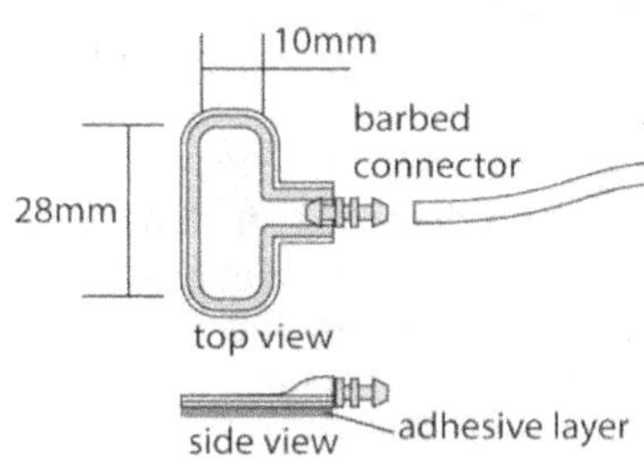

Figure 4. Design of the square-shape sticker actuator.

The prototype sticker actuator (Fig.4) contains a 28mm by 10mm rectangular pouch, made with 0.002" (2mil) thick Nylon sheets. A user simply peels off a sticker actuator from the film liner and attaches it onto the object to be actuated.

FABRICATION

Heat Bonding

Inflatable bladders/pouches are fabricated from plastic sheets through a heat bonding process. The heat seal outlines the shape of the pouches, and then an adhesive layer is applied on the back. This sealing method is commonly seen on heat sealers that seal plastic bags. The tape actuator is a series of pouches that can be cut by tearing. For sticker actuators, each pouch has a barbed tube fitting, which allows pouches to be connected to tubes during operation.

We developed a computer-controlled heat bonding machine that consists of a three-axis CNC gantry holding a heat pencil (Fig.5). The machine can draw sealing lines on thermo plastic sheets mounted on the workspace. We use a layer of high-temperature fiberglass film that covers the target PE film layers. Once the design of the actuator (a two dimensional line drawing) is made on the computer, CAM software generates G-codes from the design and sends commands to the CNC gantry. The machine then interprets the G-codes line by line and moves the heat pencil to draw the pattern.

After thermally printing pouches for the tape actuators, perforated cuts were made with knives between units in order to make pouches easily separated by tearing.

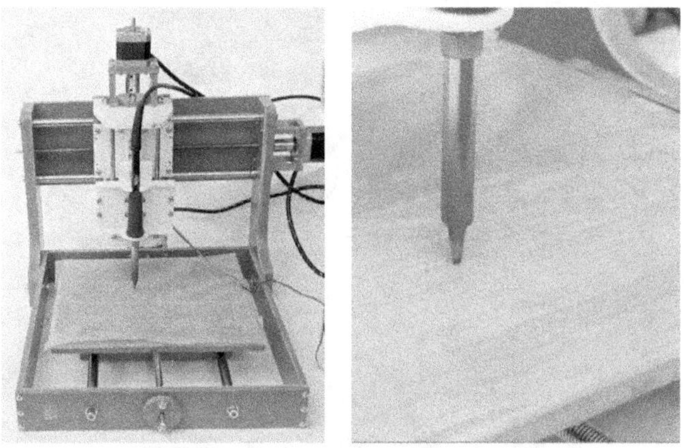

Figure 5. The CNC heat bonding machine: overview (left), and close-up of the heat pencil (right).

After printing sticker actuators, pouches were cut into individual components so that tube fittings could be connected. For each pouch, a barbed PE tube fitting was placed in between two films.

The simplicity of the fabrication process allows sticky actuators to be easily mass manufactured. In fact, the manufacturing process of plastic packaging can be applied directly to make the actuators. It can allow people to use inexpensive actuators.

Material

In order to utilize thermal bonding, the film material must be thermoplastic. In addition, film materials need to be less stretchable but flexible. For this reason, the film materials we selected are nylon films and polyethylene films with a thickness of about 0.002"–0.004" (0.051mm–0.102mm). The actuators can be applied to variety of materials such as paper, plastic, wood, and metal, depending on the performance of the adhesive layer.

CONTROL

Manual Control

We use syringes connected to the actuators by tubes for manual control. As the syringe plunger is pushed and pulled within the cylinder, the airflow inflates or deflates the actuator. The simple principle of cylinder-piston mechanism provides users intuitive interaction with the actuators and their corresponding animated objects.

Programmable Control: Teaching-Playback

We have also created a control system that the user can use to record a sequence of inflating and deflating actions. The system consists of an Arduino board, a motor driver, miniature pumps, solenoid valves, a battery, and buttons. The controller shows in Fig.6 has two large buttons with LEDs so that user can control the two channels of pneumatic inflation/deflation.

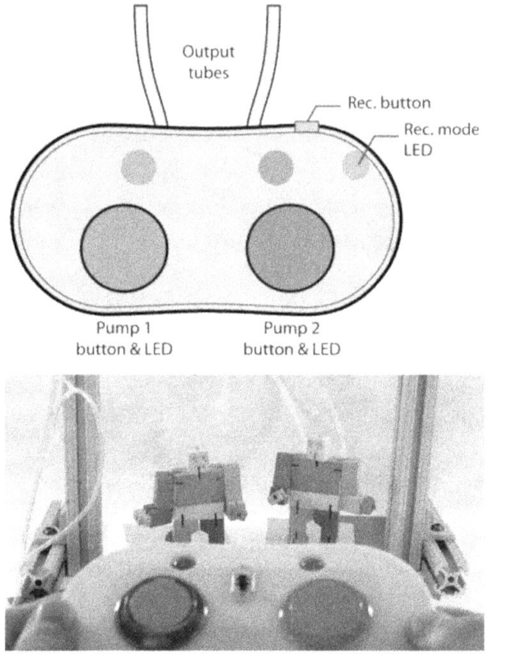

Figure 6. Design of the teaching-playback controller.

The pump vacuums air out of the pouch as the program initiates. Then, as the user pushes big pump buttons, the corresponding pump starts pumping and the LED indicators light up.

If the recording button is pushed, the green LED lights up showing the system is entering record mode. While still holding the record button down, the system records how long the user pushes each pump button, and in what sequence. Once the record button is released, the green LED goes off, and the system plays back the pump sequence that was recorded. If the recording button is pressed and released quickly again, the program will erase the recorded sequence. The control system thus allows users to choreograph the animated objects with tape/sticker actuators without complicated programming.

PERFORMANCE OF THE ACTUATOR

We performed a tension test to examine the basic properties of the tape actuator using a single-axis tension testing machine with a force sensor and a linear potentiometer. Fig.7 shows force-length relationships of the tape actuator. The sample used was a tape actuator with four pouches, which were pressure controlled at 5kPa, 10kPa, and 20kPa.

The result of the tension test shows that the tape actuator can generate tension force up to 10N at 20kPa. The observed maximum contraction ratio is 15% at 20kPa, and generated less contraction ratio at lower pressures. In the fully contracted state, the tension force goes to a minimum because the pouches are fully inflated.

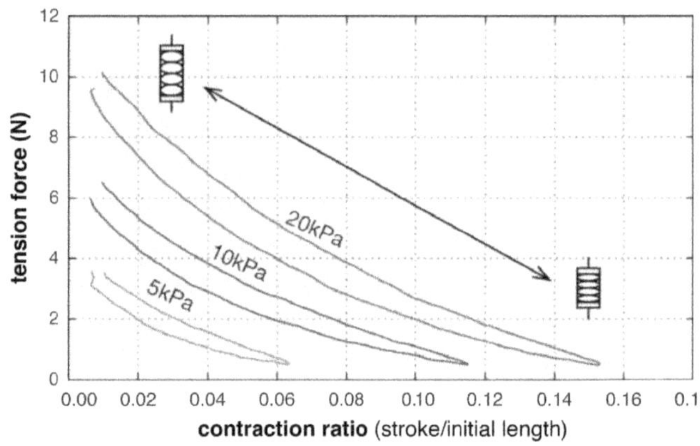

Figure 7. The measured data of the force-length relationships of the four pouches tape actuator.

APPLICATION EXAMPLES

Tape Actuator Examples

The tape actuator can easily drive the joints of objects like muscles. We put two tape actuators onto a box in order to actuate its opening. One end of each tape actuator is adhered above a folding line of the opening and the other end below, onto the side of the box (Fig.8). Once they are inflated, they contract in length and pull the covering boards outward (Fig.9).

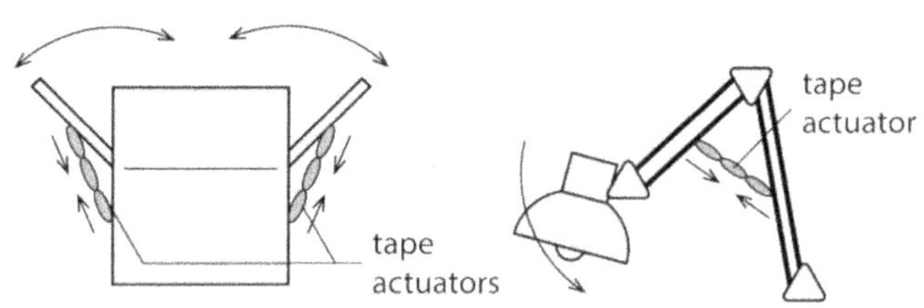

Figure 8. Applied tape actuators on the everyday objects: paper box (left) and desk lamp (right)

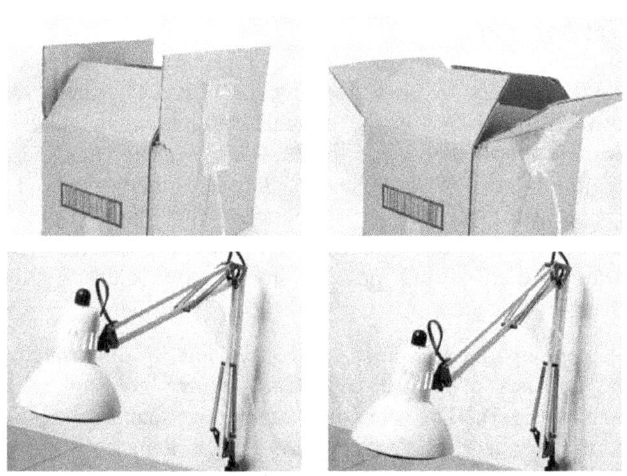

Figure 9. The snapshots of the movements: open/close the paper box (top), and swinging the lamp arm (bottom).

We can also use tape actuators to actuate motions on linkages, for example a swing-arm lamp (Fig.8). One end of the tape actuator is adhered to the horizontal arm and the other end to the vertical arm. Once it is inflated, it contracts in length and pulls the light closer to the desk (Fig.9).

Sticker Actuator Examples

Origami allows the transformation of flat sheets of paper into intricate three-dimensional artworks. With sticker actuators, they can be further transformed into "living" creatures. Here we demonstrate how to actuate motion on an origami crane and fish using sticker actuators (Fig.10).

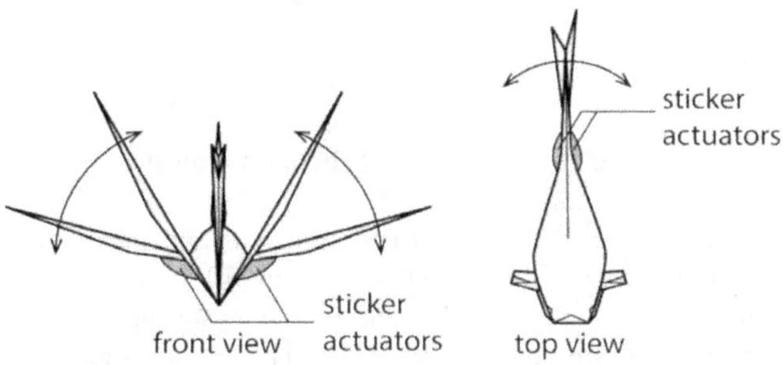

Figure 10. Applied sticker actuators on the origami objects: origami crane (left) and origami fish (right)

Figure 11. The snapshots of the movements: flapping wings (top), and swinging the tail fin (bottom).

On the origami crane, two sticker actuators are adhered under the joints of the wings. These two sticker actuators are connected to two side parts of a T-shape pneumatic connector. A syringe is connected to the other part. When the syringe is pumped, the two sticker actuators inflate and deflate at the same time, resulting in a wing flapping motion (Fig.11).

On the fish origami, two sticker actuators are adhered to the fish's tail. Each sticker actuator is connected to a syringe. When the two syringes are pumped alternatively, the tail swing from one side to the other (Fig.11).

Sticker actuators can also be used to provide other types of motion on everyday objects. For example, we attached a sticker actuator to the hinged mouth of a clay frog (Fig.12). When air is pumped into the pouch with syringe, the inflated pouch pushes the top of the head upwards, causing the mouth to open (Fig.13). When the air is sucked out of the pouch, the mouth closes due to the weight of the head.

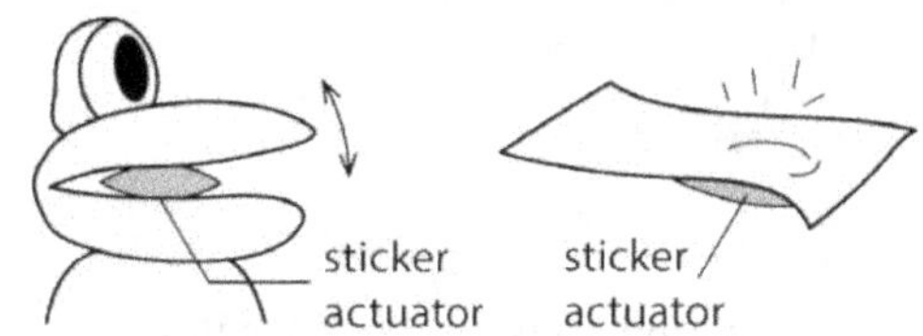

Figure 12. Applied sticker actuators on play dough objects (left) and sticky note (right)

Figure 13. The snapshots of the movements: singing clay frog (top), and beating sticky note (bottom).

We also attached a sticker actuator to the back of a sticky note (Fig.12). When inflating the pouch, bending is induced on the paper's surface. Deflation returns the paper to its original flat state. By alternating inflation and deflation, a sticky note can attract more attention from viewers (Fig.13).

Mixed Examples

Tape and sticker actuators can be used together. In this demonstration, we adhere one end of a tape actuator to the top bar of a metal frame, and the bottom to the head of the left robot. We also put sticker actuators beneath both of the robots' arms (Fig.14).

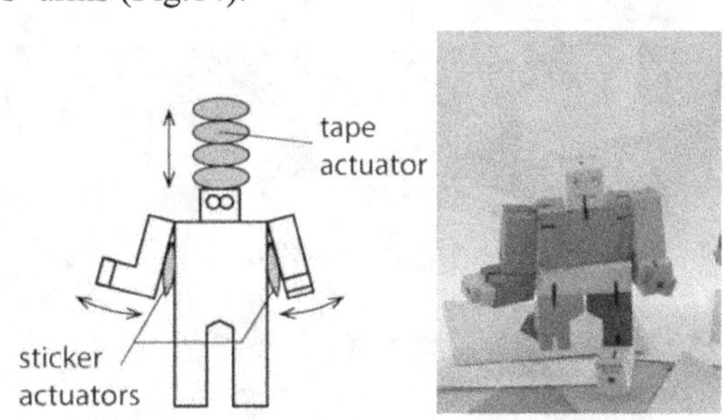

Figure 14. The example that use multiple sticky actuators: actuator arrangement (left), initial state (right)

Figure 15. The actuators is used for dancing and jumping motion: arm swing with sticker actuators (left), and jumping with tape actuator (right).

When the tape actuator is inflated, it pulls the left robot up, replicating a jumping motion. When the sticker actuators are inflated, both robots wave their arms (Fig.15).

USER STUDY

Basic Setup and Participants

Two 90-minutes animated origami workshops were held in a museum to study how children interact with sticky actuators (Fig.16). There were twenty participants at each workshop, all accompanied by their parents. The instructor demonstrated how to fold origami models and the use of sticky actuators. Then the participants were asked to make their own creations. Finally, participants presented their creations and answered a short questionnaire. Origami papers, sticky tape, syringes with tubes for manual control, and square-shape sticky actuators of variable sizes were provided to each group.

Figure 16. The animated origami workshop.

Questionnaire Results

We received twelve effective questionnaire respondents. We analyzed the answers of the following questions from the responses: 1) "What did you make today?" 2) "How did you use the pouch motor?" 3) "Please let us know if you have any other questions, comments, or requests." The distribution of subject ages is shown in Fig.17.

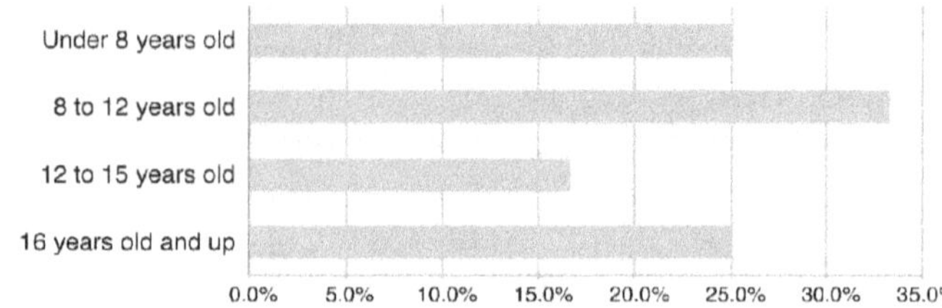

Figure 17. The age of the participants.

Fig. 18 shows the analysis of the motions and mechanisms implemented in the workshop. About 70 percent of the actuation was related to animal locomotion, such as flapping, swimming, and walking. This result shows that the free-form features and softness of the actuator are suitable for nature-inspired objects. The rotational motion (bending) is employed in 95 percent of the creation, and a few objects were controlled by pushing through inflation. This result suggests that children are interested in large straightforward motions rather than more subtle motions such as breathing or beating.

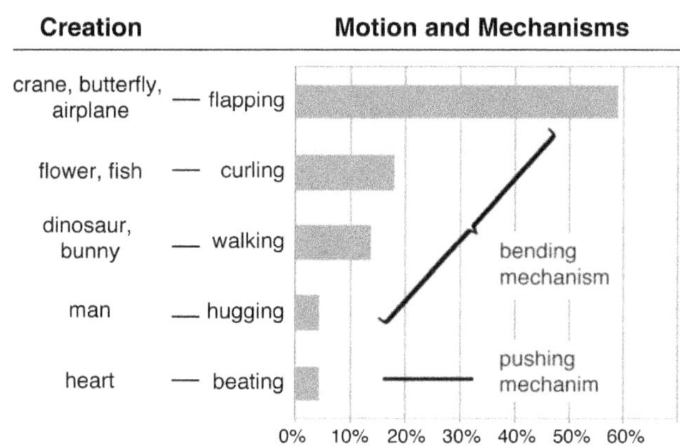

Figure 18. The analysis of motions and mechanisms of the results.

Children who were older and had prior experience with origami found the workshop interesting and were able to make innovative artwork. The difficulty of placing the pouches and actuating origami depends on the type of origami. We found most of flying birds were easy for children to play with; they put pouches either at the tip or bottom of the wings, with both positions producing pleasing results. However, when actuating origami with more complex motion, such as fish, children found it difficult to place the pouches to simulate body movements.

Animated Origami Examples

We observed that the combination of single-motion sticky actuators with a simple origami object could generate diverse behaviors and stories. Fig.19 shows animated origami objects from the workshop. As quoted from one participant, *"The actuator was very interesting, and depending on the origami, there were different challenges"*: the sticky actuator adds more challenges to the already complex art of folding origami. The actuation was even viewed as a new dimension to the origami art, as one participant mentioned: *"I definitely enjoyed it. It added a new dimension to an art I love"*.

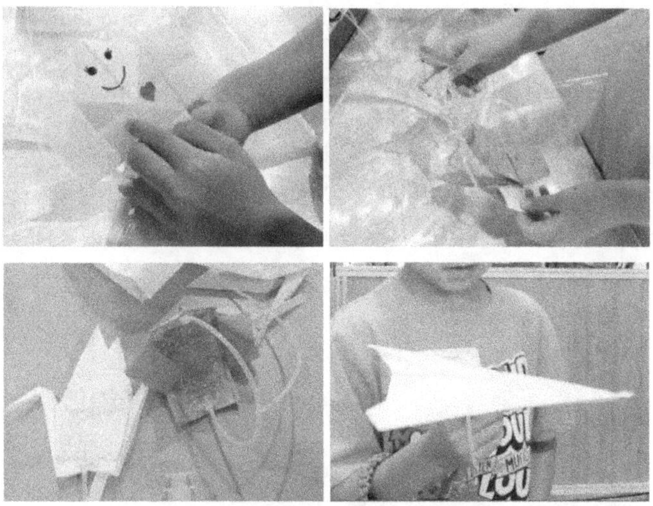

Figure 19. The examples from the workshop: a man with heart beat, a blooming flower with a flapping butterfly, a flapping crane, a hugging man, and an airplane with flaps (from upper left to lower right).

LIMITATIONS AND FUTURE WORK

We believe that the sticky actuators can offer practical features by overcoming the following limitations.

One of the limitations of the sticky actuator is the reliability and repeatability of the adhesive. It can be exhausted or may damage the target surface. A disposable feature could solve this issue as well as exploring other attachment methods.

There are many more possibilities in actuator geometries that can create a variety of motions and textures with the sticky actuator. The combination of free-form curves can generate complex motions such as corrugation in contemporary origami.

Advanced sensing and control are also possible directions for the future. Our pneumatic control system is capable of not only binary control but also continuous pressure control of the actuator. However, the current controller design is constrained to the on/off buttons. Direct interaction enhanced by embedding sensors need to be further explored. Printable and deformable electric circuit technologies can also be employed.

CONCLUSION

We proposed planar soft actuators that can be easily applied to passive objects, such as origami/clay animals, puppets, and everyday products. To facilitate mass production, we developed a fast fabrication method with inexpensive materials for the actuators. In addition to the manual control system with syringe, we also provided a programmable control system that can animate objects by using a teaching-playback method. With these beginnings, we envision a future in which soft/ flexible robotic components can quickly and cheaply expand the capability of passive objects and static environments.

ACKNOWLEDGEMENTS

This work was funded in part by NSF Grant No.1240383 and No.1138967. We are grateful for this support.

REFERENCES

1. Rasmussen, M.K., Pedersen, E.W., Petersen, M.G., and Hornbæk, K. Shape-changing interfaces. *Proceedings of the 2012 ACM annual conference on Human Factors in Computing Systems - CHI '12*, ACM Press (2012), 735–744.
2. Yao, L., Niiyama, R., Ou, J., Follmer, S., Della Silva, C., and Ishii, H. PneUI: pneumatically actuated soft composite materials for shape changing interfaces. *Proceedings of the 26th annual ACM symposium on User interface software and technology - UIST '13*, ACM Press (2013), 13–22.
3. Probst, K., Haller, M., Yasu, K., Sugimoto, M., and Inami, M. Move-it sticky notes providing active physical feedback through motion. *Proceedings of the 8th International Conference on Tangible, Embedded and Embodied Interaction - TEI '14*, ACM Press (2013), 29–36.
4. LEGO Group, LEGO Mindstorms, http://www.lego.com/
5. Raffle, H.S., Parkes, A.J., and Ishii, H. Topobo: a constructive assembly system with kinetic memory. *Proceedings of the 2004 conference on Human factors in computing systems - CHI '04*, ACM Press (2004), 647–654.
6. Oschuetz, L., Wessolek, D., and Sattler, W. Constructing with movement: kinematics. *Proceedings of the fourth international conference on Tangible, embedded, and embodied interaction - TEI '10*, ACM Press (2010), 257–260.
7. Sugiura, Y., Lee, C., Ogata, M., et al. PINOKY: a ring that animates your plush toys. *Proceedings of the 2012 ACM annual conference on Human Factors in Computing Systems - CHI '12*, ACM Press (2012), 725–734.

8. Kawahara, Y., Hodges, S., Cook, B.S., Zhang, C., and Abowd, G.D. Instant inkjet circuits. *Proceedings of the 2013 ACM international joint conference on Pervasive and ubiquitous computing - UbiComp '13*, ACM Press (2013), 363–372.
9. Olberding, S., Gong, N.-W., Tiab, J., Paradiso, J.A., and Steimle, J. A cuttable multi-touch sensor. *Proceedings of the 26th annual ACM symposium on User interface software and technology - UIST '13*, ACM Press (2013), 245–254.
10. Chibitronics, Circuit Stickers (2013). http://www.crowdsupply.com/chibitronics/circuit-stickers
11. Harrison, C. and Hudson, S.E. Providing dynamically changeable physical buttons on a visual display. *Proceedings of the 27th international conference on Human factors in computing systems - CHI 09*, ACM Press (2009), 299–308.
12. Stevenson, A., Perez, C., and Vertegaal, R. An inflatable hemispherical multi-touch display. *Proceedings of the fifth international conference on Tangible, embedded, and embodied interaction - TEI '11*, ACM Press (2011), 289–292.
13. Kim, S., Kim, H., Lee, B., Nam, T.-J., and Lee, W. Inflatable Mousee: Volume-adjustable Mouse with Air-pressure-sensitive Input and Haptic Feedback. *Proceeding of the 26th annual CHI conference on Human factors in computing systems - CHI '08*, ACM Press (2008), 211–214.
14. Niiyama, R., Rus, D., and Kim, S. Pouch Motors: Printable/Inflatable Soft Actuators for Robotics. IEEE International Conference on Robotics and Automation (ICRA), (2014), 6332–6337.
15. Martinez, R. V, Fish, C.R., Chen, X., and Whitesides, G.M. Elastomeric Origami: Programmable Paper-Elastomer Composites as Pneumatic Actuators. *Advanced Functional Materials 22*, 7 (2012), 1376–1384.

Fl.UIs : Liquid-Mediated Vision Based Touch Surfaces

Tim Campbell, César Torres, Eric Paulos
Department of Electrical Engineering and Computer Sciences
University of California Berkeley
{timcam, cearto, paulos}@eecs.berkeley.edu

ABSTRACT
Fluid User Interfaces (Fl.UIs) are liquid-based touch surfaces that use computer vision to detect and interpret a range of tactile user inputs. While Fl.UIs have less input resolution than digital touch screens, they provide an excellent low-cost solution for rapidly prototyping non-rectilinear screen designs as well as exploring novel surface interaction techniques. Fabricated on a laser cutter using low-cost materials, Fl.UIs use unique shape outlines to displace an internal colored liquid to regions-of-interest for a camera. This paper presents a set of software tools that help users rapidly design, fabricate and author interactions with Fl.UIs. The robust construction and an unpowered surface makes Fl.UIs well-suited for outdoor and public installations. Our Fl.UIs prototyping tool encourages these uncommon "screens" to emerge in complex environments (i.e. urban spaces, benches, tables, fountains, sidewalks).

Author Keywords
tangible user interfaces; computer vision; digital fabrication; urban computing

ACM Classification Keywords
H.5.m. Information Interfaces and Presentation (e.g. HCI): Miscellaneous

INTRODUCTION
Interactive surfaces are emerging in a wide variety of new environments. However, there is a natural tension between the physical constraints of current touch screen technologies and the dynamic surfaces found "in-the-wild." By reducing the requirement for high-resolution input, passive hardware designs can challenge current perceptions of touch devices and the available environments for surface interactions.

In this paper we present Fluid User Interfaces (Fl.UIs), liquid-mediated touch surfaces. In response to touch input, Fl.UIs create color changes by displacing an internally sealed colored liquid guided by the shape of the surface (Figure 1). A web-accessible computer vision system identifies these color changes and triggers action events that a designer can then use to create custom applications. The shape of the custom hardware defines how the fluid flows within the surface – thus defining the type of interaction. Fl.UIs also support a different level of pressure than more delicate capacitive touch surfaces, which allows for a wide variety of touch modalities (e.g. finger, hand, sitting, crawling, slapping, etc).

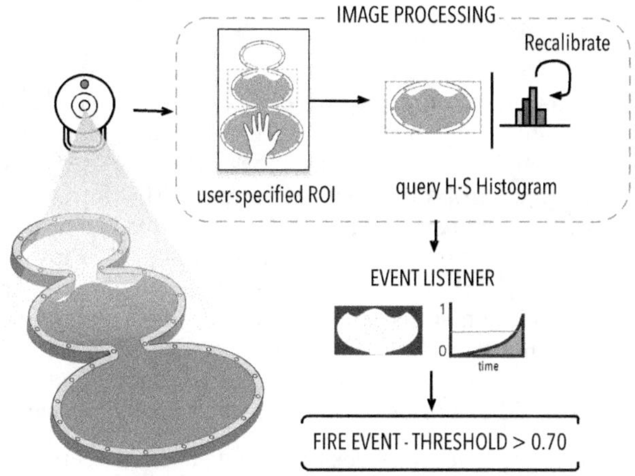

Figure 1. A webcam is positioned to observe a Fl.UI, or fluid-mediated surface. Our web-accessible computer vision system listens for changes in the distribution of colored pixels in specified regions-of-interest (ROIs). When a user applies pressure to the surface and displaces the colored liquid, our system triggers an action event.

Access to electronics prototyping and digital fabrication has redefined how we develop touch interactions [5], yet prototyping these interactions still requires off-the-shelf hardware or a fully-developed system. We present a design work-flow for Fl.UIs as a rapid prototyping tool for both hardware and software. Using a liquid to interactions challenges current forms of input and turns touch into a playful, colorful experience. Although a camera is needed to power Fl.UIs, the surfaces themselves are unpowered making them more reliable and easier to scale, maintain, and create.

RELATED WORK
Vision-based touch screens promise cost-effective, large scale interaction. In an early example of diffuse illumination, researchers built wall-sized touch interaction with a rear-projection screen [10]. The Extended Multi-Touch project extracts multi-touch input passively using a depth camera [13]. Similarly, we decouple the sensing capability from the Fl.UIs surface and offset it to a low-cost webcam.

TEI'15, January 16–19, 2015, Stanford, CA, USA.

ACM 878-1-4501-3305-4/15/01 ISBN/14/04...$15.00.
http://dx.doi.org/10.1145/2677199.2680604

Deformable surfaces have been explored in tangible interfaces [2]. Hennecke et. al. used simple marker patterns from pads to extract position, orientation and pressure on a touch surface [6]. Other system minimally augment a surface for touch detection. Frustrated total internal reflection (FTIR) uses edge-lit LEDs [3] and Moeller et. al. modified existing displays with additional hardware to enable touch capability [12]. However, many of these vision-based sensing techniques [1, 3, 7, 10] require underside or rear-mounted camera, limiting the form and environment of the system. For example, GravitySpace [1] achieved pose reconstruction from a user's contact with custom FTIR floor tiles but required an entire room underneath to place the camera sensor.

Several projects have explored the use of liquids as sensing or output mediators. Sylvester et. al. explored the use of soap bubbles as an alternative, playful, and ephemeral tangible user interface material [15]. MudPad uses magnetic fields to control stiffness in ferrofluids [8]. Harrison et. al. constructed active pneumatic UI components that used the air connection for both sensing and actuation [4]. Most similar to our work, Hilliges et. al. constructed a liquid displacement surface that masked a flexible nylon sheet with opaque ink for high precision touch and shape detection [7]. We add a robust surface construction to Hilliges' technique and then utilize fluid displacement for an *overhead* camera setup.

Though mediated surfaces have made touch detection viable, extracting meaningful information from computer vision systems remains a challenge. Fl.UIs use principles for prototyping computer vision applications to create a direct manipulation interface with a plug-in architecture [11]. Although we sacrifice 2D input, the Fl.UIs workflow is a full-featured prototyping tool for non-experts as well as professional interaction designers to create low-cost, bespoke touch surfaces.

THE FI.UI DESIGN PROCESS

In this section, we decompose the Fl.UI design process into two components: a) the physical design and construction of the Fl.UI surface, and b) computer-vision prototyping system for detecting input.

Physical Design

The Fl.UI hardware is a simple layered construction of a liquid sandwiched between two layers of plastic and sealed with a cork gasket (Figure 2). We use the outline of the hardware to guide fluid movement to a region-of-interest for the camera. Fl.UIs displace pigmented liquid away from a user's point-of-contact but still replicates the user's interaction in a principle we call *spatial redundancy*. Since vision-based system have problems with occlusion, providing alternative areas with equivalent information greatly improves the reliability of the signal.

Designing form factors

Two shapes were helpful in the design of Fl.UIs: *wells*, which are larger chambers of liquid, and *channels*, which constrict flow between wells. Figure 4 shows a "barbell" design that mimics the functionality of a button by channeling fluid from one well to another.

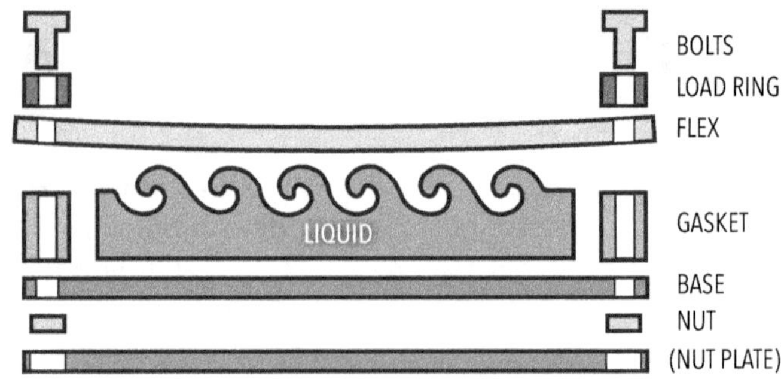

Figure 2. A top-input Fl.UI configuration. A liquid is sandwiched between a flexible (FLEX) and rigid (BASE) plastic, sealed with a cork material (GASKET) and low-profile bolts.

To facilitate rapid iteration, the required components of a Fl.UI can be extracted from a single closed Scalable Vector Graphic (SVG) path. Using the paper.js library[9], we generate the five solid layers as laser cutter-ready files from this single path. Script parameters allow a user to specify bolt sizes, material depths, and ring thickness. This approach supports design tools that produces SVG graphics, allowing users to quickly iterate on Fl.UI form factors.

Techniques for construction

In general, the construction of a Fl.UI mimics standard pressure vessels. Fluid is sealed between the base and a flexible plastic using a gasket ring and bolts spaced approximately 25 mm apart (Figure 2); a **LOAD RING** between **FLEX** and **BOLTS** ensures uniform loading.

We chose materials and processes available to the Maker community. The cutting operations used a 50 Watt laser cutter; all acrylic was 3 mm thick continuous-cast acrylic, which cuts easily and remains rigid under pressure. The semi-flexible material was 0.05" (0.127 mm) thick Mylar film. For the **GASKET** we found cork blended with a rubber compound (McMaster #9304K42, 1/16" sheets) cut well and remained tough and pliable even after extended use. To ease assembly we regularly used an optional **NUT PLATE**, which had cutouts to capture the nuts. Layers were stacked to an overall height of 12.50 mm, including low-profile M3×10 **BOLTS** and **NUTS**.

For the mediating fluid, we used either water or vegetable oil dyed with acrylic ink or oil color, respectively. Non skin-colored pigments were used to minimize ambiguities with the computer vision system. The exact volume and proportion of liquid-to-pigment was determined empirically using the CV system as feedback. Tuning the Fl.UI was made easier by inserting a hypodermic dispensing needle (McMaster #6710A26) under the **GASKET**. The material cost of each Fl.UI is approximately $15 (USD) per square foot, though overall footprint and layout efficiency matter greatly.

Software Design

In order to allow for a true plug-and-play environment, we designed a computer vision prototyping system that runs on a modern web browser (Figure 3). Using the HTML5 `getUserMedia` API, we extract video from a computer's

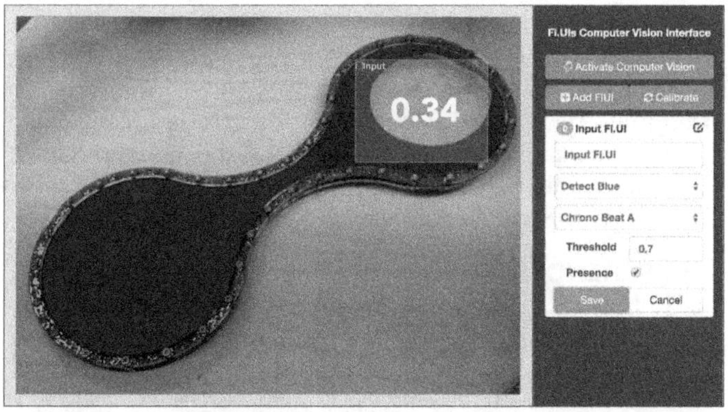

Figure 3. CV Web Interface - In this interface, the user has specified a region-of-interest (input) and a query color (blue). When the computer vision routine is activated, pixels classified as blue are overlaid with a blue pixel. This interface has one event listener observing the "input" ROI that fires when more than 70% of pixels are blue.

built-in or peripheral webcam and classify color using a color back-projection routine [14]. With this system, a user can bypass setting up and using a development environment and simply point their camera in order to interact with multiple Fl.UIs.

Our interface is divided into three modes:

- **Design**: users select areas on a webcam feed to listen for color changes. They can specify a query color as well as trigger parameters. Events are exported as JavaScript events; in our applications, we trigger sounds to play/pause or change volume.
- **Calibration**: users select sample color regions to recalibrate the system. While color backprojection does relatively well at identifying colors, changes in lighting disturb most computer systems. Pixels in the sample region are used to repopulate a hue-saturation histogram. Assuming a stable camera setup, color samples in a stable location within the environment can be used to automatically calibrate the system.
- **Active**: Pixels are classified as belonging to a distinct hue using the Hue-Saturation histograms derived from the *Calibration* mode. The system evaluates the distribution of colored pixels in each region-of-interest, which is then used to trigger user-defined events (*e.g.,* more than 70% blue pixels detected). Our system is able to provide real-time classification on five hues at 28fps with limited lag (40ms) on a modern laptop browser. Webcam pixels are overlaid with their classified colors for better system state visibility.

PROTOTYPING INTERACTIONS

In this section, we give an overview of design considerations for Fl.UIs and novel interactions that arise from fluid properties. The most salient property of a Fl.UI is the "waterbed effect," a playful interaction that occurs when applying pressure on a large, flexible portion of the Fl.UI. This property can be controlled by the a) stiffness of the FLEX material, b) thickness of the GASKET, and c) area of the region-of-contact. Additionally, the designer can tune these parameters

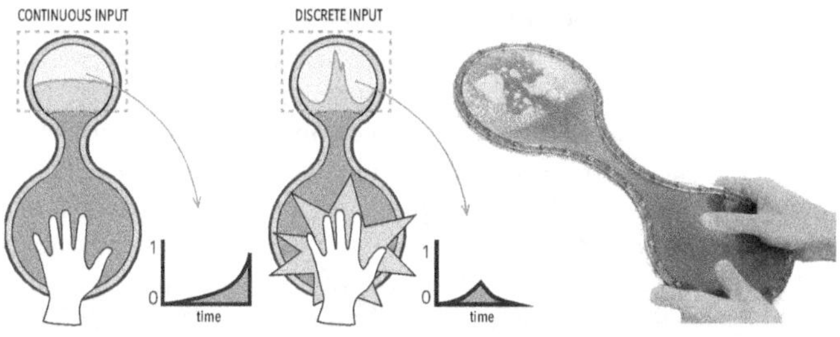

Figure 4. A barbell Fl.UI design. A single channel between two wells can be used to provide continuous or discrete feedback. Each type of feedback gives a unique input-output coincidence profile that can be used to fire action events by the computer vision system.

to change the responsiveness of the Fl.UI, from light touches to hard stomps.

Moving liquids from one well to another influences the input profile of the Fl.UI. That is, applying abrupt pressure to the liquid-filled well with a thin channel creates a turbulent jet of liquid, which can act as a momentary button. A steady press fills the receiving well linearly for continuous input, where analog resolution is defined by the region's pixel count. The width of a channel between two wells modulates the rate of diffusion. Using combinations of wells, channels and inclines we made a "barbell" construction (see Figure 4) that allows liquid to flow from one well to another. We demonstrate a multi-state input on a single Fl.UI in Figure 5 as another configuration of form. The smaller wells have been designed to fill incrementally as the user presses harder on the base. For momentary input, the liquid must return to the steady state configuration. This force is currently supplied by slightly elevating the Fl.UI ($< 15°$) or placing the Fl.UI on a vertical surface. One could also use bending or channels to mimic "latching switches," common in electronics, though this remains for future work.

The mediating liquid can also influence the type of input. In a large 600×300 mm rectangular construction mediated with vegetable oil, we found that an "oilfall" interaction could be used as a timing mechanism. Displacing a pocket of oil to the top of the Fl.UI would correspond in a slow movement down. Increasing both the fluid thickness layer and viscosity can create visceral interactions where the user must "sculpt" the fluid into the desired location.

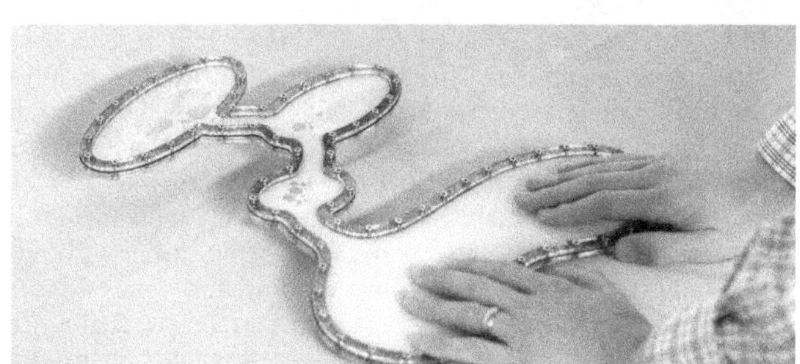

Figure 5. A top-input Fl.UI configuration using two wells to create multi-state input. When the user presses on the lower well, fluid travels to multiple upper wells.

DISCUSSION AND FUTURE WORK

The solid construction of Fl.UIs affords rougher interactions than most input devices. By decoupling the sensing capability from the surface, Fl.UIs can function unpowered and eliminate the need for complicated wiring at the point of interaction. This can promote designs that can be embedded in new, uncommon environments such as playgrounds, park benches, or even underwater. Security becomes less of a problem since Fl.UIs do not have the perceived value of consumer electronics, and the low-cost construction makes them easy to replace or repair. We can also utilize the camera's field-of-view to create input ecosystems, distributing and linking interactions amongst several Fl.UIs in a single space.

Although the camera still requires power and installation, we anticipate that the trend of cost-effective IoT cameras will act as drivers of computer vision-enabled ubiquitous computing. At this time, we explore static and grounded Fl.UI installations to focus on fluid interactions. Ideally, the Fl.UI CV system should support moving Fl.UIs, and some initial computer vision SIFT tracking prototypes show promising results in this direction.

Fl.UIs are also ideally suited for educational and STEM programs. Students learning computational design could design and fabricate their own Fl.UI and then connect their hardware for inexpensive interaction. We assume access to a laser cutter, but such tools are becoming commonplace in shops and Makerspaces.

We initially aimed at using spatial redundancy to recover accurate 2D touch input from overhead video capture. Instead Fl.UIs use shape to create a more profound displacement of liquid away from the point-of-contact. As a result, Fl.UIs forgo the accuracy found in other liquid-mediated interfaces such as [7].

Fl.UIs could additionally benefit from a material that forms a permanent colloid with a liquid. Current liquid pigments fell out of suspension after a month of non-use. Currently, our construction process favors a watertight seal over assembly time. The "barbell" construction, for example, has 40 bolts that each require hand tightening. We have explored welding our layers together to minimize assembly time. Joining only Mylar **FLEX** layers could create a flexible Fl.UI for more wearable and non-planar applications.

CONCLUSION

Fl.UIs are not designed to replace all current screen-based interaction techniques. Instead we envision Fl.UIs as a tool for prototyping "screen-like" designs that are both counter and complementary to established interfaces. Since the surface outline defines fluid flow, Fl.UIs tend towards bespoke and non-rectangular shapes. Our low-cost hardware lowers the barrier of entry and encourages exploration of liquid-mediated surfaces using web-based computer vision. Finally, we challenged the notion of a touch surface by decoupling the electronics from the point-of-interaction and constructing Fl.UIs for public settings. Fl.UI design tools have been made publicly available at `http://fluis.t-h-e.org/`.

ACKNOWLEDGMENTS

We thank Dan Armendariz, Clint Anderson, Ki Fung Chow for their collaboration on the initial Fl.UI prototypes, and Kimiko Ryokai, Laura Devendorf, Bjoern Hartmann, and the anonymous reviewers for their insightful comments and suggestions. This research was supported by the NSF Grant No. IIS-1451465 and an Adobe GEM Fellowship.

REFERENCES

1. Bränzel, A., Holz, C., Hoffmann, D., Schmidt, D., Knaust, M., Lühne, P., Meusel, R., Richter, S., and Baudisch, P. Gravityspace: Tracking users and their poses in a smart room using a pressure-sensing floor. In *CHI '13*, ACM Press (2013), 725–734.
2. Follmer, S., Johnson, M., Adelson, E., and Ishii, H. deForm: An interactive malleable surface for capturing 2.5D arbitrary objects, tools and touch. In *UIST '11*, ACM Press (2011), 527–536.
3. Han, J. Y. Low-cost multi-touch sensing through frustrated total internal reflection. In *UIST '05*, ACM Press (2005), 115–118.
4. Harrison, C., and Hudson, S. E. Providing dynamically changeable physical buttons on a visual display. In *CHI '09*, ACM Press (2009), 299–308.
5. Hartmann, B., and Wright, P. K. Designing bespoke interactive devices. *Computer 46*, 8 (2013), 85–89.
6. Hennecke, F., Berwein, F., and Butz, A. Optical pressure sensing for tangible user interfaces. In *Proc. ITS '11*, ACM Press (2011), 45–48.
7. Hilliges, O., Kim, D., and Izadi, S. Creating malleable interactive surfaces using liquid displacement sensing. In *Proc. Tabletop 2008*, IEEE Press (2008), 157160.
8. Jansen, Y. Mudpad: fluid haptics for multitouch surfaces. In *Extended Abstracts of CHI '10*, ACM (2010), 43514356.
9. Lehni, J., and Puckey, J. Paper.js, 2011.
10. Matsushita, N., and Rekimoto, J. HoloWall: designing a finger, hand, body, and object sensitive wall. In *UIST '97*, ACM Press (1997), 209–210.
11. Maynes-Aminzade, D., Winograd, T., and Igarashi, T. Eyepatch: prototyping camera-based interaction through examples. In *UIST '07*, ACM Press (2007), 33–42.
12. Moeller, J., and Kerne, A. Zerotouch: An optical multi-touch and free-air interaction architecture. In *CHI '12*, ACM Press (2012), 2165–2174.
13. Murugappan, S., Vinayak, Elmqvist, N., and Ramani, K. Extended multitouch: Recovering touch posture and differentiating users using a depth camera. In *UIST '12*, ACM Press (2012), 487–496.
14. Swain, M. J., and Ballard, D. H. Color indexing. *Int'l J. Computer Vision '91*, 1 (1991), 1132.
15. Sylvester, A., Dring, T., and Schmidt, A. Liquids, smoke, and soap bubbles: reflections on materials for ephemeral user interfaces. In *TEI '10*, ACM (2010), 269–270.

THAW: Tangible Interaction with See-Through Augmentation for Smartphones on Computer Screens

Sang-won Leigh Philipp Schoessler Felix Heibeck Pattie Maes Hiroshi Ishii
{sangwon, phil_s, heibeck, pattie, ishii }@media.mit.edu
MIT Media Lab, 75 Amherst Street, Cambridge, MA, United States

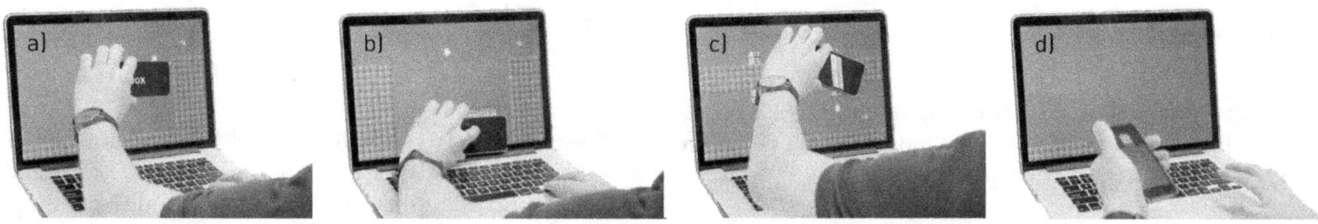

Figure 1: A smartphone screen can be used as a user interface intervening into the display space of a computer screen.

ABSTRACT

The huge influx of mobile display devices is transforming computing into multi-device interaction, demanding a fluid mechanism for using multiple devices in synergy. In this paper, we present a novel interaction system that allows a collocated large display and a small handheld device to work together. The smartphone acts as a physical interface for near-surface interactions on a computer screen. Our system enables accurate position tracking of a smartphone placed on or over any screen by displaying a 2D color pattern that is captured using the smartphone's back-facing camera. As a result, the smartphone can directly interact with data displayed on the host computer, with precisely aligned visual feedback from both devices. The possible interactions are described and classified in a framework, which we exemplify on the basis of several implemented applications. Finally, we present a technical evaluation and describe how our system is unique compared to other existing near-surface interaction systems. The proposed technique can be implemented on existing devices without the need for additional hardware, promising immediate integration into existing systems.

Author Keywords

Multi-device Interaction; Tangible Magic Lens;

ACM Classification Keywords

H.5.2 User Interfaces: Input devices and strategies (e.g., mouse, touchscreen)

TEI '15, January 16 - 19 2015, Stanford, CA, USA

ACM 978-1-4503-3305-4/15/01…$15.00
http://dx.doi.org/10.1145/2677199.2680584

General Terms

Human Factors; Design;

INTRODUCTION

A growing number of people own a smartphone in addition to their computer. The collocated interaction with those devices poses the question of how to seamlessly connect the different display spaces and their afforded interactions. Some existing systems mediate users' actions across multiple devices, however, their use scenarios are mostly focused on using a secondary device as mere a remote controller or a viewport [2, 3, 6].

To challenge this limitation, our research focuses on the spatial fusion of the two display devices through near-surface interaction. This allows to best leverage both device's affordances to create a fluid experience: The physical body of the phone affords tangible manipulation, while the screens on both devices can display virtual graphics that augment or interact with each other. If the interaction between the devices happens in close proximity, the phone's physicality and the graphics on each device in combination with our strong visual-motor skills bridges the gap between spatial reality and the digital as shown in prior research in the fields of Augmented Reality (AR) [10] and Tangible User Interfaces (TUI) [14]. The two domains are not mutually exclusive, having slightly different focuses on visual augmentation and tangible interaction respectively.

In this paper we present THAW (Tangible, Handheld, and Augmented Window), a system that enables near-surface interaction with ordinary computer displays and smartphones without any necessary hardware modifications. We present the underlying technology and provide a classification of possible interactions. The implemented applications explore scenarios to transfer digital content between two devices, novel game mechanics and map navigation with multiple users.

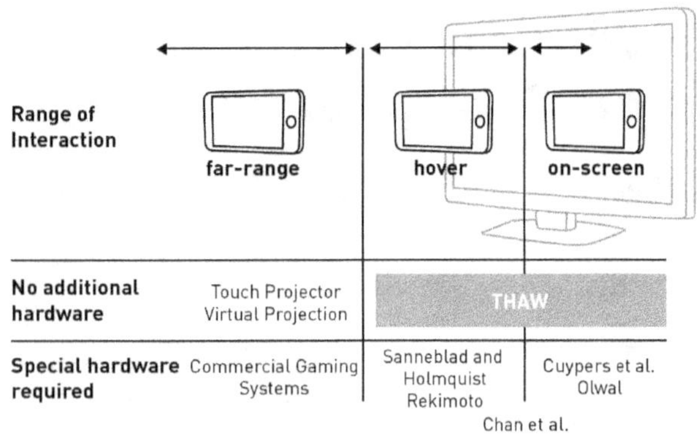

Figure 2: Systems based on tracking of handheld devices. THAW fills the void of systems that offer near-surface interaction and are easy to deploy

RELATED WORK

Prior see-through augmentation styled interaction systems explored interactions between a phone and a computer screen over a certain distance, however, none thoroughly explored near-surface (on-screen) interactions. This is mainly because the proposed tracking techniques require a certain distance between the devices to work properly or special tracking hardware / setups. (Figure 2)

Handheld Displays with Large Display

Commercially available gaming systems like the Wii U provide a game controller consisting of a small touchscreen [2]. The controller acts as a position-tracked window that can display an additional layer of information. Touch Projector [6], by Boring et al., is a system that allows manipulating digital content on a large screen through touching on live video captured by smartphones. Baur et al. presented Virtual Projection [4], simulating projections of graphics onto computer screens inferring a phone's 3D position in space. Due to the nature of the tracking techniques used in these systems, the handheld screen can be operated only from a considerable distance to the screen. Particularly in [4, 6], the graphics on the computer screen are used as a tracking pattern, which has to be updated every frame creating significant latency.

There are systems that explored closer range interactions using mobile phones on top of a larger display. Rohs et al [23], Sanneblad and Holmquist [24], and Reilly et al. [20] explored the application of digital maps. Hansen et al. [12] used a fiducial marker on a display screen for tracking the position of a smartphone hovering above it. For the purpose of their studies, they used mock up systems [20], fiducial markers printed on a map [12, 23], or a pseudo tracking setup using a commercial touch pen [24], which were at a yet preliminary stage for practical uses. Chan et al. [8] and Cuypers et al. [9] presented hardware systems that project a tracking pattern from beneath a tabletop display. BlueTable [27] tracked phones on a tabletop using external cameras. The LightSense system [16] tracked a phone's flashlight with a camera installed behind a surface or with embedded light sensors. These systems allowed continuous tracking of the phone, but are quite complex in their setup and large in size, as additional hardware is needed.

Tangible and See-through Interaction

We consider our work situated at the intersection of AR and TUI, as the use of a handheld screen on a larger display enables both tangible interactions and see-through augmentation. Here we introduce previous and current research from each domain that shares similarities with the THAW system.

Physical Tokens

Physical tokens are widely used for tabletop computing systems. Underkoffler et al. presented Urp [28], a tabletop system that utilizes physical wireframe buildings to simulate environmental behaviors for urban planning. Sensetable [18] uses magnetic gadgets that can be actuated in 2D space by a computer-controlled electromagnet array. Liang et al. [15] presented Gaussbits, magnetic tokens that can be tracked using an array of bipolar-magnetic sensors. Capstone [7], are widgets that can be stacked on top of capacitive touchscreens. While those systems all showcase the utility of physical tokens to interact with digital data, they require special hardware.

Magic Lens and Touching Through Video

Bier et al. introduced Toolglass and Magic Lens [5], a software widget controlled by the non-dominant hand, and users can touch "through" the widget with their other hand. This concept of see-through interaction has then been further explored by using handheld screen devices that would act as the magic lens. Fitzmaurice and Buxton [11], as well as Rekimoto [22] used palm top displays to reveal information based on the devices' 3D positions in space. Spindler et al. [25] did a general study on the interaction using handheld magic lens displays in a tabletop system.

Tani et al. [26] presented Object-oriented Video, a concept of touching and controlling physical interfaces through a video feed. This concept has been iterated through many recent projects: the most notable is Smarter Objects [13] by Heun et al., which allows controlling and reprogramming the behavior of physical objects by overlaying the graphical UI when looking through the display of a handheld device.

Most of the listed projects explore different techniques for location aware interaction with remote objects through the video feed of a handheld device. However, none have taken an exhaustive investigation into the combination of see-through and tangible interaction, mainly due to the lack of a reliable system for such combined interaction.

INTERACTION

In our system, the surface of a screen represents the main space for interactions. A handheld screen device is put on top of a larger screen, allowing a user to manipulate the handheld device in a very close proximity to the larger

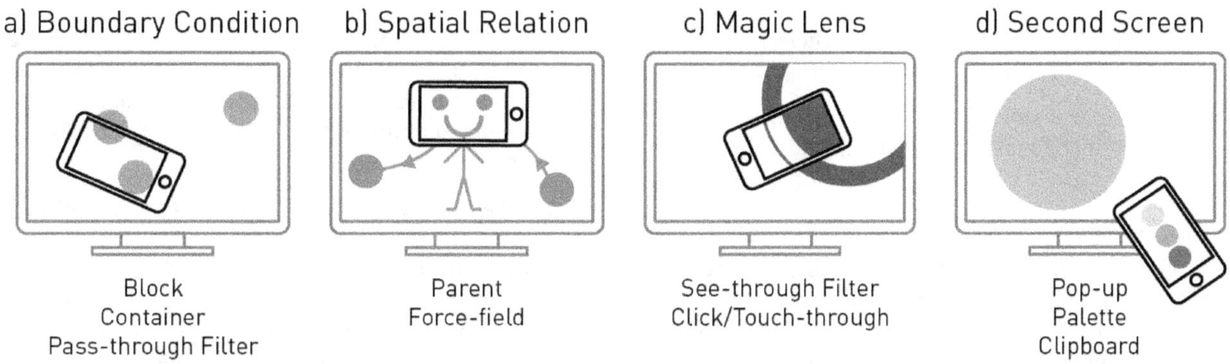

Figure 3: Classification of interaction on our system. Each represents different modes of direct, near-surface interactions.

screen. As the user moves the handheld screen, the graphics on both screens respond accordingly, right at the location of the user's action. Our strong visual-motor skills help us to make the perceptual connection between our hand's motion and the visuals on the screen, producing a believable experience of connecting both display spaces.

In this section we present our classification of possible interactions with the THAW system (Figure 3). The phone can be used as a physical token to directly interact with digital entities based on their relative positions (Figure 3(a), (b)). It can act as a lens for controlling or augmenting objects on a computer screen and also offers an additional space to be used for extended control or as a physical clipboard (Figure 3(c), (d)). The presented interactions can be building blocks for more sophisticated interactions as will be presented in next section.

Boundary Condition

Using a handheld screen device as a physical token lets us intervene "in" a larger screen and interact with its displayed graphics content. Similar to the computer game Roy Block [1], in which a virtual character needs to jump on physical blocks to solve a level. Interactions are classified based on the boundary condition that determines the entry direction into the handheld screen device. (Figure 3(a))

Block: The handheld screen device acts a physical boundary and has the ability to block and constrain elements on the screen. It can be used to manipulate objects in virtual space.

Container: The handheld screen device provides a complimentary space for containing data. The user can put data or virtual objects "into" their device, for example through drag and drop.

Pass-through Filter: Digital elements can travel "through" the handheld device in turn modifying their properties. For instance, this can be used to filter, translate, encode/decode certain data (sounds, images, etc.) as well as for compression and decompression.

Spatial Relation

This section defines the set of interactions based on the relative position of the handheld device to the graphics on the larger screen. (Figure 3(b))

Parent: The handheld device can act as a parent object providing a physical anchor for graphical elements on the larger screen.

Force-field Generator: The handheld device is able to generate a force field that affects the virtual objects on the larger screen by attracting or repelling them.

Magic Lens

Using the handheld screen device as a virtual window we can reveal certain information or content. Hidden annotations can be displayed while the users are browsing the Internet or editing a document. Additionally, the device's touch screen affords touch interactions with the displayed content. (Figure 3(c)) This enables Toolglass and Magic Lens type interaction [5].

See-through Filter: The handheld screen device becomes a lens for revealing or filtering displayed information.

Click/Touch-through: By putting the handheld screen device on items on the larger screen, users can touch or click the items through the handheld screen. Olwal and Feiner [17] provided a comprehensive study on this type of interaction using stylus and phone.

Second Screen

Here we describe the use of off-screen interactions on the secondary display space. (Figure3(d)) The handheld screen device can be used to link or store digital elements that can then be controlled or modified off-screen or from a remote location. This category aligns with Pick-and-Drop styled interactions introduced by Rekimoto [21].

Clipboard: The handheld device can be used as a mobile clipboard to collect digital elements (images, text, etc.). The handheld device can then be brought to a larger screen where the stored elements can just be swiped out of the handheld device onto the larger screen.

Palette: We imagine the handheld device to be an adaptive tool with which we can alter digital data as a painter arranges and mixes different colors on a real palette. Through making use of the handheld device's various sensors (e.g. touchscreen, accelerometer) the data can be modified. This subcategory describes a direct alteration of the data on the handheld device, in contrast to a palette example introduced by Piazza et al [19] where a phone is used as a separate controller for modifying brush strokes.

Pop-up: The phone can be linked to an element on the screen and will then constantly give updates about that element.

MIXED INTERACTION

Used in combination or sequentially, the interactions introduced in the previous section can construct more unique convolutions of tangible interaction and see-through augmentation (Figure 4). The near-surface configuration of our system allows the formerly disparate interaction styles of TUI and AR to be mixed.

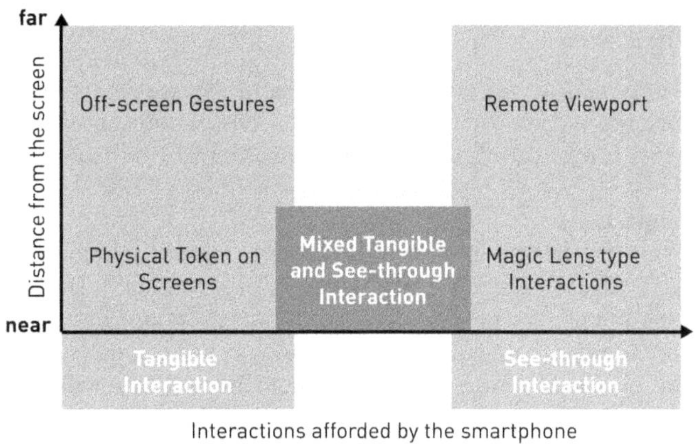

Figure 4. Near-surface interaction space allows unique combination of tangible and see-through interaction.

Magic Lens + Container: Figure 5(a) shows an example of using *'see-through'* and *'container'* interactions in combination. This combination allows selective manipulation of active foreground information (the game character) while displaying the static background information (the gray wall) through the smartphone screen. This spatially and contextually separates controllable entities from unnecessary ones. In addition to this, touch events can be used to move data across the phone (in the front) and the computer screen (in the back) (Figure 10).

Figure 5. Mixed interaction techniques used in a gaming scenario. (a) Simultaneously displaying foreground (character) and background (wall) (b) Using gestures to change the size of the character jumped into the phone (c) Changing behavior of an object by adding virtual friction

Second Screen + Container: Interactions on the phone screen allows manipulation of the data contained in it and feeding it back to the larger screen. As a result, the phone turns into an always-accessible magic box that lets users transform digital objects in a seamless manner. Figure 5(b) illustrates how using gestures on a smartphone changes the size and behavior of a game character that jumped "into" it. A more practical use of this is to apply the same adjustments to multiple files selectively by simply dragging them into the phone.

Magic Lens + Pass-through Filter: The secondary screen can be used as a moveable tangible filter that alters properties of digital elements behind it. However, it is difficult to know the filtering process without being able to see through the filter's body. In this case, see-through augmentation will greatly improve the visual cues that provide direct visual feedback to the users. Figure 5(c) shows an example of changing the speed of a moving object on the computer screen, where motion friction being applied by the phone is displayed via see-through augmentation.

IMPLEMENTATION

The very close distance from the smartphone to the screen (< 2cm) makes conventional feature-based tracking impossible due to the camera's lack of near-focusing capability and limited field of view (FOV). In our system, a computer screen displays a distinct color pattern. The phone's back-facing camera detects the pixels' color shown on the screen behind the phone. Sampled points are used to infer the phone's position from the RGB values through linear transformation. Constantly displaying the color pattern to enable tracking limits the aesthetics and readability of many applications. To minimize this interference we use a masked pattern that only shows in the camera's field of view. Its position and size are updated based on the previous frame's tracking result. (Figure 6)

For the implementation we used the iPhone 5S and 4S on a 15-inch Retina Macbook Pro as well as a 50-inch Hisense 1080p LED TV. The software is built upon openFrameworks. On the host computer, a server listens for incoming connections from the smartphone. Once a connection is established the devices exchange the calibration and tracking information. For data communication between the devices, we used Open Sound Control (OSC), an UDP-based communication library.

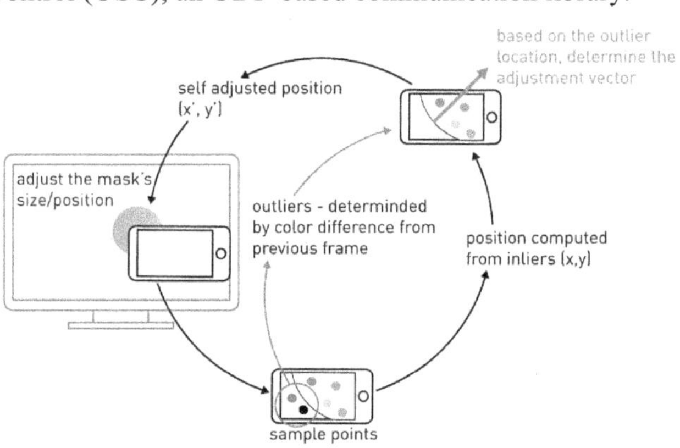

Figure 6. Sequence diagram of the tracking algorithm

Position

On capacitive touchscreens, the position of a phone can easily be tracked by attaching copper tape to the bottom of the phone to create capacitance between the two devices. Here, we focused on computer screens without capacitive touch capabilities to create a system that could potentially be applicable to any available display. We propose a method for tracking the 2D position of a smartphone relative to a computer screen using a distinct color pattern displayed on the host screen (top left is black (0, 0, 0), top right is red (255, 0, 0), bottom left is green (0, 255, 0) and bottom right is yellow (255, 255, 0)). Using the back-facing camera of the phone, we can detect the color of the pixels that appear on the screen behind the phone. Four corner points are sampled from the captured image. If there is an abrupt change in color value, the sample is regarded as an erroneous measurement and thus filtered out.

From the captured RGB values the corresponding 2D coordinate can be calculated. The mathematical relationship between RGB color and 2D coordinate can be described as:

$$\boldsymbol{x} = A\boldsymbol{c}$$

with $\boldsymbol{x} = (x, y)$ and $\boldsymbol{c} = (r, g, b)$. Due to white balance and the dynamic range of camera and screen the mapping might deviate from a linear function. However, experimentally, we found that linear mapping gives a reliable approximation. The coefficients are determined through Linear Least Squares using known measurement points $\boldsymbol{x}$ and detected color $\boldsymbol{c}$,

$$\hat{A} = \underset{A}{\operatorname{argmin}} \|\boldsymbol{x} - A\boldsymbol{c}\|$$

Since each computer display has fixed color characteristics, the calibration needs to be performed only once per device.

Orientation

The phone's orientation can be determined using the four sample points in the captured image. However, on a vertical host screen we get more precise tracking results using the phone's accelerometer and gyroscope. If the host screen is in a horizontal position, as most tabletop interfaces, we can determine the phone's orientation using its compass in combination with the color pattern.

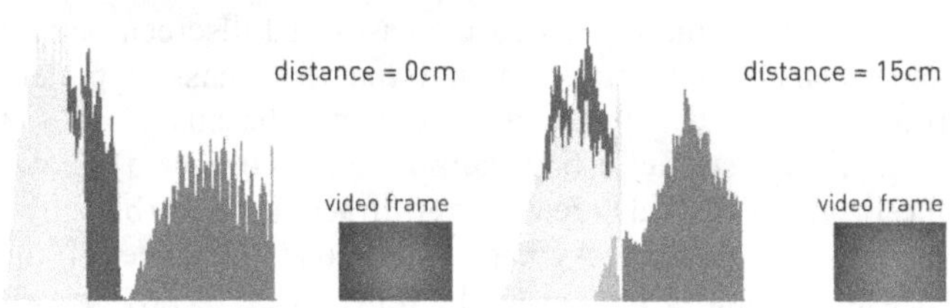

Figure 7. Proximity can be obtained via color analysis

Proximity

The distance between the computer screen and the phone can be inferred from the color delta of the video frame captured by the camera. As the computer's background is a linear color gradient, viewing it from further distance will show a larger color delta. The corresponding histogram can be seen in Figure 7. Through this we are able to get considerably reliable tracking results for up to 15 cm.

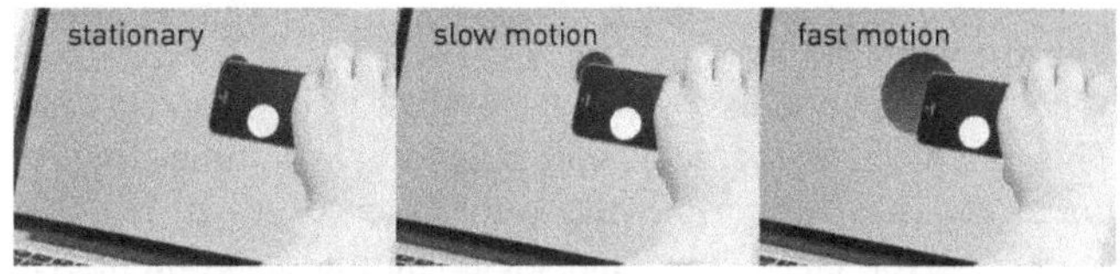

Figure 8. The masked pattern changes its size proportionally to the phone's velocity.

Updating Mask Position

To achieve continuous tracking it is sufficient for the color pattern to only be visible in the camera's field of view. Therefore we can hide the pattern in the area occluded by the phone. This allows tracking on the screen without sacrificing valuable information space.

To compensate for fast movements and the camera's relatively slow frame rate (30 fps), we constantly adjust the size of the pattern to provide a larger tracking area when the phone moves faster. (Figure 8) The initial position of the mask is found by increasing its size until the camera picks up the tracking pattern.

This masking technique not only hides the pattern behind the phone, but it also affords auto-calibration. A mismatch in color characteristics causes a spatial mismatch of the camera's location and the masked pattern. Once the camera picks up the pattern's boundary, the pattern's position is adjusted to again fit the cameras field of view. This offset could not be detected without the masked pattern, making this technique more robust.

Figure 9. Limiting the color spectrum minimizes the invasiveness of the tracking pattern.

Limited Color Spectrum

An additional method to make the tracking less invasive is to limit the color spectrum used. (Figure 9) If the display's dynamic range is high enough for fine color representation, we can choose a small range for R and G values to create the pattern (e.g.220 - 255). Limiting the color spectrum makes the pattern nearly invisible to human eyes. By adjusting the camera's exposure and white balance it is possible to get a good dynamic range within this color spectrum. However, this technique is not as reliable and requires a higher calibration effort. As cameras improve this might become a feasible technique in the future.

EXAMPLE APPLICATIONS

To showcase our system, we developed a series of example applications. Each application incorporates different interaction modes that were described earlier in this paper.

See-through Mouse

We use the phone as an advanced see-through mouse tool. This enables us to touch and drag/drop multiple files at once. At the same time the phone serves as a tangible clipboard for easy copy and paste of digital content. By placing a file inside the phone and removing it from the screen the data gets transferred to the phone. This makes it extremely simple to transfer files between two devices. This see-through mouse extends the modality of a conventional mouse as it can contain and visualize files that are being dragged. Users can select, drag/drop or delete files by direct touch gestures (Figure 10). The user can also place the phone on top of any link on the computer's screen and open it on the phone through a simple tap (Figure 11).

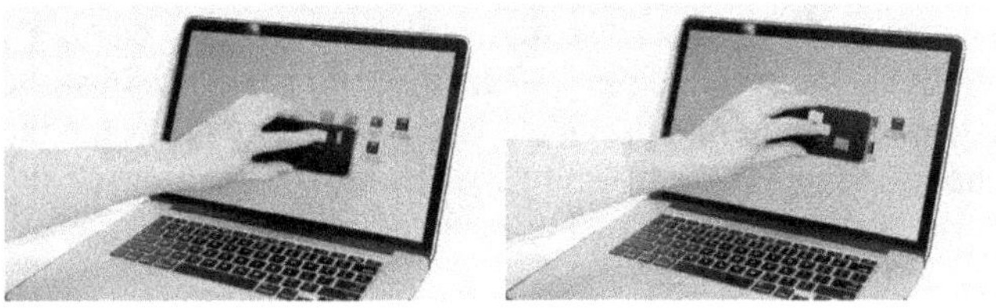

Figure 10. Seeing and touching through the smartphone. This enables easy file transfer between devices.

Figure 11. Opening a hyperlink in the smartphone

Adaptive UI Tool

Here we present an image editing application (Figure 12). The graphical UI displayed on the phone is aware of its location and context on the screen and can adjust accordingly. We use it to display functionalities only relevant to the task. Additionally, we incorporated motion gestures to manipulate image properties. Rotating the phone mimics a real lens focus ring to blur an image. Shaking the phone adds grain to the image just as if you were using a salt & pepper shaker. (Figure 12 right)

Figure 12. Images can be adjusted by using the phone's position, rotation and gesture recognition.

Navigating Maps and Buildings

To explore multiuser interaction as well as tabletop scenarios we developed a geo navigation application. On a shared tabletop map, different users can place their phone on the area of their interest to obtain different information, e.g. satellite view, traffic information, etc. In addition to revealing information through this magic lens, users can access different layers of information by changing the phone's distance to the computer screen. In this example lifting the phone can access different floors of a building. In its current state all phones are registered on the tabletop screen before starting the app. (Figure 13)

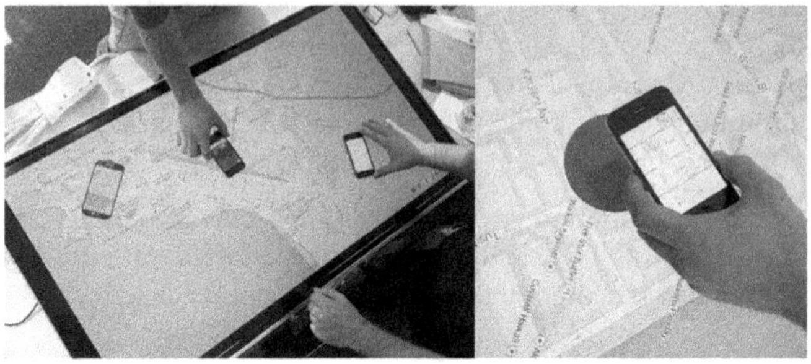

Figure 13. Multiple users can reveal additional information using their phone in this map application.

Game

We developed a simple game in which the goal is to help the character reach the flag. The smartphone acts as an active controller that can be used to physically intervene in the gameplay (Figure 1, 5). Players have to choose different strategies to clear the current stage. Each stage is designed to showcase a specific interaction or a mix of interactions we described in our classification. By combining the display space of a handheld device and a larger screen through near-surface interaction we can explore countless novel gaming scenarios.

SYSTEM EVALUATION

Tracking Accuracy

We tested the tracking accuracy by comparing the sample 2D coordinates on the computer screen to the measured coordinates from the phone. In the test, the distance between the phone and the computer screen was set to zero. We examined and compared the cases of fullscreen pattern and masked pattern. We found that the masked pattern provides better tracking accuracy because of its dynamically self-adjusting calibration. Figure 14(a) shows the result of the fullscreen pattern tracking, and (b) shows the masked pattern. Average deviations (distance of the measure point from ground truth) were 33.67 pixels (7.73mm) and 27.59 (6.33mm) pixels respectively. The maximum deviations were 98.25 pixels (22.55mm) and 56.44 pixels (12.95mm) for each. The screen's resolution was 1440x900 at 110 ppi.

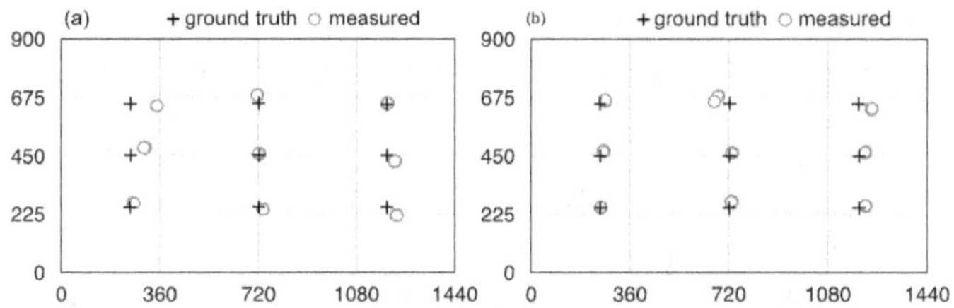

Figure 14. Tracking Accuracy. Left: without masked pattern, Right: with masked pattern.

Display's Dynamic Range vs. Tracking Resolution

As our tracking method relies on the color variation, the dynamic range of the computer display is critical for the quality of tracking. Here we examined the relationship between the display's dynamic range and obtainable tracking resolution on our 15-inch Retina display. Figure 15 shows the available color range (R-value) and the color captured by the camera from different x locations when changing the display's brightness from 100% to 25%. We found that 75% brightness provided the best range for tracking. Brightness of 100% and 87.5% will give equally good ranges of color. However, the captured color gets saturated, leading to clipping at the edges, thus limiting the effective tracking range.

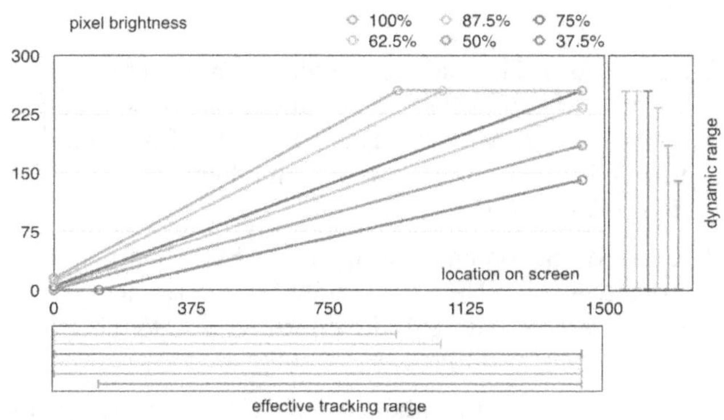

Figure 15. Screen brightness determines the effective tracking range.

Lost Tracking Behavior

To evaluate the reliability of our tracking system, we had to analyze the main factors for failure and the behavior of the system in such situation. We found that fast acceleration of the phone is the main reason for failed tracking. This is being addressed by rapidly increasing the masked pattern size, leading to a fast recovery of the phone's position. The general behavior of the masked pattern size is illustrated in Figure 16. After ~150 repetitions the average relocation time was 235ms, with a maximum of 737ms.

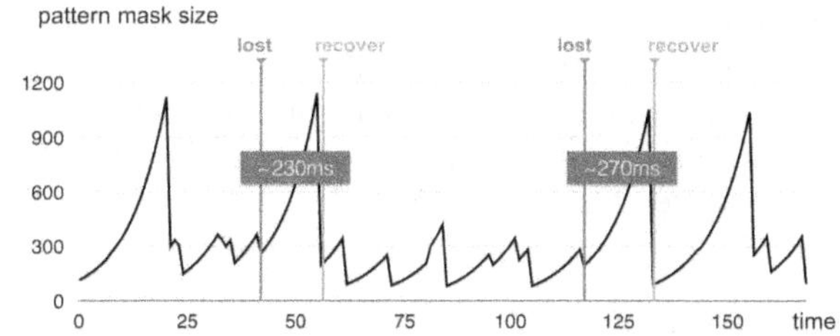

Figure 16. Rapid increase of the masked pattern size leads to fast tracking recovery.

LIMITATION

The proposed system has some limitations remaining to be solved. The use of color gradients for tracking promises easy deployment, while it still interferes with displayed content. Partial solutions of masked pattern/limited spectrum pattern are presented in this paper, however, the system needs very high dynamic range screens and cameras for reliable tracking. Another limitation is the latency caused by the relatively low framerate of the smartphone's camera (30 fps in general). To get tracking with almost no latency the system need to match the refresh rate of other human interface devices like optical mice. These are potentially resolvable by utilizing light spectrum invisible to human eyes. For example, if a distinct 2D infrared pattern is displayed on a monitor with dual infrared/visible light channel, a low resolution, high framerate infrared camera can reliably track its position much faster and more reliably.

CONCLUSION & FUTURE WORK

In this paper, we proposed an easy to deploy technology as well as interaction scenarios to better utilize the near surface space of computer screens with handheld smart devices. We show that the combination of AR and TUI enables versatile user interfaces for context aware seamless interactions. A growing number of people own computers and mobile phones, and with no need for additional hardware, the THAW system could work with those existing devices immediately. We believe this that this will open up a new space and tools for interaction designers to create fluid experiences using multiple personal devices.

A necessary step towards ubiquitous deployment of our system is to enable an effortless connection of personal handheld computing devices to any screen. One incremental step would be to develop a data protocol that allows easy and fast communication of relevant specifications between different devices. Another step forward is to expand this concept to devices with different display sizes and types (large, small, wearable, transparent, or flexible). Furthermore, a ground and more coherent taxonomy of the interactions that encompasses all different configurations would potentially benefit future multi-device applications.

ACKNOWLEDGMENTS
The authors would like to thank Professor Ramesh Raskar and everyone from 2013 Computational Camera class for valuable feedbacks during the conception of the project. We also appreciate Professor Ken Perlin and Alex Olwal for advises and inspiring inputs on the project.

REFERENCES
1. http://sebastianschmieg.com/royblock
2. http://www.nintendo.com/wiiu
3. Ballagas, R., Rohs, M., Sheridan, J., Borchers, J. The Smart Phone: A Ubiquitous Input Device. In IEEE Pervasive Computing, 5 (1), 2006.
4. Baur, D., Boring, S. and Feiner, S. Virtual Projection: exploring optical projection as a metaphor for multi-device interaction. In Proc. CHI '12.
5. Bier, E. A., Stone, M. C., Pier, K., Buxton, W., and DeRose, T. D.. Toolglass and Magic Lenses: The See-Through Interface. In Proc. SIGGRAPH '93.
6. Boring, S., Baur, D., Butz, A., Gustafson, S., and Baudisch, P. Touch projector: mobile interaction through video. In Proc. CHI '10, 2287–2296.
7. Chan, L., Muller, S., Roudaut, A., and Baudisch, P. CapStones and ZebraWidgets: sensing stacks of building blocks, dials and sliders on capacitive touch screens. In Proc. CHI '12, 2189–2192.
8. Chan, L.-W., Wu, H.-T., Kao, H.-S., Ko, J.-C., Lin, H.-R., Chen, M. Y., Hsu, J., and Hung, Y.-P. Enabling beyond-surface interactions for interactive surface with an invisible projection. In Proc. ACM UIST '10, 263–272.
9. Cuypers, T., Francken, Y., Vanaken, C., Reeth, F. V., and Bekaert, P.. Smartphone localization on interactive surfaces using the built-in camera. In Proc. Procams, pages 61–68, 2009.
10. Feiner, S., MacIntyre, B., Haupt, M., Solomon, M Windows on the world: 2D windows for 3D augmented reality. ACM UIST. p. 145-155.
11. Fitzmaurice, G., Buxton, W. The Chameleon: spatially aware palmtop computers. In Proc. ACM CHI '94.
12. Hansen, T., Eriksson, E., Lykke-Olesen, A. Mixed Interaction Space - Designing for Camera Based Interaction with Mobile Devices. In Extended Proc. CHI '05.
13. Heun, V., Kasahara, S., and Maes, P. Smarter Objects: Using AR Technology to Program Physical Objects and Their Interactions. In Extended Proc. CHI '13, 961–966.
14. Ishii, H. and Ullmer, B. Tangible Bits. Towards seamless interfaces between people, bits and atoms. In Proc. CHI '97, 234–241
15. Liang, R.-H., Cheng, K.-Y., Chan, L., Peng, C.-X., Chen, M. Y., Liang, R.-H., Yang, D.-N., and Chen, B.-Y. GaussBits: magnetic tangible bits for portable and occlusion-free near-surface tangible interactions. In Proc. CHI '13, 1391–1400.
16. Olwal, A. LightSense: Enabling spatially aware handheld interaction devices. Proc. ISMAR '06, 119–122.
17. Olwal, A, and Feiner, S. Spatially aware handhelds for high-precision tangible interaction with large displays. In Proc. TEI '09, 181–188.
18. Patten, J., Ishii, H., Hines, J., and Pangaro, G. Sensetable: a wireless object tracking platform for tangible user interfaces. In Proc. CHI '01, 253-260.
19. Piazza, T., Fjeld, M., Ramos, G., Evren Yantac, A., and Zhao, S. Holy Smartphones and Tablets, Batman! Mobile Interaction's Dynamic Duo. In Proc. APCHI '13, 10.
20. Reilly, D., Welsman-Dinelle, M., Bate, C., and Inkpen, K. Just point and click?: using handhelds to interact with paper maps. In Proc. MobileHCI '05, 239-242.
21. Rekimoto, J. A multiple device approach for supporting whiteboard-based interactions. In Proc. CHI '98, 344–351.
22. Rekimoto, J. The magnifying glass approach to augmented reality systems. In International Conference on Artificial Reality and Tele-Existence / Conference on Virtual Reality Software and Technology (ICAT/VRST), 123–132, 1995.
23. Rohs, M., Schöning, J., Raubal, M., Essl, Georg and Krüger, A. Map Navigation with Mobile Devices: Virtual versus Physical Movement with and without Visual Context. In Proc. ICMI '07, 146-153.
24. Sanneblad, J. and Holmquist, L.E. Ubiquitous Graphics: Combining Hand-held and Wall-size Displays to Interact with Large Images. ACM AVI Conference on Advanced Visual Interfaces 2006.
25. Spindler, M., Martsch, M., and Dachselt, R. Going Beyond the Surface: Studying Multi-Layer Interaction Above the Tabletop. In Proc. CHI '12, 1277–1286.
26. Tani, M., Yamaashi, K., Tanikoshi, K., Futakawa,M., and Tanifuji, S. Object oriented video: interaction with real-world objects through live video. In Proc. CHI '92, 593-598.
27. Wilson, A.D., Sarin, R. BlueTable: connecting wireless mobile devices on interactive surfaces using vision-based handshaking. In GI '07, 119-125.
28. Underkoffler, J. and Ishii, H. Urp: a luminous-tangible workbench for urban planning and design. In Proc. CHI '99, 386-393.

ATSI: Augmented and Tangible Sonic Interaction

Put a sound on it!

Roberto Pugliese
Department of Media Technology
Aalto University
roberto.pugliese@aalto.fi

Archontis Politis
Department of Signal Processing and Acoustics
Aalto University
archontis.politis@aalto.fi

Tapio Takala
Department of Media Technology
Aalto University
tapio.takala@aalto.fi

ABSTRACT
This paper presents ATSI, a system for sonic augmentation of physical objects with spatialized sounds and their control by gestural interaction. The implementation combines tracking of the users' hands and head with commodity hardware, and binaural spatialized sound rendering over headphones. The user may attach sounds to common objects and the system maintains the correct spatial auditory perspective inside the augmented scene during the actions of attaching sounds, picking and moving the sounding objects, or exploring the scene. Attention has been given to the binaural rendering of distance cues to support the above actions with perceptual realism in small scale environments and for many objects. Through a user study assessing the localization accuracy that can be achieved with the system, we show that sound rendering performance looks appropriate for applications such as auditory displays for context and object specific information, sonic design for architectural planning and interior design, and music applications.

Author Keywords
Augmented reality; tangible interaction; spatial audio; sonic interaction; user study.

ACM Classification Keywords
H.5.1 Multimedia Information Systems: Artificial, augmented, and virtual realities; H.5.2 User Interfaces: Auditory (non-speech) feedback; Interaction styles; H.5.5 Sound and Music Computing: Systems

INTRODUCTION
Augmented audio reality (AAR) systems aim to extend the physical environment with virtual auditory cues and sound information. They can be part of audiovisual augmented reality systems or purely based on audio cues, which in themselves can be mixing virtual with real sound scenes [8] or augment the environment purely with virtual sounds. AAR, in contrast to its visual counterpart, has the potential to provide non-obstructing cues, useful in many hands-free communication scenarios [12]. Most AAR systems require the location of the user with respect to its environment, in order to activate, spatialize and transmit the sound information. An early example is that which augments a tour guiding system for museums with non-linear description of artworks activated as the visitor is walking among them [1], or the one in [16] for transmission of personalized information from workstations to workers in workspaces. When the user's head orientation is tracked, then fully spatial sound techniques can be employed for the presentation of the sounds, which have been found to increase immersion, exploration and interaction with the environment [23, 27].

The ATSI system takes advantage of recent advances in spatial audio coding [18] for effective binaural spatialization of the sound sources combined with head plus hands tracking technology. A low-cost efficient implementation is realized using commodity hardware and a user study is performed to study its localization performance.

TEI 2015, January 15–19, 2015, Stanford, California, USA.

http://dx.doi.org/10.1145/2677199.2680550

RELATED WORKS
In ATSI, the user can augment physical objects with spatial sounds in a small scale environment, such as a normal-sized working space or living room and be able to move them around while listening to the sound attached to them as if it would be located in the object.

Other spatial sound design system have been presented in the last decade. Many relies on augmentation of objects by means of sensors or markers to track and register the objects (see [13] for instance as an early example). This design choice poses the constraint that the augmented objects need to be designated beforehand or custom-based designed rather than freely and dynamically chosen by the user during the exploration and interaction with the sonically augmented environment.

Other systems such as the one in [4, 17], let the user manipulate virtual sounds detached from any physical objects in an augmented environment by means of gestural interaction. Both systems require special wands with markers or haptic gloves for the manipulation of the virtual sound sources.

In contrast with these systems, in ATSI the user does not need to wear any device but headphones. Furthermore, and this is a key-differentiating factor to any previous system, the physical objects do not need to be modified in any way, as the interaction and overlaying of the virtual scene on the real scene is done by hands-tracking alone, offering a non-intrusive natural AR experience. Also, special emphasis is put to maintain the link between the physical object and the virtual sound thanks to the spatial sound rendering, offering the possibility to the user to grasp and manipulate daily and arbitrary objects and still offer the correct spatial auditory perspective. Contrary to previous AAR systems, which are based solely to adjustment of the loudness of the sounds to convey distance information, ATSI employs the additional cue of direct-to-reverberant ratio, which is an important cue on distance perception [25] and crucial for externalization of the audio scene beyond the headphones. Furthermore, due to the dimensions of the applications considered, a scalable distance rendering scheme is explored as proposed in [27].

In [7], a system for grabbing, moving and manipulating sound objects in mid-air, The BoomRoom, is presented and evaluated. This system shares many similarity with the one we present. Both systems allow listening to a 3D sound environment emitted from physical objects and manipulation through gestural interaction. Unlike the BoomRoom, our system is based on binaural sound reproduction against a 56 multichannel setup for wave-field synthesis (WFS). WFS is a natural choice for a loudspeaker-based system that can handle multiple listeners, but it requires a dedicated space, careful set-up and costly hardware requirements. Furthermore, ATSI uses affordable tracking devices, available at consumer level, compared to a multi-camera optical system. All in all, our solution is lower-end and can be installed in a normal living room. Also, from an interaction design point of view, in the BoomRoom the manipulation of the sound happens with an empty hand while the sound keeps on being rendered at the position of the object. In contrast, our system treats the sound as attached to the object, to the extent that moving the object is to move the sound.

In this respect, we follow the early propositions of Ishii and Ullmer [10] of "tangible user interfaces" (TUIs), defined as user interfaces that "augment the real physical world by coupling digital information to everyday physical objects and environments". Fiskin et al. [5] proposed a taxonomy for TUI based on two dimensions *embodiment* and *metaphor*. The ATSI system could be defined as fully embodied due to the first person perspective provided by the sound rendering (the object "emits" the sound) when grabbing and positioning of the sound in space. With respect to the *metaphor* dimension, depending on the application and the sound-object association the user decides to establish, the system can be considered as "noun" (which often refers to the shape or certain quality of an object) as in the case of sounds that are naturally produceable by the object they are augmenting (a guitar chord attached to a guitar) or "verb-like" (pouring-coffee sound attached to a cup). Also the action of attaching the sound to the object can be considered "verb-like" (attaching the sound to the object is as attaching a speaker to an object) or "full" (put a bird inside a cage or a ringing phone in a purse).

With respect to the categories listed in [22], the system could be considered as a spatial, associative, with physical to digital dynamic binding, instance of TUIs. The freedom to physically associate sounds to common marker-free objects makes the system suitable for target applications such as attaching informational sound tags to objects, sonic decoration of the environment with sounds, re-positioning of non-acoustical sound generators to the point of interaction for musical applications, transforming a cluttered environment into a musical controller. More detailed concepts are described in the discussion section.

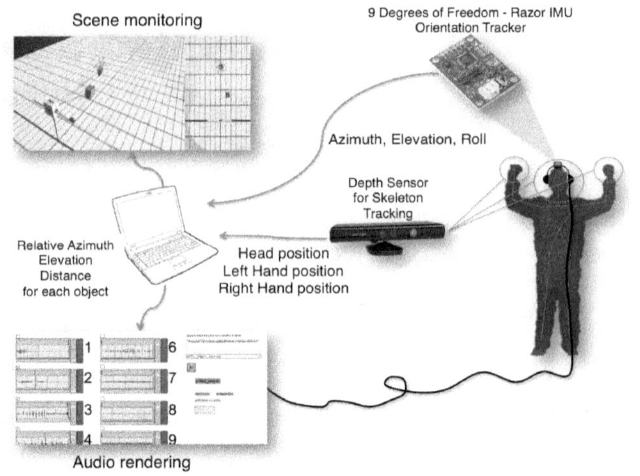

Figure 1. Schematic representation of the ATSI system in its components

ATSI SYSTEM

Figure 1 shows a schematic representation of the ATSI system in its main components. The sound rendering unit comprises the core technology of the system and it relies on two main components: the tracking module and the binaural rendering module. The tracking mechanism is based on a combination of positional and orientation tracking. The fused tracked data are fed to a module that renders the scene and offers the designer means to monitor the user interaction. Furthermore, the same module incorporates a user interface for initialization, addition, removal and re-positioning of the virtual objects that stand for the physical objects to be manipulated in the real environment. It is noted that the system can operate without any form of graphic display, however these functions in the 3D-rendering module can aid the designer in authoring and debugging tasks. Finally the relative position and orientation of each object with respect to user's head position and orientation are sent to the audio rendering module already described. For an accompaniment to the following description, the reader can view a video documentation of the system[1].

Tracking

Tracking relies on two components. The first is positional tracking of the user's head and hands based on an external device. This device registers the location of the user and of the sound objects in a world coordinate system and it extracts the positional relations between them. It is the component that aims to a) enable the interaction with the sound objects by tracking the hands, and b) ensure correct audio parallax

[1] http://vimeo.com/110463176

effect by tracking the head while the user moves inside the scene. In the present implementation this part is realized with Microsoft Kinect [2] using the OpenNI [3] skeleton tracking library. The tracking accuracy and update rate provided by such a low-cost game-oriented device is found to be adequate for most scenarios mentioned in this work. For a wider field of action than what Kinect can cover, or for accurate tracking of many users simultaneously, more professional optical tracking solutions can be used.

The second component adapts the binaural rendering to the rotation of the head as the user explores the sound scene by looking at different directions, and it is necessary both for a) a realistic audio perspective that preserves the position of the sound objects in the audio scene independently from the look-direction of the user, and b) improved sound spatialization that takes into account the changes in binaural cues from the head-rotation [2]. The head tracking is realized with an inexpensive inertial tracker mounted on the headphones. The model is the Sparkfun Razor 9DOF IMU[4] which consists of a gyroscope, three accelerometers along the cartesian axes and a magnetometer (compass). The firmware that handles the calibration and the fusion of the sensor data to extract the rotational angles is the one provided by Quality and Usability Lab, TU Berlin[5]. The tracker is connected to a bluetooth modem board that transmits the rotational angles to the computer, in the yaw-pitch-roll convention. The combination of the tracker and modem board are housed in a matchbox-size box.

Since the binaural rendering is head-centric, the directions and distances of hands and all enabled objects need to be computed with respect to the head-frame. This operation is performed using standard rotation and translation matrices, based on the combination of Kinect's head-and-hand positional tracking and the tracker's rotational data. Finally, the azimuth, elevation and distance for each head-to-object vector are sent to the binaural spatialization module for the appropriate rendering of the scene.

Binaural Rendering

To achieve a high degree of naturalness the binaural renderer should be able to provide correct perceptual cues for each object in the scene. These cues are accurate inter-aural level and time differences that relate to directional perception, and appropriate cues that relate to distance perception. Furthermore, externalization, meaning that users do not perceive the sounds as being only inside the head, common with normal headphone reproduction, is considered crucial for natural scene rendering. The directional cues are encoded in Head-Related Transfer Functions (HRTFs), which is the preferred choice for binaural panning, and they can be individualized or non-individualized [24], in which latter case elevation perception is mostly affected. Distance perception on the other hand depends on a combination of different cues at different ranges, such as sound intensity decreasing with an inverse squared-distance law, near-field spectral cues [3], the direct-to-reverberant sound energy ratio (DRR) [25], or high-frequency attenuation due to air absorption.

From this set of distance cues, the intensity cue and adjustment of the DRR were used for the current implementation, under the assumption that they are the most prominent ones for the target range of distances. Changes in intensity are very useful as a dynamic cue and a necessary step for correct translation effect in an interactive scene. They are the most commonly used way to render distance information to the user in VR applications and auditory displays. However, intensity cues alone fail to externalize the sound scene. We achieve good externalization through manipulation of the DRR, achieved as follows. Reverberation is injected to the scene according to the DRR, using a parametric Schroeder reverb [19]. All sound sources share the same reverberator which has a user adjusted constant level $0 < G_{rev} < 1$. As the k-th source moves further away to a distance d_k, its direct sound is attenuated by the inverse distance law as per $G_{dir_k} = 1/d_k$. Hence, using a simple gain per source and a shared reverb, the DRR is

$$DRR_k = \frac{G_{dir_k}}{G_{rev}} = \frac{1}{(d_k G_{rev})}. \quad (1)$$

This kind of behavior, even though not exact, approximates the behavior in a real room; the direct sound is dependent on the distance to the listener but the reverberant sound has approximately the same intensity independently of position. An intuitive way to adjust the reverberant gain G_{rev} is by defining a critical distance d_{crit} at which reverberant and direct sound energy are equal, as in

$$G_{rev} = \frac{1}{d_{crit}}. \quad (2)$$

The critical distance should depend on the application.

Instead of handling each source channel separately, the whole sound scene is spatially encoded into the popular 4-channel 3D-audio format termed B-format, including reverberation, according to [14]. For the rendering, the Directional Audio Coding (DirAC) method was employed, which is an established time-frequency analysis/synthesis method for recorded [18] or synthesized [14] spatial sound, with reproduction capabilities to loudspeakers or headphones. For this implementation, the headphone rendering version was used [15]. The DirAC module performs a time-frequency analysis on the B-format and extracts perceptual parameters, which are used in the synthesis stage to recreate the sound scene to headphones. The method uses HRTFs for the panning and appropriate rendering of direct and reverberant sound. Headphone equalization was implemented to cancel the effect of the headphones to the binaural rendering, for the set of headphones used in the test. For a more detailed description the user is referred to [15]. All stages of encoding to B-format, adjusting the DRR levels, reverberating and processing with DirAC were realized in Max/MSP, in which the sonic design parts of the

[2] http://www.microsoft.com/en-us/kinectforwindows/
[3] https://github.com/OpenNI/OpenNI
[4] https://www.sparkfun.com/products/10736
[5] https://github.com/ptrbrtz/razor-9dof-ahrs

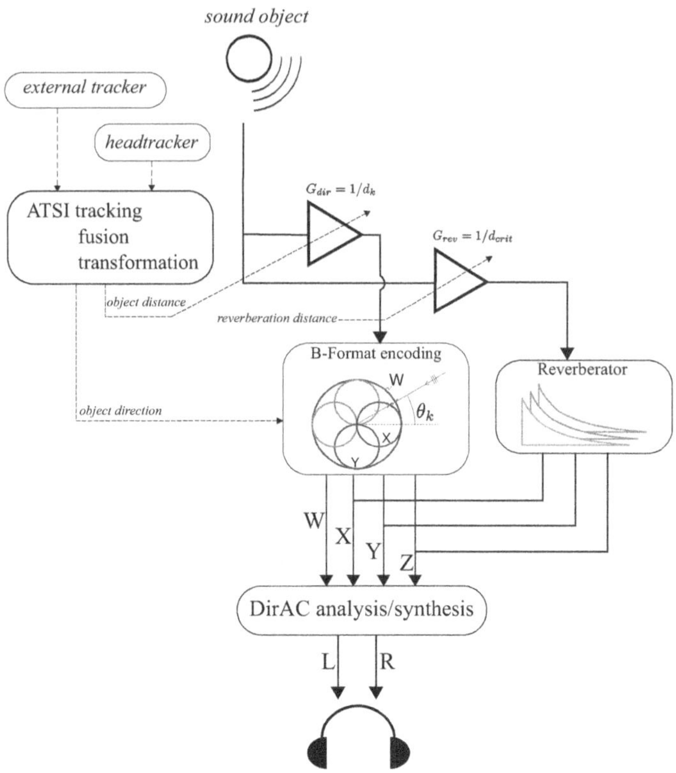

Figure 2. Audio rendering flow diagram for a single object.

system were also implemented. A schematic of the binaural rendering module is presented in Fig. 2.

Even though the distance attenuation governed from the inverse-distance law is the most natural one, it has been found that in AR applications, user-defined profiles can be more appropriate by creating artificial cues that pronounce the effect of nearby sources and attenuate or switch off sources completely far or outside some predefined distance. Such an approach was tried herein using the linear scaled-distance profile of [27] as in

$$G_{dir_k} = \frac{d_{max} - d_k}{d_{max}} \tag{3}$$

where d_{max} is a maximum distance defined by the user as the maximum range of interest in which the direct sound of the source needs to be audible. In contrast to that implementation though, in this work when sources are outside the cut-off distance, instead of being muted, their reverberated copy is still active in a lower level. Hence the user is aware that these objects are active, but they are in the far field and not localizable.

Sound Interaction Design

The system is general with respect to the sound objects associated to the physical object. A front-end of the sound rendering module implemented in Max/MSP lets the user load a library of samples. Each sample is preliminary associated to a virtual object waiting to be initialized by the user. The sound is loaded into a many-voice granular sampler and by default the sound is played back as a loop at normal speed. Nevertheless, the granular synthesis allows for a variety of sound manipulation by controlling parameters such as pitch-invariant time-stretching within certain ranges, granular re-synthesis from sub-selection of the original sample for the creation of more or less chaotic textures.

Although the selection of the samples to be used is up to the sound designer, by choosing this synthesis technique we deliberately encourage the creation of sustained textural sounds. The reason is twofold. Firstly, as long as the sound is continuous and can be looped more or less seamlessly, the user can be aware of its presence in the scene all the time. The sound is always audible in the spatialization and it can be heard depending on the user's relative position and thus controlled. Secondly, because of the strong visual and tactile cue that the interaction allows, we direct our design choice towards concrete sounds rather than synthetic. Sounds that can express the physicality of the object in terms of size, material and even shape allow object-sound mappings that can lead to meaningful and sharable associations. Thus the designer can create sustained sounds that still retain some resemblance with the real sound produced by a physical and tactile interaction with that object. As a further feature, the designer can record each sample on-the-fly using a wireless wearable or headset microphone, for instance associating voice messages to the object and creating a personal semantic association.

The use of the system is divided in two phases: **initialization** and **interaction**. During the **initialization**, the user assigns the sounds previously imported in the sound library loader to objects present in the room. As long as visible by Kinect (roughly within a box of 3x3x5 meters) every object is a suitable candidate for the association. An audio interface consisting of a female voice previews a sample and asks the user to gesturally indicate which object she wants the sound to be assigned to. The user is expected to touch the object first with one hand, then also with the second one and finally remove the second hand from the object. The audio interface notifies the user every time the object has been assigned and subsequently previews the next sample. The process proceeds iteratively until all the sound sample have been assigned. Other more natural sample selection technique could be employed and we recommend the one in [12] which is based on spatial audio and gestural interaction. We intend to adopt similar technique in further development of the present system.

In the **interaction** phase the user can move in the physical space and hear the sonically augmented object in accordance with the sound rendering scheme presented in the previous section. In order to interact with an object and also with the sound attached to it, the user may grab the object following a sequence of small gestures. Fig. 3 shows a typical sequence of interaction steps a user might follow, namely exploration of the environment, selection of the object to be moved through two-hands interaction and finally grabbing and repositioning the object. The user selects the object by touching it first with one hand and then with the second, after which the object can be moved and released by separating the hands along the line of what already done during the initialization phase. Although a perfectly natural interaction will allow the user to

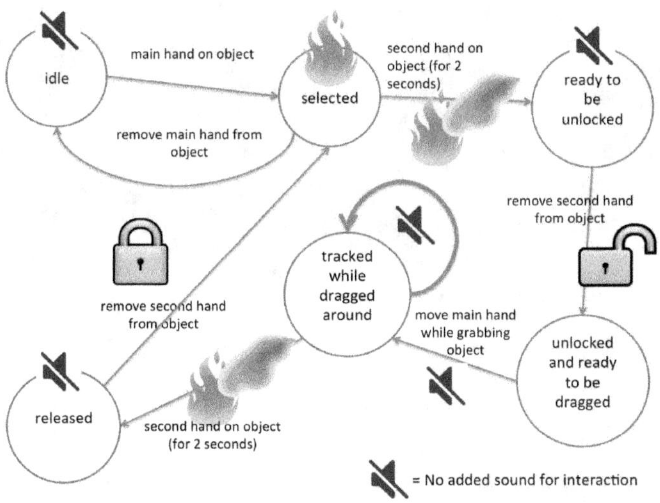

Figure 4. Transition graph of the gestural interaction and auditory icons.

simply grab and move the object, detecting a grabbing gesture of an object without apriori knowledge of its geometry is an hard computer vision problem. While the library of gestures for Kinect 2 allows detecting the "close-hand" gesture, the algorythm will not reliably work in the case of grabbing a physical object. For this we propose 2-hands interaction as a compromise between a reliable "out-of-the box" recognition technique and an intuitive interaction.

In order to engage with the object, the user's hand needs to be within a limited distance from the object. To facilitate the memorization of the gestures, provide feedback on the correctness of their execution and acknowledgment of the system, auditory icons are associated to each of these actions. Fig. 4 shows a transition graph of the state of the object during the interaction, with the actions the user can perform, the auditory icons associated and the resulting state of the object. The design of these icons was guided by the goal of creating physically informed action-sound metaphors. When inside this interaction volume the user will hear the sound of "fire" and the state of the object will change to "selected". The user places the other hand on the object while hearing the sound of "water on fire". When the fire sounds extinguished, the user can remove the second hand and hears an "unlocking" sound. The object is now ready to be moved. After repositioning it somewhere else in the environment, the user places again the second hand on the object until the "water on fire" sound vanishes. Then he removes the second hand from the object to release it confirmed by a "locking" sound. These sounds are also spatialized at the hands' location in order to improve the naturalness of the interaction and keep the focus on the object itself. Since the auditory icons are audible together with the sound object the user interacts with, their volume can be adjusted depending on the application.

One further gesture, second hand touching the head, was added to activate audio input and let the user record their voice into the object.

USER STUDY

The following experiment aims at understanding the localization accuracy achieved by the binaural sound rendering engine integrated with the tracking system. Since the system is intended for a variety of scenarios where in general more than one sound source is audible, we undergo tests involving both 1 source and also 2 sources audible at the same time as stimuli. The study does not involve evaluation of the interaction with the object, which will be tackled in future work.

Localization accuracy

We want to assess the localization accuracy of virtual sound sources when using the system in different conditions. Our hypothesis is that the combination of the HRTF rendering along with the head-tracking, the manipulation of the DRR ratio and the intensity cue based on the distance of the sound object should provide adequate directional and distance perceptual accuracy. It is additionally speculated that the scaled distance factor of Eq. 3 will help in distance discrimination if multiple objects are active. Localization performance under the condition of a second sound source present in the environment, possibly acting as an interference, is also tested.

In this task, the user needs to identify the correct position of either a female or male voice (in a randomized order) among a grid of numbered place-holders, as shown in Fig. 5. These locations are 40 cm apart in both lateral and depth separation.

Apparatus: A table (2.3 m wide, 2.4 m deep, 1 m high) is placed in an empty room. The depth sensor is placed at the end of the room facing the listener. Headphones Sennheiser HD 600 are provided to the participant.

Conditions: Two conditions are considered. In Condition 1 only one sound is presented, either male or female in randomized order. In Condition 2 both male and female voice sounds are presented. Conditions are counterbalanced across subjects following an *ABBA* design.

Stimuli: In each trial, one or two sounds are presented: a female (F) and a male (M) voice declaring the same sentence. The samples have roughly the same duration and they were chosen from the TSP speech library [11]. The sound(s) are rendered at different position on the grid for a total of 25 trial. In condition 2, also the position of the second source is randomized in a balanced way.

Procedure: A within-subjects design was used. Ten unpaid volunteers participated in the experiment, all reporting normal hearing. The listener stands in front of the table and they are free to move within an area (1m deep x width of the table). By moving the head freely the listener can take advantage of the dynamic cues provided by the sound rendering system. Each trial lasts until the participant answers or up to a time limit of 30 second, after which the participant is "forced" to declare which numbered placeholder the sound is coming from. For each trial the distance between the position of the correct placeholder and the one indicated by the participant is registered. An initial warm-up session with 10 trials is given to let the participant familiarize with the task and tracking system. The instructor indicates the right answer after each completed trial. The session acts as training

Figure 3. A typical interaction scenario with the ATSI system: an object on the table is augmented with sound rendered from the perspective of the user who explores, selects, picks and re-positions the objects.

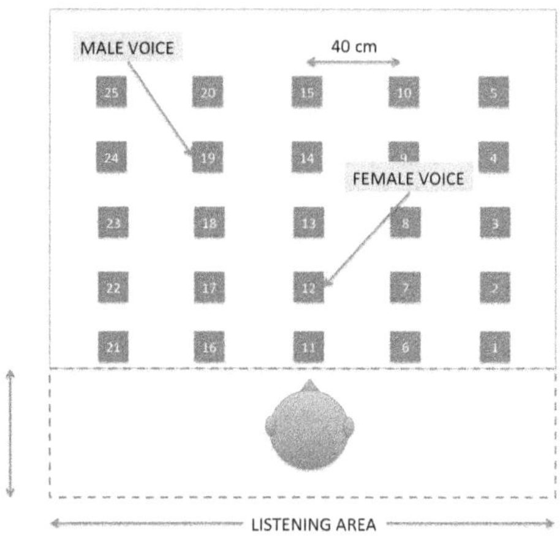

Figure 5. Setting for the localization accuracy user study: sounds are rendered at the placeholders positions

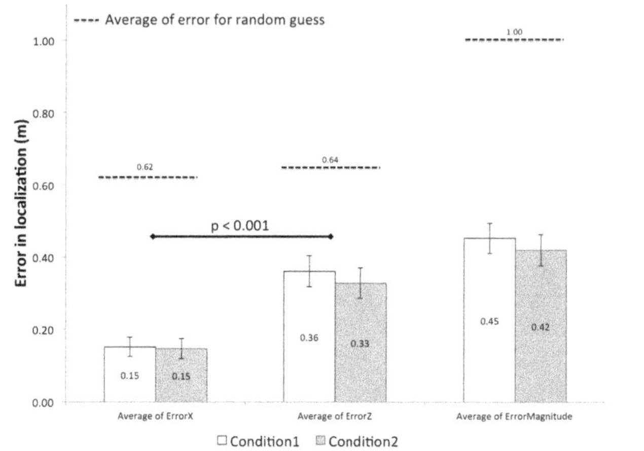

Figure 6. Average localization errors in the two conditions, with confidence intervals and random guess average error

for the participants to calibrate the intensity cue with the intended distance. In the actual test no feedback about the right answer is given.

Results

Statistical analysis was performed on the collected data by means of one-way repeated measures ANOVAs by considering the 2 conditions for each of the 4 dependent variables accounting for the localization performance: lateral error $Error_x$, depth error $Error_z$ and error magnitude $Error_{mag}$. Also we compared the lateral error vs. the depth error. All comparisons among conditions were performed with post-hoc Bonferroni tests.

Fig. 6 shows the localization error in the two conditions. There are no significant differences among the conditions with one and two sound sources. While the task might be more taxing because of the interference of one unwanted sound, the resulting localization accuracy does not decrease. A possible explanation is that with two sounds the listener can rely on relative distance cues between the two objects. This result does not necessarily generalize for more than 2 sound sources though.

We found statistical difference among the localization accuracy in the lateral dimension and depth ($F(1,499) = 119.1$, $p < .001$). The post-hoc comparison showed that lateral localization was significantly higher than depth localization (MD = .196 and SE = .018). The result is not surprising considering that localization on the azimuth plane is relatively well rendered by averaged HRTFs.

The position of the objects did not differ in height since they were all placed on the surface of the table. The situation is similar to the condition NOEL (no elevation) presented in the study of Sodnik et al. [20]. That means that beside the azimuth localization only the sound intensity decay profile learnt during the warmup session could have helped with the perception of distance to the object. Better results can be expected if different elevation cues between objects are also present. Common patterns of behavior were observed among participants. Usually the listener would try to find the correct column first (x-dimension) and afterward estimate the distance using the intensity cue. Some participants stooped and tried to get their head close to target object to additionally emphasize the contribution of the intensity cue. Many tilted their head in such a way that the head azimuth plane would roughly intersect the sound object which is an effective way to estimate depth by maximising interaural differences.

DISCUSSION

The localization accuracy achieved seems well suited for a standard operation scenario of the system, with a lateral error less than half the distance among adjacent objects and depth error less than the whole distance. We expect that longer training sessions plus the presence of the visual cue given by the tangible object should result in deeper reliance on the localization cues provided by the system. As long as these cues stay consistent in the action-sound loop the listener can acquire expertise of the augmented environment. For a discussion about the adaptation to scaled distance, non-individualized HRTFs, directional and depth perception see [9]. Furthermore, increased sound rendering realism can be reached by tuning the reverberation according to a set of real acoustic properties of the room.

Occasionally we observed wrong registration of the position of the object caused by erroneous tracking, sometimes due to the occlusion among objects, other times due to the instability of the Kinect tracking when the hands are close to each other and to the body. These accidents result in the mismatching between the position of the physical object and the sound object made evident by the conflict between visual and sound cue. Also, there are situations when an object might accidentally (by an other person) be moved without sonic interaction, leaving the associated sound as "ghost" in space. Naturally, the user can correct these problems during the interaction repositioning the virtual sound there where the physical object is, by grabbing the sound from the location suggested by the sound rendering plus the sound interaction icons.

While the position of the object is directly inferred by the position of the two hands when close to each other, no information about its orientation is currently available due to insufficient tracking information provided by the Kinect. Precise orientation of the hands can be used to infer orientation of the sound object, which can be used for implementing directivity profiles of how the object emits sound at different directions. This functionality has been already implemented and is ready to be used if orientation information becomes available.

The tracking can be improved using Kinect 2, which additionally provides the orientation of the hands. As an alternative to visual tracking, sound can be employed for estimating the location and rotation of the head based on (possibly inaudible) anchor sound sources with known positions and analysis of binaural signals [21, 6] which could possibly remove the need for an optical external tracker and the associated problems of a limited field of view. These technologies assume microphones mounted on the earphones, required also for proper blending of real sounds around the listener with the virtual ones, but they do not address the problem of hand-tracking. A potential solution can be small anchor sources mounted on the hands and tracked accordingly from the user's binaural signals, but this remains a subject for future work.

As it is, the system is suitable for a variety of applications, which we can categorize into four main groups: auditory information display, soundscape preview for urban and architectural planning, sonic interior design and electroacoustic music performance. The first is a classic scenario envisioned from the early age of augmented reality: objects we encounter and interact with on a daily basis able to capture our attention sonically and provide useful information about their status (a plant that needs some water, food that need to be eaten before the expiration date or car keys that tell us where they are when hard to find). The ATSI system provides means for designating which objects are relevant for the user and offer means to build context-aware and time-dependent information display applications.

In the case of architectural planning we refer to scenarios (even collaborative) where users preview the soundscape of an area or a building, while moving their components on a physical model. Different user can explore from their own point of view the 3d scene and affect the landscape by repositioning the object of the model. This idea can be fostered further in the case of sonic interior design where the designer decorates an environment both visually but also sonically.

Finally, music applications ranging from game-like sonic exploration and manipulation, to scenarios closer to performance, are a natural one. An obvious useful application is enhanced live-music monitoring, by redirection of synthesized or amplified live sound to the point of interaction, such as positioning the amplified feed of an electroacoustic instrument to the location of the instrument, bypassing the common case of the feed coming from the PA system. The usefulness of such a concept, employing musical instrument directivities and tracking of the instrument orientation and the musicians' hands, has been demonstrated in the context of group music performance in [26]. Similar applications are not limited to instruments but can be applied as well to any music controller.

We envision further sonic interactions, like the definition of sound trajectories over the physical object, as a path along which the sound specified by the user would move, e.g. a song spatialized across the surface of a sofa. Also we intend to explore linked sound manipulation when objects are placed close to each other, resulting in more complex behaviors.

CONCLUSIONS

We have presented ATSI, a new system that incorporates elements of audio augmented reality with tangible interaction. The binaural sound rendering engine is based on a perceptual spatial audio coding method for efficient spatialization and diffusion of multiple sound sources. Reverberation and diffusion are integrated to the binaural processing for enhanced perceptual distance rendering through manipulation of the direct-to-reverberant ratio.

ATSI is developed with low-cost off-the-shelf tracking technology and the implementation is general with respect to the tangible objects and sounds the user choses to use. This allows the user/designer to create metaphors and associations between the objects present in the physical world and a personalized sound library.

The mixed-reality environment the user can create and control can find applications in the context of interior design application, auditory displays and electroacoustic music performance. Further studies are needed to assess the user experience and the naturalness of the system in the main scenarios proposed.

ACKNOWLEDGMENTS

We want to thank Dr. Hannes Gamper for the fruitful discussions which inspired part of this work, and Dr. Mikko-Ville

Laitinen and Tapani PihlajŁmŁki for the implementation of the binaural version of Directional Audio Coding processor.

REFERENCES

1. Bederson, B. B. Audio augmented reality: a prototype automated tour guide. In *Conference companion on Human factors in computing systems*, ACM (1995), 210–211.
2. Begault, D. R., Wenzel, E. M., and Anderson, M. R. Direct comparison of the impact of head tracking, reverberation, and individualized head-related transfer functions on the spatial perception of a virtual speech source. *Journal of the Audio Engineering Society 49*, 10 (2001), 904–916.
3. Brungart, D. S., and Rabinowitz, W. M. Auditory localization of nearby sources. head-related transfer functions. *The Journal of the Acoustical Society of America 106*, 3 (1999), 1465–1479.
4. Dobler, D., Haller, M., and Stampfl, P. Asr: augmented sound reality. In *ACM SIGGRAPH 2002 conference abstracts and applications*, ACM (2002), 148–148.
5. Fishkin, K. A taxonomy for and analysis of tangible interfaces. *Personal and Ubiquitous Computing 8*, 5 (July 2004), 347–358.
6. Gamper, H., Tervo, S., and Lokki, T. Head orientation tracking using binaural headset microphones. In *Audio Engineering Society Convention 131*, Audio Engineering Society (2011).
7. Geier, M., Dicke, C., and Spors, S. The BoomRoom : Mid-air Direct Interaction with Virtual Sound Sources.
8. Härmä, A., Jakka, J., Tikander, M., Karjalainen, M., Lokki, T., Hiipakka, J., and Lorho, G. Augmented reality audio for mobile and wearable appliances. *Journal of the Audio Engineering Society 52*, 6 (2004), 618–639.
9. Hofman, P. M., Van Riswick, J. G., and Van Opstal, A. J. Relearning sound localization with new ears. *Nature neuroscience 1*, 5 (1998), 417–421.
10. Ishii, H., and Ullmer, B. Tangible Bits : Towards Seamless Interfaces between People , Bits and Atoms. 234–241.
11. Kabal, P. Tsp speech database. *McGill University, Database Version 1*, 0 (2002), 09–02.
12. Kajastila, R., and Lokki, T. Eyes-free interaction with free-hand gestures and auditory menus. *International Journal of Human-Computer Studies 71*, 5 (2013), 627–640.
13. Kato, H., Billinghurst, M., Poupyrev, I., Imamoto, K., and Tachibana, K. Virtual object manipulation on a table-top ar environment. In *Augmented Reality, 2000.(ISAR 2000). Proceedings. IEEE and ACM International Symposium on*, Ieee (2000), 111–119.
14. Laitinen, M.-V., Pihlajamäki, T., Erkut, C., and Pulkki, V. Parametric time-frequency representation of spatial sound in virtual worlds. *ACM Transactions on Applied Perception (TAP) 9*, 2 (2012), 8.
15. Laitinen, M.-V., and Pulkki, V. Binaural reproduction for directional audio coding. In *Applications of Signal Processing to Audio and Acoustics, 2009. WASPAA'09. IEEE Workshop on*, IEEE (2009), 337–340.
16. Mynatt, E. D., Back, M., Want, R., and Frederick, R. Audio aura: Light-weight audio augmented reality. In *Proceedings of the 10th annual ACM symposium on User interface software and technology*, ACM (1997), 211–212.
17. Niinimäki, M., and Tahiroglu, K. Ahne: a novel interface for spatial interaction. In *CHI'12 Extended Abstracts on Human Factors in Computing Systems*, ACM (2012), 1031–1034.
18. Pulkki, V. Spatial sound reproduction with directional audio coding. *Journal of the Audio Engineering Society 55*, 6 (2007), 503–516.
19. Schroeder, M. R. Natural sounding artificial reverberation. *Journal of the Audio Engineering Society 10*, 3 (1962), 219–223.
20. Sodnik, J., Tomazic, S., Grasset, R., Duenser, A., and Billinghurst, M. Spatial sound localization in an augmented reality environment. In *Proceedings of the 18th Australia conference on Computer-Human Interaction: Design: Activities, Artefacts and Environments*, ACM (2006), 111–118.
21. Tikander, M., Harma, A., and Karjalainen, M. Binaural positioning system for wearable augmented reality audio. In *Applications of Signal Processing to Audio and Acoustics, 2003 IEEE Workshop on.*, IEEE (2003), 153–156.
22. Ullmer, B., and Ishii, H. Emerging frameworks for tangible user interfaces. *IBM systems journal 39*, 3.4 (2000), 915–931.
23. Vazquez-Alvarez, Y., Oakley, I., and Brewster, S. A. Auditory display design for exploration in mobile audio-augmented reality. *Personal and Ubiquitous Computing 16*, 8 (2012), 987–999.
24. Wenzel, E. M., Arruda, M., Kistler, D. J., and Wightman, F. L. Localization using nonindividualized head-related transfer functions. *The Journal of the Acoustical Society of America 94*, 1 (1993), 111–123.
25. Zahorik, P. Direct-to-reverberant energy ratio sensitivity. *The Journal of the Acoustical Society of America 112*, 5 (2002), 2110–2117.
26. Zea, E. Binaural in-ear monitoring of acoustic instruments in live music performance. In *15th International Conference on Digital Audio Effects, DAFx 2012 Proceedings* (2012), 1–8.
27. Zhou, Z., Cheok, A. D., Qiu, Y., and Yang, X. The role of 3-d sound in human reaction and performance in augmented reality environments. *Systems, Man and Cybernetics, Part A: Systems and Humans, IEEE Transactions on 37*, 2 (2007), 262–272.

Catch-Up 360: Digital Benefits for Physical Artifacts

Florian Perteneder, Eva-Maria Grossauer, Yan Xu, Michael Haller
Media Interaction Lab
University of Applied Sciences Upper Austria
mi-lab@fh-hagenberg.at

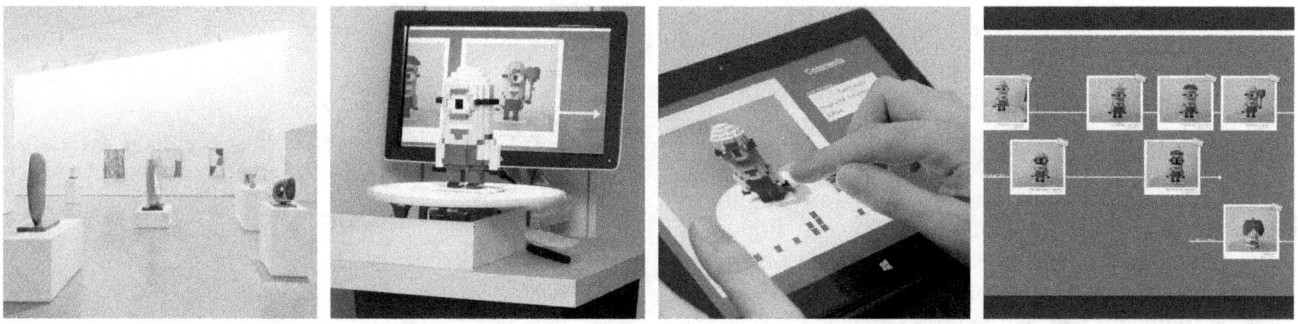

Figure 1: Left to right: We took inspiration from galleries where artifacts are put on meaningful places; Artifacts are placed on a motorized, augmented platform; A web-interface provides remote access; Captured artifacts provide a history for comparison.

ABSTRACT
Industrial designers have a tangible working style. However, compared to digital data, physical mockups are difficult to copy and share over distance. They require a lot of physical space, and earlier versions are lost once they are modified. In this paper, we introduce Catch-Up 360, a tool designed for sharing physical mockups over distance to gain feedback from remote located designers, and compare current models with earlier versions. Summarizing, our approach provides a simple, intuitive, and tangible UI that supports the use of lightweight, web-based clients by using remote manipulation of the physical objects.

Author Keywords
Tangible User Interface; Physical Mockups; Sharing Objects; History; Industrial Design;

ACM Classification Keywords
H.5.m. Information interfaces and presentation (e.g., HCI): Miscellaneous.

INTRODUCTION
Large companies, such as LEGO®, have offices at different locations and while sharing digital data works smooth, exchanging physical mockups is more difficult. Producing digital blueprints to enable the reconstruction of prototypes at different venues would be an option, but requires complex digitization and time-consuming rebuilding. The usual approach is to build two physical models and ship one to the distant place, which does not work if the recipient is on the go. In any case the development cycle is slowed down, as the feedback from fellow designers is essential for developing the next iteration of a prototype and exploring an idea further. Moreover, in this cycle it is also important to compare the current model to earlier versions. Multiple physical versions of an artifact require a lot of space. In addition, new versions of a mockup are often based on earlier iterations. Therefore, a direct comparison can become difficult.

TEI '15, January 16 - 19 2015, Stanford, CA, USA
Copyright 2015 ACM 978-1-4503-3305-4/15/01…$15.00
http://dx.doi.org/10.1145/2677199.2680564

We introduce Catch-Up 360, a system designed for sharing early-stage physical mockups over distance and capturing different iterations for later retrieval and comparison. Our goal was to provide a simple, intuitive, and tangible UI that makes sharing and recording of physical artifacts as easy as putting them up on a shelf. Our design was inspired by art galleries (see Figure 1, left), where individual artifacts are often placed on pedestals. This placement creates additional attention and gives more significance to the object. Moreover, the free positioning in the room provides different perspectives to the spectator. At LEGO, we observed that movable pedestals are used to present prototypes to colleagues. We took up the idea to place a physical mockup on a significant place in a design studio. By equipping it with a camera that streams a live video to a web-client, the spot becomes not only a local anchor point for conversations, but also allows for asynchronous remote communication.

BENEFITS OF PHYSICAL ARTIFACTS
There are a number of reasons why designers build and use physical prototypes. Jacucci and Wagner [7] point out that besides the importance of physical properties (texture, geometry, material, energy), physical artifacts are also important communication tools. Taking this classification into account and interviewing and observing industrial and

toy designers, we identified four key reasons why physical prototypes are an important part in the design process:

Haptics: When talking to designers we were surprised to hear that in many cases the haptics (e.g. texture, material) of a model is not the most important reason for building a physical prototype. Nevertheless in many cases it is necessary to touch and feel the object.

Geometric Properties (different perspectives): Building prototypes is a lot about understanding the geometric properties of an idea, such as size, scale, and proportions. One important way to perceive geometric properties is by looking at physical mockups from different perspectives.

Communication: Physical artifacts that are built or positioned within the designer's studio are important triggers for conversations [7]. Physical models trigger discussions involving a range of different perspectives and persons. Moreover, just the pure existence of physical models in the working space gives insights about the status quo in others projects and about people's expertise.

Intuitive Creation and Modification: While all other points are about perceiving, understanding, and communicating different designs, the point of creation is easily overlooked. Designers argued that crafting physical models is much more intuitive to them and provides them with a faster possibility to try and test different options, compared to digital tools.

CATCH-UP 360

The main idea of Catch-Up 360 is to provide an easy and simple way to share and record physical artifacts. Nevertheless, we tried to maintain most benefits of physical artifacts. We aim to provides each designer with the possibility to show and share early-stage physical mockups to get feedback from colleagues and to track the history of the development. We deliberately chose a concept that does not involve 3D scanning as the visual quality of automatic captured 3D meshes did not meet our aesthetic requirements. Moreover, 3D content requires more complex navigation and interaction, especially on the remote side. After discussing this issue with our users we decided to forgo this possibility.

Figure 2 depicts all components of Catch-Up 360. The mockups are placed on a *motorized turntable,* similar to devices used to make 360° product views (e.g. pamco-imaging.com, or 3d-viz-technology.com). The turntable can either be spun locally by hand or remotely via a web interface. A side-mounted *IP camera* provides the possibility to visualize the mockup remotely and to view the object from different angles, while the *capture camera* records the models to provide historic views of the models. A *touch display,* next to the pedestal provides additional information about the history of the object. Locally, annotations are created using a pen-and-paper approach. The notes are digitized instantly and displayed on the

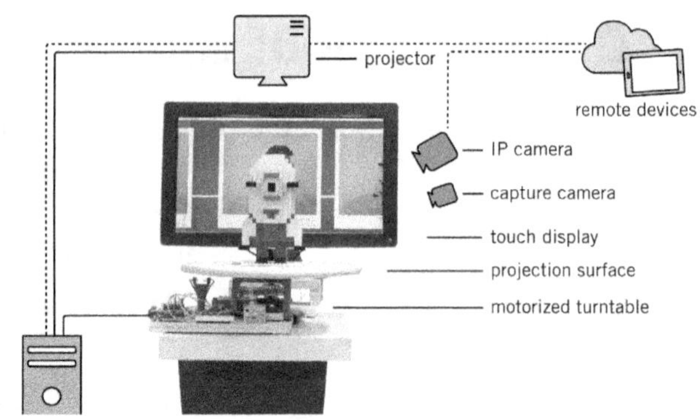

Figure 2: Catch-Up 360 components: the main parts are the spinning turntable, a projector, cameras, and remote devices.

projection surface. Another option is to add notes through *remote devices.*

INTERACTION

Placing Physical Objects & Turning the Table

Once placed on the turntable, the artifacts are identified automatically and the corresponding annotations and earlier versions of the modeling process are automatically loaded. In the current prototype, for placing an already captured artifact, the user has to align the model to ensure that comments are displayed correctly. Locally, the turntable can be spun manually to allow for an easy and more tangible interaction experience. Notes are digitized and projected on the turntable in an angle relative to the object. This angle is maintained when turning the table. Notes can be moved around the object or deleted by dragging them to the projection border. We experimented with projecting directly on the artifact but as the visual quality heavily depends on the used material, we decided against this possibility.

Remote Interaction

In order to provide remote access, we put a webcam next to the pedestal. The main idea is that the camera streams a live image of the model to a browser application (see Figure 3), where designers can have a look at the model from any location and at any time. In contrast to a pre-captured 360° scan, a live image supports synchronous discussions between multiple remote and local users as they all see the same image. To make up for the inability to take a look from different angles, a motor can be triggered to turn the object remotely by interacting directly on the live video image.

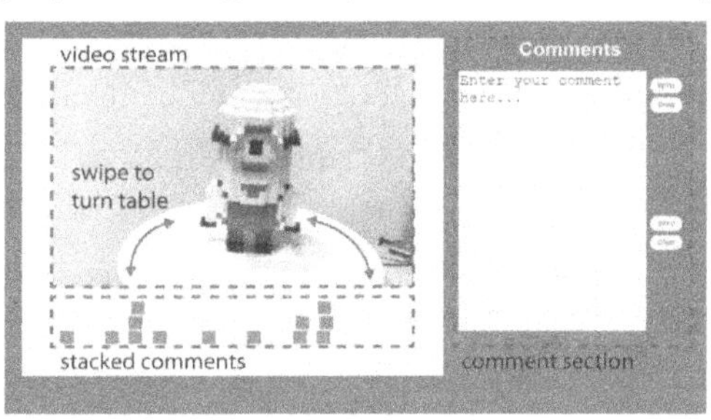

Figure 3: The remote interface and its components.

Notes and object information are synchronized and shown dependent on the current viewing angle of the artifact (see Figure 3). Following the direct interaction paradigm, notes can be created remotely by tapping directly on the desired position on the live video. The remote web-client allows users to add and view two types of notes, comments (typed text) and annotations (handwritten strokes / sketches).

Object History

When a new object or a new version of an object is placed on the turntable, a digital copy of the artifact is created fully automatically to provide a historic reference for later comparison. During the recording process, the motor turns the object stepwise around 360° while a series of roughly 70 images is shot. Iterations of an artifact are appended to the existing model history, while new artifacts start a new version history. When a known object is positioned, it is possible to swipe through previous version on a timeline that is shown on the touch screen monitor (see Figure 1, right).

Turning the physical model also spins the image of the earlier version (see Figure 4). We align the captured historic objects with the (anticipated) spectator's perspective in front of the screen by taking the angular offset between the viewing angle and the position of the camera account.

Figure 4: When spinning the turntable with the real object on it, the earlier version on the screen is rotated into the same perspective for adequate comparison.

IMPLEMENTATION

The centerpiece of Catch-Up 360 is a motorized turntable that involves sensors to detect rotation, regardless if performed by using the motor or per hand. A top projection provides an augmented surface, where notes and other information regarding the placed artifact are displayed. A touchscreen displays older versions of the artifact. Finally, an embedded RFID antenna provides an easy way to identify artifacts that are placed on the turntable.

Turning the Table

To support accurate movements, the turntable is driven by a stepper motor. As the stepper cannot be used to track manual spinning and an accurate rotation angle is essential for most features of the system, the calculation of the angle works independent from the motor. An optical rotation encoder is used to capture the continuous motion. Due to the use of a v-belt with different pulleys the final resolution is approximately 1.4°. Moreover, a photoelectric relay is triggered at a fixed position to avoid drift. All sensors and the stepper motor are controlled using an Arduino Uno board.

Object Tracking

We decided to use RFID tags to identify artifacts, as in contrast to optical markers the tags can be easily placed on the model's bottom and tracked through the wooden baseplate. However, one drawback of this approach is that the direction of an object on the turntable cannot be detected. As objects are supposed to be positioned in the middle of the turntable, the reader is best placed directly underneath the center. Due to the driving axle that is in the way here, we built our own slim antenna that surrounds the axle and attached it to the RFID reader.

Tracking Annotations

The annotations are projected on the turntable that is equipped with Anoto[1] pattern to enable direct pen-interaction. As the pattern is mounted on a rotating object, a custom driver takes the angle into account when matching the pen position with the projection. This process is one main reason for the complex angle detection as it requires an accurate angle to provide precise interaction.

Remote Connection

Besides connecting to the IP camera, the remote web-interface connects to the main computer by a separate, WebSocket based connection to trigger the motor and to synchronize table rotation, object information, and notes.

RELATED WORK

Amongst the huge amount of work that has been done in the area of remote collaboration, there are a few examples, such as MirageTable [1] and ShareTable [14] that focus on how to share physical items in remote synchronous collaboration. Peek-a-Drawer [6] is an example for simple asynchronous interaction without remote object manipulation and additional communication modalities. Unlike Catch-Up 360 all of these works share content between two similar setups, making it hard to access physical models from everywhere on the go. Our approach is more related to DIGIMUSE [5], a tele-robotic system to provide interactive remote access to 3D objects in art galleries. In contrast, Catch-Up 360 focuses on gaining feedback during the creation process. Therefore it needs to support bidirectional ways of communication.

There are different attempts to merge the digital and physical collections of designers. Cabinet [9] supports the digitization of physical objects by using an overhead camera and organizing the captured images with digital document on an interactive table. The Tangible Archive [3] supports designers with connecting one or more digital files to a physical object, tagged with RFID tags.

Tani et al. [13] is an early example where a live video image is used for direct interaction to control an industrial plant. Liao et al. [11] extend this idea by introducing multiple cameras in a conference room for remote collaboration and interaction. CRISTAL [12] provides a live video feed on a tabletop to control different devices within the living room.

---

[1] www.anoto.com

Capturing the version history of physical artifacts is also an integral part of our approach. Earlier work spans across history capture and retrieval systems for website design [10] to attempts that capture various data from unstructured, collaborative processes that take place in design workspaces [8].

DISCUSSION AND FUTURE WORK

In our work, we focused on displaying physical artifacts by using a live video stream for remote access or a series of images for viewing earlier versions. In this section we discuss how the benefits of physical artifacts are supported by our system. While our approach provides no direct *haptic* experience, the ability to turn the mockups remotely provides a practical way to experience various *geometric properties* – even though the human body-size is lost as a frame of reference. The strengths of Catch-Up 360 are clearly the manifold *communication* possibilities that support synchronous and asynchronous communication. However, most importantly, designers can keep up their *physical workflow*, while being provided with an easy way to discuss their models remotely and to compare them with earlier versions. Our intention to maintain the physical working style by extending it with digital capabilities to share and compare, was appreciated by the designers we interviewed and worked with. Despite the lack of a deployed prototype at their facilities due to security standards, we were excited to see that designers at LEGO picked up on the ideas of our prototype and manually captured models from 360° to share them with away colleagues.

To preserve more of the properties of physical models when communicating over distance, one option for future work would be to use more sophisticated devices at the remote side. 3D-scanning the object and printing it at a distant 3D printer or displaying it with a shape display [4] could provide a haptic experience. However, the reproduction speed of 3D printers is slow; just like shape displays they are bulky and cannot be used on the go. Shape displays, moreover, have a very limited resolution, which limits their capability to adequately represent design artifacts. AR displays [2] are bulky but provide a nice option to provide a highly detailed 3D image of a model. Therefore, exploring more sophisticated methods of remote object manipulation would maintain the benefit of our very lightweight remote client.

CONCLUSION

The highly tangible working style of industrial designers benefits only inadequately from today's digital ways of working and communicating. In this work, we presented an easy-to-use solution to this problem. Catch-Up 360 is a tangible interface that provides remote sharing, recording, and retrieval capabilities for physical artifacts. While there might be more technically sophisticated displaying methods to make physical models remotely accessible, our approach of controlling the real object over distance enables the use of very lightweight devices on the remote client side and therefore provides a very practical and flexible solution to the problem. Moreover, by capturing every iteration of a placed object, Catch-Up 360 provides a simple yet effective way of comparing different versions of an artifact.

ACKNOWLEDGEMENT

The presented research was funded by the European Union's Seventh Framework Programme FP7/2007-2001 under grant agreement n°318552. We would like to thank our colleagues for their support and helpful feedback.

REFERENCES

1. Benko, H., Jota, R., and Wilson, A. MirageTable. In *Proc. CHI 2012*, ACM Press (2012), 199-208.
2. Bimber, O., Fröhlich, B., Schmalstieg, D., and Encarnação, L.M. The virtual showcase. *ACM SIGGRAPH 2006 Courses*, ACM Press (2006), 48-55.
3. Binder, T., et al. Supporting configurability in a mixed-media environment for design students. *Personal and Ubiquitous Computing 8*, 5 (2004), 310-325.
4. Follmer, S., Leithinger, D., Olwal, A., Hogge, A., and Ishii, H. inFORM. In *Proc. UIST 2013*, ACM Press (2013), 417-426.
5. Goldberg, S.B., Bekey, G.A., Akatsuka, Y., and Bressanelli, M. DIGIMUSE: an interactive telerobotic system for remote viewing of three-dimensional art objects. In *Proc. SPIE 3524,* SPIE (1998), 196–200.
6. Itiro Siio, Jim Rowan, E.M. Peek-A-Drawer: Communication by Furniture. *Ext. Abstracts CHI 2002*, ACM Press (2002), 582-583.
7. Jacucci, G. and Wagner, I. Performative roles of materiality for collective creativity. In *Proc. C&C 2007*, ACM Press (2007), 73-82.
8. Ju, W., Ionescu, A., Neeley, L., and Winograd, T. Where the wild things work. In *Proc. CSCW 2004*, ACM Press (2004), 533-541.
9. Keller, A.I., Hoeben, A., and der Helm, A. van. Cabinet: merging designers' digital and physical collections of visual materials. *Personal and Ubiquitous Computing 10*, 2-3 (2006), 183-186.
10. Klemmer, S.R., Thomsen, M., Phelps-Goodman, E., Lee, R., and Landay, J.A. Where do web sites come from? In *Proc. CHI 2002* , ACM Press (2002), 1-8.
11. Liao, C., et al. Shared interactive video for tele-conferencing. In *Proc. MULTIMEDIA 2003*, ACM Press (2003), 546-554.
12. Seifried, T., et al. CRISTAL: A Collaborative Home Media and Device Controller Based on a Multi-touch Display. In *Proc. ITS 2009*, ACM Press (2009), 33-40
13. Tani, M., Yamaashi, K., Tanikoshi, K., Futakawa, M., and Tanifuji, S. Object-oriented video. In *Proc. CHI 1992*, ACM Press (1992), 593–598.
14. Yarosh, S., Cuzzort, S., Müller, H., and Abowd, G.D. Developing a media space for remote synchronous parent-child interaction. In *Proc. IDC 2009*, ACM Press (2009), 97-105.

BreathingFrame: An Inflatable Frame for Remote Breath Signal Sharing

Jina Kim, Young-Woo Park, Tek-Jin Nam
CIDR Lab, Department of Industrial Design, KAIST
291 Daehak-ro, Yuseong-gu, Daejeon 305-701, Republic of Korea
{jina_kim, pyw, tjnam}@kaist.ac.kr

ABSTRACT
We present BreathingFrame, a breath signal sharing device that supports pairwise remote communication through delivering the physical inflating movement of the other party's breathing on the surface of a digital photo frame. The results of our observational study with eight couples showed that participants could associate the other party on the frame, feel sentimental connectedness and the breathing movement from the other party, and stimulate their curiosity in a positive way. We also found that it was effective for conveying affection and making users to do natural abdominal breathing through intentional breath signal delivery. Allowing the users to share breathing at a distance by applying unconscious but partially controllable breath signals on the digital picture frame which is used in everyday lives, BreathingFrame can deliver new forms of telepresence and support emotional communication.

Author Keywords
Breath Sharing; Remote Communication; Inflatable Desk Frame

ACM Classification Keywords
H.5.2 Information interfaces and presentation: User interfaces—Input devices and strategies, interaction styles.

INTRODUCTION
As long-distance relationships among family members and couples increase, the importance of new digital devices that support feelings of closeness and telepresence has also increased. Traditionally, visual, audio, and text information have been used; currently long-distance communication is limited to these channels. To overcome these limitations, various studies in the HCI field are being undertaken to investigate new means by which to support remote intimacy. Light changes on a digital picture frame [2] and movement of feather or scent [11] have been used to deliver the sense of presence at a distance in ambient ways. In addition, there have been efforts to promote remote intimacy by providing tactile feelings of the other party's finger gestures or pressure information during voice calls [1, 6]. Recently, systems that represent and share bio-signals—such as heartbeat and breathing—through digital devices have been developed [7, 8, 10]. Rings [13] or pad-type [4] devices that can share heartbeats between lovers have been developed. Also, the mechanism of heart rate signal sharing is being studied using a design probe [8] method. It is notable that bio-signal sharing helps to form remote interpersonal intimacy and has the value of smoothing the communication by making the users to expect the other party's emotional status and response as a means for providing empathy. The current exploration of the possibilities of bio-signals as a means of communication mainly focuses on the sharing of heartbeats.

TEI 2015, January 15–19, 2015, Stanford, California, USA.
Copyright 2015 © ACM 978-1-4503-3305-4/15/01...$15.00.
http://dx.doi.org/10.1145/2677199.2680606

We noted of breath signals for ambient interpersonal communication at a distance. In comparison to other bio-signals, breath signals have the advantage that they can be managed unconsciously and with the will. Due to this feature, breath signals have been applied to provide emotional stability through conscious breathing exercise [12], control game interfaces [5] and represent seamless movements in media arts [9]. Also, because breathing information symbolizes life and is closely connected to emotional status, it has the potential to be improved as interesting interfaces that helps remote interpersonal communication. In spite of these features, breath signals have not been investigated sufficiently as a medium for communication at a distance.

Based on previous studies, we aim to identify what possibilities breath signal sharing may have for the creation of emotional communication channels that provide telepresence. To achieve this, we developed a digital photo frame-type device that can share breath signals. We observed the user experiences of this device with eight romantic couples to find whether the device could support emotional communication and the remote sharing of presence.

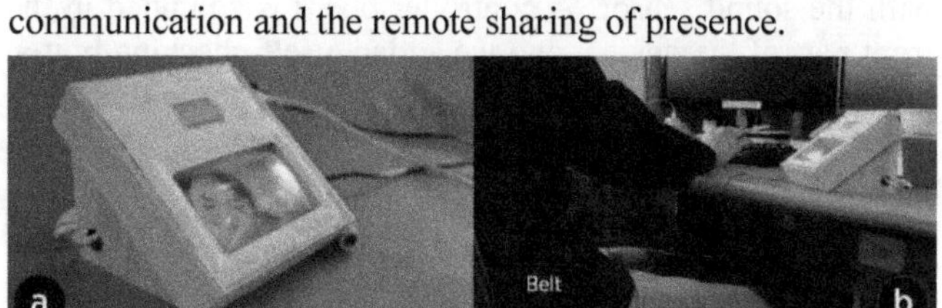

Figure 1. BreathingFrame (a) and its use on the desk (b)

BREATHING FRAME DESIGN
BreathingFrame is a breath signal sharing device that supports pairwise ambient communication by reflecting the physical inflating movement each party's breath. The key design features of BreathingFrame are as follows:

- Visual and tactile representation of breaths: It enables users to see and touch my or the other party's breath through the device. Latex-covered air-inflatable surface was used as the material of the device's surface, so that it can express the movement of breaths in a natural way.
- Breathing system in a photo frame: Breathing movements are shown on a photo frame. It can be put on a desk or a table in a domestic context or personal workspace. We considered that the photos of lovers or family members in the frame are one of the best means to make users remind and feel togetherness [2].
- Unobtrusive breath sensing: We used the belt around their waist as a breath signal sensor rather than wearing additional sensors on the chest or near the nose, because we wanted the device to be natural, ambient and not to draw high attention when used.
- Real-time breathing transmission: The breath signal sharing is delivered in real time to other party. We wanted to support synchronous sharing of the bio-signal in remote.

Implementation

Hardware

BreathingFrame consists of a main wooden frame body and a belt (Figure 2). We integrated the hardware parts in the frame than using a separate casing for the inflation control parts, because we wanted to make users to feel the device as a real inflatable photo frame not a prototype. We developed two sets of hardware to enable bidirectional communication. To detect breath signals, we inserted a stretch sensor in a length-adjustable belt intended to be worn around the waist by the user. When the belt senses the movement of the breath in the user's belly, the other party's device represents ambient breathing through movements on the latex-sheeted surface of the frame through the actuation of a soundproof-treated air pump and solenoid valve. When the first user exhales/inhales, the other party's surface inflates/deflates. Through a sound sensor attached to the frame, the device detects the ambient sound of each user's space, and the picture slowly dims and blinks in response. Through the sound absorption materials that surround the air pump and valve in the back part of the device, we could reduce noise to 48dB (i.e., an average ambient noise level within a home) and prevent interference with the sound sensor. A controller board is equipped in the front part of the device, and we added a self-checking button on the side of the frame that enables users to check their own breathing with their device. This mode can be recovered when the user pushes the button again.

Figure 2. Hardware of BreathingFrame

Software for Bidirectional Communication

The software system controls users' BreathingFrame data with client-server architecture (Figure 3). Each user's device is connected with a laptop that becomes the client. Client A's stretch sensor values are sent to the server, and then client B reads the value from the server and sends breathing output through the controller board connected to the device. The logging software is installed in the server computer.

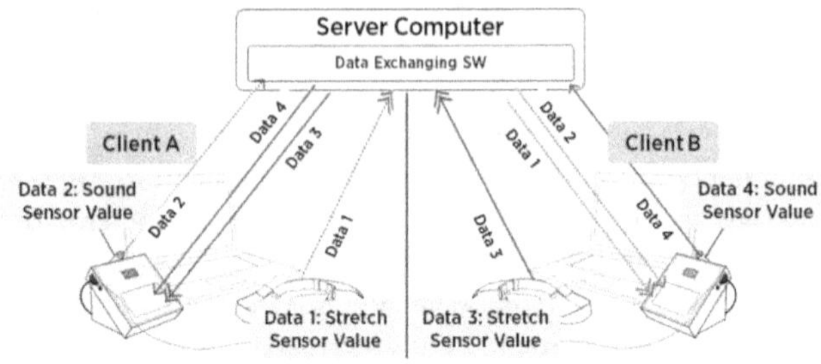

Figure 3. Bidirectional communication diagram

USER STUDY

We conducted an exploratory study to investigate the value of BreathingFrame in the context of everyday activities on a desk at home. Specifically, our question in the study were: how can the sharing of breath be used to improve emotional communication and support telepresence at a distance? Eight couples (average age is 25.5 and we are coding them as C1-F/M~C8-F/M) in their twenties participated. We recruited them because their emotional communication is more active than people in casual relationships, and also people tend to feel uncomfortable exposing their bio-signals to people who are unfamiliar to them [8]. We introduced the device and gave a 10-minute training session before starting the tasks. We taught each user how to manipulate the BreathingFrame, and each participant wore the belt and sent breath signals to the other party by following the preset instructions. Then, each participant was led to one of two separate rooms that have a table, chair and cushions like a general room in a domestic environment. We also deployed a laptop on the table with a wireless internet connection, and with the client software and Skype installed. We asked each participant to complete five different activities with their partner. These included a video call, co-online shopping, a break, reading, and filling out an e-mail survey (Table 1). The activities were carefully selected to observe the users' experiences of the BreathingFrame while they are doing typical daily activities on a desk at home.

Process (in a set like Figure 1, b)	Time
1. Video call through Skype	10 min
2. Online shopping: choosing what to wear by discussion on a Skype voice call	10 min
3. Break (Free time but still connected)	5 min
4. Reading a paper book (a chapter of an essay)	10 min
5. Filling in an e-mail survey related to the reading contents	10 min
Interview	30 min

Table 1. User study process

We video recorded all the uses, and audio recorded while conducting the interviews after participants finished the activities. During the interview, we asked about the users' impressions of BreathingFrame, including good and bad aspects, what the value of the breath sharing was, and overall usability. 240 minutes of interview data was transcribed and our research team had three iterations of grouping process using affinity diagramming method. We used the video recorded data to identify the detail uses that were conveyed through the interviews.

FINDINGS

Reflecting the Other Party on the Frame

Participants showed a tendency to project the other party's presence on the BreathingFrame. Total 12 users answered that they regarded the frame special by recognizing the fact that this device represents their lover's breathing in real-time. C4-F mentioned every time when she identifies the experience that her device reacts synchronously while she saw the other party breaths during the video call; this experience made her to recognize the device as the other party. C7-F also answered similarly: *"I already knew the frame's movement is the other party's breaths, and I became to think this as him when the device moves and feel the closeness"* In addition four participants represented BreathingFrame as *"(the other party's) belly'* during the interview. C4-M noted, *"I was able to identify the inflating part of the device with my girlfriend's belly. I felt this was more like my girlfriend during this remote situation even I cannot see her"* We expect these findings are the result of the device's feature that represents the breathing detection from the belt worn on the belly as changes in the inflatable surface.

Supporting Sentimental Connectedness

Four couples stated that they felt connected through the use of breathing frame during the break context after the Skype conversation. C6-F answered, *"(also when we are not having a skype call) I wondered if he's okay, but I felt emotional connectedness that this frame provided sentimental feeling"* C3-M also mentioned, *"It was fun and good to be able to see her breath. I felt like she was sitting next to me and holding my hand."* These findings are also similar to those of Slovak et al [8], which showed that heartbeat sharing provides a feeling of strong connectedness. Additionally, participants noted that creating their own vocabulary by using bio-signal formed strong bonding feeling. C5-F sent certain patterns of breath signals to her boyfriend consciously, expecting him to know it; she mentioned that she felt good when she received his answer. We also identified that BreathingFrame have the potential to be used as a means for feeling intimacy and presence in a private way during remote communications. C2-M mentioned that he wanted to be connected continuously via a video chat window when he is apart from his girlfriend, but video call exposes my face and background. He noted BreathingFrame allowed them to convey interests and intimacy in a private and ambient way.

The soft tactile feeling of the inflated latex surface stimulated the participants' desire to touch it. We could identify that they recognized the frame as their lover by feeling the other party's breaths by touch, and that this provided the feeling of emotional closeness. Also, C1-M and C5-F said that if the breathing came from their pet, they would want to touch the frame as they had when the breathing came from their lovers. Previous studies related to haptic interpersonal communication systems mention that simulated touch through inflation support a feeling of closeness at a distance [6].

Stimulating the Curiosity on the Other Party's Status

Similar to the findings about heartbeat sharing [8], we were able to identify that breath signal sharing stimulated participants' curiosity on the other party's status related to emotional states according to the types of breath signals they received. Interestingly, participants expressed satisfaction in terms of new information channel is provided which conveys unseen information into actual form. In particular, participants mentioned that they tended to show interests on the other party's status when the breathing movement of the frame becomes bigger or slower. For instance, C1-F stated, *"I thought 'what kind of content is he reading now?' when the belly (the device) inflated sometimes while he was reading the book."* She mentioned that this curiosity was not a serious concern but a positive response. These findings show a common point with previous remote communication devices that the restricted expressions flexibly extended the meanings [1].

Delivering Intentional Abdominal Breathing

Conveying Affection and Playfulness

The breath signal was naturally used as a means to convey affection and playfulness between the participants. C1 intentionally exhaled strongly and used it to inflate the other party's frame into a big size. C1-F stated, *"It appeared to me like he is being mischievous when my frame suddenly inflates bigger."* Most of the participants reacted to the frame's inflation from the other party by intentional breathing control during the conversation. C4-M noted by recalling the video call situation, *"If the breathing frame is next to me, I guess it will be difficult to get angry. I will feel like my girlfriend is doing as a puppy is acting charming by throwing out the abdomen"*

Making Users to Do Natural Abdominal Breathing

We identified that BreathingFrame induced natural abdominal breathing by making users to deliver regular breathing pattern or mimic the other party's breathing pattern that is represented with the device. This finding was also similar to the effect that breathing instruction provides during interpersonal communication [12]. Through the video observation of C3, we found that men encouraged women to breathe when their breathing was stopped during a focused situation. C3-F stated, *"I tend to focus on my breathing intentionally to make my breathing look even on his device.*" C4-F also noted, *"I would feel stressed if this device forced me to do abdominal breathing, but I think I used it interestingly because it does not. It will be good to do breathing exercises while doing work."* Moreover, C8-F answered, *"I began to breathe like his [C8-M's] breathing pattern when he breathed comfortably. I strongly felt like we were together at that time."*

SUGGESTIONS FOR IMPROVING BREATHINGFRAME

We also heard feedback during the interviews about ways to improve the design of BreathingFrame. First, the participants mentioned that emotional intimacy and stability is needed, and that they became more conscious of the lover's emotional state during the relaxed context than during the focused context. Thus, the design can be improved to be more suitable for a relaxed environment, and to have a softer form and material, such as a cushion, that the users can hug or lean on. Second, regarding the focused context, the participants mentioned that they want to feel the other party's breathing continuously by applying this feature on the product that has frequent skin contact (e.g. mouse, touchpad or back of chair) with subtle inflating movement that does not interfere focusing on the work. Therefore, it will be effective to be applied as delivering the lover's breath signal in an ambient way and be applied for the purpose of providing emotional stability through breathing exercise induction in the stressed working environment. Thirdly, we found that BreathingFrame can be used for identifying an individual's breathing status when used between parent and child or similar, and that in this capacity it can be used as a form of medical device. This requires the simple breath signal detection technology and could be done with a naturally wearable belt, bracelet, or glasses; furthermore the signals could be delivered in real time without the restriction of the space. Additionally, it will be more useful if precise and meaningful health status information is provided by the interpretation of the breath signal with other bio-signals at the same time.

CONCLUSION

We presented a physical breath signal sharing through a digital photo frame-like device. We also investigated the value and user experience by observing the uses of eight couples in a relationship. BreathingFrame deliver an individual's breath signals in real time through the movement changes of an inflatable display surface using breath signal detection through a simple wearable belt. It supports visual and tactile sharing of the breath signal that occurs both unconsciously and internationally. The results from the user study showed that participants tend to reflect the other party on the frame, feel sentimental connectedness and the breathing movement from the other party, and stimulate their curiosity in a positive way. We also found that the device was effective for conveying affection and making users to do natural abdominal breathing through intentional breath signal delivery. Allowing the users to share breathing at a distance by applying unconscious but partially controllable breath signals on the digital picture frame, BreathingFrame can deliver new forms of telepresence, emotional communication, and induce natural breathing from the connected remote party.

ACKNOWLEDGEMENT

This paper is based on work supported by the ICT R&D program of MSIP/IITP. [10041313, UX-oriented Mobile SW Platform]

REFERENCES

1. Chang, A., O'Modhrain, S., Jacob, R., Gunther, E., and Ishii, H. Comtouch: Design of a vibrotactile communication device. In *Proc. DIS 2002*, ACM Press (2002), 312-320.
2. Chang, A., Resner, B., Koerner, B., Wang, X. C. and Ishii, H. LumiTouch: an emotional communication device. *Ext. Abstracts CHI 2001*, ACM Press (2001), 313-314.
3. King, S. and Forlizzi, J. Slow messaging: intimate communication for couples living at a distance. In *Proc. DPPI 2007*, ACM Press (2007), 451-454.
4. Lotan, G. and Croft, C. Impulse. *Ext. Abstracts CHI 2007*, ACM Press (2007), 1983-1988.
5. Marshall, J., Rowland, D., Rennick E S., Benford, S., Walker, B. and Mcauley, D. Breath control of amusement rides. In *Proc. CHI 2011*, ACM Press (2011), 73-82.
6. Park, Y-W., Baek, K-M., and Nam, T.-J. The roles of touch during phone conversations: long-distance couples' use of POKE in their homes. In *Proc. CHI 2013*, ACM Press (2013), 1679-1688.
7. Schnädelbach, H., Irune, A., Kirk, D., Glover, K. and Brundell, P. (2012). ExoBuilding: Physiologically Driven Adaptive Architecture. ACM TOCHI 19(4), 25.
8. Slovak, P., Janssen, J. and Fitzpatrick, G. Understanding heart rate sharing: towards unpacking physiosocial space. In *Proc. CHI 2012*, ACM Press (2012), 859-868.
9. Rafael, L-H. Last Breath. *11th Bienal de la Habana*, (2012).
10. Sommerer, C. and Mignonneau, L.Mobile Feelings– wireless communication of heartbeat and breath for mobile art. *The Mobile Audience: Media Art & Mobile Tech* 5, 269.
11. Strong, R. and Gaver, B. Feather, scent and shaker: supporting simple intimacy. In *Proc. CSCW 1996*, ACM Press (1996), 29-30.
12. Vlemincx, E., Taelman, J., Van Diest, I. and Van den Bergh, O. Take a deep breath: The relief effect of spontaneous and instructed sighs. *Physiology & behavior 101*, 1 (2010), 67-73.
13. Werner, J., Wettach, R. and Hornecker, E. United-pulse: feeling your partner's pulse. In *Proc. MobileHCI 2008*, ACM Press (2008), 535-538.

LiveSphere: Sharing the Surrounding Visual Environment for Immersive Experience in Remote Collaboration

Shohei Nagai
The University of Tokyo
Tokyo, Japan
shohei.nagai14@gmail.com

Shunichi Kasahara
Sony Computer Science Laboratory
Tokyo, Japan
kasahara@csl.sony.co.jp

Jun Rekimoto
The University of Tokyo
Sony Computer Science Laboratory
Tokyo, Japan
rekimoto@acm.org

ABSTRACT
Sharing an immersive experience enhances situational awareness, enabling effective collaboration between persons in different places. The development of a head-worn camera enables us to capture the first-person view and share it as the personal experience. However, the limited viewing angle of such cameras prevents a remote viewer from obtaining a complete surrounding situation. In this paper, we propose a system called LiveSphere, which presents the entire surrounding visual environment using a head-worn system with multiple cameras. The image-stabilizing algorithm compensates image motion caused by the wearer's head movement. This enables the remote viewer to look around the environment independently from the wearer's head direction. We developed a prototype to examine how sharing the surrounding visual environment improves collaboration between persons in different places.

Author Keywords
Experience sharing; spherical image; wearable computing; remote collaboration; visual environment;

ACM Classification Keywords
H.5.m. Information interfaces and presentation (e.g., HCI): Multimedia Information Systems

INTRODUCTION
Sharing an immersive experience in real-time is a highly effective solution for collaboration between persons in different places. Such experience makes it easy to understand the situation, and provide effective guidance as if they exist in the same place. Particularly, Fussel et al. [2] suggested that sharing "visual space" could facilitate effective collaboration. Previous studies explore various approaches to share visual space utilizing video streaming with cameras [e.g. 7]. The cameras capture parts of the visual space and share them to a person in remote place.

TEI '15, January 16 - 19 2015, Stanford, CA, USA
Copyright 2015 ACM 978-1-4503-3305-4/15/01···$15.00
http://dx.doi.org/10.1145/2677199.2680549

Figure 1. The LiveSphere headgear with six cameras captures the entire surrounding scene of the wearer, without hampering the wearer's activities.

Head-mount cameras such as a GoPro [3] allow us to capture a first-person view and share that experience. In previous studies of remote collaboration, using wearable cameras is one of the primary approaches for sharing visual information. Such wearable camera can share the first-person view of an individual's environment, enabling collaboration with that individual from a remote location. That first-person view is useful for understanding the situation and providing effective guidance and instruction.

On the other hand, sharing a first-person view may introduce several issues. When the wearer moves their head and changes direction, the captured image tracks their field of vision. Often times, this movement can cause intense shaking, which may also cause motion sickness [1]. During remote collaboration, the remote viewer needs to fix their vision on specific objects, when necessary. This allows the remote viewer to understand the wearer's environment and give appropriate guidance. However, the object in question can easily go out of perspective depending on the head movement of the wearer, making it more difficult for the viewer to keep up with the situational context.

To solve these problems, JackIn [4], which is one of our research projects, proposed an approach by which a series of first person images are spatially merged to create a virtual out-of-body view. Using this technique, a remote

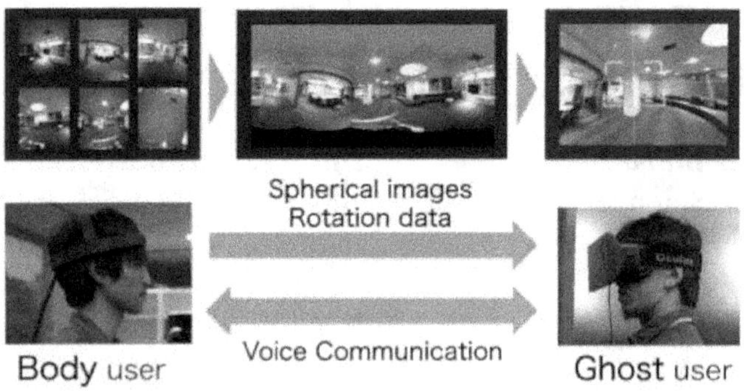

Figure 2. LiveSphere system configuration. A Body user wears the headgear capturing the surrounding visual environment and transmits it. A Ghost user can look around the environment independently from Body's head direction. The direction of Body's head is overlaid in Ghost's perspective.

viewer with the appropriate instructional expertise can observe the scene independently from the wearer's head direction. However, as it relies on the assumption that the wearer pans the environment to capture images for merging, it is not always robust.

In this paper, we propose LiveSphere, a novel remote collaboration system that shares the visual environment surrounding a wearer with a viewer in a remote location using a spherical image. The image rotation caused by a change in the wearer's head movement is compensated by rotation data. We gather this data from a nine-axis sensor recorded simultaneously with the images. That provides the remote viewer an immersive experience as if present in the real environment, and looked around independently from the wearer's head direction.

In the remainder of this paper, we use the term "Body" to represent a person who performs activity in the real environment, and "Ghost" for the person who observes the shared environment and gives guidance and instruction.

SHARING SURROUNDING VISUAL ENVIRONMENT

To provide Ghost with an immersive experience and realize effective collaboration, LiveSphere shares the surrounding visual environment. Sharing the surrounding visual environment consists of the following:

- Provide perspective ranging over a fixed scope.
- Provide independent perspective from Body's head rotation.

Perspective over fixed scope

To understand the Body's situation, Ghost needs to observe the environment from different angles and pay attention to everything related to the collaborative task. However, the perspective captured by one wearable camera is limited in fixed scope. Conventional studies have used different approaches to remove this limitation. For example, Fussel et al. [2] utilized the combination of a wearable camera and a scene-oriented stationary camera. Kashiwabara et al. [5] used an actuator to change the direction of the camera to capture wider area.

LiveSphere captures almost the entire surrounding environment visible from Body's position using six cameras directed toward the outside. This enables Ghost to look around and observe everything in the surrounding environment as if they were present. In addition, this enables Ghost to look around and observe everything around Body over the limitation of the single fixed-scope camera. That enhances Ghost's awareness of the situation surrounding Body.

Independent Perspective from Body's Head Motion

For a deeper understanding of Body's location and situation, it is important that Ghost can look around. In addition, if there is an object that should be paid attention to, Ghost can focus on it for a certain period. In the conventional wearable camera system, Body moves and turns their head of their own volition, with the resulting view dependent on head direction. Therefore, the shared perspective is suddenly turned around, and Ghost may lose perspective on an object of focus. If Ghost wants to focus on a specific object, Body must maintain their head direction toward it, which is not practical in a real activity. LiveSphere removes this limitation by combining the images captured from the surrounding visual environment with Body's head rotation. The shared images' rotation is compensated with the rotation data. That provides Ghost with perspective, which is independent from Body's head motion. This also resolves any motion sickness caused by shaky images.

Interaction through sharing visual environment

In sharing surrounding visual environment, LiveSphere can realize various applications, which are difficult in a conventional remote collaboration system. The following are possible applications on LiveSphere.

Disaster rescue

We can use LiveSphere in situations that require persons to perform an activity in a dangerous place. For example, in the case of disaster rescue, Body actually enters a disaster-stricken area (which might be dangerous) to search victims. Conversely, Ghost observes the area remotely from the perspective of Body's position using the shared surrounding visual environment. Ghost can guide Body to assist in searching for the victims. In this manner, Ghost can remain in a safe place and focus more on searching. Body, who is in dangerous place, may concentrate on moving their body.

Navigation to specific object

LiveSphere is also useful in daily cases where Body looks for a specific object in an unfamiliar place that Ghost knows well. If Body and Ghost communicate only with voice, it takes a lot of time for Body to share location details and for Ghost to communicate where Body should search. Conversely, if Body shares the surrounding visual environment with Ghost, Ghost gains a more intuitive understanding of where Body is located. This enables effective guidance using directional expressions such as "It's on your right," and deictic expressions such as "It is on that shelf."

Virtual sports experience
We can utilize LiveSphere in entertainment applications. For example, Body is a soccer player and Ghost as a spectator, shares the visual environment surrounding the player on the ground. Ghost can experience it as if they were the soccer player and played the game. Ghost can enjoy the game from literally any different viewpoint. This enables elderly or handicapped individuals who cannot play sports to enjoy them. It is also possible for Ghost to make decisions on how to move and play on the game by giving directions to Body. This can induce the feeling of participation, which makes sports more enjoyable.

PROTOTYPE DESIGN REQUIREMENT

We developed a LiveSphere prototype to demonstrate how a shared surrounding visual environment changed the performance of remote collaboration. In designing the LiveSphere prototype, besides sharing the surrounding visual environment, we listed the following:

Show Body's Situation

For a remote collaboration system where persons in different places work together, it is important to support mutual awareness [3]. To provide effective guidance and instruction, Ghost should be able to understand how Body sees the environment in addition to what they are focused on, and in this situation, what assistance is needed to achieve a task. LiveSphere should present the information, which shows Body's perspective to understand above things. This also enables Ghost to use directional and deictic expressions, which give Body a more intuitive understanding of the guidance and instruction from Ghost.

Shape of Capturing Device

Wearability is an important consideration for designing LiveSphere's capturing device. Some devices record spherical images, such as 360Heros [11]. However, it might be cumbersome in situations where Body moves their body and head dynamically due to the device's weight and high center of balance. In one of our projects where gymnasts wore 360Heros to record the spherical view from their perspective, they lost balance, and some fell when landing.

The height of the cameras is also important consideration. The captured environment should be close to Body's viewpoint. As such, the cameras need to be located near the height of Body's eyes. One reason for this is coverage of the captured visual environment. If Body wears cameras on Body's head, the top of Body's head obstructs the captured images. This causes Ghost to lose track of specific objects that Body can watch. The other reason is gaze matching. In human interaction such as face-to-face conversation and eye contact, sharing the correct scene expression depends on proximity of the gap between the camera and the wearer's eyes [6].

PROTOTYPE SYSTEM CONFIGURATION

The LiveSphere system consists of the following three parts (Figure 2): In the first part, the visual environment surrounding Body is captured and transmitted to Ghost in remote location. In the second part, Ghost is presented with the shared images as the surrounding visual environment. They can observer the shared environment as if present. In the third part, according to the shared information, Ghost and Body communicate through voice.

Capturing Visual Surrounding Environment

In LiveSphere, Body wears a head-mount device called the headgear to capture the surrounding environment (Figure 1). The headgear has six wide-angle cameras. It is designed to affix the cameras lower than the top of Body's head, close to Body's eye level. This lowers the center of balance and prevents the headgear from hampering any activities (Figure 3). This also brings the captured images close to the Body's actual viewpoint. Each of the cameras has approximately 135° horizontal angle, and 122° vertical angle of view. The cameras cover approximately 93% of the surrounding visual environment. Such wide-angle cameras tend to have barrel-shaped image distortion. Therefore, we calibrate the images captured using Zhang's method [10]. We synthesize these images into one spherical image through equirectangular projection using a GPU, which is streamed to Ghost via network in a real-time. The headgear also has nine degrees of freedom sensor to record the Body's direction of the head. We use this data for stabilizing the rotation of Body's head.

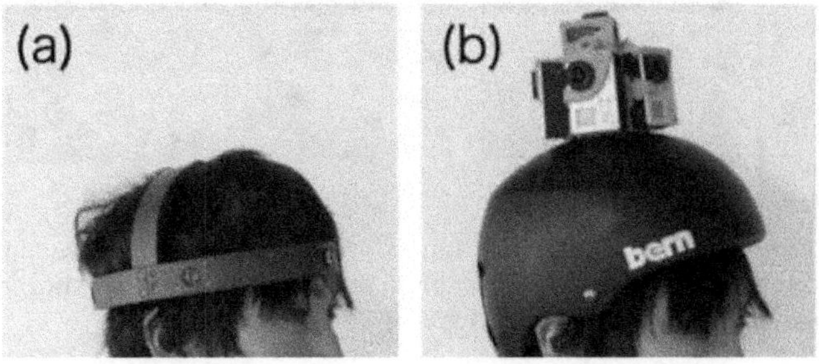

Figure 3. (a) The LiveSphere headgear, (b) 360Heros. The headgear is small and light weight. The center of balance is lower than existing devices, which capture the surrounding scene without hampering activities, and cover the area Body can see from his/her viewpoint.

Present the Shared Environment

We use Oculus Rift [8] to present the transmitted images of the visual environment surrounding Body (Figure 2). Oculus Rift is a head-mounted display, which can detect the user's head rotation and render scenes depending on it. The shared image, which was projected through Equirectangular projection on Body side, is mapped to sphere, and Oculus rift shows the perspective from the center of the sphere. When the Body moves their head, the image might be turn around. We compensate this turning by rotating sphere with the same rotation angle as the Body's rotation, which is recorded simultaneously with the images using the 9-axis sensor (Figure 4). Therefore, the user can look around in the shared environment independently from Body's head rotation as if present (Figure 5).

In the display shown by Oculus Rift, the direction of Body's head is also provided using an indicator, which is overlaid on Ghost's perspective (Figure 2, 5). This makes it easy for Ghost to understand the Body's situation, and give effective guidance.

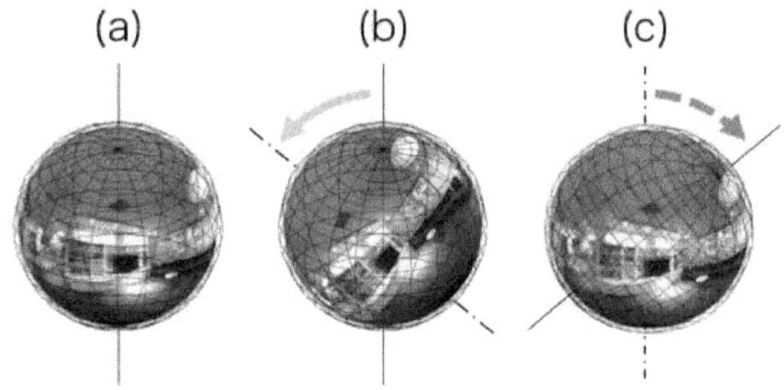

Figure 4. (a) The shared spherical image mapped on a sphere (b) Body's head rotation turns the Ghost's perspective. (c) The image rotation is compensated by turning the mapped sphere with the rotation data recorded using 9-axis sensor.

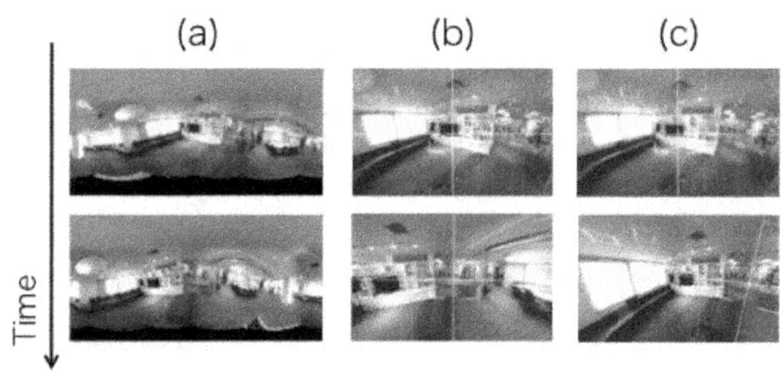

Figure 5. (a) Spherical image. (b) Unstabilized view. (c) Stabilized view. Ghost is able to look around the shared environment independently from Body's head rotation.

Guidance

Voice communication is available on LiveSphere. In the shared visual environment surrounding Body, Ghost can understand Body's situation without the constraint of Body's head direction. Ghost can even provide information about objects in directions unrelated to Body's field of vision. Because Body and Ghost share the surrounding environment, they can communicate with each other more efficiently using deictic expressions and directional expressions.

CONCLUSION AND FUTURE WORK

In this paper, we present a new approach that shares the surrounding visual environment using a spherical image, and provides immersive experiences with a person in remote location for effective collaboration. We developed the LiveSphere prototype and demonstrated its conceptual feasibility. As future work, we explore a more effective way for individuals to interact other than voice communication. JackIn utilized AR annotation by see-through head-mounted display to navigate Body to a specific point. The virtual force is also a possible approach. Rekimoto [9] proposed a small, lightweight actuator, which provides virtual force. This actuator may easily be embedded in the headgear, and does not hamper Body's head movement. Moreover, we are implementing real-time image processing for stabilization because stabilization only by motion sensor may have difficulty in synchronizing with image and sensing, which can cause jitters in the video sequence.

REFERENCES

1. Benson, Alan J. Motion sickness. *Medical aspects of harsh environments* 2 (2002), 1048-1083.
2. Fussell, S.R., Setlock, L.D., and Kraut, R.E. Effects of Head-Mounted and Scene-Oriented Video Systems on Remote Collaboration on Physical Tasks. In *Proc. CHI '03*, ACM Press (2003), 513-520.
3. GoPro Official Website, http://gopro.com/
4. Kasahara, S. and Rekimito, J. JackIn: Integrating the First Person View with Out-of- Body Vision Generation for Human-Human Augmentation. In *Proc. AH'14*, ACM Press (2014), 1–8.
5. Kashiwabara, T., Osawa, H., Shinozawa, K., and Imai, M. TEROOS: A Wearable Avatar to Enhance Joint Activities. In *Proc. CHI'12*, ACM Press (2012), 2001–2004.
6. Kondo, K., Mukaigawa, Y., and Yagi, Y. Wearable Imaging System for Capturing Omnidirectional Movies from a First-person Perspective. In *Proc. VRST '09*, ACM Press (2009), 11–18.
7. Kuzuoka, H., Spatial Workspace Collaboration: A SharedView Video Support System for Remote Collaboration Capability, In *Proc. CHI '92*, ACM Press (1992), 533-540.
8. Oculus Rift Official Website, http://www.oculusvr.com/
9. Rekimoto, J. Traxion : A Tactile Interaction Device with Virtual Force Sensation. In *Proc. UIST'13*, ACM Press (2013), 427–431.
10. Zhang, Z. A Flexible New Technique for Camera Calibration. *Pattern Analysis and Machine Intelligence, IEEE Transactions on 22.11* (2000). 1330-1334.
11. 360Heros Official Website, http://www.360heros.com

HandiMate: Create and Animate using Everyday Objects as Material

Jasjeet Singh Seehra [1], Ansh Verma[1], Kylie Peppler [2], and Karthik Ramani[1]
C Design Lab, School of Mechanical Engineering, Purdue University. [1]
The Creativity Lab, Indiana University, Bloomington. [2]
[jseehra, verma25, ramani]@purdue.edu[1], kpeppler@indiana.edu[2]

ABSTRACT
The combination of technological progress and a growing interest in design has promoted the prevalence of DIY (Do It Yourself) and craft activities. We introduce HandiMate, a platform that makes it easier for people without technical expertise to fabricate and animate electro-mechanical systems from everyday objects. Our goal is to encourage creativity, expressiveness and playfulness. The user can assemble his or her hand crafted creations with HandiMate's joint modules and animate them via gestures. The joint modules are packaged with an actuator, a wireless communication device and a micro-controller. This modularization makes quick electro-mechanical prototyping just a matter of pressing together velcro. Animating these constructions is made intuitive and simple by a glove-based gestural controller. Our study conducted with children and adults demonstrates a high level of usability (system usability score - 79.9). It also indicates that creative ideas emerge and are realized in a constructive and iterative manner in less than 90 minutes. This paper describes the design goals, framework, interaction methods, sample creations and evaluations methods.

Author Keywords
Gestural interface; Play-Value; Constructionism; Handicraft; Creativity

ACM Classification Keywords
H.5.2 [Information Interfaces and Presentation]: User Interfaces - Input devices and strategies, interaction styles; K.3.1 [Computers and Education]: Computers Uses in Education

INTRODUCTION
The easy accessibility of information and electronic technology has resulted in the availability of cheap and powerful electronic tools. This is encouraging hobbyists and tinkerers to invent and prototype, growing the culture of learning through doing [21]. A similar trend is also seen in robotics as it is becoming a popular pedagogical method. One reason for the educational appeal of robotics, is that in the pro-

TEI15, January 16 - 19 2015, Stanford, CA, USA.
Copyright © 2015 ACM 978-1-4503-3305-4/15/01$15.00
http://dx.doi.org/10.1145/2677199.2680570

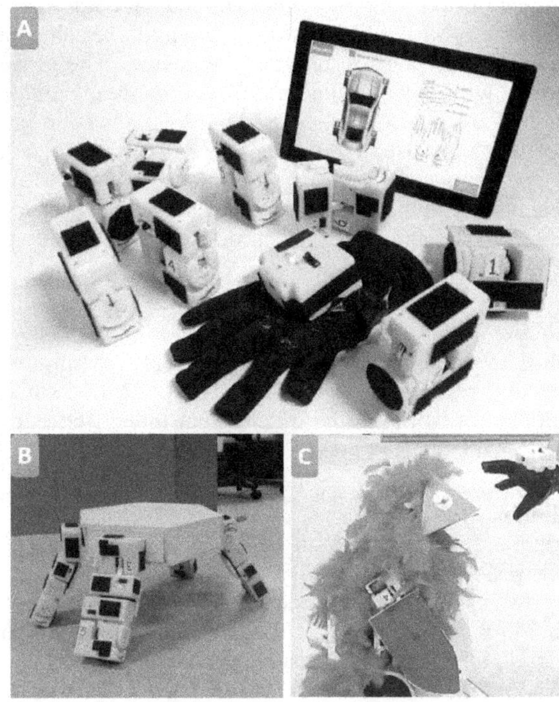

Figure 1. (a) HandiMate Kit (b) Sample creation (c) Gesture control of robot

cess of designing and programming robots, students indirectly learn important engineering, math, and computer science concepts [7]. On the other hand, handicraft objects made completely by hand or by using only simple tools, have served as a medium to express and demonstrate skills, knowledge, thoughts, experiences, perceptions and emotions [22]. The process of building and constructing functional prototypes has been shown to actively engage users, particularly when they see their creation as an extension of their self-concept [9].

Marvin Minsky explains in his book "Just as we learn to interpret certain types of changes as representing motions of objects in the physical realm, we learn to classify other types of changes as signifying mental events; these are what we call gestures and expression" [16], implying that gesture is a natural language of the brain. This suggests that a gestural user interface is an intuitive command methodology. Hence we have developed a gestural control device enabling intuitive control the user constructions.

Our goal was to create a kit that allowed the user to easily build and animate objects. We wanted this kit to allow the user to create robots using the values encouraged by handicrafting. HandiMate explores the intersection of three important trends: (a) animation of everyday objects, (b) gestural interaction with portable and personal devices, and (c) expression of user creativity through craft. The animated toys are created using everyday objects (like spoons, cardboard box, milk cartons, etc) as material and joined with modules we have designed using velcro. The modules are equipped with micro-controller, actuator, wireless communication and a battery. The modules are extensible and independent of each other. A tablet application helps the user configure the object built. The object is animated using hand gestures through a glove based input device. The glove is integrated with flex and inertial sensors that read signals to understand the pose of the hand. HandiMate thus eliminates the need for expertise in technology like motor control, packaging, communication, wiring, and programming. Moving the technology to the background encourages the user to explore and create, and at the same time broadens the age range of participation.

RELATED WORK

HandiMate draws its inspiration from crafts, configurable robots, and gestural interactions. Here we mention some of the prominent works in these fields that influenced our design rationale.

Crafting & Creativity

Crafting and making decorative articles by hand, have been given a variety of definitions, from the desire to do a job well for its own sake [25] to the celebration of social and creative explorations of material [15]. Today's crafts have been combined with DIY activity in creative subcultures across America. These DIY communities (Instructables, Dorkbot, Craftster, Ravelry, Etsy, and Adafruit) have been shown to emphasize open sharing, learning, and creativity [14]. Such discussions of the intricacies of the work, telling stories around craft, and describing the processes for others to remake or modify, has prompted further customization, creativity and reuse.

Inspired by the DIY and maker movement, we developed a platform that can allow children and adults to quickly construct and animate toys made using virtually any material.

Configurable Robots

Many researchers have explored different types of configurable robots for purposes such as smart machines capable of locomotion and transformation [19], educational tool kits that children can use to learn about programming [26], and simple toys [20]. These kits allow construction of robots using different materials such as predefined plastic shapes [2, 23], user defined plastic shapes [1], laser cut shapes [27] and a combination of craft and LEGO [24]. The control techniques in these kits generally use either a graphical programming system [2, 24], autonomous control [19] or kinetic memory - the ability to record and playback physical motion [23]. The culture of building robots using pre-defined shapes has been widely commercialized via LEGO Mindstorms [2] and EZ-Robot [1].

These kits were generally designed to make systems with few (1 to 4) motor actuated joints. A majority of these prior works tend to restrict design freedom, as they have a set of predefined physical shapes that could only be assembled in specific ways. On the other hand, crafting using everyday objects as material provides more freedom in creative exploration.

Gestural Interaction

A large amount of research has been done to exploit the idea of capturing gestures via glove-based devices. Devices implementing different sensor technologies, various patterning and placement of these sensors on the hand, and multimodal systems have been explored [6]. As a result, products like Mechdynes Pinch Glove, Mattel, and Peregrines gaming glove were introduced in the market. Recently, depth cameras supported by computer vision algorithms, have been extensively used to capture user gestures (Kinect, PrimeSense, Leap Motion device). SixthSense [17] and Omnitouch [10] illustrate a wearable on-the-move system for gestural interactions. Other wrist worn depth camera devices have been developed to detect coarse motion of fingers [11]. People have also explored hand-held [18] and shoe-worn [4] systems.

Electronic sensors provide us with high fidelity sensing in mobile applications and are reliable in robustly reading input signals. We embedded electronics sensors in a wearable glove to allow capturing multiple analog values (joint bends of the hand) in a computationally efficient manner. This motivates the use of a glove-based gestural system for our kit.

DESIGN GOALS

The design goals for HandiMate are to provide a platform for the user to easily construct and animate systems using everyday objects as materials. To this end, we attempt to take away the technical complexities, while providing more design freedom and encouraging constructionism and creativity. The framework was designed based on the following design goals:

DG1. *Accessible*: The material used for constructing the objects should be easily accessible and be assembled quickly using simple and familiar techniques.

DG2. *Easy to use*: The system should be simple enough to be used by people of all ages including children.

DG3. *Safe and robust*: As the system is to be used by people of different age groups, the device should be safe and should work reliably.

DG4. *Adequate & smooth movement*: The system should be able to recreate most motions (both fixed angle and continuous motion) smoothly to provide an enjoyable experience.

DG5. *Scalable*: In the spirit of a modular design, every individual module should be physically and computationally complete and extensible.

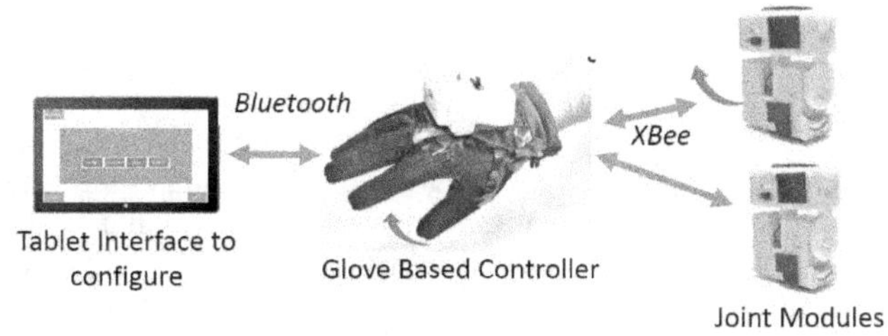

Figure 2. System overview showing flow of data

DG6. *Expressive*: Encourage exploration of a topic without prescribing right and wrong activities.

HANDIMATE OVERVIEW

HandiMate consists of a tablet application, glove-based controller and joint modules (Figure 2).

Interface Design

A simple tablet application has been developed to understand the topology of constructions made and to effectively map them for gestural control. The interface is built using the Unity3D[1] game engine. The application can be installed on any tablet or mobile device. A few basic families of constructions are made available with predefined control mappings where the user has to select the position and direction of motion of the joint modules (Figure 3). The interface also allows the user to create objects that are different from these predefined families and to assign their own user defined mapping to the object being constructed. Once defined, these mappings are transferred to the glove-based controller using Bluetooth communication. This operation has to be done only once each time the user constructs a new object.

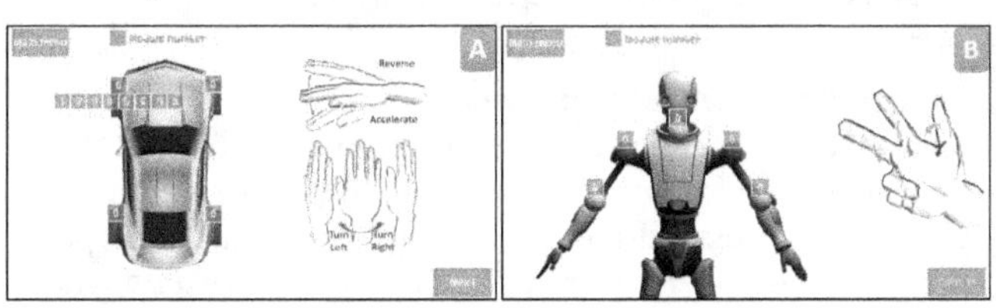

Figure 3. Tablet Interface for selecting position of the joint module (a) four wheel vehicle (b) puppet

Glove-Based Controller

The glove-based controller is used to read the hand pose of the user and control the motion of the joint modules. It consists of an Arduino Nano[2](ATmega 328, clock speed 16MHz), flex sensors[3], MPU 6050[4] (IMU), BlueSMiRF Silver[5](Baud rate 115200 bps) and XBee Series 1[6] (Baud rate 57600 bps) (Figure 4(a)). The Bluetooth device receives the joint module and hand joint mapping from the tablet interface. Flex sensors are placed on the thumb (Interphalangeal, Metacarpophalangeal joints), index and middle fingers (Proximal Interphalangeal and Metacarpophalangeal joints) due to the greater dexterity of these fingers from the rest of the hand [12]. A sensor is also placed on the pinky finger (Proximal Interphalangeal joint) for differentiating control gestures from start and stop gestures. The seven flex sensors, are multiplexed by a 16-channel analog multiplexer[7]. When the resistance of the flex sensor changes (34K to 67K ohms) by bending, the micro-controller picks up the voltage across the flex sensor based on a voltage divider circuit. These analog values are then converted into corresponding motor values. This mapping between the analog sensor value to the motor value is not directly based on the actual angle of the hand or finger, but is scaled to allow full rotation of the joint module within a comfortable range of motion of the hand or finger. This range was determined by doing a small pilot test with few people of different hand sizes. The flex sensors are also placed and calibrated in a way to prevent interference between the joints on the same finger (Figure 4(b)). In a similar manner the micro-controller also reads the angle values from the gyrometer and accelerometer in the IMU device by I^2C communication and generates the motor values. The motor values are transmitted to the respective joint modules by a PAN network created by the XBee communication device.

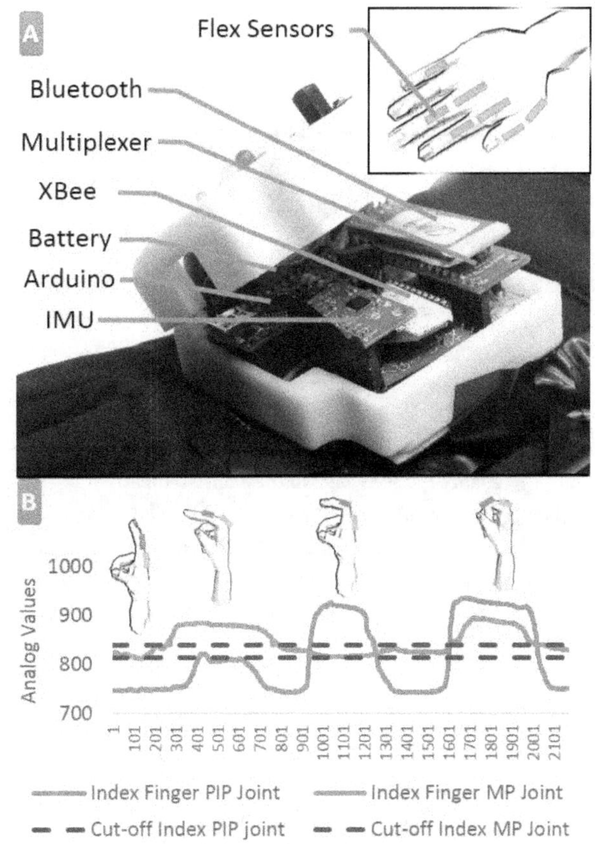

Figure 4. (a) Electronics in the Glove-based Controller (b) Analog readings of the flex sensor at Index finger PIP joint and MP joint for different finger orientations

For safety, these electronic components are enclosed in a

[1]https://unity3d.com/
[2]http://arduino.cc/en/Main/arduinoBoardNano
[3]https://www.sparkfun.com/datasheets/Sensors/Flex/flex22.pdf
[4]https://www.sparkfun.com/products/11028
[5]https://www.sparkfun.com/products/12577
[6]https://www.sparkfun.com/products/8665
[7]https://www.sparkfun.com/products/9056

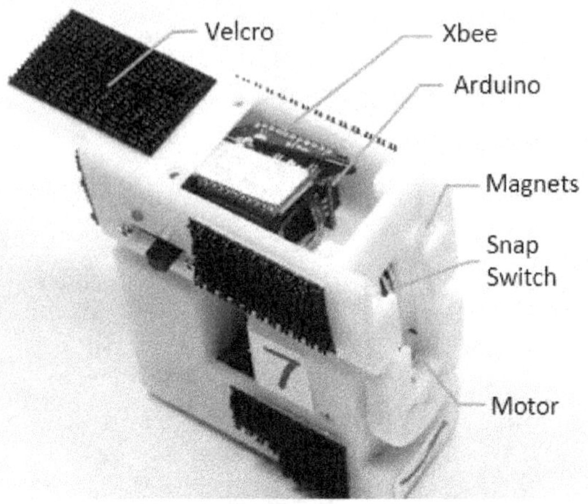

Figure 5. Electronics in the Joint Modules

shell like casing made by 3D printing. A LED based visual feedback system makes the user aware of the state of the IMU and the glove-based controller.

Joint Modules

The joints modules are used to animate the user's construction using the glove-based controller. These modules contain an XBee communication device that reads the information from the glove-based controller, a micro-controller (Arduino Nano) for interpreting this information, and Herkulex DRS-101[8] motors for motion (Figure 5). The parameters of acceleration - time ratio and power input were adjusted to obtain a smooth and non-jerky motion of the motor. The motor, wires and electronics are enclosed in a shell like casing to make the device safe for use. Each module is powered using a 9V lithium ion battery.

The joint modules are connected to each other and to everyday objects using velcro as it is a widely popular temporary fastener. These strips of velcro are provided on all sides to give users freedom to attach objects at different orientations. To allow the device to have both fixed angle and continuous rotation motions (basic forms of motion by a one degree of freedom electric joint), inserts are used. These inserts are held in place with the help of magnets. The fixed angle insert allows for rotation from -90° to 90°. It snaps into the motor connector and locks the upper and lower halves of the module. The continuous rotation insert allows a wheel like continuous motion. It is attached to the motor connector and provides a large surface area for attaching objects (Figure 6(a,b,c)). A snap switch is used to prevent damage to the module in case the fixed angle insert is in place when the joint is being used for continuous rotation. Two LED lights are used to provide the user with visual feedback of the state of the device (Figure 6(d)).

[8]http://www.robotshop.com/en/herkulex-drs-0101-robot-servo.html

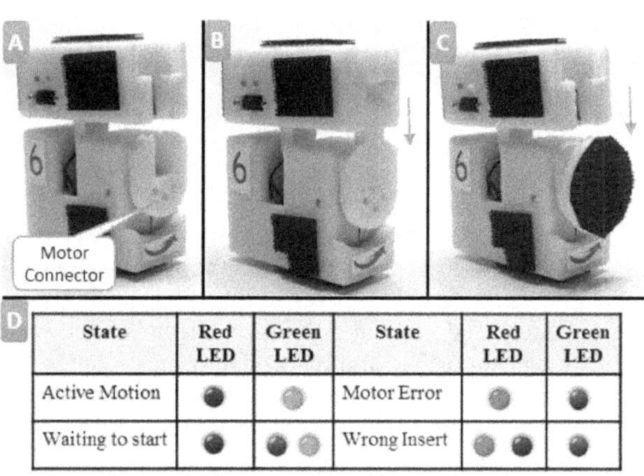

D

State	Red LED	Green LED	State	Red LED	Green LED
Active Motion	●	●	Motor Error	●	●
Waiting to start	●	● ●	Wrong Insert	● ●	●

**Note: Two LEDs in a cell indicate blinking*

Figure 6. (a) Joint module without any insert (b) Joint module with fixed angle insert (c) Joint module with continuous rotation insert (d) LED Indication

INTERACTIONS

With the help of our glove-based controller that provides us with eight analog input values, the constructions are controlled by means of hand gestures. These gestures can be classified as global and construction control.

Global Gestures

Global gestures are valid regardless of the construction made by the user (Figure 7(a)). The global gestures are:

Shake: This gesture is used to start the system. After shaking the hand, the user is expected to keep their hand flat for 100 milli-seconds. This allows the construction to always start from rest and the user to have good control over it.

Closed fist: This gesture is used for an emergency stop. When a closed fist gesture is performed in any orientation of the hand, the system comes to a complete standstill. The shake gesture is then required to restart the system.

Construction Control Gestures

These sets of gestures are used for animating the construction. The general control of each type of construction is divided into the relaxed hand state (close to a flat hand position) where the object is at rest and active hand state where the object performs the motion based on the mapping. The constructions made by the user can be of three main categories:

Articulated

The constructions of this type has a fixed angle for rotary motions. Articulated constructions are further sub divided into:

Puppet Shaped Constructions: For controlling this type, the user makes use of the thumb, index and middle finger. This mapping is similar to how hand puppets are commonly controlled [8] (Figure 7(b)). When the user moves their fingers from the rest position, the corresponding joint modules move.

Robotic Arm: As the index finger is the most decoupled finger from the rest of the hand, the robot arm is controlled using the index finger and orientation of the hand [12](Figure 7(c)). Similarly, when the user moves his hand and finger from the rest position, the respective joint modules move.

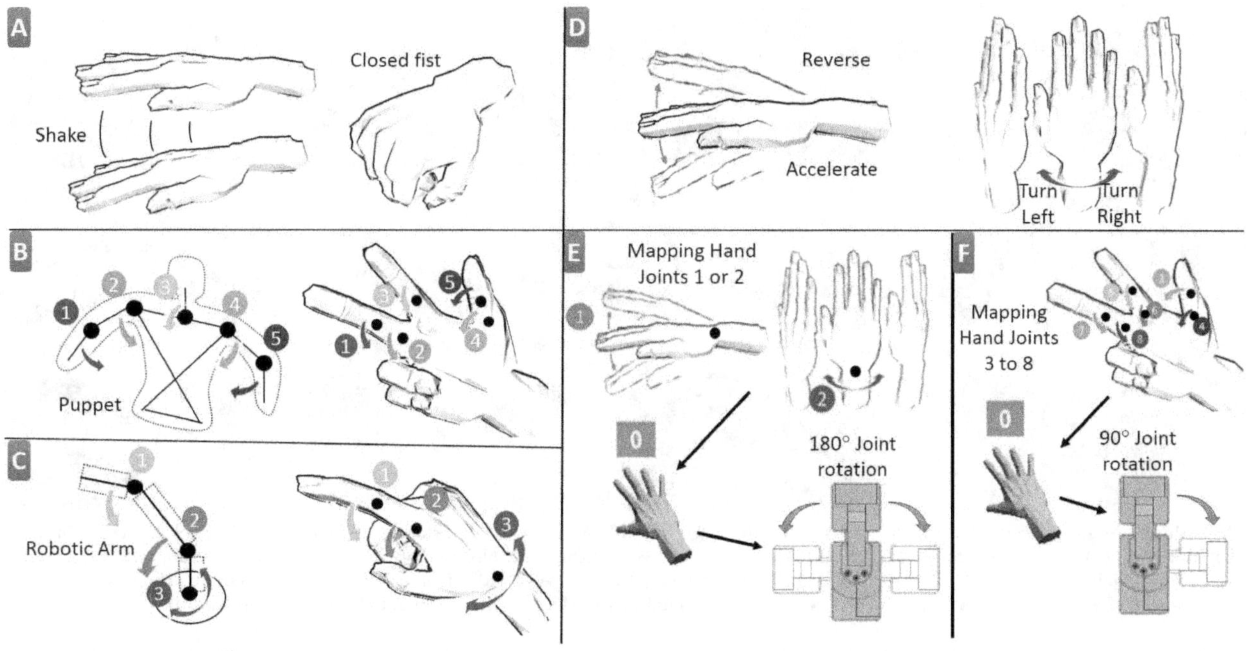

Figure 7. Interaction methods: (a) Global Gestures; Gestures for (b) Puppet Shaped Constructions (c) Robotic Arm shaped constructions (d) Vehicular constructions; User Defined gesture mapping for custom robots (e) Hand joints 1 or 2 (f) Hand joints 3 to 8

Vehicular

This type of construction consists of 2, 3 and 4 wheeled robots. The speed is mapped based on the principle of a joystick where the speed is proportional to the angular displacement of the hand from the relaxed (flat) position (Figure 7(d)). The steering mechanism for the vehicle is executed by spinning wheels on the two sides of the vehicle in opposite directions. The user is also given the option of adding the different articulated constructions mentioned above, on top of the vehicle (Figure 8(g,p,t)).

Custom Robots

The previous two categories had predefined mappings for the control technique. This category does not have any fixed mapping, but allows the user to explore and experiment with different mapping techniques, and select one which they feel is more natural. The user is given the option of choosing the modules being used and their desired motion, such as fixed angle clock wise (CW), fixed angle counter clock wise (CCW), continuous rotation (CW), or continuous rotation (CCW). Once they select the modules, they have the option of choosing the hand joint number and mapping the hand joint to the respective joint module (Figure 7(e,f)). The user has the option of mapping multiple joint modules to the same hand joint. To avoid inconsistency and confusion, the option of mapping multiple hand joints to the same joint module is not available.

As hand joints 1 and 2 allow a 180° angle hand rotation (Figure 7(e)), the joint modules controlled by these joints move from -90° to 90° when in fixed angle mode. Since joints 3 to 8 are finger controlled, the joint modules mapped to them can rotate from 0° to 90° or -90°(Figure 7(f)). When the joint module is in continuous rotation mode, the user can control the speed of the joint module rotation based on the deflection from the relaxed (flat) hand position. Joints 1 and 2 allow bi-directional speed control whereas joints 3 to 8 allow unidirectional speed control.

USER STUDY

We conducted a user study to determine the usability of our framework, observe the variety of constructions made by the user, and various control mappings used by them. The framework was explained to the participant and they were given freedom to build and construct on their own. We obtained feedback from the participants in order to evaluate, improve and come up with possible future directions.

Procedure

We recruited nineteen participants by distributing flyers at the university. We had twelve participants who were graduate and undergraduate students aged between 20 and 29 years. Seven participants were school going kids aged between 10 and 15 years of age. The participant pool consisted of six females and thirteen males; seventeen right handed and two left handed individuals. All participants had no prior experience of using the framework. The user study was conducted in two different settings.

Setting 1

This study was conducted in a closed environment with the raw materials provided by us. The raw materials consisted of kitchen ware, such as spoons, fork and pans, and craft material such as construction paper, multi-colored thread, colored craft sticks, assorted feather collection, crayons, markers, tape, glue gun, knifes, googly eyes, scissor and foam core board. For quick prototyping, precut basic 2D and 3D shapes such as rectangles, circles, triangles, hexagon, cubes, rectangular prisms and triangular prisms of foam core board were also provided. The user was also given the option of

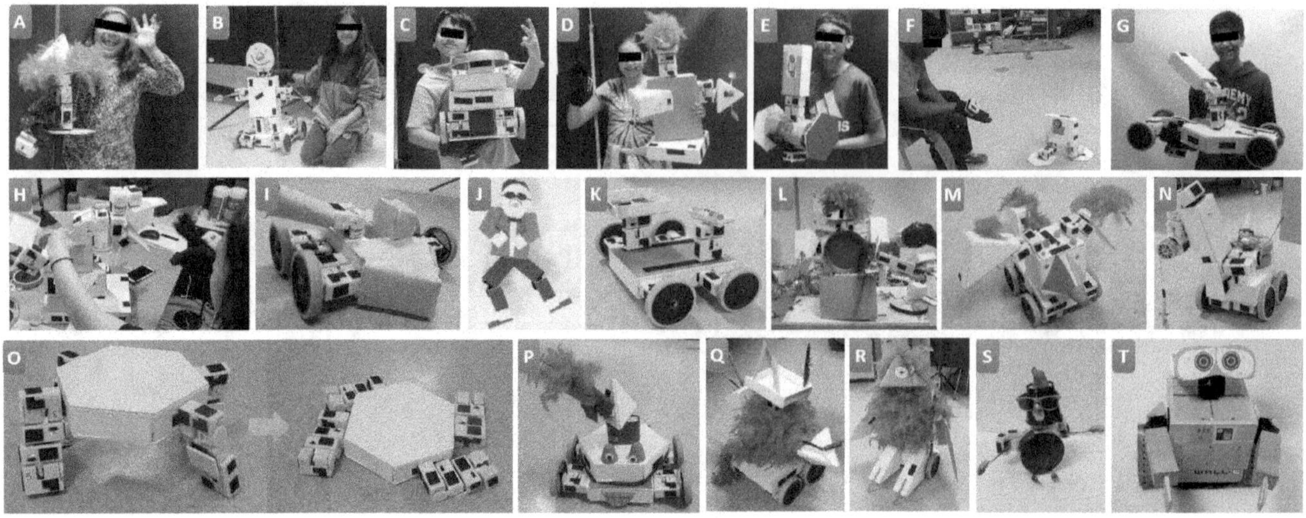

Figure 8. Different objects constructed (a) Dance arm awesome (Age 8) (b) Maddie (Age 8) (c) Bat cave moving (Age 8) (d) Pinnochio Hulk (Age 11) (e) Tie Fighter (Age 11) (f) Two legged robot (Age 11) (g) Turner (Age 14) (h) Running Chicken (Age 20) (i) Small orange boat (Age 21) (j) Gangnam Style (Age 21) (k) Tooler man (Age 21) (l) Afro-Dog (Age 22) (m) Pup on wheels (Age 22) (n) Spooner bot (Age 27) (o) QuadruBot (Age 26) (p) Preston (Age 28) (q) Indi Robot (Age 28) (r) Anxious bird (Age 29); Objects made by student of the school of arts (s) Tin Man (t) Wall-E

cutting any specific shape from the raw materials provided. Each study with each participant lasted 60 to 90 minutes. The participant was initially made aware of the HandiMate framework and was shown some basic constructions made by us. We explained to the participant the physical structure of the joint modules, tablet interface and gestural control methods of the glove-based controller. To start with, they were allowed to test the system by making a basic construction of either a 2-wheeled car or a 2-joint robotic arm, and allowed to control their construction. After this initial familiarization with the framework, the participant was asked to build their own desired construction using the raw materials and eight joint modules provided. They were allowed to sketch their idea first and then build in steps. They tested each step as they went on, or directly completed the whole fabrication and played with the system (Figure 9).

Setting 2

This study was conducted specifically with one participant from the school of arts. The study was conducted in an open environment where we explained the framework and allowed

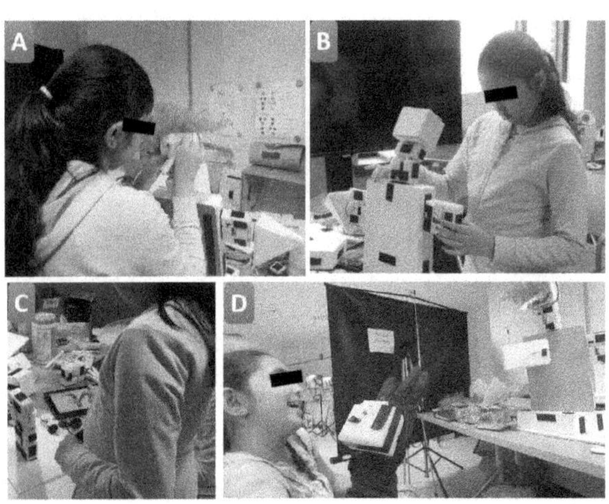

Figure 9. Steps followed during the study (a) Crafting (b) Assembly using joint modules (c) Setup on the interface (d) Play

the participant to build a small sample construction. He was given a sample joint module for dimensional reference and a period of one week to fabricate his constructions. The participant was given complete freedom to construct using any material desired. After the period of one week, he was asked to assemble his construction using the joint modules and animate them.

RESULTS & DISCUSSIONS

Design Motivations

We observed that the design motivation of the construction ranged from fantasy to challenge (Figure 8). Most of the kids tried to realize their fantasy by constructing popular characters from Star Wars or Disney characters. In adults we found a mixture of fantasy and goal motivated approach towards construction. These motivations were influenced by:

- *Personal life or current professional work*: A dog motivated by her pet (The pup on wheels), anthropomorphizing a tank (Preston, he shoots red feathers out of his cannon with a constant green smile and a leopard print nose). A student who works with robots tried to create different robotic gaits using the system (QuadruBot).
- *Task Specific*: Cart to enable users to reach objects placed far away (Tooler - man), robot with a crane like mechanism to pick up spoons (SpoonerBot).
- *Creative trends*: Samurai with an insane afro hair style (Afro-Samurai), a native american chief (Indi Robot), a attention grabbing bird that flaps its wings and squawks (Anxious Bird).

These user constructions demonstrate that the HandiMate framework supports playfulness. It embodies construction, fantasy and challenge all within it [13].

Usability

The pool of our adult participants had a range of expertise in using electronics and micro-controllers. Seven people had

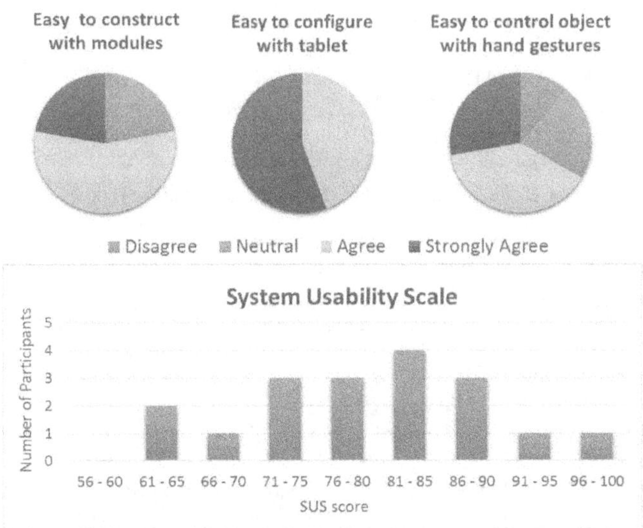

Figure 10. Results of the survey

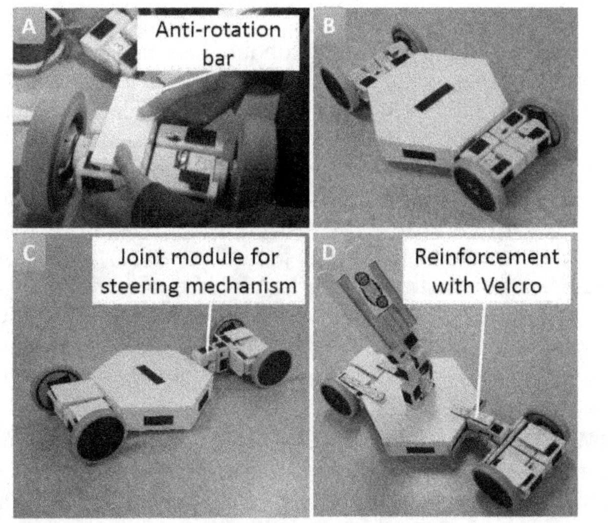

Figure 11. Learning by prototyping (a) Inserting anti-rotation bar to the two wheeled car (b) 4 wheeled car (c) 4 wheeled car with steering mechanism (d) Final 4 wheeled car with robotic arm

rudimentary knowledge in these areas whereas five others had extensively worked with them. We observed that all these participants were able to realize their design goals regardless of the extent of their knowledge constraint. Children as young as 8 years and above were extremely excited about animating the object as they felt amazed when they built something and brought it to life without implementing any electronic circuits. We observed that the student from the school of arts was able to create a variety of constructions and animate it. Thus we observed that when the participant was given more freedom of material and time he could create more artistic and well finished constructions.

The post study questionnaire consisted of a survey based on the system usability scale [5] (SUS) and a few questions specific to the system. For the survey conducted with children, few terms of the system usability scale were changed to simpler words like the word *'system'* was replaced by the word *'toy kit'*. For kids the average SUS score was 84.3 (SD - 4.94) and for adults it was 77.1 (SD - 11.11) giving an overall value of 79.9 (Figure 10). Based on the responses in the survey we believe this discrepancy in the value was due to the expectations of these different demographics. While kids were excited about the fact that the creation they made moved, adults expected better and precise control of the movements. Figure 10 also shows the distribution of the responses, on a Likert scale, of all the participants for specific questions about the ease of use of the system.

Learning by Doing

One 14 year old participant desired to make a robot mounted on a car using the system (Figure 11). Initially, he made a two wheeled car as a prototype. On controlling the car he observed that the car was not stable (system had no mechanism to prevent flipping of the body). He made an anti-rotation structure to constrain the flipping action. To further stabilize the car in order to attach a robot. He changed the car design to a 4 wheeled car. While testing this 4 wheeled vehicular system, he was not satisfied with its default turning mechanism as the turning was not smooth (because of the wheel skidding). He brainstormed to derive a method for a better turning mechanism by improving the design of his robot. He realized that by adding another module he could solve the problem. He went on to attach a module in between the body and the front axle of the vehicle, that could control the angle of rotation of the axle (like a steering mechanism). He tested the vehicle and was successful in efficiently maneuvering it. However when he attached the robotic arm to the main body of the vehicle he observed that the velcro in the single joint module link connecting the two bodies failed due to the overall weight of the system. He then reinforced the system using more strips of velcro. Thus he was able to learn basic engineering concepts of anti-rotation, robot steering mechanisms and structural stability.

A 11 year old participant wanted to make a robot with legs. For this he constructed a system with 4 joint modules. While testing the motion he realized that for the robot to remain stable it was necessary for the two planes of contact with the ground to remain parallel. By trial and error he configured the mapping to do so. On testing the system on the ground he observed that the robot always fell on its back. He realized that the weight distribution on the robot was not balanced and attached a wheel as a counter weight to prevent the robot from falling back. This made the robot squat only when he controlled the movement by slowly moving his hand. However, on moving the robot at high speed he observed that the robot fell erratically. He thus realized that the stability of the robot needed to be increased and he managed that by using bigger base structures at the legs of the robot (Figure 8(f)). In this manner, he learnt about the significance of center of mass and dynamic stability of a system.

This process of designing by iterative prototyping was also observed in the user study with adults. As the system allowed independent and complete control of each joint module, many of the participants were able to divide their overall design goal into many different steps involving building and testing. One of the participants decided to take on the challenge of designing a movable robot to pick up spoons using a crane mechanism. He used the rim of one of the wheels as a pulley, the wires we had provided as rope and magnets in a pen cap as the hook. He initially tested his 3-joint crane mechanism on a base and attached appropriate counter weights to balance the cantilever structure. To firmly attach the crane to the base he also made L-brackets out of foam core and attached it to the base joint (Figure 8(n)). These are examples of constructionism by children and adults alike, in the process of reaching their goals [3]. They identified functional problems in their system, and developed design solutions to overcome them by iterative building and testing.

LIMITATIONS AND FUTURE WORK

During the user study we saw some scope for refinements in HandiMate. Because of the size of the modules, the overall size of the robots tends to be bulky. In a more customized implementation, we would fabricate components with a smaller footprint and integrate them into a more power-efficient system with a smaller form-factor. We also observed some discontent among the users when they were trying to control the vehicle, as it would twist slightly while starting/stopping, due to the limited baud rate of XBee communication causing a delay in motion. This issue can be resolved by switching over to WIFI communication.

CONCLUSION

HandiMate is a cyber-physical construction kit that enables the user to craft functional electromechanical systems, and control them using hand gestures. Its framework consists of a tablet interface, glove-based controller and joint modules which package all the electronics. This allows the user to focus on designing and building. Using velcro we provide an easy technique to attach the joint modules to any crafted construction made from everyday objects. Our study conducted with both adults and kids reported a SUS score of 79.9. The diversity of creations made by the users shows that HandiMate encourages creativity and playfulness. The study portrayed constructionism: the iterative design processes of the users to achieve their goal by quick prototyping.

ACKNOWLEDGMENT

We would like to acknowledge support from the Donald W. Feddersen Professorship.

REFERENCES

1. Ez-robot https://www.ez-robot.com/.
2. Lego mindstorms http://www.lego.com/en-us/mindstorms/.
3. Alimisis, D., and Kynigos, C. Constructionism and robotics in education. *Teacher Education on Robotic-Enhanced Constructivist Pedagogical Methods* (2009), 11–26.
4. Bailly, G., Müller, J., Rohs, M., Wigdor, D., and Kratz, S. Shoesense: a new perspective on gestural interaction and wearable applications. In *Proceedings of the 2012 ACM annual conference on Human Factors in Computing Systems*, ACM (2012), 1239–1248.
5. Brooke, J. Sus-a quick and dirty usability scale. *Usability evaluation in industry 189* (1996), 194.
6. Dipietro, L., Sabatini, A. M., and Dario, P. A survey of glove-based systems and their applications. *Systems, Man, and Cybernetics, Part C: Applications and Reviews, IEEE Transactions on 38*, 4 (2008), 461–482.
7. Druin, A., and Hendler, J. A. *Robots for kids: exploring new technologies for learning*. Morgan Kaufmann, 2000.
8. Engler, L., and Fijan, C. *Making puppets come alive: how to learn and teach hand puppetry*. Courier Dover Publications, 2012.
9. Groom, V., Takayama, L., Ochi, P., and Nass, C. I am my robot: The impact of robot-building and robot form on operators. In *Human-Robot Interaction (HRI), 2009 4th ACM/IEEE International Conference on*, IEEE (2009), 31–36.
10. Harrison, C., Benko, H., and Wilson, A. D. Omnitouch: wearable multitouch interaction everywhere. In *Proceedings of the 24th annual ACM symposium on User interface software and technology*, ACM (2011), 441–450.
11. Howard, B., and Howard, S. Lightglove: Wrist-worn virtual typing and pointing. In *Wearable Computers, 2001. Proceedings. Fifth International Symposium on*, IEEE (2001), 172–173.
12. Ingram, J. N., Körding, K. P., Howard, I. S., and Wolpert, D. M. The statistics of natural hand movements. *Experimental brain research 188*, 2 (2008), 223–236.
13. Kudrowitz, B. M., and Wallace, D. R. The play pyramid: A play classification and ideation tool for toy design. *International Journal of Arts and Technology 3*, 1 (2010), 36–56.
14. Kuznetsov, S., and Paulos, E. Rise of the expert amateur: Diy projects, communities, and cultures. In *Proceedings of the 6th Nordic Conference on Human-Computer Interaction: Extending Boundaries*, ACM (2010), 295–304.
15. Levine, F., and Heimerl, C. *Handmade nation: The rise of DIY, art, craft, and design*. Princeton Architectural Press, 2008.
16. Minsky, M. *Society of mind*. Simon and Schuster, 1988.
17. Mistry, P., and Maes, P. Sixthsense: a wearable gestural interface. In *ACM SIGGRAPH ASIA 2009 Sketches*, ACM (2009), 11.
18. Molyneaux, D., Izadi, S., Kim, D., Hilliges, O., Hodges, S., Cao, X., Butler, A., and Gellersen, H. Interactive environment-aware handheld projectors for pervasive computing spaces. In *Pervasive Computing*. Springer, 2012, 197–215.
19. Murata, S., Yoshida, E., Kamimura, A., Kurokawa, H., Tomita, K., and Kokaji, S. M-tran: Self-reconfigurable modular robotic system. *Mechatronics, IEEE/ASME Transactions on 7*, 4 (2002), 431–441.
20. Oschuetz, L., Wessolek, D., and Sattler, W. Constructing with movement: kinematics. In *Proceedings of the fourth international conference on Tangible, embedded, and embodied interaction*, ACM (2010), 257–260.
21. Papert, S. *Mindstorms: Children, computers, and powerful ideas*. Basic Books, Inc., 1980.
22. Pöllänen, S. H. Beyond craft and art: a pedagogical model for craft as self-expression. *International Journal of Education through Art 7*, 2 (2011), 111–125.
23. Raffle, H. S., Parkes, A. J., and Ishii, H. Topobo: a constructive assembly system with kinetic memory. In *Proceedings of the SIGCHI conference on Human factors in computing systems*, ACM (2004), 647–654.
24. Rusk, N., Resnick, M., Berg, R., and Pezalla-Granlund, M. New pathways into robotics: Strategies for broadening participation. *Journal of Science Education and Technology 17*, 1 (2008), 59–69.
25. Sennett, R. *The craftsman*. Yale University Press, 2008.
26. Shaer, O., and Hornecker, E. Tangible user interfaces: past, present, and future directions. *Foundations and Trends in Human-Computer Interaction 3*, 1–2 (2010), 1–137.
27. Wu, K.-J., and Gross, M. D. Topaoko: interactive construction kit. In *CHI'10 Extended Abstracts on Human Factors in Computing Systems*, ACM (2010), 3619–3624.

TACTIC: An API for Touch and Tangible Interaction

Rafael Nunes
Universidade de Lisboa
rlnunes@di.fc.ul.pt

Fábio Rito
Universidade de Lisboa
farito@fc.ul.pt

Carlos Duarte
Universidade de Lisboa
caduarte@fc.ul.pt

ABSTRACT
Interactive surfaces, gesture recognition, object tracking, tangible interaction are increasingly moving from the research arena to the domain of commercial applications. However, the effort required to combine all these technologies is still a barrier preventing a wider adoption. In this paper, we present TACTIC, an API combining touch surfaces, tangibles, and the interaction space above the surface, in a way that allows developers to easily combine all these features, and distribute interfaces across multiple devices if required. Additionally, we present the results of a developer study showing how TACTIC is easy to learn and use.

Author Keywords
API; touch interaction; tangible interfaces; continuous interaction space; distributed interfaces; mobile devices.

ACM Classification Keywords
H.5.2. Information Interfaces and Presentation (e.g. HCI): User Interfaces; D.2.2. Software Engineering: Design Tools and Techniques

INTRODUCTION
Interactive surfaces are becoming common, mainly through the dissemination of smartphones and tablets, but larger interactive surfaces should not be dismissed. In the latter segment, the initial research efforts have paved the way to current commercial products. From the likes of DiamondTouch [4], a front-projected interactive display supporting multiple users capable of identifying which person is touching where, through TouchLight [14], with its ability to display 2D images of objects placed on the screen and supporting non-collocated interaction, or the Reactable [7] combining an interactive surface with a tangible user interface, we have arrived at matured products like the Microsoft PixelSense[1] (formerly know as Microsoft Surface), a platform combining software and hardware components that allows its users to use touch and real world objects, in a digital content sharing context. Additional research efforts have tried to complement the combination of interactive surfaces and tangible user interfaces with the possibility to use the continuous interaction space [6, 15, 10] located above the table surface. These efforts become more significant when it is now possible to take advantage of available hardware, such as Microsoft Kinect or Leap Motion, to build such interactive environments [12].

[1] http://www.microsoft.com/en-us/pixelsense/

TEI '15, January 16 - 19 2015, Stanford, CA, USA

http://dx.doi.org/10.1145/2677199.2680592

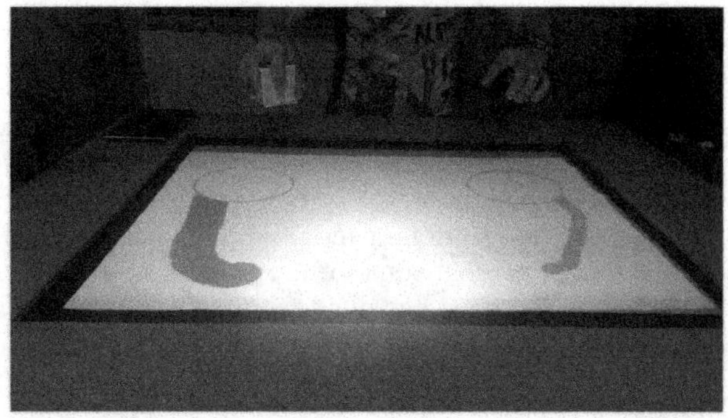

Figure 1. Objects being tracked above the surface maintaining object ID and hand distinction

The availability of hardware and software supporting interactive surfaces, mid-air gesture and object recognition above the surface, and tangible user interfaces, create exciting opportunities both for interaction research and development efforts. However, these are still impaired by the complexity in making all the components of such platforms communicate and exchange information with each other. Furthermore, having the information from each platform available in a common programming environment is another limiting factor that prevents a wider exploration of the interaction possibilities made available by these platforms.

In this paper we present an API that addresses the aforementioned limitations. TACTIC is an API supporting the exchange of information between interactive surfaces, mid-air hand and object recognition and tracking services, and tangible interfaces (Figure 1). TACTIC was developed to be used in web applications, thus being accessible to what is probably the most pervasive environment currently. Being used in a browser, it can be deployed in an interactive touch table or a smartphone. It can recognize and track tangibles on and over the interactive surface, and if these are capable of executing in a browser, it can exchange information between the tangible object and the other interactive elements connected.

To validate the proposed API we conducted a developer study, asking experienced web developers, who were not familiar with touch surfaces or tangible interaction to develop a web based painting application, that explored different combinations of touch, gesture, tangible and distributed interfaces. Study results demonstrate the API to be easy to understand and use, contributing to an efficient development work.

In the remainder of the paper, after the discussion of related work, we describe the TACTIC API, detailing its architecture and introducing its objects and events. We then present a group of sample applications to illustrate how the API can be used to build complex applications. Afterwards, we describe the developer study and discuss its results. We conclude with a discussion of the overall features of the API and the possibilities for expansion.

RELATED WORK

In recent years we have seen a proliferation of research exploring the continuous interaction space consisting of interactive surfaces and the area above them. Similar efforts were made regarding tangible interaction. Some of these works have led to the creation of APIs providing mechanisms to help developers in the creation of interactive applications. In this section we will present some of these APIs as well as other works that would have benefited from an existing API such as TACTIC.

Existing APIs

HapticTouch framework [8] allows the creation of haptic tabletop applications. While computers typically handle feedback through visual and auditory modalities, haptic interfaces give tactile feedback to users. HapticTouch has a component responsible for providing haptic feedback called Haptic Tabletop Puck (HTP), which is a tangible device with a fiducial marker indicating its position on the table. The puck changes its behaviour depending on its position. This framework allows developers to create different ways of transmitting haptic feedback and to complement visual components with haptic behaviours.

Interactive space [9] is a framework that allows programmers to develop multi-touch and gesture based applications. Similar to our API, this framework does gesture recognition through a Microsoft Kinect above the interactive surface. This framework uses the OmniTouch approach as a solution to gesture recognition. This approach can generate false positives and also has directional limitations, such as fingers only being detected while in a vertical or horizontal position.

Cross-device sharing of data allows developers to create applications that share the user interface between multiple devices. In [17], [5] and [16] three frameworks that help programmers in the development of distributed user interfaces are presented. Using Panelrama programmers have an easy way to create cross-device web applications. Their solution is to categorize device properties and dynamically optimize the user interface to these devices [17]. Similarly, the ROSS API [16] allows applications to exchange information regarding the devices they are running on and also to receive input from other devices. TACTIC also allows to distribute interfaces across devices although in a manner not as advanced the ones described in [17] and [16]. However, TACTIC gives support to interactions not possible with Panelrama or ROSS, such as tangible and above the table interactions.

Interactive surface applications

Many interactive surface applications are developed to promote collaboration among users. One example is T-Vote [11], a decision making collaborative application working on a tabletop and using tangible objects. The main goal of T-Vote is to promote collaboration among children and shared interests between them. These interests are related with a museum context.

In [13] a new interaction style that expands across mobile devices and interaction surfaces is explored to support natural interactions. To illustrate this a number of applications are proposed, ranging from a word game that allows users to assemble letters on their phone and drop them onto the shared word board. A calendar application allows users to share their calendar by tapping the surface, while the application is open on the phone.

These works would benefit from TACTIC since it could considerably reduce development time as we will show in the following sections.

TACTIC API

TACTIC (Tangible and Tabletop Continuous Interaction) is an API that supports development of web applications with touch, tangible and above the surface gestures. The API abstracts TUIO [3] protocol and mobile browser touch events making it easy to develop applications with existing technologies and setups. The RabbitMQ[2] messaging middleware, which is included in our system architecture, adds modularity allowing communication between any components (see Figure 2). Any set-up component can use RabbitMQ to publish and subscribe to events, bridging different technologies and languages. This makes it easy to add new components to your system without making changes to previous configurations.

TACTIC abstracts touch events allowing tabletop applications to run on mobile devices without the need to add or change any line of code.

A node.js module is included for communication between applications. This enables easy development of distributed interfaces. All of the information exchange is intended for use on a local network, therefore no delay is expected in any of the message exchanges.

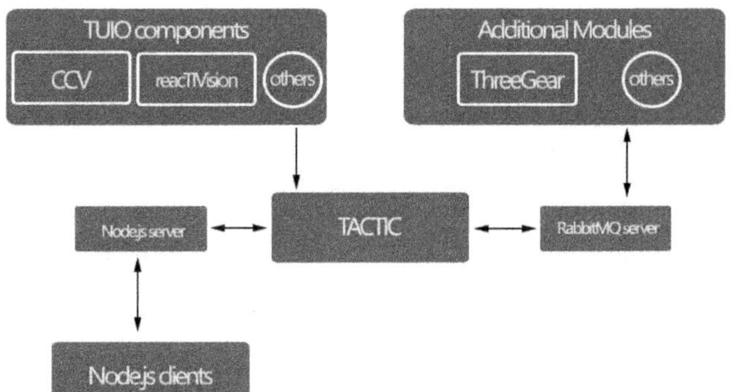

Figure 2. API underlying components and message exchanging protocols

[2] http://www.rabbitmq.com

object_added object_updated object_removed	Events triggered whenever an object **enters**, **moves** or **leaves** the surface
object.added object.updated object.removed	Events triggered whenever an object **enters**, **moves** or **leaves** an element that is expecting this event
touch.press	Event triggered whenever a **touch** is tracked **inside** an element that is expecting this event
touch.update	Event triggered whenever a **touch** already being tracked **moves** inside an element that is expecting this event
touch.release	Event triggered whenever a **touch** is **no longer** tracked inside an element that is expecting this event

Table 1. API Events

object_hovering	Event triggered when an object is **lifted** from the surface and while **moving** above it
hand_pinched	Event triggered when a hand makes a **Pinch** gesture
hand_unpinched	Event triggered when a hand unmakes a **Pinch** gesture
hand_moved	Event triggered while hand is detected detailing position
fingers_moved	Event triggered while hand is detected detailing each finger's position and ID

Table 2. ThreeGear exclusive Events

Events

The API is fully implemented in JavaScript to support building HTML client applications. It does all the heavy lifting while providing users with abstract events that contain the information needed. All of the API events will be detailed in tables 1 and 2.

The events shown in table 1 relate to on the surface interactions, while events in table 2 relate to above the surface interactions. Table 1 events are always available as part of the API. Table 2 events are only available when using a ThreeGear[3] based set-up and the jar file made available with the API[4].

Element Properties

Some properties can be easily attached to HTML elements by adding the respective CSS class to them. This way the API saves the user the trouble of making extra calculations. Next we detail a set of classes that can be added to elements and the properties they receive:

- **movable** A movable element is automatically moved by the API whenever a touch is registered inside it and movement follows. When the touch is released the element stays in the new position.
- **resizable** A resizable element is automatically resized by the API when two touches are registered inside it at the same time, followed by movement from both touches causing a pinch gesture.
- **rotatable** A rotatable element is automatically rotated by the API when two touches are registered inside it at the same time, followed by a rotation gesture in any direction.
- **resizable_above** A resizable_above element is automatically resized when a Pinch gesture is tracked above it followed by an upward or downward motion.
- **rotatable_above** A rotatable_above element is automatically rotated when an open hand is detected above it followed by a rotation motion to the right or left.
- **touchable** A touchable element receives events related to touch inside the area that corresponds to it, and can then respond to those events (**touch.press**; **touch.update**; **touch.release**) in whatever way the user wishes.
- **object-aware** An object-aware element receives events related to object tracking inside the area that corresponds to it and can then respond to those events (**object.added**; **object.updated**; **object.removed**) in whatever way the user wishes.

How does it work?

Events can be bound to elements to add functions to specific situations throughout the code. For example, if the user wishes to make an element aware to touch events the only requirement is for the element to have the class *touchable*.

```
<div class='button touchable'></div>
```

Elements that are *touchable* will receive **touch.press**, **touch.update** and **touch.release** events. These events can be handled by binding the element to the event and adding a function that works as the event handler. Events also have data associated to them. Touch events have the following data: X and Y coordinates; Hand and Finger. Object events have the following data: X and Y coordinates; ID; Angle. *object_hovering* event details: X, Y and Z coordinates; Hand holding the object; Object ID. *hand_moved*, *hand_pinched* and *hand_unpinched* have the following data: X, Y and Z coordinates and Hand. *fingers_moved* details: X, Y and Z coordinates of each finger for both hands. In case TACTIC is used on a set-up that does not support above the table interactions all Hand and Finger related data is returned as undefined allowing the API to work without any problems.

The following code could produce "Pressed at 300,200 with hand RIGHT and finger INDEX".

```
$('.button').bind('touch.press',
                 function(event, data) {
    alert('Pressed at '
```

[3]http://www.threegear.com/technology.html
[4]http://accessible-serv.lasige.di.fc.ul.pt/~tactic/

```
            + data.x + ',' + data.y
            + ' with hand ' + data.hand
            + ' and finger ' + data.finger);
});
```

The integrated node.js component allows users to send and receive messages between web applications easily without having to initiate any variables or messaging protocols. These messages can be sent in a network environment allowing applications to communicate in a cross-device setting. The following code shows how to subscribe to messages and how to send them.

```
socket.on('message', function(msg){
        console.log(msg);
});

socket.emit('message', 'hello');
```

Finally, the RabbitMQ messaging framework allows communication between different technologies and languages making it easy to add new modules to an application. Users can send information back and forth from other languages such as Java or Python to their Web applications with the following commands.

```
// Subscribing to data (example)

MQ.queue('auto',{autoDelete:true}).bind(
        'handInfo', '*').callback(
    function(m) {
            console.log(m.data);
    });

// Publishing data (example)

MQ.topic('handInfo').publish({
        //...
        //place object here
        //...
}, 'app.finish');
```

SAMPLE APPLICATIONS

We developed a set of applications in order to display some of TACTIC's capabilities ranging from multiple types of interactions and interfaces.

To test these applications we used a set-up (Figure 3) that is similar to the one presented in [12]. This set-up uses Frustrated Total Internal Reflection (FTIR) [1] to allow detection of touch input from a camera inside the table. Tangibles are tracked through fiducial markers that are identified by *reacTIVision* [2] on a second camera, also inside the table. Both of these inputs are translated into TUIO [3] protocol messages for the API to interpret. Above the surface gestures are detected using ThreeGear [**?**] which can track fingers and hands using one Kinect camera above the table.

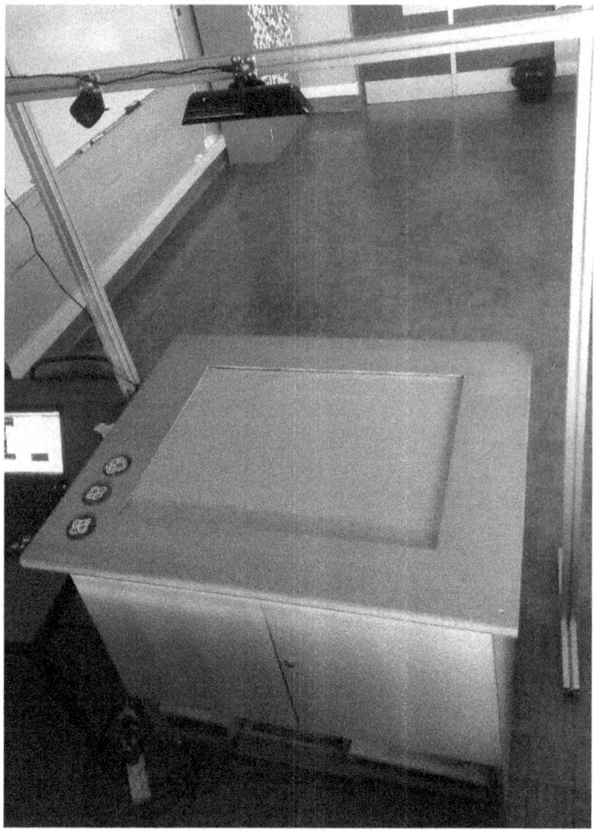

Figure 3. Set-up with two cameras inside allowing touch and tangible interaction. Kinect camera installed above to allow gesture detection above the surface

Our first sample application shows how to use TACTIC's classes and events to quickly build a functional touch application. The page's body is made of a single DIV element. By adding the **touchable** class this element is able to receive touch events. By binding a function that changes the color of the element to yellow when receiving **touch.press** (Figure 4) and another to change it back to red when receiving **touch.release**, the application gives us actual touch feedback for touches. We also add other classes to the DIV to make it react to gestures. By adding **movable**, **resizable** and **rotatable** to the DIV class, it will automatically respond to single touch dragging by moving with the finger, as well as Pinch gestures for resizing and Rotation gestures for rotating.

For our second sample application we wanted to demonstrate some of TACTIC's tangible events. We developed an object scanner for tangibles, showing feedback for each object as it is identified. Again a single DIV is placed on the page and the **object-aware** class is added to it so that it can receive tangible events. We bind a function that displays the object ID on the screen to the **object.added** event. The object ID number is matched with a previously set list of real objects to provide a textual feedback of the object. We also bind the **object.updated** event to a function that increases or decreases the text size on the screen depending on the object's angle of rotation, causing it to change in real time as the object rotates as shown in Figure 5.

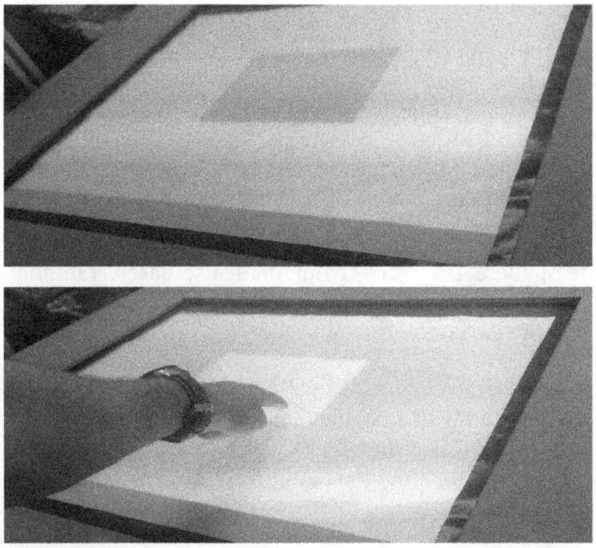

Figure 4. Upper image showing touchable element; lower image showing touchable element being pressed

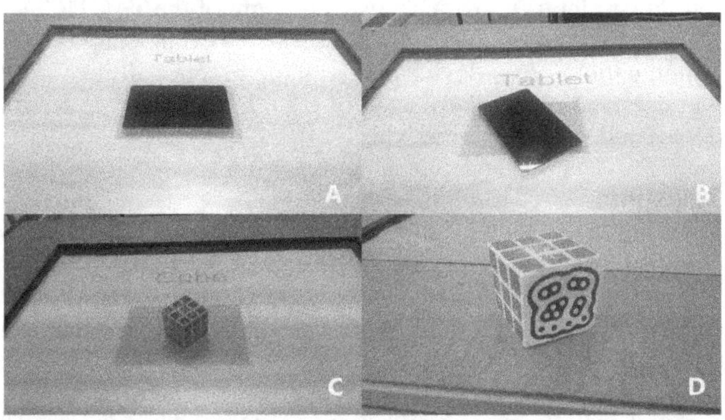

Figure 5. (A) Tablet recognized in application; (B) Tablet rotation increases text; (C) Cube being recognized in application; (D) Fiducial marker on Cube

In order to show how TACTIC keeps track of objects above the surface, our third application allows objects to paint while hovering, with a specific color assigned to each object and a specific size brush assigned to each hand. To achieve this, a canvas is created in the page's body. The canvas is bound to the **object_hovering** event, which triggers from the moment an object is lifted from the table surface and continues to trigger until it leaves the area or returns to the surface. This event contains information regarding which hand is holding which object and it can detect when the hand holding the object changes. In the bound function a set of clauses determines that if the hand holding the object is the right one, then the paint brush will be thick and if not then it will be thin. Objects are assigned colors, making the current color red for the phone and blue for the cube (Figure 6).

Finally to show TACTIC's communication capabilities and easy cross device coding we developed a table application that has random objects spread out on the surface. Mobile devices can drop on top of them and "steal" them into their screen. The user can then drop them again on the table surface, while hovering, with a touch on the phone screen. A second smart device can also come near the other device and "steal" the element from it. Three elements are randomly generated and all have the class **object-aware** in order to receive the **object.added** event when an object enters them. When this occurs the element information is sent to the page associated with the tangible ID which will be waiting for messages on the smart device. When the smart device has an element inside it, it starts to scout for other nearby objects using the **object_hovering** event. If another object gets close to it, the element is sent to that smart device's page since it is also waiting for messages. At any given time a hovering smart device can be touched, triggering a **touch.press** event to send an element inside it to the hovering position on the table (Figure 7).

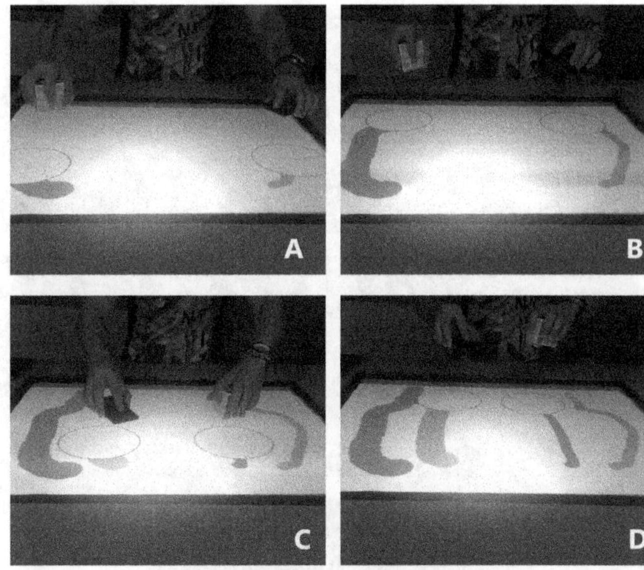

Figure 6. (A) Cube and Phone being tracked above; (B) Cube paints with blue, phone paints with red; (C) When changing hands, color is switched accordingly; (D) Brush size remains correct for each hand, big for right hand, small for left hand

DEVELOPER STUDY

A developer study was conducted to investigate ease of learning and use of the TACTIC API. In this section we describe the study followed by a discussion of its results.

Participants

Five participants were chosen (1 female, 4 male) between ages of 22 and 27 to test our API by developing a test application. All participants were experienced web developers (at least 3 years of experience). From the pool of projects all participants were involved during the last year, a total of 7 projects dealt specifically with mobile web applications. Just a single project included touch interaction that did not directly relate with mobile devices. No project involved tangible interfaces.

Tasks

Participants were tasked with developing applications that would require knowledge of different aspects of the API as

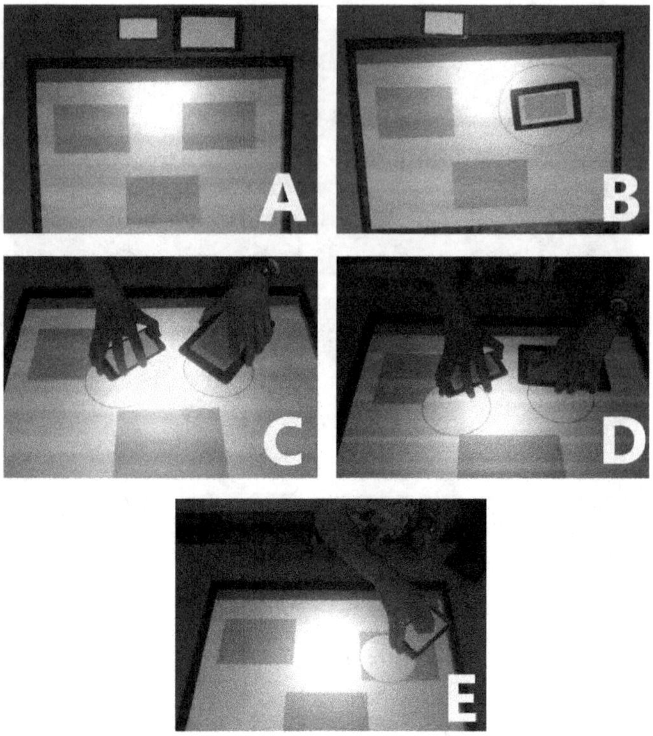

Figure 7. (A) Application with 3 elements; (B) Tablet is placed on top of element capturing it; (C) Tablet and phone being tracked above; (D) Tablet and Phone proximity caused the element to be sent from one to the other; (E) Phone being tracked above is touched, causing the object to return to the table below it

well as a few JavaScript and CSS basics. Our purpose was to understand how easily and fast users could build complex applications using TACTIC. To achieve this, users were tasked with developing a painting application that would incrementally gain complexity as well as use more API functionalities.

Task 1 - Build an HTML page that displays 3 buttons representing the colors Red, Green and Blue and 3 buttons representing Small, Medium and Big brush size. This task was designed to get users to build a standard HTML page with no required API functionality, which will allow them to work on their own code through the next tasks.

Task 2 - Add touch functionality to the previous page to build a paint application. By touching the color buttons a new color is chosen, and by touching the size buttons the size of the brush is chosen. By touching any other area, the canvas is painted with the chosen brush color and size. The goal of this task is to understand how users adapt existing pages to the API and how they use its touch events.

Task 3 - Add tangible functionality to the previous page so that all previous interactions can be done with objects as well. We wanted to study how users used tangible events and how the API promotes code recycling.

Task 4 - Add above the table interactions, requiring painting to be done above the table exclusively. This allowed us to study how users used above the table events and further understand patterns of code reuse.

Task 5 - Add cross-device functionalities building a new mobile application. When a color is chosen, it is sent to the smartphone page changing its background color and painting above is only done while touching the smartphone's screen. We wanted to study how users employed the node.js communication component to build cross-device applications, as well as the abstraction of touch events for both mobile and tabletop settings.

All of these tasks cover our main use cases, ranging from touch, tangibles, above the surface object manipulation and cross-device communication.

Procedure

Trials started with a profile questionnaire. After the questionnaire, a brief overview of the API would follow explaining the basics of the documentation and how everything worked. Next users were asked to do each one of the tasks, while task duration and written code were stored. Users had access to the API's documentation website at all times during trials.

When all tasks were completed, another questionnaire would follow to let us know what users thought of the TACTIC API. Users were asked to express how easy the event, classes, communication, cross-device and tangible functionalities were to understand on a Likert scale of 0 to 9, with 0 being terribly hard and 9 being perfectly easy.

Results

During the trials we collected the time to complete each task and snapshots of the code at the end of each task. Developers took an average of 14.3 minutes to complete the first task (SD=2.8 minutes). The second task, the first one requiring the use of the API, was completed on average in 8.3 minutes (SD=1.7 minutes). The third task was quicker, being completed in 2.9 minutes on average (SD=30.8 seconds). The fourth task was the quickest one, completed in 37.7 seconds on average (SD=23.6 seconds). The fifth and final task, which introduced a mobile device to the application, was completed in 6.4 minutes on average (SD=1.8 minutes).

In what regards the analysis of the code written, we have analyzed how many lines were changed and how many new lines were written between each task. The analysis considers all HTML, CSS and JavaScript files produced. For the initial task, developers wrote on average 63 lines of code. The second task asked developers to include the API in their page, and to perform the painting through touch. This resulted, on average, on 76 new and 6 changed lines of code. The new lines were mainly responsible for performing the painting. The changed lines introduce the touchable behaviour in existing page elements. For the third task, developers were required to introduce tangibles for painting. All developers changed exactly 14 lines of code in this task, without any further changes. In the fourth task, the painting needed to be performed through gestures above the table instead of touching. This was achieved by all developers with the introduction of a single line of code, and a change in another line of code. Finally, the last task introduced a mobile device to control the painting. This lead developers to write an average of 9 new lines of code for the page that was being displayed on

Feature	Average (Standard Deviation)
Events	8.2 (0.84)
Classes	8.4 (0.55)
Communication	8.6 (0.55)
Cross-platform	8.2 (0.84)
Tangibles	8.2 (0.84)

Table 3. Average and standard deviation of the questionnaire results from a scale of 1 to 9.

the interactive table, and a page to be displayed on the mobile device with 45 lines of code on average.

After completing the tasks, trial participants completed a questionnaire about how easy it was to understand and use the TACTIC API. We asked them classify the API's events and classes, and the API's support for communication, cross-platform development and tangible interaction. The results are summarized in table 3.

As can be seen from the results, the developer's impressions are overwhelmingly positive. Additionally we collected their opinions after the trials, which support these results. All developers expressed their happiness with how much they were able to achieve in such a short time (the longest session - D3 - took less than 40 minutes). Additionally, all participants pointed out as a positive point the fact that to use the API they were not required to learn something specific regarding the technology used to support touch, object recognition and tracking, or tangibles, and they could rely on their existing JavaScript and jQuery knowledge. Other positive factors mentioned include the intuitiveness of the names of events and classes (D2), the ease of use of the API (D2, D4 and D5) and the small amount of time required to learn it (D4).

Discussion

The user trials aimed to assess the ease of learning and use of the TACTIC API. We asked a group of experienced Web developers to incrementally build a painting application. In each iteration they were requested to incorporate further features of the API. By analyzing the written code, and through conversations with the developers, we got a better understanding of their performance in the trials.

Tasks 1 and 2 comprised building the main blocks of the painting application, which justifies their being the longest ones. In these tasks, developers had to build the elements to select brush color and size, and the code to do the painting. The API was used solely in task 2 to endow the HTML canvas and button elements with touchable behaviour.

From task 3 onwards, we expected to see the benefits of the API. In task 3, developers were asked to replace usage of touch by interaction through tangibles. Results for this task demonstrate that developers understood how to use the framework. All developers did the same thing in this step, which was simply to change the event and binding that was attached to each interactive element (6 buttons and the canvas), resulting in 14 changes to their code. This reveals they understood the way of using the framework, and furthermore, it did not take them too long to do so. On average they took under three minutes.

Task 4 asked to replace the interaction on the tabletop with interaction above the table. The fact that the longest it took one participant to complete it was 64 seconds, reveals that by this point all developers had fully grasped the API grounding concepts, and could very easily and quickly apply them. Once more, they all performed the same actions: introduced one line to start using the ability to track objects above the table, and changed one event processing line to begin responding to object hovering events.

The final task included distributing the application to another device. A mobile device was now used to control when the painting was performed, which meant the operation of the mobile device had to be communicated to the table application responsible for painting on the interactive surface. This task implied changes to the HTML page loaded on the table's browser, and the creation of a new HTML page to be loaded on the mobile's browser. Changes to the table's page were small (under 10 lines of code on average). All the changes and new code were completed in about 6 minutes, which is another sign that the API's way of operating had been well understood by this point.

Overall, from the analysis of the code and the questionnaires, the API proved to be easy to understand and use. It promoted code reuse, and enabled developers without experience with tangible interaction, distributed interfaces and object tracking, to incorporate those features in their Web applications.

TACTIC'S LIMITATIONS

Here we discuss some of our API's limitations. Browser events have been integrated into the API. However for touch enabled devices, that do not process touch input through TUIO, these events are currently ignored by the browser's own handling of input. For example, our **movable** class, along with some others, does not work on mobile browsers, since when a user moves his finger, the input is handled towards moving the page itself and does not reach our API in a way that we can handle coordinates to move the **movable** element.

Additionally, although RabbitMQ adds to our API's modularity by easily bridging different technologies, it requires users to learn an additional API to connect whatever technology they have before hand. We have been working towards passing most of the communication responsibilities to our node.js module and, ideally, we would like to dismiss RabbitMQ in favour of node.js in the future.

We also have a limited number of currently supported gestures. Our API supports *Pinch* gestures (**hand_pinched**, **hand_unpinched**, **resizable_above** class) and a Rotation gesture for the **rotatable_above** class. But it is possible for users to create their own gestures through our **hand_moved** and **fingers_moved** events, which detail the same raw data that our API receives. This means that developers can create and handle new gestures by having access to the same information we had when developing our own gestures and events. We hope this will bring more content to our API and help it grow to support more events and gestures.

CONCLUSIONS

In this paper we have presented TACTIC, an API supporting the development of web applications aware of touch events, object recognition and tracking on and above interactive surfaces, and tangible interfaces. TACTIC supports the abstraction of touch events, thus enabling the same code base to be used in interactive tables and mobile devices. TACTIC allows easily enabling digital objects with interactive behaviours, such as rotatable, resizeable and moveable, removing the need for the developer to do the back-end processing required for these behaviours. Additionally, TACTIC makes available gesture information, such as which hand and finger are being used, as part of touch and tangible events.

We have demonstrated TACTIC features through a set of proof of concept applications, and assessed its ease of learning and use through a study with five experienced web developers. Developers found TACTIC's concepts easy to grasp and use, and were able to build a web based painting application including touch interaction, tangible interaction, above the table gesture recognition, and distributing the interface of the application across an interactive touch table and a mobile device. Even without being familiar with any of these technologies, developers were capable of concluding their tasks in a short amount of time. This was possible by quickly learning to use the API, and by taking advantage of the code reuse features that TACTIC promotes.

REFERENCES

1. Frustrated total internal reflection. `http://wiki.nuigroup.com/FTIR#Links:`, Dec 2013.
2. A toolkit for tangible multi-touch surfaces. `http://reactivision.sourceforge.net/`, Dec 2013.
3. Tuio 1.1 protocol specification. `http://www.tuio.org/?specification`, Dec 2013.
4. Dietz, P., and Leigh, D. Diamondtouch: A multi-user touch technology. In *Proceedings of the 14th Annual ACM Symposium on User Interface Software and Technology*, UIST '01, ACM (New York, NY, USA, 2001), 219–226.
5. Hamilton, P., and Wigdor, D. J. Conductor: Enabling and understanding cross-device interaction. In *Proceedings of the SIGCHI Conference on Human Factors in Computing Systems*, CHI '14, ACM (New York, NY, USA, 2014), 2773–2782.
6. Hilliges, O., Izadi, S., Wilson, A. D., Hodges, S., Garcia-Mendoza, A., and Butz, A. Interactions in the air: Adding further depth to interactive tabletops. In *Proceedings of the 22Nd Annual ACM Symposium on User Interface Software and Technology*, UIST '09, ACM (New York, NY, USA, 2009), 139–148.
7. Jordà, S., Geiger, G., Alonso, M., and Kaltenbrunner, M. The reactable: Exploring the synergy between live music performance and tabletop tangible interfaces. In *Proceedings of the 1st International Conference on Tangible and Embedded Interaction*, TEI '07, ACM (New York, NY, USA, 2007), 139–146.
8. Ledo, D., Nacenta, M. A., Marquardt, N., Boring, S., and Greenberg, S. The haptictouch toolkit: Enabling exploration of haptic interactions. In *Proceedings of the Sixth International Conference on Tangible, Embedded and Embodied Interaction*, TEI '12, ACM (New York, NY, USA, 2012), 115–122.
9. Liu, Y., Weibel, N., and Hollan, J. D. Interactive space: A prototyping framework for touch and gesture on and above the desktop. In *CHI '13 Extended Abstracts on Human Factors in Computing Systems*, CHI EA '13, ACM (New York, NY, USA, 2013), 1233–1238.
10. Marquardt, N., Jota, R., Greenberg, S., and Jorge, J. A. The continuous interaction space: Interaction techniques unifying touch and gesture on and above a digital surface. In *Proceedings of the 13th IFIP TC 13 International Conference on Human-computer Interaction - Volume Part III*, INTERACT'11, Springer-Verlag (Berlin, Heidelberg, 2011), 461–476.
11. McCrindle, C., Hornecker, E., Lingnau, A., and Rick, J. The design of t-vote: A tangible tabletop application supporting children's decision making. In *Proceedings of the 10th International Conference on Interaction Design and Children*, IDC '11, ACM (New York, NY, USA, 2011), 181–184.
12. Nunes, R., Stanchenko, N., and Duarte, C. Combining multi-touch surfaces and tangible interaction towards a continuous interaction space. In *Proceedings of the 3rd Workshop on Interacting with Smart Objects* (2014), 1114.
13. Schmidt, D., Seifert, J., Rukzio, E., and Gellersen, H. A cross-device interaction style for mobiles and surfaces. In *Proceedings of the Designing Interactive Systems Conference*, DIS '12, ACM (New York, NY, USA, 2012), 318–327.
14. Wilson, A. D. Touchlight: An imaging touch screen and display for gesture-based interaction. In *Proceedings of the 6th International Conference on Multimodal Interfaces*, ICMI '04, ACM (New York, NY, USA, 2004), 69–76.
15. Wilson, A. D., and Benko, H. Combining multiple depth cameras and projectors for interactions on, above and between surfaces. In *Proceedings of the 23Nd Annual ACM Symposium on User Interface Software and Technology*, UIST '10, ACM (New York, NY, USA, 2010), 273–282.
16. Wu, A., Mendenhall, S., Jog, J., Hoag, L. S., and Mazalek, A. A nested api structure to simplify cross-device communication. In *Proceedings of the Sixth International Conference on Tangible, Embedded and Embodied Interaction*, TEI '12, ACM (New York, NY, USA, 2012), 225–232.
17. Yang, J., and Wigdor, D. Panelrama: Enabling easy specification of cross-device web applications. In *Proceedings of the SIGCHI Conference on Human Factors in Computing Systems*, CHI '14, ACM (New York, NY, USA, 2014), 2783–2792.

WoodenHaptics: A Starting Kit for Crafting Force-Reflecting Spatial Haptic Devices

Jonas Forsslund
Royal Institute of Technology
Stockholm, Sweden
jofo02@kth.se

Michael Yip
Stanford University
Stanford, CA, USA
mcyip@stanford.edu

Eva-Lotta Sallnäs
Royal Institute of Technology
Stockholm, Sweden
evalotta@kth.se

ABSTRACT
Spatial haptic interfaces have been around for 20 years. Yet, few affordable devices have been produced, and the design space in terms of physical workspace and haptic fidelity of devices that have been produced are limited and discrete. In this paper, an open-source, open-hardware module-based kit is presented that allows an interaction designer with little electro-mechanical experience to manufacture and assemble a fully working spatial haptic interface. It also allows for modification in shape and size as well as tuning of parameters to fit a particular task or application. Results from an evaluation showed that the haptic quality of the WoodenHaptics device was on par with a Phantom Desktop and that a novice could assemble it with guidance in a normal office space. This open source starting kit, uploaded free-to-download online, affords *sketching in hardware*; it "unsticks" the hardware from being a highly-specialized and esoteric craft to being an accessible and user-friendly technology, while maintaining the feel of high-fidelity haptics.

Figure 1. The completed wooden haptics device.

Author Keywords
Guides; do-it-yourself; open-source; open-hardware; spatial haptics; force-feedback; haptic device; hardware sketching; interaction design

ACM Classification Keywords
H.5.2. Information Interfaces and Presentation (e.g. HCI): User Interfaces (D.2.2, H.1.2, I.3.6) Haptic I/O

PART I: INTRODUCTION
Spatial haptic interfaces are grounded human interface devices that track a physical manipulandum (handle) in space, and provides the means of reflecting a directional force on that manipulandum and consequently the user. With the device and appropriate haptic rendering algorithms, an end-user can explore a virtual environment through virtual coupling between the manipulandum's position and a representative avatar [24]. As more applications have 3D user interfaces [1], spatial haptics becomes increasingly useful for feeling the shapes of occluded objects, collisions, object stiffness and inertias, surface textures, and so on [24]. While vibrotactile haptics are ubiquitous in all cellular phones, the 3D force-displaying counterparts, spatial haptics, are not as widely present. Devices for spatial haptics have been used for surgical simulation [3], physical rehabilitation [2] and for hand tool guidance [9]. Applications in other domains could benefit from including spatial haptics, but this requires finding a good match between the qualities of the device employed and the application. The common devices commercially available (Figure 2) represent only a limited design space in terms of fidelity, price and capabilities (e.g. workspace dimensions and maximum force). Therefore, application specific devices have sometimes been developed, such as for simulation of micro-surgical bone drilling [22]. However, engineering a haptic device is still a large commitment and only feasible in highly specialized robotics labs that have the mathematical and mechanical know-how to realize and achieve high quality haptics in their design.

Research and advances in haptics tend to be focused on technological refinements and little attention is directed towards holistic design and aestetics of the devices. As a response to this, Moussette has proposed the intersection of Design and Haptics as a new field of study [17]. This approach is centered around hands-on workshops [16], exploration, making and sketching in hardware with simple haptics [18] in order to get a heightened sensitivity to haptics. The benefits that follow from this approach can be extended to spatial haptics.

TEI 2015, January 15–19, 2015, Stanford, California, USA.

ACM 978-1-4503-3305-4/15/01 ...$15.00.
http://dx.doi.org/10.1145/2677199.2680595

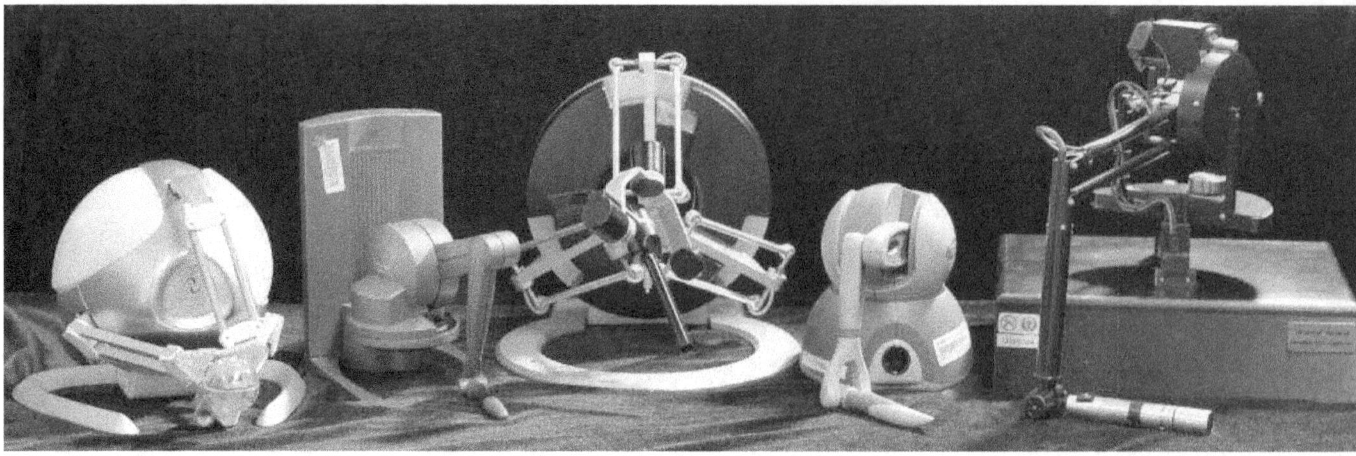

Figure 2. Common spatial haptic devices. From the left: Novint Falcon, Phantom Desktop (now 3D Systems Geomagic Touch X), Force Dimension Omega, Phantom Omni (now 3D Systems Geomagic Touch), and Phantom Premium 6-DOF (now 3D Systems Geomagic Phantom Premium).

In this paper we introduce a new spatial haptic device that is designed and packaged as a kit in a way that a designer can reconfigure or re-design it, thus adapting it to different domains or requirements. This kit, called WoodenHaptics, is designed to provide comparable haptic fidelity to commercial devices. We carefully chose to encapsulate certain technical details (e.g. the electrical system), whereas others are very visible (the mechanical structure and wire rope power transmission); this is intended to help designers focus more on designing for their application rather than problem solving through mechanical and electrical nuances and details. Through these efforts we have reduced the "stickiness" [29] of constructing spatial haptic devices to a level where a designer can design, create, assemble and modify their own version of the device. We evaluated its ease of adoption on non-specialists and first-time builders (under guidance) to show that it provides a valuable medium for "hardware sketching" in spatial haptics.

The experience of building and interacting with different motors, size of workspace, etc. greatly contributed to our own understanding of how the "material" of spatial haptics behave and the flexibility and limitations in which spatial haptic design are confined to. To promote this, the starting kit is described and released as open-source hardware with free parts lists, drawings, software and assembly guides for personal fabrication at `www.woodenhaptics.org`.

Background

With the advent of Massie's [10] force-reflecting device in 1993, spatial haptics as a multi-purpose human-computer interaction interface became popular through the commercialized Phantom series [11] still available on the market today (figure 2). While all these devices can read a spatial position and render a directional force back to the user through the manipulandum, the experience and quality of the forces/movement is quite different, something that is also reflected in the price tag that ranges from $300 to over $20,000 USD. Other devices with equivalent functionality from the user's perspective have since appeared, but the market is far from being as diverse as that of computer mice and joysticks.

A great deal of fundamental theory for building a haptic device has been described in e.g. [7] and [6]. However, bridging the gap from reading the fundamentals to constructing a fully-functional 3D spatial haptic device of the prototypical Phantom [10, 11] is still a daunting task to a common interaction designer and is only feasible for an expert roboticist. Much practical and tacit knowledge is required to actually make a high-fidelity haptic device, since it relates to making a correct combination of design choices, ranging from which type of motors, what mechanical structure, which control paradigm and even which type of screws to choose. Then the parts need to be located and purchased, which can be very time-consuming and confusing. Furthermore, the robotics literature describing the mathematics required to operate the haptic device [7, 4] might be overwhelming in scope and content to the electro-mechanical novice.

Kits and Tools for Design

Kits and tools for design through making and crafting is an active research area in TEI/HCI [5, 8, 13, 14, 25, 26]. Phidgets [5] is used to simplify development of physical interfaces through providing "everyday programmers" with a kit of pre-made electronic physical widgets. Toolkits have been described as particularily instrumental to sketching in hardware [19]. Software tools have been developed explicitly targeting designers without production training in electronics [8] and furniture design [26]. Even the notion of an "untoolkit" has been proposed as a conceptual tool to leverage existing standard materials and components in new artifacts [14]. Open source hardware designed for personal fabrication has been described as an approach to support design of different aspects of electronic products, since the designer only has to modify those parts of the design pertinent to the designers interest and still get a working product [13]. Other kits such as the Hapkit [15] is constructed with goal of teaching engineering concepts per se through hands-on experience [21, 27].

In this paper, WoodenHaptics is presented as an open source "starting kit" for material exploration, design and realization of application specific force reflecting haptic devices. This distinguishes our kit from a toolkit where combinations of

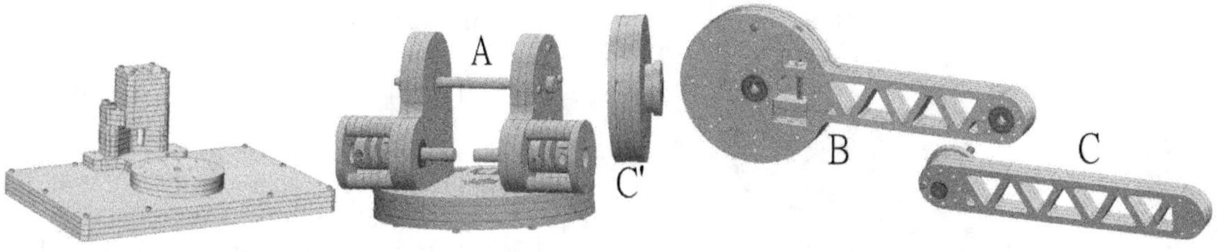

Figure 3. The parts needed to be assembled by user: the base driving the body A, that in turn drives body B and, indirectly through C', body C.

provided parts yield many designs (we only provide one reference design in the kit itself), and an untoolkit where none of the modules from the kit goes into the final design. The intended audiences for the kit are interaction design studios and HCI researchers, especially for cases where applications require different form factors (e.g. length of arms), and other properties (e.g. maximum force) that off-the-shelf devices won't meet, something we in our own practice have seen a need for. Our primary aim is to support professional design exploration of the interaction qualities that follows from modifications of the reference design. A high-quality spatial haptic interface requires careful attention to its computational and physical materials, which can *only* be experienced as a whole with a fully assembled device. Therefore, a designer who decides to deepen her engagement beyond software will have to set up a workbench for explorations. WoodenHaptics serves as a complete kit for starting such explorations.

PART II: KIT DESCRIPTION AND USAGE

A pair of interaction design researchers without training in mechanical engineering were provided with the kit consisting of a complete set of hardware components that make up a full spatial haptic device. This included all the pre-cut plywood parts, screws, bearings and all other mechanical components (Figure 4). The kit came with three motors (Maxon RE40) with pre-mounted encoders, and an electronics box (Figure 5) that connects to a 48V lab power supply and a standard PC equipped with a Data Acquisition interface (DAQ, Sensoray S826). The kit requires only a limited set of tools: hex keys, a steel wire crimping tool and snippers, a torch and an arbor press (Figure 8); a list of these tools and where to purchase them are available online. Software required to operate the device was included as well. Thus, the builder can immediately run available demo programs and proceed to application-specific development.

Assembly

The entire structural pieces are manufactured from a laser cutter out of 6 mm (or approximately 1/4 inch) plywood. To form stiff three-dimensional parts from the flat sheets, several layers are stacked and held together with screws. All holes in the plywood parts are adjusted with sub-millimeter precision such that all screws can self-tap (self-thread) the holes, allowing for quick assembly and disassembly. Stacked parts are aligned by inserting dowel pins (precision cylindrical pins) with an arbor press before adding screws. Bearings are press-fit as well using the arbor press. In fact, there is no use of

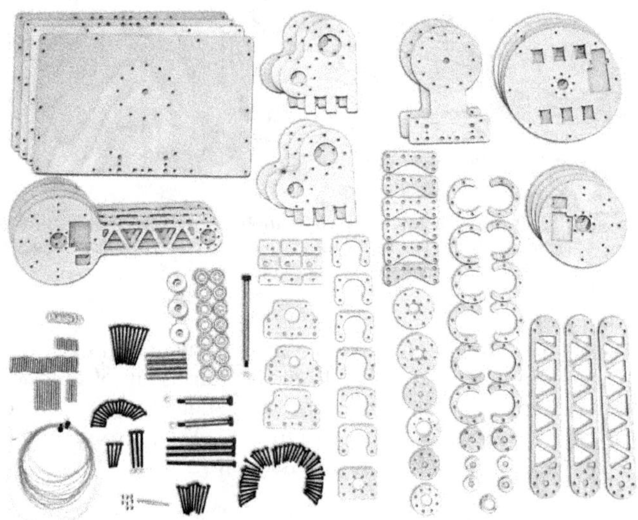

Figure 4. The parts included in the kit. Not shown here are the three motors, electrical cables and the electronics box (Figure 5), and configurable software that completes the kit.

bondants or adhesives, resulting in a visually and mechanically clean, quickly disassemble-able and reconfigurable device. The kit comes with instructions on how to assemble the main bodies, as well as video documentation.

The bodies A, B and C (figure 3) form the three links or *degrees of freedom* (DOF) that together enable the tip of the device (P in figure 6) to be moved left/right, up/down and in/out. Each DOF is coupled independently to a motor through wire rope. The angle of each DOF is a fixed ratio to the rotation of the motor shaft, and therefore the angles are measured by the *encoders* mounted on each motor (figure 5).

Cabling

The kit utilizes cable drive for all its transmissions: a strong steel wire rope transmits the power from each motor to its own respective link. Figure 5 shows a standard cable drive transmission used in all degrees of freedom. The motor shaft is attached to the *capstan*, which is a shaft for a cable to wrap around and grip. The cable makes 5 wraps around the capstan and is terminated at both ends. The cable needs to be taut to grip the capstan, which is done at the termination by either tightening or loosening a screw. For the last link, a turnbuckle is used to maintain a taut cable. Now, for each body, when the capstan is rotated with the cable gripped firmly to it, the body is then rotated; alternately, when the body is rotated, the capstan is subsequently rotated. This completes the transmission

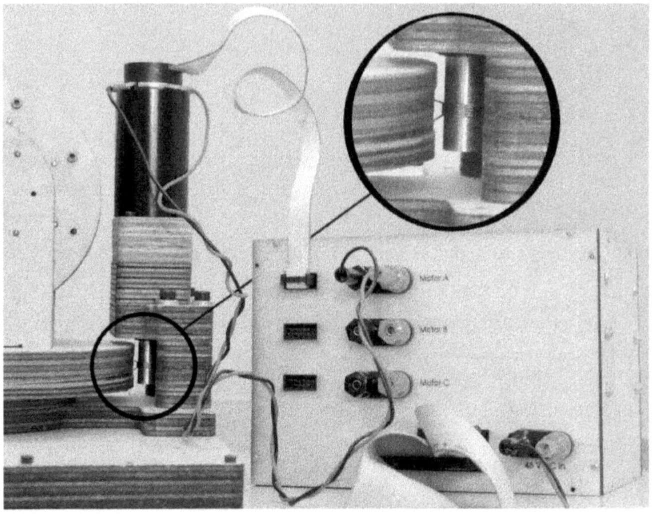

Figure 5. The first degree of freedom motor connected with power and encoder wires to the electrical interface. The close-up view shows the aluminum capstan and wire rope coupling.

assembly, allowing for the motors and the driven axis to not require collocation. This allows for gearing up of the motor torques for achieving larger forces without using gearboxes, as well for easy replacement of motors. The reasons for these design choices are further discussed in Part III.

Electrical system

The kit comes with three high-quality motors, each driving a respective degree of freedom. The designer only has to connect the encoder to the electronics box (that routes them to the computer), and each motor power cable to respective output of the electronics box (figure 5). Two ribbon cables connects the electronics box with the Sensoray S826 board on the PC.

The motors chosen are more powerful than is common in the devices pictured in figure 2. They are specified for allowing a max continuous current of 3.16A safely, and we have limited the maximum current to 3 ampere. This means that the user will not have to worry about electrical heat, burning, etc, which is the case when the motors are overdriven in short periods of time, which is common practice otherwise.

Software Configuration

The kit is complete with a working open-source software module for the mechanical design that comes with the kit. If a dimension have been changed by the user or tuning of the experience is desired, the user can easily modify a variable in a text file to represent this change. The variables of interest to change are: the diameter of each capstan and body, the length of each link and the mass and mass center of each body. This effectively is equivalent to changing the gearing of the motor, and changing the size of the workspace, respectively. The design also affords the easy replacement of motors with different motors, but the user will then need to adjust the torque/current ratio as defined by their motor datasheet. The maximum stiffness and damping of the complete device can be found retroactively by experimenting and adjusting the values accordingly.

PART III: FUNDAMENTALS AND THEORY

This section describes how the kit was developed and the design principles/considerations involved. We cover here briefly, the mechanical structure, the kinematics and control theory applied and why certain design decisions were made to support easy user fabrication and modification in particular. We are knowingly only addressing one kind of mechanical structure (the serially linked) and one control type (impedance control). Alternatives are parallel mechanical structure like e.g. Novint Falcon, and admittance control [28] that requires force sensing.

Haptic fidelity and transparency

The power transmission of a haptic device is a critical component that needs to be designed carefully as it transmits the forces and velocities from software to the hand of the user. Haptic fidelity is achieved by having *transparency* in the system – that is, desired forces and velocities defined in software accurately match forces and velocities delivered to the user. Three major contributions that reduce the transparency of a system is friction (resulting in diminished haptic perception), backlash (resulting in chatter in the motors and the device), and physical compliance (resulting in a loss of ability to perceive stiff environments).

Although motor and gearbox combinations are commercially much more common, cable drive transmission is the standard for haptic devices because it provides a near frictionless transmission and has no backlash, which no gearbox can achieve. The choice of cable is also an important factor: a cable with high flexibility will provide greater transparency as the users will not percieve the forces required to "bend" and "unbend" the cable as the capstan rolls. Therefore, uncoated stainless steel cables with high count of individual steel fibers (we use a cable of 0.54 mm diameter, with fibers in a 7×7 configuration, more is recommended if available) present a viable option. The grip of the cable on the capstan increases exponentially as the cable wraps around, and therefore even a few turns will immediately prevent the cable from slipping. In practice, 5 turns is more than enough to prevent any slipping between the capstan and the cable. This principle is also how the final link's cable transmission (using the cable loop and turnbuckle) works without slipping.

Another major design choice for achieving high haptic fidelity was to mount the second and third axis motors on body A (figure 6). This choice is highlighted by three intentional benefits: the simplified and shorter cable routing affords better transparency in the system, placement of the motors allow for easy access, removal, and installation for other motors of different sizes, and shorter cable routing reduces the chance of the transmission de-cabling. Failure in the cable transmission (e.g. cable snap or comes loose) is thereby localized to its own small section of the device, while allowing for the rest of the device to remain in working order.

The third major contribution to achieving transparency in the system is having a physically stiff device. Increasing stiffness (ie. reducing compliance) in the device's structure is done by increasing the second moment of inertia of each link (e.g. making link wider so they do not twist), improving the joint

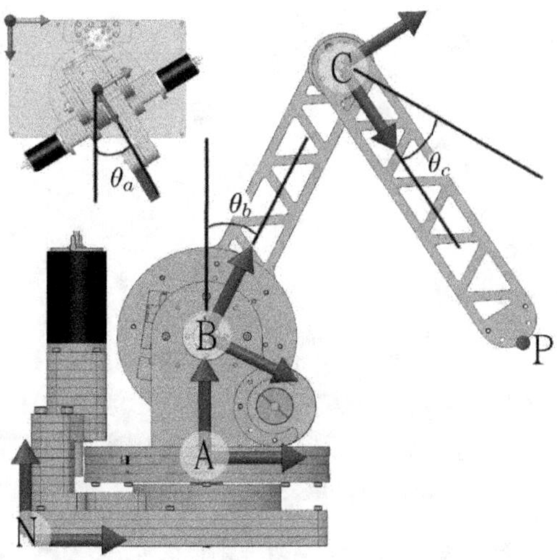

Figure 6. The device is a serially linked mechanism, where the angle of A, B and C uniquely defines point P in the base reference frame N.

stiffnesses (e.g. by increasing shaft diameters, increasing distance between shaft bearings that hold the shafts straight), and using a stiff material. Because plywood is a layered composite, it is in fact quite stiff and yet still reasonably light; it is also soft enough for self-tapping holes and very minor misalignments that all contribute to making the device more accessible and forgiving to build, without sacrificing substantial haptic fidelity.

Finally, each motor to capstan combination is connected through a flexible shaft coupler, which acts to not only reduce friction caused by misalignments in the axes of the motor and the capstan, but also serves as an easy way to swap out different motors and find the best motor for an application without performing any disassembly of the cable transmission. This serves to promote hardware sketching on the actuator side.

Mathematical description and analysis

In order for the spatial haptic interface to be useful, the position of the user's hand and thus the end-effector of the device must be known in space. This is achieved by measuring the angle of the motor shafts using encoders, and doing the forward kinematics to map motor angles to cartesian-space position. Below we provide only a very brief overview of the mathematics involved in achieving haptic feedback; all the details regarding the position and force mappings discussed in this section are derived from [4] using standard techniques for robot manipulators.We derive the manipulandum position through forward kinematics, which in this case is a classic 'RRR' configuration manipulator; that is, it has three moving links which are serially-linked through revolute(R) joints (figure 6), and can be calculated as follows:

$$\begin{aligned} P_x &= \cos\theta_a(L_b\sin\theta_b + L_c\cos(\theta_b+\theta_c)) \\ P_y &= \sin\theta_a(L_b\sin\theta_b + L_c\cos(\theta_b+\theta_c)) \\ P_z &= \quad L_b\cos\theta_b - L_c\sin(\theta_b+\theta_c) \end{aligned} \tag{1}$$

where L is the length of each body to the next and $\theta_{a,b,c}$ are the angles of respective body. To give a force $\mathbf{F}$ at the manipulandum, the body torque τ is computed as:

$$\tau = \mathbf{J}^\top \mathbf{F}, \tag{2}$$

where $\mathbf{J}$ is called the Jacobian matrix, and is the first partial derivative of the forward kinematics (1) with respect to the body angles θ [4]. A final necessity to account for is the weight of the manipulandum: without compensating for the manipulandum weight, the user will have to hold up the device's weight in their hands. To compensate for gravity, the weights of the three links as well as their centers of gravity are estimated, and motor torques to counter gravity forces are applied. For ease of use, the kit's software module allow for tuning of the link parameters while masking the mathematics involved to solve for force, position, and gravity.

Electrical system

The electrical system has two purposes: to drive the motors and to measure their angular position. The torque of the motor used is proportional to the current that is driven through it, not the voltage it is supplied. Therefore a current or torque controller (in our case Maxon ESCON 50/5) is connected between a generic power supply and the motor.

It is worth mentioning that the components used (motors, amplifiers, encoders and acquisition card) are of professional lab quality and should not be confused with hobbyist counterparts. While efforts to replace them with lower cost alternatives are very welcome, one has to be careful in preserving the precision needed. For example, the delay has to be less than 1 ms and the resolution and quality of D/A converter sufficient [23]. However, this also brings to the surface the potentials of this starting kit, as it allows users to explore what their haptic tolerance is for lower-cost alternatives.

Figure 7. Exploring designs: Mini-woody with smaller workspace and larger forces, and a different handle arm crafted using a lathe.

Variations

While the starting kit provides everything needed to complete a functioning device, the intention is to invite the designer to modification and variants of the design. Below we highlight a few interesting areas worthy of exploration:

Workspace

The user can very easily try different sizes (lengths) of the body, and experience the difference in scaling up or scaling down their reachable workspace and the haptic perception.

Figure 7 depicts a smaller version, that also, as a direct consequence, can render larger forces (table 1).

Motors and Encoders

The user can switch between using high-cost, high-quality motors and encoders, or a low-cost alternatives. This allows the designer to identify the specific factors and limits of haptic fidelity (e.g. the backlash from a geared motor versus ungeared motor, the cogging or friction from a $20 hobby shop motor versus a $300 motor). Effects of motor size can also be investigated.

Material

Plastics (such as acrylic) are as easy to cut as plywood, and comes in different colors for the designer to experiment with, but can be brittle. They also tend to be heavier, which have to be supported with more motor torque for gravity compensation. Aluminum is lightweight and stiff, but needs to be cut using special equipment (warter-jet cutter) and requires threading holes separately. Solid and composite wood choice can provide different stiffness and weight tradeoffs. Physical stiffness, the inertia of the device, and even Visual appeal can be explored by using different materials. Figure 7 shows a variant where one part is hand-fabricated from solid wood using a lathe.

Add-ons

A user may add buttons, sensors or even vibrotactile actuators on the manipulandum, which can further improve perception of textures [12]. Different grips or end-attachments that interface with the user can be explored.

PART IV: EVALUATION

Three aspects of the reference design and starting kit were evaluated. First, to what extent could someone without robotics training or access to a sophisticated lab use the kit, assemble the device and make it work? Second, how does the device compare to commercially-produced haptic devices? And finally, what are the technical properties?

Assembly Workshop

In order to investigate the feasibility of the kit, the extent it can reduce stickiness, and the level of instructions required, a workshop was held with two researchers previously inexperienced in robotics construction. While the first version of the device was built in a robotics lab (in the US), this workshop was held in a interaction design lab on another continent (in Europe). All the parts in the kit seen in figure 4 and motors, electronics box and a tool set of hex keys, cable crimper, cutter and arbor press were presented to the users. A computer with the software installed to run the completed device with a virtual environment was provided.

The instruction material was in the form of print-outs of the bodies with notations of screw location and so on. The users took turns building while being supervised by one of the authors, and guidance was provided when deemed necessary. The assembly sessions were videotaped and notes and build times recorded.

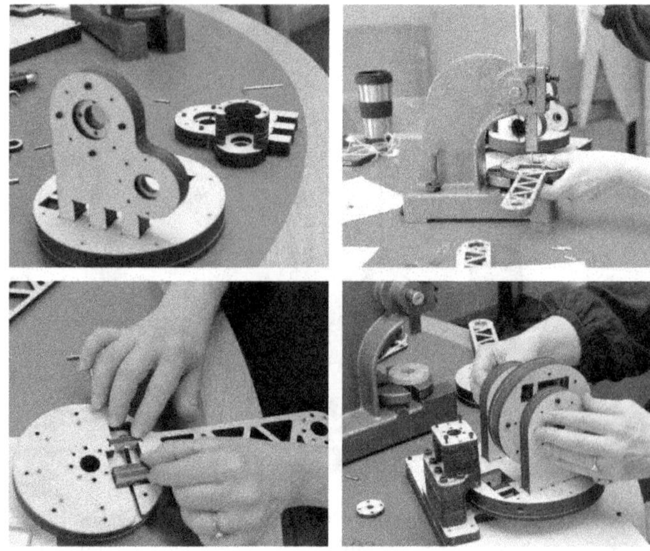

Figure 8. User assembly of the wooden haptics device as part of the evaluation of the feasability of the starting kit.

It took the users approximately 11 hours distributed over 4 sessions to successfully assemble the complete WoodenHaptics device. Most of the guidance required was initially regarding the proper use of the tools, order of insertion of pins and screws and so on, and during the process of cabling (the process of mounting the wire rope). These instructions could be readily provided in a detailed construction document as is provided in Lego® sets. Since only one copy of the kit was present and thus some errors would be irreversible, care was taken to make sure stacking of similar parts and assembly order was performed correctly. Despite that, one part got placed in a flipped direction, but could still work in a satisfactory manner. Some bearings were not inserted until parts added later made it cumbersome, and had to be mounted with mallet (with risk of damaging them). Two outer diameters were wrongly adjusted by the authors and had to be reduced with sand paper, since cutting new parts was not an option (no laser cutter in the lab, and long turn-around for ordering). Finally, some extra tools were used: a pair of tweezers during the cabling, and the mallet when the arbor press was too small. With this said, the final device worked as well as the one built previously.

Perceived quality of finished assembly

An evaluation was conducted regarding the quality of the haptic feedback, comparing the Phantom Desktop, Phantom Omni, Novint Falcon and our assembled version of the starting kit, hereafter named “Woody” for short. For this evaluation, 10 participants (5 women and 5 men, mean age 32) were recruited among students and faculty. The same virtual environment[1] was used for each device that were placed side-by-side, which enabled the user to go back and forth between the devices (Figure 9).

[1] Chai3D version 3.0 example 13 - Primitives, www.chai3d.org

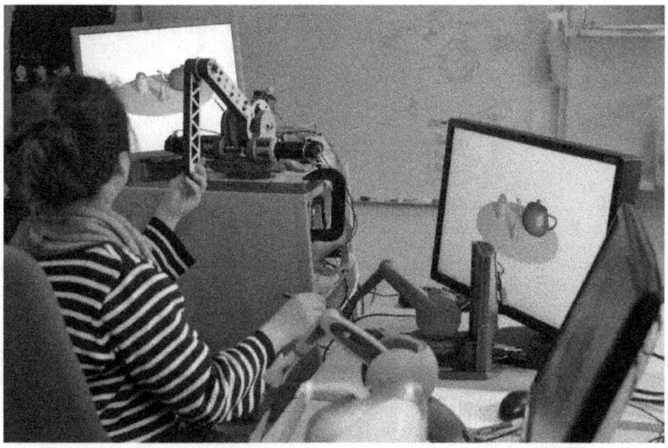

Figure 9. The setup of the evaluation showing the four different devices and the demo application used in the test.

The evaluation consisted of two parts. The participants first task was to rate the experienced quality of the haptic feedback using the devices one at a time. Experienced quality was evaluated in a questionnaire using a seven point Likert-type scale with four items asking about to what degree the haptic feedback felt being of *high quality*, *precise*, *smooth* and *distinct*. In the analysis, the four items were summed into one dimension measuring subjective experience of haptic feedback quality. The questionnaire was filled in after experiencing each haptic device respectively. In the second part, participants compared all devices again and reported which one of the commercial devices they felt most closely matched that of Woody in haptic quality on their own terms.

The results, as the average summed ratings (std. dev.) of each device was as follows. Desktop 25.8 (2.10), Omni 19.5 (5.7), Falcon 11.2 (6.3) and Woody 24.4 (3.37). The participants thus rated Woody's experience between Phantom and Omni. It resonates with the second part of the evaluation when the participants were explicitly asked to draw a line between Woody and the device they thought was most similar to Woody. The results show that 7 of the participants thought that Woody was most similar to the Desktop, 3 reported that Woody felt the most similar to the Omni.

Changing haptic properties when varying design

In order to demonstrate the ability to modify haptic performance through design, different versions of the device were constructed with the starting kit as a base. Woody (B=20 cm, C=22cm) and a "mini" variant (B=10 cm, C=12 cm) were created to explore the trade-off betweeen workspace and force-feedback properties (Figure 7). Stiffness was empirically tuned at a level where no vibrations was felt while interaction were at a maximal stiffness (5 N/mm). The results are presented in Table 1. For comparison, maximum force values for Omni and Falcon were added from [22] and friction and workspace measurements were taken for these devices as well. A lower bound for the workspace was found by placing a virtual sphere in the virtual origin and increasing its diameter while maintaining that the whole sphere can easily be touched from the outside. Peak force was found for

	Woody	Mini-w.	Omni	Falcon
workspace	200+	80+	100+	60+
peak force	9.9+	19.0+	3.3	8.9+
cont. force	9.9	19.0	0.88	8.9
friction	0.6/0.7/0.9	0.6/1.0/0.9	0.2/0.4/1.1	1.2/3.6/1.3

Table 1. Varying haptic properties through different design changes, and comparison to commercial devices.

Woody and Mini-woody by calculating, but not physically outputting, the largest force that could be applied in x, y, and z direction until at least one motor saturates. The workspace was swept and the lowest value was recorded. Since the motors were specified to handle more than 3 ampere nominally the continuous force and peak force is the same. Back-drive friction was measured using a hand-held digital force gauge (FG-5000A-232, Lutron Electronics, Taiwan) slowly moved from one side of the workspace (as defined above) to the other passing the origin, sideways, inwards and upwards. Ten measurements were taken and averaged for each direction and device. Gravity compensation was enabled if available. Omni, which lacked active gravity compensation was supported by a 2 m thin string from the ceiling in sideways and inwards measurements.

This study demonstrated the exploration of trade-offs in changing workspace dimensions with forces and friction. The commercial devices provided the static performance mark for which the modified designs were compared against. It can be seen that there is no one device that provides the largest workspace, forces, or minimum friction altogether, showing the strengths and limitations of each design and the benefit for hardware sketching.

PART VI: DISCUSSION

We have shown how the WoodenHaptics starting kit can be an engaging spatial haptics device testbed without many of the sticky issues usually involved in the craft. We have furthermore demonstrated that high haptic fidelity was achievable using WoodenHaptics, on par with commercial devices. For an interaction designer, the WoodenHaptics toolkit serves to:

- help the designer understand the fundamentals of the mechanism (e.g. it shows clearly how three motors work together to generate one force vector at the end point of the manipulandum).
- enable the designer to incorporate the device into their own projects quickly and easily without being a electro-mechanical expert.
- enable the designer to explore the user experience (by objectively changing/tuning certain parameters or replace components such as motors).
- establish a common language between designers and experienced hardware engineers. The designer can now say "can you make a device like this, but smaller?" or "what could or needs to change for us to manufacture something like this for our application?"

With WoodenHaptics, a designer can create variations of a serially-linked 3-DOF grounded spatial haptic device. The constraints imposed by the kit frees the designer from solving many electrical, computational and mechanical problems since these have already been solved; it instead allows the user to innovate in terms of motor choices, workspace dimensions, physical material, aesthetics and extended functions like buttons. As personal fabrication of parts becomes easier, e.g. through direct interaction with a laser cutter [20] or software tools [26], designers can quickly explore different variations that can optimize their haptic experience for a particular application.

Common haptic devices and application programming interfaces sometimes give wrong expectations of what experiences they actually support. For example, Mousette [17] noted that "hardware hard is relative" from his experiments with a commercial haptic device where a virtual object specified to be of maximum stiffness still yielded a sensation he refer to as "mushy hard". It is likely that he would have had a different experience with a device equipped with more powerful motors, or if the developers had used another terminology than "hardness" to describe the feature. By crafting with WoodenHaptics one can learn, experience, quantitatively define, *and alter* mushiness or other unarticulated haptic experiences.

WoodenHaptics is not intended to replace off-the-shelf devices and is not necessarily cheaper. Instead it offers unique opportunities for dedicated designers as a workbench for exploring the experiential qualities of new designs. The components mentioned here carry a cost of about 3000 USD. Future work, especially on the electronics side, will lead to significantly lower costs (e.g. use of custom circuit board).

Finally, designers are encouraged to share their experiences and designs with the community, and improve upon the kit itself. This allows them to go beyond the original constraints set by the kit and its modules when they are ready. We also expect simpler versions for e.g. 2-DOF planar device to benefit from our modules. Bringing spatial haptic device design to a larger audience allows them to share more perspectives on both what a designs should look like and how they should be evaluated.

ACKNOWLEDGMENTS

WoodenHaptics was initially developed at Stanford University. We are thankful to Reuben Brewer and Ken Salisbury for introducing many of the concepts discussed in this paper in CS235: Applied Robot Design for Non-Robot Designers. We would also like to thank Adam Leeper and Ylva Fernaeus.

REFERENCES

1. Bowman, D. A., Kruijff, E., LaViola, J. J., and Poupyrev, I. *3D User Interfaces: Theory and Practice*. Addison Wesley Longman Publishing Co., Inc., Redwood City, CA, USA, 2004.
2. Broeren, J., Rydmark, M., and Sunnerhagen, K. S. Virtual reality and haptics as a training device for movement rehabilitation after stroke: a single-case study. *Archives of physical medicine and rehabilitation 85*, 8 (2004), 1247–1250.
3. Chan, S., Conti, F., Salisbury, K., and Blevins, N. H. Virtual reality simulation in neurosurgery: technologies and evolution. *Neurosurgery 72* (2013), A154–A164.
4. Craig, J. J. *Introduction to robotics*, vol. 7. Addison-Wesley Reading, MA, 1989.
5. Greenberg, S., and Fitchett, C. Phidgets: easy development of physical interfaces through physical widgets. In *Proceedings of UIST*, ACM (2001), 209–218.
6. Hayward, V., and MacLean, K. E. Do it yourself haptics: part i. *Robotics & Automation Magazine, IEEE 14*, 4 (2007), 88–104.
7. Kern, T. A. *Engineering haptic devices*. Springer, 2009.
8. Knörig, A., Wettach, R., and Cohen, J. Fritzing: a tool for advancing electronic prototyping for designers. In *Proceedings of TEI*, ACM (2009), 351–358.
9. Lee, J. Haptic intelligentsia, http://studio- homunculus.com/portfolio/ haptic-intelligentsia-human-prototyping-machine, apr 2014.
10. Massie, T. Design of a three degree of freedom force-reflecting haptic interface. Bsc thesis, MIT, 1993.
11. Massie, T. H., and Salisbury, J. K. The phantom haptic interface: A device for probing virtual objects. In *Proc. Haptic Symposium 1994*, vol. 55, Chicago, IL (1994), 295–300.
12. McMahan, W., and Kuchenbecker, K. J. Displaying realistic contact accelerations via a dedicated vibration actuator. In *WorldHaptics*, IEEE (2009), 613–614.
13. Mellis, D. A., and Buechley, L. Case studies in the personal fabrication of electronic products. In *Proceedings of the Designing Interactive Systems Conference*, ACM (2012), 268–277.
14. Mellis, D. A., Jacoby, S., Buechley, L., Perner-Wilson, H., and Qi, J. Microcontrollers as material: crafting circuits with paper, conductive ink, electronic components, and an untoolkit. In *TEI* (2013), 83–90.
15. Morimoto, T. K., Blikstein, P., and Okamura, A. M. Hapkit: An open-hardware haptic device for online education. In *Haptics Symposium, 2014 IEEE* (Feb 2014), 1–1.
16. Moussette, C. Learn to make, make to learn: Reflections from sketching haptics workshops. *Design and semantics of form and movement* (2012), 180.
17. Moussette, C. Simple haptics: Sketching perspectives for the design of haptic interactions.
18. Moussette, C., and Banks, R. Designing through making: exploring the simple haptic design space. In *Proc. TEI*, ACM (2011), 279–282.
19. Moussette, C., and Dore, F. Sketching in hardware and building interaction design: tools, toolkits and an attitude for interaction designers. *Proc. of Design Research Society* (2010).
20. Mueller, S., Lopes, P., and Baudisch, P. Interactive construction: Interactive fabrication of functional mechanical devices. In *Proceedings of UIST*, ACM (New York, NY, USA, 2012), 599–606.
21. Okamura, A. M., Richard, C., and Cutkosky, M. R. Feeling is believing: Using a force-feedback joystick to teach dynamic systems. *Journal of Engineering Education 91*, 3 (2002), 345–349.
22. Salisbury, C., Salisbury, J., Gillespie, R., and Blevins, N. A microsurgery-specific haptic device for telerobotic medical treatment. In *ANS Joint Emergency Preparedness and Response & Robotic and Remote Systems, Topical Meeting*, vol. 6 (2008).
23. Salisbury, C. M. *Haptic hardware: evaluation, design and placement*. PhD thesis, Stanford, 2009.
24. Salisbury, K., Conti, F., and Barbagli, F. Haptic rendering: introductory concepts. *IEEE computer graphics and applications 24*, 2 (2004), 24–32.
25. Sankaran, R., Ullmer, B., Ramanujam, J., Kallakuri, K., Jandhyala, S., Toole, C., and Laan, C. Decoupling interaction hardware design using libraries of reusable electronics. In *Proc. TEI*, ACM (2009), 331–337.
26. Saul, G., Lau, M., Mitani, J., and Igarashi, T. Sketchchair: an all-in-one chair design system for end users. In *Proc. TEI*, ACM (2011), 73–80.
27. Shaver, M., and Maclean, K. The twiddler: A haptic teaching tool for low-cost communication and mechanical design.
28. Van der Linde, R. Q., Lammertse, P., Frederiksen, E., and Ruiter, B. The hapticmaster, a new high-performance haptic interface. In *Proc. Eurohaptics* (2002), 1–5.
29. Von Hippel, E. Perspective: User toolkits for innovation. *Journal of product innovation management 18*, 4 (2001), 247–257.

The Kitsch-Instrument : Hackable Robotic Music

Jiffer Harriman
University of Colorado
ATLAS Institute
harrimj@colorado.edu

Michael Theodore
University of Colorado
College of Music
michael.theodore@colorado.edu

Mark Gross
University of Colorado
ATLAS Institute
mdgross@colorado.edu

ABSTRACT
We present a modular tangible user interface system and corresponding actuators for creating music with everyday objects. Users create percussive patterns by controlling algorithmic parameters, or by directly playing the interface. Various mechanical solutions allow users to investigate physical objects as sound sources. A standalone physical interface and an associated graphical programming environment enable different levels of user engagement and hardware/software transparency. We discuss a tool space in-between open and closed design concepts, as well as the physical and software design of the Kitsch-Instrument itself. We also describe recent interactions with the interface at a public event and discuss future plans.

Author Keywords
Music, robotic actuators, NIME, sketching in hardware

ACM Classification Keywords
B.0. [**Hardware**]-General; D.1.7. [**Software**]- Programming Techniques-Visual Programming; D.2.2. [**Software Engineering**]-Design Tools and Techniques-Evolutionary Prototyping, Modules and Interfaces, User Interfaces; J.5. [**Computer Applications**]-Arts and Humanities-Performing Arts

INTRODUCTION
In recent years tools such as Arduino and Processing have lowered the entry barrier for designing with electronics and programming. Both grew out of a desire to bring the design and creative practice of technology to new populations.

The digital design and construction ecosystem today offers a wide range of entry points in terms of both learning curve and application space. However, significant gaps remain between tools such as Arduino and construction kits such as LittleBits and LEGO Mindstorms. The Kitsch-Instrument and related project modular-muse [6] offer a happy medium between these ends of the spectrum, with a design that is approachable and extensible, and that encourages exploration and creative hacking.

TEI 2015, January 15–19, 2015, Stanford, California, USA.

ACM 978-1-4503-3305-4/15/01...$15.00.
http://dx.doi.org/10.1145/2677199.2680593

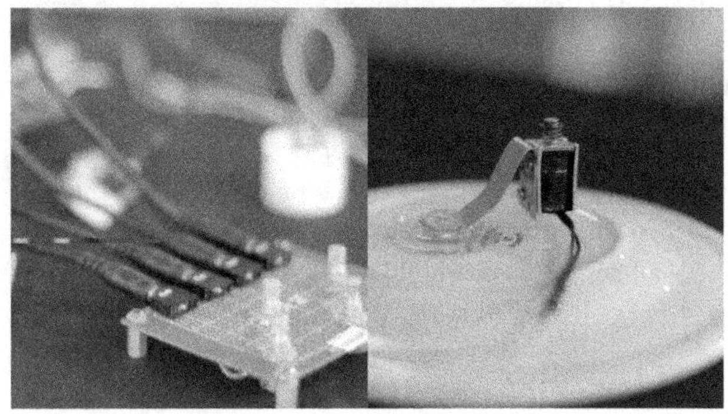

Figure 1 - Kitsch-Instrument with modular-muse knobs and solenoid affixed to a plate

The Kitsch-Instrument is a digitally mediated electro-mechanical percussive instrument with modular interface elements. Its design supports a wide range of output actuators, and enables the exploration of assorted control modalities. Various mechanical mounting attachments allow the solenoids to “play” everyday objects. The default Kitsch-Instrument algorithm (on power up) produces rhythmic beats under user control.

The Kitsch-Instrument works well in the kitchen enabling the attachment of solenoids to plates, mugs, glasses, and many other items. More generally, the kit is an engaging tool for exploring the acoustics of the world around us, as almost anything can be turned into a percussive instrument by attaching a solenoid! Additionally, users may build a control interface for the new instrument, utilizing either a set of tangible components (such as buttons and potentiometers), or a GUI that displays the construction of the custom patterns.

RELATED WORK
The Kitsch-Instrument draws on several areas of related work, including robotic percussive instruments, hardware abstraction and interaction design toolkits, and algorithmic computer music.

The field of robotic musical instruments in general has seen a recent surge of activity due to the decreasing costs of electromechanical actuators [9]. Pull solenoids such as those used in the Kitsch-Instrument have been used in a number of robotic music projects [11, 17]. Drum Duino [3] encourages the exploration of physical objects through a strap based solenoid attachment but uses a static user interface and control paradigm compared to the Kitsch-Instrument's modular, hackable approach.

Commercial music and technology kits have been a part of the landscape for some time[1]. More recently, products have appeared that can be used with digital music systems for creating customized interfaces [20, 21, 22]. These systems enable custom instruments and novel controllers, but their designs are closed, limiting extensibility and learning opportunities. Mogees and Makey Makey can be used in novel ways make use of everyday objects to create or control sound. [12, 1]

In contrast, music related open source projects such as the OWL guitar pedal [19] and Sparkpunk Sound Kit [23] from Sparkfun encourage hacking. The OWL uses C++ and offers example designs to begin from (although modification requires understanding digital signal processing), while Sparkpunk uses analog sources for sound generation.

DESIGN DETAILS

The Kitsch-Instrument

The Kitsch-Instrument enables both the actuation of various physical objects, and the exploration of different interface paradigms. The kitchen is a great place to explore different sound-making objects from plates to mugs to cereal boxes. The circuit design can also support much larger solenoids and the corresponding power supplies for more "serious" musical applications. In the interest of flexibility, we created a set of shields for the Arduino Uno to drive up to four solenoids with the modular user interface.

Modular-Muse Shield

Inspired by hardware abstraction toolkits such as the LilyPad Arduino, Phidgets and the Grove System by Seeed Studio, our modular-muse shield enables simple interfacing to a variety of sensors and allows reconfiguration of the user interface [2, 5, 20]. For example, a series of knobs may be useful for a musical performance, while a number of distance sensors might be swapped in to create a human sized mixing board for an interactive installation.

Solenoid Driver Shield

The solenoid driver shield can drive four solenoids from pulse width modulation (PWM) outputs on the Arduino. The driver circuit uses a high power N-Channel MOSFETs to power the solenoids, with a pull down resistor on the MOSFET gate, and a fly-back protection diode across the solenoid. The board has a jumper for use with either the Arduino 5V supply, or an external DC power supply (useful for larger solenoids). Solenoids can be quickly attached with two wires to terminals on the shield.

Solenoid Attachments

The other interface element is mechanical and physical, turning nearly any object into a sound source by enabling solenoid attachment. The Kitsch-Instrument employs three attachment mechanisms: A suction cup for smooth surfaces, a hanger attachment that can be hung from rims, and a cylindrical stand that allows solenoids to rest on horizontal surfaces. The various attachment mechanisms encourage investigation of different materials, and provide an element of physicality spatial dimension unavailable in speaker based systems. They also provide a tactile and tangible interaction that is pleasing to explore [9], creating endless variations by physically adjusting the solenoid elements. The system offers human performers expressive possibilities that are unavailable with fixed attachment mechanisms based robotic instruments. [10, 17]

Figure 2 – A coffee mug as an instrument

Software Design

The standalone Arduino version of the software uses chance to create an algorithmic drum beat, giving the user control over the parameters of density and tempo. An analog input corresponds to each solenoid output. At the time of each beat, a random number is generated for each solenoid. If the value read at the control input is greater than that number, then the solenoid triggers. The Pd version of this code operates in the same way, but allows users to view the algorithm in action, seeing the calculations and their effect on a particular solenoid output. This algorithm gives the user direct control over the density of each solenoid voice, and a straightforward, powerful means to conduct the solenoid "band."

DESIGN GUIDELINES

We borrow design guidelines from several sources, including those laid out by Resnick on designing construction kits for kids, and those proposed by Mousette and Dore in support of "sketching in hardware" [14,12]. This simplified list addresses some of the unique challenges of designing for a space between the open and closed ends of the spectrum, and in creating targeted yet flexible design tools.

[1] http://www.paia.com/

Our goal is to create opportunities for budding designers, artists, and students who are intimidated or uninterested in learning to program an Arduino, or who have perhaps already been discouraged by the tedium of activities such as breadboarding circuits. Although soldering and Arduino workshops have initiated many young makers into the world of technology design, how many were equally disappointed by the lack of immediacy in the process, or underwhelmed once the initial thrill of blinking an LED wore off?

Therefore, in order to create a tool for learning and exploration that can be immediately engaging, while still remaining useful to artists and musicians, we made use of the following design guidelines:

Multiple Points of Entry - The flexible nature of the Kitsch-Instrument invites a wide variety of users to become engaged.

Support transferability - The Kitsch-Instrument works well with existing systems (Arduino, Pd, etc.).

Transparency - The inner workings are visible, or at least accessible. This supports both transferability to other systems, and also education. When a learner is ready, he or she can investigate how something was made.

Hackability - By promoting "hackable design," the object becomes explicitly extensible, encouraging re-appropriation. (This is also supported by transparency.)

Multiple Points of Entry

The Kitsch-Instrument offers multiple avenues of exploration depending on the user's experience and interests. It can be used without any musical, electronics, or programming experience, but can also be used by experts. For example, in the most basic configuration, a single knob controls a single solenoid. In addition to creating an accessible interface for the uninitiated, such simple designs also free up *cognitive bandwidth*, thereby releasing musicians from the constraints of complex interfaces, and facilitating the exploration of novel elements [18].

Alternatively, the Kitsch-Instrument can be controlled from within the graphical programming environment Pure Data (Pd)[2], where users can explore and modify algorithms, as well as employ a more traditional drum sequencer paradigm for programming beats.

Support Transferability

By using the scaffolding of the Arduino platform (and optionally Pd), users can draw on existing music programming and robotic drumming knowledge within these communities. For example, the Kitch-Instrument is built on two stacked Arduino Uno shields that can each be used individually. With just a few changes of the Pd patch, the user can trigger audio samples instead of (or in addition to) the solenoids, and enable an entirely different experience. Alternatively, an experienced programmer can write code directly for the Arduino to trigger the solenoids.

Transparency

The Kitsch-Instrument exposes its components, revealing the circuit design for anyone interested in understanding the electronics. Additionally, Pd's visual programming environment enables the user to see the algorithm in action, displaying the sensor values as well as the calculations that determine when a beat will occur. In addition to supporting transparency, visual programming languages have also been shown to be accessible to those without programming experience. [7, 15]

Hackability

A device that is made transparent is not necessarily hackable. It requires both an infrastructure (comments in code, transferable hardware, example hacks) as well as an open-source aesthetic. Making a project/product explicitly hackable invites a different mindset at the outset.

Finding existing projects that meet these criteria has been surprisingly difficult; we believe it is critical that such projects find their way into the hands of budding designers.

DISCUSSION

A 2012 study found that the invention of musical instruments engaged children in many aspects of design thinking. [16] The Kitsch-Instrument offers a novel interface and musical experience, supplementing and enriching the ways in which children and adults can engage with technology.

While it is too early to draw any conclusions about its efficacy as a learning tool or a creativity support tool, early responses are encouraging. At a public event where people interacted with the Kitsch-Instrument, personal styles of pattern exploration became apparent. A visitor would typically first explore the extremes, turning the knobs all the way up and all the way down, and then find settings that they enjoyed. After this initial exploration, many moved on to physically exploring different objects as instruments, often "playing" the object by moving the solenoid around manually. Several visitors with Arduino experience inquired into the technology used and were excited at the prospect of "getting their hands" on the source code. Others were intrigued by the algorithmic drum pattern, which could be shown in action in Pd as well as experienced concretely as they turned the knobs. (Visitors often wrongly assumed there were pre-programmed beats that made it so pleasing.)

FUTURE WORK

We plan additional exploration and detailed user studies, which are scheduled for later this year in teen-centric hackerspaces and a middle school music classroom. We

[2] www.puredata.info

will look at different interface paradigms, and also compare our simple algorithmic interface to a more traditional drum machine interface. Additionally, we plan to measure impacts on computational and design thinking in order to understand how the Kitsch-Instrument and other technology mediated music design experiences contribute to both the interest and understanding of related technologies.

SUMMARY

The Kitsch-Instrument offers a novel approach to creating music, turning almost any object into a percussion instrument, while engaging new populations in technology. By using an open-source aesthetic and our design guidelines of *multiple points of entry, supporting transferability, transparency,* and *hackability*, it offers a model for a new set of tools which are immediately engaging, yet open to extension.

REFERENCES:

1. Collective, Beginner'S. Mind, and David Shaw. "Makey Makey: improvising tangible and nature-based user interfaces." *Proceedings of the Sixth International Conference on Tangible, Embedded and Embodied Interaction.* ACM, 2012.
2. Buechley, L., & Eisenberg, M. (2008). The LilyPad Arduino: using computational textiles to investigate engagement, aesthetics, and diversity in computer science education. *The SIGCHI conference on Human Factors in Computing*, 423–432.
3. De Ville, Jolien, and Jelle Saldien. "Drum Duino: a tangible interface to create rhytmic music with everyday objects." *7th International Conference on Tangible, Embedded and Embodied Interaction.* 2013.
4. Correll, N., Farrow, N., Sugawara, K., Theodore, M. The Swarm-Wall: Toward Life's Uncanny Valley, IEEE International Conference on Robotics and Automation
5. Greenberg, S., & Fitchett, C. (2001). Phidgets: easy development of physical interfaces through physical widgets. ... *annual ACM symposium on User interface Software and Technology*, *3*(2).
6. Harriman, J. "Modular-Mus: towards an interaction design toolkit for music." Proceedings of the 2014 companion publication on Designing interactive systems. ACM, 2014.
7. Harriman, J., Theodore, M., Correll, N., Ewen, H. "endo/exo: Making Art and Music with Distributed Computing."
8. Haupt, Michael, et al. "PhidgetLab: crossing the border from virtual to real-world objects." Proceedings of the fifteenth annual conference on Innovation and technology in computer science education. ACM, 2010.
9. Ishii, Hiroshi, et al. "Radical atoms: beyond tangible bits, toward transformable materials." *Interactions* 19.1 (2012): 38-51.
10. Kapur, A. (2005). A history of robotic musical instruments. *Proceedings of the International Computer Music Conference*
11. Kapur, A. "The machine orchestra: An ensemble of human laptop performers and robotic musical instruments." *Computer Music Journal* 35.4 (2011): 49-63.
12. Moussette, Camille, and Fabricio Dore. "Sketching in Hardware and Building Interaction Design: tools, toolkits and an attitude for Interaction Designers."*Proc. of Design Research Society* (2010).
13. Rasamimanana, Nicolas, et al. "Modular musical objects towards embodied control of digital music." *Proceedings of the fifth international conference on Tangible, embedded, and embodied interaction.* ACM, 2011.
14. Resnick, M., & Silverman, B. (2005). Some reflections on designing construction kits for kids. *Proceeding of the 2005 conference on Interaction design and children - IDC '05*, 117–122. doi:10.1145/1109540.1109556
15. Roque, Ricarose Vallarta. *OpenBlocks: an extendable framework for graphical block programming systems.* Diss. Massachusetts Institute of Technology, 2007.
16. Sawyer, B., Forsyth, J., Connor, T. O., Bortz, B., Finn, T., Baum, L., … Tech, V. (2013). Form , Function and Performances in a Musical Instrument MAKErs Camp, 669–674.
17. Singer, Eric, et al. "LEMUR's musical robots." *Proceedings of the 2004 conference on New interfaces for musical expression.* National University of Singapore, 2004.
18. Zappi, V., & Mcpherson, A. P. (n.d.). Dimensionality and Appropriation in Digital Musical Instrument Design, 455–460.
19. The Owl. http://hoxtonowl.com
20. Grove System. http://www.seeedstudio.com/depot/Grove-t-3.html
21. I-CubeX. http://infusionsystems.com/
22. Oplab. http://www.teenageengineering.com/products/oplab/
23. SparkPunk Sound Kit. https://www.sparkfun.com/products/11177
24. Builder DIY. http://lividinstruments.com/products/builder/

(E)Motion and Creativity: Hacking the Function of Motor Expressions in Emotion Regulation to Augment Creativity

Alwin de Rooij
Centre for Creativity in Professional Practice
City University London
Northampton Square, London EC1V 0HB, UK
alwinderooij@city.ac.uk

Sara Jones
Centre for Human Computer Interaction Design
City University London
Northampton Square, London EC1V 0HB, UK
s.v.jones@city.ac.uk

ABSTRACT
Positive emotion can help augment human creativity. To utilize this potential in an interactive system, we propose that such a system should be designed to regulate the emotions that are caused by a creative task. We argue that this can be done by hacking the function of motor expressions in emotion regulation. To this end, we have conceived and made an interactive system that is designed to regulate positive emotion during an idea generation and an insight problem solving task. The system regulates emotion by letting users interact using arm gestures that are designed based on motor expressions, choreographed in a way that enables emotion regulation. Using this interactive system we experimentally test the hypotheses that positive approaching, rather than negative avoiding arm gestures, used to interact with a system, can heighten positive emotion, and augment creativity. The findings demonstrate that an interactive system can be designed to use the function of motor expressions in emotion regulation to help people perform better on certain creative tasks.

Author Keywords
Emotion Regulation; Embodied interaction; Idea generation; Insight Problem Solving; Motor Expressions.

ACM Classification Keywords
H.5.2 Information interfaces and presentation: User interfaces - Theory and methods.

INTRODUCTION
Emotion influences how well and in what way people perform creatively in their everyday lives [2]. This provides an opportunity for designers of technologies that aim to augment creativity to develop systems that influence emotion, and via emotion, augment creativity. However, until now, the possibilities to develop such systems have been limited [20, 21, 23]. This is surprising, because creativity is often seen as the new smart, a sought after skill that helps well-being, innovation, and culture thrive [22].

TEI '15, January 16 - 19 2015, Stanford, CA, USA

http://dx.doi.org/10.1145/2677199.2680552

In this paper, we describe the conception and experimental evaluation of a system that uses embodied interactions based on the characteristics of motor expressions. This system is designed to help regulate positive emotion during two creative tasks: idea generation, and insight problem solving. To interact with the system, people use arm gestures that are designed based on motor expressions associated either with positive emotion and approach action tendencies, or with negative emotion and avoidance action tendencies. These gestures are choreographed in a way that we suppose enables emotion regulation. We demonstrate that using positive approach rather than negative avoidance arm gestures to interact with the system heightens positive emotion, and increases creativity in the tasks used. Thus, the contribution of the research presented in this paper is a demonstration that an interactive system can be designed to use the function of motor expressions in emotion regulation to help people perform better on certain creative tasks.

EMOTION AND CREATIVITY
Emotions have been defined as adaptations in the way people think and act, driven by the changing relationship between an individuals' environment and its well-being [26]. Emotions are made up of changes in a number of components, including the following: subjective evaluations of events in the individual's environment (e.g. this seems pleasant); action tendencies that guide taking appropriate action (e.g. approaching a pleasant event); somatic and neuro-endocrine changes to support these evaluations and actions (e.g. dopamine release in reward structures in the brain); motor expressions - the physical actions that form part of an emotion (e.g. smiling and approach arm movements); and feelings, which are the aspects of these changes that the individual becomes aware of, and are used to monitor emotional wellbeing (e.g. I feel happy) [26].

Creativity has been defined as the development of problem solutions or artifacts that are both novel and effective [22]. This involves executing a distinct set of information processing steps (the creative process). For instance, concepts may be combined to generate ideas, and generated ideas may be evaluated to estimate whether they should be further developed. Creativity is augmented when these steps are executed in a way that favours the emergence of novel and effective outcomes.

The relationship between *emotion and creativity* depends on the influence of the adaptive nature of an emotion on the execution of the creative process [10]. Positive emotions, and in particular those that are characterized by approach action tendencies favour creativity [2]. Positive emotion (e.g. joy or pride) is generated by the subjective evaluation that an event is conducive to the goals of an individual [26]. This stimulates dopamine release in the mesocortical and mesolimbic areas of the brain, which is associated with an increase in the flexibility with which information is relayed to other brain areas [1]. The resulting increase in flexibility makes it easier to 1) generate many and diverse ideas, a marker for creativity during the idea generation step in the creative process, and 2) gain creative insights as measured by insight problem solving tasks [2] (Figure 1). Approach action tendencies, or in other words the pursuit of a positive outcome, can further support the link between positive emotion and creativity [2].

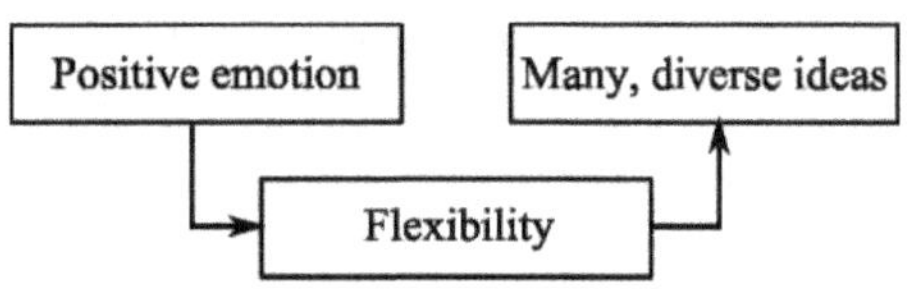

Figure 1. Illustration of the relationship between positive emotion and creative idea generation mediated by flexibility.

Interactive systems designed to influence the relationship between emotion and creativity are scarce, though some examples do exist. Emotion elicitation techniques developed in psychology have been tested on crowd-sourcing platforms within this context [20, 21]. For instance, priming positive emotion by placing a positive picture on the crowdsourcing platform during an idea generation task augments creativity [20]. Another development is using of the tendency of people to mirror each other's facial expressions to influence emotion. For instance, manipulating faces into a desired facial expression in a video feed that is used to communicate during collaborative brainstorming augments idea generation when the faces are manipulated in a positive rather than a negative facial expression [23]. From the examples above, we can see that interactive systems can be designed to influence the relationship between emotion and creativity, to help people perform better on certain creative tasks.

In this paper we focus on the relationship between positive emotion and creativity during idea generation and insight problem solving. This leads to our first hypothesis (H1).

H1: An interactive system that augments positive emotion can augment creativity during idea generation and insight problem solving.

MOTION AND EMOTION

Motor expressions are the physical actions that form part of an emotion [7, 26]. For instance, we smile when we see something nice, or we might push away the things we do not like. Motor expressions also regulate emotion [14]. This is because motor expressions are connected to the other emotion components via feedback loops [26]. Thus, changes in motor expressions influence the disposition towards having certain emotions, and the intensity of those emotions.

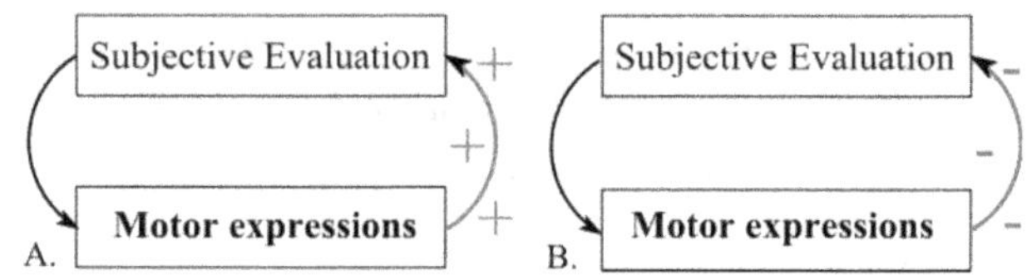

Figure 2. Motor expressions can regulate emotion by introducing A) positive feedback via congruence, and B) negative feedback via suppression.

Congruence between a motor expression and an emotion provides positive feedback to that emotion, which increases the disposition to have and intensity of that emotion (Figure 2A). This is found across the emotion components, for instance: smiling increases the pleasantness associated with pleasant pictures [27]; arm flexion increases positive feelings when it suggests pulling something towards you that you desire, facilitating approach action tendencies [6]; smiling is shown to activate reward structures in the brain [29]; and mimicking emotion expressions increases the consciously experienced feelings of these emotions [12]. *Suppression* of a motor expression can lead to negative feedback, which decreases the disposition to have, and the intensity of an emerging emotion (Figure 2B). For instance, injecting Botox to block frowning reduces symptoms of mild depression [13]. These findings show two ways in which motor expressions can regulate emotion.

There are, however, certain *conditions* that need to be met for motor expressions to help regulate emotion. We hold the view that emotions are caused by personally relevant events that happen in an individuals' environment [26]. Hence, motor expressions do not 'cause' emotion, but regulate existing emotion. For instance, approach arm movements influence emotion when people subjectively evaluate the emotion of a face, but not when they evaluate its spatial properties [25]. Therefore, we assume that motor expressions need to happen around the same time an emotion is caused. Motor expressions must also fit with an emotion in order to regulate it. For instance, when predicting the cause of future problems and opportunities, adopting an angry or sad pose only influences the prediction of future problems, not opportunities [18]. We assume that these conditions need to be met if we want to use the function of motor expressions in emotion regulation.

Interactive systems designed to use the function of motor expressions in emotion regulation are scarce. One project that uses electrical stimulation of the muscles involved in smiling as a therapeutic tool appears to augment coping

[30]. Physical positioning using an automated chair has been used to impose postures that are congruent with movie scenes, which increased the perceived intensity of some positive movie scenes [19]. Embodied interactions have also been designed based on characteristics of motor expressions (postures) that associate with high and low power [16]. Used as a way to interact with a mathematics game, it was hypothesized that this would help to combat math anxiety, but no results on this have been published until now. However, there are reports of heightened emotional engagement in computer games that enable or impose motor expressions during interaction [3, 4, 17]. This demonstrates that it is possible, in certain circumstances, to develop interactive systems that hack the function of motor expressions in emotion regulation.

In this paper we will attempt to enable the regulation of positive emotion by designing arm gestures based on expressions of positive emotion and approach action tendencies, and negative emotion and avoidance action tendencies. This leads to our second hypothesis (H2).

H2: Using positive approach rather than negative avoidance arm gestures to interact with a system augments positive emotion.

EMOTION, MOTION, AND CREATIVITY

Based on the above, we believe that motor expressions may be able to help regulate positive emotion during a creative task because as well as emotion influencing creativity, creativity also causes emotion [2, 5]. In other words, we hypothesize that when a creative task causes emotion, and the motor expression 1) happens at the same time, and 2) fits with the caused emotion, it may be able to help regulate this emotion. For instance, positive emotion can help to generate many, diverse ideas [2] and generating many, diverse ideas can increase the likelihood that a generated idea is an original idea [22] as described above. This in itself can cause positive emotion [5] (Figure 3). A positive motor expression can then help regulate that positive emotion to the benefit of creativity (Figure 4).

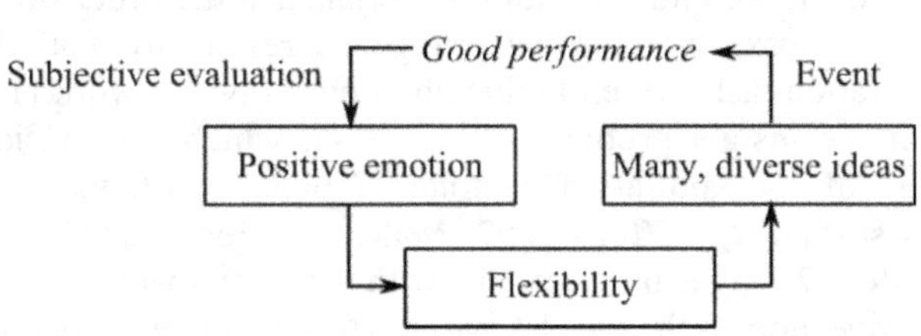

Figure 3. Illustration of the reciprocal nature of the relationship between positive emotion and creative ideation.

This way, motor expressions may influence creativity during idea generation and insight problem solving. In a previous study it has already been shown that smiling and performing arm flexion rather than frowning and performing arm extension helped regulate positive emotion, and via positive emotion, augmented creativity during an idea generation task [11]. In this paper we investigate translation of these findings into an interactive system that hacks the function of motor expressions in emotion regulation to augment creativity, which is novel in an interactive systems context.

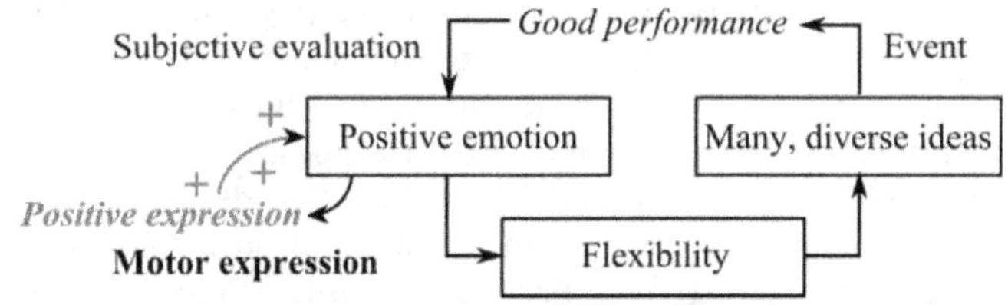

Figure 4. Illustration of how the reciprocal relation between positive emotion and creative ideation can be regulated by positive motor expressions.

We will focus on using arm expressions designed based on motor expressions of positive emotion and approach action tendencies as a means to regulate positive emotion and augment creativity during idea generation and insight problem solving. This leads to our third hypothesis (H3).

H3: Using positive approach rather than negative avoidance arm gestures to interact with a system augments creativity.

HACKING THE FUNCTION OF MOTOR EXPRESSIONS IN EMOTION REGULATION

To demonstrate our ideas we have developed a 'proof of concept' interactive system that: 1) uses arm gestures designed based on motor expressions that associate with positive emotion and approach tendencies, and with negative emotion and avoidance tendencies; and 2) uses a choreography of interaction that meets the conditions that are necessary for motor expressions to help regulate emotion.

Arm gestures

The *positive approach arm gesture* used to interact with our system is arm flexion (links to approach tendencies [6]) characterized by a centrifugal movement that starts at the side of the body and moves with a curve toward the heart, executed with a balanced level of muscle tension (links to positive emotion [7, 26]) (Figure 6A). This gesture is designed to increase positive emotion, when it occurs, via congruence, and decrease negative emotion via suppression. The *negative avoidance arm gesture* is arm extension (links to avoidance tendencies [6]) characterized by a centripetal movement that starts at the side of the body, then moves to the chest (diaphragm), and then outwards away from the body, using a slightly increased level of muscle force (links to negative emotion [7, 26]) (Figure 6B). This gesture is designed to increase negative emotion when it happens via congruence, and decrease positive emotion via suppression.

Choreography of interaction

To enable emotion regulation we designed a 'choreography' based on the conditions that enable motor expressions to regulate emotion. The arm gestures need to happen at the same time as any emotions caused during the creative task. We assume that emotions tend to happen right after an idea is generated or an insight problem is answered. These are events at which people might subjectively evaluate their creative task performance (e.g. positive: this idea was very good, or negative: again an idea of insufficient quality). If these caused emotions are positive and involve approach action tendencies, or are negative and involve avoidance action tendencies, the designed arm gestures can help regulate these emotions in an intended direction, and thereby influence creativity (Figure 5). To implement this, the arm gestures are consistently used immediately after people generate an idea or solve an insight problem.

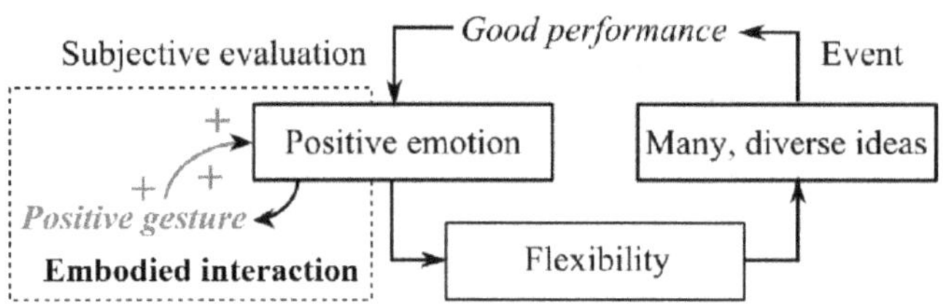

Figure 5. Illustration of how positive approach arm gestures used as part of embodied interaction can help regulate positive emotion due to the reciprocal relationship between creativity and positive emotion.

The interactive system

To test whether the arm gestures used in our proposed choreography of interaction enable us to hack the function of motor expressions in emotion regulation, we developed a basic interactive system for experimental purposes. This system is an application that hosts two creative activities, an idea generation task and an insight problem solving task. The system enables users to record their ideas or solutions with a Dictaphone by using the arm gestures.

The arm gestures are used to record an idea or solution just after it is generated, using a microphone. To start recording, the user does the arm gesture; to keep recording, the user keeps the end position of the gesture stable; and to stop recording the user releases the gesture. For the insight problem solving task releasing the arm gesture would also present the next insight problem. To meet the basic demands of the creativity tasks we present an image of the subject of the idea generation during the idea generation task, and the insight problems that need to be solved during the insight problem solving task on the screen. In case the arm gesture is used to record an idea, visual feedback is given by means of a blinking recording sign (• rec).

To enable the system to automatically trigger the recording, we use a Kinect sensor and a mechanical myograph in a classification setup. We capture the relative angles between the shoulder and the elbow, and the elbow and the wrist of the dominant arm with the Kinect; and muscle force from the biceps, triceps, flexor capri, and extensor capri is calculated by taking the root mean square of the signal of a mechanical myograph (Figure 6). We assume this captures the characteristics on which basis the gestures were designed, see [9] for further details. We trained four hidden Markov models to classify: no gesture; the start of the gesture; keeping the gesture; and releasing the gesture, using the Viterbi algorithm. The parameters were set using grid search. The user and researcher work together to record and annotate the data for the models. Classification is done using ARGMAX of a sequence on the log probability under each model. The developed models are automatically tested for performance. In case of insufficient performance (f_1-score<0.95) the researcher switches to a Wizard of Oz approach, i.e. the researcher triggers the recording him or herself when the user does the arm gesture.

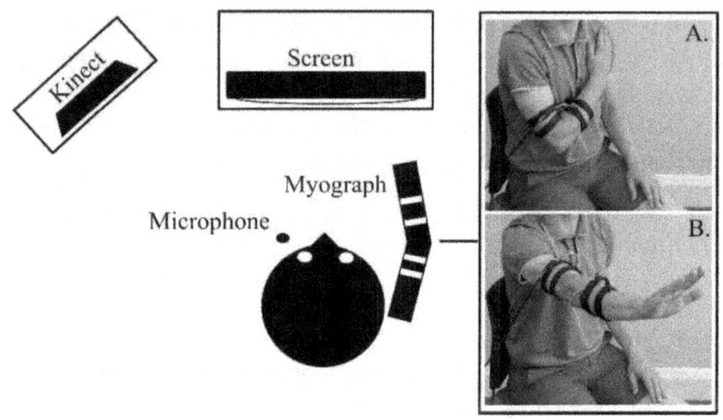

Figure 6. Illustration of the setup (left), and the end position of the A) positive approach and B) negative avoidance gesture.

METHOD

To evaluate the system, we used an experimental between-group setup with people in one group using the positive approach arm gesture, and people in the other group the negative avoidance arm gesture, to interact with the system. We favoured the between group over a within group setup because it enabled us, given limited resources, to test the interactive system with two different creativity tasks. Moreover, we chose to not counterbalance the order of the creative tasks because we prioritized results for the idea generation task, which builds upon our previous work [11], over the insight problem solving task, which we consider more of an exploration. In total 37 people participated in this study (M_{age}=32, SD_{age}=7, Males=20, Females=17, Left handed=7, Right handed=30), with 19 participants using a positive approach and 18 participants using the negative avoidance arm gesture. We switched to a Wizard of Oz mode with 8 participants in both experimental conditions. The participants were students and employees of City University London.

Creative tasks

As mentioned, we embedded two creative tasks in our application. Task 1 was the alternative uses task which was used to assess creativity during idea generation [24]. We instructed participants to generate as many and diverse original uses for a brick. They were given 5 minutes to do this. Task 2 was a verbal insight problem solving task which was used as an indicator of general creative problem solving ability [8]. We instructed participants to solve as many insight problems as they could within 10 minutes, but to try not to spend more than half a minute on each problem. Insight problems are verbal puzzles that have only one correct answer, but cannot easily be solved using the details provided in descriptions of the problems themselves, nor by step-by-step logical thinking (e.g. Q: Is it legal for a man to marry his widow's sister? A: No, he's dead.). For both tasks the participants were instructed to do their best.

Assessment of creativity

To assess creativity during idea generation, we analyzed the outcomes of the alternative uses task by counting the amount of ideas that a participant generated (fluency), the amount of semantic concepts used in the generated ideas (flexibility), and the statistical infrequency of the participants' ideas, given the ideas generated by all the participants [24]. To correct for inflation of originality for participants that were very fluent we used the percentage score, i.e. divided fluency by the count of original ideas [24]. To assess creativity during the insight problem solving task we calculated the percentage of correctly solved insight problems by dividing the amount of answered problems by the amount of correctly answered problems [8, 24].

Assessment of emotion

People self-reported their emotional state on a Likert scale (9 points) from negative to positive emotion after each task, which was part of a questionnaire.

Assessment of possible alternative causes

The questionnaire was further used to assess any possible alternative causes of variation by the designed arm gestures. To this end we asked people to self-report on the: 1) pleasantness and unpleasantness of the arm gestures themselves, 2) physical effort needed to perform the arm gestures, and 3) degree of freedom with which the arm could be moved given that there were four sensor units strapped to their arm, all by using Likert scales (9 points).

Procedure

Upon arrival, each participant was introduced to the study after which informed consent was signed. We strapped the myograph sensors to the participants' dominant arm, and calibrated the Kinect sensor. When the sensors worked correctly, the participants were given instructions to use either the positive approach or the negative avoidance arm gesture as an embodied interaction throughout the study. These were given by example by the researcher. After this, we were ready to start the recording of the arm gestures to train the arm recognition capabilities of the system. In case this did not lead to sufficient classification accuracy, we switched to a 'Wizard of Oz' approach before the two creativity tasks started. After this, we were ready to start the application for the alternative uses task (task 1) after which participants filled in a questionnaire. Then, participants used the application to perform the insight problem solving task (task 2), after which they again filled in a questionnaire. The participants were offered an opportunity to share their thoughts about the study, after which they received a £10 voucher for a large online retailer.

EXPERIMENTAL RESULTS

We first checked for possible alternate causes that could explain variation caused by the arm gestures by submitting them individually as dependent variables (DV) to a one-way ANOVA, with the arm gestures as the independent variable (IV). The results showed no significant differences between the pleasantness or unpleasantness of the arm gestures themselves ($F(1, 35)=0.38$, $p=.545$), the physical effort needed to do the arm gestures ($F(1, 35)=0.03$, $p=.866$) and the freedom with which the arm could be moved ($F(1, 35)=0.226$, $p=.638$). We will therefore not include these in further analysis.

Task 1: Idea generation

To test whether the interactive system augmented positive emotion and creativity during idea generation (H1), we correlated the assessed creativity variables fluency, flexibility, and originality, and emotion. The results show that there was a positive relationship between positive emotion and creativity during idea generation (Table 1). This relationship was characterized by no significant relationship between fluency and emotion, but rather by a significant positive relation between flexibility and positive emotion as well as originality and positive emotion. Higher positive emotion therefore related to higher flexibility and originality. This result supports H1.

	1.	2.	3.	4.
1. Fluency	-			
2. Flexibility	.739**	-		
3. Originality	.500**	.684**	-	
4. Emotion	.314	.493**	.574**	-

Table 1: Correlation between fluency, flexibility, originality, and self-reported emotion. ** is p<.005.

To test whether using positive approach rather than negative avoidance arm gestures to interact with the system augmented positive emotion during the idea generation task (H2), we submitted the assessed emotions as a DV to a one-way ANOVA with the arm gestures as the IV. The results showed that the participants who used a positive approach arm gesture rather than a negative avoidance arm gesture as a means of interaction, self-reported heightened positive emotion after the idea generation task (Table 2) in a way that is unlikely to be random ($F(1, 34)=5.97$, $p=.020$, $\eta^2=.153$). This supports H2.

DV \ IV	Positive appr.		Negative avoid.	
	Mean	SD	Mean	SD
Fluency	17.32	4.85	13.18	6.55
Flexibility	10.95	3.01	7.00	3.41
Originality	0.24	0.08	0.08	0.10
Emotion	6.89	1.24	5.81	1.34

Table 2: Means and standard deviations (SD) for the creativity and emotions assessments (DV) according to arm gesture (IV).

To test whether using positive approach rather than negative avoidance arm gestures to interact with the system augmented creativity during the idea generation task (H3), we used the same statistical approach, but with fluency, flexibility, and originality as the DVs. The results showed that participants using a positive approach rather than a negative avoidance arm gesture performed better creatively (Table 3), a result that was unlikely to be random, for fluency ($F(1, 34)=4.71$, $p=.045$, $\eta^2=.122$), flexibility ($F(1, 34)=13.62$, $p=.001$, $\eta^2=.286$), and originality ($F(1, 34)=25.52$, $p<.001$, $\eta^2=.430$). This supports H3.

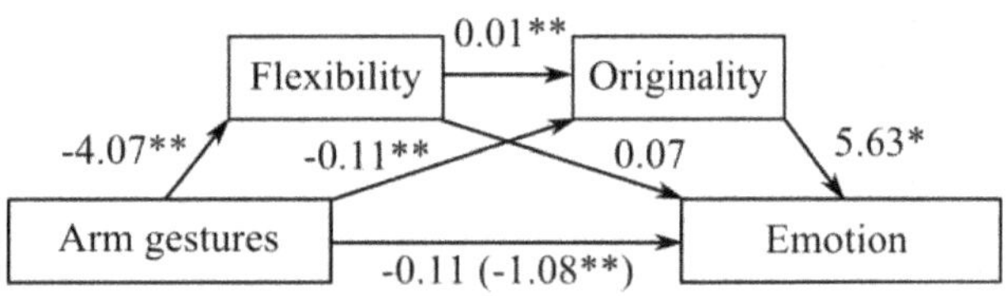

Figure 7. Conditional process model of the arm gestures, flexibility, originality, and emotion. * is p<.05, ** is p<.005.

To further explore the relationship between the arm gestures, emotion, and creativity, we performed conditional process analysis using the bootstrapping method [15]. Conditional process analysis is a non-parametric test that can be used to uncover the process or mechanisms that underlie an observed finding between an IV and DV, via other DVs (mediators). Note that the test cannot be used to test for causality between the mediators and the DV. We used this test with the arm gesture as the IV, flexibility and originality as the mediators, and emotion as the DV (Figure 7). Fluency was not included because we did not find a correlation with emotion (Table). The results showed no significant direct relationship between the arm gestures and emotion, i.e. the bounds of the confidence interval cross zero (B=0.11, 95% CI[-1.04 1.26]). Instead, the results show that the creativity parameters are conditional to the influence of the arm gestures on emotion. This conditional relationship with the arm gestures is characterized by a positive relationship between originality and emotion (B=-0.60, 95% CI[-1.51 -0.12]), and a positive relationship between flexibility, originality, and emotion (B=-0.28, 95% CI[-1.07 -0.06]), that is, the bounds of the confidence interval did not cross zero. Results for a possible relationship of the arm gestures with flexibility and emotion, without originality was not significant (B=-0.28, 95% CI[-1.26 0.17]). This provides preliminary evidence that positive approach rather than negative avoidance arm gestures help regulate positive emotion, when emotion is caused by the generation of original ideas. This supports the assumed process underlying our hypotheses (Figure 5).

Task 2: Insight problem solving

Before task 2 could be analyzed we checked whether the influence on emotion in task 1 carried over into the results of task 2. Results of a correlation showed no significant relationship between the emotions after task 1 and the percentage of correct answers ($r(1, 35)=.064$, $p=.715$). There were however, clues that emotion after task 1 carried over into task 2 ($r(1, 35)=.307$, $p=.073$). To address this issue we recoded the difference between the emotions after task 1 and after task 2 into a new variable for use in further analysis, to which we refer as emotion′, which represents the change in emotion that was observed.

To test whether the interactive system augmented positive emotion and creativity during the insight problem solving task (H1), we correlated the percentage of correct answers with emotion, and emotion′. Participants on average answered 15.47 insight problems (SD=6.94). The results showed no significant relationship between the correct answers and emotion ($r(1, 35)=.076$, $p=.659$), but did show a significant positive relationship between correct answers and emotion′ ($r(1, 35)=.335$, $p=.046$). A change toward more positive emotion relates to increased percentages of correctly answered insight problems. This supports H1.

DV \ IV	Positive appr.		Negative avoid.	
	Mean	SD	Mean	SD
Correct (%)	0.44	0.19	0.33	0.17
Emotion	6.25	1.52	5.81	1.64
Emotion′	1.45	3.69	1.31	2.98

Table 3: Means and standard deviations (SD) for the creativity and emotion assessments (DV) according to arm gesture (IV).

To test whether using positive approach rather than negative avoidance arm gestures to interact with the system augmented positive emotion during the insight problem solving task (H2), we submitted the assessed emotions and emotion′ individually as a DV to a one-way ANOVA with the arm gestures as the IV. The results showed no significant effect of the arm gestures on emotion after task 2 ($F(1, 35)=0.69$, $p=.413$) or on the recoded emotion′ ($F(1, 35)=0.12$, $p=.731$) (Table 3). This does not support H2.

To test whether using positive approach rather than negative avoidance arm gestures to interact with the system augmented creativity during the insight problem solving task (H3), we again used the same statistical approach, but with the percentage of correct answers as a DV. The results showed that positive approach rather than negative avoidance arm gestures increased the percentage of correctly answered insight problems (Table 3), in a way that is unlikely to be random ($F(1, 35)=5.09$, $p=.030$, $\eta^2=.127$). Positive approach rather than negative avoidance arm gestures increased the percentage of correctly solved insight problems. This supports H3.

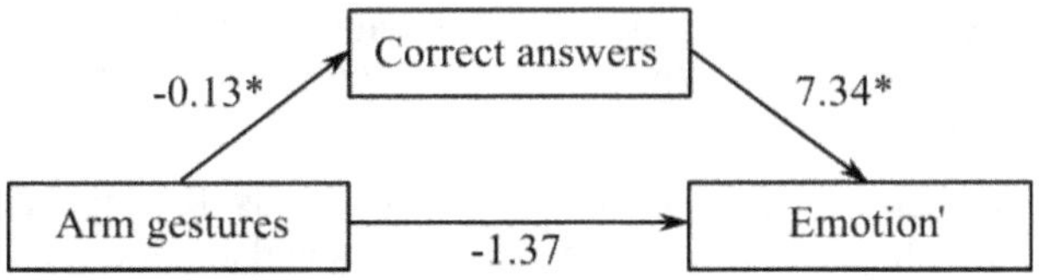

Figure 8. Conditional process model of the arm gestures, percentage of correct answers, and emotion′. * is p<.05.

Given that there was no direct relation between the arm gestures and emotion or emotion′, but there was between the arm gestures and the percentage of correct answers, and between correct answers and emotion′, it may be the case that the relationship between arm gestures, correct answers, and emotion′ follows a similar conditional process as we found in task 1. To test this we used the same statistical approach, but with the percentage of correctly answers as the mediator, and emotion′ as the DV (Figure 8). The results showed no direct relationship between the arm gestures and the emotion′, i.e. the bounds of the confidence interval crossed zero (B=-1.37, 95% CI[-3.67 0.93]). Instead, it showed a significant relation where the percentage of correct answers is conditional for positive rather than negative avoidance arm gestures to heighten positive emotion, i.e. the bounds of the confidence interval did not cross zero (*B=0.98,* 95% CI[0.07 2.41]). This provides preliminary evidence that positive approach rather than negative avoidance arm gestures help regulate positive emotion, when emotion is caused by solving insight problems. This supports the assumed process underlying our hypotheses (cf. Figure 5).

DISCUSSION AND CONCLUSION

Our findings demonstrate that an interactive system can be designed to hack the function of motor expressions in emotion regulation to help people perform better on certain creative tasks. Our findings show that when our interactive system augments positive emotion it also augments creativity (H1). This in itself is nothing new, but it validates this study within the context of previous research on the relationship between emotion and creativity. Our findings also show that when positive approach rather than negative avoidance arm gestures are used, positive emotion is augmented (H2). This finding is a novel contribution to research that aims to use embodied interaction designed based on characteristics of motor expressions to help regulate emotion [cf. 3, 4, 16, 17, 19, 30]. Finally, our findings show that using positive approach rather than negative avoidance arm gestures augments creativity during an idea generation task and an insight problem solving task (H3). This finding is a novel contribution to research that aims to develop interactive systems that influence emotion with the goal to augment creativity, as it provides a novel, embodied, approach to attain that goal [cf. 20, 21, 23]. As such, this research provides opportunities for new technologies that draw on embodied interaction to help regulate emotion, including possible applications such as such as gaming and entertainment [3, 4, 17, 19], education [16], and therapeutic technologies [30], as well as creativity support tools [20, 21, 23].

Moreover, our further exploration of the data provides preliminary evidence for a process that underlies our approach. This is indicated by the finding that there is no direct relationship between the arm gestures and emotion, but that this is dependent on an increase in originality during the idea generation task, and insight problem solving performance during the insight problem solving task. This appears to match with our ideas about the role of the arm gestures in the relationship between emotion and creativity, which is the assumption that for the arm gestures to have an influence on emotion, an emotion must be generated, and this emotion is generated when the user believes that he or she is doing well (Figure 5).

Interpretation of the results needs to be limited to the context of use in our interactive system, and the conditions posed by our experimental setup. However, the results also point toward interesting limitations in the possible utility of our approach. Whereas during idea generation the results were clear, during insight problem solving there were less pronounced relationships between the arm gestures, emotion, and creativity. Considering that the change in emotion was also characterized by relatively large standard deviations, it might be that other factors, which we did not measure, had a stronger influence on emotion during insight problem solving. However, another explanation could be that the used arm gestures are only effective for a limited amount of time due to habituation [cf. 28]. We cannot rule out the latter because we did not randomize task order.

The results also reveal a possible limitation in the effectiveness of our approach. People who used positive approach arm gestures reported more positive emotion than the people who used the negative avoidance arm gestures, but the latter people were still positive on average. It could well be that the used creative activities did not generate sufficient negative emotion for the arm gestures to help regulate these emotions, and all that we found was that positive approach arm gestures increase positive emotion, and negative avoidance arm gestures suppress positive emotion. Therefore we cannot know from these results whether the function of motor expressions in emotion regulation can be hacked for emotions other than positive ones. Previous attempts at hacking the function of motor expressions in emotion regulation suffered from similar complications [19, 30].

We believe that the latter can be investigated further by pairing embodied interactions designed based on motor expressions, with novel techniques that cause emotion. This will be addressed in future research.

REFERENCES

1. Akhbari Chermahini, S. and Hommel, B. More creative through positive mood? Not everyone!. *Frontiers in Human Neuroscience 6*, (2012), article 319.
2. Baas, M., De Dreu, C.K.W., and Nijstad, B.A. A meta-analysis of 25 years of mood-creativity research: Hedonic tone, activation, or regulatory focus?. *Psychological Bulletin 134*, 6 (2008), 779-806.
3. Bianchi-Berthouze, N. Understanding the role of body movement in player engagement. *Human-Computer Interaction 28*, 1 (2013), 40-75.
4. Bianchi-Berthouze, N., Kim, N.N., and Patel, D. Does body movement engage you more in digital game play? And why?. In *Proc. ACII 2007*, (2007), 102-113.
5. Brunyé, T.T., et al. Happiness by association: Breadth of free associations influences affective states. *Cognition 127*, (2013), 93-98.
6. Centerbar, D.B. and Clore, G.L. Do approach-avoidance actions create attitudes?. *Psychological Science 17*, 1 (2006), 22-29.
7. Dael, N., Mortillaro, M., and Scherer, K.R. Emotion expression in body action and posture. *Emotion 12*, 5 (2012), 1085-1101.
8. de Bono, E. *Lateral thinking: creativity step by step*. Harper & Row, London, UK, 1970.
9. de Rooij, A. Technical Report: Arm Expression Recognition using Acoustic Myography. http://www.alwinderooij.com/publications/acousticmyography2013.pdf
10. de Rooij, A. & Jones, S. Mood and Creativity: An Appraisal Tendency Perspective. In *Proc. C&C 2013*, (2013), 362-365.
11. de Rooij, A. & Jones, S. Motor Expressions as Creativity Support: Exploring the Potential for Physical Interaction. In *Proc. BCS HCI 2013*, (2013), article 47.
12. Flack, W. Peripheral feedback effects of facial expressions, bodily postures, and vocal expressions on emotional feelings. *Cognition & Emotion 20*, (2006), 177–195.
13. Finzi, E., and Wasserman, E. Treatment of depression with Botulinum Toxin A: a case Series. *Dermatologic Surgery 32*, 5 (2006), 645–650.
14. Gross, J.J. The emerging field of emotion regulation: An integrative review. *Review of General Psychology 2*, 3 (1998), 271-299.
15. Hayes, A.F. *An introduction to mediation, moderation, and conditional process analysis*. The Guilford Press, New York, NY, 2013.
16. Isbister, K., Karlesky, M., Frye, J., and Rao, R. Scoop! A movement-based math game designed to reduce math anxiety. *Ext. Abstracts CHI 2012*, (2012), 1075-1078.
17. Isbister, K., Schwekendiek, U., and Frye, J. Wriggle: an exploration of emotional and social effects of movement. *Ext. Abstracts CHI 2011*, (2011), 1885-1890.
18. Keltner, D., Ellsworth, P.C., and Edwards, K. Beyond simple pessimism: effects of sadness and anger on social perception. *Journal of Personality and Social Psychology 4*, (1993), 740–752.
19. Kok, R. and Broekens, J. Physical emotion induction and its use in entertainment: lessons learned. In *1st IFIP Entertainment Computing Symposium*, (2008), 33-48.
20. Lewis, S., Dontcheva, M., and Gerber, E. (2011). Affective Computational Priming and Creativity. In *Proc. CHI 2011*, (2011), 735-744.
21. Morris, R.R., Dontcheva, M., Finkelstein, A., and Gerber, E. Affect and creative performance on crowd-sourcing platforms. In *Proc. ACII 2013*, (2013), 67-72.
22. Mumford, M.D., Medeiros, K.E., and Partlow, P.J. Creative thinking: processes, strategies, and knowledge. *The Journal of Creative Behavior 46*, 1 (2012), 30-47.
23. Nakazato, N., Yoshida, S., Sakurai, S., Narumi, T., Tanikawa, T., and Hirose, M. Smart Face: enhancing creativity during video conferences using real-time facial deformation. In *Proc. CSCW 2014*, (2014), 75-83.
24. Plucker, J.A., Qian, M., and Wang, S. Is originality in the eye of the beholder? Comparison of scoring techniques in the assessment of divergent thinking. *The Journal of Creative Behavior 45*, 1 (2011), 1-22.
25. Rotteveel, M. and Phaf, R.H. Automatic affective evaluation does not automatically predispose for arm flexion and extension. *Emotion 4*, (2004), 156-72.
26. Scherer, K.R. The dynamic architecture of emotion: Evidence for the component process model. *Cognition and Emotion 23*, 7 (2009), 1307-1351.
27. Soussignan, R. Duchenne smile, emotional experience, and autonomic reactivity: A test of the facial feedback hypothesis. *Emotion 2*, (2002), 52-74.
28. Stepper, S. and Strack, F. Proprioceptive determinants of emotional and nonemotional feelings. *Journal of Personality Social Psychology 64*, (1993), 211–220.
29. Wiswede, D., Munte, T.F., Kramer, U.M., and Russeler, J. Embodied emotion modulates neural signature of performance monitoring. *PLoS ONE 4*, (2009), e5754.
30. Zariffa, J., Hitzig, S.L., and Popovic, M.L. Neuromodulation of emotion using functional electrical stimulation applied to facial muscles. *Neuromodulation: technology at the neural interface 17*, 1 (2014), 85-92.

PaperFold: Evaluating Shape Changes for Viewport Transformations in Foldable Thin-Film Display Devices

Antonio Gomes
Human Media Lab
Queen's University
Kingston, ON, Canada, K7L3N6
gomes@cs.queensu.ca

Roel Vertegaal
Human Media Lab
Queen's University
Kingston, ON, Canada, K7L3N6
roel@cs.queensu.ca

ABSTRACT
In this paper, we investigate the use of shape changes in a multi-segmented mobile device for triggering viewport transformations in its graphical interface. We study PaperFold, a foldable device with reconfigurable thin-film electrophoretic display tiles. PaperFold enables users to attach, reorient and fold displays in a mobile form factor that is thin and lightweight even when fully collapsed. We discuss how our design was informed by a participatory study that resulted in 14 preferred shape changes. In a subsequent study, we asked users to rank the utility of shape changes for triggering common view operations in map and text editing applications. Results suggest participants were able to attribute specific view operations as automated responses to folding, attaching, reorienting or detaching displays. Collated or full screen views were preferred when users collocated two displays. When adding a third display, alternative views such as toolbars or a list of apps were suggested. Showing 3D views was strongly associated with folding PaperFold segments into a three dimensional structure.

ACM Classification Keywords
H.5.2. [Information interfaces and Presentation]: User Interfaces - *Interaction Styles, Evaluation/Methodology.*

Author Keywords
Human Factors; Organic User Interfaces; Flexible Displays; Foldable User Interfaces.

INTRODUCTION
For reasons of portability, mobile devices have displays that are limited in size and constrained by weight. Despite increases in resolution, such size restrictions have resulted in sequential interaction paradigms for mobile platforms, in which apps are opened and closed one by one. By contrast, the display size of paper documents can be modulated easily through folding, tearing or combining multiple page elements. Such properties allow paper documents to be navigated and organized more efficiently, allowing concurrent access to multiple documents [19]. Paper is also very thin, durable and lightweight, perceived advantages in the mobile design space. As such, the development of electronic paper computers that adopt certain qualities or metaphors of interacting with paper documents has been an enduring research goal [9,19]. While initial research was aimed at mimicking form factors or interaction techniques of paper documents using rigid display devices [1,8], in recent years, progress has been made towards developing computers made of flexible E-Ink displays as thin and lightweight as paper [4,22].

TEI '15, January 15–19, 2015, Stanford, California, USA.

http://dx.doi.org/10.1145/2677199.2680572

Figure 1. PaperFold prototype folded into a 3D Hull.

In this paper, we investigate how thin-film, paper-like electrophoretic mobile devices [4,5,12,22] might adopt dynamic modulation of screen real estate through folding and tearing techniques in a prototype device called PaperFold[1] (Figure 1) [5]. A number of paper metaphors served as inspiration to the design of our prototype, which, like paper, allows for multiple display segments to be folded into smaller form factors. Books use folding as both a navigational and space saving technique. Paper maps use display size modulation via folding techniques of increasing shape resolution [17]. PaperFold combines the benefits of context-aware multi-display devices with paper-like thinness and familiar interaction metaphors.

Why Thinness and Light Weight are Relevant

We believe thin, flexible displays are essential when trying to mimic the kind of tactile-kinesthetic navigation, expandable screen real estate and lightweight multi-display experiences that paper offers to users. The kind of folding seen in today's mobile devices [3,20] or previous explorations [1,2,7,8] cannot be regarded as similar because the thickness of individual display segments impacts the total thickness of a folded device, while the weight of each display segment impacts overall portability. Although none of the known flexible display technologies are capable of employing creases like paper, tessellation of flexible displays allows for size modulations that approximate those of foldable paper maps. While we aim to produce more complex folds, we limited ourselves to what can be achieved with current flexible technology.

Contribution

In this paper, we evaluate the effectiveness of shape changes as viewport transformations. We present PaperFold, a prototype device consisting of 3 flexible display segments that can be combined in arbitrary configurations. We discuss interaction techniques that utilize shape changes to perform view operations, e.g. adding a display segment extends a document's view; folding segments such that they can be viewed by others produces shared views. We report on a participatory design study that resulted in 14 shapes that can be produced with PaperFold, and a subsequent study in which participants ranked view operations to changes between shapes. Results suggest participants were able to attribute specific view operations to specific shape changes. We conclude with design recommendations for matching shape changes to view operations in reconfigurable mobile devices.

RELATED WORK

While there has been research into folding displays into various form factors, most of the display technologies in prior studies were either simulations with paper mockups [14], projection [9,10,11], or thick and rigid display devices that are not particularly suitable for folding [1,2,7,8,15,18]. Other explorations focused on interactions with single displays that were stacked or placed in close proximity [4,22]. PaperFold bridges the tradeoff between portability and increased screen real estate by introducing a reconfigurable mobile display device with thin-film screens that stay within acceptable boundaries of weight and thickness.

Slate Display Form Factors

There is a large body of work on book form factors involving rigid dual-screen form factors that can orient around one axis. Pocket Edge [3] combined a tablet computer and an eBook reader in a dual-display interactive device. Sony Tablet P [20] featured interoperating hinged displays. Chen et al. [1] discussed an e-book reader featuring two displays mounted on two separate slates that can be used in side-by-side or detached configurations. Their design supported embodied navigation techniques like folding, flipping, and fanning. Their findings suggested that having additional displays offers a better support for lightweight navigation.

Multi-display Form Factors

Chen et al. [2] evaluated a multi-slate reading system, aimed at understanding how increased screen real estate across multiple devices can enhance navigation and interaction techniques in reading activities. Their results indicated that multi-slate reading systems have the potential to recapture many of the affordances associated with physical documents, while providing functionality that surpasses that of paper. Hinckley et al. [7] showed the use of tablet PCs for spanning contiguous images across multiple display surfaces. The system used simultaneous deceleration as a means for detecting connections, and was capable of performing simple view operations such as collating two displays, or spanning an image across two displays upon connection. Hinckley et al.'s [8] Codex, a dual-screen tablet computer, was an exception to the above work in that its displays are detachable and reconfigurable into various form factors. Codex can be oriented in a variety of postures to support individual work, ambient display, or collaboration with another user. The authors demonstrate interaction techniques supporting division of labor for tasks across displays. Their findings identify several benefits for detachable displays systems (i.e. *Division of Tasks between Screens; Collaboration between devices; Sidebars).* Siftables [15] demonstrated a series of networked compact devices with embedded displays that could be physically manipulated as a group to interact with digital information. Although it was able to span visuals across multiple displays, Siftables lacked connective hinges and featured thick screen objects. The rigidity and thick form factor of the displays employed in the above explorations posed real drawbacks in terms of portability and physical effort.

Thin-film Display Form Factors

DisplayStacks [4] presented a system for physically interacting with digital information via stacks of thin-film displays. It introduced tools for navigating digital documents using piles of physical display windows. DisplayStacks combined affordances of paper documents with electronic content. PaperTab [22] later featured an environment in which multiple thin-film displays work together through proximity sensing to mimic a physical paper desktop experience.

Foldable Thin-film Designs

Lee et al. [13] explored image projection on foldable materials to simulate flexible displays with variable form factors. Their findings suggested that devices that can incorporate large surfaces in a small collapsible volume offer advantages for mobile contexts. Xpaaand [10] featured a handheld device encapsulating a rollable display. The authors explored dynamic resizing as a means of interacting with digital contents. Their results indicated that having the ability to physically manipulate screen real state may effectively improve interaction with handheld devices. FoldMe [11] simulated thin-film displays on the front and back sides of a mockup device foldable along predefined hinges. Their results suggested folding navigation techniques could improve manipulation of information for portable devices. Folds in this system were limited to a pre-defined axis. Paddle [16] used projection to represent highly deformable mobile devices that can be transformed into various special-purpose controls. Their results suggested benefits over touch interaction techniques commonly used on mobile devices. We borrow from the aforementioned explorations, in designing a multi-segmented reconfigurable mobile device that can be attached and detached into arbitrary configurations along multiple axis, noting that none of the above systems used real flexible displays.

DESIGN RATIONALE

We believe that building a prototype using real flexible displays is valuable due to their unique properties in terms of thinness, lightweight and malleability. Current displays are too thick and heavy to be able to achieve the kind of shape transformations seen in our study without significant physical effort by the user. Additionally, to our knowledge there has not been a systematic exploration of three-way folding in multi-display systems. To inform the design of a multi-segmented reconfigurable mobile device, we used the following design criteria:

Use of Folding to Modulate Screen Size

Our first goal was to allow users to modulate the size of screen real estate of the device between folded conditions and expanded shapes. While there have been examples of rollable devices [10], we consider folding to be a more natural metaphor as it allows the overall form factor to be similar to that of current smartphones. We believed unfolding would typically be used to expand the size of an existing view.

Reconfigurability and Tile Geometry

Hinged displays can only be folded along one dimension. In order to increase the number of form factors, we explored attachment/detachment on multiple sides of the displays. This allows users to go from, e.g. tablet form factors to paper notebook while maintaining a simple folding interface. Unlike [1,2,8], our work explores view-transformations beyond 2 segments while preserving portability. Detachability also allows users to increase or reduce the number of displays dynamically, and implement concurrent usage scenarios with multiple displays. In particular, our design aimed to increase the subset of shapes demonstrated in previous explorations.

Orientation

The ability to alter the orientation has been used in smartphones to switch between landscape and portrait viewports. In PaperFold, orientation takes on a different role as re-orienting the device may dramatically alter the affordances of a shape, as well as visibility of information on the displays. We hypothesized that orientation of the device would therefore affect the function of the device.

Number and Angle of Tiles

The number of display segments creates a tradeoff between shape resolution and portability of the device. More display segments result in complex cable management, since currently available flexible displays are not wireless. As we will discuss in our participatory study, folding a four segment device into a one segment device alters the shape geometry of the device along two concurrent dimensions, making it more difficult for users to (un)fold the device. Shapes created by 3 segments are primarily determined by their geometry and angle of displays towards one another.

3D Shapes

Using a minimum of three displays allows users to simulate certain known display shapes through simple morphological mimicry. A flat configuration resembles a book or map form factor. Bending the displays inwards simulates a concave display that might mimic gaming or virtual reality scenarios. Bending the displays outwards, users can simulate a segment of a spherical display. A 60-degree angle between 3 displays creates a closed 3D hull. A 90-degree arrangement resembles a portion of a cube [21]. One of the questions we were interested in investigating was whether users would associate such shapes with 3D objects.

Sharing

Different orientations of display segments may cause them to be visible to the user, other users, or hidden altogether. According to Hinckley [8], configuration of tiles could be a design parameter for determining whether a shape indicated shared or private interactions.

Matching Shape Changes to Viewport Transformations

Segments of PaperFold form building blocks that can be "shaped" into an application. We investigated the relative transformation between shape states as an interaction technique. If we generalize the above discussion, we note that shape transitions in PaperFold typically appear to affect its viewport. To further investigate this, we conducted a participatory study.

USER STUDY 1: PARTICIPATORY STUDY

Our methodologies were inspired by Hinckley et al., who evaluated the affordances of pen-operated dual-display devices [8], Chen et al. [1] who compared a dual-display reader with single-display devices in typical reading tasks, and Khalilbeigi et al. [11], who studied functions that can be assigned to mockup double-sided displays with pre-defined hinges. To investigate what would be the most functional shapes of a foldable device, we conducted a participatory design session in which subjects were presented with 4 *10x15x0.15cm* 3D printed tiles without displays. Each tile contained magnets that allowed participants to interconnect as well as hold shape at right angles.

Task & Participants

To determine what configurations users would find appropriate for particular tasks, they were asked to imagine a device in which the tiles featured displays showing apps similar to those on their mobile phones. Users were told that

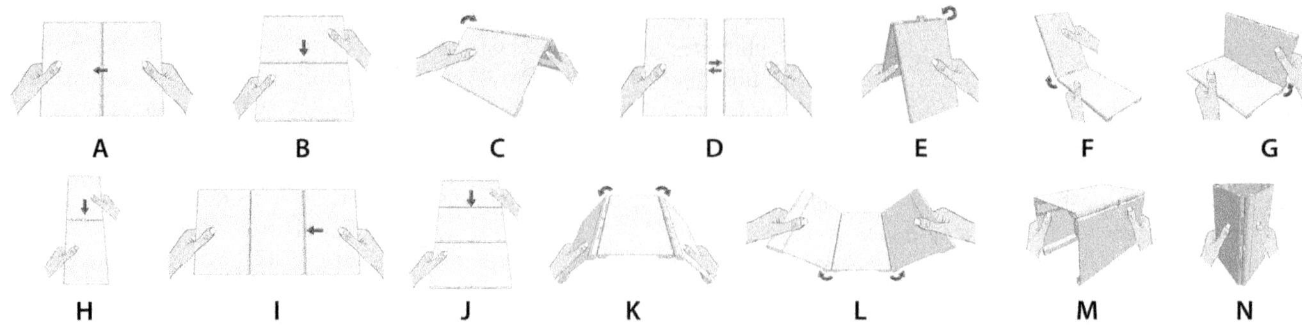

Figure 2. The 14 participant defined shape configurations used in matching shape changes to view operations.

apps could span multiple displays. They were then asked to create what they thought of as the most useful transformations of shape for a 2 display hinged/detachable device. We then repeated the exercise imagining 3 displays and 4 displays. For each shape, we asked participants to propose an associated functionality. 15 participants volunteered for this study (6 females, 9 males; mean 23 years). Subjects received $10 for 1 hour of participation.

Results

Results suggest that participants had difficulty relating to the 4 tile configurations. All participants preferred using a maximum of 3 tiles. Most participants carried multiple devices, such as smartphones, tablets and laptops on a routine basis (*Mean*: 4.07, *s.d.*: 1.16). However, they preferred to use a single device with different form factors, if this was possible (*Mean*: 4.73, *s.d.*: 0.46). Figure 2 shows the most common shape changes produced by participants for 2 and 3 tiles configurations: Holding the display in portrait (A,E,F,K,L), landscape (B,C,H,J) and 3D (M,N) orientations; Attaching displays horizontally (A,I) and vertically (B,F,J); Detaching displays (D); Bending Displays Inwards (L) and Outwards (K); Folding the displays into triangular (E,N), perpendicular (G,N) and cube-like structures (M). When asked what functionality these shapes or shape changes might have in a device, participants comments almost exclusively referred to view operations that are common in GUIs. We synthesized these comments into a list of potential view operations, shown in Figure 3.

APPARATUS

PaperFold is a foldable thin-film device with 3 detachable flexible display tiles. The design of our prototype was informed by the results of our participatory design study. Each tile consists of a flexible thin-film E Ink display, and a flexible 3D printed substrate with embedded sensors that allows the system to determine the orientation and connections of individual tiles (Figure 4).

Flexible Displays

Each PaperFold segment features a flexible 6.5" E-Ink display. Magnetic hinges allow a continuous data connection between displays. Each display is coupled to a driver board connected to a computer controlling the logic and interface graphics.

3D Printed Tiles

PaperFold's flexible 3D printed segments measure 15x10 *cm* with a thickness of 1.25*mm*. Magnetic hinges allow PaperFold tiles to be attached in a variety of configurations (Figure 4). Note that the increased thickness at the extremities of the tile is only a function of the required size of the embedded magnets. Hall Effect sensors in the tiles monitor the magnetic field in their vicinity, allowing our system to detect distinct connections among various tiles. A 9DOF IMU calculates the absolute orientation of each tile. Using this information, we are able to determine what view operations should occur upon distinct shape configurations.

Sensing Touch

E-Ink displays pose challenges to sensing touch, as their functioning requires pixels to be applied with positive or negative charges to produce the desired graphics. Readily available touch solutions have shown to interfere with the screen refresh mechanism of e-ink displays. We designed flexible printed circuit layers to sense touch input by measuring changes in capacitance between direct touch and the electrode pads.

USER STUDY 2: MATCHING SHAPE CHANGES TO VIEW OPERATIONS

In a subsequent experiment, we evaluated the use of our PaperFold prototype for effecting view operations via shape changes. We asked participants to rate the match between each shape change and the list of view operations suggested in our participatory study. Due to the nature of the participatory design session, we used a different set of participants to avoid bias towards choosing view operations our first subset of users had suggested.

Shape Changes

Figure 2 shows the 14 shape transformations used in our second study. Note that some are applied to different orientations but topologically identical. Another defining factor was the orientation of the hinge location: vertical or horizontal. To illustrate, a vertically hinged portrait display looks like a notebook. A horizontally hinged portrait display looks like a book.

View Operations

In our study, we asked participants to match the list of 12 view operations in Figure 3 to the most frequently performed shape changes derived from our participatory design session.

Figure 3. A list of view operations in GUIs suggested by participatory design session.

Task

For each shape change, we asked participants to rank each of the 12 view operations for appropriateness using questionnaire items with a 5-point Likert scale (Strongly Agree-Strongly Disagree) that answered the following question: *"When I change the shape of this device in this way, it [View Operation]."*

Experiment Design and Participants

All participants experienced all shape changes in the same order. To avoid bias, the list of view operations was presented in random order. 12 participants took part in the experiment (6 Female; 6 Male; Mean Age: 21.3). All participants received $10 for 1 hour of participation.

Procedure

During training, each of the 12 view operations were demonstrated in a GUI desktop application to avoid biasing participants with PaperFold examples. Increasing the size of the window and revealing more of an image demonstrated *Collate/Extend View*. *Show Full Screen* was demonstrated by showing a full screen window containing an entire photo. *Show Thumbnails* was demonstrated by showing thumbnails of the photo library; *Zoom In/Out* was demonstrated by zooming in and out of a photo without changing the window size. *Duplicate View* was demonstrated by showing two windows with the same image. *Show 3D View* was demonstrated by showing a 3D model of the object on the photo. Other view operations were demonstrated by showing: a keyboard; a toolbar; a phone keypad; a photo in one window and a notepad in another; and an empty window.

Participants were then introduced to the prototype, instructed on the task and given the questionnaire. A display showed a list of image transformations from which each view operation could be constructed on PaperFold. This list was similar to the images shown in Figure 3. The experimenter then loaded the first image onto the first display, after which participants were asked to make the first shape change in Figure 2: Attaching a second display horizontally. Participants were asked to go through the questionnaire and pick a favorite operation to perform upon this shape change, if there was one. They were then asked to select the images

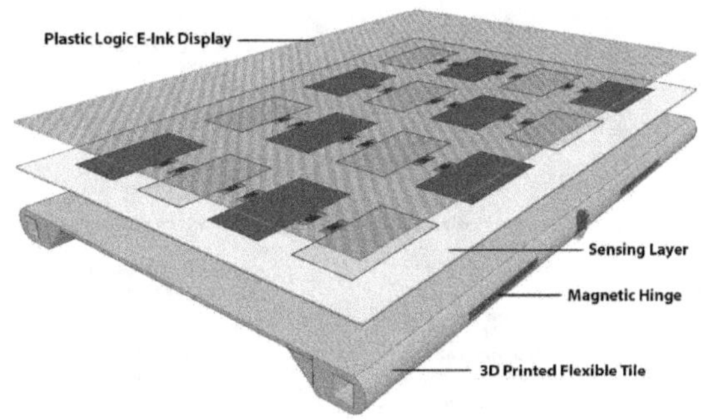

Figure 4. Exploded view of a PaperFold segment.

on the display that would best show this operation on the prototype. They then rated the view operation on the questionnaire, and were asked whether there were any operations in the list that they thought would match this shape change. If so, they were given the option to show these on the prototype and rate them.

Applications

All shapes were repeated for each of two applications: 1) A text editor showing pages of a scientific paper 2) A Google map application showing a map of London. We based our choice on applications described in previous work: [1] focused on reading activities on dual-display devices; [8] presented a pen-operated note taking application; and [11] demonstrated interaction techniques for browsing maps using mockup foldable displays. Additionally, the results of our participatory design study showed a strong user preference for these application scenarios.

RESULTS

Figure 5 shows the means and standard deviations for the scores matching view operations with shape changes, for portrait, landscape and 3D conditions in both application scenarios. A non-parametric analysis of variance (Friedman Test evaluated at $\alpha<.05$) showed significant differences between view operation scores for each shape change in the text application (Friedman's $\chi^2(11)>21.11$, $p<.05$), with the exception of *Fold 3D Triangular Hull* (Friedman's $\chi^2(11)=18.436$, $p=0.072$). In the map application, results also showed significant differences between view operation scores for each shape change (Friedman's $\chi^2(11)>23.9$, $p<.05$). Due to the exhaustive nature of possible comparisons, and because we intended our results as design heuristics, we did not perform further post-hoc tests. Instead, we assigned the highest ranked viewport for any given shape change as a best match, but only if it had a positive rating, i.e., higher than 3.0. Note that by picking the top match, we interpreted our data at the ordinal level of measurement. Approximately half our top matches in the *Text Editing Scenario* had a score above or equal to 4.0, suggesting strong preferences for these particular view operations. Optional alternative view operations, with scores between 3.0 and 4.0, are also displayed. Finally, note that in the below section, whenever we make a statement such as: "users preferred", we do not suggest such statement scientifically accurate, but rather as a trend that informs the design process.

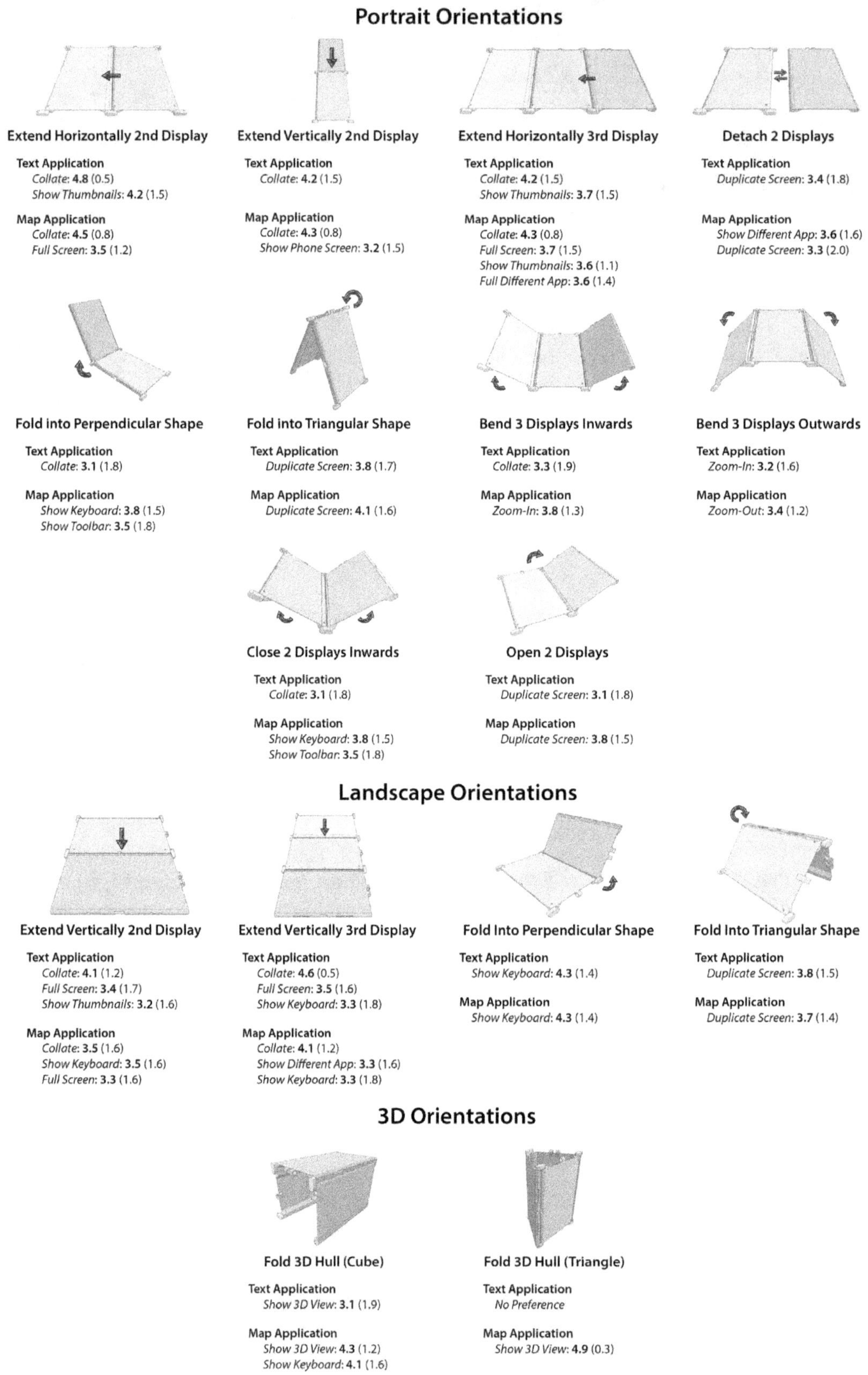

Figure 5. Mean ratings and (*standard deviations*) for matching view operations to presented shape changes for both applications

User Agreement

Since we expected multiple view operations to match any one particular shape, we decided against calculating a measure of agreement. Instead, because the Likert scale deployed does approximate an interval level of measurement, we examine the standard deviations as providing some indication of user agreement. In the text application, standard deviations, as shown in Figure 5, were low in most cases, averaging 1.33. In the map application, standard deviations averaged 1.3. This suggests users generally agreed well on rankings for both applications.

Matching View Operations to Shape Changes

Text Application

Extending the display, in both orientations, was strongly associated with the *Collate* operation. In portrait conditions, participants preferred *Show Thumbnails* as an alternative. In landscape conditions, *Full Screen* or *Show Keyboard* were suggested. Neither bending 3 displays inwards or outwards had a strong user association in the case of the text application. Bending inwards was associated with *Collate*, while bending outwards was associated with *Zoom In*. Users had a weak association with *Show 3D View* in the landscape condition. In portrait mode, there was an equally weak association with folding the display into a perpendicular shape as pertaining to *Collate*. However, in the landscape condition, there was a strong preference for *Show Keyboard*. In portrait conditions, Folding Displays into a triangular shape was associated with *Duplicate Screen*. Finally, for Detach Displays, *Duplicate Screen* was preferred.

Map Application

Extending the displays in the portrait condition was highly ranked for the *Collate* operation, in both horizontal and vertical conditions. For the third display, *Show Thumbnails, Show Keyboard, Show Different App* and *Duplicate Screen* were also ranked positively. In the landscape condition, second display, participants split their top ratings between *Collate* and *Show Keyboard*. For the landscape, third display, there was a clearer preference for *Collate*, with *Show Thumbnails, Show Keyboard* and *Show Different App* ranked positively. Bending 3 Displays Inwards, Outwards and Fold 3D Hull (Triangle) were all associated with *Show 3D View*. In the landscape condition, there was a strong preference of *Show 3D View* for Fold 3D Hull (Cube), with *Duplicate Screen* considered an alternative. In both c, there was a clear association between folding the display into a perpendicular shape and *Show Keyboard*. In both portrait and landscape conditions, Folding Displays into a shape was associated with *Duplicate Screen*. Finally, for Detach Displays *Show Different App* had the strongest rating, with *Duplicate Screen* and *Show Phone* considered weaker alternatives.

User Comments and Observations

Throughout the experiment, participants were encouraged to verbalize their thought processes, which were noted by the experimenters. Overall, participants liked having the ability to arrange PaperFold in various configurations, thus being able to dynamically alter viewports. *"I would like to be able to customize the functions of different shapes."* [P2]. There were benefits identified for using PaperFold as a multitasking system. *"I enjoyed having the ability to distribute different applications across displays and access them concurrently."* [P5, P8]. While browsing through maps, users were particularly impressed with the 3D View features of our system. *"3D shapes with multiple displays lead themselves to viewing 3D models."* [P11]. Additional benefits identified include adding peripherals [P4,P10]; thumbnails/toolbars [P3,P11]; or using PaperFold as means for distributing information, by physically detaching and sharing panels [P12].

DISCUSSION

For both application scenarios, results suggest that users associate shape changes of PaperFold's screens with specific view operations. Some shape changes are, however, more ambiguous than others. For example, extending PaperFold with a 3rd horizontal display rates above neutral on 4 different view operations. But even in those cases, generally only one or two view operations rank highly for each shape change. We will now discuss differences in trends between the two application scenarios, trying to generalize our results into design recommendations for viewport behaviors in folding multi-display user interfaces.

Horizontal Extensions

When extending the displays horizontally, the most highly ranked view operation was consistently *Collate*. In the case of the text editor, where a contextual overview of data objects is applicable, participants ranked *Show Thumbnails* higher than a *Full Screen* operation. In the map browser, which has no clear delineation of specific data objects, participants were more inclined to try and fit the data on two screens. Observations of image selections during the experiment strongly suggests that participants preferred to extend a thumbnail display with a second display showing a full screen view of the first thumbnail. Since participants chose to extend a full screen display with a collated view they overwhelmingly chose *Collated View* as the highest rated answer for both cases. Only when a third display was attached, did participants widen their options, with scores for collated views ranking lower and thumbnails higher.

Vertical Extensions

For vertical portrait extensions, *Collate* generally appears the preferred option. *Collate* is also the highest ranking option for vertical landscape extensions, where keyboard is also a strong option.

3D Shapes

Bending three displays inwards or outwards was much more highly ranked for *Show 3D View* operations in the map application, where data elements were not inherently limited to 2D. Observations confirmed that in the text editor scenarios, participants had difficulty relating any 3D operations to the inherent 2D nature of the data element. In general, folding the displays into a 3D hull was the shape change most strongly associated with *Show 3D View*. This suggests that users associate the shape of the device with known objects of similar form factor.

Detach

Detaching a screen was less easily generalizable: In the map application detaching the displays was most strongly associated with *Show Different App*. In the text editor application *Duplicate Screen* was preferred. View operations that were not ranked positively for any shape change in either application scenario included: *Zooming; Show Toolbar;* and *Show Phone*.

DESIGN RECOMMENDATIONS

We derived the following recommendations for the design of segmented, foldable, multi-display devices:

1. *Automated view operations appear to work well as responses to folding, attaching or detaching displays.*
2. *Consider a Collate operation when users extend a first display in Full Screen View with a second display.*
3. *Consider alternative views such as keyboards/toolbars or different apps when extending a 2nd display with a 3rd display.*
4. *Provide mechanisms for users to choose view operation functions, or allow them to set preferences.*
5. *Consider showing a keyboard on the lowest display when the device is folded into a perpendicular shape.*
6. *Consider mirroring the displays when the device is folded into a triangular shape.*
7. *Consider showing a 3D view of the data when users bend displays inwards or outwards, or into a 3D hull shape.*

LIMITATIONS AND FUTURE DIRECTIONS

We note that the above recommendations are based on heuristics and can be considered valid only within the limitations of the presented device and user study. We do believe that results are sufficiently clear to generalize to other application scenarios and device morphologies. We recognize that our PaperFold prototype has shortcomings that did not allow us to evaluate use by multiple users outside a laboratory environment. In particular, an important future direction is to remove the dependency on cables and extraneous equipment for what is supposed to be a mobile device.

CONCLUSIONS

We evaluated PaperFold, a mobile device with flexible display segments that can be folded into arbitrary configurations. Our design was informed by a participatory study that resulted in 14 preferred shape transformations. A subsequent study investigated the effectiveness of shape changes for viewport transformations. We evaluated how participants ranked the utility of shape changes for triggering common view operations in map and text editing applications. Results indicate that participants were generally able to select specific view operations as automated responses to folding, attaching or detaching displays. User feedback from our study indicates benefits from having multiple detachable displays. Advantages include better support for performing tasks that traditionally require multiple devices, as well as physical manipulation and sharing of views.

REFERENCES

1. Chen, N., et al. Navigation Techniques for Dual-Display E-Book Readers. *Proc. CHI '08*, 1779-1788.
2. Chen, N., Guimbretière, F., Sellen, A. Graduate student use of a multi-slate reading system. *Proc. CHI'13,* 1799-1808.
3. Entourage Edge (2013) - http://entourageedge.eu/
4. Girouard, A., Tarun, A., and Vertegaal, R. DisplayStacks: Interaction Techniques for Stacks of Flexible Thin-Film Displays. *Proc CHI '12*, 2431-2440.
5. Gomes, A., Nesbitt, A., Vertegaal, R. MorePhone. *Proc. CHI '13*, 583-592.
6. Gomes, A., Vertegaal, R. PaperFold: A Shape Changing Mobile Device with Multiple Reconfigurable Electrophoretic Magnetic Display Tiles. *Proc. CHI EA'14*, 535-538.
7. Hinckley, K. Synchronous gestures for multiple persons and computers. *Proc. UIST '03*, 149-158.
8. Hinckley, K., Dixon, M., Sarin, R., Guimbretiere, F., and Balakrishnan, R. Codex. *Proc. CHI '99*, 1933–1942.
9. Holman, D., et al. PaperWindows: interaction techniques for digital paper. *Proc. CHI '05*, 591-599.
10. Khalilbeigi, M., Lissermann, R., Mühlhäuser, M., and Steimle, J. Xpaaand. *Proc. CHI '11*, 2729-2732.
11. Khalilbeigi, M., Lisserman, R., Kleine, W. FoldMe: interacting with double-sided foldable displays. *Proc. TEI '12,* 33-40.
12. Lahey, B., et al. PaperPhone: Understanding the Use of Bend Gestures in Mobile Devices with Flexible Electronic Paper Displays. *Proc. CHI '11*, 1303-1312.
13. Lee, J.C. Hudson, S.E., and Tse, E. Foldable interactive displays. *Proc. UIST '08* (2008), 287-290.
14. Lee, S. et al. How users manipulate deformable displays as input devices. *Proc. CHI '10*, 1647-1656.
15. Merrill, D., Kalanithi, J., Maes, P. Siftables: towards sensor network user interfaces. *Proc. TEI '07*, 75-78.
16. Ramakers, R., Johannes, S. Luyten, K. Paddle. *Proc. CHI'14*. 2569-2578.
17. Roudaut, A., et al. Morphees: toward high "shape resolution" in self-actuated flexible mobile devices. *Proc. CHI '13*, 593-602.
18. Schwesig, C., Poupyrev, I., and Mori, E. Gummi: a bendable computer. *Proc. CHI '04*, 263-270.
19. Sellen, A., Harper, R. The Myth of the Paperless Office, MIT Press, Cambridge, MA, 2003.
20. Sony Corp - www.sony.co.uk/product/sony-tablet-p
21. Stavness, I., Lam, B., Fels, S. pCubee. *Proc. CHI '10,* 1381-1390.
22. Tarun, A., et al. PaperTab: an electronic paper computer with multiple large flexible electrophoretic displays. *EA CHI '13*, 3131-3134.

TorqueScreen: Actuated Flywheels for Ungrounded Kinesthetic Feedback in Handheld Devices

Martin Murer, Bernhard Maurer, Hermann Huber, Ilhan Aslan, Manfred Tscheligi
Christian Doppler Laboratory for "Contextual Interfaces"
ICT&S Center, University of Salzburg, Austria
firstname.lastname@sbg.ac.at

ABSTRACT
Handheld touch screen based devices, such as smartphones or tablets, typically provide limited haptic feedback. On current devices, what is visually perceived and what is tactile and kinesthetically felt is semantically uncoupled. In order to improve embodied interaction on handheld screen based devices, new ways to provide richer haptic feedback are required. In this paper, we present TorqueScreen, a prototypical system combining a handheld touch screen device (i.e., a tablet) with an actuated flywheel capable of imposing angular momentum onto the tablet. The TorqueScreen design allows interlinking the movement and physics of virtual objects on the screen with the torque as haptic output imposed on the tablet. We describe the design and implementation of the device, illustrate the resulting design space, and discuss future improvements and potential applications.

Author Keywords
Gyroscope; Haptic; Movement; Ungrounded Feedback

ACM Classification Keywords
H.5.m. Information Interfaces and Presentation (e.g. HCI): Miscellaneous

INTRODUCTION
In tangible and embedded computing, designs often aim to create external physical representations of something digital, connecting the digital world with the physical world in which we humans live. Hereby, the physical interaction profits from human skills that have been gained from prior experiences with physical objects in the real world. Users manipulate physical representations in physical space to easily interact with digital content. According to the theory, this kind of interaction is embodied because it relies on conceptions of movement and space, which are part of everyday interactions of humans and essential for human (embodied) cognition [7, 10].

ACM 978-1-4503-3305-4/15/01 ...$15.00.
http://dx.doi.org/10.1145/2677199.2680579

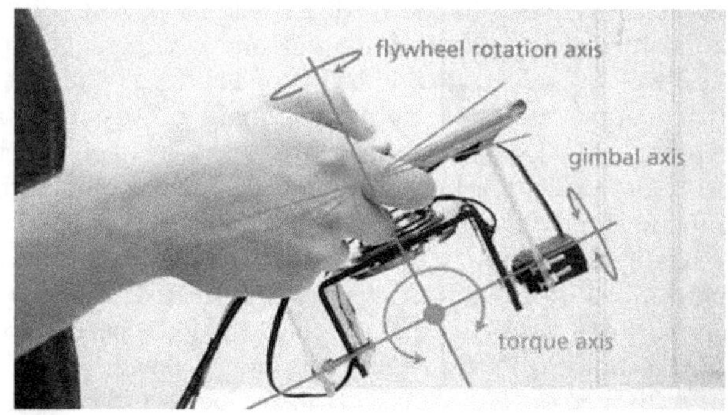

Figure 1. TorqueScreen: A gyroscopic actuator attached to a tablet. Pivoting the gimbal creates angular momentum about the torque axis, perpendicular to the rotational axis of the flywheel and the rotation of the gimbal.

Compared to physical representations, screen and pixel-based representations are visually (and emotionally) expressive but lack expressivity during physical interaction. For example, digital representations, such as images of real world objects, don't have physical characteristics such as weight. Nevertheless, when users interact with digital representations of real world objects in a drag and drop task, semantics have an impact on the interaction. The perceived semantics, such as the weight and size of a represented real world object (e.g., an apple in contrast to a car) influence how fast objects (e.g., an icon representing a car) are dragged [4]. Thus, screen technology has advanced to a level that visual representations activate bodily action tendencies. Put differently, there is a sensorimotor coupling in todays screen based interfaces.

Recently, van Dijk et al. [13] discussed different variations of Embodied Cognition, which is a theory of mind that puts emphasis on the role of the human body and the surrounding environment in human cognition. They argue for a "sensorimotor coupling" view and a "social interaction" view on embodied cognition design. The "sensorimotor coupling" view puts emphasis on the role of human senses in a continuous sense making process based on parallel actions and perceptions. Consequently, a coupling between visual and kinesthetic perceptions would serve as an ideal foundation for embodied interaction design. In this paper we present the design and implementation of *TorqueScreen*, a device that aims to harvest this potential of improved sensorimotor-coupling by combining visual representations on a handheld screen (i.e., a tablet) with haptic feedback (see Figure 1).

HAPTIC FEEDBACK

Most implementations of haptic and kinesthetic feedback require attachment to some ground or in certain cases, are body-grounded (e.g., [8]). Accordingly, screen based interfaces (especially handheld and ungrounded devices) lack physical interactive expressivity; i.e., graphical or auditve representations typically provide no haptic or force feedback and often feel "dead" or still. A widely distributed form of haptic feedback in handheld and mobile devices is vibrotactile feedback. However, the information capacity is very limited in vibrotactile feedback and not directly associated with conceptions of real space or real movement.

Richer ungrounded haptic feedback can be provided by dynamically altering physical, inertial, and kinematic attributes (e.g., weight, velocity) of a device or interface. Current implementations include weight changing (e.g., [9]), linear momentum (e.g., [3]), weight shifting, and kinesthetic inertial feedback (e.g., [11]). In contrast, torque, i.e. the angular force to rotate about an axis, is rarely utilized for ungrounded haptic feedback. Although the effect is well known from many applications of grounded devices (e.g., steering wheels) and everyday real world interactions (e.g., the force needed to unscrew a bottle), its usage in ungrounded devices has been rather limited so far. This is mainly due to the complexity of providing the required reaction force that counteracts the desired output effect.

Torque in Interfaces

Available implementations include devices that provide short-time angular momentum to handheld devices utilizing fast moving masses (e.g., provided by push-pull solenoids, [12]) or speed changes of rotating masses (e.g., [1]). In order to realise a longer lasting or continuos haptic effect an opposing reaction force is required to counteract the desired output force. One means to achieve that is based on the gyro effect, utilizing a flywheel's angular momentum, simply speaking its resistance to changes in orientation. iTorqU, for example, utilizes a metal flywheel spinning in a two-axis gimbal [14]. Similar gyroscopic actuators are well explored in domains such as controlling a satellite's orientation, with different configurations of (multiple) flywheels with (multiple) actuated gimbals providing torque to ungrounded (or floating) systems. Applications as feedback modality are discussed in detail by Antolini et al. [2]. Those implementations provide active torque feedback to handheld input devices, targeting applications such as virtual reality (e.g., impact simulation for tennis games [12]).

An initial exploration of torque feedback for handheld screen based applications has been provided by Badshah et al. [5]. Their system, GyroTab, is though limited to *reactive* torque feedback, i.e., torque that is providing varying levels of resistances to the tablets's movement. In contrast, we aimed for a system that combines screen based interaction with *active* torque feedback, i.e., a haptic effect that can be dynamically controlled by the interactive system, e.g., an application operating on the tablet providing torque based on interaction with the screen based interface.

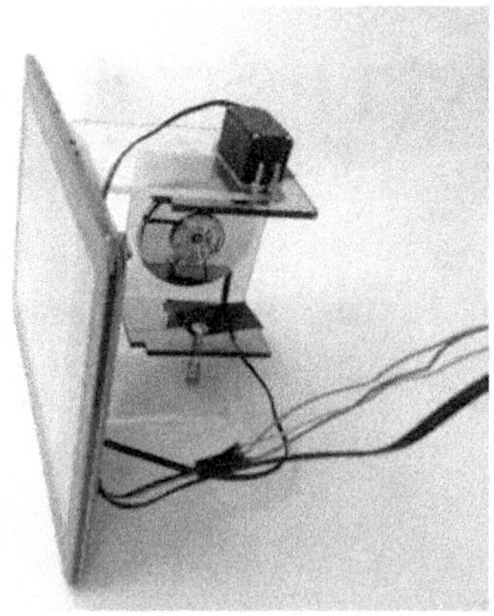

Figure 2. TorqueScreen: Prototype consisting of a tablet, a brushless dc motor driving the flywheel and a servomotor rotating the gimbal.

TORQUESCREEN

As an output modality, TorqueScreen utilizes torque to create the haptic sensation of the handheld tablet being twisted towards one direction (i.e., the torque axis, as depicted in Figure 1). This effect is created by means of a fast spinning flywheel that provides the necessary reaction force. The flywheel is mounted on a servo-actuated gimbal that allows the flywheel to pivot about one axis (i.e., the pivot axis), resulting in a rotational momentum imposed on the tablet. The current implementation allows us to explore various types of mobile interactions: haptic cues augmenting visual content (e.g., as redundant alerts in mobiles), multimodal interaction in combination with touch based interaction (e.g., haptic feedback as confirmation of touch input), and embodied interaction in form of coupling virtual representations of objects (i.e. on the screen) with matching directional torque.

TorqueScreen consists of a 10.1 inch tablet computer (Samsung Galaxy Tab 2 10.1[1]) with an attached custom torque modality based on an actuated flywheel (see Figure 1). Similar to the conceptual configuration proposed by Antolini et al. [2], the torque actuator is limited to a single flywheel rotating at a constant speed and one servo-actuated gimbal pivoting the flywheel about one axis. In our design this axis is parallel to the tablet's screen (see Figure 2). As the speed of the flywheel and the systems axial configuration is unvaried, the momentum provided on the tablet is controlled by pivoting the gimbal (actuated by the servo motor). This allows to provide angular momentum around one axis parallel to horizontal axis of the tablet. Thus, the feedback TorqueScreen can generate is the sensation of the tablet being twisted forward of backward when held in landscape orientation (see Figure 3).

Different speeds and movement patterns of the gimbal can be used to create torque feedback with varying characteristics, e.g., a constant rotation resulting in the sensation of the tablet being twisted towards a certain direction and quick rotations resulting in the sensation of some object tipping or impacting at different locations on the tablet's surface. While the form

[1]http://www.samsung.com/global/microsite/galaxytab2/10.1/

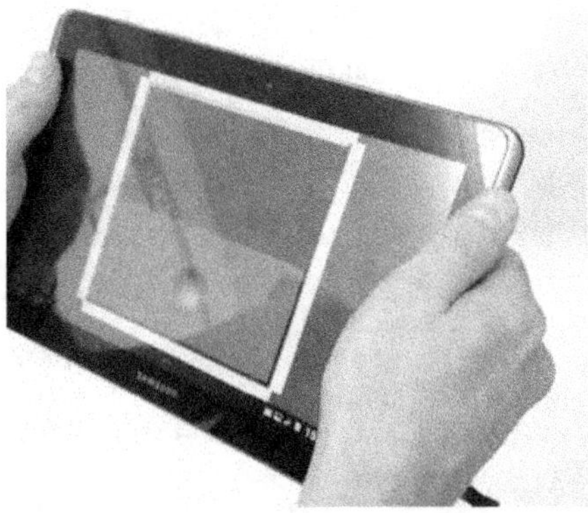

Figure 3. TorqueScreen held in Landscape mode. One example implementation allows to balance and scuttle a virtual object (i.e. a ball) in a simulated cubicle. Movements, e.g., the ball bouncing off a wall, creates torque in the according direction, creating the sensation of the tablet being twisted/tilted as the collides.

factor of the prototype together with its size and weight currently definitely limit its applicability as fully mobile device, it is a working handheld system that allows exploring potential interactions based on the combination of touch screens with torque feedback.

Implementation

The main component of our prototype is a flywheel built from a brushless DC motor; for practical reasons, it is harvested from a server-grade hard drive as this very motor type and the bearing setup provides high spindle speeds with relatively low vibration. By means of an off-the-shelf motor controller the BLDC motor is controlled and over-clocked to almost 20K rpm. This is desirable as the maximum torque is a function of rotation speed, the flywheel's rotating mass and the actuation angle. The motor and flywheel are mounted in a gimbal actuated by a server motor (see Figure 2), providing a maximum rotation of +/- 90 degrees, which accordingly limits the maximum time a torque in one direction can be created.

Both the motor controller and the servo motor are connected to an external Arduino microcontroller board[2], taking care of controlling the motor speed as well as the servo motor's position. In order to provide an accessible implementation that allows experimentation with various other components, we chose Spacebrew[3] as means to connect the prototype's behaviour to prototypical applications on the tablet. This websocket-based prototyping framework serves the purpose of quickly connecting different inputs and outputs through a web-based protocol and front-end.

TORQUESCREEN DESIGN SPACE

The current hardware configuration was implemented to explore different types of utilizing TorqueScreen by quickly building various prototypical software applications. As a result from those explorations, we will depict two types of screen based interaction with increasing complexity in the following section: torque feedback as a bidirectional output modality and TorqueScreen for embodied interaction.

[2]http://www.arduino.cc

[3]www.spacebrew.cc

Bidirectional and Multimodal Output

Adapting a framing by Antolini et al. [2] we distinguish three levels of information that can be conveyed by means of TorqueScreen: information redundancy, information transposition, and information balancing.

Information redundancy: TorqueScreen can be used to provide bidirectional cues (e.g., up/down or left/right) redundant to the visual or auditory information provided on the tablet. Potential usage scenarios include navigation tasks, alerts or notifications.

Information transposition: TorqueScreen can be used to provide information by means of torque that is usually not perceivable by the sense of touch or not related to touch input. Possible applications in that realm include confirmation of touch input, directional cues and contextual information.

Information balance: TorqueScreen can be used to reduce the amount of information conveyed visually and auditory (i.e., on the tablet) and thus, e.g., reduce the visual load or free screen real estate. This is especially promising in combination with touch input.

TorqueScreen for Embodied Interaction

In our initial exploration we studied combinations of torque on handheld devices with visual interfaces. Hereby, our intention was to make use of a sensorimotor coupling that human bodies and minds are accustomed to. Movement of physical objects and physical materials provide specific haptic feedback. There are embodied metaphors (e.g., [6]) associated with previous bodily experiences and haptic feedback. Our intention was to make use of these metaphors for sense making when interacting with handheld screens. Thus, we developed multiple explorative applications that combine digitally represented objects (i.e. objects shown on the screen) with according physical actuations (i.e. torque feedback).

One particular instantiation (see figure 3) aims to correlate the movement and behaviour of balls moving in a simulated physical environment with torque. The tablet shows a 3D simulation of a simple cubicle that changes its orientation (in the virtual space) in relation to the movement of the tablet (in physical space). Dropping objects (e.g., a ball) into this space triggers corresponding haptic reactions of the actuator, i.e. a simulated ball rolling along the cube's surface or bouncing of one of its walls creates the haptic sensation of a corresponding impact. As the *material* (i.e., the characteristics of the digitally represented object) changes, the haptic output adapts accordingly. As an example, a simulated ball made of steel creates a heavy, strong physical force, while an object of a lighter material relates to weaker haptic sensations.

Our explorations provide accounts for how torque may be used as feedback for handheld screen based devices. Based on our reflections, we came to understand that torque is a promising modality for embodied interaction design. However, our current implementation supports only a limited scope of materials and respective mappings to torque feedback.

LIMITATIONS

Our current implementation has several shortcomings that we seek to improve in future iterations. Limiting our design to a single flywheel with a single gimbal restricts the torque feedback to a single Degree of Freedom (DOF) and imposes a certain level of *reactive* torque as one alters the tablets orientation (i.e., the flywheel is resistive to movements of the tablet). Additional flywheels or multiple gimbals would increase the DOF and, thus, extend the interaction possibilities. Currently, at full speed – which equals to maximum torque – the full system draws as much as 1.2 amps at 12 Volts, which further limits feasibility as a fully mobile device due to the high power consumption.

CONCLUSION AND FUTURE WORK

In this paper, we presented TorqueScreen, a prototypical system that allows to explore the combination of torque feedback with screen based handheld devices. Our research adds to existing efforts to improve embodied interaction design with handheld, ungrounded screen based devices. Our aim was to further decrease the border between the digital and the physical. The challenge we addressed is the coupling between visually perceived semantics and tactile and kinesthetic experiences.

We coupled physical attributes of digitally represented objects, materials, and interactions with torque feedback. While our initial prototype has some limitations, it provides ways to study unexplored embodied interaction design beyond what is currently possible on handheld devices. In our future work, we aim to increase the prototype's fidelity and the according interaction space by adding multiple degrees of freedom in a desirably smaller form factor. Moreover, in a next step we aim to improve our understanding of TorqueScreen based designs and its effect on user experience through studies with users.

ACKNOWLEDGMENTS

The financial support by the Austrian Federal Ministry of Science, Research and Economy and the National Foundation for Research, Technology and Development is gratefully acknowledged (Christian Doppler Laboratory for "Contextual Interfaces").

REFERENCES

1. Amemiya, T., and Gomi, H. Directional torque perception with brief, asymmetric net rotation of a flywheel. *Haptics, IEEE Transactions on 6*, 3 (July 2013), 370–375.

2. Antolini, M., Bordegoni, M., and Cugini, U. A haptic direction indicator using the gyro effect. In *World Haptics Conference (WHC), 2011 IEEE* (June 2011), 251–256.

3. Arasan, A., Basdogan, C., and Sezgin, T. Haptic stylus with inertial and vibro-tactile feedback. In *World Haptics Conference (WHC), 2013* (April 2013), 425–430.

4. Aslan, I., Murer, M., Fuchsberger, V., Fugard, A., and Tscheligi, M. Drag and drop the apple: The semantic weight of words and images in touch-based interaction. In *Proceedings of the 7th International Conference on Tangible, Embedded and Embodied Interaction*, TEI '13, ACM (New York, NY, USA, 2013), 159–166.

5. Badshah, A., Gupta, S., Morris, D., Patel, S., and Tan, D. Gyrotab: A handheld device that provides reactive torque feedback. In *Proceedings of the SIGCHI Conference on Human Factors in Computing Systems*, CHI '12, ACM (New York, NY, USA, 2012), 3153–3156.

6. Bakker, S., Antle, A. N., and Van Den Hoven, E. Embodied metaphors in tangible interaction design. *Personal Ubiquitous Comput. 16*, 4 (Apr. 2012), 433–449.

7. Johnson, M. *The Meaning of the Body: Aesthetics of Human Understanding*. The University of Chicago Press, Chicago, 2007.

8. Lopes, P., and Baudisch, P. Muscle-propelled force feedback: Bringing force feedback to mobile devices. In *Proceedings of the SIGCHI Conference on Human Factors in Computing Systems*, CHI '13, ACM (New York, NY, USA, 2013), 2577–2580.

9. Niiyama, R., Yao, L., and Ishii, H. Weight and volume changing device with liquid metal transfer. In *Proceedings of the 8th International Conference on Tangible, Embedded and Embodied Interaction*, TEI '14, ACM (New York, NY, USA, 2013), 49–52.

10. Sheets-Johnstone, M. *The Primacy of Movement (Advances in Consciousness Research)*. John Benjamins Publishing Co, 2009.

11. Swindells, C., Unden, A., and Sang, T. Torquebar: An ungrounded haptic feedback device. In *Proceedings of the 5th International Conference on Multimodal Interfaces*, ICMI '03, ACM (New York, NY, USA, 2003), 52–59.

12. Teck, F. W. Force and torque simulation in virtual tennis. In *Proceedings of the Workshop at SIGGRAPH Asia*, WASA '12, ACM (New York, NY, USA, 2012), 143–146.

13. van Dijk, J., van der Lugt, R., and Hummels, C. Beyond distributed representation: Embodied cognition design supporting socio-sensorimotor couplings. In *Proceedings of the 8th International Conference on Tangible, Embedded and Embodied Interaction*, TEI '14, ACM (New York, NY, USA, 2013), 181–188.

14. Winfree, K., Gewirtz, J., Mather, T., Fiene, J., and Kuchenbecker, K. A high fidelity ungrounded torque feedback device: The itorqu 2.0. In *EuroHaptics conference, 2009 and Symposium on Haptic Interfaces for Virtual Environment and Teleoperator Systems. World Haptics 2009. Third Joint* (March 2009), 261–266.

DisplaySkin: Exploring Pose-Aware Displays on a Flexible Electrophoretic Wristband

Jesse Burstyn
Human Media Lab
Queen's University
Kingston, ON, Canada
jesse@cs.queensu.ca

Paul Strohmeier
Human Media Lab
Queen's University
Kingston, ON, Canada
paul@cs.queensu.ca

Roel Vertegaal
Human Media Lab
Queen's University
Kingston, ON, Canada
roel@cs.queensu.ca

ABSTRACT
Mobile devices can provide people with contextual information. This information may benefit a primary activity, assuming it is easily accessible. In this paper, we present DisplaySkin, a *pose-aware* device with a flexible display circling the wrist. DisplaySkin creates a kinematic model of a user's arm and uses it to place information in view, independent of body pose. In doing so, DisplaySkin aims to minimize the cost of accessing information without being intrusive. We evaluated our pose-aware display with a rotational pointing task, which was interrupted by a notification on DisplaySkin. Results show that a pose-aware display reduces the time required to respond to notifications on the wrist.

Author Keywords
Smart Watches; Wearable Computing; Pose Aware Display; Flexible Displays; Organic User Interfaces.

ACM Classification Keywords
H.5.2 [Information Interfaces and Presentation]: User Interfaces---*input devices and strategies*.

INTRODUCTION
When performing every day activities, people are often interested in supplementary information. Am I on time? How close am I to my destination? How far have I run? The most common method we use to access supplementary information is retrieving a smartphone. Doing so, however, requires a significant interruption in a primary activity [20]. As a consequence, we must weigh the benefit of the information against the interruption it introduces. Explorations into head mounted displays address this issue by being always visible [8]. At the same time, these devices can be socially undesirable [32] and provide no simple method of dismissing the device.

It seems the ideal design space may be somewhere in between: devices that are easier to access than a smartphone, yet less intrusive than a head mounted display. Wrist worn devices are a candidate solution, one with a great cultural and social heritage. One of their primary features is that they can be brought in and out of focal attention with great ease; they are easily accessible to quick requests for information by the user. We therefore call this class of devices *glance-based* interfaces. Glance-based interfaces do not demand a user's focal attention, and provide information to the eyes quickly and only when needed.

TEI '15, January 15–19, 2015, Stanford, California, USA.
Copyright 2015 © ACM 978-1-4503-3305-4/15/01...$15.00.
http://dx.doi.org/10.1145/2677199.2680596

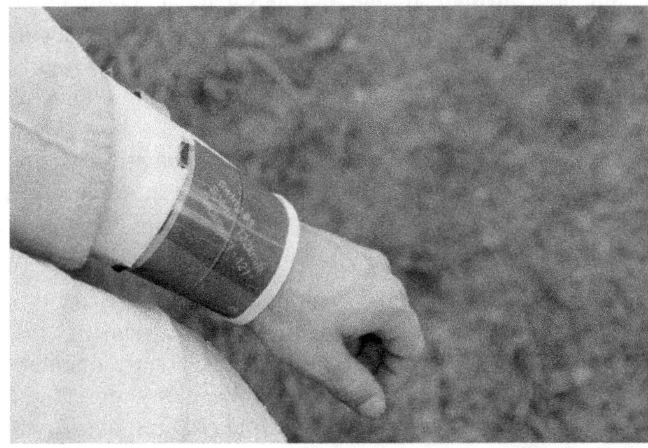

Figure 1. DisplaySkin prototype.

With the continued growth in users' exposure to contextual information, we believe the design space of glance-based interfaces is becoming increasingly relevant. For these interfaces to be more efficient, it is important that information is available as quickly as possible and with minimal disruption of primary tasks. One issue with wrist worn devices is that their small display needs to be brought into the field of view, typically by lifting and reorienting the arm. In this paper, we propose a wrist worn device with a much larger display, one that is 320° degrees around the wrist, and is aware of the user's pose. Pose-awareness allows the device to provide information directly in the field of view, regardless of the orientation of the user's arm.

As an initial exploration of pose-aware displays, we designed *DisplaySkin*, a functional prototype electronic wristband (Figure 1). DisplaySkin includes a 7.2" thin-film flexible electrophoretic display that wraps around the circumference of the wrist. It also includes inertial sensors

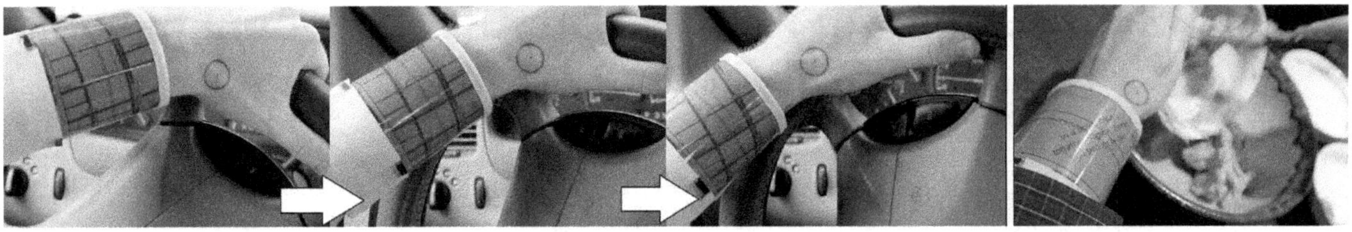

Figure 2. DisplaySkin prototype with pose-aware display.

that create a kinematic model of a user's arm and wrist. By wrapping a display around the entire wrist, DisplaySkin extends the angles from which pixels can be viewed. Using a kinematic model, DisplaySkin determines which areas of the display are visible and actively orients graphics to maximize readability (Figure 1). Figure 2 shows how combining a 320° visible screen with kinematic tracking enables DisplaySkin to provide pose-aware information in the context of everyday activities, such as driving or preparing food.

To investigate the potential benefits of pose-aware displays with DisplaySkin, we conducted an experiment that examined how fast users attend to supplementary information during a primary task. Results show that a pose-aware display can reduce the time required to respond to notifications that are secondary to a primary pointing task.

RELATED WORK

Wrist Worn Devices

A number of researchers have explored the design space of wrist worn devices. AugmentedForearm [23] is made from a row of four interconnected displays worn on the forearm. Facet [17] wraps six displays around the wrist, each acting as a window into an application. Users can rotate Facet to bring forward occluded applications, or can continually scroll to reveal virtual segments. Tarun et al. implemented Snaplet [34], a thin-film bracelet with a large display area. Snaplet's functionality changes according to its shape and the body part on which it is worn. WatchIt [25] and Abracadabra [11] expand the interaction space of wrist worn devices beyond the display using touch and in-air gestures, respectively. With Duet, Chen et al. [4] explored joint interactions with a smartwatch and a smartphone.

In addition to recent wrist worn products [9,24,26,30], Plastic Logic demonstrated a prototype smartwatch. Their prototype also used a flexible electrophoretic display, wrapped over a small portion of the wrist [26].

On Body Interaction

Rather than *attach* a device to the body, some researchers *integrate* a device with the body by interacting directly on the skin. Rekimoto explored tapping on skin for mobile interactions, leveraging skin's direct tactile feedback [29]. Nakatsuma et al. [22] detected finger position on the back of the hand using a combination of piezoelectric and infrared sensors. Makino et al. [19] detected the force and linear position of a finger between two infrared sensors placed on the arm. With Skinput, Harrison was one of the first to use skin for *both* input and output [13]. Skinput used bio-acoustic fingerprinting to locate taps on a user's forearm, but also included a body-mounted pico-projector for direct feedback. OmniTouch [10] augmented users with a projector and a Kinect sensor, enabling multi-touch interactions on everyday surfaces, including the user's own arms and hands. Harrison et al. extended this work with Armura [12], which tracked both the hands and arm posture. With Armura, users could control interfaces with arm and hand gestures.

Body Pose as Input

In addition to designing interactions *on* the body, a number of papers explored designs *with* the whole body as input. For example, Chen et al. proposed a number of new paradigms using the body as an interactive space [5], such as navigating data by moving mobile devices relative to the body. In addition, he demonstrated how users could create a mnemonic map by storing and retrieving information at chosen locations on and around their body.

Several areas in HCI leverage body pose: for rehabilitation [28], low-cost 3D modeling and rigging [43], and tracking daily activities [2]. Some solutions to detect pose embed sensors directly into clothing. Strohmeier et al. [33] put stretch sensors into sleeves to detect basic wrist motion and Gioberto et al. [7] created stitching patterns for conductive thread that estimate joint angles. The most common methods for measuring pose, however, are depth-sensing cameras [21], a series of inertial sensors [42], or by tracking infrared markers with an array of cameras [37].

Dynamic Image Rotation

Since the early 90s, researchers have suggested rotating content with the orientation of its display [35]. Today's mobile devices automatically show content in portrait and landscape modes, using accelerometers specifically included for this purpose. But if a device relies on its display orientation alone, it may make inaccurate assumptions about a user's perspective. For example, users often disable this feature when lying down [16]. Cheng et al. [6] addressed this problem by using the orientation of a user's face to adjust the orientation of a display. Their approach, iRotate, requires a direct view of the face, and like most mobile devices, it only transitions between fixed

Figure 3. Wrist worn devices. Left: Bracelet watch by Capt & Freundler (1813) [38]. Right: Samsung Galaxy Gear smart watch (2013) [30].

orientations. In contrast, Wilfinger et al. [41] used accelerometer data to smoothly rotate content on steering wheel displays.

DESIGN RATIONALE

There are varying accounts describing the invention and popularization of the wristwatch [15]. Early advertisements for wristwatches show how the bicycle and automobile were important factors; the ads tout how motorists could more easily read the time while operating a vehicle [1]. Other accounts describe military officers who found it impractical to use a pocket watch while also riding a horse and wielding a pistol. In WWI, the British Army commissioned one of the first mass-produced wristwatches because their soldiers required fast access to timepieces for coordinated attacks [39]. A common design theme runs through these differing origin stories: one of convenient access. Inspired by wristwatches, the main design goal for DisplaySkin is to allow users to more easily access information in a way that supplements their primary activity.

Designing for Non-Focal Attention

Wristwatches have come a long way since then. Indeed, wristwatches with the power of full-fledged computers are now becoming a reality in the marketplace. At the same time, wrist worn devices and computers have different motivations and we typically engage with the two classes of devices in very different ways. Designers usually assume that a computer is the primary focus of attention, the sole object a user is interacting with over an extended period of time. The design of wristwatches is quite the opposite. They are not assumed to be the focus of attention, instead supporting fleeting glances of secondary or contextual information: knowledge that complements a primary task. This means that the effectiveness of a wrist worn device should be weighed against its impact on a primary task. We believe that when designing smarter wristwatches, one should not be tempted to naively copy methods proven for standard computers. Instead, we suggest a focus on enhancing the existing affordances of the wristwatch.

Designing for Visibility

The form factor of most wrist worn devices has not significantly changed over the past two hundred years, yet the size and placement of the display is a key parameter of visibility. For example, Figure 3 shows one of the first wristwatches ever made (1813) [38] beside a Samsung smartwatch (2013) [30]. Despite the difference in their underlying technologies, their displays are in the same fixed location. This constraint limits the angles from which the display can be viewed. A flexible display, on the other hand, can be wrapped around the wrist, providing a continuous display surface with pixels always in view.

Designing for Body Pose

Our primary concern was how to compensate for the occlusions of display area that commonly occur in day-to-day activities. To address this, we propose measuring the configuration of the user's arm in relation to the rest of the body and dynamically moving information onto an area of the display that is visible. As such, a pose-aware display re-orients its content towards the user, rather than requiring the user to reorient their body towards the device. Our pose-aware display consists of two elements: a flexible display and a kinematic model of the body. By wrapping a display around the wrist, DisplaySkin has a surface with pixels always visible, independent of the rotation of the arm. By measuring the configuration of the user's arm in relation to the rest of the body, DisplaySkin can dynamically move information onto this area of the display that is visible to the user (see Figure 4).

DisplaySkin also dynamically reorients text and other content, correcting for perspective effects. This can reduce

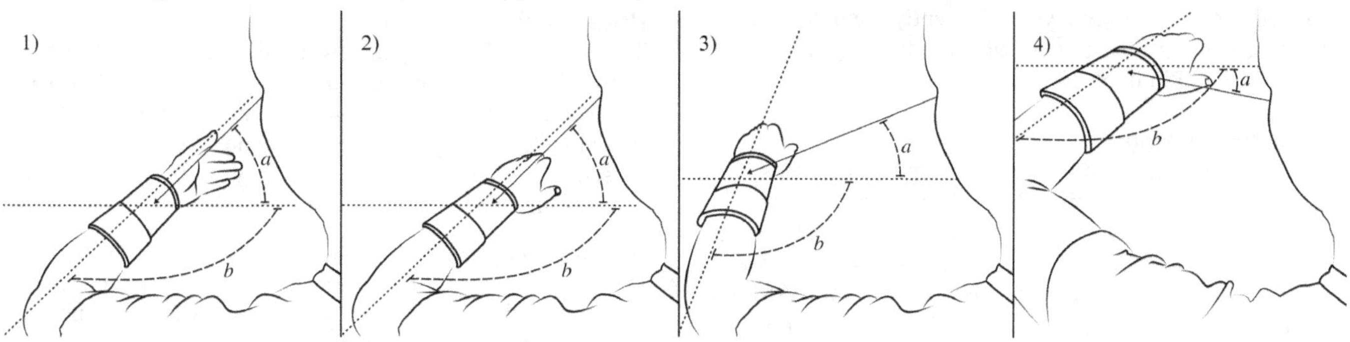

Figure 4. The kinematic model provides DisplaySkin with the angle between a user's eye and the device (*a*). DisplaySkin uses this angle to present information on visible area of the display. The model also provides the orientation of the device relative to a user's body (*b*), which is used to align the content horizontally (similar to Wilfinger et al. [41]).

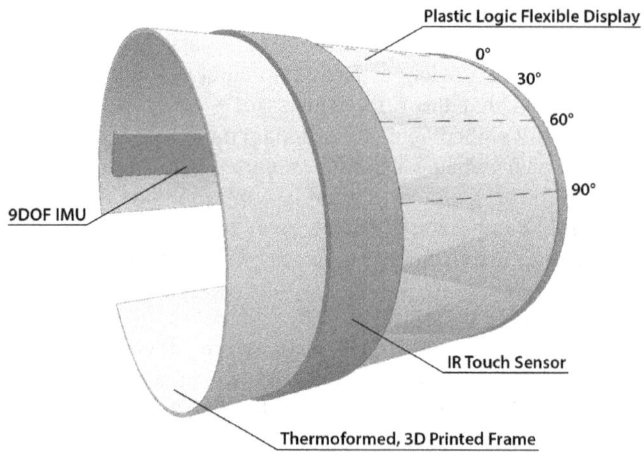

Figure 5. DisplaySkin hardware schematic.

interruption times because it improves the readability of any text displayed on the device [40]. With a pose-aware display, interfaces can be presented with a fixed perspective, regardless of how the arm is oriented. Similar to Wilfinger et al. [41], a map's north could remain upright, independent of hand orientation (Figure 2).

We also envision that future glance-based interfaces will have a degree of ambient awareness to better provide contextually relevant information. Our focus in this paper, however, was to make glancing at a device easier and less disruptive. Although a fully contextually aware device lies outside the scope of this paper, we hope our sensing platform guides future work in the area.

IMPLEMENTATION

Figure 5 illustrates DisplaySkin's components. DisplaySkin uses a flexible electrophoretic display from Plastic Logic [27] with a resolution of 354 by 944 pixels. The display is 6.5" long and 3" wide (7.2" diagonal).

Device Assembly and Form Factor

The 0.2mm thick display was inserted into a flexible 1.5mm thick 3D printed ABS frame. Once inserted, the entire device was heated and molded into a cylindrical shape. The final form factor of DisplaySkin is rigid enough to stay wrapped around the arm, yet sufficiently flexible to open and close comfortably. For added stability, a magnetic snap holds DisplaySkin in place.

Kinematic Tracking

To create the kinematic model, DisplaySkin uses two Inertial Measurement Units (IMU). One is worn around the user's upper arm and one is integrated in DisplaySkin itself. Each IMU contains a 3-axis gyroscope, a 3-axis accelerometer, and a 3-axis magnetometer. Two Arduino boards collect the data, and a sensor-fusion algorithm [18] calculates the absolute orientation of each IMU.

We use these headings to create a direct, forward kinematic model of a user's arm. The model treats a user's shoulder as the base of an open kinematic chain with two links. Each IMU represents one element in this chain and is considered a rigid body [31]. With this, we calculate the position and orientation of the user's wrist relative to their shoulder. The model assumes that a user's face is in a fixed position relative to their shoulder, an assumption that is sufficiently accurate to calculate an angle and rotation offset between the forearm and face (Figure 4). A single gyroscope would be sufficient to detect simple rotations of the arm (compare Figures 4.1 and 4.2). A kinematic model, however, is required to detect differences between more complex changes in pose (Figures 4.3 and 4.4).

Touch Sensing

To the best of our knowledge, there is no technology that can track multiple touches on the thin, flexible, and curved conditions of electrophoretic displays. As a result, we designed a sensor using infrared (IR) diodes, inspired by SideSight [3].

We placed an array of IR diodes over the bezel of the display. The diodes act as both photoemitters and phototransistors (emitting and sensing IR light, respectively). These diodes are controlled by a separate Arduino microcontroller. When a finger comes in close proximity of the display, it is illuminated, and the reflection of IR light is detected. Touch points are calculated with a custom blob-tracking algorithm. The y-position of a touch is based on blob location, while the x-position is inferred by its size and intensity.

Software

DisplaySkin's display driver is based on Holman et al.'s Flexkit [14], which runs on Plastic Logic's Hummingbird Z3. Flexkit allows DisplaySkin to run at high frame rates on the inherently slower electrophoretic display.

The two Arduino boards preprocess all the sensor data. A laptop receives the IMU data and creates the kinematic model in a Processing application. A separate Processing application consolidates the touch data and the kinematic model and updates the display. The inter-process communication was implemented in Open Sound Control.

USER STUDY

To understand how pose-aware displays benefit glance-based interfaces, we evaluated the effects of display occlusion on information retrieval. We measured participants' ability to quickly acknowledge notifications presented on DisplaySkin, while they were simultaneously engaged in a different primary task.

In this evaluation, we compared a pose-aware display to a static display (placed on the top of the wrist). Instead of comparing the two in extreme situations, we maintained ecological validity by focusing on the more interesting edge case of partial occlusion. We believe these scenarios would

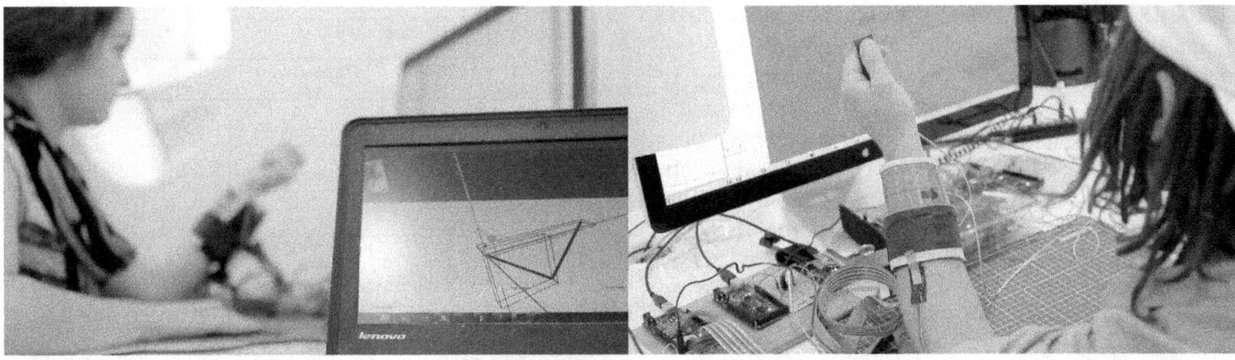

Figure 6. Experimental environment. Left: Live view of kinematic tracking. Right: Participant is interrupted and must acknowledge arrow on DisplaySkin.

reveal both the positive and potential negative aspects of a pose-aware display.

Task

As a primary task, participants performed a targeting task, similar to a one-dimensional Fitts' law pointing test. Two bars appeared on a desktop monitor and spanned the height of the screen. The bars were fixed in width and were varied in amplitude between conditions. Participants were asked to move a cursor between the two targets as quickly and accurately as possible. They controlled the cursor's horizontal position with the rotation of their left hand.

As a secondary task, participants performed an acknowledgment task on DisplaySkin. Upon completing a random trial of the primary task, the participant was interrupted by a notification: the monitor flashed red. Upon such notification, participants were instructed to look at DisplaySkin, find an arrow, and swipe in the direction indicated (Figure 6, right). Once the notification was acknowledged, participants immediately returned to the rotational targeting task.

By asking the participants to perform a task with wrist rotation, we were provided with a wide variety of wrist angles. This, in consequence, allowed us to control the level of occlusion of the top of the wrist at the moment when a notification occurred. In addition, the demands of the task required the participants' full concentration, ensuring they could not plan for interruptions.

Conditions

We used two independent variables: display type and angle. The two display types were *static* and *pose-aware*. The angles were 0°, 30°, 60°, and 90°. Figure 7 shows the position of the arm for each condition, while Figure 5 shows the corresponding position of the target on the display. In the pose-aware condition, the arrow was dynamically placed in the participant's field of view. In the static condition, the arrow was located on the top of their wrist, the standard position of a watch face. The different angles constituted varying degrees of occlusion of the arrow.

Controlling Wrist Angle and Hand Position

During a trial, the participant's left elbow and right hand were in a fixed position. The participant controlled the targeting task with their left hand and they held their right hand in a fixed position. This allowed us to specify the angle of the left forearm when the interruption occurred, as well as ensuring that the distance between the right hand and the display was consistent between participants.

Measurements

We recorded two dependent measures: homing time and resume time. *Homing time* is the time from the moment of the interruption until the participant touched the surface of DisplaySkin. *Resume time* is the time between completing the swipe to re-engaging with the targeting task, as indicated by a click on the same target that prompted the interruption.

Experiment Design

We used a 2x4 factorial within-subject design with repeated measures. Our factors were: *display type* (static and pose-aware), and *wrist angle* upon notification (0°, 30°, 60°, and 90°). Each participant performed 8 trials of the acknowledgment task per combination of factors, for a total

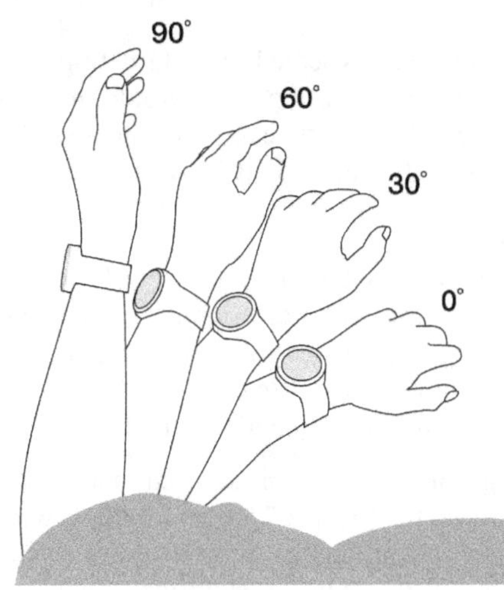

Figure 7. Wrist angles investigated. Watch face visibility indicated in yellow.

of 64 trials. Condition order was countered-balanced between participants. The experiment lasted 40 minutes, including practice. Participants practiced with each display type until they achieved less than 10% improvement between trials. Participants clicked between the vertical bars for a total of 384 targeting trials. The trials were segmented into blocks of 6, grouped by target distance (each target distance corresponding to a wrist angle). There was one interruption within each block of the targeting trials. It occurred randomly when a participant clicked on the target bar that corresponded to the desired wrist angle.

Participants

The experiment was conducted with 12 participants (9 male, 3 female) between the ages of 17-29. Most participants were right handed (9/12) and only a few currently wore a wristwatch (3/12). All participants had some familiarity with touch gestures, e.g., on a smartphone or tablet. They were paid $10 for their participation.

Apparatus

Aside from DisplaySkin, we needed additional hardware to perform the experiment. We instructed participants to place their right hand on a capacitive sensor that ensured consistent starting locations for homing locations. To select targets in the primary task, participants pressed a small push button that they grasped with the same hand (left) with which they wore DisplaySkin.

Hypotheses

We hypothesized that the pose-aware display would have faster homing times than the static display (*H1*). We predicted that participants would be able to home to the wrist faster when the arrow was dynamically placed in their field of view. We also hypothesized that, for the static display, larger wrist angles would result in slower homing times, but we would not see this effect with the pose-aware display (*H2*). We hypothesized that participants would have shorter resume times in the pose-aware display condition (*H3*).

As a control, we expected that targeting times in the primary rotational pointing task would not significantly differ between display types (*H4*), and that larger target amplitudes would result in longer targeting times (*H5*).

RESULTS

For the secondary acknowledgement task, we analyzed the collected measures by performing a repeated measures ANOVA using *display type* (2) x *wrist angle* (4) on homing time and resume time. Table 1 outlines the means and standard errors for homing and resume times.

For homing time, the analysis showed that *display type* was a significant factor ($F_{1,11}$=67.99, $p < 0.001$), with the pose-aware display resulting in shorter times than the static display. We also found a significant interaction effect between *display type* and *wrist angle* ($F_{3,33}$=3.29, $p < 0.05$).

	Homing Time		Resume Time	
	Static	Pose-Aware	Static	Pose-Aware
Overall	1.84 *(0.04)*	1.5 *(0.02)*	1.75 *(0.02)*	1.69 *(0.03)*
0°	1.69 *(0.04)*	1.55 *(0.03)*	1.74 *(0.04)*	1.90 *(0.05)*
30°	1.82 *(0.07)*	1.52 *(0.03)*	1.60 *(0.04)*	1.85 *(0.07)*
60°	1.88 *(0.10)*	1.46 *(0.04)*	1.81 *(0.05)*	1.42 *(0.05)*
90°	1.90 *(0.07)*	1.47 *(0.03)*	1.88 *(0.06)*	1.59 *(0.03)*

Table 1. Mean *(s.e.)* homing and resume times in seconds.

With respect to resume time, we observed a main effect of *wrist angle* ($F_{3,33}$=5.14, $p < 0.05$). Pairwise post-hoc tests, with Bonferroni corrected comparisons, revealed that 0° was significantly different from 90°. The analysis also showed an interaction effect between *display type* and *wrist angle* ($F_{3,33}$=15.12, $p < 0.001$).

For the rotational pointing task, we analyzed the movement times by performing a repeated measures ANOVA using *display type* (2) x *target amplitude* (4). The analysis showed that *target amplitude* was a significant factor ($F_{3,33}$=219.48, $p < 0.001$). The analysis did not show a main effect of *display type*.

DISCUSSION

Our results suggest that pose-aware displays reduce interruption times in interactions with a wrist mounted display when attending to a primary pointing task.

As hypothesized, our pose-aware display obtained significantly faster homing times than the static display (*H1*). We believe this result is because the pose-aware display presented the arrow directly in the participant's field of view, regardless of their wrist angle when the notification occurred. In addition, we confirmed our hypothesis (*H2*) that there would be an interaction between *display type* and *wrist angle*. With the static display, larger angles resulted in larger homing times.

Although we did not see a main effect of *display type* on resume times *(H3)*, we observed a significant interaction effect between *display type* and *wrist angle*. We believe the interaction effect can be explained by the different strategies we observed participants employ for small and large angles. When faced with a small angle (little to no occlusion), participants would keep DisplaySkin still and touch their left wrist with their right hand. As a consequence, their left hand remained in an ideal position to resume their primary task. Furthermore, larger angles (with larger amounts of occlusion) compelled participants to rotate their left wrist when homing with the right hand. With their left hand now in a different pose than at the start, participants were slower to resume the task.

In the pose-aware condition, participants typically swiped with a bimanual gesture. We observed that participants often let their left and right hands meet in the middle, a comfort permitted since DisplaySkin did not need to be at a specific angle. Resume times were therefore faster for the larger angles, and homing times were more efficient throughout. Swiping in the pose-aware condition was more efficient, since the right hand traveled a shorter distance to meet the left hand and there was no need to explicitly rotate the left wrist to re-orient the arrow.

Somewhat surprisingly, we found that in the 0° condition, the pose-aware display had faster homing times than the static display, a scenario where performance should be equivalent. We believe this difference is due to the dynamic nature of the pose-aware display and these differences in acknowledgement strategies. Even though the target appears at the same place, it adjusts position during the interaction: the swiping motion is more efficient when the arrow remains at an angle that is easier to reach.

In the pose-aware conditions, it appears that the 60° angle resulted in the shortest times for both homing and resume times. The result suggests that users may be naturally inclined to touch at that angle of the wrist for interactions that are not constrained by a fixed target. This result might be relevant to the design of wrist worn devices that are not pose-aware. There may be a benefit to having the display and interaction area slightly rotated facing the body, away from the 0° position, and towards the 60° position.

Although the targeting task was not the focus of this experiment, we conducted a statistical analysis of the task to ensure that the conditions were consistent across both display types. We confirmed our hypothesis that movement times did not differ between display types (*H4*) and larger amplitudes resulted in longer times (*H5*). Even though non-significant difference is not equivalence, these results are enough to suggest that the participants' focus was on the primary task.

FUTURE DIRECTIONS

Our prototype was tethered to a dedicated driver board because flexible displays are still a new technology. When given the opportunity to explore DisplaySkin before the experiment, some users noted that the cables occasionally restricted their movement. Later, they commented that for the more limited motion required in our experiment, the cables did not concern them. In the future, we aim to reduce these cables through miniaturizing the driver boards.

In our current prototype, our forward kinematic model requires users to wear, not only DisplaySkin, but also a small (8 x 36 x 2mm) secondary IMU on their upper arm. Future research in tracking algorithms may allow us to create an inverse kinematic model to remove this IMU.

One of the results revealed during our study is that there are interaction effects between wrist angle and display type; since the pose-aware display adjusts to the users movement, the effects of arm rotation are corrected for. This result presents an opportunity for further study into the ergonomics of wrist interactions.

Our tracking technology was primarily implemented to support a pose-aware display. At the same time, we feel it is a strong platform for building future context aware applications for situations that would greatly benefit from a pose-aware display. For example, to understand eating habits, one might create an application that records how many mouthfuls a meal was divided into and at what frequency the mouthfuls were consumed. A golf player could use an application that shows how hard the golf ball was hit and how well the swing was executed. The kinematic model might also learn which instruments its user plays and switch into a sheet music library, or recording mode, when the user is playing. Identifying a driving pose becomes straightforward as well, making it easy to automatically supply the driver with relevant information, such as a map (Figure 2).

In addition to our kinematic tracking, we also believe that there might be strong synergies with other sensing technologies such as the MYO [36] or Rekimoto's GestureWrist [29].

CONCLUSION

In this paper, we presented DisplaySkin, a prototype pose-aware display with a large 320° cylindrical display surface. Our prototype is the first interactive wrist worn device to adjust its display to the user's body pose. DisplaySkin is also unique in regards to its degree of curvature, flexibility, and display size.

To evaluate whether a pose-aware display helps users access information more efficiently, we designed an experiment in which users performed a rotational pointing task that was interrupted by a task on the wristband display, at varying angles. Results suggest that pose-aware displays reduce the time taken to acknowledge the notification, minimizing the overall interruption. Our results also suggest that some areas on the wrist might be more natural to touch than others and that pose-aware displays may be a useful method of exploring ergonomics of body-worn devices.

REFERENCES

1. Boettcher, D. The Development of the Wristwatch. 2006. http://www.vintagewatchstraps.com/wristwatches.html.
2. Brendel, W. and Todorovic, S. Activities as time series of human postures. *Proc. ECCV*, Springer-Verlag (2010), 721–734.
3. Butler, A., Izadi, S., and Hodges, S. SideSight: multi-touch interaction around small devices. *Proc. UIST*, ACM (2008), 201–204.
4. Chen, X.A., Grossman, T., Wigdor, D., and Fitzmaurice, G. Duet : Exploring Joint Interactions on a Smart Phone and a Smart Watch. *Proc. CHI*, ACM (2014), 159–168.

5. Chen, X.A., Marquardt, N., Tang, A., Boring, S., and Greenberg, S. Extending a mobile device's interaction space through body-centric interaction. *Proc. MobileHCI*, ACM Press (2012), 151–160.
6. Cheng, L., Hsiao, F., Liu, Y., and Chen, M. iRotate: automatic screen rotation based on face orientation. *Proc. CHI*, (2012), 2203–2210.
7. Gioberto, G., Coughlin, J., Bibeau, K., and Dunne, L.E. Detecting bends and fabric folds using stitched sensors. *Proc. ISWC*, ACM Press (2013), 53–56.
8. Google Glass. Google Glass. http://www.google.com/glass.
9. Google. Android Wear. http://www.android.com/wear/.
10. Harrison, C., Benko, H., and Wilson, A.D. OmniTouch : Wearable Multit ouch Interaction Everywhere. *Proc. UIST*, ACM Press (2011), 441–450.
11. Harrison, C. and Hudson, S. Abracadabra: wireless, high-precision, and unpowered finger input for very small mobile devices. *Proc. UIST*, (2009), 121–124.
12. Harrison, C., Ramamurthy, S., and Hudson, S. On-body interaction: armed and dangerous. *Proc. TEI*, (2012), 69–76.
13. Harrison, C., Tan, D., and Morris, D. Skinput : Appropriating the Body as an Input Surface. *Proc. CHI*, (2010), 453–462.
14. Holman, D., Burstyn, J., Brotman, R., Younkin, A., and Vertegaal, R. Flexkit: A Rapid Prototyping Platform for Flexible Displays. *Proc. UIST*, ACM Press (2013), 17–18.
15. Jaquet, E. and Chapuis, A. *Technique and history of the Swiss watch from its beginnings to the present day*. Graf Verlag, 1953.
16. Kim, S. Disabling an automatic rotation function of mobile computing devices. 2013.
17. Lyons, K., Nguyen, D., Ashbrook, D., and White, S. Facet: a multi-segment wrist worn system. *Proc. UIST*, (2012), 123–129.
18. Mahony, R., Hamel, T., and Pflimlin, J. Nonlinear complementary filters on the special orthogonal group. *Automatic Control 53*, 5 (2008), 1203–1218.
19. Makino, Y., Sugiura, Y., Ogata, M., and Inami, M. Tangential force sensing system on forearm. *Proc. Augmented Human*, ACM Press (2013), 29–34.
20. Marshall, J. and Tennent, P. Mobile interaction does not exist. *Proc. CHI EA*, ACM Press (2013), 2069–2078.
21. Microsoft. Kinect. http://www.xbox.com/en-US/Kinect.
22. Nakatsuma, K., Shinoda, H., Makino, Y., Sato, K., and Maeno, T. Touch interface on back of the hand. *Proc. SIGGRAPH*, ACM Press (2011).
23. Olberding, S., Yeo, K., Nanayakkara, S., and Steimle, J. AugmentedForearm: Exploring the Design Space of a Dis-play-enhanced Forearm. *Proc. Augmented Human*, (2013), 9–12.
24. Pebble SmartWatch. Pebble SmartWatch. http://www.getpebble.com.
25. Perrault, S.T., Lecolinet, E., Eagan, J., and Guiard, Y. WatchIt : Simple Gestures and Eyes-free Interaction for Wristwatches and Bracelets. *Proc. CHI*, (2013), 1451–1460.
26. Plastic Logic. It's a wrap! https://www.youtube.com/watch?v=5kqFlx7rSs4.
27. Plastic Logic. Plastic Logic. http://www.plasticlogic.com/.
28. Rector, K., Bennett, C., and Kientz, J. Eyes-free yoga: an exergame using depth cameras for blind & low vision exercise. *Proc. ASSETS*, (2013).
29. Rekimoto, J. Gesturewrist and gesturepad: Unobtrusive wearable interaction devices. *Proc. ISWC*, (2001), 21–27.
30. Samsung. Galaxy Gear. http://www.samsung.com/global/microsite/galaxynote3+gear/.
31. Sciavicco, L. and Siciliano, B. *Modelling and Control of Robot Manipulators*. CreateSpace, 2000.
32. Stop The Cyborgs. Stop The Cyborgs. http://stopthecyborgs.org/.
33. Strohmeier, P., Vertegaal, R., and Girouard, A. With a Flick of the Wrist : Stretch Sensors as Lightweight Input for Mobile Devices. *Proc. TEI*, (2012), 307–308.
34. Tarun, A., Lahey, B., Girouard, A., Burleson, W., and Vertegaal, R. Snaplet: using body shape to inform function in mobile flexible display devices. *Proc. CHI EA*, ACM Press (2011), 329–334.
35. Teicher, M. Orientation-sensitive display system. 1993.
36. Thalmic Labs. MYO. https://www.thalmic.com/en/myo/.
37. Vicon. Vicon. http://www.vicon.com.
38. Watch Museum of Le Locle. Times of the watch. http://www.mhl-monts.ch/en/temps_montre.php.
39. Wesolowski, W. *The Concise Guide to Military Timepieces 1880-1990*. The Crowood Press Ltd, 1996.
40. Wigdor, D. and Balakrishnan, R. Empirical investigation into the effect of orientation on text readability in tabletop displays. *Proc. ECSCW*, Springer-Verlag (2005), 205–224.
41. Wilfinger, D. and Murer, M. The wheels are turning: Content rotation on steering wheel displays. *Proc. CHI*, (2013), 1809–1812.
42. Xsense. Xsense. http://www.xsens.com/.
43. Zhang, Y., Han, T., Ren, Z., and Umetani, N. BodyAvatar: creating freeform 3D avatars using first-person body gestures. *Proc. UIST*, (2013), 387–396.

Interaction Design as a Bricolage Practice

Anna Vallgårda
IxD lab
IT University of Copenhagen
Copenhagen, Denmark
akav@iu.dk

Ylva Fernaeus
Dept. of Media Technology and Interaction Design
Mobile Life Centre and KTH
Stockholm, Sweden
fernaeus@kth.se

ABSTRACT
With this paper we propose bricolage as an interaction design practice. We make the case that bricolage promotes design qualities that are specifically tuned to tangible and material computing practices in that it is highly sensible towards the unstable physical world and proposes a non-hierarchical negotiation of forms. We further show how bricolage can aid design results with strong and rich cultural and material grounding. Finally, we argue how bricolage and mythical thinking can be proponents for new ways of thinking and using technology.

Author Keywords
Bricolage; mythical thinking; design practice; interaction design; tangible computing; material computing;

ACM Classification Keywords
H.5.m. Information interfaces and presentation (e.g., HCI): Miscellaneous.

INTRODUCTION
Conceptual design plays an important role in pivoting research in interaction design forward [27]. It changes how we see the potential of the technology and thus what we will do with it. In this paper, however, we will look at their polar opposite – the bricolage – and analyze how this practice of making can bring forward an alternative path expanding how we see and use technology. Bricolage is, as we will develop further in the paper, a way of making which draws on what is already there both culturally and materially. It is a practice that favors making connections between the tools and materials at hand rather than looking for globally optimal solutions. Bricolage is an everyday concept in many Roman languages and denotes a *builder* or a *tinker*. In this paper, however, we rely on the more elaborate description provided by the anthropologist Lévi-Strauss [17]. We find his notion of bricolage and mythical thinking offers a fundamentally different way of making compared to conceptual design.

TEI '15, January 15–19, 2015, Stanford, California, USA..

ACM 978-1-4503-3305-4/15/01...$15.00.
http://dx.doi.org/10.1145/2677199.2680594

Bricolage, in the notion from Lévi-Strauss, has previously been introduced to design thinking most notably by Louridas [18] who proposes to use bricolage as a metaphor to describe all design practice. His purpose is to draw out and discuss the relationship between design and art and design and science. Several interaction design researchers [10; 12; 14; 30; 34] also touch upon the notion most often, however, using Louridas' interpretation [18] in which design work *per se* is considered a bricolage practice. Our aim here is to look at bricolage as a particular way of practicing design – a way distinguished from that of engineering and conceptual design.

Indeed, the reason why we find bricolage a both suitable and interesting practice for interaction design, especially when working with tangible and material computing, is fourfold. First of all, the bricoleur is not curbed by the impreciseness of our physical world rather she will use it to her advantage. When working solely with graphical user interfaces we are rarely toppled by any imperfections or unpredictable events in our technology – it tends to behave as prescribed. Breaking out into the varied multitude of input and output devises, as we do in tangible and material computing, we constantly meet those imperfections. Instead of dismissing these quirks as just bumps in the road in an early prototype and polish the conceptual description, bricolage proposes to work with them – to exploit them.

Second, the bricoleur does not plan ahead but develops the project in-situ with concerns of interaction, physical form, and behavior pattern not being hierarchically ordered *a priori*. Thus, the bricolage is the result of careful negotiations in the making, which render it less skewed towards either (i.e. as we often see in co-design or technology driven design).

Third, we find how bricolage proposes interesting ways of creating more culturally grounded and material rich artifacts because it operates in-situ and not towards an imagined future.

And fourth, we find bricolage to provide fruitful ways of constraining the design space and that the mythical way of thinking provides promising ways of making new connections. Connections, which in turn can help open new design spaces and in general expand our understanding of technological potentials. However, there are also limitations to a bricolage practice, for instance, the inherently local optimal solutions and the potential conservative results.

In the first part of the paper we present a close reading of Lévi-Strauss' notions of mythical thinking and bricolage tailored to be read prescriptively. We then look at how the notion has been used in interaction design literature. Afterwards, we analyze the qualities of bricolage as a particular design practice, specifically in the context of interaction design. We go on to discuss some of the limitations of the practice. And finally, we briefly mention which areas of interaction design we believe could benefit from practicing bricolage and mythical thinking.

BRICOLAGE & MYTHICAL THOUGHT

In his book 'The Savage Mind' [17], the anthropologist Lévi-Strauss makes the argument that 'primitive cultures' seems to develop a language for and, thus understanding of, things in their surroundings even if they find them more interesting than useful. He makes the point that for them "animals and plants are not [necessarily] known as a result of their usefulness; they are deemed to be useful or interesting because they are first of all known" [17, p. 9]. This is the cornerstone in the *mythical thinking*[1] (intellectual plane) and the *bricolage practice* (technical plane) we will present here in the context of interaction design.

We are not about to compare the practice of interaction design to a 'primitive culture' rather Lévi-Strauss' point is that this way of thinking and making is thriving side-by-side with scientific thinking and engineering even in industrial and post-industrial cultures. And our point is that there are significant qualities to be found for interaction design in this immediate way of structuring events through material assemblage and modification that together signifies the practice of bricolage.

Lévi-Strauss is a structuralist and as a general worldview we would perhaps rather argue for a post-structuralistic one. We find, however, that there is little conflict between the notions of mythical thinking and bricolage and a more post-structuralistic perspective since they are both about the constant creation and re-creation of structures based on particular events. Further, we propose them here as some sort of meta-structures we can adapt and appropriate in our practice rather than a specific method.

Bricolage

Basically, there are three crucial points to a bricolage practice, which regards what the bricoleur works with, the nature of his skill-set, and especially how he works.

The bricoleur's task is to "take to pieces and reconstruct sets of events (on a physical, socio-historical or technical plane) and use them as so many indestructible pieces for structural patterns in which they serve alternatively as ends or means" [17, p. 33]. In other words, it is to make a structure of events. These events may be prior to the project and as such even occasion it. They may be intrinsic to "the course of execution itself, in the size or shape of the piece of wood" [17, p. 27]. Lastly, they may be posterior to the act of creation. For example, when the work is created to an end the bricoleur will consciously or unconsciously put himself "in the place of the person for whose use it is intended" [17, p. 27]. Thus, the bricoleur may start out with an idea of a project but the result will always be a compromise between what is already there and what is needed. "His universe of instruments is closed and the rules of his game are always to make 'whatever is at hand'" [17, p. 17]. Indeed, the bricoleur's treasury of materials and tools does not pertain to neither the current project nor any prior particular project but are the "contingent result of all the occasions there have been to renew or enrich the stock or to maintain it with the remains of previous constructions or deconstructions" [17, p. 17].

Second, the bricoleur does not "need the equipment and knowledge of all trades and professions" [17, p. 18] but operates based on interpretations of the relation between the materials and tools before him. The 'bricoleur' is adept at performing a large number of diverse tasks; but, unlike the engineer, he does not subordinate each of them to the availability of raw materials and tools conceived and produced for the purpose of the project [17]. In other words the bricoleur sometimes uses the tools (and materials) as they were used before but he is also able to reinterpret their function in the course of the execution. Further, the bricoleur rely on his own experience – his own history of events – in everything he does.

Third, the bricoleur's task is to make structure of the events before him (his treasury). The first step of execution is thus always retrospective. "He has to turn back to an already existent set made up of tools and materials, to consider or reconsider what it contains and, finally and above all, to engage in a sort of dialogue with it and, before choosing between them, to index the possible answers which the entire set can offer to his problem. He interrogates all the heterogeneous objects of which his treasury is composed to discover what each of them could 'signify' and so contribute to the definition of a set which has yet to materialize but which will ultimately differ from the instrumental set only in the internal disposition of its parts" [17, p. 18]. For example, "[a] particular cube of oak could be a wedge to make up for the inadequate length of a plank of pine or it could be a pedestal – which would allow the grain and polish of the old wood to show advantage. In one case it will serve as extension, in the other as material" [17, pp. 18-19].

[1] In The Savage Mind [17] *mythical thought* and *magic* is used seemingly interchangeably. We suspect this is specific to the English translation but we are not in possession of the French edition. For the sake of simplicity we only use *mythical thought* in this paper.

Importantly, though, the bricoleur does not start *tabula rasa* rather "the possibility always remain limited by the particular history of each piece and by those of its features which are already determined by the use for which it was originally intended or the modification it has undergone for other purposes" [17, p. 19].

Thus, bricolage is not merely about a reflective conversation with materials in a design situation [cf., 26]. Indeed, the reflective conversation with materials can be seen as aspects that engineering and bricolage have in common – much like the systematics of both mythical thought and science. Rather, bricolage differs by being an *in situ* structuring of events through material assemblage and modification – in a process with no hierarchal ordering. Where the *in situ* also adheres the restricting of tools and materials to whatever is at hand thus making the outcome both local and particular.

Mythical thought

Bricolage is the technical plane – the practice of making – that accompanies the intellectual plane of the mythical way of thinking [17]. Thus, *mythical thought* can be seen as the mind-set responsible for the nature of the structure made in a bricolage.

Mythical thought makes connections between cause and effects as they appear. It is a way of thinking that connects events, not because that would give an insight, but because these events take place there "immediately presented to the senses" [17, p. 11], at the same time or right after each other. Its reasoning is systematic and arguments coherent yet the explanations and conclusions may, from a scientific perspective, seem outlandish. Indeed, the quality of myths is the poetry that arises from these alternative connections of events and sometimes even the alternative connections *per se*. "The elements of mythical thoughts [...] lie somewhere between percepts and concepts" [17, p. 18]. Thus, mythical explanations offer a foundation for stories, wonder, and imagination. Furthermore, the mythical thought does not discriminate in layers of knowledge as scientific thought does. Rather, it approaches everything at the same level which is why it is able to bridge events differently.

For example, in a myth that connects the touch of a woodpecker's beak and toothache, "the real question is not whether the touch of a woodpecker's beak does in fact cure toothache. It is rather whether there is a point of view from which a woodpecker's beak and a man's toothache can be seen as 'going together' (the use of this congruity for therapeutic purposes being only one of its possible uses), and whether some initial order can be introduced into the universe be means of these groupings. Classifying, as opposed to not classifying, has a value of its own, whatever form the classification may take" [17, p. 9]

"For even a heterogeneous and arbitrary classification preserves the richness and diversity of the collection of facts it makes. The decision that everything must be taken account of facilitates the creation of a 'memory bank'" [17, p. 16]

The point is, that "every object made by man is the embodiment of what is at once thinkable and possible" [19, p. 17] as Manzini states in the opening of his seminal book The Material of Invention. Articulating and classifying is part of the practice of making it thinkable. Doing so from a mythical perspective rather than a scientific perspective will enable us to think and, consequently, to make differently. Further, Lévi-Strauss [17] stresses how *mythical thought* is not merely a naive predecessor to scientific thinking rather it is a way of thinking with entirely different ways and means.

This account of bricolage is not to be interpreted as a manifesto to be followed dogmatically. It is a proposal for a way of thinking and making fundamentally different than engineering and in that we find it to hold some qualities, which we will analyze after we have looked at related work.

RELATED WORK

Panagiotis Louridas' proposal [18] of metaphorically seeing design as bricolage is probably the most influential introduction of bricolage in design thinking that also found its way to interaction design. He too draws on Lévi-Strauss notion of bricolage and uses it to analyze in what ways design differs from the practices of science and art. His errand is descriptive, as opposed to our more prescriptive, in that he uses bricolage as an analytical lens to discuss the nature of design [18]. Louridas' analysis is divided between the unselfconscious designer and the self-conscious one, which he borrows from Alexander [1]. The unselfconscious one is the original bricoleur, the craftsman, who is bound by tradition and only is allowed a limited form of originality [18]. The other is the modern designer who designs for manufacturing and uses design methods [cf., 5]. This designer has the responsibility of setting up his own scene for the bricolage – create his own treasury. He is responsible for determining which events that should be included in the structure [18]. What we aim to do with this paper is to propose bricolage as a particular way of practicing design for the self-conscious designer. Thus, unlike Louridas, we argue that bricolage differs from design-by-drawing, conceptual design, or engineering which are otherwise common ways of practicing self-conscious design. The differences lies primarily in its lack of outlook – its *in situ* nature that results in local and particular structures, construed through a mythical mindset. We acknowledge that all self-conscious design is a matter of conversation with events, and through that structuring them, but it is the scope of those events the mindset behind the structuring that distinguishes a bricolage from most modern and engineer based design.

Louridas paper has inspired others to analyze interaction design practices as bricolage. Most prominent is Wakkary and Maestri's studies of the everyday designer and thus what can be seen as the unselfconscious designer [34]. Through ethnographic studies in family homes they identified and analyzed the design aspect of the families microstructures.

The Tanenbaums and Wakkary [30] later uses bricolage to articulate the practice of Steampunk design and thus emphasizing the bricolage practice's quality of remaining within the cultural and aesthetic tradition of the bricoleur.

Hazelwood *et al.* [14] bring forward bricolage in a simplified version in which they propose to use a combination of bricolage and consultancy for the design of large-scale installations. "By *bricolage* we refer to the act of making resourceful use of materials that are 'at hand' and tinkering with them" [14, p. 386]. They introduce consultancy to overcome the risk of suboptimal solutions by only relying on the skills of the bricoleur.

Fallman [10] argues how bricolage is closely related to the pragmatic and hermeneutic practice of design that, for instance, Schön puts forward with his notion of reflective conversation with the materials at hand [26]. We have argued above, however, how bricolage is somewhat more than that. Indeed, we suggest that the conversation with materials rather can be seen as one of the common traits of engineering and bricolage.

Büscher *et al.* [4] uses bricolage as an idea for a cost effective method for situated design. Their main point is that 'designing immediately' accommodates the situatedness of a work organization and, thus, helps minimize the gap so often seen between technical solution and the actual organization of work [4]. This work is interesting in that it broadens the scope of tools and materials to also include actors. It applies bricolage to a context beyond the dull artifacts to also include interactive technologies. Indirectly, this work even suggests that bricolage could be used in a practice of the more ephemeral user experience design besides the more tangible interaction design we will discuss in this paper.

Another area related to interaction design in which bricolage has played an analytical role is in creative and end-user programming practices [3]. Especially child programming has found a prominent use of the concept [11; 25]. The main take on bricolage in this body of work is based on Turkle and Papert's interpretation [31] in which bricolage becomes a way of "learning by making". Thus, the outlook is naturally limited and any making will inevitably be of the unselfconscious kind.

Finally, there are a wide range of related and semi-related work from within the maker, DIY, and hacker cultures that we will have to discuss another time. Most notably, perhaps, the Bardzels and Toombs use of *adhocism* [2] or the repair work studied by Jackson & Kang [15].

INTERACTION DESIGN AS A BRICOLAGE PRACTICE

The reasons why we find it interesting to further elaborate on bricolage as an interaction design practice are four. First, it offers a material alternative to conceptual design one that is made to cope with the imperfections of our physical world. Second, it levels the importance of all three form-elements of interaction design in its non-hierarchal process of making and thus increasing the likelihood of well-balanced results. Third, it explicitly builds on cultural references and existing material expressions with results inevitably grounded in something familiar. Thus, the results can be seen as a counterweight to the more hyper-modern kind of design. And fourth, the mythical thinking in combination with the implicit design constrains forces the bricoleur to make new connections and thus possibly open new design spaces.

Making and making do

In interaction design, and especially the tangible and material practices, we are constantly reminded of the unstableness of the physical world. We are often tempted to dismiss this trait as something to be solved with more sophisticated technology yet to come. Often, that will also be the case. Yet sometime there are interesting connections to be found in these imperfections and instabilities. Bricolage offers a way to exploit those rather than dismiss them. The bricoleur will thoroughly study the events of his treasury – explore them together and separately – in the quest for placing them in a materialized structure. And it is through this that bricolage is able to exploit the imperfections.

We use bricolage in our teaching. In an introductory course on making interactive artifacts our students are given a physical computing kit with cheap and unreliable sensors and actuators and we explicitly tell them not to pretend they are better. Instead, we force the students to find the qualities of the technology as it behaves before them – imperfections and all. We force them to 'articulate' these qualities through a series of inspirational bits [28]. Meaning, they build a series of small interactive constructs that each expresses one or more of the electronics' qualities. These constructs or bits then serve as common experience for the students to go on designing an interactive artifact for a given context. The students are later let loose in the lab with instruction to give body to their electronics. They may use all scrape materials and repurpose all discarded projects they can find. The only requirement is that it all will form a coherent working design in the end. The results may not be high-end designs, and the concepts often not too strong, but the imagination and the cunning put into the details of the solutions almost always astonish us. And it is in this we see a quality of bricolage.

Bricolage is about reflective conversations with the materials [26] and the cultural connotations of 'what is at hand' as well as it is about making the actual thing as opposed to a sketch or a prototype [5]. It is an in-situ practice of making with no plans but with an objective to create structure of what is happening through a material assembly. Bricolage it thus well suited for design situations that allow an exploratory approach or for the creation of one-offs – like in the case of the everyday designer [34], the design researcher, or possibly even the designer aiming for production if accompanied by reverse engineering. As exemplified above, it can also be used in teaching situations as means for the students to become familiar with the technology and force them to engage in a conversation with the materials and especially the unstable physical world.

Leveling the playing field

As Vallgårda [32] proposes, interaction design can be seen as a negotiation of forms: the physical form, the temporal form, and the interaction gestalt. In conceptual design practice there are often given precedence to one of these – simply by being the starting point and because planning for all three at once is a highly complex task [32]. As bricolage and mythical thinking are both non-hierarchical and in-situ at their core the negotiation of forms will only happen in the making and with an importance of each form determined only from the nature of the project as the events unfold. In essence, the interaction gestalt, the temporal form, and the physical form will all be the result of a coherent process of structuring the events.

In the previous case of the students, for example, the temporal form of the technology was only interesting from an interactive perspective. The qualities of the technology were only discerned from en experiential experience. And while the students often chose one as a starting point for giving it a physical body they went as often back to reconsider both temporal form and the interactive experience as all changed through the addition of new elements. Thus, while we can discuss the complexity of interaction design from the view of other practices [32; 33] it is inherently dissolved in a bricolage where there is no planning and all happens in-situ with no predetermined hierarchical order.

Rich cultural references and material expressions

The meticulous attention the bricoleur has to pay to 'what is at hand' both in terms of personal experiences, cultural annotations, forms, and material qualities ensures the creation of artifacts that are grounded in what we know. The result may break with both prior functionality and expression but there will always be traces of a cultural grounding. Further, it encourages the combination of cultural references (from those present in the bricoleur's treasury) and it is in this we find the likelihood of designs that exhibits rich and complex expressions. Indeed, given how design of technologies from an engineering practice tends to seek an aesthetics and cultural reference, which favor the hypermodern often liberated from any historic reference in interaction gestalts and materials [cf. 20; 23] the inherent grounding in bricolage propose an interesting alternative.

An example of a bricolage, from within the interaction design is a musical cabinet called Ajna [12]. This project clearly draws on a rich mixture of cultural references and material expressions (see Figure 1). The musical cabinet comprises a collection of more or less traditional musical instruments that are mechanically operated and digitally controlled [12]. It is the result of collaboration between two artists trained as a musician and a computer engineer respectively. The project lasted three and a half years and was the result of a combination of tinkering and scavenger hunt [12]. The project was conceived as the artists' need for a way to stand out as artists and is thus highly autobiographical [21]. Indeed, our retrospective study of the artists' practice led us to argue how it can be seen as an example of a bricolage practice [12]

"The physical frame of Ajna consists of a re-purposed old rococo vitrine cabinet made from mahogany and bought on an online auction early on in the process. Within this frame a range of mechanical parts are fitted, including three drums, two cymbals, one marimba-style instrument with 20 wooden bars, one sampler, two maracas, two bells, one murmur machine, and one horn. All these parts are digitally controlled mechanical systems, some previously served the purpose of start engines in cars, one used to be a shoe shining machine and even others are handcrafted structures. The original form factors of the cabinet shape the layout of the musical components. The large drums, for instance, are fitted in what once used to be the main doors of the cabinet, using the space behind for the sound to resonate." [12, p. 3]

The result of the project is an interactive musical cabinet drawing on a "combination of rococo, voodoo and steampunk, Ajna is a fusion of cultural and historical references that may be difficult to decode at first encounter" [12].

In a practice of repurposing and hacking what is already there it seems likely that the aesthetic style will be closer to

Figure 1. Left: Ajna, a human-sized interactive musical cabinet created by the art- and music collective *I Skogen Ibland* [12]. Right: An IKEA bricolage coffee table made from KNUFF magazine holders, a FROSTA stool, and a NASUM basket [9]

Steampunk than modernism. However, the IKEA bricoleurs, for example, provides a different aesthetic (see Figure 1) [24]. In other words, the treasury of the bricoleur, whether it is an IKEA store, old inherited furniture, or the scrape materials from other lab activities, will inevitably set the aesthetic tone of the result.

Making new connections

Finally, we will make the case that adopting a bricolage practice in interaction design can enable new interpretations of the potential of technology, new forms of use, and new material expressions. We argue thus, that bricolage is not only suited as a design practice but also as a design practice with potential to pivot the field forward – a practice suitable for design research [16].

Bricolage's predisposition for making new connections is twofold. One stems from the restrictions put on the scope of the treasury the other from the even-leveled mythical way of thinking. In both cases, however, the bricoleur must either step into the role of the researcher in order to acknowledge the significance of a new connection in a larger, if not global, context, or it may be a discovery of an on-looker (e.g. an ethnographer).

It is not uncommon in interaction design practice to find ways of putting restrictions on the design practice as means to enforce creative solutions [13; 22]. Indeed, necessity is the mother of invention. Bricolage can likewise be seen as a set of restrictions on an otherwise open-ended design practice. The restrictions comprise the immediacy of the events that are to be included in the resulting structure – the particular and local treasury, the skill-set of the bricoleur, and the in-situ making.

The mythical way of thinking that accompanies bricolage is about making sense of what is immediately before our senses. The sense making, however, does not have to comply with scientific knowledge or useful solutions. The connections between events, that inevitably will form the resulting structure, just have to be within the scope of the treasure. Like in the case of the touch of a woodpecker's beak and the toothache. Mythical thinking, in other words, is likely to form a more poetic and imaginative set of connections in the bricolage than both functional and scientific thinking would.

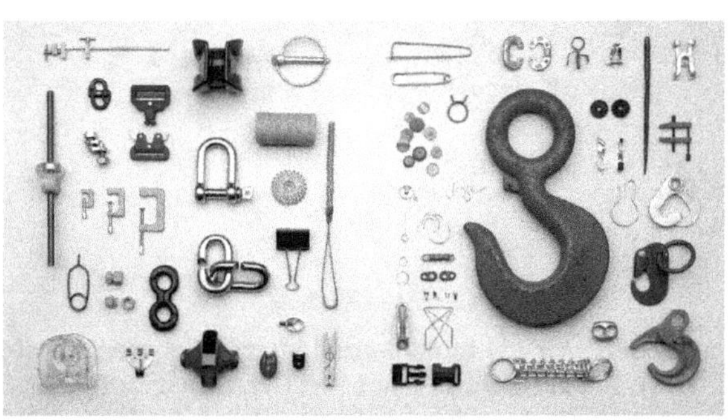

Figure 2. Collection of objects that can hold things together, from the Clivio's No Name Design exhibition in Milan 2014 [6]

As there are not yet many examples of bricolage from within the interaction design literature we have ventured to look at two recent art and design projects which both emphasize new connections in their bricolages.

The first is a peak into an intriguing treasury, and the mind of the Swiss product designer Franco Clivio [7]. Over the years he has collected numerous objects from which he now makes simple yet thought provoking juxtapositions on pictures [7] or in a display cases [6]. For example, his collection of objects that hold things together makes us to reflect on this varied technological landscape (see Figure 2). Indeed, what does it entail to keep two pieces together? How can it be done? What does the material matter? Little had we previously thought of pearl buttons, metal carabineers, and metal paper clips at the same time.

The second, and perhaps more explicitly a bricolage, is the work of the American artist Sarah Sze [29]. Her sculptures make us see ordinary objects, which we normally pay little attention to but often have a bodily experience with (like a plastic water bottle), through a myriad of transitions in complex sculptural universes (see Figure 3). Sze emphasizes transitions in her sculptures and they always seems to be somewhere between construction and deconstruction – a tension which helps or forces the audience to engage. Her sculptures destabilizes the meaning of the singular objects both in the way they are placed in relation to one another but also in how they are placed in the universe of the whole sculpture.

Indeed, the connections made through bricolage are likely to be more poetic and thought provoking than necessarily

Figure 3. Planetarium by Sarah Sze, 2013 Venice. Materials: wood, steel, plastic, stone, string, fans, overhead projectors, photograph of rock printed on tyvek, mixed media 632.5 x 548.6 x 502.9 cm [8]. Copyright: Sarah Sze

useful. However, even the artists of the musical cabinet claimed mechanical inventions in their construction of, for instance, the modified car engine solenoid drumstick structure [12].

CRITIQUE OF A BRICOLAGE PRACTICE

In a sense bricolage and mythical thinking can be seen as an attempt to romanticize the naïve. However, we would rather propose it as becoming an expert in open-mindedness. Indeed, the bricoleur can hold specialized skills and be knowledgeable in certain fields. However, it is likely that he will encounter tasks for which he has not trained and in such situations he is resourceful with what he has got and already know. Further, with interaction design being as interdisciplinary as it is and the design teams often lack one or another expertise being a bricoleur can actually prove desirable if not explicitly necessary.

Nevertheless, accepting a local outlook and restrictions on the treasury is an almost certain way of obtaining suboptimal solutions. Not seeking and making use of new technological inventions can seem counterintuitive in a field that thrives on technological invention. However, what is globally suboptimal may be good enough if not better locally. As we have argued bricolages may hold other qualities than the functionalistic ones. Their cultural and material grounding, for instance, may render an aesthetics that makes them locally superior. Still, the restricted outlook does produce the risk of conservative solutions with the starting point always being in what is and what used to be, and this even from a cultural and aesthetical perspective.

Further, interaction design is traditionally a practice with a high sensitivity for the future user and her situation. And while the bricoleur will be emphatic and consciously or unconsciously put himself "in the place of the person for whose use it is intended" [17, p. 27] it will demand some sort of experience with the context of the intended use. In other words, the bricolage is highly dependent on the personal experiences of the bricoleur. As Büscher *et al.* [4] show this could perhaps be remedied by letting the bricolage take place with the people, for which it is intended, in a sort of co-design process. These would then be included in the collection of events for which the bricoleur had to find a structure

Interaction design research has been known to produce many one-offs that are not necessarily reproducible. A bricolage is explicitly so. The musical cabinet, for instance, is not replicable – it is and will be unique. Obviously, in some cases reverse engineering may be applied to open up the bricolage and produce the necessary sketches and optimizations. However, it is more likely that a bricolage practice will tailor to situations where the unique is desired or at least accepted. In design research, bricolage practice enables *a posteriori* knowledge development through the materialization of a new connection.

Lastly, we are not trained to be limited in our outlook. We more or less do have the world at out feet with the Internet and an abundance of technologies, materials, and tools available for our purchase – often at a relatively low cost. Thus, as Louridas' points out [18], we will almost always be responsible for the extent of our treasury. We will always have to set the limit. In the case of the musical cabinet [12] the limit was defined by an artistic and autobiographical vision as well as limitations on budget and time.

Further, seeing as many interaction designers are trained as engineers adopting a mythical way of thinking may prove difficult and confusing, because it demands that they let go of the global outlook. However, with some practice it may be possible and we believe there is value to be found in designing with the mindset and constraints of bricolage.

CONCLUSION

Introducing bricolage as an interaction design practice is primary meant as an alternative to the conceptual design. As we have argued it promotes some design qualities, which are specifically attuned to tangible and material computing practices primarily due to its sensibility towards the unstable physical world. Just as the in-situ negotiations of concerns from a non-hierarchical perspective is likely to ensure coherent and well-balanced interactive design artifacts.

Further, the cultural and material grounding, which it promotes, are qualities that we find can have merits in an interaction design practice, perhaps again, primarily in material and tangible interaction. And finally, the in-situ constrains of bricolage and the leveled non-functionalistic structures of mythical thinking seem well suited in a quest for new connections. Thus a bricolage practice may very well be fruitful way of pivoting the field forward.

Indeed, with this paper we have sought to propose bricolage, not as a manifesto, or as something to be followed dogmatically, but as a design practice and a mindset highly suitable for interaction design.

ACKNOWLEDGEMENTS

This research was partially conducted as part of the Arts and Crafts project at Mobile Life Centre, funded by Vinnova in partnership with Ericsson, Microsoft, Nokia, IKEA, and Stockholm City.

REFERENCES

1. Alexander, C. *Notes on the Synthesis of Form*. Harvard University Press. 1964
2. Bardzell, J., Bardzell, S., & Toombs, A. Now That's Definitely a Proper Hack": Self-made Tools in Hackerspaces. *In Proc. CHI '14,* Toronto 2014, pp. 473-476.
3. Blackwell, A. F. Gender in Domestic Programming: from Bricolage to Séances d'Essayage. *In Proc.*

CHI'2006 Workshop on End User Software Engineering, 2006, pp. 1-4.

4. Büscher, M., Gill, S., Mogensen, P., & Shapiro, D. Landscapes of Practice: Bricolage as a Method for Situated Design. *Computer Supported Cooperative Work*. 10, (2001) 1-28.
5. Buxton, B. *Sketching User Experiences: Getting the Design Right and the Right Design*. Morgan Kaufmann. San Francisco. 2007
6. Clivio, F. No Name Design. (2014).
7. Clivio, F., Hansen, H., & Mendell, P. *Hidden forms*. Skira. Milano. 2014
8. Designboom. *Sarah Sze represents the US at venice art biennale 2013*. http://www.designboom.com/art/sarah-sze-represents-the-us-at-venice-art-biennale-2013/ (Retrieved: August 1 2014)
9. Emerjadesign. *Coffee Table*. http://www.ikeahackers.net/2014/06/new-version-of-the-coffee-table-with-knuff-magazine-files.html (Retrieved: July 30 2014)
10. Fallman, D. Design-oriented Human Computer Interaction. *In Proc. CHI'03,* Fort Lauderdale April 5-10 2003, pp. 225-232.
11. Fernaeus, Y. *Let's Make a Digital Patchwork: Designing for Children's Creative Play with Programming Materials*. PhD Stockholm University. Stockholm. 2007
12. Fernaeus, Y. and Vallgårda, A. Ajna: negotiating forms in the making of a musical cabinet. *In Proc. DIS'14,* Vancouver June 21 - 25 2014, pp. 915-924.
13. Gaver, W. W., Beaver, J., & Benford, S. Ambiguity as a Resource for Design. *In Proc. Ambiguity as a Resource for Design,* Fort Lauderdale, FL, USA 2003, pp. 233-240.
14. Hazlewood, W. R., Dalton, N., Marshall, P., Rogers, Y., & Hertrich, S. Bricolage and consultation: addressing new design challenges when building large-scale installations. *In Proc. DIS'10,* Aarhus 16-20 August 2010, pp. 380-389.
15. Jackson, S. J. and Kang, L. Breakdown, Obsolescence and Reuse: HCI and the Art of Repair. *In Proc. CHI '14,* Toronto 2014, pp. 449-458.
16. Koskinen, I., Zimmerman, J., Binder, T., Redstrom, J., & Wensveen, S. *Design Research through Practice: From the Lab, Field, and Showroom*. Elsevier. Waltham, USA. 2011
17. Lévi-Strauss, C. *The Savage Mind*. University of Chicago Press. Chicago. 1966
18. Louridas, P. Design as Bricolage: Anthropology Meets Design Thinking. *Design Studies*. 20, 6. (1999) 517-535.
19. Manzini, E. *The Material of Invention: Materials and Design*. MIT Press. Cambridge, USA. 1989
20. Microsoft. *Future Vision*. http://www.microsoft.com/office/vision/ (Retrieved: July 30 2014)
21. Neustaedter, C. and Sengers, P. Autobiographical design in HCI research: designing and learning through use-it-yourself. *In Proc. DIS 2012,* Newcastle Upon Tyne, UK 2012, pp. 514-523.
22. Pierce, J. and Paulos, E. Counterfunctional things: exploring possibilities in designing digital limitations. *In Proc. DIS'14,* 2014, pp. 375-384.
23. Rogers, Y. Moving on from Weiser's Vision of Calm Computing: Engaging UbiComp Experiences. *In Proc. UbiComp'06,* Irvine, CA 2006, pp. 404-421.
24. Rosner, D. and Bean, J. Learning from IKEA hacking: I'm not one to decoupage a tabletop and call it a day. *In Proc. CHI'09,* 2009, pp. 419-422.
25. Ryokai, K., Lee, M. J., & Breitbart, J. M. Children's storytelling and programming with robotic characters. *In Proc. C&C'09,* Berkeley 2009, pp. 19-28.
26. Schön, D. A. *The Reflective Practitioner: How Professionals Think in Action*. Basic Books. New York. 1983
27. Stolterman, E. and Wiberg, M. Concept-Driven Interaction Design Research. *Human–Computer Interaction*. 25, 2. (2010) 95-118.
28. Sundström, P., Taylor, A. S., Grufberg, K., Wirström, N., & Belenguer, J. S. Inspirational Bits: Towards a Shared Understanding of the Digital Material. *In Proc. CHI'11,* Vancouver 2011, pp. 1561-1570.
29. Sze, S. *The meaning between things*. http://channel.louisiana.dk/video/sarah-sze-meaning-between-things (Retrieved: August 1 2014)
30. Tanenbaum, J., Tanenbaum, K., & Wakkary, R. Steampunk as Design Fiction. *In Proc. CHI'12,* Austin May 2012, pp. 1583-1592.
31. Turkle, S. and Papert, S. Epistemological pluralism: Styles and voices within the computer culture. *Signs: Journal of Women in Culture and Society*. 16, 1. (1990) 128-157.
32. Vallgårda, A. Giving form to computational things - Developing a practice of interaction design. *Personal Ubiquitous Computing*. 18, 3. (2014) 577-592.
33. Wakkary, R. Framing complexity, design and experience: a reflective analysis. *Digital Creativity*. 16, 2. (2005) 65-78.
34. Wakkary, R. and Maestri, L. Aspects of everyday design: Resourcefulness, adaptation, and emergence. *International Journal of Human Computer Interaction*. 24, 5. (2008) 478-491.

Resisting Alignment: Code and Clay

Daniela K. Rosner
Department of Human-Centered Design and Engineering
University of Washington
dkrosner@uw.edu

Miwa Ikemiya
Townsquared
San Francisco, CA
mdikemiya@gmail.com

Tim Regan
Microsoft Research
Cambridge, UK
timregan@microsoft.com

ABSTRACT
Today thousands of artists, designers, and craftspeople turn to digital fabrication tools to invent and manufacture new forms. They use vector-graphics software to sketch models, laser-cutters to customize parts, and 3D printers to generate prototypes. However, how our experiences of expressivity, skill and value shift with these developments remains under-explored. This paper describes our early engagements with emerging fabrication technologies in the domain of ceramics, one of our oldest and most enduring artistic mediums. In particular, we detail a collaboration with Helen Martino that resulted in the Sound Bowl, a vessel designed to record an audio message through surface undulations, much like a vinyl record. As an example of *design as inquiry*, we developed the bowl to explore the integration of digital fabrication in ceramics production. In the process, we found new and intriguing tensions in the entanglement of code and clay: contrasting temporal frames, blurred traces of breakage, and coinciding human senses. We discuss implications of these observations on the nature and organization of embodied interaction.

Author Keywords
Craft, ceramic, clay, handwork, sound, code, digital grips.

ACM Classification Keywords
K.4.0. Computers in Society: general.

INTRODUCTION
Developing production-focused computational tools that amplify our expressive experience has become an important challenge facing design and human-computer interaction. Today makers use instructional resources to learn new techniques; physical computing hobbyists join social networks to share personal narratives of production; and design hopefuls use social media to scaffold idea generation and manufacturing. In parallel, a growing number of people use digital technologies to extend craft production: generating furniture with 3D printers, altering jewelry with laser cutters, and sewing circuitry into clothing [3]. However, we understand little about how these tools to support craft (*e.g.* laser cutters, 3D printers) account for and change people's experiences developing form and meaning. Conversely, most existing technologies for communication and collaboration around craft (e.g., social networks, blogs, tutorials) that integrate with makers' tools could help us map and extend possibilities for expressivity, engagement and value.

This paper examines emerging possibilities of *hybrid craft* [17,23] — the use of computational resources within and around traditional modes of craft activity — and how this confluence might lead to new understandings of expressivity, skill and value in TEI. By attending to the specific mediums of code and clay we focus our investigation on media that stretch the gamut of human production over time. In this exercise, we find that code and clay resist alignment due to the temporal frames they embody. We further show how tools for production uniquely shape, envelope, and coerce our ways of thinking with material.

We develop this line of inquiry through a research through design approach [8] that relies on material engagement not as an end in itself but as a way to investigate shifting practices of craft. This follows on recent design-led research by Jackson and Kang [15] proposing an integrated program of theoretical, empirical and material work. In what follows we begin by laying out some of our core theoretical foundations around embodiment, medium and craft, drawing especially on the scholarship of Tim Ingold and Karen Barad. These theorists, hailing from anthropology and feminist science studies, interrogate questions of engagement with particular attention to matter and agency. We then describe

Figure 1: Running a fingernail along the surface plays "Happy New Year," much like a vinyl record. © Miwa Ikemiya

an ethnographic interview study of pottery and ceramics, focusing on activities of people who create, use, and care for pottery on a daily basis. Lastly, we turn to a project of our own making: the Sound Bowl. This project evolved through collaborative experiments around code and clay and three stages of design: framing, modeling, and amplifying.

BACKGROUND AND THEORETICAL DEVELOPMENT

In Edmund de Waal's [6] essay "The event of a thread, the event of clay: Black Mountain College & the Crafts", de Waal suggests celebrated artist Josef Albers refused to sanction the teaching of ceramics at the Black Mountain College. He believed clay to be too resistant a material for students to handle. For a medium with significant physical malleability, this may seem peculiar, and indeed other accounts reverse Albers' objection [9]. Clay may be flattened, molded, roughened, hardened or softened. What does it mean for a medium to resist or align with another? And how might alignment change, especially with respect to the most 'malleable' material of all, software?

Here we draw primarily from anthropologist Tim Ingold [12,13] who seeks to understand how mediums of making characterize, shape and envelop worldly actions. Ingold argues, "we need to think of making in terms not of the simple, mechanical execution of complex structures, but of the form generating potentials of complex processes" [13:22]. Making consists of recognizable phases that become improvisational in character, much like walking. They do not follow each other in succession, but get drawn into relation according to a program of action. The materials brought into alignment become histories told through experienced engagement. Ingold's conception of material reappears in the scholarship of feminist sciences studies scholar Karen Barad [2] who describes *intra-actions* between the semiotic and material (neither existing before the other). In their entanglement, individual agencies precede their practices and lack an "independent, self contained" status [2:ix]. As for Ingold, meaning is material in nature, developing out of our engagements with the world. To develop this point, Ingold relates drawing to storytelling and wayfaring, wherein people produce itineraries without fixed templates or "pre-composed plots" underwriting the journey [12:75). This contrasts with modern assemblies of "point-to-point connections" [13:3] embodied in digital tools like Computer-aided design (CAD).

Turning now to digital craft, we ask what it might mean to extend material interactions with code? What forms of understanding emerge through the confluence of discourse and material, digital and non-digital, or code and clay? This paper takes up Ingold's notion of making as wayfaring — travelling with an itinerary rather than a map — and Barad's concern for entangled agencies to examine digital craft as series of guided agential alignments, each with its own appetite for change and disruption. We examine these themes in the domain of ceramics.

Over the years, ceramicists have produced some of our oldest and most cherished cultural artifacts, from teatime china to religious figurines. "A smashed and discarded ceramic pot literally kills time as it waits to be discovered," notes art historian Glenn Adamson [1]. "When unearthed, it seems to provide a direct connection to the point at which it was made or used; a cultural trace that transports a sense of immediacy across the centuries." Drawing from our first-hand accounts, we focus on this succession of changes underlying ceramics work. The observation that material is not so much an object of study as a set of situated relationships highlights the development of digital craft as part of both moral and material accountabilities. Our research extends this analytic stance by locating those accountabilities within the specific material relations of clay and code. Before we turn to our program of research and making, we wish to briefly review scholarship that set this project in motion.

Ceramics and Computing

Traditional craft materials have increasingly found their place in the worlds of digital fabrication, including developments in computing with wool [6] sand [9] and clay [20]. These hybrid forms provide opportunities for exploring the interweaving of analogue and analytical feedback. In the *Whispering Table*, made by the Green Eyl design group (thegreeneyl.com/whispering-table), museumgoers can listen to audio-recorded stories about food and tradition coming from inside the bowls and vases. The Particules Studio (particules-studio.com/objets-sans-âge.html) recently sought to bring a kind of "poetry to everyday life" by blurring the boundary between craftsmanship and technology with a series of porcelain speakers resembling bowls.

In other work, digital or computed patterns that decorate ceramics begin to shape resulting interactions as well as ceramics process. Meese and colleagues [18] collaborated with ceramic designers to create complex decorative patterns on plates and bowls identifiable by computer vision software. Jonathan Keep (ww.keep-art.co.uk) produces two categories of work each with a different digital genesis. In one Keep adapted a 3D printer to extrude carefully formulated slip to thus construct digitally formed ceramic objects, what Keep calls "Digital Pots." A different digital genesis precedes some of Keep's larger works, where the curved form of the ceramic arise from repeated sketching in the Processing visualization software. Using a similar process, Geoffrey Mann (www.mrmann.co.uk) materializes in clay that which cannot otherwise be seen, such as the flight pattern of a moth around light or the ripples created by blowing on a cup of tea. His piece *Crossfire* comprises a series of dinner table vessels representing the sound of an argument passing through them. Collectively, this work demonstrates the broad attention to digital and material sensitivities (e.g., light, touch, sound) in the ceramic medium. Our work broadens these developments by examining questions of ceramic and computational co-production.

UNDERSTANDING CERAMICS

In this section we report findings from an ethnographic interview study conducted between September 2012 and February 2013 with six artists and designers who work with ceramics as central methods or topics in their work. To develop a richer understanding of ceramic materials and processes, the second author visited four studios, four homes, and a symposium on the intersection of craftwork and networked objects. We designed our interview questions to elicit reflections on the use or potential use of clay and ceramic processes. Our interviews were guided towards the stories associated with ceramic materials, the potential future life of these materials, and techniques and obstacles around the integration of ceramics and technology.

Our work draws on interpretivist approaches that focus on the translation rather than transcription of social phenomena. Instead of seeking an objective, transparent view of these settings, we used our own subjective experiences — often closely tied to the subjects we studied — to generate intersubjective knowledge (falling "somewhere between the subjectivity of the researcher and that of the researched" [4:85]). While studying members' justification of belief, we reflected on the extent to which we resembled our subjects in background and ideology. In particular, we recognized how the second author's working knowledge of ceramic throwing, glazing and firing techniques influenced our accounts. The second author studied in both the United States and Japan over fourteen years and to a certain degree identifies as a ceramicist. In conducting our analysis, we sought to use these experiences to deepen our discussions of subsequent design activities [4].

Articulating Endurance

The longevity of ceramic materials was important to Helen, a ceramicist, who described teaching a group of school children how to create ceramics at a museum. She made the children's eyes widen when she explained that, even if the pots break, their shards would stick around through the rise and fall of civilizations. When probed further about this quality of endurance, Helen brought out four vessels she had used to capture images of four generations of her family (Figure 2).

> *"These are the bottles I made, so they are like women, and the images are from photos, so there is my mother with me, me with my daughter, my mother with my daughter, and my daughter with her daughter. So it's to do with mothers and daughters. And that's what I've drawn from the photos and made photocopies of those drawings, so you can see it's not very precise, extra spots and things happening but it's gives it a sort of freedom to be not too photographic anymore."*

Here the ceramic objects merged with the high-contrast images of intimate family portraits Helen created on a photocopier. The warped shape of the vessels reminded Helen of gestural, talking women, producing generative intra-actions [2] between the female stories and their form. Even as the photos referenced specific moments, they lost precision with their translation into clay, giving the image a kind of "freedom." This notion of freedom stands apart from the issues of clarity and accuracy Helen associated with photographic prints. Sean, who calls himself a potter, explored this through *test tiles,* small trials he used to consider the integration of different materials such as copper wire in clay. Such experiments enabled Sean to surprise himself, expanding the possibilities of clay. Though the artists we visited reported clear expectations for how their work would be communicated over time, they remained open to different ways of getting there.

Knowing Imperfection from the Inside

Like other potters, Evelyn was intimately aware of her material; so much so that she could spot small inconsistencies in industrially produced tableware that other people might overlook.

> *"I've started looking at shapes that I like from supermarkets, they are all different. They are both Churchill but they are at different times. Can you see that? Very subtle but this has a pinkier glaze and is slightly bigger."*

She spoke of enjoying their subtle differences: how the various mass-produced white plates and bowls remained unique despite their industrial heritage. Imperfections were central for Evelyn. The only plates in her collection made by her that did not get sold were the plates that had a chip, a glaze defect, or a hairline crack in the surface. All the defects became reasons for her not to sell the plates and feel that she had to keep them. The plates remained in heavy use in her kitchen alongside industrially produced tableware, which she reported caring less about. She said,

> *"It's got a chip there that I've mended. So if somebody breaks this I don't mind so much but the ones I really like I'd be so upset."*

The plates with imperfections may have been the only plates left for Evelyn's family because she sold the others. Yet, as for others we interviewed, imperfection could also be considered a virtue. Later in our interview, Evelyn described a cup (created by another potter) as being "terribly warped": *"There are things I find really wrong with it, but I still like it."* She appreciated the serendipitous way the warping seemed to occur. She then spoke about her electricity free kick-wheel designed by Bernard Leach, a well-known British potter, whose style of pottery she had studied. Having worked with this specific wheel for 25 years

Figure 2: Helen's images of a mother-daughter relationship. The warped shape was meant to reflect talking gestures.

she felt she had complete control over the tool and this part of the process, being able to make the wheel go at precise speeds (even slow speeds which are notoriously difficult to achieve on electric wheels). She felt she had reached a point where she had mastered wheel throwing defined as being able to exactly execute what she had envisioned. She threw her plates symmetrically and perfectly yet delighted over a series of plates that she unintentionally warped.

Ceramic flaws were equally relevant to other artists we spoke with. In the evolution of a style from naïve and rustic to smooth and polished, one explained, "*This is one I made at school. Do you see what I mean? About the naive painting. It's just so naive, it's before I knew anything about drawing.*" She seemed surprised to see the differences between her work now and her work at that time. The inconsistent treatment of the clay indicated that time had passed.

Our ethnographic interviews revealed a defiant quality to clay: how it resists fine control and embraces imperfection. We also saw how it can often perform the role of either a mundane object (the plates and cups used everyday) or an heirloom object (cherished and passed on from generation to generation). Many people we spoke with kept clay objects in display cases, hung them on the walls, or stored them away, while they kept other clay objects in easily accessible places.

TELLING BY HAND: BUILDING THE SOUND BOWL

To further examine these ethnographic insights, we decided to use the material of clay to build on this fieldwork and the theoretical foundations we outlined earlier. Our series of experiments would ultimately produce the "Sound Bowl," a piece of pottery created during fall 2012 and developed by the second author in collaboration with Helen Martino, a ceramicist she met in the course of fieldwork. The Sound Bowl plays back encoded sounds through ridges carved into its surface. We used the bowl to explore multiple concepts: the material process of inquiry, knowing from the inside, and alignments between code and clay. This process of de-

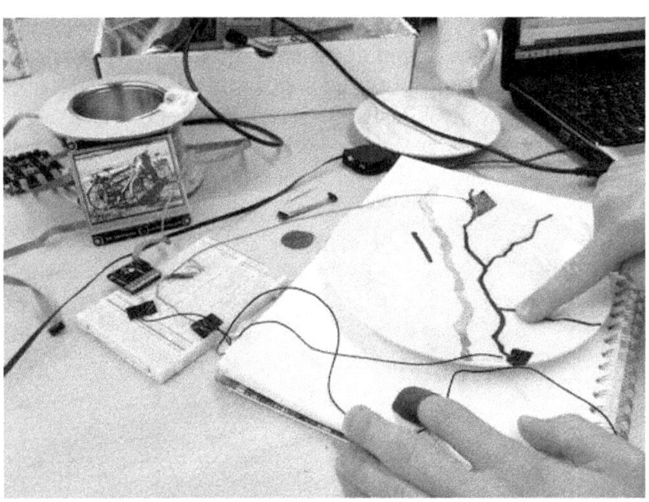

Figure 3: A line of conductive paint is used as a potentiometer to read out different levels of resistance when current travels through the finger to the microcontroller.

Figure 4: Sensing experiments: plate is coated with conductive material on the bottom and sits on a coin-sized soft conductive pad. The weight of the plate completes the connection. Additional ceramic housing for Sensing Plates (left).

sign began with a series of sensing experiments to which we now turn.

Sensing Experiments

Our initial experiments explored questions of breakage in code and clay over a period of four weeks. This focus developed from the concerns for wear and imperfection we observed in our fieldwork as well as two prior experiments: first, a series of broken probes [11] designed by members of the research team to explore the use of ceramic cracks as a material anchor for digital messages (building on Japanese concepts of *kintsugi* and *wabi-sabi*); second, a collaborative interaction with designer Tommy Dykes, who had worked the previous year with a member of the project team to build a set of interactive tea cups and saucers with conductive gilded edges. Unlike the teacups, the probes used a mobile phone application to enable people to associate digital images with specific cracks on pottery. The cracks became a unique barcode for digital annotation. During interviews, people expressed the desire to elicit the images directly by touching the cracks — focusing on the object rather than the phone as an intermediary.

Our intention for this early experimentation was to consider interactions (or intra-actions, after Barad [2]) between the meanings accrued through breakage and tactile modes of storytelling. Using a conductive material called BareConductive, a black conductive poster paint, we built a potentiometer to read out different levels of resistance when current traveled to the microcontroller through a conductive glove. We associated specific ranges of resistance with personal photographs. Touching a point along the crack yielded a specific photo on the small screen based on an arbitrary mapping between resistance values and digital photos.

Much of our process was guided by serendipitous discovery rather than particular aims for an outcome. For example, we discovered we could put a conductive finger glove on the opposite hand and use a bare finger to effectively interact with the painted line (soon indicating breakage). Following this, we tried using an aluminum circle on the plate instead of a finger glove. When we broke a plate and pieced it back together, filling the cracks with conductive paint, the interaction failed to connect to the server. We then created a second plate, reproducing the cracked lines using thick raised steams of conductive paint. This 'worked' the first day (producing photographs upon touch) but ceased to work the second day. When we inspected the plates, we found he dried paint had cracked, leaving gaps in the circuitry.

Here the *cracks* accrued a dual purpose: becoming materials for refection and traces of fracture. Though our design process was driven by the use of cracks, we had not expected to find breakage in other places besides clay. Cracks in the code left us searching for hidden bugs; cracks in the paint left us wishing we could control the process of drying paint. Cracking became a mode of aesthetic interaction, inspiring us to touch and reconnect with traces of wear. Yet, trying to determine the most stable method of conductive glazing prompted us to question how stability became a condition of this project being made. Stability invited instability: rewriting code, checking electrical connections, and letting the materials dry, crack and rub away. Grappling with these ambiguities not only pointed to the difficulties of locating the origin of breakdowns, but also suggested initial incongruences between the mediums of code and clay.

Before turning to our Sound Bowl, we wish to highlight one final phase of our sensing experimentation. As part of our early trials, we resolved to explore how the design of pottery might enable serendipitous storytelling—framing bowls or plates as tools for *telling by hand* [13]. Inspired by related work [16], we built a second system that sensed hand gestures over a ceramic plate (with or without eating utensils) to produce simple visual patterns of interactivity. The plates sat on a coin-sized soft conductive pad connected to a WI-FI enabled microcontroller that acted as a capacitive proximity sensor (Figure 4). We used the plate during meals and explored a variety of common gestures — e.g., cutting with a knife and fork, twirling and lifting a fork, and scooping with a spoon. Because the system used capacitance to read proximity, the conductivity of the items above the plate affected the visual output in the system. For instance, soupy dishes read differently from dry dishes, heavy or wide utensils read differently from light or narrow utensils, and food eaten with fingers contrasted with utensils.

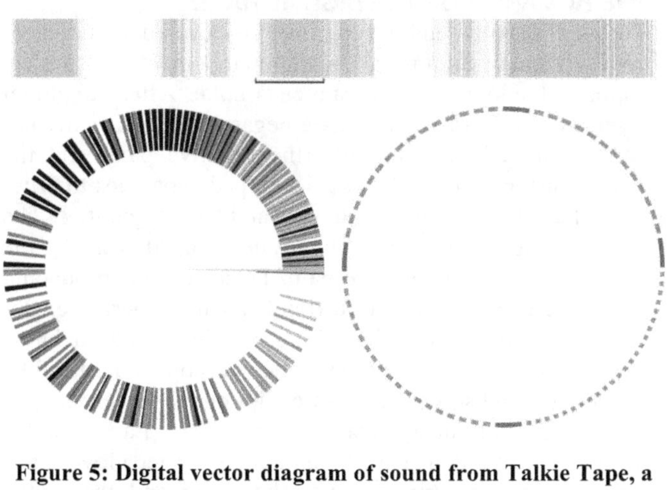

Figure 5: Digital vector diagram of sound from Talkie Tape, a piece of plastic with ridges that produces sound by running a nail across the surface, much like a vinyl record.

Figure 6: Plastic Talkie Tape (left); laser cut acrylic reproduction of the Talkie Tape (right). © Miwa Ikemiya

Although this assemblage of code and clay characterized ephemeral patterns of interaction in provocative ways, the accounts also struck us as strange. We felt differently knowing that our gestures were being captured, prompting us to become more purposeful about where we put our hands. Consequently, our search for the serendipitous and accidental got skewed. As we traced the ephemeral in code and clay, it changed the behavior we hoped to trace.

Sound Bowl

These initial sensing experiments warned us of incompatibilities between code and clay, raising tensions between the dual purpose of cracks, on the one hand, and the nature of digital ephemerality, on the other. The experiments also recalled qualities of clay we encountered in our fieldwork: the improvisational quality of working with clay and its resistance to change or capacity for imperfection. Our process of defining and building the *Sound Bowl* developed these concerns across three stages: framing, modeling, and amplifying.

Framing

Meeting and working with Helen provided an initial framing for our project. Most of the work she made came from slabs of clay stamped to create textures and hand painted to evoke time and place (by the sea, on a hill, under the moon, etc.). She explained that she does this type of *slab work* to keep her from being too 'fussy' about the forms. Her pieces include figurines, which she described as representations of people she knew in specific environments. In this way, she felt viewers could interpret the clay as personal moments, making the pieces relevant to their lives on their own terms.

During our initial discussions with Helen about her work as a potter and a ceramicist, we had interacted with a ribbon called Talkie Tape (Figure 6), a plastic strip with ridges that encodes sound much like a vinyl record. Running a fingernail along its surface audibly produced the phrase 'happy new year.' Inspired by Helen's attention to unintended, emergent form, we hoped to merge the subtle ceramic textures with unexpected meanings and functions. As we will see, this symbolic framing would prompt us to reengage with questions of accuracy around clay.

Modeling

Once envisioned, we began building the Sound Bowl by creating an illustrator file that represented the grooves on the Talkie Tape. We first rubbed ink into the ridges of the tape so that the ink was only visible in the grooves. We then scanned the tape and traced the lines in our vector graphic software, taking note of the lines that appeared darker (deeper grooves) or lighter (shallower grooves). To account for these layers on the laser cutter — i.e., shallowest to deepest cuts — we codified the cuts into four categories of color, each with its own layers within our vector graphic software (see Figure 5). Yellow is the shallowest, followed by red, purple, and finally blue. When we sent the vector graphics file to laser cutter, we adjusted the depth of cuts according to the encoded layers, varying the speed and power of the machine. To move these grooves into clay we used the acrylic as a stamp (Figure 5). Yet, the fine detail in the resulting pattern produced intersecting lines in the clay. Even as the laser cutter retained the structure of the lines, the stamp did not. The ridges became too subtle to reproduce using our laser cutter given its resolution and the depth it could carve into plastic. Thus began a process of amplifying Helen's slab technique with a digital stamp.

Unable to recreate this process in clay, we moved to a 3D printer. Though cutting acrylic proved simple on the laser cutter it became another obstacle while 3D printing. The space between the vector graphic lines remained much smaller than the minimum (3mm) required by the printer. With no hope of recreating an audible sound, we decided to simplify the form to focus on pitch (see Figure 8). The deeper blue lines became larger gaps between the different "pitches." Through modeling and printing the 3D bowl, the process became deceptively bland — introducing entirely different questions and constraints from the process we went through during our sensing experiments.

Amplifying

Helen's slab technique involved creating an even and flat area of clay and wrapping it around a ball (Figure 7). Laying out a clay slab, we cut a circle in the clay, and then created small hatch mark tests with pin tool by hand, like Sean's 'test tiles.' A paper printout of the vector graphics file guided our acts of mark making (Figure 5). Once complete, we painted directly onto clay with an underglaze in blue and drew lines into clay painted blue to highlight both the algorithmic marks and their imprecision. The impossibility of replicating the pattern faithfully offered a way out of the translation between code and clay.

Figure 7: Slab process creating the bowl.

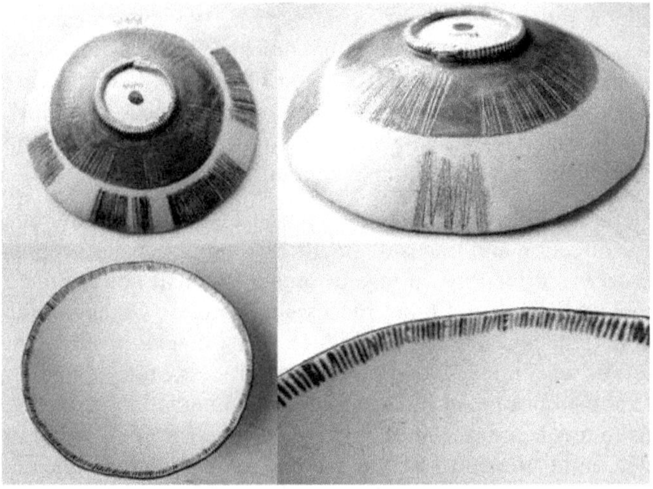

Figure 8: Resulting handmade Sound Bowl with an auditory "china mark" (top right). © Miwa Ikemiya

The rhythms of production in this setting also contrasted with our prior sensing experiments. Firing in Helen's studio took place every three months. Helen often waited until she had a good number of pieces ready before setting up to fire. Given this cycle, we expected to get only one chance to produce our bowl. As the final stage of ceramic work, the firing not only organized the pace of production, it also influenced the kind of project we could take on.

After the initial bisque firing, we painted blue underglazed area with wax and dipped the whole bowl in overglaze. We wanted to avoid having too much glaze on the lines, which would have diminished the possible sound quality. We left the areas on the outer ring where the lines without overglaze and only underglaze to create definition. The clay was also rougher in those areas, not smooth like the other parts of the bowl. We also painted patterns with words hidden on the inner rim and signed the bowl with an auditory "china mark" (Figure 8, top right). The resulting form produced scratchy but audible intonations.

THE HUMANITY OF THE DIGITAL HAND

Through making and testing, we discovered qualities of code and clay unfamiliar to all members of our project team, technologists and ceramicists alike. After our initial sessions of experimentation, we began to build a richer understanding of our materials (the resistive paint and the sensing technology). We also developed capacities to articulate their differing temperaments and tactile qualities. The code functioned at one moment and stopped working the next. The black conductive paint began to dry, producing miniscule cracks that were difficult for us to perceive. Because we applied the paint with a paintbrush, its thickness challenged uniformity and resistance became unpredictable. Despite these discrepancies, serendipitous discovery helped us develop previously unanticipated ideas. Early on, for instance, we thought we needed a snug finger glove made from conductive fabric to touch the cracks and change the image. However, we noticed the other hand with no finger glove was still able to activate the image because the electricity was passing through the user's body. This meant that a finger glove was unnecessary to touch the resistive paint with conductive fabric (Figure 3). Thus, we encountered technical barriers that prompted course corrections and afforded the possibility of creating strange and unusual forms.

However, aspects of this ad hoc assembly began to surface tensions with clay. Echoing insight from our fieldwork, clay presented surprising resistances that contrasted with our computational hacks. While gathering together existing pieces to create 'working' systems, conductive soft-circuit pads and the Arduino and WI-FI shields were easy to replace and wireless networks were easy to come by. The ceramic form and process unfolded something more precious, as exemplified by Helen's three-month cycles of kiln use. While creating the handmade Sound Bowl, we made aesthetic choices about glaze, decorative elements, shape and thickness of clay that incorporated Helen's techniques and background. Inspired by her slab technique, we sculpted the clay by hand instead of throwing clay from a wheel, purposefully emphasizing small imperfections and irregularities. While 3D printing, we uncovered need for precision and predictable material consistency that avoided clogging or other system snags. The clay used was as uniform as possible, and could not accommodate the gritty, coarse clays that helped define Sound Bowl design. As such, each bowl revealed distinct human and non-human constraints that put different emphases on care and precision.

In closing, we wish to reflect on three relations of precision and improvisation that emerged at the interface of computational and traditional craft-based production: (1) our ways of knowing through gestures, (2) our digital grips, and (3) the regression of our digital hands.

Knowing through Gestures

Our work brought about many ways of learning and understanding digital materials through gestures. Much like the mother-daughter vessels encountered in our interview study, we found clay could embody conversational movements in different ways than code. The attention to accuracy and control demanded by the sensing plate code and digitizing of the Talkie Tape failed to incorporate inconsistencies of the human hand, as apparent from the 3D printed ceramic bowl (Figure 9). Conversely, our sensitive handling of the material, our glazing techniques, and our shaping of the vessels struggled to support the rigid digital encodings.

Figure 9: 3D printed ceramic Sound Bowl. © Miwa Ikemiya

Here we find 'skill' an odd construction for this entanglement of code and clay. The quality of our interactions had little to do with competence in achieving some fixed or essential goal, but rather recognizing notable encounters along the way: feeling caught between a familiar and unfamiliar expertise, using gestures to define an emergent path, and learning to *see* the material, reminiscent of Ingold's wayfarer and the sculptural work we observed during our artisan study. This prompted us to imagine ways of providing room for engagement during the fabrication process and extending ordinary objects by actively embedding sound in their surfaces. Throughout our interactions with clay and code, gestures encouraged us to think differently about everyday artifacts and triggered us to imagine where technology might take another course.

Digital Grips

A second concern for digital craft is how the human senses may be more effectively leveraged. We found that the work of ceramics requires deep sensitivities to material form — manual modes of production that allowed the maker to notice and feel subtle inconsistencies on surfaces, experiencing the roughness of clay. We also saw that while our sensing experiments required detailed attention to breakage across two mediums (bugs in code or cracks in gilded clay), we could not attend to both at the same time.

In creating the Sound Bowl, our moves from hand to machine became quick and recursive: shifting from a machine-produced ribbon, to hand rubbed ink, to a scanned digital image, to a hand traced digital image, to a laser cut plastic. As part of these recursive moves, we acquired digital grips: ways of approaching material that enabled us to add sensitivity and sentience (after Ingold [13]) to material encodings such as the language embedded in glazed lines and the audio indentations of our custom "china mark."

Digital grips like the audio china mark involve sophisticated understandings of how human bodies experience algorithms through material form. They also build on emergent disruptions across mediums to expand opportunities for expression. How can we learn from what these encodings change to produce new kinds of stories and relations? How could we use the weight of a bowl, the texture of a surface, or the thickness of a glaze to challenge our ways of seeing through code? Sensory inputs might welcome new readings of computation and agency, refiguring our auditory, tactile, and kinesthetic capacities. Like musical rumble strips or rings on a tree, digital grips extend the varied 'propensities' [15] handwork makes possible and the layered histories they leave behind.

Regression of the Digital Hand

Today many of us buy our pottery ready-made. We sort through shelves of identical ceramic objects when we require a pot, plate, or cup. Though pottery may appear anachronistic, hidden on shelves or routinely overlooked, our experiments suggest otherwise. Ceramic techniques can operate as reminders of our agential perspectives, calling forth age-old modes of making that cast people as active citizens rather than passive consumers. "With citizenship comes moral responsibility," Ingold observes, "yet how can we be responsible for a world that comes to us ready made?" [13:122] Answering this question involves new incarnations of the digital hand. During sensing experiments, we kept track of our footprints and became more aware of where we might tread next, leaving wonderment by the wayside. While building the Sound Bowl, we found an ensemble of techniques began to shift perceived differences between code and clay.

Carrying these lessons into future work, we find resistance might have a larger role to play in our understanding of aesthetic interaction, practices that engage distinct social, ethical and emotional dimensions of information and communication media, "actively involv[ing] people's bodily, cognitive, emotional and social skills" [19:3]. What makes a sound 'crisp' may align well with what makes a ceramic form brittle. But the rigidity of clay and malleability of code became difficult, if not impossible, to seamlessly combine [5]. Investigations of tangible design might take advantage of those seams by observing how an object comes into being through this resistance, surfacing new discontinuities of the digital hand.

REFERENCES

1. Adamson, G., E. De Waal, and A. Graves. *Signs and wonders: Edmund de Waal and the V&A Ceramics Galleries*. V & A Publications, 2010.
2. Barad, K. *Meeting the Universe Halfway: Quantum Physics and the Entanglement of Matter and Meaning*. Duke University Press, 2007.
3. Buechley, L, M. Eisenberg, J. Catchen, and A. Crockett. "The LilyPad Arduino: using computational textiles to investigate engagement, aesthetics, and diversity in computer science education." In *Proc. of CHI'*08: 423-432, ACM, 2008.
4. Burrell, J., and K. Toyama. "What constitutes good ICTD research?" *Information Technologies & International Development* 5, no. 3: 82. 2009.
5. Chalmers, M., and A. Galani. "Seamful interweaving: heterogeneity in the theory and design of interactive systems." In *Proc. of DIS'04*: 243-252. ACM, 2004.
6. De Waal, E. "The event of thread, the event of clay, Black Mountain College and the Crafts." In *Starting at Zero: Black Mountain College, 1933-57*. Ed. E. M. Harris. Arnolfini Gallery, Limited, 2005: 62-73.
7. Fernaeus, Y., M. Murer, *et al*. "Handcrafting electronic accessories using 'raw' materials." In *Proc. TEI'14:* 369-372. ACM, 2014.
8. Gaver, W. "What should we expect from research through design?." In *Proc. of CHI'12*: 937-946, 2012.
9. Harris, M. E. *The Arts at Black Mountain College*. *Cambridge*, MA: MIT Press, 1987.
10. Huson, D. "The digital fabrication of ceramics by 3D powder printing." NIP26: *International Conference on Digital Printing Technologies and Digital Fabrication*. Vol. 26, 2010.
11. Ikemiya, M., and D. K. Rosner. "Broken probes: toward the design of worn media." *Personal and ubiquitous computing* 18, no. 3: 671-683, 2014.
12. Ingold, T. "Walking the plank: meditations on a process of skill." *Defining technological literacy: Towards an epistemological framework*: 65-80, 2006.
13. Ingold, T. *Making: Anthropology, archaeology, art and architecture*. Routledge, 2013.
14. Ishii, H, C. Ratti, B. Piper, Y. Wang, A. Biderman, and E. Ben-Joseph. "Bringing clay and sand into digital design—continuous tangible user interfaces." BT *Technology Journal* 22.4: 287-299, 2004.
15. Jackson, S. J., and L Kang. "Breakdown, obsolescence and reuse: HCI and the art of repair." *In Proc. of CHI'14*: 449-458. ACM, 2014.
16. Kadomura, A., K. Tsukada, and I. Siio. "EducaTableware: computer-augmented tableware to enhance the eating experiences." In CHI'13 Ex Ab., 2013:3071-3074.
17. McCullough, M. *Abstracting craft: The practiced digital hand*. MIT press, 1998.
18. Meese, R., Ali, S., Thorne, EC., Benford, S., Quinn, A., Mortier, R. Koleva, B., Pridmore, T., and Baurley S., From Codes to Patterns: Designing Interactive Decoration for Tableware. In *Proc. of CHI'13*: 931-940. ACM, 2013.
19. Petersen, M. G., Iversen, O. S., Krogh, P. G., & Ludvigsen, M. Aesthetic Interaction: a pragmatist's aesthetics of interactive systems. In *Proc of DIS'04*: 269-276. ACM, 2004.
20. Piper, B., C. Ratti, and H. Ishii. "Illuminating clay: a 3-D tangible interface for landscape analysis." In *Proc. of CHI'02*. ACM, 2002.
21. Rosner, D. K., and K. Ryokai. "Spyn: augmenting the creative and communicative potential of craft." In *Proc. of CHI'10*: 2407-2416. ACM, 2010.
22. Rosner, D. K. "The material practices of collaboration." In *Proc. of CSCW'12*: 1155-1164. ACM, 2012.
23. Zoran, A., and L. Buechley. "Hybrid reassemblage: an exploration of craft, digital fabrication and artifact uniqueness." *Leonardo* 46, no. 1: 4-10, 2013.

SPATA: Spatio-Tangible Tools for Fabrication-Aware Design

Christian Weichel Jason Alexander Abhijit Karnik Hans Gellersen
Lancaster University
Lancaster, United Kingdom
{c.weichel, j.alexander, a.karnik, h.gellersen}@lancaster.ac.uk

ABSTRACT
The physical tools used when designing new objects for digital fabrication are mature, yet disconnected from their virtual accompaniments. SPATA is the digital adaptation of two spatial measurement tools, that explores their closer integration into virtual design environments. We adapt two of the traditional measurement tools: calipers and protractors. Both tools can measure, transfer, and present size and angle. Their close integration into different design environments makes tasks more fluid and convenient. We describe the tools' design, a prototype implementation, integration into different environments, and application scenarios validating the concept.

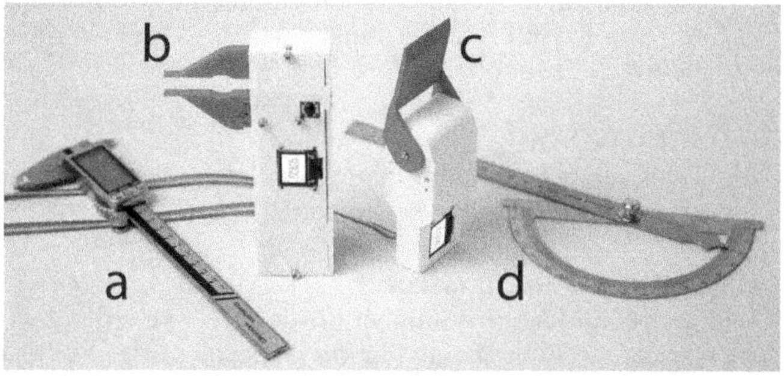

Figure 1. The two SPATA tools next to their original counterparts. (a, b) calipers for size in-/output, (c, d) the protractor for angle in-/output.

ACM Classification Keywords
H.5.2. Information Interfaces and Presentation: User Interfaces - Input devices and strategies

INTRODUCTION
Digital fabrication, such as 3D printing and laser-cutting, enables users to quickly create physical artifacts from digital files. The interfaces and environments used for designing these artifacts are typically tied to a computer screen and are thus removed from the physical world. This separates the physical nature of the fabricated artifacts, and the virtual environments in which they are designed. However, during the design of a fabricable artifact, physical features (i.e., size and angle) play an important role. The artifact will be subject to that physicality once fabricated. Further, fabricated artifacts often interact with previously existing objects e.g., to hold, encase or decorate them.

In this paper we introduce two spatio-tangible tools for fabrication-aware design (SPATA tools), a digital adaptation of two commonly used measurement tools: calipers for measuring length, and bevel protractors for measuring angle. The SPATA tools can measure their respective value (length or angle), but are also actuated so that they can actively present it in the physical world: the calipers have a self-actuated lower jaw that can physically represent length; the protractor can move its blade to output an angle (Figure 1, red parts).

Our tools can bidirectionally transfer—input and output—their value between the physical and virtual world. Users can measure a physical object, and the measured value is automatically transfered to the design environment. Conversely, length, distance, and angle measured in the virtual environment are automatically transfered to the physical world and presented by the SPATA tools. For example, to get an impression of the size of an object a user is designing, one can measure it in the design environment and have the SPATA calipers tangibly output that size in physical space.

SPATA integrates closely into virtual environments used to design fabricable artifacts, namely mechanical computer aided design (mCAD), mesh-based modeling, and 2D design. When designing new objects in these environments, we create shapes (e.g., primitives like boxes, cylinders or rectangles), manipulate them, and combine them into new forms. Those tasks, in a fabrication-aware context, often require physical measurements taken from existing objects. To reduce the need to switch between the virtual and physical world, we support those tasks in the respective design environments. By partially offloading control to the measurement tools, we can make task execution more fluid and convenient. For example, to model a box-shaped object (e.g., an enclosure) using SPATA, users can measure all three dimensions (width, height, and depth) in sequence without having to put down the SPATA calipers or manually type in measurements.

To further support the design tasks, our tools can sense their orientation, display additional information (such as estimated fabrication time or the amount of required material) and have a button built-in. We combine these capabilities to provide a more integrated and convenient design experience when designing for the physical world. In total, we make the following three contributions:

1. We present digital adaptations of calipers and bevel protractors, that can bidirectionally transfer information be-

TEI '15, January 16 – 19 2015, Stanford, CA, USA

http://dx.doi.org/10.1145/2677199.2680576

tween the physical and virtual world, providing an active tangible interface supplementing fabrication aware design.

2. The integration of both tools into three design environments commonly used for fabrication-aware design: mechanical computer aided design, mesh-based modeling and 2D design (e.g., laser-cutting or circuit board design).

3. Lastly, we demonstrate both tools and their integration in three application scenarios that highlight the benefits of the bi-directional information transfer and design-environment specific task support.

RELATED WORK

SPATA is related to digital fabrication interfaces, active tangibles and spatio-tangible design tools.

Digital Fabrication Interfaces

Interactive fabrication combines the design of an artifact with its fabrication, both situated in the physical world. Willis et al. [24] present a set of example interfaces where fabrication and design blend into one activity, always driven by physical input (e.g., movement or sound). Modelcraft proposes an iterative design process where the annotation of a physical model modifies its virtual counterpart [20]. Hybrid Carving starts with a pre-existing model that can be modified while the user physically carves it out of a block of foam [25], promoting a stronger physical engagement with the artifact. Rivers et al. promote a similar idea for large-scale objects [16]. These interfaces emphasize the physical tools that are used to design and fabricate objects. Inspired by this emphasis, we connect virtual design environments closer to physical tools.

Other systems situate the design process (instead of fabrication) in the physical world to enable the seamless integration of physical features. CopyCAD is centered around the modification of existing 2D outlines [4] projected into a 2D computer-controlled milling machine. Interactive Construction [11] extends this approach to 2D outlines and textures using a laser-cutter as drafting table. MixFab is a mixed-reality environment that enables users to integrate 3D shapes from physical objects into the design process [22]. SPATA is similar to these systems, as it also promotes the integration of existing physical artifacts into fabrication-aware design.

Physical features have also been integrated into entirely virtual fabrication-aware design environments. SketchChair uses a mannequin as size reference for the chair being designed [17]. Enclosed [21], a system to design prototype enclosures, relies on existing models of the components that are being enclosed to provide a spatial reference. Both systems assume that measurements have already been taken. SPATA integrates measuring physical objects into virtual design environments through active, tangible measurement tools.

Active Tangibles

Bi-directional physical interaction through active tangible user interfaces has been used for design tasks. The Actuated Workbench [15] is a top-projected surface on which passive, but magnetic pucks can move autonomously. Used for example to decide cell-phone tower locations, the system always maintains consistency between the projected and physical state. ZeroN [9] shows an active tangible suspended in mid-air. The commercially available Phantom Chess [3] game uses autonomous tangible chess pieces to interact with the user in two dimensions. Nowacka et al. [13] give an overview of self-actuated autonomous tangible user interfaces. The SPATA tools build on those ideas, as they can autonomously maintain a consistent state of the virtual model and it's measurement in the physical world.

Spatio-Tangible Design Tools

A variety of tangible tools for spatial input have been developed. Sheng et al. [19] present a tangible proxy for sculpting 3D models, and ShapeTape [6] enables the direct, tangible control of shape and position in a virtual environment. Other tools focus on specific measurements e.g., HandSCAPE [10] is a digital measurement tape that can transfer it's measurements to interior design applications. The commercially available Mitutoyo USB calipers [1] simulate keyboard input whenever their value changes. SPATA builds on this automated transfer, extends it to be bidirectional (from virtual to physical) and generalizes their integration.

Tangible tools have also been used in an augmented reality setting. Lau et al. enable users to create 3D shapes in their designated environment using tangible primitives [8]. ToolDevice [2] introduces tweezers, a knife and a hammer for 3D modeling. With Spatial Sketch [23], users can create 3D shapes in an embodied drawing environment. Schkolne et al. combine the users hand curvature with physical tools to create a tangible, spatially situated design environment [18]. These tools focus on the creation of shapes through tangible and embodied interaction, SPATA focuses on length and angle of 3D models, thus supplements these approaches.

Using props to navigate in 3D space has been explored early on. Hinckley et al. use a rubber ball for neurosurgeons to navigate a 3D model of the brain before surgery [7]. They did not use a realistic prop as a rubber ball can be more comfortably held. Rotating the physical prop directly rotates the model on the screen. The Cubic Mouse [5] also lets users change the models orientation using a spatially tracked prop, but adds a button for clutching. This way, the model can be rotated to any position while the prop can still be held comfortably. Both SPATA tools are spatially tracked and can serve as prop to change the view orientation. We use the button built into the tools for clutching.

SPATA TOOLS

SPATA tools are intended to become part of existing design environments. When designing new objects, designers often need to transfer a measurement into the virtual environment or visualize another measurement to help make a design decision. We go beyond the trivial step of digital acquisition of measurements and transfer to the virtual environment. Our tools provide a higher level of context-awareness to the steps of the design tasks and become integral to their progression. The specific features of the tools are:

- **Measuring and presenting physical values**: SPATA can measure length and angle, as well as present those values

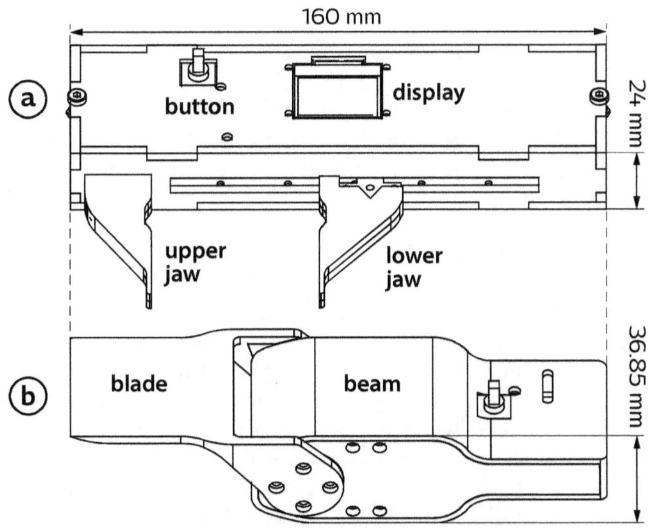

Figure 2. (a) The SPATA calipers and (b) the protractor design. Both have a fixed and actuated part, a five-way button and a display (for (b) the display is on the other side, see Figure 1).

in physical space. As both tools are actuated and computer-controlled, they can tangibly output physical dimensions.

- **Bidirectional value transfer:** Both tools automatically transfer a measurement from the virtual world to the design environment, or the opposite way. Users do not have to manually enter measured values or manually move the jaw/blade (see Figure 2) of the SPATA tools.
- **Design task integration:** We support design tasks by using transfered values in context (e.g., as correct dimension when modeling a box), and by partially offloading task control to the tools. Through the built-in display, five-way button and orientation sensing, users can navigate task steps, select modes and navigate in the 3D world.

In design practice, many different tools are used for measurements. Which tool is used depends on the type of measurement (e.g., size vs. angle) and the order of magnitude at which the measurement is taken (e.g., millimeters vs. meters). Large-scale measurements, for example using a measurement tape, have been integrated into their respective tasks [10]. Small-scale measurements, as they are typically required for personal fabrication, have yet to be integrated.

We identified tools which are important in a personal fabrication setting, through a short questionnaire among 26 personal fabrication practitioners (experience in months: $M = 29.27$, $SD = 33.98$). The results of the survey indicate that for size input, calipers are the most prominently used tool (22 out of 26 practitioners). This potentially relates to the scale of objects targeted by fabrication processes, as well as the precision afforded by the calipers. The only angular measurement tool mentioned was the protractor (4 out of 26 practitioners).

SPATA Calipers

Calipers measure length, diameter and depth. We designed the SPATA calipers to resemble their analog counterpart (Figure 1, c-d). Their size of 160×43×24 mm approximates the bounding box of traditional calipers. The jaws are shaped to support the measurement of length and inner diameter (using the thin front of the jaws, see Figure 2, a). As with the original, the upper jaw is fixed and the lower jaw can be moved from 0 mm to 100 mm; either manually or computer actuated.

Our calipers are designed so that they can be held in one hand, with the display and button being easily accessible (Figure 2, a). The display is centered and recessed into the top, giving it a prominent and easily visible position. The button can be operated with the right thumb while holding the tool, particularly when holding it with a single hand (see Figure 4).

We implemented the calipers using audio sliders as actuators. Positional feedback is provided through a voltage divider relative to the sliders position. We drive the audio slider using a dual H-bridge, controlled through a custom PID controller implemented on the microcontroller. The positioning error is less than 1.5 mm – the measurement error is less than 0.5 mm. The enclosure is made from laser-cut acrylic.

SPATA Protractor

Protractors measure the angle between two lines or surfaces. They are often used to explore or measure the slant of a surface. Bevel protractors, a common kind of protractors in mechanical design applications, consist of a beam and a blade. The beam is fixed, the blade can rotate around the center point where both intersect. We stay true to the beam and blade mechanism, with the latter attached to a servo motor (Figure 2, b). Both surfaces are co-planar in their default position (0 deg), and can assume angles from -90 deg to 170 deg.

The SPATA protractor is based on a Dynamixel AX-12A servo motor, which provides a serial interface and reports its orientation with 10 bit resolution. We can sense and actuate the angle with an error of less then one degree. A 3D printed enclosure provides the blade of the bevel protractor design, and encapsulates the electronics, including the servo motor.

Common Hardware

Both tools, calipers and protractor, are based on the same hardware platform. An ATmega328p microcontroller controls the actuator and display. It also captures the button input and accelerometer values. The latter come from an ADXL335 accelerometer that is centered on a custom circuit board. A 4D Systems μOLED-96-G2 module is used as display. Our tools connect to a communication board that supplies 5V and 9V, and provides a USB/serial interface through an FTDI based USB-serial bridge. Both tools send their measurements and orientation at a rate of 10 Hz.

Client-side Integration

We integrate the tools and the design environments using a custom middleware layer. This middleware contains the communication with the tools, the access to the design environments, and the workflow logic. Both tools are free of integration specific logic, and do not require reprogramming to be used in different environments. The same is true for the design environments, none of them contains any workflow logic; all logic is contained in the middleware layer.

We implemented the integration for three different software packages which are used by digital fabrication practitioners.

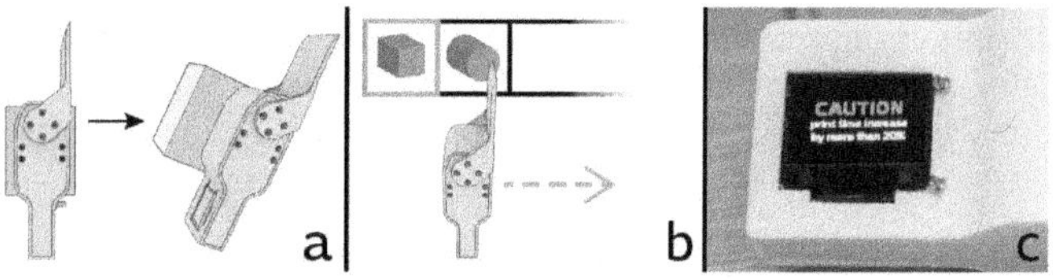

Figure 3. (a) Rotating the SPATA tool to the perspective of the model on the screen. (b) Flicking the tool to the side changes the mode of operation. (c) SPATA tools showing fabrication related information.

To integrate into Autodesk Inventor, representing mechanical CAD, we used the API that comes with the software. Blender, which represents mesh-based modeling, can be scripted with Python. Hooking into the redrawing routine of Blender, we can read commands from a file/Unix pipe and execute them in the modeling environment, thus creating our own remote control API. Because Adobe Illustrator does not provide any extension mechanisms, we simulate key-strokes and analyze screenshots to control this environment.

DESIGN ENVIRONMENT INTEGRATION

Automating the value in- and output from the physical world to the virtual design environment removes the need for manual value transfer. Existing projects and products, such as the *Mitutoyo USB calipers* [1], provide automated value input, but are not integrated with the design environments (other than simulating keyboard input). SPATA integrates into design environments, aiming to reduce the required context switches and to make the design process more convenient.

We integrate the SPATA tools into three types of commonly used design environments. Starting from a general 3D environment integration, we specialize to specific environments: mechanical computer aided design (mCAD) and mesh based 3D modeling. The former is often used for product design, the latter for more artistic, organic modeling of shapes. Lastly, we describe how our tools integrate with 2D design environments, for example laser-cutting or circuit board design.

3D Design Environments

We implemented SPATA tools suppport for two 3D design environments: mechanical CAD and mesh-based modeling. Both environments have common tasks e.g., navigation and tool selection which do not directly affect the 3D shape.

Navigation

Viewing a model from different angles, zooming in and out, as well as panning the model are essential tasks during design. SPATA supports such operations by serving as tangible proxy.

By making SPATA tools tangible proxies for the object being designed, users can change the model orientation by physically changing the orientation of the SPATA tool. This allows users to view and inspect a model from different angles (Figure 3, a). Both tools can represent a continuous variable i.e., the current zoom level. When in zoom mode, users can zoom in and out by moving the lower jaw of the calipers or changing the angle of the protractor blade respectively.

Tool Selection

While designing we need to navigate the design environments user interface to start some operation, change a value or select a tool. Often times, we need to alternate between two tools e.g., measuring or manipulating a length. Such selection tasks can be performed using quick mid-air gestures: flicking the tools to either side. Users could flick through a color swatch by quickly moving to the left or right (Figure 3, b). Manipulation/measurement modes could be changed by quickly moving forward or backwards.

Second Display

Design decisions often depend on their influence on fabrication: its impact on printing time, material cost or whether support structures are needed. This information can be displayed on the second screen of the SPATA tools. For example, when slanting a surface of a 3D model that is going to be 3D printed, beyond some slope support material is needed. Presenting this information enables users to make an informed decision whether they want to cross that threshold or not (i.e., make the angle 40 degrees instead of 45; see Figure 3, c).

Mechanical CAD

Mechanical computer aided design (mCAD) is used by engineers and designers for product design and prototyping. Mechanical CAD revolves around shapes typically found in man-made objects, such as cylinders, blocks and curves.

Modern mCAD systems e.g., Autodesk Inventor or SolidWorks, are based on 2D sketches which are extruded or revolved into solid 3D objects. When drawing sketches or creating these objects, users need to constrain different dimensions, often using physical values, such as length and angle.

Quick Primitive Creation

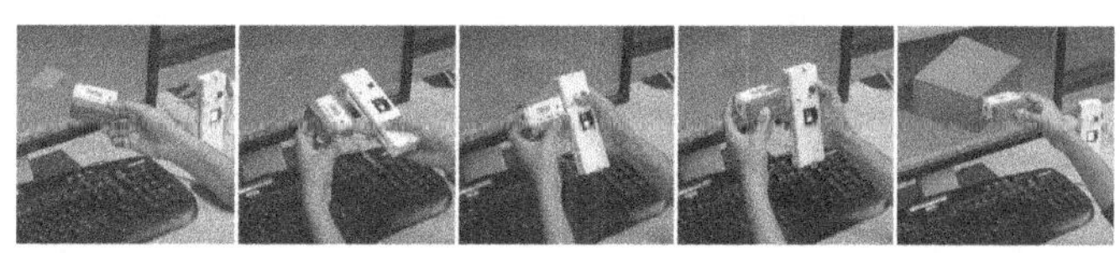

Figure 4. Creating a box (from left to right): select the ground plane, measure width, height and depth.

SPATA supports the creation of boxes from a prescribed series of real-world measurements (e.g., width, height, depth; see Figure 4). The measurements can be preformed in rapid succession using the button on the SPATA tool, thus users can create a new cube with no context switch. A similar sequence exists for cylinders: first measuring the diameter, then height. After a primitive has been created, SPATA stays in this mode enabling a series of primitives to be built on top of each other – the *broken sprocket* use-case demonstrates this feature.

Extrusion, Revolution and Holes

More complex shapes can be created by extruding or revolving more drawings. The height of the extrusion, or angle of revolution are often determined by existing physical artifacts, or by the liking of the designer; both of which are best determined in the physical world. Further, mechanical CAD systems often support semantic actions, such as creating holes. We support those tasks by providing a continuous value input: if the value of the tool changes, it's directly used as the respective design parameter (e.g., extrusion height).

This mode is particularly useful if one wants to create a hole with respect to a physical artifact. For example, if a user in a previous step measured a box, and now wants to create a hole in it, they could use the physical box in conjunction with the SPATA calipers to determine the depth of the hole.

Selection

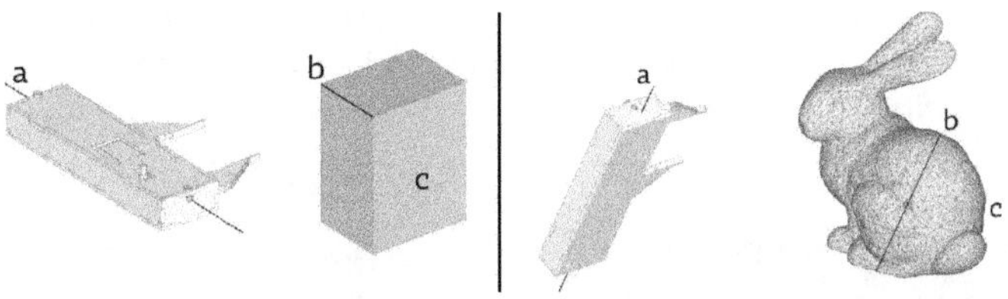

Figure 5. (left) Feature based selection. The axis of the SPATA tool (a) is aligned with a feature (b) of the virtual object (c), causing this feature (i.e., edge) to be selected. (right) Ray-based selection. The axis of the SPATA tool (a) is fixed at a pivot point inside the model (c) and rotated around it (b). The intersection points of this selection ray select vertices.

Each SPATA tool can sense it's orientation in space. When a SPATA tool is aligned with a feature e.g., an edge, hole or plane in case of the protractor, that feature is selected (see Figure 5). Once the selection mode has been enabled, the selection is updated continuously until it's confirmed using the button on the SPATA tools. Often times selection is part of another task, in which case the selection is transfered to overarching task e.g., scaling the just selected edge.

Measuring the Model

To measure the length of a feature e.g., the length of an edge or diameter of a hole, the user first selects that feature, either using the SPATA based selection mechanism or using the design environments native one. Once selected, the calipers transfer the length into the physical world. A similar process is used for measuring an angle: after the user selects two planes either using SPATA or the environments native methods, the protractor transfers that value into the real world.

Mesh-based Modeling

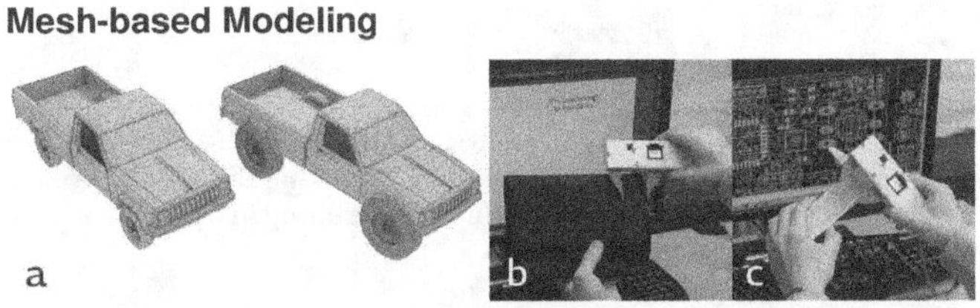

Figure 6. *Local scaling:* (a) Deforming a mesh by scaling only the selected red parts. *2D design:* (b) Placing text on a physical artifact. (c) Ensuring a PCB fit's inside an existing enclosure.

Mesh-based 3D modeling is a general-purpose modeling paradigm, that is often used for creating organic and artistic models in tools such as Autodesk Mudbox, Blender or ZBrush. The smallest unit of manipulation is a vertex or an edge of the 3D model. Modeling operations typically manipulate either a single vertex or a vertex group. Mesh-based modeling often deals with many vertices at the same time: e.g., the Standford Bunny in Figure 5 has 35947 vertices.

To create new models, designers often start with geometric primitives which are then combined, subdivided and scaled. Vertices are often directly manipulated to form the desired shape. Additionally to directly manipulating vertices, designers use tools like brushes and stamps to refine the shape. All these operations act on generic vertices and do not carry semantic information (as compared to mechanical CAD).

Selection

We use the accelerometer of the SPATA tools for selection. By rotating a line around a fixed anchor point users can select vertices or vertex groups. This selection line by default extends to one side only, but can also extend in both opposite directions to select orthogonal pairs. The anchor point of the selection line can be moved by the user (see Figure 5).

Depending on subsequent actions, the selection can be continuous so that every orientation change, modifies the selection. In this mode, we can use this selection method like a brush to create vertex groups. It can also be a one-off selection, where the selection is confirmed using the built-in button.

Scaling

We support global and local scaling. Global scaling is applied to the whole model, local scaling is applied to a specific selection of vertices or vertex groups. Scaling the whole model can be used to bring the model to a certain size based on a single dimension. Scaling a selection of vertices is often used to modify the shape locally and to articulate features of the model (see Figure 6, left). For local scaling we support a *select and scale* task, where users first select what they want to scale (using the previously described selection technique) and then perform the modification.

Measuring the Model

To measure length in the design environment, we select two vertices, or planes using the selection mechanism described earlier. We can also use built-in measurement tools (e.g., the ruler/protractor feature in Blender). To measure angle, we select two planes: two model faces, or a global plane and a model face; again using the previously described mechanism or environment specific selection techniques. In both cases the respective tool will output the value in the physical world, as well as on its display.

2D Design

2D design environments are used in many domains, such as for laser-cutting, desktop publishing (DTP) and electronic computer-aided design (eCAD). The often domain-specific design environments revolve around semantic objects such as circles, holes, text blocks and electronic components; objects that need to be arranged and scaled on a 2D canvas.

Translating, Scaling and Rotating

Most 2D design environments have a global coordinate system that spans the working area. Objects placed in the working area have an anchor-point in the coordinate system which is used as point of reference for transformations. Some design environments support snapping mechanisms with regards to that anchor point e.g., snapping to multiples of 5 mm when translating, or 45 degrees when rotating. SPATA supports such snapping mechanisms in form of tactile feedback – for example, the calipers physically snap to the underlying grid.

Translation is used to place objects in the working area; e.g., text on an existing object (see Figure 6, b). SPATA calipers can be used to place objects. Users first select the axis along which they want to place the object; this makes the calipers output the current location into the physical world. Second, any change of the calipers measurement is continuously applied as translation value along that axis, synchronously moving the object (with respect to the anchor point). Scaling is performed in the same way. After selecting the axis, the calipers output the current value and update the size with every change of measurement. During object placement, it maybe necessary to rotate an object. Entering rotation mode, causes the protractor to output the current orientation into the physical world. Changing that angle with immediately update the objects rotation around the anchor point.

Measuring the Design

We implement a feature-based measurement strategy, as most two-dimensional artifacts have semantic annotations (e.g., parts placed on a PCB or a rectangle drawn on a poster). Users first select the features they want to measure using the design environments built-in selection mechanism, which is typically mouse-based. When a single feature is selected (e.g., the outline of a printed circuit board, see Figure 6, c) the length of that feature is transfered into the physical world. When two features are selected at the same time, and they have an angle of inclination to one-another, we output that angle using the protractor.

APPLICATION SCENARIOS

We illustrate the integration of the SPATA tools into the three design environments. By walking through examples for each environment, we demonstrate the tools capabilities and how they make the design process more convenient.

Replacing a Broken Sprocket

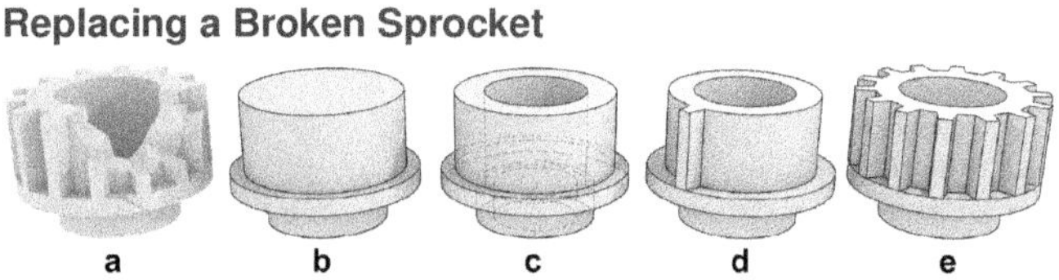

Figure 7. Replacing a broken part. (a) the broken sprocket we want to replace, (b - d) the intermediary steps for modeling the replacement part, (e) the finished part.

In this example scenario we're going to model a working replica of a broken sprocket (see Figure 7, a) in a mechanical CAD environment. Repairing broken parts with digital fabrication requires the creation of a printable model. Because the part is physically broken, we need to complete it while modeling it. In this case, 3D scanning the part is not feasible, as we require an exact geometrical representation of the object in order to complete/repair it.

As with many man-made objects, the sprocket consists of geometric primitives, primarily cylinders. We start modeling by introducing a series of cylinders (Figure 7, b). For each cylinder we first measure its diameter, then the height, confirming each value with the built-in button. In this *cylinder mode*, SPATA builds one cylinder on top of another, resulting in a configuration depicted in Figure 7, b.

Next, we add the two inner holes. We again use the *cylinder mode*, only this time we instruct the design environment to cut out the cylinders, instead of adding them. Measuring first the diameter, then height of each of the two holes, yields our second intermediary model shown in Figure 7, c.

In order to add the gear teeth, we first create a single tooth which is then replicated around the gear. Each tooth is a regular cube. Specifying it's width, height and depth fully describes the shape (see Figure 7, d). We count the number of teeth and assume a uniform distribution of teeth around the gear. Adding the according number of teeth, creates the final replacement part (Figure 7, e).

Modeling the replacement sprocket required a total of 12 sizes to be measured of the physical object. Using analog calipers, we need to not only manually type in all measurements, but also change repeatedly change context to do so (23 times if one measures the height of the sprocket teeth in CAD). The SPATA tools automatically transfer the measurements, and support creating the primitives that make up the sprocket. This way, we have to refocus our attention fewer times (6 times) and can perform the task more efficiently.

Sculpting

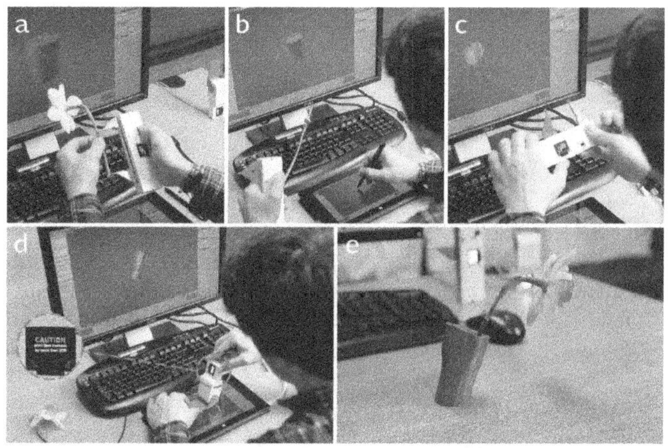

Figure 8. Creating a vase. (a) We start with a cylinder, scaled to eight centimeters using the SPATA calipers. (b) We sculpt decorative features, using the SPATA tools for orientation. (c) Checking the size of the model. (d) Exploring different flower hole angles, resulting in a print time warning. (e) The printed result object.

In this scenario we want to create a flower vase which will be 3D printed. To model that vase, we use a mesh-based design environment that supports vertex-based modeling, sculpting and constructive solid geometry. For artistic modeling often pen input is used instead of a mouse; we follow this practice.

We start the design process by creating a new cylinder. The vase needs to be correctly sized so that flowers fit in it and that it can be placed on a desk. Using the SPATA calipers and their ability to globally scale, we scale the cylinder until it is eight centimeters high. Using local scaling, we scale the diameter of the vase to 4 centimeters (see Figure 8, a).

Next, we add the decorative features by drawing on the cylinder using the pen. We use the SPATA calipers, which we now hold in our non-dominant hand, to rotate the model so that we can draw on all sides (see Figure 8, b). This way we do not have to change the mode from drawing to rotating, but use the pen to draw, the SPATA tool to rotate.

Sculpting the shape has changed it's size as well. Using Blender's built in measurement tool, we measure the vase model. This causes the SPATA calipers to output that size in the physical world (see Figure 8, c). This way we can compare the size against the flower, or get a feeling for the dimensions of the vase we are creating.

To make the vase more interesting, we want it to stand slightly angled. To explore different angles, we use the SPATA protractor. During this exploration our focus is on the SPATA tool, which gives us additional, fabrication specific feedback. When we use a too steep angle, we'll be warned when the current angle will make the fabrication take longer and be more expensive (see Figure 8, d).

Lastly, we cut off the bottom to create a flat surface for the vase to stand on and add the flower hole. We then send it to a 3D printer. The resulting vase fit's the flower as designed and does not need support structures to print (see Figure 8, e).

Desktop Organizer

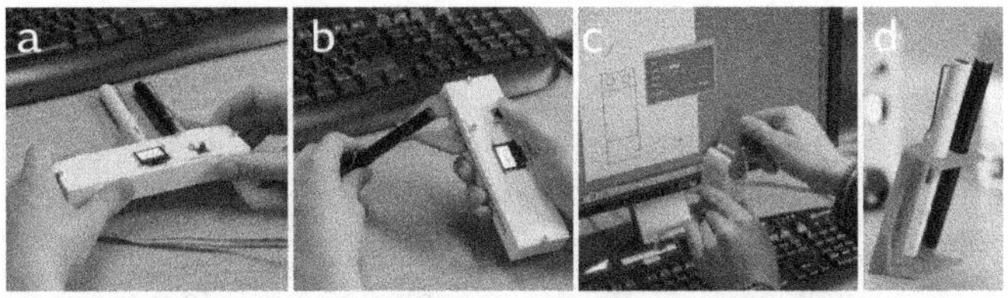

Figure 9. (a) Measuring the width of the pen holder using the pens it will hold. (b) Measuring the pen holders height. (c) The drawing used for laser-cutting the parts of the holder. (d) The final object.

This scenario demonstrates SPATA's integration into a 2D design environment, as they are often used for laser-cutting. We create a simple, laser-cut pen holder.

We start by creating the top face of the pen holder. After starting to draw a rectangle, we use the SPATA calipers to measure its width and height (see Figure 9, a). The button on SPATA tools can be used to confirm and navigate between measurement axis (width and height). Next, we create the back piece. Its width is determined by the width of the top panel, but the height is measured using SPATA. After selecting height as dimension we wish to scale, every new measurement is immediately set as new height. In this mode, we measure the height of the pen. Then we create circular cutouts much like we created the first rectangle: measuring the diameter of the pen yields holes of correct size (see Figure 9, b).

We use the protractor to explore which angle we want the pen holder to be at. After enabling rotation, the protractor assumes the current orientation: zero degrees in this case. Manipulating the protractors blade rotates the line on the screen accordingly (see Figure 9, c). Pressing the built-in button confirms the rotation. To fabricate the object, we laser-cut this drawing and assemble the pieces by acrylic-welding them. This yields our final object (Figure 9, d).

DISCUSSION

Generalizing To Other Tools

The SPATA concept, automated measurement transfer and integration into design environments, generalizes to tools other than calipers and protractors. On different scales, different tools are used. HandSCAPE [10], the digital measurement tape for example, could also output it's value using an additional motor. Alternatively, a folding ruler could be augmented to support input and output of not only length, but also angle along its joints.

Physical features besides length and angle could also be considered. For example, an integrated measurement tool for material stiffness could be used to design multi-material 3D printed objects. Techniques such as jamSheets [14] could serve as output technology. Similarly, tools for transferring elasticity or weight and volume could be built (e.g., using technology presented by Niiyama et al. [12]).

Implementing the Integration

While building the tools, we implemented their integration into Autodesk Inventor, Blender and Adobe Illustrator. We found it beneficial to contain all logic in an integration middleware layer. Many software packages support an API to extend their functionality (e.g., SketchUp has a Ruby based plugin mechanism). We further kept both SPATA tools free of design environment specific artifacts, to avoid firmware changes. When developing other tools based on the SPATA concept, we recommend a similar approach to enable quick prototyping and exploration.

Customization

We have implemented tasks commonly found in their respective environments (e.g., creating a box in mechanical CAD). However, specialists often customize their environments to better support their work. A macro editor (or other forms of end-user programming) would enable users to create their own workflows or tasks that integrate the SPATA tools. Custom jaws and blades for specific applications could also be built. For example using specialized task support and adapted tools that align well with human physique, doctors could quickly model a splint for their patient.

Applicability

SPATA is tightly integrated into digital design environments, thus their use is primarily beneficial in a digital design process. When measuring things in an analog setting, traditional tools are preferable over our prototype implementation. In their current iteration SPATA tools are tethered to a computer, restricting the environments they can be used in. Additionally, in their current iteration, the tools are not as precise as their analog counterparts. This prevents them from being used to very small parts. Further, traditional calipers have a thin depth probe to measure the depth of cavities and holes. The current implementation of SPATA calipers does not have such a depth probe, rendering depth measurements difficult.

Non-Fabrication Scenarios

The need for integrating spatial features extends beyond design for fabrication. In computer supported collaborative work (CSCW), or whenever there is a spatial/temporal division between users, SPATA could be used to transfer spatial features. For example, two spatially disconnected users could exchange the screen-size of the new tablet they've bought. In a temporally disconnected scenario, users could get an impression of the size of an object offered in an online store, or measure parts of their body to order a custom-made artifact.

CONCLUSION

In this paper we presented spatio-tangible measurement tools that aim to make the design of fabricable artifacts more efficient and convenient. By automating the measurement transfer between the tools and design environments, we make the process less error prone; by integrating the tools into the tasks found in these environments, we make the process more efficient and convenient. To demonstrate how the design process can benefit from our tools, we use our prototype implementation to walk through three application scenarios.

In future work, we plan to study how the SPATA tools benefit digital fabrication practitioners; particularly if the number of context switches can be reduced in daily practice (similar to to the first application scenario).

ACKNOWLEDGMENTS

This work was supported by the EU Marie Curie Network iCareNet under grant number 264738.

REFERENCES

1. Mitutoyo corporation: `http://www.mitutoyo.co.jp/eng/index.html`.
2. Arisandi, R., Takami, Y., Otsuki, M., Kimura, A., Shibata, F., and Tamura, H. Enjoying virtual handcrafting with tooldevice. In *Adjunct Proc. UIST* (2012), 17–18.
3. Excalibur Electronics, Inc. *Phantom Force - Auto-Motion Intelligent Response Chess*. Excalibur Electronics, Inc., Excalibur Electronics, Inc., 13755 SW 119th Av, Miami, Florida 33186 U.S.A.
4. Follmer, S., Carr, D., Lovell, E., and Ishii, H. Copycad: remixing physical objects with copy and paste from the real world. In *Proc. UIST* (2010), 381–382.
5. Fröhlich, B., and Plate, J. The cubic mouse: A new device for three-dimensional input. In *Proc. CHI* (2000), 526–531.
6. Grossman, T., Balakrishnan, R., and Singh, K. An interface for creating and manipulating curves using a high degree-of-freedom curve input device. In *Proc. CHI* (2003), 185–192.
7. Hinckley, K., Pausch, R., Goble, J. C., and Kassell, N. F. Passive real-world interface props for neurosurgical visualization. In *Proc. CHI* (1994), 452–458.
8. Lau, M., Hirose, M., Ohgawara, A., Mitani, J., and Igarashi, T. Situated modeling: a shape-stamping interface with tangible primitives. In *Proc. TEI* (2012), 275–282.
9. Lee, J., Post, R., and Ishii, H. Zeron: mid-air tangible interaction enabled by computer controlled magnetic levitation. In *Proc. UIST* (2011), 327–336.
10. Lee, J., Su, V., Ren, S., and Ishii, H. Handscape: A vectorizing tape measure for on-site measuring applications. In *Proc. CHI* (2000).
11. Mueller, S., Lopes, P., and Baudisch, P. Interactive construction: interactive fabrication of functional mechanical devices. In *Proc. UIST* (2012), 599–606.
12. Niiyama, R., Yao, L., and Ishii, H. Weight and volume changing device with liquid metal transfer. In *Proc. TEI* (2014), 49–52.
13. Nowacka, D., and Kirk, D. Tangible autonomous interfaces (tais): Exploring autonomous behaviours in tuis. In *Proc. TEI* (2014), 1–8.
14. Ou, J., Yao, L., Tauber, D., Steimle, J., Niiyama, R., and Ishii, H. jamsheets: Thin interfaces with tunable stiffness enabled by layer jamming. In *Proc. TEI* (2014), 65–72.
15. Pangaro, G., Maynes-Aminzade, D., and Ishii, H. The actuated workbench: Computer-controlled actuation in tabletop tangible interfaces. In *Proc. UIST* (2002), 181–190.
16. Rivers, A., Moyer, I. E., and Durand, F. Position-correcting tools for 2d digital fabrication. *ACM Trans. Graph. 31*, 4 (July 2012), 88:1–88:7.
17. Saul, G., Lau, M., Mitani, J., and Igarashi, T. Sketchchair: an all-in-one chair design system for end users. In *Proc. TEI* (2011), 73–80.
18. Schkolne, S., Pruett, M., and Schröder, P. Surface drawing: creating organic 3d shapes with the hand and tangible tools. In *Proc. CHI* (2001), 261–268.
19. Sheng, J., Balakrishnan, R., and Singh, K. An interface for virtual 3d sculpting via physical proxy. In *Proc. GRAPHITE* (2006), 213–220.
20. Song, H., Guimbretière, F., Hu, C., and Lipson, H. Modelcraft: capturing freehand annotations and edits on physical 3d models. In *Proc. UIST* (2006), 13–22.
21. Weichel, C., Lau, M., and Gellersen, H. Enclosed: A component-centric interface for designing prototype enclosures. In *Proc. TEI* (2013).
22. Weichel, C., Lau, M., Kim, D., Villar, N., and Gellersen, H. Mixfab: A mixed-reality environment for personal fabrication. In *Proc. CHI* (2014).
23. Willis, K. D., Lin, J., Mitani, J., and Igarashi, T. Spatial sketch: bridging between movement & fabrication. In *Proc. TEI* (2010), 5–12.
24. Willis, K. D., Xu, C., Wu, K.-J., Levin, G., and Gross, M. D. Interactive fabrication: new interfaces for digital fabrication. In *Proc. TEI* (2011), 69–72.
25. Zoran, A., Shilkrot, R., and Paradiso, J. Human-computer interaction for hybrid carving. In *Proc. UIST* (2013), 433–440.

Tiles that Talk: Tangible Templates for Networked Objects

David Bouchard
Ryerson University
350 Victoria St, Toronto,
ON M5B 2K3, Canada
david.bouchard@ryerson.ca

Steve Daniels
Ryerson University
350 Victoria St, Toronto,
ON M5B 2K3, Canada
steve.daniels@ryerson.ca

ABSTRACT

Fine art and design students face a novel set of challenges when asked to realize their creative vision with code-based projects. In this paper, we discuss the development of a system of tangible tiles and integrated software code factory that is intended to help students build bridges of understanding between proposed interactive and networked experiences and the required computer syntax, software libraries and hardware that animate those proposals. Our tiles help students see relationships between artistic concept and programmatic code by giving them intuitive tools that can be directly manipulated.

Author Keywords

Tangible interface; education; networks; programming

ACM Classification Keywords

H.5.m. Information interfaces and presentation (e.g., HCI): User Interfaces.

INTRODUCTION

Over the past decade artists and designers have increasingly integrated code-based approaches to their practice [17]. As these practices become standardized and fully integrated into university curricula, new pedagogical challenges emerge. Our experience with New Media fine art undergraduate students suggests that while they are very adept at manipulating forms and structures, they often find the transition to code based, syntax driven, modes of production challenging. The abstract effects of code are unlike the material and formal explorations that comprised much of their previous artistic study. Mixing of colors, lighting scenes or explorations with pencil for example all have immediate embodied consequences that can be linked to the construction of meaning. The effects of code however are linked to meaning abstractly through logic, not through embodiment. Exploration and understanding of code therefore comes through deduction not kinesthetics [9, 10].

Shifting to a mode of practice that depends upon logic-linked meaning construction often presents a significant hurdle for art students [17]. Consequently, novel methods for teaching code to art students are required.

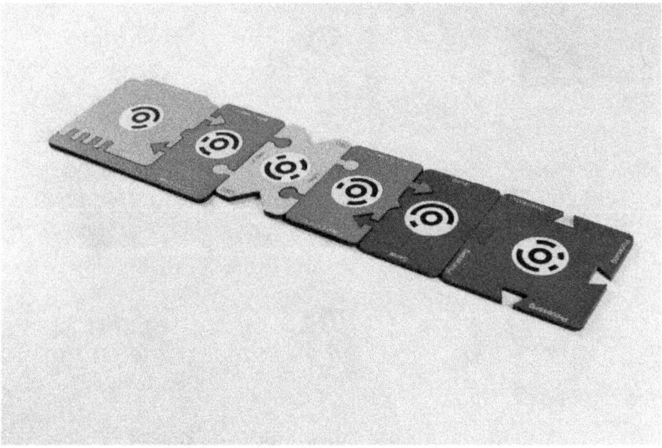

Figure 1. The *Tiles that Talk* system

Students of computer programming need to develop an integrated set of fundamental skills that merge the ability to envision relationships and behaviors (actions and outcomes) with the reading and writing of corresponding language specific syntax (programming language skills). Art students tend to excel at the former and can certainly master the latter, but they often need considerable help matching the outcomes they envision with appropriate computer syntax. This can be a deeply frustrating experience for students as their conceptual abilities greatly outstrip their technical programming skills. This internal difference in cognitive ability contrasts previous research in which children have been introduced to computer programming with tangible systems analogous to ours. In these studies, children have more evenly matched conceptualization and programming abilities [4, 12]. We have witnessed our students getting bogged down by code and quickly expressing frustration. At the early stages of their shift toward code based practice

TEI '15, January 16 – 19, 2015, Stanford, CA, USA.

ACM 978-1-4503-3305-4/15/01...$15.00.
http://dx.doi.org/10.1145/2677199.2680607

our students often find it difficult to realize their simplest creative ideas including those that may take seconds to conceptually sketch.

Given the novel needs of undergraduate art students learning to program, we have developed a hybrid learning system [5] of tangible tiles and integrated code factory that together facilitate the rapid prototyping of code based art projects. The system entitled *Tiles that Talk* consists of passive, puzzle-like tiles [6] that embody code concepts with real world phenomena. Specifically, we have developed a limited set of tiles that facilitate the prototyping of networked smart objects. Networks are relatively constrained programmatically but are creatively open-ended making them a good point of departure and the site of our initial exploration.

Figure 2. A selection of tiles from the set.

IMPLEMENTATION

Taking networked art practices [2, 8] as our starting point, our goal was to develop a tangible tile system that would help students explore, develop, and realize projects involving networked smart objects and spaces. We started with tiles that represent Processing [14] and Arduino [1], the core technologies of our interactive curriculum. We then identified communication pathways between these technological anchors. Using iterative rapid prototyping strategies and anticipating chains of up to 6-8 tiles, we created tiles to model communication paths that included microcontrollers (brain of the smart object), computers, serial and internet protocol connections (IP), software libraries for serial communication, networked servers and clients and mobile phones.

During development, successive generations of tiles were laser cut to determine scale, form, and ensure basic interlocking capabilities. The physical characteristics of the tiles operate on several levels simultaneously. The color, size and shape of a tile all reveal unique aspects of the technical communication pathways they represent. Students can use each of these characteristics to identify the correct technologies for the project they wish to develop. Color and size group tiles by technological family (eg. xBee radios and their related shields and breakout boards), communication type (serial or IP) and message protocol (raw or OpenSoundControl (OSC) [13]). Anchoring platform tiles are distinguished by their larger size and cool colors. Smaller, warm colored tiles represent intermediate software and hardware elements. Irregular shapes are reserved for Arduino shields. The interlocking shapes that give the tiles their puzzle-like quality encode communication pathways. The shapes only allow tile interconnections when the represented technologies can validly communicate. This ensures that students can only build tile chains that represent technologically possible networks.

Code Factory

In addition to the above physical characteristics, individual tiles are labeled with machine-readable tags and whole chains can be analyzed using a mobile phone application. Our application's template engine (code factory) then provides students with working code scaffolding, including any required external libraries as well as customized instructions such as how to set IP address or xBee radio configuration steps when needed. The code templates only provide a programmatic foundation for the communication path students have assembled with the tiles. Project specific behaviors must still be created and integrated by students. Through in-class challenges employing different topologies and studying their own project specific code templates, our students have gained a stronger understanding of the relationship between code syntax and structure and their own creative concepts. This allows students to quickly bootstrap their projects and spend more time focused on developing their networked experiences.

The source code, application and tile image files are available as an open source project on GitHub [3]. While our tiles were made out of laser cut wood and have their optical markers silk-screened for durability in a classroom setting, a working set could also be assembled by anyone using paper, cardboard, or other materials.

USE CASE EXAMPLE

Consider a student with some physical computing and interactive programming experience. The student is naive to the technical aspects of coding networks but wishes to control a physical object from their laptop. Using our system, the student locates the Arduino and Processing tiles. Knowing that the tiles interconnect to create networks, the student now searches for intermediate tiles that link these end nodes together. A complete set of tiles affords numerous pathways and solutions to this specific problem, including: simple serial, wireless serial (xBee), internet protocol (IP) based communication as well as sending raw (byte) data or OSC formatted communication. The tile pathways indicate software libraries and additional hardware (shields, radios) required for different solutions. Generally longer tile chains will suggest more complicated outcomes. As students become more adept with the tiles and networked ideas they grow comfortable assembling tiles into linear and branching chains that reflect desired creative outcomes and network topologies.

Figure 3. The phone application recognizing a tile chain

Once the tile chain is assembled the student can use the smart-phone app to access the code factory and obtain project-specific code templates. They can now map their planned creative layers over the communication backbone to realize their intended project.

DEPLOYMENT IN THE CLASSROOM

The *Tiles that Talk* project was initiated to support our undergraduate networked art course. Fifty sets of small (about the size of playing cards) tiles were produced for student use (more than enough for one set per student) along with several sets of larger instructor tiles. The latter have magnetic backs for attaching to classroom whiteboards. In the classroom, students and instructors can create tile chains, discuss the technologies they represent and consider creative scenarios supported by the communication pathways.

With students and instructors building tile chains together, students quickly identify how groups of technologies are related to networked art contexts. Students can rapidly identify links to their creative concerns as the tiles facilitate a deeper understanding of the relationship between specific project-supporting technologies and original creative concepts. When combined with the code factory, students can see how concepts, hardware pathways, and software work together to support the development of a creative experience.

We used our tiles system during the Fall 2013 iteration of our networking course. The experience was well received and students indicated (through exit interviews) that they found the tiles helped them understand the relationships between code and experience. They also indicated that the tiles helped them plan and develop their own works.

Subjectively, we found that students were more likely to explore novel applications of networks in their own practices. The created works were driven more by concept than available code samples as they have been in the past. Specifically, students broke away from one-to-one networks and explored branching topologies, systems with more than two physical localities and single site networks involving multiple nodes. In this first trial, students also tended to spend more time resolving material interfaces and contextualizing their user interactions rather than being burdened by parsers and pathways. We will be using the tiles again in the same course in the Fall of 2014.

RELATED WORK

There are numerous examples of tangible systems for learning computer programming that this work builds directly upon. We were initially inspired by Ubi de Feo's *From 0 to C* workshop series [15] which utilize a curriculum for code education that foregoes computers altogether. These classes rely on the use of pen, paper and handmade tangible objects to demonstrate programming concepts.

Early toolkits such as AlgoBlocks [18], the Tangible programming bricks [11] or the Electronic Block [19] establish a formal foundation demonstrating the potential of tangibles as a teaching tool for abstract concepts such as programming. Tangibles were shown to provide unique advantages such as tactile engagement, accessibility and enabling group interactions that can enhance learning. Other projects like Zuckerman's Flow Blocks [20] expand beyond representations of code into other abstract domains such as flow modeling and mathematical concepts like counting and probability.

Our project owes perhaps the most to Tern [7], a tangible computer language designed by Horn and Jacob. Unlike many of its predecessors, who relied heavily on embedded electronics within the manipulables, Tern made the case for a low-tech and low-cost approach by providing a symbolic-only representation of its programming language. This was accomplished by the use of optical markers on basic wooden blocks. Our project makes use of the optical markers developed for Tern called TopCodes [16], follows a similar low-tech approach and employs its puzzle metaphor.

The work discussed in this paper distinguishes itself from these projects in two important ways. First, our target audience is considerably older. We developed our system for undergraduate students while much of the education research done in the past on tangible programming toolkits has been aimed at younger children. Secondly, our tiles do not provide a means to write programs directly. We make the assumption that our students are already somewhat familiar with the basics of programming, as a result our tiles provide a greater level of abstraction. They are used to model high level network topologies as opposed to direct programming of algorithms. The code templates generated from the tiles become an intermediate step, rather than an end in and of themselves. Students are expected to modify the templates and use them as a point of departure to realize their vision.

CONCLUSION AND FUTURE WORK

The *Tiles that Talk* system empowers students by providing a rapid pathway from ideation to actualization of a project. Students are able to treat tiles as elements in a conceptual sketch, while the software code factory provides them immediate feedback in the form of properly structured functional code. Students can then integrate their creative vision and more rapidly experience success rather than frustration as they realize projects grounded in their own ideas. They gain confidence as they learn syntax with code samples that reflect the specific experiences they want to develop, rather than from generic code samples typical of programming textbooks.

Moving forward, we plan to extend the tile set and code factory to map connections between sensors, actuators, software, and people in order to support the development of more open-ended interactive experiences.

ACKNOWLEDGMENTS

We would like to thank the Learning And Teaching Office at Ryerson University for financial support as well as the Ryerson EDGE lab and Ryerson RTA School of Media for in-kind support. Thanks also to our research and production assistants Kathryn Hartog, Dante Nocera, Connor Crawford and Erin Brazeau.

REFERENCES

1. Arduino, http://www.arduino.cc
2. Ascott, R. 2003. *Telematic Embrace: Visionary Theories of Art, Technology and Consciousness / Roy Ascott : Edited and with Essay by Edward Shanken.* University of California Press. Berkeley, 2003, pp. 427.
3. Bouchard, D. and Daniels, S. Tiles that Talk. Github Repository. https://github.com/hex705/tiles (2013)
4. Horn, M.S., E.T. Solovey, R. Jordan Crouser, Robert J.K. Jacob. Comparing the Use of Tangible and Graphical Programming Languages for Informal Science Education, *Proc. CHI 2009,* pp. 975-984.
5. Horn, M.S., Crouser, R.J., Bers, M.U. Tangible interaction and learning: The case for a hybrid approach. *Personal and Ubiquitous Computing vol. 16, no. 4,* 2011, pp. 379-389.4c
6. Horn, M.S. and Robert J.K. Jacob. Designing Tangible Programming Languages for Classroom Use. *Proc. TEI*, 2007, pp. 159-162.
7. Horn, M.S. and Robert J.K. Jacob. Tangible programming in the classroom with Tern, Proc. CHI, 2007, ACM Press (2007) pp.1965-1970.
8. Kac, Eduardo. *Telepresence and Bio Art: Networking Humans, Rabbits and Robots.* The University of Michigan Press, Ann Arbor, 2005, pp. 311
9. Manche, A. and O'Malley, C. Tangibles for learning: a representational analysis of physical manipulation, *Personal and Ubiquitous Computing, vol. 16, no. 4,* 2011, pp. 405–419,
10. Marshal, P. 2007. *Do tangible interfaces enhance learning? Proc. TEI*, 2007, 163 - 170.
11. McNerney, T. S. Tangible programming bricks: an approach to making programming accessible to everyone [M.S. thesis], MIT Press, Boston, Mass, USA, 2000.
12. O'Malley, C, Danae Stanton F. Literature review in Learning with Tangible Technologies. *Report 12: Nesta FutureLab Series*, 2004, pp. 27
13. OpenSoundControl, http://www.opensoundcontrol.org
14. Processing, http://www.processing.org
15. Ubi de Feo, From 0 to C, http://hellosavants.com/from-0-to-c/
16. Horn, M. Tangible Object Placement Codes, http://users.eecs.northwestern.edu/~mhorn/topcodes/
17. Reas, C. and McWilliams, C. *Form and Code in design, art and architecture.* Princeton Architectural Press, 2010, pp. 176
18. Suzuki, H. and Kato, H. Interaction-level support for collaborative learning: AlgoBlock – an open programming language, Proc. CSCL 1995, ACM Press (1995), pp. 349–355
19. Wyeth, P. and Purchase, H. C. Tangible programming elements for young children, Ext. Abstracts CHI, 2002, ACM Press (2002), pp. 774–775
20. Zuckerman O., Arida S., Resnick M. (2005). Extending Tangible Interfaces for Education: Digital Montessori-Inspired Manipulatives. Proc. CHI 2005, ACM Press (2005)

VoxBox: a Tangible Machine that Gathers Opinions from the Public at Events

Connie Golsteijn[1], Sarah Gallacher[1], Lisa Koeman[1], Lorna Wall[1], Sami Andberg[2], Yvonne Rogers[1], Licia Capra[1]

[1] ICRI Cities, University College London, UK
{c.golsteijn; s.gallacher; lisa.koeman.12; l.wall; y.rogers; l.capra}@ucl.ac.uk

[2] University of Helsinki, P.O. Box 28
FI-00014 University of Helsinki, Finland
sami.andberg@helsinki.fi

ABSTRACT
Gathering public opinions, such as surveys, at events typically requires approaching people in situ, but this can disrupt the positive experience they are having and can result in very low response rates. As an alternative approach, we present the design and implementation of VoxBox, a tangible system for gathering opinions on a range of topics in situ at an event through playful and engaging interaction. We discuss the design principles we employed in the creation of VoxBox and show how they encouraged wider participation, by grouping similar questions, encouraging completion, gathering answers to open and closed questions, and connecting answers and results. We evaluate these principles through observations from an initial deployment and discuss how successfully these were implemented in the design of VoxBox.

Author Keywords
Public opinion; gathering opinions; crowd engagement; playful; tangible interaction; design research

ACM Classification Keywords
H.5: Information interfaces and presentation (e.g., HCI): H.5.2. User Interfaces; H.5.m. Miscellaneous

INTRODUCTION
Traditional ways of obtaining public opinions have largely been through marketing people approaching the general public at events or in the street with a clipboard, cold calling over the phone, or sending a text or email with a link to a webpage for people to register and then fill in a survey. More recently, tablet computers have been used to replace the clipboard. However, all of these approaches have their limitations and are susceptible to bias. The reasons include the general public being wary of people approaching them, and an increasing tendency to simply ignore unsolicited messages. Many will avert their gaze, put the phone down or delete the message. Those who do respond are often only a small number of the population and it is therefore unclear how representative they are of the general population at large [8]. An alternative approach is to design systems that gather opinions from the crowd in situ without inappropriately interrupting people or negatively influencing their positive experiences. While previous studies have introduced large screens, social media plug-ins, or simple voting systems, we aimed to design a more playful experience that gathers detailed feedback from the crowd at events such as festivals or fairs, by providing an engaging and playful tangible system that invites people to use it through its affordances. In this paper we present the design, implementation and initial deployment of a novel system, called VoxBox (Figure 1), which used a range of physical input and output devices, based on a set of core tangible design principles. We present and discuss the value of our design approach for creating such a public tangible opinion system.

TEI '15, January 16 - 19 2015, Stanford, CA, USA

ACM 978-1-4503-3305-4/15/01…$15.00
http://dx.doi.org/10.1145/2677199.2680588

Figure 1. VoxBox: a system to gather opinions from crowds.

BACKGROUND

A variety of technologies for eliciting public opinions or feedback have been developed that try to be more inclusive and approachable when placed in situ in public spaces. These include the use of large screens, mobile phones, and voting boxes. Texting or Tweeting are often used as the medium. For example, Schroeter et al. [14] developed an application for public displays to elicit opinions via text or tweet from citizens who otherwise would not have their say. Others have used more traditional input devices, such as keyboards and public telephone handsets to get the public to voice their opinions or concerns. The Opinionizer [2] comprised a large projected display that people added their opinions to via typing at a keyboard. The VoiceYourView system [17] provided an old fashioned telephone in a library to obtain peoples' views about a recent refurbishment, which were represented as colorful visual bubbles on public screens. While many people freely gave their opinions in both settings, some felt uncomfortable and self-conscious doing so. This suggests that the method by which people are asked to give their views and the setting in which they do so impacts the extent to which they will voice their opinions or take part. Taylor et al. [15] found that users did not like using mobile phones to interact with public displays, and preferred to press buttons on the device directly. Müller et al. [9] found that mobile phone interaction with public displays did not receive as high uptake as expected. More recently, MyPosition asked people to vote on local issues through gesturing in front of a public display [16]. While many people stopped to look, only one in four chose to submit an opinion.

While this new generation of opinion-based technologies can be attractive and encourage more people to participate, there is still the problem that others shy away. It is not always clear how to interact with a public display that people have never seen before, especially if it is novel. Moreover, people may not see them in the first place. Such display and interaction blindness has been found to exist for a number of public displays and billboards [7, 9]. People expect them to be advertising material they don't want to look at or that simply do not grab their attention. We would argue that the opposite is true for physical tangible objects, which do have the affordances to draw people's attention. People are drawn to something that is novel, unusual and at odds with the environment. For example, the Periscope was designed as an unusual technological device for viewing videos about the surrounding area. Situated in a woodland, it provoked children to stop, wonder and interact [13]. Houben and Weichel [4] have also found that the introduction of a curious physical object linked to a public display attracted attention and significantly increased the numbers of people interacting with the display. The physicality and tangibility of components with clear and familiar affordances, such as pressing buttons, moving sliders, and turning knobs and handles, clearly indicate that they are there to be interacted with and also they are obvious how to do so. Both curiosity and clear affordances are important, firstly, to attract passers-by attention and secondly, to help them move through the threshold of participation [2].

In this light, researchers have designed very simple physical button-based voting boxes for gathering opinions [1, 3, 5, 15]. A benefit of using such simple input devices is that they are cheap to make and can be situated in a range of public places. However, they are limited in how far they can probe people's views and opinions. The question this raises is how best to design a range of tangible input devices that people are drawn to, will find compelling, will know intuitively how to interact with, and will also not feel self-conscious when doing so, or feel that it is too childlike or too technical for them to use. Our approach was to design a large tangible interactive machine that could stand out, was obvious to interact with, was playful and would engage people to gather a diversity of responses and views. We also wanted to maintain the interest of passers-by and provoke further discussion amongst those nearby by showing the collected data in aggregated form as a real-time visualization.

DESIGN PRINCIPLES

The design of VoxBox focused on recreational events, such as festivals or fairs, and aimed to gather opinions on the 'feel good factor' of such events, e.g. do people enjoy the event, do they feel connected to the people around them, and what are the elements that are most memorable? We considered characteristics of online or paper questionnaires and also key issues that were observed with these, and employed the following design principles.

Encouraging Participation

To prevent situations that are uncomfortable for both researcher and participant, such as hassling people with a clipboard, our aim was to design a system that invited people to participate without forcing them or interrupting their event experience. At the same time, it was important to design VoxBox to be able to stand out and draw attention from competing stalls that are also often part of an event. We thus chose to create a large physical system with physical input mechanisms through which people could give their opinions, instead of using, for example, text messages or social media input. VoxBox was designed as a modular system built around a physical shelving unit that lets users move through groups of questions, module by module (Figure 1). Each module used a different input mechanism that people were familiar with and knew how to use, such as sliders, buttons, knobs, and spinners. The first module asked closed questions about demographics, the second about their current mood, the third about the crowd, the fourth about the event, and the fifth and final asked an open question. In addition the system included a transparent tube at the side that dropped a ball step by step as the question modules were completed as an incentive for completion and progress indicator. Finally, the reverse side of the system showed three real-time visualizations of the collected data on small screen embedded in portholes. The aim of our research was to make VoxBox mostly self-explanatory so that it was clear what it was and why someone would want to interact with it [7]. We further designed interactions to require no technological knowledge or skills [3], and made the system, in most cases, usable without instructions.

Grouping Similar Questions

In conventional questionnaires, related questions or questions that require the same way of answering are often visually grouped, for example by putting them on the same page, or separating them with whitespace. We employed a tangible approach to this by designing VoxBox to consist of a number of separate question modules. Each module contained groups of questions that were related, and that used the same input mechanism. In this way we created a questionnaire with a logical flow of questions, and chose to make it not visually intimidating, as grouped questions emphasized that the questionnaire was not long.

Encouraging Completion and Showing Progress

One issue with questionnaires is people dropping out during completion, which is often caused by lack of clarity about length of questionnaire or progress, along with a lack of incentive for completion. In the VoxBox design the entire questionnaire was visible all the time so that users knew how many questions they needed to respond to and how long it may take. Further, a tangible reward (a stress ball featuring the URL of the website with the results) was given to the users to encourage completion; the ball could only be obtained when the questionnaire was completed. By designing a transparent tube that dropped the ball in stages after each part of the questionnaire was completed, the ball also served as a progress indicator. Progress was also shown by lighting up the active panels one by one as the user went through the questionnaire. This light feedback, in addition to lights next to buttons and scales for each corresponding option, provided immediate feedback from the system to show that it was interactive and that it was working, in order to encourage further use [7].

Gathering Answers to Closed and Open Questions

One problem with questionnaires is a lack, or brevity, of responses to open questions. Rogers et al. [12] found that engaging participants in playful activities resulted in a greater willingness to talk, and that it triggered free thinking. Although most of the questions in VoxBox are closed questions, we specifically designed a playful input mechanism, a phone handset that rang when a user reached this panel and asked them a question when they picked up. The user could then speak their answer into the handset and hang up the phone. We hoped that through this playfulness and engagement our questionnaire would result in more willingness to answer the open questions asked.

Connecting Answers and Results

In traditional surveys there is often a divide between a respondent answering questions and the researcher gathering data and presenting these in reports or papers. Respondents often do not have access to the results of the survey or are not informed where these results can be found. To make VoxBox more enticing to use and to trigger discussions from by-standers, we decided to make the collected results visible to the users [3]. Real-time results were shown in two different ways: on the website (for which the URL was printed on the incentive balls), and on a set of visualizations on the reverse side of the system. By printing the URL on the balls that were obtained after answering questions, we physically linked the users' answers to the results website by symbolizing that the results quite literally rolled out of the system after answering questions. The data visualizations on the system offered an immediate insight into the results. We tried to encourage users to look at these through the physical design by making them walk around the side of VoxBox to collect their ball. The box where the ball dropped was angled backward to encourage users to walk further around the back to see the visualizations.

DESIGN AND IMPLEMENTATION OF VOXBOX

Inspiration for the design of VoxBox came from a number of sources including the archaic computer game 'The Incredible Machine' (in which a user solves puzzles by arranging physical objects, e.g. levers, ropes, and conveyor belts), marble tracks (in which marbles are guided through sometimes complex tracks), and mechanical devices and interactive exhibitions as seen in science museums.

We decided on a final set of questions we wanted to ask based on our own interpretations of what may influence the feel good factor, and inspired by reading through evaluation reports on several organized events [e.g. 6]. As mentioned, these questions were divided into five categories, which were shown on five separate question modules in the system. An overview of the questions that were asked in each module can be seen in Table 1. While the demographics were mainly entered through simple push buttons, for the mood, crowd, and event questions we decided on different variations of input scales, so that people could rate their agreement. Although we could have used similar interactions for each of these groups, we felt it was important to include a variety of interactions to avoid the tedium of having to answer many questions in the same way, and keep the system engaging throughout the whole interaction. For the mood questions we decided to use linear sliders with LED feedback that represented semantic differential scales [10] on which people rate their response between two opposite answers on a scale; these scales were continuous (Figure 2a). For the crowd questions we used rotary knobs with LED feedback to show the answer along the scale. These questions were rated between disagreement and agreement and the interaction provided a discrete scale

Panel	Interaction	Questions
Demographics	Push buttons, rotary knob with 5 ranges for age	What is your age? (0-24; 25-44; 45-64; 65-74; 75+; blanc) Where do you live? (greater London; nearby county;different part of the UK; outside the UK) With whom are you visiting this event? (alone; partner or family; friends; other) Are you? (female; male; other)
Mood	Linear sliders: continous scale	How do you feel? (semantic differential scales: excited – bored; surprised – unsurprised; welcome – unwelcome; inspired – indifferent; safe – unsafe)
The crowd	Rotatory knobs: discrete scale (16)	What is the current mood of the crowd? (The mood is negative – the mood is positive) How well do you feel you fit in with the crowd? (I don't fit in at all – I fit in completely) How connected do you feel to the crowd? (I don't feel connected at all – I feel strongly connected)
The event	Spinners: 5 options	How much do you feel a part of this event? (I feel excluded from this event; I feel somewhat excluded from this event; I feel neither excluded nor a part of this event; I feel somewhat a part of this event; I feel a part of this event) How is the experience provided by this event (The experience is negative; the experience is somewhat negative; the experience is neither negative nor positive; the experience is somewhat positive; the experience is positive)
Open question	Phone handset: asked one randomly selected question from set	If there was an entry fee for this event, how much would you be willing to pay? What will you most remember about this event? How would you describe this event to a friend? If the organisers could change one thing about this event what would that be?

Table 1. Overview of the questions and interaction mechanisms in the different question modules.

with 16 increments (Figure 2b). The event questions were answered through physical spinners with five options between disagreement and agreement similar to a Likert scale (Figure 2c). Finally, for the open questions, we designed a phone handset to employ a familiar metaphor for dialog in an unfamiliar setting, which we hoped would result in surprise and excitement (Figure 2d).

We developed VoxBox as a modular system with separate question modules for the different groups of questions, and incorporated mechanisms for the incentive ball to run through the system (Figure 3a). Early variations of the design imagined the ball completing a track through the physical device in which obstacles had to be removed, or the track had to be completed, by answering questions. Different questions would have different physical mechanisms behind them that would allow the ball to move forward, for example a 'yes' or 'no' question would tip a slope in a certain direction, while a Likert scale may move an obstacle out of the way. Ideas also included mechanisms for encouraging longer answers to open questions, such as gradually moving obstacles away or only running a conveyor belt while the user was still recording an answer.

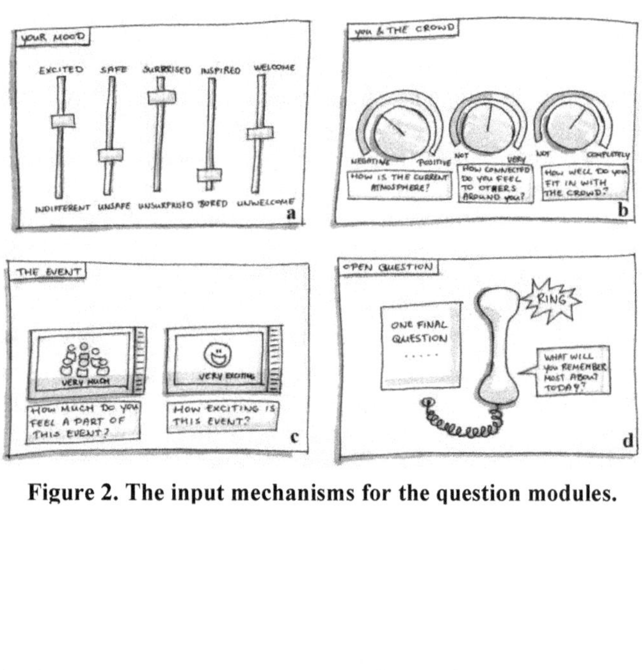

Figure 2. The input mechanisms for the question modules.

Due to feasibility reasons within the time constraints of the project, the ball track was simplified to run through the device and be controlled through physical levers after each question panel (see Figure 3b) and ultimately, replaced by an external tube that dropped the ball after each stage.

Implementation

VoxBox was implemented using three off-the-shelf shelving units to make sure it was sturdy enough to withstand many interactions and unanticipated user behavior. To allow for a flexible and modular system, we designed each question module as a drawer that was slotted into the shelving unit. In this way, question modules could be moved around and the sequence of the questions could easily be changed. Question modules were created from plywood using a laser cutter to give VoxBox an appearance that called up associations of 'a time machine' and 'a mix of Willy Wonka, the controls of the Tardis and those ornate fairground automata', according to initial responses.

Each question module contained a front panel for user interactions, which contained the sliders, buttons, knobs, spinners, or handset. A question module further contained an LED strip around the edge of the front panel that was lit up in green when a panel was active (Figure 4a), and a green submit button that was used to submit the user's answers. This button was necessary to determine when a user had made a final decision on the answers. Along with a

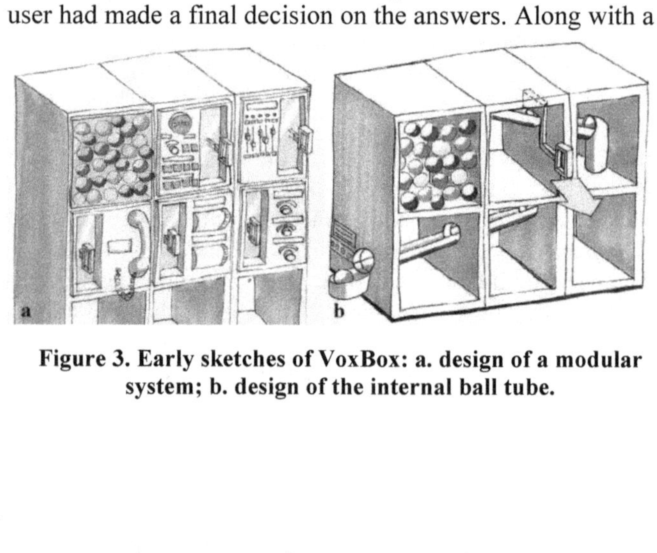

Figure 3. Early sketches of VoxBox: a. design of a modular system; b. design of the internal ball tube.

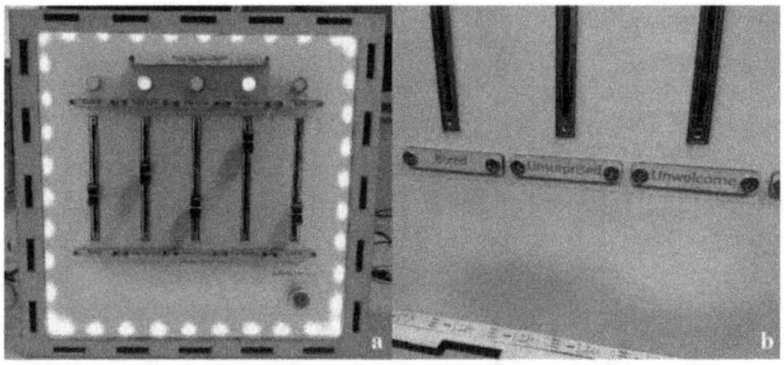

Figure 4a. Green LED strips showed that a panel was active; b. Separate question and answer labels were screwed on for easy changes.

large green start button, elements in this color were thus deliberately used to navigate the users through the system. Although buttons and sliders were fixed in the panels, questions and answers were cut from separate labels that were screwed on (Figure 4b). This allowed for questions to be easily changed (within the constraints of number and type of question in each panel) for different events where different questions may be desired. Most question panels used off-the-shelf components, for example the sliders, knobs, and buttons. We created a tailored rotary dial for age input and spinners for the event questions (Figure 5). Similar to the easily changeable question labels, the paper inlays of these spinners could also be replaced to show different answers.

VoxBox was controlled by open source Arduino technologies. To enable a modular design each question module contained its own Arduino board that controlled the I/O for that module. In addition there was a 'Master' Arduino and one to control the ball tube. The Master had overall control of the VoxBox operation and a WiFi connection to a backend server and database. On startup the Master downloaded the ordered list of currently attached question modules. It then proceeded to go through the list in sequence (Table 1), activating the next question module in the list, waiting for it to send back its data and then deactivating it again. All communication between Arduinos within the VoxBox was via I2C. Once the Master reached the end of the list it collated all the data it had collected

Figure 5. Tailor-made spinners; paper inlays could be changed to show different answers.

from the question boxes and uploaded this to the backend server and database via its WiFi link. This architecture allowed VoxBox to be easily adapted, as question boxes could be added, removed or swapped around without needing to make any changes to their code or the code inside the Master. Even extra connectors for possible additional data cables between modules were already implemented in the system. The only change required was an alteration to the ordered list of currently attached question modules in the backend server.

The ball tube was implemented by creating a tailored construction from plywood and a transparent tube (Figure 6). The tube was divided into six parts and a servo motor with a long arm was mounted in each part to stop the ball from moving through. After pressing the start button, and each of the submit buttons the servos rotated in sequence to drop the ball step by step. The ball tube was connected to a ball compartment within the VoxBox unit and although balls were fed into the tube manually in this implementation, an automatic feed was imagined for potential redesigns. The ball tube thus functioned as an incentive to complete the survey and as a physical progress bar. Because the tube consisted of separate parts that corresponded to each question module, this element of the system could also easily be adapted to account for more or fewer attached question modules.

Data that was sent from the Master Arduino to the server was used to created visualizations that were shown on the website and on the system itself. VoxBox was designed to not only allow people to share data on their demographics and views, but to also give them the opportunity to learn more about the opinions held by others. Similar public visualizations of people's perceptions have served as a talking point [e.g. 5, 16]. To enable passers-by to view and discuss the data gathered at the front side of the VoxBox, eye-catching and simple visual representations were shown on the reverse side (Figure 7a). To ensure the aesthetics of

Figure 6. The ball tube at the side of the system functioned as an incentive for completion and progress indicator.

Figure 7a. The reverse side of VoxBox showed real-time visualizations of the data; b. visualization screens were embedded in portholes.

these representations would match the look and feel of the input technology, inspiration was sought from retro display technology: flip-disc displays, the electromechanical dot matrix displays traditionally used for destination signs on buses. While these signs are originally of ultra-low resolution, recreating digital screen-based flip-disc displays allowed for the display of higher resolution infographic-like visualizations. By flipping the discs row by row, the display scrolled through real-time visual summaries of the data. By creating side panels around these digital screens, we created the illusion of a porthole via which people could look into the VoxBox (Figure 7b). Apart from protecting the screens from direct sunlight, the portholes were also meant to spark curiosity and lure people to the screens — thereby overcoming common display blindness [9].

INITIAL DEPLOYMENT

In addition to numerous people in our research institute coming by our lab to try out VoxBox, we ran an initial deployment at a one-day conference on technology concerned with the relationship between the government, digital democracy and the public (Figure 8). At this event, over 50 academic researchers, people from industry, and government organizations were present who were interested in novel technologies. VoxBox was set up in the area where coffee and lunch breaks took place, and over lunch there was a dedicated slot for interactive demos. As such, VoxBox was available for the attendees to use for a total of 1.5 hours. Around 30 people used the system, who all completed the whole survey and took an average of three minutes to complete. Below, we describe our observations on how VoxBox was used at this event. Based on these we discuss how our design principles played out in this context. We end by describing possible improvements to the design.

Overall, VoxBox was well received and gained a lot of interest. In the first break, we witnessed one person walking with a brisk pace towards our system as soon as he spotted it and immediately started interacting with it, eager to be the first one to engage with the system. On several occasions a queue formed as people waited for their turn. Others deliberately chose to watch others interact first while taking their turn afterwards. Many attendees were interested in the thoughts behind the system and how it was built, and reacted enthusiastically to its visual appearance. Small groups of attendees who knew each other often came up together and each had their turn. One person thought out loud: 'With whom did you come to this event?' 'Are you guys my friends?' which resulted in laughter from the group. The phone handset, which rang shortly after the users had submitted the answers on the previous panel, caused surprise, and many users could be seen grinning while picking up the phone. Most users answered the open question through the phone, and several gave quite elaborate answers, e.g.: 'If there was an entry fee for this event, how much would you be willing to pay?' 'I'd sell my children. And possibly my mother. But I get less money for my children – aye.' Another example of an answer was: 'What will you remember most from this event?' to which they replied, 'I'll remember the VoxBox most.'

Among many utterances of 'Wonderful, fantastic. Thank you.' and 'that was fun!' there was one attendee who questioned whether the data shown on the system was the data we were actually collecting there and then. He wondered if he was the only one who would question if the data representations were manipulated by the organizers of the event to show favorable results. He was the only one at this event to raise this concern, but it would be worth exploring further to what extent people trust the accuracy of the data visualizations. Among those that did 'believe' the data, there was substantial interest and several people remained watching the visualizations scroll through different results. One speaker teased another by commenting: '23% feel bored, that was your talk!' Users did not always immediately notice the ball dropping down the side of the system – this happened mostly in early interactions where people had not seen others use it yet, and had not yet had a chance to walk around the device. They sometimes seemed surprised that they could keep the ball but were always pleased when we informed them. One or two people opted to give their ball back to 'save us money.'

Figure 8. User interacting with VoxBox during the initial deployment at a one-day conference.

Finally, we noticed that some users did not realize that the start button needed to be pressed before any other interaction could take place. They usually figured this out quickly, or had it pointed out to them by other attendees.

DISCUSSION

Our observations based on the initial deployment confirmed that VoxBox is a novel and engaging system that succeeds in gathering opinions from crowds at events. We were interested in how our observations were able to validate the choice of our design principles for creating interactive features that were able to draw people to answer all the questions thoughtfully. From these principles we consider more generally which tangible features are effective and how to combine them to make a compelling and enjoyable experience for answering questions at other kinds of events.

Considering our first aim was to *encourage participation*, we saw that the appearance of the system was very attractive, drawing many people to it like a honey pot [2]. Although the deployment took place at an event with predominantly attendees that were excited about technology, there were also a number of attendees from industry or governing organizations that had less affinity with technology but were still very enticed by VoxBox. As researchers, we deliberately took a stand-back approach: instead of inviting people to have a go, we let them approach it by themselves. Many people took initiative and used it from start to finish. The ball tube and ball compartment appeared an unanticipated attention catcher as people were intrigued by the function of the colorful balls and by the appearance of the ball tube. The system appeared to be mostly self-explanatory although a few usability issues were observed. Users did not always notice the start button without which none of the panels were activated. We had noticed this before during informal trials in the lab and had created a large arrow to point out the start of the interaction sequence but this was insufficient to fully solve this issue. We further noticed that some users were surprised at first about the sequence of the panels, although the green light navigation helped to make this clear. Apart from these small issues, VoxBox was very effective in encouraging people to give their opinions.

As mentioned, VoxBox *grouped similar questions*, by separating them on several question panels. Although this did work well in giving the appearance of a short survey, some people got a bit confused at first about having to go through the panels in a fixed sequence. This fixed sequence was introduced in part by technology constraints, and in part by this being a common approach in traditional questionnaires. It was thus unanticipated that users would be confused by having to follow a sequence. It seems that by transposing characteristics from paper or online questionnaires to a physical device, we had created new affordances that invited different behaviors, e.g. all the questions were visible at the same time and some interaction mechanisms may have looked more enticing than others. We realize that VoxBox does not need to incorporate a fixed sequence of interaction and we can consider other ways in which the affordances of a physical system are exploited to create a more appropriate, less constrained form of interaction. Similarly, in traditional questionnaires there are often options to activate different flows of questions based on previous answers. We could think of ways in which such more sophisticated functions could be integrated in the physical design of VoxBox.

We aimed to *encourage completion and show progress*, mainly through the ball tube that provided the ball as an incentive and showed the progress in the questionnaire. In our initial observations we saw that this did not work as well as planned. Because of the location of the ball tube at the side of the system, users did not always notice straightaway that something was happening. Many users had to be notified afterwards that they had now earned their ball. We saw that once people noticed that the ball dropped after each panel they were enthusiastic about this and often stepped aside after each panel to check their progress. This issue can easily be solved by moving the ball tube forward along the side so that it is more visible while standing in front of VoxBox. Furthermore, although most users were pleased when informed that they could keep their ball, it did not seem as strong an incentive as the joy of interacting with Voxbox. Nevertheless, the ball functioned as a link to the survey results and showed the URL of our website.

A further aim was to *gather answers to open questions* by enticing people to speak their answers into a phone. This method proved to be effective as shown by the number of people who listened intently to the question and then spontaneously gave a, sometimes elaborate, verbal response after being pleasantly surprised by the phone ringing.

In showing the results of the data collection on the system, we also wanted to *connect answers and results*. As a result of the ball tube position not being ideal, the ball rolling towards the back to encourage the users to walk towards the visualizations did not work as strongly as hoped. Although plenty of users did see the visualizations (albeit sometimes prompted) and enjoyed seeing the results, it is important to consider other ways to link the data input and visualizations more strongly, for example, by not placing them at the reverse side of the system but bringing them closer to the location of the input so that users do not have to divide their attention as strongly [11]. We further considered ways in which to link data from the user more explicitly to that of the crowd so comparisons are possible between personal opinions and those of the crowd, e.g. by showing current and aggregated data on different screens at the same time. Such additions and improvements could connect answers and results more strongly than was currently the case.

Finally, privacy is an important concern when asking people to give personal information, such as their age or views, in a public place. We considered placing the VoxBox in a booth with a curtain that could be drawn by the users to prevent people looking over their shoulders. However, this would mean it would lose its attractive visibility that was central to how we envisioned it drawing people to it. We found that no-one was worried about their privacy in this context and that those using it were given a wide berth from onlookers – akin to how people stand back when waiting to use an ATM machine.

CONCLUSIONS

In this paper we have presented the design, implementation, and deployment of VoxBox, a tangible system to gather opinions from crowds at events. We have shown through an initial deployment how appealing and engaging VoxBox was considered to be, and how successful it was in drawing people in and gathering opinions in a novel way. We have extensively discussed our rationale behind designing this system and have reflected on the extent to which we have successfully implemented our design principles based on observations with an initial deployment. VoxBox opens up discussions around the design of novel systems that can encourage the sharing of opinions by engaging users in playful interactions. Our findings have shown this is an important area for researchers to explore because gauging opinions and knowing what people think is considered an increasingly important part of community engagement. Our future plans include deploying and adapting VoxBox for a variety of other events in different contexts and settings. Finally, we argue that our tangible questionnaire approach – asking people to walk up to playful and attractive life-size machine and provide answers to a set of questions about how they feel – shows much promise at getting people from all walks of life to voice their opinions.

ACKNOWLEDGMENTS

This research was funded by ICRI Cities. We further thank everyone who tried out VoxBox for their valuable insights, and our colleagues in ICRI and UCL Interaction Centre for their feedback on our ideas.

REFERENCES

1. Braun, L., et al. SkyWords: an engagement machine at chicago city hall. In *Proc. CHI '13 Ext. Abstr.*, ACM Press (2013), 2839-2840.
2. Brignull, H. and Rogers, Y. Enticing people to interact with large public displays in public spaces. In *Proc. Interact 2003*, Rauterberg, M., Menozzi, M., and Wesson, J., (eds). IOS Press, 2003, 17-24.
3. Dade-Robertson, M., Taylor, N., Marshall, J., and Olivier, P. The political sensorium. In *Proc. MAB 2012*, ACM Press (2012), 47-50.
4. Houben, S. and Weichel, C. Overcoming interaction blindness through curiosity objects. In *Proc. CHI 2013 Ext. Abstr.*, ACM Press (2013), 1539-1544.
5. Koeman, L., Kalnikaite, V., Rogers, Y., and Bird, J. What chalk and tape can tell us: lessons learnt for next generation urban displays. In *Proc. PerDis '14* (2014), 130-136.
6. Maennig, W. and Porsche, M. The Feel-good Effect at Mega Sports Events. Recommendations for Public and Private Administration Informed by the Experience of the FIFA World Cup 2006. *IASE/NAASE Working Paper Series 8*, 17 (2008), 1-28.
7. Marshall, P., Morris, R., Rogers, Y., Kreitmayer, S., and Davies, M. Rethinking 'multi-user': an in-the-wild study of how groups approach a walk-up-and-use tabletop interface. In *Proc. CHI 2011*, ACM Press (2011), 3033-3042.
8. Miller, K.W., Wilder, L.B., Stillman, F.A., and Becker, D.M. The Feasibility of a Street-Intercept Survey Method in an African-American Conmunity. *American Journal of Public Health 87*, 4 (1987), 655-658.
9. Müller, J., et al. Display Blindness: The Effect of Expectations on Attention towards Digital Signage. In *Pervasive Computing*, Tokuda, H., et al., (eds). Springer Berlin Heidelberg, 2009, 1-8.
10. Osgood, C.E., Suchard, G.J., and Tannenbaum, P.H. *The Measurement of Meaning*. University of Illinois Press, Urbana, 1957.
11. Price, S. A representation approach to conceptualizing tangible learning environments. In *Proc. TEI 2008*, ACM Press (2008), 151-158.
12. Rogers, Y., et al. Never too old: engaging retired people inventing the future with MaKey MaKey. In *Proc. CHI 2014*, ACM Press (2014), 3913-3922.
13. Rogers, Y., et al. Ambient wood: designing new forms of digital augmentation for learning outdoors. In *Proc. IDC 2004*, ACM Press (2004), 3-10.
14. Schroeter, R., Foth, M., and Satchell, C. People, content, location: sweet spotting urban screens for situated engagement. In *Proc. DIS 2012*, ACM Press (2012), 146-155.
15. Taylor, N., et al. Viewpoint: empowering communities with situated voting devices. In *Proc. CHI 2012*, ACM Press (2012), 1361-1370.
16. Valkanova, N., Walter, R., Moere, A.V., and Müller, J. MyPosition: sparking civic discourse by a public interactive poll visualization. In *Proc. CSCW 2014*, ACM Press (2014), 1323-1332.
17. Whittle, J., et al. VoiceYourView: collecting real-time feedback on the design of public spaces. In *Proc. Ubicomp 2010*, ACM Press (2010), 41-50.

Augmenting Children's Creative Self-Efficacy and Performance through Enactment-Based Animated Storytelling

Sharon Lynn Chu, Francis Quek, and Kumar Sridharamurthy
TAMU Embodied Interaction Lab
Texas A&M University
College Station, TX 77840.
[sharilyn, quek, kumarsmurthy]@tamu.edu

ABSTRACT
At around age nine when social awareness and self-evaluation heighten, children experience a precipitous slump in creative engagement. We propose an enactment-based approach grounded in embodied cognition theories to support children's creative self-efficacy and creative thinking in storytelling during the period of this slump. Our investigation of the approach with 20 children indicated that enactment-based animated authoring improves children's sense of self-efficacy in creating stories, particularly for children with low to medium extraversion, and enables children to produce richer stories, especially for children who scored low on the baseline creativity test.

Author Keywords
Creativity; Storytelling; Enactment; Embodied interaction

ACM Classification Keywords
H.5.2. User Interfaces: Interaction Styles.

INTRODUCTION
The power of the embodiment concept is not just that activity takes place in the body. It is that mind and body function as an unalloyed compound such that the activity of the body enhances the capacity, experience and potency of mind, and the machinery of mind functions in unison with the body. This paper explores how a child's enactment of story and imagination through the body may augment her her affective state in terms of self-efficacy, and her cognitive capacity in terms of creativity. Specifically, we investigate how encoding the enacted or externalized imagination as animated digital stories may support creative output and positively influence the child's self-efficacy in storytelling.

Storytelling is a significant component of elementary school curricula. It is both taught in the Language Arts subject and used as a tool for instruction in other subjects. However, many students face a daunting challenge in creative storytelling at school: creative expression, the language mechanics of writing or 'production', and knowledge of the topic that fuels the storytelling. These challenges remain whether children write on paper or type their stories on the keyboard. According to psychological research, children aged 8 to 10 are particularly vulnerable to the challenges of engaging in creative activities such as storytelling. This phenomenon is referred to as the '4th-Grade Slump' [1, 2]. We propose that the theories of embodied cognition may act as the foundation for an approach to support children's creativity and sense of creative self-efficacy in storytelling throughout the period of the 4th-Grade Slump.

TEI '15, January 16 - 19 2015, Stanford, CA, USA.

ACM 978-1-4503-3305-4/15/01...$15.00
http://dx.doi.org/10.1145/2677199.2680602

THE 4TH-GRADE SLUMP
Paul Torrance described the phenomenon of the 4th-Grade Slump as a "precipitous decrement in all creative thinking abilities near the end of 3rd grade or beginning of the 4th grade" [1, 2] observed through longitudinal studies in many countries from the United States to Norway, India and Western Samoa. This phenomenon is still of concern today, as shown by Kim's [3] study that found decreasing creativity scores among children since 1990 as opposed to steadily increasing IQ (Intelligence Quotient) scores.

There are several possible causes of the 4th-Grade Slump, but a key factor may be the increased social awareness and self-evaluation that take place in late childhood [4]. Figure 1 illustrates the process. Manifested creative activity of the child increases (A in Figure 1) until around 8 or 9 years old. This period coincidentally happens at the same time as Piaget's [5] 'concrete operational phase' (COP) when he posits that egocentric speech is replaced by socially-directed adult speech, and social awareness is ignited. During this critical period, factors like social accommodation, peer approval, and

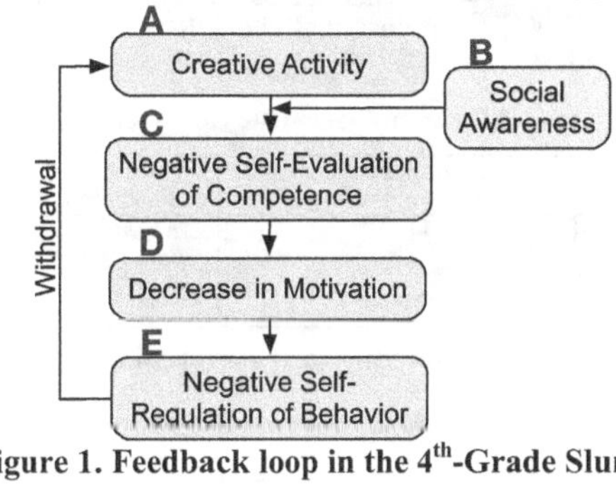

Figure 1. Feedback loop in the 4th-Grade Slump

the need for validation become important as the child experiences greater awareness of society (B). This social awareness leads a child to be more judgmental of her work, and to engage in more critical self-evaluation of competence (C). Such self-appraisals with respect to social norms and standards may lead to a decrease in the child's motivation to engage in specific creative activities (D), and eventually may lead to self-regulation of behavior, in the form of a withdrawal from creative activity in general (E). In our research, we seek to intervene at the level of the child's self-evaluation of competence (self-efficacy), taking creative storytelling as a domain of study.

SELF-EFFICACY, CREATIVITY AND EMBODIMENT

Self-efficacy has been defined as "people's beliefs about their capabilities to exercise control over their own level of functioning and over events that affect their lives" [6]. The construct has often been equated with self-confidence or self-esteem. As a carrier of meaning and valence that shapes one's perception of external events, self-efficacy influences people's feelings, cognition, and course of actions [7]. Alfred Bandura, the originator of the self-efficacy concept, argues that perceived self-efficacy triggers self-regulatory processes such that "a person with the same knowledge and skills may perform poorly, adequately, or extraordinarily depending on fluctuations in self-efficacy thinking" [6]. The ability of self-efficacy to influence one's motivation to engage in specific behaviors and tasks is generally accepted [8]. But what role does self-efficacy play in creativity? Creativity is generally defined as the generation of domain-specific, novel, and useful or appropriate outcomes [9]. The creativity-focused sense of efficacy then is the "belief that one has the ability to produce creative outcomes" [10]. A fair amount of research has shown that positive creative self-efficacy may improve creative performance and work involvement (e.g., [10-14]).

Figure 2 outlines our model of how to support or improve creative activity and self-efficacy in creating stories through embodied action. By supporting enactment-based storytelling ([1] in Figure 2), we hope to facilitate the creative process in the child[2]. We expect that such facilitation will enhance both the child's self-efficacy[3] (through process enablement where the child is better able to express story idea), and the stories produced[4]. This has the potential of a positive resonance effect as improved self-efficacy improves story quality that in turn increases self-efficacy[5]. Furthermore, self-efficacy improvements positively regulate motivation to re-engage in the storytelling process[6], thus affording the child greater practice in creating[7].

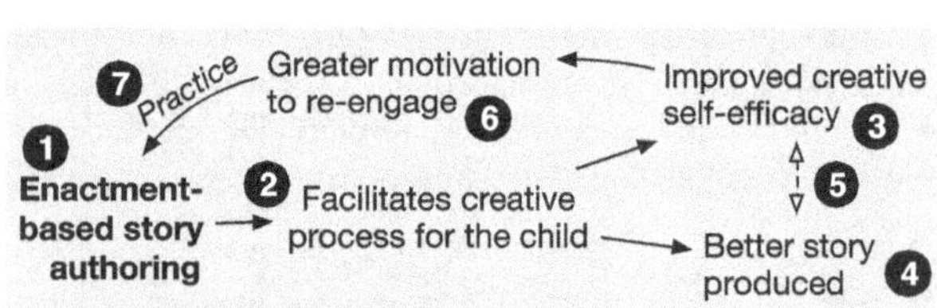

Figure 2. Model for Creative Storytelling Support

Dimension	Enactment-based animated story authoring	Video-based enactment	Theater/ Drama
Feedback	Real-time	Delayed/ Real-time	Social evaluations
Output	Cartoon animation	Video of self	Performance for others

Figure 3. Enactment-based storytelling approaches

Embodied enactment may facilitate the creative storytelling process through three mechanisms: first, telling stories through the body allows the child to draw from their previous bodily experiences in the world. The body already knows which neural pathways and muscles to activate to replicate an action that has previously been experienced. But furthermore, an action "goes beyond the physics of the movements and captures the semantics of the act in terms of meaning, goal, and/or underlying intentions" of the situation [15]. These are transferred to enactive actions, potentially enabling a child to infuse greater richness in her story. Second, enactment, as in pretend play [16], gives the child the license to imagine. It creates a 'magic circle' [17] in which disbelief can be suspended, and the child feels able to let her imagination fly, which is often difficult for children to do when approaching a blank page.

Third, body enactment allows for greater transparency in the child's expression of her imagination. According to the media naturalness theory [18], body language is essential to our communication and makes up the most intuitive medium for us. Body enactment bypasses the need to encode ideas into linear, symbolic form in order for the child to express them, as is required with language and text. It has been shown that our motor systems are intrinsically engineered to anticipate the sensory consequences of planned movements [15], thereby enabling flow of actions.

ENACTMENT-BASED ANIMATED STORY AUTHORING

In our proposed approach, a child draws on her bodily experiences (daily, recurrent or even unique) events to enact pieces of a digital story. Her enactment of the story pieces directly translates into the creation of an animated cartoon, thereby coupling physical enactment with a digital or virtual representation. This allows her to engage mentally in the creative process of digital storytelling by generating ideas through the body. Our research questions are twofold – What are the effects of enactment-based authoring of animated stories on 3rd to 4th-grade children's (i) sense of creative self-efficacy in storytelling; and (ii) quality of creative stories produced?

Figure 3 shows two key dimensions that distinguish our proposed physical-digital coupling approach from simple video-based enactment (child enacting in front of a video camera) or pure theater/drama performance in facilitating the child's creative process. Our approach provides real-time visual feedback of a child's enactment through an animated cartoon movie. In video-based enactment, the feedback can be real-time (if the child can see the video capture screen) or delayed (if the child can see the captured video only during playback), and the output is a video of the child herself. In theater/drama performances, the feedback typically takes the form of social evaluations, and the output is the performance itself as viewed by an audience.

The embodied cognition concept of externalization [19] can help us to understand the role of immediate feedback in story authoring. We offload mental concepts into the physical world and reuptake them through the perception of their material representations. This ability enables us to extend our thinking from basic functions (e.g., remembering) to higher-level thought (e.g., recombining ideas). Similarly, the real-time feedback of the enactment may enable the child to extend her thinking beyond disconnected ideas.

The creative story output in the format of a cartoon animation is critical in our approach to enactment-based storytelling: i) it sustains interest through the child's intrinsic attraction to media; ii) it allows for a lower level of self-disclosure, and this may be important for some children who may not be comfortable with an overt performance featuring themselves; iii) it provides interactivity in the form of the remote control of a virtual character; and iv) the expected lower level of fidelity of cartoon characters makes the method more 'forgiving' of deficiencies in acting skill and makes it more like play than in real-life acting or video-based enactment where 'what-you-see-is-what-you-get'.

A number of systems with similarities to our proposed enactment-based animated story authoring have previously been advanced. Figure 4 lists five systems (with their targeted users) that are closest in terms of their physical-digital coupling. Each of them uses enactment to different degrees. With 'pen-to-mime' [20], the user can map movements of a tablet pen (e.g. trajectory, speed, posture) to the walking and running motion of a 3D character. In 'Handimation' [21], the user holds two wiimotes in hand and has one attached to the head while performing gestures that maps to a 3D character. Movements are recorded on tracks that can be combined using a sequencer-like interface. In 'performance-driven motion choreographing' [22], the performer wears sensors (accelerometers) that detect her movements. The system then searches a motion database for moves that maps the closest to the movements performed. 'Prochinima' [23] allows children to project a selection of pre-made animations onto any surfaces that they can combine with live-action acting during recording. Finally, in 'shape your body' [24], the performer attempts to position her body shape so that she reflects poses of pre-rigged virtual silhouettes of human/non-human characters.

THE DIME SYSTEM DESCRIPTION

We developed the DiME (Digital Micro-Enactment) system as a testbed to study enactment-based storytelling. As shown in Figure 5A, the DiME system architecture is organized around three activity stages. The system was designed to be used in pairs, with one child acting as the 'director' and the other as the 'actor' at any one point in time.

I. Story Structuring: A story in DiME is represented as a series of 'story frames or scenes'. Story construction is pre-

#	System Name	Year	Interaction Tools	Output	Audience
1	Pen-to-Mime [19]	2004	Pen	3D	Adults
2	Handimation [20]	2008	Wiimotes	3D	Animators
3	Performance-driven motion choreographing [21]	2009	Accelerometers	3D	Adults
4	Prochinima [22]	2011	Mobile phone, Video camera	2D	Children
5	Shape Your Body [23]	2012	Body	3D	Adults

Figure 4. Prior enactment-based authoring systems

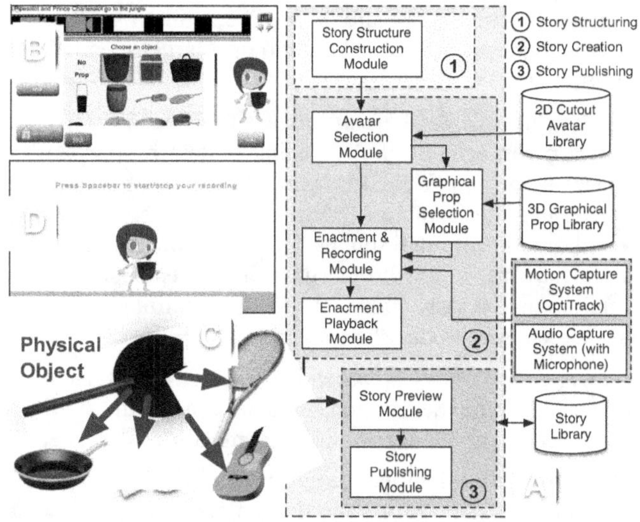

Figure 5. A. DiME system architecture; B & D: Screenshots; C. Physical object-Virtual props mapping

sented to the children through a series of blank frames that they can fill in on the 'home' screen (Figure 5B).

II. Story Creation: The children tell their stories by authoring the details of the story frames. DiME consists of three interactive modules for this activity.

Avatar selection module: A library of 2D cutout cartoon characters are made available to the children to choose for their enactment. The models are articulated and are able to mirror a child as her movements are tracked. The library has Front, Back and Side 2D cutout views of each of the characters and the sprites/images are switched based on the orientation of the child during enactment.

Graphical prop selection module: This is an optional phase where the children can pick from a variety of 3D graphical props (e.g., flashlight, bowl, sword) to use in the enactment (Figure 5B). Once the graphical prop is selected, the child is directed to pick up its control proxy in the form of a physical object with the appropriate affordances (e.g., a stick for a sword – see Figure 5C).

Enactment and recorder module: After an avatar and a graphical prop are selected, the system activates the avatar enactment subsystem. The 2D cutout cartoon characters are controlled by six 'control frames' corresponding to the head, torso, right and left hands, and right and left feet. Each control frame is specified as a solid rigid body with 3D positions and orientations. At this point, the child would be wearing tracking markers, as shown in Figure 6.

The enactment module animates the character and object by moving graphical models to reflect the tracking data streams, subject to model connection constraints. DiME performs motion tracking using a commercial motion capture system with eight cameras. Figure 7 shows the system set up in a room at an elementary school. The software tracks the body markers and the physical object, and performs the associated animations continuously in real-time during enactment (Figure 8A). The animations are displayed against a white background on a large screen display (Figure 5C).

At any time while the enactment subsystem is active, the children can activate the recording system by pressing the spacebar on a wireless keyboard. When recording is activated, an audio capture subsystem captures the co-temporal vocal utterances and sounds made by the children. This audio stream is synchronized with and embedded in the final animated story video. When the recording is stopped, the screen goes to the Playback mode.

Enactment playback module: The enacted cartoon video is played back to the children, and they have the option to save the enactment or redo the enactment for the scene.

III. Story Publishing: From the DiME 'home screen' showing the story film strip, the children can preview and publish their entire story.

Preview story module: All cartoon frames can be played back to the users in the order that they were created.

Publish story module: At the end of the story creation process, all the frames are collected, saved to the library, and output as video files.

DIME AS A RESEARCH TESTBED

A study with the DiME system was conducted at 4 different locations. An early in-lab test of the system was conducted with 2 children (one girl and one boy, aged 8 and 10 respectively) to identify obvious bugs and usability issues. A revised version of DiME was then pilot tested at a local 'Boys and Girls Clubs of America' afterschool program over two weeks with 7 children (4 girls, 3 boys, all 8 and 10 years old). This pilot study was also used to test our study protocol and instruments. These were modified to be adapted to children's cognitive and language abilities.

The main study was conducted with the modified versions of DiME and the protocols and instruments at two elementary school summer camps. Eleven children (8 girls, 3 boys) participated at the first school over two weeks, and 9 children (6 girls, 3 boys) took part at the second school the following two weeks, yielding a total of 20 children. Parents voluntarily signed up their children by completing a consent form and a personality questionnaire (Big-Five Inventory [25] — the BFI-10 that includes extraversion, agreeableness, conscientiousness, neuroticism, openness) for their participating child (underlining represents study variables).

Figure 6. Markers worn by child for tracking

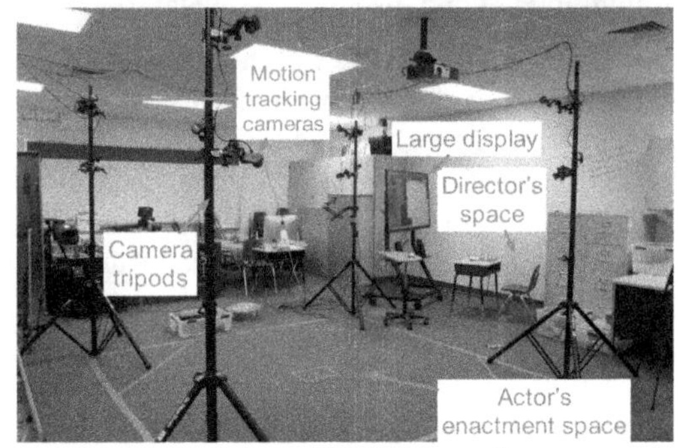

Figure 7. Setup of DiME in a classroom

At each school, randomly selected gender-matched children were paired and taken to a room where the motion tracking cameras and the DiME system was set up. Each pair took between 2 to 4 hours (approx. 3 hours on average) to complete the study, which was facilitated by two researchers. Because of an odd number of sign-ups for the study, a child at each site did not have a partner. In these cases, one of the researchers played the role of the 'partner', but the child was allowed to make all creative decisions and actions. The study followed the protocol described below:

A. Ice-breaking exercise: The researchers first engaged the two children in a simple 'In the River, On the Bank' game.

B. Minor's assent: Verbal assent was obtained from each child for her willingness to participate before the study session was formally started.

C. Pre-questionnaires: Each of the two researchers assisted one child to fill in several questionnaires —

i. Using the smileyometer [26] (5-point likert scales with smiley graphics), the first questionnaire assessed the child's pre-level of self-efficacy in creative storytelling (Beghetto's [27] 3-item 'creative self-efficacy measure' – I am good at coming up with new ideas for stories; I have a lot of good ideas for stories; I have a good imagination for stories).
ii. The second questionnaire assessed the child's visual imagery ability using Sheehan's adaptation of Bett's 'questionnaire upon mental imagery' [28] , which asks the participant to rate how clearly she can visualize various things relating to the five senses (appearance, sound, taste, etc.) on a 5-point scale (graphical versions of 'really clear' to 'not at all clear' were used).

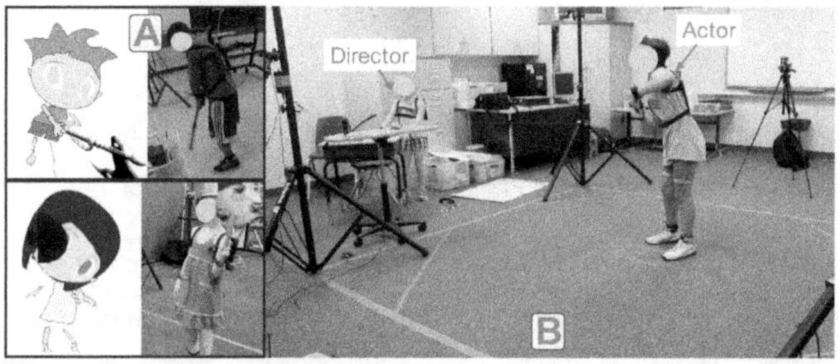

Figure 8. A. Enactment-Animation mapping; B. A pair of children enacting their story

iii. The third questionnaire assessed the child's baseline level of creativity as measured by Guilford's [29] 'alternate uses test' that asks the participant to come up with alternate uses for various objects (e.g. ping pong ball, brick, pen).

D. Control condition: We used 'comics drawing' as a control to the enactment-based intervention that is the subject of our investigation. Drawing is a common instructional tool used in the form of 'creative notebooks' to encourage storytelling in children in the classroom. After being guided through an example, the two children were asked to create a story on the theme of 'An adventure in the jungle' by drawing a 'comics'. After that, the two children were each asked to write separately the story they just made on paper.

E. Treatment condition: The researchers explained the DiME system to the two children by creating an example story of 3 scenes/frames where one researcher played the role of the 'director' to control the recording of the animation, and another played the 'actor' who enacted the scenes. The children were then asked to create a story on the theme of 'An adventure in the cave' using the system. Figure 8B shows a pair of children enacting a story scene. The children were then separated and asked to write the story they just made, just as they did in the control condition.

F. Post-questionnaires: Each child was assisted by a researcher to complete a questionnaire that assessed her:
i) General attitude towards different types of story authoring methods, including writing, keyboard typing, and enactment-based authoring, using the 5-point smileyometer.
ii) Preferences with regard to the story authoring methods using the Fun Sorter from the 'Fun Toolkit' [26], whereby the child ranks the three methods from 'Best' to 'Worst' on several dimensions (Like a lot, Is the most fun, Makes me feel happy, Is the easiest).
iii) Motivation to re-engage with creative storytelling using the different story authoring methods using the 'Again-Again table' from the 'Fun Toolkit' [26], whereby the child chooses 'Yes', 'Maybe' or 'No' to the question 'Would you like to do it again?'.
iv) Post-level of self-efficacy using different methods to author stories (measured using the same 3-item creative self-efficacy scale [27] used in the pre-questionnaire).

Owing to time constraints, 2 pairs out of the 20 children completed only the treatment condition. The rest of the pairs underwent a within-subjects study design that counterbalanced the order of the control and treatment conditions. Four pairs (including the child with the researcher 'partner') engaged in the control condition first and the treatment condition second, and 4 pairs (again including one child with the researcher 'partner') did the reverse.

DATA ANALYSIS AND RESULTS

Responses to variables measured using 5-point likert scales (personality, creative self-efficacy – CSE, visual imagery ability, general attitude) were coded and averaged into a mean score. For the baseline creativity level, alternate uses were coded according to Guilford's [29] method on dimensions of originality, fluency, flexibility and elaboration, and a mean score was generated for each child. For the ranking of story authoring methods on dimensions of liking, fun, happiness and ease-of-use, each method was assigned a score based on the rank in which it was placed by the child (e.g., first rank is assigned a score of 3, second rank a score 2, and third rank a score of 1).

The written stories provided a common creative output that could be compared across the treatment and control conditions. They were evaluated using Amabile's [30] *consensual assessment technique*, whereby a panel of experts rate creative products using their subjective understandings along several dimensions. The children's stories were retyped with all grammar mistakes corrected so that language abilities do not present biases to the evaluators. Three 'field experts' (one with expertise in HCI and two with extensive experience as elementary school teachers) were asked to rate the stories on dimensions of creativity, coherence, richness, and narrative structure using a scale of 1 (Not at all) to 5 (Very). The scores of the evaluators were averaged for each dimension, and were integrated across dimensions into a story quality score.

Quantitative Results

All scores were entered into the SPSS statistical software package. A repeated measures ANOVA test (child's personality variables as covariates) yielded a statistically significant interaction of *Time* × *Extraversion*, $F^{(1, 14)} = 5.70$, $p < .05$, with the mean post-CSE scores ($\mu = 4.52$) being higher than the mean pre-CSE scores ($\mu = 4.42$). To investigate the interaction effect further, we classified the children into three levels of extraversion from low to high based on quartiles (Figure 9.A). Improvements in creative self-efficacy scores from pre-study to post-treatment times occurred for children with low and medium extraversion levels, but not for high extraversion levels.

A repeated measures ANOVA test (visual imagery ability and baseline creativity as covariates, and the child's age and condition order as between-subjects factors) produced a statistically significant *Medium* × *Baseline Creativity level* interaction effect between the quality of the written story created from enactment-based authoring and written story quality from comics-based authoring, $F^{(1, 6)} = 6.061$, $p < .05$. Looking at the relationship between authoring methods and written story quality based on three different levels of baseline creativity level, we found that the quality of enactment-authored stories supercedes comics-authored stories only for children with low baseline creativity (Figure 9.B).

Moreover, repeated measures ANOVA tests for each story quality dimension separately, we see a *Medium* × *Baseline Creativity level* interaction for Story Creativity, $F^{(1, 6)} = 8.076$, $p < .05$, with stories from comics-based authoring having a mean score ($\mu = 2.65$) higher than those from enactment-based authoring ($\mu = 2.64$). We also see a *Medium* × *Baseline Creativity level* interaction for Story Richness, $F^{(1, 6)} = 16.714$, $p < .01$, with stories from enactment-based authoring having a mean score ($\mu = 2.59$) higher than those from comics-based authoring ($\mu = 2.52$).

A repeated measures ANOVA test (with personality variables as covariates) showed a statistically significant *Attitude* × *Extraversion* interaction effect among the children's attitudes towards different methods of story creation, including enactment-based authoring, typing and writing, $F^{(2, 36)} = 4.462$, $p < .05$ (Figure 9.C1). Categorizing the attitude scores based on extraversion levels, we found that enactment-based story authoring is least favored by children low on extraversion. Children with both medium and high extraversion viewed enactment-based authoring very favorably (Figure 9.C2).

With regard to preferences, a Friedman Test yielded a statistically significant difference in the ranks of the three story authoring methods surveyed in terms of liking ($\chi^2(2) = 12.177$, $p < 0.01$), fun ($\chi^2(2) = 17.949$, $p = 0.000$) and feeling of happiness ($\chi^2(2) = 8.380$, $p < 0.05$), but not in terms of ease-of-use (Figure 9.D1). Furthermore, a spreadsheet count tabulation of the children's responses on their willingness to re-engage in creative storytelling using the various story authoring methods showed a clear motivation (80% 'yes') to create other stories using enactment-based authoring (Figure 9.D2).

Qualitative Results

We also performed analyses of the interview comments from the children using the qualitative approach of open, focused and axial coding [31]. We wanted to find out what the children liked and disliked about the enactment-based authoring method. Phrase units (minimally codable unit of text that carries an idea or a meaning) were extracted from the interview transcripts and assigned a code. The list of codes was then grouped into themes or categories. Six themes emerged from the interview data as to why they liked the approach: *Fun & Play; Interactive control; Problem-solving; Authoring control; Actualization of real experiences; and Sustained interest in acting*. Among those, the element of fun and play that the system afforded was one of the main reasons: *"Because it was funny. Because I threw the ball so many times. And I was saying I hate you bears." [Fr11F]; "It was really fun...and...um..like how it was ... like how I kept on saying ooo la la because I was waiting for Alex to stop the recording." [Fr2F].*

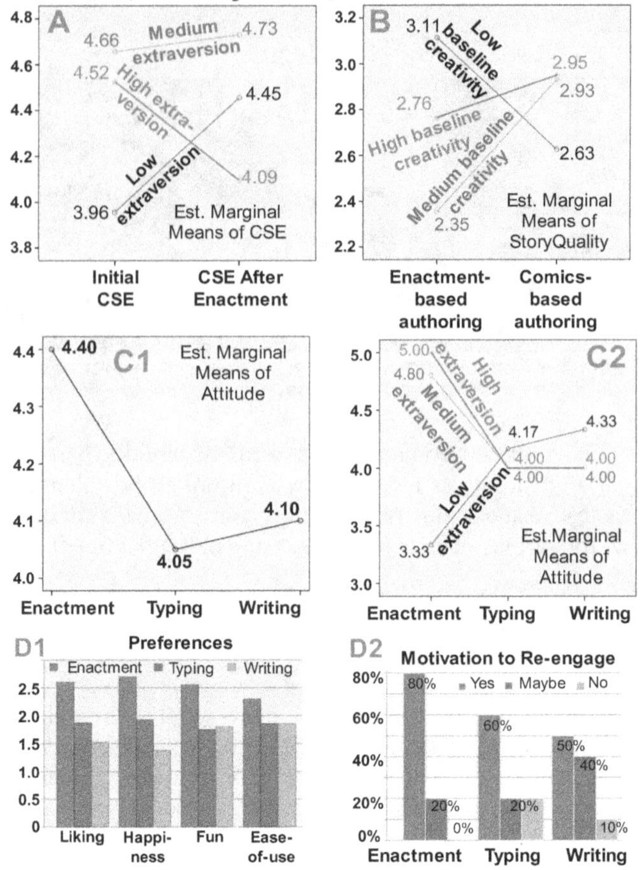

Figure 9. Graphs from study results

Another significant reason was the ability to control a character remotely in an interactive manner: *"I get to be a funny character. I could move and see what it's like." [Fr8F]*; *"I like how I can control it. And when I control it, I feel like it's a video game I mean." [Hm7F].*

An interesting reason that was mentioned was the pleasure in figuring out how to act out a particular idea, akin to problem-solving: *"I liked acting out when he (story character) figures out it was a dream. When he says 'there's the biggest diamond in the world' or something. And then the narrator is like then he woke up'. So now you got to act like he was sleeping, then he just woke up, and it was pretty fun."*

All but two children said that there was nothing that they did not like. The themes from the two children included the *constrained acting space* that was provided, *getting tired when the scene to be acted was very long*, and having *difficulty to remember lines* when acting out.

DISCUSSION

Extraversion and Creative Self-Efficacy: Children's sense of perceived self-efficacy to create stories using enactment-based authoring showed an increase over their initial level of CSE prior to the enactment-based story creation. However, this increase in self-efficacy to create seems to be affected by the child's personality, especially the degree of extraversion. Extraversion refers to the extent to which one is outgoing or sociable [25]. Our results suggest that a more reserved child experiences improved CSE with enactment-based authoring, but not a highly extraverted child. The influence of extraversion is not surprising, but the positive impact on more reserved children was rather unexpected and exciting. It may be that our approach of enactment-based authoring is directed by an objective function of creating an animation with a cartoon character, thereby presenting a form of 'transformed self' where the child is the actor, but the representation that is shared or viewed is the cartoon character. Thus it may feel less threatening for children who typically attempt to minimize social exposure, causing them to be more self-efficacious in creating stories with our system.

The lack of effect of DiME on the self-efficacy of high extraversion children may be because they gain little from the anonymity afforded by the transformed-self-effect of the cartoon output. There is evidence that self-efficacy is positively related to extraversion [32]. It could be that a single study session did not have an appreciable effect on their already high self-efficacy. Perhaps longer exposure to and use of DiME may have a measurable effect on the self-efficacy of extraverted children.

There was an interesting paradox uncovered regarding improvements in self-efficacy in low extraversion children and their favorability ratings. Although their self-efficacy in storytelling increased with DiME, low-extraversion children nevertheless indicated a stronger preference for and a more positive attitude (in terms of liking, fun and happiness) toward more traditional storytelling methods (writing and typing) over enactment-based authoring. It is likely that these children's low extraversion made them uncomfortable in the unfamiliar study condition with unfamiliar experimenters, and this discomfort caused their negative favorability ratings for the use of DiME. With long-term use, the effects of DiME on their favorability ratings may echo their positive creative self-efficacy with the system.

Story Quality with Enactment-based Authoring: In terms of outcome, children's stories created using enactment were judged as being significantly different from their stories created through comics drawings. But this difference occurred only for children with low baseline creativity levels, who produced stories of higher quality using enactment-based authoring than with comics-based authoring. Improvement in the quality of the stories occurred in terms of richness, i.e. how textured and detailed the story is. No significant positive effects were found on the other dimensions of story creativity, coherence and structure.

This may be partially explained by the novelty of the system to the children. We observed that for many of the children, especially those with high baseline creativity, the story scenes produced were strongly influenced by the graphical props available in DiME. They wanted to use the different props available, and adapted their planned stories to the props as they went on. This may be the cause of the reduced coherence and structure of the children's stories as they reconstructed them in writing, since recall and retelling became more difficult. Unlike coherence and structure however, story richness is evident within each story scene. Since a prop is chosen for and kept throughout each scene, the within-scene richness was not influenced by system choices. With greater familiarity of DiME, highly creative children may produce stories of better quality with enactment-based authoring than with other methods like drawing comics, which was already a familiar medium for them at the point of the study.

Feedback on DiME: The children's feedback on what they liked and disliked about the enactment-based method to creative storytelling provided support for the features that we included in the DiME system. The system provided fun and excitement, prompting the children to step into the 'magic circle' [17] to create through playful interactions, interactive control of virtual characters and props, and problem-solving of how to act ideas through the body. Generally, the children exhibited positive valence towards enactment-based authoring, and the majority were willing to re-engage in creative storytelling using the medium.

We make three main contributions in this paper. First, we proposed an approach to nurture children's sense of creative self-efficacy during the period of the 4th-Grade Slump, when creativity appears to drop in the child precisely because of a demotivational cycle. Reinforcing a child's confidence in being able to create leads to greater likelihood that the child will continue to engage and gain practice in the creative process. Second, we developed the DiME system as a technological innovation that can act as a research testbed to investigate the effects of embodied enactment on children's creative storytelling. Third, through an empirical study, we contributed to the understanding of how enactment-based animated story authoring can support children's creative self-efficacy, creation of rich stories, and enjoyment of the creative storytelling process. Future work is needed to study the effects of the approach with a larger sample of children and with an expanded DiME system that includes more characters, props, etc. In the long-term, longitudinal investigations that consider the effects of novelty, and work looking at ways to integrate the approach into the school curriculum have to be carried out.

CONCLUSION

The 4th-Grade Slump in children's creativity is an important phenomenon that has received little attention in the HCI community. We see it as representative of a broader human experience across domains whereby self-evaluation of our creations modulates our confidence in our abilities to further create. With the new wave of Kinects, Wiis, Leap controllers and motion capture systems, it is increasingly possible to ground digital technologies in embodied cognition. In creative storytelling, enactment-based animated story authoring represents one such technology that has the potential to augment not only children's self-efficacy in their ability to create, but also the richness of their creative output, especially for introverted children, thereby short-circuiting the negative feedback cycle of the Slump.

ACKNOWLEDGEMENTS
This work has been partly funded by NSF #IIS 1059389.

REFERENCES

1. Torrance, E.P., *Understanding the Fourth Grade Slump in Creative Thinking*, in *Cooperative Research Project.* 1967, US Department of Health, Education and Welfare. p. 444.
2. Torrance, E.P., *A Longitudinal Examination of the Fourth Grade Slump in Creativity.* Gifted Child Quarterly, 1968. **12**(3): p. 195-199
3. Kim, K.H., *The creativity crisis: The decrease in creative thinking scores on the Torrance Tests of Creative Thinking.* Creativity Research Journal, 2011. **23**(4): p. 285-295.
4. Chu, S.L., F. Quek, and X. Lin. *Studying Medium Effects on Children's Creative Processes.* in *Creativity and Cognition*. 2011. Atlanta, GA.
5. Piaget, J. and B. Inhelder, *Memory and intelligence.* 1973, London: Routledge and Kegan Paul.
6. Bandura, A., *Self-efficacy: toward a unifying theory of behavioral change.* Psychological review, 1977. **84**(2): p. 191.
7. Bandura, A., *Perceived self-efficacy in cognitive development and functioning.* Educational psychologist, 1993. **28**(2): p. 117-148.
8. Stajkovic, A.D. and F. Luthans, *Self-efficacy and work-related performance: A meta-analysis.* Psychological bulletin, 1998. **124**(2): p. 240.
9. Amabile, T.M., *Creativity and innovation in organizations*. Vol. 5. 1996: Harvard Business School.
10. Tierney, P. and S.M. Farmer, *Creative self-efficacy: Its potential antecedents and relationship to creative performance.* Academy of Management Journal, 2002. **45**(6): p. 1137-1148.
11. Gardner, H., *Creating minds.* 1993, Basic Books: NY.
12. Kirton, M., *Adaptors and innovators: A description and measure.* Journal of applied psychology, 1976. **61**(5): p. 622.
13. Tierney, P. and S.M. Farmer, *Creative self-efficacy development and creative performance over time.* Journal of Applied Psychology, 2011. **96**(2): p. 277.
14. Gong, Y., J.-C. Huang, and J.-L. Farh, *Employee learning orientation, transformational leadership, and employee creativity: The mediating role of employee creative self-efficacy.* Academy of Management Journal, 2009. **52**(4): p. 765-778.
15. Prinz, W., *What re-enactment earns us.* Cortex, 2006. **42**(4): p. 515-517.
16. Bergen, D., *The role of pretend play in children's cognitive development.* Early Childhood Research & Practice, 2002. **4**(1): p. n1.
17. Huizinga, J., *Nature and significance of play as a cultural phenomenon.* The performance studies reader, 2004: p. 117-20.
18. Kock, N., *The psychobiological model: Towards a new theory of computer-mediated communication based on Darwinian evolution.* Organization Science, 2004. **15**(3): p. 327-348.
19. Hollan, J., E. Hutchins, and D. Kirsh, *Distributed Cognition: Toward a New Foundation for Human Computer Interaction Research.* TOCHI, 2000. **7**(2): p. 174-196.
20. Oshita, M. *Pen-to-mime: A pen-based interface for interactive control of a human figure.* in *the 1st Eurographics conference on Sketch-Based Interfaces and Modeling*. 2004. Eurographics.
21. Svensson, A., S. Björk, and K.-P. Åkesson. *Tangible handimation real-time animation with a sequencer-based tangible interface.* in *the 5th NordiCHI: building bridges*. 2008. ACM.
22. Liang, X., et al., *Performance-driven motion choreographing with accelerometers.* Computer Animation and Virtual Worlds, 2009. **20**(2-3): p. 89-99.
23. Åkerman, P. and A. Puikkonen. *Prochinima: using pico projector to tell situated stories*. in *Proceedings of the 13th International Conference on Human Computer Interaction with Mobile Devices and Services*. 2011. ACM.
24. Leite, L. and V. Orvalho. *Shape your body: Control a virtual silhouette using body motion.* in *CHI'12 Extended Abstracts.* 2012. ACM.
25. Rammstedt, B. and O.P. John, *Measuring personality in one minute or less: A 10-item short version of the Big Five Inventory in English and German.* Journal of Research in Personality, 2007. **41**(1): p. 203-212.
26. Read, J.C. and S. MacFarlane. *Using the Fun Toolkit and Other Survey Methods to Gather Opinions in Child Computer Interaction* in *IDC' 06: Interaction Design and Children*. 2006. Tampere, Finland: ACM.
27. Beghetto, R.A., *Creative self-efficacy: Correlates in middle and secondary students.* Creativity Research Journal, 2006. **18**(4): p. 447-457.
28. Sheehan, P.W., *A Shortened Form of Betts' Questionnaire Upon Mental Imagery.* Journal of Clinical Psychology, 1967.
29. Christensen, P., et al., *Alternate uses test.* Beverly Hills, CA: Sheridan Psychological Services, 1960.
30. Amabile, T.M., *Social Psychology of Creativity: A Consensual Assessment Technique.* Journal of Personality and Social Psychology, 1982. **43**(5): p. 997-1013.
31. Strauss, A. and J. Corbin, *Basics of Qualitative Research: Grounded Theory Procedures and Techniques.* 1990, Newbury Park, UK: Sage.
32. Robins, R.W., et al., *Personality correlates of self-esteem.* Journal of Research in Personality, 2001. **35**(4): p. 463-482.

Eugenie: Multi-Touch and Tangible Interaction for Bio-Design

Casey Grote[1], Evan Segreto[1], Johanna Okerlund[1], Robert Kincaid[2], Orit Shaer[1]

[1]Wellesley College
Wellesley, MA, USA
caseygrote@gmail.com, esegreto@wellesley.edu,
jokerlun@wellesley.edu, oshaer@wellesley.edu

[2]Agilent Technologies
Santa Clara, CA, USA
robert_kincaid@agilent.com

ABSTRACT

We present a case study of applying TEI research to a data-intense scientific workflow that requires the exploration of large datasets through the construction of complex queries. We describe our two-year-long effort and design iterations of Eugenie, an interface for helping synthetic biologists through the collaborative and intricate process of bio-design. We introduce new interaction techniques for browsing large data sets and for constructing complex queries with active tangible tokens and an interactive tabletop. We also discuss challenges and opportunities for applying TEI to support data-driven inquiry.

Author Keywords

Physical tokens; tabletop; queries; multi-display environments; interactive surfaces.

ACM Classification Keywords

H.5.m. Information interfaces and presentation: User Interfaces---input devices and strategies, interaction styles.

INTRODUCTION

Tangible and multi-touch user interfaces offer unique opportunities for enhancing collaborative learning and discovery. Several studies indicate that horizontal interfaces support active reading [12], foster collaboration [18, 22] and facilitate external cognition [14, 18].

However, while tangible and tabletop interaction have been applied to a broad range of application domains, relatively little research has been devoted to investigating these interaction styles in the context of scientific exploration [17]. Tangible and tabletop interfaces designed for supporting scientific inquiry mostly focus on the representation and manipulation of information with inherent physical or spatial structure (e.g. proteins and molecules). Our focus is on investigating the application of tangible and multi-touch interaction to data-driven inquiry, where large and abstract data sets are accessed and manipulated. Shaer et al. proposed that applying TEI research to fields and processes involving Big Data such as genomics presents an opportunity to drive forward the theory and practice of TEI [17]. They further recalled that participants in the inaugural TEI conference panel suggested that, in the future, "more complex computation should be occurring behind the tangible interface, instead of only one-to-one input-output."

In this paper, we apply TEI research to the data-intense area of Synthetic Biology. We reflect on the design, implementation, and evaluation of Eugenie, an interface for bio-design. We describe our two-year-long effort and design iterations from a visual multi-touch interface to a tangible user interface with active tokens. This paper presents four main contributions: (1) Lessons from the iterative design, implementation, and evaluation of a multi-touch and tangible interface for querying large data sets; (2) New tangible interaction techniques for navigating large hierarchical data sets using *active* tokens; (3) Tangible interaction language for forming complex queries; and (4) A discussion of challenges and opportunities for applying TEI approaches to the exploration of large data sets. We begin with a discussion of related work.

RELATED WORK

Multi-touch Interfaces for Big Data

Several multi-touch and tangible interfaces have been created to support collaborative exploration in data intense areas. For example, Block et al. created the DeepTree exhibit for science museums [4], a multi-touch tabletop interface that allows users to explore an interactive visualization of the Tree of Life. These multi-touch interfaces support collaborative and playful exploration but limit exploration through designer-defined guided discovery scenarios.

G-nome Surfer [18] and GreenTouch [22] are tabletop multi-touch applications for collaborative exploration of genomic and phenology databases. Both applications support college-level inquiry-based learning and allow open-ended data exploration. However, in both, users cannot define and set query operators directly. Morris et al. [13] surveyed the design space of collaborative tabletop search applications, reporting that most search input

TEI '15, January 16 - 19 2015, Stanford, CA, USA
Copyright 2015 ACM 978-1-4503-3305-4/15/01...$15.00
http://dx.doi.org/10.1145/2677199.2680605

techniques have relied on touch, keyboard, and mouse input. WIMP-style controls in data-intense applications have limitations including occlusion and challenges for accurate touch due to finger size [9, 24]. Recent studies have explored novel multi-touch interaction techniques that provide advantage over WIMP-style touch controls [6]. However, these techniques often suffer from low discoverability and lack of persistence [6].

Tangible Queries

Several tangible user interfaces (TUIs) have explored the use of tokens for query formulation. Navigational Blocks [5] is an early TUI for querying a database where each block represents one query parameter, its six faces representing the possible values. DataTiles [15] combines tiles – graspable windows for digital information – on top of a horizontal display. DataTiles provides a highly expressive physical interaction language but is constrained to a horizontal surface. Ullmer et al. [21] introduced two TUIs for query formulation (TQI) that use tokens to represent query parameters. One employs "parameter wheels" for fixed query parameters: the other, "parameter bars" that can be dynamically assigned to various parameters. In both interfaces, tokens are manipulated and interpreted on a series of physical constraints. Such interaction, while highly expressive, limits the portability of tokens and possibilities for collaboration. Facet-Streams [10] combines passive tokens and an interactive surface as query parameters. Stackables [11] explores the use of active tokens arranged vertically for expressing a query. We designed a system that supports complex queries and utilizes tangible interaction with *active tokens*—programmable physical objects with integrated display, sensing, or actuation technologies [23]—which are manipulated in-air and on-bezel.

Tangible Interaction with Active Tokens

Tangible Video Editor [26] employs active tokens to represent video clips. To guide users' interaction, video clip tokens are embedded in cases that resemble jigsaw puzzle pieces. SynFlo [25] is an interactive installation for introducing Synthetic Biology concepts to non-scientists. It utilizes Sifteo cubes, microcomputers that implement various gestures including shaking, flipping, tilting, neighboring, and touching [1]. The application simulates a wet-lab bench and evokes gestures such as pouring and shaking. Valdes et al. studied user expectations of a hybrid tangible and gestural language for querying large datasets [23]. They presented a vocabulary of user-defined gestures for active tokens and a characterization of the design space. Our work draws on this study and on the previous efforts we described above.

APPLICATION DOMAIN AND DESIGN GOALS

We designed Eugenie to help synthetic biologists in the intricate and data-driven workflow of bio-design. Next, we briefly explain the application domain and the bio-design process, as well as our design strategy.

Synthetic Biology

Synthetic biology is an emerging research area that couples engineering and biology with the goal of designing organisms with new specified behaviors that are useful in particular applications, including therapeutics, environmental decontamination, and *in vivo* sensing.

The field applies engineering principles such as abstraction and modularity into biological research. Synthetic biologists often solve problems by applying a forward engineering approach: composing a specification of the behavior to be designed into an organism, and then selecting genetic elements and their regulatory architecture to achieve the functional goal. Genetic elements are treated as standardized biological parts and used like "Lego Bricks" based on data about their characterized behavior.

Design Strategy

Considering the complexity of the synthetic biology domain, our design strategy combined rigorous user-centered and participatory design methods. We established a design partnership with domain scientists from a synthetic biology lab at <*Anonymous*> University, as well as with two student teams enrolled in a synthetic biology research competition (i.e. iGEM). We also collaborated closely with the developers of the Eugene [3] synthetic biology programming language.

Over the last two years, we met with our partners regularly. We conducted three workshops in which we teamed with iGEM students, received training in the Eugene programming language, and worked together to specify a wide array of biological designs. In addition, we joined our partners' research meetings and observed them throughout the bio-design process.

Bio-design

Bio-design is a central workflow in synthetic biology. It begins with a set of functional specifications to be assembled from a set of available genetic parts, and it ends with a set of exact DNA sequences to be stitched together in the laboratory. This is a collaborative and iterative workflow that is used in most synthetic biology labs and involves investigators and both graduate and undergraduate students. Because synthetic biologists design complex systems based on uncertain biological mechanisms, the bio-design process requires large design spaces to be sampled combinatorially while applying voluminous experimental design for each design candidate. Biologists define increasingly specific design parameters with each iteration, narrowing the design space. This process typically consists of three stages: (1) Research - users search for information about the structure and function of existing biological constructs; (2) Specification - users specify the desired functionality of their biological construct (e.g. a XOR gate) and draw a generic construct using visual SBOL (Synthetic

Biology Open Language). They then constrain its structure and behavior using a set of rules (e.g. a biological construct that is a transcriptional unit must begin with a promoter and end with a terminator). Many synthetic biologists use Eugene [3], a domain-specific programming language, for constructing a set of rules that narrows the solution space; (3) Exploration - users explore concrete instantiations of their specification, sampling a large data set of permutations. Each construct consists of a set of available biological parts and satisfies the specified rules. Users then iterate on this paradigm, adding more rules until they reach desired results. These activities are often collaborative and typically take place in a conference room or an office space.

Interviews with biologists revealed that, despite the value of using Eugene for formally specifying design rules, many biologists—particularly novice researchers—are intimidated by the notion of writing code and thus reluctant to program in Eugene. We also found that the planning, execution, and tracking of experimental data and results are currently implemented using ad-hoc processes that limit the scale and complexity of biological design.

Design Goals

In collaboration with our design partners, we decided to focus on supporting novice scientists - iGEM participants and college students. We identified the following goals:

G 1. Facilitating an integrated and fluid workflow - supporting users' progress from the information currently available for them (e.g., a database of standardized biological parts) to the information they need (a concrete set of complex biological constructs) through a series of stages while facilitating a flexible iterative workflow that integrates disparate data sets.

G 2. Leveraging rule-based design with Eugene – allowing novices to leverage the power of rule-based bio-design with the Eugene programming language. Lowering the threshold for specifying complex biological constructs.

G 3. Fostering collaboration - the collaborative nature of bio-design implies that multiple stakeholders must participate in this process and agree on desired results that can be produced in the lab. Thus, a tool for bio-design needs to support co-located collaboration.

G 4. Facilitating constructivist learning - our goal is to support constructivist learning at the college level by providing an engaging environment that enables users to interact with the data through sensory and motor processes important for scientific thinking [2,7].

FIRST PROTOTYPE: MULTI-TOUCH INTERFACE

Design

Informed by these goals, we designed and implemented Eugenie - a collaborative, multi-touch interface for rule-based bio-design with the Eugene programming language. Our choice to design and implement Eugenie using a large *vertical* multi-touch surface was informed by current work practices of our users, who typically collaborate through side-by-side work on the whiteboard or a shared screen.

In order to harness the power of rule-based design with Eugene while eliminating the need to write Eugene code, we provided visual representations of 3000 biological parts that could be combined to represent various Eugene rules. The visual representations draw on the standard SBOL visual notation and were designed in close collaboration with the developers of the Eugene language. We conducted a series of pilot studies with users to assess and improve the expressive power and learnability of these representations.

The Eugenie multi-touch application consists of a *toolbox* and a *workspace*. The *toolbox* allows users to search public or private databases of biological constructs; users can choose generic (e.g. a promoter, coding sequence, ribosomal binding site, signal, terminator) or specific biological parts and either store them in the *toolbox* or drag a copy to the workspace.

The workspace is divided into four views: *structure*, *behavior*, *code*, and *results*. Each view is represented using a sliding panel. Users can move back and forth between the different views in a nonlinear fashion, keeping one or multiple panels open at any given time, and visiting and revisiting different stages of the design process (G1). The *structure* view allows users to specify structural rules using visual representations. For example, Figure 1 shows the Eugenie system and the specification of a transcriptional unit: it must start with a promoter, contain a ribosome-binding site and at least one coding sequence, and end with a terminator. The *behavior* view enables users to specify rules regarding the interaction of two parts or constructs (e.g. signal A induces promoter A). Each representation of a biological part is associated with a *property sheet* for specifying and viewing properties and additional information. Property sheets are displayed and edited upon request, thereby reducing on-screen clutter.

The *code* view presents Eugene code that is generated automatically when users specify rules in the *structure* and *behavior* views (G2, G4). When the user selects a part in the *structure* or *behavior* view, the relevant Eugene statements in the code are highlighted. Finally, the *results* view displays the query results—all valid permutations of biological constructs that satisfy the specified rules. Permutations are displayed using standard SBOL notation. Eugenie provides multiple points of entry by supporting parallel work across different panels (G3). The use of multi-touch input enables spatial and direct manipulation of biological constructs, which engages the connection between the hand, eye, and brain to support learning and facilitate "thinking through action" [2, 7] (G4).

Implementation

Eugenie is implemented on the Microsoft PixelSense device using MS SDK 2.0 written in C#. Information is drawn from the MIT Registry of Biological Parts, PubMed, Google Scholar, and the iGEM archive. We use the synthetic biology domain-specific languages Eugene [3] and SBOL for validating new designs (G2).

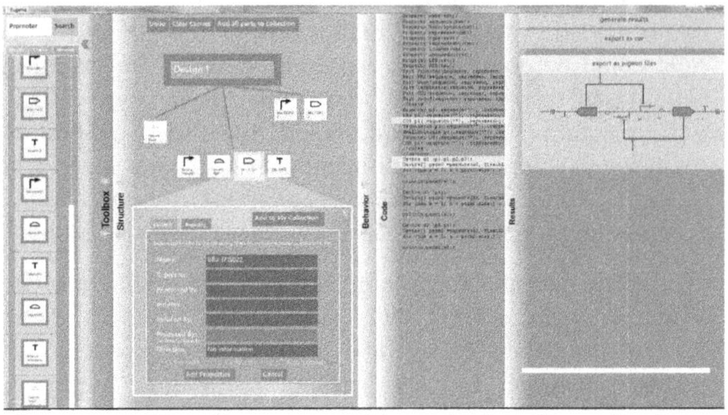

Figure 1, The Eugenie multi-touch interface displays *toolbox*, *structure*, *code*, and *results* views.

Evaluation

We conducted an observational study with 15 undergraduate science students (12 female, age 18-23). 9 students were iGEM team members, while the other 6 were majoring in life sciences. Our study focused on the *usability* of Eugenie, aiming to identify its strengths and weaknesses.

Studies were conducted in conference rooms next to users' laboratory space. In the session, we handed users written tutorial materials about bio-design, SBOL, and the Eugene programming language, which included brief paper-based practice tasks. Then, we provided an overview of the Eugenie interface, demonstrating how to specify the design of a biological construct that is functionally equivalent to an AND gate. The experimental task consisted of using the Eugenie interface to specify the design of a biological toggle switch and to explore the solution space. The task required students to: 1) search for biological parts and store them in the *toolbox*; 2) define structure rules; 3) specify relationships between parts; and 4) review results.

This task was selected, because it mirrors a real-world research task often conducted by iGEM teams. Users documented their progress and answered task-related questions. We collected data through observations and videotaped all sessions. Following the session, we debriefed the users. 12 of the users were assigned to work in dyads (total 6 dyads), while 3 iGEM students with significant Eugene programming experience worked independently.

Results

All users were able to complete the task successfully, producing biologically correct and valid designs (in some cases, with some difficulty that was resolved through collaborative work). On average, dyads spent 42 minutes working on the task, while independent users spent 41 minutes. Users' answers to a post-task questionnaire indicate that they understood the bio-design process.

Dyads collaborated effectively, mostly through side-by-side collaboration, with both users involved (physically or verbally) in the task. We observed that users used the sliding panels often and were able to easily transition back and forth between different views (G1). Users were able to specify structure rules using Eugenie without difficulties. As one user noted: "It is easier to count and relate the different parts when they are symbols rather than words. It is also easier to tell the overall structure of the system when you can see the whole thing all at once." (G4) Several users commented on the value of the *code* view. E.g.: "Seeing the code on the side and how the names were changing when you edited the properties was very helpful." (G2)

The study also highlighted several problems that led to major design iteration: (1) *Target size* – Our design incorporated WIMP-style elements such as checkboxes and textboxes within the *toolbox* and property sheets. Due to the amount of information presented, some of the controls were small; as a result, users reported difficulty in specifying properties using touch. Also, while the representations of biological parts were big enough for conveniently dragging using touch, they were still occluded by fingers. We observed that users often asked each other "which part are you talking about?"; (2) *Integrated representations* – To reduce clutter and improve the readability of visual representations, we separated the specification of structural and behavioral rules into two views. However, users noted that this separation diminished their understanding of the biological constructs designed. In addition, some users found it confusing to drag a copy of a biological part from the *toolbox* to the *structure* or *behavior* view; (3) *Persistent representation* – Our design incorporated the use of property sheets for specifying properties of biological parts. Property sheets could be displayed and edited upon request. Many users commented that some properties, such as the direction of a biological part (i.e. reverse or forward) and its size, are very important and should be represented in a persistent manner rather than hidden in a property sheet; (4) *Lack of constraints* – To allow for maximal flexibility, the representations offered by Eugenie did not utilize visual constraints. Instead, when biological parts were arranged to represent valid rules, the representations "snapped" together. Most users found it easy to specify structural rules. However, users found the specification of behavioral rules, which describe the interactions between biological parts (e.g. represses or induces) to be confusing. We think that the lack of user-guiding visual constraints in specifying the more abstract behavioral rules led to confusion regarding possibilities for action; and (5) *Aggregation* – Users expressed need for the ability to specify rules between constructs, rather than only between primitive biological parts. This requires aggregating multiple parts and rules and representing them as a single construct.

TOWARDS A TANGIBLE LANGUAGE FOR BIO-DESIGN

Design

While we could attempt to address the shortcomings described above by redesigning the existing interface, we decided to investigate an alternative approach: using tangible interaction with active tokens for constructing rules, while continuing to display Eugene code and results in a similar application to the first design on the multi-touch surface. Active tokens are programmable physical objects with integrated display, sensing, or actuation technologies that allow users to dynamically modify the tokens' associations with datasets or controls [23, 26]. We chose a tangible implementation because (1) by combining tangible active tokens with physical constraints, we attempt to provide users with persistent and integrated representations of data and with physical constraints to enforce interaction syntax (G1, G2), (2) exploring the use of active tokens on-bezel rather than on-surface allows us to design a multi-touch interface that is less cluttered and displays only essential information, and (3) tangible interaction also allows for multiple points of entry [16] (G3) as well as for direct interaction with representations through sensory and motor processes, which are important for learning [2, 7] (G4).

Our work expands on Tangible Query Interfaces (TQI) [21] and draws upon the Tangible Video Editor [26], which uses embedded active tokens in jigsaw-puzzle-inspired casings. Our design decisions were further informed by Valdes' et al. investigation of the design space of tangible interaction with active tokens combined with interactive surfaces [23]. For example, their findings indicate that users have strong preference for interacting with tangible active tokens atop a *horizontal* surface, leading us to reorient our interface horizontally. We also apply users' proposal to explore interaction *on-bezel* and *in-air* in order to free up important screen real estate. While our design implements elements that resemble tangible programming and was inspired by block-based languages, our focus is not on creating a single program; rather, we seek to allow the specification of a set of rules to query a large design space. We also incorporate dynamic bindings between active tokens and query parameters, which allows tokens to represent concrete or abstract biological parts. In the following section, we describe the interaction techniques that we developed.

Combining Active Tokens with Multi-touch Tabletop

The redesigned Eugenie application consists of a horizontal tabletop multi-touch application and a set of tangible tokens. We refer to this prototype as Eugenie++. Browsing the library of biological parts and specifying bio-design rules in Eugenie++ are performed on the tabletop bezel by creating physical configurations of tangible tokens. This allowed us to redesign the multi-touch application to include only two views: *rules* and *results*.

Eugenie++ provides two types of tangible tokens. *Active tokens*, implemented using Sifteo Cubes, represent generic or concrete biological parts that are dynamically associated by the user. The Sifteo Cubes' form factor is consistent with the synthetic biology metaphor of biological parts as building blocks. We encased each block in a cover that resembles a jigsaw puzzle piece, similar to those of the TVE [26]. The covers have connectors on the left and right, allowing pieces to interlock. Each case also has a socket on the top of the block, which is used to add operators. The active tokens can be manipulated through gestures (shake, flip), touch (swipe, click) and spatial interaction (neighbor, stack). *Passive tokens,* on the other hand, are statically bound. They represent various query operators including AND, OR, <, >, =, THEN, ALL, BEFORE, AFTER, NOT, NUMBER. These operators have sockets and plugs that indicate how they should (or should not) connect to the blocks. For example, an AND block (a binary operator) goes between two parts, while a NOT block (an unary operator) fits into the socket on top of a part. The passive tokens are shaped as symbols to indicate which operator they represent. We also use color-coding to indicate function (e.g. red for NOT).

Specifying Bio-Design Rules with Tangibles

Users specify *structure* rules by connecting active and passive tokens (G2). Users then "stamp" the physical structure within the *rules* view on the tabletop to embody the transferal of data from the pieces in the user's hand to the surface. Upon stamping, the physical representation of the rule is transformed into a digital representation in the form of a Eugene statement, which appears on the surface in the rules area. The rule is then applied to the design of the biological construct and holds unless the statement is removed from the code view. The REVERSE property is indicated by the orientation of the block. To specify behavioral rules (i.e. REPRESSES and INDUCES), users connect two parts, place them on the surface, and rotate the assembly counterclockwise or clockwise. We chose to use gestures to specify these rules, since they represent a continuous action.

Figure 2, Two users interact with Eugenie++, constructing bio-design rules using tangible tokens. Upon "stamping" a rule on the surface, a new Eugene statement is added to the *rules* panel.

Searching Hierarchical Database with Active Tokens
Active tokens can be used to search a hierarchical database: the MIT Registry of Biological Parts, which contains over 3000 parts (G1). To browse between items at the same level of the database hierarchy, users tilt the block, like manipulating a stream of menu items. Users then neighbor the tokens vertically to traverse the hierarchy. For example, when a token is neighbored below another token that displays the generic biological part "promoter", sub-categories that exist within the class "promoter" are displayed (see Figure 3). This interaction mirrors the tree-like structure of the database as the user traverses the levels.

Aggregating Representations
Users may collapse or expand biological parts displayed by different tokens into one biological construct by stacking: simpler constructs stacked atop more complex constructs collapses, while the opposite expands (see Figure 3).

Exploring the solution space
Solutions—permutations of biological constructs that satisfy the set of Eugene rules—are displayed on the surface using SBOL notation and can be manipulated through touch in the tabletop application.

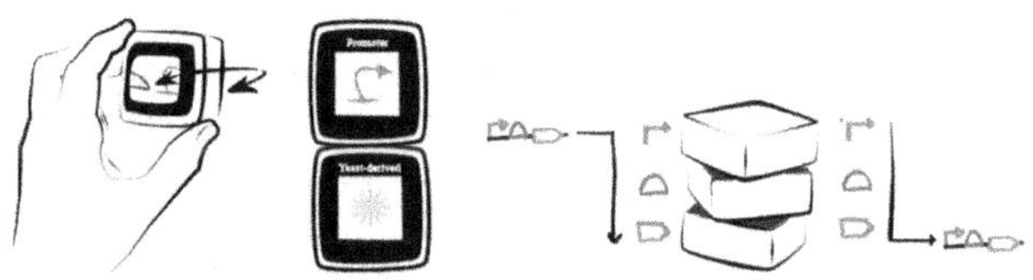

Figure 3, Illustrates tilting to search, neighboring for traversing the hierarchical database, and stacking to collapse and expand biological constructs.

Implementation
Eugenie++ uses Sifteo cubes ver. 2.0: 1.7-inch block micro-computers that interact with each other. We programmed the cubes using the Sifteo SDK and C++. The current prototype supports 8 Sifteo cubes. The tabletop application is implemented on a SUR40 device using the Microsoft Surface 2.0 SDK and written in C#. We detect the position and orientation of the Sifteo cubes and passive tokens on the tabletop using Byte Tags. We implemented Client-Server communication between the SUR40 and Sifteo applications using PyUSB, a Python module that supports USB access. Results are generated using the domain-specific programming language, Eugene [3].

Preliminary Evaluation
We conducted a qualitative study with 18 users (16 female, age 18-32) to evaluate the strengths and limitations of constructing rules and exploring a solution space using tangible interaction. One of the users is a primary investigator in the area of synthetic biology, three are iGEM students who did not participate in the previous study, 8 are undergraduate students majoring in life sciences, and 8 are undergraduates majoring in computer science. 12 of the users had some prior experience with the Eugene programming language.

Studies were conducted in the HCI Lab with users working in pairs (total of 9 dyads), sitting side by side at the tabletop surface. The study began with a warm up task that included an introduction to logic gates and required users to construct two different logical statements by combining active and passive tokens. Users were given all the physical tokens available and were asked to choose the pieces that made the most sense to them in order to build the logical construct. Following the completion of this task, users were given a brief oral and written introduction to synthetic biology, SBOL notation, the Eugene language, and the mapping between our physical tokens and Eugene. The study moderator also demonstrated how to use the physical active tokens in order to specify the design of a biological construct described in an SBOL diagram. As the experimental task, users were given two SBOL diagrams and were asked to construct the bio-design rules of the described biological constructs. Each design included between 5 and 10 biological parts and required specifying between 13 and 17 rules. This task mirrors a real-world iGEM task similar to the one used in the evaluation of our multi-touch Eugenie prototype.

Sessions were videotaped and notes were taken. Users were asked for their initial impressions following each of the two tasks and answered additional questions at the end.

Results
On average, dyads spent 36.5 minutes on the task (SD=9.3, MAX=50, MIN=23). All users were able to easily browse through a library of parts using the *tilt* gesture, and to find and select the parts that they needed. In general, users were able to figure out which operator tokens to use based on their physical form factor. Users easily identified the function of logical operators (e.g. AND, OR, <, >, =), but some found it difficult to identify the ALL and THEN operators. Groups that took longer spent more time discussing pieces and did not find some of the representations as obvious as others.

All dyads were able to specify the correct design rules for the biological devices, but in 6 cases, users attempted to use the tokens in ways different from the designed interaction syntax. For example, 4 users put the NOT operator on the side of the negated block rather than on the top, attempting to create a linear representation of the rule. 1 pair tried to rotate for REVERSE rather than turning the piece upside down, and 1 pair tried to use the = sign to specify THEN. However, in most cases (except the reverse), users were guided by the physical constraints to discover their misuses before they finalized the rule.

All pairs collaborated effectively with both members contributing physical and verbally to the task, using words, gestures, and pointing to express ideas. Users almost always designated a common space in which to place the rule in progress. 6 of the pairs lined pieces up in this common area, discussing the proposed formation before making the appropriate connections.

We also found evidence that users used the physical tokens to think. 4 pairs deliberately sorted pieces based on similar shape and moved the pieces they were using closer to them. Users also held or pointed to the piece they were considering. For example, when one user was talking about a gene that needed to be repressed, they made a counter-clockwise gesture with their hand, a gesture that mimics our representation of the REPRESS relationship.

The study drew our attention to several limitations: (1) *Limited interaction space* – While the physical tokens could be manipulated above the surface in-air, almost all users restricted their interactions to the bezel, which limited the extent to which users were able to explore the pieces. We suspect that the flat and puzzle-like form factor afforded manipulation on a flat horizontal surface rather than picking up the blocks; (2) *Rule Persistence* – While some users appreciated how the flexibility of active tokens "...allowed me to have more options with less blocks", in general, users had a hard time understanding the metaphor of "stamping" a rule on the surface. After stamping a rule, it is transferred to the surface and displayed as a Eugene statement in the rules view. The pieces can then be deconstructed and active tokens can be reused through dynamic binding. We observed that many users wanted each Sifteo cube to represent the same part for the entirety of the session. Users also left the constructed rules on the surface for later reference. Users were more likely to point to the physical structure rather than the code representation on the surface. We think that providing users with a *visual* rule representation on the surface, rather than just code could bridge the gap between the physical and digital representations, thereby helping users view stamped rules as persistent; (3) *User expectations* – While the use of physical constraints helped users to figure out syntax, user's expectations sometimes restricted their exploration of the pieces. Many users expected a more direct mapping between the physical syntax and natural (or programming) language. For example, we provide a "then" token that takes two arguments and represents "a→b". While users could easily identify the token, they also looked for an "if" piece even though it is not necessary syntactically. Several users also attempted to arrange the tokens linearly and read the rule from left to right like a sentence.

DISCUSSION

In this paper, we describe the design, development, and evaluation of two different implementations of Eugenie, a system for supporting novices in the bio-design process. While both implementations have limitations, they demonstrate the challenges and opportunities of applying TEI approaches to the exploration of large data sets through the construction of complex queries.

Some of the *challenges* highlighted by these case studies include: (1) Providing users with *rich representations* that integrate multiple facets of information (e.g. properties, structure, behavior) and are easy to manipulate. We found that in multi-touch interaction, visual clutter, target size, and occlusion could limit the effectiveness of visual representations; (2) *Closing the gap between tangible and digital representations*. We found that transforming tangible representations to digital requires visual representations that can be easily mapped back to its tangible counterpart, in order to reinforce persistent and continuous representation; (3) Supporting *aggregation* of complex configurations of digital and tangible representations into simpler representations. We learned that users want to combine complex structures representing a set of rules into a single reusable representation.

These case studies also highlight *opportunities* for TEI manipulation of large datasets: (1) *Achieving scalability* through the use of *active tokens* and *dynamic binding*. One of the core limitations of tangible user interfaces is scalability [16]. Providing tangible representations for large data sets can require a large number of tangibles that take up space and are difficult to manage. However, our tangible implementation of Eugene demonstrates that, by using active tangible tokens that can be dynamically associated by users, we can enable users to search and select subsets from a large data set (in our case, a data set of more than 3000 biological parts) with a compact set of tangibles; (2) *Utilizing new interaction spaces*. The tangible implementation of Eugenie supports interaction *on*, *in-front-of*, and *next-to* an interactive surface, by utilizing the surface bezel. In addition, active tokens can be manipulated independently of physical constraints through gestures. Designing for interactions beyond the surface helped to overcome challenges common to data-intense applications (e.g. finger size, occlusion, and visual clutter). In our study, we found that the interaction space on the bezel was too small (4 in.) to encourage exploration; this suggests a need to further consider how best to utilize the space *in-front-of* and *next-to* the surface; (3) *Enforcing interaction syntax with physical syntax*. Constructing complex queries often requires abiding to strict syntax. Physical constraints afford certain actions while preventing (or increasing the threshold for) others. We observed that, when using the tangible implementation of Eugenie, physical constraints allowed users to determine syntactic rules as well as correct errors; (4) *Thinking through action*. The Eugenie tangible user interface allows users to apply various strategies for reducing cognitive workload. For example, we observed that users sorted and arranged the tangibles around the surface, gestured with and pointed to the tangibles, and attempted various spatial configurations; and (5) Supporting *effective collaboration*. Both case studies support co-located collaboration. The multi-touch implementation provides multiple access points through parallel workspaces, allowing users to reinforce their territory or share a particular workspace. The tangible implementation provides multiple access points through the physical tokens. Both interfaces enable users to divide the problem spatially and temporally so that users can assume different roles or work together.

CONCLUSION AND FUTURE WORK

In this paper, we presented four main contributions: (1) lessons from the iterative design, implementation, and evaluation of a multi-touch and tangible interface for querying large data sets; (2) new tangible and scalable interaction techniques for using active tokens to navigate large hierarchical data sets; (3) a tangible interaction language for forming complex queries; and (4) a discussion of challenges and opportunities for applying TEI approaches to the exploration of large data sets.

Future work will include design iterations of Eugenie++ and comparative studies with isomorphs of Eugenie. We also intend to deploy and study Eugenie++ in an introductory synthetic biology course.

ACKNOWLEDGMENTS

We thank Traci Haddock, Swapnil Bhatia, Ernst Oberortner, Douglas Densmore, and the BU iGEM team. We also thank the undergraduate students that contributed to this work: Consuelo Valdes, Tiffany Chen, Catherine Guo, and Sravanti Tekumalla.

REFERENCES

1. (n.d.). Retrieved from Sifteo: https://www.sifteo.com/
2. Antle, A. N., & Wise, A. F. (2013). Getting down to details: Using theories of cognition and learning to inform tangible user interface design. Interacting with Computers, 25(1).
3. Bilitchenko L, Liu A, Cheung S, Weeding E, Xia B, Leguia M, Densmore D (2011). Eugene—a domain specific language for specifying and constraining synthetic biological parts, devices, and systems. PLoS One 6(4).
4. Block, F., Horn, M. S., Phillips, B. C., et. al. (2012). The DeepTree Exhibit: Visualizing the tree of life to facilitate informal learning.Visualization and Computer Graphics, IEEE, 18(12).
5. Camarata, K., Do, E. Y. L., Johnson, B. R., & Gross, M. D. (2002). Navigational blocks: navigating information space with tangible media. In Proc. of IUI, ACM.
6. Drucker, S., Fisher, D., Sadana, R., Herron, J., & Schraefel, M. C. (2013). TouchVix: A Case Study Comparing Two Interfaces for Data Analytics on Tablets. In Proc. of CHI, ACM.
7. Glenberg AM (2008) Embodiment for education. In: Calvo P, Gomila T (ed) Handbook of cognitive science: an embodied approach, pp 355–372
8. Hornecker, E., Marshall, P., Dalton, N. S., & Rogers, Y. (2008). Collaboration and interference: awareness with mice or touch input. In Proc. of CSCW, ACM.
9. Isenberg, P., Isenberg, T., Hesselmann, T., Lee, B., Von Zadow, U., & Tang, A. (2013). Data visualization on interactive surfaces: A research agenda. Computer Graphics and Applications, IEEE, 33(2), 16-24.
10. Jetter, H. C., Gerken, J., Zöllner, M., Reiterer, H., & Milic-Frayling, N. (2011). Materializing the query with facet-streams: a hybrid surface for collaborative search on tabletops. In Proc. Of CHI, ACM.
11. Klum, S., Isenberg, P., Langner, R., Fekete, J. D., & Dachselt, R. (2012). Stackables: combining tangibles for faceted browsing. In Proc. of AVI. ACM.
12. Morris, M. R., Brush, A. B., & Meyers, B. R. (2007). Reading revisited: Evaluating the usability of digital display surfaces for active reading tasks. In Proc. of ITS, IEEE.
13. Morris, M. R., Fisher, D., & Wigdor, D. (2010). Search on surfaces: Exploring the potential of interactive tabletops for collaborative search tasks. Information processing & management, 46(6), 703-717.
14. Patten, J., & Ishii, H. (2000). A comparison of spatial organization strategies in graphical and tangible user interfaces. In Proc. of DARE, ACM.
15. Rekimoto, J., Ullmer, B., & Oba, H. (2001). DataTiles: a modular platform for mixed physical and graphical interactions. In Proc. of CHI, ACM.
16. Shaer, O., & Hornecker, E. (2010). Tangible user interfaces: past, present, and future directions. Foundations and Trends in HCI, 3(1–2).
17. Shaer, O., Mazalek, A., Ullmer, B., & Konkel, M. (2013). From Big Data to Insights: Opportunities and Challenges for TEI in Genomics. In Proc. of TEI. ACM.
18. Shaer, O., Strait, M., Valdes, C., Wang, H., Feng, T., Lintz, M., ... & Liu, S. (2012). The design, development, and deployment of a tabletop interface for collaborative exploration of genomic data. International Journal of Human-Computer Studies, 70(10), 746-764.
19. Synthetic Biology Open Language (2011) Retrieved from http:// www.sbolstandard.org/
20. Thudt, A., Hinrichs, U., & Carpendale, S. (2012). The bohemian bookshelf: supporting serendipitous book discoveries through information visualization. In Proc. of CHI, ACM.
21. Ullmer, B., Ishii, H., & Jacob, R. J. (2003). Tangible query interfaces: Physically constrained tokens for manipulating database queries. In Proc. of Interact.
22. Valdes, C., Ferreirae, M … & Shaer, O. (2012). A Collaborative Environment for Engaging Novices in Scientific Inquiry , In Proc. ITS 2012, ACM.
23. Valdes, C., Eastman, D., Grote, … & Konkel. M. (2014). Exploring the Design Space of Gestural Interaction with Active Tokens through User-Defined Gestures. In Proc. of CHI 2014, ACM.
24. Voida, S., Tobiasz, M., Stromer, J., Isenberg, P., & Carpendale, S. (2009). Getting practical with interactive tabletop displays: designing for dense data, fat fingers, diverse interactions, and face-to-face collaboration. In Proc. of the ITS, ACM.
25. Xu, W., Chang, K., Francisco, N., Valdes, C., Kincaid, R., & Shaer, O. (2013). From wet lab bench to tangible virtual experiment: SynFlo. In Proc. of TEI. ACM.
26. Zigelbaum, J., Horn, M. S., Shaer, O., & Jacob, R. J. (2007). The tangible video editor: collaborative video editing with active tokens. In Proc. of TEI, ACM.

Immersive Simulation of Visual Impairments Using a Wearable See-through Display

Halim Çağrı Ateş cagri@cse.unr.edu

Alexander Fiannaca fiannaca@cse.unr.edu

Eelke Folmer efolmer@cse.unr.edu

Computer Science - University of Nevada

ABSTRACT
Simulation of a visual impairment may lead to a better understanding of how individuals with visual impairments perceive the world around them and could be a useful design tool for interface designers to identify accessibility barriers. Current simulation tools, however, suffer from a number of limitations, pertaining cost, accuracy and immersion. We present a simulation tool (SIMVIZ) that mounts a wide angle camera on a head-mounted display to create a see-through stereoscopic display that simulates various types and levels of visual impairments. A qualitative user study evaluates the immersiveness, usability and effectiveness of SIMVIZ versus using a smartphone based simulator. SIMVIZ enables quick accessibility inspections during iterative software development.

Author Keywords
Design Tools; Accessibility Testing; Visual Impairment; Augmented Reality; Wearable Computing; Oculus Rift

ACM Classification Keywords
H.5.1 Multimedia Information Systems: Augmented Reality

INTRODUCTION
The number of people who will be living with a visual impairment is anticipated to significantly increase over the next decade. An aging baby boomer generation is one of the main drivers of this anticipated increase, but another cause is the current obesity epidemic, as obese individuals are twice as likely to lose their sight due to cataracts or diabetic retinopathy [15]. In the US, macular degeneration, cataracts, diabetic retinopathy and glaucoma are the most prevalent eye diseases [6], which affect approximately 20 million people. There are a wide range of visual impairments, each which affect remaining vision to different extents. For example, macular degeneration typically blurs central vision and does not affect peripheral vision, where retinopathy and glaucoma reduce or blur peripheral vision but central vision remains unaffected. Such differences pose a significant challenge for interface designers when testing for accessibility, i.e., assuring that a software product or website is accessible to users with disabilities, because different visual impairments may lead to different types of accessibility problems.

ACM 978-1-4503-3305-4/15/01 ...$15.00.
http://dx.doi.org/10.1145/2677199.2680331

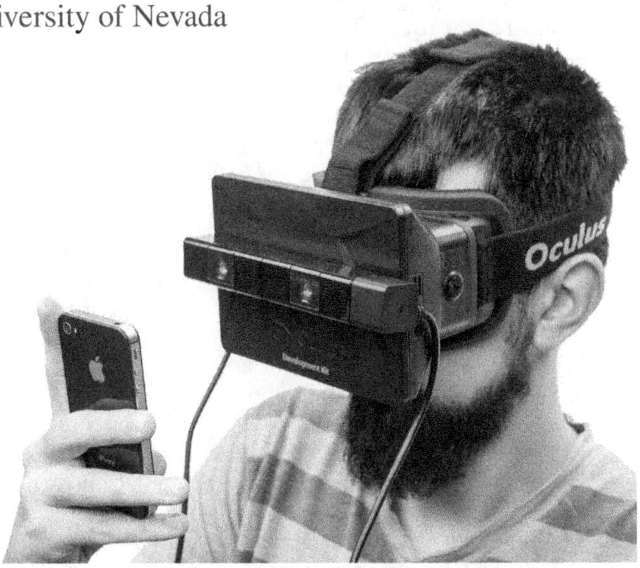

Figure 1. Accessibility inspection of a smartphone app using SIMVIZ. Our display features twin wide angle cameras mounted on a head mounted display. Designers can cycle through different types of visual impairments to quickly identify potential accessibility barriers.

Various techniques such as user studies, design guidelines, expert reviews, or automated test tools can be used for detecting accessibility problems (see [19] for a comparative analysis); however, each presents limitations in one manner or another. User studies can be time consuming and costly to perform in addition to the fact that it is difficult to recruit enough subjects to cover every type of visual impairment. User studies also tend to happen towards the end of the development cycle when it is often prohibitively expensive to fix major accessibility problems [19]. Guidelines and automated test tools require expertise on behalf of developers to be used and do not detect all accessibility problems [23]. Expert reviews are most effective for uncovering accessibility problems [19]. Test tools can be valuable for experts as well as inexperienced designers, but there is a lack of: (1) lightweight evaluation tools that support iterative design [19] and (2) tools that can visualize the experience of users with a disability [23].

In recent years, there has been increasing interest in developing visual impairment simulators in an attempt to address these limitations, This paper presents a low-cost simulation tool (SIMVIZ) built using recent advances in head mounted display (HMD) technology (Oculus Rift). SIMVIZ uses stereoscopic vision to allow for simulating visual impairments with a high degree of immersion and by using a see-through display SIMVIZ takes into account where the user is looking at. SIMVIZ addresses the need for more usable accessibility design tools [19, 23] by enabling quick accessibility inspections during iterative design.

RELATED WORK

Various simulation kits are commercially available [13, 3]. These kits typically include goggles, lenses and funnels, which –when combined– can simulate different visual impairments. Several studies have evaluated the feasibility and effectiveness of simulation goggles as an alternative to performing user studies with users who are visually impaired [24, 14]. A benefit of goggles is that they are low cost, and as they cover most of the user's field of view, they closely mimic how a visually impaired person actually sees the world. A drawback is that goggles generally allow for simulating only a few of the most common visual impairments. For quick evaluations, switching between or adjusting the level of a simulated impairment is cumbersome due to having to disassemble the goggles to switch lenses and funnels.

Various software based visual impairments simulators have been developed that can be used to provide early feedback on the accessibility of software or websites. The Evaluating Accessibility through Simulation of User Experience (EASE) tool [19] can simulate both motor and visual impairments at the OS level. This simulator supports blurring and occluding part of the screen and simulating red-green color blindness. Goodman-Deane et al. [16] presents a Windows based desktop simulator that simulates various visual impairments (cataracts, macular degeneration etc) on a loaded image. A similar simulator is available on the web [11]. NoCoffee is a plugin for the Chrome browser that simulate various impairments that are superimposed on a webpage [5]. VisionSim developed by the Braille Institute [1] is a smartphone app that simulates various types of visual impairments using filters superimposed on a video stream from the smartphone's camera. Software simulators offer larger flexibility than goggles, allowing designers to quickly cycle through various impairments and adjust the level of impairment; however, most simulators are confined to a screen. Although VisionSim [1] offers see-through functionality, it doesn't offer stereoscopic vision. Simulators further do not model where the user is looking at, but assume the user looks at the center of the screen, which may not allow for accurately identifying all possible accessibility problems.

Highly immersive, realistic stereoscopic simulations of visual impairments are possible using virtual reality (VR) environments. Maxhall et al. created a stroke simulator [20] using a HMD (640x480, 60° FOV). The user wears accelerometers to track the orientation of the hands, head and body. Users navigate a 3D model of a domestic environment by turning the wheels of a wheelchair that they are seated in. A visual impairment resulting from a stroke is modeled as a motion blur on the left side of the display. User studies found this to be an effective tool to raise empathy among caregivers. Jin et al. [17] uses a drafting table format VR display to simulate visual impairments for a virtual non-photorealistic indoor environment. This simulator simulates glaucoma, macular degeneration, and double vision. This display is at a 45° angle with users wearing shutter glasses to see stereoscopic head tracked images. By standing close to the 1024x768 display users experience a 110° horizontal FOV. This VR system is non-portable and very expensive. Lewis et al. [18] lets users navigate a photo realistic 3D model of a restaurant on a university campus. Most common visual impairments are simulated and a user study investigates performing tasks related to navigation and reading signs. Results showed an increased awareness and understanding of how it is to live with a visual impairment; however, this approach does not support stereoscopic vision and is therefore less immersive than a VR environment. Closely related to SIMVIZ is the work by Subramaniam et al. [22] which uses a see-through display using an HMD to simulate retinal prosthetic vision. Prosthetic vision is subject to various distortions, due to different prosthesis placements. A Point Grey Research Firefly webcam (480x752) is mounted on top of a Z800 3D Visor HMD (800x600, 40° FOV per eye). Because the display capabilities of current prosthesis are limited, this approach renders low resolution (60x60) (black/white) images and transformations are applied to simulate different distortions.

DESIGN OF SIMVIZ

To address the need for more usable design tools [19, 23], we developed a novel simulator platform that offers the flexibility of a software simulator, the immersion and stereoscopic vision of a VR environment, and the ability to perform real-world accessibility inspections by not being tied to a desktop of simulation goggles. SIMVIZ is an augmented reality see-through display that is created by mounting a wide angle camera on a HMD and feeding the camera feed into the HMD (see Figure 1). Filters are applied to the video stream to simulate different visual impairments. Our setup is related to [22], but because we aim to accurately simulate different visual impairment our setup is different in display resolution, camera and the application of different filters.

VR display. For our display, we used the popular Oculus Rift HMD. The Rift uses a 7" LCD display and offers a resolution of 640x800 per eye at 60Hz. The image for each eye is rendered in the panel as a barrel distorted image that is then corrected by the pincushion effect created by lenses in the headset, generating a spherical-mapped image for each eye. The distance of the lenses to the eye can be manually adjusted. Additional interchangeable lenses for dioptric correction are provided. A distinguishing feature of the Oculus Rift is its large 110° diagonal and 90° horizontal FOV which fills the users entire field of vision and creates a strong sense of immersion. The stereoscopic vision is not a 100% overlapping, which mimics human vision and makes its horizontal resolution larger than 640 pixels. Drift-less head tracking is implemented using 3-axis gyros, accelerometers, and magnetometers. The HMD weighs 379 grams.

Camera. To create a realistic see-through display, a camera was required that matched the resolution (1280x800), refresh rate (60Hz) and FOV (110°) of the Oculus Rift. We used a PlayStation 4 Camera; a motion sensing accessory which features two wide-angle cameras with an 85° FOV and which can stream two 1280x800 feeds at 60 fps. This sensor uses a USB 3.0 cable with a proprietary AUX connector, however we were able to splice a standard USB 3.0 connector to the cable. Using an adhesive the camera was attached to the front of the Oculus Rift (see Fig 1). Because it only weights 183 grams our setup does not strain the user's neck.

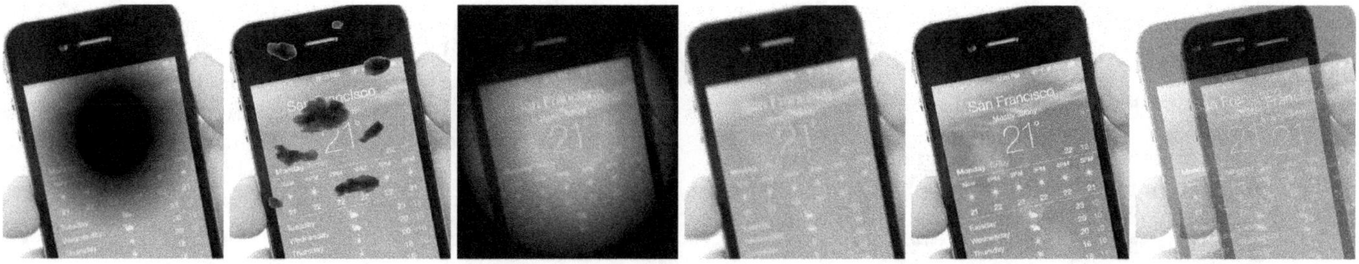

Figure 2. Visual impairments implemented in our simulator: (a) Macular Degeneration; (b) Diabetic Retinopathy; (c) Glaucoma; (d) Cataracts; (e) Color blindness (protanopia); (f) Diplopia. Filters applied to a still image in VR Player for illustration purposes.

Software. To render our video stream into the Oculus Rift we used VR Player [10], an open source VR media player which can render stereoscopic video files. VR Player is available on Windows and supports various projections and distortions, including the barrel distortion needed for the Oculus Rift. VR Player is able to play video streams using the VideoLan VLC media player plugin. VR Player supports various effects that can be defined using the High-level shading language (HLSL). We connected the Oculus Rift and PS4 camera to a high-end Desktop PC (Intel Core i7/ GeForce GTX 660) with a USB 3.0 port. We acquire a 1280x800 stream from each camera in the sensor and use VLC to combine this into a single 1280x800 MPEG stream with a fixed horizontal offset between both streams to represent the distance between lenses. We used an open source shader editor called Shazzam to create HLSL shaders to simulate different visual impairments. Though some filters, such as blurring are considered somewhat computationally intensive, we did not observe any significant latency. The user can cycle through shaders and adjust the level of their intensity using a keyboard shortcut.

Visual Impairment Simulations

Based on example photos provided by the National Eye Institute [8], we implemented the following filters (see Fig 2).

- **Macular degeneration:** this disease causes damage to the macula, which is needed for sharp, central vision. We apply a Gaussian blur and mix the pixels with black depending on their distance from the center.
- **Diabetic retinopathy:** this eye disease is caused by diabetes and changes the blood vessels of the retina. Symptoms include dark spots, blurring, and glare sensitivity. For this filter we superimpose a texture with black areas.
- **Glaucoma:** damage to the optic nerve which causes blurred peripheral vision. For this filter we apply a gaussian blur and mix each pixel with black depending their distance from the center.
- **Cataracts:** aging causes a clouding of the lens and symptoms include blurred vision. A Gaussian blur is used to simulate this condition.
- **Color blindness:** a deficiency in the development of retinal cones. A reduced sensitivity to particular colors makes it hard to distinguish between pairs of colors, e.g., red/green. For this filter, an RGB transformation is applied.
- **Diplopia:** a malfunction of extraocular muscles where both eyes cannot converge to target the desired object. Symptoms include double vision. Diplopia is simulated by rendering the same image using a small horizontal offset.

EVALUATION

A number of studies have previously assessed the feasibility and effectiveness of a simulation tool to detect accessibility problems [19, 24] or for raising awareness about living with a visual impairment [18, 20]. Evaluating whether our tool accurately simulates a visual impairment is challenging because visual impairments are subject to a large amount of inter-individual variation. Because of these constraints, our evaluation focuses on evaluating the immersion, ease of use and effectiveness of our tool versus using a smartphone based software simulator, i.e., VisionSim [1]. This evaluation is similar to [18]. We recruited 12 computer science students (2 female, average age 27.2, SD = 4.4). Subjects were divided into two groups, with the first group trying VisionSim on an iPhone 4S and the second group using SIMVIZ. After each trial each group switched to exploring using the other tool. Subjects explored three different simulations (macular degeneration, glaucoma, diabetic retinopathy and color blindness) and we explained some of accessibility barriers (small fonts, low contrast) that users with visual impairments may encounter. Subjects were encouraged to look at an email program on a 27" screen as well as an Ishihara test plate (red number on green background). Each tool was evaluated using a questionnaire with questions to assess immersion, ease of use and potential for detecting accessibility problems using a 5-point Likert scale that ranged from 1 (strongly disagree) to 5 (strongly agree). The difference in immersion, e.g., $4.67(SD = .49)$ for SIMVIZ versus $2.92(SD = 1.08)$ for VisionSim was found to be significant ($t_{22} = 2.21, p < .05$). The difference in ease of use, e.g., 4.00 ($SD = .95$) versus 4.50 ($SD = .90$) for VisionSim was not found to be significant ($t_{22} = 1.32$, $p = .20$). The difference in potential for detecting accessibility problems, e.g., $4.50(SD = .67)$ versus $3.50(SD = .52)$ for VisionSim was significant ($t_{22} = 4.08, p < .05$).

DISCUSSION

A general limitation of simulators is that they are unable to exactly model a person's visual impairment but only offer an approximation [3]. Though the correctness of certain visual impairment simulations like colorblindness can be easily verified using an Ishihara test plate, other types of visual impairments, such a diabetic retinopathy are subject to large amounts of inter-individual variation. A visually impaired user can provide a verbal description of their specific visual impairment but they may be unable to verify the correctness of the filter as they may not be able to use the HMD.

Most simulation tools therefore implement their filters based on sample images provided by the National Eye Institute [8].

With regard to usability donning our HMD may be slightly harder than using a smartphone, but the use of stereoscopy and modeling where the user is looking allows for creating more immersive simulations and may help detect accessibility problems more effectively as we verified using our qualitative study. Another benefit of SIMVIZ is that it can be used handsfree. Though visual impairments vary between individuals, the ability to adjust the intensity provides a range of impressions for that impairment.

A limitation of our tool is that the current resolution of the Oculus Rift is too low to allow for accurately being able to read text on a mobile phone with a high resolution display (text appears pixelated). This limits the usefulness of our tool as an accessibility design tool. However, recently several High Definition (HD) HMDs [4, 9] were announced that offer significantly higher display resolutions (2560 x 1440) than the Oculus Rift, and which we plan to explore in future work. Our tool improves over current software simulators as it uses a see-through display that takes into account where the user is looking at. A more accurate simulator would also track the position of the user's eyes. Current HMDs do not allow for eye-tracking because the lenses of the HMD are close to the eyes, which doesn't leave enough space to position a camera based eye-tracker.

FUTURE WORK

In addition to exploring a higher resolution HMD, we plan to investigate the following issues:

Cost. Recently approaches have been presented that appropriate a smartphone using low cost materials [2] into an HMD. This platform could offer a number of benefits in terms of lower cost and mobility over commercially available HMDs which are tethered. A limitation of this approach is that most smartphones only have a single front facing camera thus making it impossible to use stereoscopic vision.

Persuasive Technology. The current obesity epidemic is anticipated to significantly increase the number of users with visual impairments. Because obesity is considered a preventable disease [12], simulation of eye diseases caused by obesity, such as diabetic retinopathy using SIMVIZ could be used to stimulate behavioral change in obese individuals.

Magnification. Visually impaired individuals often rely on magnification software. For reading text with varying font sizes, users often lean towards the screen as this is faster than having to magnify the screen and reacquiring the location of the text they wanted to read. Leaning in is straining for the neck and back and limits how long users with visual impairments can use a computer. We plan to explore using an HMD as a monitor and which would allow visually impaired users to use head tracking to select the focus area of the magnification, without having to lean in.

Complex impairments. We plan to develop filters for dynamic visual impairments, such as, floaters, i.e., specks that float in the user's FOV as well as cortical visual impairments, i.e, visual impairments that are caused by a brain problem with symptoms that include highly variable vision. Such types of visual impairments are difficult to simulate using goggles or software simulators but could be easily simulated using our approach. Of educational interest could be to simulate how animals like a dog (limited color perception) or an eagle (20/5 vision and a 300°FOV) perceive the world.

REFERENCES

1. The braille institute: VisionSim, http://www.brailleinstitute.org/digital/mobile-applications.html.
2. Cardboard, Google Inc. http://g.co/cardboard.
3. Fork in the road vision rehabilitation services, http://www.lowvisionsimulators.com.
4. GameFace 2.5K HMD, http://gamefacelabs.com.
5. No Coffee vision simulator https://chrome.google.com/webstore/detail/nocoffee/jjeeggmbnhckmgdhmgdckeigabjfbddl?hl=en-US
6. Prevent blindness America, prevalence of adult vision impairment and age-related eye disease in america, http://www.visionproblemsus.org.
7. PS4 camera tools, https://github.com/ps4eye/ps4eye.
8. National Eye Institute: Eye Health Information, https://www.nei.nih.gov/health.
9. Oculus Rift DK2, http://www.oculusvr.com/dk2.
10. VR player, http://vrplayer.codeplex.com.
11. Web based vision simulator, http://visionsimulations.com.
12. World Health Organization: Obesity and overweight fact sheet, www.who.int/mediacentre/factsheets/fs311/en.
13. Zimmerman low vision simulation kit, http://www.lowvisionsimulationkit.com.
14. Aballéa, S., and Tsuchiya, A. Seeing for yourself: feasibility study towards valuing visual impairment using simulation spectacles. *Health economics 16*, 5 (2007), 537–543.
15. Cheung, N., and Wong, T. Y. Obesity and eye diseases. *Surv Ophthalmol 52*, 2 (2007), 180–195.
16. Goodman-Deane, J., Langdon, P. M., Clarkson, P. J., Caldwell, N. H., and Sarhan, A. M. Equipping designers by simulating the effects of visual and hearing impairments. In *Proc. of ASSETS'07*, 241–242.
17. Jin, B., Ai, Z., and Rasmussen, M. Simulation of eye disease in virtual reality. In *Proc. of EMBS'05*, 5128–5131.
18. Lewis, J., Brown, D., Cranton, W., and Mason, R. Simulating visual impairments using the unreal engine 3 game engine. In *Proc of SeGAH'11*, 201, 1–8.
19. Mankoff, J., Fait, H., and Juang, R. Evaluating accessibility by simulating the experiences of users with vision or motor impairments. *IBM Syst. J. 44:3*, 2005, 505–517.
20. Maxhall, M., Backman, A., Holmlund, K., Hedman, L., Sondell, B., and Bucht, G. Participants responses to a stroke training simulator. In *Proc. of ICDVRAT'04*, 225–230.
21. Morris, O. F. Simulation of visual impairments as a training technique. *New Outlook for the Blind 70*, 10 (1976), 417–9.
22. Subramaniam, M., Chundi, P., Muthuraj, A., Margalit, E., and Sim, S. Simulating prosthetic vision with disortions for retinal prosthesis design. In *Proc. of SHB '12*, 57–64.
23. Trewin, S., Cragun, B., Swart, C., Brezin, J., and Richards, J. Accessibility challenges and tool features: An IBM web developer perspective. In *Proc. of W4A '10*, 32:1–32:10.
24. Wood, J. M., and Troutbeck, R. Elderly drivers and simulated visual impairment. *Optometry & Vision Science 72*, 2 (1995), 115–124.

TastyBeats: Celebrating Heart Rate Data with a Drinkable Spectacle

Rohit Ashok Khot, Jeewon Lee, Larissa Hjorth, Florian 'Floyd' Mueller
Exertion Games Lab, RMIT University, Australia
{rohit, jeewon, larissa, floyd}@exertiongameslab.org

ABSTRACT

Visualizing heart rate on screen has become popular to measure physical activity performance and progress towards set health goals. However, we believe that this prevalent method of visualizing data often reduces the interaction to only reading of information. In response, we propose a new way of visualizing heart rate data through a public interactive water fountain installation we call, TastyBeats. TastyBeats engages participants in a fluidic spectacle by creating a personalized sports drink representing their heart rate data while serving the additional purpose of replenishing lost energy during physical activity. We present findings and three design strategies from the three exhibitions of this work to inform designers interested in using drinkable fluids to support the physical activity experience. Ultimately, with our work we aim to expand our understanding of the potential of interactive technology to support the energy-cycle when being physically active.

Author Keywords

Physical activity; biofeedback; fluidic interfaces.

ACM Classification Keywords

H.5.m. Information interfaces and presentation (e.g., HCI): Miscellaneous.

INTRODUCTION

Heart rate monitors are gaining popularity to monitor and support physical activity experiences [2]. By visualizing heart rate, individuals can gain better insights into their physical activity levels and make this gained knowledge actionable in terms of their health and performance related aims [19]. Currently, the most common way of representing heart rate data is on a smartphone screen or wristwatch in a numerical or graphical form. However, this predominant method of visualization often reduces the interaction to reading of information in order to make personally relevant inferences.

This work expands the view of visualizing physical activity beyond the screen by providing a fluidic representation that can also be consumed later; thereby, serving an additional purpose of replenishing lost energy during physical activity. We designed *TastyBeats* to induce an active engagement of the user with a fluidic representation of personal heart rate data in the form of a sports drink created by mixing different flavors together. Furthermore, rather than simply adding different flavors together based upon one's efforts, we explore an opportunity to create a fluidic spectacle that celebrates the experience of being physically active. Such a public rendering of heart rate data can not only be widely seen and interacted with, but can also be tasted; thus offering vivid ways of engaging with the data. We showcased our system at three international academic events where over 400 participants interacted with the system and shared their experience with us through follow-up discussions. This paper describes our system along with our findings from the public demonstrations. Later, we present three design strategies to inspire and guide designers to utilize fluidic forms of interactions to support the experience of being physically active.

RELATED WORK

Our work is concerned with the fluidic representations of heart rate data of physical activity. Therefore, we present the related work in two categories. First, we discuss the existing works concerning the representations of heart rate data. Secondly, we discuss fluidic interfaces as a representation medium.

Related work on representing heart rate data

Previously, heart rate has been used for several purposes. For instance, Nacke et al. [13] captured player's emotions through heart rate to adjust game interactions, while Nenonen et al. [14] used heart rate as a game input. Furthermore, Walmink et al. [23] and Curmi et al. [3] facilitated social experience through public display of heart rate data on cycle helmets and social networks respectively. Lately, Khot et al. [10] studied individual's relationship with physical activity through 3D printed physical artifacts created from their heart rate data. These works inspired us to explore public representations of heart rate data through other physical mediums such as fluids.

Related work on fluidic interfaces

The most popular example of a fluidic interface as a public spectacle is a choreographed musical water fountain, the Fountains of Bellagio [8]. Similarly, Currency fountain [4] shows relative currency rates using water fountain display.

In HCI, fluidic interfaces have been proposed to support tangible interactions with water: Wantabe [24] and Mine et

ACM 978-1-4503-3305-4/15/01...$15.00.
http://dx.doi.org/10.1145/2677199.2680545

al. [12] used fluidic interface for browsing and mixing of multimedia files respectively. In other works, Richter et al. [18] designed water jets for tactile feedback on virtual touchscreen elements, while Sylvester et al. [22] created a Soap Bubble Interface to control sounds and room light. Fluidic interfaces can also offer interactive play experiences through manipulation of water flow within a receptacle [9]. Additionally, Steve Mann designed various fluidic musical instruments such as Water Hammer piano [11] for interactive entertainment. Student Innovation Contest at UIST 2013 [6] also featured various fluidic interaction possibilities developed using PumpSpark water fountain kit.

These works illustrate the potential of fluidic interfaces in representing information and creating engaging experiences. However, there has not been much exploration on drinkable fluid interfaces except a system by Daisuke [5] that creates a drink from the backend web processing data. We believe that such fluid interfaces have the potential to facilitate the recovery of body fluids lost during the physical activity. Addressing this, we present a drinkable fluid interface, *TastyBeats,* as a representation of one's physical activity data.

TASTYBEATS

TastyBeats is an exploration into drinkable fluidic representation of physical activity. TastyBeats creates a personalized sports drink using the measured heart rate data of individuals during their physical activity session. With *TastyBeats* we also focus on creating a spectacle by using a familiar water fountain-based interaction to celebrate the experience of being physically active. Additionally, since heart rate vary over time and are different for different individuals [2], flavor of the created drink will be distinctly personalized and will vary with different activities.

In our system, we have divided heart rate data into four zones with the following ranges: 60-95 beats per minute (bpm), 96-130 bpm, 131-165 bpm, and 166-190 bpm, where each zone denotes the intensity levels of physical activity. Heart rate values below 60 bpm and higher than 190 bpm are discarded as they occur rarely. Earlier research suggests that color plays a crucial role in users' perception of fluids [15]. We, therefore, chose four flavors with distinct colors to highlight different zones. Figure 1 illustrates the mapping between heart rate zones and corresponding flavored sports drinks.

As an initial exploration, we have focused on short physical activity sessions, lesser than 90 minutes. Since such sessions do not require electrolyte or other supplements [20], our current system utilizes only flavored water with zero calorie content. In the future, we envision the use of specific supplements for intense physical activity sessions.

TastyBeats setup includes four containers containing flavored water along with a food-graded water pump [7] and a central glass as shown in Figure 1. These pumps shoot water into the central glass where the different flavors get mixed and are controlled by Arduino [1].

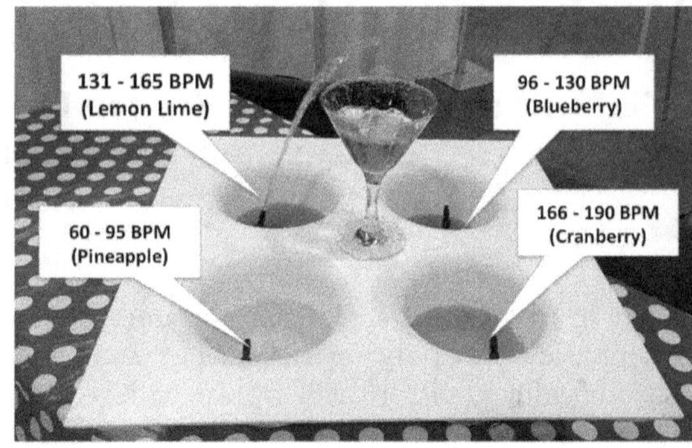

Figure 1: TastyBeats utilizes heart rate data to create a personalized drink.

We have used Pulse sensor amped [15], an Arduino compatible heart rate sensor, to record the heart rate data of an individual. The user holds this sensor between her fingers, while performing a physical activity and her heart rate data is sent to the system. Based upon the recorded value, the system identifies its corresponding heart rate zone and initiates the water pumps accordingly. Water from the corresponding container is pumped into the central glass for about 3 seconds. As long as the heart rate value stays in the same zone, pumping from that container happens only once. And when the zone shifts, water from the corresponding zone container gets pumped into the central glass (Figure 1). Thus, rapid transitions will add more flavors to the drink. This interaction continues until the central glass is filled. The user can then enjoy the drink representing their physical activity.

LEARNINGS FROM PUBLIC DEMONSTRATIONS

TastyBeats was exhibited in three different international academic exhibition events that cater to large audiences. In total, more than 400 participants directly interacted with our system, while the others around cheered up the participants. Figure 2 shows an example of *TastyBeats* being exhibited.

Figure 2: Participants were thrilled to see how their heart rate data obtained a fluidic form in the early version of *TastyBeats*.

Participants were from a diverse background of academics and professionals from engineering and HCI backgrounds. Their age varied from 18-60 years. Participants shared their experience through verbal conversations, while interacting with our system. We also had a brief discussion with about 70 participants afterwards to understand the potential of how our system could integrate into their day-to-day activity. We describe below the insights gained from observations and conversations with participants.

The overall response from the participants was positive and encouraging. Participants appreciated the novelty and playful nature of the interaction with *TastyBeats* in comparison to the routine way of checking heart rate data on a screen. Participants particularly enjoyed the fact that the interaction was not just a visualization of their heart rate data, but there was also a drinkable reward associated with it. They were able to correlate the created drink with their heart rate: "*It's really cool to see how what I just did is now somehow in the glass!*" Unfortunately, one caveat of the exhibition was that participants were not allowed to taste the created drink due to the exhibitions' policies on food regulation. Participants showed interest in knowing the ingredients, and wanted to know if they can choose their favorite flavors if they were to use the system at home.

Furthermore, dynamics of the fluid interaction provided a momentary pleasure of being physically active, while the visual and sound effects of fluids such as color and flow sounds intrigued people and motivated the use of the system. Participants were mostly excited about how many different colored drinks they can get in a glass and what activities can increase their heart rate in a short period of time. As a consequence, they were enthusiastically engaged in the interaction to beat each other's heart rate and talked over the outcomes. Participants tried different physical activities such as push-ups, jumping and running to raise their heart rate, whereas some utilized 'tricks' such as controlled breathing to achieve the same outcome. Sometimes the heart rate was also raised with emotions such as thrill and surprise related to experiencing the system socially. The audience also got involved by tickling their friends who were interacting with the system and by loudly cheering them up. As a result, the interaction became a public spectacle of someone's fitness and every attempt was encouraged and applauded by the audience.

Sometimes, due to accidental movements or low levels of fluids inside the containers, the fluid was spilled on the nearby surface of the setup. To our surprise, spilling made the interaction more dramatic. Participants considered it as a part of their performance to get the desired outcome of shooting the fluid correctly into the central glass. For example, one participant felt that she did not deserve the drink because of an average performance and that was why the drink spilled over the table surface.

Unlike a traditional method of viewing heart rate on a screen, where data is accurately communicated to user, we explored a vibrant yet abstract form of representation with *TastyBeats*. For example, although users could identify the heart rate zone in which their heart rate was falling in, they could not see the exact heart rate value. Furthermore, there was a little delay between the measured heart rate and the fluidic outcome because of the lag in reading the sensor data and initiating the water pumps. As a result, participants did not know what would happen and when: "*from where does the water come out and how much will spill?*". On one hand, the delay was sometimes frustrating as participants felt that there was something wrong with either their body or the system. On the other hand, the delay also invoked fun conversations as participants teased each other, "*You are a zombie!*", "*You don't have a heart (beat)*". But it also encouraged more efforts from the participants as they tried to increase their heart rate through different activities.

Some participants raised concerns on safety of the created drink. The interaction also challenged their notion of whether it is good to play with food (drinkable fluids). In follow up discussions, few participants also hinted towards a clean and tidy setup, where the fluid interaction could be akin to a coffee machine setup and fluid will flow downward rather than shooting upwards.

In summary, public rendering of heart rate data in a fluidic form made participants laugh, cheer, expressive and playful with their personal heart rate data and encouraged different physical activities. This suggests that there is a potential to use fluidic interaction to support the experience of being physically active. However, there are also a few concerns regarding the design and food safety when exploring the fluidic interaction with the data.

DESIGN STRATEGIES

Based on the reflections on our design process, we put forward the following three strategies to support designing drinkable representations of heart rate data.

1) Encourage playing around with drinkable fluids through spilling: In *TastyBeats,* spilling was accidental and caused mess on nearby surface. On one hand, participants welcomed it as a dramatic outcome of the playful interaction; while on other hand, it also challenged their notion of playing with drinkable fluids as for some of them food is mostly a forbidden object to play with. We believe that encouraging the users to play around with drinkable fluids provides an opportunity to facilitate immersive engagement that can further entice the user to fulfill a daily need of having appropriate fluid intake [20].

2) Harness physical creativity through public fluidic spectacle and drinkable rewards: Sheridan [21] defines physical creativity as the ability to innovate through exertion to acquire skills and agility; it involves the use of body movements for self-expression, improvisation and imaginative play. In our system, participants liked how a drink became a celebration of their physical activity along with an opportunity to express themselves in front of a large cheering crowd. As such, the fluidic spectacle of heart rate becomes a public display of self, allowing the participants to be imaginative and creative with their movements.

Designers, therefore, can utilize such interaction and public display to nurture physical creativity.

3) Support abstract visualization of heart rate data through fluids: The public fluidic display of heart rate facilitated creative and exertive self-expression among participants even when the system did not reveal the exact values of heart rate or the information about how it attains a fluidic form. For participants the dynamics of fluidic interaction were more engaging as compared to the actual information. We recommend the designers to consider abstract visualization of data using fluids by being 'secretive' (on how data gets transformed into a new representation) and 'expressive' (to support exertive self-expression and spectator engagement [17]).

CONCLUSION

TastyBeats creates a personalized sports drink where the making of and ingredients of the drink are decided upon the heart rate data sensed as part of the physical activity. By utilizing a familiar water fountain based interaction in a public space, the interaction can become a public spectacle and a celebration of personal fitness that can further incentivize physical creativity among users. We would also like to encourage design thinking towards cross model aspects of the drink such as color, flavor, and texture to support the experience of being physically active.

REFERENCES

1. Arduino. http://arduino.cc.
2. Benson, R., and Connolly, D. Heart rate training, *Human Kinetics*, 2011.
3. Curmi, F., Ferrario, M.A., Southern, J., and Whittle, J. HeartLink: open broadcast of live biometric data to social networks. In *Proc. CHI'13,* ACM (2013), 1749-1758.
4. Currency fountain. http://www.koert.com/work/datafountain/.
5. Daisuke, A. Weburette. In *Proc. SA'12*, ACM (2012).
6. Dietz, P., Reyes, G., and Kim, D. The PumpSpark fountain development kit. In *Proc. DIS'14*, ACM (2014), 259-266.
7. Food grade mini water pump. http://www.lightobject.com/High-temperature100-39C-DC-12V-185LMin-29GPH-mini-Water-Pump-Food-grade-P711.aspx.
8. Fountain of Bellagio. https://www.bellagio.com/attractions/fountains-of-bellagio.aspx
9. Geurts, L., and Vanden Abeele, V. Splash controllers: game controllers involving the uncareful manipulation of water. In *Proc. TEI'12*, ACM (2012), 183-186.
10. Khot, R., Hjorth, L., and Mueller, F. Understanding physical activity through 3D printed material artifacts. In *Proc. CHI'14*, ACM (2014), 3835-3844.
11. Mann, S., Janzen, R., Huang, J., Kelly, M., Ba, L. J., and Chen, A. User-interfaces Based on the Water-hammer Effect: Water-hammer Piano As an Interactive Percussion Surface. In *Proc. TEI '11*, ACM (2011), 1-8.
12. Mine, M. R., Barnard, D., Yang, B., and Baker, D. Thermal Interactive Media. In *Proc. SIGGRAPH'11*, ACM (2011), 18.
13. Nacke, L., Kalyn, M., Lough, C., and Mandryk, R. Biofeedback game design: using direct and indirect physiological control to enhance game interaction. In *Proc. CHI'11*, ACM (2011), 103-112.
14. Nenonen, V., Lindblad, A., Häkkinen, V., Laitinen, T., Jouhtio, M., and Hämäläinen, P. Using heart rate to control an interactive game. In *Proc. CHI'07*, ACM (2007), 853-856.
15. Pulse Sensor Amped. https://www.sparkfun.com/products/11574.
16. Ranasinghe, N., Lee, K., and Do, E. FunRasa: an interactive drinking platform. In *Proc. TEI'14*, ACM (2014), 133-136.
17. Reeves, S., Benford, S., O'Malley, C., and Fraser, M. Designing the spectator experience. In *Proc. CHI'05*, ACM (2005), 741-750.
18. Richter, H., Manke, F., and Seror, M. LiquiTouch: liquid as a medium for versatile tactile feedback on touch surfaces. In *Proc. TEI'13*, ACM (2013), 315-318.
19. Ruckenstein, M. Visualized and Interacted Life: Personal Analytics and Engagements with Data Doubles. *Societies*, (2014), 4, 68–84.
20. Sawka M., Burke L., Eichner E., Maughan R., Montain S., and Stachenfeld N. American College of Sports Medicine position stand. Exercise and fluid replacement. *Med Sci Sports Exerc.* (2007),39, 377-90.
21. Sheridan, J. When clapping data speaks to Wii: physical creativity and performative interaction in playground games and songs. In *Proc. BCS HCI'10*, ACM (2010), 299-308.
22. Sylvester, A., Döring, T., and Schmidt, A. Liquids, Smoke, and Soap Bubbles - Reflections on Materials for Ephemeral User Interfaces. In *Proc. TEI'10*, ACM (2010), 269-270.
23. Walmink, W., Wilde, D., and Mueller, F. Displaying heart rate data on a bicycle helmet to support social exertion experiences. In *Proc. TEI'14*, ACM (2014), 97-104.
24. Watanabe, J. VortexBath: study of tangible interaction with water in bathroom for accessing and playing media files. In *Proc. HCI'07*, Springer (2007), 1240-1248.

Scotty: Relocating Physical Objects Across Distances Using Destructive Scanning, Encryption, and 3D Printing

Stefanie Mueller, Martin Fritzsche, Jan Kossmann, Maximilian Schneider, Jonathan Striebel, Patrick Baudisch
Hasso Plattner Institute, Potsdam, Germany
{firstname.lastname}@hpi.uni-potsdam.de

ABSTRACT

We present a simple self-contained appliance that allows relocating inanimate physical objects across distance. Each unit consists of an off-the-shelf 3D printer that we have extended with a 3-axis milling machine, a camera, and a microcontroller for encryption/decryption and transmission. Users place an object into the sender unit, enter the address of a receiver unit, and press the *relocate* button. The sender unit now digitizes the original object layer-by-layer: it shaves off material using the built-in milling machine, takes a photo using the built-in camera, encrypts the layer using the public key of the receiver, and transmits it. The receiving unit decrypts the layer in real-time and starts printing right away. Users thus see the object appear layer-by-layer on the receiver side as it disappears layer-by-layer at the sender side. Scotty is different from previous systems that *copy* physical objects, as its destruction and encryption mechanism guarantees that only one copy of the object exists at a time. Even though our current prototype is limited to single-material plastic objects, it allows us to address two application scenarios: (1) Scotty can help preserve the uniqueness and thus the emotional value of physical objects shared between friends. (2) Scotty can address some of the licensing issues involved in fast electronic delivery of physical goods. We explore the former in an exploratory user study with three pairs of participants.

Author Keywords: fabrication; rapid prototyping; 3D printing; 3D scanning.

ACM Classification Keywords: H.5.2

INTRODUCTION

Personal fabrication tools, such as 3D printers, enable a wide range of new applications, including creating one-off physical objects [9], fast iterative prototyping (*faBrickation* [18]), creating interactive objects (*Sauron* [23]), and repairing broken parts (*Hybrid reAssemblage* [28]).

When combined with 3D scanning, 3D printing allows converting physical objects to a digital state and back. While in digital form, users can vary the shape and design of objects (*OpenFab* [26]) or even more importantly share it with others [22]. As a result, many envision a future in which any object will be available to anyone anywhere anytime [9].

Figure 1: Johannes, (front) has placed a physical necklace pendant into his Scotty unit and is now sending it to Julia (back). Each Scotty unit consists of an off-the-shelf 3D printer (MakerBot) extended with a milling machine, a camera, and an additional processor. By destroying the necklace during scanning, encrypting it during transmission, and preventing reprinting, Scotty assures that never more than one pendant can exist, thereby preserving the pendant's uniqueness throughout the relocation process.

Some researchers in psychology, however, have looked at the sharing of physical objects from a different perspective. They question whether replicating an object is always desirable, as additional copies affect the uniqueness and thus the emotional value of a physical object [10]. Consequently, they speculate whether the value of an object might not be better preserved if one were able to send the object by *"teleporting"* it, rather than by copying [11].

Unfortunately, all these studies were carried out as wizard-of-oz experiments [10] or written scenarios [19] as no functional system existed.

In this paper, we demonstrate a simple, yet functional device that allows us to relocate inanimate physical objects by means of destructive scanning, encryption, and remote 3D printing. Our prototype, currently still limited to single-

TEI '15, January 16 - 19 2015, Stanford, CA, USA

http://dx.doi.org/10.1145/2677199.2680547

material plastic objects, allowed us to carry out an exploratory study in which we interviewed participants who had just sent handmade personal objects using our device.

RELATED WORK

The work presented in this paper is related to personal fabrication, duplication psychology, destructive scanning, and digital rights management.

Replicating objects, telefabrication, and 3D faxing

Researchers have demonstrated how to replicate physical objects by combining reverse engineering and rapid prototyping [6]. They first 3D scan the object's surface and then print copies of the object on a 3D printer. Since no intermediate models, such as CAD and STL, are required for replication, Chen et al. [5] show how to output scanned geometry directly to a 3D printer.

In telefabrication, digital files are transmitted via the Internet to a remote rapid prototyping facility [17]. Combined with a 3D scanner, telefabrication setups can copy physical objects over a distance (*3D fax machine* [22]). One application scenario for such devices is to share hand-annotated physical prototypes among distributed product teams [8]. 3D faxing potentially allows bypassing shipping costs and customs [21].

Duplication Psychology

Already in the 1980s, psychology researchers studied how duplication affects the value of an object: They found that people prefer personal objects, such as their child's first baby shoes, to perceptibly identical copies even if they can't tell the difference [2]. Newman et al. [19] list possible explanations, such as that the object had physical contact with a loved person or documents a special experience (similar to what Walter Benjamin calls the *aura* of an object [3]). In their personal attachment framework [20], Odom et al. list additional reasons, such as the personal engagement with the object. Using a mock-up duplication machine, Hood et al. [10] showed that this bias already exists in young children.

Researchers also investigated whether the co-existence of the original affects the value of the duplicate. Using written scenarios, Newman et al. [19] found that scarcity affects the value of objects, i.e. participants ranked a recreated object as being of higher value when the original was destroyed.

Finally, Hood et al. [11] researched a hypothetical "teleportation" scenario, in which they evaluated how much of the physical and mental properties of a living being are thought of as being transferred to the remote location.

Encryption and Digital rights management

Digital rights management (DRM) restricts the use of digital content after sale to the number of purchased licenses. While DRM is most commonly used in the entertainment industry (e.g., Apple iTunes [24]), a patent on DRM for 3D printing [12] suggests that a similar process will soon apply to personal fabrication.

Destructive scanning

Destructive scanning is used to obtain a 3D model of an object in cases where the object contains undercuts or hidden internal features [13]. Destructive scanners use either a milling machine [16] or a grinding wheel [14]. They can scan plastic parts as well as metal parts (*CGI* [4]).

SENDING UNIQUE OBJECTS ACROSS DISTANCES

Figure 1 shows Scotty, a simple self-contained appliance that we created to allow users to send inanimate physical objects to distant locations.

Each unit consists of an off-the-shelf 3D printer (MakerBot) that we have extended with a custom-made milling machine and a camera (Figure 2), as well as a microcontroller (Raspberry Pi) running custom software for encryption and transmission.

Figure 2: The standard MakerBot carriage carries two extrusion units. To allow it to destructively scan a physical object, we added a simple mill and a camera.

Walkthrough

The following figures show a user relocating a personal object, here a handcrafted necklace pendant (Figure 3).

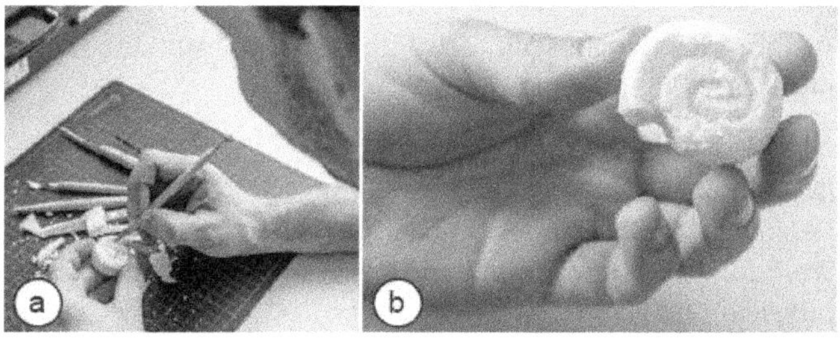

Figure 3: The handcrafted snail necklace pendant.

As illustrated by Figure 4, the user starts by (a) dipping the pendant into fast-drying black paint. This generates visual contrast for the subsequent optical scanning step, i.e. only the currently milled away surface will appear white to the camera, and the remaining part remains black. (b) The user places the pendant into the sender unit, (c) selects the Scotty unit to send to from the display, and presses the *relocate* button. This causes the sender unit to digitize the object layer-by-layer, i.e., a repeated process of shaving off a layer, taking a photo of it, encrypting it, and sending it.

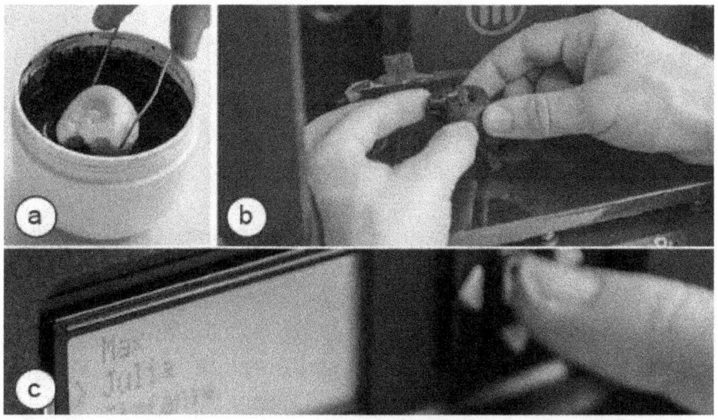

Figure 4: To relocate this pendant: the sender (a) dips it in black paint, (b) mounts it into the sender unit by placing it on double-sided adhesive tape, (c) selects the receiver name and presses the *relocate* button.

While the sender unit is still digitizing, the receiver unit starts receiving the object. It decrypts each layer and starts printing right away. Users thus see the object appear layer-by-layer on the receiver side as it disappears layer-by-layer at the sender side, until complete (Figure 5).

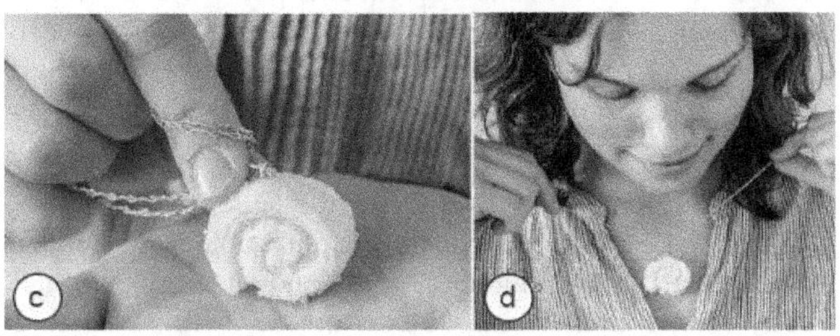

Figure 5: The received necklace pendant.

How Scotty works

Figure 6 shows Scotty's built-in milling machine shaving off a layer of material. Scotty moves the mill across the object using the same 3-axis mechanism that the MakerBot uses to move the extruder. The mill bit is aligned with the extruder heads to prevent the mill from cutting into the base plate of the MakerBot.

Figure 6: Here Scotty is digitizing an object by moving its mill across the object coated in black paint.

Between layers, Scotty lowers the base plate that holds the object. This moves the object away from the carriage, allowing Scotty's down-facing camera to take a picture of the object's top surface (e.g., Figure 7a). The object's black coating helps to provide good contrast against the object's off-white material. Scotty optimizes image quality by illuminating the object using the MakerBot's built-in LED strip. Scotty then encodes the captured image in .png format, encrypts it, and sends it to the other side.

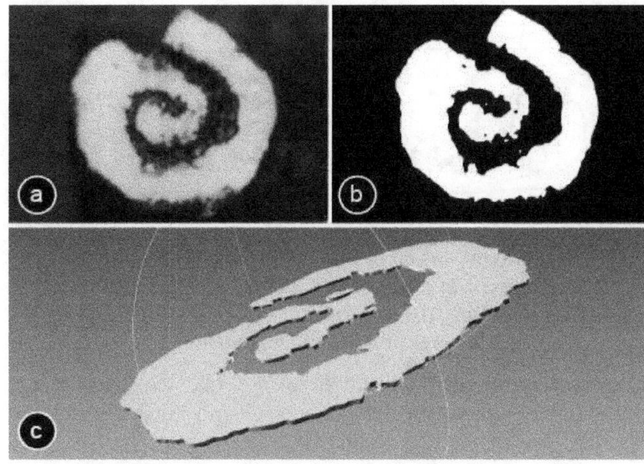

Figure 7: Scanning and 3D reconstruction process: (a) photo of one layer, (b) after thresholding, (c) reconstructed 3D model of the layer.

Figure 7b shows what happens at the receiver side. The receiver unit binarizes the image and extracts the object contour using the connected components algorithm (OpenCV). It then triangulates the 2D polygon, generates a 3D mesh of the layer by using the same polygon as top and bottom surface (Figure 7c). It then sends the 3D mesh to the MakerBot's slicer, which generates 3D printing instructions in g-code and prints them.

Preserving uniqueness using encryption

As discussed in the introduction, the key property of relocating an object is that it guarantees the uniqueness of the object, i.e., that only one instance of the object exists at all times. This means that Scotty has to guarantee that neither the sender, nor the receiver, nor any person in the middle is able to keep or produce an additional copy.

Figure 8 shows how Scotty achieves this across the three individual steps involved in relocation: *(a) scanning:* Scotty destroys the physical original during scanning. This does not only ensure that the object on the sender side disappears, but is also necessary to obtain a true volumetric scan of the object, unlike traditional (non-destructive) methods that reproduce only the façade of an object. *(b) transmission*: Scotty prevents men-in-the-middle from fabricating a copy of the object by encrypting the object using the receiver's public key. *(c) re-fabrication:* Scotty prevents the receiver from making multiple copies by maintaining an eternal log of objects already fabricated, which allows it to refuse the reprinting of objects.

Here is Scotty*'s* encryption/decryption in full detail:

Initial setup: Every relocation unit has its own public/private key pair. The private key is stored inside the unit; each unit shares its public key through a public key server.

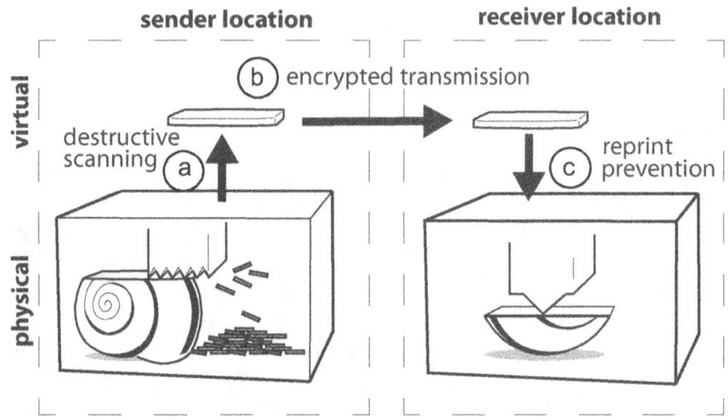

Figure 8: Scotty assures that never more than one pendant can exist at a time by (a) destroying the necklace during scanning, (b) encrypting it during transmission, and (c) preventing reprinting,

(a) Secure sending: The sender unit retrieves the receiver unit's public key from the key server and encrypts the object using this key. The sender unit also signs the object file with a hash code, which is then encrypted with the private key of the sender unit. This allows the receiver unit to verify that the object had been truly sent by the sender unit. The sender unit now securely deletes the non-encrypted object file and sends the encrypted object file to the receiver unit via a network connection.

(b) Secure receiving: The receiver unit requests the sender unit's public key from the key server and uses it to verify the signature of the file. This allows the receiver unit to confirm that the file was indeed sent by the sender unit and that the data has not been modified during transmission.

(c) Re-fabrication: To prevent objects from being fabricated repeatedly, the receiver unit looks up the hash-code in its eternal list of already fabricated objects—it only prints if the code is not contained in the list. It then adds the hash-code to the list to prevent additional copies. The receiver unit finally decrypts the object file using its own private key, prints it, and securely deletes it.

A crucial feature of Scotty is that it is an encapsulated appliance. During relocation, the object data is inherently non-encrypted (1) at the moment of scanning and before encryption and (2) at the moment of re-fabrication, i.e., after decryption. If users were able to gain access to the data at these stages, they would be able to print copies of the object, compromising its uniqueness. Scotty addresses these issues by forming a single encapsulated (and if commercially manufactured *sealed*) device, with all processing happening inside the device. This allows Scotty to perform "scanning-and-encryption" in one step inside the device and "decryption-and-fabrication" in one step inside the device, as suggested by the dashed lines in Figure 8. This prevents the undesired access, thereby protecting the object's uniqueness.

APPLICATIONS

The fact that our devices preserve uniqueness throughout the relocation process (unlike systems that *copy* physical objects) allows us to create two new application scenarios:

#1 Scotty keeps personal objects unique: As in the example shown earlier, Scotty guarantees that a personal, handmade gift remains unique when sent across distances, i.e., that there is no other copy—an important aspect that emphasizes the intimate relationship between sender and receiver.

#2 Scotty reduces licensing issues in online sales of used goods: As fabrication technology advances to the point where we can make functional copies of designed objects, replication of a purchased object starts to raise licensing issues. Imagine a seller of an online auction site, such as eBay, offers a used copy of the cleverly designed stand for a computer tablet shown in Figure 9 for sale. With instantaneous payment systems such as online banking already in place, the buyer may want to *receive* the object the very moment he or she completes the auction—by receiving the object electronically and fabricating it locally.

This raises licensing issues since the particular design of the iPad stand is currently sold on the web for $15. If a user replicates the object using $2 worth of 3D printing material, the designer misses out on being paid for the $13 worth of "design" contained in the object. This point will get raised more often as the debate around the intellectual property and licensing of 3D objects is heating up [12] and it will make it difficult to switch from slow postal delivery to fast electronic delivery based on local personal fabrication.

Scotty addresses this issue. When the seller *sends* the object through Scotty, the system guarantees that the seller's object ceases to exist the moment the buyer receives it, i.e., Scotty allows transferring objects quickly without infringing on designers' rights to be paid for their designs.

Figure 9: Application scenario 2: Selling a designed iPad stand on an online auction site. By relocating the object to the buyer using Scotty, the buyer receives the object quickly and prevents the seller from infringing on the designer's rights.

Note that Scotty only prevents licensing issues associated with the *transfer* of the object—users may still try to reproduce objects at other times, e.g., by scanning the object's façade (which works for objects without cavities and no internal mechanisms).

CONTRIBUTION

We make a technical contribution by demonstrating how to actually implement physical relocation. We have created two functional units including software and hardware and we demonstrate how to use them to send objects across. To help other researchers replicate our design, we provide a detailed description of our design (see section "Implementation Details" below).

By engineering an actual solution, we take the question of physical relocation out of the mock-up space, where it has traditionally been handled in psychology and other disciplines and into the space of engineering where we can actually operate and test.

The engineering of functioning units also allowed us to conduct an exploratory study in which participants used an actual functioning system rather than a mock-up.

Finally, the fact that our devices preserve uniqueness throughout the relocation process allows us to create two new application scenarios.

Design decisions and limitations

Unlike the aforementioned research in psychology that used mock-ups to create an impression of relocation, Scotty is a real-existing, functional system. However, this also causes it to have real-existing, functional limitations.

First, since the 3D printers used in our current prototypes print only single-color ABS of comparably low resolution, only coarse objects made from that specific type of off-white ABS plastic will look the same after being relocated. However, the set of objects that remain indistinguishable will increase with future versions of Scotty as we employ high-resolution printing, full volumetric color, and mixed materials (e.g. Objet500 Connex3 [25]).

Second, unlike the mock-ups, we deliberately designed Scotty to expose its inner workings. In particular, we allow users to see that the received object is fabricated from a roll of ABS string and that the sent object is being destroyed and sucked into a shop vacuum cleaner. This design choice has two implications.

(1) Users know that the received object is not made from the same atoms as the sent objects. This clarifies that even if the received object should look identical to the original, it is not physically the same object. Consequently, one would *not* expect users to feel that the received object "*is*" the sent object.

(2) Users witness the original object being irrevocably destroyed. For objects to which users attribute a "soul", such as a wedding ring, this can make a difference. In psychology research, these types of objects are called *attachment objects* and it is still an open research topic why people prefer these to perceptibly identical copies even if they can't tell the difference [10].

Designers of future versions of Scotty may thus choose *not* to expose the inner workings (e.g., by simply using opaque blinds) resulting in a system that allows users to make up their own conceptual model of what happened (similar to how the mock-up studies in psychology research allowed for this). For our current version of Scotty, however, our goal was not to trick users into believing in a super-natural process, but to deliver a working mechanism for relocating physical objects.

QUALITATIVE EXPLORATIVE USER STUDY

We conducted a small-scale qualitative user study to explore the use of Scotty in the first of our two application scenarios, i.e., sending objects of personal emotional value between couples and close friends. (Whether our second use case—online sales—becomes relevant in the future seems to be more a matter of legislation than of user experience, we thus chose not to user test it).

Our goal was to study whether the fact that Scotty preserves an object's uniqueness allows it to preserve the emotional value of the object better than a regular 3D printer that allows for duplication. Unlike existing studies on this topic in psychology research, all of which had to rely on hypothetical cases such as text scenarios [19] or mock-ups [10], Scotty allowed us to test in a situation where participants *witnessed that and understood how* the object was being relocated.

Study set-up

We set up a *sender* and a *receiver* unit in two different rooms in our institution. Participants could not see the respective other room with the second device. To allow both sides to witness the sent object disappear, we added a webcam to the sender unit and displayed the image on an iPad on the receiver side.

Studies were conducted with two participants at a time, i.e., a sender and a receiver participant.

Each study began by the sender participant handcrafting a personal object to be gifted to the receiver (Figure 10). To assure that the object would be worth giving, we required senders to spend 60 minutes on creating it. We enforced good design process, i.e., we required sender participants to create multiple ideas and to sketch them before picking one design to execute. After they made a choice, sender participants carved the object from an off-white block of hard foam material using the carving tools we had provided. Senders then placed the object into the sender unit and relocated it to the other participant.

Receiver participants waited in the room containing the receiver unit. We told receiver participants that the respective sender participant had handcrafted an object for them as a personal gift and that it would be sent to them using the device.

The process of transmitting the object took 2-3 hours, depending on the size of the object. In order to not over tax participants' time, we brought receiver participants in only for the last 30 minutes of the transmission. For additional context, we asked receiver participants to also rewind the webcam transmission so as to watch the object starting to disappear on the sender side. Upon completion, receiver participants took out the received object.

Finally, receiver participants filled in a questionnaire. The questionnaire asked receiver participants to rate the value of the received object and rate how its value would be affected by different ways how Scotty might have allowed copies to be made along the way.

Overall, the study took about 4 hours per participant pair.

Participants

We recruited six participants (3 female) in the form of three pairs. Each pair was selected so as to know each other well, i.e. was either a couple or close friends. From each pair, we assigned one participant the role of *sender* (2 male, 1 female) and one the role of *receiver* (2 female, 1 male). Participant's ages ranged between 22 and 26 (mean=25, s=1.53).

Findings

Figure 10 shows the handcrafted gifts sender participants made: (a) the grazing alpaca the couple had recently seen, (b) the van the couple had used to travel the US, and (c) a foot as a memento of the moment he had given her his own shoes and continued to walk barefoot.

Figure 10: Each sender participant hand-carved a gift and send it to the receiver participant using Scotty: (a) the grazing alpaca the couple had recently seen, (b) the van the couple had used to travel the US, and (c) a foot as a memento of the moment he had given her his own shoes and continued to walk barefoot.

Figure 11 shows the corresponding objects as received by the receiver participants after relocation through Scotty.

Receiver participants rated the value of the received object through Scotty as very high (7, 7, 6 on a 7-point Likert scale). Receiver participant p2 rationalized this as "it is one-of-a-kind, it is specifically made for me and nobody else will ever have an exact replica".

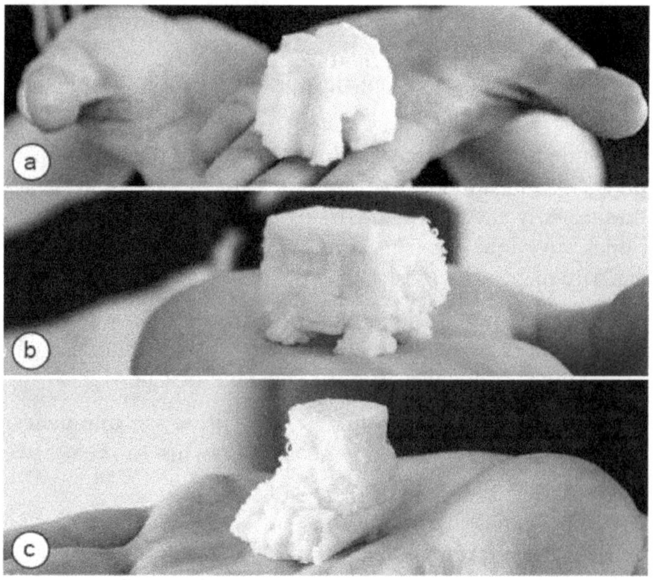

Figure 11: Receiver participants showing off the objects they had received by means of relocation.

To investigate the value of object uniqueness, we asked receiver participants three questions, each of which investigated the value of one of the three arrows from Figure 8.

(1) Sender side uniqueness: Had the Scotty device *not* destroyed the object, receiver participants rated that this would have made the received object less valuable (3, 2, and 1 respectively on a 7-point Likert scale with 1 meaning "less valuable" to 7 meaning "more valuable"). Participant p3 explained: "In that case, mine would just be a replication and the other person would posses the original". Participant p2 said "it's about a moment we shared with each other early in our relationship and if the original was given to someone else [...] that would make me associate my object with them."

(2) Man-in-the-middle uniqueness: Had the Scotty device allowed a man-in-the-middle to tap the transmission and fabricate additional copies, receiver participants rated that this would essentially not affect the value of the received object (4, 4, and 3 respectively on a 7-point Likert scale). Participant p2 explained: "it would not be completely unique anymore, but that would not really matter. My boyfriend made it only for me." Participant p1 said: "The idea of my *unique object* stays unique [...]—the object *is* made for me."

(3) Receiver side uniqueness: Had the receiving Scotty device stored a digital copy of the received object, allowing the receiver participant to fabricate additional copies when necessary, receiver participants rated that this would have made the object *slightly* less valuable (4, 3, and 2 respectively on a 7-point Likert scale). Participant p1 explained: "I can't reprint my feelings. My emotional state will be different when I get the 'same' object again. The object won't be the same actually."

Discussion

Our results suggest that users do care about uniqueness, when it comes to sharing among close friends and partners. Overall, the social effects we learned about in our exploratory study are congruent with what psychology researchers had hypothesized based on their mock-up experiments [10]. However, previous studies in psychology were limited to very young children that could be made to believe in mock-ups. In contrast, we conducted our study with adult participants who interacted with a functioning prototype. In summary, our results are encouraging and afford additional studies with a larger sample size.

IMPLEMENTATION DETAILS

To help readers replicate our system design in order to build their own Scotty units, we now present the technical details behind our design.

Figure 12 offers a look under the hood. (a) A RaspberryPi processor board runs Scotty*'s* software. (b) A USB hub connected to the RaspberryPi contains the cable for the MakerBot, the camera, and (c) the Arduino that controls the mill. (d) A switch-mode power supply for powering the mill. All components are mounted to the bottom of the MakerBot. Normally, all components are enclosed in the MakerBot's bottom casing; the photograph was taken with this cover removed.

Figure 12: The Scotty hardware enclosed in the bottom of the MakerBot: (a) RaspberryPi (b) USB hub with camera, MakerBot and (c) Arduino for controlling the mill, (d) mill power supply, (e) Ethernet cable.

Digitization using mill and camera

Figure 13 shows an exploded view of the carriage extension that holds our digitizing apparatus consisting of a custom mill and a camera. We rigidly coupled the second carriage [1] to the MakerBot's standard extruder carriage; this allows Scotty to actuate the mill using the same mechanism that moves the extruder heads. To minimize friction, the carriage rests on four linear ball bearings (LM8SUU). A custom laser cut assembly attaches the milling head and the camera (model: MSLifeCam) to the top of the carriage.

The mill itself uses a fast-turning, low-torque brushless motor (KV890) as they are commonly used in quad copters. In Scotty, it drives a two-sided flat milling head.

The 3D printed nozzle on the left of Figure 13 allows connecting a shop vacuum cleaner. The 3D printed part redirects the suction to the mill head to provide cooling and to make sure milled-off chips are removed from the object's top surface before Scotty captures the next picture.

Scotty moves the milling head by sending g-code commands to the MakerBot API. Scotty uses that same API to move the object into the focus plane of the camera and to control the MakerBot's LED strip.

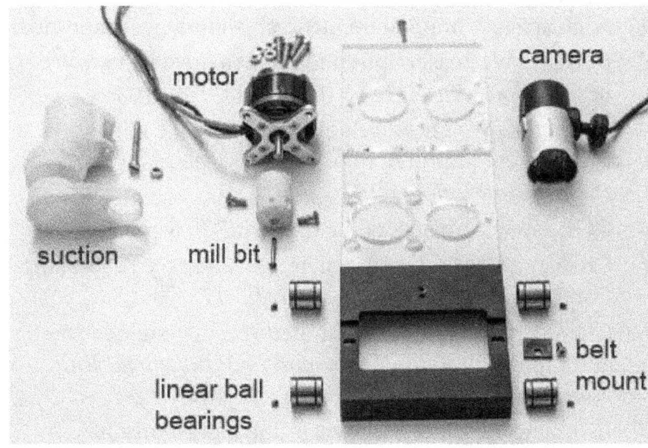

Figure 13: Exploded view of the milling carriage.

Encryption and transmission

Scotty encrypts the thresholded binary image using the ecliptic curve cryptography implementation of the libsodium library [15]. Scotty transmits the data via a TCP connection to the receiver (for easy control we use a TCP abstraction layer called zmq4 [27]). For decryption, Scotty again uses the libsodium library.

Re-fabrication

Scotty converts the threshold image into a 2D polygon using OpenCV's contour detection. It then triangulates the 2D polygon using Seidel's algorithm from the poly2tri library [7]. Scotty's code then triangulates the polygon and transforms it into a 3D object using the polygon as the bottom and top surface and closing the space between with a triangle strip. The generated 3D mesh is written into an .stl file, which Scotty sends to the MakerBot's slicer (called *miraclegrue*). Scotty overwrites the slicer's default z-position (normally the base of the platform) so as to reflect the number of layers already printed.

Transmit at once

Objects with overhanging structures require support material in order to be printed. To support such objects, Scotty offers a *"transmit as a whole"* option in the MakerBot display. If this option is active, Scotty delays 3D printing until the entire object has been received, allowing the receiver unit to generate support material.

CONCLUSION

In this paper, we presented the design and implementation of simple, yet functioning relocation units that allow relocating inanimate physical objects to remote locations. We discussed two application scenarios, i.e., sharing unique personal objects among close friends and preventing licensing issues in online sales. The findings of our exploratory study suggest that users do care about uniqueness, when it comes to sharing personal objects among close friends and partners. As future work, we plan to create high-definition versions of Scotty that allow transmitting objects in much higher fidelity and to study users' conceptual models in study conditions where we do not reveal the mechanism.

REFERENCES

1. AluCarriage: http://shop.raffle.ch/shop/alucarriage-dual/
2. Belk, R. W. Possessions and the extended self. *Journal of Consumer Research,* Vol. 15, '88, 139–168.
3. Benjamin, W. The Work of Art in the Age of Mechanical Reproduction. *CreateSpace Independent Publishing Platform,* 1936.
4. CGI, www.cgiinspection.com/Pearl700.aspx
5. Chen, Y., Li, K., Qian, X. Direct Geometry Processing For Tele-Fabrication. *Proc. ASME '12.*
6. Chen, Y.H., Ng, C.T. Integrated reverse engineering and rapid prototyping. *Computers & Industrial Engineering*, Vol. 33, No. 3-4, '97, 481-484,
7. Domiter, V., Žalik, B. Sweep-line algorithm for constrained Delaunay triangulation. *International Journal of Geographical Information Science '08,* Vol. 22, No. 4, 449-462.
8. Galantucci, L.M., Percoco, G., Spina, R. Telemanufacturing of reverse engineered parts: A case study. *Journal of Engineering Manufacture,* Vol. 217 No. 5, '03, 727-731.
9. Gershenfeld, N. Fab: The Coming Revolution on Your Desktop From Personal Computers to Personal Fabrication. *Basic Books,* '07.
10. Hood, B.M., Bloom, P. Children prefer certain individuals over perfect duplicates. *Cognition '08,* Vol. 106, 455-462.
11. Hood, B.M., Gjersoe, N. L., Bloom, P. Do children think that duplicating the body also duplicates the mind? Cognition, Volume 125, Issue 3, '12, 466–474.
12. Jung, E.K.Y. et al. Manufacturing control system. *U.S. Patent 8286236*, filed January 31, '08, issued September 10, '12.
13. Lan, H. A re-configurable cross-sectional imaging system for reverse engineering based on a CNC milling machine. *International Journal of Advanced Manufacturing Technology 37 (3-4),* '08, 341-353.
14. Lee, W.C., Chen, L.W. Design and fabrication of a general purpose 3D digitizer based on grinding technique. *Materials Science Forum*, Vol. 594, '08, 7-14.
15. Libsodium Encryption Library, https://github.com/jedisct1/libsodium
16. Liu, Z., Wang, L., Lu, B. Integrating cross-sectional imaging based reverse engineering with rapid prototyping. *Computers in Industry 57 (2),* '06, 131-140.
17. Luo, R.C., Lee, W.Z., Chou, J.H., Leong, H.T. The development of Internet accessible rapid prototyping system. *Proc. IECON '99,* 1498-1503.
18. Mueller, S., Mohr, T., Guenther, K., Frohnhofen, J., Baudisch, P. faBrickation: Fast 3D Printing of Functioning Objects by Integrating Construction Kit Building Blocks. *Proc. CHI'14*, 3827-3834.
19. Newman, G.E., Bloom, P. Art and Authenticity: The Importance of Originals in Judgements of Value. *Journal of Experimental Psychology '11.*
20. Odom, W., Pierce, J., Stolterman, E., Blevis, E. Understanding why we preserve some things and discard others in the context of interaction design. *Proc. CHI'09,* 1053-1062.
21. Paul, C. Fluid Borders: The Aesthetic Evolution of Digital Sculpture. *International Sculpture Center, Web Special.* http://www.sculpture.org/documents/webspec/digscul/digscul6.shtml
22. Reyes, R. World's First 3D Fax Machine. '91. https://webspace.utexas.edu/reyesr/self/3D_fax.htm
23. Savage, V., Chang, C., Hartmann, B. Sauron: embedded single-camera sensing of printed physical user interfaces. *Proc. UIST'13,* 447-456.
24. Sharpe, N. F., Arewa, O.B. Is Apple Playing Fair? Navigating the iPod FairPlay DRM Controversy. *Journal of Technology and Intellectual Property* 5.2, '07, 331-349.
25. Stratasys, 3D printer: Objet500 Connex3, http://www.stratasys.com/Objet500Connex3
26. Vidimče, K., Wang, S.-P., Ragan-Kelley, J., Matusik, W. OpenFab: A Programmable Pipeline for Multi-Material Fabrication. *ACM Trans. Graph* 32 (4), '13.
27. ZMQ4 TCP library, https://github.com/pebbe/zmq4
28. Zoran, A., Buechley, L. Hybrid reAssemblage: An Exploration of Craft, Digital Fabrication and Artifact Uniqueness. *Leonardo Journal '13,* Vol. 46, No. 1.

Mirror Puppeteering: Animating Toy Robots in Front of a Webcam

Ronit Slyper
Media Innovation Lab
The Interdisciplinary Center
Herzliya, Israel
rys@cs.cmu.edu

Guy Hoffman
Media Innovation Lab
The Interdisciplinary Center
Herzliya, Israel
hoffman@idc.ac.il

Ariel Shamir
Computer Science
The Interdisciplinary Center
Herzliya, Israel
arik@idc.ac.il

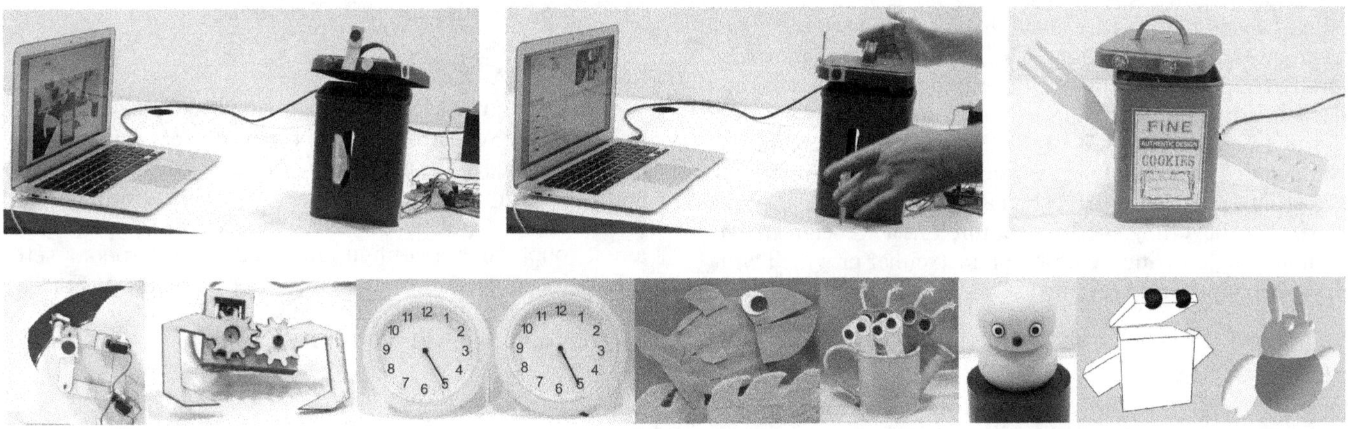

Figure 1. Mirror Puppeteering is a system for creating gestures for a robot by moving its limbs in front of a webcam. First, a robot tagged with markers self-calibrates in front of a webcam, building up a map between motor angles and camera-space marker locations (*top left*). The user then creates animations by puppeteering the robot's limbs in realtime (*top middle*). Animations are played back by the stand-alone robot (*top right*), or can be transferred to control animated characters. We demonstrate our system on a variety of homemade robots, the commercial toy My Keepon, and two virtual characters (*bottom row*).

ABSTRACT

Mirror Puppeteering is a system for easily creating gestures ("animations") for robotic toys, custom robots, and virtual characters. Lay users can record animations by simply moving a robot's limbs in front of a webcam. Makers and hobbyists can use the system to easily set up their custom-built robots for animation. Gamers and amateur animators can real-time control or save animations for virtual characters. Our system works by tracking circular markers on the robot's surface and translating these into motor commands, using a calibration map between marker locations in camera space and motor angles. New robots can be quickly set up for Mirror Puppeteering without knowledge of the robot's 3D structure, as we demonstrate on several robots. In a user study, participants found our method more enjoyable, usable, easy to learn, and successful than traditional animation methods.

TEI '15, January 16 - 19 2015, Stanford, CA, USA
Copyright 2015 ACM 978-1-4503-3305-4/15/01...$15.00
http://dx.doi.org/10.1145/2677199.2680548

Author Keywords

robotics; puppeteering; animation; gesture authoring

ACM Classification Keywords

H.5.1 Information interfaces and presentation (e.g., HCI): Multimedia Information Systems—*Animations*

INTRODUCTION

With the increasing accessibility of robot kits, microcontroller platforms, home manufacturing methods, and cheap actuators, more people are building and buying simple low-cost robots than ever before. Some of these are commercial, such as the Karotz robotic companion, My Keepon, or the Jibo family robot, while others come in the form of assembly kits, such as the CrustCrawler construction set or the Robotis Bioloid series. In addition, hobbyists and "makers" are increasingly building their own robots using 3D-printed and laser-cut parts and sharing their creations online.

A major element in the appeal of these robots is the expressivity of their movement and gestures, which need to be carefully designed to evince emotion and intention. However, designing expressive robot motion is challenging. It lies mostly in the realm of professionals, depending on meticulous programming, or techniques from 3D animation, which come with a significant learning curve. In contrast, we are interested in low-end amateur motion generation: animation of toy robots by lay users with no technical background.

This paper presents a novel approach and system we call *Mirror Puppeteering*, which allows makers and lay users to create expressive animations for simple robots at home, by directly puppeteering them in front of a webcam. Our system does not depend on knowing the 3D model of the robot, nor does it require high-end hardware on the robot or the user's PC. Instead it is a software system that only needs a webcam and cheap actuators with no position feedback.

We make use of the fact that many home-made or store-bought desktop robots are small, have a stationary base, and have few degrees of freedom. This makes such a robot structurally simple enough that if it could merely "take a look at itself in a mirror", it should be able to figure out what motion it is undergoing. We provide such a mirror, and the computation to translate the mirror image into a direct puppeteering system. From a technical perspective, our method works by converting markers captured in a webcam image to motor angles using a calibration map either provided with the robot or generated by the user.

DESIGN GOALS

Our aim in designing "Mirror Puppeteering" was to bring the expressive power and direct manipulation of puppeteering to low-cost robotic toys and lay users.

Puppeteering—the process of animating virtual characters and robots by moving a real-world physical model—has long been a useful technique in the toolbox of both animators and robot motion designers. Using the body and gestures to explore the animation space is an intuitive and rich way to express movement, allowing the quick and easy creation of complex motions that would be tedious to keyframe or to describe numerically.

However, today's puppeteering systems rely on high-end motion capture systems, custom waldos, mechanical proxies, or sensor-equipped actuators, making these methods more appropriate for professional and semi-professional settings.

In contrast, we want to allow the use of out-of-the-box low-cost puppets for which anyone can quickly create expressive motions. This should ideally be as easy as playing with the robot itself.

This leads us to the following design goals:

- **Easy to Learn and Use** — The system is intended for lay users, with no technical background, and for hobbyist makers. It should be easy to learn and use. It should work out-of-the box with direct manipulation and one-click controls.
- **Fits Low-cost Robotic Toys** — To work with commercial robotic toys and home-made robots, the system should not rely on motor sensors, position feedback channels, or sophisticated robot hardware.
- **Makes Use of Existing Hardware** — For wide acceptance, we aim for a software-only system that does not require high-end computing hardware on the user's side either.
- **Robust** — Given the low-cost hardware and consumer-grade computing requirement, the method should be robust enough to be feasible for home use.
- **Customizable for new robots and toys** — To make this appealing for makers, the system should be easily adapted to new custom-made robots. Makers should be able to quickly set it up with no more complexity than building and programming their simple robot.

USER SCENARIOS

We illustrate how "Mirror Puppeteering" addresses these goals by presenting scenarios of three kinds of users (Fig. 2): The novice user generates animations for the robot by puppeteering it out of the box in a set position in front of the camera. A more sophisticated user can set the robot in a different robot-camera configuration and run the robot's self-calibration procedure with the press of a button. Finally, "makers" can build their own robots and quickly set them up to be animated with Mirror Puppeteering.

Novice (Puppeteering only)

In the simplest use-case, the novice user buys a toy robot, which comes with a number of preset gestures and expressions, but also with the capability of authoring new gestures using "Mirror Puppeteering". To do so, the user places the robot in front of a webcam, the robot's "mirror", in one of a choice of preset positions indicated by outlines drawn on the camera video view. The user then presses "Record" and starts puppeteering the robot by moving the desired limbs in realtime. The user can also layer movements one limb at a time (i.e., animating one part, rewinding the timeline and then animating others). When puppeteering is completed, the user presses the "Stop" button, and the robot can save and play back the animation without the need for a camera.

Advanced User (Calibration + Puppeteering)

As mentioned above, the robot would ship with a number of pre-set camera positions for animation. However, an advanced user might want to set up the robot in a different position, for example to use two robots at once in a robot theater scene. To do so, the advanced user places the robot in the desired position and runs a firmware self-calibration routine with a single press of the "Calibrate" button. The robot moves its motors through all degrees of freedom to generate an up-to-date calibration for the new position. The new configuration is stored, and used for as many puppeteering sessions as the animator likes.

Maker (Design + Calibration + Puppeteering)

For "makers", Mirror Puppeteering allows rapid prototyping of new home-made robots. The maker builds a robot using robotics kits, 3D-printing, or laser cutting, in combination with hobby servos or stepper motors controlled through a micro-controller board. Once the robot is built, the maker

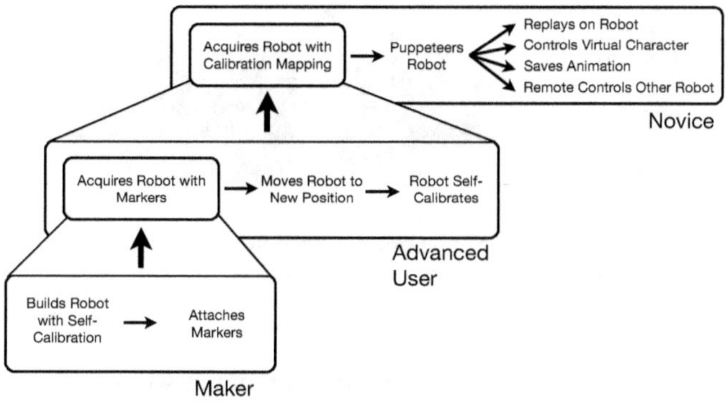

Figure 2. Three uses of Mirror Puppeteering. Novice users can simply puppeteer and playback (top row); advanced users can create new calibration maps in different scenarios (middle expansion); makers can quickly prototype new robots (bottom expansion).

simply attaches temporary markers to the robot's exterior and includes a short self-calibration routine as part of the robot's firmware.

Relation to Design Goals

These use-cases, in combination with our user study, demonstrate the way "Mirror Puppeteering" addresses our design goals. We evaluate ease of learning and use in a user study involving novices with no prior gesture animation experience. We find that participants rate continuous puppeteering more usable, easier to learn, more successful, and more enjoyable to use than traditional keyframing.

To demonstrate the feasibility of our system for consumer-grade robotic and PC hardware, we apply it to a low-cost robotic toy, My Keepon. We also run the software for all our demo robots using a standard MacBook laptop.

Our computer vision algorithm is designed for robustness, with the home user in mind. Marker detection is done per-frame, not tracked over time, thus vision errors do not accumulate and markers can pass in and out of occlusion. Our formulation of the matching algorithm is robust to detection failure and ignores excess markers in the background.

Finally, the self-calibration routine means that new robots can immediately use our system; the user need not import or specify the joint hierarchy or 3D model. In fact, we have been able to build five different custom robots, each in a few hours, and use our system to animate them without altering the software in any way. We also used the system with a store-bought robot toy, demonstrating the use case of a hacker retrofitting a commercial product.

Figure 1 and the accompanying video clip show the generalizability of Mirror Puppeteering through the variety of robots we animated using our system. The robots include, among others, a 2-axis robotic drawing machine, a robotic gripper, four dancing felt snakes, and a soft commercial robotic toy. We also used our system to control and animate two virtual characters.

RELATED WORK

Methods for animating robots present tradeoffs between the level of control over the final animation, and the ease and naturalness of the animation process. At the highest level of control, robot motion is programmed numerically in code. A step forward in usability is designing the motion in 3D animation software and then exporting the generated motion into motor space. The process is time-consuming but allows a fine level of control, making it mostly appropriate for highly trained professionals.

In contrast, using human motion to animate a robot is accessible even to non-professionals, and enables a high level of naturalness by taking advantage of the embodied coordination of the human body. In previous work, data from motion capture systems has been retargeted to animate complex robots and characters [14, 19]. Human motion for animation can be captured more cheaply, but with fewer degrees of freedom, using video [7], accelerometers [16], depth cameras [9], force sensors [10], and multitouch input devices [17]. Proxy objects, such as the sensing stuffed toy used in Sympathetic Interfaces, can also be used [12]. Motion retargeting, however, comes with a price: robots can have markedly different morphologies than humans, and in the transfer of the motion to the robot physiology, small-scale motion fidelity is lost. Our work, instead, works by directly puppeteering the robot.

Direct puppeteering takes advantage of the identity of input and output, while still allowing direct embodied control over the motor trajectories. This method generally relies on actuator proprioceptive sensors. In previous puppeteering work, a sensing robot spine for dancing stuffed animals [3] uses the Robotis Dynamixel line of servos with serial-readable encoders. Other actuated sensing platforms include an active puppet [20]; Curlybot, a toy that can replay motion [8]; and Topobo, a construction set with kinetic memory [15]. In contrast to our system, they all come with position-readable actuator hardware, usually not found in low-end robotic toys. Although it is possible to hack the latter to get encoding feedback, the servo must be powered (thus non-backdrivable) to read the encoder, so this trick is not viable for puppeteering.

A related field, also using sensor-equipped robots, is "learning by demonstration" (see [4] for a survey). Training examples are created for the robot, e.g. by teleoperation, human motion capture, or kinesthetic teaching, where a human guides the robot to show it how to point to an object [13], perform a task [2], or gesture [6]. In contrast to ours, the application domain for these is mostly industrial and concerned with movement generalization for high-end robots.

Using an external camera to record motion presents a tempting alternative to sensors, as cameras are cheap, reusable, and noninvasive. Puppeteering systems can track 2D paper cutouts using an overhead camera [5], and 3D objects using a depth sensor [11]. Motion capture systems have been used to calibrate robot motors [18]. None of these, however, have used a webcam to directly puppeteer a robot.

SYSTEM DESCRIPTION

"Mirror Puppeteering" works by converting markers to motor angles using a calibration map either provided with the robot or generated by the advanced user. This mapping is a lookup table from markers on the robot viewed in camera space, to motor angles; it is thus generated once per robot and camera position.

The method consists of three stages: self-calibration, puppeteering, and playback. In self-calibration, the robot moves each of its limbs through its full range, streaming the limb's current motor commands to the computer. Simultaneously, the moving markers are detected in the webcam frames, allowing the software to build up a calibration map between motor angles and camera-space markers. This stage needs to be done only once per camera-robot configuration, and can be done ahead of time as part of the robot's factory settings. In puppeteering, the animator moves the robot through its desired trajectories, and our software detects markers in the camera image. For each frame, the system scans through the limb's map, to find the entry with markers in a similar position as the current camera frame. Once a match is found, the corresponding motor angles are added to the animation timeline. In playback, the robot uses the stored motor commands to recreate the movement. This stage does not require markers or a camera. Replay can be duplicated and transferred to a different robot, or to a virtual character.

Note that, at no stage, did we need to give the software any knowledge of the robot's geometry, joint hierarchies, input limits, or self-collisions. Instead, we maintain the paradigm that it is the robot that embodies self-knowledge; our "mirror" is a hardware-agnostic tool for the robot to look at itself. Any new robot with the right calibration routine can be used out-of-the-box, without altering the mirror software.

We split the description of the system into four parts:

1. **Self-Calibration** we describe the automatic calibration stage, including marker placement and tracking.
2. **Puppeteering** we describe puppeteering in realtime continuous mode and tracked keyframing mode, and detail the matching algorithm and graphical user interface.
3. **Playback and Beyond** we describe ways in which the data collected during Mirror Puppeteering can be used, beyond direct playback.
4. **Prototype** we describe the hardware setup we used in our Mirror Puppeteering prototype.

Self-Calibration

In the self-calibration stage, our software tracks markers placed on each of the robot's limbs. We use markers consisting of dark circles on a light background. We chose these markers not only for their traceability, but also because they can be easily incorporated into a robotic puppet, e.g. as eyes.

We identify markers in realtime using OpenCV; with a webcam resolution of 1280x720, median blur and marker detection are actually the speed-limiting part of our software, running at circa 18 fps on a 2GHz quadcore processor. We experimented with using QR codes and various marker shapes and colors to provide identification and orientation information, and found circles to be the only shape whose tracking is robust to the significant amount of motion blur.

Figure 3. The cookie jar robot calibrating its head, with the calibration map visualized as a colored overlay onscreen.

The markers need to be placed such that in any given robot pose, at least one marker will be visible at the end of every motor chain. For this purpose, we define a *motor chain* as an ordered set of motors from the robot base to an end effector. When referring to motors, we use the notation

$$chain_i \equiv (motor_{i_1}, motor_{i_2}, \dots, motor_{i_N})$$

Motors can belong to more than one chain; for instance, if motors are arranged in a "Y" configuration, the base motor belongs to two chains, and is therefore both $motor_{1_1}$ and $motor_{2_1}$. The angle of $motor_{i_j}$ is denoted θ_{i_j}.

One marker visible in the 2D camera view is sufficient to characterize a two-motor chain. In a chain of length $N > 2$, each additional $motor_{i_j}, j \leq N - 1$, added to the base of the chain, requires a marker to always be visible on the robot limb between $motor_{i_j}$ and $motor_{i_{j+1}}$.

We do not track marker trajectories over time, nor label the markers; each frame provides only a set of marker locations and sizes. Our philosophy is to build a stable system by making use of the parts of computer vision that are very accurate: blob (marker) finding in a single frame is mostly repeatable and mistakes do not accumulate; in contrast, attempting to label markers over time as they come in and out of occlusion is more error prone.

We will use $\{(x_k, y_k, r_k)\}$ to refer to the set of markers, with x and y coordinates *in camera frame space* and radii r (as a proxy for z position), detected in a given frame k. During the calibration phase we compute which markers are in motion. We maintain a one-second buffer of marker sets; to compute whether a marker in the current frame is moving, we look one second earlier and check if there was a marker in the same location and size as the current marker. If not, the marker is defined as moving.

To calibrate the robot, it is positioned in front of the webcam as shown in Figure 3. By clicking on the "Calibrate" button in the interface, a signal is sent to the microcontroller to begin the calibration routine. In this routine, the microcontroller takes each chain in turn, and moves the chain through every combination of angles it can assume. With each change in angle, the microcontroller sends the list of motors in the chain, and their current angles, to the software for recording. As the software receives the angles over serial for each $chain_i$, it simultaneously finds the markers $\{(x_k, y_k, r_k)\}$ that are moving in the current camera frame. The software then stores this combination as one calibration map entry in $calib_i$, matching the angles and the moving markers:

$$calib_i[(\theta_{i_1}, \theta_{i_2}, \ldots)] = \{(x_k, y_k, r_k)\} \quad (1)$$

Calibration for the cookie jar robot seen in Figure 1 takes roughly 5 minutes. The arm is moved from its lowest position to its highest, in increments of $\sim 1°$. For each $3°$ yaw of the head, the head does a full up-down sweep. For chains of length $N > 2$, it is important to work backwards from $motor_{i_N}$ in the outer loop to the base motor, $motor_{i_1}$, in the innermost loop. With the base motor always moving, *all* markers on the chain will be moving, and they can thus be isolated from other chains.

Along with the calibration map, we save a sample frame and its motor angles; when the user reloads a map, we present the frame overlayed on the current live video stream so that the robot can be positioned accurately.

Puppeteering

After the calibration step, or by loading previous calibration data and aligning the robot, the animator can start animating.

Matching Algorithm

The matching algorithm selects the motor signals that would create the robot pose currently seen by the webcam. Marker locations are captured by the webcam and matched against entries in the calibration map. A chain can have many calibration poses with similar marker sets; our matching function will choose between them by checking for continuity with previously computed angles. Thus, we track the robot throughout a user's session, whether or not the data is being recorded. We initialize the matching algorithm with the angles from the sample calibration frame.

In our matching algorithm we look at each motor chain independently. For each $chain_i$, we run through all entries in $calib_i$. The entry we are seeking will be an accurate subset of the markers (moving or not) in the current camera frame. A distance function uses this metric, looping over each marker (x_k^c, y_k^c, r_k^c) in the calibration entry and adding the distance to the nearest marker in the camera frame (from the set $\{(x_k, y_k, r_k)\}$). By matching from the calibration set to the current frame, spurious markers in the background, and markers in other chains, do not hinder matching.

When calculating the distance function, we penalize motor jumps greater than 10 percent. This enforcement of motor continuity is key to our being able to use indistinguishable circular markers. For example, the cookie jar looking 90 degrees right with a marker on the left side of its lid, and looking straight with a marker in front center of its lid, both present identical (x_k, y_k, r_k) marker locations; however, the penalty ensures only the pose closest to the previously computed one is chosen.

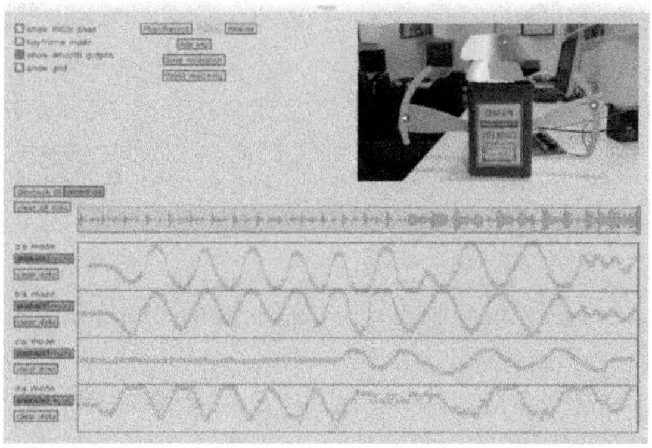

Figure 4. The interface showing a puppeteered animation.

Graphical User Interface

Our GUI, shown in Figure 4, presents a timeline with audio visualization and motor graphs along the bottom of the screen, and button controls in the upper left. A live view of the camera is in the upper right. The view is overlayed with the calibration data and a realtime view of the matching results (white lines between detected markers and the calibration markers that matched to them).

We support two Mirror Puppeteering techniques in the GUI: *continuous puppeteering* and *tracked keyframing*. During *continuous puppeteering*, the robot's movements are recorded in realtime with the timeline playhead advancing continuously. The animator toggles motors back and forth between "record" and "playback" mode. When the animator hits "play" to puppeteer the robot, motors set to "record" will continuously record, and motors set to "playback" will move of their own accord. Thus the animator can layer animation, animating one limb, and subsequently replaying the motion at the same time he is animating another limb. In *tracked keyframing*, the software tracks the robot as the animator moves it; but only discrete poses are recorded. The animator moves the playhead to a given position, poses the robot, and clicks "add keyframe" to add the pose to the graph. For the purpose of evaluating our system with respect to traditional methods (see below), we also include an option for *traditional keyframing*, where no tracking is used and the animator clicks on graphs representing each limb's position to create, delete, and adjust keypoints.

Playback and Beyond

Playback can be done away from the camera; at this point, the systems knows all the motor positions in the animation. Markers are usually part of the robot's "costume", but if temporary markers were attached to the robot, they can be removed at this stage.

The "mirror" we have created produces a fairly generic mapping: markers visible in the camera to motor positions. Mirror Puppeteering thus has capabilities in addition to the recording and playback of a single robot.

Without any modification, our system supports realtime show control. A user with two physically identical robots can pup-

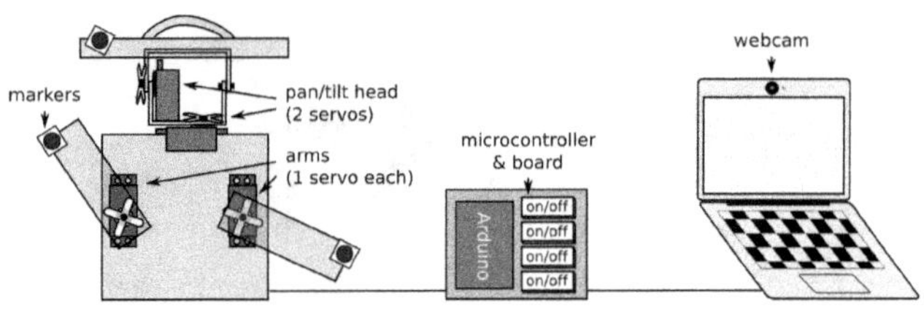

Figure 5. Our prototypes consist of a robot made up of servos, a microcontroller with a circuit board, and a laptop with a webcam.

peteer one robot "behind the curtain" while simultaneously playing back the animation on the second robot; we show this technique in the accompanying video using the clock robots. The control robot can also be a smaller proxy of a larger animated robot on stage. Our software can also function as a more general motion capture tool. For example, after calibrating the cookie jar robot's arm, one could attach a marker to one's own hand, and animate the robot by waving one's hand along a similar path.

Finally, an animator can use the system to drive a virtual character by puppeteering a physical robot. Our software streams out motor angles simultaneously to USB and to a named pipe, allowing both custom hardware and animation software to link easily into our system.

Hardware Prototype

Mirror Puppeteering works on any robot with position controlled actuators which can be back-driven when switched off. In our prototypes, we tested the system on My Keepon, a toy robot with DC gear motors, and several robots we built ourselves, actuated with hobby servos.

In our prototyping setup for homemade servo robots, the robot's custom calibration routine is loaded on the Arduino microcontroller acting as the robot's firmware. The circuit board attached to the microcontroller cuts/gives power to the servos to switch them between "record" and "playback" modes (Figure 5). We build two development boards. The manual board contains flip switches to control power to each servo individually. The automatic board contains relays which are controlled by our software "record" and "play" toggles.

The Arduino and computer communicate over USB. During calibration, the Arduino streams the current motor angles to the computer. During animation playback, the computer sends power control signals and motor angles in realtime to the Arduino and the Arduino moves the motors.

EVALUATION

We evaluated our system using the 4-DoF cookie jar robot shown throughout this paper. We measured the system's accuracy by comparing original motor positions to reconstructed motor positions for several motion trajectories. We measured user experience in a user study comparing continuous puppeteering, tracked keyframing, and traditional keyframing.

Accuracy

To evaluate the accuracy of our system we took puppeteered dance animations from participants in the study described below, and played them back on the robot. Simultaneously, we used our matching algorithm to reconstruct the motor positions.

We measured the mean error in degrees for each motor over three 15-second animations, sampled at 1000Hz. Mean errors were 3.2° for the left arm, 3.0° for the right arm, 2.7° for the head pan, and 3.1° for the head tilt. Fast movements were the greatest source of error, as they create motion blur which can cause tracking failure.

User Study

To evaluate the usability of our system as compared to traditional robot animation, we ran a user study comparing three methods: continuous puppeteering, tracked keyframing, and traditional keyframing. Participants used the cookie jar robot in a preset configuration setup, simulating the use-case of a novice user animating a commercial robot.

Participants were given fifteen seconds of a piece of dance music, and asked to design a dance for the robot. The dance could be on-beat or off-beat, detailed or not. For each of the three methods, used in randomized order, the experimenter explained the method, the participant worked on a dance "until they were satisfied" (usually around 10 minutes), and then the participant completed a survey.

The survey contained four Likert scales, each the mean of two items: quality of results ("I was satisfied with the quality of the animation I created.", "The result of this method was close to what I originally had in mind."); enjoyment ("I had fun animating using this method.","This method was annoying to use (reversed scale)."); usability ("I could easily get the robot to move like I wanted it to.","I found this method inefficient (reversed scale)."); and learning curve ("I understood how to use this method easily.","I became productive quickly using this method."). These correspond to our design goals. Each item was rated from 0 (strongly disagree) to 7 (strongly agree). At the end of the survey were two optional open-ended questions asking the participant to write one good and one bad thing about the method.

Eighteen participants, 11 male, 10 female (3 participants were pairs), ages 10 to 39, participated in the study. Four had experience with an animation software such as Maya, but none were expert animators. All participants seemed entertained by the experience of programming a robot, no matter which method.

Results

From subjective observation, we note that each of the three methods requires a different mental approach to animating; the experimenter observed that participants would often "get" one method most intuitively.

We found support for this observation in the participants' open question remarks. Most participants used the word

	mean (std dev)		
	continuous puppeteering	tracked keyframing	traditional keyframing
Results	**5.7 (1.3)**	5.2 (1.1)	**4.3 (1.9)**
Enjoyability	**6.4 (0.9)**	*5.6 (1.5)*	***4.0 (2.0)***
Usability	**5.6 (1.4)**	5.1 (1.3)	**4.2 (1.7)**
Learning Curve	**6.2 (1.1)**	5.4 (1.2)	**5.2 (1.5)**

Table 1. Participants rated continuous puppeteering and traditional keyframing significantly different along all four scales (bold). Tracked keyframing was significantly different (italics) only in "enjoyability" against traditional keyframing.

"fun" to describe the puppeteering interface; but while some found it "easy to use" and "more interactive", and one liked the "unmediated feel to the animation process", several others complained that it required too much coordination. Some found that tracked keyframing, "allows you to easily stay on beat" and "be more exact", but others had trouble with the thinking process, because "you need to remember what you already made the robot do in order to make a good dance. You have to focus, which makes it more difficult", and "you don't really know how it will all come together". When using the traditional keyframing interface, some participants happily created an interesting curve on the graph, and extensively fine-tuned it, with little regard for what it would actually look like on the robot; others focused intensely on mentally mapping locations on a motor graph to corresponding motor angles. The traditional keyframing interface was thus both "straightforward and pretty simple" and "quicker", as well as "far less intuitive" and "exhausting".

Likert Scales

Table 1 shows the results of the four Likert scale measures. One-way ANOVA revealed significant differences between groups in all four scales: scale Results, $F(2,51) = 3.97, p < .05$; Enjoyment, $F(2,51) = 12.36, p < .001$; Usability, $F(2,51) = 4.03, p < .05$; and Learning Curve, $F(2,51) = 3.68, p < .05$. Post-hoc Bonferroni-corrected pairwise comparisons revealed that puppeteering was significantly different from traditional keyframing on all four metrics ($p < .05$). Tracked keyframing was significantly different only in the "enjoyment" scale, compared with traditional keyframing ($p < .05$).

LIMITATIONS

The primary limitation of our algorithm, which restricts us to low-DoF robots, is that the number of combinations of angles in the calibration sequence must be tractable. As each motor chain is calibrated independently, the robot can have a large number of limbs, but to be computationally feasible, each limb must be restricted to two degrees of freedom. A limb can have more degrees of freedom if each motor covers a small range. For example, in the accompanying video we add ears to the lid of the cookie jar robot, creating three DoF chains; however, we restrict the range of the ears to three discrete positions (left-middle-right).

Robots must have a stationary base. While this does not make our system appropriate for mobile robots, in practice, many of the expressive robots designed in the last decade do actually have a stationary base. Some examples include MIT's Leonardo and AUR; iCat; Jibo; Georgia Tech's Travis and Shimon; Keepon; and Karotz.

Very fast puppeteering can cause markers to motion blur in the camera frame. We overcome the ambiguity among similar marker sets in calibration entries by looking for temporal motor angle continuity. However, if—for example—-we rotate the cookie jar head too rapidly from left to right, causing motion blur during the transition, our tracking algorithm will fail, as both sides look similar. We can alleviate this problem by offsetting the markers so they do not end up in identical camera frame locations. Note in Figure 1 that the center marker on the cookie jar's head is raised relative to the side markers. Future work could include additional disambiguation cues such as marker color.

Robots must be designed so that one limb cannot fully occlude all the markers in another limb. A possible solution in case of occlusion is to place the markers on an extension for calibration and puppeteering. In the snakes robot in Figure 1, for example, the front snakes fully occlude the rear snakes; we added antennae to hold the rear markers.

The relationship between the camera and the 3D marker movement affects the precision of tracking. Marker movements that are co-planar or near co-planar to the image plane are most readily tracked. Movements which are largely towards or away from the camera are not as easily distinguished, but this limitation is ameliorated by factoring in the radius of the markers. Naturally, the higher the resolution of the camera, the less sensitive the system is to this issue.

The robot must be in precisely the same camera alignment during calibration and animation. In practice we found it often faster to take the role of the "advanced user" and let the robot run self-calibration whenever placing it in front of the camera.

CONCLUSION AND FUTURE WORK

This paper presented Mirror Puppeteering, a direct puppeteering system that enables lay users to create expressive animations on toy robots. Robots in this class tend to be small and structurally simple, an ideal opportunity for a vision-based system. We use markers on the robot, which can be embedded in the robot's design, and track these markers to recover motor positions. Our system is agnostic to the 3D structure of the robot, allowing new robots to quickly use the software as-is. This makes our system a candidate to be web-deployed and generic enough for a large number of toys.

Mirror Puppeteering can also be used to control robots in realtime, control virtual characters, and record animations for them. In this paper and the accompanying video, we demonstrate these possibilities on a range of small robots and virtual characters.

Our user study showed that puppeteering at this scale is understandable by the naive user, useful, and, moreover, enjoyable. Although the optimality of continuous recording versus poses is task dependent [1], participants' preferences in even our single task were divided among all three methods, encouraging their inclusion in future puppeteering systems. Moreover, several participants suggested that the ideal animation software would be a combination of puppeteering and traditional keyframing: puppeteering to lay down the rough animation, and keyframing to fine-tune it. This workflow is possible in our current software, although it would be tedious to adjust each point in the dense curves created by puppeteering. An intuitive way to modify these curves at different scales would be a useful addition to our software.

Future work could make the system simpler still, eliminating the need for even the robot's firmware to know its joint hierarchy and motor limits in advance. Similar to the self-calibration step, the robot could look at itself in the mirror, tracking marker locations, to figure out what its structure and limits are.

Given the increasing popularity of both toy robotics and amateur 3D animation, the fact that Mirror Puppeteering is specifically designed for consumer-grade webcams and low-cost motors, and is designed to work easily out of the box, makes this a promising candidate for real-world usage of puppeteering as a home animation technique. Novices can thus use both hands, and the richness and fluency of their embodied motion, to bring their robots and 3D characters to life.

REFERENCES

1. B. Akgun, M. Cakmak, K. Jiang, and A. Thomaz. Keyframe-based learning from demonstration. *International Journal of Social Robotics*, 4(4):343–355, 2012.
2. B. Akgun, M. Cakmak, J. W. Yoo, and A. Thomaz. Trajectories and keyframes for kinesthetic teaching: a human-robot interaction perspective. In *ACM/IEEE International Conf. on Human-Robot Interaction*, pages 391–398, 2012.
3. J. Allen, J. Young, D. Sakamoto, and T. Igarashi. Style by demonstration for interactive robot motion. In *ACM Designing Interactive Systems Conf.*, pages 592–601, 2012.
4. B. Argall, S. Chernova, M. Veloso, and B. Browning. A survey of robot learning from demonstration. *Robotics and Autonomous Systems*, 57(5):469–483, 2009.
5. C. Barnes, D. Jacobs, J. Sanders, D. Goldman, S. Rusinkiewicz, A. Finkelstein, and M. Agrawala. Video puppetry: a performative interface for cutout animation. *ACM Transactions on Graphics*, 27(5):124:1–124:9, 2008.
6. S. Calinon and A. Billard. Incremental learning of gestures by imitation in a humanoid robot. In *ACM/IEEE International Conf. on Human-Robot Interaction*, pages 255–262, 2007.
7. J. Cole, D. Grimes, and R. Rao. Learning full-body motions from monocular vision: dynamic imitation in a humanoid robot. In *IEEE/RSJ International Conf. on Intelligent Robots and Systems*, pages 240–246, 2007.
8. P. Frei, V. Su, B. Mikhak, and H. Ishii. Curlybot: Designing a new class of computational toys. In *ACM Conf. on Human Factors in Computing Systems*, pages 129–136, 2000.
9. P. Goebel. Skeleton tracker teleoperation package for mobile robot, 2013. `www.ros.org`.
10. S. Ha, Y. Bai, and K. Liu. Human motion reconstruction from force sensors. In *ACM SIGGRAPH/Eurographics Symp. on Computer Animation*, pages 129–138, 2011.
11. R. Held, A. Gupta, B. Curless, and M. Agrawala. 3d puppetry: a kinect-based interface for 3d animation. In *ACM Symp. on User Interface Software and Technology*, pages 423–434, 2012.
12. M. Johnson, A. Wilson, B. Blumberg, C. Kline, and A. Bobick. Sympathetic interfaces: Using a plush toy to direct synthetic characters. In *ACM Conf. on Human Factors in Computing Systems*, pages 152–158, 1999.
13. A. Lemme, A. Freire, G. Barreto, and J. Steil. Kinesthetic teaching of visuomotor coordination for pointing by the humanoid robot icub. *Neurocomputing*, 2013.
14. N. Pollard and J. Hodgins. Optimizing human motion for the control of a humanoid robot. In *International Symp. on Adaptive Motion of Animals and Machines*, March 2003.
15. H. Raffle, A. Parkes, and H. Ishii. Topobo: a constructive assembly system with kinetic memory. In *ACM Conf. on Human Factors in Computing Systems*, pages 647–654, 2004.
16. R. Slyper and J. Hodgins. Action capture with accelerometers. In *ACM SIGGRAPH/Eurographics Symp. on Computer Animation*, pages 193–199, 2008.
17. Y. Sugiura, G. Kakehi, A. Withana, C. Fernando, D. Sakamoto, M. Inami, and T. Igarashi. Walky: An operating method for a bipedal walking robot for entertainment. In *ACM SIGGRAPH Asia Emerging Technologies*, pages 79–79, 2009.
18. Y. Takase, H. Mitake, Y. Yamashita, and S. Hasegawa. Motion generation for the stuffed-toy robot. In *SICE Annual Conf.*, pages 213–217, 2013.
19. K. Yamane, Y. Ariki, and J. Hodgins. Animating non-humanoid characters with human motion data. In *ACM SIGGRAPH/Eurographics Symp. on Computer Animation*, pages 169–178, 2010.
20. W. Yoshizaki, Y. Sugiura, A. Chiou, S. Hashimoto, M. Inami, T. Igarashi, Y. Akazawa, K. Kawachi, S. Kagami, and M. Mochimaru. An actuated physical puppet as an input device for controlling a digital manikin. In *ACM Conf. on Human Factors in Computing Systems*, pages 637–646, 2011.

Comparing Pictorial and Tangible Notations of Force Image Schemas

Jörn Hurtienne
Würzburg University
97074 Würzburg
joern.hurtienne@uni-wuerzburg.de

Diana Löffler
Würzburg University
97074 Würzburg
diana.loeffler@uni-wuerzburg.de

Patty Gadegast
HS Magdeburg
39114 Magdeburg
pattygadegast@googlemail.com

Steffi Hußlein
HS Magdeburg
39114 Magdeburg
steffi.husslein@hs-magdeburg.de

ABSTRACT
Force image schemas (FIS) are cognitive representations of our naïve understanding of physical force dynamic events in the world. Designers have been struggling to apply FIS in their design processes, because their deliberate use has been made difficult by applying too abstract notations. In this paper we try to advance FIS as a possible theoretical framework for tangible design and present new pictorial and tangible notations of FIS that aim to be more directly applicable. The new notations were tested by asking non-experts to (1) match pictorial and tangible FIS representations to force image schema names and (2) to develop design ideas based on these pictorial or tangible representations. While the group working with the pictorial notations was more correct in assigning FIS names to FIS representations, design ideas tended to be more tangible and interactive in the group working with the tangible FIS notations.

Author Keywords
Tangible interaction design; force image schemas; design guidelines; image schematic metaphors; haptic interaction.

ACM Classification Keywords
H.5.2. Information interfaces and presentation (e.g., HCI): User Interfaces – Theory and methods.

INTRODUCTION
Many studies of tangible interaction design use image schemas and their metaphorical extensions as tools for inspiration. Image schemas as introduced by Johnson [13] are abstract representations of recurring dynamic patterns of bodily interactions that structure the way we understand the world. Image schemas exist beneath conscious awareness what makes them interesting for designing intuitive interactions [7, 9]. They integrate information from multiple modalities and can be represented visually, haptically, kinesthetically or acoustically. Depending on the author, about 30 to 40 of such image schemas are distinguished [5, 13]. Hurtienne [7] organizes these into seven groups: basic image schemas like SUBSTANCE and OBJECT; space image schemas like CENTER-PERIPHERY and UP-DOWN; containment image schemas like FULL-EMPTY and CONTAINER; multiplicity image schemas like SPLITTING and COLLECTION; process image schemas like ITERATION and CYCLE; attribute image schemas like BIG-SMALL and HEAVY-LIGHT; and, finally, force image schemas, like ATTRACTION and BLOCKAGE.

http://dx.doi.org/10.1145/2677199.2680553

The actual strength of image schemas lies in their metaphorical extensions to structure abstract concepts. Examples of such metaphorical extensions include: ACTIVITIES ARE CONTAINERS, as in: *she used to delight in washing clothes;* UNPROBLEMATIC IS SMOOTH – PROBLEMATIC IS ROUGH, as in: *Top management faces a potentially rough ride. Don't interfere with the smooth running of our love life;* HAPPY IS UP – SAD IS DOWN, as in: *I'm feeling up. He is really down these days.*

Tangible interaction design can use image schemas as topological, spatial and object attributes to inspire new physical-to-abstract mappings. Previous research, for example, has shown that metaphorical mappings of object attributes to a large extent follow image-schematic metaphors proposed from linguistic analysis [12, 15] and can also be found in the spontaneous use of tangible artifacts and full body interaction [1, 2, 3]. Combined with the linguistic analysis of user's utterances image-schematic metaphors can also inspire the design process of full-scaled graphical and tangible user interfaces [7, 9, 11, 14] with original and novel designs that at the same time are intuitive to use.

In this paper, the focus is on force image schemas (FIS) – cognitive representations of our naïve understanding of physical force dynamic events in the world. FIS are promising for tangible interaction design – whether used in their physical instantiations or as instantiations of their metaphorical extensions. From previous studies we know that FIS can be a challenge to apply because of their too abstract notations. Hence, we devised new sets of image schema representations – one pictorial, one tangible – and tested these for their effectiveness in analysis and design.

FIS*	Definition	Original notation [13, 19]	UI Example (Physical or Abstract)	New pictoral notation
AT	A (passive) object exerts a force on another object, to pull it toward itself, mostly acting from a distance.	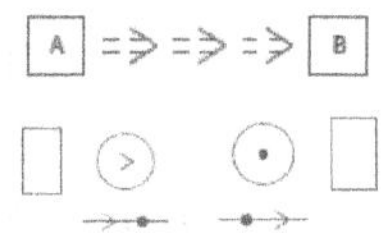	If the seatbelt is not fastened in the car, then a beeping sound is activated to alert the driver.	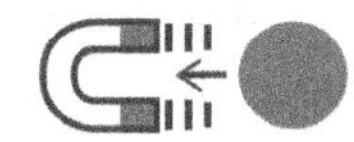
BA	Forces and/or weights counteract/ balance off one another. Meta–phorically, there is equilibrium, not too much and not not enough.	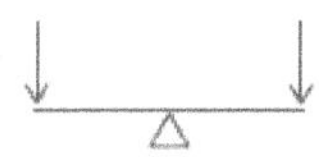	Countersteering when slowly riding a bicycle.	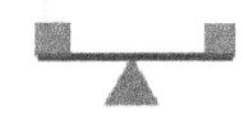
BL	A force/movement is stopped or redirected by an obstacle.	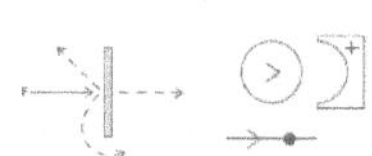	The car driver pulls on the handbrake to prevent inadvertent rolling.	
CP	An external force causes some passive entity to move.		The car driver steps on the accelerator and the car accelerates.	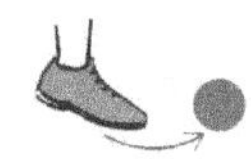
CF	The active meeting of opposing forces that are equally strong. Both forces collide; there is no further movement.		The plane pilot struggles against the autopilot about changing height. The plane neither descends nor ascends.	
DI	Forces that meet and produce a change in direction or force vectors (at least one).	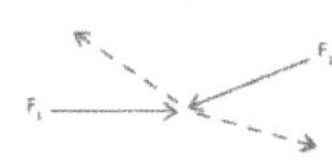	A ringing phone diverges the user from doing her actual task.	
EN	Having the power to perform some act or a potential force (vector) and the absence of BL, RS, CF or CP	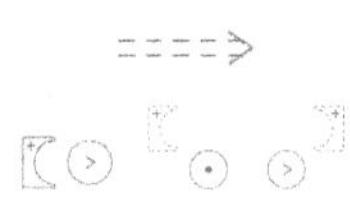	When the car is taking a bend, the cornering light actively lights into the bend where the driver needs to look. (active EN)	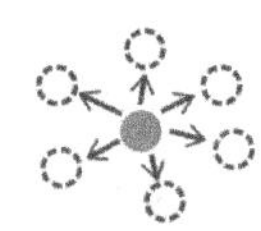
MO	The tendency of an object to maintain the actual state of motion (or rest) if there is no influence of another agent.		The progress indicator of an mp3-player is moving as long as the song is playing or until stopped.	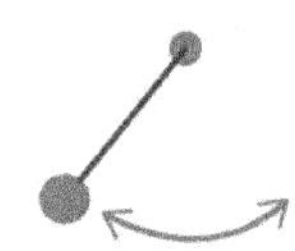
RP	A (passive) object exerts a force on another object, to repel it, mostly acting from a distance.	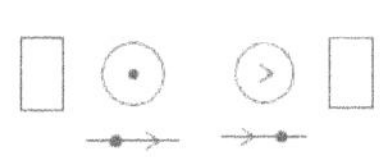	A sudden loud noise from the anti-theft device is repelling the thieve.	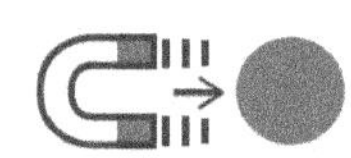
RS	A force that tends to oppose or retard the motion of another entity.	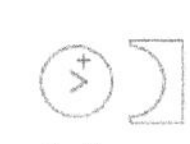	A heavily embellished font slows reading.	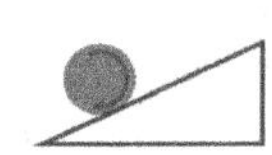
RR	The removal of a barrier to the action of a force, or absence of a barrier that was potentially present.	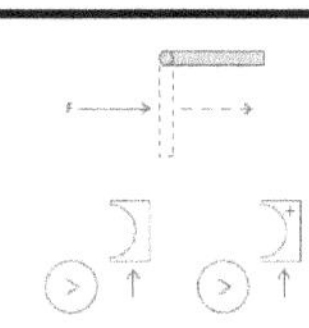	The car driver releases the handbrake to move off.	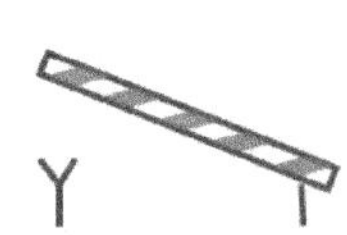
SM	A resting entity starts moving without any forces acting on it.		The backing up of data is taking place automatically.	

Table 1: Force image schema definitions, notations and examples. The last column contains the new FIS icons.
***ATTRACTION (AT), BALANCE (BA), BLOCKAGE (BL), COMPULSION (CP), COUNTERFORCE (CF), DIVERSION (DI), ENABLEMENT (EN), MOMENTUM (MO), REPULSION (RP), RESISTANCE (RS), RESTRAINT REMOVAL (RR), SELF MOTION (SM)**

FORCE IMAGE SCHEMAS

What are Force Image Schemas?

The idea of a special group of force image schemas originates in cognitive linguistics [13, 19]. Force image schemas are cognitive representations of our naïve understanding of physical force dynamic events in the world. Accordingly, language specifies only selected aspects of a force dynamic scenario and heavily abstracts from other dimensions of experience: "[Force dynamics] presents an extremely simple representation of causality, one that marks few distinctions and lumps together ranges of diversity. This representation abstracts away, for example, from particularities of rate, scope of involvement, manner of spread, and the like." ([19], p. 92). More concretely, most force interactions that are encoded in language can be reduced to the following properties ([19] p. 97): two forces are involved – not one, and not three or more; the two forces are opposing each other – not acting in concert in the same direction; the two forces are opposing each other 180° head on – not coming at each other at some other angle; a force is acting along a straight line – not along a curved line, not concentrically outward or inward; there is a constant force tendency in the Agonist (the focal force tendency) – not one that varies; this force tendency has two values: toward either action or rest – not one of multiple or continuous value; the resultant state in the Antagonist (the opposing force entity) is also two-valued: either action or rest – not one of multiple or continuous value.

Talmy points out that these characteristics form the conceptual naïve physics of force dynamics that is reflected in language, because the same pattern can be seen across different unrelated languages. He delivers a first set of force image schemas, i.e. ATTRACTION (AT), BLOCKAGE (BL), COMPULSION (CP), ENABLEMENT (EN), RESISTANCE (RS), and RESTRAINT REMOVAL (RR) that all follow the above characteristics [19]. Other force image schemas, albeit with a looser understanding regarding their characteristics were introduced by Johnson [13]: COUNTERFORCE (CF), BALANCE (BA), and DIVERSION (DI). On the basis of strong psychological evidence [4, 17], we added MOMENTUM (MO) and SELF-MOTION (SM) to the group of force image schemas. An overview of the force image schemas is given in Table 1 along with definitions and user interface examples.

As with other image schemas, in tangible interaction design, force image schemas can be used physically and metaphorically. When applying FIS to design, it is useful to differentiate the Agonist from the Antagonist in the force interaction. Several possibilities exist: (1) The user is the Agonist, the technology is the Antagonist. (2) The technology is the Agonist, the user is the Antagonist. (3) Users are Agonists and Antagonists, where the technology has a mediating or representing role. (4) Other agents are Agonists and Antagonist and the user interface is a representation of their force dynamic processes.

Force image schemas can always be useful design aids when representing or mediating real physical forces through the user interface (e.g. control rooms in factories and chemical plants). The type of instantiation may differ: from providing physical force feedback to a visualization of movement trajectories.

FIS can also be used in metaphors to express abstract information. The most common application areas include the representation and manipulation of causality, e.g. starting, stopping, and letting physical and abstract processes. FIS can be used to express social forces, as in *She pushes us to our limits* (COMPULSION), or *My doctor has forbidden me to drink alcohol* (BLOCKAGE). This can be extended to the modeling of rules and regulations in business processes, processes of negotiation and argumentation, as well as diplomatic or even military conflicts. FIS can also be used to represent metaphoric psychological forces, e.g. emotions, as in *I am moved by this poem* (COMPULSION) and inner-psychic conflicts as in *He is wrestling with his feelings* (COUNTERFORCE).

Although FIS have been used in previous tangible interaction research [1, 11], their use, compared to other image schemas, remains rather limited. The reasons could be that FIS are harder to detect and categorize than other groups of image schemas. Much of this has to do with their dynamic and transient nature. Whether something is UP or DOWN, IN or OUT, BIG or SMALL is obvious and can be easily detected. Whether something is ATTRACTING, RESISTING or BLOCKING something else may be subtler to identify. Space, attribute and containment image schemas are often instantiated by static entities. FIS like COMPULSION, MOMENTUM, and DIVERSION, in contrast, are instantiated by the more transient dynamics of two or more interacting forces that may be more difficult to detect in the fleeting moment. Furthermore, FIS can be instantiated in both physical (e.g. blocking the movement of a lever) and abstract ways (e.g. blocking an un-authorized user from accessing a website) – the variety of instantiations makes it difficult to detect the underlying pattern.

To sum up, although the potential of FIS for TUI is great, there seem to be some hurdles to their application in interaction design that have to do with teaching and identifying FIS in action. We propose that looking at FIS notation systems might eventually provide a solution to bring FIS closer to those designers that are not image-schema experts.

Original FIS notations

Talmy [19] also developed a notational system for the force image schemas he proposed. Its basic elements are shown in Figure 1. In this system, there is always an Agonist and a stronger or weaker Antagonist. Agonists have either an intrinsic tendency toward rest or toward motion. In Talmy's notational system, the Agonist is indicated by a circle and the Antagonist by a concave form. Further, the Agonist's intrinsic force tendency, the resultant of the force interaction, and whether an entity is stronger or weaker than the other is coded in the notation. In the example of the notation of the blockage image schema, for example (see Table 1), the Agonist's tendency is towards action, but it is held back by a stronger Antagonist so that the Agonist is kept in place.

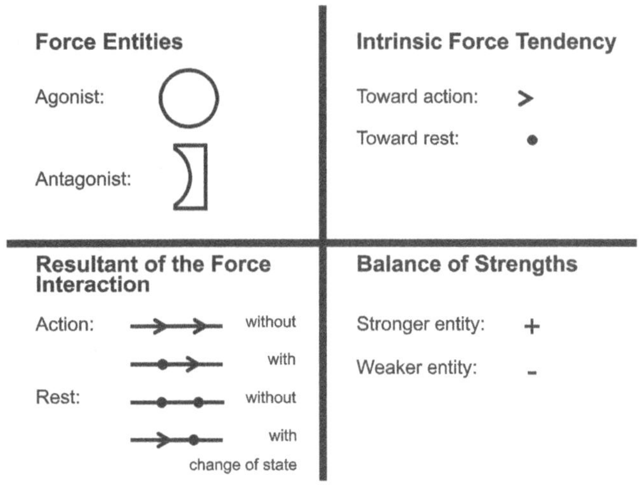

Figure 1. Elements of Talmy's [19] notation of force-dynamic elements.

Johnson's [13] notational system is rather informal and intuitive and depicts the meeting of forces and their resultants as movements on straight paths. Both notations are included in the overview of force image schemas in Table 1.

In a previous study [8], four designers familiar with force image schemas were provided with Johnson's and Talmy's notations and categorized 80 short force-dynamic episodes describing human-technology interactions (e.g. *The driver released the handbrake* as an example of restraint removal) into ten FIS categories (AT/RP, BA, BL, CF, CP, DI, EN, MO, RR, RS). The results show that while 73% of classifications were correct, many category confusions occurred. Confusions were more likely when image schema definitions overlapped. Some FIS differ only in degree of force strength (e.g. the increasing degree of Antagonist strength from RESISTANCE to COUNTERFORCE to BLOCKAGE) or are the precondition or consequence of another image schema (e.g. a BLOCKAGE, RESISTANCE, or COUNTERFORCE is the precondition of RESTRAINT REMOVAL; ENABLEMENT is a direct consequence of RESTRAINT REMOVAL; DIVERSION is a likely consequence of COMPULSION, ATTRACTION/ REPULSION, BLOCKAGE, COUNTERFORCE, and RESISTANCE). From the results of the study a number of suggestions for the training of image schema coders were derived. However, if image schemas are to be used in daily design processes, a specialized FIS training would not be feasible and we would need other ways of teaching.

The previous study has also shown that useful results can already be achieved with an introduction to FIS that lasts as long as 30 minutes. We, however, believed that neither the highly systematic notation of FIS by Talmy nor the informal sketches by Johnson would be of much help in quickly learning the definitions of force image schemas and making them easily applicable in practice. Therefore we devised two new sets of notations, one pictorial, the second tangible, based on force-dynamic prototypes. The aim was to see whether people could easily match the new FIS representations to FIS definitions and whether their design ideas based on these notations differed in any remarkable sense.

NEW FIS NOTATIONS: PICTORIAL AND TANGIBLE

Designing FIS Icons as a New Pictorial FIS Notation

Seventeen image schema experts were asked to create sketches that illustrate the core concept of each FIS. All of the experts professionally worked with image schemas for 0.5-6 years, mainly due to participation in a related research project. The experts were provided with the name of each FIS and a definition. They were allowed to draw as many sketches as they wanted to. Altogether, a total of 301 sketches were collected for eleven force image schemas (AT, BL, RS, CP, DI, BA, CF, EN, RR, MO, SM). Each sketch was decomposed in single elements, which were categorized as active/passive and object types involved. The final step of the analysis consisted of determining the most frequent characteristics of each FIS and creating a final iconic representation out of these elements (see Table 1, last column). For example, a swinging pendulum visualizes the FIS MOMENTUM and a rolling ball being slowed down by a ramp visualizes the FIS RESISTANCE. The icon for the missing FIS REPULSION was added after this study as a direct opposite of ATTRACTION.

In an informal test, five image schema novices were asked to describe the newly developed icons as well as the notations by Johnson [13] and Talmy [19]. Language analysis of the subjects' speech revealed that their language was consistent with the intended image schemas with the newly developed icons, e.g., 'the ramp impedes the balls movement' (RESISTANCE). However, the subjects in almost all cases were not able to understand and describe Johnson's and Talmy's notations.

Designing FIS Dials as a Tangible FIS Notation

The second attempt in developing 'tools' to support understanding and learning of FIS involved creating physical interactive prototypes. Designers should be enabled to grasp force image schemas in the literal sense (cf. [16]) with the idea that a tangible representation is more conducive to conveying force image schemas than a visual representation.

After collecting and exploring a variety of example FIS instantiations in animation, interactive simulation and early interactive physical prototypes we designed a set of twelve FIS prototypes and one neutral reference model. The prototypes were made very similar to each other to enable direct comparisons between different FIS. Each FIS was instantiated as interactions between a user and a physical rotatory dial. The prototypes were kept free of any applied context, to enable focusing on the FIS themselves. Each prototype consists of a neutral front with a rotary dial, a functional backside, and a side panel with some information regarding the FIS (Figures 2 and 3).

Figure 2. FIS-dial, generic front view (left). Interacting with a FIS-dial (right).

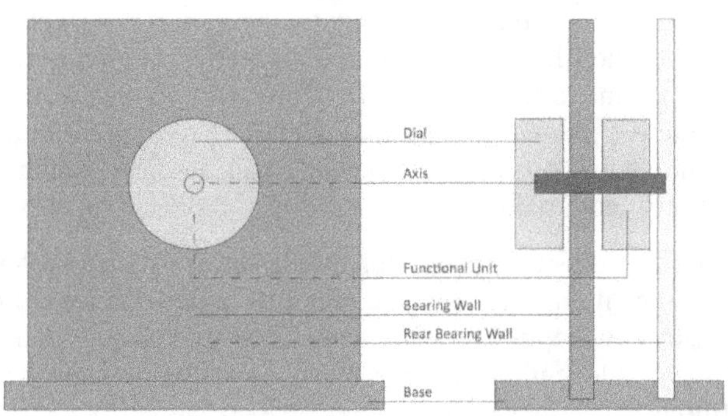

Figure 3. Generic design of FIS-dials.

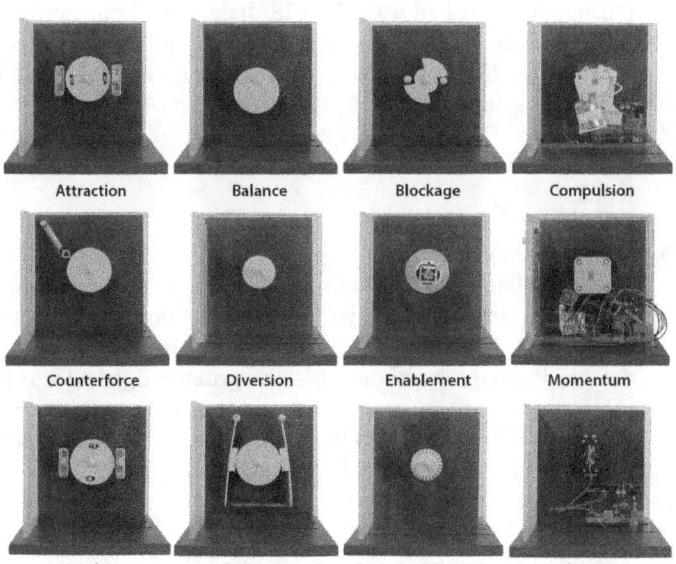

Figure 4: FIS-dials, rear view.

When interacted with, the dial on the front exhibits force image schematic behavior. The backside contains the functional part, implementing an active or passive force feedback mechanism. Passive models give haptic force feedback that is implemented by simple mechanics. Active models contain sensors and actors to perform movements of the dial. They were controlled by Arduino microcontroller boards. Figure 4 gives an overview of the functional backsides of the FIS dials.

ATTRACTION: When the user rotates the dial, a force attracts the dial to certain positions. Implemented with Neodym magnets in the dial and the bearing wall.

BALANCE: After turning the dial it re-assumes its original position. Implemented by a dial that rotates off-center.

BLOCKAGE: When the user rotates the dial, the motion is suddenly stopped. Implemented by wooden sticks hindering the movement of the dial.

COMPULSION: When touching the dial, the dial moves the users' hand. Implemented by sensing contact with a capacitive sensor (aluminium parts in the dial and axle), a simple electric circuit on the Arduino and a geared motor.

COUNTERFORCE: When rotating the dial, the user feels a counteracting force getting gradually stronger until the user can't move the dial further. Implemented with a strong spring attached to the dial and the bearing wall.

DIVERSION: When the user rotates the dial, it moves towards the user on the z-axis. Implemented by two complementary wave shapes. If the wave peaks touch, the dial is in its outer position, if wave peak and trough touch, the dial is back at its normal position.

ENABLEMENT: The existence of a dial that can be rotated already instantiates passive ENABLEMENT. This dial can be sunk into the wall where it cannot be rotated (thereby disabling it). Implemented using a stove knob with a spring mechanism.

MOMENTUM: The dial keeps its state of movement until the user changes it. When the dial does not move and the user rotates it, the dial will continue this rotational movement. When already rotating, the user can stop the dial or change the direction of the rotation. Implemented with a rotation sensor, an Arduino board, and a stepping motor.

REPULSION: When the user rotates the dial, the dial is repelled from certain positions and the user is not able to keep the dial at these positions. Implemented similar to the attraction dial by inversing the magnets' poles.

RESISTANCE: When rotating the dial, the user feels a continuous force that resists his movements. Implemented by using friction between two rubbers and wooden spatulas. A spring connecting the spatulas keeps a constant pressure.

RESTRAINT REMOVAL: This dial can only be moved when the user pulls it out. Implemented by two cogwheel shapes, pushed together by a spring. By pulling the dial the cogwheels are decoupled and the dial can be rotated.

SELF MOTION: This dial spontaneously moves with different speeds and directions. The user cannot influence the movements. Implemented with a modified servomotor and an Arduino board.

COMPARING NOTATIONAL SYSTEMS

We conducted a workshop to evaluate whether the newly developed FIS icons and FIS dials improve the correct identification and distinguishability of FIS by designers freshly introduced to force image schemas (part 1) and to gauge their usefulness in supporting designers to brainstorm design ideas for specific contexts (part 2).

Method

Fifteen students from a course on User-Centered Design at the University of Würzburg (10 male, mean age = 22 years) participated in a workshop as part of their course fulfillment. They received a 30-minute introduction to definitions and examples of the twelve FIS. Then they were randomly assigned to the FIS-dial (n = 7) or FIS-icon group (n=8) that worked in separate rooms. They were told that they were now tested on how good they could match the FIS dials to FIS names, or, in case of the other group, how good they could match FIS icons and FIS names. The dials and icons were displayed on tables and each participant according to his or her route card went to each 'FIS station' in sequence and identified the FIS instantiated by the FIS dials or icons. Multiple answers were allowed. Additionally, participants rated on a 4-point Likert scale how confident they were with their choices (1 = uncertain to 4 = certain). The sequence of FIS icons/dials was randomized and participants had two minutes time for each FIS instantiation.

In the second part of the workshop, the same participants were asked to brainstorm design ideas for all FIS. They were randomly assigned to the application contexts of a driver assistance system (DAS) or a smart phone application (APP). They worked through each FIS in random order and had four minutes time at each FIS. They were required to create sketches and short descriptions of their ideas. The ideas could describe either new or already existing designs.

After they had completed the task (that took about one hour), participants filled out a questionnaire providing demographic data and subjective ratings (6-point Likert scales, 1= strongly disagree to 6 = strongly agree) on how well they understood FIS, whether they were able to apply the FIS in design, whether FIS were helpful in creating design ideas and whether they found FIS important for interaction design.

Results

Image Schema Identification

A trial was counted as 'correct' when participants only chose the correct FIS. It was counted as 'partly correct' when the participants chose the correct FIS among other FIS, and as 'incorrect' when the correct FIS was not chosen at all. An independent samples t-test, $\alpha = 0.05$, revealed that participants in the FIS-icon group ($M = 0.69$, $SD = 0.44$) had more correct matches on average than the FIS-dial group ($M = 0.38$, $SD = 0.44$), $t(178) = 4.74$, $p < 0.001$, Cohen's $d = 0.76$. Unambiguousness of FIS identification was operationalized as the number of answers for each task. Participants in the FIS-icon group ($M = 1.19$, $SD = 0.39$) did choose on average fewer FIS in each matching task than the FIS-dial group ($M = 1.58$, $SD = 0.90$), $t(108.701) = 3.67$, $p < 0.001$, $d = 0.62$. Both groups did not differ in their confidence ratings, $p > 0.1$.

Design Exercise

On average, participants in the FIS-dial group created $M = 20.14$ ($SD = 5.27$) design ideas, whereas the participants in the FIS-icon group created $M = 30.39$ ($SD = 10.64$) ideas. The resulting total of 366 design ideas were rated by an author of this paper according to the criteria correctness (whether the FIS was instantiated correctly, on a scale from 0 to 2), innovation (on a scale from 0 to 3), interactivity (interactive/passive), haptic feedback (haptic/not haptic), visual feedback (visual/not visual) and auditory feedback (auditory/ not auditory).

Figure 5 shows the results for the driver assistance system. Although slight advantages for the FIS-dial group regarding interactivity, haptic feedback and auditory feedback seem to be seen, independent samples t-tests revealed no significant differences for these variables.

Figure 6 shows the results for the smart phone application. Participants that had used the FIS-dials when brainstorming design ideas created designs that were more interactive, $t(137.67) = 2.01$, $p = 0.046$, $d = 0.33$; more haptic, $t(78.84) = 3.45$, $p = 0.01$, $d = 0.66$; more visual, $t(146.256) = 2.50$, $p = 0.01$, $d = 0.36$, but less auditory, $t(161.073) = 3.59$, $p < 0.001$, $d = 0.48$ than the design ideas created from the FIS icons.

Post-Study Questionnaire

The FIS-dial and FIS-icon groups did not significantly differ in their subjective judgment how well they understood FIS and whether they were able to apply FIS in design. Participants in the FIS-icon group judged FIS to be more helpful in creating design ideas, $t(13) = 2.32$, $p = 0.04$, $d = 1.29$, and FIS to be more important for interaction design, $t(13) = 3.29$, $p = 0.006$, $d = 1.82$, Figure 7.

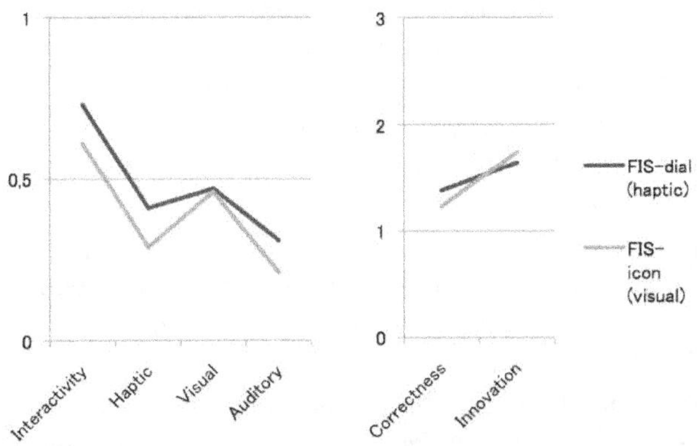

Figure 5. Rating FIS design ideas for driver assistance systems.

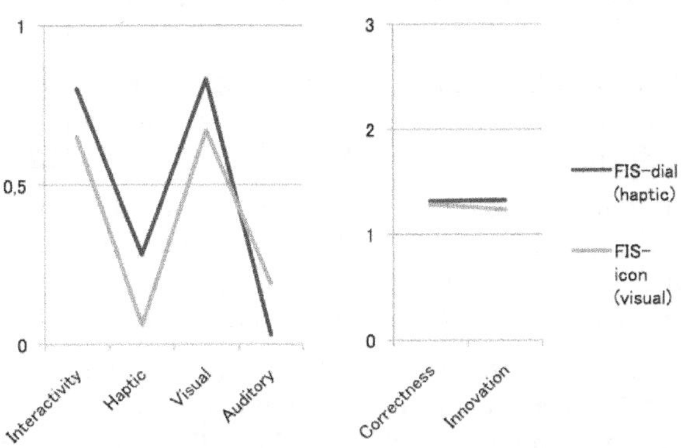

Figure 6. Rating FIS design ideas for the smartphone app.

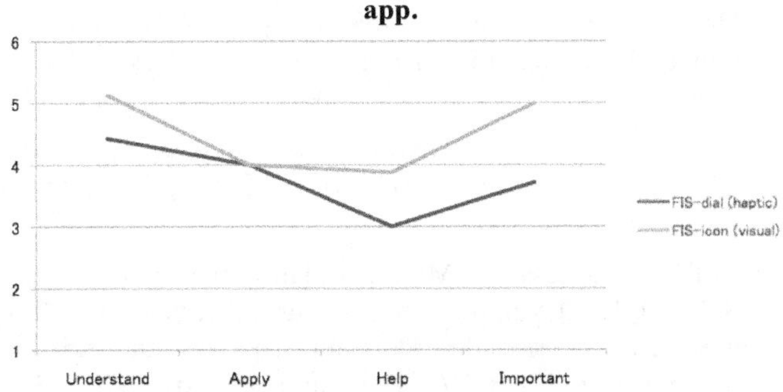

Figure 7. Results of post-study questionnaire.

Discussion

On the one hand, the results seem to demonstrate a clear advantage for the FIS-icon pictorial notation over the FIS-dial tangible notation. Workshop participants were more likely to correctly categorize FIS when using the FIS icons than when using the FIS dials. Thus, equipped with the FIS icons, designers could attain similar FIS recognition rates as the FIS experts in a previous study [8]. Participants in the FIS-icon group also categorized FIS less ambiguously than participants in the FIS-dials group. They also created more ideas in the design exercise. Participants found FIS more helpful and more important for interaction design when they had interacted with FIS icons before. They, however, did not differ in their judgment whether they had understood force image schemas and whether they were able to apply FIS in interaction design.

On the other hand, there seems to be a slight advantage for the FIS-dial tangible notation, when it comes to the quality of design ideas. Participants who used the FIS dials tended to have (in one task even significantly so) more interactive, more haptic and more visual design ideas than participants who used the FIS icons.

Thus, can we draw the seemingly paradox conclusion that, if one wants to achieve a clear understanding of force image schemas, one should use a pictorial notation like the FIS icons rather than a tangible notation like the FIS dials to support learning? And if one likes to inspire tangible interaction (although at the cost of FIS correctness), one should take a tangible representation like the FIS dials? What do these results tell us about the power of tangibles to teach abstract concepts? The answers to these questions cannot be clear-cut as the specific circumstances of this study needs to be taken into account.

First, while the FIS icons were unconstrained in what they visualized, the FIS dials were created with the aim to make the FIS comparable to each other. To the participant they all looked the same (the functional backsides of the prototypes were covered throughout the experiment). It thus seems that focusing attention to the tactile channel at the cost of visual distinctiveness might not be very helpful in learning FIS (cf. [17]). Second, by applying visual constraints to the design of the dials, some FIS, e.g. BALANCE, would not be instantiated in the most suitable way.

Third, while the FIS icons represent a precise snapshot of a continuous action, it is difficult to isolate a precise moment of force feedback in the tangible interaction prototypes. Therefore, some of the FIS dials could represent more than one FIS to the user. For example, the transition between RESISTANCE, COUNTERFORCE, BLOCKAGE and RESTRAINT REMOVAL is gradual and probably needs to be interpreted in relation to an anchor stimulus. Although it was available, the participants rarely consulted the neutral dial prototype. The correct identification of ENABLEMENT and COMPULSION was low, because participants had difficulty discovering that the ENABLEMENT dial had to be pushed to become available and the COMPULSION dial sometimes initiated movement by itself when a participant had a high body voltage and came near the device (creating a possible confusion with SELF MOTION).

Fourth, whereas with the FIS icons a quick look at the pictorial notation was enough to bring the image schema to mind, participants spent more time interacting with the FIS dials. As a result the FIS-dial group had less time left to actually brainstorm design ideas.

Fifth, the FIS dials only communicated one direction of effect: the user as Agonist, the FIS dial as Antagonist, whereas the FIS icons assumed a more neutral stance and showed different actors as Agonists and Antagonists. In the FIS-dials group this one-way focus may have led to fewer design ideas and the feeling of a limited use of FIS as seen in the questionnaire results.

Finally, the participant sample is very small, so that these effects may be due to the specifics of the participants and the situation so that further studies employing larger sample sizes seem to be necessary.

CONCLUSION

This paper introduced force image schemas as a promising group of image schemas for tangible interaction design. Like other image schemas FIS can be used to convey physical and abstract metaphorical meaning via the user interface. In the light of a previous study, it was asked how the analytic understanding of force image schemas by designers who are not image-schema experts might be enhanced. The current systematic notation by Talmy did not seem helpful. Therefore two design aids, a pictorial and a tangible, were derived and tested with image schema novices. It was found that the pictorial representation of force image schemas let to better image schema learning than the tangible representation, while the tangible representation was more likely to produce more tangible and interactive design ideas. The findings open up new areas of thinking about the usefulness of tangible representations for learning abstract concepts. Several problems have been discussed and need to be pursued in further research adding to previous findings about the benefits and drawbacks of using tangibles for learning [10, 16, 18]. In particular, this research has shown that in comparison to pictoral sketches the concreteness of tangibles sometimes may constrain the expression of a pure idea in a way that this idea at the same time becomes less flexible (only one particular stance is presented) and more ambiguous (due to irrelevant affordances, also cf. [6]). There also remains the interesting possibility that tangibles are just too interesting to explore that might stand in the way of solving tasks efficiently. Further research needs to clarify whether these speculations hold true for tangibles under other circumstances.

REFERENCES

1. Antle, A.N., Corness, G. & Droumeva, M. Springboard: exploring embodiment, balance and social justice. In *CHI EA '09*, ACM, New York, 2009, 3961-3966.
2. Antle, A.N., Droumeva, M. & Corness, G. Playing with the sound maker: do embodied metaphors help children learn?. In *IDC '08*, ACM, New York, 2008, 178-185.
3. Bakker, S., Antle, A. N., & van der Hoven, E. Identifying embodied metaphors in children's sound-action mappings. In *IDC'09*, ACM, New York, 2009, 140-149.
4. Gibbs, R., & Colston, H. The cognitive psychological reality of image schemas and their transformations. *Cognitive Linguistics*, 6, 1995, 347-378.
5. Hampe, B. *From Perception to Meaning: Image Schemas in Cognitive Linguistics*, Berlin: Mouton de Gruyter, 2005.
6. Hornecker, E. & Dünser, A. Of pages and paddles: children's expectations and mistaken interactions with physical–digital tools. Interacting with Computers, 21(1-2), 2009, 95–107.
7. Hurtienne, J. *Image schemas and design for intuitive use. Exploring new guidance for user interface design.* Doctoral dissertation, TU Berlin, 2011.
8. Hurtienne, J. Inter-coder reliability of categorising force-dynamic events in human-technology interaction. *Yearbook of the German Cognitive Linguistics Association,* 1, 2013, 59-77.
9. Hurtienne, J. & Israel, J. H. Image schemas and their metaphorical extensions – Intuitive patterns for tangible interaction. In *TEI'07*, ACM, New York, 2007, 127-134.
10. Hurtienne, J., & Israel. J.H. PIBA-DIBA or How to blend the digital with the physical. Workshop on Blended Interaction at CHI Paris. http://hci.uni-konstanz.de/downloads/blend13_hurtienne.pdf
11. Hurtienne, J., Israel, J. H. &Weber, K. Cooking up real world business applications combining physicality, digitality, and image schemas. In *TEI'08*, ACM, New York, 2008, 239-246.
12. Hurtienne, J., Stößel, C., & Weber, K. Sad is Heavy and Happy is Light - Population Stereotypes of Tangible Object Attributes. In *TEI'09*, ACM, New York, 2009, 61-68.
13. Johnson, M. *The Body in the Mind: The Bodily Basis of Meaning, Imagination, and Reason*. Chicago: University of Chicago Press, 1987.
14. Löffler, D., Hess, A., Maier, A., Hurtienne, J., & Schmitt, H. Developing intuitive user interfaces by integrating users' mental models into requirements engineering. In *BCS-HCI'13*, London: BCS, 2013, Art. 15.
15. Macaranas, A., Antle, A.N. and Reicke, B. Bridging the gap: Attribute and spatial metaphors for tangible interface design. In *TEI'12*, ACM, New York, 2012, 161-168.
16. Manches, A. & O'Malley, C. Tangibles for learning: a representational analysis of physical manipulation. *Personal Ubiquitous Comput.* 16, 4 (2012), 405-419.
17. Mandler, J. How to Build a Baby: II. Conceptual Primitives. *Psychological Review* (99) 4, 1992, 587-604.
18. Marshall P. Do tangible interfaces enhance learning? In *TEI'07*, ACM, New York, 2007, 163-170.
19. Talmy, L. Force dynamics in language and cognition. *Cognitive Science* 12, 1 (1988), 49–100.

Tactile Teacher: Sensing Finger Tapping in Piano Playing

Chih-Pin Hsiao [1,3], Richard Li [1,2], Xinyan Yan [1,2], Ellen Yi-Luen Do [1,2,3,4]

[1]ACME Lab, GVU Center Georgia Institute of Technology

[2] College of Computing Georgia Institute of Technology

[3] College of Architecture Georgia Institute of Technology

[4] CUTE Center National University of Singapore

{chsiao9, lichard49, voidpointer, ellendo}@gatech.edu

ABSTRACT

In a piano lesson, a student often imitates the teacher's playing in terms of speed, dynamics, and fingering. While this learning model leverages one's visual and even audial perception for emulation, it still lacks an important component of piano playing – the tactile sensation. We seek to convey the tactile sensations of the teacher's keystrokes and then signal the student's corresponding fingers. We implemented an instrumented fingerless glove called Tactile Teacher to detect finger taps on hard surfaces. Since finger taps generate acoustic signals and cause vibrations, we embedded three vibration sensors on the glove and use machine learning algorithms to analyze the data from the sensors. After a brief training procedure, this prototype can accurately identify single finger tap in a very good performance at above 89% accuracy, and two finger taps resulted in accuracy around 85%.

Author Keywords

Sensing; Piano Learning; Tactile Sensations; Wearable Computing

ACM Classification Keywords

H.5.m. Information interfaces and presentation (e.g., HCI): Miscellaneous.

General Terms

Human Factors; Design; Measurement.

INTRODUCTION

In a piano lesson, the teacher instructs the student by demonstrating the physical playing of the piece. The student observes by watching the teacher's hands, following along in the score, and listening to the minute details of the sounds produced by the teacher. Clark et al. describes these common representations when conveying motor skills as the common ground [3] in which novices (e.g. students) usually benefit from different sensory inputs produced by masters (e.g. teachers). For instance, in a real piano lesson, a teacher would tap his or her fingers on the palm or on the back of the hands of the students so they would experience the sensation of the finger taps from the teacher. This real life example inspired us to create Tactile Teacher to capture the teacher's fingering, and enhance the learning experience for the students. The result is an implementation that adds an additional medium – touch sensation – for assisting students in learning piano.

TEI '15, January 15–19, 2015, Stanford, California, USA.

http://dx.doi.org/10.1145/2677199.2680554

In this paper, we start by discussing the importance of sharing common representations for learning motor skills. Based on the experiences of other researchers, we explore the possible designs and implementations of Tactile Teacher, a device that can detect finger taps without covering or hindering the fingers. As shown in Figure 1-right, the fingerless glove employs three piezo vibration sensors mounted on the back of the user's hands. With a micro-controller and a machine-learning program on the host computer, we obtained accurate results when tapping one finger (89%) and two fingers simultaneously (85%). We conclude the paper with discussions about the potentials of this implementation in addition to enhancing learning in a piano lesson.

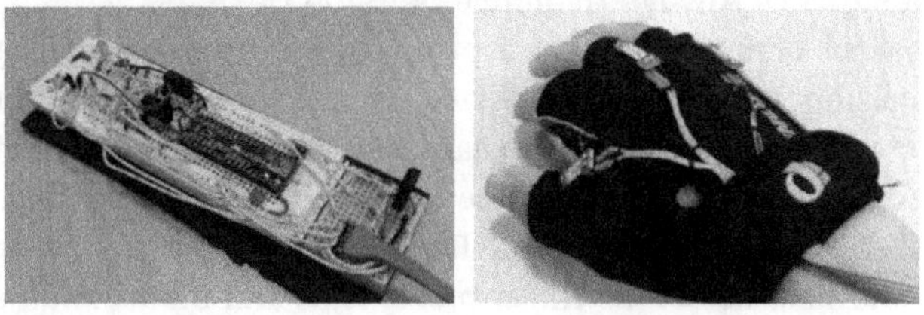

Figure 1. Tactile Teacher Prototype with a microcontroller (left) directly connected to an instrumented glove (right)

RELATED WORK

Sharing Tactile Sensations

Sharing common representations is crucial in learning, especially for motor skills [3]. Sharing haptic feedback for communication and learning is particularly interesting because touch sensation is invisible and difficult to convey through verbal descriptions. Thus, researchers have created prototypes that employ preset haptic stimuli to enhance the learning procedures of various motor skills, such as handwriting [14], memorizing force sequences [10], and remembering finger patterns [6,13].

Chellali et al. argues that real-time haptic communication will dramatically improve the learning curve for motor skills [2]. Typically, the haptic communication channel needs to be coupled with verbal or visual channels to maximize the effects [1]. It would be beneficial to engage in a multi-modal experience to enhance the learning of motor skills, especially with the experience of haptic communication. However, very few projects (e.g. [11]) discuss the types and means of sharing tactile representations in real-time learning scenarios, especially for those applications that require immediate responses.

Haptic Feedback for Guidance and Learning

Several researchers employ haptic or tactile guidance for providing additional information and improving the usability when using multi-touch devices, e.g. [8,15]. However, our task of assisting the piano learning process also requires the sensing of speed, dynamics, and fingerings on the originating hand and then rendering these sensations on the receiving hand. Mobile Music Touch (MMT) [6] employs various vibration motors to convey the tactile sensations for piano teaching purposes. The MMT glove addressed the rendering side of our task, and demonstrated the passive learning effects. However, the data used for vibration output is hardcoded in the program and lacks the spontaneity as well as the artistic aspects of timing and the force of hitting the piano keys that are demonstrated by the pianist (e.g., a teacher or a virtuoso). Therefore, in addition to building a piano glove that renders the finger tapping for students, we designed a sensing glove to capture the piano fingering from the teachers

Designs of Always Available Sensing Devices

Instead of instrumenting a piano with sensors, the design decision was made to provide an always-available input device for capturing finger taps that can be applied to any regular piano or hard surfaces. Various approaches can be taken to achieve this goal. For instance, computer vision could help detect the finger movements and the location of the fingers [4]. This approach would require intensive computation and is error prone without rigorous configurations. An alternative method is to wear sensors on hands or arms for detecting motion. We have seen many different efforts in this approach. Sensing muscle movements by using EMG is one feasible method for detecting finger movements as an always-available input device [12]. However, EMG sensors cannot accurately recognize the timing of finger tapping on hard surfaces, which is crucial to piano playing. The other approach is to wear an array of vibration sensors on arms for detecting bio-acoustic signals on the skin [5]. In this implementation, users need to train the system every time before use since the locations of the sensors can vary when wearing the armband. In addition, this implementation is not capable of sensing multiple finger taps simultaneously. Therefore, we implemented a lightweight sensing glove with a fun and engaging way to train the system to distinguish fingers and recognize the strength of the finger taps.

HARDWARE DESIGN AND SENSING

Glove Design

Designing the Tactile Teacher glove was a challenging task. Pianists would not appreciate wearing a glove that would affect dexterity. Thus, the traditional pressure-sensing glove that employs piezo pressure sensors on the fingertips is not appropriate. We also needed to avoid additional materials on the fingers and employ as few sensors as possible. We initially employed only two piezo vibration sensors (MiniSense 100, Measurement Specialties, Inc.) on the back of the hand. Table 1 Column 1 shows that this configuration is capable of classifying the signals from one-finger taps (93%), but with very bad results when testing two-finger taps (< 50% recognition rate on average). To improve the results of recognizing two-finger taps, we added a third sensor. We experimented with many different sensor placements with these three sensors. Placing the sensors on the wrist (Figure 3B) would remove the burden of wearing a glove, which would be ideal for the pianist. However, putting the sensors on the back of the hand - closer to the fingers - returned better results. In the following sections, we describe the sensor placements and the training of the machine learning classifier.

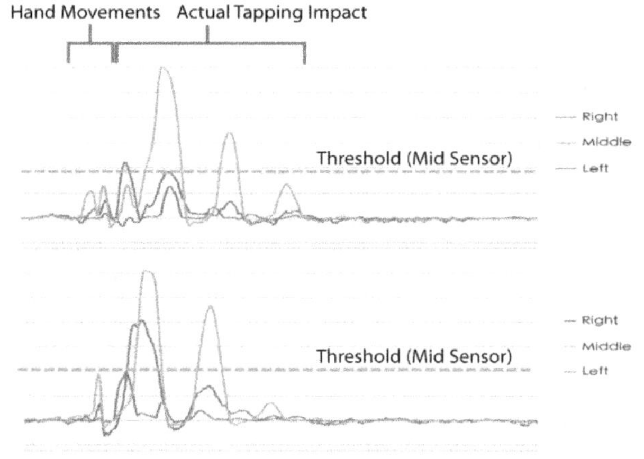

Figure 2. Top: signals of index finger tapping. Bottom: tapping of index-ring finger combination.

The Waveform from Different Finger Combinations

Figure 2 shows sample data received by the host computer with the sensor placements in Figure 3-D. The blue, green and red lines represent signals received from the right, middle and left sensors, respectively. These signals exhibit characteristics that would impact the machine learning results. For instance, in the upper chart of Figure 2 (one-finger tap), the tallest spike in the green line appears before the tallest spike in the blue line while the lower chart (two-finger tap) depicts how the tallest spike in the blue line happens only slightly before the tallest spike in the green line. This relationship is due to the smaller distance from the right sensor to the tapping finger (ring finger) in a double-finger tap than a single-finger tap – the vibration needs to travel from the index finger to the right sensor. Likewise, in a ring-finger tapping event, the tallest spike in the blue line would appear before the tallest spike in the green line, in reverse order of the spikes shown in the upper chart of Figure 2.

Hardware and Data Processing

As shown in Figure 1, we employ a Maple Mini board (from LeafLabs) [7] to sample three ADC channels at 6.5KHz from piezo vibration sensors and send the data to a computer for further data processing, before running a machine-learning program for classification. This data processing includes exponential smoothing and filtering. When the smoothed data from one of the three channels exceeds a triggering threshold, the subsequent samples from all of the channels are considered as a tap event. Likewise, if the samples fall under the threshold, the signal is considered to have exited the tapping session. As shown in Figure 2, each tap comes with the tallest spike and few shorter spikes, each of which lasts for about 12-17ms (58-83Hz). To ensure that the samples influenced by a tap event are filtered, the key parameters, such as the threshold, smoothing factor, and number of samples around the exceeding time, are tuned.

After smoothing and filtering, 174 features can be extracted from each three-sensor-input event for machine learning purposes. These features include the three averages and square averages of each channel, as well as the three ratios and square ratios between the 2-combinations of the three channels, totaling to twelve features. The system also computes a 256-point Fast-Fourier Transform (FFT) for transforming input from the time domain to the frequency domain. Because the frequency of the tap waveform is roughly between 50 to 100 Hz, only the lower nine bins (23 Hz each) are used for computing the normalized decibels; FFT is also applied to the log10 of the sensor data, totaling 162 features from FFT. Finally, peak time difference and peak value ratios are calculated for each 2-combinations of the three sensors' waveform, giving six features. The 174 features are then classified using the Support Vector Machine (SVM) package from Weka [9]. The latency of computing the data for each tap event, from receiving the data on the host computer to finishing the computation, is about 128ms on an Intel® Core™ i5 processor.

Training Procedure

Since people have different sized hands, the system requires an initial training of the machine-learning model by playing the well-known tune "Ode to Joy". This procedure not only makes the training session more enjoyable than simply repeatedly tapping on the same key multiple times, but it also gives the machine learning algorithm a chance to observe the natural variations of finger movement that may only occur when the player is tapping the key organically. During the training session, the program records all of the data from the three vibration sensors to build the model described above. Since the program knows the finger taps required for the tune, it can map the set of features to each finger as it progresses.

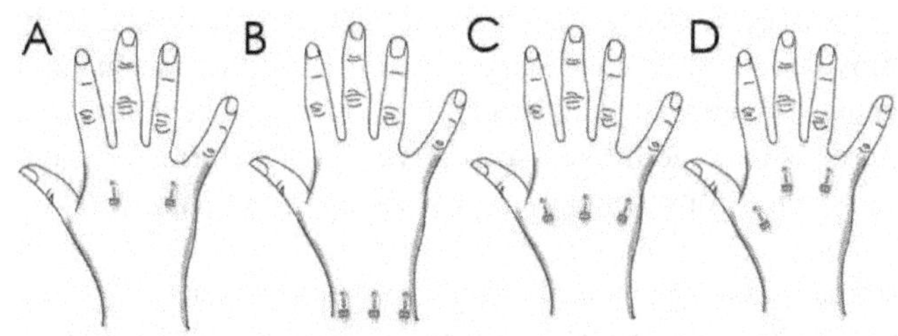

Figure 3. Different sensor placements and orientations

Table 1. Sensor placements versus tap accuracy percentage.

Finger	1	2	3	4	5	Single Avg.	1-3	2-4	3-5	Total Avg.
Pl.A	100	100	90	85	90	93	70	20	60	76.875
Pl.B	100	100	50	75	45	74	55	60	70	69.400
Pl.C	75	55	50	35	55	54	80	65	70	60.600
Pl.D	95	100	90	70	90	89	100	75	85	88.125

Results from Different Sensor Configurations

In order to find the best sensor placements, we have conducted the experiments with the machine learning classifier described above. The experiment results were obtained by the following procedure: after the model-training procedure, 20 taps for each finger and finger combination were performed, and each tap's correctness was verified. Sensor locations were changed between trials for experimenting results from different sensor placements. We picked four example placements as shown in Figure 3, and reported the results in Table 1, where finger numbers 1 through 5 correspond to the thumb, pointer, middle, index and pinky fingers, respectively.

As predicted, the best result is derived from sensors placed on the back of the hand in a radial fashion. (Figure 3-D). In our observations, the orientations of the sensors are also important. Specifically, the placements of the sensors aligned toward the spreading directions of the fingers obtained maximal sensibility. The optimal placement is to align one sensor in the same direction of the middle finger, and the other two sensors placed facing towards the in-between directions of the rest of the fingers (i.e., between thumb and index finger, between ring finger and pinky).

CONCLUSION

We are excited that Tactile Teacher can capture teacher's finger tapping with high accuracy. We have demonstrated the prototype to a piano teacher in a demo session who responded with positive feedback and showed enthusiasm about the prototype and its idea. While she would refuse to wear a complete glove with fingers covered, she believes she could wear our fingerless glove in piano playing and teaching that could benefit novice piano learners.

In the future, we would explore capturing more of the embodied experience of piano playing for a more engaging kinesthetic learning. For instance, a pianist may use body movements to increase the dynamics of the music, and achieve complex, multi-limb movements. Eventually we may also use additional sensors worn on the arms or other body parts for detecting and conveying these supplemental features. These sensors may also provide data from which we can more intelligently filter the vibration sensor signals, rather than the currently rudimentary approach of setting a threshold through experimental data.

In addition to complementing piano lessons, we believe this prototype can lead us to many other applications that were not possible before, especially those that require fine dexterity and a high level of motor skills, such as learning other (musical) instruments that also require finger movements. This prototype can also be extended and applied to the rehabilitation procedure, including regaining the capability of using hands of a post-stroke patient.

SUMMARY

In this paper, we have described an implementation of a light weight fingerless glove to recognize the finger taps in piano playing with only three vibration sensors placed on the back of the hand. These sensors, passed into a machine learning classifier, provide sufficient results of both keystrokes by a single finger (89% accuracy) and by two fingers tapping (85% accuracy) simultaneously. These results are encouraging and give us the confidence to test the prototype in a real world setting with a real pianist giving a lesson. We conclude the paper with the positive feedback from a pianist and the many rich possibilities derived from this glove configuration.

ACAKNOWLEDGEMENT

We thank our collaborators in the Contextual Computing Group, especially Prof. Thad Starner and Scott Gilliland, for feedback and supports on the initial developments of the Tactile Teacher, members of ACME Lab for thoughtful insights, and the support from the National Research Foundation, Prime Minister's Office, Singapore.

REFERENCES

1. Chellali, A., Dumas, C., and Milleville-Pennel, I. Influences of haptic communication on a shared manual task. *Interacting with Computers 23*, 4 (2011), 317–328.
2. Chellali, A.M., Dumas, C., Milleville-Pennel, I., and others. WYFIWIF: A haptic communication paradigm for collaborative motor skills learning. *Proceedings of the Web Virtual Reality and Three-Dimensional Worlds 2010*, (2010), 301–308.
3. Clark, H.H. and Brennan, S.E. Grounding in communication. *Perspectives on socially shared cognition 13*, 1991 (1991), 127–149.
4. Erol, A., Bebis, G., Nicolescu, M., Boyle, R.D., and Twombly, X. A Review on Vision-Based Full DOF Hand Motion Estimation. *Computer Vision and Pattern Recognition - Workshops, 2005. CVPR Workshops. IEEE Computer Society Conference on*, 75–82.
5. Harrison, C., Tan, D., and Morris, D. Skinput: appropriating the body as an input surface. *In Proc. SIGCHI '10*, ACM (2010), 453–462.
6. Huang, K., Starner, T., Do, E., et al. Mobile music touch: mobile tactile stimulation for passive learning. *In Proc. SIGCHI '10*, ACM (2010), 791–800.
7. LeafLabs. The Maple Mini. http://leaflabs.com/.
8. Ledo, D., Nacenta, M.A., Marquardt, N., Boring, S., and Greenberg, S. The HapticTouch Toolkit: Enabling Exploration of Haptic Interactions. *In Proc. TEI '12*, ACM (2012), 115–122.
9. Machine Learing Group at the University of Waikato. Weka. http://www.cs.waikato.ac.nz/ml/weka/.
10. Morris, D., Tan, H.Z., Barbagli, F., Chang, T., and Salisbury, K. Haptic feedback enhances force skill learning. *In Proc. WHC '07*, (2007), 21–26.
11. Sallnäs, E.-L., Rassmus-Gröhn, K., and Sjöström, C. Supporting Presence in Collaborative Environments by Haptic Force Feedback. *ACM Trans. Computer-Human Interaction 7*, 4 (2000), 461–476.
12. Saponas, T.S., Tan, D.S., Morris, D., Balakrishnan, R., Turner, J., and Landay, J.A. Enabling always-available input with muscle-computer interfaces. *In Proc. UIST '09*, ACM (2009), 167–176.
13. Seim, C.E., Quigley, D., and Starner, T.E. Passive Haptic Learning of Typing Skills Facilitated by Wearable Computers. *In Proc. CHI '14 Extended Abstracts on Human Factors in Computing Systems*, ACM (2014), 2203–2208.
14. Yoshikawa, T. and Henmi, K. Human skill transfer using haptic virtual reality technology. *experimental Robotics VI 250*, (2000), 351–360.
15. Zimmermann, S., Rümelin, S., and Butz, A. I Feel It in My Fingers: Haptic Guidance on Touch Surfaces. *In Proc. TEI '13*, ACM (2013), 9–12.

Mapping Place: Supporting Cultural Learning through a Lukasa-inspired Tangible Tabletop Museum Exhibit

Jean Ho Chu[1], Paul Clifton[1], Daniel Harley[2], Jordanne Pavao[2], Ali Mazalek[1,2]
Synaesthetic Media Lab
Georgia Institute of Technology[1] Ryerson University[2]
Atlanta, GA, USA Toronto, ON, Canada
{jeanhochu, paulgclifton}@gmail.com, {dharley, jordanne.pavao, mazalek}@ryerson.ca

ABSTRACT
Museums are exploring new ways of using emerging digital technologies to enhance the visitor experience. In this context, our research focuses on designing, developing and studying interactions for museum exhibits that introduce cultural concepts in ways that are tangible and embodied. We introduce here a tangible tabletop installation piece that was designed for a museum exhibition contrasting Western and African notions of mapping history and place. Inspired by the Lukasa board, a mnemonic device used by the Luba peoples in Central Africa, the tabletop piece enables visitors to learn and understand symbolic and nonlinguistic mapping concepts that are central to the Lukasa by creating and sharing stories with each other. In this paper we share our design process, a user study focusing on children and learning, and design implications on how digital and tangible interaction technologies can be used for cultural learning in museum exhibits.

Author Keywords
Tangible interaction; interactive tabletop; interaction design; cultural history; museum exhibit; storytelling; collaboration; learning.

ACM Classification Keywords
H.5.1. [Information Interfaces and Presentation]: Multimedia Information Systems---*Animations*; H.5.2. [Information Interfaces and Presentation]: User Interfaces---*Input devices and strategies*, *Interaction styles*; H.5.3. [Information Interfaces and Presentation]: Group and Organization Interfaces---*Collaborative computing*; K.3.1 [Computers and Education]: Collaborative learning.

General Terms
Design; Human Factors.

INTRODUCTION
Emerging digital interaction technologies are increasingly used in museums. In this context, multi-touch tabletops and tangible interfaces can offer collaborative experiences that assist the learning process through hands-on interactions with the subject matter. Interactive tabletops and tangible media have been used in museums to promote cultural and historical knowledge, but the learning effects of such endeavors require further investigation. Similar systems that teach STEM subjects are well-documented, and many lessons can be applied toward teaching the humanities. We identify a broad opportunity for the HCI community to develop an understanding of how tangible interactions can be effectively used to support learning and comprehension of cultural heritage.

TEI '15, January 15 - 19 2015, Stanford, CA, USA
Copyright 2015 ACM 978-1-4503-3305-4/15/01…$15.00
http://dx.doi.org/10.1145/2677199.2680559

Figure 1: Lukasa-inspired tangible tabletop installation in the *Mapping Place* museum exhibition.

We worked with the Robert C. Williams Paper Museum in Atlanta, GA on an exhibition titled *Mapping Place: Africa Beyond Paper*. The museum holds special exhibitions and hosts workshops about papermaking and paper-related arts for school groups, especially elementary and middle school students. The *Mapping Place* exhibition (held from February 28 – June 6, 2014) invited visitors to contrast Western notions of mapping and maps of Africa with the way African cultures conceptualize and represent their own history and place.

Our part in the *Mapping Place* exhibition involved the design and development of an installation piece that aimed to re-envision and convey African notions of mapping history and place through digital and tangible media. Our goal as researchers was to better understand how tangible interaction technologies can be designed and situated within the museum context in a way that supports learning and comprehension of cultural and historical concepts.

The design of our piece was inspired by the Lukasa from the Luba peoples of Central Africa. The Lukasa, or memory board, is a hand-sized wooden tablet that is studded with beads and shells and/or carved with ideograms [18]. The beads, shells and carvings are used to represent pieces of stories and thus serve to record the history, genealogy and cosmology of the Luba peoples. A board can only be interpreted by its creator and by specially trained members of the tribe. In our digital version of a large scale Lukasa, visitors create stories through a combination of tangible objects and multi-touch tabletop interactions (see Figure 1). With the authentic Lukasa inside glass case in the *Mapping Place: Africa Beyond Paper* exhibition, our piece aimed to give students a tangible way to explore the abstract concepts of the Lukasa through collaboration, story construction, and storytelling. To inform the design of the tabletop installation piece, we researched museum installations, tangible user interfaces (TUIs) for learning, and tangible narratives. We describe our design process as well as a user study conducted to understand how the context of the installation supports learning and sensemaking. Based on our results, we draw design implications for museum exhibits that use tangible technologies to support learning about history and culture.

RELATED WORK

Tangible interactions are increasingly used in museums to promote engagement and learning for visitors. Researchers are developing novel approaches to explore scientific concepts, math and programming, sustainability, interactive narratives, and historical and cultural heritage through interactive digital applications. We provide a brief overview of research and design in three areas: interactive museums, TUIs and learning, and tangible narratives.

Interactive Museums

Cultural museum exhibits are traditionally comprised of static historical artifacts, existing in physical spaces that are often far removed from their original environments. These artifacts cannot be touched, and their original uses must be imagined. Interactive exhibits seek to bridge the gap between the visitor and the exhibit though hands-on interaction, and are designed to give visitors the opportunity to engage with a variety of subject matter.

Much of the research that investigates the benefits of technology and learning focuses on STEM subjects [14], and indeed science museums have been early adopters of interactive installations. For example, an exhibit at the Boston Museum of Science encourages non-linear constructivist learning of computer programming through “passive tangible interfaces,” a combination of powered and unpowered components designed for low cost and durability [10]. Another tabletop application for museums teaches children about programming concepts by encouraging collaboration and storytelling, and uses puzzle pieces and blocks to mitigate the difficulty of interface interaction [16].

Although the learning objectives for interactive tabletops that are used to communicate cultural subject matter are less discussed in the literature, interactive tabletops are becoming more common in museums. Notable examples include those developed by firms such as Potion Design. Many of Potion Design’s installations explore history and cultural heritage, enabling visitors to interact with archival photos, videos, or 3-D reconstructions [17].

These types of interactive exhibits will continue to interest museum patrons, as technologies with tangible input devices and digital augmentation tend to reach a wider audience than traditional exhibits [11]. At the same time, research suggests that if the purpose of the technologically enhanced exhibit is not immediately understood, social discussion around the exhibit will deal more with the mechanics of the interaction rather than the content [12]. A closer look at how interactive technologies can be designed to promote positive effects of learning and comprehension is therefore necessary.

TUIs and Learning

Although many TUIs that aim to promote learning focus on STEM subjects, we believe that certain benefits associated with these TUIs may also be relevant for systems that strive for cultural learning. Specifically, we looked at tabletops that promote learning through collaboration or play.

Researchers have studied how the physical structure and shape of tangible interfaces enables exploratory learning and content creation. For example, TellTale [1] used a toy caterpillar whose body segments can record and play back audio clips to allow children to experiment with and learn about the structure and content of oral stories. Oh et al. [16] used puzzle blocks as tangibles in order to help young children with the difficulty of navigating interface interaction. The use of puzzle blocks as constraints further serves to clarify the purpose of their actions.

Multi-touch tabletop applications can also foster collaborative learning. Harris et al. [9] suggest that children engaged in multi-touch surface interactions will discuss the tasks at hand more than the children engaged in single-touch interactions. Benford et al. [4] analyze the design of interactive storytelling technologies, KidPad and Klump, as platforms for collaborative learning and development among young children. They suggest that TUIs can promote “shoulder-to-shoulder” collaboration; that is, with TUIs children benefit from watching the progress of their peers, which can in turn increase cumulative learning potential.

The interaction design and game mechanics applied to a multi-touch tabletop application can be structured to achieve collaborative learning. Multi-touch collaborative games, such as Futura [2] and Youtopia [3], aim to foster an understanding of urban planning and the environment through a series of choices and actions that have environmental consequences. In games like these, the learning comes from conditional constructs, where the consequences of a player's actions are clear. In YouTopia and Futura, the game mechanics also foster collaboration where actions can be co-dependent, giving children different but complementary goals to discuss [3].

The tangible objects of the *Mapping Place* installation are an entry point for interaction as well as a way to direct the focus of each visitor. The form factor of the tabletop, situated in a large space, enables collaborative learning by creating an opportunity for multiple visitors to see and discuss each other's use of the system.

Tangible Narratives

A number of researchers have explored the use of tangible interfaces to afford natural physical interactions with digital stories. Many tangible narratives allow the personalization of users' experiences through creative storytelling. Tangible Viewpoints [15] employed tangible pawns on an interactive tabletop to navigate a multi-viewpoint story space, resulting in different story experiences based on the interactive choices made by the user. Tangibility also allows multiple users to simultaneously interact with a story, leading to a cooperative and social experience. As storytelling is a social experience, it enables development of language and communication skills and collaborative learning. TellTable demonstrated that children using a multi-touch storytelling application took inspiration from one another's stories, and planned their stories in advance, creating more complex and cohesive stories [5].

An important aspect of storytelling with tangible narratives is the absence of imposed linearity. The affordances designed for the applied technology will naturally create constraints, but these constraints can also be considered the tools of the storyteller, and a platform for imagination. In Triangles [8], users connected triangles to form patterns recognized by a computer. The Triangles were used as non-linear storytelling tools, with each configuration potentially generating visual or audio feedback. Conversely, when direct meaning is applied to the tangible objects, there is a sense of authorial control, even when the user's ability to sequence the objects suggests non-linearity. Essentially, the user is able to actively explore the story rather than openly construct the story. This is the case with RENATI [7] as well as The Reading Glove [20], each of which used RFID tags to trigger audio clips assigned to physical objects.

The *Mapping Place* exhibition draws on tangible narrative research in two ways. First, since it remediates a traditional storytelling artifact, we draw from tangible narrative techniques in order to create a successful storytelling platform. Second, we capitalize on the learning and comprehension implications of tangible narratives in order to create a piece that promotes learning, not only about the story that is constructed, but also about how stories themselves can be constructed and what those constructions mean to different cultures.

PROJECT GOALS AND EXHIBITION OVERVIEW

Our goals were (1) to create an interactive installation that remediates traditional African notions of mapping history and place through digital and tangible media and (2) to better understand how digital and tangible interaction technologies can support learning and comprehension of cultural material and concepts within a museum context.

The installation piece was part of the *Mapping Place: Africa Beyond Paper* exhibition, which also included European representations and maps of Africa on paper, from the late 16th to the 20th century, along with an authentic Lukasa on loan from the Royal Museum for Central Africa in Tervuren, Belgium (see Figure 2). The exhibition invited visitors to explore the ways that the changing representation and projection of space has shaped Western approaches to Africa. By bringing the mnemonic tradition of Central Africa to an engaging storytelling activity, the tabletop installation helped to bridge the gap between certain aspects of Western and traditional Central African cultures. The piece's implied story structure, tangible objects, and physical and contextual space were designed to cohesively function to enable children to create and share stories of their own.

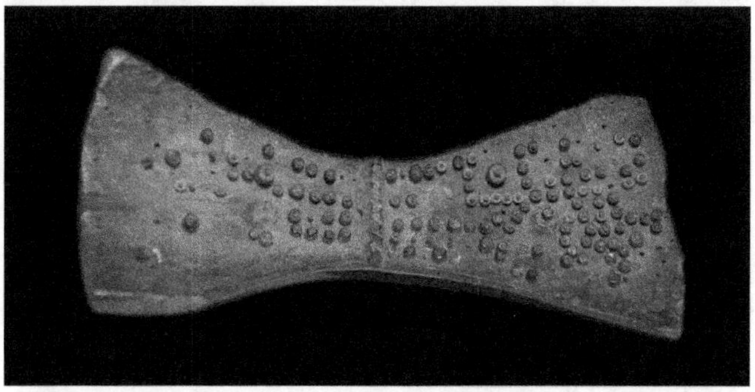

Figure 2: Lukasa board loaned by the Royal Museum for Central Africa for the *Mapping Place* exhibition. Photo taken by Sidarth Kantamneni for the Robert C. Williams Museum of Papermaking.

INTERACTIVE INSTALLATION OVERVIEW

The design of the interactive tabletop installation was inspired by the nonlinguistic symbolic mapping practices related to the making and reading of the Lukasa board. There are three steps involved in the tabletop interaction: making, mapping, and telling stories. Making stories involves drag-and-drop interaction of virtual beads to icons around one's tangible story shell on the interactive tabletop. Mapping stories involves arranging and visualizing the connections between story elements with the help of visual animations on an adjacent wall display. Telling stories happens through oral performance as visitors narrate their stories to one another around the table.

The installation consists of a multi-touch tabletop with tangible shells and two wall mounted projections. As visitors approach the table, they see digital beads scattered around the surface and a collection of physical objects shaped like shells on the edges. A visitor can pick up a shell and place it on the tabletop display to start building their digital story. The tangible shells are meant to encourage participation and storytelling by helping visitors differentiate their stories. Their shell becomes the central node of their story, and seven icons appear in a circular "menu" around it, representing possible components of a story about family and place: man, woman, boy, girl, pet, home, and city (see Figure 3). The visitors can arrange digital beads around the tangible shell by dragging them onto the icons to assign meaning to them. For example, if a visitor wants to tell a story about their mother and aunt, they can drag two beads onto the "woman" icon one after another. They may choose to represent their mother with a red bead and their aunt with a yellow bead in order to distinguish them.

Figure 3: A circular menu of icons (left) appears around a tangible shell when it is placed on the tabletop (right)

As each bead is assigned meaning, a corresponding animation begins to play on a wall adjacent to the table (see Figure 4). When more beads are added, the animations are layered to create a story scene. The visitor can arrange the position of the elements in their scene as desired by moving the assigned beads around the central shell. The story is completed when the visitor removes the tangible shell from the table and the "menu" of icons disappears. Only the final arrangement of assigned beads remains and the visitor can verbally share their story with others around the table.

Figure 4: Visitor dragging beads to icons around a tangible shell (left); wall animation (right)

The visitors complete the interactive session by sharing their stories with one another around the table, accompanied by the playback of the animated scene on the wall. Multiple visitors can create stories on the table at the same time, each with their own tangible shell, resulting in a larger "story map" of the group's shared experience.

As each group completes their session, their tabletop "Lukasa" is captured as a digital image and stored in an archive of all visitors' creations. These conceptual maps, which represent the stories shared by visitors, are displayed in a slideshow on screens at the back of the exhibition space. As with the Lukasa, without the original creators to give meaning to these maps by narrating the stories they represent, the recorded images remain little more than abstract symbols to subsequent viewers.

DESIGN PROCESS

The design of the piece was guided not only by the overarching goals for the project, but also by audience and site-related factors. Given that the piece was created for a museum setting, we anticipated that visitors would typically interact for five minutes or less. Furthermore, we expected the main audience to be primary or middle school children on school field trips. As a result, we realized it would be necessary to convey the Lukasa-inspired story-mapping concept through a short interaction that was both engaging and easy to understand. We considered storytelling and collaboration as important elements for learning about the Lukasa and developed our piece focusing on these aspects.

We considered three different ways of learning:

The first is to *learn by doing*, since the system's mechanics enable visitors to learn the underlying rules through interaction. We designed the system to resemble the meaning making process of the Lukasa board, where meaning is created through the selection and placement of beads on the wooden board. In our piece, visitors drag and drop virtual beads to icons in order to make their stories.

The second is to *learn by creating*. The system provides open-ended interaction, which allows visitors to decide their own ways to symbolize their story elements by using the components of the system. Visitors gain an understanding of the arbitrary, yet personal, symbolization process by devising their own ways to remember and tell the pieces of their stories.

The third is to *learn through interaction with others*. Visitors learn each other's ways of symbolizing story elements as they construct their stories side-by-side and share them with one another through oral performance.

The interaction, visual, and physical elements of the installation piece were designed to support these different ways of learning.

Interaction Design

The system design was inspired by the creation and storytelling process of the Lukasa board.

Embodied Interaction as Meaning Making

The drag-and-drop interaction resembles the meaning making process of the Lukasa board, where beads are assigned meaning as the creator selects them and arranges them together on the board. Similarly, virtual beads are scattered around the table as unclaimed story elements. Visitors can look at the different beads and push them around the table using multi-touch interaction; the beads respond with fluid movements, guided by physics. When a bead is dragged and dropped onto an icon, it connects to the central story shell and becomes a piece of one's story.

Personal Symbolization

The interface has four components that each visitor can incorporate to symbolize pieces of their story: color, icon, location, and movement. These story elements are reflected on the wall animation. The animations on the wall reflect the colors and story elements of the assigned beads, and can be arranged to create a scene by moving the corresponding beads around the central shell. By creating a composition of story elements, a visitor can differentiate his or her pieces of animation from others and also find his or her own ways of symbolizing story elements.

Personal Story-Map

The interaction with the tabletop results in a personal story map. We were informed by the original Lukasa board in which the spiritual capital is represented through beads centered around a cowrie shell. A tangible story shell becomes the center of each visitor's digital Lukasa, holding all the pieces of their story. As beads are attached to the shell and positioned around it, a thin line between bead and shell shows the association. Lifting the tangible story shell reveals and completes the story map.

Collective Storytelling

The entire tabletop becomes the group's digital Lukasa, holding multiple visitors' stories. Since sharing of the stories represented by the Lukasa was a tribe's ritual and performance, we wanted the stories to be shared as a collective experience. The wall animation visualizes the stories and encourages sharing with others. By looking at the wall, the visitor can point to, move, or change their story elements, making the experience performative.

Visual and Physical Design

The visual and physical design of the piece draws on Luba art in general and the Lukasa in particular. Inspired by the cowrie shells and studded beads typical to the Lukasa, we decided to design story elements as story shells and beads. The shells and beads are made in five different shapes and colors adopted from Luba art. The tabletop screen shows a texture of old wood, and the hourglass shaped table is made out of wood carved with geometric patterns. These design choices are intended to help people perceptually connect the digital tabletop to the Lukasa (see Figure 5).

The visual materials such as icons and animations are intended to help people visualize and share their stories. These are meant to be general enough so that they can fit to any type of story. The table is placed diagonally towards the center of the two display walls in the gallery to encourage visitors to look at the wall animation while interacting. Instructions are placed on each side of the table to inform visitors how to interact, and what each icon represents. Figure 6 shows a group of visitors interacting with the table during the *Mapping Place* exhibition.

Figure 5: Tangible objects (left); tabletop (right)

Technical Implementation

The tabletop uses diffused surface illumination (DSI) to evenly light the surface with infrared (IR) light. It runs the Community Core Vision (CCV) engine to recognize touches and ReacTIVision [13] fiducial markers on the bottom of the shells. CCV stitches the images from four Playstation™ Eye cameras modified to see IR, which enables us to create a large interactive surface that can more consistently recognize smaller objects and fingers.

The front-end application was developed in Unity3D. The Unity scene stretches across three projected screens: the table surface and two projectors aimed at the walls. Unity3D controls the physics of the beads on the surface and the behaviors of the animations. Unity3D and CCV communicate using the TUIO protocol.

The animations were drawn and rendered in Adobe Flash and Adobe After Effects. Each frame was exported as an image to be colored and layered in Unity3D upon interaction.

The form of the table and the tangible shell objects were designed in SolidWorks. The table was cut at the Advanced Wood Projects Lab at Georgia Tech from plywood using a CNC (computer numerical control) router. The tangible shell objects were 3D printed on a Dimension SST 768 in the GVU (Graphics, Visualization and Usability) Prototyping Lab. The objects were then finished by sanding and painting the plastic.

EVALUATION

We conducted a user study to understand how the interaction with the tabletop primes students for learning abstract concepts, and how the understanding of such concepts affects interaction. Based on the goals of the exhibit and our background research, we developed the following research questions:

- Priming for learning – Does the interactive experience prime and affect understanding of the subject matter?
- Supporting sensemaking – Are visitors able to apply their knowledge to the experience? Does grounded knowledge affect how the visitors interact with the piece?

- Encouraging group interactions – Does the application support collaborative activities in groups?

Figure 6: Interaction around the tabletop

Participants and Evaluation Sessions

The user study involved fourteen participants 8-13 years old, four female and ten male. Eight were homeschooled children and seven were primary school students. We arranged the students in four groups of 2-5 students to visit the museum and participate in a focus-group interview. The user study took place at the gallery where the exhibition was held.

We started the user study with a pre-task activity asking students about their storytelling practices, and to share a story with the other participants. The pre-task activity was meant to prime students to think about stories and find out if they had prior knowledge about the Lukasa. We contrasted two different ways to teach students about the Lukasa board, with a lesson either before or after the tabletop interaction. Two groups of participants had the lesson first, interacting with the tabletop later, while the other two groups used the tabletop first. The ten-minute lesson was given by the researchers in a classroom and explained the socio-cultural background, the usage, and the cultural meaning of the Lukasa board. The lecture was accompanied by slides containing texts, images, and a video. The lesson was followed up by a mid-task interview to assess the participants' understanding of the Lukasa board. The mid-task interview was in the form of a semi-structured discussion. We asked participants to explain what they had learned, and to compare and contrast the Lukasa board to other storytelling practices and artifacts such as books, maps, or oral narration. For the ten-minute interaction session with the tabletop, we asked participants to make stories about their family and neighborhood. The interaction was followed with interview questions asking about the ways participants used the table to make stories. Once the participants had been exposed to both the lesson and the tabletop, we ran a post-task interview to investigate how the tabletop influenced the sensemaking process for learning about the Lukasa. We asked participants to discuss the similarities and differences between the tabletop application and the Lukasa board.

Methods

During the interaction session, participants were asked to talk aloud while we recorded video and took field notes. We transcribed the video and evaluated the data from the interactions and interviews by coding based on grounded theory. We compared the two groups to understand the learning effects of the lesson and the tabletop interaction, and their influence on one another. Grounded theory is a qualitative analysis method often used in social science research involving discovery of theory through analysis of data [6, 19]. Our use of grounded theory was primarily to discover a metric for coding emerging data and to find repetitive patterns. The codes were grouped into similar concepts, and into categories. This method was appropriate for our study as we did not have a theoretical framework to test but rather wanted to understand the meaning of our observed data. We used the analysis software NVivo to code and analyze our data. We eventually narrowed down the codes and categories as summarized in Table 1.

	Category	Codes
Priming for Learning	Definition	Object, Use of, History,
	Memory	Cultural Memory, Memory Aid
	People	Exclusive Knowledge, Oral Performance
	Symbolic Representation	Symbolic, Iconic, Nonlinguistic, Movement
	Literal Representation	Visual Representation, Storytelling
Supportive of Sensemaking	Storytelling	Intentional, Random, Frustration
	Symbolic Representation	Color, Movement
	Literal Representation	Visual Representation, Icons, Location, Time
Supportive of Group Interactions	Collaboration	Joint Action, Joint Attention, Communication

Table 1: Codes and categories extracted from the data.

Results

We conducted qualitative analysis of our coded data based on our goals and the research questions mentioned above. Deeper observation and patterns in the data that emerged during coding gave us insights into the use and effects of the interactions.

Priming for Learning

Based on our analysis, it appears that the interactive experience does affect understanding and does prime students for learning the concepts in the lesson. Students who interacted with the table first drew on that experience during the lesson.

"In Lukasas, the symbols represent things, and based on probably visual similarities. They probably make the

symbol look similar to what they are explaining.” – Participant with interaction first

Students who received the lesson first also applied the lesson to the interactive session, contextualizing the experience.

“It [The tabletop application] helped me understand how something could symbolize things. Like for example, this boy icon can symbolize something but then I can tell different stories out of it.” – Participant with lesson first

Some design elements of the application led to unintended interpretations of both the interactions and the content in the group who interacted with the installation first. Since our application visualized the story compositions through animations and characterized icons, participants who interacted with the tabletop first were more likely to interpret the visual components of the symbols literally instead of using them as abstractions of more specific meanings. Even though they still learned about the Lukasa, they understood the idea of symbolization based on visual similarities rather than abstraction of story elements.

Supportive of Sensemaking

We found that having contextualized knowledge supports sensemaking through interaction. That is, grounding the interaction with a prior lesson helped participants focus their interaction in order to grasp the concept. In our study, participants who received the lecture first were able to abstract and symbolize their story elements and use color to indicate relatives, groups, and emotion to tell their stories during their interaction.

“I put the lady into red because she got really angry at the baby for crying so loud.” – Participant with lesson first

In contrast, those without the prior lesson did not try to symbolize story elements and made literal interpretations of the visual elements such as how the animation looks to explain their story.

“The man is trying to kill the cat so it is running away. Poor cat.” – Participant with interaction first

Supportive of Group Interactions

The collaborative activities of those who received the lesson first were limited to learning how to use the system without further effort for collaborative story construction. Because the Lukasa is a personal story construction device, knowledge of the Lukasa board appeared to constrain the interaction and individualized the story construction. Conversely, participants who completed the interaction first demonstrated a greater tendency to collectively explore the system and collaborate on story construction.

“I have a dad and a boy, you have a mom and a dad. You have a cat and I have a cat. So I am going to get rid of my dad. We have so many cats! Now what can we do with everybody’s cats?” – Participant with interaction first

Limitations

The museum setting introduced its own set of limitations. The museum we worked with and the teachers of visiting school groups were not able to significantly alter the curriculum they provide to focus on the Lukasa and mapping concepts due to both schedule and curricular constraints. These factors limited both the pool of subjects and the curriculum we were able to work with for our study and made it impossible to conduct our study with visiting school groups.

As a result, we recruited participants separately from school groups, running a focused small-group one-time-visit user study. Admittedly, group dynamics and user diversity affected our observation. Recruiting a larger number of participants would mitigate such concerns and generate quantifiable data for analysis. Expanding the curriculum or conducting follow-up studies could provide additional insights. In addition to the lecture, other activities such as drawing or crafting a personal Lukasa could be done jointly with tabletop interaction.

DESIGN IMPLICATIONS

The evaluation produced implications for interactive technology design for museum exhibits.

Learning through Sensemaking

A culture’s embodied practices and perspectives can be taught through an interactive system that embeds that culture’s logic and structure. Digital technologies can enable visitors to perform and realize the ideas behind conceptual and historical practices through engaging and playful interactions.

However, in order to support effective learning through a short interactive experience, these interactions should be based on contextualized knowledge. Effective sensemaking happens through interaction and reflection of meanings. Through hands-on experience, visitors can reconstruct and personalize the content they have learned. Without such knowledge, the interactions risk remaining simply a fun experience that provides limited understanding of the concepts at hand.

Storytelling for Collaborative Learning

For children, tangible narratives are an opportunity to create a dialogue where cultural ideas and values can be shared. Tangible narratives have been shown to encourage exploration, play, and collaboration through storytelling. Multiple users are able to simultaneously interact with a story, leading to a cooperative and social experience. This can be a good method to encourage learning and foster a collaborative learning environment in cultural museums.

Contextualized Use of Technology

Interaction and visual design should reinforce learning goals and actively attempt to avoid implying unintended meanings. Aligning an installation with learning goals is a good way to give students a way to critically engage with certain types of content, especially if it is part of a larger curriculum. However, without some grounding, design decisions can mislead students and lead them to make unintended interpretations of the content.

CONCLUSION AND FUTURE WORK

The Lukasa-inspired interactive installation demonstrates one way in which emerging digital interaction technologies can be used to revisit and support learning about historical and cultural concepts in ways that are tangible, embodied, and performative. The implied story structure, tangible objects, and physical and contextual space of our piece were designed to cohesively function to enable children to create and share stories of their own. Our user study showed that grounding the experience in contextualized knowledge can enhance comprehension of abstract concepts and subject matter. Future work can explore the how a system's design reflects the content and context of cultural interactions, highlighting how design for the humanities may compare or contrast to design for STEM subjects. There is still much to be done to understand how tangible technologies can best support learning in cultural museums and our future directions include further design, development, and evaluation work in order to generalize our results across a broader range of subject matter and a larger participant pool.

ACKNOWLEDGMENTS

We thank: the Robert C. Williams Paper Museum for holding the exhibition and letting us run the user study; the Royal Museum for Central Africa and Brygg Ullmer for lending Lukasa boards; our collaborators Ken Knoespel, Teri Williams, Yuanyuan Lin, Chris DeLeon, and the other students in the Synaesthetic Media Lab; the user study participants for their time and valuable feedback. This work was supported by: the Ivan Allen College at Georgia Tech as part of the Africa-Atlanta project, the Robert C. Williams Paper Museum, and the SSHRC CRC Program.

REFERENCES

1. Annany, M. Supporting Children's Collaborative Authoring: Practicing Written Literacy While Composing Oral Texts. In *Proc. CSCL '02*, ACM (2002), 595-596.
2. Antle, A.N., Bevans, A., Tanenbaum, J., Seaborn, K., and Wang, S. Futura: design for collaborative learning and game play on a multi-touch digital tabletop. In *Proc. TEI 2011*, ACM (2011), 93–100.
3. Antle, A.N., Wise, A.F., Hall, A., et al. Youtopia: a collaborative, tangible, multi-touch, sustainability learning activity. In *Proc. IDC 2013*, ACM (2013), 565–568.
4. Benford, S., Bederson, B.B., Åkesson, K.-P., et al. Designing storytelling technologies to encouraging collaboration between young children. In *Proc. CHI 2000*, ACM (2000), 556–563.
5. Cao, X., Lindley, S.E., Helmes, J., and Sellen, A. Telling the whole story: anticipation, inspiration and reputation in a field deployment of TellTable. In *Proc. CSCW 2010*, ACM (2010), 251–260.
6. Charmaz, Kathy. Constructing Grounded Theory: A Practical Guide through Qualitative Analysis. SAGE Publications Ltd; 1 edition, 2006.
7. Chenzira, A., Chen, Y., and Mazalek, A. RENATI: recontextualizing narratives for tangible interfaces. In *Proc. TEI 2008*, ACM (2008), 147–148.
8. Gorbet, M.G., Orth, M., and Ishii, H. Triangles: tangible interface for manipulation and exploration of digital information topography. In *Proc. CHI '98*, ACM /Addison-Wesley (1998), 49–56.
9. Harris, A., Rick, J., Bonnett, V., et al. Around the table: are multiple-touch surfaces better than single-touch for children's collaborative interactions? In *Proc. CSCL 2009*, International Society of the Learning Sciences (2009), 335–344.
10. Horn, M.S., Solovey, E.T., and Jacob, R.J.K. Tangible programming and informal science learning: making TUIs work for museums. In *Proc. IDC 2008*, ACM (2008), 194–201.
11. Hornecker, E. and Stifter, M. Learning from interactive museum installations about interaction design for public settings. In *Proc. OZCHI 2006*, ACM (2006), 135–142.
12. Hornecker, E. "I don't understand it either, but it is cool"-visitor interactions with a multi-touch table in a museum. In *Proc. TABLETOP 2008*, IEEE (2008), 113–120.
13. Kaltenbrunner, M. reacTIVision and TUIO: A tangible tabletop toolkit. *Proc. ITS 2009*. ACM (2009), 9-16.
14. Marshall, P. Do tangible interfaces enhance learning?. In *Proc. TEI '07*. ACM (2007), 163-170.
15. Mazalek, A., Davenport, G., and Ishii, H. Tangible viewpoints: a physical approach to multimedia stories. In *Proc. MM 2002*, ACM (2002), 153–160.
16. Oh, H., Deshmane, A., Li, F., et al. The digital dream lab: tabletop puzzle blocks for exploring programmatic concepts. In *Proc. TEI 2013*, ACM (2013), 51–56.
17. Potion Design. Future Energy, Memory Pool, Ware and Peace Table. http://www.potiondesign.com/projects/.
18. Roberts, M. N. and Roberts, A. F., Eds. (1996). *Memory: Luba art and the making of history*. New York, Museum for African Art.
19. Saldaña, J. "An Introduction to Codes and Coding." From *The Coding Manual for Qualitative Researchers*. Los Angeles: Sage, 2009. 1–31.
20. Tanenbaum, K., Tanenbaum, J., Antle, A.N., Bizzocchi, J., Seif el-Nasr, M., and Hatala, M. Experiencing the reading glove. In *Proc. TEI 2011*, ACM (2011), 137–144.

TIMMi: Finger-worn Textile Input Device with Multimodal Sensing in Mobile Interaction

Sang Ho Yoon, Ke Huo, Vinh P. Nguyen and Karthik Ramani
C-Design Lab, School of Mechanical Engineering
Purdue University, West Lafayette, IN 47907, USA
{yoon87,khuo,nguye131,ramani}@purdue.edu

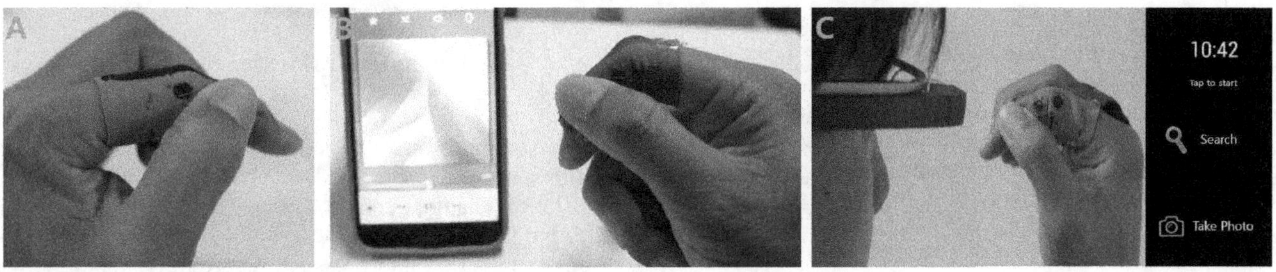

Figure 1: (a) TIMMi provides multimodal sensing through a single layer of textile (b) Controlling music player in smartphone (c) Navigating user interface in smartglasses

ABSTRACT
We introduce TIMMi, a textile input device for mobile interactions. TIMMi is worn on the index finger to provide a multimodal sensing input metaphor. The prototype is fabricated on a single layer of textile where the conductive silicone rubber is painted and the conductive threads are stitched. The sensing area comprises of three equally spaced dots and a separate wide line. Strain and pressure values are extracted from the line and three dots, respectively via voltage dividers. Regression analysis is performed to model the relationship between sensing values and finger pressure and bending. A multi-level thresholding is applied to capture different levels of finger bending and pressure. A temporal position tracking algorithm is implemented to capture the swipe gesture. In this preliminary study, we demonstrate TIMMi as a finger-worn input device with two applications: controlling music player and interacting with smartglasses.

Author Keywords
Tangible and wearable interface; mobile interaction; sensing; smart textile; finger; prototyping

ACM Classification Keywords
H.5.2. [Information interfaces and presentation]: User Interfaces - *Input devices and strategies; Interaction styles.*

TEI '15, January 16 - 19 2015, Stanford, CA, USA
Copyright 2015 ACM 978-1-4503-3305-4/15/01$15.00
http://dx.doi.org/10.1145/2677199.2680560

INTRODUCTION AND RELATED WORK
Mobile interaction with various sensing techniques has been drawing interest from researchers and developers [8]. Weiser metaphorically suggested the smart textiles as a next generation of the human computer interface with his vision of computers that "weave themselves into the fabric of everyday life" [14]. However, the sensing techniques in the smart textiles are more focused on a single modal sensing [2]. Recent works including Teleglove [9] and Beartek Glove[1] provide sufficient numbers of input trigger for the mobile interaction. These devices still require embedding sensors in multiple layers of the fabric which diminish the tactile feedback due to the stacked layer thickness. FIN[2] and FingerPad [3] provide rich interactions while maintaining a small form factor using optical and magnetic sensing. Inspired from these works, we use the smart textile for an interaction medium to achieve softness and thinness with a small form factor. We present TIMMi, a textile interface which utilizes finger pressing, bending, and swiping as input metaphors for the mobile interaction.

TIMMi brings both strain and pressure sensing capabilities from a single layer of textile. We employ a two-phase and a polynomial regression analysis to model the relationship between magnitudes of pressure and strain against applied finger pressing and bending. By using a multi-level thresholding, we differentiate input signals from the pressure and strain sensing. The swipe gestures are captured via implementing the temporal position tracking algorithm. TIMMi only requires a single layer with stitched conductive threads which alleviates sensitivity issues due to the thickness of the device [1]. The prototype consists of soft materials to pre-

[1]Beartek Glove: `http://www.beartekgloves.com/`
[2]FIN: `http://www.wearfin.com`

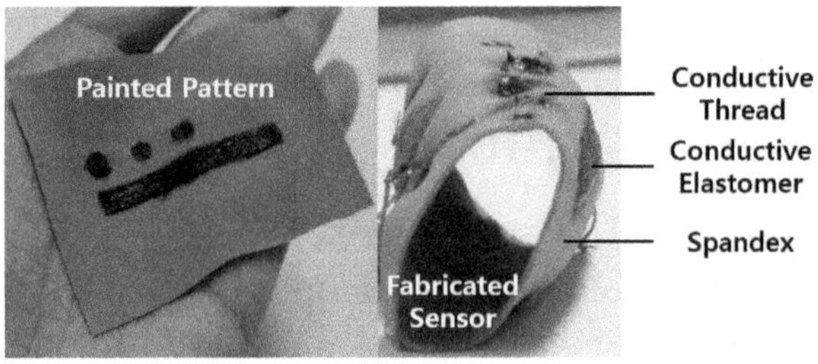

Figure 2: TIMMi prototype composition

serve the tactile sensing and improve the wearability compared to attaching hard and rigid sensors. We intend to explore: 1) A smart textile with multimodal sensing capability for mobile interaction, 2) Utilizing multimodal sensing for capturing user intent from finger bending, pressing, and swiping, and 3) Implementing applications including music player and smartglasses as applications.

DESIGN RATIONALE

- *Input Metaphor*: The thumb and index finger possess the most frequent interaction area, the greatest range of pinch strength in the hand, and are most digit-wise independent [7, 10, 11]. These fingers support pressing, rubbing, and bending as input modalities for mobile interaction. Thus, we decided to adopt interactions between thumb and the index finger.
- *Multimodal Sensing & Wearability*: Smart textiles provide various sensing metaphors based on different compositions and structure [4]. Moreover, a thin layer of fabric and conductive thread provide sensory comfort [1]. In our prototype, the discrete distribution of carbon elastomer allows capturing bending and pressing concurrently.
- *Understanding multimodal inputs*: We utilize a time-based algorithm due to its ability to differentiate finger pressing and swipe gesture. Two-phase and polynomial regression models have been used for estimating magnitudes of pressure and strain [5, 6]. These regression models in combination with the temporal tracking algorithm allow TIMMi to support numerous input modalities.

SYSTEM DESIGN

Our system design aims for three goals: 1) achieving a simultaneous pressure and strain sensing, 2) capturing different levels of finger pressing and bending as well as swipe gesture, and 3) fabricating thin, soft, and small form factor prototype. We apply flexible and soft materials to form the entire system.

Sensor Fabrication

TIMMi consists of elastic fabric painted with conductive carbon elastomer[3] and conductive threads stitched on the fabric (Figure 2). Nylon-Spandex fabric (80% Nylon and 20% Spandex) is selected due to the exceptional elasticity. The diluted conductive elastomer is painted using a stencil and a brush. We selected the conductive elastomer due to its rebound elasticity (52%). The painted fabric is cured at 120 °C

[3]Wacker LR3162: http://www.wacker.com/

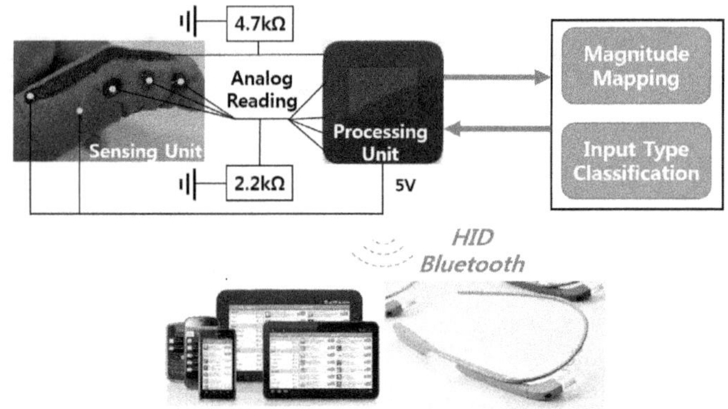

Figure 3: TIMMi schematic workflow

for 10 minutes. Combined Spandex and customized ink exhibits a good piezoresistive properties (0.15mm thick, resistance change of $50\Omega/in^2 \sim 40k\Omega/in^2$ due to pressure, gauge factor of 5). The design of two separate sensors allows detecting strain and pressure accordingly: a single line with 5mm width and three dots with 5mm diameter (Figure 2). While strain sensing is addressed with normal stitching, cross stitching into the front and back surfaces applies for pressure sensing [13].

Hardware

Analog readings are transmitted to a microprocessor through a customized fabric connector ($< 0.2\Omega/cm$). Instead of metallic wires, the customized fabric connector is used to keep the softness of the prototype. The processing unit comprises a chip sized microcontroller[4] (ATmega328, clock speed 16MHz), Bluetooth module (115200bps), and 3.3V lithium-ion battery. We select $2.2k\Omega$ and $4.7k\Omega$ resistors for pressure and strain sensor based on the voltage divider calculation(Figure 3). HID Bluetooth module passes input via standard communication protocol to the device. The total weight of the system is under 50g.

Multimodal Sensing

The analog outputs from the piezoresistive fabric are processed with two different regression models. A multi-level thresholding and a temporal position tracking algorithm are used to create different input commands.

Simultaneous Pressure and Bending Sensing

We performed initial tests on pressing and bending with TIMMi which were investigated to confirm the capability of fabricated piezoresistive fabric in recognizing both finger pressing and bending discretely and simultaneously. The virtual manipulation illustrates real-time performance of the prototype (Figure 4).

Magnitude Mapping

The bending and pressing magnitudes levels are defined by the regression analysis. The resistance changes are plotted against applied pressure and finger bending angle. The zero-calibration is performed before each trial to compensate for

[4]Microview: `https://www.sparkfun.com/products/12923`

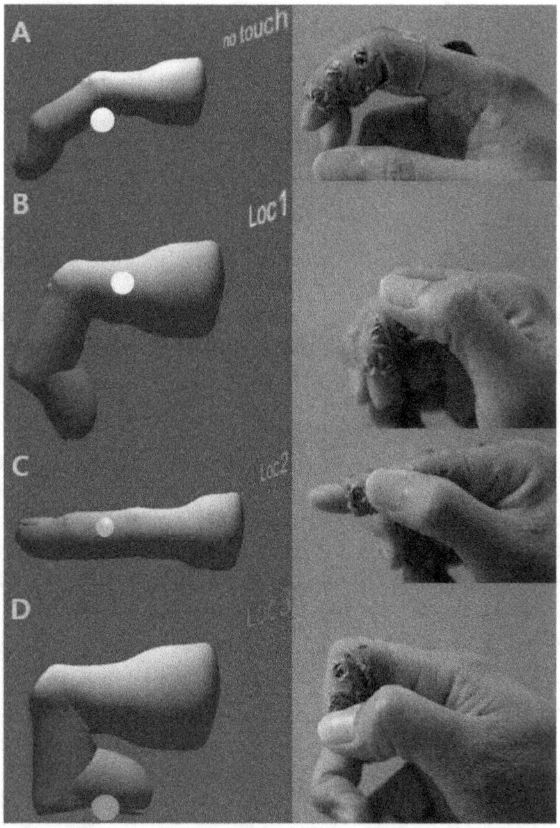

Figure 4: Real-time manipulation of virtual finger model with TIMMi (a) slight bending, (b) slight bending with tapping, (c) pressing gently, and (d) full bending with pressing firmly

variations in finger-worn conditions. For pressure, we use a two phase regression model which encompass linear and exponential characteristics of the sensor output. For finger bending, we employ a polynomial regression model which could predict magnitudes between 0∼90° of proximal interphalangeal joint bending. Magnitude mappings are primarily carried out since mapped values are used as a reference in recognizing different levels of the input signal.

Two-phase Regression Model:

$$y_i = mx_i + b,\ for\ x \leq 0.7N/cm^2 \tag{1}$$

$$y_i = \alpha x_i^{\beta},\ for\ x > 0.7N/cm^2 \tag{2}$$

Polynomial Regression Model:

$$y_j = \sum_{i=0}^{n} a_i x_j^i + \epsilon_j \tag{3}$$

These magnitude models show average accuracy of 97.3% (pressing) and 90.6% (bending). Plots illustrate the raw data and the developed regression models (Figure5).

Capturing Input Types

TIMMi utilizes mapped magnitude models to capture input types. In this preliminary work, we dissect pressure and bending magnitudes into three regions which can distinguish more

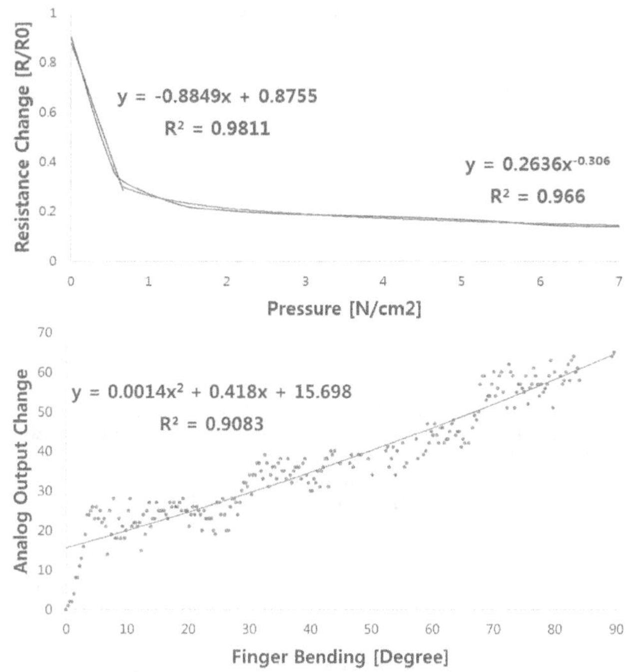

Figure 5: Magnitude model using two-phase regression model for finger pressing (Top) and polynomial regression model for finger bending (Bottom)

than an on/off status. The segmentation levels can be adjusted according to applications. We employ a temporal position tracking method to detect the swipe gesture and differentiate between discrete pressing and swiping. If users trigger two different painted dots with small amount of pressure, the algorithm counts the time gap between two events. The whole event is recognized as a swipe gesture only if the time gap falls within a specific constant for which we use 0.5 seconds.

We conducted a small pilot test to confirm the input classification performance of TIMMi. It involved 7 participants where we asked them to execute every input type designed in the prototype such as different levels of pressing and bending as well as swiping with both directions. The zero-calibration was carried out with a straight finger posture prior to each test. Figure 6 illustrates the confusion matrix of different input types. Pressing and bending magnitude detection exhibited average accuracy of 97% and 92% respectively while swipe gestures detection gave 80% accuracy. Less accuracy was observed in swipe gestures due to different swipe velocities among users.

IMPLEMENTATION

In this study, TIMMi is implemented as a new input device for smartphone and smartglasses.

Eyes-free Mobile Input Metaphor

Multimodal sensing provides intuitiveness in controlling the default music player application in Android OS. Our design focuses on providing comfort for wearing in order to not restrict natural finger motion. In general, the eyes-free interaction is motivated to enhance the controllability while visually

Presented \ Selected: class	1	2	3	4	5	6	7	8	9	10	11	12	13	14
1	**67**	4	0	0	0	0	0	0	0	0	0	0	4	0
2	2	**66**	1	0	0	0	0	0	0	0	0	0	0	3
3	1	0	**69**	0	0	0	0	0	0	0	0	0	0	5
4	0	0	0	**68**	3	0	0	0	0	0	0	0	1	1
5	0	0	0	2	**66**	0	0	0	0	0	0	0	0	0
6	0	0	0	0	1	**70**	0	0	0	0	0	0	1	0
7	0	0	0	0	0	0	**68**	0	0	0	0	0	3	2
8	0	0	0	0	0	0	2	**68**	1	0	0	0	1	1
9	0	0	0	0	0	0	0	2	**69**	0	0	0	6	0
10	0	0	0	0	0	0	0	0	0	**70**	2	0	0	0
11	0	0	0	0	0	0	0	0	0	0	**63**	9	0	0
12	0	0	0	0	0	0	0	0	0	0	5	**61**	0	0
13	0	0	0	0	0	0	0	0	0	0	0	0	**54**	0
14	0	0	0	0	0	0	0	0	0	0	0	0	0	**58**

(1) Tap (2) Press gently (3) Press firmly on outer pressure dot
(4) Tap (5) Press gently (6) Press firmly on middle pressure dot
(7) Tap (8) Press gently (9) Press firmly on inner pressure dot
(10) 0°(11) 45° (12) 90° finger bending
(13) Inner direction (14) Outer direction swiping

Figure 6: Confusion matrix of different input types. Rows indicate presented inputs and columns refer to selected inputs.

distracted from mobile devices [15]. Our approach is to suggest a wearable device with passive haptic experience where users utilize somatosensory tactility for mobile interaction.

Socially Acceptable Interface

TIMMi works as an input device for the smartglasses. The tactile input interface for conventional smartglasses is located on the frame which requires publicly noticeable gestures. The social acceptance of the interaction can improve with less noticeable gesture [12]. We aim to enhance the social acceptability by utilizing a single finger interaction. This approach is expected to reduce the extra noticeable gesture since users can manipulate fingers accurately with a subtle motion.

DISCUSSION

Implemented applications and conducted pilot test show that rich interactions can be accomplished in a single finger by broadening input modalities. A thin and soft layer of prototype provides the multimodal sensing without adversely affecting the user wearability. Incorporating a smart textile as a wearable device for mobile interaction illustrates that the embedded and embodied interactions can be merged into a single device. In TIMMi, the piezoresistive sensing technology is embedded while users interact using embodied gestures like finger pressing, bending, and rubbing (swiping). We hypothesize that exploiting these embodied gestures within a small embedded system improve the eyes-free performance and social acceptability. To explore this further, we intend to conduct physio-psychological user studies.

We only used conductive threads to provide a soft conductive path in our current design. It will be interesting if we imprint highly conductive ink over the conductive elastomer for future work. To improve a classification, we will consider Support Vector Machine (SVM) method. During follow-up user studies, we expect to figure out quantitative and qualitative results on eyes-free performance and social acceptability as well.

CONCLUSION

We present TIMMi, a finger-worn textile input device with multimodal sensing capabilities for mobile interaction. By painting carbon elastomer and stitching conductive threads, we implemented pressure and strain sensor on a single layer of fabric. We employed multi-level thresholding for magnitude detection and temporal position tracking algorithm for capturing different finger gestures. A pilot test showed participants were able to effectively use TIMMi for triggering various inputs. The applications shown in this paper imply the potential enhancement of current mobile interaction. We expect that our work will be helpful in exploiting smart textiles as a multimodal input device.

ACKNOWLEDGMENTS

This work is partially supported by the NSF IGERT on Sustainable Electronics (DGE 1144842), and the Donald W. Feddersen Chair Professorship support from the School of Mechanical Engineering. Any opinions, findings, and conclusions or recommendations expressed in this material are those of the authors and do not necessarily reflect the views of the sponsors.

REFERENCES

1. B. Behera et al. Comfort properties of fabrics woven from ring-, rotor-, and friction-spun yarns. *Journal of the Textile Institute*, 88(3):255–264, 1997.
2. L. M. Castano et al. Smart fabric sensors and e-textile technologies: a review. *Smart Materials and Structures*, 23(5):053001, 2014.
3. L. Chan et al. Fingerpad: private and subtle interaction using fingertips. In *Proc. of UIST*, pages 255–260. ACM, 2013.
4. G. Cho. *Smart clothing: technology and applications*, chapter 9. CRC Press, 2010.
5. C. Cochrane et al. Design and development of a flexible strain sensor for textile structures based on a conductive polymer composite. *Sensors*, 7(4):473–492, 2007.
6. Z. Del Prete et al. A novel pressure array sensor based on contact resistance variation: Metrological properties. *Review of Scientific Instruments*, 72(2):1548–1553, 2001.
7. F. Gonzalez et al. A framework for the classification of dexterous haptic interfaces based on the identification of the most frequently used hand contact areas. In *World Haptics Conference*, pages 461–466. IEEE, 2013.
8. K. Hinckley et al. Sensing techniques for mobile interaction. In *Proc. of UIST*, pages 91–100. ACM, 2000.
9. K. Huber et al. The making of the teleglove: crafting interactions for basic phone use in the cold. In *Proc. of TEI*, pages 241–244. ACM, 2014.
10. S. N. Imrhan. Trends in finger pinch strength in children, adults, and the elderly. *Human Factors: The Journal of the Human Factors and Ergonomics Society*, 31(6):689–701, 1989.
11. J. N. Ingram et al. The statistics of natural hand movements. *Experimental brain research*, 188(2):223–236, 2008.
12. C. S. Montero et al. Would you do that?: understanding social acceptance of gestural interfaces. In *Proc. of MobileHCI*, pages 275–278. ACM, 2010.
13. M. Shimojo et al. A tactile sensor sheet using pressure conductive rubber with electrical-wires stitched method. *Sensors Journal, IEEE*, 4(5):589–596, 2004.
14. M. Weiser. The computer for the 21st century. *Scientific american*, 265(3):94–104, 1991.
15. B. Yi et al. Exploring user motivations for eyes-free interaction on mobile devices. In *Proc. of CHI*, pages 2789–2792. ACM, 2012.

Tangible Interactive Microbiology for Informal Science Education

Seung Ah Lee, Alice M. Chung, Nate Cira and Ingmar H. Riedel-Kruse
Department of Bioengineering, Stanford University
318 Campus Drive, Stanford, CA 94305, USA
{salee30, amchung, ncira, ingmar}@stanford.edu

ABSTRACT
We present an interactive platform that enables human users to interface with microbiological living cells through a touch-screen, thereby generating a tangible interactive experience with the microscopic world that is hidden to most people. Euglena gracilis, single-celled phototactic microorganisms, are imaged and optically stimulated via a microscope setup equipped with a projector and a touch-screen display. Users can directly interact with these organisms by drawing patterns onto the screen, which displays the real-time magnified view of the microfluidic chamber with the motile euglena cells. The drawings are directly projected onto the chamber, thereby influencing the swimming motion of the cells. We discuss the architecture of the system and provide exploratory user testing results in a facilitated setting, which shows engaging nature of our system for children and the general public. In conclusion, our tangible interactive microscope allows artistic expression and scientific exploration with the ease of "child's play."

Author Keywords
Tangible interactive microbiology; Interactive biology; Biotic games; Biotic processing unit; Tangible microscope

ACM Classification Keywords
H.5.2. User Interfaces; K.3.m Computers and education

INTRODUCTION
Modern life sciences and its technology increasingly affect our society, driving the need for new media and approaches to educate the general public and (future) professionals. The educational potential for interactive devices is well demonstrated for electronics from the early home-computers to the latest touch-pads [17, 21]. In this work, we present a new medium that enables humans to tangibly interact with living biological systems via an interactive microscope based on consumer-electronic devices (Figure 1). Users can interact with photo-responsive microorganisms by drawing patterns onto a touch-screen device displaying a magnified view of these microorganisms (Figure 2). The user's drawing is then projected onto the microorganisms as light beams, which the cells can sense and respond to by changing their swimming motion and morphology. Such optical feedback can be achieved by integrating a commercial movie projector into a webcam-enabled microscope, both of which are spatially synced and controlled by a touch-screen laptop computer. This interactive microscope enables users to actively play with microscopic living organisms in real-time.

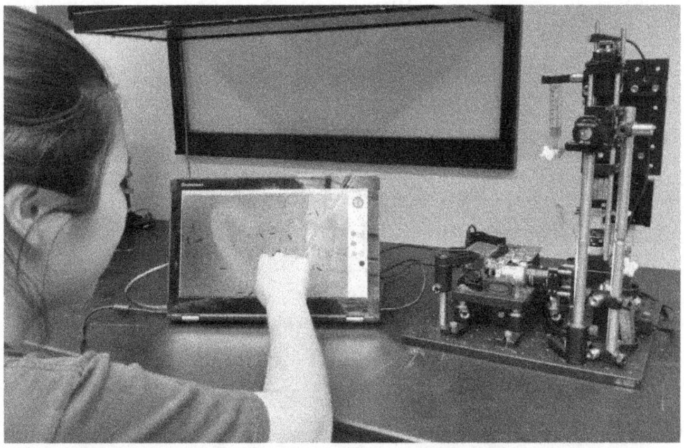

Figure 1. We developed an interactive system that enables free-form human interaction with microbiological organisms through a touch-screen electronic device (left) and optical hardware (right). We see significant educational potential for this type of tangible biology experience.

The development of this platform is motivated by the persistent need for formal and informal science education (in general as well as with regard to modern life-sciences) [1, 29], by the human tendency to toy around with objects leading then to secondary educational effects [33], and by the enabling power of emerging electronic, biotechnological and hybrid technologies [31, 32, 39]. We were also inspired by the recent development of augmented reality systems that extends the physical world with virtual reality techniques [2, 7]. In addition, 97% of teens play digital games [19], tablets are increasingly used in education [3]. Both media have been shown significant educational promise, in particular through increase in

TEI '15, January 16 - 19 2015, Stanford, CA, USA

http://dx.doi.org/10.1145/2677199.2680561

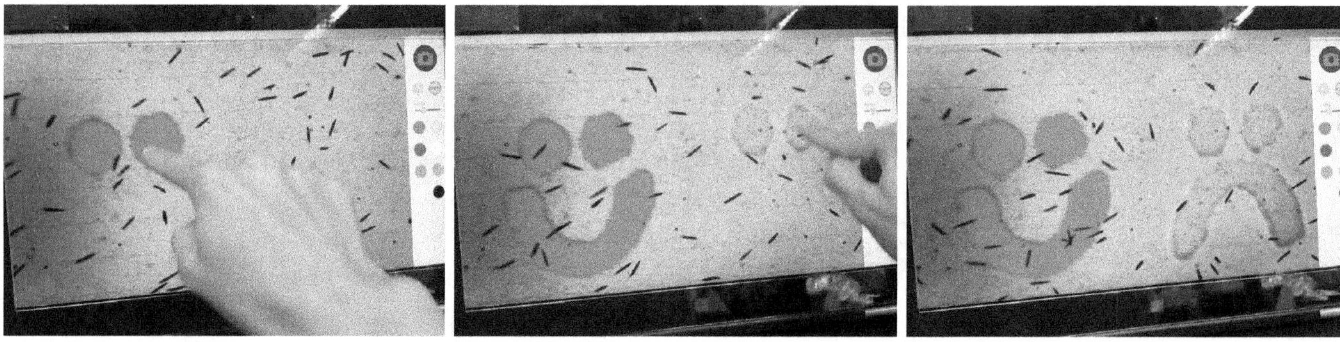

Figure 2. Tangible interaction with phototactic euglena cells. The patterns drawn onto a touch-screen is projected onto motile microorganisms (euglena) inside a microscope, which is then conveyed to the user in real time. The differently colored faces demonstrate how the cells (black elongated objects) are attracted to one color (red) while avoiding the other (blue).

motivation and engagement [15, 26, 28]. This platform is also coherent with the emerging efforts in human computer interaction (HCI) field to integrate biological systems into the interaction design, where living matter becomes a part of the hardware system that senses, controls and responds to the human user [12, 14, 18, 25, 37, 38].

If we turn to microbiology we notice that such interactive experiences are essentially lacking [32]. Microscopes are usually the only equipment used for microbiology education and usually limited to passive observation. The report by United States national research council [34] described among its key items for science learning in informal settings to "Experience excitement, interest, and motivation to learn about phenomena in the natural and physical world (motivation)." Based on these issues, we were interested in creating a platform for microbiology that is similarly versatile and expressive, that provides a tangible experience with this microscopic world with expected educational value for all ages and – most importantly – allows for true interaction rather than just observations as with traditional microscopes. The system can be easily applied to various applications by modifying its software, without the need for biological knowledge and experimental skills. Our setup enables users to: playfully explore, plan experiments, and be expressive with microbiology.

IMPLEMENTATION

Biological background

Our microorganism of choice is *Euglena gracilis*, a photosynthetic single-celled protozoan commonly found in fresh-water ponds. Euglena shows phototactic behavior and their response varies with different colors and intensities of light [4, 9, 22, 23, 40]. Under natural conditions, they move away or towards increased light levels to position themselves for effective photosynthesis while avoiding ultraviolet damage [4]. The mechanism of light-responsive motion is known to originate from a subcellular photodetecting organelle, which has strong absorption in the blue wavelengths [4]. Thus, for same intensities of irradiation, colors that better match the absorption spectrum of their photodetector will stimulate the cells more strongly. Their phototactic turning is caused by electrochemical signal transduction from the photodetector to the flagellum [19].

The phototactic responses of euglena is instantaneous, allowing for real-time interaction with human users. However, the level of response varies among individual cells, that is, some cells are more sensitive than others. The phototactic behavior is dependent on the relative illumination intensities between background, stimulus, as well as the outside environment. For the present system we chose light conditions where we would get consistent and clear responses to particular colors (Figure 2) – blue light is too intense such that most cells shy away from blue region, whereas red and green is moderate but brighter for the cells than the background such that the cells prefer.

Euglena gracilis are biologically safe, easy to culture and has been widely used in educational settings [20]. We maintain a stable batch culture in a vial at room temperature under a static illumination. The batch culture is connected to the microfluidic chamber via tubes and valves and is stable for multiple weeks without human intervention. The cells in the microfluidic chamber are flushed out every 6-8 hours to maintain the cell concentration and their phototactic responses.

Essentially, any phototactic motile microorganism can be used with our system – we have tested and are currently optimizing our system with other organisms such as Chlamydomonas and Paramecea.

Hardware

The architecture of this system follows design principles that would enable wide distribution, adoption, and educational effectiveness for other media (Figure 3): The core part is a biotic processing unit (BPU) [32] consisting of a microfluidic chip [39] providing an automated and stable culture of the organisms. This microfluidic chip is sandwiched between a projector and a camera, which constitute high-dimensional input and output devices. The BPU itself is controlled by a conventional computer with a touch-screen monitor that enables the human to observe and interact at the fingertips.

Conceptually, the interface that the human visually experiences on screen contains 3 layers (Figure 4): The light projection, the microscopic fluidic world including organisms, and the overlaid virtual objects. Here the ~50-µm long Euglena cells are magnified to the scale of a human finger (~5 cm) on the screen, thereby bridging 3 orders of magnitude to enable a human tactile experience. This bridging is afforded by electronics and optics, where optics is used both for manipulation and viewing. (Stimuli other than light such as chemicals or fluid flow could be considered in the future.)

The setup is constructed with consumer electronic devices and conventional optical components for microscopy. We used microscope objective lenses to relay the movie projector's display screen onto the microfluidic chamber (2 4×/0.10 infinity-corrected objectives, Nikon), and to image magnified view of the microfluidic chamber and the light stimulus pattern onto the camera (4×/0.10 finite conjugate objective, Edmund optics). For imaging, we modified a webcam (Logitech) by removing the lens module and placed it at the back focal plane of the imaging objective lens. A commercial pico-projector (Incredisonic) is integrated on the other side of microfluidic chamber. We used a digital light processor (DLP)-based projector with 3-light emitting diode (LED) lamps, also modified by replacing the original projection lens system with our 2-objective relay system. A neutral density filter of 1 optical densities were placed between the relay objectives to decrease the projector's simulation intensity. The optical setup measures approximately 12 × 12 × 18 inches, which makes a table-top device (Figure 1). With customized design and mass-produced optical parts, we can further scale down the form factor and the cost of our system.

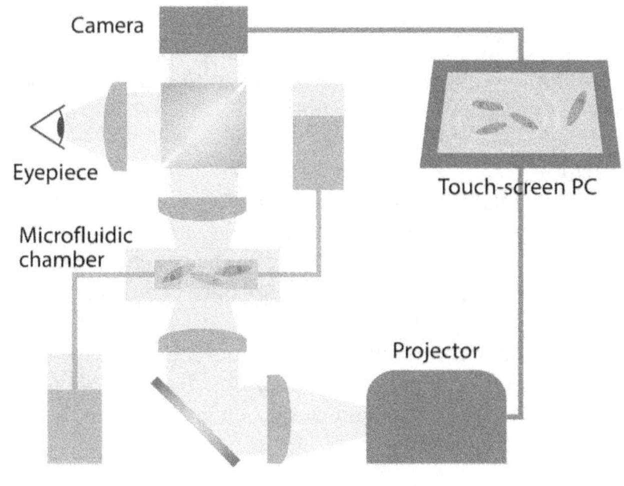

Figure 3. Schematics of the hardware setup. A projector projects light patterns onto a microfluidic chamber, in which light responsive cells (euglena) are housed. A camera captures the cells incl. the projected stimulus live and displays the resulting image onto an interactive user interface, on which additional virtual objects are overlaid.

The imaging resolution of the microscope is ~1 µm, and the projected pixel size of the projection is ~7 µm, which, in

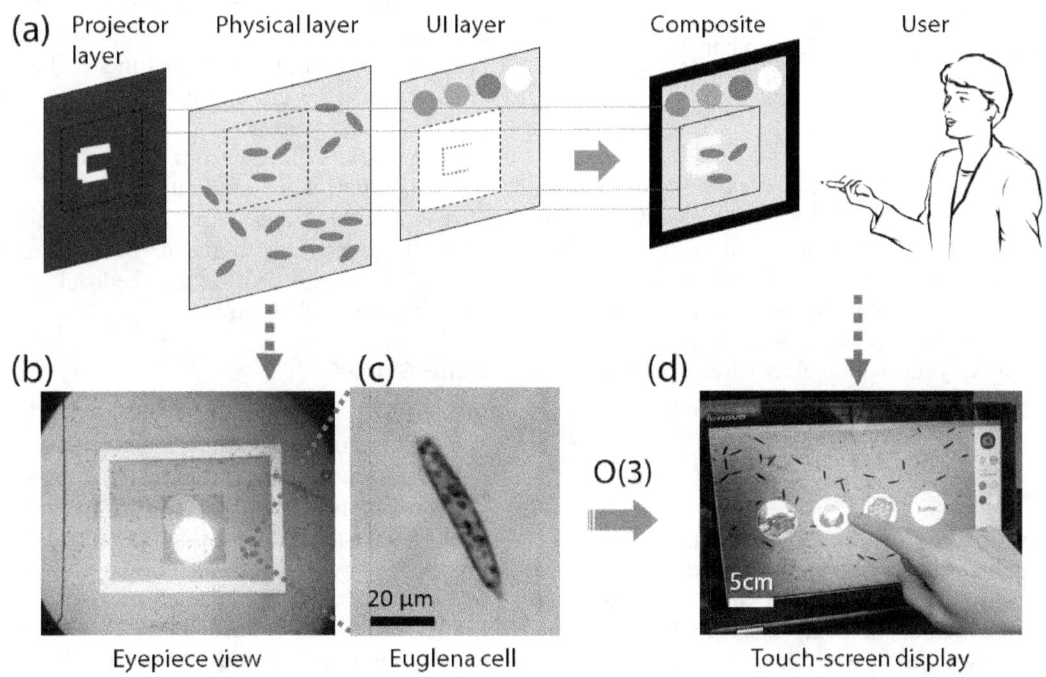

Figure 4. (a) Schematics of the three layers that the user effectively experiences (projector, physical, and user interface). (b) View of the physical layer seen through the eyepiece. (b-d) The system bridges the length scale of three orders of magnitude difference between euglena (c) and human finger (d).

principle, even allows subcellular stimulation of euglena. All these parameters can be customized with different optical arrangements. A magnified view of the microorganisms and the light projection is displayed on the touch-screen device for real-time interaction. Alternatively, the user could look through the eyepiece (Figure 3) to observe both the projected image and the euglena directly. A beam splitter cube is inserted in the tube of the microscope to show display the images to both the camera and the eyepiece at the same time.

Software

The user interface and the hardware for imaging and projection is are written in Processing [30]. Based on the user input (touch information) from the touch-screen, the drawings of selected color and intensities are displayed on the projector display. Simultaneously, the camera captures the real-time view of the microfluidic chamber, which is displayed on the touch-screen monitor. Both displays are refreshed at video rate and the touch information is also continuously updated.

The program provides a multi-step paradigm consisting of the following components (Figure 5): (1) A freehand drawing canvas with the instruction "doodle" (Figure 5a, b); (2) a canvas displaying three overlapping color circles with the question "What color do they like?" (Figure 5d) (3) a "mini-game" where a bright blue colored river is displayed (which Euglena do not cross) with the instruction "help euglena across the river", and (Figure 5e) (4) a "mini-game" that would ask to get as many euglena as possible in a virtual box displayed on the screen (Figure 5f). The program launches with the freehand drawing canvas, and the user can select options from the toolbar menu to start the color quiz or other mini-games (Figure 5c). This arrangement encourages users to get familiar with the system before playing the games.

The program starts by tapping on the "doodle" button at the center of the screen (Figure 5a). Here, the user interface is designed to maximize expressive drawing without interruptions, adopting the familiar interface designs of conventional touch-screen drawing software. (Figure 5b). On the toolbar, we provide 8 color choices (red, green, blue, white, orange, pink, yellow and black) that the user can simply pick. The user also has an option to clear the screen and use an eraser tool to correct/erase out his/her drawings. The line width of the drawings can be chosen from 2 to 20 projector pixels.

As the user drags his/her finger on the screen, the user can see the lines of selected color and width drawn on the monitor. The drawn line is the projection of the pattern, which is optically imaged from the physical layer, rather than rendered graphics on the UI layer. (Figure 4). The camera's field-of-view and the projector's field-of-projection is pre-aligned and scaled according to the magnifications of the optical system and the display resolution. The actual intensities and colors for the background and the stimuli were calibrated to provide stable and clear phototactic responses of the euglena. We also made a version with a full color/intensity control for the background and the stimuli, only for internal uses to investigate and optimize the system.

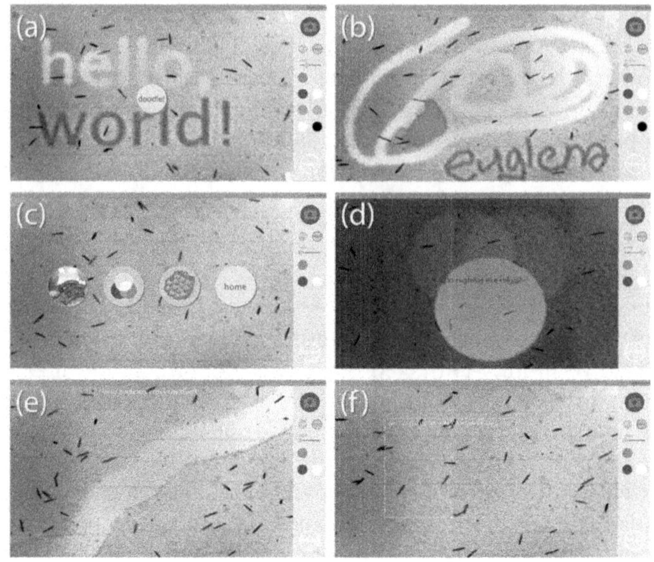

Figure 5. User interface the system. (a-b) Canvas for free-hand drawing. (c) Main menu with options for selecting mini-games and quiz (d) mini-game to build colored bridges to make euglena cross the blue "river". (d) Controlled experimentation for color responses of euglena. (e) Mini-game to concentrate euglenas in a virtual box.

In the mini-games (Figure 5e, f), the intensities were calibrated such that the cells would avoid blue color, while red and green will likely attract them – hence depending on what color the users chose (and how fast they chose that color), it could be shown that the children and students transferred knowledge from the free exploration into the test condition. For simplicity, we only allowed 4 colors (red, green, blue and white) for the mini-games and quiz. There were no time limits or "correct answers" to these games. Also, the scoring or feedback had not yet been implemented in these mini-games.

USER STUDY

Procedure

We undertook exploratory qualitative user studies to understand the general affordance of the system, as part of an iterative process to refine the technology: The initial study consisted of 21 interactions with individuals or groups (many of them as families) ranging from ages 3 to 50. The study was conducted at a local science museum (San Jose Tech museum) and the people were either invited to or voluntarily visited our setup. The interactions were supervised and facilitated by two researchers; i.e., we guided the users through the activities, motivated the users with open-ended questions and answered the questions

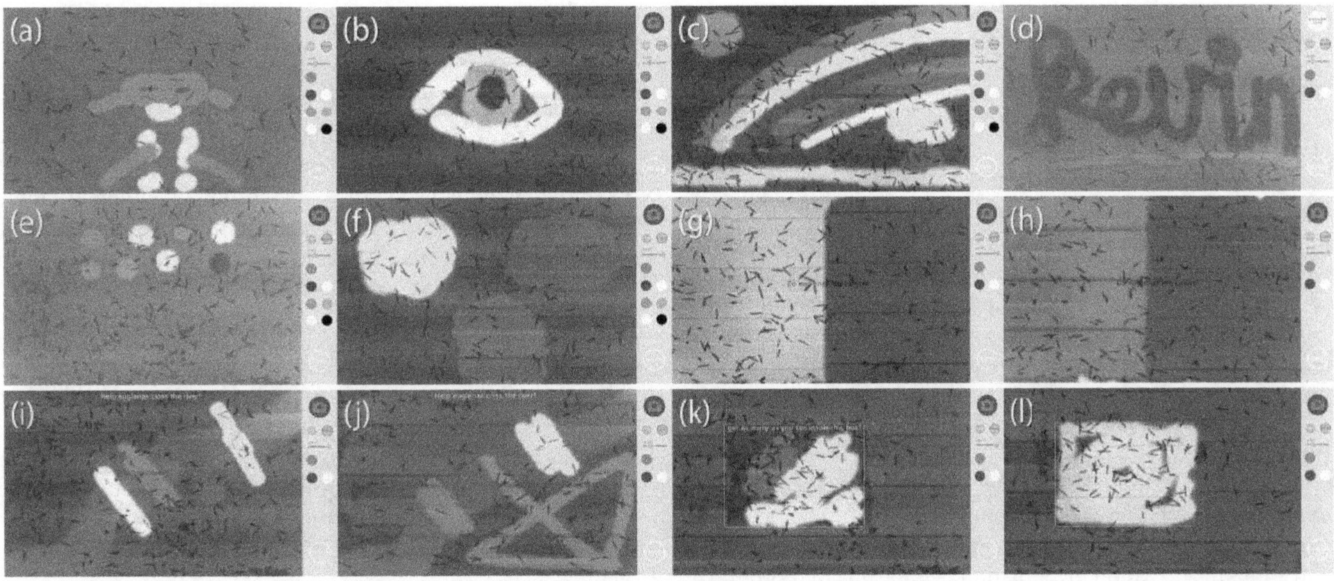

Figure 6. Examples of user interactions. a-d) Examples of what people drew and explored. e-h) Users perform experiments to test color preference of organisms. i-l) Mini-games to test for knowledge transfer about color response. i,j) "Get euglena across the river" and k,l) "Get as many as possible inside the box".

users asked during the activities. In the beginning, we prompted the users with the question "Do euglenas like colors?" Then, we passively observed the users actions, occasionally prompting questions to the user, or answering questions when asked by the user. We introduced mini-games (Figure 5d-f) to the users who stayed longer than 2 minutes and showed active engagement with the system. We informally asked all users at the end about their experience, and inquired the ages. For documentation, we captured screenshots of the software (both monitor and projector displays) every 5 seconds while the users were interacting with the system. We also had the whole system encased in a transparent plastic housing such that the users are able to see the individual components, which we also labeled.

Engagement

Our main findings were that people were directly drawn into the system – especially children started doodling and drawing right away (including 3 year olds). The average dwell time was 4.9 minutes. Out of 21 interactions, less than 2 groups stayed less than a minute and 4 groups spent more than 10 minutes drawing and exploring, which speaks for the engaging nature of the system. These dwell time can be considered successful for a museum setting [6, 16] and are likely also mediated by the fact that many users were familiar with handheld touch pads including games and doodling programs.

When multiple people were in front of the system (usually parents with their kids, or groups of children) they started discussing with each other. Overall participants said that this system was "really cool". Many teenagers and adults made comments and asked question on about the organisms and the system, indicating that the system not only prompts questions about biology but also about technology in broader terms. Hence people of all ages are certainly very excited and have a direct connection (affordance) to the system, especially children and adults engage with each other.

In our study, we observed that the mini-games (Figure 5e, f) and the quiz (Figure 5d) promote stronger engagement to the system. For the users who were prompted the mini-games, the average dwell time was 7.7 minutes with the average gaming time of 4 minutes. All participants have successfully transferred their experience and findings about the system and the organisms. People showed active engagement during mini-games with active discussion among the groups and questions about the organisms and the system. More controlled user studies will follow in the future to investigate the effect of mini-games on engagement and learning outcomes.

Perception

We wondered whether the users comprehend what they see on the screen, in particular whether they grasp the concept of microscopic scale. We found that using an eye-piece (Figure 4b), through which the organisms as well as the drawn patterns could be observed, significantly helped the conceptual understanding of what the interaction was about. The eyepiece view has larger field-of-view than the camera display, and intermediate magnification between the actual chamber and the camera view. When introduced to the eyepiece, some users (especially children) looked back and forth between the screen and the microscope as they were drawing on the screen. This allows the users interpret the "layers" in the system, especially that the drawings shown on the screen is "real" and actually projected on the physical layer, not on the UI layer.

Most users noticed on their own that there were cells swimming across the screen, prompting questions what they are. For younger children (typically below 10 years), this seemed primarily as an engaging doodling program, and only when asked specific question by their parents or us pointing to the swimming cells they started noticing and got engaged into discussion. With increasing age the children seemed to make increasingly more sophisticated connections, calling the Euglena "fishies", "bugs", "germs", and "bacteria", respectively. Many adults asked "What are they?" or "Are they bacteria?"

Patterns of activity

Ultimately, we found that the system is versatile and expressive enough to enable the scientific method from exploration, discovery, hypothesis, controlled experiments, and transfer to another situation – all on the order of minutes. We classified the participants' activity patterns into three categories; free exploration, controlled experimentation and gaming, according to the purpose and the form of activities.

Free exploration

Many people began their interaction with the program by exploring the setup/interface and free-drawing various clips on to the screen. The examples include; simple patterns (lines and dots), more complex drawings (face, eye, rainbow, Figure 6a-c) and writings (name, Figure 6d). In these examples, people were being expressive and used multiple colors and line widths to polish their drawings. Users in a group asked each other they are drawing and also commented about the drawing. During these initial exploration stage, many people have noticed (by accident) and commented on the phototactic behavior of the euglena cells.

Controlled experimentation

Some users (either on their own or after question from us) explored the euglena's color responses more systematically. In the freehand-drawing canvas, these users attempted to perform (semi) controlled-experiments by drawing the same pattern with different colors or filling the screen with sections of different colors (Figure 6e-g). Rather than polishing their drawings, users spent more time observing the swimming motions of the euglena; such as accumulation/evacuation of cells in colored regions and phototactic turning of single cell upon the incident of light stimulus. During this stage, most discussions and questions were about the euglena's response to light and/or possible methods of experimentation.

Gaming and playing

For the user groups who had been successful with previous stages of the activity (doodling and experimentation), we introduced them to our mini-games. When confronted with the mini-games, users did not have problems providing working solutions to the games. The game was simple enough that everyone interpreted what the goals of the games were without additional explanations. In the testing, we got different answers to the mini-games (Fig 6.k-m). For example, people used different colors to either attract or push the cells, furthermore used different drawing speeds to guide or gather cells. Some users commented on the time limit or scoring (as there were none), which we plan to implement in the future.

To summarize, the platform is versatile and expressive to trigger and stimulate open-ended exploration and to showcase the scientific paradigm to lay people ("everyone is a natural born scientist"); no previous hands-on biology procedural knowledge is required to do so, and biotic games [32] have educational potential by connecting and drawing learners attention towards the biological context in a playful way.

CONCLUSION

In conclusion, this interactive setup provides a flexible constructivist medium [5, 24] for many applications; the user studies we presented here represents only the beginning – much of its potential awaits to be explored and discovered raising novel questions for HCI (or rather human-biology –interaction, HBI) [27].

Although current version of the system was tested with public users in the presence of a facilitator, we envision that the system will eventually become a stand-alone interactive "micro-aquarium" [22] with minimum human intervention. The user experience can be designed to provide a natural and intuitive flow through different types of activities that the system can support. The organisms inside the chip are stable for weeks, then changing organisms and chip requires only a few minutes, i.e., the system maintenance of this system is very low. These organisms, including euglena, are also widely used in school education and are easily obtained from educational suppliers [20], which overall addresses any safety and logistic issues regarding wider dissemination. Ethical concerns potentially raised regarding this type of biological manipulation are also refutable [13].

That fact that users of diverse age groups can naturally make meaningful and open-ended investigations also fits well with the formal learning content of many school curricular, such as the new science standards in the US that emphasizes biology in 7th grade, and scientific investigations in the middle school in general [36]. The microfluidic chip [10] used here is a very simple device, and in the future we can expect increased structural complexity and versatility, such as microscopic mazes or the integration of other actuators such as chemicals and flow, and where for this type of technology we can expect commercial development and price drops along the line the integrated circuits took [11]. The affordability of this system such as a consumer product or interactive school microscope is in reach given that the technology primarily consists of a webcam and a pico-projector (with adjusted optics to project onto a 5-mm chamber instead of a 2-m screen), leading to a cost estimate of less than $250 in line with other mass-market electronics.

A commercial setup also promises significant utility as research tool, such as in the growing optogenetic field [8, 31] where light is used to control and interrogate complex neural activity. A setups like this would be usable with similar effort and cost as the early personal computers [21], current tablets [17], arcade games [35], museum exhibit [16], and interactive school and DIY microscopes - with similar significant potential for formal and informal education as their electronic counterparts [1, 34].

ACKNOWLEDGMENTS

The authors are grateful to the Riedel-Kruse lab members for participating in initial user tests and providing valuable comments. We thank San Jose Tech Museum for arranging the user test and providing useful resources. We also thank Mr. Engin Bumbacher and Professor Paulo Blikstein from Stanford School of Education for their helpful suggestions. This research was supported by the National Science Foundations (grant on cyberlearning #1324753) and Stanford BioX (interdisciplinary seed funding).

REFERENCES

1. Alberts, B., Prioritizing Science Education. *Science*, *328*, 5977 (2010), 405.
2. Azuma, R.T., A survey of augmented reality. *Presence*, *6*, 4 (1997), 355-385.
3. Banister, S., Integrating the iPod Touch in K–12 Education: Visions and Vices. *Computers in the Schools*, *27*, 2 (2010), 121-131.
4. Barsanti, L., V. Evangelista, V. Passarelli, A.M. Frassanito, and P. Gualtieri, Fundamental questions and concepts about photoreception and the case of Euglena gracilis. *Integrative Biology*, *4*, 1 (2012), 22-36.
5. Blikstein, P., Gears of our childhood: constructionist toolkits, robotics, and physical computing, past and future, in *Proceedings of the 12th International Conference on Interaction Design and Children*.(2013), ACM: New York, New York.173-182.
6. Boisvert, D.L. and B.J. Slez, The relationship between exhibit characteristics and learning-associated behaviors in a science museum discovery space. *Science Education*, *79*, 5 (1995), 503-518.
7. de Souza e Silva, A. and G.C. Delacruz, Hybrid Reality Games Reframed: Potential Uses in Educational Contexts. *Games and Culture*, *1*, 3 (2006), 231-251.
8. Deisseroth, K., Optogenetics. *Nat Meth*, *8*, 1 (2011), 26-29.
9. Diehn, B., Phototaxis and Sensory Transduction in Euglena. *Science*, *181*, 4104 (1973), 1009-1015.
10. Duffy, D.C., J.C. McDonald, O.J.A. Schueller, and G.M. Whitesides, Rapid Prototyping of Microfluidic Systems in Poly(dimethylsiloxane). *Analytical Chemistry*, *70*, 23 (1998), 4974-4984.
11. Frederickson, R.M., Fluidigm. Biochips get indoor plumbing. *Chemistry & biology*, *9*, 11 (2002), 1161.
12. Hamidi, F. and M. Baljko, Rafigh: a living media interface for speech intervention, in *Proceedings of the 32nd annual ACM conference on Human factors in computing systems*.(2014), ACM: Toronto, Ontario, Canada.1817-1820.
13. Harvey, H., Havard, M., Magnus, D., Cho, M., & Riedel-Kruse, I. , Innocent fun or microslavery? : Public Responses to and Ethical Analysis of Biotic Games. *Hasting Center Report*, *44*, 6 (2014), 38-46.
14. Hertz, G., Cockroach controlled mobile robot. *Garnet Hertz-Http://conceptlabcom*, (2008).
15. Hilton, M. and M.A. Honey, *Learning science through computer games and simulations*. 2011: National Academies Press.
16. Horn, M., Z.A. Leong, F. Block, J. Diamond, E.M. Evans, B. Phillips, and C. Shen, Of BATs and APEs: an interactive tabletop game for natural history museums, in *Proceedings of the SIGCHI Conference on Human Factors in Computing Systems*.(2012), ACM: Austin, Texas, USA.2059-2068.
17. Karsenty, T. and A. Fievez, The iPad in education: uses, benefits, and challenges. (2013).
18. Lamers, M.H. and W.v. Eck, Why simulate? hybrid biological-digital games, in *Proceedings of the 2012t European conference on Applications of Evolutionary Computation*.(2012), Springer-Verlag: Málaga, Spain.214-223.
19. Lenhart, A., J. Kahne, E. Middaugh, A.R. Macgill, C. Evans, and J. Vitak, Teens, Video Games, and Civics: Teens' Gaming Experiences Are Diverse and Include Significant Social Interaction and Civic Engagement. *Pew Internet & American Life Project*, (2008).
20. Littleford, R.A., Culture of Protozoa in the Classroom. *The American Biology Teacher*, *22*, 9 (1960), 551-559.
21. Mertens, M. and T.O. Meißner, *Wir waren Space Invaders: Geschichten vom Computerspielen*. 2006: Katrin Blumenkamp.
22. Ozasa, K., J. Lee, S. Song, M. Hara, and M. Maeda, Two-dimensional optical feedback control of Euglena confined in closed-type microfluidic channels. *Lab on a Chip*, *11*, 11 (2011), 1933-1940.
23. Ozasa, K., J. Lee, S. Song, M. Hara, and M. Maeda, Euglena-based neurocomputing with two-dimensional optical feedback on swimming cells in micro-

aquariums. *Applied Soft Computing*, *13*, 1 (2013), 527-538.

24. Papert, S., *Mindstorms: children, computers, and powerful ideas*. 1980: Basic Books, Inc. 244.
25. Parkes, A. and C. Dickie, A biological imperative for interaction design, in *CHI '13 Extended Abstracts on Human Factors in Computing Systems*.(2013), ACM: Paris, France.2209-2218.
26. Pivec, M., Editorial: Play and learn: potentials of game-based learning. *British Journal of Educational Technology*, *38*, 3 (2007), 387-393.
27. Preece, J., Y. Rogers, H. Sharp, D. Benyon, S. Holland, and T. Carey, *Human-Computer Interaction*. 1994: Addison-Wesley Longman Ltd. 775.
28. Prensky, M., Computer games and learning: Digital game-based learning. *Handbook of computer game studies*, *18*, (2005), 97-122.
29. Ramey-Gassert, L., H.J. Walberg, and H.J. Walberg, Reexamining connections: Museums as science learning environments. *Science Education*, *78*, 4 (1994), 345-363.
30. Reas, C. and B. Fry, Processing: programming for the media arts. *AI & SOCIETY*, *20*, 4 (2006), 526-538.
31. Rein, M.L. and J.M. Deussing, The optogenetic (r) evolution. *Molecular Genetics and Genomics*, *287*, 2 (2012), 95-109.
32. Riedel-Kruse, I.H., A.M. Chung, B. Dura, A.L. Hamilton, and B.C. Lee, Design, engineering and utility of biotic games. *Lab on a Chip*, *11*, 1 (2011), 14-22.
33. Salen, K. and E. Zimmerman, *Rules of play: Game design fundamentals*. 2004: MIT press.
34. Schweingruber, H.A. and M. Fenichel, *Surrounded by Science:: Learning Science in Informal Environments*. 2010: National Academies Press.
35. Sellers, J., *Arcade fever: the fan's guide to the golden age of video games*. 2001: Running Press Book Publishers.
36. Stage, E.K., H. Asturias, T. Cheuk, P.A. Daro, and S.B. Hampton, Opportunities and Challenges in Next Generation Standards. *Science*, *340*, 6130 (2013), 276-277.
37. van Eck, W. and M.H. Lamers, Hybrid Biological-Digital Systems in Artistic and Entertainment Computing. *Leonardo*, *46*, 2 (2013), 151-158.
38. Wessnitzer, J., A. Asthenidis, G. Petrou, and B. Webb, A cricket-controlled robot orienting towards a sound source, in *Proceedings of the 12th Annual conference on Towards autonomous robotic systems*.(2011), Springer-Verlag: Sheffield, UK.1-12.
39. Whitesides, G.M., The origins and the future of microfluidics. *Nature*, *442*, 7101 (2006), 368-373.
40. Wolken, J.J., Euglena: The Photoreceptor System for Phototaxis*. *The Journal of Protozoology*, *24*, 4 (1977), 518-522.

TaraScope: Controlling Remote Telescopes Through Tangible Interaction

Trevor Hogan[1] Dylan Goveas[2] Rebecca Noonan[2] Luke Twomey[2]
Dept. of Media Communication, Crawford College of Art and Deign, Cork Institute of Technology, Bishopstown, Cork, Ireland.
(1) trevor.hogan@cit.ie (2) {dgoveas2, rebecca.noonan, luke.twomey}@mycit.ie,

ABSTRACT

In this paper we present TaraScope, a multimodal installation that enables student groups, participating in workshops at a Space Observatory in Ireland, to remotely manipulate and capture images from a robotic telescope situated in San Francisco, California. This project is developed as part of an international initiative between Blackrock Castle Observatory (BCO), Ireland and Chabot Space & Science Center, California, with the aim of connecting the two locations while also stimulating interest in astronomy, science, technology, engineering and math. We describe the design rationale and implementation of the installation, which is based on creating an inviting, apprehendable, inexpensive and engaging system that supports inquiry-led learning and group interactions. Furthermore, we present several initial observations on the user experience of the system that we gathered through a series of evaluations that we conducted at the Observatory.

Author Keywords

Tangible Interface, Museum, Installation, Astronomy.

ACM Classification Keywords

H.5.2 [Information Inter- faces and Presentation]: User Interfaces - Haptic I/O

INTRODUCTION

Gazing at celestial objects in the night sky has been a fascination for humans for many millennia. Regarded as one of the oldest sciences, there is evidence to show that the practice of Astronomy was embedded in many cultures, from the pre-historic Mesopotamian, Egyptian, Babylonian and Chinese civilizations, through the middle-ages and the Renaissance, right up until modern times when the invention and further refinement of the telescope enabled casual astronomers to peer beyond what is visible to the naked eye and back into time [1].

Although the availability of consumer refracting telescopes is relatively widespread today, and most of which are far more powerful than the earliest working models, which appeared in early seventeenth century Netherlands, there is an attraction, especially in children, attached to being able to look further and deeper into space at objects such as stars, galaxies, planets, and nebulae that are beyond the reach of these telescopes. In this paper we present TaraScope, a project situated in a public Observatory in Cork, Ireland, that can used by school children during workshops conducted to stimulate their interest in and learn about astronomy. TaraScope comprises of a tangible interface, digital displays and analogue output, which connects to and harnesses the power of a live robotic telescope located in California. In the following, we describe the background to this project, the design concept, development process and our initial observations gathered during a series of evaluations that were conducted to test the use of TaraScope.

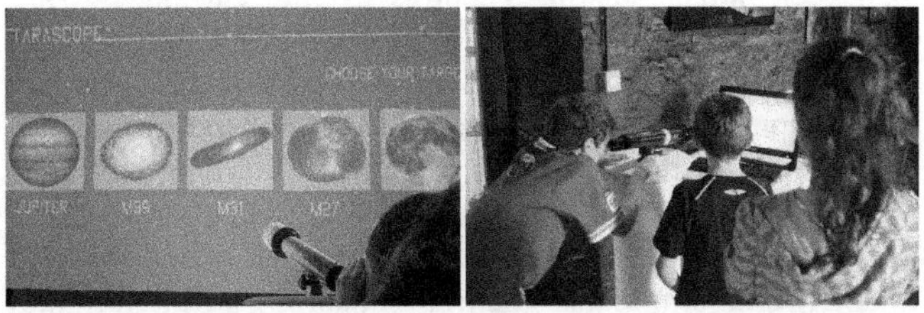

Figure 1. (Left) The telescope interface of TaraScope, (Right) TaraScope in use at Blackrock Castle Observatory during the evaluation study.

BACKGROUND AND RELATED WORK

The research described in this paper was conducted within the context of the Tara Project[1], which is an initiative that was set up following a workshop facilitated by Blackrock Castle Observatory (BCO), Ireland and Chabot Space & Science Center, California. This workshop taught students (11-16 year olds) how to explore the night sky and make astronomy images from data captured by a telescope located at Ormondale Elementary School (OES), California. The aims of the initiative were twofold, (1) to connect these remote locations by enabling visitors to BCO to control and take images in real time using the telescope located in OES; and (2) to stimulate interest in science, technology, engineering and math (STEM) and learn about astronomy.

[1] For more details about the Tara Project see http://www.projecttara.com/

TEI '15, January 16 – 19, 2015, Stanford, CA, USA.
Copyright 2015 ACM 978-1-4503-3305-4/15/01…$15.00.
http://dx.doi.org/10.1145/2677199.2680562

Organized school trips to cultural, heritage and science museums (including space observatories and planetariums) are a common occurrence for many schools. However, only recently have these institutes received proper recognition for their role in formal education [2]. Research has suggested that these environments facilitate an exposure to the subject matter in a way that is difficult to achieve in a classroom environment, and it allows the student to integrate their experience and knowledge gained in the museum into the curriculum delivered in school [8]. It has also been noted that these centres extend learning beyond cognition toward aspects such as attitudinal change, affective responses and social understanding [11]. Unlike the learning environment facilitated within the classroom, where the priority is placed upon formal learning based on an agreed standard curriculum, museums today are challenged with attracting and engaging children in a manner that stimulates them to absorb information and learn in new and unique ways [4]. An approach that has been utilized by many museums to achieve this goal is the integration of digital technology and offering novel forms of interaction to access information in the museum space. It is a commonly accepted belief that interactivity is a key factor to provide children with an environment where they can enjoy learning. In their mission to engage, inspire, and open minds, science museums have been at the forefront of innovative interaction design for children [5].

In our review of existing cases that use digital technology to enhance the visitor experience and facilitate learning within cultural, heritage and science museums we observed three main categories. We should note that this was not an exhaustive review, instead we present it here to help contextualize our work in the broad field of research aimed at enhancing science museums through digital technology and novel interfaces. The first category that we classified includes projects that use mobile technology or personal handsets to access and deliver information to the visitor. These applications aim to enhance the learning process by providing a dynamic and personal experience for each visitor or groups of visitors to the museum. One such example [9], utilizes both mobile and wearable technology to enhance the students' and teacher's experience when visiting a science museum. Students activities, before and after the visit are supported and the system enables them to visualize invisible phenomena during the visit.

The second category includes applications that augment the physical space with virtual objects, mainly to transpose the visitor to the time and place where the artifacts was found or alternatively to let the visitor engage with objects that may not exist anymore or may be too fragile to hold. In the context of a science museum [10] created an augmented reality system with a laser projection device as a hands-on that provides virtual information, which learners can control for a visual explanation about an exhibited item.

The third category, in which we situate our research, includes exhibitions that allow the visitor to physically interact with objects to reveal information and to enrich the interaction between the visitor and the exhibits. In their evaluation of a digitally-augmented exhibition, Hornecker & Stifter [6] show evidence of the usefulness and appropriateness of this type of interface within the context of museum. They also state that haptic input devices with computational augmentation are effective in arousing interest in unfamiliar topics and attracting children and are the most popular installations in terms of overall usage during runtime. An example of such a mode of interaction is [5]. Situated in Boston Museum of Science, this system introduces children to the basic logic of computer programming through a tangible interface consisting of wooden blocks shaped like jigsaw puzzle pieces that represent actions for the robot to perform.

DESIGN CONCEPT

The basic functionality of the system described here allows students to remotely connect to a robotic telescope, located in California, from a workstation in BCO, Ireland. Once connected, students can send a request to the telescope to point at a particular spot in the sky. Once the telescope has reached this heading, it captures an image and sends it back to BCO for the students to view. This system infrastructure, which was initially controlled and viewed through one desktop computer and LCD display, was in place prior to our team joining the project. Upon joining the project we were challenged with enhancing the interaction and facilitating an intuitive, engaging and playful learning experience. Our team, which comprises of an interaction designer, user-experience designer and a user-interface designer, commenced the design process by analyzing the present setup and discussing its use with students who had already operated it. Based on this analysis, the team completely redesigned the front-end while also adding extra functionality into the system.

When formulating the design criteria for the new setup we decided to follow those developed by Horn et al. as described in [5]. Here they suggest that to increase the potential for a Tangible User Interface to be successful for children in a museum setting the design artifact should be *inviting*, *apprehendable* and *engaging*. It should *support group interactions* while being *inexpensive and reliable.* Alongside these considerations we also envisaged that the system should support inquiry-led learning, where the students inquire about a set of phenomena through investigatory activity and draw conclusions based of these activities [7]. Alongside these criteria, a key conceptual theme that influenced the design of the interface was multi-modality. We sought to facilitate learning by supporting different sensory modalities that could engage multiple senses - tactile, auditory, and visual - by means of tangible inputs, audiovisual content and tactile output.

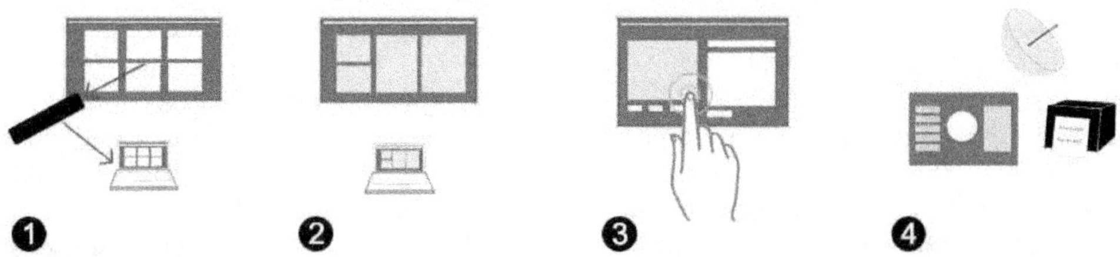

Figure 2. The system design of TaraScope: (1) The user selects a celestial object by pointing the telescope at an image onscreen and pressing a button. (2) While the system is retrieving the image from the Californian telescope (typical duration 4 minutes) the users are presented with audio/visual information. (3) The image captured by the telescope is presented on a touch-screen, the users can now edit this image by drawing over it. They can also compile a message to be sent into Space. (4) Users can view past images created by other people, they can also choose to send their message to Space and they receive a printed receipt that includes this message.

TaraScope

Taking into consideration the design criteria discussed above, a multi-station installation was created that would facilitate group interaction and would involve multimodal input and outputs. The space was divided into two main sections. Firstly, students are directed to an area where they can choose which celestial object they would like the remote telescope to capture an image of. The old system required the students to input a numerical heading, which we observed to be difficult to understand and control. This also meant that the student could aim the telescope at any point in the sky, which regularly resulted in images of empty space. During a series of design exercises we explored various ways of selecting points in the sky by using physical objects, these included: mobile handsets, slingshots, bow and arrows and an assortment of wooden implements. We finally decided to use a small consumer telescope that we augmented with a laser pointer and an inertial measurement unit (IMU). The rationale for choosing this as the input devise was to mimic, as close as possible, the actual interaction that would occur if the remote telescope were situated on-site. However, instead of allowing the students to choose any point in the sky, we offered a selection of six predefined objects that could be selected by pointing the telescope at a projected image in the exhibition space (see Fig. 1.(left)). Once they have selected an object, a display within the space presents the students with audiovisual information about their chosen object. The rationale for including this presentation was not only to facilitate learning about their selected celestial object; we also wanted to keep the students engaged while the remote robotic telescope adjusts its heading, captures the image and transmits this image back to BCO. This process usually took between 3 and 4 minutes to complete.

When this is complete the students are directed to move to another workstation where they can view the image. This image is displayed on a touch screen device where the students are allowed to draw over the image and tag it with their names and a short text message. When they submit their edits, they can choose to send their message to space. A 1-meter radio telescope, located in BCO, which is fitted with a 4.7MHz transponder, adjusts to the heading that they have previously selected and transmits this message back towards the object that they have just viewed. This content is also archived on a public website. The final part of the installation includes a thermal printer, which outputs the student's name, their message and the URL of their submission. We incorporated this to provide the students with a memento of their time as well as encouraging them to log on to the website to view their message alongside submissions completed by other student groups.

USER EVALUATION

Throughout the design and development of TaraScope we employed various methods to evaluate the use and functionality of the system. In the early stages, the tests were typically conducted within the lab, testing each of the interfaces and workspaces separately and we mostly focused on addressing issues related to the usability of the system. Once we were satisfied that of the separate elements of the system were working and communicating to one another we decided to deploy TaraScope in Blackrock Castle Observatory to evaluate the system in use by groups of students and members of the public. The objective for carrying out this series of evaluations was to explore whether or not the system met the criteria that was set out during the design phase.

Procedure

TaraScope was deployed in BCO over the course of two weekends. During this period we carried out two evaluation sessions, firstly a group evaluation, which was followed by a public evaluation. The first session involved three groups of five children, fifteen in total (11-16 years old), who were invited to use the system. Following a short introduction by a researcher - where the group were shown how to use the system – each group were allowed to use the system for as long as they wanted to (average: 24-minutes). A researcher facilitated each of these sessions, but they only engaged with the participants if they needed assistance or questions answered. The main role of the researcher was to observe the children's interaction with the system as well as observing the dynamics within the group while they were using TaraScope, for example turn taking. After they had used the system we carried out a brief informal interview with the group. These sessions were also recorded using video and audio equipment for future analysis. The following weekend we conducted a study that was open to public visitors to the observatory. During this period, approximately one hundred visitors used the system, their ages ranged from 5 to 70 years old. A researcher was in place at all times to assist the participants and interactions were captured using a video camera and digital audio recorders. Although the analysis of both studies is not fully complete, below we collate and present some initial observations from both studies.

Observations

During the group evaluation we focused our inquiry on whether TaraScope *supported group interaction* and whether or not it was *apprehendable* to the participants, while the purpose of the open session was to focus on whether the installation was *inviting* and *engaging*. During the group session we observed all members of the group actively engaging with the system throughout the process, while at times different members would take charge. We noticed that a different member would lead the team at the various stations and that this would change when the group moved to the next part of the installation. We found that the majority of participants demonstrated a clear understanding as to what they have completed and were able to articulate the complexity of the operation with the aid of the receipt that they had printed out. The responses we gathered during the public evaluation were very positive. While in use at BCO TaraScope was the most popular installation that was open to the public, we also observed numerous visitors returning to use the system again once they had visited the other installations in the Observatory. The part of the installation that proved to be most popular was the interaction with the telescope, children spent most of the time looking through the view-finder to select an object for the telescope to capture. One participant remarked: *"I really like the way you have to use the telescope to pick, because it's like you're actually using a real one to look into space, but this one looks into space in America"*. We also observed that some continued to look through the telescope to view the audio-visual presentation. Equally popular was the tool to send a message to space, referring to this one child enthusiastically said: *"I'm so excited, I'm actually sending a message to space!"* Although the general consensus was that this aspect was exciting, some questioned how they would know if it was received by someone or even whether the message would be sent at all.

CONCLUSION

In this paper we presented TaraScope, a multimodal installation based in Cork, Ireland that captures real-time images from Space using a remote telescope situated in San Francisco, California. The installation allows visitors to the observatory to control what the remote telescope captures through a tangible interface, while also displaying information about the captured objects and providing them with a token to remember the experience. Over the course of two weekends we observed and interviewed groups of children and members of the public while they engaged with the system. Our initial observations indicate that the installation meets the criteria laid out in the early stages of the design process: inviting, apprehendable, engaging and supportive of group interactions. Following completion of the analysis of these studies, our future work will focus on extending the tangible interface to include a natural form of interaction for sending messages to Space, early prototypes include a slingshot, a message in a bottle and throwing an object into the air. We are also investigating more engaging ways to present information to the users as they wait for the images to be returned from the telescope. We envisage that these amendments will enhance the overall experience of TaraScope.

REFERENCES

1. Berry, Arthur (1961). A Short History of Astronomy From Earliest Times Through the Nineteenth Century. New York: Dover Publications, Inc.
2. Black, G. (2005). The Engaging Museum. London, Routledge. Cabrera.
3. Dindler, C., et al. Participatory Design at the Museum - inquiring into children's everyday engagement in cultural heritage. In Proc. of OZCHI '10 (2010), 72–79.
4. Hooper-Greenhill, E. Communication and communities in the post-museum: from metanarratives to constructed knowledge. In the Nordic Museums Leadership Programme. University of Leicester, 2001.
5. Horn, M.S., et al. Tangible Programming and Informal Science Learning : Making TUIs Work for Museums. In Proc. IDC'08 (2008), 194–201.
6. Hornecker, E. and Stifter, M. Learning from interactive museum installations about interaction design for public settings. In Proc. of OZCHI '06, (2006), 135-142
7. Kuhn, D., et al.. (2000). The Development of Cognitive Skills To Support Inquiry Learning. Cognition and Instruction 18(4), p. 495-523.
8. Rennie, L.J. & McClafferty, T.P. (1996). Science Centres and Science Learning. Studies in Science Education 27, p. 53-98.
9. Sotiriou, S., Anastopoulou, S., Rosenfeld, S., and Milrad, M. Using advanced technologies to connect schools to science museums. In Proc. of WMTE'06, (2006), 169–170.
10. Takahashi, T.B., et al. Making a Hands-On Display with Augmented Reality Work at a Science Museum. In Proc. of SITIS'14, (2013), 385–390.
11. Vavoula, G., et al. Myartspace: Design and evaluation of support for learning with multimedia phones between classrooms and museums. Computers & Education 53, 2 (2009), 286–299.

Universal Threshold Object: Designing Haptic Interaction for Televised Interactive Narratives

Jean Ho Chu[1], Paul Clifton[1], Hank Blumenthal[2], Abhishek Nandakumar [2], Balasubramanium Ganapathi[2], Janet Murray[2], Ali Mazalek[1]
Synaesthetic Media Lab[1] & eTV Lab[2]
Georgia Institute of Technology
Atlanta, GA, USA
jeanhochu@gmail.com, paulgclifton@gmail.com, hankblumenthal@gmail.com, abhishekn@gatech.edu, balasubramanyam@gatech.edu, jmurray@gatech.edu, mazalek@gatech.edu

ABSTRACT
The 'Universal Threshold Object' is a tangible device for television-like interactive narratives based on the TV show *American Horror Story*. The project uses gestural interactions with a tangible controller that provides haptic feedback as an interaction strategy to augment the narrative pleasures of immersion and dramatic agency. We leverage a branching scenario and story-driven gestural interaction with haptic feedback to provide limited sets of interactivity suitable for a television platform. From our research, design goals, and design process, we provide design implications for interactive narratives that employ gestural and haptic interactions.

Author Keywords
Tangible interface, haptic feedback; gestural interaction; interactive television; expressive interaction; threshold object.

ACM Classification Keywords
H.5.2. [Information Interfaces and Presentation]: User Interfaces---*Haptic I/O, Input Devices and Strategies*; K.8.0. [Personal Computing]: General---*Games*.

General Terms
Design; human factors.

INTRODUCTION
Emerging interactive TV platforms offer enhanced interactivity and new possibilities for providing engaging experiences. Looking beyond conventional remote controllers used for channel navigation, more experiential and intuitive interactions are in demand as television converges with more interactive media forms such as websites and games. However, current television program formats remain unisequential, limiting interaction to synchronized second screen polls and informational enhancements. Our research focuses on designing tangible and embodied interactions for next-generation television, which we are assuming will retain its episodic form while allowing for more integrated story-driven interactivity [11].

TEI '15, January 15 - 19 2015, Stanford, CA, USA
Copyright 2015 ACM 978-1-4503-3305-4/15/01...$15.00
http://dx.doi.org/10.1145/2677199.2680563

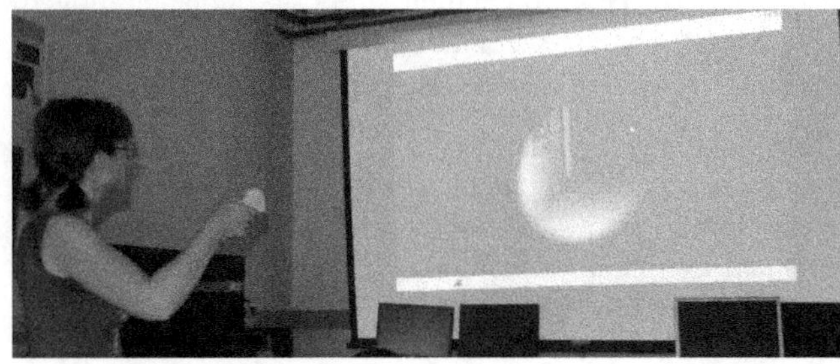

Figure 1: Interaction with the Universal Threshold Object.

The Universal Threshold Object (UTO) is a haptic handheld controller for participatory viewing of an interactive television narrative (see Figure 1). We demonstrate its potential with the TV show *American Horror Story*. The project is based on our previous work, *Don't Open That Door,* which examined in-air gestural interaction with interactive TV narratives [2]. The results of *Don't Open That Door* indicated that using a tangible device might enhance interactivity by providing nuanced information on when to interact, how to interact, and the result of interaction. In order to maximize the narrative pleasure coupled with haptic interaction, our goals were to realize key narrative decisions through physical interaction, to use haptic feedback as a storytelling technique, to prolong emotional decisions, and to reinforce physical presence of the narrative through a tangible interface.

To inform the narrative design, we researched elements of interactive narratives and haptic interactions. Based on our research, prototype design, and user testing, we formulate design considerations for tangible/haptic interfaces for televised interactive narratives: designing interactive narratives for television, providing goals and guidelines for interaction, designing interface and interactions, and designing haptic feedback.

RELATED WORK
The design and implementation of the UTO builds on: (1) interactive narratives particularly within the context of interactive television, (2) tangible and embodied

interactions for narrative progression, and (3) haptic interfaces that augment the narrative experience.

Interactive Television and Interactive Narrative

Storytelling in television is changing as traditional formats converge with new digital media technologies, leading to increasing experimentation with interactivity [7, 10]. Most industry innovation has focused around social media and "transmedia" applications, but a few examples exist of interactive television narratives that allow viewers to interact with stories while they are being told. Storymap is a second screen application that provides tightly synchronized, context sensitive, and character-focused information to enhance comprehension of the series *Justified* [12]. This application supports understanding of the complex character relationships and past episodes for first-time viewers of a late season episode.

There have been explorations on employing interactor's interaction and engagement to lead the narrative progression. The *Gormenghast Explore* prototype, produced by the BBC, enabled viewers to create their own sequences of clips from the popular miniseries, navigating from a 3D model of the Octagonal Gallery in Gormenghast castle. Viewers were able to choose among characters and spaces to develop a unique perspective from which they could comprehend the mystery of the castle [15]. Other examples of interactive television include a prototype for *Battlestar Galactica* episodes created by the AFI Digital Content Lab (2003) that allowed viewers to toggle between watching the television show and being a space pilot defending the ship [9].

While the idea of interactive television seems promising for enhancing viewer engagement, it is challenging to implement due to its complexity for production and requirements for appropriate technical support. If programs progress in a branching narrative, the plot being determined by viewer's interaction in open ended choices, it has to be edited in real time, at the time of viewing [17]. Since software and the interaction replace post-production, the complexity of each program and narrative system has to be planned ahead. The composition, rendering, and delivery requires the viewer's set-top box or computer to have software with processing power to handle the interaction.

With the UTO project, in order to provide interactivity within the constraints of the television broadcasting system, we provide interactions from a first person point of view from the main character of the narrative. The viewer occupies the role of a known character, allowing them to make decisions that affect the lives of characters critical to the show's narrative and motivating them to interact with the narrated environment.

Tangible Interactions with Narrative

Watching television has been perceived as a lean-back (passive) activity, but the rise of interactive television has brought lean-forward (active) viewing experiences, in which viewers assume more involved and social roles. Lean-forward is a term usually used to denote social or second screen interaction and we would like to put forth the term "lean-into" to describe an interaction in a liminal space that is at the diegetic level [6] and part of the unfolding story. The goal is a first person immersion in the dramatic story arc. This viewing experience has potential advantages in that a first person embodied experience may be more immersive, therefore more compelling and pleasurable, and also provide novel storytelling affordances to explore creatively. However, the way this interaction is implemented has been recognized as a potential distraction that prevents viewers from focusing on the linear content. Researchers find that the user interface and interactions need to be designed for fewer interruptions and accommodate a lean-back experience. Vatavu and Zaiti propose using leap gestures for interactions with television [18]. They find that gesture types using hands are more appropriate in the context of lean-back versus lean-forward interaction paradigms with television than are large body movements. Experiments have also been done on using one's palm as a remote control since it eliminates the need to look away from the screen to perform interactions [5].

However, the interactions implemented in the above-described research employ binary or numeric interactions leaving the interactor's performance distinct from the story world. Tangible interface techniques provide gestural or object-based interaction to invite the interactor to be part of the narrative. The Reading Glove [16] uses a glove interface with which interactors pick up different physical objects and hear pieces of stories. As they pick up the objects, they gradually see more information about the story. The physical objects allow the story to progress in diverse ways and also connect the story world with the interactor's physical space. Tangible Comics [14] uses full-body gestural interaction to create a narrative performance and storytelling environment. The gestures the interactor makes and their effects are clearly visualized on-screen through iconic animations. The interactor can also use everyday tangible objects to aid the story's progress. Some researchers have also explored touch and haptic interaction for increasing immersion and involvement, and argue that there are possibilities for employing haptic interaction in home entertainment to enhance engagement with broadcast content [2, 13].

Our UTO project draws on tangible narrative research to design interactions that conform to the narrative, yet strives to tightly couple the input with haptic feedback through the tangible control device to enhance immersion. We provide a single handheld device with haptic interaction, which aims to enhance immersion without distracting from the viewing of the content.

Haptic Interfaces

Haptic feedback as an output method provides feedback for the interaction with the virtual object by applying force or tactile stimulation to the interactor. Haptic feedback has been widely used in movies and games to augment the narrative experience. Danieau et al. finds ways to record video and physical motion to provide haptic effects of motion during movie viewing [4]. The physical motion of activity is translated into force feedback through a Novint Falcon device. A pen, which the interactor can hold, is connected to the torque that gives force feedback. Lemmens et al. made a tactile jacket to make movie viewing more emotionally immersive [8]. Vibrotactile actuators are distributed over the jacket to create patterns that simulate emotional bodily reactions such as goose bumps or shivers down the spine. Alam et al. integrated a haptic jacket, sofa, and wristband with an e-book to provide reading experience with haptic feedback [1]. The system supports three basic emotions: love, joy, and fear. It also incorporates real life scenarios such as bike riding, driving, flying on an airplane, holding hands, and hugging. O'Modhrain and Oakley propose methods to provide rich interaction with broadcast content in the Touch TV project [13]. The system consists of a haptic remote control with a two degrees of freedom actuator, and a couch-shaker for displaying the haptic channel. The work suggests two possible interactive scenarios representing physical actions through haptic interaction. One scenario is authored and reactive haptic interaction with children's cartoons, and the other is real time haptic content of live sports broadcasting.

UTO employs tangible/gestural input together with haptic output to provide emotional or physical feedback for a given scene. The UTO project further explores haptic interaction as a way to affect the narrated plot and enhance emotional engagement with the story world.

BACKGROUND AND DESIGN GOALS

Our research focuses on designing tangible and embodied interactions for a televised interactive narrative. While the technology for interactive television enables viewers to explore diverse narratives, existing televised narrative content is most often structured in an episodic format, where individual episodes have a self-contained plot that provides narrative closure. In order to fit within existing television industry structures, a "lean-into" interactive televised experience should thus adhere to the episodic format of existing shows. Also, to lower the barrier of viewing, it is necessary for those who don't know how or don't want to interact to still be able to view the interactive televised narrative as if it were an ordinary TV show. To meet these requirements, we formulated the following design requirements: (1) The narrative should be segmented and diversified within a self-contained and coherent plot; (2) The story should be able to continue even after failure of the interaction; (3) The interactor should be scripted with expectations to know when and how to interact; (4) The physical actions should be simple, allowing lean-into interaction.

In our previous project *Don't Open That Door* [2], we created a Kinect-based gestural interaction for an interactive narrative based on the horror-drama television series *Supernatural*. We scripted the interactor with verbal and visual cues so that the interactor would know when and how to interact. Despite these visual and verbal cues, we found that interactors were often confused about when to and how to interact, and were unsure of whether or not their interaction was successful. Based on these observations, we hypothesized that tangible controllers coupled with gestural interaction could solve some of these problems by closing the loop between the interactor and the narrative scenario, providing more refined and immediate feedback.

In designing the physical interface for the interactive narrative, we were inspired by Murray's description of a "threshold object" [10]. She argues that an object in the real world, like a game controller or a teacup, can take the interactor across the boundary to the virtual world, and increase immersion by reinforcing belief in the virtual world. Murray further explains dramatic agency as a state with maximized story power, which can be created when the interactor's actions are integrated with the story content. The design of the tangible controller should thus be grounded in the narrative and provide interactions and feedback that are tightly coupled with the narrative.

Based on the insights from our previous project and our research, we designed the narrative, interface, and interactions to meet the following design goals.

- Realize key narrative decisions through physical interaction that results in dramatic agency.
- Tightly couple haptic feedback as a storytelling technique and define a haptic/visual integrated grammar.
- Allow prolonged emotional decision-making in a first person experience.
- Reinforce the physical presence of the narrative through a threshold object and the entering of a liminal space that is part of the diegetic story.

THE UNIVERSAL THRESHOLD OBJECT (UTO)

The UTO is a tangible device for interacting with televised interactive narratives. As an interface, the UTO acts as a changing threshold object, its liminal presence assuming the affordances of key objects in the narrative to reinforce the physical presence of the storyworld in the interactor's embodied space. Narrative decisions are thus realized through physical interaction, which is designed to sharpen dramatic agency by the interactor. The interface provides emotional and physical haptic feedback as a storytelling technique coupled with visual and narrative cues. The haptic interaction also augments immersion by prolonging emotional decisions that the interactor performs.

We chose the 2012 Emmy award-winning series *American Horror Story* as our source for a narrative environment because of its well-established genre elements and its popularity. The horror genre provided us with story patterns that are immediately familiar to members of our target audience and that provide dramatic points of inflection to address with maximum dramatic agency. The horror genre also benefits from haptic experience due to creation of suspense through visual tropes like haunted and dark spaces that have a direct correlation to embodied senses.

The events in the series are tied to dramatic family relationships and conflicts such as a cheating husband whose young lover haunts the married couple. We reconfigured the story elements and situated the interactor in the point of view of the betrayed wife inside of the romantic triangle. Our narrative scenario repurposes the ending of the last episode where the husband is hanged and then reunited with his wife in the afterlife.

The Synlab and eTV lab at Georgia Tech co-designed the device, narrative, and interactions in a collaborative and iterative process. The eTV lab focused on the narrative scenario and visual/embodied grammar, programmed the interactions with the narrative, and shot/edited the interactive video. The Synlab designed the tangible interface and physical interactions. Storyboards, flowcharts, wireframes, foam models, and prototypes were used to share and communicate ideas during the collaborative work process.

Walkthrough

The flow of the scenario/experience is shown in Figure 2. The interactor assumes the role of Vivien, one of the main characters of the show. The video begins with an exposition in the form of Vivien's dream that reveals her continuing to feel disturbed, as she is unable to forgive her husband Ben for cheating on her with his student Hayden. The interactor sees a flashlight being grabbed from a table, and the UTO device vibrates. Then the interactor sees a flash of Ben being hanged and a shot of hands grabbing a rope. There is a close-up of the flashlight on the table and the device vibrates again. The close-up shot of an object combined with vibration of the UTO device is used as an aesthetic grammar to indicate what the threshold device will become.

The video then shows Vivien waking up from her sleep. As she is getting up, Vivien is startled by a glimpse of a ghostly figure. She grabs the flashlight next to her table, and the device vibrates in the user's hand as a confirmation that it is active. The video shows the flashlight in Vivien's hand from a point of view shot to indicate that the interactor is now in control. As Vivien opens her bedroom door the shot fades into a hallway seen from a first-person point of view. Vivien walks down the hallway to find out what is happening.

The hallway sequence starts with the flashlight pointing forward and this creates the onscreen sensation of walking forward (see Figure 3, left). As the interactor points toward each door in the hallway, "she," the interactor, sees different objects through the doors such as jars containing scary objects, a man hanging in a rubber suit, gothic paintings, and bloody graffiti. The UTO vibrates with a heartbeat-like pulse to emulate Vivien's heartbeat and connect the interactor to the space. Pointing the flashlight forward, Vivien arrives at a door at the end of the hallway, and Ben's screaming can be heard.

Onscreen the interactor's point of view is through the door's keyhole as Vivien sees a faint image of Ben being hanged just like in the dream sequence. A close-up of the rope and a hand is shown to indicate the threshold device is becoming the rope (see Figure 3, right). The device starts vibrating continuously to make the interactor quickly realize that it is Vivien who has grabbed the rope. The constant vibration of the device is an indication that she feels the pressure of the rope holding Ben at the other end. Shots of Ben struggling are alternated with shots of hands on the rope. Depending on how the interactor applies or releases pressure on the device, the rope grows tauter (keeping him hanging), gradually looser (slowly lowering him to the ground), or very loose (slipping through the fingers and dropping him quickly to the ground). The scene

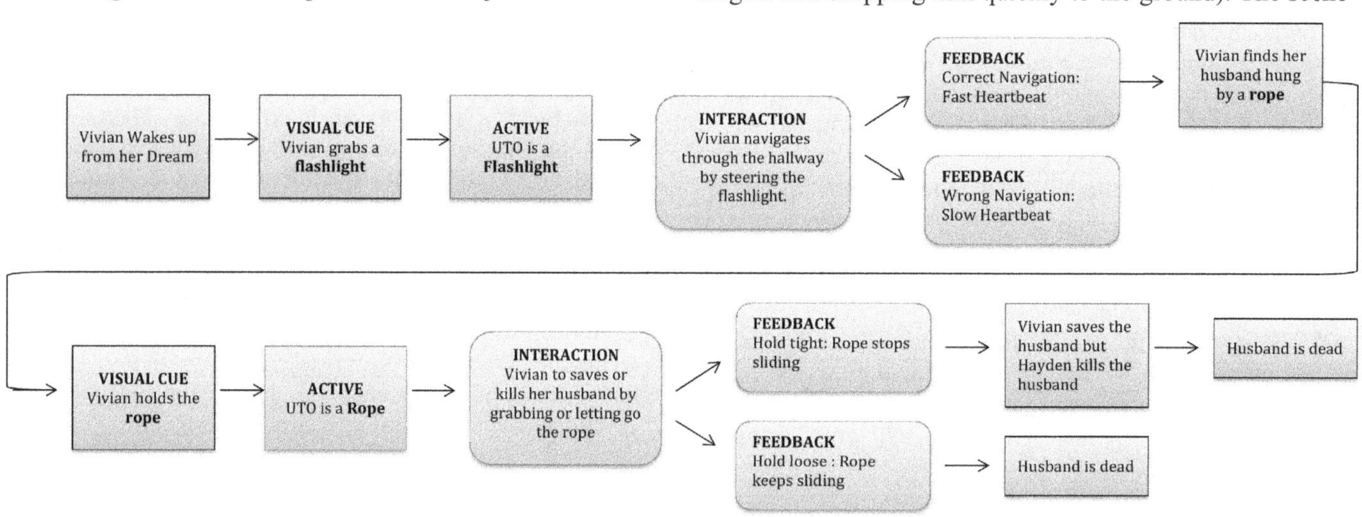

Figure 2: Scenario flow chart

is edited dynamically in response to the interactor's pressure. Haptic responses are paired with visual confirmations in the form of shot sequences that are edited on the fly based on an algorithm responding to the interactor's physical interaction as Ben drops quickly or slowly to the ground. This threshold event places the interactor into the climax of the story with the ability to exert maximum dramatic agency. It is also meant to dramatize Vivien's ambivalence toward Ben, whom she may or may not want to save. The choice is not meant to be logical but rather embodied and immediate as the interactor's actions are given a haptic and visual response.

If Ben hangs to death, we see a shot of his student Hayden, who died previously on the show, feeling satisfied that he too is dead like her. If Ben falls to the ground, we see him die immediately while seeing Vivien feeling shattered. If Ben is brought down slowly and is able to survive, we see Vivien forgiving him. But Hayden then appears suddenly and stabs him to death. Therefore, the end result of the interaction maintains dramatic agency, while making sure that Ben ends up dying in any case, as in the series finale.

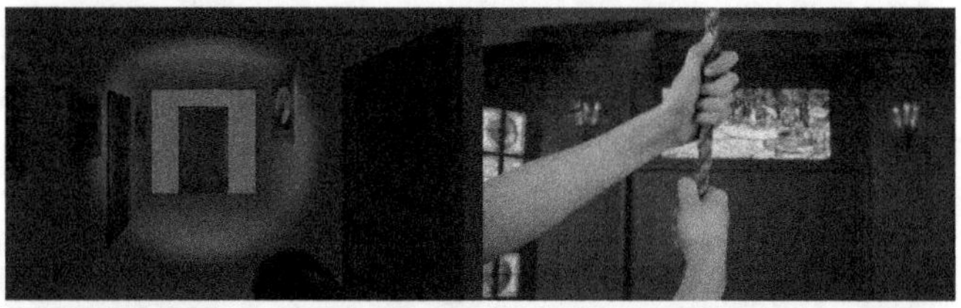

Figure 3: Video of the scenes when the interactor is using UTO as a flashlight (left) and a rope (right)

System Design

To fulfill our design goals, we set the following system and story requirements: (1) the interactor should be informed about when/how to interact so that s/he can form reasonable expectations, (2) the UTO should be a single handheld multifunctional device to avoid distraction, (3) objects should be situated to play key roles in the narrative, and (4) the story should progress in a first-person point of view.

To script the interactor with narrative expectations, we structured the initial scene as a passive introduction to the story and interactions. The sequence indicates the upcoming events and interactive grammar that will unfold, complete with haptic confirmations in concert with various shots. Scenes such as flashback, dream, and glimpse are used to provide expositions with visual and narrative cues about what will happen and how to interact without disrupting the narrative. In Vivien's dream, the flashback of her husband's betrayal provides background narrative information and sharpens the dramatic stakes. The dream scene of Vivien's husband being hanged prepares the interactor for the key event that will happen during the show.

When the scene is passive, the story progresses as it would normally in a TV show. When the scene is active, we use visual and haptic cues to signal the interactor, such as a sequence of shots with a close up of a threshold object, first person point of view shots of the character grasping the object, and synchronous vibration of the UTO device (see Figure 4). The scene changes into a first-person point of view in the active scenes. When the UTO is ready to be used, it is set to vibrate while the flashlight or the rope appears in the video.

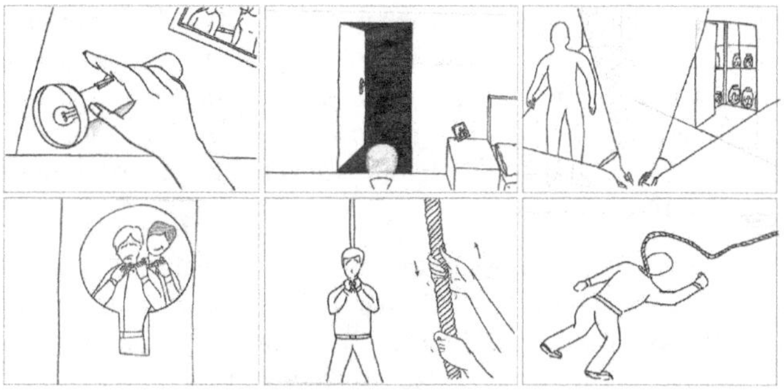

Figure 4: Storyboard for the interactive video

We designed the UTO as a single handheld device with multiple functionalities to prevent interactor distraction (e.g., having to select between different objects to interact with) and to make the haptic interaction useful as a storytelling technique. The form of the device is neutral and generic so that the interactor can mentally connect it to many different objects while holding it. The cylindrical shape of the UTO allows it to be held comfortably with one hand. It can be used as a variety of different objects, e.g. for aiming, grabbing, or pulling, as with the flashlight or rope in our scenario. To provide physical and emotional feedback for the interaction, the UTO vibrates in five different patterns, two for the pulsing heartbeat while holding the flashlight and three for the friction and resistance of holding the rope. The interactor's gestural actions such as steering or grabbing serve as input to change the content of the video and the UTO device provides the corresponding haptic feedback. This closes the loop between the interactor and the narrative and helps the interactor focus on the story without getting distracted by searching for devices or feedback/response in the video.

We progress the story in the first-person point of view of the betrayed character to enhance dramatic agency. The haptic experience provides emotional cues of fear, spookiness, suspense and revulsion. As the interactor continues walking through the hallway, her emotion rises with anxiety, urgency, and suspense and the device vibrates like a beating heart in a pattern that is meant to represent both the pulse rate of the character and the character's nervousness while walking forward in the dark. The haptic experience of the heartbeat helps the interactor empathize and identify with Vivien.

We create dramatic agency by having the interactor realize a key narrative and emotional decision through the physical interaction of squeezing or releasing the UTO as a rope. The amount of force applied by the interactor on the device corresponds to how hard the character holds onto the rope in the narrative. The device vibrates differently depending on the amount of pressure applied, replicating the feeling of a rope sliding through the hand through a coded interaction of pulses to denote different actions.

To provide a prolonged emotional decision, the interactor is required to hold the rope for a certain amount of time, 5 seconds, which consist of dynamically edited shots coupled with haptic feedback in order to proceed. While having to wait and continue, the prolonged emotional decision becomes augmented to a maximal degree. The vibration also stays on during this time to support the prolonged emotional decision.

To keep the interactive plot self-contained and consistent with the series, Vivien's husband must die even if Vivian decides to save him, which is then done by Hayden. This additional irony is also meant to add to the immersive emotions of the haptic experience.

System Implementation

To create the video, we cut footage from various episodes of the first season of *American Horror Story* to provide a bank of shots from which to create clips for our invented events. When we could not match our storyboard with existing shots, we shot additional footage, with and without green screens. The green screen footage allowed us to insert visual elements from the sets of the actual series, creating continuity with the diegetic world. Videos are segmented and can be played in an HTML5 web browser.

To accurately represent the interaction of navigating through a hallway with high-fidelity representation, we used the Unity3D engine. We tasked the Unity application with interpreting the gestures and allowed it to call the correct JavaScript functions in the web browser using the Unity WebPlayer along with the HTML5 video. The hallway space was built as a 3D environment to work with the Unity player and create a space with additional interactive affordances such as looking in doors and peeking around corners.

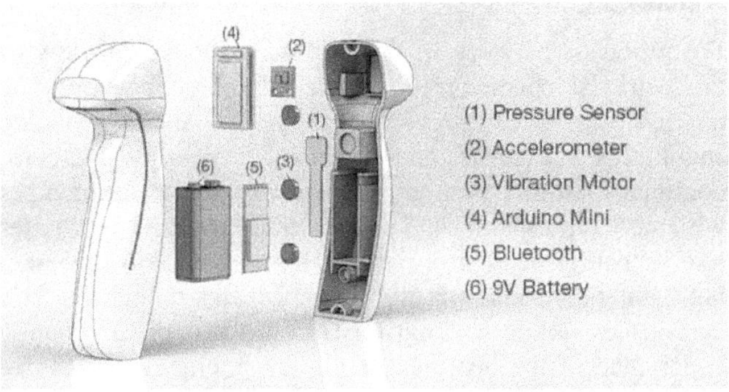

Figure 5: UTO device diagram

The physical interface of the UTO was modeled in Solidworks and fabricated with a 3D printer (see Figure 5). The interface contains a microprocessor, Bluetooth module, battery, vibration motors, as well as a pressure sensor and a gyroscope. The gyroscope is used for the flashlight to be steered and the pressure sensor is used as the rope is grabbed. The controller has three vibration motors placed in a row to create different patterns of haptic experience. The Bluetooth module sends binary signals that are parsed by the server application.

We used Arduino to program diverse vibration patterns. In order to create patterns, we emulate the tactile feedback of a heartbeat and the sensation of holding a rope with a heavy load at the end. By turning on and off the three vibration motors or running them at different speeds, we create rhythmic patterns (see Figure 6). To imitate the pulsing pattern of the heartbeat, three motors are turned on shortly and turned off, alternating in high speed and low speed. To give the feeling of a rope sliding through the hands, we turned on and off each of the motors in a sequence. To depict the horrible moment when the rope is taut and loaded with the weight of the husband who is struggling to live, we run the motors at high speed in a distinct pattern.

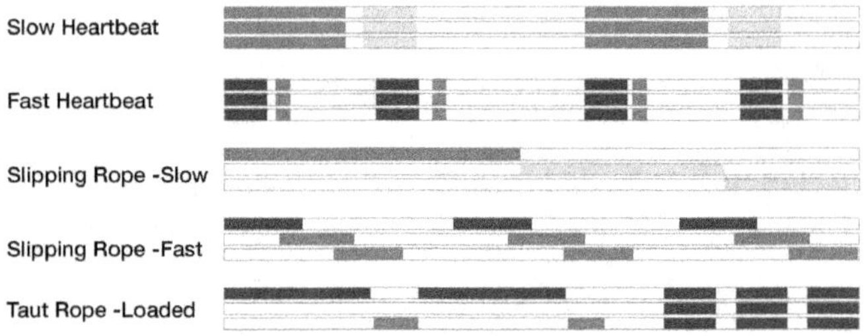

Figure 6: Haptic vibration patterns (the darkness of the color bar indicates the speed of the vibration motor)

The setup requires a computer paired with the UTO interface via Bluetooth and a screen the interactor can view. The computer application consists of three parts: the HTML5 application, the Unity Web Player application and the Server application. The server application sends the serial data it receives from the device to the Unity application, which in turn translates the binary data and calls the correct JavaScript function in the HTML5 application to seek to the correct position in the video.

FEEDBACK AND DISCUSSION

We first showcased the project in December of 2012. We had thirty participants for our pilot user test where they provided us with feedback about their experience using the UTO device. Some of the participants also answered a short exit questionnaire after they interacted with the system. After getting feedback about the first version, we made revisions and released a second version. We report our findings based on feedback about both versions.

The narrative was understood clearly and the initial narrative exposition thus proved to be very effective, as most users had not seen the show before and felt the exposition provided them with sufficient context for the interactions. Almost all the users understood that they had taken the role of Vivien as they saw the dream progress.

Even though we added narrative cues and some visual cues for when and how the UTO should be used, it appeared that some interactors were unable to connect how the interface should be used in regards to the onscreen object. The ambiguous shape of the universal object appeared to be confusing with respect to how it should be held. Even though all the users held the device in the upright vertical position as we intended for the rope sequence, some users also held the device in an upright position for the flashlight sequence, instead of holding it horizontally. Furthermore, the technical constraints required the device to be initially calibrated when held in a correct horizontal position while entering the hallway. When held at a wrong angle, the device calibrated incorrectly, resulting in the character moving in an unproductive direction in the hallway.

Some visual cues appeared to be interpreted incorrectly, and we learned that verbal cues are sometimes more efficient. Some participants felt that the movement of hands in the video of the rope sequence seemed to suggest that the rope could be released by moving the device instead of decreasing pressure on it. Some users did not see sufficient feedback to believe they were in control of the rope, and as a result let the rope sequence play back through its default path. We added a voice over of Ben screaming "lower me gently" to improve this interaction.

In the case of the hallway sequence, which provided freedom to explore, interactors were sometimes lost in the middle. It appears that visual and verbal cues are necessary to inform interactors where they are supposed to go and what their goals are. In our first round of testing, some users did not focus on the door at the end of the corridor, and did not point the flashlight in that direction, which was the input that triggered simulated movement toward the door, where the next dramatic action took place. We added dramatic emphasis in the form of flickering lights and shaking of the door, with audio of Ben asking for help. The second trial, with these changes, was successful in cueing the interactors to point the device straight ahead.

The haptic experience and the threshold object coupled with the narrative gave pleasure to the interactors. Though some found it initially confusing, once they saw the shot sequence of Vivien grabbing the flashlight they felt that the device's vibration worked well to confirm their expectation of being in control of the device. Also, interactors found the squeezing and releasing gesture from the rope scene appealing. It seemed to present a good emotional match for the action onscreen.

We were limited to providing haptic feedback as iconic vibration patterns rather than realistic representations of tactile sensations, due to limitations of our development period and resources. The haptic feedback we designed was initially not clearly interpreted as intended physical or emotional feedback by interactors. The prototype device mapped different patterns of vibration to events that the interactor controlled in the narrative, but it was difficult for interactors to distinguish between the changing vibration patterns associated with different events and actions. Our revisions intensified the differences in speed, intensity, and rhythms, which made the patterns easier to differentiate.

DESIGN CONSIDERATIONS

Our research suggests that using a tangible device with an interactive narrative can create dramatic agency and provide narrative pleasure to the interactor. The interactor realizes emotional choices through physical interaction as s/he empathizes and struggles with the character. The haptic interface as a threshold object reinforces the liminal and physical presence of the story world, employing haptic feedback as a storytelling technique.

Designing Interactive Narratives for Television

Interactivity on television expands plot varieties. However, the existing episodic structure and content creation and distribution models are not capable of multiple conclusions and require coordination of a branching interactive narrative within a linear television series. There could be several different techniques to extend the plot while adjusting the ending to be consistent. Choosing each character's perspective to view in a scenario or focusing on specific parts of the narrative are some ideas. Coupling these with the affordances of the tangible interface can add the pleasures of interactivity and narrative exploration.

Providing Goals and Guidelines for Interaction

Interactivity provides agency and pleasure while watching television. However, interactivity can also confuse the interactor about how to interact and what to do. Adding cues and feedback in the video and the haptic interface to imply how to interact can minimize confusion and increase clarity in this new story space. This includes visual, verbal and haptic cues about when to interact, what to do, how to hold the interface, and what gestures to make, as well as about what the haptic feedback means in the story context. Also, it is possible that repeated exposure to this new type of narrative haptic grammar would improve intuitive understanding of the interactions and the cues.

Designing Interface and Interactions

The direct mapping of the interface to the form and function of the object in the narrative helps the interactor understand how to interact. We explored several different forms and interactions that can be expressed through a single handheld interface. We explored a set of actions, such as pulling, grabbing, swinging, triggering, and aiming, which correspond with threshold objects such as rope, rod, sword, gun, and flashlight. During our brainstorming sessions, we used green foam to experiment with diverse possibilities for forms and functions that can be connected to the object. Using green foam let us test how it would be held in the hand and allowed us to explore different poses. We finally chose a combination of flashlight and rope to tie in with the narrative scenario we were developing.

Designing Haptic Feedback

The haptic experience could be improved through refining the haptic feedback and using different materials for the interface. We were limited to providing iconic vibration patterns but there can be other ways to provide more realistic vibro-tactile feedback. In this project we used only vibration motors, but other methods of stimulation such weight shifting, or electro-tactile feedback could give different results. Our interface was made out of 5mm plastic. The thickness and rigidness of the material diminished the sensitivity. Using thin or flexible material for the interface could improve sensitivity.

CONCLUSION AND FUTURE WORK

Our research suggests that tangible objects can create an experience of dramatic agency and increased immersion when integrated with regular television programming. By extending objects from the narrative world to have a physical presence in the interactor's space as threshold objects, we were able to create engaging interactions that reinforced the interactor's immersion in the story. Interactors were willing to accept that a neutrally-shaped handheld haptic device could represent different objects at different points in the narrative.

We see many other areas for productive research in the growing area of interactive television. We plan to extend the project by investigating how the system would work with different genres of stories, or longer and more complicated narratives. In our prototype, the interactor was constrained to a single point of view, but if we let interactors switch points of view, how would this affect dramatic engagement? Although the UTO remains a speculative design rather than a commercial product, it is a useful framework for exploring the evolving design space at the convergence of interactive computing and television storytelling.

ACKNOWLEDGEMENTS

We thank Tawny Schlieski from the Intel Interaction and Experience Research Group for support and collaboration. We also thank our collaborators on the project: Derek Young, Yuan Yuan Lin, and Erin Hennessy from the Synaesthetic Media Lab (Synlab) and Patrick Coursey, Amrutha Krishnan, Benjamin Pincus, Pratik Zaveri, Laurie Marion, Sarah Fox and Toby Smith from the eTV lab. *American Horror Story* Season 1 was produced by 20th Century Fox who holds the copyright.

REFERENCES

1. Alam, K.M. et al. Mobile haptic e-book system to support 3D immersive reading in ubiquitous environments. *ACM TOMCCAP*, 9, 4 (2013), No. 27.
2. Cha, J. et al. A Framework for Haptic Broadcasting. *IEEE MultiMedia.* 16, 3 (2009), 16–27.
3. Clifton, P. et al. Don't open that door: designing gestural interactions for interactive narratives. *Proc. TEI '13*, ACM (2013), 259–266.
4. Danieau, F. et al. Framework for enhancing video viewing experience with haptic effects of motion. *Proc. HAPTICS '12*, IEEE (2012), 541–546.
5. Dezfuli, N. et al. PalmRC: imaginary palm-based remote control for eyes-free television interaction. *Proc. Euro iTV '12*, ACM (2012), 27–34.
6. Genette, G. and Lewin, J.E. *Narrative discourse: An essay in method.* Cornell University Press (1983).
7. Jenkins, H. *Convergence culture: where old and new media collide.* NYU Press (2006).
8. Lemmens, P. et al. A body-conforming tactile jacket to enrich movie viewing. *Proc. World Haptics '09*, IEEE (2009), 7–12.
9. Lu, K.Y. *Interaction design principles for interactive television.* MS Thesis, Georgia Tech (2005).
10. Murray, J.H. *Hamlet on the holodeck: The future of narrative in cyberspace.* Simon and Schuster (1997).
11. Murray, J.H. (2012). Transcending Transmedia: Emerging Story Telling Structures for the Emerging Convergence Platforms. *Proc. Euro iTV '12*, ACM (2012), 1-6.
12. Nandakumar, A. and Murray, J. Companion apps for long arc TV series: supporting new viewers in complex storyworlds with tightly synchronized context-sensitive annotations. *Proc. TVX '14*, ACM (2014), 3–10.
13. O'Modhrain, S. and Oakley, I. Touch TV: Adding feeling to broadcast media. European Conference on Interactive Television: from Viewers to Actors (2003), 17–41.
14. Samanci, Ö. et al. Tangible comics: a performance space with full-body interaction. *Proc. ACE '07*, ACM (2007), 171–178.
15. Sussner, J. et al. 3D Navigable Interface for Interactive Movie Gormenghast Explore. *Proc. AXMEDIS '06*, IEEE (2006), 242–250.
16. Tanenbaum, J. et al. The Reading Glove: designing interactions for object-based tangible storytelling. *Proc. AH '10*, ACM (2010), No. 19.
17. Ursu, M.F. et al. Interactive TV narratives: Opportunities, progress, and challenges. *ACM TOMCCAP*, 4, 4 (2008), No. 25.
18. Vatavu, R.-D. and Zaiti, I.-A. Leap gestures for TV: insights from an elicitation study. *Proc. TVX '14*, ACM (2014), 131–138.

SWARM: An Actuated Wearable for Mediating Affect

Michele A. Williams[1,2], Asta Roseway[2], Chris O'Dowd[2], Mary Czerwinski[2], Meredith Ringel Morris[2]

[1]UMBC
Baltimore, MD, USA
mawilliams@umbc.edu

[2]Microsoft Research
Redmond, WA, USA
{astar, v-chriso, marycz, merrie}@microsoft.com

ABSTRACT

We present SWARM, a wearable affective technology designed to help a user to reflect on their own emotional state, modify their affect, and interpret the emotional states of others. SWARM aims for a universal design (inclusive of people with various disabilities), with a focus on modular actuation components to accommodate users' sensory capabilities and preferences, and a scarf form-factor meant to reduce the stigma of accessible technologies through a fashionable embodiment. Using an iterative, user-centered approach, we present SWARM's design. Additionally, we contribute findings for communicating emotions through technology actuations, wearable design techniques (including a modular soft circuit design technique that fuses conductive fabric with actuation components), and universal design considerations for wearable technology.

AUTHOR KEYWORDS

Wearable technology; accessibility; universal design; affective computing; emotions; stress management

ACM CLASSIFICATION KEYWORDS

H.5.m. Information interfaces and presentation (e.g., HCI).

INTRODUCTION

Identifying and reacting according to one's own emotional state is vital for physical and mental well-being (e.g., stress management). It is also critical to identify others' emotions for successful communication. Devices for measuring emotion (using signals like heart rate and perspiration) are becoming cheaper and more reliable; the emerging category of "smart watch" products is already beginning to integrate heart rate sensing (e.g., the Samsung Galaxy Fit). Within a few years, wearable affect monitors such as multi-purpose smart watches or specialty devices (e.g., Spire [spire.io]) may be as ubiquitous as fitness bands are today.

Our work extends current emotion detection techniques by introducing a wearable device to aid in interpreting and/or enhancing one's personal emotions and alerting the wearer of others' emotions; the device is designed to respond to signals gathered from various sensors (via Bluetooth). While this is potentially valuable for everyone, both areas of personal and group emotion management have particular implications for people with disabilities. People with vision or hearing impairments, for instance, may not receive important visual or verbal cues of others' emotions. Thus, universal design (making the device inherently accessible for many types of users) was central to our project.

TEI '15, January 16 - 19 2015, Stanford, CA, USA
Copyright 2015 ACM 978-1-4503-3305-4/15/01…$15.00
http://dx.doi.org/10.1145/2677199.2680565

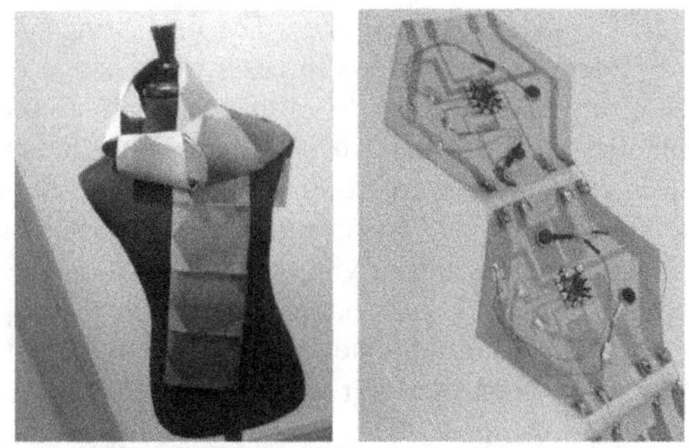

Figure 1. Our modular cotton scarf houses canvas modules with conductive fabric circuitry designed to control heat, vibration, and audio actuations.

We iteratively designed, built, and tested a wearable technology, SWARM, involving target stakeholders for user-centered feedback at various stages. After discussing related work, we expound on the iterative design of our scarf from a low-fidelity prototype to a final working design, including lessons learned and novel techniques developed regarding the fabric, hardware and software design, as well as user perspectives on wearing a device that reacts to emotions. We close by discussing the implications of our findings for wearable technology as a means of emotion management.

RELATED WORK

Affective Computing & Quantified Self

Quantified Self [quantifiedself.com] is a movement of using technology (primarily sensors) to provide people with quantitative data about their everyday activities, generally physical (such as using a pedometer). The data has also been applied to affective computing (using technology to determine one's emotional state), not surprising given the correlations between mental and physical health [13, 16, 25].

Affective computing is accomplished using many techniques, including biosensors, audio and text analysis, and facial recognition [6, 7]. Work is also being done to outfit the environment with sensors, such as pressure sensors in keyboards and computer mice, and implicit patterns of device use [8, 23]. From the raw numbers provided by the sensors, algorithms can determine a person's affective baseline and indicators of a change in emotion [4]. Researchers are studying how best to present this data to end users, ranging from data visualizations on a mobile application to environmental displays for everyone to see [3, 18].

Our work extends this line of affective computing research to explore two additional avenues. The first is intervention, where a system not only alerts the user of a change in their emotions, but also attempts to mitigate negative emotions and enhance positive ones in real-time using actuations. Similar interventions were recently proposed, though not yet implemented, in [9], whose authors proposed actuations for relieving stress while driving such as cooling the car's temperature. Our work goes beyond the proposals in [9] by involving a spectrum of emotional states and creating a prototype of the actuations to receive user feedback.

The second focus of our research is group detection, where the system conveys the emotional state of others, either individually or in aggregate (assuming a prevalence of wirelessly available sensor data per person). For example, as a person approaches a conference room where an important business meeting is taking place, her SWARM scarf might actuate to let her know if the mood in the room she is about to enter is tense or relaxed. This is particularly relevant for people with disabilities.

Affective Computing & People with Disabilities

Due to the nature of certain disabilities, many people have difficulty identifying emotions – either their own and/or those of others. As a result of an Autism Spectrum Disorder, for instance, a person may have difficulty recognizing and articulating their emotional state, as well as difficulty interpreting and reacting to the emotions of others [2]. For people with vision or hearing impairments, identifying another person's emotional state may be difficult without being able to see or hear the visual or verbal cues associated with communicating emotions [10].

Prior accessibility research has explored specific aspects of emotion awareness for these populations. For instance, many systems attempt to teach children with ASD how to identify emotions based on body language (e.g., [15]). Researchers have explored using vibration feedback on a glove to emulate information from facial expressions for those with vision impairments [11]. Work has also been done to ensure automated American Sign Language systems include emotion expressions in the signing avatars as well as emotional states in captions [12, 20]. However, no prior work has sought to combine emotional interpretation suitable for use by people with varied disabilities into a single system.

(Wearable) Affective Objects

An important aspect of affective computing is the affective object: "...any physical object which has the ability to sense emotional data from a person, map that information to an abstract form of expression and communicate that information expressively, either back to the subject herself or to another person" [19]. In evaluating the type of affective object to create, we explored a design space that would allow for real-time, on-body interventions. Thus our focus rapidly and firmly pointed towards a wearable object.

The ability for wearables to blend in with typical fashion designs is important, as it has implications for people with disabilities. Assistive technology that looks drastically different from mainstream devices draws unwanted attention to a person's disability and perpetuates a stigma often associated with disability [21]. Creating a wearable that looks fashionable and conveys information subtly to the user was therefore a key design criterion for our project.

Two notable projects inspiring our work were the modular scarf built in [1] and scarf, bracelet, and vest built in [24]. Designed for people with ASD to help relieve anxiety, both projects used wearable technology to embed many actuations into garments including haptics, cooling, and air compression. These projects helped bring awareness to the types of actuations that may be useful for users with autism. We extend this work by exploring additional actuations (to facilitate various affect interpretations) and employ a modular design for personalization (to address universal design for many types of users).

SWARM: INITIAL DESIGN

In the first phase of our project, we identified which aspects of affective computing we wanted to address, designed the actuations, built a low-fidelity prototype, and presented the initial design to users for feedback. We named the project SWARM (Sensing Whether Affect Requires Mediation).

Form-Factor

We designed SWARM as a scarf for several reasons. Firstly, we were inspired by weighted vests used in ASD therapy [22]. While there is some controversy over its usefulness, many people with autism use pressure as a means of helping to focus and relieve the stress of sensory overload [5]. A scarf could be wrapped around the wearer in a vest-like manner if such comfort were desired.

Secondly, as mentioned, previous work in [1] presented a promising modular and versatile scarf design that appeared viable for housing several different actuations in one garment. The vast number of ways in which a scarf can be folded further motivated using this style of garment.

Lastly, scarfs are currently fashionable and worn as an everyday garment, addressing our desire for a discreet design that does not draw unwanted attention as an assistive device [21]. Because many fashion items are gendered (in the U.S., "indoor" scarves are more commonly worn by women), we tailored our design and evaluation for adult women users.

Mood	Actuations
Stressed	Cool body temperature Hear/Feel soothing music Use stress relief balls Apply pressure (ASD)
Sad	Warm up body temperature Hear/Feel cheerful or somber music See soothing visualizations
Calm	None (scarf is dormant)
Happy	Maintain body temperature Hear/Feel cheerful or upbeat music See soothing visualizations
Excited	Cool body temperature Hear/Feel cheerful music See festive visualizations
All	Vibration alert notification: (a) Short buzzing for personal notification (b) Varied patterns to relay group emotions

Table 1. Six actuations for the personal emotion awareness scarf included vibration, heat, cooling, music, weights, lights.

Actuations

In selecting SWARM's actuations, we first limited the emotions addressed by the garment to five from Russell's circumplex model of affect: stressed, sad, calm, happy, and excited [17]. These gave us a balance of positive and negative emotions common enough to be familiar to our participants. We identified six actuations inspired by prior work such as [9] but also thought to be accessible and provide a rich, multimodal language for conveying emotion – heat, cooling, music, weights, vibration, and lighting (Table 1).

We imagined the overall scenario around the scarf's use as someone (or everyone) wearing biosensors (such as heart rate monitors) that send readings via Bluetooth to the scarf.

Reacting to One's Own Emotions

Table 1 shows our initial design for how SWARM would react upon receiving a particular emotion notification about the wearer. For instance, in response to an excited state, SWARM could play upbeat music, or in response to stress, users could add weights to the scarf (analogous to weighted vests sometimes used in ASD therapy). We chose weights that could serve a dual role as embedded stress relief balls. Depending on a user's needs, SWARM's utility could be customized towards the goal of either reflecting a user's current emotional state (e.g., minor-key music when feeling sad) or the goal of transitioning to a new state (e.g., upbeat music when feeling sad).

Indicating the Mood of Others

For alerting of others' emotional states, we designed only two classes of actuation due to our accessibility and discretion concerns: vibration and lighting. These would activate as a distinct pattern such as longer vs. shorter vibration pulses, or varying colors and patterns. To promote discretion for lighting, users could wear the scarf in a configuration that reduced visibility to others; alternatively, subtle color changes in the scarf could be considered aesthetically pleasing and fashionable by observers, who need not be aware that they encode information for the wearer.

Actuation	Hardware
Alert	Vibration motors soldered to battery pack
Heat	12V heating coil soldered to battery pack
Cooling	Columbia Freezer Zero ™ Neck Gaiter fabric
Music	Adafruit MP3 Shield on Arduino Uno
Weights	(a) Fabric bean bags used in weighted vests (b) Balloons filled with sand
Lighting	(a) Battery-powered fabric ribbon LED strip (b) Adafruit NeoPixel Matrix on Arduino Uno

Table 2. Initial prototype's hardware components

While users with no vision would not be able to view the lighting, many visually impaired people have some usable vision, particularly for coarse, low-resolution color or brightness changes such as those we designed for SWARM's embedded LED display. Also, the vibrations could accompany the visualizations to ensure accessibility.

We did not want the scarf to speak the emotions of others, not only because of the accessibility concerns for those who are deaf but also because we did not intend for the wearer to constantly wear headphones, nor would it be discreet to have sound over speakers.

Hardware Design

For initial prototyping, we explored low-fidelity items that would work well enough to present the concept to users, even if they were not lightweight enough for all-day wear. Our goal was to elicit reactions to the overall concept as well as each proposed actuation to determine whether the design was desirable before pursuing further development. We used the Arduino prototyping platform due to the extensive availability of lightweight hardware options; we also purchased ready-made components as well as nontechnical items to complete the initial design (Table 2).

Fabric Design

We wanted to include each actuation as its own interchangeable module to provide personalization and customization (for instance, the ability to remove lighting modules for users without vision). In considering scarf designs, a hexagon shape emerged as a way to add visual appeal to the scarf while facilitating interlocking modules. Like the actuations, the design also became part of the initial user study to see how users reacted to SWARM's appearance.

After paper prototyping and then laser cutting felt designs, we decided on a honeycomb pattern with a higher-elasticity fabric between the shapes to allow for stretching the scarf around the body (Figure 2). In total there were 27 modules (three rows of 9-5"x6" pods with 1" of space in-between) to mimic the size of a typical scarf. We only needed eight modules for the technology we wanted to demonstrate (Table 2), so the others were empty placeholders for potential duplicate modules or to store weights. We designed the modules as pockets to insert either electronics or weights.

We also tested different fabrics, exploring both front-facing and inner-lining fabrics. The most important consideration was being thick and sturdy enough to house the electronic components such as the MP3 player shield and controller.

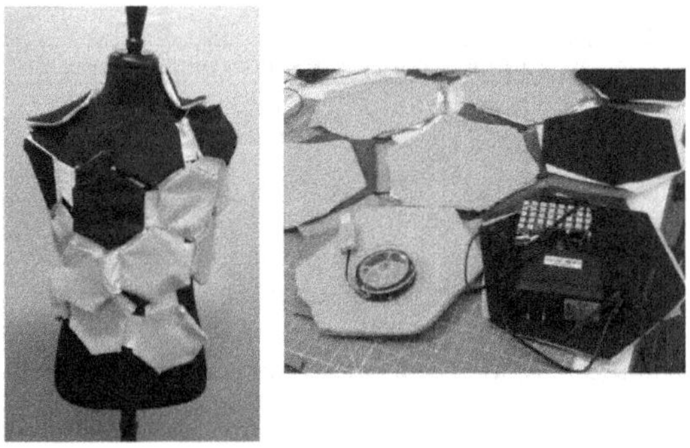

Figure 2. Cotton fabric scarf includes detachable hexagon-shaped modules enclosing hardware such as battery-powered vibration modules and heat coil pads

While we realized this did not represent the final design (which would have smaller, lighter components) we wanted the scarf to be comfortable enough to try-on. We also wanted a breathable texture (since many of the electronics would heat up when powered), as well as one that was soft and comfortable to wear (since this would rest against the skin, and users with ASD with sensory sensitivities might find rough fabrics particularly uncomfortable). We also didn't want the fabric to wrinkle too easily during stress ball use.

Ultimately, we preferred cotton for the outer layer because of its breathability and softness; we disregarded color. We used a denim knit to house most of the electronic components using no lining, and used a mid-weight knit lined with polyurethane for the modules that were either empty or included only the LED ribbon strip (Figure 2). We used a stretchy jersey knit between the modules and Velcro to seal each module as well as attach the knit between the modules. This allowed for fast assembly and would later be useful when demonstrating the modules to users.

USER FEEDBACK ON SWARM'S INITIAL DESIGN

To help refine our design, we conducted a user study of the preliminary garment. Our goal was to get feedback on users' desire to have a garment that reacts to and/or relates emotions, the fashion design, the appropriateness of the actuations, and ideas for future features and improvements. For this initial round we focused on recruiting people with disabilities to confirm our motivating scenarios and ensure the features were accessible.

Our participants were eight adults aged 20 to 62. We had one participant who was both hard of hearing and low vision, four visually impaired participants, two auditory impaired participants, and one with high functioning autism. Though SWARM's aesthetics are targeted for women, we had two male participants in this initial group, one with a visual impairment and the other with autism. Their feedback was valuable to the project, since it confirmed that, as suspected, our design was better-suited for female users.

We used a semi-structured interview along with a written questionnaire to gather our data. The interview included gathering the participants' current strategies on handling their emotions, walking through each actuation to collect impressions, discussing the personal vs. group emotion awareness features, and having participants draw their preferences for where to place the actuators on a body diagram.

Overall Reactions to the Scarf

Participants found the overall concept of having a reactionary garment appealing. On a 1 to 7 scale of "Not Useful" to "Very Useful", survey scores averaged 5.0 for interest in a garment that reacts to emotions and 5.38 for one that displays and reacts to the emotions of a group. They found the preliminary scarf design too bulky and heavy to be comfortably worn, however, likening it more to a blanket.

Overall, participants found the vibration alerts useful and a logical first step prior to any other actuations taking place. They felt the heating element was soothing and would change a somber or stressed mood. As our autistic (male) participant stated, *"If I'm stressed or feeling sad I wouldn't mind having a warm hug."* They felt the idea of fabric cooling them was just as helpful, but many wondered if having both heat and cooling were redundant.

The stress balls were liked, though one participant said they preferred a gel to the sand we used in our balloons. One of the Deaf participants also mentioned she would use them to massage her hands since she uses sign language to communicate and it leads to cramping. When introducing the dual function of the stress balls as weights, our autistic participant said he had never heard of weighted vests. Thus, while participants speculated that weights may be a useful feature for some, there was no one to attest to its true value.

All of the participants said some sort of auditory feedback would be useful but two participants mentioned they would want an alternative to music such as environmental sounds or talking (e.g., a talk radio show). (Our hearing-impaired participants had hearing aids that could pair with personal sound systems to allow them to hear audio.)

The LED lights were most controversial and had mixed reactions mostly regarding whether to publically share their emotional state. Three participants (all female) said they would like to have a visual display but only when they were in a good mood, not a bad one. The remaining participants did not want their emotions shown due to privacy concerns. For instance, one (deaf female) participant said she wouldn't want people to *"take advantage"* of that information. That same participant viewed the LEDs more as a back up to the vibrations in case she didn't feel them.

In terms of placement on the body, participants generally agreed – the heat, cooling, and vibrations were preferred around the neck, the MP3 player either near the neck or near the hands (depending on how the scarf was worn), and the LED lights throughout the scarf.

Displaying Others' Emotions

We explored not only a personal emotion device but also group detection to address the perceived accessibility issues surrounding detection of others' emotions. Participants with more severe hearing and visual impairments confirmed they had difficulty detecting other people's emotions due to missing verbal and non-verbal cues. Our autistic participant said he did not have trouble detecting emotions, but explained that he was "high functioning," and thus did not have as severe symptoms as others.

When told about the group emotion detection concept in general, reactions were overall reluctant but willing. Four participants had concerns about the privacy implications of being able to detect the emotions of other people using technology. Two participants thought it would be better to limit the usage to certain scenarios (a classroom or meeting) and people (the teacher or boss). Only two participants explicitly wanted to use this feature for themselves - our autistic participant and one of the female visually impaired participants. The autistic participant explained that while he can detect emotions, he has a problem producing empathy and felt this would give him a cue. The rest of the participants saw this as being more useful for "someone else" but not themselves. The "others" included police officers, therapists, and people with autism; thus, they were willing to concede that certain monitoring of emotions to benefit others was worthwhile.

Initial User Feedback: Summary of Key Points

By involving users from target demographics at this point in our design process, we learned that participants liked the idea of a scarf form-factor, with many mentioning they liked the modularity as well. Based on the questionnaire rankings, the vibration alerts, heat, cooling, and stress balls emerged as favorite actuations. The MP3 player was not as popular overall, but those participants who favored it felt it was vital to changing their emotional state. Being able to wrap one's self with the scarf and using it as a weighted garment were not as important as initially thought. No one mentioned additional actuations they would like to see included in the scarf. From these findings we began to refine our design to create a working, lightweight, slender scarf.

SWARM: FINAL DESIGN

In this second phase of our project, we used the user feedback to refine the appropriate hardware and fabric to produce an updated, fully functional, comfortable scarf.

Actuations

From the user study, we removed lighting (due to users' privacy concerns) and cooling (as heat was more favored and we agreed might be redundant to cooling)..We ultimately removed the stress balls, also, due to the circuitry and fabric design outcomes, as described in sections below. We continued our focus on five basic emotions: stressed, sad, calm, happy, and excited. We also continued to focus on both personal and group emotions given users' interests.

For personal emotion actuation the designs were fairly straightforward: we envisioned two short vibrations that would alert the wearer of a change, followed by heat (if they were stressed or sad), and music playing (in all cases, with the song choices varying from slow to fast) While simple in its execution and design, the concept was substantial because it would elicit feedback on a wearable technology receiving notifications about a change in one's emotions and automatically reacting to that information.

For group emotion actuation, we took a cue from our participants as well as prior research (for instance, [11]) and explored varying vibration patterns as a means of relaying emotion. Accordingly we programmed nine patterns, varying both the number of vibrations (between two and three) and length (from 250ms to 1000ms). Most patterns had a consistent duration, but one pattern toggled long and short. The patterns were meant to be enough to demonstrate the concept to the participants and begin a discussion of what types of patterns they would desire.

Cell Design

As we began the actual fabrication, modularity was a focus because participants in the first study liked the customization it afforded, and also because it facilitated easier replication of the fabrication processes for future explorations.

Initially, we explored printed circuitry and electronics such as inkjet printers and conductive pens. However, paper and Kapton film are the only sensible outlets, making the cell rigid and less supple for wearability. This led us to the soft circuitry work of Wilson [14], whose hard-to-soft component techniques inspired us to work with conductive silver ripstop fabric and felt. After several failed attempts to laser cut the circuits and adhere them to felt, we decided to invert the process by adhering the conductive fabric onto a large section of the felt first, then used a raster setting to cut out the negative space. This resulted in a successful soft circuit pattern. While the felt worked, we opted for cotton canvas to achieve more flexibility, with some regret since the felt provided a stronger support for the components.

We therefore created "soft cells" or fabric modules that each contained their own microprocessor (in our case a Beetle [dfrobot.com], a miniaturized version of the Arduino Leonardo). The Beetle accompanied by an actuator could, in theory, stand alone, but when linked could create a "chain" of cells to generate a suite of actuation (Figure 1b). We generated two unique cell circuit designs for vibration and heat (Figure 3), which was followed by one music cell, and a master cell that would be used to control them all with the I2C protocol and power them with a 3.7V by 800 MAH battery. We were unable to find a flexible 6-watt heater so we generated our own heat cell by including a coil of 40-gauge wire connected on the backside. They required additional power, and therefore we added a 3.7V by 800 MAH lithium battery in each module. In total the SWARM scarf consisted of 12 cells, 10 functional and 2 empty (due to the desired length of the scarf) (Figure 1a).

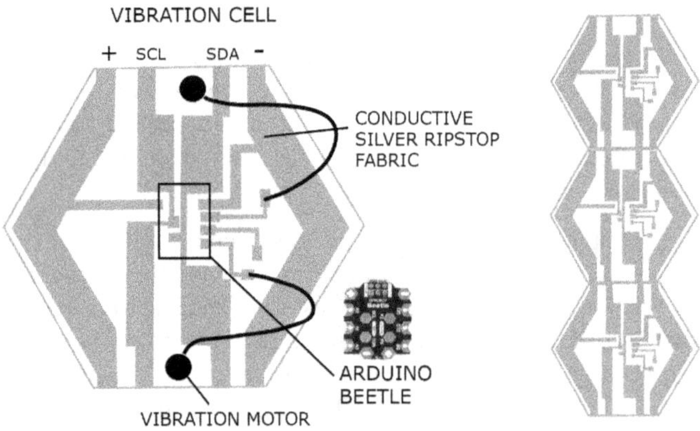

Figure 3. Circuit diagram for vibration and chain of cells

Adding hard components such as microprocessors or actuators to fabric is not a trivial task, so we initially used CircuitWorks® conductive epoxy [chemtronics.com] but this resulted in undesirable higher resistive connections. We then switched to Z-Tape [3m.com], a conductive adhesive transfer tape that consists of silver nanospheres embedded onto a 2D array in an adhesive surface that act as conductive double-sided tape. While this did work for attaching hard components, we discovered that over time the consistency of the connection started to fail as the silver spheres were absorbed into the fabric. To ensure secure connection to the haptic motors, we soldered copper shim stock pieces to wires and secured them with the Z-tape.

Finally, we needed a way to connect all the cells. Initially, for simplicity, we attempted to connect them with a metal agent such as safety pins or hooks and eyes, but found these connectors moved too much and interfered with the consistency of the power. Some of the loss in power was also due to the Z-tape coating being absorbed by the fabric, which also occasionally lost connection with the board. These types of issues in connecting hard and soft components are not new problems [18]. We were not able to route consistent power over multiple cells and resorted to hardwiring the cells together to ensure quality testing and omitted the master cell in exchange for a USB connection to a laptop. While this wasn't ideal, it still enabled some modularity that would resonate with users later in the studies.

Fabric Design

In creating a soft fabric covering for the circuits, we found lightweight woven cotton that had a visually appealing black-to-white gradient (Figure 1a). We wanted to continue incorporating the hexagon but did not want the honeycomb shape for the scarf overall. Given we could not confirm the usefulness of the large design that mimicked a weighted vest and our multiple rows led to the undesirable bulky design, we only included one row of modules. We played upon the gradient in the fabric to cut 12-5"x6" rectangles and adhered 5"x5.75" hexagons in an inverted gradient atop the rectangles on both sides. Initially we included a fusible interfacing on the rectangles but removed it because the double-sided adhesive on the hexagons served as a stabilizer as well and we were concerned about stiffness.

The rectangles were left open at each end to ensure that the cells could be inserted and moved if needed. While safety pins did not work for our circuitry design, we found them useful for connecting the fabric as they allowed for a connection that was hidden from view but easily adjusted and flexible. To prevent additional time hand sewing a blind stitch, we laser cut the fabric to the correct dimensions, sewing on the sides of the rectangles and used anti-fraying products on the top and bottom. Despite having two cells empty of circuitry, we removed the stress balls for fear of jarring the circuitry and because the fabric wrinkled.

USER FEEDBACK ON SWARM'S UPDATED DESIGN

Recruiting a new set of participants, our goal for this study was to again gather feedback on the scarf's overall concepts and fashion design, but also more detailed feedback on the actuations, placement, and wearability of our soft circuits. Participants were nine women, ages 18-61. Two participants were visually impaired, three auditory impaired, one was autistic, and three had no disabilities at all (to test the universal suitability of the technology).

We again used a semi-structured interview plus written questionnaire to gather data. We presented concepts in the second user study in phases, much like the first study. Users were introduced to affective computing overall, then shown the scarf and asked to put it on, evaluating each concept then concluding with the human diagram drawing. As mentioned in the prior section, we needed to mitigate some of the circuitry and fabric complications encountered. Thus, we demonstrated that the scarf was able to heat up and vibrate, gathering overall reactions to those actuations. Unfortunately only the first five participants experienced the heat directly as the heating element stopped working during the study. For the patterned vibration actuations we had a separate set of vibration motors for users to hold and analyze, and the music was played through headsets connected to a mobile phone for demonstration.

Overall Reactions to the Scarf

Participants again found merit in the scarf. On a 1 to 7 scale of "Not Useful" to "Very Useful", survey scores averaged 5.56 for interest in a garment that reacts to emotions, and 4.78 for one that displays and reacts to the emotions of a group (lower than the prior study due to the inclusion of people without disabilities). Participants found the scarf lightweight, often forgetting they had it on at the conclusion of the study. Participants with disabilities appreciated the discreet aesthetics of the design.

The heating module, even when not fully demonstrated, was again a highly desired feature. A few participants pointed out this would be helpful as long as the surrounding temperature was not also hot (a point made more prominent by our summer timeframe). The music player was also found to be a fun feature and, as one participant noted in her questionnaire, one that would motivate everyday use. Overall, participants did not readily associate the vibration patterns with emotions. Generally any method of vibration only meant alert, primarily associated with phones ringing.

Interestingly our 7th participant (who was hard of hearing) mentioned heat would be a better indicator of mood than vibration as she could envision the scarf's heat indicating stress levels or the overall intensity of someone's state. When mentioned to the 8th (hard of hearing) and 9th (autistic) participants in subsequent interviews, they both agreed this would be an even more discreet, distinctive, and distinguishable actuation. P9 also mentioned two concerns specific to people with autism: that vibration might be too much stimulation or it might be misinterpreted as an alert of incorrect behavior rather than of someone else's emotions.

Participants again agreed on placement with the heat and vibrations preferred around the neck and near the shoulders, and the MP3 player either near the neck or near the hands.

After the first five participants, the scarf began to fray in some places as well as wrinkle; we gathered that either stitching or leaving the interfacing would have prevented this. As a result, we re-sewed a commercially-purchased, jersey-knit scarf into a tubular shape. During the 6th interview, we placed the circuitry into this tubular scarf housing after the participant commented that the grey scarf looked stiff. That participant and the remaining three participants subsequently wore the inner circuitry with the jersey-knit scarf and found it very comfortable, although it was a little restrictive when tying it around their necks due to the hexagon shape of the inner circuitry pods and the USB cables.

User Feedback: Summary of Key Points

Participants in this round of feedback found high value in being alerted of their change in emotions, as they might not be aware of certain stressors, for instance. Overall interest in using the garment as an everyday item was less in this study than the previous study, however, particularly among the participants without disabilities. This was partly due to the design and form of a scarf in that it would not coordinate with all their outfits or be appropriate in the summer, but also because it appeared to be more useful in specific circumstances. For instance, three participants mentioned it being useful for people who could not otherwise convey their emotions (including elders in general, one participant's aunt who was wheelchair bound and not able to speak, and one participant's autistic son). Another participant mentioned she could see it used for law enforcement (a comment mentioned in our prior study as well). Notably our autistic participant did indicate she would find it useful for confirming emotional states and that she could see herself wearing it every day (though the exterior of the scarf would need to be interchangeable so that wearing the same scarf every day would not draw undue attention).

Unlike the first study, only one participant mentioned privacy concerns with detecting a group's emotions, explaining that people may not want to have their emotions detected. Most participants, however, envisioned the sensing would be optional if worn on-body or simply similar to the use of cameras today if sensed in the environment.

Utilizing the tubular knit scarf in the study produced the idea of having interchangeable outer shells to allow for matching in everyday wear. The knit fabric also allowed more movement than the woven cotton modular design. In addition, when asked to draw where on the body they would want the actuations, participants were almost unanimous in their responses, seeming to lessen the need for modularity over flexibility in how the scarf could be worn.

Participants did feel the heat and music were mood-changers, as we envisioned, and appreciated the vibrations as an alert of their *change* in emotions. The varying vibration patterns for *distinguishing* emotions were not received as intuitive, however, with the suggestion of using heat instead an avenue for future exploration.

DISCUSSION

This project assumes accurate physical sensing devices that can detect and project emotions wirelessly. We recognize this is not the current state of emotion detection technology; however, the advancements in this field led us to envision what could result from such accurate and detailed devices. Though our scarf did not actuate to the full capabilities we envisioned for the second study, we were still able to receive valuable feedback, including confirming interest in group emotional awareness using sensing technology and future uses for personal and group actuations (such as using heat as an indicator of emotional state). This combines previously segmented work in many areas such as wearable computing, affective computing, and assistive technology.

The scarf design also accomplished discreet emotion awareness, broadening the prior use of specialized clothing as a therapeutic device for people with ASD to a fashionable, more universal technology. The form factor also led to a lightweight, flexible fabric circuitry wearable technology contribution.

The sleeve we ultimately created proved useful for the final design; having an interchangeable outer shell addressed the everyday wearability issue participants expressed. Also, modularity and customization (a desired feature given the individual preferences for actuation, particularly from the first study) could still be accomplished through attaching the inner electronic components more permanently, and then simply changing the wrapping to match other garments and the weather. Preferences for modules were not seen as specific to any particular user group (such as all participants with visual impairments) but instead were individualized, further motivating the idea of completing several modules then allowing a choice of inclusion.

Participants with disabilities saw the scarf as most useful. Participants without disabilities did not make a personal connection with the intended use of the scarf. Certainly our probe is not in-depth enough to make strong conclusions; however, this does indicate the need for more investigation into future uses of emotion detection systems.

CONCLUSION & FUTURE WORK

SWARM is meant to compliment a user's current strategies for coping with their emotions, and also provide more information that may not be available, particularly for users with disabilities. We pushed this boundary by exploring scenarios beyond personal emotion detection to that of interpreting others' emotions.

People already use technology to regulate their emotions – our participants mentioned listening to music, driving, and calling others when experiencing emotions from stressed to excited. Thus, envisioning explicitly combining emotional reactions into one device is not inconceivable. As indicated by our participants, one's emotional state is not necessarily something people want broadcast, but more personal awareness (as in the Quantified Self movement) was desired. We propose systems for reflecting on and increasing awareness of one's own and others' emotional states as a future area of accessibility research that might be also useful for everyone as we move towards a smarter, sensor-filled world that knows how people are feeling and can help people address this context.

As part of our future work, we are recreating the soft circuitry using copper fabric and rivets to secure hardware components. We are also sewing additional fabric scarfs for the outer shell. Lastly, we are updating the software to create a wireless solution that will eventually integrate with physical sensing devices such as a heart rate monitor to generating a full emotion detection system.

ACKNOWLEDGEMENTS

We thank Cati Boulanger, Paul Johns, and the MSR Hardware Lab for their ideas and contributions to this project.

REFERENCES

1. Bonanni, L., et al. TapTap: A Haptic Wearable for Asynchronous Distributed Touch Therapy. *CHI EA 2006*. 580 - 585.
2. CDC Autism Spectrum Disorder: Signs and Symptoms. http://www.cdc.gov/ncbddd/autism/signs.html
3. Davis, F., et al. Actuating mood: design of the textile mirror. *TEI 2013*. 99-106.
4. Eaton, K. *Does Your Phone Know How Happy You Are? The Emotion-Recognition Industry Comes Giddily Of Age.* Fast Company (2012).
5. Grandin, T. (1992) Calming Effects of Deep Touch Pressure in Patients with Autistic Disorder, College Students, and Animals. *Journal of Child and Adolescent Psychopharmacology*, 2, 63-72.
6. Healey, J.A. and Picard, R.W. Detecting stress during real-world driving tasks using physiological sensors. *ITSC 2005*. 156-166.
7. Hernandez, J., et al. Call Center Stress Recognition with Person-Specific Models. *ACII 2011*. 125-134.
8. Hernandez, J., et al. Under Pressure: Sensing Stress of Computer Users. *CHI 2014*. 51-60.
9. Hernandez, J., et al. AutoEmotive: Bringing empathy to the driving experience to manage stress. *DIS 2014*. 53-56.
10. Knapp, M. L. (1972) *Nonverbal communication in human interaction.* New York: Holt, Rinehart & Winston.
11. Krishna, S., et al. VibroGlove: An Assistive Technology Aid for Conveying Facial Expressions. *CHI EA 2010*. 3637-3642.
12. Lee, D.G., et al. (2007) *Emotive Captioning*. Computers in Entertainment-Interactive TV. Vol 5, Issue 2.
13. McEwen, B. S. (1998) Protective and Damaging Effects of Stress Mediators. *New England Journal of Medicine*, 338:171-179.
14. Mellis, D.A., et al. Microcontrollers as material: crafting circuits with paper, conductive ink, electronic components, and an "untoolkit". *TEI 2013*. 83-90.
15. Park, J.H., et al. A Framework for Designing Assistive Technologies for Teaching Children with ASDs Emotions. *CHI EA 2012*. 2423-2428.
16. Picard, R.W. (2000) *Affective computing*. Cambridge: MIT Press.
17. Russell, J.A. (1980) A circumplex model of affect. *Journal of Personality and Social Psychology*. 39:1161 1178.
18. Sanches, P., et al. Mind the Body!: Designing a Mobile Stress Management Application Encouraging Personal Reflection. *DIS 2010*. 47-56.
19. Scheirer, J. and Picard, R. (2000) Affective objects. *MIT Media Laboratory Perceptual Computing Section Technical Report No. 524*.
20. Schnepp, J.C., et al. Combining emotion and facial non-manual signals in synthesized American Sign Language. *ASSETS 2012*. 249-250.
21. Shinohara, K. and Wobbrock, J.O. In the Shadow of Misperception: Assistive Technology Use and Social Interactions. *CHI 2011*. 705-714.
22. Stephenson, J. and Carter, M. (2009) The Use of Weighted Vests with Children with Autism Spectrum Disorders and Other Disabilities. *Journal of Autism and Developmental Disorders*, 39, 105-114.
23. Sun, D., et al. MouStress: Detecting Stress from Mouse Motion. *CHI 2014*. 61-70.
24. Vaucelle, C., et al. Design of Haptic Interfaces for Therapy. *CHI 2009*. 467-470.
25. Wilkins, J. and Eisenbraun, A. J. (2009) Humor Theories and the Physiological Benefits of Laughter. *Holistic Nursing Practice*, 23, 349-354.

Button Matrix: how Tangible Interfaces can Structure Physical Experiences for Learning

Emily S. Cramer & Alissa N. Antle
Interactive Arts and Technologies, Simon Fraser University
Surrey, British Columbia, 250-13450 102 Avenue
{ecramer, aantle}@sfu.ca

ABSTRACT
Physical experiences are frequently used to represent mathematics to children. However, students sometimes fail to transfer performance to symbolic representations of problems. In this paper, we suggest that tangible interfaces can promote transfer by structuring physical experiences. We realize our concept in a system, Button Matrix, that uses coupled tactile, vibration and visual feedback to a) *highlight* features of a physical experience that represents arithmetic concepts and b) cue *reflection* on the links between the physical experience and mathematical symbols.

ACM Classification Keywords
H.5.2. [Information Interfaces and Presentation]: User Interfaces-- *input devices and strategies.*

INTRODUCTION
Tangible user interfaces (TUIs) and physical materials (e.g. Diennes Blocks) are frequently used to teach children abstract concepts, as in science and mathematics [7,8]. These media are popular because children often demonstrate knowledge through physical interaction that they cannot in words or in pictures [6,10], and may solve problems better when physically "working them out" [6,7]. However, in many situations, children do not transfer performance with physical to symbolic representations of problems [8]. What is needed are features that promote transfer. Two ways to promote transfer may be: highlighting conceptually relevant physical features [7], and cueing reflection on the links between physical and symbolic representations [10]. Here, we describe how tangible interfaces might accomplish these goals.

THEORETICAL BACKGROUND
Mathematical concepts can be represented in various ways [7], including symbols, graphs, and objects. Generally, students find concrete representations, such as pictures and objects, easier to understand than symbolic representations. [7,8]. However, mathematical aptitude requires fluency with symbolic representations [9]; training students to translate between different representations is a goal of mathematics education [9,4].

Translating between representations presupposes knowledge of the concepts' essential, or 'representation-independent' features [10]. Because concepts must be introduced via a representation, a question in mathematics education is which representation to use? The ideal representation allows students to understand mathematics using knowledge they already have, without downplaying the concepts' essential features, or introducing inessential ones [7,5].

Nunez and Lakoff propose that because mathematics derives from physical experience, teachers should introduce mathematics via physical objects or gesture [6]. This allows students to understand mathematical concepts, such as division, as physical actions, such as partitioning sets of objects. The rationale is that because physical constraints on this action reflect mathematical rules, (one cannot evenly partition an odd set, or divide an odd integer), students can apply such "physical knowledge" to other representations.

Applications of Lakoff's view have met variable success. When learning through physical experience, students are more engaged [7,8], and demonstrate problem-solving strategies they do not in writing or speech [5]; however, students rarely transfer performance to symbolic representations [8].

Failure to transfer knowledge from one representation to another could suggest deficiencies in the representation itself, (it misrepresents some, or cannot represent all, conceptual features), or in learners' comprehension of its relations to the concept. In the latter case, our goal is changing how students experience the representation, versus changing the representational mode.

There is evidence supporting this latter alternative. Goldin-Meadow investigated which factors predicted transfer from gestural to symbolic representations of balance problems; the gesture was intended to highlight a mathematically viable strategy [5]. As a group, the gesturers' pre-post test

TEI '15, January 16 - 19 2015, Stanford, CA, USA.

http://dx.doi.org/10.1145/2677199.2680566

performance improved more than non-gesturers, and they seemed to use the strategy the gesture represented. In support of Lakoff's view, this suggests that physical experiences can develop transferable knowledge. However, not all gesturers improved; those who did could verbalize the strategy the gesture represented. Because *telling* students the strategy did not improve performance, Goldin-Meadow hypothesized that gesture only benefited students inclined to experience the gesture mathematically, i.e., they attended to mathematically relevant features, and interpreted them as mathematical concepts [5].

The question then becomes how to encourage mathematical ways of experiencing physical representations? Goldin-Meadows' work suggests that verbally conveying the relations between representation and concept is insufficient. By Nunez and Lakoff's view, "mathematical ways" of experiencing would also develop through physical experience. Entertaining this perspective, we urge designers to create physical experiences that *encourage* mathematical ways of experiencing them.

Recent work suggests two strategies: a) *highlight* mathematically relevant physical features and b) *cue reflection* on their connections with symbolic representations [7,9]. Both promote transfer in more students. For example, Walkington et al found that "full-bodied" gestures, which highlighted mathematical constraints by mapping them to salient biomechanical constraints, produced transfer in more students than "hand-only" gestures, which did not [13]. However, transfer still depended on students' apprehending mathematically relevant gestural features, such as the "length" of an imaginary hypotenuse [13]. More recently, Gerofsky mapped "full-bodied" gestures to functions, and highlighted relevant gestural features, e.g, extrema and roots, acoustically [4]. She found transfer in all students; however, she measured transfer to graphic representations alone. It thus remains unclear how to help all students apprehend mathematically relevant features, and to relate them to *symbolic* representations. In the following sections, we describe how programmable tangible interfaces could accomplish both goals.

The first goal is highlighting mathematically relevant physical features. "Dually coding" such features in stimuli of another modality, one that is salient and related to the physical action, could help students apprehend them [3]. Programmable interfaces, which 'know' the relevant mathematical features, could control these additional stimuli. Consider the representation "division is partitioning physical sets", in which case "indivisibility" is subset inequality. A programmable interface, which "knows" the set size and current divisor, could require more force to partition indivisible than divisible sets. Students may be more perceptive to the core relation between set size, subset equality and number of subsets when the requisite force to partition correlates it.

Although many modalities could dually-code the relationship between physical action and mathematical concept, work on human motor learning suggests that tangible (e.g., texture, resistance), as opposed to non-tangible (vision and sound) feedback, is ideal: non-tangible feedback may distract learners from their physical experiences [2] and prevent them from learning the concepts the experience represents. Tangible stimuli may also have an advantage because they can directly constrain physical actions, e.g., the increasing resistance of an exercise band directly constrains the ease with which I can stretch it apart. Non-tangible stimuli, by contrast, constrain action indirectly (e.g. "red light" makes us stop because of an additional rule). Stimuli that directly constrain physical action may better reflect how mathematical properties (e.g., divisibility of m by n) constrain mathematical actions (can I evenly partition m objects into n subsets?) [12].

While strictly tangible feedback may meet our first design goal (highlight the action's mathematically relevant features), our second, promote reflection on the connections between different mathematical representations, requires visual-symbolic representations, i.e., of expressions like "2 x 3 =6". Ullmer and Ishii [10] suggest that 'coupling' tangible and visual representations promotes their integration; in most investigations of physical mathematical experience, however, students are exposed to symbolic representations *after* the experience [4,12,7]. Work on multimodal perception may support Ullmer's view: stimuli are integrated better when presented simultaneously, presumably because the common time-course makes them seem related [1], and because students' memories of the stimuli experience less decay [1].

We therefore encourage designers to use coupled tangible and visual (symbolic) materials to highlight mathematically relevant features of physical experience, and promote integration between physical and symbolic representations. In the remaining section, we show how designers might realize both ideas via describing our initial proof of concept, "Button Matrix": a tangible system for learning arithmetic.

DESIGN RATIONALE AND IMPLICATION:

"Button Matrix" is a tangible system that uses coupled physical (texture and vibration) and visual feedback to highlight features of an action (pressing sequences of buttons) that represent basic arithmetic (addition, subtraction and multiplication). Basic arithmetic seemed a fitting domain because it has been targeted by various other tangible systems [7,8] and because students' core problems (appreciating commutativity and the recursive definition of integers [9]) are well-defined.

There are general criteria for a physical experience that represents mathematics and the system that supports it. The 'physical experience' must map unintuitive mathematical to intuitive physical procedures [10]. The system must be easy to learn and use. It must provide interpretable feedback, and allow students to offload 'irrelevant' cognitive load (e.g., keeping track of where they are in the problem) [11]. Every salient feature should be mathematically relevant, and no feature should convey *erroneous* ideas. A successful system must withstand "rough" button presses, and conceal electronics. It should be small enough to sit on students' desks, but large enough to hold students' attention. We advocate additional criteria: a successful system highlights physical features that represent mathematical concepts and promotes on-line reflection on their relation to symbolic representations.

DESIGN SOLUTION

Button Matrix maps arithmetic to action via Nunez and Lakoff's metaphor of "journeying" along a number line [6]. It is intended for grades 1-2. Students duplicate on-screen integer steps in arithmetic problems (e.g. 2+5) by pressing buttons in a continuous sequence along a 3 by 3 matrix; this captures a recursive definition of integers (1 or 1+ an integer) as decomposable sets, which extends grade 1-2 students' knowledge of counting and patterns [9,10], and may be useful in later grades, when students 'balance equations' by identifying integer operands' missing components (e.g. 7+3=5+X) [5].

Button Matrix maps an unintuitive idea (different symbolic expressions, such as 2x3, 3+3, 7-1, are mathematically equivalent) to an intuitive physical fact (moving up 4, then 2, brings me to the same place as 2, then 4, or 3, then 3). Here, we describe how we used coupled tangible and visual feedback to highlight this physical feature (the equivalence of different journeys) and its relation to the mathematical analogue (various procedures can achieve equivalent results).

TECHNICAL FEATURES

The system is an Arduino microcontrolled button matrix that communicates with laptop-run software. The software displays a screen that the microcontroller updates; the software sends each problem to the microcontroller. Button Matrix sits on students' desks; to promote engagement, it covers the desk. A foamcore box hides the electronics. The caps and buttons are fused with modelling clay, and reinforced with wood glue.

INTERFACE FEATURES AND FUNCTIONALITY

The software allows teachers to specify sequences of addition, subtraction and multiplication problems with operands between 0 and 16; the program displays the problems in sequence.

Button Matrix represents problems in steps. Each step is an integer. Addition and subtraction problems have two steps (one for each operand); multiplication problems (mxn) have n steps, each of which is m.

Students complete steps by pressing a number of buttons equal to the integer. An integer begins one button past where the previous terminated. At the end of the problem, students press a button that represents the result. Each press represents a one unit change in the accumulating result; buttons represent different integers. Adding is moving forward; subtraction moving backward.

The screen represents the student's progress in mathematical symbols. It has 3 components: the Stepper, which displays the current step, surrounded by a rectangle, and all steps that preceded it; the accumulator, which displays the current sum that the students' journey represents, and the solution, which appears when students complete the problem, and displays the problem expression, along with the equals sign and the result (e.g., 2x5=10).

The form of the expressions reinforced the equivalence of different arithmetic procedures, and the relationship between these expressions and the physical experience. For example, the Stepper conveyed a key idea- multiplication is iterated addition- by representing the steps of a multiplication problem (nxm) as $n_0+n_1+...n_m$; students only see it as nxm upon completing the problem, when the solution (nxm=nm) appears. This was intended to provide grade 1-2 students, who do not know multiplication or the symbol "x", a grounding of multiplication as "iterated addition" [9]; it also related multiplication to the physical procedure of executing an additive journey some number of times. For results >9, the accumulator provided an additional representation: the current sum in base 9 (e.g., 11=9x1+2). The base 9 representation reflects the physical action that produces results >9. Because the matrix has 9 buttons, every 9 buttons, students return to the first button; conveying these longer "journeys" as units of 9, or "times around the matrix", reinforces the connection between multiplication and addition, and between the physical and arithmetic procedures. The on-screen display and physical matrix were coupled. All screen components updated immediately after the physical interface issued tactile feedback; this highlighted and promoted reflection on the links between all symbolic and physical representations of the students' progress through the problem.

The matrix supplied two forms of tactile feedback. The first attributed a pager motor, which signaled correct and incorrect button presses. Correct presses elicited a 50ms pulse; incorrect presses elicited a continuous buzz that ceased when the user pressed the correct button. The second attributed the button's textures. Each button had a unique texture. Because our matrix was 3 by 3, we represented integers texturally in "base 3 notation". Each button had 1 to 3 small and 0 to 2 large beads. The large beads represented "one 3"; thus, only the second and third column had large beads (1 and 2 respectively). Like the accumulator's representation of results >9 as "times round a 9x9 matrix", the base 3 notation highlighted how journey segments <=9 could be represented as "times up a column".

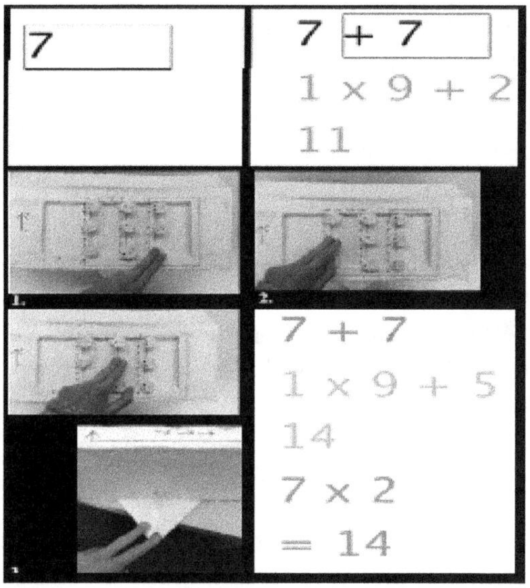

Figure 1: stepping through the problem "7x2=14".

We spaced the beads such that, using two fingers to depress the button, students felt the small and large beads on separate fingers. The short pulse focused students' attention on the feel of the current button, while the sustained pulse washed it out.

The distinctly textured buttons highlighted the physical feature, that various journeys achieve the 'same destination', that represented the arithmetic concept, that various operations achieve the same result. Because of the distinctly textured buttons, mathematically equivalent procedures *feel* the same. Different procedures with equal results (6-2, 2+2), end on the same button; that button feels unique. Because subtraction "goes backward", while addition moves forward, subtraction "feels like" reversing addition. Forcing students to wait until they feel the short pulse prevents them from "rushing" through the journey and promotes attention to the mathematically relevant textures.

USE SCENARIO

Button Matrix is an in-class supplement for grade 1-2 students. We envision students alternating between Button Matrix and paper and pencil to solve arithmetic drill problems. Instructors should specify sets of problems that emphasize equivalence (e.g., 2x3=3+3=4+2=2+4) and are appropriate to the child's skill level. While the instructor should explain and provide examples of how to use Button Matrix, students should be able to complete problems alone.

CONCLUSION

We have articulated a rationale for representing mathematics in physical experiences, and the need for interfaces that promote transfer from physical experiences to symbolic representations. Button Matrix is one realization of our core idea, that by highlighting mathematically relevant physical features, and cueing reflection on their connection to mathematical symbols, tangible interfaces can promote learning through physical experience. Our next step is using Button Matrix to test our ideas. In the meantime, we hope that this conceptual piece inspires designers to consider new requirements for systems supporting embodied learning experiences, and new ways of mapping tangible to conceptual features.

REFERENCES

1. Bara, F., Gentaz, E., Colé, P., & Sprenger- Charolles, L. (2004). The visuo-haptic and haptic exploration of letters increases the kindergarten-children's understanding of the alphabetic principle. *Cognitive development*, *19*(3), 433-449.
2. Casile, A., & Giese, M. A. (2006). Nonvisual motor training influences biological motion perception. *Current Biology*, *16*(1), 69-74 .
3. Clark, J. M., & Paivio, A. (1991). Dual coding theory and education. *Educational psychology review*, *3*(3), 149-210.
4. Gerofsky, S. (2010). Mathematical learning and gesture: Character viewpoint and observer viewpoint in students' gestured graphs of functions. *Gesture*, *10*.
5. Goldin-Meadow, S., Alibali, M. W., & Church, R. B. (1993). Transitions in concept acquisition: using the hand to read the mind. *Psychological review*,*100*(2), 279.
6. Lakoff, G., & Núñez, R. E. (2000). *Where mathematics comes from: How the embodied mind brings mathematics into being*. Basic books.
7. Manches, A., O'Malley, C., & Benford, S. (2010). The role of physical representations in solving number problems: A comparison of young children's use of physical and virtual materials. *Computers & Education*, *54*(3), 622-640.
8. McNeil, N. M., Uttal, D. H., Jarvin, L., & Sternberg, R. J. (2009). Should you show me the money? Concrete objects both hurt and help performance on mathematics problems. *Learning and Instruction*, *19*(2), 171-184.
9. Sovchik, R. J. (1996). *Teaching mathematics to children*. Longman.
10. Ullmer, B., & Ishii, H. (2000). Emerging frameworks for tangible user interfaces.*IBM systems journal*, *39*(3.4), 915-931.
11. Uttal, D. H., O'Doherty, K., Newland, R., Hand, L. L., & DeLoache, J. (2009). Dual representation and the linking of concrete and symbolic representations.*Child Development Perspectives*, *3*(3), 156-159.
12. Walkington, C., Srisurichan, R., Nathan, M., Williams, C., Alibali, M., Boncoddo, R., & Pier, L. (2012). Grounding Mathematical Justifications in Concrete Embodied Experience: The Link between Action and Cognition.

Simply Spinning: Extending Current Design Frameworks for Kinesthetic Empathy

Shannon Cuykendall, Ethan Soutar-Rau, Karen Cochrane, Jacob Freiberg, Thecla Schiphorst

School of Interactive Arts and Technology, Simon Fraser University
102 Avenue Surrey, British Columbia
V3T 0A3 Canada
{*scuykend, esoutarr, kcochran, jfreiber, thecla*}*@sfu.ca*

ABSTRACT
We describe design considerations in *Serpentine Dance, Refocused* (SDR), an interactive movement installation that pays homage to Loïe Fuller's mesmerizing creations of light and motion. Our design goals were inspired by kinesthetic empathy research. Fuller created the *Serpentine Dance* (1891) at a time when many artists turned to abstraction as a way for audiences to engage with the essence of motion rather than narrative plots. We sought to heighten the feeling of kinesthetic empathy through creating an interactive environment where audience members could physically engage and reflect on the sensation of spinning, a prominent action in the *Serpentine Dance*. Through our analysis of SDR we found that our design intentions relating to kinesthetic empathy were not addressed by current design frameworks for kinesthetic interactions. Based on kinesthetic empathy research, we restructure and extend these frameworks into an evaluative and generative framework for interactive systems. We propose that kinesthetic empathy is the center of all movement interactions. This broader definition of kinesthetic empathy can be used to evaluate and generate a wide variety of movement interactions. We discuss the design of SDR through the lens of our evaluative framework.

Author Keywords
Kinesthetic Empathy; Interaction Design; Audience Engagement; Kinesthetic Experience; Kinesthetic Awareness

ACM Classification Keywords
J.5 Computer Applications: Arts and Humanities—*Performing arts*; H.5.2 Information Interfaces and Presentation: User Interfaces—*Interaction Styles, Theory and Methods*

General Terms
Design, Human Factors

ACM 978-1-4503-3305-4/15/01 ...$15.00.
http://dx.doi.org/10.1145/2677199.2680567

INTRODUCTION
Movement is extremely complex, and the interactions that can be created for movement are even more complex. Not only do designers need to consider the multiple aspects and dimensions of movement, but they must also take into consideration what motivates users to move, how to measure this movement, and decide on the best environment for these interactions to play out. We examine design frameworks that have been created to aid in generating and evaluating interactive systems for movement. We discuss our design considerations for the interactive movement installation *Serpentine Dance, Refocused* (SDR). The design and artistic motivation behind SDR is inspired by kinesthetic empathy research; however, many of our design intentions were not addressed in current frameworks for movement interaction. Based on kinesthetic empathy research and SDR design considerations, we restructure, combine, and extend current frameworks. We create an evaluative and generative framework for kinesthetic interactions that can apply to a broad range of movement interactions and help simplify the numerous design considerations one must take into account when designing for movement. We propose that kinesthetic empathy lies at the center of all movement interactions and suggest design principles be considered in relation to kinesthetic empathy.

BACKGROUND
What is Kinesthetic Empathy?
Kinesthetic empathy has caught the attention of researchers and artists in many diverse fields including dance, theatre, film, sports, therapy, music, photography, participatory performances, and interactive environments [18]. Its definition is ever expanding, making it a challenging concept to clearly define. Generally, it refers to the phenomenon of experiencing a first person sensation of observed movement. John Martin was one of the first to write about this phenomenon in the 1930's,"We shall cease to be mere spectators and become participants in the movement that is presented to us, and though to all outward appearances we shall be sitting quietly in our chairs, we shall nevertheless be dancing synthetically with all our musculature" [12].

Mirror neurons may be one possible neurological explanation for kinesthetic empathy [18]. Mirror neurons are activated in the brain both when observing and performing movement. Calvo-Merino et al (2006) found heightened brain activity in those who had physical familiarity with movement they were observing and less brain activity in those who had only visual familiarity with the movement [2]. This research suggests a strong link between our physical experiences and perception of movement.

In the *Watching Dance Kinesthetic Empathy Project*, Dee Reynolds and Matthew Reason interviewed dance audiences in order to understand why they enjoy watching dance. They found audiences connect with movement in multiple ways. Audiences reported engaging with virtuosic components, effortful qualities, and the gracefulness and ease of the movement they watched. Some audience members described imagining performing the movement themselves or described their own embodied responses while watching the performance [17]. Many of these responses suggest that audience members *feel* movement they observe in addition to *seeing* it.

This research demonstrates that one does not need to move or mimic actions in order to have a kinesthetic response to movement. However, in dance therapy studies, researchers have suggested that physically mirroring another's actions can enhance empathy [13]. McGarry et al (2011) define mirroring as, "When two people make similar body movements that are coordinated or slightly echoed in time" [13]. Expert movement observers, trained in Laban Movement Analysis (LMA), also mime movement in order to form a deeper understanding of the actions they observe. Mentis (2013) describes this process, "In using her own body to see the movements she is exposing the link between feeling the movement through her own bodily ability and seeing the movement as it resides in another's body" [14].

Many elements of kinesthetic empathy remain ambiguous, such as its relationship to mirror neuron research, affective accounts of movement, and cognitive experiences [18]. This ambiguity makes kinesthetic empathy a challenging theory to test and many questions remain open for investigation. What is the boundary between affective and kinesthetic responses? Can enjoyment and engagement levels be linked to our ability to kinesthetically empathize with movement? How does our brain activity relate to our empathy towards movement? Can kinesthetic empathy occur during movement interactions?

Kinesthetic Empathy and Interactivity

There is a long history of artists and designers that have created interactive movement systems. Our focus, for the purposes of this paper, brings to light those artists that have specifically mentioned how kinesthetic empathy plays a role in their design choices. In interactive environments the role of kinesthetic empathy has many avenues, and often its role is blurred. When does the audience member become a performer and how does this separation affect the experience of kinesthetic empathy? In reference to kinesthetic empathy, dance researcher Sarah Whatley proposes that an interactive immersive environment, where users both embody and partner with an avatar, "invites a different kind of kinesthetic engagement" [19]. In contrast, we argue this engagement is a heightened form of kinesthetic empathy.

Choreographer Brian Knoth explored how audiences experience kinesthetic empathy when watching interactive, multisensorial, immersive performances. Through audience surveys Knoth found that many audience members engaged with how the music, sound and visuals aligned. Audience members also felt particularly connected to the performer during the audience participation portion of the work [11]. In a similar study, Kirsch et al (2003) found when audience members have had physical experience with the movement they watch, they also have increased enjoyment levels [10]. Kirsch et al (2013) encourages interactive performances stating, "The first step in getting spectators more interested in watching dance might be to get them up and moving themselves" [10]. Audience participation and closely integrating movement with sound and visuals may be one way to enhance kinesthetic empathy in performances.

Kinesthetic Empathy and Interactive Design Frameworks

Jin Moen created a design framework for kinesthetic movement interaction (KMI) [15, 16]. As a starting point for empirical inquiry, Moen relays five methods of creating meaning in movement that were first presented by Lynne Anne Blom and L. Tarin Chaplin in *The Moment of Movement* [15, 16]:

- *Kinesthetic Awareness*: expanding the range of bodily perception and sensation
- *Phrasing*: contextual grouping of movements
- *Forming*: patterning and organizing movement
- *Relating*: experiencing another's movement to create empathy
- *Abstracting*: simplifying a movement to the essence of an experience

Moen, inspired by modern dance techniques, used these five themes to design a study for gathering information on participants' experiential accounts of movement. Through conducting in-depth interviews and building a prototype, Moen found four important aspects designers should take into account when designing for full-body movement interactions [15]:

- *Movement Literacy*: Designers must have physical knowledge of the movement they are designing for. They need to understand both the visual or observed qualities of the movement and the physical sensations they bring forth. According to Moen, movement literacy is gained through movement exploration and reflecting on these experiences.
- *Personal Interaction Space*: Designers should consider the user's physical range of movement and the size required for their personal space. Some questions to consider are: How far can the user extend out into space? How close should the user be to another object or user? What directions and levels can the user move in?
- *Imitate-React-Express*: Allow users to create a back and forth dialogue with the system and give users the chance to both direct the conversation and react to it in a natural way.
- *Social Acceptability*: The social contexts and physical environment influence how one moves and interacts with a system; therefore, designers should design for specific contexts and scenarios.

Fogtmann et al (2008) took a slightly different approach than Moen and created a conceptual framework to evaluate kinesthetic interactions for interactive sports equipment. This framework defines three main design goals of movement interactions [7]:

- *Kinesthetic Development* improves or develops specific bodily skills
- *Kinesthetic Means* uses movement to reach a goal that is not related to increasing bodily skills
- *Kinesthetic Disorder* challenges and transforms one's kinesthetic experience

Fogtmann et al (2008) further defines design parameters in relation to these themes [7]:

- *Engagement*: encourages exploration of bodily movement
- *Sociality*: creates a sociable experience that promotes users to interact with one another through active participation or observing
- *Explicit Motivation*: directly informs the user how to move and interact with a system and limits the types of interactions that can occur
- *Implicit Motivation*: allows the user to explore and interact with a system in an open, unrestricted manner
- *Movability*: refers to how the body is free to move while using the system
- *Expressive Meaning*: transpires when the goals of the system correspond to the kinesthetic interaction
- *Kinesthetic Empathy*: creates an environment where users can anticipate and react to another user's movement

In this framework kinesthetic empathy is narrowly defined as a design parameter relating to action prediction. Maiken Hilerup Fogtmann expands on this definition in other works, and distinguishes between *joint kinesthetic empathy interaction* and *opposing kinesthetic empathy interaction*. In joint kinesthetic empathy interaction users work together to achieve a goal and in opposing kinesthetic empathy interaction two users compete against one another to achieve the same goal [5]. Fogtmann lists further design considerations specifically for these kinesthetic empathy interactions [6]:

- *Decision Making*: facilitate many movement interactions and allow users to decide what action to execute in many differing contexts
- *Anticipation*: encourage users to predict another user's movements
- *Degree of Difficulty*: the ability to adjust the level of difficulty as kinesthetic skills increase
- *Interpersonal Feedback and System Feedback*: highlight user-to-user interaction instead of user-to-computer interaction

Although Fogtmann's framework is already quite extensive, design is continuously expanding. Fogtmann states, "This is not to be understood as the finalized list, but should rather be seen as design concerns that are known at this point in time" [6].

These frameworks deal specifically with systems where participants must move beyond everyday computer movements, such as clicking a mouse. In contrast, Cuykendall et al (2014) defined interaction categories for heightening kinesthetic empathy in interactive, online movement works. Designers from Ohio State University created the interactive website *Synchronous Objects* [8] which breaks down the choreographic structure of William Forsythe's *One Flat Thing, reproduced* (2000). Users navigate this website through point and click interactions. Through a close reading analysis of this unique work, Cuykendall et al (2014) defined three categories of interaction that support kinesthetic empathy [3]:

- *Instructional Interaction* simplifies movement through abstraction, making it more familiar to broader audiences. Interaction is restricted to focus attention on components of the movement deemed important by the designer.
- *Exploratory Interaction* gives authorship to the users and allows them to explore concepts in a more personalized context. Interaction and user agency is increased.
- *Translational Interaction* recontextualizes movement into a new form. In *Synchronous Objects* these interactions serve as a way to attract audiences through novelty.

Each interaction category affords different amounts of explicit interaction to increase engagement and focus attention. Cuykendall et al (2014) suggest these interaction categories increase kinesthetic awareness, which in turn supports kinesthetic empathy [3].

In summary, Fogtmann's framework for kinesthetic empathy focuses on how to design systems to help users anticipate and predict another human's actions. In contrast, Cuykendall et al (2014) discuss how kinesthetic empathy can be supported through increasing kinesthetic awareness. Moen, inspired by movement themes related to empathy, focuses on understanding actions through exploration and reflection. When presented together these frameworks create an overwhelming list of criteria that is challenging to comprehend and apply to design. We consolidate these frameworks and propose kinesthetic empathy is the center of all movement interactions.

Our Definition of Kinesthetic Empathy

Our definition of kinesthetic empathy is the result of our attempts to acknowledge and combine the many varied directions the research surrounding this phenomenon has taken. Through widening the scope of kinesthetic empathy we can more easily see how the design frameworks described above overlap and relate to one another. We propose that action prediction and action understanding are both a part of the ever expanding definition of kinesthetic empathy. Following dance therapy research, we propose that physically mirroring and engaging in movement can heighten kinesthetic empathy [13]. In opposition to Fogtmann, we suggest kinesthetic empathy is not just a human-to-human phenomenon, but can occur with motion in any context or even in still images where motion is implied. Freedberg and Gallese (2007) found that "physical traces" of an artist, such as brush strokes, can evoke a kinesthetic connection [9]. This research suggests that it is possible to create kinesthetic empathy with abstract forms and without necessarily having human-to-human interaction.

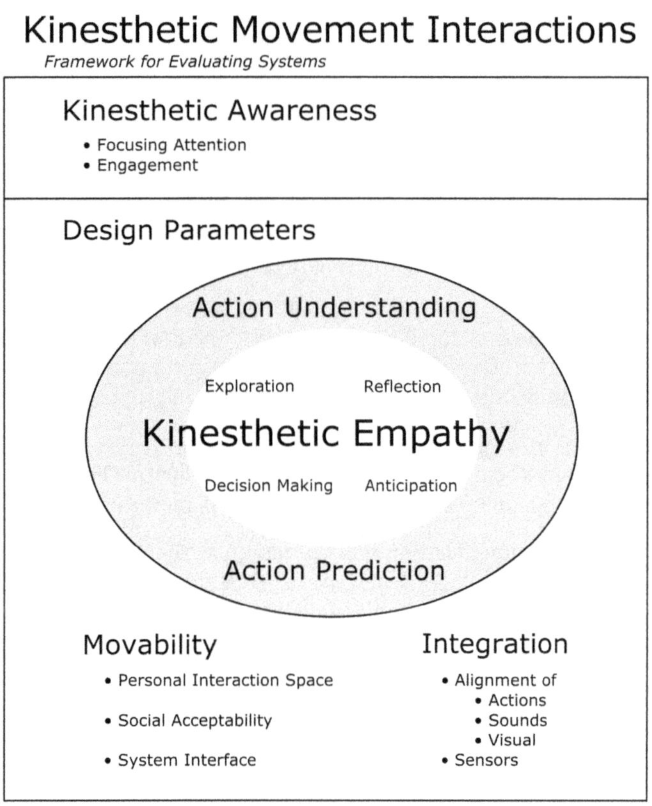

Figure 1. Restructured KMI Evaluative Framework

RESTRUCTURED KMI FRAMEWORKS

We propose an evaluative and generative framework for KMI. These frameworks are a culmination of previous KMI frameworks. We borrow terminology from these previous frameworks and apply the same definitions, unless otherwise noted. In our evaluative framework we place kinesthetic empathy as the center and primary facilitator of all movement interactions (See Figure 1). We suggest that kinesthetic empathy can only occur in movement interactions after kinesthetic awareness has been established. Kinesthetic awareness is established through focusing the user's attention and creating an opportunity for the users to engage with the work. Our use of "engagement" is slightly different than Fogtmann et al (2008). We suggest engagement does not have to include bodily movement, but can relate to many varied ways participants can immerse themselves in the work. Once kinesthetic awareness is established, we suggest four major themes of kinesthetic empathy: *Exploration*, *Reflection*, *Anticipation*, and *Decision Making*. These themes are not discrete and designers can choose to highlight one or all of these themes. "Exploration" and "Reflection" are inspired by Moen's KMI framework that focuses on action understanding. According to Moen, movement literacy is increased through exploring movement and reflecting on these experiences [15]. "Anticipation" and "Decision Making" derive from Fogtmann's framework [6] related to action prediction. Surrounding kinesthetic empathy we list two main design parameters that can help develop the themes of kinesthetic empathy: *Movability* and *Integration*. We expand the definition of "Movability" provided by Fogtmann et al (2008) [7] and list components from Moen's framework [15] that directly relate to how the user is able to move within the system: *Personal Interaction Space* and *Social Acceptability*. We add *System Interface* as a third design component to consider. This component of the framework was inspired by our design considerations in SDR. Lastly, "Integration" was inspired by Knoth's findings [11], which suggest closely aligned sound, movement and visuals can heighten kinesthetic empathy. We also add *Sensors* as another important aspect to consider for integrating the user's movement with the system.

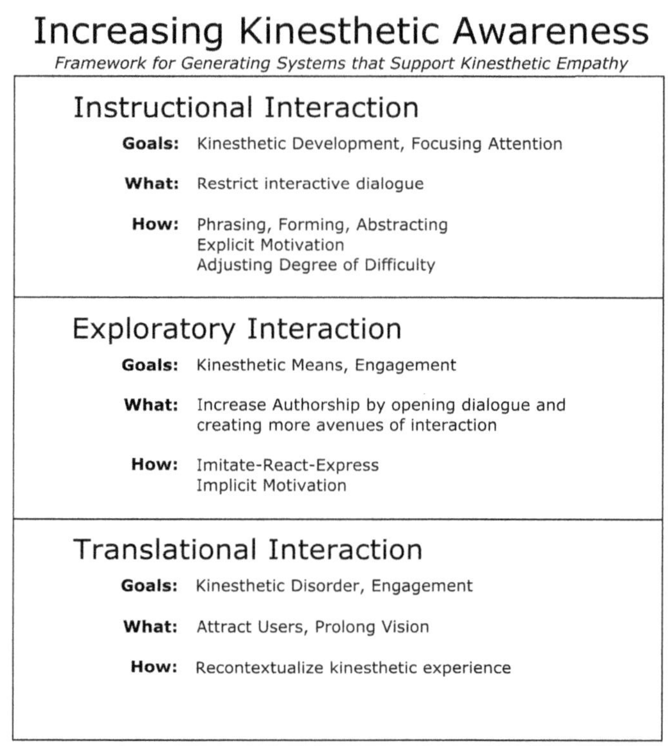

Figure 2. Generative Framework to establish kinesthetic awareness and support kinesthetic empathy

In our generative framework we propose specific interactions that can support kinesthetic empathy by increasing kinesthetic awareness (See Figure 2). We link the goals described by Fogtmann et al (2008) of *Kinesthetic Development, Means and Challenges* [7] with the concepts of *Instructional, Exploratory and Translational Interaction*, developed by Cuykendall et al (2014) [3].

In creating a system for Kinesthetic Development we suggest focusing the user's attention through Instructional Interaction design techniques. In instructional interactions, interactivity is restricted and awareness is formed through simplifying and bringing attention to important aspects of the kinesthetic sensation. Simplification can be accomplished through *Phrasing*, *Forming*, and *Abstracting* movement. We borrow these terms from Moen's interpretation of movement themes developed by Blom and Chaplin [15]. Fogtmann's ideas of *Explicit Motivation* [7] and adjusting the *Degree of Difficulty* [6] can also be utilized in instructional interactions.

Exploratory Interaction design techniques are useful for creating a system for Kinesthetic Means. In these types of systems it is important to build awareness through engaging the user. In exploratory interactions, interactivity and agency are increased through opening up the dialogue between the system and the user. We suggest Moen's concept of *Imitate-React-Express* [15] and *Implicit Motivation* put forth by Fogtmann et al (2008) [7] are ways to develop these types of interactions.

Lastly, Translational Interaction can be used to create a system for Kinesthetic Disorder. In translational interactions, designers recontextualize the kinesthetic experience to attract users and sustain engagement. We propose that Instructional, Exploratory, and Translational Interactions can be designed in concert with one another to guide users through kinesthetic experiences. These interactions can help build kinesthetic awareness from multiple perspectives and in turn support and heighten kinesthetic empathy.

SERPENTINE DANCE, REFOCUSED

SDR first premiered on April 10, 2014 at the exhibition *Medium: Play* in Vancouver, BC Canada. The artistic design was created by Shannon Cuykendall, the mechanical design was created by Jacob Freiberg, and the physical computing design was created by Karen Cochrane. Video images were projected onto a 20' x 10' white sheet using a short throw projector. The surface of the screen gently rippled in response to a fan (see Figure 3). SDR explores relationships between experiencing and perceiving movement, while also questioning the boundaries between chaos and clarity. We invited participants to take a spin on a chair while watching Loïe Fuller's (1862-1928) famous *Serpentine Dance* (1891). We further abstract the *Serpentine Dance* into psychedelic swirling images of color and motion and entice participants to spin continuously, which is a prominent action in Fuller's choreography. Through spinning, the human form and original video of the *Serpentine Dance* is revealed. A preview of SDR can be viewed online: http://vimeo.com/95478604.

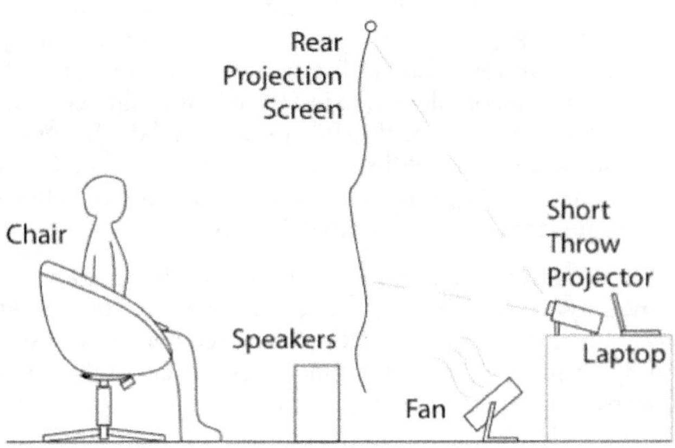

Figure 3. Setup of SDR installation

We centered SDR around Fuller's *Serpentine Dance* because of its historical significance and ground breaking approach to enhancing and increasing audience engagement of abstract dance. Fuller is known for her liberating approach to movement and creating abstract representations of the body in motion. In the *Serpentine Dance* Fuller concealed her body with a flowing silk gown that enveloped her as she twisted and turned in space. In each hand, hidden beneath layers of silk, she held a long stick to manipulate and control the fabric. Symbolist poet Stéphane Mallarmé (1842-1898) comments on the *Serpentine Dance*, "The suspense of the dance, a contradictory fear or desire to see too much and not enough, demands a transparent prolonging" [1]. Art historian Nell Andrew further describes,"The visual effects that Fuller created through motion engaged her viewers with a new experience of vision"[1]. In SDR we sought to extend this "new experience of vision" and intensify "prolonging" by concealing and revealing Fuller's dance in response to the participant's movement.

The main goals in SDR were to 1) heighten kinesthetic empathy by breaking the fourth wall between the audience and performer and 2) entice "out of control" spinning to demonstrate how clarity can arise out of chaos. Although these goals were often at odds with one another, we used our evaluative framework to find compromises so that both could be adequately achieved.

DESIGNING FOR KINESTHETIC AWARENESS IN SDR

Focusing Attention

Following dance therapy research, that suggests physically mirroring movement can enhance empathy [13], we sought to bring more kinesthetic awareness to Fuller's movement by inviting participants to partake in a similar action. There are many features of movement we could have focused on, such as the spatial positioning, timing, or dynamic qualities. Inspired by our artistic motivations, we focused on bringing attention to the sensation of spinning. In order to bring more awareness to this kinesthetic sensation we centered our installation around a twenty-second clip of the *Serpentine Dance* from *Création de la Serpentine* (1908), a film directed by by Segundo de Chomón, that features Loïe Fuller [4]. In this segment a group of dancers spin continuously, creating a mesmerizing visual display of twirling fabric in mid-air (See State 3 in Figure 4). We abstracted the sensation of spinning by inviting participants to sit on a swivel chair that allows for 360 degrees of rotation. The participant's movement was restricted to a chair in order to focus the installation on a particular kinesthetic aspect (which in this case was spinning) and not overwhelm the audience with the complexities of Fuller's movement.

Engagement

In SDR we recontexualized the *Serpentine Dance* through blurring, compositing, and manipulating the color space of the video, producing a multi-colored psychedelic display (See State 1 in Figure 4). When the chair was stationary the obscured video randomly changed between twenty-eight different color combinations every three seconds. These images helped attract audience members to the installation site, and many stood and watched these images for extended periods of time.

Our main challenge in SDR was to entice audience members into the chair. Some of the users did not spin or even sit in the chair at all. In the current iteration of SDR there is no system feedback when participants sit in the chair. This was overlooked due to our focus on one of our main goals–to entice the user to spin rather than sit still. However, we realize now that limiting the feedback can create periods of disengagement. This hinders the user's ability to move on to the next stage of the work and experience kinesthetic empathy.

DESIGNING FOR KINESTHETIC EMPATHY IN SDR

In SDR we provided audience members the opportunity to reflect on the action of spinning through experience and observation. Our design choices were centered around the kinesthetic empathy theme of *Reflection*. We realized through our evaluation the need to create more opportunities for *Exploration* in order to guide participants into a reflective state.

Movability

Overall, SDR was designed to have limited movability so that participants could reflect on the particular action of spinning.

Personal Interaction Space

The chair was placed approximately 10' from the screen in a pool of light from a spotlight above. Two speakers were placed directly in front of the screen on the right and left side. The space around the installation was open, allowing for observers to see participants in the chair. The spotlight above the chair helped highlight the chair's significance in the interaction. As stated previously, the chair restricts the user's movement to the horizontal plane and a seated position to focus the user's attention on the action of spinning. In our original idea of SDR we planned to partially encircle the user with projection screens in order to guide the user to turn in the chair. However, this complicated the technical design of the work tremendously. In future iterations of SDR we plan to reconsider this option and also explore other methods to entice spinning. For example, incorporating surround sound may help increase immersion and movability within the space.

Social Acceptability

An important conceptual aspect in SDR was to combine third person and first person perspectives of spinning. As stated previously, the space surrounding the chair remained open so that onlookers would be welcome to spend time and passively observe. This design choice may have inhibited some users from fully engaging in the spinning action. We observed that many users at the exhibition did not spin in the chair at all, but sat respectfully watching the obscured images change before them on the screen. This may have been due to the social acceptability aspect of the design. Many of the users were professional adults amongst their colleagues, making it hard to completely lose control and spin wildly. Other adverse effects associated with spinning, such as motion sickness, may have also inclined users not to spin. In future iterations we plan to create space for the participant to adjust to the installation by creating more opportunities for exploration and providing more feedback. This added feedback can gradually and comfortably guide the user to spin while also increasing the range of movement the system recognizes and responds to.

System Interface

The system interface in SDR is an IKEA brand Skruvsta rotating chair. This interface affords spinning and restricts movability to focus the participant's attention. We chose this chair because it is safe and sturdy to spin in. The chair spins easily, and with one push-off users can rotate multiple times. Overall the chair provides a safe way for a broad range of users to experience the sensation of spinning "out of control."

Integration

Actions, Visuals, Sound

In order for us to ultimately achieve our goals relating to kinesthetic empathy, users of SDR must see and understand the relationships between the projected image and the action of spinning. In the current iteration of SDR, when the chair is stationary, swirling obscured video images of Fuller's *Serpentine Dance* are projected on the screen. As the chair rotates, the blur in the video decreases, the color fades out, and the original black and white video is revealed. In order to create this effect we created three video states (See Figure 4). The first state of the video corresponds with a stationary chair. As the user begins to rotate, the video transitions into the second state. The third state of the video corresponds to a continuously rotating chair. The faster the user spins, the more quickly the user will pass through each video state. We found that timing the interaction to allow for smooth video transitions, while maintaining the appearance of authorship proved difficult. Once users began spinning, many of them did not stop the chair long enough for the transition from state three to state one to complete, making the relationship between the visuals and movement difficult to understand. In future iterations of SDR we will shorten the transition time between the video states to strengthen the integration between the projected images and the participant's actions.

In addition to visuals, the music for the installation, composed by the first author, mimicked the effects of the video. The music was pre-recorded and featured flautist Rachel Bittner. During the first state of the video, layers of the melodic line overlapped, forming many echos and blurred impressions of the melody. During the second and third state, the music cross-faded into a single melodic line, increasing its clarity. In future iterations of SDR we plan to spatialize the sound in order to strengthen the integration of sound and actions.

Sensors

Only one action in SDR was intended to transform the video–out of control spinning. However, we found that actions other

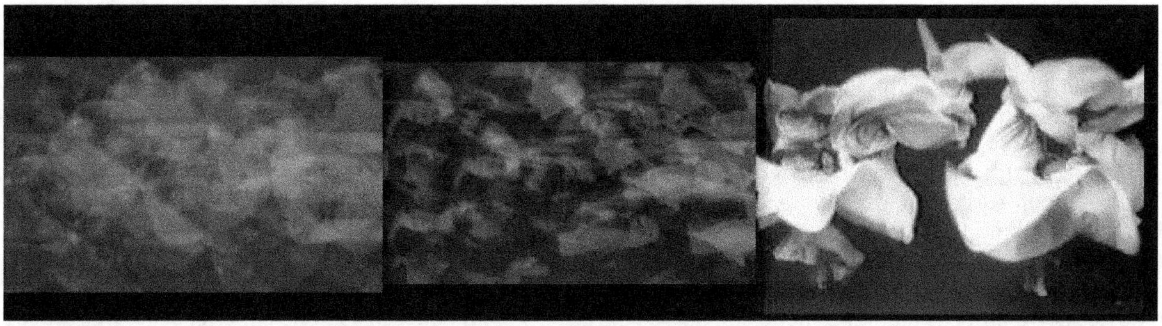

Figure 4. Left (State 1): screenshot of abstracted video image ©Shannon Cuykendall, Middle (State 2): screenshot of transitional video image ©Shannon Cuykendall, Right (State 3): screenshot from *Création de la Serpentine* (1908) film directed by by Segundo de Chomón, featuring Loïe Fuller [4]

than spinning, such as rocking the chair back and forth, also changed the video states. In the first iteration of SDR, we used a 12-step rotary encoder to count the chair's rotations. We chose the rotary encoder because it allowed the installation to be integrated and presented within a wide variety of spaces and was designed to easily measure rotations. We briefly considered tracking the chair's rotations with a camera; however, decided against this method due to uncontrollable interferences that affect camera tracking, such as lighting or accidental obstruction of the camera's view. The rotary encoder was also very stable when the chair was not moving so that it would not send spurious signals at rest.

In the first iteration of SDR, a decision was made to measure the rotational speed of movement and to ignore the direction of rotation. This became very consequential later when the work was presented. In practice, this meant that any changes in the signal coming from the rotary encoder would be interpreted as spinning, including small back and forth rocking movements. In the current iteration of SDR, both direction and rotational speed are factored into the interaction. Additionally, we conducted an analysis and created a taxonomy of movement interactions that participants executed during the first exhibition of SDR. In the following section we describe our decision to change the sensor to an accelerometer based on this analysis. By changing the sensor to an accelerometer, we can measure more nuanced interactions, which allows us to more closely integrate the participant's actions with the projected images. Through strengthening the integration of actions and visuals, we can increase exploration within the system and heighten kinesthetic empathy.

ANALYSIS OF SDR INTERACTIONS

The movability in SDR may have been restricted to the affordances of a chair, but this did not stop users from finding many expressive ways to move. In order to understand the users' interactions, we coded video footage taken at the installation site. Through member checking and agreement we created a taxonomy of interactions:

- *Swivel*: Turning while keeping feet planted on the ground
- *Rock*: Moving back and forth with feet planted on the ground
- *Step*: Rotating step by step, keeping contact with the ground and controlling speed
- *Planted*: Sitting without rotating, feet on the ground
- *Glide*: Rotation following a push off or a step and allowing the chair to come to a natural stop
- *Push Off*: Propelling the chair in one direction with the feet
- *Kick*: Moving legs rapidly in the air to propel the chair
- *Full Rotation*: Rotating around in a complete circle and stopping facing the original direction
- *Partial Rotation*: Rotating to a face a new direction

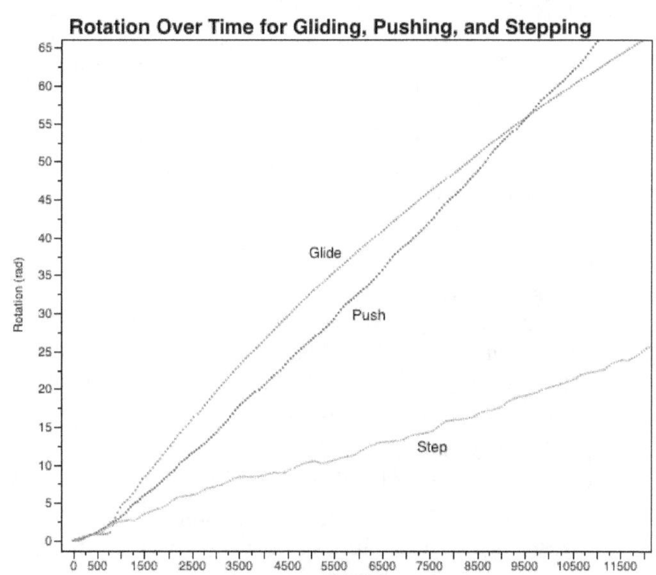

Figure 5. Styles of movement in the chair have recognizable patterns. When pushing off, users maintain speed by periodically pushing with their feet. Stepping creates slower jerky motion. Gliding creates smooth motion as the chair naturally comes to rest.

Not only did we observe these actions, but we also found these expressive actions can be detected in accelerometer data (See Figure 5). Based on this analysis, in the current iteration of SDR we use an accelerometer to measure and recognize these nuanced interactions.

CONCLUSION

In summary, we created an interactive movement installation, SDR, that was inspired by kinesthetic empathy research. In recreating the *Serpentine Dance* in an interactive context, we created a "new experience of vision" and aimed to heighten kinesthetic empathy through physical engagement. Current design frameworks in KMI do not easily apply to our design intentions regarding kinesthetic empathy. Therefore, we extended these frameworks into an evaluative and generative framework, applicable to a wide range of interactions, systems and devices. We propose that kinesthetic empathy is the center of all design decisions relating to movement interactions after kinesthetic awareness is established. In future iterations of SDR we will continue to enhance design features relating to Movability and Integration in order to heighten kinesthetic empathy. We will also work towards enticing users to sit and move in the chair through Exploratory and Instructional Interaction design considerations. In our analysis of SDR we found many movement interactions can be detected in accelerometer data indirectly. This finding allows us to create a more expressive movement system within the boundary of our artistic intentions.

ACKNOWLEDGEMENTS

We thank Malcolm Levy for his guidance in creating SDR and the first participants that interacted with SDR at the exhibition *Medium:Play* in Vancouver, BC Canada. We also thank the anonymous reviewers for their helpful feedback and comments on a previous version of this paper.

REFERENCES

1. Andrew, N. The medium is a muscle. In *Film, Art, New Media: Museum Without Walls?* Palgrave Macmillan, Basingstoke, 2012, 57–77.
2. Calvo-Merino, B., Grèzes, J., Glaser, D. E., Passingham, R. E., and Haggard, P. Seeing or Doing? Influence of Visual and Motor Familiarity in Action Observation. *Current Biology 16*, 19 (2006), 1905 – 1910.
3. Cuykendall, S., Schiphorst, T., and Bizzocchi, J. Designing interaction categories for kinesthetic empathy: A case study of synchronous objects. In *Proceedings of the 2014 International Workshop on Movement and Computing*, MOCO '14, ACM (New York, NY, USA, 2014), 13:13–13:18.
4. de Chomón, S. Création de la serpentine. https://archive.org/details/CrationDeLaSerpentine, 1908.
5. Fogtmann, M. Kinesthetic empathy interaction -exploring the possibilities of psychomotor abilities in interaction design. *Second International Workshop on Physicality*, September (2007), 2–3.
6. Fogtmann, M. H. Kinesthetic empathy interaction: Exploring the role of psychomotor abilities and kinesthetic empathy in designing interactive sports equipment. In *Kinesthetic empathy in creative and cultural practices*, D. Reynolds and M. Reason, Eds. Intellect, Bristol, 2012, 57–77.
7. Fogtmann, M. H., Fritsch, J., and Kortbek, K. J. Kinesthetic interaction. In *Proceedings of the 20th Australasian Conference on Computer-Human Interaction Designing for Habitus and Habitat - OZCHI '08*, ACM Press (New York, New York, USA, 2008), 89.
8. Forsythe, W., Palazzi, M., and Zuniga Shaw, N. Synchronous objects. http://synchronousobjects.osu.edu/, 2009.
9. Freedberg, D., and Gallese, V. Motion, emotion and empathy in esthetic experience. *Trends in cognitive sciences 11*, 5 (May 2007), 197–203.
10. Kirsch, L. P., Drommelschmidt, K. A., and Cross, E. S. The impact of sensorimotor experience on affective evaluation of dance. *Frontiers in Human Neuroscience 7* (2013).
11. Knoth, B. Interactive multimedia performance and the audience's experience of kinesthetic empathy. In *Kinesthetic empathy in creative and cultural practices*, D. Reynolds and M. Reason, Eds. Intellect, Bristol, 2012, 283–300.
12. Martin, J. *Introduction to the dance*. Dance Horizons, New York, 1978.
13. McGarry, L. M., and Russo, F. A. Mirroring in dance/movement therapy: Potential mechanisms behind empathy enhancement. *The Arts in Psychotherapy 38*, 3 (2011), 178–184.
14. Mentis, H. M., and Johansson, C. Seeing movement qualities. In *Proceedings of the SIGCHI Conference on Human Factors in Computing Systems*, ACM (2013), 3375–3384.
15. Moen, J. *KinAesthetic Movement Interaction : Designing for the Pleasure of Motion*. PhD thesis, KTH, Numerical Analysis and Computer Science, NADA, 2006. QC 20100913.
16. Moen, J. From Hand-held to Body-worn: Embodied Experiences of the Design and Use of a Wearable Movement-based Interaction Concept. TEI '07, ACM (New York, NY, USA, 2007), 251–258.
17. Reynolds, D., and Reason, M. Kinesthesia, Empathy, and Related Pleasures: An Inquiry into Audience Experiences of Watching Dance. *Dance Research Journal 42*, 2 (2010), 49–75.
18. Reynolds, D., and Reason, M. *Kinesthetic empathy in creative and cultural practices*. Intellect, Bristol, 2012.
19. Whatley, S. The poetics of motion capture and visualisation techiques: The differences between watching real and virtual dancing bodies. In *Kinesthetic empathy in creative and cultural practices*, D. Reynolds and M. Reason, Eds. Intellect, Bristol, 2012, 265–279.

Scarfy - Augmenting Human Fashion Behaviour with Self-Actuated Clothes

Luisa von Radziewsky, Antonio Krüger
German Research Center for Artificial Intelligence (DFKI)
Saarbrücken, Germany
(firstname.lastname)@dfki.de

Markus Löchtefeld
School of Computing and Communications,
Lancaster University
Lancaster, United Kingdom
m.loechtefeld@lancaster.ac.uk

ABSTRACT
Our clothes are objects we interact with constantly. They represent our attitude and the circumstances we live in. In the following we will present an example of how this information can be used. *Scarfy* is a system based on a scarf which augments the natural interaction between a person and her clothes. *Scarfy* is able to detect the way it is tied and it can deliver information by shape-change and vibration. In this paper we explore the technical and fabrication approaches of technologically extended clothes and their input and output generation and discuss future applications.

Author Keywords
self-actuated clothes; scarf; clothing; shape-changing; wearable devices

ACM Classification Keywords
H.5.m. Information Interfaces and Presentation (e.g. HCI): Miscellaneous.

INTRODUCTION
Clothes are one of the few goods people interact with from the very first day of their life onwards. The style and amount of clothes worn is often based on the social and geographic background, but it also serves different physical purposes. While they can be used as a protection from weather or different surfaces, their most unique trait is that they can also be used to express ones personality, mood, attitude or current feelings. What we wear and also how we wear it depends on how we feel, what we want to do on a day, and on external circumstances like the weather or the people who surround us.

Interactions with clothes include the opening and closing of buttons and zippers as well as the way a scarf or a cravat is tied. With today's technology it is possible to integrate sensors into the clothes to measure such interactions. Users are familiar with the idea that clothes combine both a functional and a representative side. We use clothes to keep us warm when it is cold outside or dry when it is raining. At the same time we show our attitude and our social affiliations through them. This makes clothes a natural choice for a computing interface.

TEI 2015, January 15–19, 2015, Stanford, California, USA.
Copyright © 2015 ACM 978-1-4503-3305-4/15/01 ...$15.00.
http://dx.doi.org/10.1145/2677199.2680568

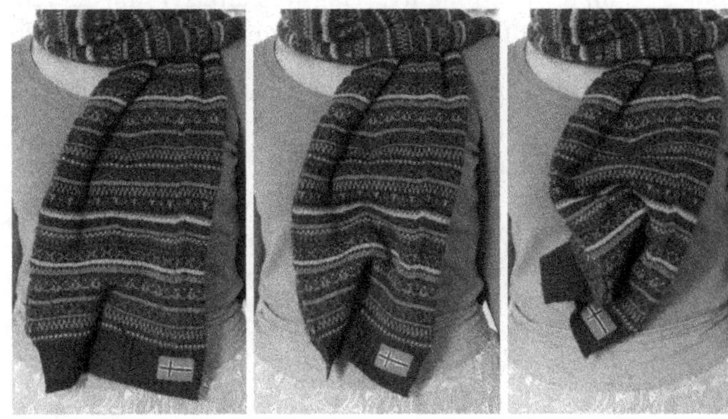

Figure 1. ***Scarfy*** **a system based on a scarf which augments the natural interaction between a human and his clothes. It can deliver information by vibration and self-actuated shape-change.**

In this paper we present a system – called *Scarfy* – that allows to augment the natural interaction between a person and her clothes. In particular, *Scarfy* exploits the way a scarf is tied, to create an interface which can be used in conjunction with different devices and in various processes. Furthermore *Scarfy* allows to deliver information by vibration and self-actuated shape-change, which can be used for notification as well as for fashionable purposes (see fig. 1).

RELATED WORK
We found that there are two main ways in which clothes can be technologically extended.

- The first and most often adapted way is the functional one. Since clothes are normally the objects we wear closest to our body, using them to measure health or fitness parameters is a widely applied approach. There are many different examples of the use of functional wearables in the form of clothing. By sensors physiological signals can be monitored, which can lead to better healthcare for elderly people, people suffering from chronic diseases, and people working in risk situations [12]. Haptic communication between people can be recorded and reproduced [2].

Even the probability of comfort eating can be detected by recording heart rate, skin conductance and movement [3].

- The second way is representational. In this case the ability of clothes to represent emotions and attitude is exploited. There are examples of clothes that are getting more transparent the more data their wearer produces in the internet [5], dresses which move when detecting fear or anxiety [7] or skirts which decrease or increase in length at the will of the wearer [8].

Scarfy is designed as an interface which can be used for both purposes. It uses the interaction between a user and her clothes as input functionality. This was already considered by Ye et al. They distinguished between wearers of a jacket by measuring their heart rate [12] and used support vector machines (SVMs) to classify these measurements. Lee introduced *Hatching Scarf* a scarf which moves if the user reaches into an attached pouch for food [6]. Hartman created *(re)connect*, a garment which creates vibration along the back if the user hugs himself. The hugging is recognized through the connection of different patches of conductive fabric which are sewed onto different points of the garment [11].

In *Scarfy* we wanted to adapt a subliminal way of output. The idea of changing the overall appearance of clothes and using this as output seems promising. Berzowska et al. created dresses which use shape memory alloys to move and change in organic, continuous motions [1]. Perocich et al., on the other hand, used a pneumatic approach to lift garments and, therefore, change the appearance of clothes [8]. Another way of achieving output that is perceivable only for the user is to create haptic feedback via coin vibration motors or solenoids. This form has been used by Bonanni et al. to stimulate tactile perception [2]. Our approach combines vibration motors and shape memory alloys to allow for different notifications as well as for fashionable purposes.

DESIGN AND MOTIVATION

Scarfy is meant to use the natural way in which a person interacts with her clothes to create a fabric interface.

For the input functionality we use the possibility to discriminate between different ways of tying a scarf. An application can trigger an event if *Scarfy* is tied in a specific way or use the information for any other input reasons. For output functionality we use shape-change as one method. The goal is to move the ends of the scarf in such a way that they lift when being addressed. Shape memory alloys already have been used for shape-changing in clothing [1]. Only a very limited space is needed for performing a suitable amount of movement in the fabric (see fig.1). Since there are certain ways to tie a scarf that would make it hazardous to tighten the fabric around the neck while it is worn, we also implemented two vibration motors as an alternative notification tool.

In some settings a user might wish not to use shape-change for output, which may happen because of fashionable reasons or if the shape-change can't be seen as for example in the tying *Parisian Knot* (see fig.4). Also specific users might prefer different ways of tying a scarf for different occasions. Therefore applications which use *Scarfy* as an interface always should provide the user with the ability to define her own personal settings for the output and input functionality.

Figure 2. Concept sketch of a shape-changing scarf

Scarfy can be used for supporting functional purposes like the interaction with other devices or for representational purposes.

Applications for representational purposes: We use fashion for representing our identity [9]. Therefore it is useful for our clothes to provide functions that support us in changing our appearance (see fig. 2). In *Scarfy* we use self-actuated shape-change to allow the user to change the appearance of her scarf automatically. This allows the scarf to adapt to the user's context and location.

- An application could simply use the shape-changing ability of *Scarfy* when worn in a specific way. Also GPS data from a smart phone could be used for adapting the appearance according to the users location.

Applications for functional purposes: We considered different kinds of functional purposes by using *Scarfy* as an interface. There are several applications that might take advantage from the use of *Scarfy* . We present a subset of examples in the following:

- An application which uses the input functionality of *Scarfy* to inform social networks about the status of the user, for example if she can be disturbed or should not be.

- An application that uses *Scarfy* as interface for a smart phone. It can notify its wearer of calls or text-messages. Even if the phone is not kept close to the body or it's vibration patterns can not be felt because of thick closing, *Scarfy* still makes it possible to get informed in a discrete way through vibration or shape-change. The user can operate her smart phone by using different ways of tying. Even if the phone rings during a meeting it is possible to switch it off without anyone noticing simply by adapting the way *Scarfy* is tied.

- The vibration motors of *Scarfy* could be used to create

a massage scarf, different massage settings could be replayed through different ways of tying *Scarfy*.

IMPLEMENTATION

Scarfy consists of an Arduino LilyPad, a Sparkfun Bluetooth Mate Silver, a 3.7V Polymer Lithium Ion Battery, nine Flex Sensors 10k, two shape memory alloys (9V Battery as external power supply for the actuation of the shape memory alloys), two vibration motors and small parts like transistors or resistors necessary for the circuit.

Input Functionality The main ability of *Scarfy* is the recognition of different ways of tying it. To achieve the necessary sensing to get analysable data for the recognition, we sewed flex sensors lengthwise into the fabric. These sensors measure the bending rate and directions when the scarf is being tied in a specific way. Our initial tests showed that the approach already worked well using five sensors, but in the final design nine sensors were sewn in approximately 10-15 cm apart from each other (see fig. 3). Additionally, we added plastic filling to ensure a constant resistance while bending and tying the scarf. This also allows to generate meaningful sensor data as a continuous bending is achieved when tying *Scarfy*. After finding a way of producing recognizable sensor data, the actual recognition had to be achieved. We use support vector machines with radial basis kernel functions and the C-SVC approach as classification tool. With the help of this model, new sets of data can be assigned to one of the trained classes and, in this way, be recognized. The LIBSVM tool is utilized for the SVM training implementation and the scaling of the training data [4]. Since the actual recognition should be executed by the Arduino on the scarf we re-implemented the classifier with radial basis kernel for the Arduino to extend the LIBSVM implementation. Before classification, the measured data is scaled. For recognition, the classification described by Chang and Lin [4] with a C-SVC approach and radial basis kernel functions is used. For multi-class classification, we use the one-versus-one approach. This means that for a set of data that should be recognized, each class is compared to every other class. For each pair of classes, the one the data matches more is determined. By repeating this procedure for each pair, a score list is generated. The classifier simply assigns the class of highest score to the given measured data. Even if we still need a computer for the training of *Scarfy*, this allows us to do the recognition of the different ways of tying using just *Scarfy* without the need of being connected to a more powerful device which performs the recognition. This makes it possible to use *Scarfy* for an independent application as described above. Of course, the ATmega328 chip which is used by the Arduino constrains the number of classes (ways of tying) which can be recognized, since it only has a very limited Flash memory of 32k bytes. For the recognition the necessary support vectors, trained kernel coefficients, and other data has to be stored. So far, we have had no problems with storing the data in tests with six to eight ways of tying. But, of course, the number of data-sets that has to be stored for the model on the Arduino also depends on how well the different classes can be distinguished and the number of training instances used. Therefore the size of memory in an ATmega328 chip always has to be considered when working with this implementation. We will make our implementation of the LIBSVM extension for Arduino publicly available under the following URL: `https://github.com/radzilu/Arduino-SVM`

Figure 3. The implementation of flex-sensors in *Scarfy*

Output Functionality: For the shape-change of *Scarfy* one pull string of Nitinol wire on each side of the scarf was attached to perform the actuation. This results in a very low shape resolution [10]. The movement of the fabric by shape memory alloys (SMAs) at the ends of the scarf only works in one direction. Therefore the ends have to be pulled back down by hand once they are lifted up. This has the advantage that even after the battery of *Scarfy* died the notifications would still be visible. Still, it might be helpful to try different diameters for the SMAs and other implementation ways to create the movement.

Texture of the Garment and Fabrics: To provide a flexible structure of the scarf, we tried to avoid the use of bigger solid circuit structures. The Arduino and the Bluetooth adapter had to be sewn onto the fabric. Apart from this all necessary resistors, transistors, diodes, sensors, actuators and wires were soldered in a flexible way. A problem while working with the flex sensors is that the parts of fabric between the sensors bend easier than the sensors and, therefore, in the beginning the fabric creased only in these areas. To correct this behaviour we sewed plastic pieces in the form of the flex sensors in all spaces. Through this the scarf got slightly stiffer but was still flexible enough. To protect the user's skin from the circuit, a second layer of fabric was added by partly sewing it and partly connecting it by press buttons on top of the circuit. Now it is possible to use the scarf normally but it is still easy to get access to the circuit.

EVALUATION

To evaluate the chosen classification system we ran recognition tests using *Scarfy* and LIBSVM with data-sets of 8 test persons. With their help we collected data of five different ways of tying. Four of these ways were trained by the participants – drape, once around, twice around, and parisian knot – (see fig. 4) and a fifth set of data was collected by measuring while the scarf was simply lying straight. Every binding is represented by a set of 30 measurements. The data was collected by asking the participant to tie the scarf in a

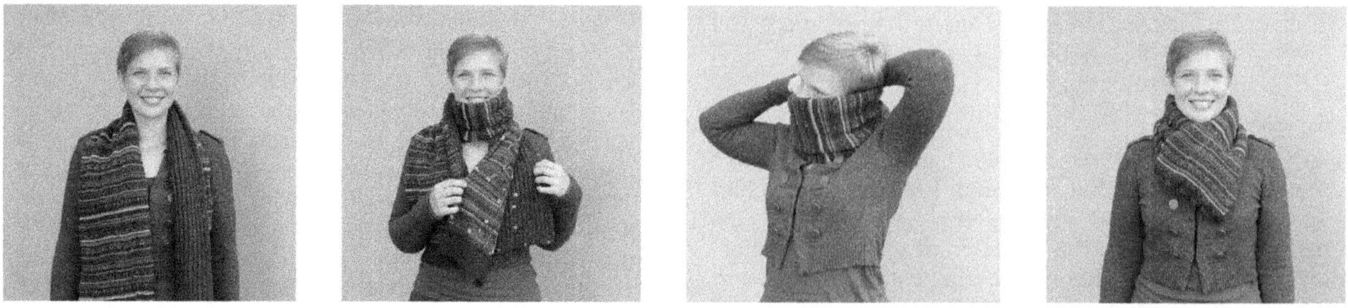

Figure 4. Different ways to tie *Scarfy*
From left to right: drape, once around, twice around, and parisian knot

specific way, when she had done so we measured the flex-sensor values the first time, then the participant was asked to move the binding twice, after each movement we measured again. After these three measurements, the participant had to open the scarf completely and tie it again. Each participant repeated this procedure 10 times for each way of tying. For evaluation we first trained the SVM with the data-sets of only one participant.

By 10-fold cross validation we measured an average recognition rate of 96,59 % (MD 97,51%, SD 2,74%). Secondly we trained the SVM with the data of all participants and validated the recognition accuracy by 10-fold cross validation. The result was a recognition rate of 94,70%. In the last test we wanted to know how the recognition would be if *Scarfy* is trained by data-sets from other people than the ones using it. Therefore we trained the SVM with the data-sets of first 3 then 5 then 7-participants and let the model predict the bindings of one of the data-sets not used for training. It appears that the recognition rate increases with the number of training sets used. With 3 sets we measured an average recognition rate of 79,93% (MD 78,17%, SD 6,80%). With 5 sets an average recognition rate of 81,33% (MD 81,10%, SD 7,42%) and with 7 sets an average recognition rate of 84,20% (MD 84,65%, SD 7,17%). This gives us reason to believe that the results from the 7 to 1 approach can be improved by using more training data. The tests made clear that recognition works sufficient when the training is performed using data-sets that are not personalized, but improves with the use of personalized data.

FUTURE WORK AND CONCLUSION

In this paper we have presented *Scarfy*, a system based on a scarf that uses the natural interaction between a user and her clothes to create a fabric interface. It has the ability to distinguish different ways of tying with the help of support vector machines and can deliver information by self-actuated shape-changing and vibration. The main task for the future is to implement different applications on different devices that use *Scarfy*. In these applications the functional use of *Scarfy* and its fashionable use should be considered. The improvement of the actuation of *Scarfy* is left to a future prototype. To achieve this, different implementations of the shape memory alloys in the ends of the scarf should be considered. *Scarfy* could also be extended by adding more shape-change possibilities through the whole length of the scarf so that it can be pulled together automatically when it is cold outside and provide a better warming ability through the increased density.

REFERENCES

1. J. Berzowska and D. Mainstone. Skorpions: Kinetic electronic garments. In *ACM SIGGRAPH 2008 Talks*, SIGGRAPH '08, pages 46:1–46:1, New York, NY, USA, 2008. ACM.
2. L. Bonanni, C. Vaucelle, J. Lieberman, and O. Zuckerman. Taptap: A haptic wearable for asynchronous distributed touch therapy. In *CHI '06 Extended Abstracts on Human Factors in Computing Systems*, CHI EA '06, pages 580–585, New York, NY, USA, 2006. ACM.
3. E. Carroll, M. Czerwinski, A. Roseway, A. Kapoor, P. Johns, K. Rowan, and M. Schraefel. Food and mood: Just-in-time support for emotional eating. In *Affective Computing and Intelligent Interaction (ACII), 2013 Humaine Association Conference on*, pages 252–257, Sept 2013.
4. C.-C. Chang and C.-J. Lin. LIBSVM: A library for support vector machines. *ACM Transactions on Intelligent Systems and Technology*, 2:27:1–27:27, 2011. Software available at `http://www.csie.ntu.edu.tw/~cjlin/libsvm`.
5. X. Chen and P. G. C. Oliveira. x.pose. https://www.behance.net/gallery/17256769/xpose, July 2014.
6. Y. Lee. Hatching scarf: A critical design about anxiety and persuasive computing. In *Proceedings of the 8th International Conference on Tangible, Embedded and Embodied Interaction*, TEI '14, pages 321–322, New York, NY, USA, 2013. ACM.
7. H. Lin. Envella: Making space personal. In *Proceedings of the 17th International Symposium on Electronic Art, ISEA2011*, 2011.
8. L. Perovich, P. Mothersill, and J. B. Farah. Awakened apparel: Embedded soft actuators for expressive fashion and functional garments. In *Proceedings of the 8th International Conference on Tangible, Embedded and Embodied Interaction*, TEI '14, pages 77–80, New York, NY, USA, 2013. ACM.
9. M. E. Roach-Higgins and J. Eicher. Dress and identity. In *Clothing and Textiles Research Journal*, 10, 1-8, 1992.
10. A. Roudaut, A. Karnik, M. Löchtefeld, and S. Subramanian. Morphees: Toward high "shape resolution" in self-actuated flexible mobile devices. In *Proceedings of the SIGCHI Conference on Human Factors in Computing Systems*, CHI '13, pages 593–602, New York, NY, USA, 2013. ACM.
11. S. Seymour. *Fashionable Technology, the intersection of design, fashion, science, and technology*. SpringerWienNewYork, 2008.
12. C. Ye, B. V. K. V. Kumar, and M. T. Coimbra. Human identification based on ecg signals from wearable health monitoring devices. In *Proceedings of the 4th International Symposium on Applied Sciences in Biomedical and Communication Technologies*, ISABEL '11, pages 25:1–25:5, New York, NY, USA, 2011. ACM.

An Accessible Platform for Exploring Haptic Interactions with Co-located Capacitive and Piezoresistive Sensors

Adrian Freed
CNMAT - UC Berkeley
1750 Arch Street,
Berkeley, CA 94709
adrian@cnmat.berkeley.edu

David Wessel
CNMAT - UC Berkeley
1750 Arch Street,
Berkeley, CA 94709
wessel@cnmat.berkeley.edu

ABSTRACT
This paper introduces an open research platform for exploring haptic interactions with co-located, capacitive and piezoresistive sensors. The solution uses readily available material, hardware and software components and allows for experiments on many system levels from low-level material concerns up to high-level sensor fusion software. This provides the HCI community with a platform to accelerate explorations of the many applications that have opened up of sensor fusion in haptic interaction.

Author Keywords
Haptic Interaction; Sensor Platform; Piezoresistive Sensing; Capacitive Sensing; Sensor Fusion

ACM Classification Keywords
H.5.2. User Interfaces: Haptic I/O; Input devices and strategies; Prototyping

INTRODUCTION
The massification of portable touch screen devices in the last decade has precipitated a surge in investment in research and development of surface sensing techniques. One common theme has emerged in this work: the co-location of multiple sensing techniques. Many patents have been issued [17] and filed around combining capacitive and resistive sensing in particular [6] [7] [1] [16] [15].

Unfortunately, the mass manufacturing techniques used in modern, touch-screens are not readily accessible to laboratory experimenters and vernacular engineers (a.k.a. DIY, makers, bricoleurs). Also vendors are often reticent to share low-level access to their sensor streams preferring instead to wrap their innovations in high level, black-boxed Application Programmer Interfaces (API). The platform described in this paper enables many interesting explorations of the interaction potential of hybrid surface sensing without requiring exotic materials or challenging construction techniques. "Off-the-shelf" materials are used for the physical aspects and all the software required is freely available.

TEI '15, January 16 – 19, 2015, Stanford, CA, USA.

ACM 978-1-4503-3305-4/15/01…$15.00.
http://dx.doi.org/10.1145/2677199.2680571

STRUCTURE AND CONTRIBUTION
After a description of the platform, some prototypes are introduced with an elaboration of some experiments associated with them. Apart from the contribution of the platform itself, this paper points to the value of using sensor fusion to leverage the temporal aspects of sensor measurements and broaden the sphere of use of tangible sensing systems.

CO-LOCATED SENSOR PLATFORM

Sensor Components
Sensor components are assembled from readily available conductive materials or piezoresistive sensors from Interlink. In the first device we present, a round sensor (model number 30-81794) is switched between resistive and capacitive modes. For the second device, the interdigitated conductors of a square FSR (30-73528) were separated from the piezoresistive backing material and stacked onto a piezoresistive track pad (54-00031). These configurations correspond to the two major design patterns seen in the literature and prior art: 1) shared, switched components and 2) stacked layers with fixed-function capacitive and resistive sensing.

Microcontrollor Data Acquisition
The Freescale MK20DX256 microcontroller was chosen for this work because it includes dedicated capacitance measurement hardware, two 16-bit ADC's, and it provides a dozen I/O pins that can be dynamically switched among many functions: digital output, digital input, input with pull-up resistors, analog voltage input and capacitance sensing. This microcontroller is available in a compact board (Teensy 3.1) for which a free, multi-platform software development environment is available (Arduino and Teensyduino).

Sensor Fusion and Signal Conditioning
The platform includes:

- A Freescale 96MHz ARM 32-bit microcontroller that can perform sensor fusion computations and run gesture analysis and estimation algorithms. For development purposes, it is mostly used for data acquisition, time stamping and to transmit the measurands to a more powerful host computer via USB or Ethernet.

- The o.io component [3] of the odot system running on the host computer in the freely-available PD or commercially-supported Max/MSP/Jitter programming environments. This is used to display, process and map the sensor data. Mappings to sound facilitate experiments on the temporal aspects of gesture leveraging the particular capabilities of the human auditory system.
- The expression language of the "odot" system [4] provides arithmetic operations on high resolution time stamps allowing, for example, the computation of velocity estimates of touch and motion parameter vectors.

CASE STUDIES

Switched Modality

This example employs a single sensing system and rapidly switches between resistive and capacitive measurement modes.

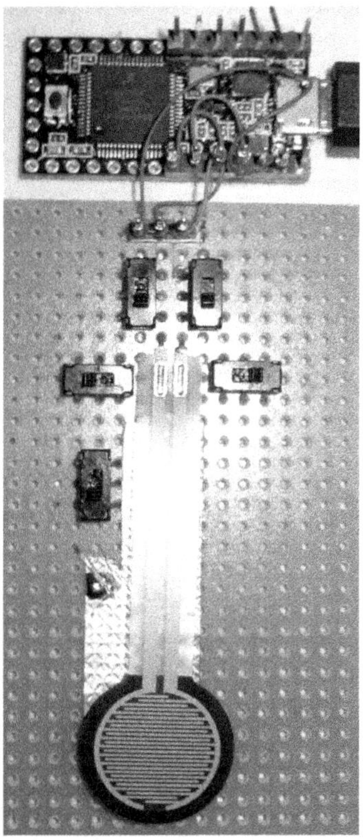

Figure 1. Microcontroller, Fault-simulating Switches and FSR.

The round Force Sensing Resistor (FSR) at the bottom of Figure 1 is made from an interdigitated array of printed silver ink conductors separated from a semiconducting, piezoresistive substrate by an air gap. Displacement (from the press of a finger) brings the conductive and semiconducting substrates into contact. These FSR's thereby combine a switching action and a compression-sensing action. Other researchers and suppliers use this common design pattern. The separating function has been implemented in various devices by exploiting the mechanical properties of the plastic layers involved, using trapped air [10], sparse arrays of elastomeric dots [2] or porous fabric nets [11].

While the conductive elements are separated from the resistive material, they can be used as plates for capacitive sensing. One of the interdigitated conductors is grounded. The other is connected to two different input pins of the Teensy microcontroller board. One of those pins is switched between capacitive and voltage measurement modes; the other provides a "pull-up" resistor to the 3.3v supply rail that is only enabled during voltage measurements. This provides the current source needed to estimate electrical resistance values from the measured input voltages.

Switching between sense modalities is determined by the actual values obtained in each mode: sudden large increases in measured capacitance signal the closures of the switching action of the sensor. This precipitates the transition to resistive measurements. Jumps to high voltage values, measured during resistive mode, signal the separations from the resistive material, prompting a return to capacitive measurements.

The simple prototype of Figure 1 was developed to learn whether capacitance sensing could serve as a degraded-performance backup of a resistive sensor system subject to wear and failures [8]. The dark slide switches allow simulation of broken leads to the sensor, shorts to ground and shorts between the leads. We have confirmed that a finger press on the sensor can be detected in all the fault scenarios except (as we expected) for the case of both leads shorted to ground or both leads broken. We were, in those cases, able to establish and report the nature of the fault.

We learned from this prototype that the proximity of the resistive surface to the conductors produces a significant shunt capacitance that shapes the e-field and reduces sensitivity of the capacitive sensing to a usable range of 4mm from finger to surface.

Stacking a special-purpose sensor on top of a resistive sensor allows for a reduction of capacitive coupling and increased sensitivity and dynamic range for proximity estimation. This is explored in the following section.

Stacked Concurrent Sensors

The sensor system of Figure 2 includes a piezoresistive track pad that senses position and pressure of a single finger touch or stylus point. It has a thick protective upper layer to resist wear from pens in "point of sale" applications. The interdigitated conductors glued on top were taken from a square FSR from Interlink. Its original resistive layer was peeled off and put aside leaving just the conductors that are used primarily as a proximity sensor, complementing the position and pressure sensing of the track pad underneath.

Figure 2. Stacked Track Pad and Interdigitated Surface Sensor

It is well known that the accuracy of position and pressure measurements in piezoresistive materials decreases at low contact pressures–a problem partially addressed using complex machine learning techniques that require calibration tasks [14]. Capacitive proximity measurements provide an alternative approach to ameliorate this situation by giving more accurate temporal information about the points of arrival and departure of touch gestures. This is especially useful in musical-instrument applications, for example, where moderate latencies of a few milliseconds can be introduced to make time to extrapolate pressure information to transition events and thereby absorb jitter in the overall gesture/sound synthesis signal path.

The key to this non-linear sensor fusion is the availability of accurate time stamps for transition events and acquired pressure events. These are provided in the "OSC for Arduino and Embedded Devices" library used to encode measured data and send it as SLIP-wrapped, OSC-encoded bundles to the host application.

As well as exploiting increased temporal fidelity for surface touch events, capacitive sense data can be used to estimate arrival and departure velocity profiles of objects interacting with the surface. This technique was used in the Mathews/Boie Radio Drum [9], a music controller that measures proximity by coupling radio waves from transmitting batons to a specially structured receiving antenna array. On the Radio Drum a reference plane is established based on signal strength and velocity is estimated by sampling the rate of change of proximity as a baton passes through this reference plane. This method is susceptible to changes in environment conditions. Using the surface interaction timing data available in our devices more precisely establishes a reference plane to which velocity profiles can be anchored.

If reliability is the primary concern it makes most sense to glue the capacitive sensor array (of Figure 2) conductive-ink side down. This would protect the ink from the corrosive effects of skin contact. However, for experimentation we found it more interesting to glue it conductor-side up allowing us to explore the use of resistive sensing through the skin of an impinging finger to estimate very light pressure values before the FSR tablet underneath is able to. This increases the temporal precision of touch and release time estimates and produces an affordance for gentle stroke gestures that don't involve the track pad at all.

We found a usable proximity measurement range of 0-16mm with the stacked arrangement of Figure 2.

From Prototypes to Platform

The prototypes discussed so far are accessible because they are constructed from commercially available sensors that require so little preparation. Unfortunately, such screen-printed sensors are only available in a small number of different sizes and shapes. Custom sized, flexible printed circuits boards are now within reach for well-funded projects such as the multi-touch resistive arrays from Sensitronics, but it is the recently availability of conductive and resistive ink pens, ink jet cartridges, paper, textile threads and yarns that creates the opportunity for the accessible, affordable and scalable designs researchers need. Our platform includes a selection of all of these materials because they synergistically work together. For example, silver-based conductive ink pens can be used to quickly create conductive patterns but conductors will break across folds in plastic or paper substrates. We solve this by using conductive thread at these hinge points attached to conductive ink pen traces using conductive epoxy.

Textile processes can be slower and more technically demanding than sketching with conductive ink, but textiles offer degrees of freedom of movement unavailable to the developable surfaces provided by sheet materials, e.g. sheer and stretch.

Figure 3 shows a prototype that combines custom-built e-textile position and pressure sensors with commercial sensors. The substrate surfaces in this case are the diaphragms of loudspeakers, an example of co-located sensing and actuation typical of haptic feedback scenarios. Fabric was particularly useful in the case of the large, round speaker because off-the-shelf devices can accommodate neither that shape nor size.

FUTURE WORK AND CONCLUSION

An obvious avenue for future work is to address the challenge of translucency so that sensing can be co-located with displays. The requisite materials and processes are becoming more accessible for desktop use as printing techniques for organic conductors and semiconductors improve and the performance of the devices produced also grows.

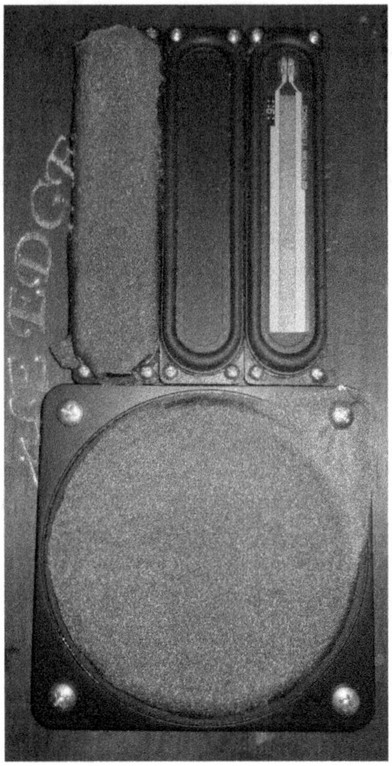

Figure 3. Haptic Speakers, fabric (top left and bottom) and commercial FSR (top right).

Meanwhile we use top projection as a reasonable approximation – one that is especially convenient as we explore scaling to large-scale surfaces such as floors and walls.

As suggested in recent publications on specific projects [12] [5] [13], the platform components presented here can be composed into a wide variety of interesting experimental prototypes for tangible interaction design. We look forward to enabling new projects as we further share our platform and techniques–especially as they move from our core focus of musical instrument controllers to other application spaces where collocated sensing is valuable.

DEDICATION
In memory of Professor David Wessel, his generous mentorship and enumerable contributions to tangible and embodied interaction.

SUPPORT
This work was supported in part by TerraSwarm, one of six centers of STARnet, a Semiconductor Research Corporation program sponsored by MARCO and DARPA.

REFERENCES
[1] Antila, M., Raemoe, T. and Karhiniemi, M., Touch sensor and method for operating a touch sensor, WO 2008155409 A2, 2008.

[2] Eventoff, F.N. and Christiansen, T., Digitizer pad, US4739299, 1988.

[3] Freed, A., DeFilippo, D., Gottfried, R., MacCallum, J., Lubow, J., Razo, D., Rostovtsev, I. and Wessel, D. o.io: a Unified Communications Framework for Music, Intermedia and Cloud Interaction *ICMC*, IMCA, Athens, Greece, 2014.

[4] Freed, A., MacCallum, J. and Schmeder, A. Composability for Musical Gesture Signal Processing using new OSC-based Object and Functional Programming Extensions to Max/MSP. *NIME 2011* (June). 308-311, 2011.

[5] Freed, A., Uitti, F.-M., Mansfield, S. and MacCallum, J. "Old" is the new "New": a Fingerboard Case Study in Recrudescence as a NIME Development Strategy *NIME*, Daejeon Korea, 2013.

[6] Fricker, J.P., Alou, M. and Kasser, B., Resistive and capacitive touchpad, US20010013855 A1, 2001.

[7] Griffin, J.T., Touch-sensitive display with capacitive and resistive touch sensors and method of control, US8179376,2012.

[8] Kent, J. and Wilson, G.D., Dual sensor touchscreen utilizing projective-capacitive and force touch sensors, US6492979, 2002.

[9] Mathews, M.V. and Oberheim, T.E., Baton and X, Y, Z, position sensor, US6222522,2001.

[10] Murphy, J., Kapur, A. and Burgin, C., The helio: A study of membrane potentiometers and long force sensing resistors for musical interfaces. *New Interfaces for Musical Expression*, (2010), 459-462.

[11] Roh, J., Freed, A., Mann, Y. and Wessel, D., Robust and reliable fabric, piezoresistive multitouch sensing surfaces for musical controllers. in *New Interfaces for Musical Expression*, (2011), 11.

[12] Rowland, J. Flexible Audio Speakers for Composition and Art Practice. *Leonardo Music Journal*, *23*. 33-36, 2013.

[13] Rowland, J. and Freed, A. Colocated Surface Sound Interaction *SigCHI*, Paris, France, 2013.

[14] Schmeder, A. and Freed, A. Support Vector Machine Learning for Gesture Signal Estimation with a Piezo-Resistive Fabric Touch Surface *NIME*, Sydney, 2010.

[15] Serban, B., Boyer, P. and Hoyer, D., Method of generating input data, WO 2009021837 A1, 2009.

[16] Serban, B., Boyer, P. and Schoos, A., Input device, WO 2008009687 A2, 2008.

[17] Wilson, G.D., Borgnis, V.E., Kent, J., Lewis, M., Loucks, D., Roney, J. and Patti, M.B., Touch confirming touchscreen utilizing plural touch sensors, US6504530, 2003.

Lightwear: An Exploration in Wearable Light Therapy

Halley P. Profita
Dept. of Computer Science
University of Colorado Boulder
halley.profita@colorado.edu

Asta Roseway
VIBE Group
Microsoft Research
astar@microsoft.com

Mary Czerwinski
VIBE Group
Microsoft Research
marycz@microsoft.com

ABSTRACT
We present "Lightwear", a series of garment-based, lightweight, light-emitting wearables designed to administer light therapy for on-the-go treatment of Seasonal Affective Disorder (SAD). Bright Light Therapy (BLT) has been used to treat SAD for more than 25 years. While light boxes continue to serve as the predominant method of treatment, it often requires a user to sit at a dedicated location for a sustained period of time (30-60 minutes), rendering therapy inconvenient and resulting in unsatisfactory compliance rates. To date, there have been few successful products developed for wearability and portability to ease the uncomfortable nature of light box treatment. However, new low-profile, light-emitting sources yield opportunities for less cumbersome textile integration and wearability. We explore the integration of light into textile substrates that focus on fashion-forward wearables which can, in turn, address BLT efficacy, usability, and convenience.

Author Keywords
Bright Light Therapy; Seasonal Affective Disorder; Wearable Technology; Fashion

ACM Classification Keywords
H.5.m. Information interfaces and presentation (e.g., HCI): Miscellaneous.

INTRODUCTION
Seasonal Affective Disorder (SAD), also referred to as winter depression [10], is a disorder that causes the onset of depressive-type symptoms, typically during the fall and winter months [8]. This mood disorder is often linked to limited sunlight exposure [4], resulting in biochemical changes in the brain [12]. It often presents in regions further from the equator that have shorter daylight hours and affects approximately 5% [8] of adults in the United States alone, with women at a higher risk (4:1) for onset [8, 23]. Bright Light Therapy (BLT), the most common form of SAD treatment, uses light boxes that emit artificial light

TEI '15, January 16 - 19 2015, Stanford, CA, USA
Copyright 2015 ACM 978-1-4503-3305-4/15/01...$15.00
http://dx.doi.org/10.1145/2677199.2680573

Figure 1. Fiber optic light-emitting scarf.

(simulating natural light) to offset depression-related symptoms associated with SAD. Such symptoms include hypersomnia, increased appetite and weight gain, fatigue, irritability, and social disengagement [23, 24]. Light boxes are commercially available and come in a number of configurations to meet the specific needs of the individual. While light boxes have been clinically proven to help in the treatment of SAD, research has indicated that users often find them to be burdensome: 69% considered light boxes to be inconvenient due to extended sitting and up to 19% admittedly abandoned treatment [1]. Our motivation for researching mobile treatment options comes from low adherence rates around using light boxes. New light-emitting materials and smaller hardware profiles permit for the exploration of novel, wearable form factors that can serve as alternative light therapy treatment options.

RELATED WORK
A number of studies have ascertained that exposure to bright light could chemically 'trick' the brain into counteracting the depression-like symptoms associated with winter depression (SAD) [4, 10, 16, 23, 24, 26]. Since then, a number of studies have been conducted evaluating the efficacy of different light spectra [14, 15, 21], lux ratings [7, 9], treatment durations [20], time-of-day treatments [4, 11], placebos [4], as well as alternative treatment options such as dawn simulation [1] or negative ion exposure [24], pharmacotherapy [8], or combinations of these treatments [8, 24]. Light visors, hats or visors with lights embedded on the underside of the brim that shine towards one's face, have also been researched as a portable alternative to light

box treatment [7, 13, 16, 19, 21]. As referred to in [13], various studies have found light visors to be effective in treating SAD, however, some studies failed to find a significant difference in the efficacy of BLT administered via light box versus a light visor. Light visors are of interest as they have been attributed as being more convenient than light boxes as they mediate the need to stay situated in a fixed position [19]. While light visors solve the problem of portability, they are still not as prolific as light box usage (findings from our initial survey revealed that none of the participants used a light visor to treat their SAD-related symptoms), suggesting other factors at play, such as efficacy, acceptability [2], and comfort. In addition, users are unlikely to think of wearing a visor when it is dark and cloudy outside. To date, we have found little research exploring other form factors or more wearable options that serve as alternatives to light visors. Given the advent of new materials such as fiber optic fabric, conductive textiles, and flexible 3D printed media, we explore how new form factors can be designed to address the noncompliance issues surrounding current BLT options.

Bright Light Therapy for SAD

Bright Light Therapy (BLT) has been used to successfully treat a number of conditions, including SAD, non-seasonal depression, jet lag, sleep disorders, dementia, skin disorders (psoriasis), and night shift work schedules[1]. BLT for SAD has historically entailed the use of full spectrum, white light (UV filtered out) administered using a light box. Light boxes can range in size from portable handheld devices to torso-length units and commonly range in price from $180 to $500 USD [8]. Standard bright light therapy entails a user being situated in front of a white, fluorescent lamp or light source producing 10,000 lux [8]. Users should be located within a certain range of the light box (typically 12 to 18 inches) [8] for approximately 30-60 minutes in the early morning [5]. The administration of light in the early morning is essential for proper treatment, as light administered later in the evening can severely impact sleep. The main criterion for treatment to have a beneficial effect is that one's eyes must be exposed to the light so that the light strikes the retina, however, a user is not required to look directly at the light. This often becomes a limiting factor as it prevents users from attending to other tasks.

Light visors have been developed to address this issue, however, visor usage is often met with significant tradeoffs. While a light visor solves the issue of portability, a user's eyesight often remains obstructed either due to the brightness of the light or the physical protrusions of the visor. Thus, users are cautioned to perform minimal, non-hazardous activities. Furthermore, prior research suggests that treatment efficacy is a function of total irradiated

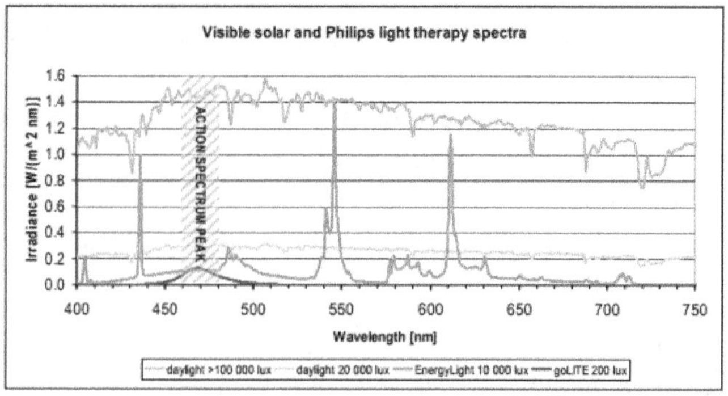

Figure 2. Action spectrum-blue light vs. other light sources [18].

energy. Similar effects can be obtained at exposure to higher intensities for shorter periods of time, and lower intensities for proportionally longer durations. For example, a standard treatment session of white light at 10,000 lux for 30 minutes is comparably effective to treatment at 2,500 lux (appropriate for the visor's distance from the face) administered for 2 hours [20], increasing treatment time substantially. Continuous exposure to a light source can be known to result in a number of side effects including irritability, headaches, eye strain, and nausea [8, 12]. Studies have also referred to the link between BLT used for melatonin suppression, with the result of treating winter depression [5, 17]. The association between the effects of light on circadian rhythm, melatonin levels, and SAD-symptom relief merit continued research. New research suggests that short wavelength light (blue) is significantly effective for melatonin suppression [27] and for alleviating SAD-symptoms [5]. This has prompted the development of new BLT products, such as the Philips goLite BLU energy light[2], that specifically harness blue light to treat SAD-related symptoms.

Light Spectrum

Various studies have tried to distill the appropriate spectrum of light for BLT [14, 15, 21]. While some studies yield conflicting results, full spectrum white light (with filtered UV) has consistently been used for BLT. New research on blue light has demonstrated beneficial effects on SAD-related symptoms [5, 18]. Additionally, applying blue light-emitting diodes for melatonin suppression has been found to yield more efficient levels of melatonin suppression in the 446-477 nm spectrum [27]. This research is promising yet is also proving to be somewhat controversial as high intensity blue light with wavelengths between 435-445 nm wavelengths may pose hazards to the retina [5]. Since the action peak for BLT appears to occur at around 470 nm (see Figure 2), light sources should have an energy concentration around this wavelength.

[1]http://www.mayoclinic.org/tests-procedures/light-therapy/basics/why-its-done/prc-20009617

[2]http://www.usa.philips.com/c-p/HF3332_60/golite-blu-energy-light

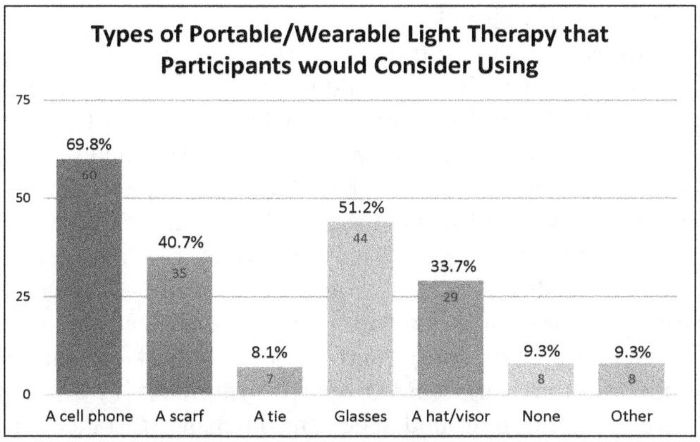

Figure 3. Reported wearable form factors that participants would consider wearing for light therapy.

Online Survey

1) For how many years have you had Seasonal Affective Disorder or exhibited SAD-related symptoms?
2) Do you currently participate in any form of bright light therapy?
   ☐ Yes ☐ No
3) Have you found bright light therapy to be beneficial?
   ☐ Yes ☐ No ☐ Somewhat
4) Do you find the use of a light box to be convenient or inconvenient?
   ☐ Yes ☐ No ☐ Neutral ☐ Other:__________
5) Have you ever stopped using a light box due to inconvenience?
   ☐ Yes ☐ No
6) Roughly how often do you use your light box during the fall/winter?
   ☐ Daily ☐ Weekly ☐ Monthly ☐ Less Than Monthly
7) Light therapy has been shown to have beneficial effects on mood for individuals with SAD-related symptoms. Would you be open to the possibility of using a portable or wearable form of light therapy treatment?
   ☐ Yes ☐ No ☐ Perhaps
8) What types of portable or wearable light therapy might you consider using? *(Check all that apply)*
   ☐A Cell Phone ☐A Scarf ☐A Tie ☐Glasses ☐A Hat/Visor ☐None ☐Other:_
9) What types of concerns might you have about using a more portable or wearable form of light therapy treatment? *(Check all that apply)*
   ☐ Battery Life ☐ Comfort/Discomfort ☐ Obstructions Caused by the Device
   ☐ Brightness of Light ☐ Heat ☐ Any Resulting Symptoms
   ☐ General Nuisance of the Device ☐ Social Awkwardness
   ☐ I Have No Concerns ☐ Other:___________

Figure 4. Select questions from the online survey.

USER-CENTERED DESIGN APPROACH

We decided to employ user-centered design methods to explore the design space of wearable BLT. Here we describe our online survey used to inform our design explorations.

Method

Multiple forms of user data collection were employed in order to gather pertinent information regarding the design of the wearable prototypes. A preliminary online survey was administered to those with SAD or SAD-related symptoms to assess current treatment methods and attitudes toward wearable forms of therapy. This data was used to inform the design of the wearables that were prototyped and evaluated with a pilot study to garner participant attitudes and contribute to overall prototype refinement. A larger, follow-up user study was conducted (currently under review) yielding insights for overall prototype wearability, convenience, user experience, and usability. Overall results complement the initial, qualitative findings we obtained and report here.

Recruitment

Online Survey

To capture feedback pertaining to Bright Light Therapy for Seasonal Affective Disorder, a global survey was administered to collect attitudes and experiences from individuals in regions (northern latitudes) with a higher incidence of SAD. Specific target audiences included individuals located in Washington, USA, New York, USA, the United Kingdom, Ireland, Finland, and Scandinavia.

Online Survey Results

We collected data on 101 individuals (42.6% female) between the ages of 18 and 70. Approximately eighty-five percent (86 individuals) of these participants were either clinically diagnosed with SAD or expressed SAD-related symptoms associated with autumn and winter seasons. Of interest to us were individuals who use or have used a light box to treat their SAD-related symptoms. Twenty-one individuals reported current (17) or prior (4) light box usage to treat their symptoms. Of the 21 light box users, 9 (42.9%) individuals indicated that they found a light box to be inconvenient. Additionally, of those individuals who currently used a light box, 76.5% percent indicated that they have stopped using a light box due to inconvenience. This aligns with prior research reporting that 69% of those with SAD found light boxes to be inconvenient [1]. These figures also reinforce our motivation to explore new wearable, light-emitting treatment options. Reasons surrounding the inconvenience of light boxes were cited as having to remember to use it, lack of portability, bulkiness, having to remain in front of it for an extended period of time while essentially doing nothing, knowing how to set it up and angle it appropriately, and having to switch work locations where the light box is not located. We also used the survey to garner attitudes regarding the possible use of wearable/portable alternative treatment options for their SAD. From the 86 participants who identified as having SAD or SAD-related symptoms, 93% responded 'Yes' or 'Perhaps' to the possibility of using a portable or wearable form of light therapy. We surveyed the types of form factors that individuals might be interested in wearing to treat their SAD. The popular items were a cell phone (69.8%), glasses (51.2%), a scarf (40.7%), and a hat/visor (33.7%) (see Figure 3).

We used this data to inform the design of our wearables and to create form factors that we hoped were both convenient to wear and appropriate for emitting light toward the face/retina. A cell phone was excluded from our design as we were solely focused on wearable/textile options and it was considered highly unlikely that an individual would dedicate their phone to 30-60 minutes of daily BLT. In addition to collecting user feedback on receptivity toward particular wearable form factors, we polled participants on their existing concerns for wearable devices of this nature (as shown in Figure 4). Social awkwardness was the primary reported concern (79.1%), followed by comfort/discomfort (68.6%), general nuisance of the device (61.6%), obstructions caused by the device (52.3%) and battery life (41.9%). Of interest were the top 4 rated concerns as they also closely correspond to existing barriers related to BLT adoption. Thus, this feedback was dually noted for the prototyping phase and can be used to inform future wearable technologies in this design space.

DESIGN

Given the data collected, we were encouraged to create a wearable light therapy experience that users would want to use, or even enjoy using. There are a number of design considerations in the development of a wearable form of bright light therapy. We used these considerations to drive the development of our wearables, however, relaxing guideline #3, as we were strictly focused on prototyping wearable form factors and not conducting clinical trials:

1) Light must strike the retina, preferably from the peripheral view as opposed to a direct viewing angle.
2) Beneficial full-spectrum white light ranges from 2,500-10,000 lux [20], however, blue light has been shown to be effective at 200 lux [18].
3) Light intensity, radiance, and duration should be specific to Bright Light Therapy.
4) Proximity of the light and the wearable form should not interfere with daily routine and should be at a safe distance.
5) Light should be administered in the early morning.
6) User preference should be optimized for the location-based administration of light.
7) Heat dissipation and power tradeoffs must be managed.
8) Social/contextual appropriateness of a wearable device must be considered.
9) Form factors must be designed for comfort and wearability.

Given the need for light to strike the eyes, the wearable prototypes were designed for the upper chest and head regions. Data collected from the online survey was used to guide which form factors (hats, glasses, and scarves) to develop for our study. The light-emitting and other unconventional materials also drove the concept development as they permitted for malleability, form exploration, and alternative integration techniques. A total of 6 prototypes (2 scarves, 2 hats, a hooded neck piece, and glasses) were developed for evaluation. These wearables were designed to align with the current cultural fashion trends of the time (or to be deemed classical) and often were gender specific. Despite one's gender, all participants were asked to explore each wearable and to stack rank the prototypes based on preference.

Light-Emitting Materials

A number of light-emitting materials were used to explore the manner in which light could be embedded into wearable prototypes. These light sources include Philips LUXEON Rebel Color (blue) Lumileds[3], a light strip made up of WS2812 LEDs[4], Sparkfun Fiber Optic Fabric[5], and Corning Fibrance Light Diffusing Fiber[6]. The Corning Fiber was also accompanied by a ThorLabs Blue (470nm) Fiber-Coupled High-Power LED[7] and ThorLabs T-Cube LED Driver[8]. These light sources were specified at the peak wavelength (470 nm) shown to support melatonin suppression and offset SAD-related symptoms [5, 27]. We exercised caution around spectrum, intensity, distance, and lamp and lighting standards (IEC 62471:2006, section 4.3.3) [6], to ensure that our prototypes were safe for user testing. Beyond that, all light sources were purposefully diffused for added protection. These light sources were embedded in fashionably-oriented attire to strive for social appropriateness. Users could then hopefully employ light treatment at their discretion for contextually appropriate therapy scenarios.

Wearable Prototypes

Our design goal was to achieve desired form factors while incorporating light in a manner that was appealing. Thus, our wearables were designed for the purposes of fashion and utility, as certain prototypes enabled light to emanate from below the neckline, above the brow, or at one's periphery. For the overall design, it was important to have a relatively equal number of gender-oriented garments for testing purposes. This is one reason as to why there are duplicate items (two hats and two scarves). Early renditions of the prototypes were developed in an open work space for preliminary feedback. While the fascinator hat, hood, and teal cowl (scarf) were designed with a female user in mind (and the brown golfer's hat and fiber optic scarf with a male user in mind), initial feedback from passersby and external members of the research team revealed that many individuals gravitated toward prototypes geared to the opposite gender. We ascertained that while some prototypes were clearly not gender neutral, we could benefit from having pilot study participants evaluate all of the prototypes as there might be aspects from one form factor that could be applied to another, more preferred form factor.

Many of these wearable items featured season-appropriate designs, thus, the form factors leveraged the fact that most of these wearables would typically be worn in the fall and

[3] http://www.philipslumileds.com/products/luxeon-rebel/luxeon-rebel-color
[4] http://www.adafruit.com/datasheets/WS2812.pdf
[5] https://www.sparkfun.com/products/12712
[6] http://www.corning.com/specialtymaterials/advanced_optics/specialty_fiber/products/light_diffusing_fiber/index.aspx
[7] www.thorlabs.us/thorproduct.cfm?partnumber=LEDD1B
[8] www.thorlabs.us/thorproduct.cfm?partnumber=LEDD1B

winter months – the key time for SAD onset. One participant commented that a light visor fails conceptually in that the functional design of a visor is intended to be worn during a sunny day to keep light out of one's face (and yet it's being leveraged to mount light sources and administer light to an individual). While our prototypes maintained season appropriateness, we realize that a number of these items, such as the hood or a scarf, are traditionally worn outside. We developed wearables that aligned with both indoor and outdoor usage to garner user preference and also to permit for items that could be worn as one readies themselves for the day (e.g., worn eating breakfast or on one's public commute to work) as BLT is most effective when administered in the morning hours. Additionally, all of the prototypes were developed with generic operation (on/off) methods so that the users could report their insights into how they envisioned the prototypes working (using a timer, interaction methods, etc.).

1. Glasses

The glasses were chosen due to their gender-neutral aesthetic and because their larger frames support hardware integration. This prototype was 3D printed on an Edin 260V Objet printer and used Philips Lumileds embedded in the temples for peripheral illumination. Two layers of striated 3D printed clear PLA were placed in front of the LEDs so that it would diffuse the light over a larger surface area (to maximize exposure) and also not overwhelm the eye. Due to the close proximity of the light source to the eye in this particular prototype, lights were placed in one's peripheral vision as opposed to the rim above the eye so as not to trigger an upper lid drop (thus reducing the efficacy of light reaching the eye) [3].

2. Fiber Optic Scarf

The fiber optic scarf incorporated fiber optic fabric on one side of an existing cashmere gray scarf. Thus, one side has the appearance of a standard scarf while the opposing side has the mounted fiber optic material. Two blue Philips Lumileds were embedded on either side of the scarf with a standard on/off switch for operation. When not illuminated, the fiber optic fabric blends into the wearable relatively well as it has the appearance of stiffened gray fabric with small fiber optic cables running through it. When one side of the scarf is wrapped up and around one's neck, it creates a cowl that then casts the light up towards the user's face. The malleable rigidity of the fiber optic fabric lends to a scarf that can retain a semi-self-supporting structure, permitting the scarf to maintain its shape for continuous, directed light. This type of open-ended scarf permits for flexibility in how the item is worn. Some individuals wrap scarves up and around one's neck, while others prefer to wrap the scarf up and over the head, producing a hood-like effect that shields one from the elements. Designing a wearable with this flexibility in mind shed insight on the functional benefits of such as form factor as well as to how a user might choose to wear such a light emitting device.

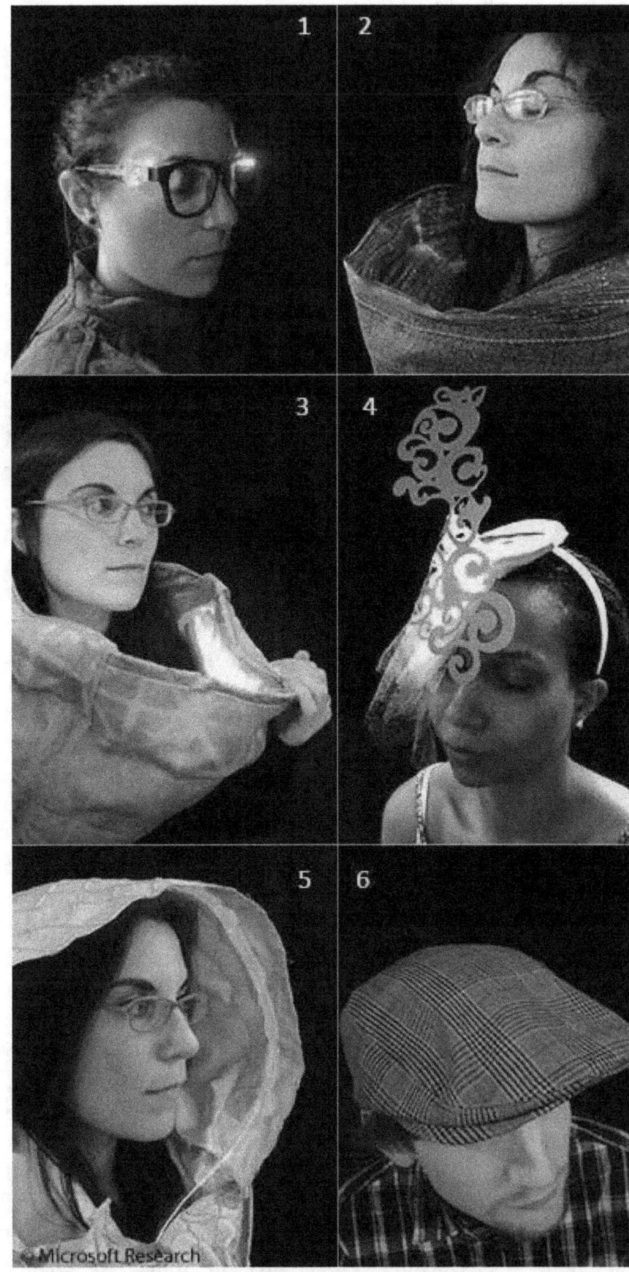

Figure 5. Wearable light-emitting prototypes – Glasses (1), Fiber Optic Scarf (2), Teal Cowl (3), Fascinator Hat (4), Hood (5), and Classic Golfer's Hat (6).

3. Teal Cowl/Scarf

The cowl entailed a neck piece prototyped out of foam and fabric and reinforced with light weight metal ribbing so that the scarf could be reformed to permit for a change in light angle, height, and envelopment. The metal ribbing also contributed to a self-supporting structure that could easily remain in place on a user post-adjustment. This differed from the fiber optic scarf, which could be repositioned in a number of configurations. This discerning feature was employed to understand if participants preferred a set-it-and–forget-it form factor (the teal cowl stays in place), or a wearable that permitted a higher degree of reconfiguration.

Blue light LED strips[4] embedded in the cowl were used to simulate light emitted from below the neckline, allowing us to assess if users preferred light cast from below.

4. Fascinator Hat
A fascinator hat and veil were used as a way to administer light in front of the face. This form factor was chosen due to the advantageous property of the veil extending up and over one's face. In this manner, fashion guided function. However, recently published research has found that blue light administered to animals for melatonin suppression was as effective when administered in one eye versus two eyes [25]. Such a parameter invites new usage scenarios for SAD management, and can be leveraged in both the fascinator hat and the glasses. The convenience of treatment dedicated to one eye might minimize any potential nuisance or distraction caused by the light, but needs further validation in humans. The veil was constructed out of Mistyfuse, a thermoplastic polymer resin fusible used for soft, strong fabric bonding, as initial prototyping phases showed that it was well suited at diffusing light throughout the body of the veil – covering a larger surface area in front of the face. A Philips blue Lumiled was embedded in the outer ornamentation between the headpiece and the veil. An on/off switch and 2032 coin cell battery used to power the device were embedded in the anterior diskette of the hat.

5. Hood
The hood was an extension of the cowl, permitting for light to be cast from two directions: the collar region below the face and the enveloping hood that extends up and over the forehead. We chose to solely embed lights in the hood region so as to disambiguate feedback from that which might be associated with light emanating from a neckpiece. Corning Fibrance Light Diffusing Fiber was integrated into the underside of the hood. This light source is light weight, channels uniform, continuous bright light, and can curve and contour with fabric, making it advantageous for this application. The hood was created to be both soft and malleable, with inner conduits permitting for a guided integration of the Corning Diffusing Fiber. These conduits also help the Corning Fiber stay in place to ensure continuous exposure to the lights.

6. Brown Golfer's Hat
A classic golfer's hat was repurposed with Philips blue Lumileds embedded in the brim to project light toward the eyes/face from above. From a fashion standpoint, this hat differed from the other prototypes due to its familiarity, and was also used to ascertain the differences in which individuals experienced light cast on the face (e.g., the golfer's hat projecting from above and the fascinator hat projecting from the front-side). Mistyfuse was layered over the Lumiled to diffuse the intensity of the light and spread it out over a larger surface area. A switch and a 2032 coin cell battery (used to power the device) were housed inside the hat above the brim.

PRELIMINARY FINDINGS

Pilot Study
We conducted a small pilot study consisting of four participants (1 male, age range 26-45) to gather preliminary feedback on the six wearable form factors. Participants were recruited from the greater Seattle area and had exhibited SAD-related symptoms for at least 3 years. Participants either currently participated in Bright Light Therapy (used a light box) or had participated in BLT in the past. No participants had reported using a light visor. For the pilot study, participants were introduced to the wearable items individually in a randomized order. The prototypes were first presented to the participants on a mannequin so as to gain an overall impression of the wearable. Next, participants were encouraged to explore and interact with each prototype (a mirror was provided to use for feedback and appearance) and to talk aloud throughout the process. Participants were then instructed to fill out a questionnaire pertaining to each item.

User Feedback
Initial feedback revealed that all of the participants were rather receptive to the idea of wearable light therapy, noting the inconvenience of light boxes (in particular, themes emerged around dedicated sitting and remembering to use the box). In general, participants liked the convenience of the brown hat and the glasses. User commentary reflected both function and fashion as advantageous attributes of the prototypes:

P1: "[Glasses] Super convenient. Don't need to adjust it myself and try to figure out what the best angle is for light to enter my eyes."

P2: "[Golfer's Hat] I like that it is stylish...comfortable, easy, and something that I would wear"

P2: "[Fiber Optic Scarf] I like the scarf a lot. It's different without being out there. It's something that I can accept. It's eye-catching."

P3: "I have a knit poncho that would be perfect for incorporating light therapy into.

P3: "[Hood] I wouldn't wear this hood but if this were built into my favorite hoodie I would wear it all the time."

Of particular interest was a wearable that was fashionable (yet not too extreme) that could simultaneously administer light therapy. Two participants liked the idea of embedding lights in a hood or a scarf; however, due to personal stylistic preferences they seemed to prefer retrofitting their existing favorite hoodie or scarf with the lights as opposed to using the options presented to them.

Much to our surprise, participants did not feel that the social awkwardness of an illuminated device was an issue. One participant did mention light as being more flattering from below versus above and cited this as a concern. Participants were also asked to envision different scenarios of operating the prototypes. Three of the four participants highlighted existing, natural interactions with attire as a recipe for prototype operation. Examples include tapping a hat brim to turn the light on and off *(P4),* outfitting the hoodie with drawstrings that can be pulled to activate the light *(P2),* or wrapping the scarf to initiate illumination *(P1).*

DISCUSSION

In this work, non-traditional light emitting materials were used to explore wearable light treatment options as an alternative to traditional light box therapy for SAD. It is important to note that this initial phase of research was specifically an exploration of the design space surrounding attitudes toward wearable light therapy form factors. A formal user study investigating the user experience, usability concerns, and wearability factors related to these prototypes was conducted, with the findings currently under review, but complementary to what we initially report here. The wearable light sources that were used seemed optimal for seamless integration of light therapy into garments in order to simulate and study the preferences associated with light on and around the face. While light sources were used to recreate the light box experience, this study did not scientifically test the efficacy of these wearables on melatonin suppression or SAD-symptom reduction. Although, to our knowledge, there is no concrete link between melatonin production and SAD-onset, existing studies have demonstrated consistent findings when using blue narrow-band light-emitting diodes to offset melatonin production [27] and SAD-symptoms [5]. We see these scientific validation efforts as the next line of research, in addition to conducting long-term usability studies of the wearables themselves. Of particular interest is the exploration of the specific interaction techniques, use cases, and social appropriateness of these factors longitudinally, as they are expected to change with time.

For overall light garment development, there were a number of design tradeoffs that one had to take into account. A balance of gender-specific and gender-neutral designs was a priority, as well as form factors that could easily administer light toward the eyes and face. Some of the wearables were liked due to their multi-purpose function in the winter months – e.g., a hood provides protection from the elements and can adequately administer light to the front of the face. However, participants did indicate that garments strictly worn outdoors could lose their utility once indoors (2 participants were not inclined to wear a hood once inside a building). This reinforces the importance of modularity in design (e.g., a hood/neckpiece where the hood can be doffed while the neckpiece remains on the user and continues to administer treatment). This was complemented by one participant who indicated that she liked the fact that her need for light therapy gave her an excuse to wear a fashion-forward item that she typically wouldn't wear otherwise. This insight places emphasis on the advantages of designing garments with aesthetic qualities in mind to appeal to different user preferences.

With the design of such wearables there are still marked limitations with respect to power and heat dissipation. While the Philips Lumileds could operate off of 2032 coin cell batteries, the power draw requirements meant that continuous operation was capped at 5-6 hours. This could support anywhere from 4 – 24 treatments depending on therapy intervals. In such an instance, making the device rechargeable would eliminate excessive battery waste. The other light sources had different power requirements (i.e., constant current drivers instead of voltage drivers). For the purposes of testing, we were fine using tethered, off the shelf componentry. In order to make these prototypes truly usable and wearable, we would have to create custom designed power boards to reduce the weight and size of the power sources. These light sources would also have to be properly designed to account for heat dissipation through creative use of heat sinks. While heated clothing during the fall/winter may be seen as a benefit, care should be taken so as not to cause discomfort to a user during warmer months.

CONCLUSION

This work presents "Lightwear," an exploration of light-emitting wearables designed for the purposes of Seasonal Affective Disorder treatment. Developments in unconventional light-emitting materials have made it possible to study questions related to what it means to put light on the body for therapeutic purposes and continuous wear. These materials have also facilitated integration into wearable form factors, redefining our notion of Bright Light Therapy to account for portable, convenient, and fashionable items that can more easily accommodate the users' needs and address treatment noncompliance.

ACKNOWLEDGEMENTS

We would like to acknowledge Dr. Marcel Gavriliu, Chris O'Dowd, and Dr. Tom Blank for their guidance and support on the hardware and electronics design of the wearable prototypes. A special thank you is extended to Dr. Joel Kollin, Dr. Kevin Larson, Dr. David Sliney, and Dr. James Sheedy for their assistance on lamp, lighting, and optical properties of light. Finally, we would like to thank Microsoft Research for sponsoring this work.

REFERENCES

1. Avery, D. H., Eder, D. N., Bolte, M. A., Hellekson, C. J., Dunner, D. L., Vitiello, M. V., and Prinz, P. N. Dawn simulation and bright light in the treatment of SAD: a controlled study. Biol. Psychiatry, 50(3) (2001) 205-216.

2. Costa, G., Kovacic, M., Bertoldi, A., Minors, D., and Waterhouse, J. The use of a light visor during night work by nurses. Biol. Rhythm Research, 28(1) (1997).

3. Deaver, D. M., J. Davis, and D. H. Sliney. Vertical visual fields-of-view in outdoor daylight. Ophthalmic Literature 50, no. 1 (1997).

4. Eastman, M., Young, L., Fogg, L., Liu, L., and Meaden, P. Bright light treatment of winter depression a placebo-controlled trial, Arch Gen Psy. 55 (1998), 883-889.
5. Glickman, G., Byrne, B., Pineda, C., Hauck, W. W., and Brainard, G. C. Light therapy for seasonal affective disorder with blue narrow-band light-emitting diodes (LEDs). Biological Psychiatry, 59(6) (2006), 502-507.
6. International Standard IEC 62471, CIE S 009:2002, First edition 2006-07 "Photobiological safety of lamps and lamp systems".
7. Joffe, R. T., Moul, D. E., Lam, R. W., Levitt, A. J., Teicher, M. H., Lebegue, B., Oren, D. A., Buchanan, A., Glod, C. A., Murray, M. G., Brown, J., and Schwartz, P. Light visor treatment for seasonal affective disorder: A multicenter study. Psy. Research 46 (1) (1993), 29-39.
8. Kurlansik, S. L., and Ibay, A. D. Seasonal affective disorder. *Indian Jour. of Clinical Practice* 24.7 (2013).
9. Levitt, A. J., Joffe, R. T., and King, E. Dim versus bright red (light-emitting diode) light in the treatment of seasonal affective disorder. *Acta Psychiatrica Scandinavica, 89*(5) (1994), 341-345.
10. Levitt, A. J., and Lam, R. W. *Canadian consensus guidelines for the treatment of seasonal affective disorder*. Clinical & Academic Pub, (1999).
11. Lewy, A., Bauer, V., Cutler, N., Sack, R., Ahmed, S., and Thomas K. Morning vs evening light treatment of patients with winter depression, Arch Gen Psychiatry 55 (1998), 890-896.
12. Light Therapy. Mayo Clinic. http://www.mayoclinic.org/tests-procedures/light-therapy/basics/definition/prc-20009617. Last retrieved Jul.25, 2014.
13. McIntyre, I.M., Johns, M., Norman, T.R., and Armstrong, S.M. A portable light source for bright light treatment. sleep 12/2 (1990), 272-25.
14. Meesters, Y., Beersma, D. G., Bouhuys, A. L., and van den Hoofdakker, R. H. Prophylactic treatment of seasonal affective disorder (SAD) by using light visors: bright white or infrared light? *Bio. Psy., 46*(2) (1999), 239-246.
15. Oren, Dan A., Brainard, G. C., Johnston, S. H., Joseph-Vanderpool, J. R., Sorek, E., and Rosenthal, N. E. Treatment of seasonal affective disorder with green light and red light. *Am J Psychiatry* 148.4 (1991), 509-511.
16. Rosenthal, N. E., Moul, D. E., Hellekson, C. J., Oren, D. A., Frank, A., Brainard, G. C., Murray, M. G., and Wehr, T. A. A multicenter study of the light visor for seasonal affective disorder: no difference in efficacy found between two different intensities. *Neuropsychopharmacology, 8*(2) (1993), 151-160.
17. Rosenthal, N. E., Sack, D. A., Gillin, J. C., Lewy, A. J., Goodwin, F. K., Davenport, Y., Mueller, P. S., Newsome, D. A., and Wehr, T. A. Seasonal affective disorder: a description of the syndrome and preliminary findings with light therapy. *Archives of General Psychiatry* 41, (1) (1984), 72-80.
18. Safety of Light Boxes and Light Devices. Philips. http://www.p4c.philips.com/cgi-bin/get?url=/sca/sca/110614/110614133710_75542.pdf &ofn="Safety of Blue Light Devices.pdf"
19. Stewart, K.T., Gaddy, J. R., Benson, D.M., Byrne, B., Doghramji, K., Brainard, G.C. Treatment of winter depression with a portable, head-mounted phototherapy device. Prog Neuropsychopharmacol Biol Psychiatry 14 (1990), 569-578.
20. Tam, E. M., Lam, R. W., and Levitt, A. J. Treatment of seasonal affective disorder: a review.*The Canadian Journal of Psychiatry/La Revue canadienne de psychiatrie* (1995).
21. Teicher, M. H., Glod, C. A., Oren, D. A., Schwartz, P. J., Luetke, C., Brown, C., and Rosenthal, N. E. The phototherapy light visor: more to it than meets the eye. *American Jour. of Psychiatry, 152*(8) (1995),1197-1202.
22. Terman, J., Terman, M., Lo., E., and Cooper, T. Circadian time of morning light administration and therapeutic response in winter depression, Arch Gen Psychiatry 58 (2001), 69-75.
23. Terman, M., Terman, J. S., Quitkin, F. M., McGrath, P. J., Stewart, J. W., and Rafferty, B. Light therapy for seasonal affective disorder. Neuropsychopharmacology, 2(1) (1989), 1-22.
24. Terman, M., Terman, J., and Ross, D. A controlled trial of timed bright light and negative air ionization for treatment of winter depression, Arch Gen Psychiatry 55 (1998), 875 – 882.
25. Walsh, C. M., Prendergast, R. L., Sheridan, J. T., and Murphy, B. A. Blue light from light-emitting diodes directed at a single eye elicits a dose-dependent suppression of melatonin in horses. The Veterinary Journal, 196(2) (2013), 231-235.
26. Wesson, V. A., and Levitt, A. J. Light therapy for seasonal affective disorder. *Seasonal Affective Disorder and Beyond. Light Treatment for SAD and Non-SAD Conditions. Amer. Psy. Press, Washington DC* (1998).
27. West, K. E., Jablonski, M. R., Warfield, B., Cecil, K. S., James, M., Ayers, M. A., Maida, J., Bowen, C., Sliney, D., Rollag, M. D., Hanifin, J. P., and Brainard, G. C. Blue light from light-emitting diodes elicits a dose-dependent suppression of melatonin in humans. Journal of Applied Physiology, 110(3) (2001), 619-626.

Fusilli: Translating the Exploration of a Product Customization Space from Digital to Physical

Clement Zheng
National University of Singapore
4 Architecture Drive, Singapore 117566
clement.zheng@nus.edu.sg

Figure 1. Fusilli variants fabricated via SLS.

Figure 2. Interacting with Fusilli with hand gestures and display.

ABSTRACT
Fusilli is a natural interface developed for end-users to explore and customize the design of a parametric wrist accessory. The natural interface utilizes bare-hand interactions, designed to enable end-users to control the parameters of wrist accessory, and export designs for additive manufacturing. This paper describes the interaction concept and design details of the interface, as well as a preliminary evaluation of this interface against a control interface utilizing sliders to affect the parameters. This paper concludes with the evaluation results, along with a discussion of the insights uncovered from the user study.

Author Keywords
Parametric Design, Bare-hand Interaction, Customization.

ACM Classification Keywords
H5.m. Information interfaces and presentation (e.g., HCI): Miscellaneous.

TEI '15, January 16 - 19 2015, Stanford, CA, USA
Copyright 2015 ACM 978-1-4503-3305-4/15/01...$15.00
http://dx.doi.org/10.1145/2677199.2680574

INTRODUCTION

Fusilli is a natural interface developed for end-users to customize the design of a parametric wrist accessory. The wrist accessory (Figure 1) is designed to be fabricated in polyamide via selective laser sintering (SLS), an additive manufacturing (AM) technology. It is defined by a series of periodic mathematical formulae, which control five different parameters of the accessory's design. The interface enables end-users to explore these parameters and design their own variation of the wrist accessory. This interface (Figure 2) consists of physical space which detects the movement of the user's hands via a Leap Motion device, using the hands' coordinates in space to define the various accessory parameters. This is translated in real-time to an updated 3D model of the accessory displayed on a screen. Simple hand gestures allow users to fine-tune, as well as export their designs for digital fabrication.

This project explores an interaction model for digital product customization via a natural interface, where consumers can move fluidly between exploring the possibilities of the design, to actively specifying their design preference.

Digital Fabrication
AM technologies, commonly labelled "3D Printing" by the media, have gained significant public attention over the past few years. Observers have proclaimed 3D printing to bring about a paradigm shift in the way products are fabricated

and consumed, the Economist magazine even heralded it as the "Third Industrial Revolution" [2]. A key difference between these relatively newer fabrication technologies, and the conventional mode of manufacturing, is that the former fabricates on-demand, while the latter mass-produces. This ground-up approach of digital fabrication reduces the barriers that designers and consumers face in producing their own designs. Gershenfeld reflects in his article [1], that digital fabrication is good for personalization and "producing products for a market of one person". This is also evident in the emergence and increasing accessibility of 'fab labs' in different places around the world [3]. Digital fabrication disrupts the traditional route which a product is designed and distributed into the market. It also blurs the line between designer and consumer, as more fabrication tools become accessible for amateurs [4].

Digital fabrication, and the new dialogue between designer and consumer, frames the context for my research described in this paper.

Product Customization via Digital Fabrication

Product customization can be organized as a spectrum, with pure standardization on one end, and pure customization on the other end [15]. 3D Printing and other digital fabrication tools, enables a greater degree of customization of many products due to the made-to-order nature of the process. Atkinson, in The Design Journal [4], points out technology's role in blurring boundaries between professional and amateur designers, contrasting the end-user as an 'agent of design' rather than a passive consumer. In the *Automake* exhibition, his team created a process where the designer designs a product logic which the user interacts with to generate a personalized product [7]. Designer and user establish a 'co-design' relationship, with the digital interface as the medium.

A common heuristic for customization enabled by digital fabrication, is to break the design down into its parameters or generative logic [5], thereafter designing an interface for end-users to manipulate those parameters. This falls into the area of tailored customization as organized in the customization spectrum [15]. In particular, design studio Nervous System [10] creates apps for designing fashion accessories based on various parametric and generative algorithms. Control over the outcome is relinquished to the consumer as the 'agent of design' [4], who interacts with the app and who eventually purchases the outcome through an AM service provider like Shapeways.

This disrupts the current product retail paradigm whereby consumers pick from a displayed selection of products [5]. I see the designer's role in product customization via digital fabrication, as one who sets the boundaries and rules of a sandbox, within which the user is free to explore.

Interaction Design Dilemma

Hermans [5] describes product customization as a balance between the authority of the designer and the autonomy of the consumer. Currently, many of these digital customization interfaces exist as screen-based apps, a reasonable constraint given the Web context they are found in. The interactions are outcome-driven, while the interface design follows current graphic user interface (GUI) conventions, mostly to allow users to vary the design parameters set by the designer, such as the use of sliders, point and click mechanisms, and text fields (Figure 3).

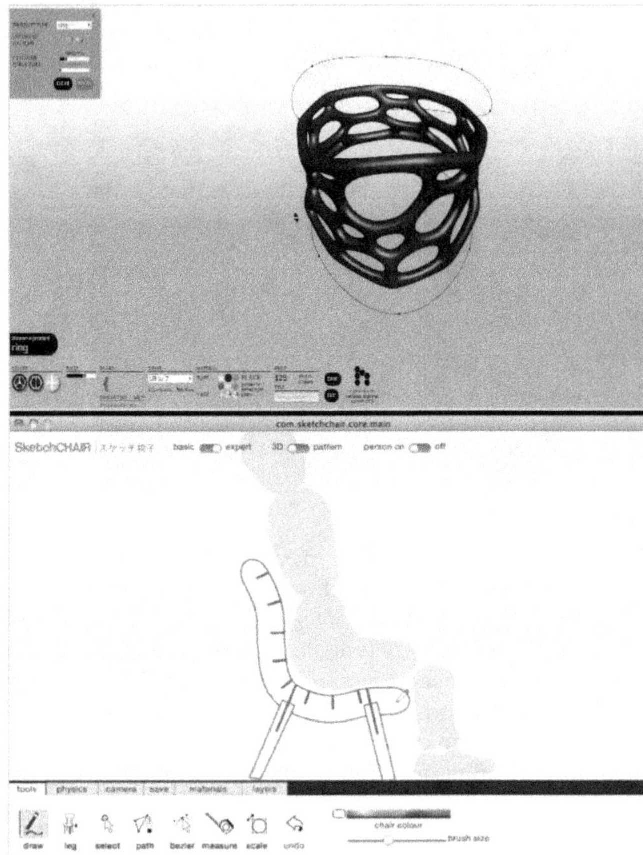

Figure 3. Cell Cycle Ring Creator by Nervous System, and Sketch Chair by Saul et al [6].

Such interfaces place consumers in the position of having to make an active decision on the different product specifications; a position which puts consumers in the shoes of designers. This is an unfamiliar and uncomfortable scenario for many consumers [5]. In the case studies outlined, consumers are placed in this role of active decision making right from the start (Figure 3).

This affects the customization space, which is to provide for consumer needs that diverge the most [8]. In Hermans' study [5], participants faced with active design decisions referred to an existing 'ideal design', and has the fear of regretting the decisions they make. This resulted in a perceived lack of variation in the customization space provided, an important aspect of product customization which I term as 'significant variation'.

Bare-Hand Human-Computer Interaction

There has been a lot of research carried out in the area of natural human-computer interaction (HCI), driven by the motivation to break free from the conventions of the GUI, keyboard and mouse. We see the increasing embodiment of natural interfaces in commercial products, such as the Nintendo Wii, the Xbox Kinect and the Leap Motion device. These interfaces commercially have changed the gaming paradigm for consumers, as well as their perception of HCI.

Bare-hand HCI [9] is an area within natural interfaces. 'Bare' refers to not having a device in contact with the body, while the computer analyses and interprets the human movement via computer vision algorithms [9, 10]. Bare-hand HCI has progressed to detect larger objects, including the whole body (i.e. Xbox Kinect), down to precise movements like finger joints (i.e. Leap Motion). Bare-hand HCI enables the user to interface spontaneously with the computer, with minimal preparation.

RESEARCH GOAL

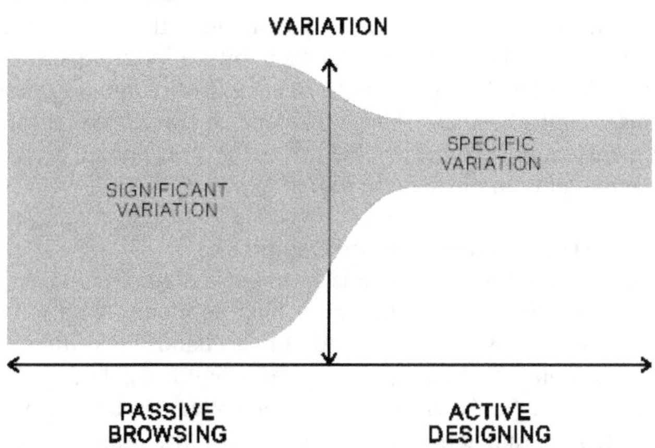

Figure 4. Fusilli's customization interaction model.

As with earlier research [4, 5], I see a need to address the role of the consumer in the context of product customization and digital fabrication. I see an opportunity in reducing the barrier for end-users interacting with digital product customization systems, by introducing 'passive browsing' into such systems; in contrast to placing end-users in an active designing mode right from the start. I propose an interaction model (Figure 4) where end-users can fluidly move between browsing through the full extent of the customization space (significant variation), and actively specifying design details (specific variation).

This research aims to design a natural interface for digital product customization based on bare-handed interactions. The interface should provide a greater degree of fluidity for consumers to move between 'passive browsing' and 'active designing'. The design would be evaluated based on how well it supports the interaction model proposed above (Figure 4).

RELATED WORK

There has been research conducted in this intersection of natural interactions, digital fabrication and customization. One of the earliest works found describe the interactive creation of digital ceramic artwork via special gloves connected to the computer [11]. More recently, separate projects describe a similar digital pottery experience controlled by bare-hand interactions via a Leap Motion device [12] and via a structured light scanner [13]. Both researches sought to digitally replicate the actions of real-world pottery experience. 'Interactive fabrication' [14] describes the concept of real-time control of digital fabrication devices via alternative natural interfaces. In one example, a wire was bent in real-time according to the sound picked up by a microphone, which was eventually crafted into a unique set of earrings.

While the works above are concerned with the broader area of designing interactions for digital fabrication, this research is focused specifically on digital product customization. A key difference to highlight between the works above, and the research described in this paper, is the level of abstraction between the outcome and the interaction. For the examples above, the interactions were semantically designed to replicate real world conceptual models, for example the potter's wheel and hand [12, 13, 14]. This research proposes an abstraction between the interaction and outcome. This abstraction is hypothesized to serve the interaction of 'design exploration' or 'browsing' better, in contrast to placing the end-user into the role of a 'craftsman'. In addition, this abstraction is potentially more versatile as it can be applied to different designs.

IMPLEMENTATION

Parametric Design

The interface was designed for the customization of the parametric design of the Fusilli accessory (Figure 5). The archetype of a wrist accessory was chosen as the customization medium as users would be more concerned with the "look and feel" of the product, than its function. This would allow for less constrained user exploration.

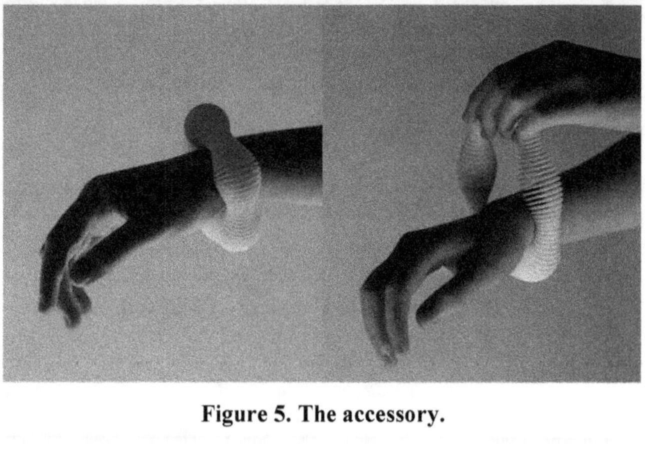

Figure 5. The accessory.

The interface designed through this research allows end-users to vary the five parameters detailed below (Figure 6).

Param.	Visual Description	Variation
1	Number of blobs	8
2	Size of the blobs	~4
3	Density of waves	8
4	Density of spikes	8
5	Height of waves and spikes	~4

Figure 6. Accessory's customization parameters.

Parameters 1, 3 and 4 are discrete values, while parameters 2 and 5 are continuous as they control the size of the other parameters. Based on a visual evaluation, parameters 2 and 5 were estimated to have 4 visually significant steps.

A combination of these five parameters results in approximately 8,120 variations of the wrist accessory (Figure 7). This is the customization space which the interface would need to address. While the parameters are all linear, they affect the outcome multi-dimensionally. Two requirements for the interface were defined:

1. The interface should afford the multi-dimensional exploration of the full extents of the different parameters and their contribution to the design (significant variation).
2. The interface should also afford individual parameters to be varied in isolation. This gives finer control over the specific parameters of the design (specific variation).

Figure 7. Visual extents of variations. Row 1: Varying blobs only. Row 2: Varying waves and spikes only. Row 3: Varying blobs, waves and spikes.

Hardware & Programming Platform

The Leap Motion controller was evaluated to be the ideal bare-hand sensor for this interface. As a sensor, it has sufficient resolution to recognize multiple hands and fingers in a space well sized for individual interaction. It is a commercial product that is affordable (~$100), and it has good customer and developer support. This is important especially since the research targets mass market consumers. Setup is straightforward. The Leap Motion device is connected with a computer running either Mac or Windows, and requires a display for the GUI, either via a screen or projection.

The interface was designed with the Processing platform. Implementation for the Leap Motion device was done with the Voidplus leap motion library, while the STL mesh creation for 3D Printing was done with the help of Toxiclibs' library.

INTERACTION AND INTERFACE

Conceptual Model

The interactions were built on the concept of exploring a physical space to affect the accessory's digital solution space. An imaginary box, defined by the space detectable by the Leap Motion device, contains all the possible variations of the accessory. As such, by exploring this 'box' with their hands, users can move multi-directionally, and thus control the five different parameters multi-dimensionally. Figure 9 illustrates the conceptual model, and mapping of physical to digital exploration.

Hand Tracking and Gesture Design

The coordinates of the hands in the space are translated to the five different parameters. This is done simply by extracting the x, y and z fields of the hands' coordinates, and mapping them to a parameter (Figure 8). Using this method, six fields can be easily controlled via both hands. Related parameters are affected by the same hand. Specifically, parameters mapped to the left hand affect the density, sharpness and height of the waves on the accessory, while the parameters mapped to the right hand affect the density and height of the blobs on the accessory.

Left Hand		Right Hand	
x	Number of waves	x	Number of blobs
y	Height of waves and spikes	y	Height of blobs
z	Number of spikes	z	-

Figure 8. Mapping of coordinates to parameters.

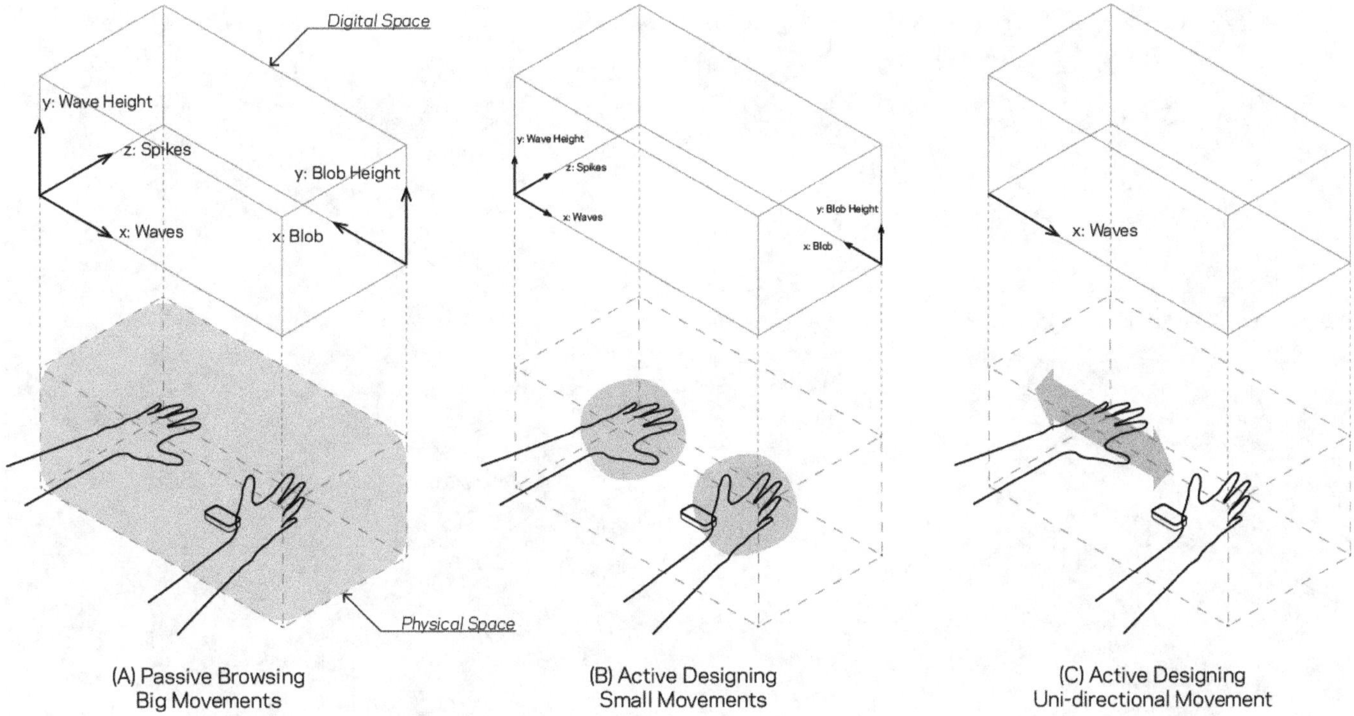

Figure 9. Conceptual model, and hand movements in relation to 'browsing' and 'designing'.

In essence, the hands function as sliders in the three Cartesian directions with this mapping, a common control element found in many web-based product customization interfaces as discussed earlier. However, as shown in Figure 2 and 9, there are no directional guides, only a space for the user's hands to move within. The hand movement is thus not bound by any direction, enabling users to freely 'browse' within the space (A). At any particular point, the user can choose to narrow their explorations simply by limiting their hands within a smaller space (B). A single parameter can also be varied in isolation by moving the hand in the respective direction (C).

This aims to address the two requirements, namely multi-dimensional exploration, as well as fine control of individual parameters. Both modes of interaction can transit fluidly as they exist in the same interface state with no change in control, removing the barrier between exploring with significant variation and designing with specific variation (Figure 4).

A simple gestural rule was designed to support the interaction.

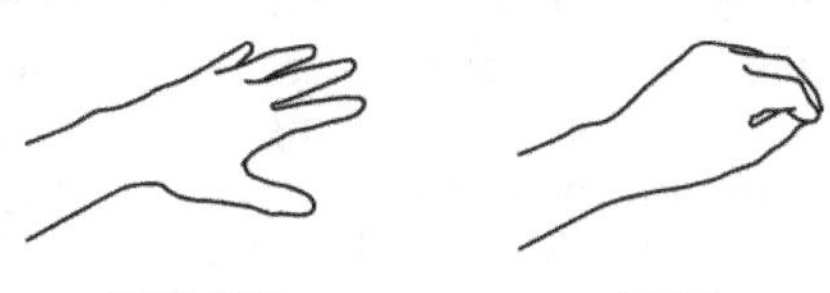

Figure 10. Gestural rule.

An open hand affects the different design parameters, whilst a pinched hand disables the variation of parameters. To elaborate, pinching the right hand while keeping the left hand open would allow only the left hand's parameters to be varied. This improves the user's control over specific variations.

Graphic User Interface

The GUI follows a simple layout, organizing the space to side menus and a main workspace (Figure 11). The user has the options of viewing the hand-parameter mapping (Y), exporting the outcome to an STL file (X), as well as viewing the exported outcomes in a gallery (W). Detected hands appear as colored pointers on the screen.

Button Selection

Buttons on the GUI can only be called by a pinched hand, separating clearly the customization actions from button actions. Hovering a pinched hand over a button selects it. To prevent accidentally calling an action, the user has to keep the pinched hand in place while the action 'loads' (X), after which the action is called.

Hand-tracking Map

The hand-parameter map (Z) labels the user hands' position in physical space and their corresponding parameter value. Besides the information feedback, the visualization can potentially help users to understand the correlation between their hand movements and the outcome.

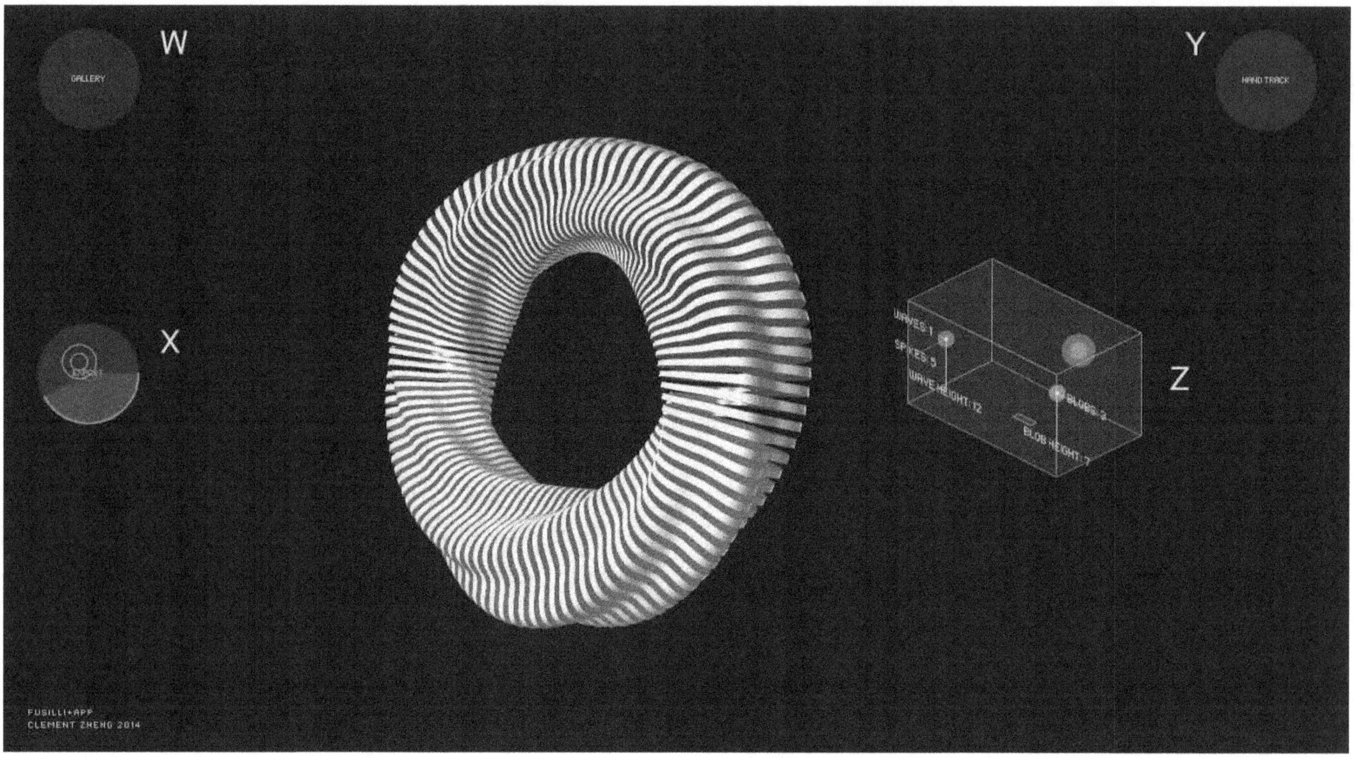

Figure 11. Graphic User Interface for Leap Motion interaction.
W: Gallery button. X: Export Button and loading action. Y: Hand-tracking button. Z: Hand-tracking map.

EVALUATION AND DISCUSSION

A within-group study was carried out with eight users. The bare-hand interaction interface (Figure 11) was tested against a control interface which uses on-screen sliders to affect the accessory's parameters (Figure 12). For the user study, the hand-parameter map (Z) was not displayed to the users, in order to provide a consistent comparison between the bare-hand interaction method and the slider method.

Two sessions were conducted with each user for the two separate interfaces, with a one week gap between the sessions. During each session, users were left alone for 10 minutes to interact with the interface. Four users started with the bare-hand interaction interface, while the other four users started with the slider control interface.

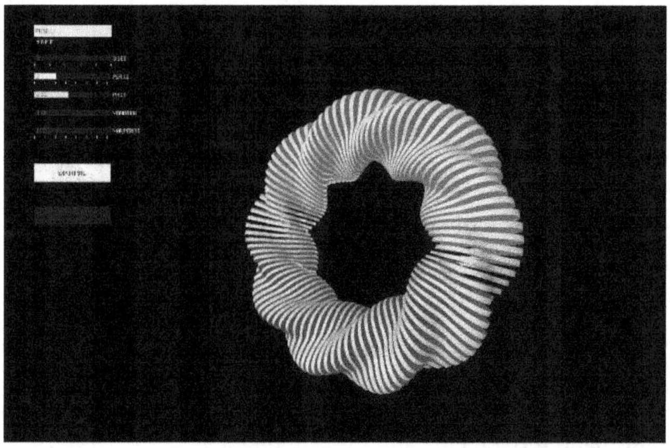

Figure 12. Graphic User Interface for Slider control.

Movement Tracking

While the users interact with the interfaces, data corresponding to their movements and the five different parameters are recorded and analyzed.

Dynamism

In this evaluation, dynamism is defined as the speed at which parameters were varied over the duration of the session. From the data gathered, there was a significant difference between the dynamism of movements of the two interfaces across all users. The bare-hand interaction was at least 4 times more dynamic than the slider control; one particular user was 27 times more dynamic with the bare-hand interaction. This can be clearly seen from Figure 13, which visually compares the movements between the slider control and bare-hand interaction of two users.

Discovery

The variants viewed by the users during the sessions were also tracked. Across all users, the bare-hand interaction allowed them to view a larger extent of the variants possible with this parametric design. On average, users viewed 2.5 times more variants with the bare-hand interaction than they did with the slider control, as highlighted in the visualization (Figure 14) comparing a user's sessions. In addition to this, the bare-hand interaction afforded more discoveries. For the bare-hand interaction, 13% of all moves on average led users to a variant they have not seen before, while for the slider control, 4% of all moves on average led users to a new variant.

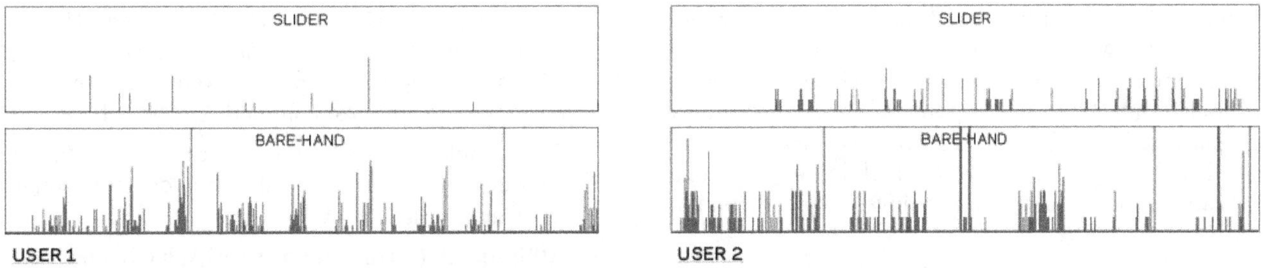

Figure 13. Comparing change in parameter values (vertical axis) over duration of interaction (horizontal axis).

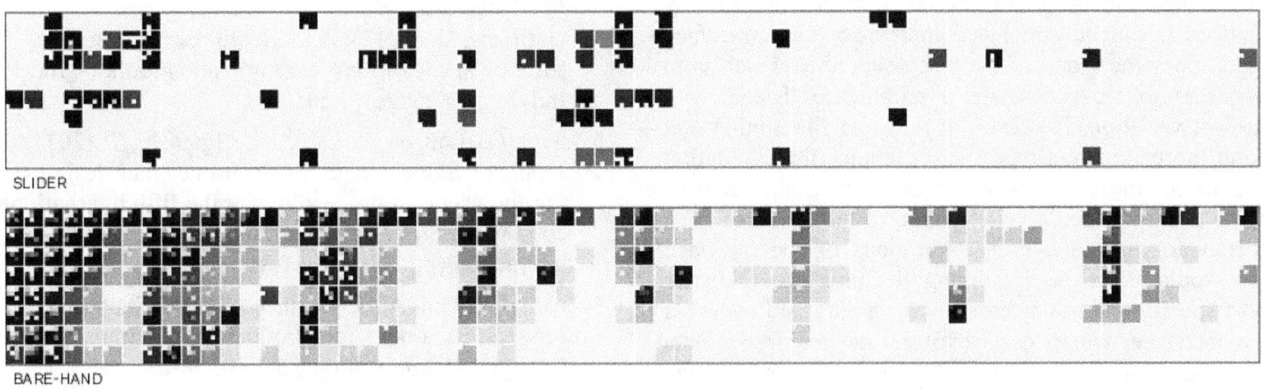

Figure 14. Comparing variant set (represented by filled squares) seen by a user within the total set of variants.

Insights

Users were interviewed on their experience at the end of each session, and these, along with the data recorded from their interactions, uncovered a few insights regarding the interactions evaluated.

Multi-dimensionality

In comparing the bare-hand interaction with the slider control, the amount of dimensions that could be varied at once was a key factor affecting the user's experience. Users unanimously agreed that the bare-hand interaction supported their browsing experience better. Many users developed their own movement logic when interacting with the bare-hand interface. Quoting a user, "wilder and larger movements allow me to vary the design more, while smaller movements allow me to fine-tune the design." Another user mentioned, "I did not like the design when my right hand was too high, so I kept it low subsequently." In contrast, the slider control which allowed only one dimension to be varied at a time did not elicit such responses; rather, it generated some confusion. A few users found some sliders to "have no effect at times". These were in fact the parameters which had to work in tandem with other parameters to create a visual change, such as the number of blobs and the blob height (Figure 6). These observations were supported by the data collected (Figure 13), and highlights the advantage that the bare-hand interaction have over the slider control, in terms of providing for a more fluid interaction with the parameters.

Some users also found it easier to get back to previous variants with the bare-hand interaction compared to the slider control. These users remembered the previous hand locations, and simply moved the hands back to that location to return to a previous variation; in contrast, they felt it was "difficult to remember 5 different values" with regard to the slider control.

Parameter Limits and Values

Being aware of the limits of the different parameters affecting the design was important to all users tested. In comparing the bare-hand interaction to the slider control, many users mentioned that the bare-hand interaction space was "indefinite", "ambiguous" and "loose", while the extents provided by the sliders clearly demarcated each parameter's limits. Even though the bare-hand interaction supported the exploration better than the slider, users were uncertain of the 'box' which they should explore in.

To a lesser extent, values were helpful to the users in interacting with the parametric design. Some users drew a correlation between the variant they see on screen with the values of the parameters of the sliders, and that gave them "more control over the accessory's design."

Conceptual Models and Engagement

This evaluation was the first time all users used a leap motion device, and they were in general unfamiliar with bare-hand interactions. In contrast, many of them have used sliders as a control element in other software and websites. As such, learning to use the slider control interface was easier than the bare-hand interaction.

Despite the initial learning curve, all but one user found the bare-hand interaction more engaging than the slider control.

In observing the users at the end of the allocated interaction time, all users were still engaged with the bare-hand interaction interface, while most users have stopped for the slider control interface. A user remarked that she enjoyed being "surprised" by the different designs possible as she moved her hands around, again highlighting personal interpretation and meaning users invest in this natural interface.

REFLECTION AND FUTURE WORK

From the data and insights gathered from this preliminary evaluation, it can be concluded that the natural interface designed does meet one of the research's aim, which is to allow users to freely browse a parametric design with significant variation. However, in terms of fine-tuning and defining the parameters (specific variation), the evaluation has revealed more insights for consideration, such as allowing users to have a better gauge of the limits of each parameter for instance. Future iterations of the interface design would focus on improving the interface to better support specific variation; possibly designing and testing a hybrid interface, where users explore and export variants via bare-hand interactions, and fine-tune the parameters via conventional control methods such as sliders. Other parametric designs could also be tested with this interface, to evaluate the versatility of porting the same interface across different digital product customization.

The physicality and bare-hand nature of this natural interface, in contrast to its slider counterpart, does pose some food-for-thought about the future scene of digital product customization. At a week-long exhibition in a local high school showcasing the Fusilli natural interface, many passersby briefly interacted with the interface; often simply waving their hands above the leap-motion device to watch the design change. Not just individuals, but groups of people often crowd around the interface, moving four, five, six hands all over, excitedly watching the visuals on screen morph. In my opinion, this low interaction barrier that natural interfaces afford, in particular bare-hand interactions, would certainly challenge the web-based paradigm of digital product customization interfaces; even opening opportunities to bridge the gap between our traditional brick-and-mortar retail shops, and the digital online marketplace.

ACKNOWLEDGEMENTS

The author would like to thank the Division of Industrial Design of the National University of Singapore for providing the resources for implementing the interface, as well as Mr. Patrick Chia, Prof. Yen Ching-Chiuan and Prof. Ellen Do, for their advice throughout the course of this research.

REFERENCES

1. Gershenfeld, N. (2012). How to make almost anything: The digital fabrication revolution. Foreign Aff., 91, 58.
2. Markillie, P. (2012, April 21). A Third Industrial Revolution. *The Economist, Special Report: Manufacturing and Innovation.* Retrieved from http://www.economist.com/node/21552901.
3. Gershenfeld, N. (2008). Fab: the coming revolution on your desktop--from personal computers to personal fabrication. Basic Books.
4. Atkinson, P. (2010). Boundaries? What boundaries? The crisis of design in a post-professional era. The Design Journal, 13(2), 137-155.
5. Hermans, G. (2012). A model for evaluating the solution space of mass customization toolkits. Int. J. Ind. Eng. Manage, 3, 205-214.
6. Saul, G., Lau, M., Mitani, J., & Igarashi, T. (2011, January). SketchChair: an all-in-one chair design system for end users. In Proceedings of the fifth international conference on Tangible, embedded, and embodied interaction (pp. 73-80). ACM.
7. Ertu, U., Paul, A., & Justin, M. (2008). Automake Physics: Random Craft Production. Computer-Aided Design and Applications, 5(1-4), 58-65.
8. Salvador, F., De Holan, P. M., & Piller, F. (2009). Cracking the code of mass customization. MIT Sloan Management Review, 50(3), 71-78.
9. Von Hardenberg, C., & Bérard, F. (2001, November). Bare-hand human-computer interaction. In Proceedings of the 2001 workshop on Perceptive user interfaces (pp. 1-8). ACM.
10. Weichert, F., Bachmann, D., Rudak, B., & Fisseler, D. (2013). Analysis of the accuracy and robustness of the leap motion controller. Sensors (Basel, Switzerland), 13(5), 6380.
11. Korida, K., Nishino, H., & Utsumiya, K. (1997, September). An interactive 3D interface for a virtual ceramic art work environment. In Virtual Systems and MultiMedia, 1997. VSMM'97. Proceedings., International Conference on (pp. 227-234). IEEE.
12. Ramani, K., Lee Jr, K., & Jasti, R. (2014, April). zPots: a virtual pottery experience with spatial interactions using the leap motion device. In CHI'14 Extended Abstracts on Human Factors in Computing Systems (pp. 371-374). ACM.
13. http://www.unfold.be/pages/projects/items/l%E2%80%99artisan-electroniqu
14. Willis, K. D., Xu, C., Wu, K. J., Levin, G., & Gross, M. D. (2011, January). Interactive fabrication: new interfaces for digital fabrication. In Proceedings of the fifth international conference on Tangible, embedded, and embodied interaction (pp. 69-72). ACM.
15. Lampel, J., & Mintzberg, H. (2012). Customizing customization. Sloan Management Review, 38(1): 21-30.

Better Posture Awareness through Flower-Shaped Ambient Avatar

Jeong-ki Hong **Sunghyun Song** **Jundong Cho** **Andrea Bianchi**
Sungkyunkwan University
Suwon, Gyeonggi-do, Korea, Republic of
{ burnness1, boss.ssong, jdcho07, andrea.whites }@gmail.com

Figure 1. The flower avatar can emulate the users' postures with great level of details by bending the stem up to 50° (A, B, C). Colors and flashing lights are also used to indicate both incorrect postures (A, B, C) and long sitting sessions (D). Finally, the stem animation suggests users that they should perform a stretching exercise (E).

ABSTRACT
Incorrect postures and long sitting sessions are among the main causes of back pain and discomfort, a problem affecting a growing portion of office workers. In the past, researchers have suggested possible ways to notify with alerts those users who sit improperly, but often such notifications are perceived as intrusive and tend to be ignored. In this paper, we present a flower-shaped physical avatar that subtly and pleasantly (through motion, colors and sounds) provides an ambient feedback to users about their postures. Compared with similar previous work, the flower-avatar described in this paper presents, through better sensing and fine-grain output capabilities, a more expressive ambient media platform that showcases the potential of media ambient avatars in health-care scenarios.

Author Keywords
Ambient media; physical interface; flower; back posture.

ACM Classification Keywords
H.5.2. Information interfaces and presentation: User interfaces.

TEI 2015, January 15–19, 2015, Stanford, California, USA.
Copyright 2015 © ACM 978-1-4503-3305-4/15/01...$15.00.
http://dx.doi.org/10.1145/2677199.2680575

INTRODUCTION
Poor sitting postures for prolonged period of time are responsible for the development and perpetuation of stiffed neck and back-pain related conditions [13]. As the average office worker spends approximatively 50,000 hours seated at the desk in front of a computer throughout his/her career, it is not surprising that 40% of all office workers are considered at risk of back-related discomfort or injuries [5] - a figure that in the next decades might just worsen.

The proliferation in recent years of mobile phones, small computers, sensors and wearable devices have helped researchers to find possible solutions for this problem, by sensing users incorrect sitting postures and providing notification alerts to warn them [e.g., 5, 14]. Although these approaches are promising, in practice most users who deal everyday with an increasing amount of notifications on multiple devices, each requiring a share of their attention, tend to ignore such alerts or to consider them invasive [5]. Depending on the nature of the interrupted task, even notifications meant to safeguard users' health could be perceived as disruptive, adding stress to the users and ultimately causing frustration rather than pain relief [1, 3].

For such reasons, many researchers have envisioned alternative strategies to notify users in more subtle ways, for example using peripheral displays [11], wearable devices [2], or ambient media - static or actuated physical objects [12], avatars [8], or places [7] which display information without requiring immediate users' attention. This last class of interfaces is also known as calm technology [6], as it allows users to smoothly shift the focus of their attention from background to foreground tasks. For example, with Jeremijenko's Live Wire (Xerox Park, 1995), users could keep focusing on their primary task, while remaining aware of the network traffic condition represented by the motion of a spinning wire in the office [6]. The major benefit of using ambient physical media like a spinning wire is that, when compared to graphical alerts or haptic feedback, physical objects are considered the most informative but less invasive form of notification [5].

In this paper we present a novel ambient system, which, through an array of sensor modules, recognizes users' posture and activities when seated in front of a computer, and then uses a physical avatar shaped as a flower to subtly inform whether users are sitting properly or they are jeopardizing their back-health. Though previous work [5] had a similar objective and used a flower-shaped display as a binary notifier (good/bad posture), our work is different because proposes a much richer sensing system capable to discern among four different problematic sitting behaviors, and a much more expressive mechanical output display, capable of rendering uniquely and with multiple degrees of freedom each of the particular conditions affecting the user. We believe that the increased expressiveness of our multi-sensory system for both the input and output channels could enable researchers to envision new possible usage scenarios for physically actuated ambient media, such as for example, applications for healthcare.

RELATED WORK

Ambient media are those interfaces that allow users to smoothly transfer the focus of their attention from peripheral background information represented in the environment to a foreground task [6]. A prominent early example of ambient media space is the ambientROOM [7]. It is a physical room in which visual displays (e.g., lights and water ripples, shadows on the ceiling), sound through speakers, room temperature, airflow, and physical objects (e.g., clock and bottle) are all together used to represent background information (e.g., activities of a distant loved one, or physical presence of others) and to respond to users' actions (e.g., uncorking the bottle releases information in the room). The main advantage of ambient media, compared for example with explicit notification systems [5], is that they subtly provide information for background processing rather than enforcing them to users (calm technology). Other examples of ambient media include animated information (e.g., collages with news stories) on peripheral monitors [11], personal and wearable displays for near-eye notifications [2], physical and customizable avatars to represent instant messaging contacts' activities [10], and a physical commercially available Internet device such as the Nabaztag [8] that allows, among other features, to handle remote phone calls.

Another approach to ambient media is advocated by Poupyrev et al. [12], suggesting that a combination of tangibility and motion can further enhance the design of physical ambient media. The authors introduce several examples, starting from the Vaucanson duck (18th century), which is the oldest documented mechanically actuated ambient media [12]. Since then, a myriad of physical actuated devices were developed, including shape displays, pneumatic interfaces, tactile arrays [12], and even flower-robots capable of multiple degrees of freedom [9]. Highly related work from Haller et al. [5] features a simple flower-like notification system based on shape memory alloys that mimics the user's posture. However, due to the hardware limitations, this actuated flower is only capable to render two states (correct vs incorrect posture), resembling more a notification system than not an ambient display.

PROTOTYPE

Typical sitting posture problems appears in the neck and lumbar region of the back and are often related with the degree in which the trunk is bended forward [13], and the amount of time the user remains statically seated [5]. Moreover, great changes of posture are also a good indicator of discomfort and potential problems [13]. Our prototype uses two different sensor modules to track the back curvature and the user proximity to the computer monitor (e.g., some users tend to lean toward the monitor to better see screen text). Moreover, it tracks the rate of changes of posture and the amount of time the user remains seated. It uses this information to determine the overall sitting behavior, and, through a flower-shaped actuated physical ambient avatar, it constantly provides a feedback to the user. In the following sessions, we describe the hardware for the input modules, the flower avatar, and the software to determine the user's posture.

Sensors input

A module (5 x 5.5 x 2 cm width/depth/height) with a six-axis gyro+accelerometer sensor-board (MPU-6150) and a micro-controller (Arduino Pro Mini) is pinned to a user's back (e.g., shirt's collar) to track the degree in which the user's trunk lean forward (Figure 2). The micro-controller reads the data from the sensor (such data is filtered and processed by the on-board Digital Motion Processor library), and custom code determines the user's back posture through a state machine with five states (from correct posture to fully bended back). The user's current state is then sent by bluetooth communication (HC-06 module) to a remote PC running the application controlling the flower avatar. All the module parts are powered with a

Figure 2. System overview with sensors and avatar.

3.7V lithium battery and are connected with jumper wires on a mini breadboard.

The second module (8 x 5.5 x 2 cm width/depth/height) is used to track both the user's proximity to the computer monitor and the time the user remains seated. A Sharp GP2Y0A02YK0F infrared proximity sensor is attached to the computer case, pointing toward the user and tracking his distance. Similarly, a 4x4 cm Force Sensitive Resistor (FSR) is positioned on the chair's seat and acts as a switch to detect the user's presence. Both sensors are connected to an Arduino Uno, which, through a USB cable, sends data to a PC hosting the main application.

Flower avatar

We built a custom-made mechanical avatar shaped like a flower to represent the user's posture and provide a feedback about potential sitting problems. The flower avatar is composed by an actuated stem and a pot where the controller and communication units are located (Figure 3).

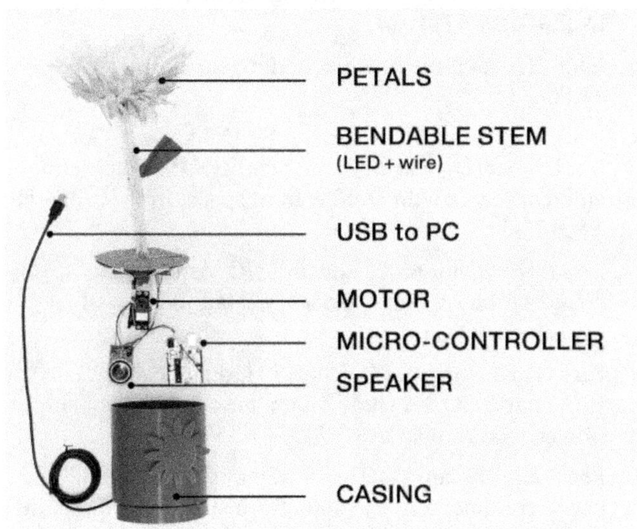

Figure 3. Exploded view of the mechanical flower avatar.

The stem is made by a bendable silicon tube (20 cm long, outer/inner diameter 18mm/10mm) containing a strip of 13 small RGB color LEDs, and a nylon wire that causes the stem to bend when pulled. The tip of the stem is decorated with fake petals, to resemble a blossoming sunflower.

The pot is a cylinder case (15 cm height by 14 cm diameter) designed in Rhino3d and 3D printed on a Cube X 3D printer. It encloses a small servomotor (capable of 4.3 kg-force-cm torque at 6V) responsible of pulling the wire, an Arduino Uno serially connected through USB interface to a PC, and a small audio speaker.

Software

The flower avatar and the sensor modules are all connected to a PC running a custom software written in Java. Using the sensor data, a state-machine determines the user's posture, and according to the result, it instructs the avatar how to operate. There are several output modalities, including LED color changes, stem bending, sounds and stem animations. We describe how sensory input and avatar operations are blended together in the next session.

APPLICATIONS

Using the input/output platform described above, we envisioned four different types of application to help users maintaining a correct posture when seated at a work-desk in front of a computer. Such applications are aimed to track typical sitting problems and provide an immediate but subtle feedback to the users through the actuated flower-shaped avatar. The system is also capable to determine whether the user is constantly ignoring the ambient feedback, and in case of critical but unaddressed posture problems, it can generates explicit notifications to correct the user behaviors. Finally, because these applications are multi-modal and might result in high cognitive load, users can decide, according to their preferences, to run them all simultaneously or selectively in any combination.

1) Tracking back posture

When a user sits incorrectly at the desk, the gyroscope module pinned on the user's back determines the degree of curvature of the cervical region, then computes the corresponding user's posture (state) and wirelessly transmits it to the PC controlling the flower avatar. When the flower receives a request to change state, within a second the motor inside the pot pulls the wire so that the stem bends of an amount proportional to the user's back curvature. Moreover, also the color of the stem changes depending on the curvature: when the flower is vertical, the stem color is green, an analogy of the flower's good health. A bended stem is represented with shades of yellow, signifying that the flower is becoming unhealthy. When the flower is completely bended, it shows a red stem, to indicate that it is dry (Figure 1.A-C).

Differently from previous work that presented a bending flower avatar capable of displaying either the user's correct or incorrect position (2 states) [5], our prototype can describe the user's position with much richer details, hence better helping users to identify not only if they are sitting in the incorrect posture, but also the degree of their mistakes. Specifically, the flower stem can bend up to 50° according to five different states (from vertical to completely bended), each state accounting for 10°.

2) Tracking sitting time

Long sitting sessions without exercise or pauses are among the most common causes of back pain [5]. To encourage a healthier behavior our software tracks the amount of time in which the user remains seated, using the FSR sensor located on the chair seat. When the user is seated, every 5 minutes one of the 13 LED in the stem turns blue, from bottom to top, similarly to a progress bar (Figure 1.D). The color blue was chosen to resemble the color of the flower pot (also blue), an analogy that subtly indicates that the flower is "turning into a static object" because of the user's lack of motion. When the stem is completely blue (after 65 minutes), the system plays a short melody and the blue lights blink, signaling that the user should take a walk for few minutes. If the user returns to his seat after 5 or more minutes (a customizable threshold), the flower resets to the neutral state.

3) Tracking proximity to the screen

Users tend to bend toward the monitor whenever reading small fonts on the screen. We used a proximity sensor mounted on the computer case to track the distance of the user from the monitor. For our purpose, we only distinguish among three different states (normal, near, very near). If the user is near to the screen, the LED lights encased in the stem start blinking to signal that the user is getting too close, but if the user gets even closer to the screen also a sound melody is played through the speaker inside the case.

4) Tracking posture changes

Continuous posture changes are a symptom of discomfort and potential problems, but this situation can be improved by practicing simple back exercises [13]. Using our state machine the system can track the rate of change of postures per minute. If such rate is higher than a configurable threshold, the flower animates with motions of the stem and its color changes to purple (an analogy of bruises), signifying that the user should practice a short physical exercise (Figure 1.E). After a 10 seconds stretching exercise (sensed by the gyro-module), the flower avatar goes back to the neutral state.

CONCLUSION AND FUTURE WORK

Physical ambient media is becoming a well establish model for discretely presenting background information to users [6]. Examples usages include peripheral displays [2, 11], objects in a room [7], and physical avatars [5, 9, 10]. More recently, physical ambient media that can also be mechanically actuated are becoming prominent [12]. In this paper we contribute to the corpus of literature that describes new types of physical and actuated ambient media. Specifically, in this paper we presented an actuated flower-shaped avatar that through colors, sounds, motion and animations of a bendable stem provides a continuous feedback about the posture of users seated in front of a computer. The final goal of this work is to subtly inform users about wrong postures, encouraging physical exercises and adjustments that could help avoiding possible back pain and injuries. Future work includes testing this system with real users in a longitudinal study, and building additional input sensors and output modalities. Finally, we plan to extend this work by seeking other applications for this avatar to promote healthy behaviors in working places, and by exploring different physical form factors.

ACKNOWLEDGMENTS

This research was supported by the Ministry of Trade, Industry and Energy (MOTIE), Korea, through the Education Support program for Creative and Industrial Convergence (Grant Number N0000717).

REFERENCES

1. Adamczyk, P.D., and Bailey, B.P.: If not now, when?: the effects of interruption at different moments within task execution, in proceedings of CHI '04, 271-278.
2. Costanza, E., Inverso, S.A., Pavlov, E., Allen, R., Maes, P.: eye-q: eyeglass peripheral display for subtle intimate notifications, in Proc. of MobileHCI '06, 211-218.
3. Cutrell, E., Czerwinski, M., Horvitz, E: Notification, disruption, and memory: Effects of messaging interruptions on memory and performance, in INTERACT '01, 263-269.
4. Gellersen, H., , Schmidt, A., Beigl, M.: Ambient media for peripheral information display, in Personal Technologies, 1999, 3(4), 199-208.
5. Haller, M., Richter, C. Brandl, P., Gross, S., Schossleitner, G., Schrempf, A., Nii, H., Sugimoto, M., Inami, M.: Finding the Right Way for Interrupting People Improving Their Sitting Posture, in INTERACT'11, 1–17.
6. Ishii, H.: Tangible bits: beyond pixels, in Proc. of TEI'08, 15-25.
7. Ishii, H., Wisneski, C., Brave, S., Dahley, A., Gorbet, M., Ullmer, B., Yarin, P.: ambientROOM: integrating ambient media with architectural space, in Proc. of CHI '98, 173-174.
8. Lund, K., Coulton, P., Edwards, R.: Ambient conversations using a physical avatar, in Proc. of MindTrek '09, 11-14.
9. Park, H.K., Jung, S.M., Choi, J.H., Park, S.H., Yoon, C.H., Park, J.O.: A study on the moving mechanism for flower robot, in ICCAS'07, 2514-2518.
10. Peek, N., Pitman, D., The, R.: Hangsters: tangible peripheral interactive avatars for instant messaging, in Proc. of TEI'09, 25-26.
11. Plaue, C., and Stasko, J.: Animation in a peripheral display: distraction, appeal, and information conveyance in varying display configurations, in Proc. of GI '07, 135-142.
12. Poupyrev, I., Nashida, T., Okabe, M.: Actuation and tangible user interfaces: the Vaucanson duck, robots, and shape displays.\, in Proc. of TEI '07, 205-212.
13. Vergara, M., Page, A.: Relationship between comfort and back posture and mobility in sitting-posture, Applied Ergonomics, 33(1), 2002, 1-8.
14. Zheng, Z., Morrell, J.B.: A vibrotactile feedback approach to posture guidance, in IEEE Haptics Symposium 2010, 351–358.

Designing Wearable Haptic Information Displays for People with Vision Impairments

Marlon Twyman, Joe Mullenbach, Craig Shultz, J. Edward Colgate, Anne Marie Piper
Northwestern University
{marlont2, mullenbach, craigdshultz}@u.northwestern.edu, {colgate, ampiper}@northwestern.edu

ABSTRACT
With the ubiquity of wearable computing, an important and emerging challenge is to understand how to design wearable information displays for non-visual, non-auditory interaction. This is particularly relevant to the design of accessible technologies for people with vision impairments. Working towards this aim, we developed a smartwatch prototype that uses variable friction surface haptics to test initial design concepts. Through interviews and iterative prototyping with seven blind users, we identified three key use cases for a haptic smartwatch as well as embodied conceptual models for presenting haptic information. We found that a physical clock face, compass, and numerical keypad are productive representations for presenting information haptically, and these models build on existing tactile and spatial understandings of our target user group.

Author Keywords
Blind; surface haptics; watch; variable friction

ACM Classification Keywords
H.5.2. User Interfaces: Haptic I/O, Screen Design

INTRODUCTION
In recent years, wearable devices have been gaining popularity in the consumer market, with smartwatches, activity tracking wristbands, and other on-body computing accessories becoming more pervasive in everyday life. Past work examines novel interaction techniques for wearable devices and the integration of haptics as a feedback mechanism (e.g., [13,17]). Additionally, a growing body of research focuses on designing wearable devices and mobile computing for people with disabilities, particularly for individuals with vision impairments [1,3,6,7,19,20].

This paper describes a formative study to understand the design and presentation of tactile information on a haptic smartwatch for people with vision impairments. The technology used is a Motorola smartwatch instrumented with a variable friction touchscreen surface (e.g., Tactile Pattern Display) [10,11]. Unlike vibration or vibro-tactile feedback, variable friction surface haptic displays render localized force feedback to the fingertip. As a user's finger slides across the display, the friction between their fingertip and the touchscreen can be dynamically adjusted to give the perception of complex textures and shapes.

While most research on wearable devices focuses on input or interaction techniques, this paper examines the design of *information presentation* on a small, wearable, haptic display, particularly for blind users. Designing embedded computing experiences for everyday objects can be informed by our embodied and cultural practices with familiar physical devices [9]. During the study, we identify three contexts for watch-based haptic interaction (time telling, navigation, and quantification of activity). Using iterative design and prototyping, we develop an understanding of how to present information through haptics in these contexts. The present work focuses on design for people with vision impairments, but all users stand to benefit from eyes-free, non-auditory access to wearable displays.

RELATED WORK
This research draws on theories of embodiment and related work on wearable and haptic displays to inform the design of a haptic watch for people with vision impairments.

Embodiment and Non-Visual Interaction
Theories of embodiment [2] are particularly relevant when designing information displays for people with vision impairments, who rely on tactile and auditory cues for interaction. William James introduced the concept of the sequential nature of touch and the simultaneous nature of vision. He described that a "seeing baby's eyes take in the whole room at once" in order to discern objects, but the blind child "must form his mental image of the room by the addition, piece to piece, of parts which he learns to know successively" [5]. Such sequential interaction is pervasive in the current design of computing technologies for people with vision impairments. Screen readers (e.g., Apple VoiceOver), which improve non-visual access to graphical displays, rely on sequential auditory cues to help a user build a model of the spatial layout of the display.

In addition to auditory cues, haptic feedback is an important channel through which people with vision impairments come to understand the physical world. Just as a blind person's cane becomes part of their body and sensory experience [12], so too could new haptic technologies. The design of haptic information displays can be informed by

ACM 978-1-4503-3305-4/15/01···$15.00
http://dx.doi.org/10.1145/2677199.2680578

examining the embodied nature of interactions. For example, analyzing how blind children produce gestures, including to their blind peers, can indicate their emerging conceptual understandings that may not be visible through talk alone [4]. Similarly, work by Quek and McNeill [15] examines the embodied nature of learning mathematics and how the lack of visual access to the instructor's embodied, spatiotemporal mathematical explanations affects learning for blind students. Based on this analysis, they suggest vibro-tactile gloves and joysticks as feedback displays to help students understand embodied representations in math learning. This phenomenological view guides our work on understanding how to design wearable tactile information displays for people with vision impairments, including our analysis of how users interact with the prototype system.

Wearable and Haptic Displays

Wearable displays present challenges of designing for small screens, noisy environments, and mobile usage scenarios [13,14,16]. For example, Pasquero et al [13] introduced a haptic watch prototype, in which actuators on the bottom of the watch touching the wrist would provide eyes-free haptic communication with an adjacent mobile device. Ye et al. [20] examined the potential of on-body interaction for people with vision impairments by focusing on a wearable wristband prototype to control the screen reader for a linked mobile device. We build on this work through a focused exploration of a haptic watch prototype with localized tactile feedback directly on the display surface.

With respect to haptic interaction, several studies have examined vibro-tactile feedback on mobile phones to increase accessibility [1,3,6], and this work suggests that visually impaired users may outperform sighted users with haptic feedback. The TeslaTouch system [18], which uses electrostatic vibration, demonstrated that blind users were able to sense and create 2D tactile images on a haptic display. Similarly, variable friction surface haptics enabled by tactile pattern displays (TPad) have been explored for improving touchscreen usability [10] and affective communication [11], and the present study examines surface haptics in a mobile context for blind users.

TPAD WATCH HARDWARE

To enable exploration of wearable haptics, we introduce the TPad Watch (Fig. 1), which uses a Motorola MOTOACTV smartwatch with a display of 220 x 176 pixels that runs Android 2.3 Gingerbread. This prototype was developed based on the TPad Tablet technology [10,11]. The haptic surface is a glass plate with an array of piezoelectric actuators along the side. The actuators vibrate the glass at ultrasonic frequencies, causing the fingertip to periodically break contact and reduce the coefficient of friction. This plate is mounted to the watch screen and the level of friction reduction is controlled in real time by a program running on the watch. A more complete description of the TPad system can be found in previous research [11]. The TPad Watch enables new explorations of how to design

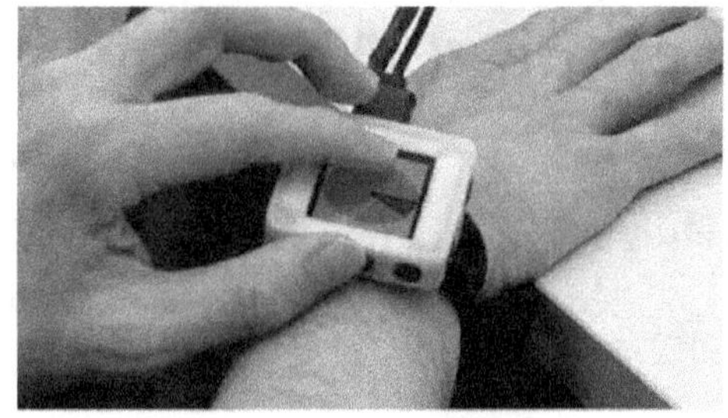

Figure 1: Blind participant using TPaD smartwatch.

programmable surface haptics on a wearable digital display. Using the openly available Android SDK for the TPad (www.tpadtablet.org), we developed multiple example applications to understand initial usage scenarios for a haptic watch as well as dedicated haptic visualizations (Fig. 2, right) to explore various techniques for presenting information to users with vision impairments.

METHOD

Seven people with vision impairments (ages 20-62; 2 female; legally blind to light perception only) and two experts in assistive technology who work with people with vision impairments were involved in this study. Two visually impaired people and the two experts participated in early discussions, using initial applications (Fig 1). We then employed an iterative design process. With five visually impaired people, the research team conducted a total of five semi-structured interviews, two paper prototyping activities (Fig. 2, center), and three technology testing sessions. Some participants were involved in more than one session. All visually impaired participants demonstrated how they interact with their current mobile devices and watches.

The TPad Watch prototype was both a probe for understanding potential usage scenarios and a platform for testing early design ideas. Our design process focused on: (1) information gathering about mobile accessibility through discussions and interviews, (2) creating paper prototypes with participants and then developing haptic visualizations for testing, and (3) obtaining feedback on the TPad watch prototype and interface designs. During all parts of the study, the research team took notes to understand current practices, inform design, and capture reactions to early prototypes. Five interviews or prototype testing sessions were audio/video recorded and transcribed. Each session was between 60 and 75 minutes. The research team iteratively coded all notes and transcripts for themes.

FINDINGS

After the early discussions and interviews, we identified three use cases to explore for a haptic watch. While testing our applications, we learned how our participants interact with the TPad Watch. We also uncovered embodied conceptual models to inform the design of a haptic watch.

Use Cases and Value of a Wearable Haptic Display

Three primary use cases for exploration were suggested in early discussions: time telling, navigation, and quantification of activity. During the course of research, engagements with participants supported these use cases. Time telling with haptic interaction is unsurprising since the watch form factor is already associated with this task. All seven visually impaired people saw value in telling time through a tactile interface, particularly when in environments where auditory information may not be appropriate [7]. P2 said, "*When I learned to tell time...I usually use braille watches, then when speech technology came along I would sometimes use a combination [tactile/audio] watch. I've never been one of those people who likes an audio only watch because, every time I want to check the time, the world hears it...*" P3 described similar benefits to haptic only feedback: "*A lot of people have gone to talking watches or they carry some device in their pocket... I'm still old school as far as the watch is concerned... That's why I have my braille watch. I don't have to worry about loud environments.*" For time telling alone, two participants said they would prefer their existing braille watch (Fig. 2, left) to a digital haptic watch.

Building on prior work [7,19], navigation was also an important use case to all seven visually impaired participants: *P4: "It's very important that you have an accessible GPS system because it's how you tell where you are and where you're going and what you want to do."* A haptic watch can provide immediate access and privacy [20]. Finally, quantification of activity was supported as a third area of exploration due to observations of participants' existing practices of counting steps for navigation and counting landmarks to understand spatial layouts. Quantification could work with a compass-like navigation tool to track progress toward a destination or more private data about physical activity (e.g., pedometer or Fitbit feedback). Initial prototypes included percentage-based representations (e.g., screen coverage or pie chart, Fig 2g,h) to represent quantification, although displaying the raw numerical value emerged as an important theme.

Understanding Initial Usage

We observed that physical reference points for device usage were essential for participants during testing. Participants were eager to learn the location of the power button, which served as a marker to properly orient the device on their wrist. All of our interface designs were orientation dependent, and all users successfully learned to orient the device based on physical hardware buttons. When exploring the screen, they tended to start at the top left of the screen, then move up/down or side-to-side rather than a circular motion as we expected based on braille watch usage. Even after lifting a finger, they returned to exploration by starting in this corner. The participants used the hardware as a physical guide for on-screen interaction inside the watch casing similar to descriptions in prior work [8]. Adding physical indentations strategically around the edge of the display (e.g., midpoints) would aid accessibility.

When learning how to detect and interpret the on-screen haptics, one participant offered parallels to prior learned haptic experiences, referencing Optacon and braille. P2 said, *"I guess I'm using the same approach as I would with braille,"* describing his behavior of reading the screen from left to right. This illustrates the sequential nature of exploring inherently spatial haptic representations.

Embodied Conceptual Models for Design

In contrast to the linear presentation of information through a screen reader, with which all participants were familiar, we prototyped a variety of spatial haptic representations to understand which concepts would be most appropriate. An analog clock was a familiar spatial representation for time telling (Fig. 2a-c show clock hand variations) and may work for navigation. P4 uses a clock face as a conceptual model for orientation: *"As I navigate, instead of forward, down, left, and right. I'm thinking in terms of blindness, which would be 12, 3, 6, and 9 [o'clock]."*

In addition to the clock face, all participants understood the concept of a compass and mentioned exposure to an accessible physical compass (e.g., braille magnetic compass). P1 said, *"One of my orientation and mobility instructors had a raised one with raised markings."* For the navigation prototypes, we observed the need to highlight the direction of interest with a textured area near the edge of the display (Fig. 2d-f).

Another spatial representation of which participants had an embodied understanding is a numerical keypad (e.g., on a phone). In the context of activity quantification, presenting information using the spatial layout of digits on a number pad (Fig. 2i) was more appealing than a pie chart representation (Fig. 2h). There were nine positions (1-9) on the number pad, and the strong texture was the "tens" value while the weak texture had the "ones" value. Spaces with textures could be added resulting in a numerical range from zero to 99. In Fig. 2i, the black texture occupies the "6" position and is worth 60, the gray texture is at "3" and is

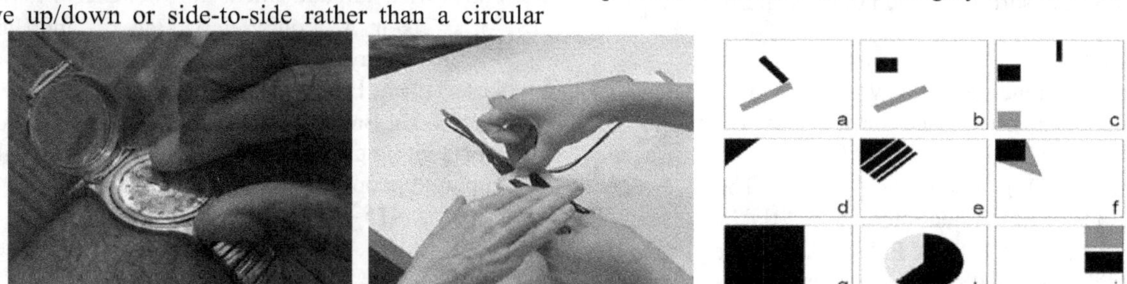

Figure 2: ***Left*: Blind participant telling time with braille watch. *Center*: paper prototyping haptic representation for the navigation context (i.e., direction of compass). *Right*: Haptic visualizations for clocks (a, b, c), compass navigation (d, e, f), and activity quantification (g, h, i). Black is stronger haptic texture and gray is weaker.**

worth 3 totaling a value of 63. When asked, participants displayed a general preference for the presentation of numerical information on a number pad rather than graphical figures. P2 described his difficulty in learning graphical concepts, *"I can't interpret things that way. Even if you described it, my brain doesn't think that way because there's no technology that allows me to think that way."* Although further evaluation is required, in our initial prototype testing two blind participants were able to discern all nine sections (70 x 50px each) representing a number pad on the watch. While the participants preferred the number pad for reading quantitative values, some appreciated the idea of creating an alternate summary of activity (e.g. percent completed). In our broader discussion, using the concept of a number keypad helped participants orient to the location of haptic areas or targets on the watch.

Naturally, participants' success in understanding the haptic representations depended on their exposure to these visual concepts. One participant excelled in all scenarios, correctly identifying the time on the clock, directions on the compass, and detecting the circular pie chart. This participant had education at a young age in visual reasoning and concepts. In order to draw on embodied conceptual understandings to improve design [2,9], these concepts must be current and well known among the target user group. For example, P2 said, *"I learned math on an abacus...I would not be able to do that now... If someone asked me to do it today I wouldn't know what to do. I'd say give me a calculator."*

CONCLUSION

We have presented an initial exploration of how to design haptic information displays on a smartwatch for people with vision impairments. This work lays the foundation for subsequent development and evaluation of more robust prototypes, providing productive embodied conceptual models for designing for this user group. With the growing ubiquity of wearable computing, understanding how to present information in non-visual, non-auditory contexts is an important research challenge that affects all user groups.

ACKNOWLEDGMENTS

We give special thanks to Michael Jastram for building the TPad Watch. We also thank Michael Peshkin for continued support of the TPad Project. NSF Grant 0964075 and the National GEM Consortium funded this research.

REFERENCES

1. Azenkot, S., Ladner, R. E., & Wobbrock, J. O. Smartphone haptic feedback for nonvisual wayfinding. In *Proc. ASSETS '11,* 281-282. ACM.
2. Dourish, P. (2001). Where The Action Is: The Foundations of Embodied Interaction. MIT Press.
3. Galdón, P.M., et al. (2013). Enhancing mobile phones for people with visual impairments through haptic icons: the effect of learning processes. Assist Tech. 25(2):80-7.
4. Iverson, J.M., and Goldin-Meadow, S. (1998). Why people gesture as they speak. Nature 396, 228.
5. James, W. (1890). *The principles of psychology.* Holt.
6. Jayant, C., Acuario, C., Johnson, W., Hollier., J, and Ladner, R. V-braille: haptic braille perception using a touch-screen and vibration on mobile phones. In Proc of ASSETS '10, 295-296.
7. Kane, S. K., Jayant, C., Wobbrock, J. O., & Ladner, R. E. Freedom to roam: a study of mobile device adoption and accessibility for people with visual and motor disabilities. In *Proc. ASSETS '09,* 115-122.
8. Kane, S. K., Morris, M. R., & Wobbrock, J. O. Touchplates: low-cost tactile overlays for visually impaired touch screen users. In *Proc. ASSETS '13*, 22-29.
9. Klemmer, S. R., Hartmann, B., and Takayama, L. How bodies matter: five themes for interaction design. In *Proc. DIS '06,* 140-149.
10. Levesque, V., Oram, L., MacLean, K., Cockburn, A., Marchuk, N. D., Johnson, D., Colgate, J.E. and Peshkin, M. A. Enhancing physicality in touch interaction with programmable friction. In *Proc. CHI '11,* 2481-2490.
11. Mullenbach, J., Shultz, C., Colgate, J. E., & Piper, A. M. Exploring affective communication through variable-friction surface haptics. In *Proc. CHI '14,* 3963-3972.
12. Noë, A. (2010). Out of Our Heads: Why you are not your brain, and other lessons from the biology of consciousness. Hill and Wang.
13. Pasquero, J., Stobbe, S. J., & Stonehouse, N. A haptic wristwatch for eyes-free interactions. In *Proc. CHI '11,* 3257-3266.
14. Perrault, S. T., Lecolinet, E., Eagan, J., & Guiard, Y. WatchIt: simple gestures and eyes-free interaction for wristwatches and bracelets. In *Proc. CHI '13,* 1451-1460.
15. Quek, F., and McNeill, D. Embodiment Awareness, Mathematics Discourse, and the Blind. Ann N Y Acad Sci, 1093: 266-279.
16. Tam, D., MacLean, K. E., McGrenere, J., & Kuchenbecker, K. J. The design and field observation of a haptic notification system for timing awareness during oral presentations. In *Proc. CHI '13,* 1689-1698.
17. Xiao, R., Gierad, L., and Harrison, C. Expanding the Input Expressivity of Smartwatches with Mechanical Pan, Twist, Tilt and Click. In *Proc. CHI '14,* 193-196.
18. Xu, C., Israr, A., Poupyrev, I., Bau, O., and Harrison, C. Tactile display for the visually impaired using TeslaTouch. Extended Abstract. In *CHI'11,* 317-322.
19. Yatani, K., Banovic, N., & Truong, K. SpaceSense: representing geographical information to visually impaired people using spatial tactile feedback. In *Proc. CHI '12,* 415-424.
20. Ye, H., Malu, M., Oh, U., & Findlater, L. Current and future mobile and wearable device use by people with visual impairments. In *Proc. CHI '14,* 3123-3132.

Manual Manuals: Media Reflexivity in Reading Through Tangible Artifacts

Jamie Allen
IXDM Critical Media Lab (Basel) / (CIID) Copenhagen Institute of Interaction Design
Jamie.Allen@fhnw.ch / J.Allen@ciid.dk

ABSTRACT
Reading is a manual activity. The touch hands are ever-present: holding, turning, pointing, scrolling, clicking and scribbling are physical practices that engross people in the printed word. The project "AIME Tiles" began by thinking about how systems of ideas can be translated into hybrid physical-concept tools. Further, the project attempts to resituate the scholarly activity of reading *as a practice* with its own material culture and media affordances. AIME Tiles, their design intent and construction are described as a modest sketch of tactile tools for scholarship— game pieces for playing with ideas while reading.

Author Keywords
Tactile; reading; scholarship; publishing.

ACM Classification Keywords
H.5.m. Information interfaces and presentation: Misc.

MANUAL(LY) READING
The history of manual and mnemonic instruments accompanying reading is both rarefied and intriguing. The English word "manual" refers both things done with one's hands, as well as a media-literary form for instruction. Scholarship, and reading more generally, has moved from being the sole purvey of a privileged and divinely ordained social strata (royalty and the clergy), first into the lives of courtiers and university scholars and then as a popular pursuit of professional and working classes. Designing materials for the development, support and augmentation of reading follow this expansion.

The prayer bead is a technology of reading and recitation which appears in many forms. Although there is a presumed first intent of these wooden and seed-based strings of elements to help the devotee remember a sequence of tasks, names or expressions their significance as ornamental and ritual devices for announcing (to oneself and to others) the kinds of thinking or reading taking place becomes an at least as important function. The cognitive benefit of not having to remember sequence in the recitation of a prayer or reading, are thought to 'free the mind' toward meditation or revelation on larger ideas and broader problems. (In Islamic traditions, a 99-bead "misbaha" is used, corresponding to the Names of God in Islam, while in Christian traditions "rosary" beads are used to count recitations of prayers).

TEI '15, January 16 – 19, 2015, Stanford, CA, USA.

http://dx.doi.org/10.1145/2677199.2680580

The material-cultural history of reading is likewise populated by a host of devices for optical amelioration. Starting in the 1st Century, monks and scribes suffering from presbyopia used reading stones as magnifying glasses, proto-eyeglasses. Made of beryllium or quartz, the form and significance of these stones went far beyond optical magnification. These smooth, polished, tactile objects were cherished by the men who's task it was to elucidate the sacred, esoteric texts. Reading stones were themselves indubitably imbued with individualized interpretative powers.

There are subtler effects of reading-with-artifacts related directly to tactility. These align with Sonneveld's [9] conclusions. "Touching an object appears as a factor in calming somebody and enhancing concentration." [4] Touch would also seem to lead to more intimate experiences, and more sensuous, embodied relations to knowledge. "Our sense of touch tells us whether we can trust the thing or not, whether it is valuable." [4] Haptic-attention, for Benjamin, underpins modern experience more broadly, through "Tactile appropriation". [1]

The AIME Tiles prototype extends the material history of loops, reading rulers, books stands and other sensible rubrics for hands and bodies in the act of reading. It develops a tactile-manual analog to a conceptual framework laid down by Bruno Latour in "An Inquiry Into Modes of Existence." [5] With this, it opposes homogenization of the material cultural of reading into samey 'platforms' and tablets. Be it through the uniformity of print-on-demand volumes, the devaluation of unique editions, the glassy and glossy encapsulation of reading experiences via the Kindle or iPad—the manual and tactile experience of reading at present reinforce tendencies toward tactile and haptic senses as "mediocre conductor[s] of thought." [6] Latour's intellectual project, as a history and actuality of how veracity and knowledge are derived from human and non-human interactions seems particularly appropriate fodder for the sketch.

MEDIA REFLEXIVITY IN READING
The ascension of digital literature [2] as an area of hybrid media and technology research, helps to develop a sense that the substrates and 'media' of information greatly

influence the overall experiential message or 'content' conveyed (see K. Hayles [3]). These are fruitful reflections on media forms and content that highlight the longstanding presence and potential of physical tools for thinking.

The book is a medium that has for over half a millennium served as our primary knowledge transduction artifact. In communities purporting toward knowledge (particularly in the Humanities), it remains an artifact and talisman so powerful and ubiquitous, that it goes largely unnoticed. This inattention to, and invariability of, media forms has grave repercussions for the possibility of alternative, new forms of knowledge creation and archiving. Those steeped in philosophical and literary traditions seldom have occasion to reflect on the media-specificity of the forms in which they traffic. Readers have less media-specific criticality Hayles has called for through "comparative media studies." [3] Traditional humanities seem in perennial shock where media-reflexivity is concerned: "You mean this is a *book* I've been reading all along?!"

AIME Tiles, a resolutely material tool set, rekindle tactility in relation to a specific theoretical framework. This brings the mediations taking place in learning, thinking and scholarship to the fore. With it we try to remind ourselves how "thinking is a practice," [8] full of process and artifact.

THE AIME TILES

The AIME Tiles are an implementation of a design for the manipulation of ideas from Bruno Latour's 2013 AIME project [5]. Each of the 15 'modes' presented is a domain of human activity with its own truth conditions and practices (e.g.: "[POL]" refers to politics). A laser-cut hexagonal wooden tile was created for each of these modes, which reveal themselves best relationally—that is, in relation to other modes. As a use-example, having two tiles in-hand while reading through the volume, reinforces which are being held in relief within the text (Figure 1).

Figure 1 - The AIME Tiles as used in reading.

The AIME Tiles therefore act as 'Scrabble Tiles' for the modes of existence in the book to be used as mnemonic and conceptual tools while undertaking close-readings of the volume. The pieces are laser-cut from a textural, wood-grained plank, with etched characters intended to be felt as much as seen. The pieces are provided to readers in a small canvas bag, which also provides comforting and sensual feedback (Figure 2). Each piece, and each set of 15 pieces is hand-sanded, prepared and bagged, creating a poetic, tactile counterpart to the AIME online digital-humanities project and its published monograph.

Figure 2 - The AIME Tiles as produced and given to readers.

ACKNOWLEDGEMENTS

AIME Tiles were produced in collaboration with Catherine Descure at CIID. Thanks to textile and fashion designer Merja Hannele Ulvinen for obligingly creating beautiful canvas bags. Thanks to the Sciences Po AIME project team, and Sara Krugman for their enthusiasm at the 2014 Copenhagen Business School workshop. Special thanks to Bruno Latour for his reconstitution of practice and theory as conjoined modes of both existence and experience.

REFERENCES

1. Benjamin, Walter (1936). The Work of Art in the Age of Mechanical Reproduction. http://www.marxists.org/.
2. Berry, D. M. (2012). Understanding Digital Humanities. Palgrave Macmillan.
3. Hayles, N. K. (2012). How We Think. University of Chicago Press.
4. Jeon, E. (2011). Enriched Aesthetic Interaction through Sense from Haptic Visuality. Curtin University of Technology, IDA Congress Education Conference.
5. Latour, B. (2013). An Inquiry Into Modes of Existence. Harvard University Press.
6. Marinetti, F.T. (1921) The Manifesto of Tactilism. Milan. http://peripheralfocus.net/poems-told-by-touch/.
7. McDonagh, D.,et. all. (2004). Design and Emotion. Taylor & Francis. P. 262.
8. Rancière, J. (2008). 'Jacques Rancière and Peter Sloterdijk debate Aesthetics and Modernity'. Podcast, Warwick University. http://www2.warwick.ac.uk
9. Sonneveld, M. H. (2010). The meaning of nonfunctional touch, KEER2010, Paris, March 2-4 2010, 257-267

Bloctopus: A Novice Modular Sensor System for Playful Prototyping

Joel Sadler[1], Kevin Durfee[2], Lauren Shluzas[1], Paulo Blikstein[3]
[1]Mechanical Engineering Department
[2]Electrical Engineering Department
[3]School of Education and Computer Science Department
Stanford University, Stanford, CA 94305-9035 USA
{jsadler, kdurfee, larenino, paulob}@stanford.edu

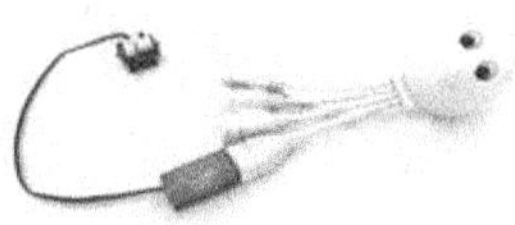

ABSTRACT
Tangible prototyping enables designers to rapidly iterate design concepts, gather feedback, and learn quickly from mistakes. However, when a higher level of functionality is needed with sensors, novices struggle with technical implementation. Existing novice electronics toolkits, such as Arduino, have lowered the threshold to electronic experimentation, but still require manual creation of circuits and software programming ability. We present Bloctopus, a modular electronic prototyping toolkit that allows direct electrical interfacing over USB, and physical interfacing with LEGO blocks. We present the stand-alone sensor model, where each module can directly interface with either a computer or microcontroller, using musical message passing over MIDI. We show that the modules can be programmed with a simplified data flow model in a web-based visual programming interface. Finally, we present a prototyping case study that demonstrates the expressivity of devices that can be created using LEGO pieces, combined with functional electronic modules.

Author Keywords
Toolkits; Prototyping; Hardware; Embedded Sensors.

ACM Classification Keywords
H.5.2. User Interfaces: Input devices and strategies; Interaction styles; Prototyping; User-centered design.

INTRODUCTION
It is challenging for technical novices to create functional electronic prototypes. A high-school student attempting to prototype a hand-held temperature sensor, a wearable pedometer, or a musical input controller, can benefit from a tangible mock-up of the idea. By adding electronic sensors and actuators to these prototypes, we can further enrich the interaction design process and provide tangible feedback around critical design features [1]. However, (i) making circuits, and (ii) programming, can be significant barriers during prototyping.

ACM 978-1-4503-3305-4/15/01...$15.00
http://dx.doi.org/10.1145/2677199.2680581

Existing electronics toolkits for novices tend to present either a simplified abstraction, such as LEGO Mindstorms [2], or require some combination of circuit building with textual programming, such as with Arduino [3]. A recent trend in this field has been the development of toolkits that inhabit the space in between those extremes [4]. This research explores this space, and attempts to find a way to bridge this gap between simple electronic ideas, and creating a working prototype. *The goal of our research is to better understand how we can enable novices to create electronic prototypes with improved design toolkits.* We present here the *Bloctopus* system, a modular electronics prototyping toolkit that builds on the lessons learned from prior novice toolkits, and focuses on presenting a path to transition from novice to expert.

Three Guiding Insights
In conducting this research we interviewed experts in the areas of design, prototyping, education, and embedded systems, to get a better sense for what was lacking in current electronics prototyping tools, and also examined the literature in the field [1, 2, 4, 5, 6, 7, 8, 9]. We uncovered three important trends that heavily influenced our design decisions:

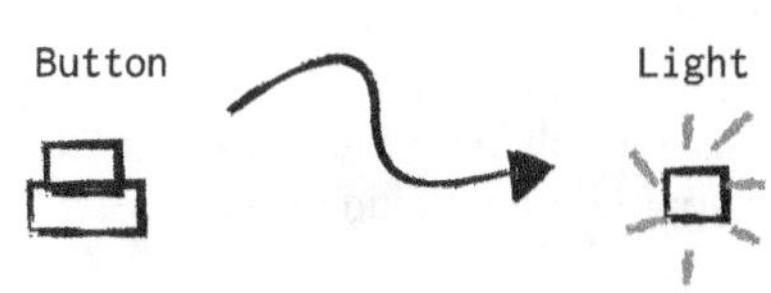

Figure 1. Example of a simple interaction that may have a complex electronic implementation.

1. Most Ideas are Simple Interactions
While a design may eventually become complex in implementation, a large number of electronic prototype ideas revolve around a set of simple *interactions.* The core element of an idea may be commonly expressed as a simple mapping of a sensor's events to control an output, e.g. *"when the button is pressed, turn the light on."* The actual implementation of mapping an analog sensor to an output is relatively more complex, as it may require technical knowledge. Since these direct input-output interactions are common, we wish to have a system that reduces the implementation burden, freeing the designer to think about

the interaction, rather than the implementation. The authors have found that exposing implementation details can significantly reduce prototyping output and creative confidence with electronics [11].

2. Feedback First

When holding a mysterious new sensor, a common first question to ask is *"does it work?"* and *"what do the raw values look like?"* These are questions that both novices and experts wish to answer before integrating a component to the larger system. Since initial sensor discovery and interrogation is a critical first step, we aim to make this feedback loop as immediate and direct as possible.

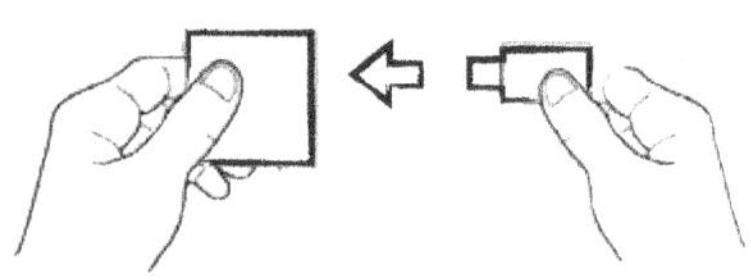

Figure 2. Plug-and-play interaction.

3. Making Interfacing a One-Step Process

Once a component is in hand, how do we connect this with other components and author some logical behavior? Each toolkit presents some set of steps one must take before a component can be activated and interfaced with other components. If one has to connect many wires and add supporting circuitry before plugging in a sensor, this adds additional friction to the process of trying out new components. As much as possible, we wish to have a single fluid step for adding and removing components. For example, a plug-and-play LED module is preferable to a raw LED component that must be plugged in a specific orientation. The author's previous work has found that modular plug-and-play tools are critical for frictionless electronics prototyping [11,12].

BACKGROUND

This research focuses on two existing fields of research: (i) hardware toolkit design for electronics novices and (ii) programming models (visual, textual, and event-driven) specifically applied to embedded systems.

Novice Hardware Toolkits

Novice Microcontroller toolkits, such as Wiring and Arduino [7, 3], have helped lower the barriers to entry, by providing an integrated experience with hardware and a software IDE, as well as a vibrant community of enthusiasts and support resources. By staying at the circuit level, prototypers are not limited by a ceiling of fixed-functionality black boxes. This makes the modifiability of the system high, and it is possible to add and remove components at a raw circuit level. The creators of Arduino, which was a derivative of the Wiring platform [7], argue that there is significant potential learning benefit to being exposed to raw circuitry [3]. However, encouraging manual circuit creation comes at a cost of a higher technical barrier to entry. On the other side of the spectrum are more modular toolkits that give novices a set of pre-fabricated, and functionally rigid, building blocks. The hardware blocks in these toolkits may have companion software to encourage novice programming, for example the LEGO Mindstorm's [2] drag-and-drop programming environment. Other toolkits may encourage building simple circuits without programming, such as LittleBits [5], an approach that has been particularly successful for young prototypers at the elementary school level. While a building-block approach may reduce technical barriers to entry, it comes at a cost of making it harder to modify the system. The core trade-off is that adding modules tends to reduce the flexibility of modifying the system. Prior research systems such as d.Tools [1], or Phidgets [6], demonstrated the advantages of using modules in a hardware prototyping system, but neither provided a novice friendly way to program behavior in the system. For a detailed literature review on the history and design of microcontroller-based toolkits for novices, the authors recommend Blikstein's 2013 review of microcontrollers, and their use with technical novices in education [4].

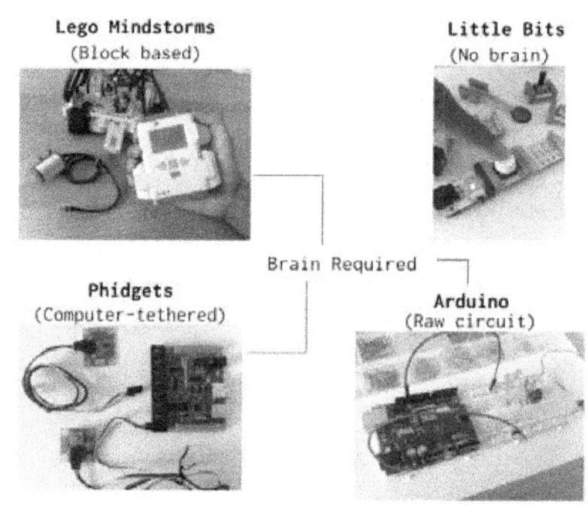

Figure 3. Existing novice electronics toolkits provide simplified models, or may require circuit building and programming.

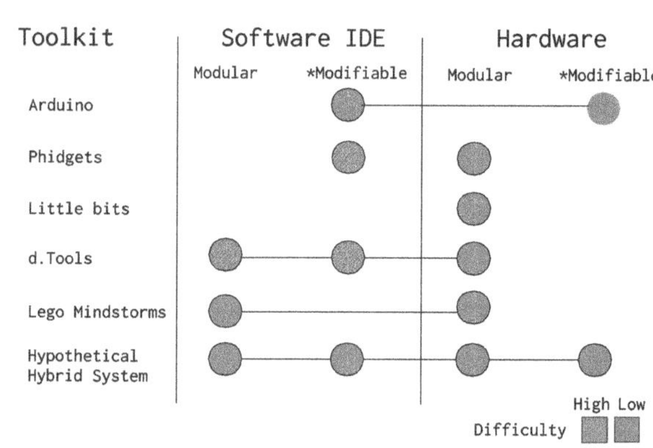

Figure 4. Comparing the modularity and the ability to add new functionality(modifiability) of different toolkits.

In the robotics community toolkits, such as roBlocks [9] and Cublets [10], have shown the benefit of using snap-together blocks with novices. However these systems tend to be physically bulky and not suited for prototyping sensitive form factors, such as hand-held or body-worn devices. As a general trend, most hardware toolkits require some form of interface "brain" to be a hub that components centrally connect with. This hub is commonly a microcontroller with pin interfaces exposed through several connectors. This means that to interface with a single component, one must always have a "brain" on hand before getting feedback about the module state. The design presented here attempts to avoid requiring a specific hub, by making each sensor "smart" enough to interface with any USB capable device. To our knowledge, except for products in the realm of scientific sensing, no prototyping system has enabled a hybrid interface that allows sensors to plug in directly with either a computer or a microcontroller.

Novice Programming Tools

A review of novice programming interfaces appears in Kelleher & Pausch [13], revealing many of the strategies for reducing the difficulty threshold, and increasing the functionality ceiling. Many attempts to simplify the programming experience center around giving the programmer simplified syntax, and direct visual feedback on the program's current structure. At least two common groups of novice programming interfaces exist: those that focus on augmenting text-based programming, and those that incorporate visual programming. Visual programming environments, such as Scratch [14] and Alice [15], have achieved notable levels of adoption in educational communities, but do not explicitly encourage hardware interfacing. In contrast, text-based tools such as Arduino and Processing [16] focus on augmenting the traditional text-based programming environment, allowing for greater transferability of common programming skills, e.g. C or Java, while sacrificing the intuitive direct manipulation interface of the graphical tools.

Recent systems, such as Modkit [8], have demonstrated in-browser programming of microcontrollers, with both graphical and textual code representation. However, Modkit has two key limitations: (i) Code is not executed dynamically (programs are statically compiled and reloaded into the microcontroller with every incremental change, similar to LEGO Mindstorms) and (ii) the textual and visual code representations are divided into separate modes, forcing the user to be exclusively in one mode or the other. Our insight is that some programming concepts are more naturally expressed visually, such as input-output connections, while other concepts such as mathematical transformations (e.g. *light=light/2+50*), are more naturally expressed in the text domain. To the authors' knowledge, few tools have demonstrated both live execution of code, and a simultaneous visual and textual programming in a hybrid interface.

Research Contributions

This research presents the *Bloctopus* prototype system, a modular toolkit for novice electronic prototyping. Specifically, this work makes the following contributions to the fields of prototyping and novice electronics toolkits:

- Demonstrates the feasibility of a system with self-contained plug-and-play USB MIDI modules with **direct interfacing** with a computer or microcontroller.
- Demonstrates that programming devices is possible with a web-based visual programming model, that is **executed live** , and with **hybrid visual-textual** programming.
- Evaluates some of the modular tradeoffs on system performance
- Shows a prototyping case study illustrating that diverse prototypes are possible in a short time frame with this modular hardware model.

THE BLOCTOPUS SYSTEM

Recalling the guiding principles of *simple mapping*, *feedback first* and, direct *one-step interfacing* we created the *Bloctopus* system. The system combines (i) a plug-and-play module architecture with (ii) a musical instrument communication model and (iii) a visual software programming system.

An Octoblock as a Stand-Alone USB Module

A core concept is to have each module in the system be a directly pluggable USB device that appears as a standard MIDI device uniformly across PCs and mobile devices. Physically each module consists of a head that contains a sensor or actuator, a flexible neck, and a base. Hartmann et. al. showed that module form factor is a critical feature of a prototyping system and large monolithic modules limit the kinds of prototypes that can be made by the designer [1]. As with modular systems, such as Phidgets and LEGO Mindstorms, there is a separation of the sensor/actuator from the main body. This reduces the physical area and volume in the critical region around the head so that modules can be attached more flexibly, and closer together on the target prototype.

Figure 5. Octoblock smart USB-MIDI module that interfaces directly to a computer's USB ports.

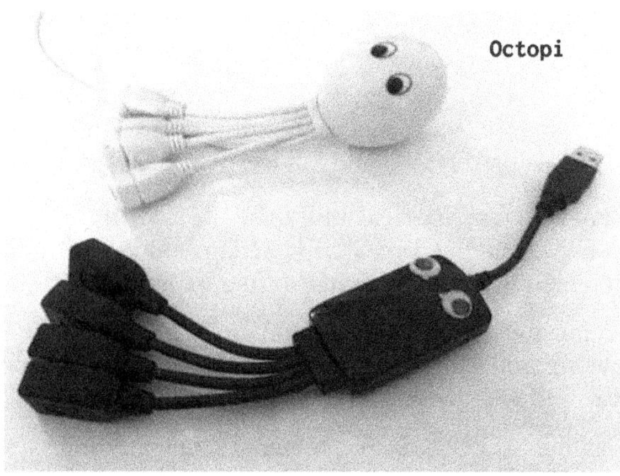

Figure 6. Octoblocks can plug into an optional USB hub for ease of interfacing directly with a computer.

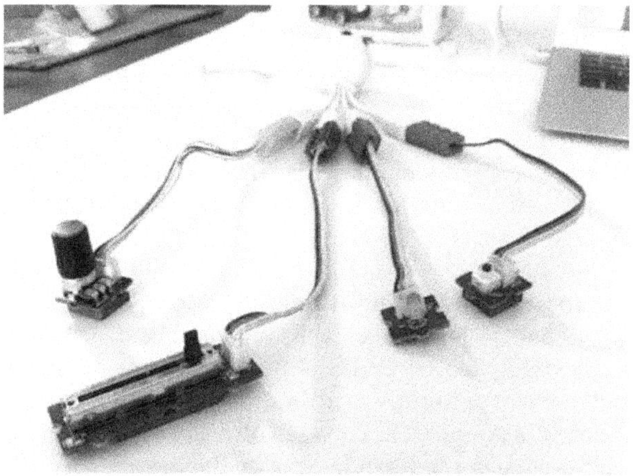

Figure 7. Multiple modules plug into an octopus-like form-factor.

The base contains the circuitry for USB connection inside of a 3D printed LEGO block form factor. The LEGO interface was chosen to give the system a playful feel, and to allow mechanical interfacing with the physical LEGO systems. Modules can then be connected directly to a computer over USB, or to a standalone microcontroller hub that has USB host functionality. In the current prototype the brain is a four-port USB hub with eyes added to suggest that the prototype is a living electrical organism. The components of a single module are shown in Figure 5.

Module-to-Module Communication with MIDI

Module systems, such LEGO Mindstorms and d.tools, allow modules to be chained together on an electrical bus. A bus-based approach has the major advantage that modules are uniquely identifiable and chained together on a small set of predefined wires. This is in contrast with Arduino-based prototyping with a breadboard, where each component typically needs to be physically connected to distinct pins of a microcontroller, and manually identified via software pin mappings declared in code. However, for a bus-based system there must be a predefined protocol for how the modules will communicate (e.g. four-wire I^2C protocol) and this communication protocol may not be universally compatible with all devices. We choose to use MIDI, a communication protocol for musical devices, as a standard method for modules to communicate. This has the following advantages:

- **Universal Support**: MIDI devices are supported on a wide range of devices. MIDI has existed for decades (since the 1980's) and most computers already come with preinstalled drivers. Even resource-constrained devices such as tablets, e.g. Apple's iPad tablet, support MIDI devices directly.
- **Designed for Interactivity**: Having been designed as a way for musicians to interface their electronic instruments with each other, MIDI is a good choice for a low-latency way to transport human input, such as key presses, into MIDI compatible software.
- **Many Software Interface Options**: Software that supports MIDI is a good candidate for directly interfacing with sensors. Visual programming environments, such as MaxMsp and PureData, were designed specifically for musical interfacing and have been shown as effective rapid prototyping environments with sensors [17]. By having many interface options, it becomes more probable that the prototyper will find a way to access sensor values and create new interactions. For example, *Bloctopus* modules will generate audible feedback in music software that may be preinstalled on the users operating system, such as Apple's Garageband. In general, the authors note that music authoring software often encourages flexible mapping to hardware controllers.

Electrical Design: A Minimal USB Module

The head of an Octoblock module contains an off-the-self "dumb" module, already mounted on a PCB with supporting circuitry. These modules are "dumb" in the sense that they contain only the minimum circuitry necessary to function, but do not contain hardware necessary to automatically identify presence or communicate over an electrical bus. The current *Bloctopus* prototype uses the Seeed Studio Grove Modules as a collection of simple barebones modules that are ready to connect to a microcontroller over 4 wires (signal1, signal2, power, ground). The electrical design of the USB base circuit uses a modified USB logging circuit AVR-Stick (DEV-09147) made by Sparkfun Electronics. This circuit exposes a male USB edge connector so that the user can directly plug in the device to a standard USB port without needing an extra cable. A schematic of the USB circuit is shown in Figure 8. It is notable that very few components are needed to recreate this schematic. When using the Attiny85's internal 16.5MHz oscillator the required components are only the microcontroller and a few discrete components.

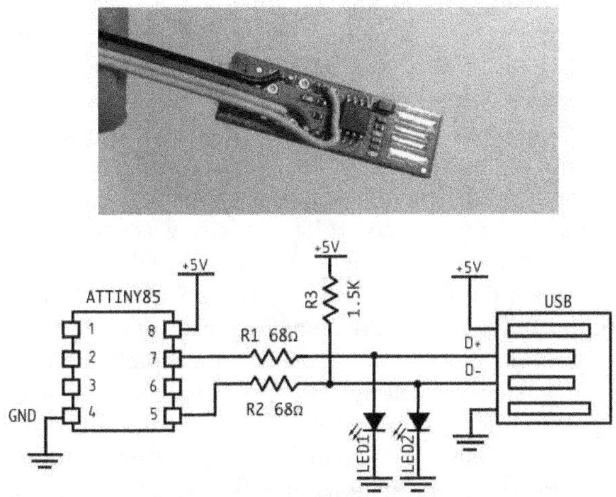

Figure 8. Electrical schematic of a USB circuit that forms the base of a module (AVR-Stick Sparkfun Dev-09147).

The total cost of the USB system can be below $2, including the PCB fabrication in 1000 unit volumes. The lowering costs of such USB compatible components makes incorporation of full USB compliant hardware into each sensor-actuator module an increasingly feasible solution for cost effective plug-and-play modules.

The firmware of the AVR-stick is replaced with a custom combination of two core *Bloctopus* system features:

(i) Virtual USB: A software implementation of a class compliant USB device with an Atmel Attiny85 microcontroller running using V-USB by Objective Development [18]. This allows relatively inexpensive microcontrollers, such as Atmel's Attiny85, to add USB functionality to every *Bloctopus* module.

(ii) Bootloader: A small 2KB bootloader (Micronucleus v1.11) [19] runs on startup, and allows new programs to be loaded over USB. Systems such as Arduino showed that a bootloader is a critical feature for novice toolkits, since they allow users to load new code into the microcontroller without special hardware or a proprietary compiler. As the prototyper transitions from a novice to an expert, this feature enables new functionality to be added to each module.

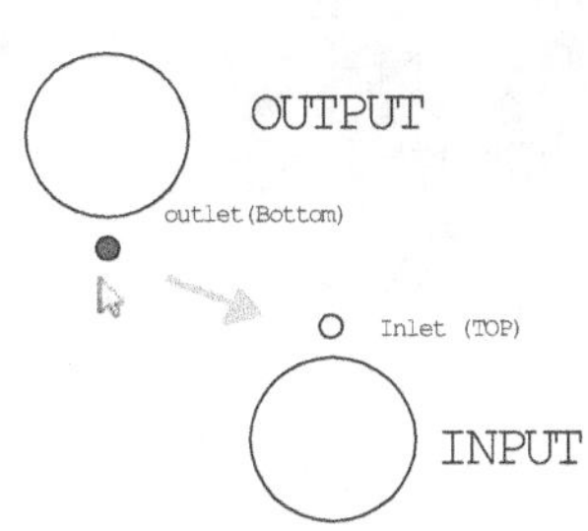

Figure 7. Simple input-to-output visual model.

Web-Based Visual Programming

In order to give the prototyper a fast way to (i) query the module state (ii) make simple input to output mappings. We implemented a proof of concept web-based programming tool in HTML/Javascript. By combining a plugin for MIDI support (Jazz Plugin, Java Applet) with standard web technologies, the Bloctopus system can be visualized in a lightweight manner without requiring the user to download and install a new programming environment. Hardware elements are represented visually as a nodes on the screen. Every node falls into one of 2 types (i) inputs and (ii) outputs, corresponding to sensors and actuators/emitters respectively. The domain of each node is either discrete (e.g. buttons are either on or off), or continuous (e.g. knobs have a range of values). When hardware is plugged in over USB, the browser automatically detects the presence of an octoblock as a MIDI device, and displays the node on the screen. The state of each module is continuously synchronized over USB, and visually updated as MIDI events are generated. To connect two modules, we use a data flow model with output sources on the bottom of a node, or inputs sinks at the top node. For example, programmatically connecting a button to a buzzer is achieved by wiring the button-output to the buzzer-input. Any MIDI messages are then routed between connected nodes.. All blocks output a single value from 0-100 to any connected blocks downstream. A web-based approach to prototyping is distinct from prior systems, like d.Tools or Phidgets, since *Bloctopus* programming does not require any prior experience with existing developer tools, but gives an avenue for textual programing over time. By using the browser, novices can eventually transition from simple input-output wiring, to textual programming, using an interpreted programming language such as Javascript. More complex control flow structures and arbitrary data transformations are possible using special code-block textboxes that evaluate standard Javascript input.

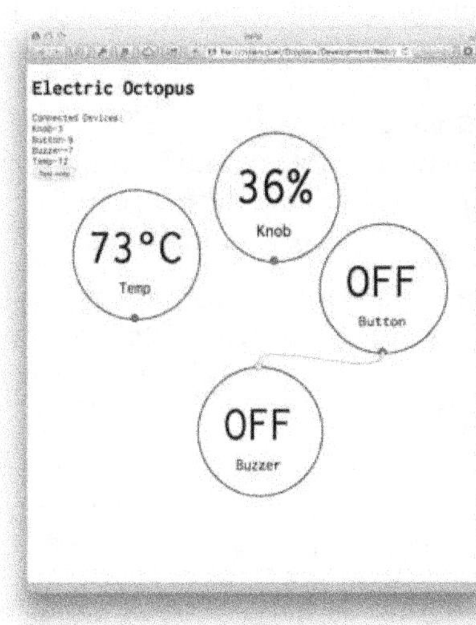

Figure 8. Web interface with visualization and programming behavior by connecting nodes.

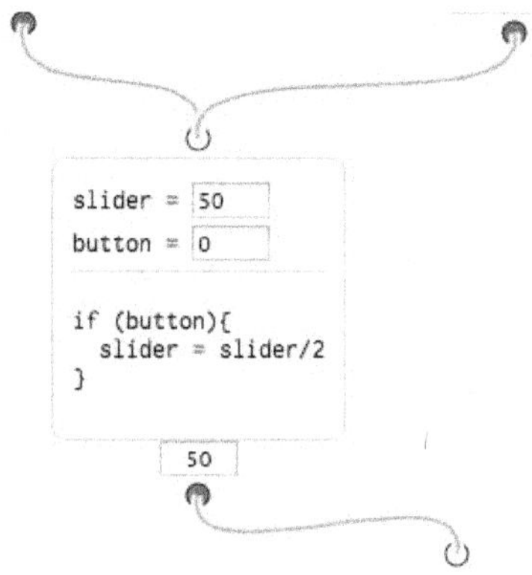

Figure 9. A close-up view of a code-textbox allowing data transformation the output of any connected blocks .

When components are connected to a code-block, input arguments are automatically created inside the block, and code is visually updated in real-time with each new sensor event. By using a standard language like Javascript, the prototyper can be gradually exposed to common textual programming elements such as variables, conditional statements, and loops. A full analysis of the textual programming features, are outside of the scope of this paper, since the authors focus here on the initial novice experience before any textual programming. In the next section we show that this simple input-output mapping is sufficient to produce a range of functional electronic devices.

EVALUATION

In order to evaluate the system design we present some initial qualitative and quantitative metrics of system performance. Because the purpose of the system is to enable novice rapid prototyping, the ultimate test lies in robust user studies that are outside the scope of this initial work. Here we present a case study of a variety of devices prototyped with the system to give a sense of what is possible. Secondly we look at the quantitative performance of the system in response to user input.

Prototyping Case Study

Using the Bloctopus System with a collection of LEGO bricks we prototyped three different device ideas in under 30 minutes to test the expressiveness of the system.

i. **Fever detector**: "A hand-held temperature probe that detects if your temperature is at a dangerous level and then buzzes if your temperature is too high."

ii. **DJ Controller**: "A musical controller that plays songs and speeds up the music with higher levels of ambient light."

iii. **Ergonomic Wrist Warning System**: "Buzzes when my wrist is at a bad angle while typing."

A photo of each prototype is shown in Figures 10 and 11. We found that the hardware was flexible enough to try out diverse forms, and that making basic functional mappings was sufficient in the web-based programming tool. By using low-resolution materials such as LEGOs, it was possible to express many alternative physical forms. When combined with the electrical blocks, the modular affordance of swapping out different components sparked new ideas. For example, the music controller initially was just a button and a slider for fading between songs, with the MIDI controls mapped natively in a DJ software (Djay, by Algoriddim). By trying different combinations of devices over USB, we were able to try multiple alternative interactions such as tilting, blowing on the device, and using gestures to control volume. While making the wrist flex sensor, we initially mounted the tilt sensor to measure wrist motions in pronation and supination, but later reasoned that is was more important to measure flexion and extension to better prevent repetitive strain injury. Because each sensor was mounted on a LEGO base, it was possible to rotate through various sensor positions in order to find a more effective orientation. Swapping out a buzzer for a vibration motor took a few seconds and allowed us, as the designers, to focus on the high-level interaction (e.g. *"how should we give feedback on wrist position?"*), rather than on the technical details.

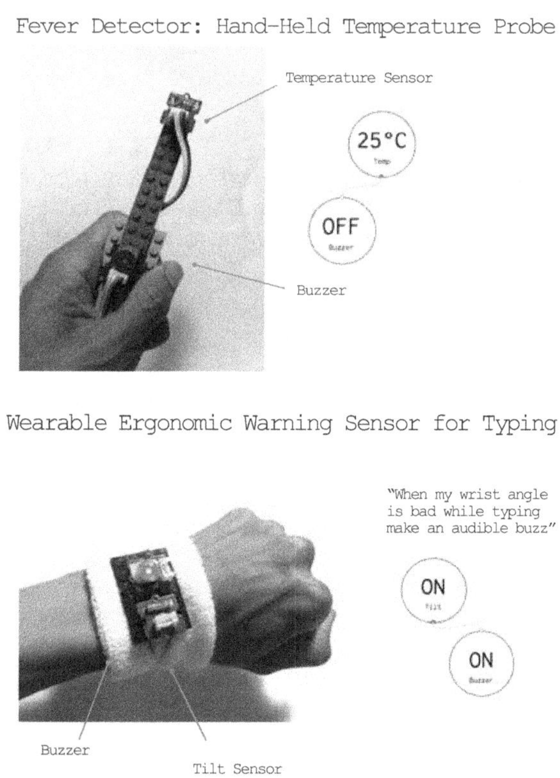

Figure 10. Example hand-held and wearable prototypes made with the Bloctopus system.

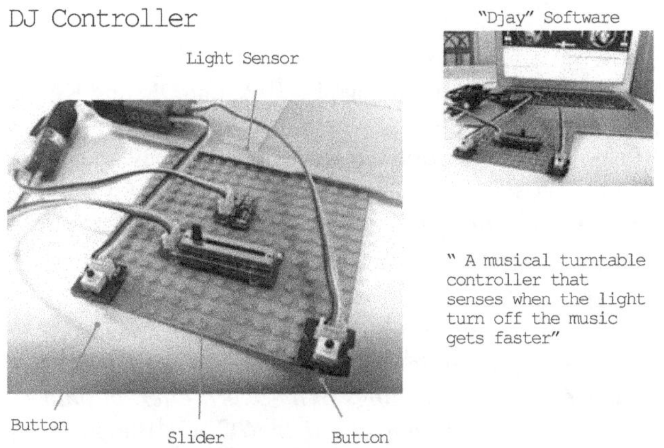

Figure 11. Example DJ-controller prototype made with the Bloctopus system.

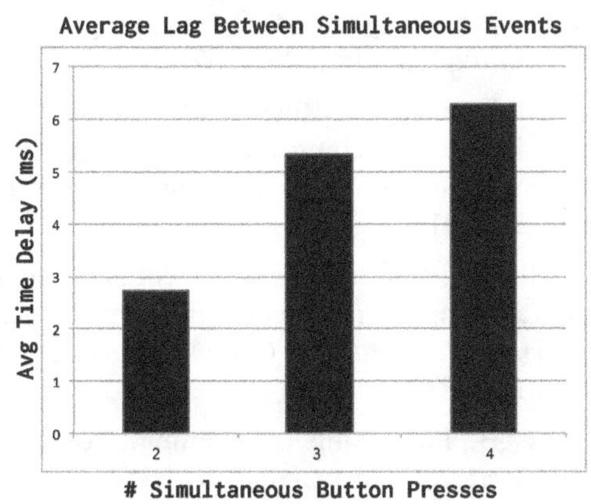

Figure 12. The event recognition lag between 4 simultaneous button presses over repeated trials

System Performance

By using USB for each module we introduce some extra overhead compared with the method of direct wiring to a microcontroller. The user experience is impacted since there is (i) a time delay introduced from module to module communication, and (ii) possible robustness issues due to lost messages. Using an oscilloscope we measured the round trip time from a user input (button press) to an output response (LED turning on). Additionally we measured the time lag between events when up to four buttons are pressed simultaneously by connecting each module to a single shared button. The results are as follows:

- We found that the average round trip time between a single input connected to an output was 13.3 ms (σ = 2.64, N = 12). This means then the time between when a user presses a button on one module, and then sees a response on a second module, is well within the typical limits of human perceptible lag [20].
- With N = 88 simultaneous button presses, 100% of the events were generated and received by the computer. No messages were lost.
- In the case of four simultaneous button presses, the one-way arrival times of each event were staggered by an average of 6.27 ms (σ = 1.2, N =88).

The above measurements suggest that the overhead of using USB MIDI modules in an interactive prototyping system is within the limits of human perceptible lag, and event transmission and detection is robust with many simultaneous inputs.

FUTURE WORK

The primary goal of future work will be to evaluate the prototyping experience through user studies. Following the work of Hartmann et al. [1] we aim to build a classroom level quantity of units (N = 25), and test each unit with a group of prototypers at the college or high school level. Based on our prototyping case study presented, we will iterate on the module design, and further explore the effects of (i) reducing the physical form factor and (ii) reducing the presence of physical wires – for example by adding wireless communication. Finally, we plan to iterate on the visual programming model of the system to better understand the limits of what can be expressed with a hybrid textual and visual programming model.

CONCLUSIONS

We present *Bloctopus*, a novice electronics prototyping system that allows modular prototyping with sensors, actuators, and LEGO blocks. We show a novel sensor model that treats each sensor as a self-contained USB-MIDI device that can be directly connected to a computer or microcontroller with no additional components. We discussed the modular tradeoffs in the system compared to prior work and found a tradeoff between modularity and modifiability. We found that a simple visual programming model can cover a wide range of prototype ideas, and demonstrated that using a web-based programming interface can allow an initial programming experience without textual code. The resulting system was used to make multiple types of devices in under 30 minutes in a prototyping case study. System performance, in terms of response time, lag, and simultaneous events, was well within typical perceptible human limits. Future work will focus on user studies and further enhancements aimed at developing a playful prototyping toolkit for electronics novices.

ACKNOWLEDGMENTS

The Authors would like to acknowledge the technical support and mentorship of Philip Levis. We give a special thanks to Amichi Amar for helping with data collection and system debugging. We are grateful for the financial support of this work under a grant from the Hasso Plattner Design Thinking Research Program.

REFERENCES

1. Hartmann, B., Klemmer, S. R., Bernstein, M., Abdulla, L., Burr, B., Robinson-Mosher, A., & Gee, J. Reflective physical prototyping through integrated design, test, and analysis. *In Proceedings of the 19th annual ACM symposium on User interface software and technology*, ACM (2006), 299-308.
2. Mellis, D. A., Banzi, M., Cuartielles, D., & Igoe, T. Arduino: An open electronics prototyping platform. *In Proceedings of the Conference on Human Factors in Computing (alt.chi)*, ACM (2007).
3. Lego Mindstorms, LEGO ® (2014). (www.lego.com)
4. Blikstein, P. Gears of our childhood: constructionist toolkits, robotics, and physical computing, past and future. *In Proceedings of the 12th International Conference on Interaction Design and Children*, ACM (2013), 173-182.
5. Bdeir, A.. Electronics as material: littleBits. *In Proceedings of the 3rd International Conference on Tangible and Embedded Interaction*, ACM (2009), 397-400.
6. Greenberg, S., & Fitchett, C. Phidgets: easy development of physical interfaces through physical widgets. *In Proceedings of the 14th annual ACM symposium on User interface software and technology*, ACM (2001), 209-218.
7. Barragán, H. *Wiring: Prototyping physical interaction design*. Interaction Design Institute, Ivrea, Italy, 2004.
8. Millner, A., and Edward B.. "Modkit: blending and extending approachable platforms for creating computer programs and interactive objects." In *Proceedings of the 10th International Conference on Interaction Design and Children*, ACM (2011).
9. Schweikardt, Eric, and Gross, M. "roBlocks: a robotic construction kit for mathematics and science education." *Proceedings of the 8th international conference on Multimodal interfaces*. ACM (2006).
10. Modular Robotics Inc. Cubelets website. http://www. modrobotics.com, 2012.
11. Sadler, J., Aquino Shluzas, L., Blikstein, P., and Katila, R. Creative Chunking: Modularity Increases Prototyping Quantity, Creative Self-Efficacy and Cognitive Flow. To appear in the *Proceedings of the Third International Conference on Design Creativity (ICDC)*, Bangalore, India, (2015).
12. Analytis , S. , Sadler, J., and Cutkosky, M.. Paper Robot: A Design Activity to Increase Beginner's Prototyping Confidence With Microcontrollers. To appear in the *Proceedings of the Third International Conference on Design Creativity (ICDC)*, Bangalore, India, (2015).
13. Kelleher C., Pausch, R., Lowering the barriers to programming: A taxonomy of programming environments and languages for novice programmers. *ACM Computing Surveys* (2005), 37(2):83–137.
14. Maloney, J., Resnick, M., Rusk, N., Silverman, B., & Eastmond, E. The scratch programming language and environment. *Transactions on Computing Education TOCE,* ACM (2010), 10(4), 16.
15. Sykes, E.R., Determining the effectiveness of the 3d alice programming environment at the computer science level. *Journal of Educational Computing Research*, (2007), 36(2):223–244.
16. Reas,C., Fry,B., Processing: programming for the media arts. *AI & Society*, (2006), 20(4):526–538.
17. Berdahl, E., & Ju, W. Satellite CCRMA: A musical interaction and sound synthesis platform. In *Proceedings of the International Conference on New Interfaces for Musical Expression,* (2011), 173-178.
18. Micronucleus Bootloader, Jenna Fox (2014, January). Github repository URL: https://github.com/micronucleus/micronucleus
19. Objective Development V-USB , (2014). URL:http://www.obdev.at/products/vusb/index.html
20. Card, S. K., Robertson, G. G., & Mackinlay, J. D. The information visualizer, an information workspace. *In Proceedings of the SIGCHI Conference on Human factors in computing systems,* ACM (1991), 181-186.

Sensing Touch Force using Active Acoustic Sensing

Makoto Ono, Buntarou Shizuki, and Jiro Tanaka
University of Tsukuba, Japan
Tennoudai 1-1-1, Tsukuba, Ibaraki, Japan 305-8571
{ono, shizuki, jiro}@iplab.cs.tsukuba.ac.jp

ABSTRACT

We present a lightweight technique with which creators can prototype force-sensitive objects by attaching a pair of piezoelectric elements: one a vibration speaker and one a contact microphone. The key idea behind our technique is that touch force, in addition to the way the object is touched, can also be observed as different resonant frequency spectra. We also show that recognition of a touch and estimation of the touch force can be implemented by using the combination of support vector classification (SVC) and support vector regression (SVR). An experiment with an additional pressure sensor revealed that our technique might perform well in estimating touch force. We also show a tool for machine learning based on our technique that uses an animated guide, allowing creators to give the system both the training data and the labels for training machine learning needed for dealing with continuous-valued output such as SVR.

Author Keywords

Prototyping; pressure; tangential force; acoustic classification; tangibles; machine learning; support vector machine; support vector classification; support vector regression; piezoelectric sensor.

ACM Classification Keywords

H.5.2 [Information interfaces and presentation]: User Interfaces - Graphical user interfaces; Input devices & strategies.

INTRODUCTION

While techniques for prototyping touch-sensitive objects such as [6, 17, 13, 8, 3, 14] give creators the chance to prototype objects with touch interaction including grasp, the capability of sensing touch force, e.g., pressure and tangential force, will further enrich the vocabulary of touch interaction, allowing creators to prototype objects with a rich set of touch interactions.

In this paper, we explore a lightweight technique with which creators can prototype force-sensitive objects by attaching a pair of piezoelectric elements, one a vibration speaker and one a contact microphone. This technique is based on our active acoustic sensing [14], which is a technique to make existing objects touch-sensitive. The previous technique utilizes the fact that the resonant property of a solid object is sensitive to the way the object is touched; that is, the resonant property changes depending on how the object is touched. Since these changes are observed as different resonant frequency spectra, it is possible to estimate how the object is touched by analyzing the spectra.

The key idea behind our technique is that touch force, in addition to the way the object is touched, can also be observed as different resonant frequency spectra. More specifically, we utilize the fact that strengthening/weakening a touch to a solid object smoothly changes the spectra. Therefore, observing how the spectra changes in real-time can be done to estimate how the object is touched and even the touch force. In this paper, we show that recognition of a touch and estimation of the touch force can be implemented by using the combination of support vector classification (SVC) and support vector regression (SVR).

TEI '15, January 16 - 19 2015, Stanford, CA, USA

http://dx.doi.org/10.1145/2677199.2680585

RELATED WORK

To enrich the vocabulary of touch interaction on surfaces such as touchpads and touchscreens, various attempts have been made to form force-sensitive surfaces.

Resenberg et al. used a matrix of force-variable resistors to build UnMousePad [16], which is a pressure-sensitive flexible multi-touch touchpad. Such a matrix had been used to build a thin flexible pressure sensor [11]. Rendel et al.'s PyzoFlex [15] used a ferroelectric material to form a pressure-sensitive bendable surface, which can sense even hovering interaction. While these devices can perform a wide range of stable pressure-sensing on surfaces, the sensitive area is the devices themselves. In contrast, our technique makes the surface of an object touch- and force-sensitive.

A vision-based technique was also devised. RetroDepth by Kim et al. [9] used a stereo camera and retro-reflective surfaces to precisely estimate the 3D contours of interacting objects on and above the surfaces; the precision is so high that subtle changes in the 3D locations of fingertips can be identified when the user presses the surface of a malleable object to estimate the touch pressure. In contrast, our technique can sense touch force on solid objects.

Pressure Sensing based on Resonant Property

Sensing force on the basis of the resonant property of objects is not new; a resonant pressure sensor [1] uses a diaphragm having a variable self-resonant frequency characteristic, a drive transducer to vibrate the diaphragm, and a

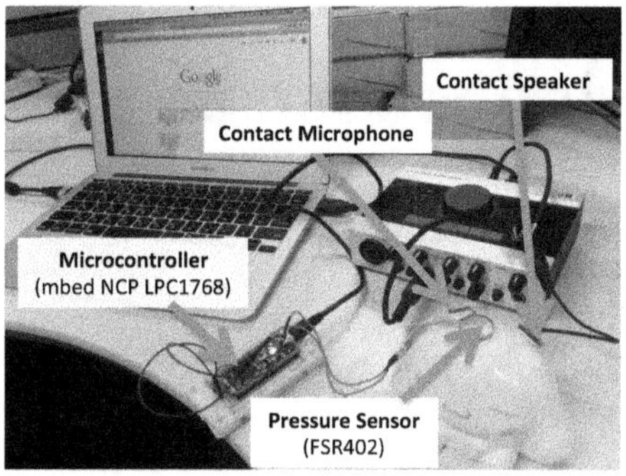

Figure 1. Experimental system. Note that pressure sensor used just for this experiment, i.e., no pressure sensor necessary in actual prototyping.

pickup transducer to capture the vibration. We use the same sensing principle to make the surface of an object touch- and force-sensitive.

Pressure Estimation using SVR

Estimating pressure by using SVR was also tried in a different context. For example, Iswandy et al. [7] used SVR to estimate the cylinder peak pressure values of three-cylinder-engines from the raw sensor data.

EXPERIMENT

To examine whether and how the idea described in INTRODUCTION works, we built an experimental system, shown in Figure 1. Note that the pressure sensor in this system was used just for this experiment, i.e., no pressure sensor is necessary in actual prototyping and only attaching a pair of piezoelectric elements is enough to sense both touch and the touch force.

Experimental System

The experimental system consists of two modules: a module for observing the resonant frequency spectra by using active acoustic sensing and a module for machine learning to recognize touch and estimate touch force.

Observing resonant frequency spectra by using active acoustic sensing

This module is almost identical to the one used in [14]. It consists of a pair of piezoelectric elements (one a vibration speaker and one a contact microphone) and a computer running software for signal processing.

As the two piezoelectric elements, we used a bimorph piezoelectric element (THRIVE K2512BP1, 25 mm × 12 mm × 0.23 mm) by cutting it into halves to reduce the footprints. Both elements were attached to an object by using double-sided adhesive bonding tape (3M SPG-12). The signals current to/from the elements were amplified and connected to a computer (Apple MacBook Air, CPU: Intel Core i7 1.7 GHz, RAM: 8 GB) via an USB audio interface (Native Instruments Audio Kontrol 1).

The computer plays sinusoid sweep signals repeatedly from 20 kHz to 40 kHz, whose frequency increases linearly in 20 ms, at a 96-kHz sampling rate through the speaker. In parallel, the computer also converts the signal captured from the microphone into the resonant frequency response by using FFT.

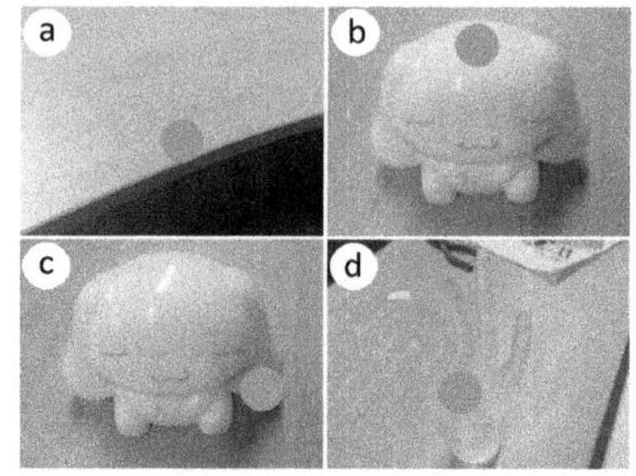

Figure 2. Conditions tested in our experiment: a) wood desk, b) head of plastic toy, c) right hand of plastic toy, and d) acrylic object. Red circle in each figure represents place where pressure sensor was attached.

Machine learning to classify touches and recognize their force

This module recognizes a touch and estimates its force in real-time by using the combination of SVC and SVR. The recognition consists of two stages. At the first stage, the module uses a SVC classifier to identify the current touch among the trained set of touches by using a SVC model, given that the model is trained beforehand. The module then uses the classification result to select one SVR model, which corresponds to the identified touch. At the second stage, the module uses a SVR classifier to recognize the touch force by using the selected SVR model.

Therefore, if a creator wants to make her/his force-sensitive prototype to recognize n kinds of touches, the creator first attaches the pair of piezoelectric elements and then touches the prototype with each kind of touch with various levels of force. As the result of this training, the module has one SVC model and n SVR models.

We implemented this module by using the C-SVC and ϵ-SVR of LIBSVM [2]. In our current implementation, we used the RBF kernel with its default parameters as a kernel function for SVC and the default parameters of ϵ-SVR. The 400-point features extracted by using FFT were passed to these algorithms every 20 ms.

In addition to the sensor necessary in prototyping, we used a pressure sensor (Interlink FSR402, 0.45-mm thick, 12 mm in diameter) for this experiment. The aim of using the pressure sensor was to systematically label the resonant frequency response according to the touch force. That is, to train a SVR model, we used the value from the pressure sensor as the label of the force. This enabled us to measure how accurately the SVR can estimate touch force. In our implementation, the value of the pressure sensor was transmitted to the computer by using a microcontroller (NXP Semiconductors, mbed NCP LPC1768) via USB as an integer ranging from 0 to 99, which means the maximum value that the pressure sensor can sense.

Setup

We tested our technique under the four conditions by using the three objects illustrated in Figure 2. The plastic toy was hollow (1.5-mm thickness), and the other ones were non-

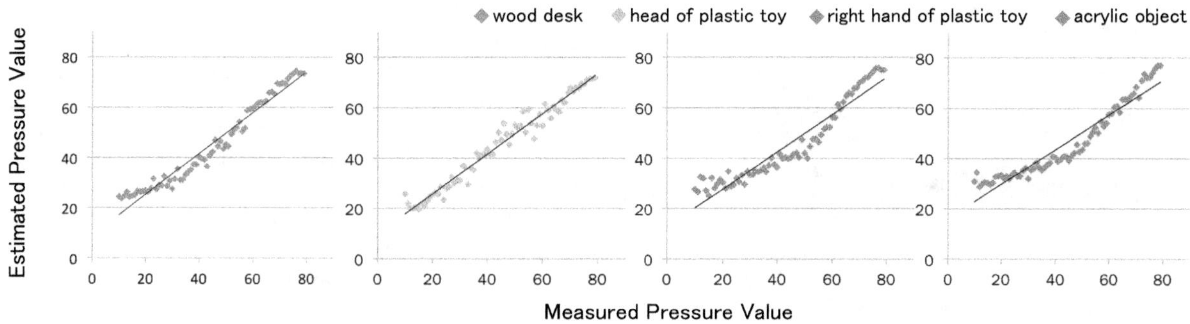

Figure 3. Results: a) wood desk, b) head of plastic toy, c) right hand of plastic toy, and d) acrylic object.

hollow. The plastic toy and the acrylic object were fixed to the desk with double sided tape so that they did not move by touch. For each condition, we attached the pressure sensor at the place annotated with a red circle, and the experimenter, i.e., the first author, touched there with the index finger during this experiment.

For each condition, we trained the classifiers first; the experimenter touched the sensor with a finger, continued the touch while varying the touch force, and detached the finger from the sensor. At the same time, the experimental system collected 10 samples of resonant frequency response for each touch force ranging from 10 to 79, i.e., 700 samples in total in each condition, to train the classifiers. We used the range because the values under 10 were unstable (even gently touching the objects with minimum pressure generates values over 9) and because values over 79 were not observed even if we pushed the pressure sensor strongly under all conditions.

Results and Discussion

Figure 3 shows the results; each subfigure is a scatter plot for each condition with a regression line, where each plot represents the mean of estimated pressure values for a measured value by 10-fold cross-validation. As the regression lines indicate, our technique shows good performance in estimating touch force.

To measure the accuracy of our technique, we also calculated the root mean square error (RMSE) between the estimated pressure values with the measured pressure values and its coefficient of determination (r^2). The result was consistent with the above observation that all these conditions exhibit strong correlations. The r^2 values ranged from 0.833 to 0.869; the RMSE ranged 7.441 to 8.704.

Although the number of tested conditions was four, these results suggest that our technique might perform well in estimating touch force. Moreover, while we used the default parameters of the SVR classifier in this experiment, the accuracy will be improved by tuning the parameters through a grid search.

TOOL FOR PROTOTYPING WITH ANIMATED GUIDE

We also designed a tool for machine learning for our technique, as shown in Figure 4. One challenging goal in designing a system for prototyping based on machine learning is how to let creators give the system both the training data and labels easily. This is especially open with a machine learning dealing with continuous-valued output such as SVR.

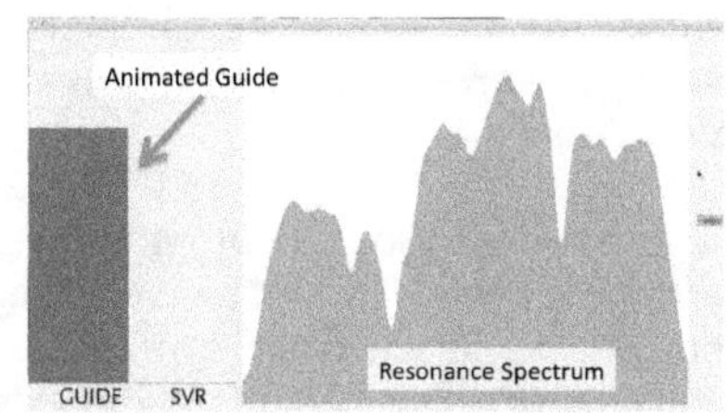

Figure 4. Tool for machine learning with animated guide. In this tool, GUIDE shows the animated guide, SVR shows the estimated force at runtime, Resonance Spectrum shows the current resonant frequency response as visual feedback.

To achieve the goal, we developed a tool that adopts an animated guide, which is the blue bar in Figure 4. This guide allows a creator to interactively give the system both a training datum, i.e., resonant frequency response, and the corresponding label, i.e., a pressure value, simultaneously. The guide begins to stretch upward once the system recognizes that the prototype is touched (this recognition is achieved by continuously comparing the difference between the resonant frequency response with that obtained when the system starts; if the difference exceeds a certain threshold which should be assigned manually in our current system, then the system recognizes that the prototype is touched). When it reaches the top of the GUI window, it disappears and appears again from the bottom of the window. The system repeats this cycle periodically, prompting the creator to perform the touch and to strengthen the touch according to the length of the guide repeatedly. Usually, repeating this cycle three or four times is enough to obtain training data. When the creator stops the animation by pressing a key, the system then begins to train the both classifiers by using the obtained data.

A great advantage of the animated guide is that it requires no pressure sensor, such as the one we used in our experiment, to train the classifiers. This allows creators to make their prototypes touch- and force-sensitive by using only a pair of two piezoelectric elements.

We tested this tool by using the same conditions illustrated in Figure 2, except that we pushed the object with an index finger at the place annotated with the red circle instead of

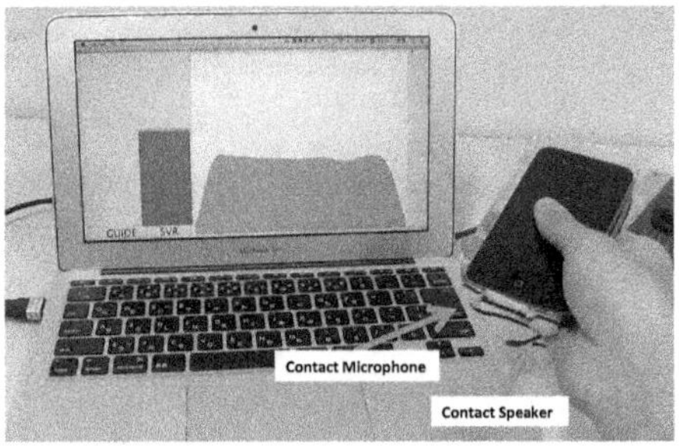

Figure 5. Prototyping smartphone with tangential force sensing.

attaching a pressure sensor. As far as we observed, the system could estimate the pressure, although the accuracy was degraded more than the results of the experiment described in the previous section.

To further test this tool, we used it to prototype a smartphone that can sense force tangential to the touchscreen, similar to [5, 10]. To do this, we attached the two piezoelectric elements to the outside of a plastic smartphone case as illustrated in Figure 5. We used a case slightly larger than the smartphone to make the case sensitive to the force exerted to it in terms of resonant frequency response. We also coated the bottom of the case with a rubber sheet to stabilize the response. Although the tangential force of this prototype is limited to be one-directional, after training, which took approximately 15 seconds, the prototype could roughly estimate the tangential force exerted onto the touchscreen in real-time.

DISCUSSION

One limitation of our technique is that it requires objects to be solid, such as the ones used in our experiment, as this approach utilizes the vibration of objects. It does not work on soft objects such as cotton or gel because of the absorption of vibration, which is the same as [14]. However, our technique still works on a wide variety of objects including flexible ones and bendable ones made of plastic.

Until now, our technique works robustly to ambient noise such as the human voice in an office environment. We have observed such noise did not interfere with the recognition. However, further in-depth investigations, especially under various outdoor conditions, are necessary in future work.

CONCLUSION AND FUTURE WORK

We presented a lightweight technique with which creators can prototype force-sensitive objects by attaching only a pair of a vibration speaker and a contact microphone as a sensor. The key idea behind our technique is that touch force, in addition to the way the object is touched, can also be observed as different resonant frequency spectra. The recognition can be implemented by using the combination of SVC and SVR, whose recognition consists of two stages. We also showed a tool for machine learning based on our technique that uses an animated guide, allowing creators to give the system both the training data and the labels for training machine learning dealing with continuous-valued output.

Our future work includes refining the accuracy in force estimation. Specifically, the parameters of the kernel in SVR were default ones; these can be tuned through a grid search to improve the accuracy. Moreover, until now, we also observed that rubbing a smooth object, i.e., moving a finger on the smooth surface of the object with a constant amount of pressure, differently changes the resonant frequency response of the object from strengthening/weakening a touch to the object, even if the gestures produce no audible sound; thus, we are trying to develop an algorithm, which is different from that of Stane [12] and Scratch Input [4], to detect rubbing gestures over smooth objects on the basis of active acoustic sensing.

REFERENCES

1. W. C. Blanchard. Resonant pressure sensor, 1973. US Patent 3,745,384.
2. C.-C. Chang and C.-J. Lin. LIBSVM: a library for support vector machines., http://www.csie.ntu.edu.tw/cjlin/livsvm
3. N.-W. Gong, J. Steimle, S. Olberding, S. Hodges, N. E. Gillian, Y. Kawahara, and J. A. Paradiso. PrintSense: A versatile sensing technique to support multimodal flexible surface interaction. In *CHI'14*, 1407–1410.
4. C. Harrison and S. E. Hudson. Scratch input: creating large, inexpensive, unpowered and mobile finger input surfaces. In *UIST'08*, 205–208.
5. S. Heo and G. Lee. Force gestures: Augmenting touch screen gestures with normal and tangential forces. In *UIST'11*, 621–626.
6. S. E. Hudson and J. Mankoff. Rapid construction of functioning physical interfaces from cardboard, thumbtacks, tin foil and masking tape. In *UIST'06*, 289–298.
7. K. Iswandy and A. König. Hybrid virtual sensor based on RBFN or SVR compared for an embedded application. In *Knowlege-Based and Intelligent Information and Engineering Systems*, LNAI 6882, pages 335–344. Springer, 2011.
8. Y. Kawahara, S. Hodges, B. S. Cook, C. Zhang, and G. D. Abowd. Instant inkjet circuits: Lab-based inkjet printing to support rapid prototyping of UbiComp devices. In *UbiComp'13*, 363–372.
9. D. Kim, S. Izadi, J. Dostal, C. Rhemann, C. Keskin, C. Zach, J. Shotton, T. Large, S. Bathiche, M. Nießner, et al. RetroDepth: 3D silhouette sensing for high-precision input on and above physical surfaces. In *CHI'14*, 1377–1386.
10. B. Lee, H. Lee, S.-C. Lim, H. Lee, S. Han, and J. Park. Evaluation of human tangential force input performance. In *CHI'12*, 3121–3130.
11. C. F. Malacaria. A thin, flexible, matrix-based pressure sensor. *Sensors Magazine*, 1998.
12. R. Murray-Smith, J. Williamson, S. Hughes, and T. Quaade. Stane: synthesized surfaces for tactile input. In *CHI'08*, 1299–1302. ACM, 2008.
13. S. Olberding, N.-W. Gong, J. Tiab, J. A. Paradiso, and J. Steimle. A cuttable multi-touch sensor. In *UIST'13*, 245–254.
14. M. Ono, B. Shizuki, and J. Tanaka. Touch & Activate: Adding interactivity to existing objects using active acoustic sensing. In *UIST'13*, 31–40.
15. C. Rendl, P. Greindl, M. Haller, M. Zirkl, B. Stadlober, and P. Hartmann. PyzoFlex: Printed piezoelectric pressure sensing foil. In *UIST'12*, 509–518.
16. I. Rosenberg and K. Perlin. The UnMousePad: An interpolating multi-touch force-sensing input pad. In *SIGGRAPH '09/ACM Trans. Graph*, volume 28, pages 65:1–65:9. ACM, 2009.
17. V. Savage, X. Zhang, and B. Hartmann. Midas: Fabricating custom capacitive touch sensors to prototype interactive objects. In *UIST'12*, 579–588.

Flutter: An Exploration of an Assistive Garment Using Distributed Sensing, Computation and Actuation

Halley P Profita, Nicholas Farrow, Nikolaus Correll
Dept. of Computer Science
University of Colorado Boulder
{halley.profita, nicholas.farrow, nikolaus.correll}@colorado.edu

ABSTRACT
Assistive technology (AT) has the ability to improve the standard of living of those with disabilities, however, it can often be abandoned for aesthetic or stigmatizing reasons. Garment-based AT offers novel opportunities to address these issues as it can stay with the user to continuously monitor and convey relevant information, is non-invasive, and can provide aesthetically pleasing alternatives. In an effort to overcome traditional AT and wearable computing challenges including, cumbersome hardware constraints and social acceptability, we present Flutter, a fashion-oriented wearable AT. Flutter seamlessly embeds low-profile networked sensing, computation, and actuation to facilitate sensory augmentation for those with hearing loss. The miniaturized distributed hardware enables both textile integration and new methods to pair fashion with function, as embellishments are functionally leveraged to complement technology integration. Finally, we discuss future applications and broader implications of using such computationally-enabled textile wearables to support sensory augmentation beyond the realm of AT.

Author Keywords
Assistive technology; e-textiles; distributed computation; wearable interfaces; haptics; fashion

ACM Classification Keywords
H.5.m. Information interfaces and presentation (e.g., HCI): Miscellaneous. C2.4 Computer Communication Networks: Distributed Systems.

General Terms
Design; Human Factors; Algorithms

INTRODUCTION
Textile-based wearable computing systems have the ability to assist and augment the human sensory network by leveraging their close proximity with the skin to provide contextual information to a user. Textile applications offer a notable platform for materials augmented with sensing, computation and actuation since fabric facilitates dense hardware integration and housing [1-5,8,10,11,13-16]. Applications for such wearable computing systems include informational displays, interfacing to other body-worn devices or the environment, and augmenting the human senses [1, 14]. We see such smart garment interfaces as lending to sensory augmentation that can benefit everyone, and especially those with disabilities. For this design exploration, we chose to focus on supplementing hearing loss as it is a common disability that often goes unaided [7], placing individuals at a significant disadvantage when navigating their environment. Flutter (Figure 1) uses a network of microphones to resolve directionality to noises in the environment (e.g., a car horn honking that one with auditory loss otherwise might not hear) and relays the directional information back to the user by means of a network of vibration motors also embedded in the garment.

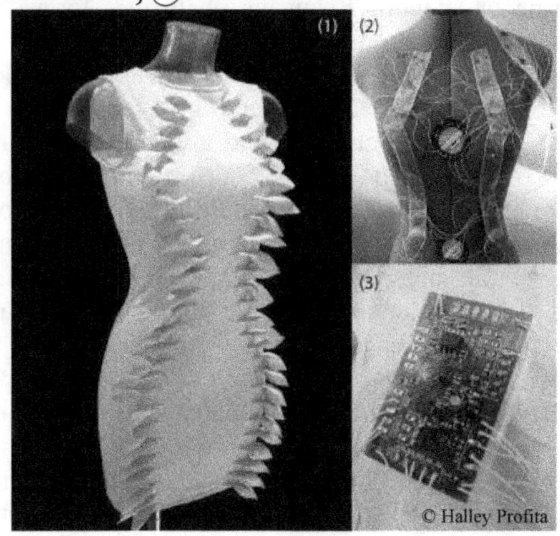

Figure 1: Flutter (1), robotic node network (2), pcb node (3).

When developing such assistive garments, continual aid is of priority. Thus, methods should be implemented which minimize single points of failure. To date, hardware constraints have hindered the development of fully functional, aesthetic, seamless assistive computing garments. However, recent developments in "robotic materials" – incorporating tiny networked microcontrollers with sensors, and actuators – permit for a distributed, modular system that can span the entire garment, can support a number of scenarios, and can provide continuous feedback while remaining inconspicuous and robust to total system failure. Moreover, we see such low-profile hardware as contributing to more aesthetic approaches in wearable AT design in the hopes of addressing current abandonment issues by minimizing social stigma to encourage adoption.

TEI '15, January 16 - 19 2015, Stanford, CA, USA

ACM 978-1-4503-3305-4/15/01…$15.00
http://dx.doi.org/10.1145/2677199.2680586

BACKGROUND

In the USA, 56.7 million people suffer from some form of disability[1]. While AT has the ability to improve one's standard of living by augmenting the senses [7], users often abandon AT due to functional, aesthetic, or stigmatizing shortcomings [7]. Textile forms of wearable computing can prove beneficial for AT as they can move throughout the environment with the user, providing continuous monitoring or support. Recurring challenges for wearable AT, and wearable computing in general, reside with cumbersome hardware constraints (i.e., making technology integration untenable and wearability impractical [1]), social acceptability/stigma [7], and user friendly interfaces [14]. We believe recent developments in miniature modular distributed networking systems could be leveraged for AT as such systems incorporate sensing, and actuation and are ideal for textile integration. Smart Dust [6] popularized the concept of fully autonomous, cubic millimeter-sized agents capable of networked sensing and communication while Pushpin Computing [9, 12] explored amorphous computing principles for surface-based distributed sensor networks to create scalable networks using omnidirectional infrared communication. Our work builds on the concept of scalable networks while also using tethered communication between nodes. Further, hardwired connections enable nodes to infer spatial configuration by imposing a deformable coordinate system defined by the shape of the garment.

Exploring infrastructures using e-textiles gained traction in the late 1990s as the desire to create wearables capable of sensing and computation was met with the challenge of trying to incorporate hardware with textiles [5, 10]. Gorlick experimented with integrating a bus system into clothing using e-textiles [4]. Lehn et al. expanded on this concept with "e-TAGs," a modular network of PCBs, sensors, and actuators that could be attached to a multi-bus architecture within a garment [8]. Bus-based approaches are limited by the number of the devices they can support. They are also susceptible to total failure resulting from single points of wire/conductor failure, while individual malfunctioning nodes may block the bus – issues we've managed to avoid through our decentralized system approach. Moreover, multiple connections to every node provides redundant access to power (i.e., power supplies can be distributed and located anywhere in the network). By using surface mount technology, we were able to reduce the hardware size and power requirements to allow us to seamlessly implement our system in a wearable textile substrate.

DESIGN CONCEPT

'Flutter' integrates function and fashion to inconspicuously and non-invasively facilitate sensory augmentation for those with hearing loss. If a loud alert is detected, such as the honk of a horn, the winglets of the garment will begin to 'flutter' in the direction of the signal for vibrotactile notification. It is common for those with hearing loss to navigate their outdoor environment unaided, despite the number of options available to users, including hearing aids, guide dogs, and cochlear implants. In fact, hearing aids remain one of the top forms of rejected AT with up to a 75% abandonment rate [7], considerable given that nearly 7.6 million individuals have some degree of hearing loss in the US[1]. This is attributed to the fact that hearing aids offer mixed reliability (e.g., limited in their ability to provide directional information and recurring amplification issues, making noisy public spaces overwhelming), call attention to one's disability, and are costly. Flutter was developed with the 'unaided' user in mind given that many individuals choose to do without their AT, leaving them susceptible to potentially dangerous situations. The aesthetic approach to Flutter was pursued to encourage use of one's assistive device by appealing to one's stylistic preferences and to 'de-emphasize' the assistive nature of AT. Additionally, often is the case that AT promotes high expectations that go unmet, leading to disillusionment and abandonment [7]. We see Flutter as providing 'just enough' contextual information to support a user without overwhelming or obstructing other senses. A distributed network of robotic materials support this design goal by facilitating a wearable, non-invasive, fashion-forward assistive garment that can be programmed to notify users of pertinent environmental cues while attempting to filter unnecessary information.

Usage Scenario

Imagine you are a female with severe hearing loss in one ear. You start off the day by donning Flutter. As you walk to work, you take caution to look both ways when crossing major intersections. The crosswalk signal indicates that you have the right of way. As you step out into the street you hear ambulance sirens but it is difficult for you to localize the direction that they're coming from. Then, the portion of the garment located over the front right shoulder begins to vibrate vehemently. As you look to the right you see the ambulance approaching and quickly return to the sidewalk so you are out of the ambulance's immediate path.

IMPLEMENTATION

Physical Design

Inspired as a garment for assistive applications and unobtrusive sensing, 'Flutter' seeks to address many of the challenges central to AT adoption and wearable technology usage. A recurring issue with AT is that it often lacks aesthetic appeal and can call attention to one's disability - stigmatizing the user and ultimately leading to AT rejection. This remains a challenge for wearable computing as well since hardware is often too cumbersome to integrate seamlessly into a garment [3, 10] calling attention to the device and making the user feel socially awkward. Computational nodes address this by employing lightweight low-profile PCBs capable of seamless textile integration.

[1] http://www.census.gov/prod/2012pubs/p70-131.pdf

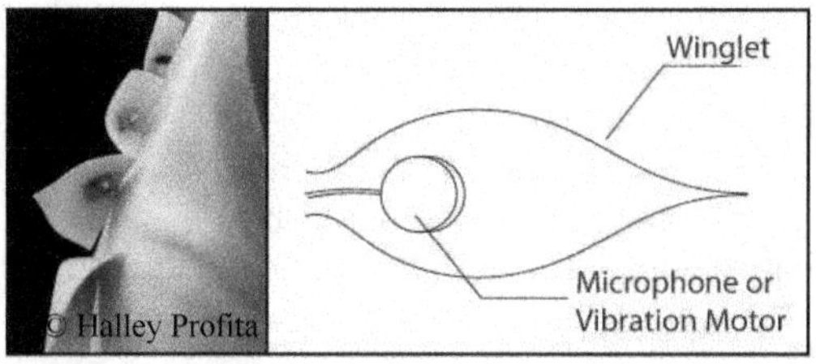

Figure 2: Winglets (left) and winglet schematic (right).

Flutter permits for node incorporation anywhere in the garment (as opposed to being forced to design around cumbersome hardware). Rather than deterring from the aesthetic appeal of the dress, small networked nodes enable configurations that can be married with fashion-forward designs. In this instance, Flutter embeds vibration motors in the anterior embellishment (winglets) to demonstrate how aesthetic ornamentation can yield a utilitarian purpose (as the winglets deliver the haptic feedback). This ornamentation also serves to mask the hardware, thus, for future smart garment designs it should be noted that fashionable embellishment can be functionally leveraged to enable and complement technology integration. This particular advantage of attire merits further exploration.

For a wearable such as Flutter, embellishment is used in a manner that supports the technology yet does not interfere with the 'wearability' of the dress. The winglets span the vertical length of the dress, increasing the volume of hardware integration to enhance the dress's utility. Each row of winglets contains two microphones and eight vibration motors connected to microcontroller nodes. The nodes located on the back of the garment are placed near the shoulder blades to measure posterior sounds. Each PCB node is networked together, lending to a decentralized system in constant communication with nodes evenly distributed throughout the garment. The fashion-forward design was created to elicit a positive emotional association with the garment (versus negative emotions commonly associated with unsightly AT). Taking fashionably-oriented properties into account can help to encourage adoption. Moreover, the fact that Flutter is a form of AT goes unrealized to outside parties, potentially eliminating stigma.

Hardware

Flutter incorporates six identical PCB nodes (four in the front, two in the back) that sense and respond to the presence and direction of auditory cues. A single on/off switch controls the device. Node placement was specifically chosen to help resolve front-back and left-right ambiguity, a common problem reported by hearing aid users. Each node is composed of an ATxmega128A3 microcontroller, a microphone for sensory input, and up to four coin vibration motors (1 cm diameter) for haptic feedback. The vibration intensity may be modulated enabling more precise feedback to the user. The microphone circuit is connected to the PCB's on-board ADC, drastically minimizing the circuit complexity for size reduction. We chose the Xmega line of processors for their large number of built-in hardware serial ports (USARTs). Six ports are used exclusively for independent communication channels between nodes, which allow arranging the nodes in a triangular-hexagonal lattice. A seventh serial port is available for interfacing the garment to a computer for programming purposes. All connected nodes propagate any program updates in a viral fashion, meaning the user only needs to access a single node to interface with the entire network. This facilitates a garment that can be reprogrammed to adapt to the changing needs of the user, a common issue for AT users [7]. Node-to-node interconnects also support power transfer so that batteries need only be attached to the distributed power and ground bus to ensure the entire garment receives power. The absence of central components dramatically facilitates wiring, and easily permits including extra nodes or power sources at any time.

Sound Measurement, and Direction Estimation

The microphone amplifier circuit provides some acoustical signal filtering prior to ADC measurement to remove infra- and ultra-sonic frequencies, noises people wouldn't normally hear. The PCB continuously samples the audio signal, recording a series of audio frames into a double buffer (256 samples in 4.1 ms). While one buffer is being filled, the other is being processed. The spectral components of the frame are calculated using a Fast Fourier Transform. This facilitates further processing (e.g., bandpass filtering and cross-correlation) because these operations are much faster in the spectral domain than in the time domain. For an assistive device, only transient signals in the environment are of interest as background noises should be ignored. The PCBs maintain an estimate of the local ambient noise by averaging the audio frames over time. Each node that detects a transient signal communicates with neighboring nodes to compute the direction of the incoming sound. Flutter uses the sound intensity differential between nodes to determine which node is facing the signal and, in turn, actuates the corresponding motors.

DISCUSSION

Wearable haptic interfaces for sensory deficits are not novel [1]. While we chose to use haptic feedback for Flutter, we see our true contribution lying in our design exploration of how tightly embedded low-profile electronics and especially distributed and local computation can take assistive, computationally enhanced attire to the next level by forgoing bulky and failure prone centralized components. Implementing the same functionality with conventional technology, i.e., Raspberry Pi and associated microphone stack, would require excessive hardware and wiring to route analog signals along the body, digitize them and process them in parallel. Such system requirements make seamless textile integration untenable. Our work supports a number of daily living scenarios (e.g., temporary sensory occlusion caused by earbuds that impede hearing). and presents new opportunities where existing AT continues to fall short. This work was originally presented at a Design Exhibition [13]. Although we were unable to test with users, we did receive relevant feedback at the Exhibition and from the online hearing loss communities. Commentary highlighted the existing concerns with abandoned hearing aids, as even hearing aid users admittedly remove their aid for outdoor activities. Moreover, one individual with partial hearing discussed difficulties in localizing sounds well. Of interest were the positive reflections on attire geared toward accessibility, alluding to an unmet need for AT users:

"the dress is just so interesting... there are so many who are potentially wanting new resources (and clothes! :-) that assist us — that make the world accessible to all" [17]

In order to substantively evaluate these claims, future testing still needs to be done to understand how well the system works in different contexts, if users would actually wear it, other preferred wearable form factors, and fabrication for washing and daily wear. We see Flutter as just one physical instantiation of how fashion can enhance assistive devices (as opposed to a blanket solution for all hearing aids). The beauty lies in the ability to create a highly customized, fashion-oriented wearable for the user's needs and preferences. Feedback also revealed many possible research directions for 'Flutter', as well as a sizable spread of applications for the technology in other domains. In addition to environmental navigation, we see opportunities to explore how somato-sensory stimulation can supplement aural processing of the environment for individuals with hearing loss. Additionally, a smart garment could be reprogrammed to map spectral information as spatial feedback. A new mapping between the environmental audio spectrum to physical vibrations in the torso would be equivalent to putting a vibrotactile spectrograph on the chest, with higher frequencies actuated higher on the chest, while lower frequencies would be mapped to the abdomen. This could be used to assist a user in enjoying music or other interesting sounds. We are also interested in how such an on-body system could be paired with existing assistive technologies, such as hearing aids to enhance sound capture and provide more accurate spatial resolution and ambient noise filtering. We would like to look at different sensors and feedback mechanisms to bring smart garments to diverse user communities. Exploring hardware integration and clothing ornamentation can lend to new developments for textile-based wearable computing. Furthermore, new hardware and fabrication techniques could yield fully networked reams of fabric that could be premade and cut to size for the application.

CONCLUSION

We presented "Flutter," an instance of a wearable, assistive platform that tightly integrates function and fashion to explore wearable computing design and to address existing AT concerns. By harnessing the benefits of distributed sensing, computation and actuation, we are able to create wearables capable of augmenting the human sensory network. Such a garment leverages inconspicuous hardware integration and the surface area of the human skin to create aesthetic, wearable interfaces capable of continuous user support. Such smart garments are scalable, amorphous, reconfigurable and reprogrammable by design, permitting for flexibility with end users and application scenarios.

ACKNOWLEDGEMENTS

This work is supported by the NSF, award #1153158, and the DARPA WarriorWeb Program, contract #W911NF-14-C-0057. We extend a special thank you to Asta Roseway for her helpful discussion in documenting this work.

REFERENCES

1. Alahakone, A. U., and Senanayake, S, A. "Vibrotactile feedback systems: Current trends in rehabilitation, sports and information display." *AIM.* IEEE, 2009.
2. Basu, S., Schwartz, S., and Pentland, A. Wearable phased arrays for sound localization and enhancement. In *Proc. ISWC,* IEEE (2000), 103-110.
3. DeVaul, R., Sung, M., Gips, J., and Pentland, A.S. Mithril. Applications and architecture. *ISWC* '03.
4. Gorlick, M. Electric Suspenders: A Fabric Power Bus and Data Network for Wearable Digital Devices. In *Proc. ISWC 1999*, IEEE (1999), 114–121.
5. Jones, M. T., and Martin, T. L. 6 Hardware and Software Architectures for Electronic Textiles. *Smart Clothing*. CRC Press, Boca Raton, FL, USA, 2010.
6. Kahn, J.M., Katz, R.H., and Pister, K.S. Next century challenges: mobile networking for "Smart Dust". In *Mobile computing and networking*. ACM Press (1999).
7. Kintsch, A., and DePaula, R. A framework for the adoption of assistive technology. *SWAAAC: Supporting Learning Through Assistive Tech.* '02, 1-10.
8. Lehn, D., Neely, C., Schoonover, K., Martin, T., and Jones, M. e-TAGs: e-textile attached gadgets.*CNDS '04.*
9. Lifton, J., Seetharam, D., Broxton, M., and Paradiso, J. Pushpin computing system overview: A platform for distributed, embedded, ubiquitous sensor networks. In *Pervasive Computing,* (2002), 139-151.
10. Marculescu, D. et al. Electronic textiles: A platform for pervasive computing. *IEEE, 91*, 12 (2003), 1995-2018.
11. Nakad, Z., Jones, M., Martin, T., and Fawaz, W. Networking in E-textiles. *Comp. communications*, *33,* 6(2010).
12. Paradiso, J.A., Lifton, J., and Broxton, M. Sensate media—multimodal electronic skins as dense sensor networks. *BT Technology Journal*, *22*, 4 (2004), 32-44.
13. Profita, H., Farrow, N., and Correll, N. Flutter. In Adjunct Proc. *ISWC 2012*, IEEE (2012), 44-46
14. Ross, D.A. Implementing assistive technology on wearabe computers. Intel. Sys. IEEE 16.3 (2001), 47-53.
15. Van Laerhoven, K., Schmidt, A., and Gellersen, H. W., Multi-Sensor Context Aware Clothing. In *ISWC* (2002).
16. Zimmerman, T.G. Personal area networks: near-field intrabody communication. *IBM Sys. Jour*, *35*(3.4) 1996.
17. Interview with CCA Captioning representative. http://ccacaptioning.org. Last retrieved 9/19/2012.

cArVATAR – A Novel Remote Control For Toy Cars

Shachar Geiger
Interaction Lab, Holon Institute of Technology
52 Golomb St. Holon, Israel
s.geiger.s@gmail.com

Michal Rinott
Interaction Lab, Holon Institute of Technology
52 Golomb St. Holon, Israel
michalrin@gmail.com

ABSTRACT
We describe a novel controller for a remote controlled (R/C) car. The controller is a small car-shaped toy which is used for controlling the larger toy car. In this avatar-inspired relationship between controller and controlled, operations performed on the small car are implemented by the larger car. The cArVATAR addresses limitations of the traditional R/C, and is proposed as an alternative allowing younger children to use R/C toys. Details of the prototype and observations from an exploratory study performed with five children aged 6 to 7 are presented, and possible applications to other products and domains are discussed.

Author Keywords
cArVATAR; Remote Control; Tangible Interfaces; Mimicry

ACM Classification Keywords
I.2.9 Robotics: Operator Interfaces
H.5.2 User Interfaces: User-Centered Design

INTRODUCTION
In the early years of life, children play in elaborate ways with objects: examining them and manipulating them directly [1]. As their knowledge grows, they give these objects symbolic properties: a toy car turns from an object to bang on a table to something that is moved on the floor while making engine sounds [2].

When first attempting to use a remote-controlled vehicle, children need to adopt new abstraction of play. They need to discover and master the relationship between the controller and the controlled in order to achieve a rewarding play experience. The division between cause and effect, as well as the sensory-motor skills required for control, are challenging. For some, this is a joyful process of mastery; for others, a frustrating one.

TEI '15, January 16 - 19 2015, Stanford, CA, USA
Copyright 2015 ACM 978-1-4503-3305-4/15/01$15.00
http://dx.doi.org/10.1145/2677199.2680589

TRADITIONAL CONTROLLER CHALLENGES
There are three main types of traditional remote controllers for toy vehicles. The simplest controller has four buttons for forward, backward, left and right functions. The more advanced controller has two sticks, one for forward and backward control, the other for orientation control (turning the wheels). A third controller type, specific to toy cars, has a circular knob for orientation control and a trigger button for forwards and backwards control. Focusing on the two-stick controller, since it is the most commonly used for R/C cars, we identify a number of challenges for beginner users:

1. **Functional separation:** the controlled car is a single object, able to move only to one direction at a time; however, the controller has two sticks, suggesting two separate functions. Users need to process these two dimensions simultaneously in order to control the car.
2. **Mapping:** while forwards and backwards movements of one stick map quite directly to movement of the controlled car, the second stick works differently! It moves right and left, but does not cause the car to move unless the other stick is being used.
3. **Relativity:** driving and turning are relative to the car's orientation: when the car front is facing the child, pushing the forward/backwards stick upwards (forward) causes the vehicle to approach the child, and pushing the left/right stick to the right makes the vehicle turn to the child's left. This relative control scheme requires children to adopt a non-egocentric point of view.
4. **Fine motor skill:** the sticks require fine motor skills, especially in controllers where the measure of stick movement translates to the speed or turn radius of the controlled car. Also, gaining full control requires coordination between the hands.

ALTERNATIVE CONTROL METHODS
Recent research has looked into alternative control methods in which the relationship between controller and controlled is made more direct.

Dang and Andre [3] compared the traditional remote controller with a gestural control method: both hands turn an imaginary steering wheel left or right, and push it forward or pull backward to drive forward and back. The article describes the users' difficulty in orientation, due to the relative nature of the controls: the user's forward direction often differs from that of the car.

Various projects have explored control interfaces that employ repetition of a series of motions [4,5,6]. In these projects, however, there is a sharp distinction between a "recording" phase and an "execution" phase. The concept of mimicry was explored by Guo et al [7], who compared two control techniques for robots: the first was based on toys which were of physical resemblance to the controlled robots; the second was graphical representations of the robots presented on a touched screen. The robot was controlled by setting a new position and orientation to its matching controller (toy or graphical representation) on the screen, thus initiating an autonomous motion of the robot to its new position. Most users strongly preferred the tangible interface to the touch surface.

In our project, we employ an object of physical and functional resemblance to the controlled object: a car avatar, or cArVATAR. Through it we explore the use of mimicry in real-time control, addressing the disadvantages of traditional controllers, especially for younger children. We aim for an easier point of entry to the interaction, and for a high level of play value.

THE CARVATAR

The cArVATAR is a small plastic toy car with two pairs of hinged wheels that roll forward and backwards but do not rotate to the sides. The cArVATAR controls an off-the-shelf R/C car with four-wheel drive. The cArVATAR is similar to the controlled car in having a car's prototypical form, and is thus a good model of the controlled car. However, it differs in scale and in the central affordance of non-turning wheels. The partial resemblance between controller and controlled allows the implementation of different control schemes.

For this exploratory study we implemented a simple control scheme for cArVATAR, keeping a high degree of similarity between the traditional controller and the cArVATAR functions. The control functions are:

- Forward and backward movement: rotation of the controller wheels is translated to motor force of the controlled car. The faster the controller wheels are rotated, the car accelerates more and stops accelerating at higher speeds.
- Orientation: changing the controller orientation while the car is in motion causes the controlled car to make the same change in angle.

An inherent feature of the cArVATAR interaction is that it requires a surface on which to move. This can be the floor, an elevated surface like a table, and even body parts like an arm.

Interesting limitations arise regarding the mapping of motion from the controller car to the controlled car. The main issues are:

- Slow forwards and backwards movements of the cArVATAR can be faithfully mapped to the controlled car. However, due to limitations in the acceleration of the controlled car, very fast gestures of the cArVATAR controller create shorter and slower movements.
- In the simple plastic car model of the cArVATAR, orientation can be changed by simply lifting and turning the whole toy car; however in the controlled car - as in all cars - orientation can be changed only while driving, and the turn radius is limited by the car wheels' degree of rotation.

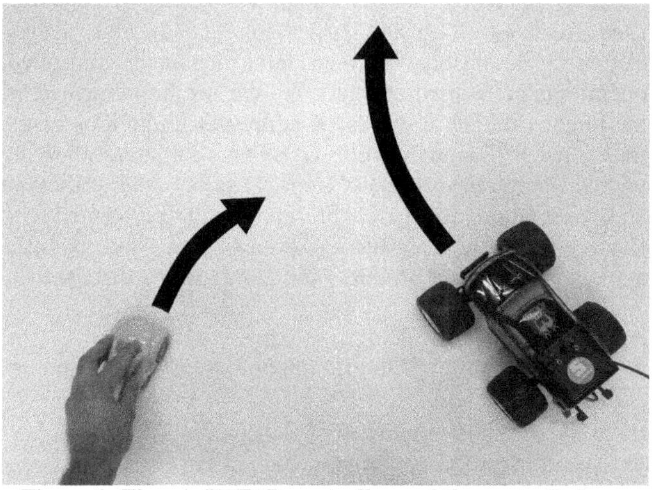

Figure 1: The cArVATAR controller and the controlled car, with motion trajectories

Expected advantages and challenges of cArVATAR

We expect cArVATAR to simplify learning and increase playfulness in controlling the car.

The main expected advantages are:

1. **Unity of control:** all functions of the controlled car are performed with a single object and gesture, removing the need for cognitive coordination between two functions.
2. **Simpler mapping:** high physical resemblance - and partial affordance resemblance - to the controlled car should enable the children grasp the functional mapping faster.
3. **Flexible orientation:** the problem of differing points of view of the controlled car and user can be easily alleviated by turning the toy car controller so that it heads in the same direction as the controlled car. In this way, drive and turn gesture directions become mapped naturally.
4. **Gross motor control:** the cArVATAR works with more gross motor skills (large gestures of the arm and shoulder) than fine ones, which fits well with younger children's capabilities.

Technical Implementation

The toy car used for the cArVATAR controller was fitted with an Arduino board, an XBee transceiver for communication with the controlled car, a rotary encoder used for sensing the rotation of the wheels and a compass module for sensing the controller's absolute orientation.

The controlled car's electronics were hacked and programmed with an Arduino board. The car was equipped with a 9 degrees of freedom sensor for sensing orientation, a rotary encoder for allowing tight control over the speed and rotation of the wheels and an XBee transducer.

PLAY SESSIONS

We conducted play session with cArVATAR in which a single child used a traditional remote, and then the cArVATAR, to control the same toy car. We chose to include the traditional controller to have an impression of children's abilities with it; however, we focus on the children's use of the cArVATAR and point to significant differences from the traditional remote when relevant. Because all children reported at least partial familiarity with the traditional remote, we chose to present it first in all sessions, followed by the novel cArVATAR.

The sessions were conducted in an empty room measuring 4 by 7 meters. Five children, aged 6-7 (3 boys, 2 girls) took part in this exploratory study. Each session, which lasted 20 minutes, consisted of the following four parts:

1. Traditional controller: A quick demonstration followed by free play
2. Traditional controller: play challenges
3. cArVATAR: A quick demonstration followed by free play
4. cArVATAR: play challenges

The play challenges were:

1. Drive slowly on the straight line marked on the floor (controlled car facing forward)
2. Drive backwards on the straight line marked on the floor (controlled car facing backwards, towards the child)
3. Drive along the tight arc marked on the floor (controlled car on the beginning of arc, facing forward)
4. Drive along the tight arc (controlled car at the end of arc, facing backwards)
5. As in challenge 3, this time along the loose arc
6. As in challenge 4, this time along the loose arc
7. Drive to a tower of blocks and knock it over

At the start of each challenge the child stood at the starting point of the curves, with the car placed before them.

Observations

We first present observations related to the basic driving functions performed in the challenges; we then present additional observations related to play value.

Driving forward and backward

All children were able to immediately start using the cArVATAR and to perform the basic forwards and backwards driving gestures simply and directly. There was no hesitation or confusion in these functions, and they were performed with the simplicity and spontaneity of playing with a toy car.

The length of an arm span was not sufficient for performing the long drive of Play Challenge 1 with the cArVATAR. In this case, the children tended to move their body to the place where their hand had reached, in order to push the car from there onward. They did not spontaneously employ the option of lifting the controller and placing it back next to them (somewhat similarly to a computer mouse at the edge of the mousepad). In this aspect cArVATAR differs significantly from the traditional controller, in which long drives do not require added effort, creating a different play pattern.

Moving precisely along the drawn line was challenging with the cArVATAR. Small unintentional changes of orientation were implemented by the controlled car, causing it to steer away from the line. In this case the traditional remote's separation of control functions makes forwards and backwards driving more precise.

Turning

In the free play session with cArVATAR, all children performed gestures composed of both straight driving and turning. In this free movement scenario, there was no gap of understanding of the basic mapping between gesture and outcome, regardless if driving straight or turning. This is different from the traditional controller, in which the basic mapping between the two sticks was not inherently clear to the children, and they tended to break their driving movements into separate forward driving and turns.

Play challenges 3,4, 5 and 6 required making a turn directly from a stationary position. Here most children tried, at first, to turn the stationary controller to the desired orientation and then drive it straight forward, rather than turning the controller while driving it forward. When they discovered this did not work, they learned to turn the controller while it is moving.

Opposing view positions

As previously described, situations in which the car is facing a different direction than the child make control more difficult, requiring the child to mentally rotate her viewpoint to that of the car, or to move to a position where the viewpoints are aligned.

All children spontaneously discovered the option of turning

the cArVATAR controller to the same heading as the controlled car. They used this solution often in Challenges 4, 6 and 7. It seems to be a natural and successful solution to the complexity of relative direction control.

Reaching a target

Challenge 7 was designed to require the combination of the different skills described above, and to provide a goal that is more gratifying and playful in nature.

While this challenge was difficult with both controllers, the level of success was lower with cArVATAR than with the traditional remote. We attribute this to two issues: the problem of straying aside due to small unintentional orientation changes, and a technical problem that caused a deviation from the path while driving backwards.

When using the cArVATAR, children were markedly more expressive than with the traditional controller. This was especially apparent in this challenge, and most pronounced in the final gesture of knocking over the block tower: the gesture was not only that of guiding the car forward, but moving foreword with a force and a gesture of enthusiasm, as if actually knocking over the tower.

Play value

Children reacted with surprise and delight when the relationship between cArVATAR and the controlled car was demonstrated to them. They were eager to try it. During the free play session, they explored the relationship, enjoyed performing large and expressive gestures such as large arcs and other round gestures like the figure 8.

The similarity between controller and controlled prompted the children to create physical contact between the two cars: three of them pushed the controlled car with the controller, making it 'escape'. One child placed the small car on the large car, trying to make it move in that configuration.

CONCLUSIONS AND FUTURE WORK

Our observations were exploratory in nature, but point to significant potential in this novel control model. The direct mapping, especially in the forward and backwards motion, was clearly an 'easy way in' to this relationship between controller and controlled, and points to cArVATAR as a model that enables young children a faster introduction into using remote controlled toys. The playful nature of the controller makes it a promising source of enjoyment.

Improving a number of implementation issues can increase the precision of cArVATAR. We plan to filter small orientation changes, informed by the attributes of the involuntary movements seen in this study, to facilitate more precise straight driving gestures.

For improving turning gestures, we plan to try an "absolute" control scheme for the next cArVATAR version. In this scheme, changing the orientation of the controller will be implemented by the controlled car as a series of short and tight arcs for aligning its orientation to the absolute orientation of the controller.

cArVATAR can be viewed as a new controller category altogether, or as a transitional model for smaller children on their way to the traditional controller. After this study, we view it more as a new category of its own. Each controller affords different play scenarios and promotes different kinds of skills. The traditional controller develops sensory-motor coordination and fine motor skills through its two sticks. Children play with it standing up, and can move large distances. cArVATAR is used mostly in a sitting or crouching posture, in a smaller area, with more potential contacts between the controller and controlled car and more expressivity in the control gestures. We plan to explore these new play opportunities through implementation improvements and further studies with children.

While mimicry is not a new concept – it has been used, e.g. in the context of robotic teleoperation - cArVATAR shows the potential of this type of interaction for young children. The simplicity of the mimicry mental model may be even more advantageous in more complex interactions of this type: for example, R/C toys with additional degrees of freedom, such as a bulldozer or excavator, in which the child can control the blade or bucket directly by moving it!

As the use of robots within the home environment grows wider, the avatar-inspired relationship of controller to controlled can be considered an interesting alternative for users and tasks where a simple entry level is more important than high levels of expertise. Furthermore, this model may be relevant to simple household objects that are out of reach, such as controlling the direction of the air conditioning vents or the speed of a ceiling fan.

REFERENCES

1. Hughe, P. (ed.). *Children, Play, and Development.* Sage, 2009.
2. Goswami, U. *The Wiley-Blackwell Handbook of Childhood Cognitive Development*, Wiley-Blackwell, 2013.
3. Dang, C.T., Andre, E. TabletopCars – Interaction with Active Tangible Remote Controlled Cars. In *proc. TEI 2013,* ACM Press (2013), 33-40.
4. Frei, P., Su, V., Mikhak, B., Ishii, H. Curlybot: designing a new class of computational toys. In *proc. SIGCHI 2000*, 129-136
5. Jain, A., Klinker, L., Kranz, M., Stoeger, C., Blank, D., and Moesenlechner, L. Sketch-A-Move - Design Inspired Technology for Children. Proc. Of UbiComp 2006 (video).
6. Raffle, H.S., Parkers, A.J., Ishii, H. Topobo: a constructive assembly system with kinetic memory. In *proc. SIGCHI 2004*, ACM Press (2004), 647-654.
7. Guo, C., Young, J.E., Sharlin, E. Touch and Toys. In *proc. SIGCHI 2009*, ACM Press (2009), 491-500.

Motors, Music and Motion

Jakob Bak
Copenhagen Institute of Interaction Design
Copenhagen 1253, Denmark
j.bak@ciid.dk

Bill Verplank
CCRMA
Stanford University
Stanford, CA 94305 USA
verplank@ccrma.stanford.edu

David Gauthier
Copenhagen Institute of Interaction Design
Copenhagen 1253, Denmark
dviid@gauthiier.info

ABSTRACT
Over the past four years the authors have conducted classes and workshops in design of systems for real-time digital synthesis of sound and haptic response. In response to current trends in Interaction Design education focusing on visual feedback and touchscreen interactions, the classes were developed to provide foundations for design students to leverage the potential of non-visual modes of interaction and provide them with tools and skills to develop complex multimodal, embodied experiences. These classes have been held in various institutions, have formed the basis for short workshops at conferences as well as provided tools for collaborations with external partners.

In this paper we describe for the first time the extent of the project and reflect on this particular field of Interaction Design education.

Author Keywords
Haptics; Interaction Design; Multi-modal; Toolkit; Hardware; Audio; Education

ACM Classification Keywords
H.5.2. Haptic I/O

INTRODUCTION
Having been involved with interaction design since the dawn of the discipline [10] and with work in Computer Research in Music and research in Haptics, Bill Verplank, together with David Gauthier, was invited in 2011 to start a course at Copenhagen Institute of Interaction Design (CIID) that fused the three fields.

Using The Hand [22] as a specific context of interaction students were asked in a one week workshop to prototype new experiences that combined sound synthesis and force-feedback through simple real-time physical modeling algorithms.

TEI '15, January 16 - 19 2015, Stanford, CA, USA

ACM 978-1-4503-3305-4/15/01…$15.00
http://dx.doi.org/10.1145/2677199.2680590

Utilising Planks [20], Arduino boards, sensors and electrical components for driving motors, the students created projects that simulated flying a kite [5], for example, or the buoyancy of a block of ice [7] – see Figure 1. The resulting installations were then accompanied by audio synthesized in response to the interactions with Max/MSP.

For the two following years a dedicated Motors & Music hardware platform was developed that integrated microcontroller components with motor drive, sensor inputs and audio circuit that allowed for easy connections between the hardware components (Planks and motorized sliders) and more importantly allowed for self-contained projects that could function without being connected to a computer – see Figure 2.

Jakob Bak joined the project in 2012 with a lightweight basic audio synthesis engine developed for the Arduino platform [9] that allowed sound to be generated on-board in immediate response to sensor inputs and chosen force-feedback algorithms.

In 2013 we were invited to run workshops at TEI'13 [19] and at Resonate'13 [15], where short one-day, hands-on workshops introduced the platform to a range of designers and technologists from academia and industry with great feedback for the project and introducing the platform to an external research project.

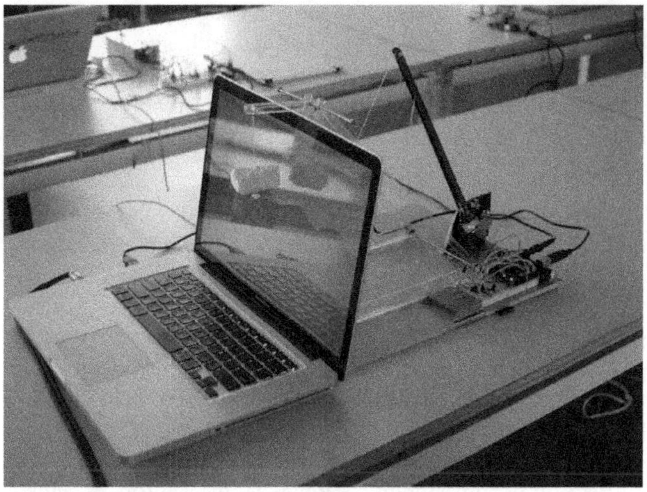

Figure 1 - Student setup from first Motors & Music class

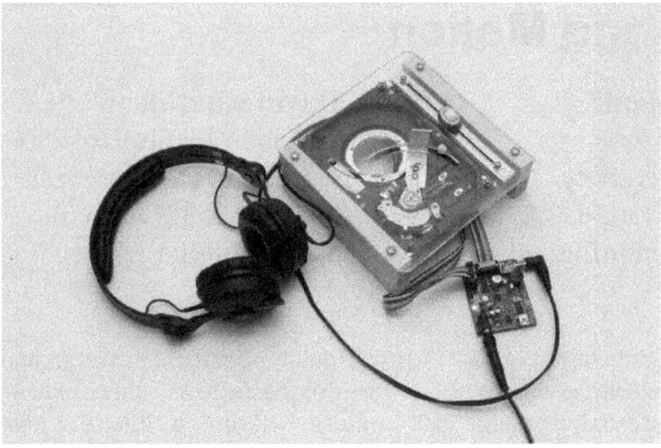

Figure 2 - Second iteration of hardware platform

In addition to the yearly class at CIID the project did a one-week workshop with interaction design students at Umeå Institute of Design (UID) in Sweden, testing a new version of the hardware running on the Arduino compatible Teensy 3.1 microcontroller platform [18]. This new version of the hardware was used again in 2014 with extensions to its audio library – see Figure 3.

MOTIVATION FOR THE PROJECT

The Motors & Music project originated from Stanford's CCRMA course "Physical Interaction Design for Music." This course was mainly targeted to music students with the aim to teach them to design haptic interfaces for musical expression. The motivation of Motors & Music, however, differed from the Stanford course in two key ways. Firstly, its targeted student population was interaction design students at the Copenhagen Institute for Interaction Design (CIID) who required little to no musical or technical expertise. Secondly, the project consisted of a one-week workshop, instead of a full semester. This could in some cases be seen as a limiting factor for the course, but in this case, rather than being a constraint, these differences helped focus the main objectives of the project: to teach students basic techniques and require them to produce prototypes quickly, without too much theory. As such, the class spans basics in haptics and digital audio synthesis, as well as offering a basic introduction to algorithmic modeling of simple physical systems, all within the general teaching framework of fast, iterative, design-led, studio culture education.

There are a number of other projects that share common aspects with Motors & Music. On the one hand, projects [1] and [3], for example utilize the same motorized slider device that is employed in Motors & Music, yet are not specifically tailored as material for teaching haptics to design students, but rather focus on the production of musical instruments. Simple haptics projects such as [11] [12], on the other hand, share the common goal of Motors & Music of producing design materials suited for interaction design students. However, the Motors & Music project differs from this project as it focus on dynamic force feedback devices with higher temporal resolution than the ones utilised in this project. Most similar to Motors & Music are projects relating to the Haptic Paddle described in [13], [4] and [16], leading to Stanford's Hapkit [6]. As does Motors & Music, these projects feature educational material aimed at introducing haptics to graduate students. The main difference with this initiative relates to its focus on educating mechanical engineering students. Motors & Music's focus is centered on the design of haptic experiences within a particular context while the Hapkit focuses on the science and techniques of motorised feedback and physical simulations.

The prime motivation behind the Motors & Music project is introducing a dedicated course in design of non-visual interactions with a focus on programming and physically prototyping cross-modal feedback systems. These foundations are then embedded in a classic interaction design process (iterations of context analysis, concept generation and experience prototyping), which emphasizes the experience of the user rather than the technical functioning of the system.

PROJECT MATERIALS

Below we will introduce in detail the various elements that come together in the classes; Hardware, Software and the didactic format employed. The most recent version of the platform can be accessed at the code repository Github [8].

Hardware

For the first iteration of the Motors & Music classes the main design materials consisted of a set of electronic components (mainly an H-Bridge and connected passive components) arranged on a breadboard, which then connected to an Arduino microcontroller board. The Arduino board was programmed from a connected computer, and through the Arduino's serial port the students triggered Max/MSP patches to play back samples or synthesize audio in response to the behavior proposed by the students' design of the system.

Figure 3 - Third iteration of hardware platform

Figure 4 - Hall-effect sensor on Plank

As their first haptic interface the students were introduced to the Plank [20]. The Plank is a repurposed hard disk drive, where the motor coil of the reading head has been connected to the outputs from the H-Bridge. Connecting a PWM signal from the digital outputs of the Arduino board to the inputs of the H-Bridge, one can obtain real-time adjustable voltage outputs and hence finely controlled current output to the motor coils. With a Hall Effect sensor fixed to the reading head, and placed between two Neodymium permanent magnets, an analog input of the Arduino board can read the position of the reading head and adjust the PWM output to the H-Bridge in a real-time feedback loop, providing precise control of position and directed force of the interface. Physically interacting with the reading head (see Figure 4) creates a force-feedback loop, which can be controlled by simple physical modeling algorithms, e.g. mass-spring-damper systems.

As a one-degree of freedom interface the Plank is surprisingly versatile, with a resolution of its force output that enables the user to feel pressure feedback over a broad range. In some setups the Plank is further equipped with a pressure sensor at the point of interaction, allowing the force-response to be tied to the orthogonally applied force from the user.

The second iteration of the hardware focused on integrating the used components into a single surface mount PCB – adding an on-board audio circuit consisting of a 12bit DAC and a headphone amplifier. The components used corresponded to surface mount versions of the Arduino board with H-Bridge and surrounding components (see Figure 5). This made it possible for the authors to stay within the Arduino IDE for programming which the students were familiar with.

In addition to the Plank the second iteration of the classes saw the use of motorized sliders, commercially available at reasonable costs, allowing for a different type of user interaction (linear, rather than arched, and with a longer throw).

Both types of interfaces was wired up with ribbon cable and connectors that allowed for easy connection to the M&M board, creating a unified interface for the students who could then concentrate on designing the surrounding materials and program the dynamic behavior of the system.

Figure 5 - Close-up of surface mount M&M board

The move to a single integrated platform for both audio and haptic feedback generation meant a severe decrease in available synthesis methods for sound especially, and issues with a limited amount of cycles for computation of outputs for both modalities. The audio synthesis engine developed for the platform (see section Software) was therefore kept intentionally simple and lean, to allow for enough overhead to run physical modeling code.

This turned out to be a welcome restriction, in that the available synthesis method was then simple enough for the students to get a sufficiently in-depth understanding over a short period of time and was able to experiment with it. It also meant that the overall developed projects could be stand-alone installations, disconnected from laptops or other computational equipment, maximizing their experiential impact and encouraged tighter integration between sound and haptic interactions.

The integration also meant that the board size itself could

Figure 6 - Stand-alone student project containing M&M board, Plank, motorized slider and speaker

be considerably smaller than the first iteration of the platform, essentially enabling all functional components to fit into confined spaces (see Figure 6).

The third iteration of the hardware platform (see Figure 3) saw the move back to through-hole components for increased ability for interested parties to produce the hardware themselves. The project embraces an Open Hardware approach to its designs and wish for students as well as other developers to experiment with building their own instances of the platform.

For increased computational capacity we chose to employ the Teensy 3.1 platform as the microcontroller unit in the system. Based on a Freescale Cortex M4 processor, the Teensy is programmable through the Arduino IDE, but being 32 bit and running at up to 96MHz, allowed for additional overhead that enabled a broader range of synthesis possibilities. Having a dedicated microcontroller board to plug into the platform also meant we could source a critical component of the platform from the outside without compromising its functionality.

Software

The software side of the platform has developed substantially since its inception. While the first iteration of the class employed writing all code in the Arduino IDE (using a couple of generic libraries), and creating Max/MSP patches for audio synthesis, the second iteration platform employed custom-made libraries that handled audio synthesis and output at fixed interrupts, as well as simple functions for controlling the force and direction of the motor outputs [9]. Physical modeling code was still written directly in the Arduino IDE as the focus of the class was developing the students' understanding of programming the cross-modal interactions, while audio synthesis could be approached as setting a range of parameters.

For the audio part, the engine developed initially was a simple three-oscillator, 15KHz sample-rate, wavetable synthesis setup with no filtering. Functions for individual frequency, gain and waveform selection, note triggering, a simple audio-rate ADSR envelope and final mixing stage, provided a conceptually simple framework for the students to experiment with (see Figure 7). Sixteen 8-bit waveforms were available as well as a 12-bit sine-wave option, which provided less noisy output.

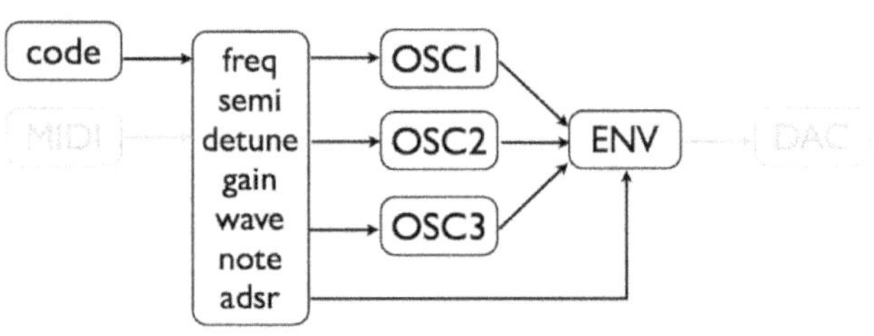

Figure 7 - Overview of first version of audio engine

Addition of a basic MIDI implementation (through serial communication with a Processing sketch on a connected computer) let the students explore from external software the sonic possibilities the limited set of parameters provided. As can be seen in Figure 7 though, the intention with the audio part of the class was to strengthen the students ability to write procedural code that would control the various parameters of their sound design without the use of externally connected software.

The Motor part of the software consisted of a set of functions with microcontroller level C code that would enable the student to write simple commands to the attached actuators. The line, for example,

```
MotorA.torque(-512);
```

will make the Plank push backwards with the maximum force, without having to worry about which pins were connected to which inputs, etc. The internal microcontroller resolution of the PWM output was bi-directional 9-bit (-512 to 511), allowing for very fine-grained control of the H-Bridge outputs, although the mechanical resistance and inertia of the Plank and motorized sliders in effect resulted in a lower physically experienced resolution.

In addition to these libraries a number of tutorial Arduino sketches demonstrating the capabilities of audio synthesis, motor control and physical modeling was included with the project's codebase to help the students get started quickly.

Finally a Processing sketch visually demonstrating the concept of a mass-spring-damper system was developed to facilitate the introduction of physical modeling and the effect of changing parameters in the equations governing its dynamic response (see Figure 8).

The third iteration of the hardware platform saw changes mainly to the audio engine. With the increased performance of the Teensy microcontroller there was now amble room for more complex calculations. This has resulted in FM capability of all three oscillators with an additional

Figure 8 - Processing sketch visualising mass-spring-damper system running on M&M board in real-time

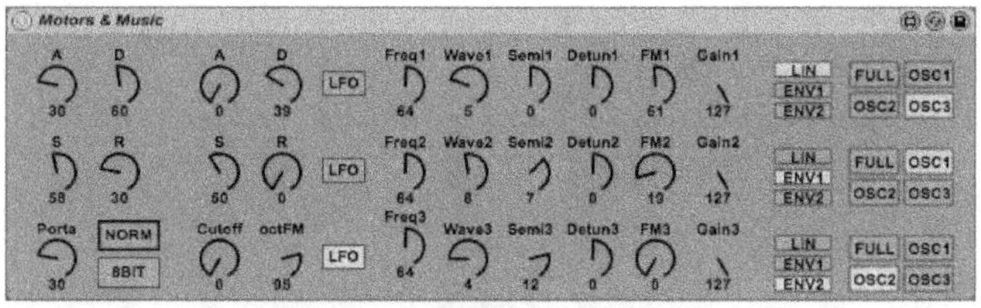

Figure 9 - Max For Live interface to the Motors & Music platform

envelope, and a FM routing scheme that lets each oscillator be modulated by any of the others, including itself. Additionally LFO capability and portamento has been introduced to provide greater sonic design possibilities (see Figure 9).

The lack of a dedicated floating point ALU on the microcontroller though means the FM implementation is fairly light on the processor's resources, resulting in some rather idiosyncratic behavior that, combined with 8-bit waveforms, can give a certain rugged identity to its sonic output.

The motor control and physical modeling implementation has been ported to the new platform but essentially remains the same.

For the fourth class at CIID in 2014 the audio engine has been extended with an a set of digital filtering techniques as the platform pushes forward into more elaborate DSP territory [8]

Workshop Format

The class and workshop formats put forth in this project adhere to both a focused one-week class and one-day workshop. Despite the short time frames (compared to classes running a full semester), the sprint-like format lends itself amiably to the hands-on and studio based nature of the design process. Rather than extensively covering the foundational theory underpinning the science of motorized haptics, Motors & Music articulates fragments of theory and practice, where core concepts of haptics design are exemplified through exercises and tutorials. Presentations are interspersed with 'live coding' sessions, where code examples are developed on-screen in front of the participants, to facilitate a "learning-by-doing" process.

Figure 10 - Gone Fishin' by Marthinus Oosthuizen and Harsha Vardhan Ramesh Babu

The syllabus is segmented into three main parts entitled Motors, Music and Motion. In the Motor part of the workshop, students learn how to drive both the voice coil of the Plank and the DC motors of the sliders while being introduced to the theory of dynamic force-feedback. The Music part focuses on examples and descriptions of digital sound synthesis, with an emphasis on synthesis performed on embedded microcontrollers. Finally, the Modeling part of the class focuses on developing simulations of physical models such as pendulums and spring-based systems. The Motors and the Music parts of the workshop can work as standalone separate topics, while the Modeling part fuses topics of both Motors and Music. In doing so, students are asked to put into correspondence both motor driving logic and sound synthesis, with the aim at creating sound based haptic prototypes (such as the sound of friction for example, or the pluck of a string).

After the introductions to the general framework of the project, participants are given a design project brief from which they develop their own prototypes, fusing in the best way possible haptics, sound and an engaging experience design. In one-week classes the introductions usually take 1.5 days, with 2.5 days of dedicated prototype development time and 0.5 day of student presentations. In the one-day workshop format the introductions are compressed down to half a day, and the design phase consist of a more free experimentation session to make a unique interactive instrument.

Throughout each design phase the teachers are present to help troubleshoot or further elaborate on the available resources to enable the participants to steer the developing concepts towards a meaningful and illustrative prototype.

SELECTED PROJECTS

Below we present a selection of projects from classes to illustrate some of the potential of the course so far.

Gone Fishin'

This project [14] was developed during the first Motors & Music class in 2011 and consisted of a playful interaction with a fishing rod connected through a Plank to model of a fish. Trying to raise the fish out of the water the participant will feel the resistance of the fish accompanied by a reactive sound composition done in Max/MSP. See Figure 10.

The Mutic Box

The Mutic Box [21] was also developed during the first Motors & Music class in 2011 and recreated the feel of a mechanical music box through digitally synthesized haptic and audio feedback. A DC motor provided rumble as force feedback and played back piano samples from MAX/MSP as the central wheel passed conductive elements past a sensor. See Figure 11.

Figure 11 - The Mutic Box by Daim Yoon and Yufan Wang

Duojam

Developed during the second Motors & Music class in 2012, Duojam [2] explores what happens when two musicians are playing the same instrument. The instrument has one tone whose frequency is determined by an average of two motorized sliders. Each player's distance from the average slider position is output in their slider as increasing force feedback and thereby elicit the two players to engage in a negotiation which alternates between collaboration and playful resistance as they try to 'jam' with the playback of a musical composition. See Figure 12.

Hapticket

The 2013 class of Motors & Music focused on 'micro interactions' and designing decoupled, but meaningful tangible interfaces for them with digitally synthesized audio and haptic feedback.

Hapticket approached the transport ticket validation micro-interaction and infused it with a haptic response, which subtly but intuitively indicated a payment by slightly resisting the move of a transport card through a slot. See Figure 13.

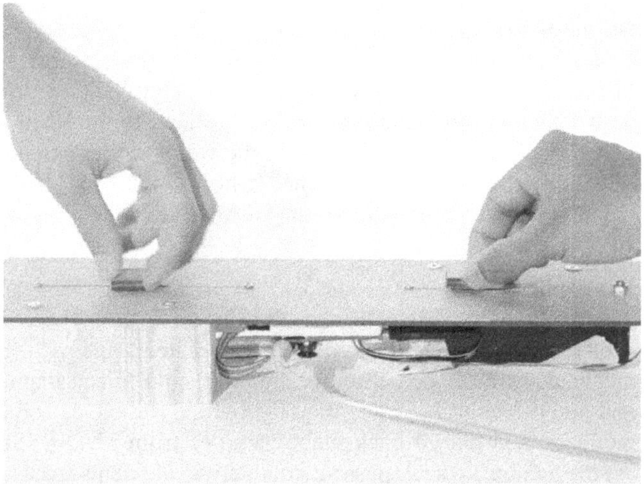

Figure 12 - Duojam by Martin Malthe Borch and Umesh Janardhanan

Figure 13 - Hapticket by Jane Kate Wong and Ankkit Modi

"As the user swipes their card through the slot, the resistance increases towards the bottom, providing immediate indication that a larger amount is being debited from their card. Soft "bumps" are felt in the hand as the card passes downwards in the slot, which correspond to the levels of money being charged. The addition of audio feedback through incrementing notes for each payment level further assists users to understand that the transaction has been made." [23]

Aether

For the 2014 class of Motors & Music the topic was on fully autonomous vehicles and redesigning the driving experience when direct control has been removed from the people being transported.

Aether focusing on the "vehicle as a membrane to the surrounding environment" designed a way for the passengers of an autonomous vehicle to experience and reconnect with the airflow around the vehicle through a tangible interaction with a digitally controlled simulacrum. See Figure 14.

"We chose to shy away from using a fan in our prototype as it would have been too much of a one-to-one association. Instead we experimented with different materials that might create the same tickling or vibratory sensations typically associated with the action. By attaching strips of straws to 'The Plank' that would vibrate and move according to a slider, the user could control the speed of the car in motion.

Figure 14 - Aether by Akarsh Sanghi, Bethany Snyder, Chia Yu Hsu and Myoungeun Kim

The more the user 'accelerated', the faster the motor vibrated which in turn generated a wind noise provided by a Max patch. This all worked in tandem with a Servo motor that adjusted the angle of a screen located above the straws to guide the user in the wave-like pattern we aimed to replicate." [17]

CONCLUSION

Motors & Music brings together two different domains that hitherto have had little connection, and the conjunction of which elicits reflection. As a technological domain, haptics has a long history of highly specialised techniques which each have carved out interesting fields for future technological research and development. These fields though come with demands of highly specialised knowledge and technological acumen, demands that can be hard for designers to meet. Design, on the other hand, brings a range of sensitivities that help develop new perspectives within established structures, new ways of using touch and haptic technology that may lie outside of the current technological focus of the domain.

In fusing the two fields, we have focused on teaching and developing new, easy to access prototyping materials that minimize the learning curves and background knowledge needed to engage with haptics research and practice. We have carefully structured hardware, software and curricula and made trade-offs in resolution, force and precision to allow for prototyping materials that fit the cognitive, temporal and financial limitations of short introductory level classes in haptic design.

Through the four years of teaching Motors & Music, we have developed and produced:

(1) introductory material for learning active force-feedback and simple audio synthesis, (2) hardware and software platforms (plank and fader) that are Arduino compatible and easy to work with, (3) sets of exercises and tutorials tailored to each platforms and addressed to interaction design students, and (4) designs and prototypes demonstrating the potential of our platform.

Part of the learning expectations we set ourselves for the project was for students to develop a critical perspective on tangibility in regards to the development of user interfaces and products. In retrospective, this goal was achieved in many ways as students are able to question current products claiming to address the sense of touch (smartphones, tablets, surfaces, etc.). Motors & Music has equipped them with basic haptics and sound synthesis vocabulary to evaluate such products and claims while provided them with enough knowledge and know-how to carry out haptic design and research work that can challenge the status quo in the design of tangible interfaces.

ACKNOWLEDGMENTS

We extend our greatest thanks to the staff and faculty at Copenhagen Institute of Interaction Design for supporting the Motors & Music workshops throughout the last four years, as well as Camille Moussette, Stefania Serafin, Dan Overholt, Stefano Trento, Francesco Grani, Mathias Willerup and Allan Koudal for sparring and collaboration.

REFERENCES

1. Berdahl, E., and A. Kontogeorgakopoulos. "The firefader: Simple, open-source, and reconfigurable haptic force feedback for musicians." *Computer Music Journal* 37.1 (2013): 23-34.

2. Borch, M. M. and Janardhanan, U. *Duojam*

   http://ciid.dk/education/portfolio/idp12/courses/motors-music/projects/duojam/

3. Gabriel, Romain, et al. "BounceSlider: actuated sliders for music performance and composition." *Proc. TEI 2008.*

4. Gassert, R.; Metzger, J.; Leuenberger, K.; Popp, W.L.; Tucker, M.R.; Vigaru, B.; Zimmermann, R.; Lambercy, O., "Physical Student–Robot Interaction With the ETHZ Haptic Paddle," *Education, IEEE Transactions on*, vol.56, no.1, pp. 9-17, Feb. 2013

5. Gillet-Kirt, A., Lyckegaard, M. and Gopalakrishnan, H. *Haptikite*

   http://ciid.dk/education/portfolio/idp11/courses/motors-music/projects/haptikite/

6. Hapkit

   http://hapkit.stanford.edu/about.html

7. Lyhne Jensen, M. T. and Liao, W. *Iceflake*

   http://ciid.dk/education/portfolio/idp11/courses/motors-music/projects/iceflake/

8. M3T3

   https://github.com/videomusik/M3T3

9. M-M-M

   https://github.com/gauthiier/M-M-M

10. Moggridge, B. (2006). *Designing Interactions*. MIT Press Books.

11. Moussette, C., S. Kuenen, and A. Israr. "Designing haptics." *Proc. TEI 2012.*

12. Moussette, C., and R. Banks. "Designing through making: exploring the simple haptic design space." *Proc. TEI 2011.*

13. Okamura, A. M., C. Richard and M. R. Cutkosky, "Feeling is believing: Using a Force-Feedback Joystick to Teach Dynamic Systems" *ASEE Journal of Engineering Education,* vol. 91, no. 3, pp. 345-349, 2002

14. Oosthuizen, M. and Babu, H. V. R. *Gone Fishin'*

   http://ciid.dk/education/portfolio/idp11/courses/motors-music/projects/gone-fishin/

15. Resonate 2013 - Belgrade New Media Festival http://resonate.io/2013/education/

16. Richard, C.; Okamura, A. M.; and Cutkosky, M. R. 1997. "Getting a feel for dynamics: using haptic interface kits for teaching dynamics and controls." *American Society of Mechanical Engineers, Dynamic Systems and Control Division* 61:153–157.

17. Sanghi, A., Snyder, B., Hsu, C. and Kim, M. *Aether* http://ciid.dk/education/portfolio/idp14/courses/music-motors/projects/aether/

18. Teensy 3.1: New Features https://www.pjrc.com/teensy/teensy31.html

19. Verplank, B., Gauthier, D. and Bak, J. "TEI 2013 studio: motors and music." *Proc. TEI 2013*.

20. Verplank, B., M. Gurevich, and M. Mathews. "The Plank: designing a simple haptic controller." Proc. NIME'02.

21. Yoon, D. and Wang, W. *The Mutic Box* http://ciid.dk/education/portfolio/idp11/courses/motors-music/projects/the-mutic-box/

22. Wilson, Frank R., *"The Hand"*, Vintage Books, 1999.

23. Wong, J. and Modi, A. *Hapticket* http://ciid.dk/education/portfolio/idp13/courses/motors-music/projects/hapticket/

BodyPods: Designing Posture Sensing Chairs for Capturing and Sharing Implicit Interactions

Dimitris Papanikolaou
Harvard University
48 Quincy Street
Cambridge, MA, 02138
dpapanik@gsd.harvard.edu

A.J. Bernheim Brush
Microsoft Research
One Microsoft Way
Redmond WA 98052
ajbrush@microsoft.com

Asta Roseway
Microsoft Research
One Microsoft Way
Redmond WA 98052
astar@microsoft.com

ABSTRACT
Today, it is not uncommon to find ourselves remote from those we care about. Despite the impact of mobile and social technologies on connectedness, recent studies suggest that it could be these very technologies that exacerbate a sense of loneliness. In attempt to help people feel more connected, we designed and created BodyPods, a remotely paired set of communicating chairs that facilitate a sense of presence by leveraging implicit actions such as sitting to communicate that someone you care about is home. Each BodyPod consists of a flexible surface with six pressure-sensitive and light-emitting pads that adjusts its shape to the body anatomy. As a person's body moves, limbs exert different pressure on each pad creating a live digital "bodyprint" that is mapped on the pads of other BodyPods through color and light. Findings from a 10 person user study suggest bodyprints may be distinctive, particularly among small groups of people with different body types.

Author Keywords
Furniture; Connectedness; Implicit Interaction; Ambient Display; Kinematic Transformation; Tangible Interface

ACM Classification Keywords
H.5.2 [User Interfaces]: Prototyping

INTRODUCTION
People create and leave behind implicit traces of their activities through their interactions with objects. For example, if John and Sarah live in the same apartment and John returns home after Sarah has left, he may infer that she spent time on the sofa based on the arrangement of cushions or even feel warmth if she was sitting there recently. Furniture provide particularly interesting tangible media from which to capture implicit interactions because people spend a significant portion of their day interacting with them. Capturing and sharing these implicit interactions could offer remote loved ones a similar sense of awareness that John and Sarah experience from living together and seeing traces of each other's activities.

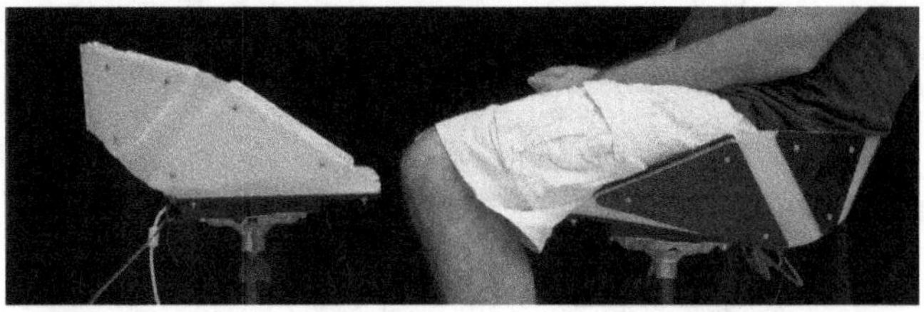

Figure 1. Each BodyPod senses the bodyprint of a person and maps it to its paired BodyPod through color and light.

Inspired by the notion of object-based implicit communication, we created BodyPods, a pair of remotely connected chairs that can sense the "bodyprints" of their users and share them as mappings on each other's surface (Figure 1). Analogous to a footprint, a bodyprint manifests in real time the sitting posture of a person as a distribution of the pressure that their body and limbs exert against the cushions of the seat. Each BodyPod consists of a flexible surface of six pressure-sensing and light-emitting pads. The surface adjusts its shape to the body anatomy, ensuring consistent contact with the sensing pads during different postures. When a person sits on one BodyPod, his/her bodyprint is reflected on the pads of the other BodyPod through color and light. Each BodyPod has a unique color ID. If two users sit on their BodyPods concurrently, their colors blend in each pad based on their relative pressures. If a user leaves, his/her bodyprint fades away with time. We selected chairs as the first type of a series of furniture due to their frequent and intimate relationship with the human body during daily activity: we sit during work, dining, leisure, and social interaction.

We conducted a formative study with ten participants with a range of body types to gather two types of data. The first type is a quantitative collection of bodyprints across five postures to evaluate differences between them. The second type is a qualitative feedback from participants on the concept of sharing implicit interactions with furniture for

TEI '15, January 16 - 19 2015, Stanford, CA, USA

ACM 978-1-4503-3305-4/15/01...$15.00
http://dx.doi.org/10.1145/2677199.2680591

connectedness through a semi-structured interview after they had used BodyPods. Results from our visualizations of participants' bodyprints suggest that they are distinct for people of differing heights and weights. For connectedness scenarios where the number of people using a chair is limited, like family members, BodyPods may be able to uniquely identify the sitting person based on the bodyprint and allow the remote chair to display a unique color conveying visually who is using the chair. Likewise, BodyPods may be able to recognize specific body postures with interesting applications as embodied gestural interfaces.

PRIOR WORK

Object-based social connectedness is a well-established area in HCI and TEI, particularly for couples in long distance relationships. One common theme in past research is the explicit, deliberate character of interaction that augmented paired objects allow. For example, using *Cubble* [8] a person can author "tap patterns" to send to their partner. Similarly, pushing the semi-transparent button of the *FeelLight* [13] prototype changes the color of all the remotely connected buttons. In *LumiTouch* [1], squeezing one picture frame causes its remote twin frame to color-illuminate based on where, how hard, and how long the frame was squeezed. In *Casablanca* [7], researchers created a Lamp and Curtain through which people can explicitly share their availability for communication. In contrast to these explicit interactions we focus on implicit interactions people have with furniture in their daily lives. For example, LumiTouch frames also include motion sensors that detect ambient presence around their remote frame.

Another common theme in past research is the synchronous aspect of interaction. For example, the *Cubble* system also includes "mutual handshakes" where cubes heat up when remote partners simultaneously squeeze them. *ComTouch* augments voice communication using a vibrotactile device sleeve on a mobile phone [2]. *The Bed* prototype recreates remotely the experience of sleeping in the same bed by utilizing pillows that exchange heat and vibration and a swaying curtain that indicates breathing rate [4]. Tollmar et al. also explored the concept of virtually living together through user research and several prototypes [14]. Most closely related to our work, their SoftAir inflatable chair senses weight and movement and represents them on a remote chair through embedded lights and sounds allowing users to simultaneously interact. While BodyPods allow synchronous interaction, we are particularly interested in exploring their ability to connect people asynchronously by capturing, sharing, and playing back animated bodyprints. Often, couples live in different time zones making synchronous interactions unlikely.

A third common theme in past research and most related to our work is body posture recognition through pressure-sensing seats. Typically such directions focus on retrofitting the back and seat of existing seats with pressure sensing units with the objective of minimizing the number, location, cost, and computational complexity of input measurements [10,15,16]. For example, Mutlu et al. focused on the problem of optimizing number and locations of analog pressure sensors concluding to 31 units (they eventually used 19) with which they recognized 10 different postures [15]. Ashgar et al. used 8 binary pressure sensors (switches), a RFID reader, a digital compass, and a RFID grid for detecting 8 body postures, user identity, and chair's orientation and position respectively [16]. Mota built a static posture recognition system using two grids of 42x48 pressure sensing units distinguishing between 9 different postures [10]. In contrast to these works we are interested in how to design a seat to better sense postures rather than how to best place sensors on an existing chair. By rethinking the form of the seat we managed to use only six pressure sensing units for posture detection. Furthermore, we are interested in visually communicating postures among humans rather than computationally recognizing them. Also, in contrast to [16], we were motivated by the theory of affordances [17] to use pressure for user identification because it is a modality that we believe sitting affords better.

Our main contributions can be summarized as follows: (1) We present a novel kinematically deformable seat design that uses only six pressure sensitive units to capture body postures. (2) We introduce the concept of bodyprint as a means to visually communicate, synchronously or asynchronously, seated postures and potentially identify users. (3) We discuss findings from design, material and fabrication explorations for interactive and kinematically flexible seats that can be useful to designers and researchers in the field of TEI interested in augmented furniture. In the rest of this paper we discuss the motivation, design process, technology, and early tests of our work.

DESIGN AND PROTOTYPING PROCESS

Concept

During early conceptualization phase we considered both how connected seats could detect and exchange bodyprints and how connected tables could allow users to exchange tap signals by knocking on their surfaces. We proceeded with the former because of the richer tactile interaction and design exploration the direct contact with the human body allows.

Next, we considered the input/output modalities strategy. Instead of retrofitting an existing chair and dealing with problems of sensor placement and resolution, we decided to rethink the design of a seat as a kinematic mechanism that directs exerted pressure in predetermined sensor locations. Recognizing posture from a flat-surface sensor matrix is a non-trivial computational problem. By tailoring instead the geometry of the seat to closely follow the anatomy of the body we can place the sensors closer to the body parts that we want to use as input reference points. This way we can

Figure 2. Form explorations (from left to right): donut-shaped form; lounge chair; rolled tessellated surface; tailored paper model.

significantly reduce the number of required sensors and the computational complexity of dealing with input. To match the resolution of the sensors to the body anatomy we decided to place the sensors not inside the cushions as grids as prior works did [10,15,16], but instead under their rigid supporting surfaces turning effectively each cushion into large pressure sensor. We furthermore decided to color illuminate the cushion pads to visually express exerted pressure as a bodyprint.

Design Goals and Constraints

Our design constraints and decision tradeoffs were balanced between developing a technology to prove a concept and designing a seat ergonomically comfortable and sturdy enough for people to use it. On one hand, we wanted a prototype that could be easily reproduced in our lab for field experiments. This meant easy fabrication using standard equipment of a fab lab (e. g. laser cutting, CNC milling, 3D printing); easy manual assembly with minimum skills, effort, and time; easy transportation for deployment in homes for future experiments; and minimum waste of materials for affordable cost. On the other hand, we wanted a customizable design, tailor-made to the body types of different individuals: if the seat feels too large, the sensors will not provide consistent input; if instead the seat feels too small, the sensors' input will saturate. Furthermore, we wanted a seat that would be light-weight, flexible, and structurally efficient during deformations: if the seat is too flexible it will not support the body weight; if it is too rigid it will not follow the body anatomy during postures.

We initially explored two forms. The first was a donut-shaped form consisting of eight components made out of bent rolled sheets that would deform and spring back during sitting to cuddle the human body like a nest (Figure 2, left). Body posture could be inferred by sensing the pressure under each component, like an old-fashioned joystick. However, early prototypes showed that adjusting the flexibility of each part based on the thickness, radius, and geometry of the sheets was too difficult to control. The second approach was a lounge chair consisting of a flexible rectangular surface of six pressure-sensing and light-emitting pads (Figure 2, middle-left). This approach was easy to fabricate, however it did not provide enough contact points around the body to detect the variety of siting postures that we wanted. The chosen design direction was a combination of the two (Figure 2, middle-right). A rolled flexible surface consisting of six rigid pads: two triangular pads on each side and two quadrilateral pads for the bottom and back. The geometry is such that the side pads create hinges that spring back, allowing the seat to deform and fold, adjusting to multiple positions of the torso (Figure 3, right). Furthermore the form is structurally self-supporting: as the back pad leans, the side pads gently squeeze the torso preventing the back pad from leaning further (Figure 3, left). The benefits of this design are that it is lightweight, easy to assemble, has minimal volume, and consists of parts that can be laser-cut.

Fabrication Tools and Methods

We used CAD/CAM modeling and CNC fabrication methods due to the high level of customization of out parts, precision in assembly, and complexity of our geometric design requirements. We considered lasercutting and CNC milling in combination with planar flexible materials like plastic sheets and plywood as a rapid, low cost, and customizable fabrication technique. Our hardware lab is equipped with an Epilog 32"x18" laser cutter, which constrained the maximum size of our parts for the assembly. We also found 96"x48" CNC mills from subcontractors, however, their machining speed, cost, availability, and distance from our lab made this option unattractive. We therefore decided to use our laser cutter and modify our design assembly accordingly.

CAD Modeling and Parametric Customization

We used Rhino 3D and Grasshopper as CAD modeling tools. We wanted a parametrically customizable 3D model while guaranteeing that each of its instances consists of developable surfaces (e. g. single-curved surfaces like cylindrical or conic components) so that we could easily

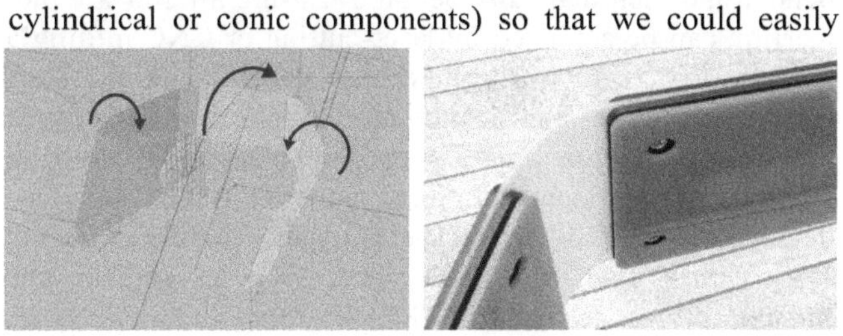

Figure 3. CAD parametric model for kinematic analysis (left); assembly detail of final Nylon/Delrin prototype (right).

Figure 4. Building the pressure sensing and lighting in the pads. From left to right: early prototype "bricks" to experiment with lighting behavior; wiring inside a pad; assembled pads; mounted pads with cushions on the Nylon chair form.

fabricate it by rolling/folding planar sheets. Furthermore we wanted to reduce the curvatures in few strategic locations to avoid jigs or complicated formwork during bending. Finally we wanted to ensure the geometry could fold during structural deformation without having its own rigid parts collide or intersect. To study the above constraints we developed a parametric model in Grasshopper, in which we customize length, width, slope, and a total of 11 parameters. The model (Figure 3, left), which was also used for kinematic and collision analysis, allows us to tailor-make customized seats for different body types reducing considerably the time for design iteration.

Materials and Forming

We explored a number of materials including plastics and wood based on their availability, cutting and molding ability, flexure properties and degree of translucency for lighting. Nylon sheets are practically unbreakable, flex back to their initial shape, can be thermoformed easily, and can be laser cut in thicknesses below 1/8" (e.g. 1/16" and 1/32"). Delrin sheets are also flexible and difficult to break (although less than Nylon) but they are springier and have better laser cutting quality than Nylon. Acrylic sheets cut nicely but are brittle. Polycarbonate sheets are flexible and unbreakable but they cannot be cut in the laser cutter. We also considered plywood, however it burns during laser cutting, it is structurally less efficient than Nylon or Delrin, and it requires expert skills and significant labor time for bending/forming (e.g. steaming, laminating, or scoring).

We tested a number of bending techniques including thermoforming, Kerfing or Dukta cutting patterns [5], and lamination. Thermoforming can be used in thermoplastics by locally heating the material with a heat gun or heat-bender and then manually bending it using a jig or a mold. Kerfing can be achieved by laser-cutting or CNC milling a surface to create spring-like perforated patterns. Kerf patterns decrease significantly the structural efficiency of the material while increasing the machining time, a significant cost consideration. After multiple tests, we decided to use 1/16" Nylon sheets for the flexible substrate, 1/8" Delrin for the panels, and ½" Acrylic for the translucent core to house the LED lighting and electronics. To bend the Nylon we used a heat gun together with small jigs and a heat-bender.

Early Prototypes

We crafted 10 prototypes in various scales (1/4, ½, full) exploring different forms, sizes, material properties, and lighting techniques. During early explorations we tailored a draft prototype by cutting and connecting paper patches with tape directly on a human body (Figure 2, right). The resulting prototype was used to determine proportions, dimensions, and helped us simplify the geometry during the CAD modeling process. We next developed few ¼ scale models using Nylon and Delrin to explore bending strategies as well as the degree of material flexibility. We also developed a full scale Delrin model to test bending techniques with the heat gun and structural deformation during sitting. Finally, we developed two full-scale prototypes from cardboard, one for finalizing the size, and a second for testing the electronic circuitry after optimizing the CAD geometric model.

Actuation and Circuitry

Early explorations included heating pads and mechanical actuation. Heating pads or Peltier tiles [11] could be combined with thermo-chromic paint to reveal or conceal shades of body prints. However, the time it takes for the thermo-chromic paint to change compared to how noticeable the effect is and the required power wattage and heat sinks for the thermal (Peltier) pads made this option unattractive. We considered mechanical actuation using a simple linear actuator to make the donut-shaped chair to contract/expand like a flower or the lounge chair to bend based on input from sensors. However the required electric current draw was too high and the resulting design felt too rigid. We decided to use color illumination in combination with pressure sensing. RGB LEDs can be programmed to associate unique color IDs to individuals. Figure 4 shows the initial bricks we built to test different lighting options, and how we built the pressure and lighting into the pads.

Electronic parts and circuitry was a challenging constraint, as they should withstand repetitive strain during bending while remaining functional. Our first approach was to avoid cables and instead embed the electric connections inside the Nylon using copper tape. When we tested this idea in a full-scale cardboard model we discovered that copper tape cracks under repetitive strain. Ideally we wanted to print the circuitry directly on the Nylon structural substrate with copper inkjet FLEX technology, turning the substrate into a

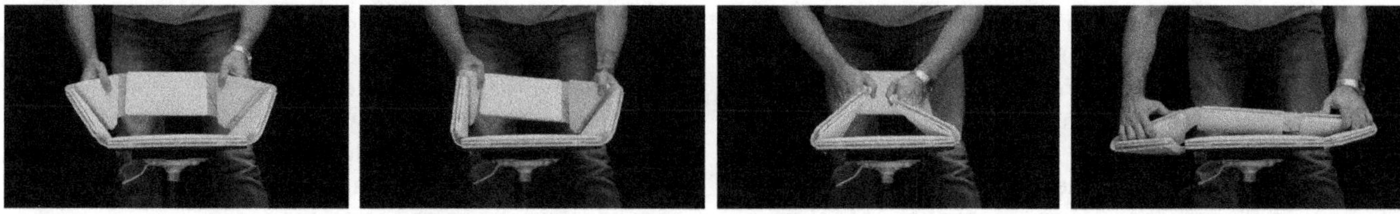

Figure 5. Each BodyPod consists of a flexible surface with six pressure-sensing and light-emitting pads that can deform and fold.

large printed circuit board (PCB), however this was unfeasible due to time constraint and instead we used cables with connectors.

BODYPOD PROTOTYPES

The final prototype consists of a tessellated surface of six Delrin pads bolted on a flexible Nylon substrate. This combination allows the seat to easily deform under applied load (Figures 5 and 6). From outside to inside, the stacked assembly of each pad consists of: an external layer from Delrin; the flexible Nylon substrate that holds all 6 pads together; a translucent case made out of ½" sanded Acrylic that houses the LEDs and electronics; an layer from Delrin upon which the FSR sensor is mounted with a small cushion. These 4 layers are hold together with nuts and bolts (Figure 3, right). A fifth layer, the cushion pressure-sensing pad, consists of Delrin, foam, and upholstered Vinyl with hot glue. The cushion pad is structurally connected to the 4-layer stack with double-sided VHB tape allowing both relative movement and detachability. The FSR sensor is squeezed between the cushion pad and the 4-layer stack and is calibrated by adjusting the size, thickness, and rigidity of the VHB cushions. For the base of the seat we used a turnaround base from IKEA which comes on wheels. The FSRs connect to 10KΩ pull-up resistors. We used daisy-chained RGB Neopixels for the LED lighting (3 in each triangular pad and 4 in each quadrilateral pad). The electric connections inside each pad were instrumented by copper tape and soldered cables. Each pad has 4 pins (analog input from the FSR, digital output for the RGB Neopixels, 5V power, and ground), which connect through male-female cable connectors to an Arduino Micro, housed under the seat. After several iterations, we reduced the size and weight of the seat to the minimum that would allow us to prove our concept at an acceptable cost. For this reason, our final design is a hybrid between a stool and a chair providing a small back support for a person. We built two BodyPods, a white one and a black one (Figure 1).

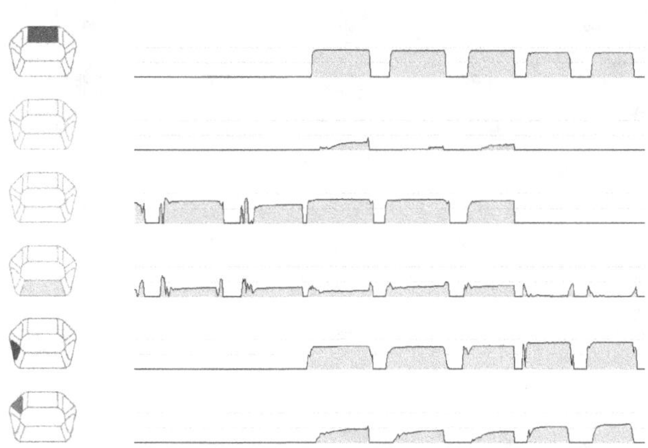

Figure 7. To help with development and testing we developed a time-series area graph of the pressure readings.

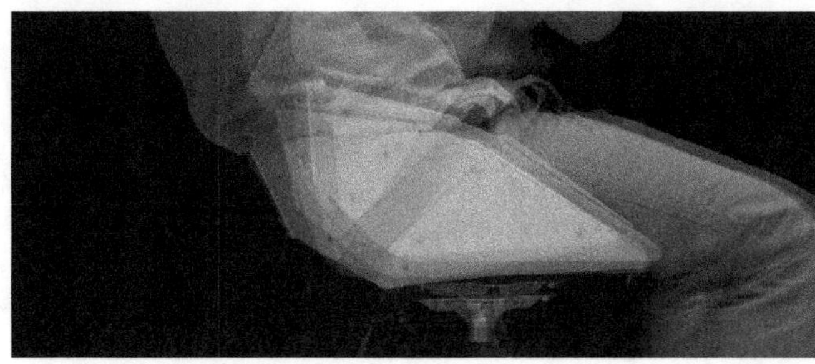

Figure 6. Kinematic adjustment of a BodyPod to body postures.

Remotely connecting the BodyPods

To remotely connect the BodyPods we integrated them with the Lab of Things (LoT) platform [9]. LoT is a flexible open platform for experimental research that uses connected devices in homes and beyond. The Arduino Micro in each chair communicates with a PC running the LoT Home Hub software over a serial connection which also powers the chair's sensors and lighting. Using the built-in data streaming capabilities of LoT, we wrote a LoT application that sends and receives data from the remote chair. With LoT integration, BodyPods can communicate with each other from anywhere in the world with network access, simplifying field study deployments and data collection.

Visualizing Data Sensed by BodyPods

To visualize pressure data, we used Processing, an open-source Java-based programming language. We developed two visualizations: a time-series area graph of the exerted pressure on each of the six pads in real time (Figure 7) and an icon pressure graph that visualizes pressure as shades of grey for each pad (Figure 8). We used the second visualization as a real-time visual feedback to visualize bodyprints and to calibrate the sensors.

USER STUDY

To gather feedback on the BodyPods and explore how bodyprints differ across people and postures we conducted a formative user study with ten participants (5M, 5F). Each study session took about 30 minutes and participants received a $5 café coupon. We selected participants with different heights and weights to gather feedback from people with different physical characteristics. Participants came to our lab space where the two BodyPods were setup. We first explained the design motivation of sharing implicitly captured data to support connectedness and showed participants how the chairs illuminate based on data sensed either from their own sensors, the other chair, or the combination. We then gave participants time to sit in a BodyPod, use it and observe the behavior of the paired BodyPod. Our first set of semi-structured interview questions focused on connectedness, whether participants had remote people they would like to stay connected with, their reactions to furniture as a media for connectedness, or other ways they might like to interact with remote people.

In second half of the study, we gathered data to create bodyprints for five different sitting postures: Sit Straight, Lean Left, Lean Right, Lean Forward, Lean Backward. Participants sat in each posture for 10 seconds and repeated the posture three times. While BodyPods were particularly effective in capturing other postures such as Lean Back-Left or Lean Back-Right we did not include these postures in the study as they seemed rather unnatural. We concluded with another semi-structured interview session asking participants to comment on the possible design improvements for BodyPods, other input or output modalities that would be of interest to them and suggestions for other applications for the chair beyond supporting connectedness.

Bodyprints

We created bodyprints for each person based on their sensed data, shown in Figure 8. To create a person's representative bodyprint for a posture, we average sensor readings from the three repetitions of the posture. For each repetition, we manually identified the stable region of the ten second recording window (e. g. the middle 5 seconds) to ignore sensor noise as participants entered and exited the posture. Pressure sensors readings vary from 0 – 1023, after averaging we have six values in this range, one for each pad. To visualize the data, we map the pressure data to 0-255 and show the grayscale values for each pad in the Figure. The darker the image, the more pressure the participant was exerting against the pad.

Figure 8 illustrates the bodyprints of people in our study. The rows show the differences in bodyprints for participants in the same posture. People of similar weight have the most similar bodyprints. As weight and height vary, the bodyprints become more different. For example, when sitting straight (bottom row) pressure data is sensed only by the bottom pad for participants M2, M3, M5, F3, F4, F5, based on how they sit. However, heavier participants exert more pressure as we would expect. Bodyprints also capture differences in how participants sit straight. For example, M1 exerts pressure on all the pads and F1 sits with her back touching the backrest.

These images represent an initial analysis across stylized postures and ideal data collection conditions. Future analysis is necessary, particularly during naturalistic use, before we fully understand the uniqueness of bodyprints across people. However, these images suggest that particularly in a home setting with a relatively small number of people who may have different height and weights, BodyPods may be able to differentiate between people. This would allow assigning each person a unique color and provide the ability to send additional information to the paired chair about who was using the remote chair.

We were also interested in how bodyprints for the same participant would vary across different postures. The columns of Figure 8 show, as we would expect, that for the same person different postures have different bodyprints. This is most obvious for Lean Left and Lean Right, as force is exerted on the side the participant leans toward. However, differences in the other positions are also visible and we are interested in exploring whether someone

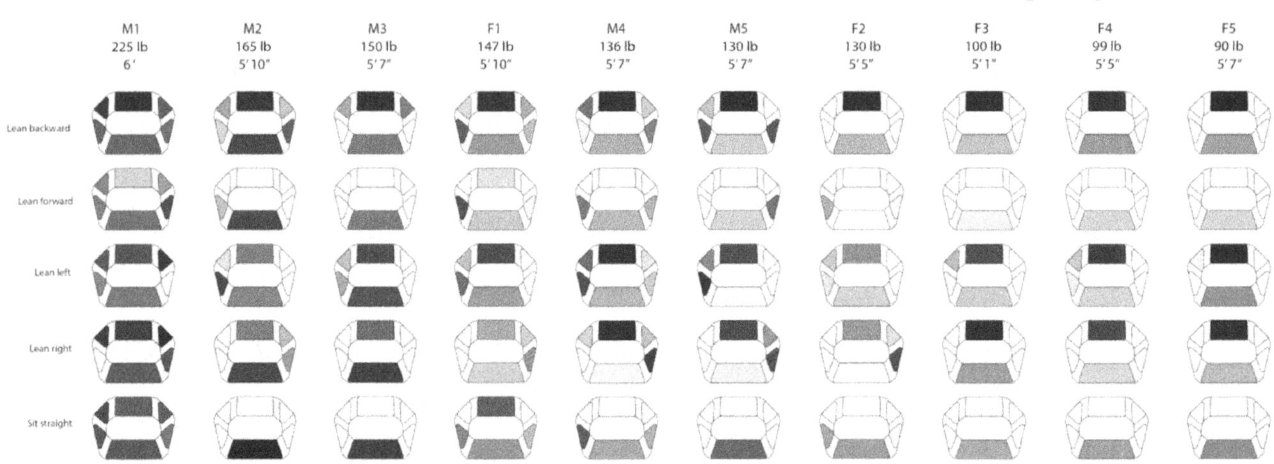

Figure 8. Participant's bodyprints for five postures. The darker the pad, the more pressure the participant exerted against it. To illustrate the pressure exerted, we mapped the average pressure values per pad ranging from 0 – 1023 to 0 - 256.

observing the mapped bodyprints on the remote chair can identify different postures and whether such richness gives them more context about what activity the person in the remote chair might be doing (e. g. eating, reading a book).

Qualitative Feedback

We elicited feedback through semi-structured interview questions from participants on the concept of sharing implicit data for connectedness, design improvements for BodyPod and possible applications beyond connectedness. Broadly speaking, the notion of staying connected with remote family or loved ones was attractive to 8 of the 10 participants. Each of these participants gave us examples of specific people they wanted to be more connected with. For example, several mentioned family in other countries. Three participants highlighted the value of asynchronous sharing, one mentioning that a 12 hour time difference between him and his parents makes synchronous interactions challenging.

Regarding BodyPods as a medium for connectedness participants highlighted aspects they felt worked well and places for improvement. Seven participants gave positive feedback about the use of ambient light to display pressure information. For example, M4 commented that ambient light worked well because it is not disruptive. However, four participants highlighted the inability to see color lighted displayed when they were sitting in the chair. As M1 said, "the chair is giving me feedback I can't see." Participants noted this was a problem for synchronous use of the chair. Hindsight suggests lights being placed closer to the edges of the chair or enabling them to show on the back exterior sides of the panels.

Participant feedback on the flexible nature of the chair was mixed. F5 and M1 commented positively about how the chair would squeeze them when they leaned back. F1 thought the flexibility made the chair more comfortable and playful and F2 called the flexibility "neat and different." On the other hand, four participants expressed concern about whether the chair would support them, particularly as they performed the leaning posture. For example, M5 commented that the lean felt unnatural and scary. F3 worried about breaking the chair and commented it was bending too much. Leaning concerns, particularly for leaning back, may be related to a feeling that the back part was too low, mentioned by six participants. M3, one of our larger participants, told us the back was too low and he felt he would destroy something if he leaned back. Another issue raised related to the low back pad was that it might lead to fatigue if people sat in the chair for a long time.

The time spent constructing a parameterized model that would allow BodyPods to be constructed in multiple sizes was validated by feedback of our participants about the size of the chairs. Two of our smaller participants (F3, M5) found the chair too large for them, while taller and heavier participants worried about breaking it. Building BodyPods in multiple sizes would be valuable.

Although we designed BodyPods for connectedness, we were interested in participant's thoughts about other applications. Seven participants mentioned sensing posture and alerting people to change their positions. F2 also highlighted that for people with some types of paralysis, a flexible pressure sensing chair that could be customize for specific body types could provide valuable feedback about how they sit, which they may be unable to feel. Other past research has found force-sensitive chairs can alert users for their posture in real-time to help prevent injuries [3]. Four participants suggested exploring applications in gaming and three were interested in security applications, for example if BodyPods could recognize a user and unlock a computer.

DISCUSSION

Our design and fabrication explorations as well as the user feedback suggest considerations for further research.

BodyPod Improvements

Results from user study encourage our initial decision to create a parametrically customizable production scheme for BodyPods. This can be combined with a better measuring system of user's anatomy such as 3D scanning. We also plan to increase the height of the back pad and use large-bed CNC routers instead of the smaller-size laser cutters. Furthermore, we observed that with one sensor, the bottom cushion pad had occasionally difficulties detecting near-edge sitting postures. This can be improved by either rearranging the sensor under the cushion pad or by introducing a second sensor (one in the front and one in the back edge of the seat). Other areas of future research include the development of learning algorithms for training BodyPods to recognize postures from bodyprint data.

Symmetry and Pairing of Connected Objects

We began our exploration of sharing implicit traces of interaction with a pair of identical chairs. We believe the symmetrical nature of the chairs and ability to use them both synchronously and asynchronously is appealing and has a clear mental model. Identical objects, e.g. picture frames, cubes, etc., have been commonly used in past connectedness research [e. g., 1, 2, 4, 13, 14]. However, there are other non-symmetrical options we think would be valuable to consider too. For example, having two versions of the chair in different scales, one in physical size for implicitly sensing input and one in miniature –doll house-size for displaying output. Having separate objects for local input and remote output could make it easier to support asynchronous interactions. The small chair could constantly be displaying a summary of the last several hours of data from the remote chair. This may be valuable for people trying to feel connected to others in different time zone.

Another area for exploration is whether connected objects are explicitly paired to only a single remote object or to multiple connected objects. Multiple connected chairs, perhaps each with their own color or set of unique colors per users, which share implicit data might be an interesting way to support connectedness across extended family members or close friends. We believe studies that help understand whether people prefer a 1-1 pairing for connected objects (e. g. this chair tells me about interactions with the one at my parents' house) or if an object can display implicit traces from many objects (e. g. this chair tells me about use of chairs at my parent's and sister's house) is a question for further research.

Beyond Connectedness

In addition to the aforementioned home connectedness scenarios we believe BodyPods may appeal for office use applications. For example, in their research studying chairs as input modalities, Probst et al. identified the use of tilting chair gestures as a valuable additional input modality for opportunistic, hands-free interactions in office settings [12]. The bodyprints created from user study data suggests BodyPods could recognize these types of tilting gestures. Probst et al. also experimented with bouncing gestures which may have a distinct signature in the pressure data collected by BodyPods, although we have not tested this.

CONCLUSION

DIY and Maker culture has, in the last few years, exploded across disciplines while promoting a new wave of non-verbal, tangible and embedded experiences that prefers the tactile over the virtual. We embraced the fabrication process to quickly generate multiple form factors and we tested their durability, functionality, and aesthetics. Additionally, microprocessors such as Arduino facilitated communication between objects therefore realizing this scenario. It is easier than ever to build and experiment with connected objects. Given the recent promise of Smart Home technologies and cloud connected experiences, it is plausible to assume that our furniture could become recipients, and broadcasters of our data. While this exploration started with chairs, we are curious to seek out other ways in which average household objects could implicitly connect us remotely. Telepresent technologies, and mobile communications may still serve as our primary mode of contact, but they require effort and time. A simple gesture, such as laying on a sofa and reading could suggest to another that you are home and resting. Perhaps that is all that is needed to feel closer across distances. We plan to continue to study the level of context that people wish to share with others as we further evolve the notion of connected pieces.

ACKNOWLEDGMENTS

We thank Tom Blank, Jason Goldstein, Chris O' Dowd, Mike Sinclair, and Patrick Therien for their helpful consultation during the prototyping and design process.

REFERENCES

1. Chang, A., Resner, B., Koerner, B., Wang, X., and Ishii, H., LumiTouch: an emotional communication device. *Ext. Abstracts CHI '01,* 313-314.
2. Chang, A., O'Modhrain, S., Jacob, R., Gunther, E., and Ishii, H., Comtouch: design of a vibrotactile communication device. *Proc. DIS 2002*, 312–320.
3. Daian, I., van Ruiten, A. M., Visser, A., and Zubic. S., Sensitive chair: a force sensing chair with multimodal real-time feedback via agent. *Proc. ECCE 2007*, 163-166.
4. Dodge, C., The bed: a medium for intimate communication. Ext. Abstracts CHI 1997, 371-372.
5. http://www. dukta. com/en/referenceprojects. html
6. Griffin, Jo, The Lonely Society? UK Mental Health Foundation, Accessed Aug. 2014, from: http://www. mentalhealth.org. uk/content/assets/PDF/publications/the_lonely_society_report. pdf
7. Hindus, D., Mainwaring, S., Leduc, N., Hagström, A., and Bayley, O., Casablanca: designing social communication devices for the home. *Proc. CHI 2001*, 325-332.
8. Kowalski, R., Loehmann, S., and Hausen, D., cubble: a multi-device hybrid approach supporting communication in long-distance relationships. *Proc. TEI 2013*. 201-204.
9. Lab of Things, http://www. lab-of-things. com/
10. Mota, S., "Automated Posture Analysis For Detecting Learner's Affective State", MIT MS Thesis, Sept. 2002.
11. Peltier Tile, http://www. explorecuriocity. org/ DesktopModules/CC_VideoPlayer/wfrm/wfrmPrintDocument. aspx?contentid=2657
12. Probst, K., Lindlbauer, D., Haller, M., Schwartz, B., and Schrempf., A., A chair as ubiquitous input device: exploring semaphoric chair gestures for focused and peripheral interaction. *Proc. CHI '14*. 4097-4106.
13. Suzuki, K., and Hashimoto, S., Feellight: a communication device for distant nonverbal exchange. *Proc. of the ACM SIGMM ETP 2004 workshop*, 40-44.
14. Tollmar, K., Junestrand, S., and Torgny, O., Virtually living together. *Proc. DIS 2000,* 83-91.
15. Mutlu, B., Krause, A., Eorlizze J., Guestrin C., and Hodgins, J., Robust, low-cost, non-intrusive sensing and recognition of seated postures. *Proc. UIST'07. 149-158.*
16. Asghar A., Shirehjini N., Yassine A., and Shirmohammadi S. Design and implementation of a system for body posture recognition. *Multimedia Tools and Applications 70*, 3 (2014), 1637-1650
17. Gibson, J. *The Ecological Approach to Visual Perception.* Psychology Press, Boston, MA, USA, 1986

Cube-in: A Learning Kit for Physical Computing Basics

Hyunjoo Oh
ATLAS Institute
University of Colorado
Boulder, CO, USA
hyunjoo.oh@colorado.edu

Mark D. Gross
ATLAS Institute
University of Colorado
Boulder, CO, USA
mdgross@colorado.edu

ABSTRACT

We present *Cube-in*, a kit designed to help beginners learn about fundamental concepts in physical computing. Through play and observation, Cube-in users can investigate digital and analog signals, inputs and outputs, and mapping between inputs and outputs before they work on electronics and construct circuits. By simplifying interaction methods, Cube-in provides an accessible entry point to key physical computing concepts.

Author Keywords

Tangible Learning; Physical Computing; Digital Craft

ACM Classification Keywords

H.5.m. Information interfaces and presentation: Miscellaneous. K.3.m Computers and Education: Misc.

General Terms

Design; Human Factors

INTRODUCTION

Today's maker culture is becoming blended with computing components. An increasing number of maker events, workshops, and classes call attention to this emerging genre of digital craft. Accordingly, many institutions also offer introductory physical computing classes, many of which start with teaching students how to use the Arduino microcontroller [1] with sensors and actuators. Although students use electronic devices every day, in this introductory class many lack knowledge of basic electronics. Fundamental concepts such as input and output, or power (Vcc) and ground, can overwhelm students and inhibit more advanced learning.

Cube-in is a learning kit for those beginners, a first steppingstone to understanding basic electronics. By inserting physical component cubes in Cube-in's base cube, a learner can observe and grasp fundamental concepts in physical computing, such as digital and analog signals, inputs and outputs, and functional mappings between inputs and outputs. Through simple tangible interactions, learners build a solid foundation of knowledge before they begin working with microcontrollers and electronics components to build designs.

TEI '15, January 15–19, 2015, Stanford, California, USA.

http://dx.doi.org/10.1145/2677199.2680597

Figure 1. A simple interaction with the Cube-in kit: it consists of one base cube and four types of nine component cubes

In the following sections, we briefly review relevant literature; describe the key concepts that Cube-in is intended to convey, system configuration, and design consideration of Cube-in; conclude with discussion about potential future work.

RELATED WORK

Although more basic, Cube-in is similar in spirit to several previous tangible learning kits. The Topaoko [7] construction kit comprises a microcontroller, sensors, actuator, and hardboard pieces. It allows users to build their own embedded-circuit kit and play with kit components. With roBlocks (now Cubelets) [4], people build robots by assembling sensor, action, and operator blocks, and learn basic robotics. It also engages users to play with each type of block and construct modular creations. The Cubement [5] mechanical movement design tool kit comprises seven types of cubes: motor, bevel gear, gearbox, crank, jumper, breadboard and support cubes. Through constructing diverse mechanical systems users can quickly grasp the fundamentals of mechanisms. Whereas these various kits are intended to enable users to construct designs, Cube-in provides a more elementary pre-constructed kit in which users play, observe, and learn about basic electronics concepts by simple interaction.

The littleBits [2] kit of preassembled circuit boards helps people create electronics prototypes by snapping modules together. It lets users build circuits with the components. LightUp [6] also enables users to design their own circuits, but it includes a mobile app that recognizes the circuit behavior and gives live and interactive graphic feedback using Augmented Reality technology. Similarly, Conradi et al.'s tabletop system [3] recognizes one's behavior and provides immediate feedback. Users explore virtual circuit building on the table surface before working on physical circuits. Squishy Circuits [8] a circuit building kit that uses conductive and non-conductive play-dough also supports learning circuit-building. Instead of soldering or using breadboards, the malleable nature of clay allows users to rapidly prototype circuits. Despite the different forms of each device, these kits help users to exploring circuit building—we simply aim for users to explore fundamental concepts underlying such circuits.

The Cubes project [9] presents a set of 20 cubes that each combines an input and an output. Each cube is a complete experience and the transparent material lets people see the mechanics of the sensing and actuation. Whereas the Cubes project allows users only to experience within the limited set of cubes, Cube-in lets users interact with diverse pairs of inputs and outputs to grasp the fundamental concepts.

CUBE-IN: THE LEARNING KIT

Conveying Concepts

The Cube-in experience is designed to convey three fundamental concepts in physical computing: the difference between digital and analog signals, the difference between input and output, and the functional mapping between inputs and outputs.

Difference between digital and analog signals

To demonstrate the difference between analog and digital signals, the kit provides two types of output cubes. Digital output cubes are actuated by a binary signal (ON or OFF); analog cubes vary actuation continuously. For example, with the digital output cubes the user can only turn a device (the vibrator motor or LED) on or off. On the other hand, with the analog output cubes the user can continuously vary a servo position, LED brightness or a melody's tempo through a piezo actuator.

Although every analog output can be also driven with a digital signal, we deliberately distinguished separate digital and analog cubes in order to unify the interface of all types of component cubes and the base cube. The coherent layout for connecting magnets for ground, power, and signal is essential to make the Cube-in experience simple and accessible.

Relation between (analog) input and output

Another key concept is the relation between inputs and outputs. Connecting the values received by input cubes directly to the output values enables users to see how input signals influence output signals. Various sensors support different interactions to enhance the engagement and support learning concepts within the limited number of component cubes. Specifically, users can control the amount of light reaching the light sensor by shading it with their hands; the potentiometer provides a familiar rotation input using a knob; and the user can squeeze and press on the pressure sensor. While interacting with the input cubes, users observe the connection with the output cubes, and see how values received from different types of sensors (inputs) can be transmitted to various types of actuators (outputs).

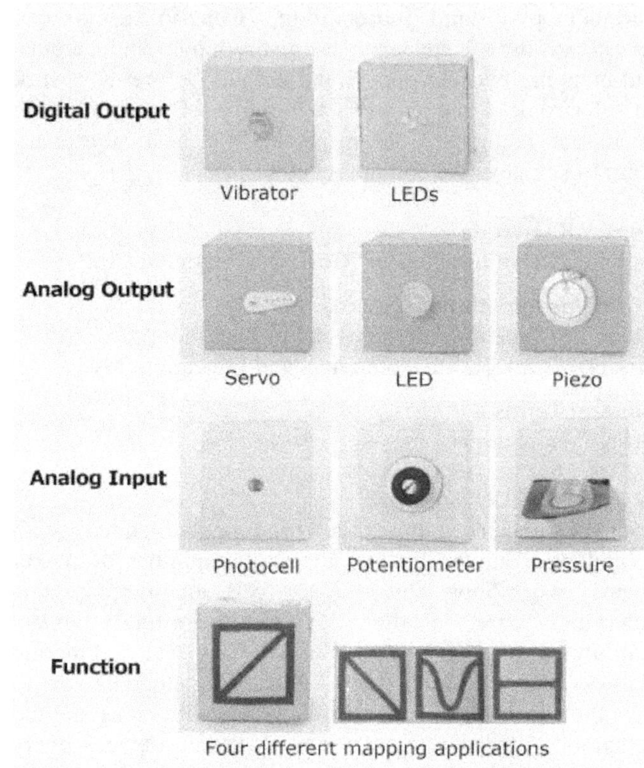

Figure 2. Four types of the component cubes: each color indicates different identities of the cubes.

Changing the input and output mapping

Lastly, the function cube demonstrates mapping. By switching its orientation, the four sides of the function cube enables users to apply one of the four mappings to change the way input values map to output values. The four mappings (depicted on the cubes as a graph) are

'direct' (output = input),

'inverse' (output = (- input)),

'sine' (output = sine (input)) and

'constant' (output = 100).

For instance, when a photocell sensor and a LED are applied to the input and the output respectively, shading the light sensor results in one of four different outcomes depending on the mapping type. With direct mapping, shading the sensor makes the LED dimmer) and with inverse mapping shading the sensor makes the LED brighter. The sine application makes the LED dim faster than the inverse one and become bright again. With the constant 'mapping' the output gets no influence from the input. The LED remains dim. The purpose of the function cube is to reinforce the idea of the input-output relation. It adds a layer to the user's understanding of how one quantity can be mapped to another.

Figure 3. The Cube-in play: by inserting component cubes in its base cube, users can turn the device on (top). Simple interactions with input cubes such as squeezing the pressure sensor or shading the light sensor show how input signals influence output signals (bottom).

System Configuration

The Cube-in hardware consists of one base cube (4.5in) and four types of nine component cubes (1.5in). Each type of component cubes is matched to the four faces of the base cube, which houses the programmed Arduino and its batteries. While the Arduino uses one connection to receive signals from the input cubes, it uses independent connections for each analog output cube. The ways to transmit signals between the Arduino and the output cubes, and the scope of possible values to control the output components vary according to the type of actuators and sensors used.

The function cube includes magnets for the top and the bottom edges, so that the four different orientations trigger different reed switches to apply different mappings. That is, each switch triggers one case of the Arduino program, and the applied formula can be modified simply by reprogramming the Arduino. Unlike other type of component cubes, which are connected to the base cube via magnets on the surface, the function cube connection via magnets and reed switches on the top and the bottom was relatively weak. To strengthen the connection, we applied magnets inside the function cube and base cube surfaces in opposite directions.

Design Consideration

All component cubes connect to the base cube through ¼" neodymium magnets. People playing with magnets tend to experiment attaching one to another and trying other directions to experience magnetic force. We applied opposite polarity magnets to Vcc and ground, and the opposing polarity prevents the user from connecting the cubes incorrectly and damaging the electronics. Wires from the sensors or the Arduino are attached to the magnets with conductive copper foil tape. When component cubes are attached to the base cube, the current flows. Along with the use of the polarity enforcement and physical connection through magnets, we used craft materials to build the Cube-in.

All materials and supplies we used are commonly available inexpensive craft materials and require little expertise. This enables those who want to build their own Cube-in kit to teach themselves. For the same reason, we designed the basic unit of the kit as a cube. As a cube is relatively easier to replicate and customize than other primitive figures, we expect that cube units can also reduce the effort in building one's own kit and adding more component cubes with different sensors and actuators.

In order to visually highlight the different functionality of the various Cube-in components, we applied colors of different saturations and hues. Pastel colors (pink, light blue, light yellow, and light green) differentiate each type of component cubes and vivid colors (red, white, and black) encircle the connecting magnets on all component cubes and the base cube. By doing so, we intend to encourage users to play with the Cube-in simply matching the colors without further instructions. (See Figure 4)

Figure 4. Four faces of the body cube with component cubes: users can play with the Cube-in kit simply by matching colors.

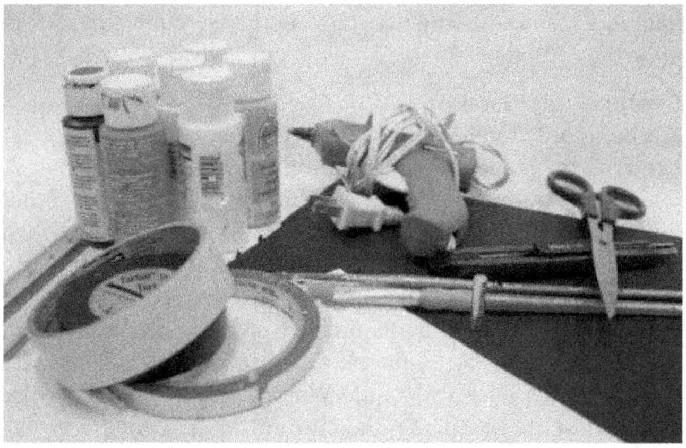

Figure 5. Supplies and materials to build the Cube-in: we built all component cubes using paper and colored with acrylic paints.

FUTURE WORK

We plan to extend Cube-in's functional flexibility. The current Cube-in has two types of output cubes; by refining the framework of interface design, we plan to make output cubes that accept both digital and analog signals. Similarly, we are interested in exploring the relation and potential feedback loop between input and output. For example, a photocell sensor as input can be used to control LED brightness as output. However, the LED brightness can again influence the input value received by the photocell sensor. Then, the LED becomes the input for the photocell sensor, a reversal of the original arrangement. By adding another base cube module, we expect to enable users to place input and output cubes freely to see how they affect each other. This greater functional flexibility will let users grasp a broader view of fundamental concepts—digital and analog, inputs, outputs, and mappings—than the current prototype.

As a parallel, we plan to develop the prototyping process as a detailed document and test with potential users such as undergraduate students in an introductory level physical computing course. We consider that this can validate how the Cube-in play can enable students to clarify basic electronic concepts. Furthermore, we plan to investigate whether students can build their own kit using our document and how the hands-on building experience can enhance their learning.

ACKNOWLEDGMENTS

We thank Michael Eisenberg at the Craft Technology Lab, Michael Theodore at the ATLAS Institute of University of Colorado, Ian Oakley at the Ulsan National Institute of Science and Technology, and anonymous reviewers for their helpful feedback.

REFERENCES

[1] Arduino. http://www.arduino.cc/

[2] Ayah Bdeir, and Paul Rothman. 2012. Electronics As Material: littleBits. In *Proceedings of the 6th International Conference on Tangible, Embedded and Embodied Interaction* (TEI '12). ACM, New York, NY, USA, 371-374. http://doi.acm.org/10.1145/2148131.2148220

[3] Bettina Conradi, Verena Lerch, Martin Hommer, Robert Kowalski, Ioanna Vletsou, and Heinrich Hussmann. 2011. Flow of electrons: an augmented workspace for learning physical computing experientially. In *Proceedings of the ACM International Conference on Interactive Tabletops and Surfaces* (ITS '11). ACM, New York, NY, USA, 182-191. DOI=10.1145/2076354.2076389 http://doi.acm.org/10.1145/2076354.2076389

[4] Eric Schweikardt, and Mark D. Gross. 2006. roBlocks: A Robotic Construction Kit for Mathematics and Science Education. In *Proceedings of the 8th International Conference on Multimodal Interfaces* (ICMI '06). ACM, New York, NY, USA, 72-75. http://doi.acm.org/101145/1180995.1181010

[5] Jeeyong Chung, Kyungeun Min, and Woohun Lee. 2014. CUBEMENT: democratizing mechanical movement design. In *Proceedings of the 8th International Conference on Tangible, Embedded and Embodied Interaction* (TEI '14). ACM, New York, NY, USA, 81-84. DOI=10.1145/2540930.2540933 http://doi.acm.org/10.1145/2540930.2540933

[6] Joshua Chan, Tarun Pondicherry, and Paulo Blikstein. 2013. LightUp: An augmented, learning platform for electronics. In *Proceedings of the 12th International Conference on Interaction Design and Children* (IDC '13). ACM, New York, NY, USA, 491-494. http://doi.acm.org/10.1145/2485760.2485812

[7] Kuan-Ju Wu, and Mark D. Gross. 2010. TOPAOKO: interactive construction kit. In *Proceeding CHI EA 2010 Extended Abstracts on Human Factors in Computing Systems* (CHI EA '10), ACM, New York, NY, USA, 3619-3624. http://doi.acm.org/10.1145/1753846.1754028

[8] Matthew Schmidtbauer, Samuel Johnson, Jeffrey Jalkio, and AnnMarie Thomas. 2012. Squishy circuits as a tangible interface. In *CHI '12 Extended Abstracts on Human Factors in Computing Systems* (CHI EA '12). ACM, New York, NY, USA, 2111-2116. DOI=10.1145/2212776.2223761 http://doi.acm.org/10.1145/2212776.2223761

[9] Michal Rinott, Shachar Geiger, Eran Gal-Or, and Luka Or. 2013. Cubes. In *Proceedings of the 7th International Conference on Tangible, Embedded and Embodied Interaction* (TEI '13). ACM, New York, NY, USA, 397-398. http://doi.acm.org/10.1145/2460625.2460711

Empowering Occupational Therapists with a DIY-toolkit for Smart Soft Objects

Argyro Moraiti[1,2] **Vero Vanden Abeele**[1] **Erwin Vanroye**[3] **Luc Geurts**[1]

[1]KU Leuven – e-Media Lab
Andreas Vesaliusstraat 13,
3000 Leuven, Belgium

[2]University of Paris-Sud
Rue Georges Clemenceau 15,
91400 Orsay, France

[3]PXL University College
Guffenslaan 39,
3500 Hasselt, Belgium

argyro.moraiti@gmail.com, {vero.vandenabeele, luc.geurts}@kuleuven.be, erwin.vanroye@pxl.be

ABSTRACT
We present an evaluation of a DIY-toolkit, designed to empower caregivers to create tailor-made, unique assistive solutions for their clients. More specifically, the toolkit aims to enable occupational therapists to turn everyday soft objects into smart devices that can be programmed to recognize certain manipulations. These smart objects can then be used to control applications or to play certain games. Our evaluation reveals that occupational therapists were able to make use of the toolkit without the aid of a technical expert. The therapists hacked everyday objects such as cushions, socks, cuddly toys and repurposed them for therapy. They computationally augmented them and tailored them to clients' needs and desires. From our evaluation, we also derive five guidelines that can inform others when creating DIY-toolkits for assistive technology.

ACM Classification Keywords
H.5.2 Information Interfaces and Presentation

Author Keywords
Tangible interaction, solutions for occupational therapy, DIY toolkit, assistive technologies, organic interfaces

INTRODUCTION
Within the field of physical rehabilitation and assistive technology, there has been a call for empowering individuals with Do-It-Yourself Assistive Technology [10,11,12]. The term DIY refers to a movement of creating, modifying or repairing objects without the need for substantial training or professional assistance [13]. Within the field of assistive technologies (AT), the argument is made that when clients, caregivers, family and friends, are able to create or adapt assistive technologies themselves, these technological solutions are better tailored to the complex needs of the individual with disabilities. Some advocates of DIY-AT even argue that 'user self-production' can lead to disruptive innovation in rehabilitation engineering [4].

TEI 2015, January 15-19, 2015, Stanford, CA, USA

http://dx.doi.org/10.1145/2677199.2680598

Current high abandon rates of assistive technologies, ranging from 8 to 75% [17,18,22], indeed suggest that assistive devices and services often fail to meet the needs of end-users. Lack of user involvement has repeatedly been listed as the main factor associated with assistive technology discontinuance [19]. Other factors that contribute to abandonment of AT are suboptimal performance, high barriers to procuring the device, and finally inadequate flexibility to adapt the technology to changes in ability, needs and lifestyles [17]. Caregivers have the most intimate knowledge of the specific needs of their clients. If they would be given the means and knowledge to participate in the design of AT, perhaps these limitations of poor performance, restricted delivery or improper fit can be avoided. By *"making the making accessible"*, perhaps these high abandonment rates may be mitigated [11].

In this paper we provide an account how we evaluated a DIY-AT toolkit, designed to empower caregivers, and more specifically occupational therapists, to create tailor-made, unique assistive solutions for their clients.

Occupational therapy as a creative practice
Occupational therapists (OTs) aim to remediate impairments and functional limitations [26], in order to maximize a person's ability to perform activities of daily living such as dressing, cooking, bathing, toileting, writing, and other common household and work-related tasks. While definitely not exclusive, occupational therapy often focuses on activities involving the upper body, and frequently includes activities to improve manual dexterity and bimanual skills [24]. As clients differ with respect to their disability, the context they live in and the daily activities that are significant to them, therapeutic procedures need constant adaptation and innovation [23]. Therefore, OTs spend significant effort in finding the right tools and adapting equipment. Another core element of the work of an OT is to increase a client's motivation for adherence to the therapy [24]. Although most clients look forward to spending time with the therapist [1], the actual motivation for executing repetitive and boring exercises is often lacking. Hence, OTs often search for interactive tools and games, as a means to add immediate feedback and fun to the therapy [7,15].

Occupational therapy is known to be a creative profession, both as a practice and in its use of fun, challenged to show creativity in applying functional activities for the benefit of clients [8,23,25]. However, while OTs are without doubt professionals in designing and tailoring therapeutic procedures, they do not have an engineering background. Therefore, with respect to creating assistive *technologies* they should be considered as non-professionals [13]. Hence, OTs in particular could benefit from DIY technology that enables them to tailor solutions to the abilities of the individual client, and that allows to add immediate feedback and fun to the therapy.

The Skweezee system

Within the domain of Tangible Interaction (TI) it is common practice to augment daily objects with computational power by using appropriate sensors, electronics, microprocessors and actuators. This opens up opportunities for OTs, since their clients typically have difficulties manipulating objects. Embedding sensors in physical objects allows for monitoring and for providing feedback which may increase the clients' motivation to practice. In our project we started from the work of Vanderloock et al. who presented the Skweezee system [27]. Skweezees are soft objects that are filled with conductive wool (see figures 1 and 3). Inside the wool electrodes are dispersed. By compressing the wool the resistance between a pair of electrodes drops, which allows to measure the deformation of the object, and to recognize preprogrammed deformations through machine learning algorithms. Consequently, this technology has the potential to respond to actions like pushing, grasping, pinching and squeezing the object.

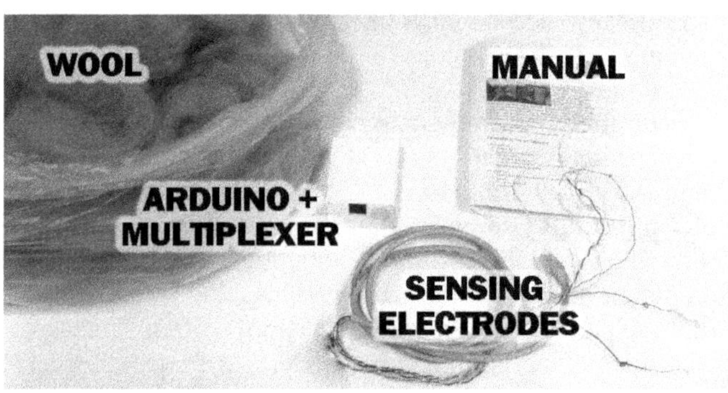

Figure 1. An overview of the hardware materials of the Skweezee, as used in the DIY-toolkit.

In this research study, we investigated how and whether this Skweezee system can be extended in order to enrich the set of tools that OTs use in their practice. First, we provide an overview of related work in the field of tangible interaction, assistive technology and DIY practices. Next we discuss the components of the DIY-AT toolkit. Finally, we present and discuss an evaluation of the DIY-AT toolkit by OTs. We analyze their creations and interviews, and describe themes that emerged from the observations. We hope these results may inform other researchers to create similar DIY-tools for assistive technology.

RELATED WORK

In order to empower OTs to create tailor-made solutions, we need to combine elements from the domain of *tangible interaction* with typical practices of the *DIY movement* and the needs of *OTs*.

First, we look at existing applications that combine **tangible interaction with a DIY approach**. A notable example is "Makey Makey" [3], a platform for improvising tangible user interfaces using physical and digital objects. Textile interfaces were presented in [16], where diverse materials and fabrics are used to handcraft fabric electronics. "Midas" [21] is a toolkit to support the design, fabrication, and programming of flexible capacitive touch sensors for interactive objects. This is also where the Skweezee system situates itself, a flexible and open system for designing and developing squeeze-based interactions. Skweezees aspire to make interactive devices of everyday soft objects and to provide the DIY community with a means for rich gestural squeeze interactions. However, in [27] no real end users were involved and no concrete applications were proposed. Rather, the technology is described, and the robustness of the system is tested via experiments. While participants could define their own squeeze gestures, they were not capable of creating their own Skweezee. Designing this toolkit, the ambition is to move beyond the DIY community and exploit tangible interfaces in the domain of assistive technologies.

Secondly, numerous applications exist that combine **tangible interaction with occupational therapy**. "NoiseBear" [9] for example, is a malleable multiparametric tangible interface that can be used by children with limited mobility or learning disabilities. "PhysiCube" takes advantage of tangible interactions and games to provide motivating physical training for the upper limbs [28]. In [14], a table-top game supporting the treatment of children with Cerebral Palsy is presented. In [2], the authors present a sensing and tangible interaction environment for post-stroke and upper limb rehabilitation. However, in the aforementioned examples, the DIY aspect is lacking. Solutions are often created by technical developers, and although these solutions offer the possibility for adaptation and customizations [7], they do not provide the means to end-users to fabricate their own solutions.

Lastly, we explore services and technologies that combine the **DIY mentality with assistive technology**. Several books have this as a topic, e.g. Willkomm, sometimes referred to as the McGyver of AT, has written a book on how to create *"assistive technology solutions in minutes"* [29]. Other similar specialists websites [30,31] and online communities [32] have arisen, where people can find and share ideas and designs for making (therapeutic) tools themselves. However, generally, these are low-tech solutions. Hurst and Tobias (in [12:16]) remark that *"manufacturing techniques are limited by what can be made without electricity and using found objects. [...] These limitations may impact the adoption rate and potential for long-term use solutions."*

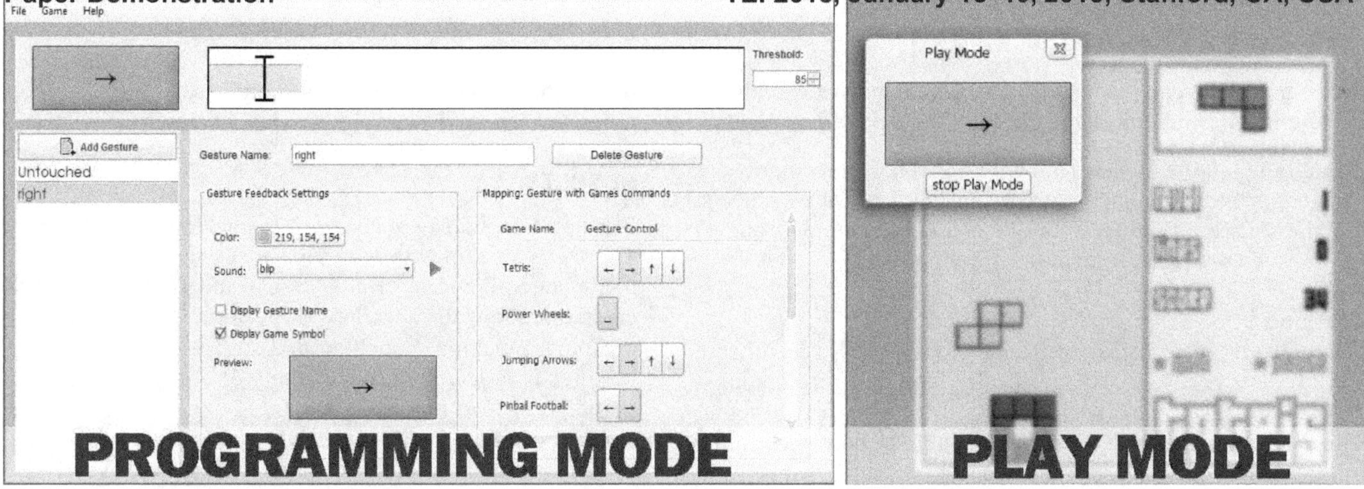

Figure 2. Two main modes of the software that accompanies the toolkit and allows to program the soft object and to play games via the manipulation of this object.

Notable exceptions do exist, e.g. diyability.org, founded by Schimmer and Cohen [33], aims to encourage more people to think creatively about technology and disabilities. They as well as Hurst et al. [11,12] suggest that DIY and personal digital fabrication techniques can and should be adopted by therapists. In sum, although there are clearly efforts to empower OTs to create their own DIY-solutions, it is not always clear to what extent these devices allow for tangible (as in computationally enhanced) interaction. Embedding sensors and electronic circuitry might discourage OTs from creating true TI solutions.

The DIY-AT toolkit evaluated in this paper can be positioned at the intersection of tangible interaction, assistive technology and the DIY approach. Its aim is to enable OTs to create their own assistive technologies involving the manipulation (pinching, bending, pushing, squeezing etc.) of soft materials.

Research questions

Currently, little work has explored how to design such a system at the cross-section of tangible interaction, occupational therapy and DIY practices. Our goal is to evaluate this DIY-AT toolkit and to find answers to the following questions:

1. Are OTs able to create solutions without the help of a technical expert?
2. Are the solutions that can be built with the DIY-AT toolkit useful for the daily practice of OTs?
3. What kind of solutions do OTs create and for what purposes?
4. What suggestions do OTs have for the improvement or extension of the toolkit?
5. Finally, from our evaluation, what recommendations arise for building DIY-AT toolkits in general?

METHODS AND MATERIALS

Materials

We started with the materials available in the traditional Skweezee System (see Figure 1). The hardware consists of an Arduino Uno board extended with a custom-made multiplexer shield. However, we decided to encapsulate these in a white box, in order not to expose them as 'electronics' to the therapists. In addition, users were provided a stripped UTP cable containing eight wires that serve as sensing electrodes, and conductive wool. We did not provide a soft object, participants should find or make their own, connect electrodes to it and fill it with conductive wool [6] to create a smart soft object.

In addition to the hardware, a new standalone software program was created. The challenge was to create a user-friendly tool that offers all needed functionality but hides all the technical complexity. Therefore, the requirements and functionality for this software were defined during two separate participatory design sessions with two OTs. This software allows OTs to test their creation, define and record different gestures, and link each gesture to a keyboard or mouse command. In this manner, other applications can be controlled by manipulating the smart object. A game, for example, normally controlled with the arrow keys, can now be played with the soft object. All settings can be saved in a file for later use.

The main screen of the software is shown in Figure 2 ("PROGRAMMING MODE"). In this example, two gestures are recorded: 'Untouched' and 'right'. Each gesture can be given a name (e.g. 'right'), linked to a color (pink in the example), a symbol (arrow pointing to the right), a sound (blip), a keyboard command (right arrow key), and can also be deleted again. The OTs can immediately test their smart object and the settings. The length of the bar on the top of the screen reflects the amplitude of the deformation, which is another element of immediate feedback. The bar becomes longer, the harder you press on the smart object. From the software, a game or application can be launched and played ("PLAY MODE"). Several games are included in the software, but OTs can also link to external games or applications.

Finally, a website was created *projects.groept.be/~skweezee/* containing details about the fabrication tutorials, software user guide several examples that could inspire therapists. These details are considered outside the scope of this paper.

Summing up, the DIY-AT toolkit consists of 1) the hardware materials and components needed to fabricate smart objects, 2) the software to program gestures and control apps, and 3) a website containing tutorials and examples.

Method

Participants were found by sending out a call to healthcare institutions and schools, specifically targeting occupational therapists. Overall 16 persons replied but due to conflicting time schedules, only 8 persons were able to take part in this stage. For a detailed overview of participants and background, see Table 1. We held both individual participatory design sessions (one participant and one researcher), as well as workshops in groups. Prior to the individual sessions and work-shops, participants were asked to have a specific client/ activity context in mind. All sessions consisted of a brief introduction to the DIY-AT toolkit, followed by a brainstorm discussion to generate and discuss ideas. Participants took the toolkit home and continued with it in their own environment. Participants were instructed to document their creations by means of notes and pictures. After a couple of weeks participants were invited back for an evaluation of the toolkit by means of a semi-structured interview.

	Sex	Age	Background
P1	M	45	Senior OT therapist, combining pediatric practice experiences and teaching
P2	F	23	OT student (intern in care facility)
P3	M	24	OT graduate (just completed internship)
P4	F	24	OT student (intern in special needs school, collaborated with P5)
P5	M	22	OT student (intern in special needs school, collaborated with P4)
P6	F	27	OT with private practice
P7	F	21	OT student, doing internship with P6
P8	F	43	ICT coordinator in OT facility, supporting OTs to find the right equipment.

Table 1. Overview of participants

During the interview we discussed their creations, and polled for their opinions on the DIY-toolkit. Questions were related to their experience of creating smart objects and using the software, how they envision the use of their solutions in their daily practice with clients, and we also asked for suggestions for improvements.

A wealth of qualitative data was gathered throughout the sessions, workshops and interviews. These interviews were transcribed at verbatim, and the data were organized and analyzed using *NVivo 10*© in order to categorize the most important results into themes. One researcher did a first exploration and coded all transcripts, notes and images.

Initially 10 themes emerged that focused on benefits, limitations and future improvements. The coding and themes were then discussed with two other researchers. A second round of axial coding was conducted, and 5 themes remained. These themes are presented below.

RESULTS

Theme 1: A diversity of solutions to tailor a diversity of clients

The OTs came up with numerous ideas and potential uses for therapeutic devices. Being soft and deformable, their creations allow for a variety of gestures such as squeezing, grasping, pinching, punching and stretching. This variety of gestures is reflected in the diversity of objects created by the participants (see Figure 3, A-L). OTs built smart objects to conduct physical exercises such as strength exercises for fine or gross motor disabilities (J,L), flexibility exercises for movement (A,G) and balance and coordination exercises (A,K). We observed that OTs used gestures ranging from full-body interaction (A,E) to bi-manual interaction (H,I) and even fine fingertip pinching (G).

Some participants created smart objects consisting of two parts, one for each hand (C,J,K,L). We were also surprised that some therapists built more than one Skweezee. P8 created smart socks (J,K,L), a pillow (E), gloves (F) and a bear (not included in Figure 1). P6 created an interactive duck (I) and an interactive floor mat(A). P1 created the spook (G,H) and the soft balls (C). The diversity of solutions and the need for variation in occupational therapy were also mentioned by some participants:

P1: *"There are many kinds of smart objects people can use in therapy: on your head, on your feet, in your clothes, as a toy. It's the variation that you need to bring to your therapy."*

P3: *"The children can choose what kind of Skweezee to use, so they will be more motivated to use it".*

P6: *"First I wanted to make a star, but then I went to look in some stores and I found the duck. The other Skweezee I came up during the presentation of the toolkit. I thought "why only train fine motor skills if you could train other motor skills as well as balance, jumping." So I came up with a big cross to lay on the floor where the children could jump on."*

Most OTs designed for and tested with young clients, and stressed that the toolkit was suited for this age group. But they added that it could also useful be for adults, especially for muscle strengthening and balance exercises.

P1: *"I will use it as a reward for children with motor problems or disabilities. For adults you can use it for strength. Also if they have high risk of falling, it would be good to use it."*

P5: *"It is appealing for children. Also the visual feedback is a motivation for kids, you can use it for training. [...] I also did an internship in the MS (Multiple Sclerosis) hospital and we worked with hand functions, so they did exercises like two times opening your hand, two times closing your hand, and I think that if you use the system there, it would also motivate people. Yeah, I think it would be useful in that situation."*

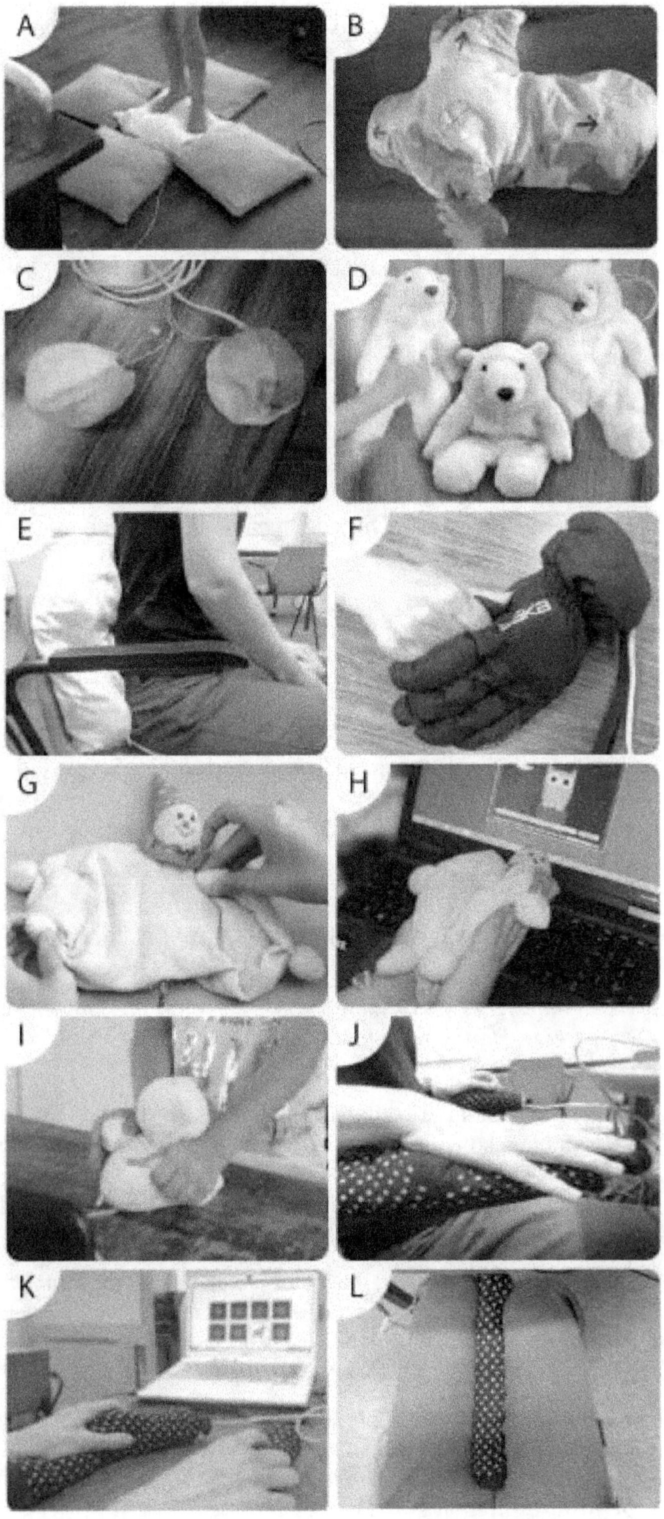

Figure 3. An overview of the different creations made by occupational therapists, with the toolkit: A - an interactive floor mat, B - a cross-controller, C -, D - polar bear, E –pillow for posture control, F- interactive gloves, G – a ghost for fine motor training, I – duck for squeeze gestures, J,K,L – socks that were turned into interactive armrests, or used for squeezing thighs.

In addition, based on the profile of their clients, the therapists introduced variety and personalization by customizing the *software* offered with the toolkit. OTs pointed out that one smart object can be used for different clients, simply by 1) changing the number or type of gestures, by 2) adding different audio-visual feedback and by 3) choosing different games to be played.

P3: "I would not make a smart object for each child, but I would change the games."

P4: "For my clients I added two gestures to the smart object but I will add two more when they improve."

P6: "I used the interactive floor mat for two different clients. So I changed the game, one difficult and one easy game. I also change the feedback. For the older boy (12 years old), I added only color feedback so it is more difficult and he will improve his concentration skills. For the younger boy (8 years old), I also used text/words that describes the move."

P8 created interactive armrests; by attaching socks to a wheelchair's armrests (J) the client could interact by applying pressure with his forearm (in different positions) while being in the wheelchair. However, the same socks were also used for strength exercises in the thigh area (L) as well as for bi-manual interaction with the computer (K).

These observations suggest that the flexibility of the DIY-AT toolkit meets the needs of OTs to bring variation in the therapy, and to tailor the therapy to the diverse and complex needs of people with disabilities.

P1: "It's a non-traditional input device and it's a new way of playing game, it allows you to be very creative in whatever way that you are going to use it, whatever kind of smart object you will create, either for gross motor or fine motor gestures, or a combination."

Theme 2: Exploiting affordances of everyday objects

The smart objects built by the therapists elicited gestures that are supported by the natural tactile feedback afforded by the soft materials. Participants reported that they did select the shape and size of their object based on gestures for specific exercises. Therapists carefully thought about the physical form and manipulability, in order to convey how to handle an object. For example, P1 who wanted to treat a client with fine motor skills disabilities, and created a ghost (G,H) with small balls at the end.

P1: "I see a lot of children in my head using my spooky (ghost) for fine motor exercises, for example the pinch grip. So I installed a small ball at each corner. The gestures are 'taking a ball with the pinch grip'."

The creativity that the DIY-AT toolkit offers to the therapists is that they can select or create any shape, color, size, texture and appearance of their physical creation. All the participants except one, created their smart objects repurposing everyday objects (plush toys, socks, pillows, etc). Most of our participants used materials that they found in their home or at work. They were also pleased that only relatively cheap materials were needed. Only the "controller" shown in figure (B) was made from scratch.

Many of the OTs created a smart object that was formed either by an old plush toy or looked like a plush toy children already owned. This increased the familiarity of the clients with the tool and so their motivation. Therapists often relied on metaphors to trigger existing mental models from other devices and to elicit the desired gesture. Both P3 and P6 created a kind of cross-controller:

P3: *"If they (young clients) have an old bear that they do not use anymore, they could make a game controller with that. So they will be not afraid of their own object."*

P4: *"We choose the polar bear because it resembles many cuddly toys. They are not afraid of it."*

Whereas the authors of this paper only thought of standalone objects, some OTs took advantage of the physical environment of the and used the toolkit to augment it. For example, P6 created an interactive floor mat (A) that was used for balance exercises, jumping from one part of the floor to the other.

Theme 3: Iterative design and tinkering

Assistive solutions have to be fitted to the clients' profile and their complex needs, therefore this calls for an iterative design and evaluation process. In our observations we found evidence of this iterative process where OTs first conducted some initial tests with the client and then re-adjusted their prototypes to ensure a successful therapy session.

P2: *"I was not sure how much wool to add. My client has serious gross motor disabilities. I needed to test it with him, otherwise my gesture with the balls could be very hard for him to squeeze."*

Being able to solve small problems without help and being able to tinker is important within a creative process. We found that participants felt confident to tinker with the toolkit and fix small problems that they encountered. Participants also experienced the limitations of the system. For example, because of the limited number of electrodes (eight), the 'sensitivity' of a smart object to certain gestures can be an issue.

P3: *"Also, I had a problem with the recognition [...] I opened my smart object and I clipped some of the length of the wires, and then it was fine. I think I was using too much wool. I solved it myself."*

P8: *"I first designed the glove for wearable gestures but that didn't really work. So then I found out that I can program pinch gestures for fine motor disabilities. So I changed it."*

However, our participants demonstrated self-efficacy, they were confident in their own ability to create and program their smart objects, to tinker and tailor their creations to the clients.

P6: *"You don't need to think 'how should I do it'. You can learn the procedure very fast, and easily and remember it for the next time."*

Theme 4: Meaningful feedback for playful motivation

As mentioned before, the software allows to control applications or play games using the smart objects as controller. Certainly children see this as a reward; interacting with a computer has a lot of added value for them.

P6: *"It's not as boring as some of the common treatments of fine motor skills, and they get to work with a computer, so it makes it less 'therapeutic'."*

An additional motivation was given to the clients due to the uniqueness and playfulness of common objects that serve as a game controller.

P1: *"It's a new way of playing game and it's a non-traditional input device."*

P4: *"When I was explaining how the soft controller is working, they were grabbing it and trying to use it".*

The system turned out not to be suitable for fast-paced games. The response time of the system is too long for such games. However, this was not a big concern for the majority of our participants, because they preferred games that did not require quick reactions, also as seen in [30]. Moreover, for some clients fast-paced games would not be appropriate for therapy.

P5: *"The system didn't always respond on time, so if you squeeze the objects it takes some time to respond. So, it is not like you do it on a keyboard that reacts immediately"*

P8: *"When they know there is time pressure, their muscles are freeze. In the school that I work, most of the children have problems with controlling their muscles."*

OTs like to include cognitive challenges in the exercises for their clients, so educational or puzzle games can also be very suitable. There should be a variety in the complexity offered by the games, starting from very simple and easy games for most cognitively impaired children.

P8: *"Games should take into consideration mental disabilities. The difficulty of a game is also related to the number of gestures needed. Tetris (five gestures) requires a lot of motor coordination and cognitive load."*

All participants strongly requested to have a set of embedded therapy games. These games should have a limited number of game commands that would translate into a low number of gestures in their smart object.

Theme 5: Platforms to learn and share, and build upon

One of the key factors in DIY culture is a community [20] to create a sense of identity, but also to enable learning, sharing and building on other's works [13]. While obviously we could not offer OTs an established community, we implemented a website that contained tutorials and examples of solutions (made by us) in order to facilitate the creations with the toolkit. OTs expressed a need for these tutorials and problem solving on demand. From the OTs' comments – *"Great tutorials but too much!"*– we realized however that the provided tutorials should be briefer, containing only the basic tip that would apply to a given case without going into too technical details. Problem solving support should be given to the therapist on demand. Participants emphasized this need: *"Could I ask feedback from the community when I had a question?"*

Moreover, a DIY project does not have to be a significant undertaking every time. Sometimes, it is enough to add something small or tweak existing components [5]. OTs suggest to provide good defaults or examples to start from.

P5: "It would be interesting to have some standard models, in case you do not have a lot of time."

This observation lead us to believe that in order to accommodate the therapists, the website that accompanies the toolkit should be extended, and include briefer tutorials, tailored to address specific issues. In addition, we should provide a small number of ready-to-use templates that can be ordered from the site.

DISCUSSION

While the DIY community is characterized by amateurs looking for ways of self-expression, the OT community consists of professionals who are motivated to find solutions for their clients. Hence the meaning of DIY for OTs is not driven by a culture of "rebelliousness or anti-consumerism" [13]. Rather, OTs are driven by empowering clients with complex needs in their daily life activities. OTs constantly adapt and repurpose object to help clients. Hence, OTs do embrace DIY, yet computational augmentation of physical objects is still a hurdle for many [1]. As one of our participants explained:

P6: "We are creative as OTs and we learn to make tools that will help the clients. But we cannot connect them with the computer."

Revisiting the aforementioned research questions mentioned above, we can conclude that OTs were able to build solutions without the aid of technical experts. We observed a variety of creations, illustrating on one the hand the need of OTs to find solutions for very different types of exercises, and on the other hand the flexibility of our DIY-AT toolkit. Certainly clients that are more difficult to motivate welcome the playful interactions. Finally, OTs suggested the availability of brief tutorials and ready-to-use templates.

CONCLUSION

It was our aim to bring DIY to occupational therapists with our toolkit, but equally to aspire other researchers. Reflecting back on the five themes that emerged from our evaluation, we believe these can also be considered as guidelines for designing any successful DIY-toolkit within the field of '*assistive therapies*'.

Firstly, a DIY-AT toolkit should ensure that it can *deliver a diversity of solutions to tailor a diversity of clients*. No person with special needs is alike, and even with one client there is a constant need for adaptations during rehabilitation or due to degenerative processes. If a therapist is going to invest time and energy in building an assistive solution, it should be easy to reuse, adapt and extend this. Hence our evaluation confirms the need for flexibility to adapt the technology to changes in ability, needs and lifestyles [17].

Secondly, occupational therapists are creative in making tools. They see affordances for therapy in the diversity of everyday objects. Therefore, DIY-AT toolkits should support this creativity and *allow for hacking and repurposing these everyday objects*. Obviously, this reduces the cost, and can reduce barriers to procuring such a device.

As aforementioned, OTs do embrace DIY, yet computational augmentation of physical objects is a hurdle for many. Therefore, any toolkit should aim to *provide therapists with the confidence that building these solutions is easy*. We took great care in designing user-friendly software and avoiding 'engineering language'. Also we didn't expose the hardware as 'electronics' but we encapsulated it in a box. We believe these decisions in part gave the therapists self-confidence and stimulated them in tinkering. Tinkering also supports an iterative process which in turn is necessary to support the first guideline mentioned; solutions should be easy to adapt and extend.

Fourthly, toolkits should include means to *offer meaningful feedback*. The initial Skweezee system was simply an input device that didn't provide any motivation for interaction (other than its form). Assistive tools in therapy need a 'purpose'. Being able to give clients a challenge and meaningful rewards is essential to any therapy.

Finally, not surprisingly, *provide an online support platform*. We felt that therapists welcomed an online community not so much to be part of an ideology or for self-expression, but rather for more practical reasons. Therefore, rather than a community, one should provide a platform that provides answers to technical issues, as well as examples and templates that promote the OTs creativity.

We hope that the above guidelines can inform the designers of future DIY-AT toolkit to empower therapists and ensure that 'in vivo' generative design takes place, hence to *make the making more accessible*.

REFERENCES

1. Annema, J.-H., Verstraete, M., Vanden Abeele, V., Desmet, S., and Geerts, D. Videogames in Therapy: A Therapist's Perspective. In *Proc. Fun and Games 2010*, ACM (2010), 94–98.
2. Boulanger, C., Boulanger, A., de Greef, L., et al. Stroke Rehabilitation with a Sensing Surface. In *Proc. CHI 2013,* ACM (2013), 1243–1246.

3. Collective, B.M. and Shaw, D. Makey Makey: Improvising Tangible and Nature-based User Interfaces. In *Proc.TEI 2012*, ACM (2012), 367–370.

4. De Couvreur, L. and Goossens, R. Design for (every)one: co-creation as a bridge between universal design and rehabilitation engineering. *CoDesign 7*, 2 (2011), 107–121.

5. Gauntlett, D. Media Studies 2.0: a response. *Interactions: Studies in Communication & Culture 1*, 1 (2009), 147–157.

6. Geurts, L., Deville, J., Abeele, V.V., Saldien, J., and Vanderloock, K. Skweezee Studio: Turn Your Own Plush Toys into Interactive Squeezable Objects. In *Proc TEI 2014*, ACM (2013), 377–380.

7. Geurts, L., Vanden Abeele, V., Husson, J., et al. Digital Games for Physical Therapy: Fulfilling the Need for Calibration and Adaptation. In *Proc.TEI 2011*, ACM (2011), 117–124.

8. Graham, J. Occupational Therapy: Is it the Creative Problem Solving Process which the Profession claims? *Australian Occupational Therapy Journal 30*, 3 (1983), 89–102.

9. Grierson, M. and Kiefer, C. NoiseBear: A Wireless Malleable Multiparametric Controller for Use in Assistive Technology Contexts. *Ext. Abstracts CHI 2013*, ACM (2013), 2923–2926.

10. Hook, J., Verbaan, S., Durrant, A., Olivier, P., and Wright, P. A Study of the Challenges Related to DIY Assistive Technology in the Context of Children with Disabilities. In *Proc. DIS 2014*, ACM (2014), 597–606.

11. Hurst, A. and Kane, S. Making "making" accessible. In *Proc. IDC 2013,* ACM (2013), 635-638.

12. Hurst, A. and Tobias, J. Empowering Individuals with Do-it-yourself Assistive Technology. In *Proc ASSERS 2011*, ACM (2011), 11–18.

13. Kuznetsov, S. and Paulos, E. Rise of the Expert Amateur: DIY Projects, Communities, and Cultures. In *Proc NordiCHI 2010*, ACM (2010), 295–304.

14. Li, Y., Fontijn, W., and Markopoulos, P. A Tangible Tabletop Game Supporting Therapy of Children with Cerebral Palsy. In *Proc. Fun and Games 2008*, Springer-Verlag (2008), 182–193.

15. Malone, T.W. and Lepper, M.R. Making learning fun: A taxonomy of intrinsic motivations for learning. *Aptitude, learning, and instruction 3*, (1987), 223–253.

16. Perner-Wilson, H., Buechley, L., and Satomi, M. Handcrafting textile interfaces from a kit-of-no-parts. In *Proc.TEI 2011*, ACM Press (2011), 61.

17. Phillips, B. and Zhao, H. Predictors of assistive technology abandonment. *Assistive Technology 5*, 1 (1993), 36–45.

18. Riemer-Reiss, M.L. and Wacker, R.R. Assistive Technology Use and Abandonment among College Students with Disabilities,3(23). I*nternational Electronic Journal for Leadership in Learning 3*, 0 (1999).

19. Riemer-Reiss, M.L. and Wacker, R.R. Factors Associated with Assistive Technology Discontinuance among Individuals with Disabilities. *The Journal of Rehabilitation 66*, 3 (2000), 44.

20. De Roeck, D., Slegers, K., Criel, J., et al. I Would DiYSE for It!: A Manifesto for Do-it-yourself Internet-of-things Creation. In *Proc. NordiCHI 2012*, ACM (2012), 170–179.

21. Savage, V., Zhang, X., and Hartmann, B. Midas: Fabricating Custom Capacitive Touch Sensors to Prototype Interactive Objects. In *Proc. UIST 2012*, ACM (2012), 579–588.

22. Scherer, M.J. *Living in the State of Stuck: How Assistive Technology Impacts the Lives of People With Disabilities*. Brookline Books, Brookline, Mass., 2005.

23. Schmid, T. Meanings of creativity within occupational therapy practice. *Australian Occupational Therapy Journal 51*, 2 (2004), 80–88.

24. Söderback, I. *International Handbook of Occupational Therapy Interventions*. Springer, 2009.

25. Estes, J., Pierce, E.D. Pediatric therapists' perspectives on occupation-based practice. *Scandinavian Journal of Occupational Therapy 19, 1 (2012), 17-25.*

26. Townsend, E.A. and Polatajko, H.J. Advancing an occupational therapy vision for health, well-being, and justice through occupation. *Ottawa, ON: CAOT Publications*, (2007).

27. Vanderloock, K., Vanden Abeele, V., Suykens, J., and Geurts, L. The Skweezee System: Enabling the design and the programming of squeeze interactions. In *Proc. UIST 2013,* ACM (2013).

28. Vandermaesen, M., de Weyer, T., Luyten, K., and Coninx, K. PhysiCube: Providing Tangible Interaction in a Pervasive Upper-limb Rehabilitation System. In *Proc. TEI 2013*, ACM (2013), 85–92.

29. Willkomm, T. *Assistive Technology Solutions in Minutes: Make a Difference Today!* ATECH Services, 2005.

30. Vanden Abeele, V., Geurts, L., Husson, J., Windey, F., Annema, J.-H., Verstraete, M., Desmet, S., Designing Slow Fun! Physical Therapy Games to Remedy the Negative Consequences of Spasticity. In *Proc. Fun and Games 2010*, ACM (2010).

31. Tots 'n' Tech, http://tnt.asu.edu/.

32. Assistive Technology, *Instructables.com*. http://www.instructables.com/group/Assistive_Tech/.

33. DIYAbility, *DIYAbility*. http://www.diyability.org.

Cord UIs: Controlling Devices with Augmented Cables

Philipp Schoessler[1], Sang-won Leigh[1], Krithika Jagannath[2], Patrick van Hoof[3], Hiroshi Ishii[1]

[1]MIT Media Lab
75 Amherst St
{phil_s, sangwon, ishii}@media.mit.edu

[2]Harvard Graduate School of Education
Cambridge, MA 02138 USA
krj444@mail.harvard.edu

[3]MIT Sloan
Cambridge, MA 02142 USA
pvanhoof@mit.edu

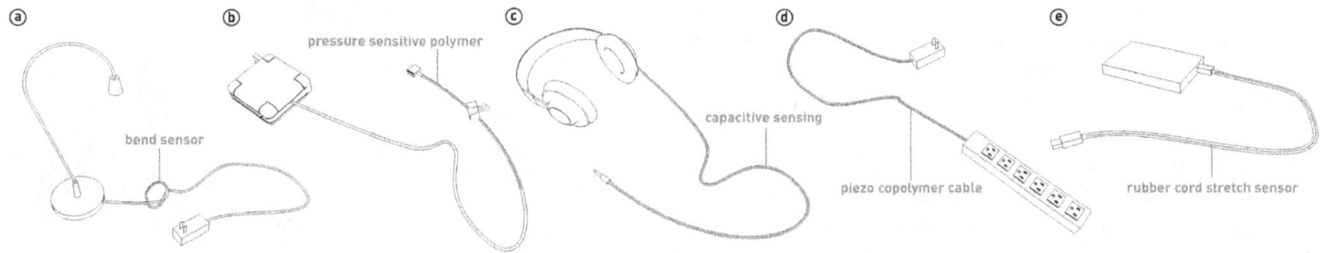

Figure 1: a) tightening the knot dims the lamp. b) attaching a clip on the power cord puts the computer to sleep. c) squeezing the headphone cable temporarily mutes the headphones. d) kinking the power strip's cord toggles it on/off. e) stretching the USB cord safe-ejects the hard drive.

ABSTRACT

Cord UIs are sensorial augmented cords that allow for simple metaphor-rich interactions to interface with their connected devices. Cords offer a large underexplored space for interactions as well as unique properties and a diverse set of metaphors that make them potentially interesting tangible interfaces. We use cords as input devices and explore different interactions like tying knots, stretching, pinching and kinking to control the flow of data and/or power. We also look at ways to use objects in combination with augmented cords to manipulate data or properties of a device. For instance, placing a clamp on a cable can obstruct the audio signal to the headphones. Using special materials such as piezo copolymer cables and stretchable cords we built five working prototypes to showcase the interactions described in this paper.

Author Keywords

Tangible Interface; Ubiquity; Touch Sensors; Seamless Interface; Sensing Technology.

ACM Classification Keywords

H.5.2 User Interface, B.4.2 Input/Output Devices.

TEI '15, January 16 - 19 2015, Stanford, CA, USA
Copyright is held by the owner/author(s). Publication rights licensed to ACM. ACM 978-1-4503-3305-4/15/01 $15.00
http://dx.doi.org/10.1145/2677199.2680601

INTRODUCTION

Traditionally, electrical devices are dependent on cords, either for power or data-transmission. Cords are often times considered a nuisance and wireless technologies have advanced to a point where they can be used to charge small devices over short distances. However, technology has not yet reached a point where we can imagine a cord free future for all of our electrical devices. This is mainly due to the exponential power loss over distance. Most recently researchers have accomplished to transmit 209 W of power at 8% efficiency over a distance of 5 m [4]. Wireless data transmission technologies are more advanced, however, they still suffer from inherent vulnerabilities and security threats and it usually takes considerable effort to setup.

Despite the intensive research on wireless technologies, cords are not going to disappear in the near future. Among their vast ubiquity cords hold unique properties, which make them a interesting tangible user interface. They offer diverse material properties and form factors (flexible, rigid, flat, round, spiral); they can be used to offload interactions from the device and can offer quick and eyes-free interactions (e.g. Figure 1c). Moreover, one of the underlying principles of tangible interface design is to augment everyday objects with technology aimed at exploiting real-world metaphors. Most interactions we describe in this paper evolved from the idea to regard the cord as a water hose and data or power as water flowing in this water hose. We propose simple interactions that involve pinching, stretching, kinking, attaching objects, or making knots with our augmented cords.

The goal is to take advantage of the richness of human intuition and handling skills developed over time through interaction with these objects. In our opinion, cords exemplify this principle, since humans have been interacting with strings and ropes for thousands of years.

REALTED WORK

In the field of human-computer interaction, cords have not yet been extensively explored. The most relevant work is by Schwarz et al. [7] who were the first to describe a cord-like multi-DOF input-device to control mobile devices. Wimmer et al. [9] explore Time Domain Reflectometry to sense input and present an application that let's users adjust the volume of music by touching the headphone cord at different locations. Nokia published a patent [2] that describes ideas to use cords as an input device. Minguet [5] augmented a rope with flex sensors to detect knots, which can be used creatively to generate visuals and sounds on an attached iPhone. Sousa and Oakley [8] investigated how cords and a bead in clothing can be used as discrete input control. Yao et al. [10] explored ropes and how its common affordances can be used to design a novel gaming interface. Balakrishnan et al. [1] describe ShapeTape, a cord-like sensor that allows to precisely tracks its current shape and orientation and, among other things, can be used to manually and precisely manipulate Bezier curves in CAD programs.

These projects use the unique properties of a rope or cord to explore different interactions. However, we believe that the affordances and especially metaphors of cords are not adequately investigated. The main contribution of this paper is the exploration of novel metaphor-rich interactions and applications with augmented cords and all kinds of electrical devices. We consider the cord as an alternative input device for simple specialized tasks that comes naturally with the device and not as an additional versatile/sophisticated interface for complex tasks as [7][1].

INTERACTION

Most of the presented interactions lend strongly from the metaphor of regarding the cord as a hose and the power and data as liquid flowing in that hose. Additionally we explore other metaphors and analogies ("breaking a connection", "pulling something out of something") that create a strong conceptual model that can help to make interactions more understandable.

Cords offer endless possibilities of manual manipulation that could be used for interaction but are better performed with other devices that offer easier multi-DOF control. Hence, we decided to focus on interactions that are simple and could potentially be performed eyes-free.

We decided to classify the interactions with cords into three categories (Touch, Knot, Objects). For each category we list several application scenarios of which we chose to exemplify five through physical prototypes described later in this paper.

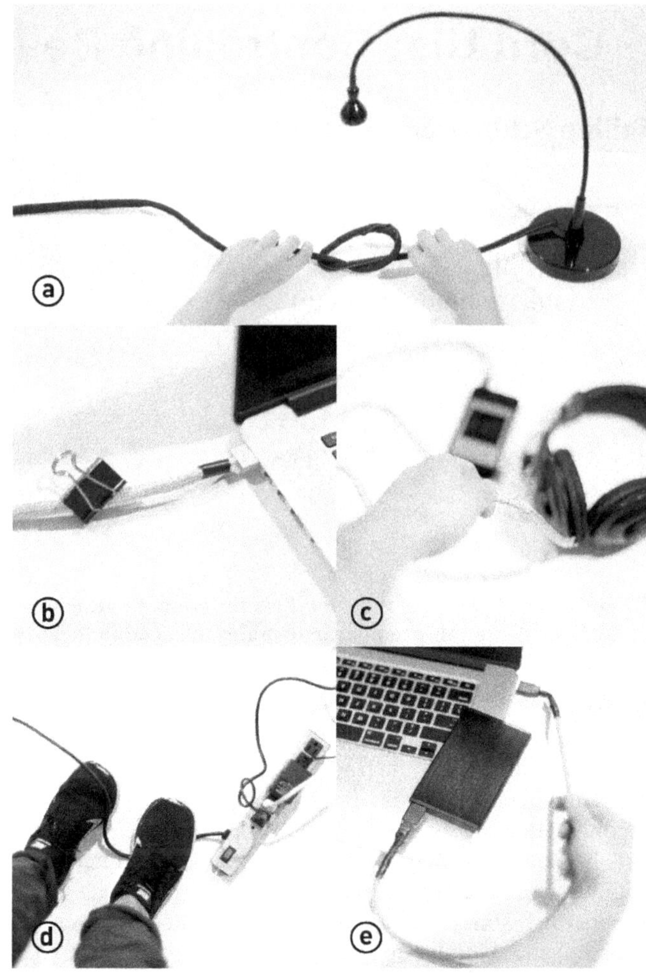

Figure 2: The five prototypes. a) embedded bend sensor detects knot's tightness. b) we can sense the clamp's pressure using conductive polymer. c) conductive yarn woven into the cord sleeve senses touch and pressure. d) special piezo copolymer cable can detect kinks. e) stretchable cord with rubber resistive cord to sense pulling.

Touch

We touch or apply pressure to the augmented cord to manipulate various parameters of the device to which it is connected. A cord's form factor lends itself for multiple types of touch interaction (sliding, pinching, twisting, swinging, stretching or kinking). Pinching the cable and varying the pressure applied, could alter the volume or speed of the music played. We imagine that people could pinch the cable of their headphones to mute the music temporarily to listen to in-flight announcements or their cab driver. This application is exemplified in our prototype (Figure 2c).

Further touch interactions that explore different metaphors are the kink and stretch. Kinking a cord back and forth in a certain frequency could be used to set a certain parameter (e.g. speed of a fan). Moreover, kinking a cord can be used to "break" a connection to the device. In our prototypes we demonstrate a power strip that switches off as soon as you kink the cable (Figure 2c). "Un-kinking" would switch it on again. The advantage hereby is that the whole cable acts a sensor and the power strip can be easily switched using the feet or hands. Power strips are often at hard to reach locations whereas large parts of its cord are usually accessible.

A stretching interaction on a cord can be an analogy to pulling out of something. In our prototype (Figure 2e) we use a stretchable cord on a portable hard- drive that can be used to indicate that a user would like to disconnect it from the computer, instead of having to use the mouse and click the eject/safe-remove button before one can pull off the hard-drive.

Knots

Tying knots in our augmented cords can manipulate a specific parameter of an appliance. For example, the tightness of a knot determines the level of data or power flow. In one of our prototypes, a simple overhand knot in the cord connected to an LED table lamp controls the intensity of the light; the looser the knot the brighter the LED light while tightening the knot dims the light until it switches off completely (Figure 2a). This is based on the analogy that a knot constricts or cuts-off the flow of something (light, volume, data, etc.) depending on how it is tied.

One key difference of using a knot over one of the touch interactions as control mechanism is that it provides visual feedback about the state it is currently in and is therefore better suited for controlling analog settings than binary ones. A further feature is that a knot can be moved along the whole length of the cord. The device's control could so be moved to most suitable position. We also imagine the possibility for multiple knots to control a number of independent parameters of a device. For instance, three knots could represent the red, green, or blue value of an RGB-LED lamp, respectively. Knot detection could be implemented using the technology described in [1].

Another, more poetic application idea lends from the old tradition of tying a knot in a handkerchief to remember something important. We imagine a cable - connected to a computer - in which the user ties a slipknot. This action automatically creates an event reminder in the user's calendar or a task in the To Do list. Upon completion the knot can be removed and the event or task is automatically checked off. The cord then acts as a tangible representation of the digital data.

Considering the countless types of knots there are more potential applications to be explored in future work.

Objects

Another way of interacting with appliances is using small objects, each having their own set of affordances, on an augmented cord. For example, users can attach and slide clips on the cord to change the volume of music. Different clips could be used to control different parameters. The shape and position of the clip provides immediate visual and tangible feedback about the type and level of control. Objects also have the advantage of maintaining a continuous state. In our prototype, for example, we show how to use a clip to put your computer into sleep mode (Figure 2b). As soon as the clip is removed, the computer starts up again. It is possible to place a multitude of objects (mug, water-bottle, paperweight, etc.) onto the cord to switch off any device. Another application could be an office telephone that cannot be called as soon as you place an object on its cord. Thinking more advanced we can imagine a cord that, e.g. via RFID, can distinguish between objects placed on or near it and switches functionality accordingly. For instance a speaker placed near the cord would eavesdrop into the flow of data and play it back.

TECHNICAL IMPLEMENTATION

To explore some of our proposed interactions we built five prototypes that work by augmenting the whole cord or parts of it. In all prototypes we use commercially available materials, sensors and cables. Sensor reading is done using the Arduino microcontroller.

Lamp (Figure 1a and 2a)

To detect a knot in a cord, and use it to adjust the brightness of a lamp by altering its tightness, we embedded a Flexpoint 2.2" bend sensor into wrap-around isolation together with a four-strand cable. Two of the strands were used to read out the sensor data. The other two strands were used to power the lamp. We used the microcontroller to read out the analog resistance value and to control the brightness of the light accordingly.

Laptop (Figure 1b and 2b)

We augmented a MacBook power cord with conductive polymer sandwiched between two sheets of heavy copper foil. When applying pressure the resistance between the two copper sheets decreases. Since the power cord doesn't offer the possibility to send any signals to the laptop we decided to send a long pulse (1000ms) by switching the power cord on/off using a relay. Using AppleScript we listen for this rising-edge "signal" by checking if the computer AC power is connected or not. We then issue the command to go to sleep or wake up.

Headphone (Figure 1c and 2c)

We use conductive yarn that we wove into the fabric of braided cable sleeving. The micro-controller detects touch via a large resistor (~1 MOhm) placed in series, which responds to any resistance changes following contact with the human body and ground. It can also detect the amount of pressure that is applied to the cord, since the resistance is inversely correlated to the area of human skin touching the cord. By temporarily shorting ground to the microphone input on an audio cable we can toggle the pause/resume functionality in an iPhone. We chose to use capacitive sensing over pressure sensors to detect pinching, to avoid accidental triggering in through cable stress.

Power Strip (Figure 1d and 2d)

Alongside the power cord we placed a Piezo Copolymer Coaxial Cable from Measurement Specialties™ to detect kinks and switch on/off the power strip. The piezo polymer generates a voltage that is proportional to the amount of compression or stretch that is put on it. Piezo cables are often times used in traffic counting. To switch the power on/off we implemented a relay into a power strip that is controlled by a microcontroller.

Hard Drive (Figure 1e and 2e)

For the easy-eject hard drive we augmented a stretchable cord with a stretch sensor (resistive rubber) that decreases its resistance when expanded. We use a a special stretchable cord which is often used in robotics where it can help to reduce a lot of wear and tear caused by the moving robots. This cable can usually only be stretched up to 30% of its original length but by removing the curled strands from their original sleeving and threading it in rubber tubing we increased the stretch to more than 50%. To interpret a stretch and eject the hard drive we used openFrameworks in combination with AppleScript.

CHALLENGE AND FUTURE WORK

As future work, we plan to explore more sophisticated technologies for linear shape and input sensing like Optical Domain Frequency Reflectometry or Swept Frequency Capacitive Sensing [6] to obtain more exact touch location readings and reliably detect different gestures. However, we believe that the gestures and interactions themselves should stay simple.

Another potentially interesting area for further exploration is the actuation of cords. Cord UIs could be used as output rather than only input. Similar to [3] this could allow for ambient, audio, visual or haptic feedback about events or interactions. For example, a cord could indicate suffering by wiggling and cringing when a data connection gets weaker. Or, similar to a fire hose when water pressure changes, a cord's stiffness could change when the connected device draws a lot of power.

Moreover, there needs to be more investigation into the diverse form factors cords come in (spiral, thick, thin, flat, etc.) and what different interactions these afford. To then better evaluate the findings a user study needs to be conducted.

CONCLUSION

This paper presents the idea of interacting with cords to manipulate parameters of connected devices through touching or making shapes. As a proof of concept, we developed five prototypes to demonstrate how cords could be used to control 1) the intensity of light in a lamp, 2) temporarily mute a media player 3) put a computer to sleep 4) switch on/off a power strip, or 5) eject a portable hard drive.

There are challenges that need to be addressed before we will see Cord UIs used in everyday devices. However, we believe the possibility of Cord UIs can inspire product designers to outfit everyday cords with sensors, giving their products new interaction and design possibilities. These cords will not be seen as a nuisance anymore, but will offer an interesting alternative interface for the appliances they are connected to.

REFERENCES

1. Balakrishnan, R., Fitzmaurice, G., Kurtenbach, G., Singh, K., Exploring Interactive Curve and Surface Manipulation Using a Bend and Twist Sensitive Input Strip. *Symposium on Interactive 3D Graphics, 1999*, ACM Press (1999).
2. Colley, A., Kosonen, J., User Interface. (Apr. 2013). Patent No. 0102361, Filed Oct. 24th.
3. Jeremijenko, N. Live Wire. July 2014. http://www.nyu.edu/projects/xdesign/mainmenu/archive_livewire.html
4. Lee, S., Gyu-Heyong, C., Chun, R., Innovative 5m-off-distance Inductive Power Transfer Systems with Optimally Shaped Dipole Coils, *IEEE 2014*.
5. Minguet, M. Knot(e)–Sound and Visual Interface for iPhone (ECAL). July, 2014. http://www.creativeapplications.net/sound/knote-by-matthieu-minguet-rope-as-sound-and-visual-interface-for-iphone-ecal/
6. Sato, M., Poupyrev, I., Harrison, C. Touché: Enhancing Touch Interaction on Humans, Screens, Liquids, and Everyday Objects. In *Proc. CHI'12*, ACM Press (2012).
7. Schwarz, J., Harrison, C., Hudson, S., Mankoff, J. Cord input: an intuitive, high-accuracy, multi-degree-of-freedom input method for mobile devices. In *Proc. SIGCHI*, ACM Press (2010).
8. Sousa, C., Oakley, I. Integrating Feedback into Wearable Controls. In *Proc. INTERACT'13*.
9. Wimmer, R., Baudisch, P. Modular and Deformable Touch-Sensitive Surfaces Based on Time Domain Reflectometry. In *Proc. UIST'11*, ACM Press (2011).
10. Yao, L., Dasgupta, S., Cheng, N., Spingarn-Koff, J., Rudakevych , O., Ishii, H. Rope Revolution: tangible and gestural rope interface for collaborative play. In *Proc. ACE'11*, ACM Press (2011).

Relationship Tunnel Vision: Altered Social Interaction Using Eye-Tracking

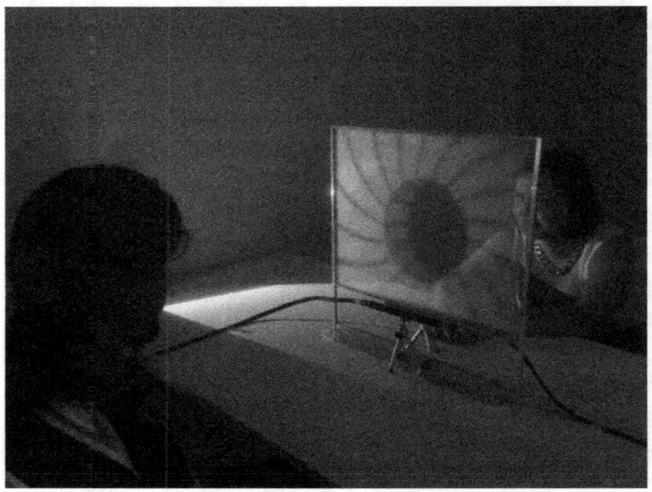

Mon-Chu Chen
Madeira-ITI
University of Madeira
Funchal, Madeira 9020 PORTUGAL
monchu@m-iti.org

Bong-Keum Jeong
Madeira-ITI
University of Madeira
Funchal, Madeira 9020 PORTUGAL
bongkeum.jeong@m-iti.org

Victor Rivera
Madeira-ITI
University of Madeira
Funchal, Madeira 9020 PORTUGAL
varz86@gmail.com

TEI '15, Jan 16-19 2015, Stanford, CA, USA
ACM 978-1-4503-3305-4/15/01.
http://dx.doi.org/10.1145/2677199.2690868

Abstract
We present a gaze-based installation enabling two participants to experience cycles of relationship "destroyed" by tunnel vision. The installation comprises a holographic projection screen and two eye-trackers. The trackers allow us to identify the gaze positions and onset of eye contacts. The holographic screen makes it possible to block out the eyesight by projection and to see through without projection. Two participants sitting on both sides of the screen will encounter series of artificial tunnel vision and blindness.

Author Keywords
Gaze-based interaction; eye tracking; eye contacts; tunnel vision; social interaction.

ACM Classification Keywords
H.5.m. Information interfaces and presentation (e.g., HCI): Miscellaneous.

Introduction
Tunnel vision refers to the phenomenon when one's peripheral vision is lost and the field of vision is constricted to a circular tunnel-like shape. While it refers to a medical condition, the term is often used as a metaphor to characterize the unwillingness to consider alternatives to one's preferred line of thought. In the beginning of a romantic relationship, couples feel

Figure-1: The holographic projection screen and the two EyeTribe eye trackers.

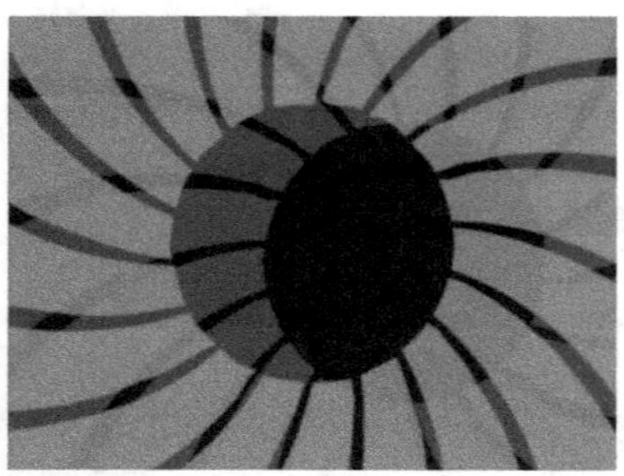

Figure-2: The positions of the pink and blue spiral patterns are controlled by eye gaze.

Figure-3: The projection is inverted to block the eyesight after prolonged eye contact.

enchanted by the affection and tend to rationalize any unfavorable traits of the partner. When the relationship becomes sour later, any negative quality turns into the only focus of attention. The relationship continues to struggle until both parties become totally blind about the person they fell in love in the beginning.

The goal of this project is to let participants experience the artificial tunnel vision and fabricated blindness in an accelerated rate. Hopefully, throughout cycles of this experience, it could inspire, stimulate and provoke thoughtful conversations between people in relationship currently or in the past.

Implementation

A freestanding projection screen was built using aluminum, acrylic and 3M CLEAR transparent projection film (Fig-1). Two EyeTribe eye trackers are attached to two networked Mac computers, and placed on both sides of the screen. One mac is in charge of connecting two eye trackers and generating projection graphics. The projector is placed not perpendicular to the projection surface, so either of the participants will not see the shining lights directly from the projector.

Two rotating spiral patterns (in pink and blue) follow the gaze positions of each participant respectively. The pattern allows people to see through the central black area, while the periphery is blocked (Fig-2). When eye contacts happened, participants will be able to see each other through the projection screen (Fig-4). After roughly 3 seconds of eye contacts, the projection is inverted so the screen becomes opaque to mimic being blinded (Fig-3, 5). The participants continue the looped experience as the projection reverses back to the artificial tunnel vision after about 5 seconds.

Figure-4: Participants can see each other.

Figure-5: Participants are blinded after a prolong tunnel vision in their relationship.

Sootoid: Generative Art Drawing by Flame of Candle

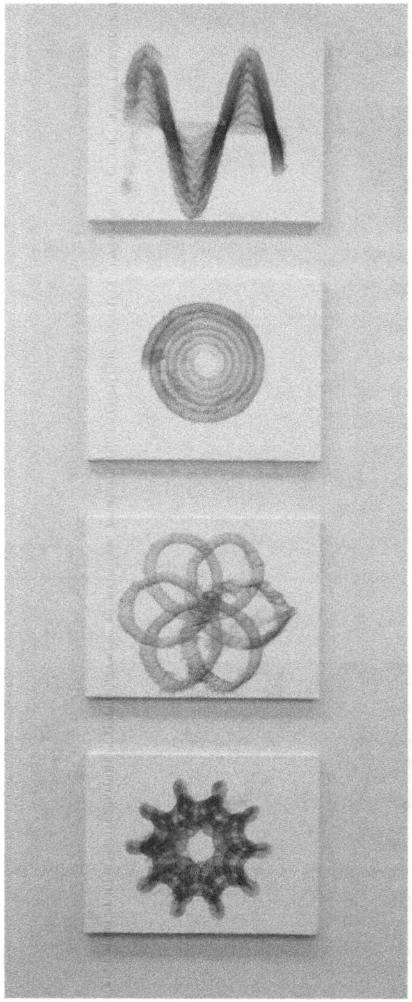

Figure.1 4 types of curve: sootoid pictures.

Hisakazu Hada
School of Media Science, Tokyo University of Technology
1404-1 Katakura-machi, Hachioji, Tokyo, Japan
hadahskz@stf.teu.ac.jp

Daisuke Tozuka
School of Media Science, Tokyo University of Technology

Sho Kamei
School of Media Science, Tokyo University of Technology

Tatsumi Hasegawa
School of Media Science, Tokyo University of Technology

Fuhito Morita
School of Media Science, Tokyo University of Technology

Shuntaro Ootsuki
School of Media Science, Tokyo University of Technology

Akito Nakano
Graduate School of Media and Governance, Keio University
Endo 5322, Fujisawa, Kanagawa, Japan
akito@sfc.keio.ac.jp

TEI '15, Jan 16-19 2015, Stanford, CA, USA
ACM 978-1-4503-3305-4/15/01.
http://dx.doi.org/10.1145/2677199.2690869

Abstract
Sootoid is a symphonic art created by collaboration between human, computer and flame of candle. While the major generative art pictures are drawn in a computer display, Sootoid creates a generative art drawing on a linen canvas by candle soot. Movement of candle is controlled by pre-programmed algorithm, making airflow and flickering of candle flame each time it moves to create unique soot line and color.

Author Keywords
Generative art, Drawing machine, algorithmic drawing

ACM Classification Keywords
J.5. Arts and humanities, Fine arts

General Terms
Design, Performance

Introduction
Soot painting is one of the major drawing methods to create drawings by attaching candle soot on a canvas material such as paper[1,2]. Most previous soot painting use airflow to create desirable appearance. Generative art is Computer Graphic (CG) art created by autonomous system or computational algorithm[2], mostly showing the calculated graphics on a computer

Figure 2. Drawing by Sootoid

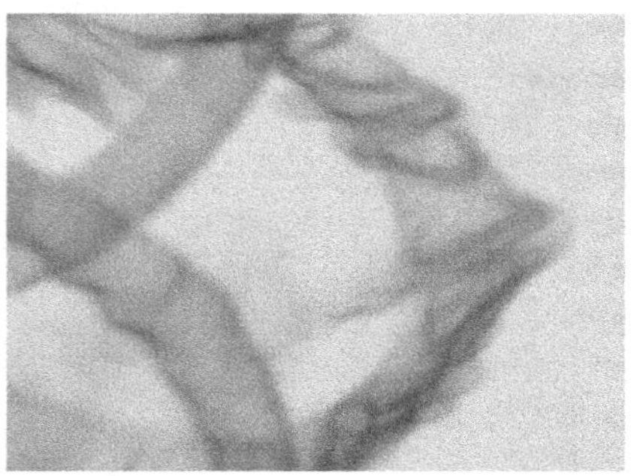

Figure 3. Effect of airflow

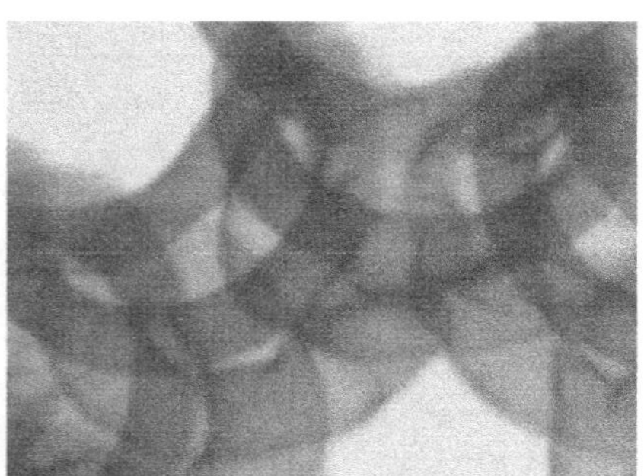

Figure 4. Effect of soot layers

display. The authors propose a new generative art drawing method Sootoid: A soot painting by a motion-controlled candle.

Sootoid

Sootoid uses motion-controlled candle as a pen to create soot painting by attaching the produced soot on a canvas material as Figure 2. This method produces twofold uniqueness.

I) Flickering of candle flame

A candle flame naturally flickers when it burns. The painting Sootoid produces reflects not only the soot caused by such natural flicker, but also the movement of a candle and wind produced by the move. It therefore produces organic and unique outcome each time even if the painting was drawn using same computational algorithm. A slight hand made airflow given in the drawing process would add elegant effect to the line. Figure 3 shows the effect given to the drawing.

II) Gradation of color by soot layers

Density of a soot color is defined by the speed of candle move, that is, faster move will add lighter color, and slower move will add darker color on the canvas. In Figure 4, soot layers are giving gradation of darker lines with foggy frame, which is a different layering expression compared to that of color paintings.

Implementation

Sootoid consists of 3axis machine with stepping motors for candle control, and programming environment based on Processing for simulation. Figure 5 shows the simulated image on a display(right) and the obtained image on a canvas(left). Medias such as linen canvas and cardboard will be set above Sootoid.

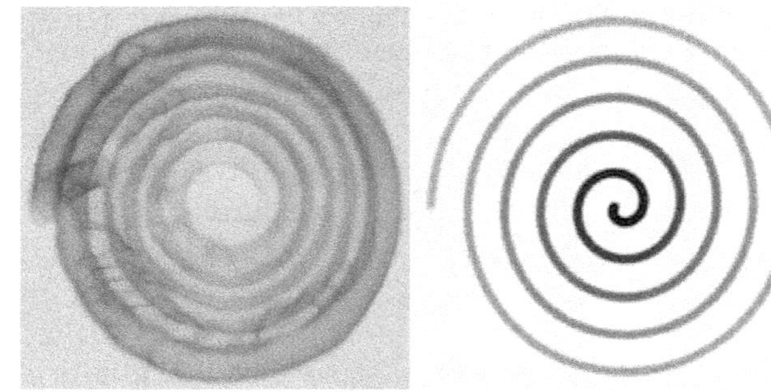

Figure 5. Sootoid image vs simulated image

Pictures

4 types of trigonometric functions based curves are shown in Figure 1. Top figure is layers of various sine curves. Second figure is a spiral. Third and last figures are the trochoid drawn using different parameters. Complexity is increasing as the canvas goes down from top to bottom.

Sootoid creates fusion of calculated image and organic nature on a canvas. Sootoid platform extends the potential of calculated image expression, and eternalize a slice of moment that will never come again.

References

[1] Fire Paintings: Artist Draws With Flames And Soot, http://www.boredpanda.com/soot-art-fire-paintings-steve-spazuk/ (2014)

[2] Etsuko ichikawa: Aquagraph, http://www.etsukoichikawa.com/Artist-Detail.cfm?ArtistsID=252

[3] Matt Pearson, Generative art a practical guide using processing, Manning Publications (2011)

What Things Dream Of

Min-Ji Ku
Hongik University
2639 Sejong-ro, Jochiwon-eup
Sejong, South Korea
reisklee@gmail.com

Bo-Kyeong Kim
Hongik University
2639 Sejong-ro, Jochiwon-eup
Sejong, South Korea
kbg1379@gmail.com

Younghui Kim (advisor)
Hongik University
2639 Sejong-ro, Jochiwon-eup
Sejong, South Korea
ihongik@gmail.com

TEI '15, Jan 16-19 2015, Stanford, CA, USA
ACM 978-1-4503-3305-4/15/01.
http://dx.doi.org/10.1145/2677199.2690870

Abstract
The everyday objects stand very still as always, fixed at the same place. People just let them pass by without noticing them. In our everyday lives, the things we spend time together might be seeing or dreaming far more than we think. The project, 'What Things Dream Of' has started with a series of questions such as; how are water glasses seeing us when we drink water feeling thirsty? How do we look to the eyes of the clock at the moment when we check for the time? The team has created six everyday objects, each embedded with sensors and tiny cameras. When these objects are not being used - therefore we imagined them to be sleeping, their dreams are being displayed as a series of moving images through the perspectives of everyday things. Their dreams are related with memories with their possessors and interconnected with other objects. When a thing is waken up by touching and using, it stops dreaming and look at us with their unusual sight of ourselves through the small camera embedded in each objects. Each of their view of us replaces its dream sequences playing on the screen.

Author Keywords
Interactive art; Interface/Experience Design; Embedded Sensors / Displays

ACM Classification Keywords
H.5.m. Information interfaces and presentation (e.g., HCI): Miscellaneous.

Concept
As living people we are not that aware of how everyday things could be. However, if you look at the things carefully, they contain a lot more than we expected. Like even a simple book might contain a long process

and memory to be on my desktop, we were curious how different it could be when our everyday lives are seen through their eyes. As a result, we have personified selected everyday objects and gave them eyes to look at us in their perspectives. We have imagined that the object that is being used is looking at us in reality and still objects are dreaming. Like we dream based on our own experiences, we imagined that objects are dreaming based on their memories of being used by the possessors. Furthermore, visual dream sequences of these objects are related with each other through their possessor, therefore in these movie sequences, their dreams are interconnected with the possessor's activities with them.

Through this project, the artists are offering to experience the new perception and conversion to one's everyday life experience. The everyday common objects we use can wake up and see us in their own perspectives and we can quietly see how people are portrayed in their dreams and realty.

Interaction

Six everyday objects including a desk lamp, laptop, clock, ukulele, camera and water glass are on the desktop casually and they are dreaming with snoring sounds. Behind the desktop, there is a projection display where their dreams are being played in sequences. It would be obvious for the viewer to figure out which sequences are which object's. When a visitor grabs any object, it wakes up and dreaming sequence stops playing. Immediately the object will look at the visitor in its own camera embedded and the projection will be replaced with the visitor's appearance in real-time. When each object wakes up, each has different sound of waking up. As an example, when a visitor grabs a water glass, there is water-pouring sound and if one touches the camera on the desktop, there would be a shutter sound.

The visitor can observe how the objects see him/her by touching or using them. When there is no interaction, real-time projection stops and it goes back to dreaming sequences.

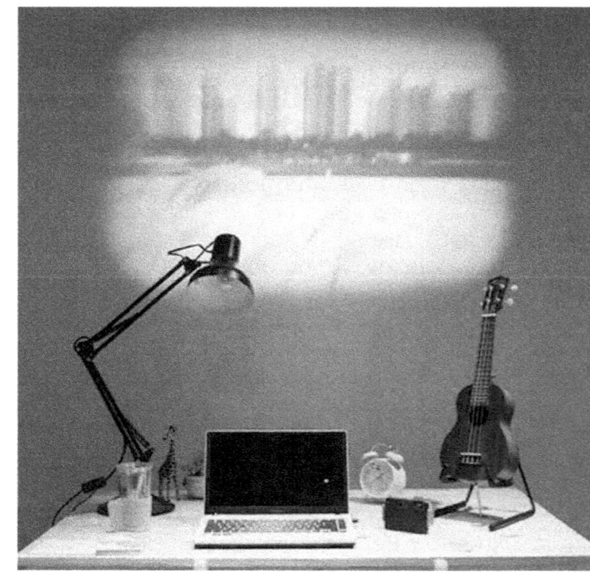

Figure 1. Six everyday objects and their dreams

Technologically, this project has used Q113 touch sensor, conductive thread and paint, small webcams and other electronic parts with Arduino and Processing.

References

[1] Annette Schäfer, Wir sind, was wir haben : die tiefere Bedeutung der Dinge fur unser Leben , 2012
[2] Royal Opera house : Audience. https://vimeo.com/1920188
[3] 'Dream of Pictures' documentation http://vimeo.com/28943705
[4] Pinokio http://vimeo.com/53476316

Pattern Stations - Extending Textile Materials through Tangible Interaction

Bert Bongers, Cecilia Heffer
Interactivation Studio
University of Technology Sydney
Faculty of Design, Architecture and Building
PO Box 123 Broadway
NSW 2007 Australia
bertbon@xs4all.n

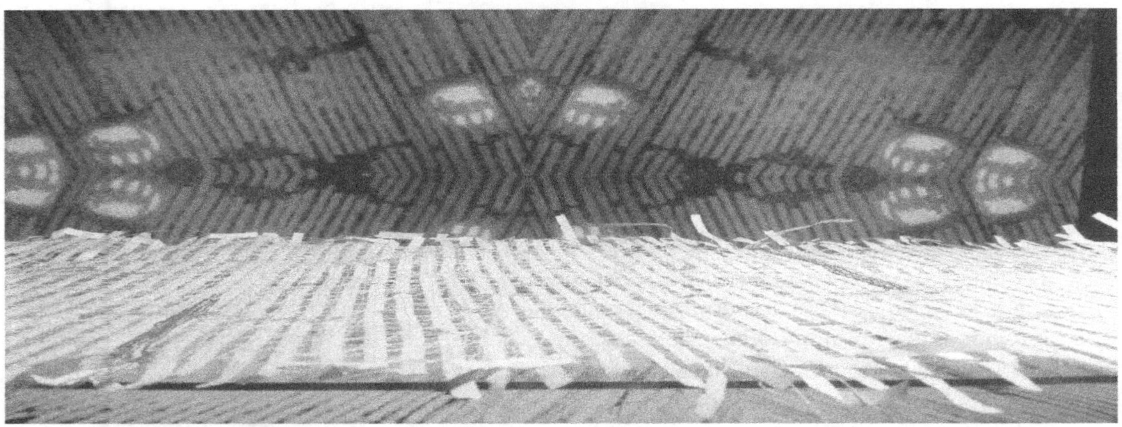

figure 1. Close-up image of Pattern Station #1; paper, textile, video screen and projection

TEI '15, Jan 16-19, 2015, Stanford, CA, USA.
ACM 978-1-4503-3305-4/15/01.
http://dx.doi.org/10.1145/2677199.2690871

Abstract

Pattern Stations is a collaborative project between textile designer and artist Cecilia Heffer and interface designer and interaction researcher Bert Bongers. The interactive installations create patterns, extending the textile patterns through sensors, cameras and computation. The tangible patterns installation is developed specifically for the TEI conference, and aims to give the audience an experience of manipulation of physical objects and materials.

Background

A pattern station is a stand alone interactive video installation, which extends and enhances textile patterns through video manipulations and physical objects with embedded sensors. The textile material pattern (contemporary lace) is placed on a horizontal video screen, hovering above it, slightly raised on one or more clear acrylic surface(s), creating a spatial effect. A video camera suspended above the screen picks up the textile pattern, and through interactive software displays the manipulated images on a screen below the textile material layer, which is picked up by the camera resulting in a feedback loop of colours and patterns. This pattern is further extended through an algorithm of fragmentation, rotation, mirroring, stretching and magnification resulting in endlessly

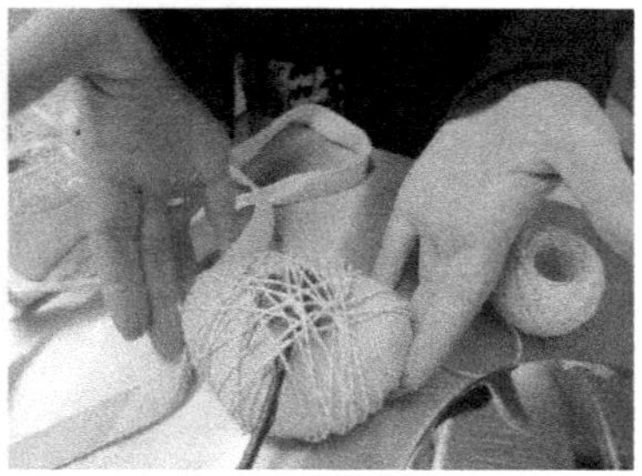

figure 2. Preparation of the rock and sensor controller

figure 3. (below) Pattern Station #1 at Craft ACT exhibition, Canberra, July - August 2014

changing kaleidoscopic facets. These processes are influenced by the audience through the manipulation of physical objects with embedded sensors. There is a conceptual link between the lace patterns, the sensor objects, and the video material, in that they all refer to Australian landscapes and elements. In one of the works the sensor is attached to a 600g rock (Fig. 2), which relates to the notion of physical effort in our research.

Earlier work

Earlier collaborations include the InterLace spatial interactive installation in the international Love Lace exhibition, held at the Sydney Powerhouse Museum from 2011 - 2013 (which received a "highly commended" award). The InterLace installation was necessarily more gesture based, which encouraged us to develop the Pattern Stations as more physical and intimate interactive installation. The first one, the SilkScreen extended landscape piece (Fig. 4), was a

commission for the end-of-year show of the UTS Design School in December 2011. Pattern Station #1 was selected for the Embracing Innovation exhibition at Craft ACT, Canberra's Craft and Design centre, in July 2014 (see Fig. 3, and vimeo.com/user5234451)

Conclusion

The Pattern Stations each consist of combinations of lace pieces and a computer screen presenting video images, expanding textile patterns through interactive responses influenced by the audience through a variety of sensors. Each pattern station has its own character, with a carefully designed response algorithm. The video responses aim to extend, counterpoint, resonate and open an intricate dialogue between material and video. We envision many possibilities, and have experimented with a range of variations in sensor set-up, textile materials and interactive capabilities to enable emerging narratives between the lace and video that will evolve during the exhibition. Pattern Station #2, Tangible Landscapes, invites the audience to create patters through several interactions and explorations including textile manipulations.

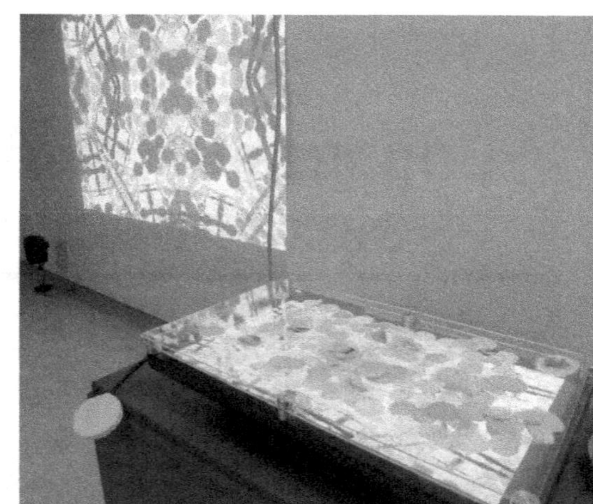

figure 4. The Silkscreen installation with felt material controllers

Vector Field, Activated Space and Inverse Interaction

Conor Peterson
New Mexico Highlands University
901 University Avenue
Las Vegas, NM 87701
conor.p.peterson@gmail.com

TEI '15, Jan 16-19 2015, Stanford, CA, USA
ACM 978-1-4503-3305-4/15/01.
http://dx.doi.org/10.1145/2677199.2690872

Abstract
Vector Field is a sound installation that offers a meditation on space, light and interactivity. It combines a polyphonic drone with a network of sensors to create a space that is sensitive to disruption. Viewers who break a laser beam cause the installation to fall silent; the work reflects on this tension and the "activated space" it articulates.

Author Keywords
Installation art; sound art; activated space; interactive work; autonomy; sculpture

ACM Classification Keywords
• **Applied computing~Fine arts**
• *Human-centered Computing~Human computer interaction*

Artwork Description
The installation consists of five freestanding sculptural forms, each equipped with acoustic resonators and a beam system that links it to the others. During normal operation the installation produces a continuous, harmonic drone through electromagnetic stimulation of steel wire. The size of the installation combined with the evolving sonic texture of the drone creates an acoustically immersive space through which viewers are encouraged to wander.

Vector Field inverts the usual human-computer interactive relationship: any disruption to the overhead network of laser beams causes the entire installation to power down, temporarily silencing the drone. This feedback mechanism requires viewers to weigh their natural desire to interact with the beams against the social consequences of doing so. In this manner, Vector Field produces an activated space, in which viewers' awareness of the interactive component enhances tension and supports the association between the sound, light, and space.

Figure 1. Vector Field, installation view.

Technical Details

The drone is produced by a set of 20 resonant panels. Each panel is equipped with a hand-wound electromagnet and a steel wire held under adjustable tension. The mechanical vibrations of the wire are transferred to U-shaped sounding panels by means of an acoustic bridge. The electromagnets are driven at fixed musical frequencies through standard H bridges.

Each audio signal is a pulse train generated by a microcontroller, essentially a custom Arduino clocked at 20 MHz. The controller further gates the signal with a coarse layer of pulse width modulation (PWM) to create low frequency oscillation (LFO) effects. Ten notes are produced in real-time to cover slightly more than one octave of the C-sharp minor scale, chosen for its aesthetic qualities and general sense of mystery.

Figure 2. Detail of sensor and mirror system.

The beam systems consist of 532nm diode-pumped solid state (DPSS) laser modules, identical to those found inside low-cost green laser pointers. To sense incident beams a CdS cell is mounted inside a circular housing capped with diffusion material. A first surface mirror mounted on a double-L gimbal permits alignment of the beam.

Acknowledgements

The author extends his deep gratitude to Russell Bauer, Nina Dubois, Lauren Kenward and Natasha Ribeiro for their support in fabricating this work.

Scented Pebbles: Interactive Ambient Experience with Smell and Lighting

Cao Yan Yan
Keio-NUS CUTE Center
Graduate School of Media Design
Keio University
Yanyan.cao@gmail.com

Naohito Okude
Graduate School of Media Design
Keio University
okude@kmd.keio.ac.jp

TEI '15, Jan 16-19 2015, Stanford, CA, USA
ACM 978-1-4503-3305-4/15/01.
http://dx.doi.org/10.1145/2677199.2690873

Abstract
Scented Pebbles is a collection of interactive lighting objects to create multisensory ambience of light and smell. When it senses people's movement and touch, the networked objects will generate dynamic ambience. The pebbles emit smells and control the lighting conditions to create your unique ambience such as Hawaiian Sunset or Japanese Onsen. Experience the orchestra of smell and light play and let your mind run free. The paper presented interactive approach to evoke sensorial imagination through multisensory interactions including olfactory sense.

Author Keywords
Multisensory Interactions, Sensory Ambient Environment, Mental Imagery

ACM Classification Keywords
H.5.m. Information interfaces and presentation (e.g., HCI): Prototyping

Introduction
Scented Pebbles is a collection of interactive lighting objects to create multisensory ambience of light and smell. It is designed to evoke sensorial imagination through multisensory interactions including olfactory sense. Human beings have the abilities to form sensorial imagination known as mental imagery process as a cognitive function. Mental imagery is "*perception-like*

Figure 1. The inner view of *Scented Pebbles* with the accelerometer, Arduino Fio, LED strip and top compartment for storing liquid scents.

Figure 2. *Scented Pebbles* was showcased at Art Science Museum, Singapore as Sunday Showcase.

experience" without the sensory input accordingly [1]. It can be in the form of multiple sensations.

Scented Pebbles map user's behavior to the change of ambience, allowing them to explore the ambience and make sense of it. Users will experience multisensory scenarios such as Hawaiian Sunset or Japanese Onsen made up of multiple smells. As they explore the objects by touching, movement or gestures i.e. tilt, shake, wave, they can unleash a variety of smells that are blended at different times to give an impression of a particular theme.

Scented Pebbles are made from modular lighting and smell diffusing units that are networked together to react to user's touch and movement. Sensors such as accelerometers, capacitance sensors are embedded in each unit to gather data such as motion, gestures to reflect user's behaviors. The multisensory stimulation of lighting and smell are designed according to specific themes, to evoke imaginations or mental imageries.

Special attention is made to the casing of the prototype to give it a sense of whimsical appearance. Experiments have been carried out with wax, 3D Printing, the final prototype for 3D printing layered with wax to achieve the desired outcome.

My research project Scented Pebbles integrates digital technologies to facilitate multisensory interactions in creating mental imagery. It creates experience that focus on feelings and imaginations through multisensory interactions. Anthony Dunne [2] argues that digital artifacts can go beyond "package for technology". Wright and John McCarthy [3] defined Enchantment using digital technology - "being charmed and delighted" "connotation of being bewitched and delighted and caught up and carried away". Peter Wright and John McCarthy explicitly call for the integration of all senses to realize enchantment technology. Scented Pebbles is built upon the sentiments that interactive technology will be able to affect emotions and engage with our mind through imaginations and multiple senses.

Video

The link to the Scented Pebbles video: https://vimeo.com/110558914

Acknowledgements

This research is supported by the National Research Foundation, Prime Minister's Office, Singapore under its International Research Centre @ Singapore Funding Initiative and administered by the Interactive & Digital Media Programme Office.

References

[1] Kosslyn, Stephen Michael. Image and mind. Harvard University Press, 1980.

[2] Hertzian Tales, Anthony Dunne, 1998

[3] McCarthy, John, Peter Wright, Jayne Wallace, and Andy Dearden. "The experience of enchantment in human–computer interaction." Personal and Ubiquitous Computing 10, no. 6 (2006): 369-378.

Remnance of Form: Altered Reflection of Physical Reality

Sang-won Leigh
MIT Media Lab
75 Amherst St
Cambridge, MA 02139 USA
sangwon@media.mit.edu

Asta Roseway
Microsoft Research
One Microsoft Way
Redmond, WA 98008 USA
astar@microsoft.com

Ann Paradiso
Microsoft Research
One Microsoft Way
Redmond, WA 98008 USA
annpar@microsoft.com

Figure 1. The shadow can be shaped programmatically, into any shapes.

Abstract
Remnance of Form is an interactive installation that explores the dynamic tension between an object and its shadow. By fusing light, projection, and motion technologies, the shadow can now detach itself from its former role. This creates a new narrative that challenges our perception of reality, what's real and what's not.

TEI '15, Jan 16-19 2015, Stanford, CA, USA
ACM 978-1-4503-3305-4/15/01.
http://dx.doi.org/10.1145/2677199.2690874

Author Keywords
Shadow; Augmented Reality, Interactive Art Installation

ACM Classification Keywords
H.5.m. Information interfaces and presentation (e.g., HCI): Miscellaneous.

Introduction
Digital technology has seeped into every corner of our existence, allowing myriad forms of mediated reality to become increasingly accessible, sophisticated, and robust. As a result, we expect to see a correlating evolution in our perception and experience of reality as we examine and challenge long-standing concepts surrounding our relationship to space, time, light, shadow, and physical objects. This is also well reflected in the technical communities. There have been systems that allow for altering the functions or visual appearances of objects and space, by fusing concepts across paradigms including Tangible User Interfaces (TUI), Augmented Reality (AR), and Ubiquitous Computing (UbiComp).

The shadow is a perfect medium for communicating the meta-state of a physical object, as it is a direct projection of the object to the physical space. This fact encouraged artists to utilize shadows as a mean for creative expression through the manipulation of it.

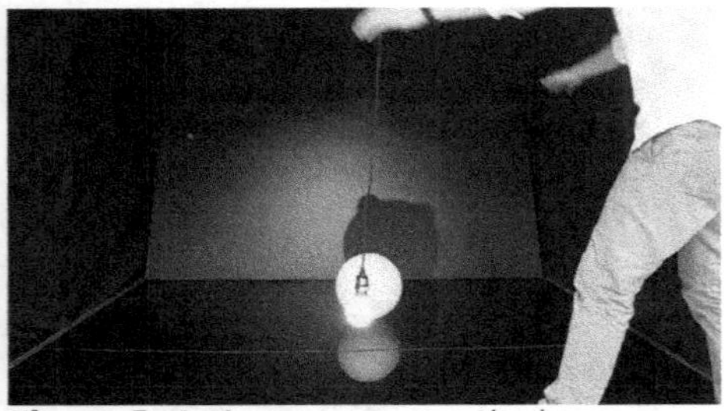

Figure 2. A viewer can scare the bear-shaped ball away.

Figure 3. By manipulating the light bulb, different aspects of the shadow can be discovered.

Figure 4. The shadow shows different degree of fear based on its viewer's body posture.

There have been light/object sculptures that explore the tension between an object and its shadow [3, 6]. *Treachery and Sanctuary* [2], *Shadow Bag* [5], and *Shadow Inverted* [4] demonstrated more dynamic use of the shadow metaphor. They captured viewers' body silhouette and displayed a fake, distorted shadow of the viewers. A recent work, *Parade* [1], tracked the fake light source's motion to create seemingly impossible shadow animation according to the light source's kinetic motion.

In this work, *Remnance of Form*, we take a step forward, by more dynamically modulating and distorting the relationship between simple, mundane objects and their shadows. Through the ambient augmentation of shadows happening in the periphery of the viewer's attention [7], we try to shift and extend the perceived nature of the object. On a technological note, the highly calibrated AR system devised for this work allows for simulating the reality very precisely. As a result, the digitally altered reality, the shadow in our case, becomes indiscernible from the pure reality. We hope to deliver the notion that a sufficiently mature AR system would be capable of making direct alteration to the reality, more than a mere visual graphics overlaid onto the actual reality.

Envisioned Exhibit

The entire installation was set up in a cubic structure of 8 feet x 8 feet x 8 feet. Three entities (a white ball, a light bulb, and a shadow) are presented to the viewers. Using Kinect and Pointgrey cameras, we track the viewers' activities as well as the position of the ball and the light bulb. The shadow's size/position are computed based on tracked positions of the ball and the light bulb; therefore, moving either of them will change the size/position of the shadow. A high-lumen projector is used to create lighting and shadow effects.

The proposed setup allows direct manipulation of the light bulb. It is notable that, as the light bulb starts to swing like a pendulum, the computer-generated shadow becomes much more realistic because our mind automatically picks up the synchronized motions of the light bulb and the shadow. This, combined with the viewers' presences and body postures, allows the interaction between the viewers and the ball with its shadow to become more playful and perceptively appealing.

Through five unique vignettes - *Disappearing, Showing Fear, Changing Shape, Dream of Flying, and Possessing the Ball*, we demonstrate a series interactions that involve varying degree of whimsical behavior, tweaking of the shadow's shape, and viewers' engagement into the narrative.

References

[1] http://dpt.co/en/parade-2/

[2] http://milk.co/treachery/

[3] http://www.kumiyamashita.com/light-and-shadow

[4] http://www.majapetric.com/portfolio/shadow-inverted/

[5] http://www.snibbe.com/projects/interactive/shadowbag/

[6] http://www.timnobleandsuewebster.com/artwerks.html

[7] Ishii, H., Wisneski, C., Brave, S., Dahley, A., Gorbet, M., Ullmer, B., and Yarin, P. ambientroom: integrating ambient media with architectural space. Proc. of CHI '98.

Monarch: Self-Expression Through Wearable Kinetic Textiles

Kate Hartman
OCAD University
100 McCaul Street, Toronto
ON M5T 1W1, Canada
khartman@faculty.ocadu.ca

Hillary Predko
OCAD University
100 McCaul Street, Toronto
ON M5T 1W1, Canada
hpredko@gmail.com

Jackson McConnell
OCAD University
100 McCaul Street, Toronto
ON M5T 1W1, Canada
jmcconnell@faculty.ocadu.ca

Izzie Colpitts-Campbell
OCAD University
100 McCaul Street, Toronto
ON M5T 1W1, Canada
izzieccampbell@gmail.com

Boris Kourtoukov
OCAD University
100 McCaul Street, Toronto
ON M5T 1W1, Canada
boriskourt@gmail.com

TEI '15, Jan 16-19 2015, Stanford, CA, USA
ACM 978-1-4503-3305-4/15/01.
http://dx.doi.org/10.1145/2677199.2690875

Abstract
Monarch is a wearable and muscle-activated kinetic textile. It consists of textile forms attached to the shoulders that expand and contract in response to the movement of the wearer's muscles. By physically extending natural body language, Monarch explores how wearable technologies can be used as a form of personal expression, as well as how and when they can begin to feel like a visceral extension of self.

Author Keywords
wearable technology, body language, kinetic textiles, electromyography sensors

ACM Classification Keywords
H.5.2 [Information interfaces and presentation (e.g., HCI)]: User Interfaces.

Introduction
Monarch enables the wearer to amplify, extend, or exaggerate their natural body language. By tensing and relaxing their arm the wearer can express enthusiasm, excitement, assertion, aggression, mischievousness, or even flirtation. It can be used as non-verbal communication or to accentuate a point in conversation.

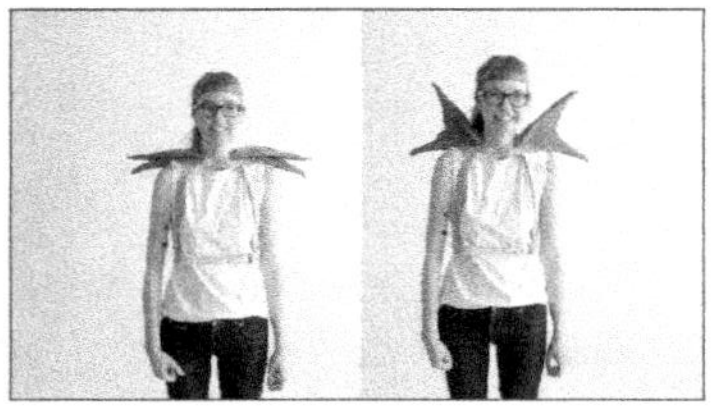

Figure 1: Monarch in down [left] and up [right] positions

Figure 2: Hyperbolic paraboloid paper prototype

Figure 3: Textile design with digitally printed fabric

Form and Material Design

Monarch takes the form of a leather harness with pleated textiles that rest on the shoulders. When in the down position the textile forms resemble shoulder pads or epaulets. When expanded they reveal a colorful and visually complex pleated interior. The positioning of the form frames the wearer's head and amplifies the presence of their body.

The pleated textile design is modeled after the structure of hyperbolic paraboloids [2]. The first iteration was constructed of laser cut acrylic felt fused with a flexible denim substrate. The second iteration was created using digital fabric printing on cotton poplin. This reduced production time, provided more freedom in visual design and color choice, and resulted in a textile form that was lighter weight and more easily manipulated by the servo motors.

Sensing and Actuation

The circuit that drives Monarch includes a muscle sensor [1], microcontroller, and two servo motors. The muscle sensor uses electromyography (EMG) to detect changes in electrical signals produced by muscles. The servo motors rotate wire arms embedded in the textile forms allowing them to control the expansion and contraction of the textiles.

Interaction Modes

Intentionality is key to the experience of wearing Monarch. The belt of the leather harness contains a control panel that can be operated by the wearer. The panel includes an on/off switch, a calibration knob (to adjust the sensitivity), and a mode switch.

Three main modes were created for operating Monarch.

Mode A is a toggle-on / toggle-off interaction. It allows the up state to be held for a prolonged period of time. Mode B requires the wearer to maintain muscle tension above a threshold in order to keep the textile forms raised. This allows for finer gesture control while still enabling the wearer to hold the textiles in an expanded state for sustained periods of time. Mode C maps the EMG sensor readings to a specific set of values along a curve. As the wearer flexes their muscle, Monarch mimics the movement as directly as possible. This mode requires more focus but allows for more control as well as a gradual fluttering movement.

Conclusion

Monarch presents new tangible and embodied ways for the wearer to interact with wearable technologies. Through continued use, the wearer has the opportunity to augment body language and develop new forms of expression.

Video

`http://vimeo.com/89654806`

Acknowledgements

We would like to thank Jamie Sherman and Rickee Charbonneau for their insights and contributions to this project. This research was funded by the Intel Experiences Group.

References

[1] Advancer technologies: Muscle sensor v3. `http://www.advancertechnologies.com/p/muscle-sensor-v3.html`.

[2] Demaine, E. D., Demaine, M. L., and Lubiw, A. Polyhedral sculptures with hyperbolic paraboloids. *Bridges: Mathematical Connections in Art, Music, and Science* (1999).

Metamorphosis

Younghui Kim
Hongik University
2639 Sejong-ro, Jochiwon-eup
Sejong, South Korea
ihongik@gmail.com

Kyungmee Kim
Hongik University
2639 Sejong-ro, Jochiwon-eup
Sejong, South Korea
kimeekm@gmail.com

Sanghwa Hong
RECT2ELLIPSE
Mapodaero 7 gil 22, Mapo-gu
Seoul, South Korea
Doublebind8306@gmail.com

Kwanu Park
Hongik University
2639 Sejong-ro, Jochiwon-eup
Sejong, South Korea
manifest30@naver.com

TEI '15, Jan 16-19 2015, Stanford, CA, USA.
ACM 978-1-4503-3305-4/15/01.
http://dx.doi.org/10.1145/2677199.2690876

Abstract

Drinking custom varies in different cultures as much as dining manners and etiquettes. The wearable project, '*Metamorphosis*' is an artistic commentary toward Korean drinking culture in wearable technology. In Korea, drinking is like a social ritual for both personal and professional relationships from friends to colleagues. '*Metamorphosis*' is a female garment created during 5 day Wearable Hackathone held by Art Center Nabi in June, 2014. It has a sensitive alcohol sensor embedded at the tip of the collar near mouth, which detects the level of the alcohol consumption from the wearer's breath and expresses in different colors and kinetic movements of the garment. Wearable, applied with culture and technology, can be a new media platform to express how social members of community feel or see.

Author Keywords

Wearable; Kinetic; Social Interaction

ACM Classification Keywords

H.5.m. Information interfaces and presentation (e.g., HCI): Miscellaneous.

Introduction

Garments are one of essential surviving elements for human beings along with food and shelters. Both food and garments are deeply related with culture, tradition and social communication. Wearable, applied with culture and technology, can express how social members of community feel or see. For social gatherings in Korea, drinking is like a social ritual for many levels of communities from family to friends and colleagues. Drinking alcohol socially means a great deal as if a course dining is an essential social ritual for other communities. For an example, when someone invites one to drink with, the invitee would anticipate for something serious to be discussed. Among friends, an invitation of social drinking is a common activity to build up friendship. In office environment, an after-work drinking occasion often means a continuing professional duty to build up career opportunities.

Metamorphosis

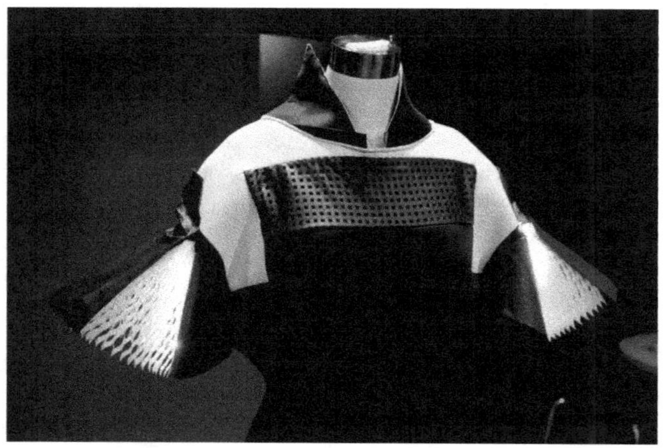

Figure 1. *Metamorphosis*, alcohol level 3, sleeves opens up in pink light.

The wearable project, '*Metamorphosis'* is an artistic commentary on Korean drinking culture and the customary obligation to drink when invited. Its concept has perceived in order to represent social Interaction through Wearable Expression. In Korea, drinking gathering is one of the most important social interactions in both professional and personal relationships. Social drinking gatherings can create strong bonds among office members but, at the same time, it results unwanted drinking obligation that are embedded into formality. For this female kinetic wearable, it expresses how alcohol brings up one's self-confidence and how it reveals ones mind by opening up its sleeves with changing colored lights. Using an alcohol sensor and a condensed microphone, and other electronics such as motors and RGB LEDs, it is programmed to react according the alcohol consumption levels that were set based on traffic violation law in South Korea. There are three different stages in interaction: by default, the garment has blue lights on its flat sleeves and as the wearer's breath is condensed with alcohol, it changes into tipsy green and then finally happily-drunk pink. When the wearer is sober, the sleeves automatically close down turning back to blue light. This concept of wearable art piece is applied to such a formal society where acceptance toward other members of society matters most. There could be a misinterpret for different manner for different culture but, as an expressive art form, this wearable lets everyone know how drunk one is visually and asking others to pace drinking.

Acknowledgements

We thank Art Center Nabi, Hongik University and everyone who has supported the project.

References

[1] Art Center Nabi http://www.nabi.or.kr

[2] Nabi Wearable Hackathon Dress It Up, 2014 http://www.nabi.or.kr/english/academy/current_read.nab?idx=309

[3] Doosan Encyclopedia, Traffic Law and Alcohol Level Detections http://m.terms.naver.com/entry.nhn?docId=1223385&cid=40942&categoryId=31693

Solar Pink Pong: Street Video Game

Assocreation and
Daylight Media Lab
1919 Green Rd.
Ann Arbor, MI 48109 USA
mail@assocreation.com

Roland Graf
University of Michigan
Stamps School of Art & Design
2000 Bonisteel Blvd.
Ann Arbor, MI 48109 USA
rolgraf@umich.edu

Surat Kwanmuang
University of Michigan
Department of Mechanical
Engineering
2350 Hayward Street
Ann Arbor, MI 48109 USA
suratkw@umich.edu

TEI '15, Jan 16-19 2015, Stanford, CA, USA
ACM 978-1-4503-3305-4/15/01.
http://dx.doi.org/10.1145/2677199.2690877

Abstract
Solar Pink Pong is an art installation that translates a video game into the physical space of the street. In this installation, a computer controlled color mirror reflects sunlight to the asphalt in the form of a neon pink spot. Through motion sensing technology, pedestrians can interact with the animated circle of sunlight. They can kick it with their feet or hit it with the shadows of their hands. They can volley it back and forth with a partner or bounce it off a boundary such as a curb or road marking. The device that makes this game possible works autonomously and completely off the grid. It can be mounted on utility poles or building sides. *Solar Pink Pong* aims at pushing the boundaries of video game culture and technology outside of the living room changing the way humans interact with outdoor environments and see daylight through the lens of technology. Video documentation of this work is available at: https://vimeo.com/111312495

Author Keywords
Interactive Art; Street Video Game; Motion Capture; Augmented Reality; Autonomous Machine; Solar Power

ACM Classification Keywords
H.5.1 [Multimedia Information Systems]: Artificial, augmented, and virtual realities; H.5.2 [User Interfaces]: Interaction styles; I.2.1 [Applications and Expert Systems]: Games

Figure 1. Autonomous, solar-powered device with computer controlled color mirror mounted on utility pole.

Figure 2. Player of this game can interact with the animated pink sunlight reflection on the street using their bodies and shadows.

Street Video Game

We are physical beings and for most part of human history we have played outdoors in bright daylight. Yet, many of our most popular games today are limited to screens and the dimmed light conditions of the living room.

The idea of *Solar Pink Pong* is to take a street and transform it in bright daylight into an interactive immersive environment. In this environment, pedestrians can play video games as physical beings unencumbered by screens or controller. Free from input devices and exposed to sunlight, players find both their bodies and shadows present in the game. The computer-generated graphic of the game – an animated pink circle of sunlight – coincides with the built and natural environment. Unlike the steady light of a screen or video projector, it is the ephemeral nature of daylight [1] that defines the quality of this street video game. I fact, the game's dependency on sunlight counters homo ludens' disconnect from outdoor environments – a disconnect that in the video game world is also known as "the battle of the living room". With the playtime fully determined by the course and availability of the sun, *Solar Pink Pong* shares the transient character of a natural phenomenon that can't simply be controlled by an on-off switch.

Solar Pink Pong references one of the first mainstream video games *Pong* [2] and builds on Myron Krueger's early artificial reality concept *Videoplace* [3]. It manipulates sunlight with a custom designed dichroic mirror that makes sunlight almost magically appear as a colorful spot on the street like an animated pixel on a screen. However, this game is not supposed to end at the boundaries of a screen as we know it. It explores the aesthetic dimension of play and augmented reality in bright daylight without the use of a *Goggle Glass*.

Technical Description

Two servomotors mounted inside a weatherproof box control the moving mirror through a push-pull mechanism. A geared stepper motor turns the box towards the sun for solar panels' best performance. A color camera with wide-angle lens is installed below the mirror. All control software is built on ROS, an open-source robot operating system. A computer vision module processes video stream from camera to distinguish humans and shadows from background. A pong game module sends desired sun spot position to mirror control module. Using position and time from GPS module on top of the box, the module can calculate current sun position with very high accuracy and then sends commands to servomotors. The system is equipped with a 3G modem to allow users to monitor its status and watch live gameplay over the Internet. For the web interface see: www.solarpinkpong.com

References

[1] Döring T., Sylvester A., and Schmidt A. A design space for ephemeral user interfaces. In Proc. TEI '13, ACM Press (2013), 75-82.
[2] Kent, S. "And Then There Was Pong". Ultimate History of Video Games. Three Rivers Press (2001), 40–43.
[3] Krueger, M. Videoplace. http://90.146.8.18/en/archives/center_projekt_ausgabe.asp?iProjectID=11224 ACCESSED ON 10-17-2014.

Acknowledgments

Part of this work was funded by the University of Michigan, Office of the Vice President for Research and by the Penny W. Stamps School of Art and Design.

Spiky Starfish: Exploring 'Felt Technology' Through a Shape Changing Wearable Bag

Young Suk Lee
Informatics and Computing
Indiana University
Bloomington, IN 47408
yaltieri@umail.iu.edu

Figure1. *Spiky starfish,* an interactive computational bag that critically explores expressive computing and embodied interaction.

TEI '15, Jan 16-19 2015, Stanford, CA, USA
ACM 978-1-4503-3305-4/15/01.
http://dx.doi.org/10.1145/2677199.2690878

Abstract
In HCI there are attempts to create expressive computing by exploring emotional engagements through a wide range of shape-changing interfaces including experimental art, fashion, architecture, furniture, etc. These approaches range from hedonic design purposes, which represent novel ideas and materials to more informative design spaces, which allow users to interact with a visual interface in order to persuade users' behavior. By bridging these explorations, I present *Spiky Starfish, a computational wearable bag,* which utilizes "felt experience with technology" to influence user bodily interaction tactically and visually. It is designed to explore how expressive shape-changing interface create a disruptive interaction when peoples' habitual behavior triggers.

Author Keywords
Tangible user interface, Affective computing, Digital crafting, Bodily interaction

ACM Classification Keywords
H.5.2. Information interfaces and presentation.
J.5. Arts and Humanities.

Introduction
Spiky starfish is an interactive cigarette bag, which aims to show how "expressive computing" affectively shapes

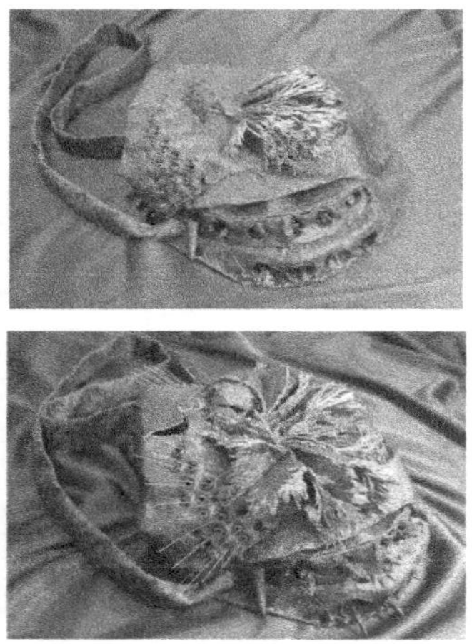

Figure2. Before-After Interaction

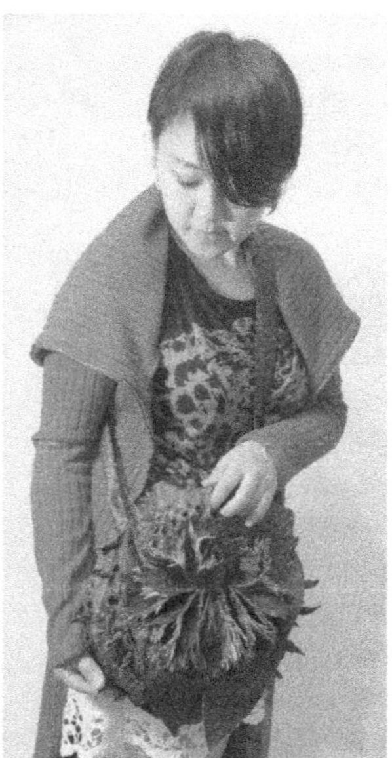

Spiky Starfish 2014

our experience as a computational wearable interface. The Spiky Starfish reacts and offers a bodily engagement as a mediator to recognize self, desire, and habit through the embedded and wearable interface. Ultimately, it is designed to explore the correlation between 1) how the interactive texture and shape trigger emotional arousal, and 2) how this expressive computing evokes meaningful interactions in peoples' lives through the bodily interaction.

Felt technology through the shape-changing interface

As Lisa et al. suggested, affective computing platforms can encourage expressive possibilities within novel forms of technology and fashion [3]. The combination of computational elements and craft enables to create textural transformations through the shape-changing interface, such as a pair of bird wings that turn into an angry starfish with spikes, which simulates life forms that are threatened by people's approaches. It reveals the metaphorical personal traits by expressing aggressive visual language that aim to create a disruptive interaction when people try to take the cigarettes from the bag.

Bodily aesthetic interaction

Spiky Startfish expresses a dynamic relationship between embodiment and aesthetic interaction as a persuasive art, which explores the correlation between phenomenological experiences and psychological affect. The design goal is to bring the notion of "felt experience with technology" [1] into a mundane object by artistic methods in order to provoke a self-reflective awareness, which can be experienced through the multimodal elements of Spiky Starfish. It is intended to create a dialogue visually, tactically with the users when their habitual activity triggers a response.

As Djajadiningrat al. introduced the aesthetics of coupling which explored "violation of unity principles and animism" [4]. When users interact with Spiky Starfish they 1) encounter a moment of conflict between pursuing their desire to get the cigarette or an offer of an alternative substitute (nicotine gum), while the artifact tries to intentionally disrupt the habit loop. Moreover, 2) if the user continually tries to open the pouch, the dynamic life-like behavior occurs with variable shape-changing elements, which elicit visceral organs that are damaged by cigarette consumption. This visual and tactical interface is intended to evoke people's emotion by providing an experience of unpleasant forms and texture when the user's vice is desired [3]. "Through emotional design, it suggests that aesthetic communication can be used to provoke paradoxical responses, by creating a narrative between then body, garment and society" [2]. In a similar vein, the interaction with Spiky Starfish is designed to reflect habits, activity, values, and personal desire.

Acknowledgements

Thanks to the support from Kay Connelly during the summer independent study.

References

[1] Hohn Macarthy, and Peter Wright, Technology as Experience, Cambridge, MA:MIT,2004.

[2] Lisa Stead al, The Emotional Wardrobe, Ubiquit Comput 2004

[3] Majken al, Shape changing interfaces: A Review of the Design Space and Open Research Questions, CHI2012

[4] Tom Djajadiningrat al, Easy doesn't do it: skill and expression in tangible aesthetics, Ubiquit Comput, 2007.

Tele Echo Tube: beyond Cultural and Imaginable Boundaries

Hill Hiroki Kobayashi
Assistant Professor
Center for Spatial Information Science,
The University of Tokyo, Japan
kobayashi@csis.u-tokyo.ac.jp

Akio Fujiwara
Assistant Professor
Graduate School of Agricultural and Life Sciences,
The University of Tokyo, Japan
akio@uf.a.u-tokyo.ac.jp

Kazuhiko Nakamura
Project Researcher
Center for Spatial Information Science,
The University of Tokyo, Japan
k_nakamura@csis.u-tokyo.ac.jp

Kaoru Saito
Professor
Graduate School of Frontier Sciences,
The University of Tokyo, Japan
kaoru@nenv.k.u-tokyo.ac.jp

Kaoru Sezaki
Professor
Center for Spatial Information Science,
The University of Tokyo, Japan
sezaki@csis.u-tokyo.ac.jp

TEI '15, Jan 16-19 2015, Stanford, CA, USA
ACM 978-1-4503-3305-4/15/01.
http://dx.doi.org/10.1145/2677199.2690879

Abstract
Tele Echo Tube (TET) is a speaking tube installation that acoustically interacts with a deep mountain echo through the slightly vibrating lampshade like interface. TET allows users to interact with the mountain echo living at 1,200 meter elevation in The University of Tokyo Forests (35°94'N,138°80'E) in real time through an augmented echo sounding experience with the vibration over a satellite data network through the position of Von Uexkull's 'Umwelt'. This novel interactive system can create an imaginable presence of the mythological creature in the undeveloped natural locations beyond our cultural and imaginable boundaries. In doing so, TET discovers the cultural cognitive processes of our imagination mechanism. Such a discovery would help us design an interactive system that leverages the boundary of the real and virtual worlds by engaging a culturally cognition to perform a nonhuman-centric interaction with a culturally imaginable creature.

Author Keywords
HCBI (Human Computer Biosphere Interaction), Nature Interface, Sustainability, Sustainable

ACM Classification Keywords
H.5.m. Information interfaces and presentation (e.g., HCI): Miscellaneous.

Figure 3. TETremote system placed in Cyber Forest project site, located 1,200 m above sea, The University of Tokyo Forests, Japan (35°94'N,138°80'E).

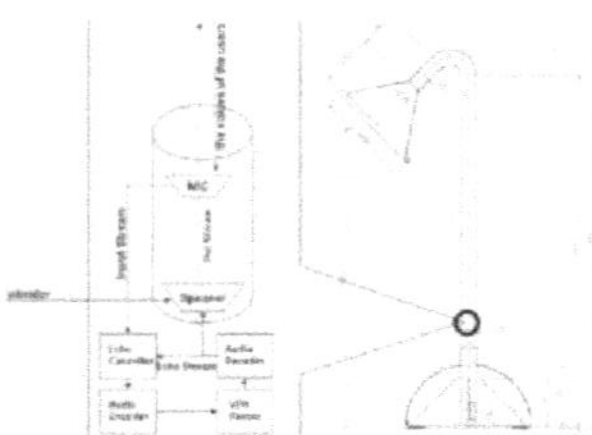

Figure 4. Tele Echo Tube Local system. [1]

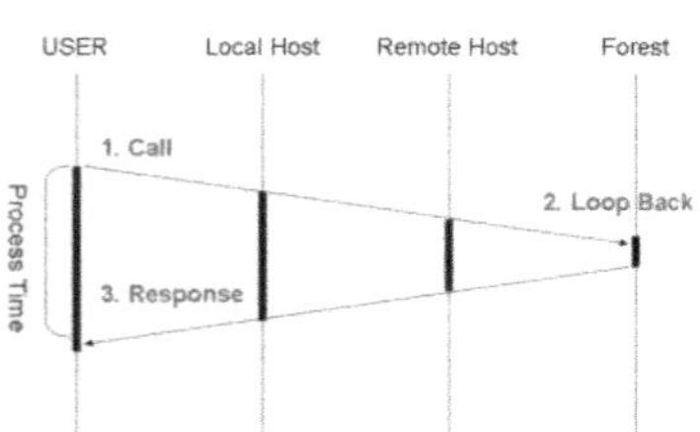

Figure 5. Diagram of non-verbal Interaction between user and echo [1]

Description

Figure 1. Tele Echo Tube (TET) local interface @ Hill Hiroki Kobayashi (**<u>the chair is not a part of this interface</u>**)

TET consists of local and remote speaking tube systems (**Figure 1,3,4**) with one-way echo canceller through a full duplex audio I/O system over the globe. The remote and local systems perform a remote interaction to create an echo sounding and experience with "Mr. Yamabiko" (ECHO, Mountain Nymph in Greek mythology) in **Figure 2** through its live sound pipe through the satellite networked internet.

[1] To interact with the "Mr. Yamabiko", users can sing out "YO-HOOOOO!" very lively from the local speaking tube to the speakers on the mountain on the remote site, as described in **Figure 5**. The loopback call at the remote host occurs because the playback sound from the speaker is captured and transferred to the user by the remote host with spontaneous network delay. When the users hear the loopback call, "their voices within

Figure 2. Mr. Yamabiko, ECHO in Japanese mythology. Left: "Yamabiko" in a collection of pictures in Hyakkai-Zukan(Suushi, 1737) . Right: The Illustrated Night Parade of A Hundred Demons (Kadokawa Shoten Publissing, 2005.)

the soundscape" from the mountain with the slight vibration by their hands through the interface in **Figure 1**, they recognize that the initial voices did actually travel through the mountain environment. This echo-sounding loop, which transfers live sounds bidirectionally from the remote and local sites, creates an echo sounding effect, and in doing so, gives the user the opportunity to interact with the presence of "a fickle ECHO" on the deep mountain remotely. Those acoustic interactions indicate the non-linguistic believability in a form of mythological metaphor of the mountain echo. with high degree of excitement. TET has been exhibited in ACM MM'13 full paper [1] and art exhibition sessions. The artist interview with Andrea Ferreiro is available [2] during a year 2010 exhibition in MUAC, in Mexico.

References

[1] H., Kobayashi, M., Hirose, A., Fujiwara, K., Nakamura, K., Sezaki, and K., Saito. Tele echo tube: beyond cultural and imaginable boundaries. In *Proc of ACM MM '13*. ACM Press (2013), 173-182.

[2] A.,Ferreiro. "TELE ECHO TUBE Hill H. Kobayashi." Online video clip. YouTube. YouTube, 18 Sept. 2010. Sun.26 Sept . 2014. https://www.youtube.com/watch?v=KDIQG92_zhQ

Redeform: Participatory 3D Printing in Public Spaces

Laura Devendorf
School of Information
University of California, Berkeley
Berkeley, CA 94720 USA
ldevendorf@ischool.berkeley.edu

Kimiko Ryokai
School of Information
University of California, Berkeley
Berkeley, CA 94720 USA
kimiko@ischool.berkeley.edu

TEI '15, Jan 16-19 2015, Stanford, CA, USA
ACM 978-1-4503-3305-4/15/01.
http://dx.doi.org/10.1145/2677199.2690880

Abstract

Redeform presents an alternative vision of 3D printing that complicates common divisions between human/machine, abstract/concrete, and high/low tech. It invites people to perform the functions of a 3D printer in order to collaboratively construct digital models from everyday materials in everyday spaces. At TEI, Redeform will serve as a site for discussion about values in digital fabrication design.

Author Keywords

3D printing; participatory art; hybrid fabrication.

ACM Classification Keywords

H.5.m. Information interfaces and presentation (e.g., HCI): Miscellaneous.

Introduction

"The machine is not an *it* to be animated, worshiped and dominated. The machine is us, our processes, an aspect of our embodiment."

– Donna Haraway, *A Cyborg Manifesto* [1]

Consider two scenarios: In one scenario a person meticulously follows a knitting pattern and translates text instructions into specific stitches in order to produce a garment. In the other, a computer-numeric controlled (CNC) knitting machine takes a digital model

Figure 1: Top. A 1:10 scale model of the proposed project made using Jellybeans. Bottom. The laser guide used to guide maker(s) along 3D printer paths.

as input, translates it to a list of text commands, and mechanically creates stitches in a garment. Which of these scenarios describes digital fabrication? Which is more technically sophisticated? What is a person able to experience and express in each scenario? The way that we, as researchers and designers in HCI, respond to these questions has important implications for the kinds of making and makers that are included in a growing maker movement. Redeform attempts to provoke discussion and/or debate on these questions through the construction of an alternative system for 3D printing.

Redeform is a system that guides a human in building objects by following the instructions typically given to a 3D printer. As a functional system for making, it allows for the construction of digital models from everyday materials, in public places, and at scales that are still difficult for 3D printers to support. What is lost in precision and control is replaced by opportunities to collaborate with other makers and realize unexpected forms. As a critical art piece presented at TEI, Redeform invites researchers and designers of human-machine systems to experience an alternative to 3D printing and contribute to a conversation about the trade-offs that emerge with each configuration of humans, machines, materials, and context in making activities.

The Mechanics of Redeform

The core functionality of a 3D printer is the ability to take a digital model of 3D object; slice is into layers, and split those layers into paths. A 3D printer consists of a programmable head that draws those paths with materials in order to reproduce a 3D form. Redeform mimics a 3D printer by using an actuated laser pointer to communicate the position of a 3D printer head [figure 1]. It invites people to physically follow the pointer while "extruding" materials. Following the laser pointer guides the maker along the exact paths of a 3D printer and over time a physical version of the digital model emerges. The interaction can be conceptually understood as a 3D version of connect-the-dots.

At TEI, Redeform will be showcased as a participatory performance art piece that invites participants to construct a human-scale physical instantiation of the Stanford bunny using balloons. The Stanford bunny is a historic test bench model used to compare the efficacy (usually in terms of precision, resolution, and speed) of 3D printers. When conference attendees visit Redeform, they will be invited to blow up balloons and use markers to label them their desired heuristic for evaluating 3D printers (i.e. expressivity, cost, precision, discovery, sustainability). Then they will be invited to become the 3D printer and follow the pointer with the balloons they inflated and marked. Over the course of the exhibition a large physical version of the Stanford bunny will emerge from the collective breath and opinions of the exhibition attendees. We hope it will complicate human machine binaries, serve as a site for reflection on values in digital fabrication design, and prompt discussion about possible futures of 3D printing.

Acknowledgements

This work was developed with support of the Autodesk/ Instructables.com Artist-in-Residence program.

References

[1] Haraway, D. *Simians, Cyborgs, and Women: The Reinvention of Nature.* Routledge, 2013.

Tangible Data, a Phenomenology of Human-Data Relations

Trevor Hogan
Bauhaus-Universität Weimar, Fak. Medien,
Bauhausstr. 11, D-99423 Weimar, Germany
hello@tactiledata.net

ABSTRACT
This paper presents an overview of the research that I have conducted as part of my PhD studies. The objective of this research is to describe and better understand how embodiment influences and augments an audience's experience of data representations. It explores, through creative practice, whether embodying data in alternative modalities contributes to an audience's capacity to construct meaning and empathize with the data source.

Author Keywords
Tangible User Interface, Physicalization, Representation Modality, Qualitative Analysis, Phenomenology, Psycho-phenomenology, Elicitation Interview Technique. Repertory Grid Technique

ACM Classification Keywords
H.5.2 [Information Inter- faces and Presentation]: User Interfaces - Haptic I/O

RESEARCH SITUATION
I am a self-funded external PhD student at the Bauhaus-Universität, Weimar and have just finished my 3rd year of a 4.5-year PhD program, under the supervision of Professor Eva Hornecker. My work is strongly interdisciplinary and may be situated in the field of Interactive Design, at the intersection of Tangible Computing, Human-Computer Interaction and Information Science. Over the past 3 years I have conducted 5 main studies, and I am in the process of planning a final study that will draw together what I learned to round off my thesis.

From attending the Graduate Student Consortium I hope to get senior advice on how to strengthen my argument that embodying data in different modalities influences and augments people's experience of the data representation. Recommendations and feedback on the methodological approach of my further study designs are also highly appreciated.

CONTEXT AND MOTIVATION
In contemporary society, data representations are now an integral part of every aspect of our daily lives. The amount of digital information that is available to us is not only constantly increasing but it is also ubiquitous. The discussion of information visualization as a tool has vastly expanded from the economic and scientific communities to the humanities and the arts and has long entered our everyday life. With this trend, the audiences or target groups that visualizations are designed for are no longer just domain experts or analysts but also everyday people who are confronted with data representations on a daily basis on the newspaper, in advertisements, at the museum, the library or other public spaces.

My research is based on the belief that new insight and meaning can be achieved by representing data beyond the visual modality, which can be touched, felt, heard, held, or even possessed. Consequently, these artifacts act as the embodiment of the data source. They capture the imagination and engage the interpretative and perceptive power of its audience through both their experiential, tactile or artistic qualities. The focus and motivation of my research is to represent data in a manner that exposes insight and affective responses that may be difficult to uncover when using traditional methods such as one-dimensional static graphs and charts. I argue that the use of modalities such as haptic, tactile, auditory - or any combination of these - to represent data can facilitate an experience for people that causes them to empathize with, and be affected by, the data source, in a manner that is significantly different when only the visual modality is used.

BACKGROUND AND RELATED WORK
My research is also motivated by recent literature that emphasizes the felt experience of interaction [8], as well as the re-emergence of phenomenology within the HCI community as an approach to better understand people's experience of technology (cf. [1]). I also seek to build upon theoretical and practical developments in the field of Information Visualization over the past two decades.

The exploration and use of alternative modalities to represent data began with the emergence of visualizations such as Ambient Displays [9]. This approach has been further developed through novel information visualization subfields that include Information Aesthetics [6], Artistic Visualization [13] and Data Art [7]. There has also been recent theoretical investigation into alternative approaches, such as Zhao and Vande Moere [14] who defines the concept of data sculpture and establishes a model of embodiment to analyze the connection between data and representation. Vande Moere followed up this research by introducing different levels of data physicality, which affect how data is mapped and perceived by human senses [11]. My research seeks to build upon this foundation,

TEI '15, January 15–19, 2015, Stanford, California, USA.

http://dx.doi.org/10.1145/2677199.269160

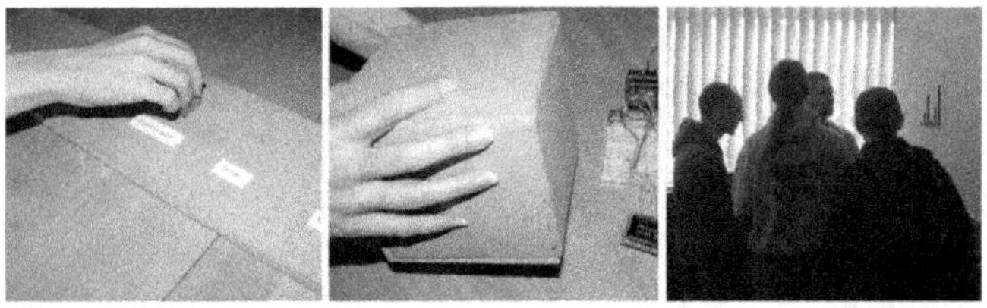
Figure 1 The same data source represented through different modalities. Left: SonicData (auditory), Middle: DataBox (Haptic), Right: Bar Graph (visual)

while focusing more closely on the role that representation modality plays in people's experience and perception of data.

STATEMENT OF THESIS OR PROBLEM

To date, the majority of published research on the evaluation of data representations predominantly address questions regarding user performance, usability, and visualization algorithms; studies that shed light into more open-ended questions regarding insight and discovery and experiences with visualizations are relatively rare (cf. [5].) One possible reason for this is that we still lack evaluation methods that can derive reliable and rich data on experience, insight generation, and discoveries. A goal of my research is to extend the present evaluation framework to include user-experience and, in particular, affective responses when evaluating the quality of data representations. My approach attempts to fill this research gap in order to support work that seeks to represent raw data using alternative modalities. I have a number of research questions, that, over the course of my studies, I have attempted to answer using a number of different methodologies:

- What influence does representation modality have on our experience of data-driven artifacts and how does this affect the way information is accessed and received by the audience?
- What meaning is made from the data, and what are the participative levels of engagement with data artifacts?
- How does embodying data beyond the visual modality, using for instance tangible metaphors contribute to an audience's capacity to construct meaning at its interface?
- How can a better understanding of people's experience of data representations inform future designs?

RESEARCH GOALS AND METHODS

My research attempts to explore the role embodiment plays when experiencing data representations. The approach I take involves designing and producing multiple data representations, each of which have alterations, such as the representation modality (see Fig 1. for example). Through a process of evaluation I aim to expose how these alterations have affected people's experience of the different artifacts.

I further describe my research approach as phenomenological oriented, developing findings inductively. The purpose is to reveal a general description of people's experience of data representations as well as eliciting a detailed description of the unfolding of this experience. My phenomenologically based studies, which include methods such as the Repertory Grid techniques [3] and Vermersch's Elicitation Interview technique [12], are designed with the aim of revealing this first-person experience, along with the cognitive effects and affective responses when interacting with bespoke data-driven artifacts.

DISSERTATION STATUS

At TEI'15 I will have just completed the 3rd year of a 4.5-year PhD program and I plan to start writing up in the summer of 2015. Over the past 3 years I have conducted a number of studies. In the following I provide a brief overview of these studies in chronological order. I then discuss my plans for a final study that will draw together all the knowledge gained in the previous studies.

Study 1. Representation Modality and the Repertory Grid Technique

The first major study I conducted as part of my doctoral studies involved producing several data-driven artifacts that represent the same data source using different levels of modality. Of the three artifacts created, DataBox used haptic feedback in the form of knocking to represent the raw data, SonicData represented it through auditory feedback, while the same dataset was also represented using a traditional bar graph (see Fig. 1). To investigate the affect these modalities had on people's experience of the data we carried out an adapted Repertory Grid Study. Findings indicate that the modality and modality combinations used to represent data do influence the users' experience and affective responses [2].

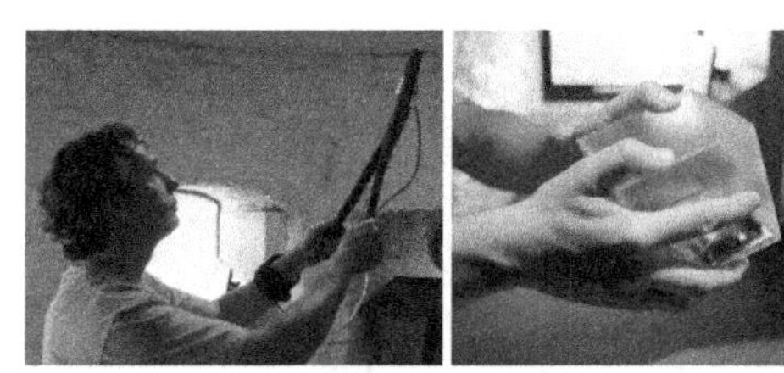
Figure 2 (left): Solar Radiation Dowsing Rod. (right) H^3

Study 2. Experiencing Live Data

Using some of the findings from the previous RepGrid study, I collaborated with Blackrock Castle Observatory, Cork, Ireland and the Irish National Space Centre to represent live streams of astronomical data. We created two cross-modal data driven artifacts H^3 ('Hydrogen cubed') and a Solar Radiation Dowsing Rod, to stimulate curiosity, intrigue and awareness of scientific data in a casual non-expert audience (see Fig.1.) These devices were presented as demos at TEI'13 in Barcelona [3]. To observe their use and assess the user-experience we deployed the devices in Blackrock Castle Observatories visitor centre. Over the course of one week approximately one hundred visitors used the devices while we conducted observations and some informal interviews. The focus of this study was not to expose any usability issues relating to the use of the devices, but to observe people's responses and to probe them about how they felt while interacting with them. We found that the devices stimulated imagination, and provided a 'tangible' direct experience of the otherwise abstract data from outer space.

Exploring and Extending Methodologies

Data representation is a popular tool to help sense-making, discovery and communicating insights. However, evaluating the impact of these in all their ubiquity is still a challenge [5]. In particular, we are lacking techniques to help us understand how representations are interpreted and experienced by people on an individual and personal level; important aspects when it comes to understanding how insights and discoveries are facilitated (or not) by data representation. Over the course of my PhD studies I have utilized and adapted two techniques to better understand people's experience as well as the insight that is generated by them as they interpret data representations.

Study 3. Blending the Repertory Grid Technique and Focus Groups

In a previous study [2] we used the Repertory Grid (RepGrid) Technique to compare and contrast people's experience of representation modality. During this study we found the RepGrid to have some limitations. Taking these into account, we designed a study to explore the benefits of blending the traditional application of the RepGrid technique with focus groups. In [3] we demonstrated the potential of this blended approach by conducting two empirical studies that investigate the same artifacts, using two different approaches. The first study follows the classic RepGrid approach, while the second adapts this by utilizing the RepGrid in a focus group session. Since the inception of the RepGrid technique, no adaptation has been purported to produce rich qualitative data during a group session. We showed how this blended approach has potential to equip a designer or researcher who wishes to better understand people's experience of designed artifacts while also revealing rich design relevant information.

Study 4. From Phenomenology to Psychophenomenology

Following our exploration of the RepGrid technique we started to look for other methods that would allow us to gather more fine grained accounts of experience as well as revealing insight about the unfolding of this experience over time. The method we chose was Vermersch's Elicitation Interview technique. The interview technique is a form of retrospective interviewing grounded in psychophenomenology. In contrast to traditional interviews, this technique is non-inductive but directive where the focus of the interview remains on a particular experience; the participant reaches and maintains a state of evocation that enables them to re-live their experience while minimizing post-reasoning. Following a number of training sessions in Paris, France with Claire Petitmengin, a key practitioner of the technique, we conducted a study to illustrate how the Elicitation Interview technique can be used to gather accounts of people's experience with data representations, and to highlight the type of insight it can provide about people's experience of data visualizations, how these experiences unfolded over time and how key moments manifest themselves as part of the exploration of the visualization *(Article Title: "Introducing the Elicitation Interview Technique to Capture People's Experiences of Data Representations" in review at IEEE Transactions on Visualization and Computer Graphics)*. In this article we presented a study that interviewed 10 participants about their experience with a static data visualization and examined the transcripts using thematic analysis. We believe that there is evidence to show that this technique offers us an evaluation tool to collect reliable and rich accounts of experience that uncover issues that go beyond common comprehension or usability aspects. In particular, we show that the elicitation technique could bring to the fore details about the formation of meaning, the construction of personal connections to the represented data, and the establishment of a dialogue between the person and the data or creator of the representation.

A Design Space for Multisensory Data Representation

As well as design and evaluation studies presented above, I have also conducted theoretical explorations, one of which was aimed at establishing a design space for multisensory data representations. Over the course of 18 months I surveyed 85 existing examples of data representations that require more than one sensory channel to fully interpret and understand the data. Based on this review we establish the design space along three axes of dimensionality: *use of modalities, representation intent and human-data relations*. The purpose of this study was not only to inform our own research, but to also draw the attention of the wider research and design community to aspects of data representation that have been hitherto either ill-defined or underexplored. The contribution of this study is threefold. Firstly, we attempted to define, for the first time, "multisensory data representation". Also, from 85 existing examples, we surveyed the state-of-the-art in multisensory data representation. Finally, we shed light on theoretical and practical considerations and point toward research challenges and questions that are presently underexplored.

The Final Study

To round off my thesis, I am planning a final study that will draw together the design and evaluation techniques that I have used thus far, to explore, in greater detail, peoples experience of interpreting and perceiving data representing through various modalities (auditory, vibro-tactile and visual.) To accomplish this I have created three tangible interfaces that measure and represent the levels of Carbon Dioxide in indoor air through sound, vibration and visuals (see Fig 2.) Up to this point in my PhD studies, the artefacts that I have produced were either interfaces produced for the sole purpose of exploring representation modality [2] or bespoke designs to be used within a public museum [3]. However, these latest objects were designed for the home or workplace, which will offer us the opportunity to explore peoples everyday experience of data represented through different modalities. We

Figure 3. (A) CO_2 Auditory Interface, (B) CO_2Vibro-tactile Interface, (C) CO_2Visual Interface

have already conducted a pilot study, which deployed the devices into homes and workplaces to gather initial observations about their use in real environments. From this we learnt that the devices are intuitive, participants had no difficulties operating them and in some cases they were appropriated for situations that we had not envisaged.

The next phase of this project will involve using our adapted RepGrid technique alongside an Elicitation Interview study to gather and analyze fine-grained accounts of people's experience of the different modalities and how this experience unfolded overtime. We hope that these methods will allow us to establish a general description of people's experience of the various representation modalities under investigation.

EXPECTED CONTRIBUTIONS

Recently there has been a dramatic rise in the amount of research focusing on the storage and retrieval of data. We have also seen a rise in the movement to democratize data, as well as new attempts to explore the use of modalities beyond the visual paradigm to represent data (cf. [9]). Questions that have been somewhat ignored include: *how the general public engages with, interprets, and experiences the represented data? What role does representation modality plays in people's experience of data? and What qualities are important to people when describing their experience of data representation?* The main contribution of this research will emerge from answering these questions. However, we also see process of answering these question as important and valuable as the answers themselves. Over the course of the last 3 years we have adapted a relatively underexplored techniques (the RepGrid) and demonstrated how it could be used to elicit rich design relevant insight. We also extended our repertoire of elicitation techniques through the use of Vermersch's elicitation interview. We hope that the work we have conducted on these methods will contribute to the TEI and wider HCI research community; by offering new approaches to reveal rich accounts about people's experience with technology that will inform the design of artifact that represent data beyond the visually modality.

REFERENCES

1. Fallman, D. In Romance with the Materials of Mobile Interaction: A Phenomenological Approach to the Design of Mobile Information Technology. Doctoral Thesis. Umea University, Sweden (2003).
2. Hogan, T., Hornecker, E. How Does Representation Modality Affect User- Experience of Data Artifacts? Proc. of HAID'12. Lund, Sweden. Springer, (2012).
3. Hogan, T. and Hornecker, E. In Touch with Space : Embodying Live Data For Tangible Interaction. *TEI 2013*, (2013), 275–278.
4. Hogan, T. and Hornecker, E. Blending the repertory grid technique with focus groups to reveal rich design relevant insight. In Proc. of DPPI'13. ACM 2013, 116-125.
5. Lam, H. et al. Empirical Studies in Information Visualization: Seven Scenarios. IEEE Transactions on Visualization and Computer Graphics, 18(9):1520–1536, 2012.
6. Lau, A., Vande Moere, A. Towards a Model of Information Aesthetics in Information Visualization. In Proc of Information Visualization. IEEE (2007) 87-92.
7. Manovich, L. The Anti-Sublime Ideal in Data Art. http://www.manovich.net/DOCS/data_art.doc, (accessed: May 2011)
8. McCarthy, J. & Wright, P. 2004. Technology as Experience. The MIT Press.
9. Swaminathan, S., et al. Supporting the design and fabrication of physical visualizations. In Proc. of CHI '14, ACM, 3845–3854.
10. Wisneski, et al. Ambient Displays: Turning Architectural Space into an Interface between People and Digital Information. Proc. of CoBuild. 1998, 22-32.
11. Vande Moere, A. Beyond the Tyranny of the Pixel: Exploring the Physicality of Information Visualization. In Proc. of IV'08 (2008), IEEE, 469–474.
12. Vermersch, P. Lentretien dexplicitation. ESF, 1994.
13. Viegas, F., Wattenberg, M. Artistic Data Visualization: Beyond Visual Analytics. Proc. of HCII 2007.
14. Zhao, J., A. V. Moere. Embodiment in Data Sculpture: A Model of the Physical Visualization of Information. Proc of Digital Interactive Media in Entertainment and Arts, (2008).
15. Zimmerman, et al. Research through design as a method for interaction design research in HCI. Proc of CHI '07. ACM, 493-502.

Authenticating Experience: Curating Digital Interactive Art

Deborah Turnbull Tillman
Director, New Media Curation
PhD Research Candidate
Creative Robotics Lab, NIEA
UNSW Art & Design,
Sydney NSW Australia
deborah@newmediacuration.com

A/Prof Mari Velonaki
Director, Creative Robotics Lab
NIEA, UNSW Art & Design
Sydney NSW Australia
mari.velonaki@unsw.edu.au

Dr. Petra Gemeinboeck
Deputy Director
Creative Robotics Lab, NIEA
UNSW Art & Design,
Sydney NSW Australia
petra@unsw.edu.au

Abstract

This paper focuses on curating interactive art in experimental ways. It takes the experiment outside labs and into institutions and cityscapes in the form of prototype exhibitions to be evaluated through the medium of audience engagement. The PhD research focuses on authenticating the audience's experience of interactive art; first defining parameters for authenticity within fine arts and creative robotics, then examining how, through the application of evaluative frameworks to iterative exhibition processes, one might capture and utilize experience as a medium in itself. The exhibitions for examination are/will be produced by PhD researcher Deborah Turnbull Tillman through her research initiative New Media Curation (NMC).

Author Keywords

Authenticity; prototyping; curating; action research; criteria; audience experience; interactivity; creative robotics.

ACM Classification Keywords

Design; Documentation; Experimentation; Human Factors; Measurement; Theory; Verification

Introduction

The main research question focuses on the issue of authenticity as investigated within the context of digital interactive art whilst emphasizing the prototyping process. It will also query the audience's role in eliciting reciprocity from digital and computational systems and the ability to analyze this phenomenon via evaluation. Situating this study across traditionally disparate media and creative and making practices will help in establishing specific criteria. These criteria will be informed by the contemplation of different definitions for authenticity across interdisciplinary inquiry. Together these outcomes will assist in establishing a common language for the experience of this hybrid art form.

As per PhD protocol, first the gaps in knowledge regarding the field of digital curating digital interactive art will be identified, along with gaps in the related fields of action and practice-based research, audience evaluation, creative robotics and creating/curating digital interactive works. A literature review will be provided encompassing contemporary practice and positing solutions based on refining the methods utilized in a case-by-case analysis of three of the exhibitions produced by the research initiative New Media Curation (NMC).[1] The outcomes will be varied. Events, exhibitions and happenings will be evaluated using the frameworks below. These evaluations will establish a set of criteria that extends the current knowledge of what it means for an audience member who engages with digital interactive art to have an *authentic experience in the context of interactive art*.

In defining the parameters of an *authentic experience*, this research will draw from the relevant fields of fine art and creative robotics. Where authenticity in fine art may include traditional curatorial practices of care and storage, authenticity in creative robotics may require the ability to replicate expressive authenticity via computer science and engineering. Authenticity across these fields means establishing a provenance precluding a genuineness and truthfulness about the work; however, in drawing on the work of Julienne Greer (Senior Lecturer in Theatre) and Sherry Turkle (PhD in Sociology & Personality Psychologist), authenticity also means a successful transmission, a pleasurable experience and an emotional connectedness at the conclusion of an engagement or interaction (Turkle, 2007) (Greer, 2011).

[1] www.newmediacuration.com. Accessed 29 February 2012, 08:43.

ACM 978-1-4503-3305-4/15/01…$15.00
http://dx.doi.org/10.1145/2677199.2691602

There is an opportunity within the prototyping process to better understand the design and making of digital interactive art. When prototyping is extended to the curatorial process, different, but equally engaging processes will have the opportunity to emerge. As with any the realization of any creative product, the production stage starts once the idea for the artefact (an artwork/play/digital component) has to be thought through but before it is publically exhibited (think of prototype-ish events such as soft launches, dress rehearsals or usability studies). In relation to art, and by extension curating art, prototyping becomes particularly significant when dealing with interaction. The audience is enacted as part of the work itself, with technology becoming a sort of enabler for this transmission of a designed and digital aesthetic. The artwork is thus completed by the audience. New media curators need to allow for this in their process in a way that traditional curators have not needed to (Graham and Cook, 2010). In a way it is not surprising that the practice of curating digital interactive art would follow a similar trajectory to the making of the art itself. The curator now takes on a sort of production role, shifting between the traditional role of caring for objects in a collection, to becoming an artist's collaborator, evaluation specialist, iterative expert, and finally, director.

To date, a key problem in this field of inquiry is the meaning of *authenticity* itself. Universities, such as the Institute of Aesthetics in Denmark,[2] are beginning to utilize the philosophical definition of authenticity [being true to one's own experience in relation to external forces, pressures, and influences which are different from, or other than, oneself] and applying it to courses on digital art (Wood, et al. 2008). In Lotte Philipson's course, students are encouraged to understand all definitions of authenticity and apply them to the digital medium (Philipsen, 2010). Drawing on the work of Dennis Dutton, two closely examined definitions in his writings are *nominal* and *expressive* authenticity. Nominal authenticity is more in line with traditional curatorial techniques. It follows the practical history of a work, correctly identifying materials, authorship, provenance, and origins when its practices are applied. Expressive authenticity is more about critiquing experience through emotions that act as a marker of the artist's society or an individual's belief (Dutton, 2003). Where the nominal definition is useful in terms of taxonomy, the expressive definition would be more difficult to evaluate. In relation to digital interactive art, evaluating *affect* would be more advantageous as it "refers to the *experience* of feeling or emotion" and "is a key part of the process of an organism's interaction with stimuli" (VandenBos, 2006). Most interesting is that this "...word also refers sometimes to *affect display*, which is "a facial, vocal, or gestural behavior that serves as an indicator of affect..."" (Ibid). As evaluative markers, it would be simpler to identify and capture *expression* than it would to capture *emotion*.

[2] http://www.au.dk/en/facultiesdepartmentsetc/humanities/aest-fag/. Accessed 29 February 2010, 13:41.

The Context

The problems associated with digital interactive art include its immateriality and repositioning of time and space, thus making the act of authenticating one's interaction with it problematic. As discussed in Graham and Cook (2010), these problems place a particular need on the curator to revise traditional practice. Relevant recent work in this field includes that of Ernest Edmonds' research group the Creativity and Cognition Studios. Through their work in Beta_space, a publicly housed laboratory at the Powerhouse Museum, Sydney, they have set up an infrastructure, a methodology for measuring experience and emotion in digital interactive art. The writings about this work form an important basis for my research. Reports on the curatorial practice of Lizzie Muller, Matthew Connell, and Deborah Turnbull Tillman all detail the making and evaluating of interactive art at various iterative phases in a public laboratory. Lizzie Muller's PhD and related writings report the core research that forms the background to this study (Muller, 2010). The significance of the Creativity and Cognition Studios work was innovation in:

1] bringing the work out of a university lab and into the public domain before it was finished (Muller, L., Edmonds, E. and Connell, M. (2006);

2] establishing a set of criteria for measuring audience experience (Bilda, Z., Candy, L., and Edmonds E. A. (2007))(Costello, B. (2007));

3] offering this process to the public as an exhibition on display for public consumption (Turnbull D. and Connell, M. (2011) p. 79-93).

4] taking these processes out of the realm of culture and into the community as creative practice for corporations and institutions as well as artists and curators (Muller, L. et al, (2006)(Turnbull, D. (2011)).

5] producing three models for curating digital interactive art, two of which hold preliminary criteria for exhibiting digital and interactive art (Turnbull, D. and Connell, M. (2014) p. 221-241).

These activities are best captured en masse in Candy and Edmonds' book *Interacting: art, research and the creative practitioner* (Libri, UK: 2011). This publication not only details the methodologies followed during the seven years

Beta_space was actively programmed in the museum, but provides a history of digital interactive art, with Candy and Edmonds outlining the current categories, aesthetics, influences, paradigms, creative spaces, and cultural shifts in relation to the artist and audience; the producers and consumers of art.

Inside these creative spaces New Media Curation (NMC) was launched. This research initiative, established in 2008 with curator Deborah Turnbull Tillman, technical advisor Aram Dulyan and artist Ian Gwilt, takes an experimental approach to curating interactive artworks. Rather than gathering research in a lab, work was taken further afield, partnerships with corporations such as Ausgrid, the Sydney Olympic Park Authority and the Australia Council for the Arts were established. Here NMC experimented in the public domain by pushing the boundaries of traditional arts creation and curating, often bringing techniques to light in reacting to the wants and needs of the institutions and artists supported, documenting via text, photography, and video; publishing these activities where possible. Though operating within academic constraints, NMC set out set out to push the boundaries of refined practice, to provide evocative social dialogue via the medium of exhibition in relation to curating digital interactive art. Three of these case studies will serve as a cultural analysis of curatorial research in the context of this thesis:

1] Memory Flows, Sydney Olympic Park Authority (May 2010) http://www.newmediacuration.com/projects/past

2] Grid Gallery, Ausgrid (June 2010) http://www.newmediacuration.com/projects/past

3] genart_sys, the Australia Council for the Arts (Jan 2011) http://newmediacuration.com/genartsys/ |@genart_sys

This research will authenticate these experiences as media that ignite the artwork for the audience, making them feel engaged in the exchange between them and an art system. Their experience could potentially be authenticated based on what their expectation of reciprocity is from the art system and if it is fulfilled. An *authentic experience* would then be one that established itself as a work of art in some true or genuine way, but also gave the person experiencing it some measure of a successful transmission in the form of an insight or understanding, followed by a feeling of pleasure and connectedness with the work. In simple terms, this might be best gauged by a subject repeatedly returning to a certain engagement, to complete the design and architecture of the work in the form of human interaction (Greer, 2011). By contrast, an *inauthentic experience* might be better defined by a breakdown in the design, architecture or embodiment of one of these variables, resulting in the subject abandoning the engagement.

The PhD study by Turnbull Tillman proposes to reflect on these exhibitions, treating them as curatorial prototypes for analysis in order to form the foundation of a larger iterative cycle involving practice-based research and curatorship. This analysis becomes important in relation to the question of authenticity and accessibility when a curator is faced with issues like a second iterative cycle of the same group of artworks. If one wanted to re-create the conceptual message of original exhibitions in another space, analysis of the first iterative cycles would assist in curating the next cycle, which would lend to an authentic experience of the artworks via a stronger transmission of their message. The results of this formal analysis will inform 2 new case studies featuring the below framework and methodology:

-> a time-based and distributed performance in Sydney, Australia featuring emergent/professional practitioners from UNSW | Art & Design's student body and staff. Audience experience will be measured, data collected and analysis performed in the below way:

Lecture and work with the emergent and professional artists in their courses and studios -> watch the way they work to produce artefacts & ideas -> perform evaluation on their prototype pieces -> act by providing feedback in terms of conceptual and physical design for the spaces where the works will be exhibited -> allow for development and revision of these ideas -> plan themes and exhibitions based on the end results of these studios -> exhibit the works as planned -> document this exhibition via photography and video -> evaluate the audience's experience of these works -> collate and analyze this evaluation -> establish a set of criteria for performing these tasks in future -> repeat these tasks in a second case study with an improved knowledge of the experience

The methodology to be employed for the case studies will be practice-based, drawing upon the action research approach (Stringer, 2003). Stringer's approach of LOOK -> THINK -> ACT is based in social reform and draws on Lewin's "spiral of steps" that attempt to depict "comparative research on the conditions and effects of various forms of social action, and research leading to social action." (Smith, 1996). Johnson, a social scientist from the 1970s, has revised Lewin's spiral utilizing words such as UNFREEZING -> CHANGING -> REFREEZING.

Conclusion

The proposed outcomes of this study will be a set of criteria for curating digital interactive artworks, taken from exhibitions, events and happenings, and distributed via publication. These criteria will be determined by applying an iterative and action-based approach to analyzing experimental curatorial practice within the contexts of experimental fine art, creative robotics research. The main aim is to assist artists, curators, and institutions to dispel their fears around engaging with new media art practice at any stage in its iterative cycle, encouraging the recreation of experience authentic to the moment an audience engages with a work. This will ultimately provide practitioners with innovative methodologies that can be successfully embedded in the action research of New Media Curation.

Acknowledgements
I would like to thank my two thesis supervisors, Mari Velonaki and Petra Gemeinboeck for their continued input, support and inspiration. I am eternally grateful to my long time mentors, Ernest Edmonds, Matthew Connell, Lizzie Muller and Linda Candy for being brave, taking risks and generally being influential. Finally, I would like to thank my partner, Arron Tillman, for his endless support, humor, and patience.

References
[1] Bilda, Z, Candy, L, and Edmonds E. A. An Embodied Cognition Framework for Interactive Experience. *CoDesign: International Journal of Co-Creation in Design and the Arts 3, 2* (2007) 123-137.

[2] Candy, L. and Edmonds, E.A. *Interacting: art, research and the creative practitioner.* Libri Publishing, UK, 2011.

[3] Costello, B. A Pleasure Framework, *Leonardo Journal,* 40,4 (2007) 370-371.

[4] Dutton, Dennis. Authenticity in art, in Levinson (ed.): *The Oxford Handbook of Aesthetics* (2003) Oxford University Press | Accessed 29 February 2012 http://www.denisdutton.com/authenticity.htm

[5] Graham, B. and Cook, S. *Rethinking Curating: Art after New Media.* MIT Press, Cambridge, MA, USA, 2010.

[6] Greer, Julienne. Digital Companions: Analyzing the emotive connection between players and the NPC companions in video game space. Part 4, Article 1 in *Exploring Video Games* (2013). Eds. Webber, Nick and Daniel Riha. E-book with Inter-Disciplinary Press: ISBN 978-1-84888-240-9.

[7] Muller, L., Edmonds, E. and Connell, M. Living Laboratories for Interactive Art. *CoDesign: International Journal of Co Creation in Design and the Arts*, Special Issue on Interactive Art Collaboration, 2,4 (2006) 195-207.

[8] Muller, L. *The experience of interactive art: A curatorial study.* PhD Thesis, University of Technology, Sydney, 2010.

[9] Philipsen, Lotte. Authenticity and in art in the digital age. Course offered in 2010 by the Department of Aesthetics, Universiy of Aarhaus | Accessed 29 February 2012: http://artandauthenticity.wikidot.com/

[10] Smith, M. K. Action research, *the encyclopaedia of informal education* (1996; 2001, 2007): www.infed.org/research/b-actres.htm.

[11] Stringer, E.T. *Action Research in Education,* Prentice Hall, 2003.

[12] Turkle, Sherry. Authenticity in the age of digital companions. *Interaction Studies,* 8,3, (2007) 501-517. John Benjamins Publishing Company, Philedelphia: USA.

[13] Turnbull D. and Connell, M. Prototyping Places: the museum. *Interacting: Art, Research and the Creative Practitioner.* (Eds) Linda Candy and Ernest Edmonds. Libri Publications, UK, 2011, 79-93.

[14] Turnbull, D. and Connell, M. Curating Digital Public Art. *Interactive Experience in the Digital Age.* (Eds) Linda Candy and Sam Ferguson. Springer Publications, UK, 2014, 221-241.

[15] Turnbull, D. New Media Curation, 2008. www.newmediacuration.com. Accessed 29 February 2012, 08:43.

[16] VandenBos, Gary R., ed. Affect. *APA Dictionary of Psychology.* Washington, DC: American Psychological Association, 2006, 26.

[17] Wood, A. M., Linley, P. A., Maltby, J., Baliousis, M., Joseph, S. The authentic personality: A theoretical and empirical conceptualization, and the development of the Authenticity Scale.*Journal of Counseling Psychology, 55*, 385-399.

Exploring Perceptual and Motor Gestalt in Touchless Interactions with Distant Displays

Debaleena Chattopadhyay
School of Informatics and Computing | Indiana University | Indianapolis
535 W. Michigan Street, Indianapolis, IN 46202, USA
debchatt@iupui.edu

ABSTRACT

Markerless motion-sensing promises to position touchless interactions successfully in various domains (e.g., entertainment or surgery) because they are deemed *natural*. This naturalness, however, depends upon the mechanics of touchless interaction that remains largely unexplored. My dissertation first aims to deconstruct the interaction mechanics of touchless, especially its device-less property, from an embodied perspective. Grounded in this analysis, I then plan to investigate how visual perception affects touchless interaction with distant, 2D displays. Preliminary findings suggest that Gestalt principles in visual perception and motor action affect the touchless user experience. User interface elements demonstrating perceptual-grouping principles, such as *similarity of orientation* decreased users' efficiency, while *continuity* of UI elements forming a perceptual whole increased users' effectiveness. Moreover, following the *law of Prägnanz*, users often gestured to minimize their energy expenditure. This work can inform the design of touchless UX by uncovering relations between perceptual and motor gestalt in touchless interactions.

Author Keywords

Gestalt psychology; Touchless interaction; Visual perception; Interaction design; Embodied interaction.

ACM Classification Keywords

H.5.2 [User Interfaces]: Interaction Styles; Theory and methods.

INTRODUCTION

Markerless sensing of whole-body movements has propelled the emergence of touchless interaction in a variety of domains, such as entertainment, surgery, interactive visualization, or collaboration. Because touchless interactions can essentially draw on existing gestures that we use in our everyday life, they are characterized as Natural User Interfaces (NUI). NUI researchers are actively exploring different touchless gestures [8], user-interface elements [2], and interaction techniques [1] that can contribute toward the naturalness of touchless interaction. Equally relevant, but little explored are the interaction mechanics or sensory-motor details that can affect the touchless user experience.

TEI '15, January 15 – 19, 2015, Stanford, CA, USA

ACM 978-1-4503-3305-4/15/01$15.00
http://dx.doi.org/10.1145/2677199.2691603

To deconstruct its sensory-motor connections, we can view touchless interaction from an embodied interaction perspective [5]. Prior work used embodied perspective to discuss touchless interactions based on Merleau-Ponty's lived-body view of individual experiences and Wittgenstein's socially organized view of action [10]. But their interaction mechanics remain unexplored. For example, compared with other interaction modalities, such as touch-based or tangible computing—touchless interaction is *device-less*. Hence, there is no embodied conception of a tool—no transition of an input device from *present-at-hand* (an object of activity) to *ready-to-hand* (absorbed in the fabric of the activity) [5].

I argue that this device-less property of touchless interactions creates unique sensory-motor connections while interacting with distant, 2D displays, thus affecting the touchless user experience. This argument can be grounded in ecological psychology that views cognition as a construct involving the ability of an entity, action, and the environment [6]. For example, a chair affords sitting to a human, but not to an entity inappropriate for sitting (e.g., a fish). In touchless interactions, the absence of a device (and its constraints) and the use of our whole body (or body-parts) imply availability of all our physical abilities toward realizing affordances of any touchless system. So while interacting with a distant 2D display, we can use our hands or fingers to push, pull, roll, or make directional strokes in mid-air as interaction commands. However, I argue that the accessibility of all these physical abilities (that we use in a 3D world) to interact with a 2D display that lacks a 3D worldview violates how *seeing* and *acting* is related in our familiar 3D environment [6]. Thus, I further argue that the psychological principles affecting visual perception will have a significant effect on touchless motor action. Moreover, the sole presence of 2D visual feedback and proprioception in touchless interactions would amplify typical properties of motor control (e.g., motor planning, or motor learning).

During the last two years of our work on touchless interactions with large displays, we observed that users' performance were often solely affected by certain visual properties of the UI. Moreover, users tend to make holistic oblique gestures instead of decoupled orthogonal hand movements. These findings—albeit ad hoc—can be explained using the Gestalt theory. Gestalt psychology—a popular proponent of *holism*—has played an illustrious role in providing theoretical foundations toward visual perception [11], and very recently motor action [7]. Inspired by preliminary findings, my aim is to conduct mixed-method studies to explore how gestalt principles in visual perception and motor action can drive the design of touchless interactions (i.e., to conduct quantitative studies to evaluate the effect of gestalt principles and qualitative studies to understand users' conscious experiences). This work on touchless, situated at the confluence of perceptual and motor gestalt, can also provide new insights to Gestalt researchers.

BACKGROUND

Touchless Interaction

Innovative applications of touchless systems are proliferating across domains, such as entertainment, surgery [10], patient-centric health settings [9], collocated collaboration, information visualization, or public spaces [10]. These systems' feasibility, adoption, or user experience is an active line of research. Another research direction deals with understanding naturalness of touchless interactions. To that aim, elicitation studies explore touchless gestures that users report natural as interaction commands. Fewer works have looked into understanding touchless interactions beyond the interface-centric view [10], or operationalizing the intuitiveness (or naturalness) of touchless interfaces [3]. With the current focus on investigating touchless UX from users' self-reports, we may be overlooking other implicit sensory-motor factors affecting touchless UX, such as visual aspects of the UI, or properties of motor action unnoticed by users.

Embodied Interaction

Touchless interactions are distinctively characterized by the absence of a device—we engage with the system without a tool. Then from Heidegger's phenomenological view (later also developed in HCI), at no point in touchless interactions we have a *present-at-hand* device, such as a mouse or a pen, as the object of an activity [5]. Thus, in the context of interacting with computers, touchless interaction may be called as the ultimate form of Merleau-Ponty's lived-body experience—the body playing the crucial role in perception.

Specifically in visual perception, ecological psychology deals with the deep connection between *seeing* and *acting* [5, 6]. This connection becomes pertinent to touchless interactions and worthy of investigation, because in certain scenarios (e.g., interacting with distant, 2D displays), users see a 2D UI but act with their whole body (or parts) that they are familiar engaging in a 3D environment with haptic feedback. This mismatch between visual perception and motor action in touchless interactions remains unexplored.

Gestalt Psychology

Gestalt psychologists argue that perceptual experiences and motor actions are inherently holistic, rather than a composite of unrelated structural units. A centennial review on Gestalt research showed how different methodological shortcomings of this research program have somewhat been addressed [11]. Specifically, the gestalt principles of perceptual grouping in vision, such as proximity, similarity, or continuity, have been quantified [11]. Another recent review analyzed reaction-time results from previous studies and argued that four fundamental Gestalt principles in perception also apply to the control of motor action—holism, constancy, mutual exclusivity, and grouping in apparent motion [7]. For example, certain motor actions, such as articulating a syllable during speech or making quick taps indicate the presence of motor gestalts (chunks). However, neither perceptual nor motor gestalt has been investigated in the context of touchless interactions.

Interacting with 2D touchless UIs using freehand gestures violates our familiar mental model of interacting with the 3D environment, and the effects of such a mismatch can be explained using Gestalt psychology. Specifically, I argue that gestalt principles in visual perception and motor action can provide a theoretical foundation to drive the next-generation touchless UX with distant displays.

PRELIMINARY FINDINGS: 'ON UNNOTICED SENSATIONS AND ERRORS OF JUDGEMENT'

We began studying touchless interactions as part of the Wall Display Experience Research (WADER) program, which aims to identify critical factors that are necessary to design next-generation interaction techniques to support collaboration around wall-size displays. While conducting controlled experiments to study visual feedback [4], interaction primitives [3] and command-selection techniques [2] for large-display touchless interactions, we observed certain performance trends that were unnoticed by users. Visual elements of the UI affected users' effectiveness (e.g., aiming a menu for command-selection) and efficiency (e.g., time taken to select a menu-option). Also, users always made similar errors while performing certain interaction primitives (e.g., pull-to-deselect). Interestingly, all our findings could be explained by gestalt principles of perceptual grouping: similarity by orientation, continuity, and the gestalt law of *Prägnanz*.

Across our experiments, users sat about 1.5 – 2.5 m away from a large display (4 x 1.5 m) and were tracked by Kinect sensors. In what follows, I briefly describe the findings that led to the conception of this dissertation proposal, some limitations of our experiments and the future research plan.

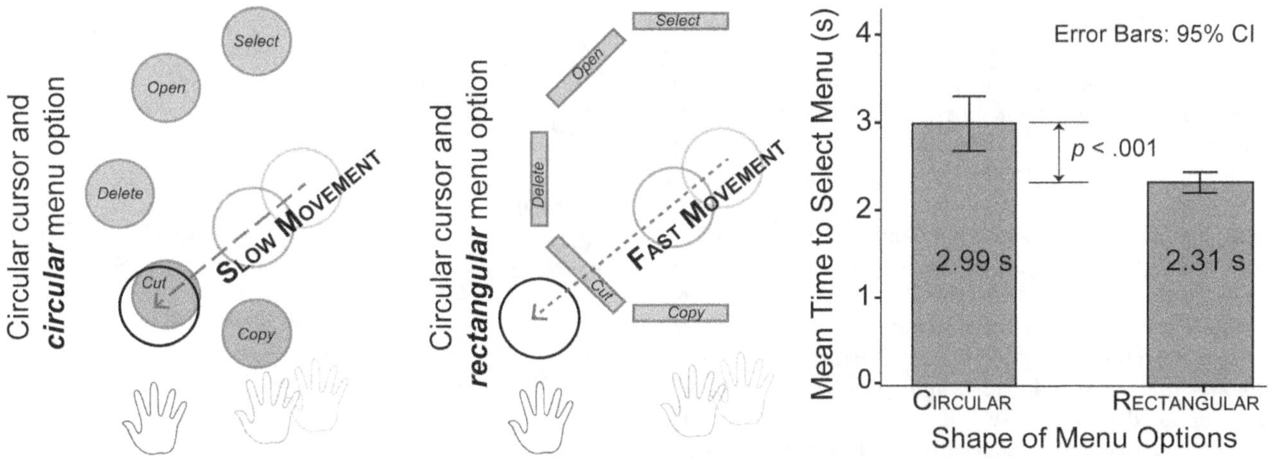

Figure 1. Perceptual grouping by *Similarity of Orientation* principle affected the efficiency of touchless interaction: Expert users were faster when *crossing-to-select* a rectangular menu option than a circular menu option with a circular cursor.

Similarity of Orientation affects Interaction Efficiency

To relieve users from strictly complying with system-defined postures as interaction commands, we introduced a command-selection technique using mid-air strokes—Touchless Circular Menus (TCM) [2]. To trigger the contextual TCM, users would land on the target folder, and to select a command, users would simply cross the menu option (Figure 1). In our early iterations, the menu options (230px) were circular, isomorphic to the cursor (256px). During pilot testing with three expert users, we found them slowing down while crossing the menu-option. When the cursor was over the menu-option, users would tend to slow down as if they were placing the cursor over the menu-option, rather than crossing it (in spite of prior instructions and practice trials). The menu options were about 800 pixels away from the folder (13.7 cm in control space). When the menu options were modified to rectangles (at the same distance), users became significantly faster. This occurred in spite of users essentially traversing the same distance: For circular options, users had to move across half the menu-option, and for rectangles cross the entire menu-option. Shape of the menu options (circular, M=2.99s, SD = 2.0; rectangular, M=2.31s, SD = 0.76) significantly affected efficiency (Log_{10} reaction time) with a small effect size, n = 161, $t(160) = 4.19, p < .001, d = .33$.

This finding can be explained using the gestalt principle of perceptual grouping by *similarity of orientation*: all else being equal, the most similar visual elements in orientation tend to be grouped together [11]. Our results suggested that users must have perceived the circular cursor and the circular menu-option as a group—at least momentarily—and thus slowed their motor action to discriminate between the object of action (the circular menu option) and the symbolic referent of their action (the circular cursor).

Continuity affects Interaction Effectiveness

For another experiment that explored user performance of mid-air directional strokes [3], users performed the following task. As they reached a landing circle on the display, a direction and a target line appeared (Figure 2A). To complete a trial, users stroked in that given direction across the target line. Although this experiment used the same gesture primitive as TCM (a mid-air directional stroke), we found a significant difference in users' effectiveness. Across the same individuals who participated in both of these experiments (mid-air strokes and TCM), we found that angular error for 23.5% of the trials was more than ± 22.5° in the first experiment, compared with only 2.7% of such erroneous trials in the second. The distance between the target line (or a menu option) and the landing circle (or a folder) was about 800 pixels. This finding can be explained by the structure of the TCM that was absent during the mid-air stroke experiment—a semi-circular

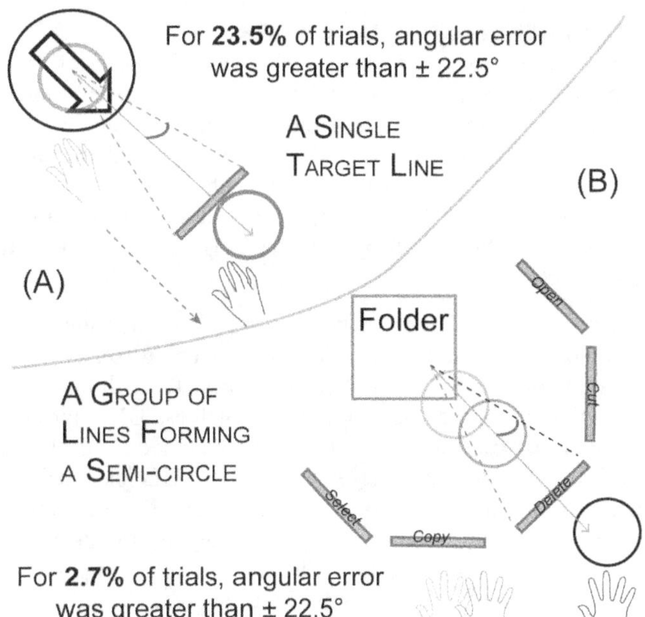

Figure 2. Perceptual grouping by *Continuity* affected the effectiveness of touchless interactions: Experimental results from two studies suggested that users were less precise when aiming an isolated rectangular target (A) compared with a rectangle as part of a semi-circular arrangement (B).

arrangement (Figure 2B). This exemplifies the gestalt principle of perceptual grouping by *continuity*: all else being equal, elements tend to be grouped together when they are aligned with each other [11]. Users were more precise with the TCM than the single line segment as they were aiming for a wider structure in TCM—a semicircle.

Prägnanz affects Intuitiveness of Gesture Primitives

In another study, we explored *push-to-select* and *pull-to-deselect* gestures [4]. In a drag-and-drop task on a large display, we observed users often trying to select targets by following the shortest, oblique path, instead of a set of orthogonal paths. Similarly, when pulling to deselect, instead of a decoupled set of orthogonal movements (parallel to the display for translation and perpendicular for action), users intuitively made oblique motions toward the center of their torso (Figure 3). Such tendencies exemplify motor planning routines that seek to minimize our metabolic energy costs [3]. Overall, the holistic nature of this oblique motion can be explained by the concept of physical Gestalten or motor gestalt [7], which is derived from a more general *Law of Prägnanz*: all physical systems, when left alone, tend to achieve a state of maximum equilibrium with minimum energy expenditure [11].

Limitations

Our findings are posteriori arguments and are limited by our tracking sensors. Other limitations include not explicitly controlling for the index of difficulty in the crossing-based trials, and a small sample size. I plan to address these limitations in my future work.

CONCLUSION AND FUTURE WORK

This dissertation proposal aims to deconstruct the interaction mechanics of touchless from an embodied perspective. Specifically, I argue that the device-less property of touchless violates our familiar mental model of *seeing* and *acting* when interacting with 2D displays using freehand gestures. And the effects of such a mismatch can be explained by gestalt principles of visual perception and motor action.

As future work, I am designing controlled experiments to test how the gestalt principles of visual perception (e.g., closure, or symmetry) and motor action (e.g., holism, or grouping of apparent motion) affect touchless UX. Findings from these experiments will create the knowledge necessary to design the next-generation of touchless UIs and gesture primitives. I also plan to use these guidelines to design a touchless system for interacting with "beyond-the-desktop" visualizations on large displays (e.g., large-scale scatterplots, heat maps or graphical networks).

ACKNOWLEDGEMENTS

I would like to thank my advisor, Prof. Davide Bolchini, for his guidance and UITS AVL for the use of their facilities. This work was partially supported by an IUPUI RSFG.

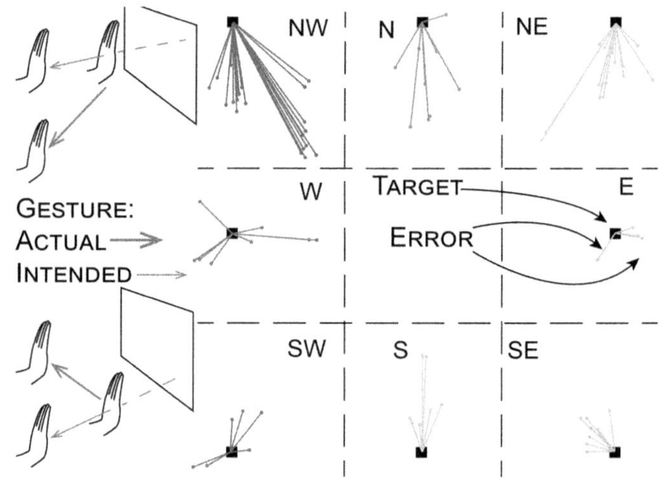

Figure 3. A holistic motor gestalt exemplifying the *Law of Prägnanz* affected gesture intuitiveness: When intending to make mid-air movements perpendicular to a vertical display, such as a pull gesture, users repeatedly made oblique motions toward the center of their torso—to optimally reach static equilibrium, thus minimizing their body's energy expenditure.

REFERENCES

1. Bailly, G., et al. (2011). Comparing free hand menu techniques for distant displays using linear, marking and finger-count menus. *Proc. INTERACT*, 248 – 262.
2. Chattopadhyay, D., & Bolchini, D. (2014). Touchless circular menus: toward an intuitive UI for touchless interactions with large displays. *Proc. AVI*, 33 – 40.
3. Chattopadhyay, D., & Bolchini, D. (2014). Motor-Intuitive Interactions Based on Image Schemas: Aligning Touchless Interaction Primitives with Human Sensorimotor Abilities, *[Special Issue on Intuitive Interaction] Interacting with Computers* (to appear).
4. Chattopadhyay, D., et al. (2014). Understanding Visual Feedback in Large-Display Touchless Interactions: An Exploratory Study. [Research Report] IUPUI Scholar Works, Indiana University.
5. Dourish, P. (2004). *Where the action is: The foundations of embodied interaction*. MIT press.
6. Gibson, J. J. (1979). *The Ecological Approach to Visual Perception*. Houghton Mifflin.
7. Klapp, S. T., & Jagacinski, R. J. (2011). Gestalt principles in the control of motor action. *Psychological bulletin, 137(3)*, 443.
8. Morris, M. R., et al. (2014). Reducing legacy bias in gesture elicitation studies. *Interactions*, *21(3)*, 40 – 45.
9. Mullaney, T., et al. (2014). Positional acts: using a Kinect™ sensor to reconfigure patient roles within radiotherapy treatment. *Proc. TEI*, 93–96.
10. O'hara, K., et al. (2013). On the naturalness of touchless: putting the "interaction" back into NUI. *TOCHI, 20(1)*, 5.
11. Wagemans, J., Elder, J. H., et al. (2012). A century of Gestalt psychology in visual perception: I. Perceptual grouping and figure–ground organization. *Psychological bulletin*, *138(6),* 1172.

Exploring the Potential of Physical Visualizations

Simon Stusak
Human-Computer Interaction Group
University of Munich (LMU)
simon.stusak@ifi.lmu.de

ABSTRACT

Although physical objects have been used for information presentation for a long time, physical visualizations only recently started to attract interest in the HCI and InfoVis communities. While physical visualizations have the quality to evoke user fascination and curiosity, our understanding of their benefits regarding data exploration and the creation of effective representations are still limited. This paper describes several projects in the area of physical visualizations, all with the goal to explore their potential and limitations. First findings show that a promising direction of physical visualizations is the area of personal data, where they can offer a more creative and mindful way to look and reflect on ones' data.

Author Keywords

physical visualization; information visualization; digital fabrication; tangible user interaction.

ACM Classification Keywords

H.5.m. Information Interfaces and Presentation (e.g. HCI): Miscellaneous

General Terms

Human Factors; Design; Experimentation.

INTRODUCTION

The emerging interest in digital fabrication and the technical progress in research areas such as shape-changing interfaces lead to the questions how such novel techniques can be integrated into everyday life and how they can complement traditional 2D displays. While technologies for shape-changing interfaces are rapidly evolving, our understanding of their clear benefits is still limited.

This thesis focuses on the area of information visualization with the goal to investigate how information can be visualized in a material form and uncover its potential but also highlight challenges and limitations. Artists and designers have produced physical representations of data in various forms and companies already used them in the early 20th century [2]. While it is widely recognized that they engage playful exploration and can foster curiosity, their analytical value and the creation of effective physical visualizations remain to be explored.

TEI '15, January 15–19, 2015, Stanford, California, USA..

ACM 978-1-4503-3305-4/15/01...$15.00.
http://dx.doi.org/10.1145/2677199.2691604

This paper starts with a short introduction into related work and a specification of the main research questions. The main part describes several projects in which material representations for a range of different data sets and in various form factors based on several materials were designed and built. All had the goal in common to explore how physical visualization can be designed, to investigate how people use and interact with them and to establish a basic understanding of their potential and limitations. First findings revealed the area of *calm* or *slow visualizations* to be a promising field for further research, since the nature of physical visualizations as long lasting and "always on" objects seem to offer a more mindful and reflective look at data, especially in the case of personal data.

RELATED WORK

Hiroshi Ishii [3] developed the vision of Tangible User Interfaces (TUIs). He argues that people have sophisticated skills for sensing and manipulating the physical environment. However, most of these skills are not employed in interaction with the digital world. TUIs are built upon those skills and provide physical form to digital information. Physical visualizations are part of this vision as they offer to explore and receive information through multiple sensory channels

Jansen et al. [5] present the first information visualization study comparing physical to on-screen visualizations. They compared physical 3D bar charts to their on-screen counterparts and showed that moving visualizations to the physical world can improve users efficiency at information retrieval tasks. The ability to be touched and the perfect visual realism of physical objects seem to be an essential cognitive aid. Their findings provide empirical motivation for further studies, which focus on other modalities (e.g. paper or touch-screens) and different tasks. In addition they extended the information visualization pipeline model by adding further levels to integrate beyond-desktop visualizations such as shape-changing displays and physical visualizations [4].

Vande Moere and colleagues [11, 12] reviewed and discussed a large variety of data sculptures. They point out the limitations of the screen medium and the advantages of information presentations that can be touched, carried or even possessed. He argues that physical visualizations can address a broader audience and extend the area of casual and ambient information visualization.

A first model of physical representation of data was developed by Zhao et al. [13]. Their data sculpture domain model is split into four relevant areas: *information visualization*, *tangible user interfaces*, *visualization art* and *interactive art*. The model is defined by the two attributes *focus (artistic - functional)* and *manifestation (virtual - physical)*.

METHOD AND RESEARCH QUESTIONS

The main goal of this research is to investigate how physical visualizations can contribute to the process of data exploration and what value they have dependent on different tasks and goals. What are the design challenges for visualizations in material form and what are the key points to create effective physical visualizations? This further leads to questions about the interplay between physical and traditional digital visualizations, their individual strengths and how they could complement one another. How for example should visualization systems be designed that try to take advantage of a multisensory approach and use vision and haptics to communicate information?

I started with a practical approach, inspired by the research through design method [14], by designing and building material representations for a range of different data sets and in various form factors. The intention and expected final output is a series of prototypes and a documentation of the design process, which can help to specify a problem space, context of use and set of target users.

To consider suitable approaches to evaluate physical visualizations and to find first indications for possible benefits a literature research was conducted. Besides areas from computer science, such as *information visualization*, *tangible user interaction* or *projection augmentation*, I also looked into research fields from psychology, e.g. *memory and cognition* or *motivation and persuasion*.

PROJECTS

This section describes several projects I am currently working on. For the fabrication a laser cutter and a 3D printer were used, which both enable rapid prototyping of physical visualizations with an adequate precision. Various materials from paper and cardboard, to wood and acrylic glass, to plastics were used for the data-driven artifacts. So far, we focused on static physical visualizations to keep the design and creation process rather simple.

Beyond Physical Bar Charts [7, 8]

To investigate the creation of effective and usable physical visualizations we used an iterative design process. We started with sketches on paper, created first low fidelity prototypes out of cardboard and built the final visualizations with acrylic glass and a laser cutter. Figure 1 (left) shows the static variation of the so-called *thread star plot*, which combines a bar chart and a star plot, both well-known 2D visualizations, into one compact physical object. Furthermore we built an interactive type by attaching hook-and-loop fastener at the edges of the acrylic glass (figure 1 right) to enable filtering and reordering of the data. A conducted user study revealed that a mature design is crucial if the physical visualizations are aimed at supporting analytical tasks. Especially stability and affordances are essential properties. [7]

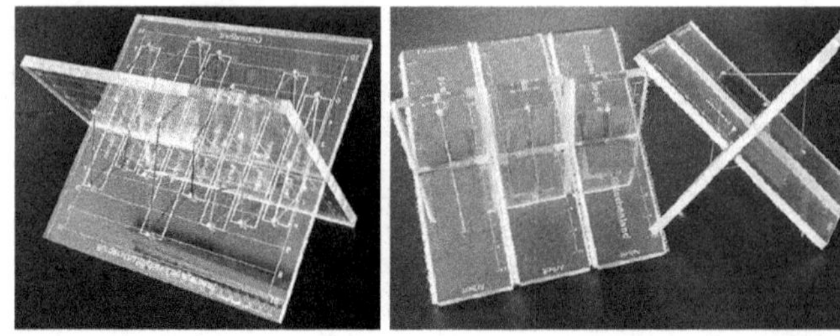

Figure 1. Static thread star plot (left); Interactive thread star plot (right) [7].

We furthermore examined to which extent physical visualizations can support well-know analytical tasks from the domain of information visualization. An analysis based on the taxonomy of Amar et al. [1], which lists tasks such as "filter", "sort" or "determine range", showed that many analytics tasks can be supported by physical visualizations. However, to support all analytical tasks more sophisticated physical visualizations that offer for example mechanical manipulation are required. [8]

Paper-Based Visualizations

The goal of the paper-based visualization projects was to explore which effects come into play, when people build their own physical visualizations. We developed three paper-based visualizations using the data of the TEI 2014 conference (see figure 2 left) and included them into the conference bags. Although the qualitative feedback during the conference was positive, the number of completed questionnaires were marginal.

Figure 2. Paper-based visualizations for the TEI conference 2014 (left) and the soccer world championship 2014 (right).

In similar spirit we designed a visualization for the soccer world championship 2014 (see figure 2 right). The result of each game is represented by two paper pyramids colored in the corresponding national flags. The scored goals of each team are visualized by the height of the pyramid. We shared pictures and source files through social media. While again the qualitative feedback was positive, nobody tried to build the visualization for themselves or developed it further to realize, for example, a different data mapping.

Augmenting Physical Visualizations [6, 10]

Physical visualizations are often limited by their fixed appearance and lack interactivity. To minimize these disadvantages we tried to fuse the digital world with the physical.

One project combined physical visualizations and interactive tabletops. The general motivation here was to use the physical visualization for a first overview of the data and to awaken interest and than use the tabletop to show further information or details on demand. Placing and manipulating the physical visualization (e.g. repositioning or rotating) on the tabletop enables a deeper exploration and interaction of the data set. [6]

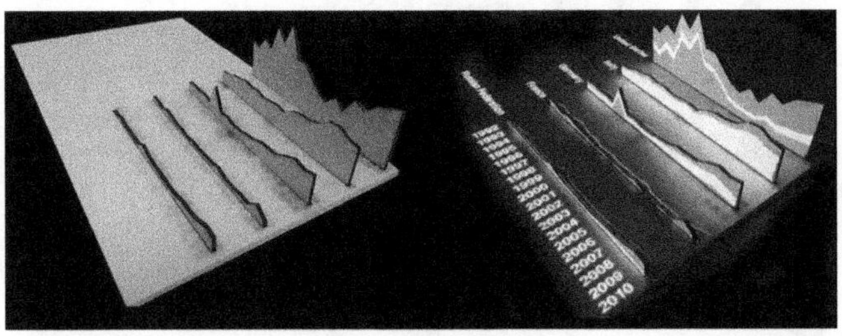

Figure 3. Physical Area Chart (left); Projection Augmented Physical Visualization (right) [10].

Another project investigated the potential of augmenting physical visualizations with projections. Figure 3 shows a concrete prototype of a wooden physical area chart (left) and its augmentation (right). The creation process revealed some initial insights as the importance of the accuracy of the physical model and the resolution of the projection. The exploration showed that projection augmentation can enhance physical visualizations, by for example projecting guides that help to overcome problems which arise through perspective distortion. As the design of projection augmented physical visualizations involves multiple dimensions such as the visualization itself (e.g. material, fabrication), the projection (e.g. position, purpose) and the input modality (e.g. touch, disassemble and reassemble, remote) our early prototype is just a starting point for a more systematic exploration of this fascinating design space. [10]

Activity Sculptures [9]

The *Activity Sculptures* project explored the impact of physical visualizations on running activity. Figure 4 shows four examples how the final sculptures looked like. The sculptures were modular, rewarding each running session with a part of the sculpture. The sculptures had in common that with better performances the size of the single pieces increased. Furthermore the performance influenced their shape, going from an angular and sharp appearance to appearing smoother and in our opinion more aesthetically pleasing. As underlying data standard measurements of running activity such as average speed, duration and distance were used.

Figure 5 offers an overview of the process we used to produce the sculptures. The running data was tracked with a popular mobile tracking application (Endomondo, Runkeeper, Nike+ Running and Runtastic) and saved in the cloud (fig. 5-1). The data was then gathered either through an export on the according website and mail (fig. 5-2a) or by API calls (fig. 5-2b).

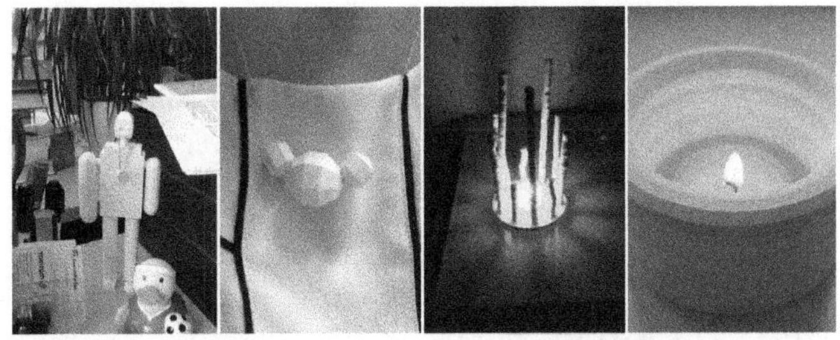

Figure 4. Four Activity Sculptures of running activity: a figure, a necklace, a lamp and a jar [9].

Based on the captured data, a digital version of the sculptures as 3D printable STL files were generated by using web technologies. We then used an Ultimaker Original to 3D print the single parts of the sculptures (fig. 5-3). Each piece of the Activity Sculptures was either handed out in person (fig. 5-4a) or by letter (fig. 5-4b).

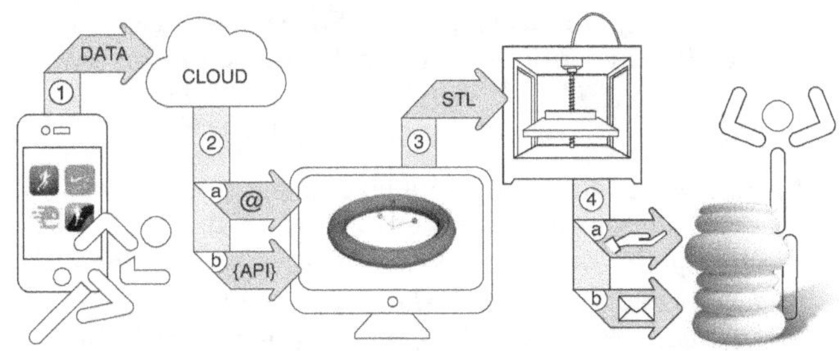

Figure 5. The fabrication pipeline of the Activity Sculptures [9].

A three-week field study with 14 participants with various levels of running activity was conducted. Semi-structured interviews at the beginning and end of the study revealed a great acceptance of the general idea of the Activity Sculptures. Most of the participants were convinced of their ability to improve motivation and self-reflection. We further observed their potential to offer a more creative view at ones activity (playfulness), as participants started to change their running habits in order to impact the shape and aesthetics of the final sculpture pieces.

FUTURE WORK

As the area of personal data representation seems a promising field for the use of physical visualizations we are thinking about a follow-up work on the Activity Sculpture project. One idea is to reward runners of public events such as marathons with physical visualizations. Another one is changing the concept of one sculpture for each person to one sculpture on which more people collaborate, which could be espeically interesting for running teams.

Haptic memory refers to the recollection of data acquired by touch and thus seems to be a promising direction for further research in the area of physical visualizations. We are planning an experiment to compare digital and physical visualizations regarding interpretation accuracy and long-term recall.

We are also working on physical visualizations with more sophisticated mechanical constructions and would like to experiment with non-rigid, elastic parts or even liquids.

REFERENCES

1. Amar, R., Eagan, J., and Stasko, J. Low-level components of analytic activity in information visualization. In *Information Visualization, 2005. INFOVIS 2005. IEEE Symposium on*, IEEE (2005), 111–117.
2. Dragicevic, P., and Jansen, Y. List of physical visualizations. tinyurl.com/physvis, 2013. [Online; accessed 04-Sep-2014].
3. Ishii, H. Tangible bits: Beyond pixels. In *Proceedings of the 2Nd International Conference on Tangible and Embedded Interaction*, TEI '08, ACM (New York, NY, USA, 2008), xv–xxv.
4. Jansen, Y., and Dragicevic, P. An interaction model for visualizations beyond the desktop. *Visualization and Computer Graphics, IEEE Transactions on 19*, 12 (2013), 2396–2405.
5. Jansen, Y., Dragicevic, P., and Fekete, J.-D. Evaluating the efficiency of physical visualizations. In *Proceedings of the SIGCHI Conference on Human Factors in Computing Systems*, ACM (2013), 2593–2602.
6. Stusak, S. Interacting with layered physical visualizations on tabletops. In *Work-In-Progress in conjunction with the 8th ACM Conference on Tangible, Embedded and Embodied Interaction (TEI '14), February 16-19, 2014, Munich, Germany*, TEI '14, ACM (New York, NY, USA, 2014).
7. Stusak, S., and Aslan, A. Beyond physical bar charts: An exploration of designing physical visualizations. In *CHI '14 Extended Abstracts on Human Factors in Computing Systems*, CHI EA '14, ACM (New York, NY, USA, 2014), 1381–1386.
8. Stusak, S., Tabard, A., and Butz, A. Can physical visualizations support analytical tasks? *IEEE Conference on Information Visualization (INFOVIS)* (November 2013).
9. Stusak, S., Tabard, A., Sauka, F., Khot, R. A., and Butz, A. Activity sculptures: Exploring the impact of physical visualizations on running activity. *Visualization and Computer Graphics, IEEE Transactions on 20*, 12 (2014), 2201–2210.
10. Stusak, S., and Teufel, M. Projection augmented physical visualizations. In *Proceedings of the 2Nd ACM Symposium on Spatial User Interaction*, SUI '14, ACM (New York, NY, USA, 2014), 145–145.
11. Vande Moere, A. Beyond the tyranny of the pixel: Exploring the physicality of information visualization. In *Information Visualisation, 2008. IV'08. 12th International Conference*, IEEE (2008), 469–474.
12. Vande Moere, A., and Patel, S. Analyzing the design approaches of physical data sculptures in a design education context. *Visual Information Communications International (VINCI09)* (2009).
13. Zhao, J., and Vande Moere, A. Embodiment in data sculpture: a model of the physical visualization of information. In *Proceedings of the 3rd international conference on Digital Interactive Media in Entertainment and Arts*, ACM (2008), 343–350.
14. Zimmerman, J., Forlizzi, J., and Evenson, S. Research through design as a method for interaction design research in hci. In *Proceedings of the SIGCHI conference on Human factors in computing systems*, ACM (2007), 493–502.

Mediating Group Experiences – Designing the In-Between

Stoffel Kuenen
Umeå Institute of Design
Umeå University, Sweden
christoffel.kuenen@umu.se

ABSTRACT

In this paper I present ongoing design research that explores mediating group experiences. The objective of the paper is to introduce subject matter and design research approach, to provide material for an in depth discussion of challenges.

Several research designs are presented that yield insight in theoretical and conceptual aspects of remote group interactions. Themes emerging from them concern the concept of embodiment, in particular regarding the conceptualization and expression of groups through the mediating system, as well as embodiment of the system for the individual, in the sense of both incorporation and extension of action-perception capacities. To further articulate and express such themes, ongoing and proposed research is presented. Difficulty is brought forward in bringing the various research designs together as one body of work, particularly in relation to theoretical framework, related work and ultimately articulating contributions.

Author Keywords

Crowd interaction; embodiment; mediation; emergent behavior; practice; theory; research through design

ACM Classification Keywords

H.5.2. User Interfaces: Theory and methods. H.5.m. Information interfaces and presentation (e.g., HCI): Miscellaneous

INTRODUCTION

Picture yourself in the middle of a 'Mexican wave' in a sports stadium filled with fans. As you are rising up and throwing your hands in the air, you cannot see the wave itself. The effect of your action combined with those of all around you, can only be seen when viewed from outside. You see the wave on the other side of the stadium. Your individual action, and the actions of others in the crowd, of another scale then the overall behavior, the emergent behavior, of the crowd.

My research concerns the design of technological systems that mediate group interactions. In particular I attempt to bring the dynamics of groups to expression in and through individual interactions with such a medium.

When we shake hands with a person, we have an immediate impression of what that person may be like. That impression comes not just from the sweatiness or firmness of the handshake, also the subtle exchange in the mutual coordination and negotiation of movements is telling.

Many of the interactions we have with remote others are technologically mediated. Such communication media are mostly designed for the intentional exchange of explicit information, in the form of i.e. speech, text, images or video, between two people. Some media also support aspects of our interaction that relate to more subtle, implicit aspects of our interactions and awareness of the presence of others. The rise of the internet and social networking services in particular, enables an exchange of information between groups of people. To some extent participating in such communities makes us aware of the social structures we are part of.

In my work I approach technologically mediated group interactions from the perspective of the kinds of experiences that being part of emergent or behavior, like the 'Mexican wave', brings about. How to design for such interactions to be as rich as shaking hands? What impressions of the crowd and our role in it could we gain?

RELATED WORK

Many people have proposed remote interaction systems intended to offer more embodied ways to engage with others. Some approaches strive for tele-presence by mimicking real world situations through high-bandwidth video systems [23], sometimes in combination with robotic avatars [24]. Others look for expressions and awareness of presence by poetic means [11,21], or tangibly, using haptic force-feedback technology [4]. Some work explicitly explores the influence of bandwidth of the medium on the sense of presence and/or emotional experience of the interaction [2,15].

When it comes to the design of interaction media for large groups, some mediate remote interactions, others augment interactions in collocated groups and crowds.

Online social networks (e.g. Facebook, LinkedIn) and their iterations on mobile devices (e.g. Twitter, Instagram), provide a platform for people to take part in some form of virtual community. Such communities can offer individuals some insight in their position and role in their social context

TEI '15, January 16 - 19 2015, Stanford, CA, USA

ACM 978-1-4503-3305-4/15/01...$15.00
http://dx.doi.org/10.1145/2677199.2691605

[3]. But the largest interest in the design of these media is from research concerning complex systems. Aspects such as network topology and the propagation of information through them have implications for e.g. Internet stability, public health and epidemiology [1,7]. In some cases motivations for studying aspects of design of social media have been questioned [13].

Interfacing large groups of collocated people with computing platforms has been an interest from the perspective of Human Computer Interaction for quite some time. Such settings often consist of an audience or spectator crowd [6,18]. More recently conceptual aspects of such settings for 'crowd computer interactions' [5] are explicitly explored in order to inform the design of other kinds of situations [17,20].

METHODOLOGY

I approach the subject of my research from an experiential rather than an analytical perspective. I build on what is often called practice based research or research through design [8,9,12]. In my practice this means I make iterations of systems that enable multiple people to interact with each other simultaneously. These designs provide platforms for reflection, insights and invention on multiple levels: conceptually, technologically, experientially and theoretically. This kind of design research practice allows for a way of working that is similar to design practice, where the idea of what is being designed co-evolves with the actual expressions of the idea, or in research terms, where the precision of research question (or program) co-evolve by probing possible answers (design spaces). [10,14]. Expected outcomes of this way of working are expressions of what such mediating systems could look, feel and be like, what they could mean, as well as articulation of conceptual and practical aspects that are relevant for design.

GRASPING THE IN-BETWEEN: RESEARCH DESIGNS

Sliders

The first group-mediating system *Sliders*, consists of a number of networked linear actuators (motorfaders). When one person moves a local slider, this is reflected in movements or forces in the other sliders, which in turn can be felt by people interacting with their remote sliders. The topology of the network (what slider influences the position and force of another slider) and the mapping between sliders (how actions on one slider in movement/force of another) are under software control.

The system is inspired by an experiment in mediated interaction from the perspective of social cognition [15]. With that experiment minimal conditions for one person to experience the presence of another is explored.

With *Sliders* an initial finger could be put on what it means to interact with multiple others. It provided conceptual and practical insight in expression of actions of multiple others in a minimal point-of-interaction. It provided insight in and experience with aspects of mediated interactions; conceptually e.g. content completeness (see *Ohlala*) and interaction dynamics; practically e.g. technological aspects of force-feedback (delay, jitter, hysteresis) and networking (topology, propagation).

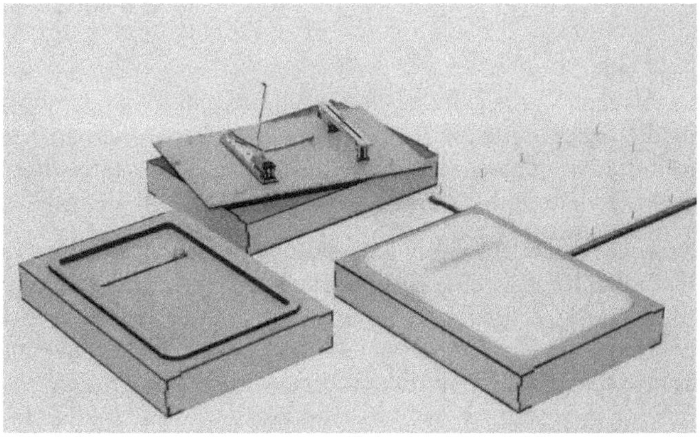

figure 1. *Sliders* in various stages of assembly

Ohlala

Ohlala is an articulation of some insights from *Sliders*. It consists of software on networked computers with which a proposed novel dimension for communication media can be explored, that of content completeness, ranging from non-content to hyper-content. It is an interaction system where the symmetry and richness of the connection can be varied by the introduction of Transformative Behaviors (mappings) in the mutual influence of the two "loci of interaction". Thus it allows exploration of the influence of the mapping, thus of the content completeness dimension, on the (emotional) experience of the interaction [16].

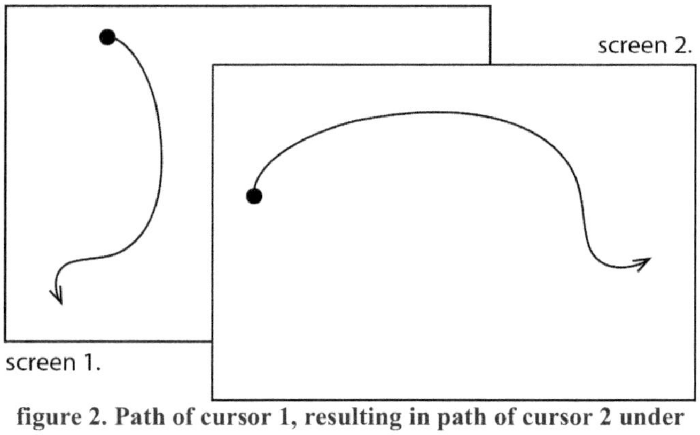

figure 2. Path of cursor 1, resulting in path of cursor 2 under Transformative Behavior (Rotate and Scale).

DiffractMe!

DiffractMe! consists of an array of movable, light-diffracting elements (prisms) networked with two actuated interaction surfaces that swivel around one axis. When one person moves the local surface, the other surface follows as well as some of the light-diffracting elements, causing a rippling effect in the array [22]. *DiffractMe!* provides for an interaction space that is richer than *Sliders* and *Ohlala*. It is the result of a design process explicitly exploring the design of interaction qualities in relation to the kinds of dynamics of the interaction process [19].

With this prototype concepts of representation and expressiveness of people's actions are explored, articulating the concept of embodiment of joint action.

figure 3. First Iteration of *DiffractMe!* installation.

OPEN RESEARCH QUESTIONS

The research designs discussed so far have realized some form of group interactions. They begin to reveal what interacting with multiple others could feel like. They provide handles on practical and conceptual aspects of such systems.

Of particular interest in my project is the way a group or crowd is conceptualized, e.g. is the crowd seen as an entity with overall behavior or a number of individuals and collection of (inter-)actions? Such conceptualization comes to expression in the way the crowd *is embodied* in the system design, and -reciprocally and inherently- how an individual *feels embodied* in the system. Practically this concerns the presentation or expression of the aggregated, collection of individual actions at the point of interaction. At the same time it concerns the qualities of interaction an individual experiences at that point of interaction. A central concept therefore is *embodiment*, in the basic sense of how something is given physical form, but also with its phenomenological connotations from cognitive science, perception theory and HCI and TEI; It concerns the intertwining of: embodiment of the crowd (dynamics); embodiment of the individual (actions) in the system; and embodiment of the system by an individual in the sense of incorporation and of extension of the body's action-perception capacities.

ONGOING AND FUTURE WORK

Sliders, *Ohlala* and *DiffractMe!* focus on aspects somehow close to the individual and of a rather minimalist form. In ongoing and future research designs, I will explore and unpack embodiment: as a theoretical concept, which has an immaterial, cognitive science ring to it; but also in a very real, physical sense, as us having a body of flesh, mass and volume in our social environments.

So far interactions between few more than two people were mediated. Large groups or crowds give rise to other kinds of dynamics and emergent behaviors. Further explorations are of forms where large numbers of people can be engaged with more easily. One opportunity lies with mobile computing platforms and another with groups of people gathered for other purposes, e.g. sports events, concerts, conferences or raves.

Spots

The initial -pilot- version of *Spots* allows people to experience a sense of mutual touch through a mobile phone. In its most simple version, a person using *Spots* experiences a vibration when the location of her finger on the screen overlaps with the touching-location of a finger of a remote person using *Spots*. The touching actions leave fading traces on the screen, locally as well as remotely.

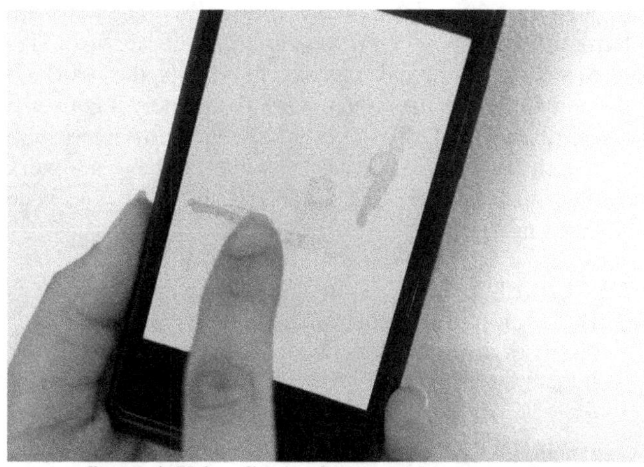

figure 4. Using *Spots* with several remote others.

Spots is easily scaled for interactions between more people. It allows for quick iterations and variations of how the touch-activity of one person is mapped to that of many others and vise versa, i.e. explorations of individual and crowd embodiment as discussed previously. *Spots* will allow exploration of the concept of mediated physicality and the illusion of body through such meagerly tangible devices as touchscreen-computers. For theoretical grounding collaboration is sought with researchers in the field of situated and embodied cognition, psychology and sociology.

Mirror

For a situation where a large number of people are gathered in the same place, I am currently developing the technology of *Mirror*. This design consists of a camera aimed at the crowd and a projected image presented to the people of the crowd. The image presented can be a filtered version of the camera's view or (combined with) dynamic imagery generated based computational processing of the camera image.

Mirror allows exploration of such concepts as 1st and 3rd person perspective on the crowd experience, inside/outside, identifiability of an individuals' action in relation to the overall dynamic. Another line of inquiry concerns self-organization and crowd-intelligence; this exploration involves initial repetition of similar experiments performed by others, which consequently will be redesigned iteratively.

CONCLUDING REMARKS

In this paper I have discussed the physical objects and theoretical and conceptual reflections I work with. I have briefly introduced the approach I take to this work. Central themes begin to emerge from the research and I have begun to formulate open research questions, or program, and proposed research designs for probing those.

A challenge posed in my way of working is how to bring together the first set of research designs and the next. The way my research designs are presented together will determine in what light my research can be viewed. This concerns the theoretical context in which the work is presented as well as the related work. Ultimately it concerns the contributions of this work to the field of interaction design and TEI. It is in such aspects that I believe my work provides material for discussion at the TEI Graduate Student Consortium.

REFERENCES

1. Barabási, A.-L., Gulbahce, N., and Loscalzo, J. Network medicine: a network-based approach to human disease. *Nature reviews. Genetics 12*, 1 (2011), 56–68.
2. Bihan, G. Le, Lenay, C., Tixier, M., and Mara, J. Touch through: experiencing remote touch across different modalities. *Extended Abstracts CHI'13*, ACM Press (2013),1629–1634.
3. Borovoy, R., Martin, F., Vemuri, S., Resnick, M., Silverman, B., and Hancock, C. Meme tags and community mirrors. *Proceedings CSCW '98*, ACM Press (1998), 159–168.
4. Brave, S. and Dahley, A. *inTouch: A Medium for Haptic Interpersonal Communication.* Extended abstracts CHI'97, ACM Press (1997), 363.
5. Brown, B., O'Hara, K., Kindberg, T., and Williams, A. Crowd computer interaction. *Extended abstracts CHI '09*, ACM Press (2009), 4755.
6. Feldmeier, M. and Paradiso, J.A. Giveaway wireless sensors for large-group interaction. *Extended abstracts CHI '04*, ACM Press (2004), 1291.
7. Fowler, J.H. and Christakis, N.A. Dynamic spread of happiness in a large social network: longitudinal analysis over 20 years in the Framingham Heart Study. *Bmj*, (2008).
8. Frayling, C. Research in Art and Design. In *RCA research papers Volume 1*. 1993.
9. Frens, J. and Hengeveld, B. To Make Is To Grasp. Proceedings of *IASDR'13*, (2013), 1–8.
10. Hallnäs, L. and Redström, J. *Interaction Design: foundations, experiments.* Textile Research Centre, Swedish School of Textiles, Unversity College of Borås and Interactive Institute, Borås, Sweden, 2006.
11. Hausen, D., Boring, S., and Lueling, C. StaTube: facilitating state management in instant messaging systems. *Proceedings of TEI'12* (2012), 283–290.
12. Koskinen, I., Binder, T., and Redström, J. Lab, Field, Gallery, and Beyond. *Artifact 2*, 1 (2008), 46–57.
13. Kramer, A.D.I., Guillory, J.E., and Hancock, J.T. Experimental evidence of massive-scale emotional contagion through social networks. *PNAS*, (2014): 201320040
14. Kuenen, C. and Redström, J. The wickedness of design research practices: Methodological issues in bringing knowledge to expression through design. *Proceeding of IASDR'13*, (2013), 1–10.
15. Lenay, C. " It's So Touching ": Emotional Value in Distal Contact. *International Journal of Design 4*, 2 (2010), 15–25.
16. Levy, P., Kuenen, S., Overbeeke, C.J., Uchiyama, T., and Yamanaka, T. Ohlala: Content-completeness, Communication and Emotional Experience. *proceeding of IASDR'11*, Delft University of Technology (2011), 323–326.
17. Ludvigsen, M. and Veerasawmy, R. Designing technology for active spectator experiences at sporting events. *Proceedings of OZCHI '10*, ACM Press (2010), 96.
18. Maynes-Aminzade, D., Pausch, R., and Seitz, S. Techniques for interactive audience participation. *Proceedings. Fourth IEEE International Conference on Multimodal Interfaces*, IEEE Comput. Soc (1994), 15–20.
19. Peeters, J., Kuenen, S., Trotto, A., and Hummels, C. Diffract Me!–Using a Skills-Based Approach in Design Practice. *KEER2014*, (2014).
20. Reeves, S., Sherwood, S., and Brown, B. Designing for crowds. *Proceedings of the 6th Nordic Conference on Human-Computer Interaction: Extending Boundaries*, ACM (2010), 393–402.
21. Strong, R. and Gaver, W.W. Feather, Scent, and Shaker: Supporting Simple Intimacy. *Proceedings of CSCW*, (1996), 29–30.

Exploring Effects of Full-body Control in Perspective-based Learning in an Interactive Museum Data Display

Jessica Roberts
University of Illinois-Chicago
1240 W. Harrison St. Ste 1570, Chicago, IL 60607
jrober31@uic.edu

ABSTRACT
Many factors are known to mediate museum visitors' learning during their interactions with exhibits, including designed elements of the exhibit itself, the other visitors present in the space, and visitors' own backgrounds and prior knowledge. Research indicates that learners' use of a first-person *Actor* perspective may confer agency to the learner and allow him to more easily reason about otherwise abstract concepts. Our preliminary research shows that full-body interaction with museum exhibits (specifically, an exhibit presenting a rich interactive data visualization), seems to promote both perspective-taking and improved data reasoning. This research builds on that work to clarify the affordances of perspective taking in mediating learning in this environment by comparing two methods of control of the interactive exhibit – full-body and handheld – in order to understand how each condition can support perspective taking and data reasoning.

Author Keywords
Museums; interactive technology; data visualization; perspective taking

ACM Classification Keywords
K.3.1 [**Computers and Education**]: Computer uses in Education – *collaborative learning*

General Terms
Human Factors; Design;

INTRODUCTION
As complex data sets are increasingly the product of modern science, museums are seeking ways of displaying them in engaging ways, often through visualizations. These visualizations help present the data, but even familiar representations (for example, data maps) can be difficult for visitors who may not be able to make connections between their prior knowledge and the data being displayed. Technology-based exhibits have great potential to scaffold these connections for users by customizing the experience: if visitors can select aspects of a dataset that are relevant or interesting to them and then dynamically control the visualization of those data subsets, they may be able to see the exhibit as representing "them." This shift in perspective – helping visitors "be" the data – can grant agency to the visitors, allowing them to reason about otherwise abstract data from the viewpoint of their own lived experiences.

The *CoCensus* exhibit studied here (See Figure 1) seeks to encourage reasoning about the spatial, temporal, and quantitative properties of the data through a customizable, interactive multi-user exhibit. Visitors first answer four questions from the U.S. census on a kiosk and then view a large display depicting a scaled centroid ("bubble") map showing the number of people in the local geography (New York City) who answered each question the same way as the visitor. Multiple visitors can interact simultaneously to change the decade of data being viewed, the aggregation level of the data (census tract, borough, or city-wide), and which question is being viewed. Each visitor can control the visualization of his or her own unique dataset, allowing users to look at their own data in isolation or in comparison to that of their co-visitor.

Figure 1. Students interacting with the CoCensus exhibit

One means of distributing control to multiple simultaneous users is through *full-body control* in which users move and

TEI '15, January 16 - 19 2015, Stanford, CA, USA

ACM 978-1-4503-3305-4/15/01...$15.00
http://dx.doi.org/10.1145/2677199.2691606

gesture in order to manipulate the visualization. This novel mode of interaction is appealing to social, informal learning environments like museums, where it can engage participating visitors as well as spectators. The effects of such control on learning, however, are not yet well understood and are the subject of this research. Our prior research suggests that embodied control may have an effect on the *perspectives* users bring to their interactions with data – in particular, that by situating the control of the visualization within the physical body of the users, they are more likely to adopt a first-person *Actor* perspective towards the data they control, which may in turn affect how users reason about the data. This research proposes to examine these putative connections.

BACKGROUND

This research views learning as a form of *mediated action,* which places focus not on individual cognition but on the interactions among the learners, the learning context, and the tools simultaneously [20, 18]. Using a mediated action perspective assumes that visitors' learning is mediated not only by the exhibit, but also by the other learners in the space and the interactions among them; collaboration and social interactions are key components of the museum learning experience, and learning is socially-facilitated [12].

Mediated Action and Cultural Tools

To study learning as a mediated activity, one must attend to the cultural tools mediating the interactions. Wertsch [20] provides a range of examples of what can be considered cultural tools, from the pole in pole-vaulting (what [19] would call a "technical tool"), to the vertical syntax of multiplication problems (a "psychological tool"). Wertsch explains that a multiplication problem (e.g. 343 x 822) is easier for most people to solve when the numbers are written vertically than horizontally, because the familiar vertical syntax is itself doing some of the "thinking," thus mediating the problem-solving activity [20].

In this research I view perspective taking — the act of positioning oneself in a particular viewpoint relative to the data being interpreted — as a cultural tool similar to that of the mathematical syntax. Each different perspective has unique affordances for data interpretation and can mediate the sensemaking experience differently.

Perspective Taking and Learning

This research is concerned with two perspectives that can be taken by visitors during their interactions: *Actor* and *Onlooker* [1]. If a visitor sees himself and his co-visitors as represented in the data, he may demonstrate the connection by using first and second person pronouns when talking about the data, for example saying, "You're along the Lake and I'm not." This phrasing suggests he is positioning himself as an *Actor* in the scene. By contrast, a visitor who does not experience such a connection might adopt an *Onlooker* perspective and use exclusively third-person pronouns, in statements such as, "They are all spread out."

Perspective and its effects on learning and cognition have been studied in a variety of contexts. The spontaneous use of first person pronouns to describe external phenomena has been observed in physicists discussing particles [14] and in students working to understand friction in a classroom [5], and the resulting perspectives "created a qualitatively different set of resources from which to reason and were found to be productive in model and theory building" [5]. Lindgren [10, 11] has found that the perspective taken by a learner can affect the learning processes taking place during an activity and that the design of a simulated environment can influence this perspective. The research presented here examines how "being the data" by invoking the *Actor* perspective may impact visitors' reasoning and investigates the affordances of two control conditions in facilitating this perspective taking.

PILOT ANALYSES

Research around the CoCensus exhibit has examined embodied allegories for control of the display [3], visitors' use of space in collaborative exploration of the display [16], embodied metaphors for visitor control [17], and design considerations for the visualization [15, 4]. Two of those studies [16, 17] have explored the emergent phenomenon of perspective taking. Upon incorporation of distributed individual control of the visualization, compared to preliminary testing of a non-interactive prototype [15], some visitors were found to spontaneously adopt the first-person *Actor* perspective when discussing the data display [16]. Interestingly, the use of this *Actor* perspective occurred in conjunction with visitors' body-based control movements within the interaction area, and the pair of visitors demonstrating the highest frequency of *Actor* perspective taking were highly engaged in the data interpretation, making inferences about populations and posing questions about relationships between their data sets over time [16].

The phenomenon of perspective taking was further explored in [17] within a study comparing two embodied metaphors for control of a timeline dictating the decade of data being displayed in the exhibit. Naturalistic interactions of pairs of children visiting the museum were recorded in order to analyze the affordances of each with respect to data interpretation and collaborative meaning making. One facet of the dialogue analysis was visitors' use of perspective and its relation to data interpretation remarks. In both conditions, a significant positive correlation between an individual's use of the *Actor* perspective and his or her frequency of data reasoning remarks was found [17].

RESEARCH QUESTIONS AND FOCUS

In combination, these two analyses suggest there may be a meaningful relationship between perspective taking, embodied control, and meaning making, but several key questions remain unanswered. Specifically, the data interpretation statements analyzed in [17] attended to the type of interpretive statements made by visitors, but did not take into consideration differences in the quality and complexity of those statements: a surface-level, descriptive statement was treated as equal to a rich inference. In order to understand how perspective taking may have mediated their reasoning, a more nuanced analysis of the dialogue is necessary. Furthermore, though occurrences of the *Actor* perspective only manifested after the full-body control was implemented, we cannot conclude whether the full-body nature of the control instigated this change or whether any kind of dynamic control – embodied or not – would show similar results with respect to both perspective taking and data reasoning. This shortcoming can be addressed by comparing two interaction conditions: *full-body control* in which the display reacts to visitors' movements and *handheld control* in which visitors each use an individual handheld device to manipulate the display. Thus my ongoing research investigates the following questions:

1. Across both conditions, what are the affordances of perspective taking for mediating visitors' collaborative reasoning about interactive data representations?
2. How does means of control – full-body versus handheld – impact visitors' data reasoning remarks, interactions, and use of perspective?

METHODS

This study will be conducted *in situ* at a mid-sized urban hands-on science center and include groups of museum visitors engaging in naturalistic interactions with one of two versions of the *CoCensus* exhibit. In one version, a motion tracking system consisting of RFID antennae and a Kinect camera will allow visitors to manipulate the decade of data being displayed by stepping into marked areas on the floor [2] and the category and aggregation levels through gestures. An alternative version will let each user perform the same manipulations through a handheld controller. This comparison will show whether the full-body control is facilitating perspective taking and/or data reasoning among visitors, or whether these phenomena occur around the exhibit regardless of control type.

Analysis of perspective taking will follow the framework utilized by [16, 17] analyzing dialogue to ascertain visitors' perspectives. Data reasoning analysis will draw upon graph interpretation literature in order to frame three kinds of behaviors involved in graph comprehension: translation, interpretation, and extrapolation [7]. In the context of a data map display, *translation* statements include instances of a user simply describing or restating what is shown on the display, i.e. using words to translate what the map is "saying." *Interpretation* statements go beyond translation to recognize patterns and relationships present in the data, requiring the use of more than one piece of information, for example comparing two pieces of data or two geographic locations. *Extrapolation* statements go even further and integrate data from the display with outside knowledge in order to pose inferences, questions, and hypotheses. Preliminary analysis of transcripts from earlier studies on *CoCensus* indicates that these three categories adequately capture the types of statements made by visitors during their interactions.

ANTICIPATED OUTCOMES

Situating control in multiple users' bodies through movements and gestures has the potential to engage multiple participants [9] as well as bystanders, who get direct visual access to the state of the data set and control actions, creating a shared learning experience [13]. However, a lack of familiarity with novel interaction techniques can result in an inability to map the locus of the interaction (i.e. the user's body, doing a gesture or movement) with the focus (the screen, enacting an effect) [3], making it difficult or frustrating to engage meaningfully with the content. A handheld controller with a familiar interface (e.g. buttons) mitigates these challenges but reduces the physical engagement of the participants and concurrently relegates bystanders to the periphery [8]. Both conditions, therefore, have inherent affordances and challenges. I predict that the full-body control condition will allow visitors to actively "be" the data and will therefore result in more usage of the *Actor* perspective than the handheld condition, thanks to the physical connection between the locus and focus of interaction. Furthermore, because of the active, engaging, and visible nature of the embodied condition, I anticipate more dialogue among visitors (both participants and bystanders) in this condition compared to the handheld condition. However, after controlling for perspective taking, I have no reason to anticipate significant differences between the two conditions in frequencies of deep reasoning statements (*interpretation* and *extrapolation* remarks).

This research also addresses the relationship between perspective taking and reasoning. Prior work indicates that an actor perspective may have value for comprehension [5, 14] and performance on procedural tasks [10, 12] and in simulations [11]. Lindgren [11] suggests that a first person or actor perspective may be valuable in learning tasks when that perspective affords a particular point of view that provides an advantage for completing the task, for example giving a novice the opportunity to "see" like an expert. I predict that the advantage of such a perspective in this case is the ability to help a visitor connect with the data, because rather than looking at abstract representations, the visitor is seeing "himself." This connection provides an access point to the complex data and may confer agency to the visitor, allowing him to talk about himself rather than an abstract population. Thus, I anticipate that the *Actor* perspective will be associated with deeper reasoning statements, both at the individual level for those visitors directly utilizing this perspective and for the entire group in the interaction in which the *Actor* perspective is used. The frequency of *translation* statements is unlikely to vary significantly regardless of perspective taking, but I anticipate a higher occurrence of *interpretation* and *extrapolation* statements in conjunction with *Actor* perspective taking.

SIGNIFICANCE

As advances in motion-sensing technology proliferate, museums are presented with unique opportunities to engage visitors through motion rather than more traditional inputs. However, the impacts of this novel mode of interaction on learning are currently not well understood. By comparing an embodied control condition with a more traditional handheld control experience, this research can parse out effects, both positive and negative, of full-body control on visitors' dialogue and interactions. Analysis of data reasoning statements will illuminate the affordances of each condition – and potential differences between the two – in mediating learning talk. Understanding how perspective taking manifests in the dialogue will contribute to theories of the role of perspective in mediating learning, including how it can be harnessed to engage users in deeper engagement with data. Findings will benefit interaction designers as well as docents and teachers seeking to facilitate learning in similar contexts. In combination, the research questions addressed here can contribute to an understanding of how interaction design can better aid learners in interpreting and reasoning about complex data sets in both formal and informal environments.

ACKNOWLEDGMENTS

This material is based upon work supported by the National Science Foundation under NSF INSPIRE 1248052.

REFERENCES

1. Brunyé, T. T., Ditman, T., Mahoney, C. R., Augustyn, J. S., & Taylor, H. A. When you and I share perspectives pronouns modulate perspective taking during narrative comprehension. *Psychological Science, 20*(1), (2009), 27-32.
2. Cafaro, F., Panella, A., Lyons, L., Roberts, J., & Radinsky, J. I See You There! Developing Identity-Preserving Embodied Interaction for Museum Exhibits. In *Proc CHI 2013*, ACM Press (2013), 1911-1920.
3. Cafaro, F., Lyons, L., Radinsky, J., Roberts, J., Kang, R., Vogt, K. Framed Guessability: Using Embodied Allegories to Increase User Agreement on Gesture Sets. In *Proc TEI 2014*. (2014), 197-204.
4. Cafaro, F., Lyons, L., Roberts, J., & Radinsky, J. The uncanny valley of embodied interaction design. In *Proc DIS 2014* (pp. 1075-1078). ACM.
5. Enyedy, N., Danish, J. A., DeLiema, D. Constructing and Deconstructing Materially-Anchored Conceptual Blends in an Augmented Reality Collaborative Learning Environment. *In Proc CSCL2013*. (2013)
6. Falk, J. H., & Dierking, L. D. Learning from museums: Visitor experiences and the making of meaning. Altamira Press, 2000.
7. Friel, S., Curcio, F., & Bright, G. Making sense of graphs: Critical factors influencing comprehension and instructional implications. *Journal for Research in Mathematics Education*, *32*(2), (2001), 124-158.
8. Heath, C., & Vom Lehn, D. Configuring 'Interactivity:' Enhancing Engagement in Science Centres and Museums.Social Studies of Science,38(1), 2008, 63-91.
9. Hornecker, E. The role of physicality in tangible and embodied interactions. *Interactions*,*18*(2), 2011, 19-23.
10. Lindgren, R. Perspective-Based Learning in Virtual Environments. ProQuest LLC. 789 East Eisenhower Parkway, PO Box 1346, Ann Arbor, MI 48106, (2009).
11. Lindgren, R. Generating a learning stance through perspective-taking in a virtual environment. *Computers in Human Behavior*, *28*(4), (2012), 1130-1139.
12. Lozano, S. C, Hard, B. M., & Tversky, B. Perspective taking promotes action understanding and learning. Journal of Experimental Psychology: Human Perception and Performance, 32(6), (2006), 1405-1421.
13. Lyons, L., and Roberts, J. Scaffolding Collaborative Interpretation of Data in a Museum Exhibit. In Leilah Lyons (chair) Synergistic Scaffolding of Technologically-enhanced STEM Learning in Informal Institutions. Symposium conducted at ICLS 2014.
14. Ochs, E., Gonzales, P., & Jacoby, S. "When I come down I'm in the domain state": grammar and graphic representation in the interpretive activity of physicists. *Studies in Interactional Sociolinguistics*, *13*, (1996). 328-369,
15. Roberts, J., Lyons, L., Radinsky, J., Cafaro, F. *Connecting Visitors to Exhibits through Design: Exploring United States census data with CoCensus. In Proc ICLS 2012*. (2012).
16. Roberts, J., Cafaro, C., Kang, R., Vogt, K., Lyons, L., & Radinsky, J. That's Me and That's You: Museum visitors' perspective-taking around an embodied interaction data map display. In *CSCL 2013*. (2013), 343-344.
17. Roberts, J., Lyons, L., Cafaro, F., Eydt, R. Interpreting Data from Within: Supporting Human-Data Interaction in Museum Exhibits Through Personalization. *In Proc IDC 2014* (2014).
18. Rowe, S. and Bachman, J. "Mediated action as a framework for exploring learning in informal settings." In *Putting Theory into Practice*, pp. 143-162. SensePublishers, (2012).
19. Vygotsky, Lev S. "The collected works of LS Vygotsky. Vol. 1." (1987).
20. Wertsch, J. V. Mind as action Oxford University Press, USA. (1998).

Designing the "Things" of the IoT

Tom Jenkins
Georgia Institute of Technology
Digital Media Program
Atlanta, GA 30332, USA
tom.jenkins@gatech.edu

ABSTRACT

Building objects that question implicit assumptions of common systems can help to reframe technological artifacts. This work builds on an inexpensive prototyping platform that augments everyday objects in minimal ways as an early move towards engaging with the Internet of Things as a site for contestation in interaction design. These intend to account for a broader understanding of design as generating political objects—design things—that draw from the work of Bruno Latour and Studio Atelier. Finally, it introduces the concept of *object ecologies* as a way to both analyze existing ecosystems of design objects and generate new, speculative ones.

Author Keywords

Prototyping; Internet of Things; IoT; design; ecology

ACM Classification Keywords

H.5.2 [Information Interfaces and Presentation]: User Interfaces—prototyping; J.5 [Art and Humanities]—design

BACKGROUND

I'm a PhD student in Digital Media at Georgia Tech's School of Literature, Media, and Communication. My research interests focus on developing systems that explore different kinds of interactions with technology, attempting to create systems that are themselves ideological and that support particular kinds of aesthetic perspectives illustrating alternative values to existing, corporatist technological practices.

My approach to critical technical practice draws from three research contexts. First, Science and Technology Studies offer a historical, textual approach to understanding how meanings and uses of technologies are constructed socially. Broadly speaking, the framework that guides my research can be called *Critical Technical Practice* [1]. A critical technical practice operates simultaneously in two spheres: on the one hand producing technical work, but on the other taking that work and treating it as both a subject for criticism as well as a site for larger cultural critique. Building devices to up-end traditional understandings of device-making engages traditional engineering and art practice to produce real, functional objects: it attempts to transcend what's out there and postulates provocative new ways to get things done. At the same time, the assessment aspect of critical technical practice, where critical theory meets evaluation, hermeneutical implication, and personal experience, can be understood as a period of interpretation that informs later production.

TEI '15, January 16 - 19 2015, Stanford, CA, USA

ACM 978-1-4503-3305-4/15/01...$15.00
http://dx.doi.org/10.1145/2677199.2691608

PROTOTYPING THE INTERNET OF THINGS

"The Internet of Things" describes a trend advocating that all sorts of physical artifacts become connected to and controllable from the Internet. According to this vision, a coffeepot might be controlled alongside a thermostat to have a home warm and the coffee on when a person wakes up; or sensors in the basement might email you if your basement is flooding. While this all seems very sanguine, current IoT technologies rely on centralized servers, well-defined APIs, and black-boxed electronics for the end-user, and are built only to be used in specific, condoned ways.

My project is to develop small, low cost, low-power, prototyping platforms to try to solve problems in everyday life. These systems offer very little: they have four bits of input and output, no analog capability, and must be programmed in assembly. While the assumption might be that these devices are hard to use, the simplicity of the chip and its low capability means that for any number of applications, a solution can be cobbled together quickly: has the mail been delivered? Do I need to cut my lawn? Is there a slot available at that bike rack? Unlike more complicated and expensive platforms like the Raspberry Pi and the Arduino (each approximately 7-10 times more costly than the current system), this prototyping platform is built to explore the possibilities, both aesthetic and prosaic, of ubiquitous minimalist computing.

The Internet of Things without the Internet

I'm using these prototypes begin to sketch out an alternative vision of the Internet of Things. This IoT is bottom-up rather than centrally controlled; it emphasizing material/computational/ human collaboration rather than the parameterization of the everyday world from a central authority, and most notably, does not require the Internet. I intend to construct devices for small-scale, human-

Figure 1. The minimalist prototyping platform with a variety of sensors for prototyping.

evaluated interactions between things; or more complicated, communication-driven emergent interactions that still requires humans for assessment. In these concepts, the system's output stays *in situ*, and people around them draw any relevant conclusions for themselves.

The lower cost that comes with using very simple hardware is a huge benefit. It becomes much more feasible to create many different kinds of smart things, with little regard to whether adding a microcontroller to something makes sense in the short term. It will be possible to build infrastructure-less sensing devices that become cheap, ubiquitous, computational material objects—from a spoon that tells you when your soup is cool enough to consume, to postboxes that make it clear the letter carrier has been by. At that point, we will find ourselves in a situation where the experiences that everyday objects have are translated only partially to the language of the observer.

While prototyping, I've had to take a new look at how people live: what simple, measurable opportunities exist that could become a site for intervention or problem solving. To that end, one unforeseen outcome of developing a platform like this is enforcing a kind of "algorithmic lifestyle" on a prospective user. This has led to a set of research questions around constructing a speculative IoT: What parts of experience can be offloaded into a device? How can we support novelty, play, and other kinds of emergent aesthetic experiences while also supporting effective, useful applications and allowing for satisfying material interactions?

INTERACTION DESIGN AS A PLACE FOR THINGS

Postulating these new kinds of socio-technical "things" has always been a part of design generally, but also of computing specifically. Computational artifacts provide an opportunity to produce objects that also serve as rhetoric, imagining new kinds of participation for both people and artifacts. As an example, Julian Bleeker's concept of *Design Fiction* moves towards postulating entire social spheres of interactive objects that have a point of view: "This is a different genre of design. Not realism, but a genre that is forward looking, beyond incremental and makes an effort to explore new kinds of social interaction rituals. As much as science fact tells you what is and is not possible, design fiction understands constraints differently. Design fiction is about creative provocation, raising questions, innovation, and exploration" [3]. The critical design of Tony Dunne and Fiona Raby offers another example of the design space creating speculative technological futures. In their work, they create devices and systems that emphasize the nature value-laden objects, running the gamut from electronic objects in a home that as a whole seek to protect the residents from the hypothetical dangers of electronic waves [7] to manifests for speculative design objects that interrogate complex, and frequently negative, emotional spaces [5,6].

Bill Gaver has also been producing work that could be called a part of the Internet of Things, even if many of the systems predate common use of the term. The *Home Health Horoscope*, for example, was built to be a "smart home" system, but without representational understandings of its users [9]. Instead of sensing residents and trying to predict their needs, the *Home Health Horoscope* kept a "fuzzy" understanding of what was happening around it. Every morning, residents of the house where it was installed would receive a slip of thermoprinted paper—a horoscope for that day generated from a suite of sensors placed around the house to try to assess emotional valences: whether the medicine cabinet had been opened could indicate that someone was feeling ill, more pressure sensors on the couch being active might represent a homeowner entertaining.

At a larger scale, the *Presence Project* [15] was a project to increase awareness of an elderly population in a housing project called the Bjilmer, in the Netherlands. While perhaps best known in the HCI community as the origin of the popular cultural probes method [8], the *Presence Project* produced a workbook of proposed environmental technologies as well as a set of working prototypes. These include "slogan furniture," such as bus benches that display snippets of emotionally charged text and curated images from the elderly into the broader public sphere of the Bijlmer.

Finally, the useful qualities of ubiquitous computing as a design discipline have been evident across material boundaries, inviting new kinds of perspectives and collaborations between things and people. Kuznetsov et al, for example, have made an effort to understand the nature of the thing as a means of creating public engagement through their work in urban settings. In *Participatory sensing in public spaces: activating urban surfaces with sensor probes* [13], small, nonfunctioning "sensor objects" are distributed to various publics, including young parents, the homeless, and bicycle enthusiasts enlisting them to place smog sensors, or bio-hazard sensors on objects in their everyday experience. What and how these populations chose to instrument emphasizes particular values that they have, illustrating matters that concern them, and especially the differences between groups, even from the same sensor object. Similarly, in *Ceci n'est pas une pipe bombe: authoring urban landscapes with air quality sensors* [12], these same communities were given real sensor packages outfitted with GPS monitoring to track how and where they were placed, creating a map of social interests as well as serving to create a feeling of public participation in a conversation around air quality.

All of these objects, social interests, plant material, sensors, elderly shut-ins, vague feelings around health practices, guilt, joy of hobbies, and so on are intrinsically parts of their respective systems, but are not usually well accounted for in system design. One way of beginning to take this broad variety of objects and values into account in HCI research in general and interaction design research in particular is to consider these kinds of complex relationships as being *things*.

DESIGN AND AN EMPHASIS ON THE THING

The "thing" is one way that designers and theorists have contemplated the role of objects in sociotechnical systems. At its roots, the "thing" comes from the term *ding*, an ancient Germanic word for particular kinds of gatherings. As described by Heidegger in [11]:

...the Old High German word thing means a gathering, and specifically a gathering to deliberate on a matter under discussion, a contested matter. In consequence, the Old German words 'thing' and 'ding' become the names for an affair or matter of pertinence. They denote anything that in any way hears upon men, concerns them, and that accordingly is a matter for discourse.

This understanding of things as a shift from an object in space to a site for contested political action is expanded by Bruno Latour in *From Realpolitik to Dingpolitik* [16]. This is Latour's proposal of thing-centered or "object oriented" democracy. This "tentative set of experiments" is constructed not to define fully define what an object-oriented view of politics actually is, but rather, to consider the kind of attributes that a politics that takes the perspectives of objects into account would have. In the early 21st century, Latour believes, it has become clear that the enlightenment model of political activity based on some sort of commonly understood mutual goal and founded upon an agreed-upon set of facts is no longer taking place, if it ever was. Instead, he wants to take political actions *as they are*, and rather than some sanitized narrative of consensus-building, examine the messy nature of alliances and allegiances based around particular situated values. "We might be more connected to each other by our worries, our matters of concern, the issues we care for, than by any other set of values, opinions, attitudes, or principles." To Latour, objects become battlegrounds for differing perspectives on matters of concern: "*every one of these objects, you see spewing out of them a different set of passions, indignations, opinions, as well as a different set of interested parties and different ways of carrying out their partial resolution.*"

To Latour, the concept of an issue and an object get mixed together in a productive way: objects are issues that have enlisted actants that care about them. Beyond simple, objective statements that can be demonstrably true or demonstrably false, political decision-making is dependent on contested realities, as multiple perspectives on objects can be debated, discussed, and brought to closure. These contested objects are things in themselves, in that they are materialized issues that simultaneously embody multiple political perspectives; but are also the locus of another kind of assembly for those who have a vested interest in that thing. The thing becomes a site for contestation as well as a representation of a perspective on the issue. In the case of the *Home Health Horoscope*, for example, its vagueness as a device that had been designed to create reflection provides tension by subverting expectations around how and what "smart home" devices should do. Refusing to be straightforwardly understandable places the system at the center of an ongoing process of contextual interpretation and shifting reinterpretation.

Latour also emphasizes how the political contestation inherent to things is distinct from governance. Traditional political action takes place exclusively in capitol buildings or parliamentary houses, defining useful political behaviors as being those that lead to resolutions, laws, and other kinds of legal structures. This object-centered political action takes a different tack. "Procedures to authorize and legitimize are important, but it's only half of what is needed to assemble. The other half lies in the issues themselves, the *matters* that matter, in the *res* that creates a public around it. They need to be represented, authorized, legitimated, and brought to bear inside the relevant assembly." This "being brought to bear" is what takes place in *Ceci n'est pas une pipe bombe*, described above. In encouraging different stakeholders to engage with the terrain of the city through installing sensor packages in sanctioned and un-sanctioned ways, the packages themselves become the site of contestation for thinking about air quality. Authoring the city with devices that make claims about Latour considers the political engagement of things as a primary motivator for objects taking a place in political dialogue. These objects become the "things" that do work'—in some ways implicitly: they operate through organizing and assembling actants into dialogs around contested issues.

Studio Atelier have taken this framing of thing as an assemblage to flesh out the idea of a *design thing*, a designed object that enacts multiple roles in the context of the process of design [2]. Unlike design projects which have well defined boundaries, design things are messy, supporting many different values and viewpoints. Borrowing from Latour the concept of actants working inside a network [14], the design thing "aligns humans and nonhuman resources into to move the object of design forward, to support the emergence, translation, and performance" of the design object through "participation, intervention, and performance in this sociotechnical thing."

As with Latour, Studio Atelier recognises the ability of the object to align various interests. To them, the object of design becomes a point of contention and contestation between many different factions. On the one hand, the design object is part of a lasting record of process: the designers build into the object a history of decisions and compromises. At the same time, the designed object is still an active space for current controversy and consequently, future decision-making.

From this perspective, the Internet of Things changes from suites of consumer products or objects that exist for people to be used exclusively in the here and now into speculative social configurations: they postulate systems to create possible encounters between people, objects, and values. As the role of interaction design has expanded generally—often through nebulous categories of work like "user experience"—the work of interaction design seems more allied with the idea of the design thing than it does making prototypes and wireframes.

OBJECT ECOLOGIES AND THE IOT

Reading the Internet of Things as a complex web of alliances and shadowy political intent casts the work of the designer as being very different at different times. I'm currently writing my dissertation proposal on "object ecologies," taking this wider theoretical framing of things and building out a way to analyze and generate ecologies of objects. I believe that this is a way to generate provocative design systems that are both rooted in the plausible while still offering a rich vein of speculation to mine for producing interesting prototypes. A method for producing speculative design without spectacle.

One example of this can be found as part of Bogost's thing-centered, object-oriented research. He advances what he calls "carpentry", or the production of devices and systems that do philosophical work [4]. Because of the nature of ubiquitous computing as a discipline of technical production, carpentry is inherent to research systems and platforms, whether or not it's acknowledged.

TEI GRADUATE STUDENT CONSORTIUM

The TEI graduate student consortium offers an exciting opportunity to meet, share ideas with, and collaborate with other researchers and practitioners who are operating on different subjects from a similar perspective. I struggle with questions around evaluation and impact. How can we evaluate and create impact from speculative design systems? Can they affect mainstream technological production in worthwhile ways? Interacting with peers undergoing analogous struggles with their own research and production processes will be very helpful in terms of framing my own interests in the Internet of Things and its discontents.

REFERENCES

1. Agre, P. Toward a critical technical practice: Lessons learned in trying to reform AI. In *Social Science, Technical Systems and Cooperative Work: Beyond the Great Divide*. Erlbaum, 1997.
2. Atelier, Binder, T., Michelis, G. de D., et al. *Design Things*. The MIT Press, 2011.
3. Bleeker, J. Design Fiction: A Short Essay on Design, Science, Fact and Fiction. 2009.
4. Bogost, I. *Alien Phenomenology or, What it's Like to Be a Thing*. University of Minnesota Press, Minneapolis, 2012.
5. Dunne, A. and Raby, F. *Design Noir: The Secret Life of Electronic Objects*. Birkhäuser, Berlin, 2001.
6. Dunne, A. and Raby, F. *Speculative everything: design, fiction, and social dreaming*. MIT Press, 2013.
7. Dunne, A. *Hertzian Tales*. MIT Press, 2006.
8. Gaver, B., Dunne, T., and Pacenti, E. Design: Cultural probes. *interactions 6*, 1 (1999), 21–29.
9. Gaver, W. et al. Enhancing Ubiquitous Computing with User Interpretation. *Proc. CHI '07*, ACM (2007), 537–546.
10. Gaver, W.W.et. al. Ambiguity as a resource for design. *Proc. CHI '03*, ACM (2003), 233–240.
11. Heidegger, M. The Thing. In *The object reader*. Routledge, London; New York, 2009.
12. Kuznetsov, S.et al. Ceci n'est pas une pipe bombe: *Proc CHI '11*, ACM (2011), 2375–2384.
13. Kuznetsov, S. and Paulos, E. Participatory sensing in public spaces. *Proc. DIS '10*, ACM (2010), 21–30.
14. Latour, B. *We have never been modern*. Harvard University Press, Cambridge, Mass., 1993.
15. Royal College of Art (Great Britain). *The presence project*. Royal College of Art, London, 2001.
16. Weibel, P. and Latour, B. *Making things public: atmospheres of democracy : [exhibition], ZKM, Center for art and media Karlsruhe, 20.03.-03-10.2005*. (Mass.) : MIT press, Cambridge, 2005.

Material & Meaning in Tangible Interactions

Shad Gross
Indiana University
919 E Tenth St
Bloomington, IN 47401 USA
shagross@indiana.edu

Abstract
Tangible interactions have incorporated new materials into interaction design as well as new perspectives on how those materials can be made useful. The dissertation research I discuss in this paper examines materials and forms in terms of how they both mediate information but also can represent meanings in their own right. My work emphasizes these meanings as an important aspect of the experience of tangible interactions.

Author Keywords
Materiality; Material Culture; Form; Experience

ACM Classification Keywords
H.5.2 Information interfaces and presentation (e.g., HCI): User Interfaces – theory and methods

Introduction
In the design of tangible interactions, it is materials that are used to give physical properties to computational devices. While these materials can be productively considered in terms of making systems more intuitive through affordances, there are also new concerns and opportunities that come with the introduction of new materials and forms [10]. Looking at such devices in terms of experience, it becomes increasingly important to consider how the different properties of materials contribute to experiential aspects of interaction.

Building off of my previous work, my dissertation will focus on materiality in HCI, specifically examining the material culture of the physical forms of computation, particularly in tangible interactions, as they pertain to concepts of quality, value, and meaning and how these affect user experience. Here I present an initial investigation—through the design and deployment of three critical designs—into how formal qualities of designs can be used to add new and possibly contradictory meanings to artifacts, as well as how users make sense of these elements. The goal of my work, both broadly and in the case described, is to *advance understanding of how the sensual aspects (that is, the aspects that can be seen, touched, smelled, or tasted) of tangible interactions affect the experience of both interacting and living with such devices*.

ACM 978-1-4503-3305-4/15/01...$15.00 .
http://dx.doi.org/10.1145/2677199.2691609

Context and Motivation
In their seminal work on tangible interactions, Ishii and Ullmer describe Tangible User Interfaces (TUIs) as "an attempt to bridge the gap between cyberspace and the physical environment by making digital information (bits) tangible" [11]. This process emphasizes how physical objects can serve as both controls and representations of data. In this sense, materials can be seen as furthering the functioning of tangible interactions as well as serving as a medium for informational content. This functioning, however, may not be as clean as simply applying affordances to interaction – with physical materials giving the perception of interactions that may not be supported by the system they control [10]. Similarly looking at the relationship between materials and perceptions, Horn et al. describe the use of *cultural forms* – "social constructions or conventions that are linked to recurrent patterns of activity" [9]. Taking "form" as the "visual, physical, or temporal appearance of a design" [12], physical materials can be seen as related to the social constructions and conventions of cultural forms. Rather than trying to make devices that function transparently, such designs emphasize the "presence" of materials, forms, and the artifacts that they compose [8]. Such concerns are an important part of making computational devices that emphasize the creation of experiences in addition to the completion of tasks.

Materiality has been presented as a lens with which to examine digital devices [14, 2, 12]. Of particular relevance, Wiberg points to "material culture" as a means of examining "meaning" in interaction design: "While wholeness can be understood from a perspective that accounts for what something contains, the notion of meaning is about how this container is perceived and understood" [14]. More specifically, meaning here refers to "a subjective interpretation about qualities and values of a material artifact, indicating how material artifacts are experienced and understood in personal and social life" [12]. Thus, material culture offers a means to examine the physical form of tangible interactions in terms of what that form itself means in terms of quality, value, and situation within a user's life, giving materials a dual role as mediator and active participant in the experience of interaction [2]. My previous work examines the material culture of tangible interactions, including how medium-specificity can be used as a lens to examine material as a medium for informational content [4,5,6], how style makes meaningful connections between materials and values by connecting artifacts and their creators [7], and how functional forms can become stylistic as skeuomorphs, connecting artifacts across time [3]. Across this work, meaning and value relate material form, informational content, and function in interaction experience.

Research Focus

Broadly, my work seeks to further investigate this question: *In what ways have tangible interactions come to propose a unique set of materials, meanings, and values over time, and how can these concepts be continued and challenged as part of a generative design process?* Unpacking that question, in addition to serving as functional controls and mediation of information content, materials and forms develop senses of value and meaning. My previous investigations have looked at how theories of medium-specificity and style can be useful for analyzing materials in terms of meaning. Moving beyond this, the next step is to explore how these theories can be applied to a generative design process.

Research Goals and Approach

Drawing insight from the description of research through design as an approach to examining materiality in HCI [2], my approach to researching these issues of material culture is through constructive design research – "design research in which construction — be it product, system, space, or media — takes center place and becomes the key means in constructing knowledge" [13]. In short, my ambition is to create artifacts that both embody and confront concepts of value, quality, and meaning in tangible interactions and use them as a means to further develop these concepts through the reactions of others.

In addition to constructive design research as a general approach, the issue of meaning can be described in terms of interpretation [12]. With respect to this, I adopt a critical approach in my work, using critical design [1] as a specific form of constructive design research. This means that the artifacts created are not necessarily presented as a solution to a specific problem, but rather as a means of raising issues and initiating discussions surrounding tangible interactions.

Critical Design for TEI Research

The three artifacts described here were created to critically examine the role of technology in self-tracking. In addition to tracking the activities of their users through photos and video, the forms of these artifacts were designed with particular attention to conveying meanings and experiences that could somehow augment or even contradict the function of tracking.

The Candy Camera (CC) is a candy machine that has been augmented to take pictures when candy is dispensed. The machine's normal function – dispensing candy through the turn of a crank- has been augmented so that it causes a camera on top of the machine to capture an image, store it to a Raspberry Pi board in the base, and then push saved images to an LCD screen in the machine's bowl. The formal aspects of the device are at once a reference to a nostalgic piece of Americana as well as a contradiction to the notion of transparency in the design of digital artifacts. The design's form is predominantly based off of a Carousel gumball machine, reminiscent of the kinds of coin-operated candy machines common to the streets of mid twentieth century America. It is a kind of nostalgic kitsch – something so common that at its original time it faded into the background and now serves as a reminder of a bygone period. Digitally augmenting this device only serves to heighten this anachronism, particularly in the way that the camera, screen, and connective wires all are visible, but blended into the form of the design. The formal qualities of the machine, particularly its color and shape, not only refer to a bygone era, but also that era's sense of what is fun and child-like. As a device that tracks users' candy consumption through pictures, this approach contradicts the tendency of designing artifacts that emphasize function minimally in the name of transparency [4]. This design, then, can be seen as both modifying an odd object digitally, but also emphasizing form to enhance an enjoyable experience.

The Melody Bot (MB) takes video captured by a custom web camera and uses it to generate custom music videos. The custom camera connects to the user's computer where video is analyzed and stored. Once enough video has been collected, the user can upload songs that the MB application analyzes and then combines with automatically cut video clips to make a custom music video. The MB application is, for the most part, very standard and based off of the GUI options that are a part of the Processing environment with which it is built. However, the physical component of the design - the web camera - more actively engages form. Similar to the Candy Camera, the web camera takes on a playful form – a three inch tall, stylized and cartoonish human form with the actual camera embedded in it's television-shaped head. Clear epoxy resin makes the

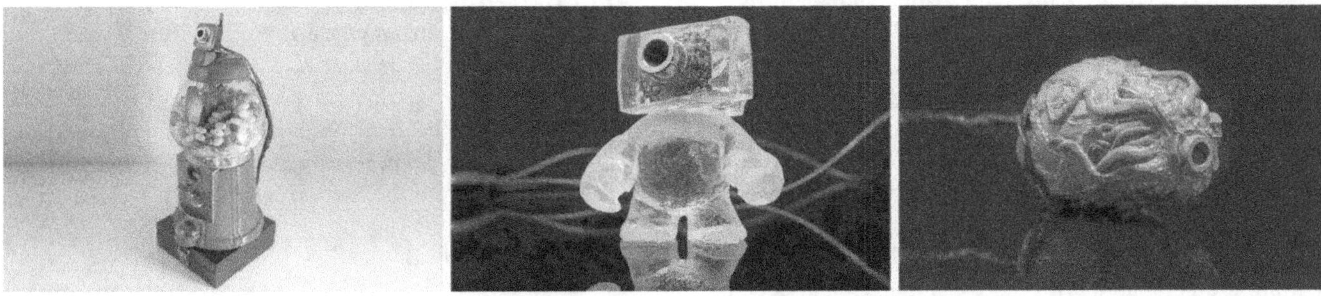

Figure 1 Candy Camera, Melody Bot , Fractured View

functional circuits of the web camera's PCB visible, using it as an aesthetic element, rather than something to be covered up. Unlike the Candy Camera, which takes an object and augments it digitally, this can be seen as emphasizing the "presence" [8] of the application. Instead of adding digital elements to a pre-existing object, this takes different elements of toy design to extend the application into the physical world.

The Fractured View (FV) is a camera that is activated by squeezing. Inside the custom cast latex shell, sensors detect when the device is squeezed, resulting in a camera capturing an image that is then distorted based on the strength and duration of that squeezing. The design is presented as a kind of stress ball that creates beautiful or exploded images when it is used. The form of the FV has less of a point of reference in trends of industrial design and more of a metaphoric relationship with its functioning. Given that the design "explodes" images, it was desirable to represent this explosive quality in the form as well. However, explosions frequently carry with them a connotation of destruction, which would emphasize only one particular facet of the designs use (destroying a photograph as opposed to making it different). An organic, plant-based form was chosen to represent this duality – the cracks in the surface representing either the internal destruction of the plant, or the bursting forth of a pod to disseminate seeds as a source of new life. In this case, natural metaphors of form situate the design in relation to concepts by means of connection to natural phenomena.

Making the Designs Public

The designs were deployed into the field in six households for six months each. The designs were deployed in two pairs – the CC and MB for three households and the CC and FV for three. This was done to encourage greater engagement with the theme of self-tracking while avoiding taking up too many USB ports on the participant's computers. Data was collected through monthly, unstructured interviews, culminating in a final structured interview after the sixth month.

For the households that received the CC and MB, the designs were frequently described in terms of fun over functionality. Speaking to the MB, Leslie, a middle-aged administrator and photographer who shares her home with her teenage son remarked: *I thought it was kind of interesting. It made it more interesting to be on the computer and have the little bot, like, looking at me.* While playful, there was also an element of simplicity conveyed by the forms of the designs as Kelly, an early 30s interaction designer who shares a household with her husband Andrew, points out: *I think it appears more child-like in nature, both devices actually.* This perceived simplicity carried over to the functioning of the design. For Leslie, this meant that the MB would best be used to capture happy memories rather than simply tracking activity at her computer. Sarah, an early 30s student who shares a household with her husband Dale, on the other hand used it as a tracking system but found it limited: *I'm hoping that the camera sitting there will make me more productive. I almost wish that as soon as the computer turned on the camera would automatically start capturing image. I feel like it would be more of an accountability tool for me.* What is perhaps most interesting about this response is the desire to have less control. It's presence was sufficient to serve as a reminder, but giving it greater autonomy, as if the computer were actually a person watching, is presented here as being something desirable rather than detrimental.

For the households that received the CC and FV, a different relationships between the designs emerged. For Jessica a single mother and administrator, the devices fell along the lines of good and evil with their forms disguising their true intentions – *that [CC] looks friendly and playful but I think that's evil and that [FV] looks evil but its actually friendly and playful.* For Jessica the form and functionality of the designs are a mismatch, but not accidentally. Rather, the designs are evaluated as good or evil because of an attempt to make something undesirable – loss of control of the photo – seem fun in the CC, while the FV conceals a fun activity within an off-putting form. Similarly, Jack, a mid thirties freelance designer and office manager who shares a household with his wife Laura and their three children saw the FV and CC as playing off each other – *one [CC] takes a nice clear picture and gives us candy when we turn the crank. It's already setup and plugged in. The other one, the Fractured View, you have to interact with it longer and the more, the longer you interact with it, the worse the image gets. Or maybe the more fractured it gets.* Rather than speaking to the form of the device itself, here the form of the information captured, the photos as a medium, are compared with the CC's images and accompanying candy serving as a reward, and the destruction of the FV's image a kind of punishment for interaction. For Ben, a writer in his 60s who lives with his wife Karen, the comparison was subtler: *think about the tiny screen on the Candy Camera—who can use something that small... the Fractured View images are way cool, but I don't really care.* Neither design fulfilled a functional need for Ben, but in spite of this there still was an emphasis on the strange-looking Fractured View as being fun and cool. In these cases, it's not only the forms, but the informational content and function of the designs getting compared. However, as especially notable in Jessica's response, no single one of these elements is deterministic, rather they all, to varying degrees, affect the experience of interaction.

Conclusion

Responses to these designs varied regarding value and meaning across participants, but they are unified in how interpretations were made in reference to prior designs and, when those were insufficient for making connections, across the deployed designs themselves. New uses of materials became situated through these connections and how forms reinforce or confront expectations. Moving forward, I will continue to examine this process of meaning-making through (dis)connection in terms of how it can be applied to generate new design forms. As TEI examines the use of novel materials in the construction of interactions, in terms of function and cultural situation, such an understanding becomes increasingly important to the creation of new experiences of using and living with tangible interactions.

As an attendee of this consortium, I will benefit from feedback from senior TEI researchers and fellow students as I continue from the substantive theoretical foundations developed in my qualifying exam into the development of my dissertation research project. Additionally, I hope to explore the practical issues of combining theory and practice in TEI with consortium attendees. In return, I offer the consortium attendees my experience in bringing together critical and social science methods and my theoretical background in art and media theory as it pertains to tangible interactions.

Acknowledgements

I would like to thank my advisors, Shaowen Bardzell and Jeffrey Bardzell, for guidance. Work presented in this paper was supported in part by NSF IIS CreativeIT (#1002772) and the Intel Science and Technology Center (ISTC) for Social Computing program.

References

[1] Bardzell, J., & Bardzell, S. (2013). What is critical about critical design? In Proc. CHI'13, ACM: New York.

[2] Fuchsberger, V., Murer, M., & Tscheligi, M. (2013). Materials, materiality, and media. In *Proc. CHI'13.* ACM: New York.

[3] Gross, S., Bardzell, J., & Bardzell, S. (2014) Skeu the evolution: skeuomorphs, style, and the material of tangible interactions. In Proc TEI'14. ACM: New York.

[4] Gross, S., Bardzell, J., & Bardzell, S. (2014) Structures, forms, and stuff: the materiality and medium of interaction. Pers. Ubiquit. Comput., 18(3), 637-649.

[5] Gross, S. (2013). Glitch, please: datamoshing as a medium-specific application of digital material. In Proc. DPPI'12. ACM: New York.

[6] Gross, S., Pace, T., Bardzell, J., & Bardzell, S. (2013). Machinima production tools: a vernacular history of a creative medium. In Proc. CHI'13. ACM: New York.

[7] Gross, S., Bardzell, J., & Bardzell, S. (2013). Touch style: creativity in tangible experience design. In Proc. C&C'13. ACM: New York.

[8] Hallnäs, L., & Redström, J. (2002). From use to presence: on the expressions and aesthetics of everyday computational things. TOCHI, 9(2), 106-124.

[9] Horn, M. S. (2013). The role of cultural forms in tangible interaction design. In Proc. TEI'2013. ACM: New York.

[10] Hornecker, E. (2012). Beyond affordance: tangibles' hybrid nature. In Proc. TEI'2012. ACM: New York.

[11] Ishii, H., & Ullmer, B. (1997). Tangible bits: towards seamless interfaces between people, bits and atoms. In Proc. CHI'97. ACM: New York.

[12] Jung, H. and Stolterman, E. (2012). Digital form and materiality: propositions for a new approach to interaction design research. In Proc. NordiCHI'2012. ACM: New York.

[13] Koskinen, I., Zimmerman, J., Binder, T., Redstrom, J., & Wensveen, S. (2011). Design Research through Practice: From the Lab, Field, and Showroom. Elsevier.

[14] Wiberg, M. (2014). Methodology for materiality: interaction design research through a material lens. Pers. Ubiquit. Comput., 18(3), 625-636.

Designing Tangible Interfaces to Support Expression and Sensemaking in Interactive Narratives

Jean Ho Chu
Department of Digital Media
Georgia Institute of Technology
85 Fifth Street, Atlanta, GA 30308
jchu35@gatech.edu

ABSTRACT

Tangible and embodied interactions can provide a means to bring performative and participatory activities that have a physical presence in the real world into the narrated story world. This research investigates how to employ tangible narrative interfaces for learning about and reflecting on cultural practices. The research is informed by tangible interface frameworks, narratology, and existing cultural practices around storytelling with physical objects. The goal of this research is to design interfaces that are cohesively coupled with narrative content and that support meaningful interaction. I adopted tangible manipulation and expressive representation as guiding principles to explain the role of tangible media. Design guidelines are proposed and tested in preliminary research.

Author Keywords

Tangible Interaction; Interaction Design; Storytelling.

ACM Classification Keywords

H.5.2. [Information Interfaces and Presentation]: User Interfaces---Input devices and strategies, Interaction styles.

General Terms

Design; Human Factors.

INTRODUCTION

Storytelling is a social activity. Stories are shared in every culture as a means of entertainment, education, cultural preservation, and to communicate moral values. Through storytelling, children learn about literacy, and about how to understand the environment around them [3]. Storytelling can be effectively used as a method to reflect upon and engage with cultural practices and artifacts in museums. Tangible media and digital technology can be used to support the process of making and telling stories. The goal of my research is to design tangible interactions that support expression and sensemaking in narratives. The work refers to previous approaches that have focused on tangible manipulation or expressive representation in interactive narratives. I propose that the interaction should be meaningful to both the story and the physical context.

This work is informed by previous work on tangible narratives, narratology [4, 15], and cultural practices. Throughout history, different cultures have used artifacts and gestural interaction to support storytelling. Physical practices can enhance reflection on the cultural practices they engage. Based on the role of tangible media in storytelling, I propose design guidelines for appropriation and for creating tangible stories. Future directions will focus on extending theoretical concepts, investigating cultural practices, and improving the interaction design of preliminary works.

TEI '15, January 16 - 19 2015, Stanford, CA, USA

http://dx.doi.org/10.1145/2677199.2693161

BACKGROUND

Tangible Interactions within Interactive Narratives

Studies on tangible interactions within interactive narratives have explored the design of physical structures to support making or telling of stories. Prior work on tangible narratives can be positioned and classified along three dimensions (Figure 1). The first axis positions tangible narrative works based on whether they focus on the generation or on the navigation of stories. The second axis distinguishes whether character or the plot leads the narrative progression. The final dimension describes whether the mapping of the physical interaction to the narrative is symbolic or mimetic. Tangible narrative projects can be mapped in this way in order to understand their design space and goal.

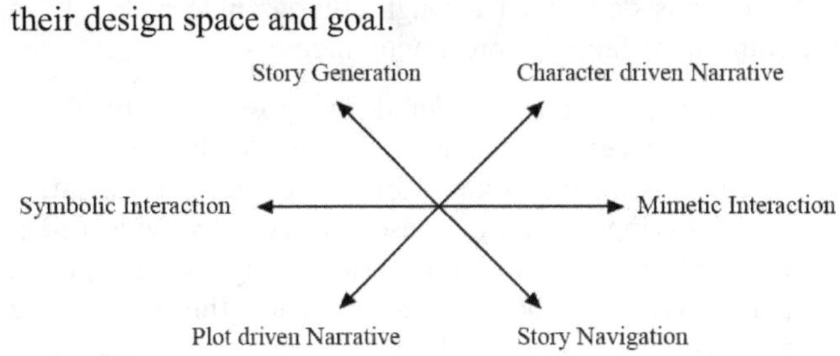

Figure 1. Framework for Tangible Narrative Interface

Telltale [1] is an example of a tangible interface that is oriented to plot-leading narrative generation. Its interface is a symbolic physical representation of the story structure. It provides structures for plots to progress during story construction and lets users reconstruct oral stories by recording and playing them in a linear order. Users can also reorganize segments of the stories. Another project, Triangles [6], supports the creation of non-linear stories. Each triangular piece can hold story elements, which can be reorganized to construct and navigate a non-linear story. The interfaces in these projects direct users to generate the story first and let them navigate it afterwards. However, these platforms, which mainly focus on plot generation, do not provide a means to create causal links between events or character relationships.

In contrast, some projects create stories based on characters, providing guidance on story generation by showing causal links between character actions. The interface in these works holds pre-rendered story elements, which can be reconstructed into a story. Telestory [8] is a platform that uses Siftables for storytelling. The cubes are preloaded with graphics and sounds, and show corresponding animations on a parallel HD screen when needed. These cubes can detect and link to other cubes placed adjacent to each other. For example, placing a prop cube to the right or left of a character cube will trigger a new episode to play on the HD screen. Similarly, Tok [16] is an interface consisting of tangible story blocks and a screen playing animations. It encourages children to put together story elements into a threaded narrative. A story block has pre-defined narrative elements such as environments, characters, and events. By combining different elements, different stories are created.

The aforementioned projects do not expressly link physical interactions to the narrative content. Researchers have also attempted to provide contextualized interactions that would align with existing social and cultural storytelling practices. Storymat [3] provides an open-ended environment for child-driven storytelling play. When children tell stories by playing with certain toys, the system records their stories and also plays back previously recorded stories associated with the same toys. Storymat thus aims to provide children with inspiration for new stories. Memorybeads [14] is a project to support cultural activities such as oral storytelling and collective memory of an indigenous community. The interface was developed through ethnographic research on the cultural artifacts for preserving memory.

Researchers have also explored the possibility of using tangible interfaces to represent characters or key objects of a narrative as active tokens for navigating the narrative space or driving the plot. These interfaces provide open-ended fluid interactions with stories. Tangible viewpoints [11] lets viewers choose the character through whose perspective they navigate the story. Since each character has a different point of view, the choice leads to different expressions, and changes the way the story unfolds.

One of the strengths of a tangible interface is that it can hold meanings that influence narrative expectations and cultural assumptions. In this case, the interface works as a boundary object, both connecting users to the story world and connecting the narrative to the physical space of the interaction. The Reading Glove [17] provides objects that act as narrative elements that can be discovered and investigated. Visitors interact with the objects and experience stories through their interaction. Since the objects hold cultural meaning and expectations, they augment the story upon interaction.

TUI AND NARRATIVE RESEARCH

Motivation

I contribute to the existing tangible interface literature by showing how tangible interfaces can support sensemaking and expression in narratives. I further investigate how tangible interaction and storytelling can support understanding of cultural practices. Storytelling provides a means for learning by encouraging one to establish and share ideas and perspectives. This learning experience can be enriched through tangible interaction. Sensemaking and expression are key elements of storytelling that can help explain how and why tangible storytelling can be effective for learning. Sensemaking is the process of discovering the meaning of the interactive experience, while expression is the personalization process through which one interacts with the story in one's own voice. Through physical engagement and story (re)construction, the interactor can realize their perspective and express their voice.

Goal

The goal of this research is to understand the role of tangible media in supporting narrative expression and sensemaking. By designing, building, and testing tangible interfaces that engage specific cultural storytelling practices, I aim to better understand the methods and benefits of using tangible media to support narrative expression and sensemaking. Drawing on tangible and embodied interaction theories and narratology, I propose design guidelines for tangible narratives that are informed by social and cultural practices. I plan to apply this knowledge to the design of tangible media experiences to enable interactors to learn about and share cultural stories in an informal environment.

The Role of Tangible Media

Hornecker's framework [7] for tangible interaction has four elements: tangible manipulation, spatial interaction, embodied facilitation, and expressive representation. My research relies on this framework because storytelling is a social activity and the framework focuses on the material and social aspects of tangible interaction. Of the four elements, I adopt tangible manipulation and expressive representation to explain how tangible media supports a narrative experience.

Tangible Manipulation

Hornecker [7] describes tangible manipulation as being derived from bodily interaction with material objects. In tangible narratives, physical visualization of the narrative elements and states encourages engagement and participation in the process of telling and creating stories. Also, by actively manipulating story elements, one can comprehend the causal relationships between elements, diverse narrative modes, and structures.

Piagetian developmental theory explains that physical interaction helps children's thinking [10, 13]. Similarly, board and tabletop game players benefit from being able to externalize and physically manipulate the states and strategies of the game. A tangible interface can serve better than a GUI in collaborative problem solving. Antle et al. [2] showed that children using a TUI were better at solving manipulation puzzles than children who used a GUI. Papert extends Piaget's ideas by arguing that being able to interact with and reconstruct physical models is effective in learning abstract concepts [12]. Rather than passively listening to stories, being able to reconstruct and express one's creativity supports active learning of the content.

Expressive Representation

Hornecker and Buur [7] explain expressive representation as expressiveness and legibility of the physical representation of data or objects. Through perceived coupling and externalization, tangible interfaces become physical tokens embodying the system state. Expressive representation can support personalized meaning-making through our bodily engagement with physically represented narrative elements.

Dourish [5] contends that embodiment is a "property of our engagement with the world that allows us to make it meaningful" (p. 126). Reading Glove [17] is an example of an object as a gateway for embodied narrative meaning. Tanenbaum et al. [17] explain that the meaning occurs when users become aware of the association between the interface and the embodied content. Van den Hoven and Mazalek [9] stress the importance of gesture in communicating meaning, and claim that more expressive mappings between tangible gestures and the resulting effects may exist.

Examples of expressive representation already exist in cultural practices and in artifacts conveying narrative. Historical cultural artifacts such as beaded necklaces, charms, and craft products were sometimes created as expressive representations of stories. These artifacts helped people to remember and tell stories. Reitsma et al. [14] explain that cultural artifacts that represent indigenous knowledge provide a symbolic framework that informs the community members of the value and the system of the culture. Employing culturally rich and situated objects in the design of tangible narrative interfaces may help users understand the narrative content.

Design Guidelines

Based on the understanding of expression and sensemaking through tangible media, I propose the following guidelines for tightly coupling TUI with interactive narratives.

1. Externalized story: Interaction should affect and be affected by the story world and narrative expectations.

2. Embodied meaning making: Narrative interaction should employ meaningful gestures or physical experiences in the real world. It can also be personalized.

3. Shared artifact: The interface and story should be manifested as shared artifacts, such as maps, animations, or sounds.

PRELIMINARY RESEARCH

I have participated in the following projects, which exhibit the above-mentioned properties of tangible narratives.

Universal Threshold Object (UTO)

Universal Threshold Object (UTO) is a haptic controller for televised interactive narrative experiences based on the television show "American Horror Story" (Figure 2, left). The interactor takes the role of the main character and engages with their physical and emotional states through a tangible interface. Emotional decisions are made through gestural interaction, which leads to different narrative endings. The project provides an understanding of how tangible interfaces can be used as a boundary or threshold object to connect the narrative and the physical space of the interactor. Haptic feedback is used to represent different states of the narrative and the emotions of the character. Employing tangible and gestural interactions to make narrative decisions enhances immersion.

Mapping Place

This tangible tabletop application supports learning about a cultural artifact from central Africa called a Lukasa through embodied interaction and storytelling (Figure 2, right). A

Figure 2. Universal Threshold Object (left); Mapping Place (right)

Lukasa is a mnemonic device studded with beads that hold cultural meaning such as genealogical history and cultural identity. The performance of holding and touching the beads while telling oral stories was a method of connecting memories and recounting history. The interaction and form of the digital tabletop was designed to resemble the concept, usage, and form of the Lukasa board. In Mapping Place, tangible interaction and storytelling supports an understanding of the symbolic and nonlinguistic mnemonic process. It was installed at a museum exhibit and its usage was studied to explore sensemaking and storytelling.

FUTURE WORK

Extension of the Concept

In both of the projects, the understanding of how tangible objects support sensemaking and storytelling can be further explored. Further research can be done to better understand how the tangible interaction affects people's engagement with and reaction to the story. Interacting with tangible objects can provide a means to actively change between narrative modes such as point of view, narrative voice, and time. Being able to switch between different narrative modes and express one's reactions in a narrative form can provide an experience that supports critical understanding. Further research needs to be done to understand how cultural activities, including storytelling, are reflected and reinforced through physical interaction with artifacts.

Recommendation of Design Approach

After testing the projects, we learned that it is challenging to design an interface and interactions that match the interactor's expectations and also align with the narrative context. Gestural interactions were specifically designed for each narrative situation, and the interactors had to learn when and how to interact to achieve expected results. Even though the actions and mappings were designed to reflect and convey meaning, they were not universal and were at times perceived to be confusing by interactors. Sometimes users did not understand what each element meant or why one should interact in a certain way, and thus required guidance. One way to extend the current work is to seek generalizable approaches for tangible interaction design that can be easily conveyed and easily understood.

CONCLUSION

The expected contribution of this research is in providing an understanding of how tangible media can support sensemaking and expression in an interactive narrative, especially for learning about cultural practices. I adopted tangible manipulation and expressive representation as guiding principles to explain the role of tangible media. Design guidelines are proposed and tested in preliminary research. Future work will extend the theoretical concepts and interaction design approaches.

ACKNOWLEDGMENTS

I thank my advisor Ali Mazalek for her support.

REFERENCES

1. Annany, M. Telling Tales: Supporting written literacy with computational toys. Unpublished Master Thesis. The MIT Media Laboratory, Cambridge, MA (2001).
2. Antle, A.N. et al. 2009. Hands on what?: comparing children's mouse-based and tangible-based interaction. *In Proc. IDC 2009,* ACM (2009), 80–88.
3. Cassell, J. and Ryokai, K. Making space for voice: Technologies to support children's fantasy and storytelling. Personal and ubiquitous computing (2001), 169–190.
4. Chatman, S.B. Story and discourse: Narrative structure in fiction and film. Cornell University Press. 1980.
5. Dourish, P. Where the action is: the foundations of embodied interaction. MIT press. 2004.
6. Gorbet, M.G. et al. Triangles: tangible interface for manipulation and exploration of digital information topography. *In Proc. CHI 1998,* ACM (1998), 49–56.
7. Hornecker, E. and Buur, J. Getting a grip on tangible interaction: a framework on physical space and social interaction. *In Proc. CHI 2006,* ACM (2006), 437–446.
8. Hunter, S. et al. Make a Riddle and TeleStory: designing children's applications for the siftables platform. *In Proc. IDC 2010,* ACM (2010), 206–209.
9. Van den Hoven, E. and Mazalek, A. Grasping gestures: Gesturing with physical artifacts. Artificial Intelligence for Engineering Design, Analysis and Manufacturing. 25, 03 (2011), 255–271.
10. Marshall, P. Do tangible interfaces enhance learning? *In Proc. TEI 2007,* ACM (2007), 163–170.
11. Mazalek, A. et al. 2002. Tangible viewpoints: a physical approach to multimedia stories. *In Proc. ACM MM 2002* (2002), 153–160.
12. Papert, S. Mindstorms: Children, computers, and powerful ideas. Basic Books, Inc. 1980.
13. Piaget, J. and Cook, M. 1952. The origins of intelligence in children. 1952.
14. Reitsma, L. et al. StoryBeads: Preserving Indigenous Knowledge through Tangible Interaction Design. Culture and Computing, 2013 International Conference (2013), 79–85.
15. Ryan, M. L. Narrative across media: The languages of storytelling. University of Nebraska Press. 2004.
16. Sylla, C. et al. A Digital Manipulative for Embodied "Stage-Narrative" Creation. Entertainment Computing. (2014).
17. Tanenbaum, J. et al. 2010. The Reading Glove: designing interactions for object-based tangible storytelling. *In Proc. Augmented Human International Conference* (2010), 19.

From Movement to Mechanism: Exploring Expressive Movement Qualities in Shape-change

Matthijs Kwak
Designing Quality in Interaction Group
Eindhoven University of Technology
Dept. of Industrial Design
P.O. Box 513, 5600 MB,
Eindhoven, the Netherlands
m.kwak@tue.nl

Joep Frens
School of Design
Carnegie Mellon University
frensjw@andrew.cmu.edu
&
Designing Quality in Interaction Group
Eindhoven University of Technology
Dept. of Industrial Design
j.w.frens@tue.nl

TEI '15, Jan 16-19 2015, Stanford, CA, USA
ACM 978-1-4503-3305-4/15/01.
http://dx.doi.org/10.1145/2677199.2683580

Abstract
This one-day studio revolves around the exploration of expressive movement qualities in shape-change by means of physical sketching and prototyping. It is a hands-on studio where participants first explore expressive movement qualities and interaction scenarios with a generic shape-changing platform and then abstract the explored movement qualities to model them in detail using cardboard modeling techniques combined with an Arduino controlled actuator (the advanced cardboard modeling platform). We recognize and want to zoom in on the potential of the expressiveness of shape-change in the context of human-product interaction as an emerging field in HCI research. In this studio we aim to both acquaint participants with new, low threshold platforms for exploration and give them insight in and a vocabulary of expressive movement qualities in shape-change.

Author Keywords
Prototyping, Design, Expressive movement qualities, Tangible interaction, Rich interaction.

ACM Classification Keywords
H.5.2 User Interfaces: Prototyping.

Introduction

Shape-changing interfaces are set to revolutionize human-product interaction but while technologies for shape-changing interfaces are rapidly evolving, our understanding of the design space of such interfaces is still limited [1].

Central to this studio is the exploration and synthesis of expressive movement qualities in shape-change by physical sketching and prototyping [2]. More specifically, it revolves around gaining insight in and developing a vocabulary of such movement qualities to be able to work towards an understanding of how to design for them. To this end the studio has two aims: (1) it presents low-threshold tools for the exploration of shape-changing interfaces and (2) it presents the notion of expressive movement qualities in shape-change and explores the subtleties required in form, interaction, function and resulting behavior. First we introduce the notion of expressive movement qualities in shape-change, then we present the advanced cardboard modeling tools for the exploration of interactivity and lastly we present the studio itself.

Expressive movement qualities in shape-change

We describe shape-changing interfaces as interfaces that use "*physical change of shape as input or output. We follow earlier work that has used self-actuated change as a defining characteristic [...]. Additionally, we require that the self-actuation must be controllable so that the object can return to its initial state and repeat the shape-change*" [p1, 1].

In an earlier publication we explored the design space of shape-changing interfaces [3] and found that people describe their experience with shape-changing interfaces in expressive terms that are similar to personal characteristics (or 'qualities') that we use to describe ourselves or (our interaction with) other people [4]. These expressive movement qualities are the result of a complex interplay between form, interaction, function and resulting behavior in which subtle differences can have a big impact on the user experience.

We see a potential in making use of the apparent expressiveness of shape-changing interfaces to further the field of human-product interaction. Expressive movements add a new layer of communication that can be used for non-iconic, non-anthropomorphic expressions of affect [5] and thereby invite for novel ways of interaction between humans and computers [6] and thus novel ways of interaction between humans and products; addressing perceptual-motor, cognitive, emotional and social skills. In the short term this can lead to compelling continuous interaction rather than discrete interaction through, for example, buttons. In the long term this can lead to more engaging interfaces as behavior can adapt to use, new functionality or trends.

A growing concern we have is that the behavior of shape-changing interfaces and other dynamic interactive products and systems is designed as an afterthought and as such misses out on the potential expressive movement qualities offer in terms of user experience. We would like to encourage people working with shape-change to explore these expressive movement qualities and attune themselves to the subtleties in form, interaction, function and resulting behavior by offering them low-threshold platforms and accompanying methods.

Advanced Cardboard modeling tools

The advanced cardboard modeling platform combines advanced foam-core and cardboard modeling techniques with Arduino controlled sensors and actuators. It emphasizes the mechanical and physical aspects of interaction and offers the possibility to experientially explore interactivity and synthesize interactive prototypes in the early phase of the design process.

The advanced cardboard modeling tools were introduced in a studio at TEI'14 in Munich [7] in response to two points of criticism on existing tools: (1) sensing has priority over actuating and (2) the integration of form, interaction and function [8] is not recognized as a carrier of meaning and expressivity [7].

In this studio we go further and chart new territory for the use of early phase exploration tools and aim for the exploration of shape-changing interfaces that are capable of integrating form, interaction, function and resulting behavior. We introduce a generic shape-changing platform that requires no programming skills and allows to quickly sketch expressive movements using a technique similar to programming by example. To go from a generic to a unique design this platform is complemented with the advanced cardboard modeling tools as a means to elaborate, fine-tune and synthesize movement. Under the guidance of the studio organizers participants will abstract expressive movement qualities from the generic sketches and translate these from a generic to a unique design using advanced cardboard modeling; building on more than eight years of teaching and numerous workshops on cardboard modeling [9].

Detailed studio setup

The studio has place for sixteen participants and presents a generic shape-changing platform and advanced cardboard modeling tools for the exploration of expressive movement qualities. It builds on cardboard modeling skills and on Arduino programming skills. While we do not require previous knowledge and skills it would be helpful if participants have some prior experience, particularly with programming the Arduino microcontroller.

The one-day program of the studio is as follows:

(1) The studio starts with an introduction of our generic shape-changing platform as a tool to explore expressive movement qualities.

(2) A range of explorations is made using the shape-changing platform, exploring expressive movement qualities. To guide this step, participants are given a list of expressive qualities from which one is chosen as a starting point to create 'Wizard of Oz' interaction scenarios.

(3) An introduction to cardboard modeling is given. We focus on integrating actuators into foam-core models and using mechanisms to decrease the number of servos required to create specific expressive movements.

(4) A quick introduction to the Arduino platform is given together with example code.

(5) A range of explorations is made, exploring a chosen 'expressive movement quality' in detail. One of the explorations is chosen and elaborated into a 'museum quality' prototype having both qualities in the physical and in the digital.

(6) The explorations are presented.

Please note: the participants work in pairs. The participants need to bring a laptop computer with the latest Arduino (www.arduino.cc) and Processing (www.processing.org) software pre-installed.

Next to this we bring the generic shape-changing platforms, Arduino boards, motor shields and other electronics that are not covered in the studio fee. These need to be returned after the studio. An open-source building plan for the generic shape-changing platform will be made available after the studio.

Learning goals

1. Explore the concept of expressive movement qualities in shape-change and gain a vocabulary to discuss it.

2. Discover the advanced cardboard modeling tools as a platform for exploration of interactivity: Acquire new exploration skills.

Studio Supporting Web Documents

http://www.cardboardmodeling.com.

Acknowledgements

The research leading to these results has received funding from the European Union Future and Emerging Technologies Seventh Framework Programme FET FP7/2007-2013 under grant agreement n° 309191 for the GHOST project.

Citations

[1] Rasmussen, M.K., Pedersen, E.W., Petersen, M.G., and Hornbæk, K. (2012). Shape-changing interfaces: a review of the design space and open research questions. In Proc. CHI (pp. 735–744). ACM.

[2] Buxton, B. (2010). Sketching User Experiences: Getting the Design Right and the Right Design: Getting the Design Right and the Right Design. Morgan Kaufmann.

[3] Kwak, M., Hornbæk, K., Markopoulos, P., & Bruns Alonso, M. (2014). The design space of shape-changing interfaces: a repertory grid study. In Proceedings of the 2014 conference on Designing interactive systems. ACM.

[4] Feixas, G., Geldschläger, H., and Neimeyer, R.A. (2002). Content analysis of personal constructs. In Journal of Constructivist Psychology 15, 1 (pp. 1–19).

[5] de Rooij, A., Broekens, J., & Lamers, M. H. (2013). Abstract Expressions of Affect. International Journal of Synthetic Emotions (IJSE), 4(1), 1-31.

[6] Taylor, A. S. (2009, April). Machine intelligence. In Proceedings of the SIGCHI Conference on Human Factors in Computing Systems (pp. 2109-2118). ACM.

[7] Frens, J., & van Campenhout, L. (2014). Advanced cardboard modeling: exploring the aesthetics of the third way. In Proceedings of the 8th International Conference on Tangible, Embedded and Embodied Interaction (pp. 349-352). ACM.

[8] Frens, J.W. (2006). Designing for Rich Interaction: Integrating Form, Interaction, and Function. Unpublished Doctoral Dissertation, Eindhoven University of Technology, Eindhoven, the Netherlands. (retrievable from http://www.richinteraction.com.)

[9] Frens, J. (2011). Cardboard modeling studio: a designerly exploration tool for rich and embodied interaction. In Proceedings of the fifth international conference on Tangible, embedded, and embodied interaction (pp. 365-368). ACM.

Integrating Theories of Mind with Tangible and Embedded Interaction Design

Ilhan Aslan
Verena Fuchsberger
Manfred Tscheligi
Christian Doppler Laboratory for "Contextual Interfaces"
ICT&S Center
University of Salzburg
Salzburg, Austria
firstname.lastname@sbg.ac.at

Jelle van Dijk
Industrial Design
Eindhoven University of Technology
Eindhoven, The Netherlands
jelle.vandijk@hu.nl

TEI '15, Jan 16-19 2015, Stanford, CA, USA
ACM 978-1-4503-3305-4/15/01.
http://dx.doi.org/10.1145/2677199.2683581

Abstract

Theories of how the human mind works have inspired but also constrained –negatively and positively - interaction design. Today's interfaces can potentially take any (physical and digital) form. Therefore, there is a need to prevent users from learning necessities for every single interface. To address the issue, interaction designers increasingly constrain their design decisions based on their conceptions of users' capacities and skills that already exist and are based on prior interactions with the real world. These skills, such as hand-eye coordination, are essential for tangible interfaces, and directly relate to cognition.

In this one-day workshop, we will discuss the role of theories of mind in contemporary human-computer interaction research, as those might provide us with a substantial understanding of cognition and human skills. The focus will be on embodied and situated theories and possible consequences of adopting an embodied and situated perspective on the design and analysis of tangible and embedded interaction.

Keywords
Theories of mind; Embodied cognition; Design Approaches

ACM Classification Keywords
H5.m. Information interfaces and presentation (e.g., HCI): Miscellaneous.

Workshop Theme

The vision of ubiquitous computing has inspired tangible and embedded interfaces. However, with interfaces taking novel (physical, digital and thus temporal [8]) forms and being embedded in our natural environment, conceptions of the "computer interface" are dated. Today, there is not one specific (representation of a) computer interface and not one specific context in which computer interfaces are used, but computing is becoming a "material", which is used in composites with physical materials [8], augmenting our existing natural environment.

Today's researchers in tangible and embedded interaction struggle with this situation in which many design problems are under-constrained in terms of the availability of various design materials. Designers not only design interaction with a given interface but also can radically redesign the interface itself (e.g., give any physical and temporal form to the digital interface). In addition, different kinds of interfaces can be designed for different contexts of use.

In all the dynamics that need to be considered by designers, capacities and skills that users have gained from prior interactions in reality [9] influences greatly design decisions while exploring new forms and possibilities. Conceptions of the nature of human capacities and skills are constraints for interaction design and can provide creativity some beneficial friction [7]. However, it is crucial that designers have an informed conception of human capacities and skills.

Rather than designing how users should interact with an established interface, nowadays, we as designers aim to improve how a user *interfaces* with interactive artifacts, and even more important, with the world through a new physical or digital form. Consequently, we need to be informed about how humans (evolutionary) interface through their bodies with their natural environment. Furthermore, we need to improve our understanding of how social and physical circumstances during interaction "influence" interaction.

This is where embodied and situated theories of mind [2] can provide insights on how users integrate their physical and social environments in everyday practices. If these theories are taken seriously, the environment is part of our cognitive system and through augmenting our environment we might even augment cognitive (physical and social) abilities or interfere with them.

> "... meaning and thought emerge from our capacities for perception, object manipulation, and bodily movement." [10]

According to Mark Johnson, human capacities constrain and define our conceptual thinking. Perception, object manipulation, and bodily movement are key characteristics of tangible and embedded interfaces. In tangible and embedded computing, physical form is given to "digital material" and through movement, object manipulation, and parallel perception users interact through "external representations" with the digital material.

> "The theory of embodied cognition offers us new ways to think about bodies, mind, and technology. Designing interactivity will never be the same." [6]

For David Kirsh [6], designers have to deal with cognition, as they have to deal with invention and conception. Embodied situated theories of mind can possibly guide design activities, however, as already highlighted by Van Dijk et al. [3], issues designers face might also be related to conceptions and theoretical issues with embodied cognition itself. Theories of mind do not provide a system of rules, which can be applied easily when designing human-computer interaction. Rather, as researchers, we need to critically explore the meaning of these theories for the design of tangible and embedded interfaces. Thus, in line with Harrison and colleagues, we consider theory as „[...] a resource for making sense of what is happening at the site of interaction." [5]

In order to better understand the consequences of adopting an embodied and situated perspective, we will address the following questions in the workshop:

- How have theories of mind influenced interaction design? Do embodied theories of mind influence contemporary interaction design in the same way?
- What users' physical (or bodily) skills do designers take into account? Do designers relate these skills with embodied cognition (and how do they relate them)?
- If cognition is social and carried out cooperatively, what could that mean for future (multi-user) interfaces?
- What consequences might embodied and situated theories of mind have on the actual act of engineering and designing?

Through discussing scholars' and practitioners' experiences on these questions, the workshop aims to find out how current tangible and embedded design research can benefit from embodied and situated theories of mind. The organizers of this workshop have experiences in designing and analyzing tangible and embedded interfaces (e.g., [1] [3]), in theoretically reflecting on design and design materials (e.g., [4]), and relating their research to the ongoing discussion on cognition and theories of mind.

Workshop Topics to be covered

After an introduction to the general workshop topic by the organizers, the workshop will be centered on the participants' experiences. The participants (including the organizers) will briefly present themselves and their stance regarding theories of mind and how they integrate (or have integrated in the past) theories with tangible and embedded interaction design. Example topics, which will be addressed, are cognition (i.e., sensorimotor couplings) in movement-based interaction, (shared) cognition during collaborative activities, and body schema and tool absorption.

Workshop Learning Goals

With this workshop we aim to increase awareness towards embodied and situated theories of mind. Moreover, it focuses on how adapting an embodied and situated perspective may influence resulting designs, how design activities are performed, and how designs can be analyzed.

Acknowledgements

The financial support by the Austrian Federal Ministry of Science, Research and Economy and the National Foundation for Research, Technology and Development is gratefully acknowledged (Christian Doppler Laboratory for "Contextual Interfaces"), as is the Austrian project – Assist 4.0 – funded by the Austrian Research Promotion Agency (FFG).

References

[1] Aslan, I., Murer, M., Fuchsberger, V., Fugard, A., and Tscheligi, M. 2013. Drag and drop the apple: the semantic weight of words and images in touch-based interaction. In Proceedings of the 7th International Conference on Tangible, Embedded and Embodied Interaction (TEI '13). ACM, New York, NY, USA, 159-166.

[2] Chemero, A. (2009) Radical embodied cognitive science. MIT Press.

[3] Van Dijk, J., van der Lugt, R., and Hummels, C. 2014. Beyond distributed representation: embodied cognition design supporting socio-sensorimotor couplings. In Proceedings of the 8th International Conference on Tangible, Embedded and Embodied Interaction (TEI '14). ACM, New York, NY, USA, 181-188.

[4] Fuchsberger, V., Murer, M., and Tscheligi, M. 2013. Materials, materiality, and media. In Proceedings of the SIGCHI Conference on Human Factors in Computing Systems (CHI '13). ACM, New York, NY, USA, 2853-2862.

[5] Harrison, S., Sengers, P., and Tatar, D. Making epistemological trouble: Third-paradigm HCI as successor science. Interacting with Computers 23, 5 (2011), 385 – 392. Feminism and HCI: New Perspectives.

[6] Kirsh, D. Embodied cognition and the magical future of interaction design. ACM Trans- actions on Computer-Human Interaction (TOCHI) 20, 1 (2013).

[7] Löwgren, J., and Stolterman, E. Thoughtful interaction design: A design perspective on information technology. The MIT press, 2004.

[8] Vallgårda, A. and Redström, J. 2007. Computational composites. In Proceedings of the SIGCHI Conference on Human Factors in Computing Systems (CHI '07).

[9] Jacob, R.J.K., Girouard, A., Hirshfield, L.M., Horn, M.S., Shaer, O., Solovey, E.T., and Zigelbaum, J. 2008. Reality-based interaction: a framework for post-WIMP interfaces. In Proceedings of the SIGCHI Conference on Human Factors in Computing Systems (CHI '08). ACM, New York, NY, USA, 201-210.

[10] Johnson, M. The Meaning of the Body: Aesthetics of Human Understanding. The University of Chicago Press, Chicago, 2007.

Un-Crafting: Exploring Tangible Practices for Deconstruction in Interactive System Design

Martin Murer
Christian Doppler Laboratory for "Contextual Interfaces"
ICT&S Center, University of Salzburg, Austria
martin.murer@sbg.ac.at

Anna Vallgårda
IxD Lab
IT University of Copenhagen
Copenhagen, Denmark
akav@itu.dk

Mattias Jacobsson
Mobile Life @ SICS
Box 1263
Kista, SE-164 29, Sweden
majac@sics.se

Manfred Tscheligi
Christian Doppler Laboratory for "Contextual Interfaces"
ICT&S Center, University of Salzburg, Austria
manfred.tscheligi@sbg.ac.at

TEI '15, Jan 16-19 2015, Stanford, CA, USA
ACM 978-1-4503-3305-4/15/01.
http://dx.doi.org/10.1145/2677199.2683582

Abstract
With this studio-workshop we aim to explore and debate how disassembling computational things can yield a potential for design practices. We believe there are significant qualities to be found in extending the mundane 'taking things apart' into an elaborate practice of *un-crafting*. The studio workshop comprises a series of collaborative disassembly activities with the aim of beginning to identify the key qualities and issues at stake. We also hope to have a diverse crowd, whose interdisciplinary viewpoints will enable us to ground an un-crafting practice in a diverse set of contexts.

Keywords
Deconstruction; design decomposition: reverse-engineering; disassembling; taking things apart; un-crafting

ACM Classification Keywords
H5.m. Information interfaces and presentation (e.g., HCI): Miscellaneous.

Introduction

In her opening keynote [2] at the 2014 CHI conference, science fiction author Margaret Atwood talked about taking things apart as a practice to make sense of the world surrounding her. In her childhood, she had felt an almost *bodily urge* to understand the inner workings and the functions of everyday objects (e.g., the moving eyes in one of her dolls) and so she had developed a habit of disassembling them.

We too recognize this almost bodily urge to become familiar with things through disassembly, a particular tangible enterprise familiar to anyone concerned with practices of making, tinkering, or crafting technology. The motivations are manifold: we disassemble appliances as a necessary step for repair [6], as means to harvest components [10], as essential part of iterative design or circuit bending [7], or simply driven by a curiosity to uncover a technological mystery [8]. With this studio-workshop, we aim to explore and debate how taking computational things apart yields a potential for design practices.

We believe there are significant qualities to be found in extending 'taking things apart' into an elaborate practice of *un-crafting*. Indeed, when understanding the design of computational things as a form-giving practice it is easy to conjecture how un-crafting can aid in getting an embodied sense of the physical form, the temporal form, and the interaction gestalt [11]. Through a series of collaborative disassembly activities at the studio-workshop, we hope to begin identifying the key qualities and issues at stake.

Related work

Others have acknowledged the values of disassembling things. Most prominently through practices in the realm of reverse engineering for the purpose of design recovery and as means to identify some system's components and their interrelationships [3]. In most cases, these activities are aimed at enabling an understanding of a particular system, its components and their interrelations in order to replicate its construction or production process and, thus, are less design oriented than we believe an un-crafting practice could be.

Moving beyond reverse engineering, the relevance of disassembling was proposed as valuable for educational science, following Seymour Papert's constructionist learning. For example, Griffin et al. argue that there is a "ying/yang interplay of the two learning modalities of Constructionism (learning by building) and Deconstructionism (learning by taking apart)" [4]. Specifically, they have proposed *Deconstruction Kits* that seeks to creatively engage learners in STEM education, problem solving, and critical thinking – while being taken apart.

Regarding the design of interactive systems, as demonstrated by two of the coordinators' earlier work [8], the collaborative act of taking apart an unknown, mystery device can be a powerful means to bootstrap explorative design exercises. Moreover, they argue that disassembling an appliance of unknown function can help an interdisciplinary design team to build common ground and a shared terminology. Taking computational things apart is, however, not limited to physical properties and aesthetic qualities of artifacts. Approaches such as inspirational bits [9] demonstrated

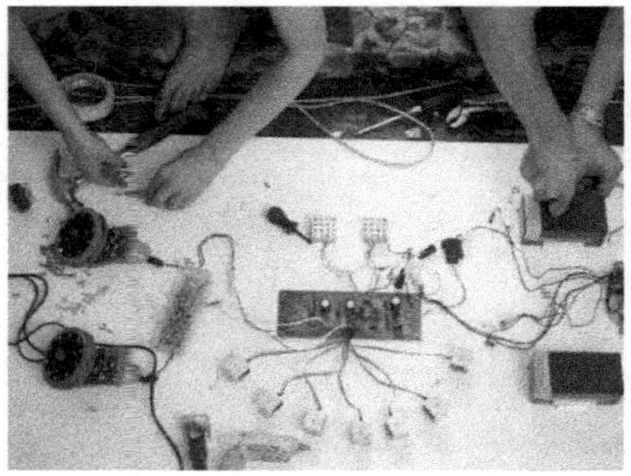

Figure 1: A robot being disassembled by one of the coordinators, keeping its circuit and function intact, while radically transforming its expression by altering its physical form, i.e., nailing the individual components to a plywood board.

how design might benefit from practices that aim to expose the *dynamic* properties of digital design materials by dissecting them in a crafty way. For the conceptual design of interactive artifacts Hallnäs and Redström [5] propose a methodological exercise that turns the classical leitmotif "form follows function" upside down in order to discover functionality in expressions. Taking things apart might be one of the more suitable practices to actually achieve this goal of rediscovering "the hidden aesthetical choices in the expressiveness of things in use." [5]

Studio-Workshop Proposal

A current rise in interest of diverse socio-technological phenomena around Maker and DIY cultures have lead to a re-emergence and re-evaluation of handcrafting skills and practices in our research field. This can be seen in past years conferences and most recently, stressed by the 2014 conference on Designing Interactive Systems (DIS), themed "Crafting Design" [1]. The corresponding research on design processes is primarily concerned with the synthesizing aspects of making; with giving form to interactive artifacts through putting things together. Consequential, this is reflected in the practical experiences offered to Studio attendees at the previous TEI conferences, focusing on a diversity of practices, techniques, and skills for creating, making, crafting, and building. The format of studio-workshops introduced this year offers the great opportunity to complement those experiences with a dedication to un-crafting; an explorative journey around the various tangible practices and techniques applied when taking things apart, as well as their present and future applications at various stages of a design process.

As stressed by the term *un-crafting,* we consider the thoughtful, reflective process of disassembling to be a very particular style of tangible activity. We see un-crafting as a something which could be developed into a practice that – not unlike other studio crafts – requires particular skills, involves specific ways of reflection, and develops and according set of terms and framings; a practice that may allow one to strive for mastership. We also see how it must start with the bodily urges of our childhood and those small mundane practices of playfully exploring and tinkering with everyday artifacts that are widely spread across cultures so nearly anyone can relate to them. Thus, we encourage a diverse audience to participate in our studio workshop, with no particular prior skills required.

Consistent with the reflexive nature of disassembling, the studio workshop will tightly intertwine hands-on activities (i.e., taking things apart) with reflections in action and academic debate. The anticipated interdisciplinary perspectives of the participants, together with the material gained throughout two days of collaborative experience, will allow participants to identify, explore and debate various facets of un-crafting: practical, methodological, and theoretical considerations.

Topics to be covered

In order to build common ground while provoking as fruitful a debate as possible, the studio workshop will cover the following topics that all aiming to identify, explore, and debate how un-crafting as a very particular reflective practice may contribute to design: un-crafting for repair, un-crafting for learning, collaborative un-crafting, and un-crafting for design. This outline will allow participants to explore and discuss the particularities of taking computational things apart, e.g., different remembrance or documentation strategies for later reassembling, in order to explore its potential for design. A final phase will encourage participants to *make* an artifact, e.g., a piece of art, or an interactive piece like the one made from robotic materials in Figure 1, that repurposes all or parts of the material gained in the previous stage. We hope the openness of the stages will inspire participants to further incorporate un-crafting into their design and research practices.

Goals & Discussion Objectives

The primary goal is to begin articulating the potential qualities of an un-crafting practice based on the tangible acts of taking a series of computational things apart. Through discussions and reflection among a hopefully diverse group of participants we further aim to begin identifying contexts for which an un-crafting practice yields potential.

Acknowledgements

The financial support by the Austrian Federal Ministry of Science, Research and Economy and the National Foundation for Research, Technology and Development is gratefully acknowledged (Christian Doppler Laboratory for "Contextual Interfaces").

References

[1] DIS '14: Proceedings of the 2014 Conference on Designing Interactive Systems (New York, NY, USA, 2014), ACM. 608146.

[2] Atwood, M. Robotics in my work and life. In *CHI EA '14*, ACM, pp. 13–14.

[3] Chikofsky, E., and Cross, J.H., I. Reverse engineering and design recovery: a taxonomy. Software, IEEE 7, 1 (1990), 13–17.

[4] Griffin, J., Kaplan, E., and Burke, Q. Debug'ems and other deconstruction kits for stem learning. In *Integrated STEM Education Conference (ISEC)*, 2012 IEEE 2nd (2012), pp. 1–4.

[5] Hallnäs, L. and Redström, J. Abstract Information Appliances - Methodological Exercises in Conceptual Design of Computational Things. In *Proc. DIS2002*, London, UK 2002, pp. 105-116.

[6] Jackson, S. J., Ahmed, S. I., and Rifat, M. R. Learning, innovation, and sustainability among mo- bile phone repairers in dhaka, bangladesh. In *Proc DIS '14*, ACM.

[7] Mellis, D. A., Jacoby, S., Buechley, L., Perner-Wilson, H., and Qi, J. Microcontrollers as material: Crafting circuits with paper, conductive ink, electronic components, and an "untoolkit". In *Proc. TEI '13*, ACM, pp. 83–90.

[8] Murer, M., Jacobsson, M., Skillgate, S., and Sundstroöm, P. Taking things apart: Reaching common ground and shared material understanding. In *Proc. CHI '14*, ACM, pp. 469–472.

[9] Sundström, P., Taylor, A., Grufberg, K., Wirstroöm, N., Solsona Belenguer, J., and Lunden, M. Inspirational bits: Towards a shared understanding of the digital material. In *Proc. CHI '11*, ACM, pp. 1561–1570.

[10] Verplank, B., Gauthier, D., and Bak, J. Tei 2013 studio: Motors and music. In *Proc. TEI '13*, ACM, pp. 431–434.

[11] Vallgårda, A. Giving form to computational things - Developing a practice of interaction design. *Personal Ubiquitous Computing*. 18, 3. (2014) 577-592.

Tangible Meets Gestural: Comparing and Blending Post-WIMP Interaction Paradigms

Leonardo Angelini
University of Applied Sciences and Arts Western Switzerland
Fribourg, Switzerland
leonardo.angelini@hes-so.ch

Denis Lalanne
University of Fribourg
Fribourg, Switzerland
denis.lalanne@unifr.ch

Elise van den Hoven [1,2]
[1] Faculty of Design, Architecture & Building, University of Technology, Sydney, Australia
[2] Industrial Design Department, Eindhoven University of Technology, the Netherlands
elise.vandenhoven@uts.edu.au

Ali Mazalek [3,4]
Synaesthetic Media Lab
[3] Ryerson University, Toronto, ON, Canada
[4] Georgia Institute of Technology, Atlanta, GA, USA
mazalek@ryerson.ca

Omar Abou Khaled
University of Applied Sciences and Arts Western Switzerland
Fribourg, Switzerland
omar.aboukhaled@hes-so.ch

Elena Mugellini
University of Applied Sciences and Arts Western Switzerland
Fribourg, Switzerland
elena.mugellini@hes-so.ch

TEI '15, Jan 16-19 2015, Stanford, CA, USA
ACM 978-1-4503-3305-4/15/01.
http://dx.doi.org/10.1145/2677199.2683583

Abstract
More and more objects of our everyday environment are becoming smart and connected, offering us new interaction possibilities. Tangible interaction and gestural interaction are promising communication means with these objects in this post-WIMP interaction era. Although based on different principles, they both exploit our body awareness and our skills to provide a richer and more intuitive interaction. Occasionally, when user gestures involve physical artifacts, tangible interaction and gestural interaction can blend into a new paradigm, i.e., tangible gesture interaction [5]. This workshop fosters the comparison among these different interaction paradigms and offers a unique opportunity to discuss their analogies and differences, as well as the definitions, boundaries, strengths, application domains and perspectives of tangible gesture interaction. Participants from different backgrounds are invited.

Keywords
Tangible interaction; gestural interaction; physical gestures; embodied design; tangible gestures.

ACM Classification Keywords
H5.2. Information interfaces and presentation: User interfaces, Interaction styles, User-centered design.

Introduction

Since Weiser's vision of ubiquitous computing [14], many branches of Human-Computer Interaction (HCI) have tried to obtain a seamless and digitally augmented interaction with the physical world. Jacob et al. formalized the transition from the Windows Icon Mouse Pointer (WIMP) paradigm to the post-WIMP era with Reality Based Interaction (RBI), which takes advantage of human natural skills to interact in the real world [7]. Tangible interaction and gestural interaction both benefit from the RBI theme Body Awareness & Skills [10] and allow moving the interaction beyond the screen. Since the origins of tangible interaction, many researchers considered gestures as a communication means in Tangible User Interfaces (TUIs). Fitzmaurice's PhD thesis on graspable user interfaces states: "By using physical objects, we not only allow users to employ a larger expressive range of gestures and grasping behaviors but also to leverage off of a user's innate spatial reasoning skills and everyday knowledge of object manipulations" [4]. A few years later, Fishkin wrote that tangible interfaces "all share the same basic paradigm—a user uses their hands to manipulate some physical object(s) via physical gestures; a computer system detects this, alters its state, and gives feedback accordingly" [3]. Still in Radical Atoms [6], Ishii's latest vision of tangible interaction, gestures and direct manipulation are the two modalities that allow the users to control the system. Similarly, gestural interaction is often associated to the manipulation of physical objects. Gesture can animate objects such as the Nintendo WiiMote or the Sony PSMove, "reinventing" the identity of the controller [13]. Ferscha et al. [2] framed tilting gesture with different types of physical artifacts, while Song et al. [11] showed how different grips and touch gestures could be used to change the inking mode of a pen.

The relative influences of the two paradigms suggest that it is possible to blend tangible interaction and gestural interaction in richer interaction paradigms that exploits at the same time our ability to communicate through gestures and our ability to manipulate objects of the real world. Vaucelle and Ishii theorized this new paradigm for the first time in 2008 as Gesture Object Interfaces [13]. In 2010, Van den Hoven and Mazalek [5] defined tangible gesture interaction at the intersection of gestural interaction and tangible interaction, bridging both our ability to think and communicate through our bodies and our manipulative skills. Van den Hoven and Mazalek [5] gave several examples and application domains of tangible gesture interaction. In order to explore the design space of gesture with objects, Valdes et al. [12] and Angelini et al. [1] have conducted two user elicitation studies. Both studies found a large variety of possible gestures, respectively with active tokens and the steering wheel, but they also noticed a strong influence of gestures typical of smartphones and tablets, such as swiping and tapping. This is consistent with the recent theory of blended interaction [8], which suggest that users blend concepts not only from their knowledge of the physical world such as in RBI [7], but also from their previous knowledge of existing interactive systems. Although smartphone gestural interfaces are more intuitive and richer than WIMP interfaces, they still do not support our ability to manipulate objects and they generally exploit only one or two fingers. Obviously, this perspective worries the TEI community and indeed this TEI'15 workshop aims at demonstrating that tangible gesture interaction can offer a richer experience to users than traditional GUI based interaction. Within this context, this workshop offers an opportunity to discuss the current trends of tangible and gestural interactions, evidencing the advantages and limitations offered by both paradigms and the possibilities and risks that arises by blending them in tangible gesture interaction.

Workshop Proposal

The workshop aims at gathering around 15-20 participants. We encourage the participation of young practitioners but also more experienced researchers from different backgrounds (design, engineering, computing, arts, social sciences, neurosciences, ergonomics, etc.), with previous experience in tangible interaction or gestural interaction, or both. Workshop participants are invited to submit 3 to 6 page position papers that cover one or more topics suggested in the call for papers. In the first part of the workshop, the participants will briefly present and discuss their contributions. The following parts of the workshop will benefit of engaging hands-on design experiences to reason about tangible interaction, gestural interaction and tangible gesture interaction. Those design challenges aims at enhancing everyday objects with interactive capabilities. The participants, divided into small groups, will design simple tangible or gestural interfaces for digital interaction with everyday objects. This activity will take the form of a design competition in order to stimulate participants' involvement and creativity. Workshop organizers will rate the designs according to the number of interactions, their quality and the originality of the application; a live ranking updated each 15 minutes will help stimulate creativity. The analysis of the hands-on phase results will allow participants to find analogies and differences between the two interaction paradigms. Then, after a second design competition, similar to the first one but applied to tangible gesture interfaces, participants will try to blend the two interaction paradigms and will discuss the definition, boundaries, strengths, limitations, application domains and perspectives of tangible gesture interaction.

Workshop Topics to be Covered

The topics of the workshop and of the participants' papers could include, but are not limited to:

- Theory and ground knowledge that frames gestural and tangible interaction
- Application of existing post-WIMP frameworks in tangible and gestural interaction
- Comparison of gestural and tangible interfaces (user performances, cognitive load, fatigue, learnability, skill development etc.) in specific application domains
- Expressivity of tangible and gestural interfaces
- Physical and psychological implications of human senses and skills involved in tangible and gestural interactions
- Feedback and feedforward for tangible and gestural interaction
- Novel applications for tangible gesture interfaces
- Theory, frameworks and future visions on tangible gesture interaction

- Techniques for mixed gesture and object recognition

Workshop Learning Goals

This workshop aims at building a community around the emerging field of tangible gesture interaction. The workshop will allow participants to see different points of view about gestural and tangible interaction from people with different backgrounds, enriching not only their personal experience but also the community's knowledge as a whole. Indeed, the insights generated during the workshop will support the advancement of the field of tangible gestural interaction and the results of the workshop will be shared with the scientific community. Moreover, the hands-on phases will allow tinkering with tangible gesture interfaces, individuating new applications for interactive objects.

Workshop Supporting Web Documents

A dedicated website at www.tangiblegestures.com will provide all the relevant information to the participants and will host the accepted workshop papers. The website will be a point of reference for the community and will publicize other future events on the topic of tangible gestures.

References

[1] Angelini, L., Carrino, F., Carrino, S., et al.: Gesturing on the steering wheel: a user-elicited taxonomy. *Proc. AutoUI'14.* (2014). *(To appear)*

[2] Ferscha, A., Resmerita, S., Holzmann, C., Reicho, M.: Orientation sensing for gesture-based interaction with smart artifacts. *Computer Communications*. 28, 1552–1563 (2005).

[3] Fishkin, K.: A taxonomy for and analysis of tangible interfaces. *Personal and Ubiquitous Computing*. 8, 347–358. (2004).

[4] Fitzmaurice, G.W.: *Graspable User Interfaces*. Ph.D. Thesis, Dept. of Computer Science, University of Toronto, (1996).

[5] Hoven, E., Mazalek, A.: Grasping gestures: Gesturing with physical artifacts. *Artificial Intelligence for Engineering Design, Analysis and Manufacturing*. 25, 255–271. (2011).

[6] Ishii, H., Lakatos, D., Bonanni, L., Labrune, J.-B.: Radical Atoms : Beyond Tangible Bits, Toward Transformable Materials. *Interactions*. XIX, 37–51 (2012).

[7] Jacob, R.J.K., Girouard, A., Horn, M.S., Zigelbaum, J.: Reality-Based Interaction : A Framework for Post-WIMP Interfaces. *Proc.CHI'08*. 201–210 (2008).

[8] Jetter, H.-C., Reiterer, H., and Geyer, F. Blended Interaction: understanding natural human–computer interaction in post-WIMP interactive spaces. *Personal and Ubiquitous Computing*, (2013). Vol. 18, Iss. 5, pp 1139-1158.

[9] Mazalek, A., van den Hoven, E.: Framing tangible interaction frameworks. *Artificial Intelligence for Engineering Design, Analysis and Manufacturing*. 23, 225 (2009).

[10] Poor, G.M., Tomlinson, B., Guinness, D. et al. Tangible or Gestural : Comparing Tangible vs . Kinect ™ Interactions with an Object Manipulation Task. *Adjunct Proc. TEI'13.* (2013).

[11] Song, H., Benko, H., Guimbretiere, F., Izadi, S., Cao, X., Hinckley, K.: Grips and gestures on a multi-touch pen. *Proc. CHI'11*. pp. 1323–1332. ACM (2011).

[12] Valdes, C., Eastman, D., Grote, C., et al. Exploring the design space of gestural interaction with active tokens through user-defined gestures. *Proc. CHI '14*, (2014), 4107–4116.

[13] Vaucelle, C., Ishii, H.: Picture this!: film assembly using toy gestures. *Proc. UbiComp'08*. (2008).

[14] Weiser, M. The computer of the 21st century. *Scientific American September*, (1991), 94–100.

Costumes and Wearables as Game Controllers

Joshua Tanenbaum
Donald Bren School of Information and Computer Sciences
Department of Informatics
University of California, Irvine
Irvine, CA 92697-3440, USA
joshua.tanenbaum@uci.edu

Karen Tanenbaum
Center for Games & Playable Media
University of California, Santa Cruz
Santa Cruz, CA 95064
karen.tanenbaum@gmail.com

Katherine Isbister
Game Innovation Lab
New York University
Brooklyn, NY 11201, USA
Katherine.isbister@nyu.edu

Kaho Abe
Game Innovation Lab
New York University
Brooklyn, NY 11201, USA
info@kahoabe.net

Anne Sullivan
Play Crafts
Santa Cruz, CA 95060, USA
anne@play-crafts.com

Luigi Anzivino
Scientific Content Developer
The Exploratorium
San Francisco, CA 94111, USA
lanzivino@exploratorium.edu

TEI '15, Jan 16-19, 2015, Stanford, CA, USA.
ACM 978-1-4503-3305-4/15/01.
http://dx.doi.org/10.1145/2677199.2683584

Abstract
There has been a significant increase in commercial interest in wearable technologies, spearheaded by Google's Glass project, and also by the success of a new generation of fitness oriented biosensors such as the Fitbit, the Bodymedia Fit, and the Misfit Shine. Concurrently, there has been a proliferation of embodied interfaces for digital games such as Nintendo's Wii, Sony's Move controller, and Microsoft's Kinect. These technologies often only scratch the surface of the design possibility space, overlooking nuances of social and emotional experience for wearers/players that are important in other areas of design, such as theatrical costuming and fashion. We propose a studio that offers participants the chance to create wearable game controllers that afford a playful exploration of this design terrain, encouraging transformation, collaboration, and enjoyment of rich spectacle.

Keywords
Wearables; Game Interfaces; Hacking; DIY;

ACM Classification Keywords
H.5.m. Information interfaces and presentation (e.g., HCI): Miscellaneous.

Wearing Google Glass is an expressive act – it has come to signify participation in a value-laden discourse around technology, privacy, and wearability.

Games like Kaho Abe's *Hit Me!* make use of player postures and movements to explore social dynamics and create engaging spectacle.

Introduction

There has been a significant increase in commercial interest in wearable technologies, spearheaded by Google's Glass project and also by the success of a new generation of fitness oriented biosensors such as the Fitbit, the Bodymedia Fit, and the Misfit Shine. However, although there is a good deal of optimism and excitement about the future of wearable technology, the design space currently occupied by these new wearables is actually quite narrow. We would argue that this is in part due to a preoccupation with individual-focused, data-driven *function* of the wearable devices among technology designers, and – consequentially – a lack of attention to the ways in which these device shape the social interactions, emotional experiences and identities of wearers. Google Glass has received significant media attention, not just because it enables a new mode of interaction with computational devices, but also because it visibly alters the social identity of its user [e.g. 8]. Wearable technologies are different than handheld technologies in part because of the ways in which clothing, costume, and fashion are used as expressive social performances in the world. Incorporating an understanding of the expressive and social dimensions of wearability opens up new design possibilities for this technology.

Concurrent with the rise in fitness and lifestyle focused wearables, in the last 10 years there has been a proliferation of embodied interfaces for digital games, including systems such as Nintendo's Wii, Sony's Move controller, and Microsoft's Kinect, as well as independent 'indie' experimentation with custom controllers. These devices afford a range of new playful experiences, in part by circumventing the entrenched literacies associated with the handheld video game controller – literacies that exclude many potential gamers who have not mastered the arcane feats of manual dexterity required by such interfaces. Embodied interfaces have opened up a whole new design space for games [e.g. 4, 7]. It is evident that interfaces that reshape the body of the player in meaningful ways are capable of using the body as an expressive channel for narrative meaning [10]. Performing an avatar/player character physically and socially can increase the sense of identification and immersion the player feels, as well as heighten social engagement and involvement for both players and spectators [3]. There is a growing 'indie' movement that has increasingly taken up embodied interaction (e.g. Kaho Abe's games, [1], including the Costumes as Game Controllers project [2]). We draw upon this work in the proposed studio.

Taking inspiration from theatrical costuming and fashion design, we plan to host a studio that enables participants to create wearable game controllers that include costuming elements. In theatrical and dance practice, costumes and masks are frequently used to elicit specific character behaviors in performers. Improvisational theater theorist and Mask practitioner Keith Johnstone describes masks as a source of *outside->in* transformation [5]. Stanslavski, the father of Method acting, wrote about the power of masks and makeup to elicit powerful new experiences of the self [9]. Schools of outside->in method acting have long held that it is possible to use external stimuli including costumes, choreography, and tangible props to elicit transformative experiences in a performer.

Fashion aficionados similarly use the clothing they select to inhabit an identity and to project that identity in social contexts and interactions with others. What takes place in a bounded 'magic circle' of gameplay with costuming, we believe also has relevance outside this sphere and in the realm of everyday life. We can see the beginnings of the modulation of wearables into fashion with experiments like Google's collaboration with Diane von Furstenberg putting Glass on runway models [6]. The proposed studio will allow participants to reflect upon the transformation of wearables into fashion objects in their own right, toward anticipating and designing these aspects of such devices.

The "Costumes and Wearables as Game Controllers" studio aims to explore how researchers within the tangible and embodied interaction community can expand the expressive possibilities inherent in wearables and embodied interfaces by applying inspiration from costuming and fashion design.

The MaKey MaKey supports quick, lightweight prototyping of simple interactions by mapping the closure of a circuit in the physical world with common keystrokes. Any conductive objects connected to it become interactive touch pads. (http://www.makeymakey.com/ image used with permission.)

Studio Proposal

We plan to assemble a simple kit for quickly hacking together wearable game controllers, so that participants can focus on the expressive possibilities of designing new wearable game interfaces. We propose a very simple hardware platform comprised of conductive fabric, alligator clips, and the MaKey MaKey interface board, which we will provide to teams of participants to facilitate rapid prototyping of wearable controllers. For more advanced and ambitious participants we will also provide an assortment of Arduinos, accelerometers, flex sensors, and other off the shelf sensors. Participants are encouraged to source and supply their own specialized hardware if they desire to work with any particularly esoteric sensors or devices.

In addition to providing an easy-to-use hardware prototyping platform, we will also provide a wide assortment of clothing, costume pieces, and accessories for participants to modify and transform into wearable game controllers. Participants will be invited to bring any costume or prop items that they would like to contribute to the shared group pool, so long as they understand that these items may well be modified and re-appropriated during the studio.

Prior to the start of the studio, the organizers will curate a selection of free-to-play online games that we believe will lend themselves to this type of expressive interface design. A list of these games will be provided to the participants prior to their arrival at the conference, to help them plan possible new interactions ahead of time, but participants are also encouraged to suggest and provide other games that they are interested in designing new interfaces for.

Expected skills:

- Passing familiarity with games and embodied interaction.
  An understanding of basic electronics prototyping will be helpful, but is not required.

Expected preparation:

- We will expect participants to bring a laptop computer capable of connecting to a MaKey MaKey via USB and the internet via WiFi.
- Participants are expected to take the time to familiarize themselves with the provided list of games and with the basic workings of the MaKey MaKey ahead of time.
- Optionally, participants are encouraged to bring any hardware, software, tools, and

prototyping supplies they wish to contribute, particularly if they have a specialized design idea that they wish to realize.

Studio Topics to be covered

- Embodied interaction and embodied game interfaces, characters and avatars.
- Basics of method acting and "outside->in" theatrical techniques.
- Cultural perspectives on clothing, fashion, and wearability.
- The importance of shaping *experience*, *identity*, and *sociality* in addition to *individual-focused function* when designing wearable interfaces.

We anticipate that exposing participants to these interdisciplinary perspectives will support ongoing explorations of meaningful wearable interface design, beyond the confines of the studio itself.

Studio Learning Goals

Our studio will broaden participants' perspective on design criteria and objectives for wearables and embodied interfaces, encouraging them to incorporate aesthetics, strategies, and values from costuming and fashion. The studio should provide valuable food for thought for participants interested in the future of the wearables and embodied interaction design space, shifting their approach to design values and process.

Acknowledgements

Thanks to Eyebeam gallery for support of the initial Costume as Game Controllers project in NYC, and to Jay Silver and the staff at JoyLabz for the donation of MaKey MaKeys for the studio.

References

[1] Abe, K. (2014). http://kahoabe.net

[2] Abe, K. and Isbister, K. (2014). Costumes as Game Controllers project, http://fashion.eyebeam.org/projects/the-lighting-bug-game

[3] Isbister, K. (2006). Better Game Characters by Design: A Psychological Approach. Morgan Kaufmann

[4] Isbister, K. (2012). How to Stop Being a Buzzkill: Designing Yamove!, A Mobile Tech Mash-up to Truly Augment Social Play. Keynote presentation, abstract included in Proceedings of MobileHCI 2012, San Francisco, CA.

[5] Johnstone, K. *Impro: Improvisation and the Theatre*. Theatre Arts Book, New York, 1987.

[6] Krupnick, E. (2012). Diane Von Furstenberg's Google Glasses Bring Geek-Chic To Fashion Week (PHOTOS). Huff Post Style, 20 August 2014, http://www.huffingtonpost.com/2012/09/10/diane-von-furstenberg-google-glasses-fashion-week_n_1870234.html.

[7] Mueller, F. and Isbister, K. (2014). Movement-Based Game Guidelines. In Proceedings of CHI 2014, Toronto, Canada.

[8] Shuster, D. The Revolt Against Google 'Glassholes', New York Post, 14 July 2014, http://nypost.com/2014/07/14/is-google-glass-cool-or-just-plain-creepy.

[9] Stanislavski, C. *Building a Character*. A&C Black, 2013.

[10] Tanenbaum, J. and Bizzocchi, J. Rock Band: A Case Study in the Design of Embodied Interface Experience. ACM Press (2009), 127–134.

Interactive Infrastructures - Towards a Language for Distributed Interfaces

Bert Bongers
Interactivation Studio
University of Technology, Sydney
Faculty of Design, Architecture and Building
PO Box 123 Broadway
NSW 2007 Australia
bertbon@xs4all.nl

figure 1. The background image of the workshop web site – extending a textile work of Cecilia Heffer, of a joint project extending the networked lace pattern through interactive media. It is placed here merely to fill the large empty space in the template, but also because of its resonance with the workshop topic.

TEI '15, Jan 16-19, 2015, Stanford, CA, USA.
ACM 978-1-4503-3305-4/15/01.
http://dx.doi.org/10.1145/2677199.2683585

Abstract
An interactive infrastructure allows people to have access to the parameters of an interactive environment in real time, potentially leading to an increased productivity, decrease of energy and material consumption, and generally greater satisfaction and experience. However, there is a need for a universal communication language between the elements of such an infrastructure and the real world. A language that can connect the Internet of Things, media contents, and people. The workshop will bring together a number of participants from the field of Tangible and Embedded Interaction, who have ideas, insights and experience in developing communication languages. Rather than a symposium or mini-conference format, the format for the day is that of a working group consisting experts and contributors. This working group will establish the groundwork for the interactive infrastructures language.

Imagine walking into a room, and being able to access all the parameters of the space (light levels, colours, temperature, music, video, etc.) from your own personal interface. The room will present all its parameters (and the ranges of each) to your personal interface device, which you can then map to the individual sensors on your device.

Introduction

The aim of the workshop is to bring together researchers, practitioners and creators, to explore the development of unified protocols and languages for distributed interaction. Due to the increased interactive capabilities of our environments, with embedded digital elements, wearable and mobile devices, a language could provide more than just the sum of these parts. In many cases applications, appcessories, devices, the Internet of Things, etc. speak their own (often proprietary) language. Sometimes there are commercial reasons for this (FitBit owns your data in their Cloud), but many applications are open and could be connected in new scenarios of use. In the early 80s the MIDI protocol started a revolution in music making with many unforeseen applications and even new kinds of music, and many new instruments [5, 12]. It provided a universal and widely implemented communication language between musical devices, based on musical performance parameters. There are many protocols and languages developed to connect elements of the digital world, and rather than proposing to develop yet another language, from an HCI point of view it makes sense to develop a protocol based on human factors and parameters from the physical world. Technically this is not complicated, but the big conceptual challenge is to describe the real world parameters in a meaningful way - and this is something the HCI and particularly the TEI communities are good at.

Background

The importance and presence of infrastructures in our environment has increased over the years.
Infrastructures provide access and control of electricity, data networks, light, water, air-conditioning etc. It is an essential part of the architectural structure because it directly relates to its inhabitants. The infrastructure is the part of the technological environment that the inhabitants interact with. However, the interaction possibilities are often severely limited due to inadequate user interfaces. The design of infrastructures is often not regarded as an essential part of architectural or building engineering practices, while it is important for the way the building operates. An increased awareness of the importance of sustainability and preserving our natural environment has led to an increase in attention for the design of the infrastructure, part of an emphasis on more holistic, integrated and inclusive design approaches. In order to do this a structured interaction language and protocol is needed, facilitating the reuse and incremental development of interaction modules. Based on the layers of solid technical developments and protocols, this proposed language is firmly based on real world parameters and human factors. The first steps towards the development of this language are explored in this workshop, based by theoretical frameworks and practical approaches, and examples projects as case studies.

Many successful projects have been established in this field, often based on ad-hoc networks of interaction. While these function perfectly well at a proof-of-concept level, as convincingly shown in many demonstrators and experimental set-ups, in order to develop a potential for wider applicability further integration of the elements would be beneficial. This proposal is complimentary to existing proposals and projects, which exchange data in more 'raw' form and the meaning is established at other layers [1, 11]. It would also relate to existing interface description protocols such as Instrumental Interaction [2], CHAI3D [8] and TUIO [9, 10].

A Design Space for Physical Interfaces

In engineering literature, but also to an extent in HCI it is common to describe and categorise sensors and actuators by their physical working principle, such as light, ultrasound, or magnetism. For the purpose of analysis of interaction and design of interfaces it is more appropriate however to categorise in terms of human factors. For instance, a human movement can be tracked through an infrared light sensor or an ultrasound sensor, and although there are subtle differences associated with each sensing technique, what is important in HCI is the human movement rather than the technology. Based on experiences in designing interfaces ranging from electronic musical instruments, interactive architecture, live video performances and installations, a framework was developed for physical interface design using the terms *range*, *precision* and *haptic feedback*, in relation to each Degree-of-Freedom of movement. This Physical Instrument Design Space (PIDS) has been applied in the design of physical interfaces, but can also be used in the analysis of existing interfaces. It enables the comparison between interfaces and interface elements in quantitative measures [3]. The design space is related to the issue of mapping, which is about the relationships between the computer's input, behaviours and parameters of its processes, and output. The importance of mapping can not be emphasised enough in design, and when applied with sophistication this is the most crucial area of the craft of designing for interaction.

Interaction Infrastructures Protocol

Following from the notion of Ubicomp and the electronic ecology, the need for a unifying interaction language is identified. Such a language or protocol will enable all the elements in what we can call an interaction infrastructure to communicate with each other. Most distributed computing and Internet of Things projects have some form of language but many are based on technical descriptions and ad-hoc devised languages. It is proposed to develop a language based on real-world parameters and the other dimensions of the physical interfaces design space (PIDS) as presented in the previous section. In order to be relevant and applicable, this language needs to be firmly based on human factors, movement parameters, and other physical measures of the environment. With this level of meaningful description, the other levels of connection and protocol can be filled in. A modular design approach is proposed [3, 6, 7], and multiple interaction modalities need to be addressed [4].

It is proposed that the protocol operates independently of the new or existing technical layers, conform the multilayered OSI model. There is a range of hardware/ software standards (USB, Firewire, Ethernet, WiFi, Bluetooth, Zigbee etc. generally accredited by the IEEE) that can form the lower layers. There are a number of languages, including those related to the performance arts, that in a way sit between this top level (human factors) language level and in some cases include low level software and hardware protocols. Examples are DMX (theatre lighting), X10 (home automation), CAN (automotive), I2C, Dali (lighting), CBus, ANT+ (commercial wearable sensors), IrDA (infrared remote controls), CoAP (and other web based protocols including XML), MQTT (telemetry), IFTTT (if this than that), OSC (real time performance data) [13], and of course MIDI.

With such a protocol in place, manufacturers and research groups have an incentive to join this open standard.

Conclusion

In this workshop proposal we have outlined the need and opportunities for interactive infrastructures. We are aiming to bring together partners from technical R&D, human sciences, design research, and industry together in joint projects to investigate these issues further and explore the opportunities. The aim of this workshop is to encourage further collaborative research, assessing the proposed approaches and develop further insights and practical applications.

More information can be found on the web site about the project, www.bertbongers.com/TEIworkshop

References

[1] Baalman, M., H. C. Smoak, C. L. Salter, J. Malloch, M. M. Wanderley. Sharing Data in Collaborative, Interactive Performances: the SenseWorld DataNetwork. *Proceedings of the NIME* conference on New Instruments for Musical Expression (2009) 131-134.

[2] Beaudouin-Lafon, M. Instrumental Interaction: an interaction model for designing post-WIMP user interfaces. *Proc. ACM CHI Conference on Human Factors in Computing Systems* (2000) 446–453.

[3] Bongers, A.J. & Harris, Y.C. The Video-Organ, A Structured Instrument Design Approach. Proceedings of the NIME conference on New Instruments for Musical Expression, Dublin, Ireland (2002) 86-91.

[4] Bongers, A.J. & Van der Veer, G.C. Towards a Multimodal Interaction Space: categorisation and applications. *Journal of Personal and Ubiquitous Computing*, vol. 11, no. 8, (2007) 609-619.

[5] Bongers, A. J. Electronic Musical Instruments: Experiences of a New Luthier, *Leonardo Music Journal*, Vol. 17 (2007) 9-16

[6] Bongers, A. J., Multimodal Interaction in Protospace In: *Hyperbody - First Decade of Interactive Architecture*, Kas Oosterhuis (Ed.). Jap Sam Books NL, 2012

[7] Bongers, A. J., Smith, S. T., Donker, V. and Pickrell, M. Interactive Rehabilitation Tiles. Work in Progress paper, TEI 8th International Conference on Tangible, Embedded and Embodied Interaction, München (D), 2014

[8] Conti F, Barbagli F, Morris D, Sewell C. CHAI 3D: An Open-Source Library for the Rapid Development of Haptic Scenes, IEEE World Haptics, Pisa, Italy, March 2005

[9] Kaltenbrunner, M. & Bovermann, T. & Bencina, R. & Costanza, E. TUIO - A Protocol for Table-Top Tangible User Interfaces", *Proceedings of the 6th International Workshop on Gesture in Human-Computer Interaction and Simulation* (2005), Vannes (France)

[10] Kaltenbrunner, M., Bencina, R.: reacTIVision: A Computer-Vision Framework for Table-Based Tangible Interaction. *Proceedings of the TEI conference on Tangible and Embedded Interaction*. Baton Rouge, Louisiana, 2007

[11] Luyten, K. and K. Coninx. Distributed User Interface Elements to support Smart Interaction Spaces. *Proceedings of the ISM*. 2005

[12] Paradiso, J. New Ways to Play: Electronic Music Interfaces. *IEEE Spectrum* 34/12 (1997) 18-30.

[13] Wright, M., Freed, A., Momeni A.: OpenSound Control: State of the Art 2003. *Proceedings of the NIME Conference on New Instruments for Musical Expression* Montreal, Canada, 2003.

Making Storytelling Personal: Finding Your User in Your Story

Barbara A. Karanian, Ph.D.
Mechanical Engineering Design
Stanford University
Stanford, CA 94305
karanian@stanford.edu

Erica S. Savig, M.Arch.
Center for Design Research
Cancer Biology Program
School of Medicine
Stanford University
424 Panama Mall
Stanford, CA 94305 USA
esavig@stanford.edu

TEI '15, January 16–19 2015, Stanford, CA, USA.
ACM 978-1-4503-3305-4/15/01.
http://dx.doi.org/10.1145/2677199.2683587

Abstract
Have you ever asked yourself if we blur the lines between the *Who* in our user's story and the *Me* in our personal story? This Workshop is based on the premise that finding our personal stories enhances our capacity to step into our user's shoes for deeper insights that fuel design.

Discover engaging parallel stories using a variety of validated processes. Through a thought-provoking, psychodynamic and design-thinking approach, we will detangle each other's stories to reveal tangible translations on multiple levels. The active workshop will consist of planned imaginative prompts and an assortment of expressive modes such as one-minute interviews, drawing, prototype writing, and simulations.

The overall process will draw us closer to our users and to ourselves, while creating necessary distance as we discover story overlaps. Each of us will leave with fresh insight into the *Why* we are designing, and more clarity into the potential impact of our design initiatives.

Author Keywords
Storytelling, Engagement, User-Centered Design

ACM Classification Keywords
K.m. Computing Milieux: Miscellaneous

Storytelling For Designing Interactive Technologies

Our minds are built to remember stories. So how can we harness the power of storytelling ideation for making creative pivots for innovation? In this three-hour studio-workshop, we center our efforts on our users, an important factor of awareness when designing interactive technologies [8]. Our time together will combine elements of Action, Reflection and Discussion.

Action

Discover, design, and surprise with your storytelling capacity through a variety of validated processes that yield actionable design results [3,5-7]. We will join in a quest to discover each of our own stories, those of our users [2], and their parallels. Participants will engage in iterative activities around organizing questions and imaginative prompts like, "Draw a picture depicting when you were inspired by a user. This is a quick sketch. If you have drawn more than stick figures, you have spent too much time."

Group engagement is an important facet of our storytelling. We will benefit from having a variety of perspectives to analyze and untangle our stories. Through group feedback, we will learn personal areas for improvement in ambiguity readiness and vulnerability, in an effort to increase our creative capacities [5]. Most uniquely, group efforts will teach us to find our personal stories, while our techniques will truly inspire and foster group Intergy [7], a shared symbiotic energy, supporting our efforts to discover new insights and directions for our design work.

Reflection

We will not only create our stories, but will iteratively analyze them for commonalities and differences that help us predict: ways to deliver an effective experience, whether we should always tell a user story, who are successful artifact producers yet hate to speak in public, how we can maximize vulnerability to create a safe storytelling experience and amplify engagement, and who tells vivid and compelling stories. Between activities, questions will be posed, like: What engages an audience to respond to a story? What is an effective or ineffective story? Does finding our personal story facilitate finding our user's story? How does it enhance our capacity for empathy? These reflections will help reveal personally motivating impact opportunities for our design initiatives, research, classes and ventures.

Discussion

We will elaborate on the posed topics during the discussion portion of the studio-workshop. There, we will make headway in understanding and furthering these new techniques for making creative pivots for innovation. We will consider how the analytical discoveries we make can be combined with theories and tools for successful storytelling to create stories that realize inventive action.

Learnings from the storytelling experience and working sessions will then be modeled into a set of business practices and used as a prototype for new applications. Suggested translations for successful storytelling to show collaborative company value will also be brainstormed.

Goals and Lessons Learned

In our workshop, we follow a storytelling based learning approach [13] where proven methods are used to gain personal insights that are subsequently applied to user-centered design. Lessons will be learned through key components of empathy, episodic memory, and collaboration, while participants filter story criteria for examination and tangible translation by exploring a series of reflective questions and planned prompts.

This studio-workshop has goals on multiple levels. We will each make developments in our own personal stories and in those of our users. Our group-oriented storytelling process will demonstrate to us how we can foster design team and audience engagement, while being reminded of our levels of ambiguity readiness and vulnerability [14]. Most importantly, we will gain empathy for our users, and discover new insights that will inspire our future design work, and will leave with a variety of techniques that we can continue to use again and again in multiple settings, as we face innovation pivots in the future. Lastly, we will discuss ways to further develop these new techniques and apply them in various design settings.

Preparation

No prior skills are required. Simply bring your designer self and any budding or formed ideas about your user population. If you wish, bring along a preferred tool for sketching, writing or painting.

While the significant work is done in the moment within the studio-workshop, we request that you bring an artifact - one thing that shows the group something you love about you or your user's story.

References and Citations

[1] Doody, S. Why we need storytellers at the heart of product development. UX Magazine. April 2011.

[2] Doody, S. A Matter of Character: Knowing your users and their stories. UX Magazine. March 2013.

[3] Eskandari, M., Pincheira, F. E., Krauthamer, R., Aggarwal, A., Forouhar, P., Dua, J., Peng, C., Kress, G., Karanian, B. Open Process for Entrepreneuring Team Collaboration: Story Parallels from an Academic Design Team to the Studied Start-Up, ASEE, Entrepreneurship and Innovation Division, 2012.

[4] Gabriel, Y. Seduced by the Text: The Desire to Be Deceived in Story, Memoir and Drama. Tamara J of Critical Org Inquiry. Jan 2008.

[5] Karanian, B.A., Eskandari, M., Liao, J., Ahmed, Z. The Power of First Moments in Entrepreneurial Storytelling. ASEE 2013.

[6] Karanian B.A, Cox, J., Green, D., Ike, D., Kress, G., Nass, C. Analyzing Engineering Design Stories – Predicting Engagement in Inventive Action. ASEE/IEEE Frontiers in Ed, 2010.

[7] Karanian, B., Kress, G., Sadler, J. Telling Design Stories: The Result of the Entrepreneuring Investigation. Int Conf on Eng Design, 2009.

[8] Kelley, D.M., Kelley T. Creative Confidence. Crown Pub Group: New York, 2013.

[9] Kim, J., Lund, A., Donbrowski, C. Mobilizing Attention: Storytelling for Innovation. Interactions. March-April 2010.

[10] Stefik, M., Stefik, B. Breakthrough. MIT Univ Press: Cambridge, 2004.

[11] Sutton, R. and Rao, H. Scaling Up Excellence: Getting to More Without Settling for Less. Crown Bus: New York, 2014.

[12] Taylor, S.S., Karanian, B.A. Working Connection: The Relational Art of Leadership. Aesthesis. 2008.

[13] Karanian, B; Eskandari, M; Taajamaa, V. Start-up Storytelling Based Learning: Vulnerability Amplifies Engagement. In progress for, ASEE, June, 2015.

[14] Brown, B. Dare to be Great: How the Courage to Be Vulnerable Transforms the Way We Live, Love, Parent, and Lead. Gotham, 2012.

Acknowledgments

Many thanks to Amber Malinowski, our student intern who thoughtfully contributed to ideation.

TEI 2015 Studio Interactive Inflatables – Amplifying Human Behaviors

Kristin Niedlinger
SENSOREE, Inc.
1320 6th Ave
San Francisco, CA 94122 USA
Kristin@sensoree.com
01 415 235 9553
sensoree.com

Edwin Dertien
University of Twent,
Drienerlolaan 5
Enschede, Netherlands 7500AE
e.dertien@utwente.nl
+31 (0) 53 489 2778
www.ce.utwente.nl/e13

TEI '15, Jan 16-19, 2015, Stanford, CA, USA.
ACM 978-1-4503-3305-4/15/01.
http://dx.doi.org/10.1145/2677199.26835849

Abstract

In the Interactive Inflatables studio, participants will create bio-responsive inflatable structures to amplify human behaviors. Methods to concept and craft unique expansive designs will be taught. The interactive inflatable structures will respond to special and biological sensors. The studio is organized in stages and will involve and introduction of materials and media, concept generation, hands on making within partners, and a display of new tangible embedded and embodied interfaces.

Author Keywords

Wearable, Inflatable, Sensor.

ACM Classification Keywords

B.1.m Hardware: CONTROL STRUCTURES AND MICROPROGRAMMING, Miscellaneous

Introduction

We will create conceptual interactive inflatables that respond to human bodies systems like heart rate or proximity of human movement. A variety of materials will be present and based on concept of project we can accommodate slow or quick response inflatables. The participants will design and build the inflatable and assemble electronics programmed with behaviors.

Studio Proposal

This workshop will design new concepts to animate space and human expression with inflatable architecture.

We will workshop new concepts to animate space and human expression with inflatable architecture. In this one day workshop participants will learn techniques to animate the body with responsive technology.

Activities include sewing, fusing plastic, inflating, and programming the Arduino interface. Participants are welcome to bring their own projects too add to or create something new.

We will be fusing recycled plastic, sewing kite fabric, or taping plastic to create inflatables.

Our Studio will evolve in five phases: introduction activity, materials introduction, group concept activity, pairing build, sharing and presentation.

Hour 1 – Introduction hour: we will gather and the coordinators will provide an introduction of materials and participants will introduce themselves how they see themselves embodied and interacting tangibly.

Hour 2 – Hands on with materials containing (if desired) a short introduction workshop in physical computing (Arduino, sensors, control).

Hour 3-5 – Make! Participants will be assisted by the instructors on individual projects.

Hour 6 - Show and Tell! Select and refine creations to wear during the following days of the conference. Participants might take their creations with them in return of the costs of the used materials.

No prior skills required. Basic Arduino programming and pattern drafting skills would be helpful, but not necessary. We will teach basics and offer an easy kit of the electronic components.

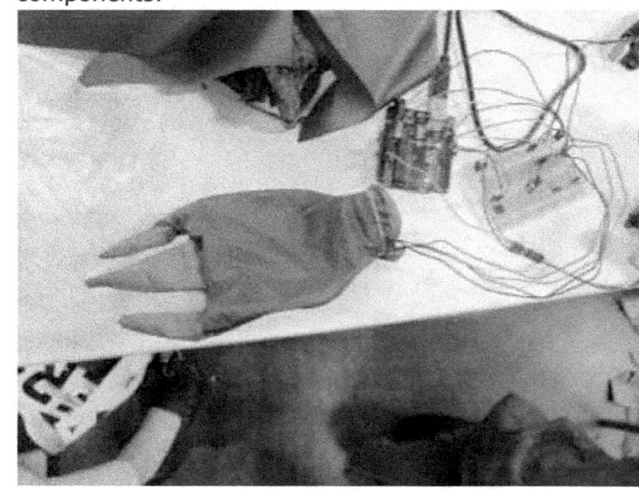

figure 1. Inflatable pocket protector student project from Interactive Inflatables workshop.

Studio Topics to be covered

- Concept generation
- Introspection of intangible moments
- Electronic components for sensory inflation
- Plastic fusing techniques
- Basic programming for Arduino
- Pattern drafting and draping
- Rapid prototyping

Studio Learning Goals

The goals of the studio are to evoke imagination and animate otherwise intangible interactions of the body. Participants are encouraged to heighten their senses during concept phase. They will gain new skills of programming, hands on pattern drafting and draping, and construction of new materials, the inflatables.

Studio Supporting Web Documents

We plan to create an Instructable and make electronic kits with basic components for sale on the Sensoree website as well as available at the workshop. (http://www.instructable.com, http://www.sensoree.com)

Acknowledgements

We would like to thank UTwente for supporting our first workshop in 2014. Met with great enthusiasm, we are excited to expand the material to the TEI community.

Input/Output: Paper Prototyping for the Future

Joselyn McDonald
Parsons, MFA Design & Technology
332 East 74th Street
New York, New York 10021
josmcdos@gmail.com

Nicole Yi Messier
Parsons, MFA Design & Technology
454 Myrtle Ave. Apt 3
Brooklyn, NY 11205
nicoleyimessier@gmail.com

Abstract
The I/O: Paper Prototyping for the Future studio will be a hands-on experience that combines art, design, and technology. Participants will learn through a series of escalating exercises how to introduce interactivity via computational crafting techniques to paper in order to heighten the paper prototyping experience.

TEI'15, January 15–19, 2015, Stanford, California, USA.
ACM 978-1-4503-3305-4/15/01
http://dx.doi.org/10.1145/2677199.2683589

Keywords
Soft-circuits, prototyping, paper engineering, simple circuits

ACM Classification Keywords
H.5.2 User Interfaces (D.2.2, H.1.2, I.3.6): User-centered design; Prototyping: OPEN LOOK

Introduction
Paper prototyping has long been a staple in design and technology realms as a way for cheap accessible concept development. This studio aims to advance participants' abilities in the realm of paper prototyping through applied paper engineering techniques, simple and soft-circuit methods, and integration of shape-memory alloys for movement. By the end of the studio, participants will be able to make paper artifacts - sculptures, interactive objects, prototypes, etc. - that have advanced interactivity.

Studio Proposal
I/O Paper Prototyping for the Future will be a studio-based work session. Upon commencement, the attendees will be introduced to global notable advanced paper interaction precedents in the field of tangible and embedded interaction. Next, participants will be introduced to a series of paper folding techniques that

allow for a broader understanding of the flexibility and adaptability of the medium. They will then build simple circuits using paper as the base and explore how folded edges can create or break circuits, while constructing paper circuit switches. Attendees will be asked to demonstrate their projects with the group so that individual (or team) breakthroughs could be shared more broadly.

For the latter half of the studio, we will integrate shape-memory alloy in order to introduce controlled movement into paper structures. Attendees will build paper objects, or models, and will include shape-memory alloy techniques so that with simple electrical pulses, they will be able to make the paper representations come to life. The conclusion of the workshop will be group presentations on their crafted moving paper projects and take-aways from the studio session.

Studio Topics to be covered

Cohesion of Prototyping, Paper Engineering, and Soft-Circuits & Simple Circuitry

Prototyping:
Prototypes are widely used to convey design ideas and concepts during a design process and materialize in different forms ranging from paper prototypes to digital models. Paper prototypes are often used to express a number of components within a design, but their ability to replicate movement and real case scenarios are often limited. Combining paper engineering with soft circuits and simple circuitry expands the usefulness and accuracy of a paper prototype by providing higher fidelity forms and models with realistic movement.

Paper Engineering
Paper Engineering uses folding techniques to transform 2-D paper into flexible three-dimensional forms that replicate natural movements.

Soft-Circuits & Simple Circuitry
Soft-circuits use alternative materials to build simple circuits, which are often constructed with flexible conductive threads and fabrics in coordination with electronic elements including batteries, lights, sensors, and speakers. This workshop will cover soft-circuits and simple circuitry using copper tape, shape-memory alloy (Flexinol), arduino, resistors, paper, and diodes.

Studio Learning Goals

1. Introduce a range of emerging technologies and techniques regarding advanced paper prototyping.

2. Instruct attendees in the realms of simple circuit building and integration of shape-memory alloys into folded paper to heighten art-practice or prototyping techniques.

3. Review projects completed in-studio and discuss troubleshooting techniques.

Studio Supporting Web Documents

"Folding Techniques for Designers: From Sheet to Form", Paul Jackson

"Many designers use folding techniques in their work to make three-dimensional forms from two-dimensional sheets of fabric, cardboard, plastic, metal, and many other materials. This unique book explains the key techniques of folding, such as pleated surfaces, curved folding and crumpling. An elegant, practical handbook, it covers over 70 techniques explained by clear step-by-step drawings, crease-pattern drawings, and specially commissioned photography."

Acknowledgements
We thank High-Low Tech at MIT Media Lab for their advancements in the realm of paper engineering.

Wearable Computing, 3D Aug* Reality, Photographic/Videographic Gesture Sensing, and Veillance

Steve Mann
University of Toronto
Toronto, Ontario, Canada
www.eyetap.org

Ryan Janzen
University of Toronto
Toronto, Ontario, Canada
veillametrics.com

Steve Feiner
Columbia University
New York, NY, USA
graphics.cs.columbia.edu

Jayse Hansen
Meta Company
San Mateo, California
jayse.tv

Soren Harner
Meta Company
San Mateo, California

Stefano Baldassi
Stanford University
Stanford, California

Mir Adnan Ali
University of Toronto
Toronto, Ontario, Canada
www.eyetap.org

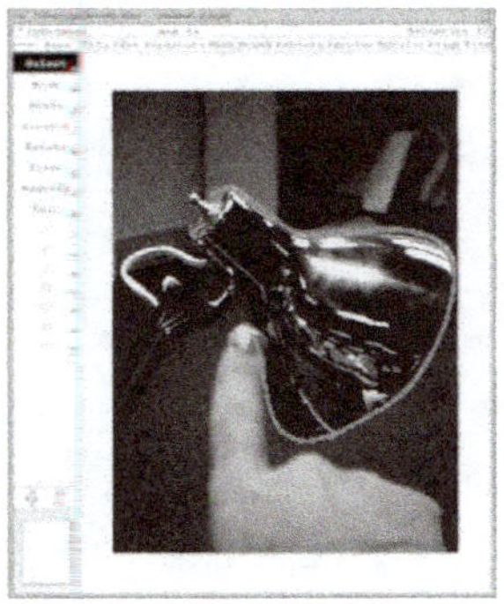

Figure 1: "SixthSense" Gesture-based 3D AR Wearable Computing, S. Mann, 1997[5]

Figure 2: "Soul Portraits". The eye is the window to the soul and this ayinograph ("sightpainting") is a new kind of expressive portrait that also happens to embody a new kind of eye test whose results are immediately comprehensible. It is also a new easthetic and artistic form. Each participant can make an ayinograph, useful for custom-calibration of wearable computing and 3D AR Spaceglases.

Abstract
Wearable computers and Generation-5 Digital Eye Glass easily recognize a user's own gestures, forming the basis for shared AR (Augmediated Reality). This Studio-workshop presents the latest in wearable AR, plus an historical perspective with new insights. Participants will sculpt 3D objects using hand gestures and create Unity 3D art+game objects using computational lightpainting.

Participants will also learn how to use 3D gesture-based AR to visualize and understand real-world phenomena, including being able to see sound waves, see radio waves, and see sight itself, through abakographic user-interfaces that interact with "sightfields" (time-reversed lightfields). Participants will also surveilluminescent devices that change color when watched by a camera. Long exposure photographs made with such devices generate "sightpaintings" that show what a camera can "see".

Author Keywords
Wearable Computing, Gesture-based 3D AR, Abakography, Ayinography ("sightpaintings").

ACM Classification Keywords
H.5.m [Information interfaces and presentation (e.g., HCI)]: Miscellaneous.

TEI 2015, Jan 16–19 2015, Stanford, CA, USA.
ACM 978-1-4503-3305-4/15/01.
http://dx.doi.org/10.1145/2677199.2683590

Figure 3: Abakographic User Interfaces allow us to **sense sensing** and **visualize vision** itself. Priveillance (privacy, surveillance, and sousveillance) becomes a new medium of artistic experession.

Wearable Computing: 3D Gesture-based AR

Wearable Computing is a quickly growing field, especially when combined with AR (Augmediated/Augmented Reality) [7] Vision-based wearable computing is known as Personal Imaging [5], e.g. *Synthetic Synesthesia of the Sixth Sense* (abbreviated *Sixth Sense*) [3]. See Fig. 1.

We present the theoretical and philosophical foundations and axioms of 3D gesture-based Wearable Computing, along with hands-on demonstrations in which participants build their own 3D mobile and wearable computing environmnts using various approaches and systems, such as Qualcomm's Vuforia, Meta-View's Spaceglass SDK, Unity 3D (Unity Technologies), and Mann's VideoOrbits [6]. We will also introduce meta-sensory tools in the world of 3D vision-based AR, including abakography and ayinography == tools that were introduced as a form of visual art in the 1980s [1, 2]. See Figs. 5 and 4.

Participants will learn how to reproduce some of these results from the early days of wearable computing in the 1970s, e.g. how to find hidden cameras using a vacuum-tube-based video feedback abakographer, as well as how to do this using Meta Spaceglasses and more modern equipment.

Each participant will have the opportunity to make their own "Soul Portrait^{TM}" (ayinograph^{TM}) == a self-portrait that allows you to see sight itself, i.e. if the eye is the window to the soul, then this is a new way of seeing ourselves (as well as a useful eye test that we can see and understand more clearly than the Latin text and numbers of a traditional eye test). See Fig. 2. Artistically, this work touches on issues of priveillance (Privacy, Surveillance, and Sousveillance). See Fig 3.

Abakographic User Interfaces

Abakographs [8] are 3D (three-dimensional) photographs made by moving one or more light sources through space during an actual or simulated long-exposure 3D photograph. They are free of self-occlusion, and therefore lend themselves well to simple image-based rendering to create virtual, mediated, and augmediated 3D gesture-controlled worlds and interactive environments. We present visual art forms in which abakographs are situated in a photographic or videographic AR world using Digital Eye Glass. Example applications include visual art, sensory visualization, gaming, and physical fitness in which players wearing DEG (Digital Eye Glass) attempt to sense each other, and sense the sensing of each other.

The word "photography" comes from the Greek words "phos" ("light"), and "graphis" ("stylus" or "paintbrush"). Literally, the word "photography" means "drawing or painting with light" [4, 9].

Abakography focuses on this "drawing with light", where we use physical motion of light sources over a real or simulated long exposure derived from one or more photographs or frames of video, supplemented in some cases, with additional sensor information (3D camera, intertial measurement units, etc.). In this work, we computationally extend the concept of *light painting*.

Participants will learn how to make hand gestures in mid-air using tactile feedback from real physical objects.

We will introduce abakography as a 3D AR user-interface == a form of sculpting that uses real physical objects, such as an array of light sources.

Figure 4: Historical context: abakographic "paintbrush" with wearable computing and sensors to visualize radio waves, sound waves, etc.: wearable computing and computational photography [1, 2].

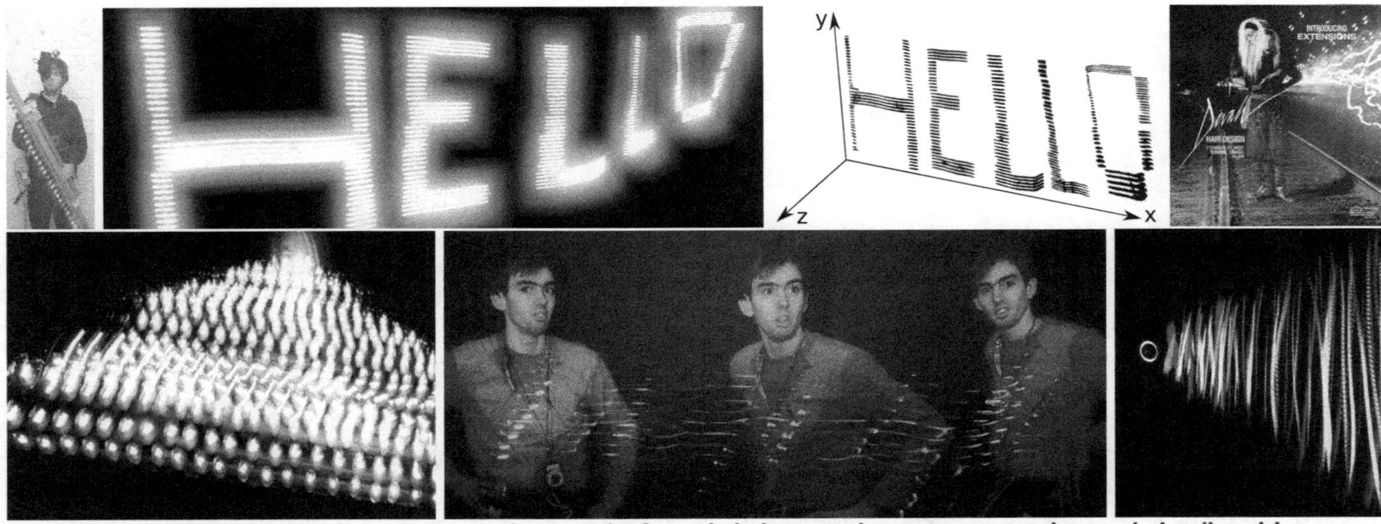

Figure 5: Historical context: long exposure photographs for artistic intervention, to sense sensing, and visualize vision. Cygraphy™(Cybernetic Photography). "Hello World" abakograph and abakogram examples. Top right: using the SWIM (Sequential Wave Imprinting Machine) to visualize circularly polarized radio waves, used in commercial photography, 1985. Bottom left: S. Mann, self portrait, sightfield of right eye (left hand held over left eye, right hand on SWIM) This "sightpainting" visualizes what the eye can see. Bottom middle: wearable computer LED shirt used to visualize sound waves and sweep for audio bugs through long-exposure photography and acoustic feedback in the early 1980s. Bottom right: video bug sweeper using video feedback to locate hidden cameras and visualize their sightfields. Red indicates strong surveillance field, green medium, and blue, weakly present.

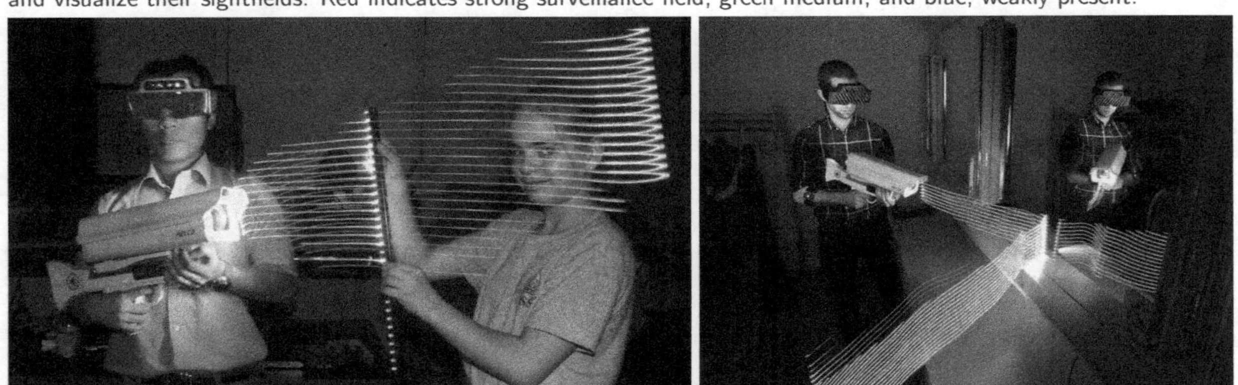

Figure 6: CameraGun game: Left: A player attempts to shoot with the camera gun, but the other player wins by being "quick on the draw" with a bugbroom to sweep for bugs and "rat out" the person with the camera gun. Right: Shooting into a mirror allows for some more advanced game play. Players need to anticipate multiple reflections and the effect they might have when the trigger is pulled.

Vuforia, Meta SDK, and Gaming

Vuforia and Unity provide extensive gaming opportunities. Each participant will have an opportunity to construct their own abakographs, and various gameplay possibilities will be presented. One such example is the CameraGun, a gun that is a camera. It gives rise to a game based on sensing sensing itself (i.e. sensing the capacity of sensors like the camera). A player wins by "shooting" an opponent with the camera, (i.e. a recognizable picture of their face is taken), but the shooter loses points if they are caught taking a picture, i.e. if the opponent detects that a "shot" has been fired from the camera. Thus the surveilluminescent light stick serves as a shield to protect from the camera in this sense, as it will "rat out" an opponents attempt at "shooting" with a camera. See Fig. 6.

References

[1] Steve mann. *Campus Canada, ISSN 0823-4531, p55 Feb-Mar 1985, pp58-59 Apr-May 1986, p72 Sep-Oct 1986*.

[2] Cynthia Ryals, describing the work of Steve Mann. Lightspace: A new language of imaging. *PHOTO Electronic Imaging 38*, 2 (1995), 14–16.

[3] Geary, J. *The body electric: An anatomy of the new bionic senses.* Rutgers University Press, 2002.

[4] Langford, M. *Story of Photography: From its beginnings to the present day.* Focal Press / Elsivier, Woburn MA, 1997.

[5] Mann, S. Wearable computing: A first step toward personal imaging. *IEEE Computer 30*, 2 (1997), 25–32.

[6] Mann, S. *Intelligent Image Processing*. John Wiley and Sons, November 2 2001. ISBN: 0-471-40637-6.

[7] Mann, S. Wearable computing. In *Encyclopedia of Human-Computer Interaction*, M. Soegaard and R. F. Dam, Eds. The Interaction Design Foundation. Available online at http://www.interaction-design.org/encyclopedia/wearable_computing.html, 2012.

[8] Mann, S., Janzen, R., Ai, T., Yasrebi, S. N., Kawwa, J., and Ali, M. A. Toposculpting: Computational lightpainting and wearable computational photography for abakographic user interfaces. In *Proceedings of the IEEE CCECE*, IEEE (2014).

[9] Mehl, R. *Playing with Color: 50 Graphic Experiments for Exploring Color Design Principles.* Rockport Publishers, 2013.

Designing for Humans in a Digital Age: Building Wearable Technology to Convey Information and Emotions

Billie Whitehouse
Wearable Experiments, LLC.
155 W 21 ST
New York, NY 10011
billie@wearableexperiments.com

Stanley He
Wearable Experiments, LLC.
155 W 21 ST
New York, NY 10011
stanley@wearableexperiments.com

TEI '15, Jan 16-19, 2015, Stanford, CA, USA.
ACM 978-1-4503-3305-4/15/01.
http://dx.doi.org/10.1145/2677199.2683591

Abstract
The purpose of our studio is to inspire attendees on what are the most important issues to think about when designing wearable technology products that provides meaningful experiences.

During the studio, attendees will have the chance to discuss the best approach to design wearable tech products that can convey both meaningful information and emotions. Attendees will also build a prototype for a wearable technology product that solves a real problem, in a team setting. We will encourage attendees to think beyond well-known wearable technology categories such as smart watches, fitness bands, and smart glasses, but rather envision products that fit our body in newly imagined ways, creating new product categories altogether.

The agenda of the studio will include discussion of "10 Principles of Good Design" by Dieter Rams, and case studies that shows the importance of invisible, unobtrusive design in wearable technology. A majority portion of the studio will be hands on, where attendees will design and prototype their own conceptual wearable tech product.

The studio will be led by Billie Whitehouse, the co-founder and design director of Wearable Experiments. Since the company's takeoff in 2013, Billie has led multiple innovative wearable technology projects, such as Fundawear and Alert Shirt, which have won a Cannes Lion and Clio Sports Award respectively. Billie has recently made the list of 2014 Silicon Alley 100 by

Business Insider. With a strong background in fashion and design, it is Billie's goal to put more intelligence into the clothes we wear every day.

Keywords
Prototyping, wearable technology, design thinking, design, product design, invisible

ACM Classification Keywords
B.0 Hardware: GENERAL; D.0 Software: GENERAL.

Studio Proposal
"Wearable technology (WT)" has been one of the fastest growing tech product category in recent years. While most of the consumer facing wearable tech products focuses on functions around fitness, health with a quantified-self approach, Wearable Experiments is on the path of discovering potential WT products that focuses on building empathy between people and their digital life through meaningful, physical interaction. In our proposed studio, we challenge the attendees to create a prototype for a WT product that can explore the opportunities to do that.

During the workshop, the attendees will identify a problem that can be solved with WT, come up with a solution, and build a prototype through electronics and molding materials.

This studio is suitable for people at any level of technical knowledge. We do encourage people to come with a creative problem solving mindset.

Studio Topics to Be Covered

One major category of topic that will be covered during the workshop is design principles. Design principle is the main factor that differentiates one designer or company from another. In this workshop, we will be covering the design principles that Wearable Experiments is founded upon.

- **Dieter Rams 10 Principles of "Good Design" and Wearable Technology**: What can we learn from a legendary designer in the 20th century when designing products for the future? During the workshop, we will introduce Dieter Rams 10 Principles of Good Design to aid attendees in designing their WT prototype. [1] (Reference: https://www.vitsoe.com/us/about/good-design)

- **Technology Should Be Unobtrusive and Empathetic:**
  How can we design for a more human experience in an increasingly digital era? We believe technology need to become unobtrusive to our time, space and state of mind. It could also become a communication tool that not only carries data and information, but also human emotions. During the workshop, we will talk about examples of how this notion has been experimented and what is up next in this school of thoughts.

- **Importance of Invisible Wearable Technology:**
  Wearable Experiments firmly believes that technology, especially wearable technology should be invisible. People want to feel connected to people and the world, but without feeling like a robot.
  At Wearable Experiments, we have made all our wearable tech project look like normal garment without indication of technology from a visual perspective. During this workshop, we will cover why we believe this is imperative. (Reference: currently many wearable technology companies believe the future of WT

is invisible WT.
http://www.fastcodesign.com/3019157/innovation-by-design-conference/the-invisible-future-of-wearables-according-to-jawbone)

Another topic to be covered is how to effectively prototype for wearable tech. This will be done through hands-on experience during the workshop.

- **Being Considerate of the Human Body**
  Because a WT product stays on the body, the physical needs to be very carefully considered to be felt natural to the wearer. Through the workshop, attendees will learn to consider attributes such as tones, textures, colors, weight, balance, proportion and silhouette into the design of their prototype.

- **Prototyping with Modeling Material and Electronics**
  Workshop attendees will be building a WT prototype using modeling clay and electronic.

Studio Learning Goals

During the studio, attendees will:

- Understand the design principles that are essential in building a great WT product

- Work with a team to solve a problem through a wearable technology solution

- Experience hands-on prototyping with modeling materials and electronics

- Think about how the design of a product can add or take away the "human" factor in the user experience

Supporting Web Documents

Attendees should familiarize themselves with the following online resources before the workshop to understand the context and background of the topics that will be covered.

- **Dieter Rams: Ten Principles for Good Design**
  (https://www.vitsoe.com/us/about/good-design)

- **Wearable Experiments**
  (http://wearableexperiments.com/)

- **Articles Related to Invisible Wearable Technology**

  - http://www.fastcodesign.com/3019157/innovation-by-design-conference/the-invisible-future-of-wearables-according-to-jawbone

  - http://nypost.com/2014/07/14/is-google-glass-cool-or-just-plain-creepy/

About Billie Whitehouse As award-winning designer, and co-founder of Wearable Experiments [WE:EX], Billie is invigorating the fashion industry and transforming it into a business focused on improving the quality of our lives. Billie was brought up in the design industry, working from the early age of 16 at Australia's leading tertiary design school, Whitehouse Institute of Design, Australia. Billie has been recognized for her work on FUNDAWEAR with a Silver Lion at Cannes Lions International Festival of Creativity, and with the CLIO Sports Award for her work on AlertShirt.

Billie is an aesthetic specialist with a naturally inquisitive nature towards technology and innovation. As a garment engineer she strongly believes people should not have to look like the technology that they have grown to love and depend on. Billie's designs are sharp, experimental, naturally confident and subtly feminine in appearance integrating the latest technology. Design principals of color, line, shape, proportion, tone, silhouette and texture are being brought to the wearable technology industry by Billie Whitehouse.

About Wearable Experiments [We:eX]

Wearable Experiments (We:eX), co-founded by Billie Whitehouse and Ben Moir, is a socially driven wearable technology company. Its mission is to bring together fashion and technology with a functional design aesthetic, and use creative problem solving to help people live well and have a better quality of life.

Wearable Experiments aim for the community's feedback on our projects to ensure it is giving the people what they want and making their lives easier. We:eX believes that people are not ready to become computers, but they are growing more interested in being connected all the time – whether they're connecting with information, people or retrieving personal data. People's clothes are an untapped resource that, together with technology, can help them stay more connected and use their fashion in a more practical way.

References

[1] Dieter Rams: ten principles for good design https://www.vitsoe.com/us/about/good-design

[2] Brownlee, John. "The Invisible Future Of Wearables, According To Jawbone." Co.Design, 2 Oct. 2013. Web. 20 Oct. 2014. http://www.fastcodesign.com/3019157/innovation-by-design-conference/the-invisible-future-of-wearables-according-to-jawbone

[3] Schuster, Dana. "The Revolt against Google 'Glassholes'" *New York Post*. New York Post, 14 July 2014. Web. 20 Oct. 2014. http://nypost.com/2014/07/14/is-google-glass-cool-or-just-plain-creepy/

Rapid Prototyping for Wearables

Mark Billinghurst
HIT Lab NZ
University of Canterbury
Ilam Road
Christchurch, 8041, New Zealand
mark.billinghurst@hitlabnz.org

Daniela Busse
Citi Ventures
Global Innovation Network
260 Homer Ave Ste 101
Palo Alto, CA, 94301
Daniela.busse@gmail.com

TEI'15, January 15–19, 2015, Stanford, California, USA.
ACM 978-1-4503-3305-4/15/01.
http://dx.doi.org/10.1145/2677199.2683592

Abstract
This half-day hands-on studio will teach how to design and develop effective interfaces for head mounted and wrist worn wearable computers through the application of user-centered design principles. Attendees will learn gain the knowledge and tools needed to rapidly develop prototype applications, and also complete a hands-on design task. They will also learn good design guidelines for wearable systems and how to apply those guidelines. A variety of tools will be used that do not require any hardware or software experience, many of which are free and/or open source. Attendees will also be provided with material that they can use to continue their learning after the studio is over.

Keywords
Wearable Computing; User Interface; Interaction Design, Head Mounted Displays

ACM Classification Keywords
H.5.2 User Interfaces

Introduction
After twenty years in research laboratories [1], wearable computing is about to enter the consumer space with products like Google Glass [2] and Moto360 [3] coming to market. There are projections that wearable devices and applications will become a billion dollar global industry within several years, but in order

for this to occur there needs to be more HCI practitioners and researchers that have experience with wearable interface design and development. Wearable computers have an intimate interface that is always on and always accessible and so are more difficult to design for than traditional mobile and desktop interfaces. Thus there is a need to go beyond traditional interface design and to learn new skills in designing for on-body technology. It is especially important that researchers and developers can learn rapid prototyping skills that they can used to clearly communicate the wearable experiences they are developing.

This studio draws on years of experience and research results from leading wearable researchers and developers to teach the skills necessary to rapidly prototype compelling wearable computing experiences. The studio will show how some desktop prototyping tools can be used for wearable applications, as well as introduce attendees to a range of different tools specifically designed for wearable systems.

Studio Proposal

The course will teach how to create compelling user experiences for wearable computers focusing on design guidelines, prototyping tools, research directions, and a hands-on design experience. These topics will be presented using both head mounted wearable platforms such as Google Glass and Vuzix M-100, and wrist mounted wearables such as the Moto 360 smart watch.

This is an entry-level studio with no hardware or software skills required. Participants should be familiar with the basics of user centered interaction design principles, but apart from this will be taught everything they need to know. During the studio attendees will be introduced to visual design tools such as proto.io [4] and Glassware Flow Designer [5], and basic programming tools such as WearScript [6] and Processing [7]. They will also be given templates and software that can be used to develop more complex systems. The most important participant skill will be a willingness to learn and to express their design ideas.

Studio Topics to be covered

The studio will cover the following topics:

- *Technology Overview/History of Wearables:* A brief introduction to wearable devices, their origins and key attributes.
- *Design Guidelines:* User centered design guidelines for developing effective wearable experiences.
- *Exemplar Applications:* Example applications showing how to apply wearable design guidelines.
- *Prototyping Tools:* Different tools that can be used to prototype wearable experiences, ranging from sketched interfaces to high fidelity mock-ups.
- *Design Session:* Hands-on session where attendees can use the prototyping tools to create their own mock-up wearable interfaces.
- *Research Directions:* Active areas of research that will enable new wearable experiences.
- *Resources:* A review of resources available to support attendees after the studio, such as software tools, websites, books, etc.

These topics will fit together to give attendees both an appreciation of where wearable devices have come from, to an understanding of how to rapidly prototype for current devices, and what future technology will be coming that may affect future designs.

Studio Learning Goals

The studio will have the following learning goals:

- To provide an introduction to wearable computers and the historical background to the technology
- To give an understanding of wearable technology and the key elements of wearable systems
- To describe key design principles/interface metaphors that can be used to create wearable systems
- To learn examples of good wearable design
- To provide an understanding of how to use a variety of rapid prototyping tools
- To give an overview of active areas of wearable computing research and future technology

Participants will leave the course knowing how to use several tools for rapid prototyping of wearable experiences. They will also have completed a simple design task to get hands-on experiences with these tools, and have learnt design guidelines that can be applied to ensure effective wearable interface design. They will also be provided with the resources that they need to continue developing wearable applications after they leave the studio.

Studio Supporting Web Documents

There are a number of online tools that will be used in the course, including the GlassSim visual mock-up tool [8], Glassware Flow Designer [5], proto.io [4], Processing [7] and Android Wear [9] and Glass interface guidelines [10]. In addition to these online tools, the course material, research papers and supporting videos will be made available on the ARforGlass website after the studio is over (http://www.arforglass.org/).

Conclusion

As computing moves onto the body there is an opportunity for developing Tangible, Embedded and Embodied Interface methods can be used to interact with them. For example, using eye-gaze or hand-gesture as input methods, or tangible objects such as rings. However designing and rapid prototyping for wearables is very different than for creating desktop or other mobile interfaces. With wearable systems the focus is on enhancing the users engagement with the real world around them, rather than improving interaction with on-screen digital content. This studio will provide attendees with all the skills they need to get started in this exciting and fast growing area.

References

[1] Mann, S. (1997). Wearable computing: A first step toward personal imaging. Computer, 30(2), 25-32.

[2] Google Glass http://www.google.com/glass/

[3] Moto 360 https://moto360.motorola.com/

[4] proto.io http://www.proto.io/

[5] Glassware Flow Designer https://glassware-flow-designer.appspot.com/

[6] Wearscript http://www.wearscript.com/

[7] Processing http://www.processing.org[

[8] GlassSim http://www.glasssim.com/

[9] Android Wear design guidelines
http://developer.android.com/design/wear/

[10] Google Glass interface guidelines
https://developers.google.com/glass/design/

Prototyping Social Interactions with DIY Animatronic Creatures

Cesar Vandevelde
Ghent University
Graaf Karel de Goedelaan 5.
8500, Kortrijk
cesar.vandevelde@ugent.be

Jelle Saldien
Ghent University
Graaf Karel de Goedelaan 5.
8500, Kortrijk
jelle.saldien@ugent.be

Maarten Vanhoucke
Ghent University
Graaf Karel de Goedelaan 5.
8500, Kortrijk
m.vanhoucke@ugent.be

Abstract

For some time now, robotics research has shifted its attention from robots that function within their own predefined space to robots that coexist with humans in the human's natural habitats. This evolution has not only driven interest in robot safety and compliance, it has also resulted in the subdomain of Social Robotics, which is concerned with natural interaction between robots and humans. In this studio, we will offer participants the chance to create their own animatronic creature using modular building blocks derived from Ono, our low-cost Do-It-Yourself social robot. In the first part, we will help participants to conceptualize a context and scenario for their social robot. Then, using craft materials (e.g. cardboard, glue, fabrics, foam, etc.) in combination with custom connectors and our animatronic modules, participants will build the physical embodiment of their creature. Finally, they are brought to life by connecting the modules to our electronics platform (Raspberry PI), which is then programmed using an easy to use library.

Keywords

Social Robotic Platform, Embodied Human-Robot Interaction, Animatronics

TEI '15, Jan 16-19, 2015, Stanford, CA, USA.
ACM 978-1-4503-3305-4/15/01.
http://dx.doi.org/10.1145/2677199.2687146

ACM Classification Keywords

I.2.9 Robotics, H.5.2 User Interfaces: Input devices and strategies, Prototyping

Introduction

A growing trend in robotics is that robots are no longer confined to spaces that were specifically designed for them, such as an industrial robotic arm that operates in an enclosure at a factory. Instead, robots are starting to show up in the living and working spaces of humans. Examples include Roomba [1] (a robotic vacuum cleaner), Paro [2] (a therapeutic seal-like robot for hospitals and nursing homes) and Baxter [3] (a robotic factory worker that can safely work alongside its human coworkers). Influenced by this trend, we created another social robot, named Ono [4], aimed primarily at children, with a focus on therapeutic applications such as the treatment of autism spectrum disorder. Different from other social robots in research, Ono was designed with low-cost materials and DIY techniques in mind, resulting in a low-cost, modular robot that can be produced in any common FabLab. Owing to the robot's modular construction, it can be repaired more easily, and the modules can also be recombined to quickly create radically different looking social robots. This aspect is very useful in the treatment of autism in particular, as therapeutic tools sometimes need to be adapted to fit the specific needs of each child. This approach is not only advantageous in our specific context; it also facilitates the process of building social robots for completely different applications. In this studio, we will show how our modules can be used to prototype an animatronic creature in a quick and iterative manner.

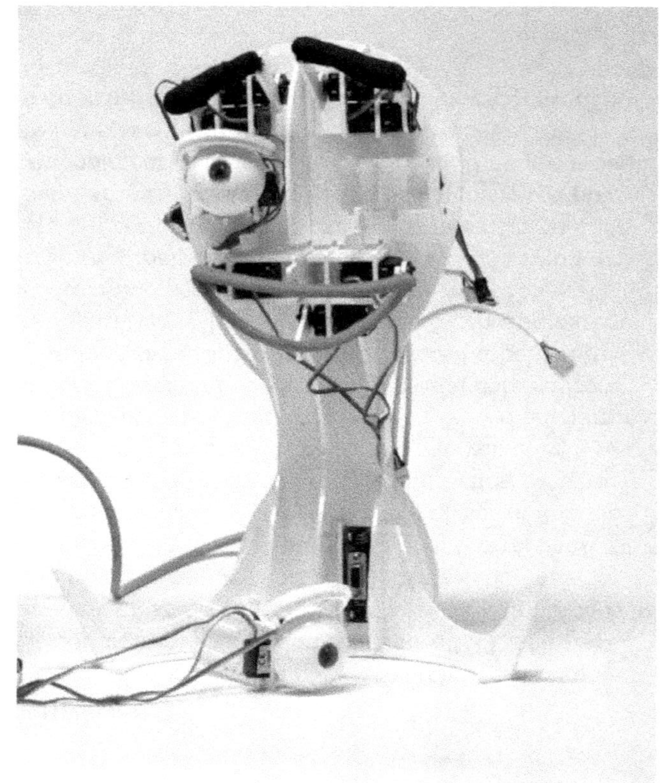

figure 1: Inside view of social robot Ono, with one eye module detached.

Studio Proposal

The goal of our studio is to enable participants to design and prototype their own robotic creature. Participants will be split up into four groups of four, and each group will build one robot. The workshop is divided into four parts:

Part 1: Concept Generation
We will start the studio session with a brief overview of social robotics. We will shortly discuss the history and inspirational examples of human-robot interaction. We will demonstrate the social robot Ono and briefly describe the design philosophy behind it. Finally, we will introduce participants to our social robotics toolkit and go over the possibilities and limitations of the kit. Participants will then be given time to come up with a concept and scenario for a new social robot.

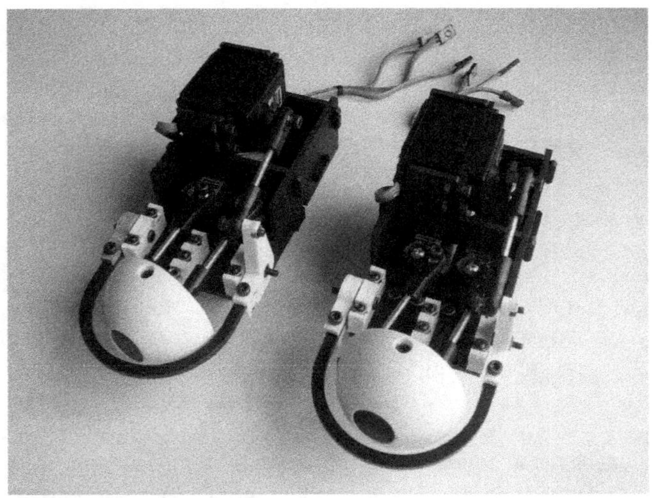

figure 2: The eye modules of the toolkit.

Part 2: Embodiment
In the second phase, we will give participants the tools and materials to turn their chosen concept into a working prototype. We will provide (1) our toolkit, which contains modules for eyes, eyebrows, mouth and neck and (2) craft materials to create the shape of the robot. The craft materials include , cardboard plates (2 mm and 5 mm), foam sheets, hot-melt glue, double-sided tape, fabrics, ... We chose these materials because they allow quick design iterations with minimal effort.

Part 3: Creating Interaction
Once the embodiment of the robot has been built, we will provide each group with a set of electronics to bring the creatures to life. Our platform consists of a Raspberry Pi with a custom add-on board. This add-on board allows the Raspberry Pi to control RC servos (used by the different modules) as well as to read analog and digital inputs. Because the Raspberry Pi is an embedded computer (as opposed to a microcontroller), interpreted languages can be used. For this workshop, we will use the Python programming language, so participants will need to be familiar with it. As part of our platform, we will use a Python module (API) to interface with the hardware.

Part 4: Demos and Reflections
When every team has completed their animatronic prototype, groups will be given the opportunity to demonstrate their robot to their peers. A short movie of each human-robot interaction scenario will be recorded. We will stimulate discussion to see what participants thought of during the design process and to find out if our lo-fi prototyping approach could be useful in other researchers' work.

Required Prior Skills
Part 3 of our studio requires some basic programming experience in order to use our platform to the fullest. We will use Python in our studio session, though knowledge of other languages is also relevant. We will try to divide the groups so that each group has at least one person has some experience with programming.

Additionally the course organizers will offer support to all teams that need help to program their envisioned interaction.

We will use simple, low threshold prototyping techniques throughout the session, so some affinity with craft techniques is helpful, though not necessary.

Studio Topics to be covered

In the process of prototyping social interactions with robots, participants will be introduced to a number of different concepts. The topics covered in our studio include:

1. Introduction to social robotics, with a special focus on embodiment.
2. Quick, low-fidelity prototyping techniques.
3. How to use our modular system for social robots.
4. Design strategies for the creation of "hackable" toolkits.
5. How to use the Python programming language on Raspberry Pi to program basic interations.

Studio Learning Goals

The main aim of our studio is to introduce participants to social robotics through a hands-on approach. It is our goal to demonstrate a quick and practical way to prototype social interactions with robots, and we think this approach could be useful for other technologies as well. We feel that there is a large overlap between social robotics and tangible interaction, and as such the topics covered in this studio should be of interest to the TEI conference's audience.

Studio Supporting Web Documents

A main overview of the Ono project is available at [5]. Source files of social robot Ono can be found on GitHub [6], source files of the modules and the electronics platform will be uploaded to GitHub at a later time. Pictures and videos of the robots built and interactions during the workshop will be made available online after the conference's end.

References

[1] iRobot Roomba Vacuum Cleaning Robot http://www.irobot.com/us/learn/home/roomba.aspx.

[2] Kidd, C.D.; Taggard, W.; Turkle, S. A sociable robot to encourage social interaction among the elderly. *Proceedings of the 2006 IEEE International Conference on Robotics and Automation* (2006).

[3] Baxter | Redefining Robotics and Manufacturing | Rethink Robotics http://www.rethinkrobotics.com/products/baxter/.

[4] Vandevelde, C., Saldien, J., Ciocci, M. C., & Vanderborght, B. *Systems Overview of Ono.* Proceedings of the 5th International Conference on *Social Robotics,* Springer International Publishing (2013), 311-320.

[5] Social Robot Ono http://www.industrialdesigncenter.be/ono.

[6] cesarvandevelde/Ono2 - GitHub https://github.com/cesarvandevelde/Ono2.

Engaging Encounters: Sketching the Future of TEI

Caroline Hummels
Designing Quality in Interaction group
Department of Industrial Design
Eindhoven University of Technology
P.O.Box 513
5600 MB Eindhoven,
The Netherlands
c.c.m.hummels@tue.nl

TEI '15, Jan 16-19, 2015, Stanford, CA, USA.
ACM 978-1-4503-3305-4/15/01.
http://dx.doi.org/10.1145/2677199.2687147

Abstract
As part of the one-year project "Engaging Encounters: Sketching the Future together", this studio-workshop will explore hands-on how the work and ideas of TEI can influence our interaction with the world in the upcoming decade. It explores the character of the different paradigms underlying the TEI community and their potential influence on our future society and as well as on our TEI community. Especially for this TEI'15 conference, six personal 1,5-hour encounters with TEI participants are organised to discuss, explore and sketch the future of TEI. The results of these encounters will be included on a blog, book and movie about the overall Engaging Encounters project, as well as in a special publication about the future of TEI. Through all the encounters and 'publications', this project aims at inspiring people in their work and perspective on the world, including TEI, and their contribution in shaping the future together.

Author Keywords
Tangible interaction; paradigms; embodied sensemaking; vision; future of TEI.

ACM Classification Keywords
Miscellaneous. H.5.2. Information interfaces and presentation: User Interfaces: Evaluation / methodology; Interaction styles; Theory and method)

Introduction

Be part of the ambitious project called Engaging Encounters: Sketching the Future together. During this one-year project, I will visit 50 inspirators around the world, including visionary politicians, innovative researchers, inspiring educators, dare-deviling business(wo)men, NGO and NPO do-gooders, imaginative designers, ingenious artists, and other creative, wise and inspiring people. During a hands-on workshop-based encounter, we will envision together what the future can be at the cross-section of our expertise. By sketching this future together and creating a joined vision, I aim at bridging our worlds in action. Through these encounters, I like to be inspired by the expertise, work and vision of the inspirator and inspire him or her by showing examples of "embodied perception theories"-inspired work from our DQI group (dep. of Industrial Design, TU Eindhoven, the Netherlands) and other interaction design work, and reveal what design could bring; and I like introduce them to the ideas and vision of the other inspirators by connecting the results of all encounters. This way I hope all participants get new insights and can grow, which might even create potential ground for further collaboration. Moreover, I hope that the overall result, documented in a blog, book and a movie, will inspire others in their work and perspective on the world.

Especially for the TEI conference, I offer six personal encounters with individual TEI participants to discuss, explore and sketch the future of TEI. Every encounter will take 1,5 hour, and the results of the six encounters will not only be included in the book and movie about the overall project, but also be included in a special publication about the future of TEI.

Studio-workshop Set-up and Topics

I receive individual participants for a 1,5 hour private studio-workshop "Engaging Encounters: Sketching the Future of TEI". This studio-workshop will run maximally 6 times during Thursday and Friday, January 15 and 16, making use of the mobile Design and Sensemaking Studio (D&S Studio) [1].

Figure 1: The first prototypes of the D&S Studio.

The studio-workshop will go through four phases: getting acquainted, setting the stage, sketching the future of TEI, and wrapping up.

00:00-00:10 *Getting acquainted:* In order to get engaged and work at an empathic level as quickly as possible, every encounter starts with a brief introduction session using Engagement Catalysers [2], to explore and visualise which values drive us in our work and life.

00:10-00:20 *Setting the stage:* We will start by each of us placing two to three items on the stage that we have selected before the start of the studio-workshop, based on the theme "sketching the future of TEI" (and which will be exchanged before the start of the studio-workshop). We will briefly explain to each other what we have brought and why.

00:20-01:20 *Sketching the future of TEI:* Thereupon we have one hour to explore, discuss and sketch the future of TEI, as tangible as possible. During the encounter we can try out each other's work, demos, techniques, tools etc. As the TEI-community is based a various paradigms, this encounter scrutinises differences in our underlying paradigms; do we use for example a phenomenology-inspired design way towards TEI, an artistic approach, or what we loosely call a Cartesian computer science and engineering-based way towards TEI? Since a multiplicity of perspectives is highly desirable for a healthy and mature TEI community, we will explore during the encounter how the different paradigms meet, how we can learn from each other, and how we can bring the field forward. Moreover, we will explore during this encounter how TEI can influence the interaction with the world in the next decade, and what we see beyond that decade.

The encounter makes use of the mobile D&S Studio, which was especially designed for this project based on embodied perception theories, and more specifically the concept of embodied sensemaking [1].

The D&S Studio consist of a stage with an integrated Ideating in Skills toolset that was especially developed to trigger ideation and creating scenarios through skill-based interaction. Moreover, it the stage contains a set of small Inspiration & Assessment Cards to trigger ones imagination [3]. To enhance the social sensemaking process, the D&S Studio supports the participants to connect digital content to physical scaffolds using a RFID Scaffolding toolset, which includes RFID scanners, stickers and a handheld printer. A set of iPads and iPods is used to access digital information and record the entire session, and a local server and a special database is developed to store and retrieve digital content related to the encounters, including the recordings made. These recordings (audio, video, and RFID time-stamped markers) are for use during the session as well as afterwards to inspire others and for ones own recollection. The input and results will be connected throughout the different sessions, making participants indirectly part of each other's sessions.

01:20-01:30 *Wrapping up:* We finalise the encounter, by concluding and summarizing the finding of the session.

The overall results will be documented in a blog, and be a part of a book and a movie about the entire project Engaging Encounters: Sketching the Future together. Through all the encounters and 'publications', this project aims at inspiring people in their work and perspective on the world, including TEI, and their contribution in shaping the future together. Moreover, the project aims at helping to bridge the communication gaps between the different worlds of research, politics, commerce and living, and the different world within research, e.g. design, art, engineering and social science.

A while after every encounter, every participant receives his or her own trace of the whole session, existing of 1) a few photos of the overall setting/trace, and 2) an URL to the digital database of that specific encounter, if feasible also with the time-stamped audio recording. In case preferred, the participant can also order a small luxury box with cards that are related to every scaffold used during the encounter and a booklet showing the overall results of the TEI studio-workshop. This way every participant gets scaffolds that they can use again to show and discuss their envisioned future with their colleagues and friends.

No prior skills are required for this studio-workshop. The participants are asked up front to collect a few items (e.g. photos, videos, prototypes, sketches, tools, articles, books or websites) to bring along to the encounter and boost the exploration, based on their perspective on TEI.

Studio-workshop Learning Goals

This studio-workshop aims at exploring hands-on how the work and ideas of TEI can influence our interaction with the world in the upcoming decade(s), and how people from different paradigms underlying the TEI community envision our future society and prefer to build our TEI community together.

The studio-workshop aims at inspiring participants to reflect on their work and the underlying paradigms; to reflect on the future society, their potential role in it and the role of TEI in it.

The studio-workshop aims at showing what design, based on embodied perception theories, can bring the TEI community.

The studio-workshop aims at helping to bridge the communication gaps between the different worlds of research, politics, industry, commerce and living, and the different worlds within research, e.g. design, art, engineering and social science.

By connecting all encounters, the entire project aims to be a breading ground for new insights, ideas and potential collaboration, to learn from each other and to sculpt the future together.

Supporting Web Documents

The dedicated website and blog for the "Engaging Encounters: Sketching the Future together" project can be found at: http://dqi.id.tue.nl/ee. A special TEI section on this website will provide additional materials for the studio-workshop: http://dqi.id.tue.nl/ee/TEI.

Acknowledgements

I like to thank Chet Bangaru, Harm van Hoek, Jaime van Hummel, Brandon Yeup Hur, Ambra Trotto, Jelle van Dijk, Less or More and the students from the IiS module for helping me realise the D&S Studio.

References

[1] Hummels, C. and Van Dijk, J. (accepted). Seven principles to design for embodied sensemaking. TEI'15 Conference, Stanford, 15-19 January 2015.

[2] Trotto, A. & Hummels, C.C.M. (2013). Engage me, do! Engagement Catalysers to ignite a (design) conversation. In: *Proc. of DPPI '13*. (Newcastle, September 3-5), 136-145.

[3] Hummels, C.C.M (2004). Educating interaction, experience and diversity. In: The changing face of design education; *Proceedings of the 2nd IEPDE Conference* (Delft, NL, September 2-3), 247-254.

Re-Orientating Time in Product Design: A Phenomenology-inspired Perspective

Jelle Stienstra
j.t.stienstra@tue.nl

Bart Hengeveld
b.j.hengeveld@tue.nl

Caroline Hummels
c.c.m.hummels@tue.nl

Designing Quality in Interaction group
Department of Industrial Design
Eindhoven University of Technology
Den Dolech 2
5612 AZ, Eindhoven, The Netherlands

TEI '15, Jan 16-19 2015, Stanford, CA, USA
ACM 978-1-4503-3305-4/15/01.
http://dx.doi.org/10.1145/2677199.2687890

Abstract
This paper presents a work in progress design case that is used to exemplify how a phenomenology-inspired perspective on *time* can impact the design of highly interactive systems and products. The design presents a calendar with a re-orientated layout that is based on a bodily relationship with time, rather than on the more established linear chronological layout found in most products and systems. The presented design offers a promising perspective as well as emergent technical issues and questions. With this work we hope to inspire interaction designers to consider embodied mechanisms.

Author Keywords
Interaction design; phenomenology-inspired design; time

ACM Classification Keywords
H.5.2. [Information Interfaces and Presentation]: User Interfaces — Theory and Methods, User-Centered Design

Introduction
Most interactive products and systems build upon a strict definition of time in terms of frames, seconds,

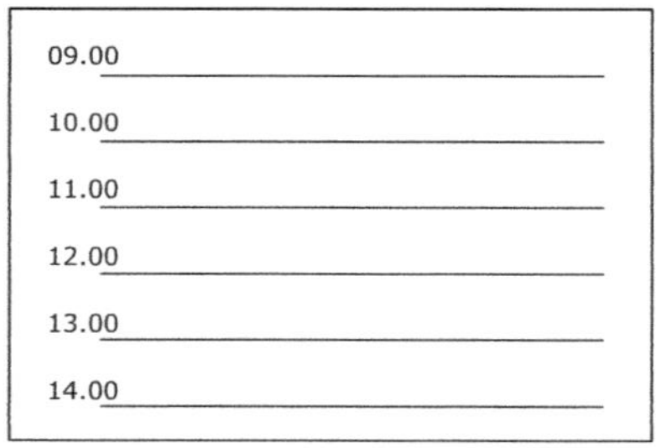

Figure 1. Mainstream orientation of time in calendars.

minutes and hours and to a larger scale in terms of days, weeks, months and years (i.e., clock time). Events are mainly defined as discrete interpretations of time (e.g., time blocks), as such directing our day-to-day life equally discretely, through our engagement with clocks and calendars.

This well-established chronological and sequential approach to time overshadows an alternative *subjective take* on time in the systems and products we engage with in our education; in our common thinking [1]. In other words, we tend to ignore that at times we experience things as fast or slow; that we grab food when we are hungry instead of waiting for the clock; and that we keep snoozing till we are actually up for it. Experience of time is embodied (i.e., it is bound to our bodily activity in the world), flexible (i.e., it sometimes is fast or slow), subjective (i.e., it is different for people) and contextual as well, and perhaps deserves technologies (and in the first place mind-sets) that better cope with it. As Martin Heidegger would frame it: we do not exist inside time, *we are time* [4].

In our work we take a phenomenological stance towards designing interactive products and systems [5][7], which respects uniqueness and our human capabilities from an embodiment of meaning [3][8], as well as a contextual experience perspective [6]. Successive to earlier work, we here aim to explore some of the arising the consequences of a phenomenological approach [2] towards designing for systems that interweave in the social fabric of our lives.

Taking *time* from a phenomenological perspective (e.g., a perspective that centralizes ones subjective experience, embodiment and contextuality) has several implications for designing. Within this paper we present a single (re-)design case that highlights what this different perspective can bring about in designing. This design case builds upon embodiment (i.e., an unification of body and functionality) in particular. After presenting this design case we identify several other phenomenological notions related to *time* that could have implications on the way products and systems come about and how people will engage with them.

We acknowledge that both approaches to time, a more linear/conventional and a more contextualized one are meaningful (e.g., some people benefit from fixed structured planning while others thrive on the turning of the world and their 'spontaneous bodily needs'). As most systems exclusively utilize the linear kind, we deliberately explore the consequences of the other perspective and hope to inspire design by doing so.

Body and Time

For our design case we take the simple phenomenology-inspired notion that *time* is not something outside us but that it is something we are [4]; that it can not be separated from our being, from our body and engagement with the world. The body (in its being) in the world brings together the past and future in the qualitatively experienced present, whereas the past brings along the awareness; the future brings along the anticipation of potential engagement [6] i.e., we use our experience and anticipation to perform actions in the moment.

Todes [8] points out that the orientation and directedness towards the world follows the structure of the active body and has diverse functions. In short, the horizontal field people engage with concerns 'the order

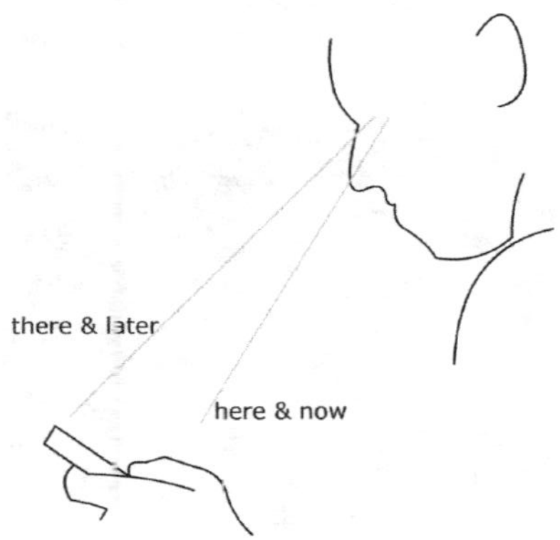

Figure 2. Person looks at calendar on smart-phone.

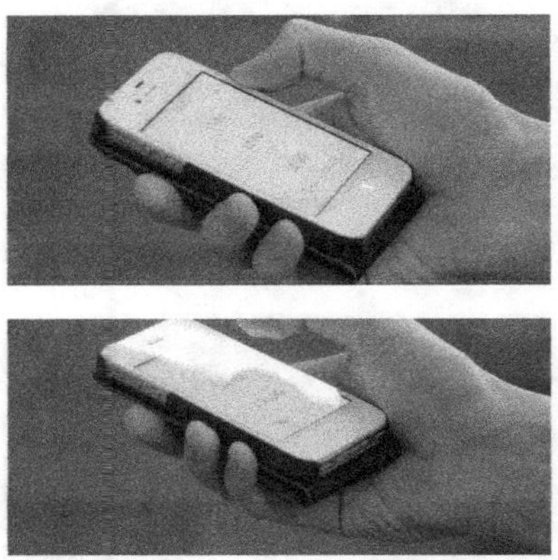

Figure 3. Time and thus the events come closer while time passes. On the top image it is about to be 11.00, in the bottom image it is about to be 13.00. The time came closer to the body.

of things' (i.e., to find orientation) presenting us with the action-possibilities. The front-back asymmetry of the body is affective in what actively lies ahead; the vertical field concerns the ability to bring action-possibilities closer. Thus, according to Merleau-Ponty and Todes, the past lies behind us, the present is in reach and the future lies ahead of us (fig. 2). The farther something is away, the longer it takes to reach it to bring it to the now.

Design

We decided to tackle the interaction design of a digital calendar, as calendars profoundly dependent on the notion of time. A redesign of this would thus most likely reveal several consequences of taking a different point of departure. The relatively simple (re-)design we present here is no more than a re-orientation of the calendar's layout. In most calendars time is represented from top to bottom (fig. 1) with on the horizontal axis the days, weeks and months. The clock, with its circular representation of time, is similarly detached from the embodiment of time in terms of its form (even though its idea is rooted in the movement of the sun and consequently shadow). Both the rotating pointer and the flat fields on the calendar have little connection to actual movement of the body through or within time.

People tend to hold their phone's calendar in horizontal manner, and not perpendicular to the viewpoint. Therefore, our design utilizes the upper space as far (in both space and time) and the bottom more closer to the body as 'now' (fig. 2). In other words, time is laid out from here to there; from now to later, and meetings on that calendar will come closer as time passes by (fig. 3).

By bringing the top of the phone closer to the body, it is possible to see closer to the now. By turning the top of the phone closer to the body (e.g., vertical) it is possible to see further in time. Additionally, the meetings that thus come closer can be pushed away: and thus postponed.

The calendar and upcoming events can be explored through changing the inclination of the screen. It is somehow possible, poetically speaking, to engage with time and meetings by uncovering time and meetings in interaction (fig. 4).

Opening Design Space

The presented design case that illustrates a simple alternative to calendars when taking a phenomenological perspective so far uses just one of the elements incorporated in the philosophy (e.g., an embodied relation to time in the perspective of space and distance). Phenomenology holds several other considerations that could provide alternative products that emphasize the subjectivity of people and their engagement with the social world. In the following part we pose two more phenomenology-derived claims that deserve to be considered when designing products that are anchored in *subjective time*. What is to be looked at when designing these products and systems if they are to be designed from a phenomenological perspective instead of a Cartesian one?

Overthrowing units

Microsoft's Exchange, Apple's iCal, Google's Calendar but also our paper date books are systems that facilitate with streamlining the flow of daily and business activities. But these calendars pay little attention to our reasoning that time as we experience

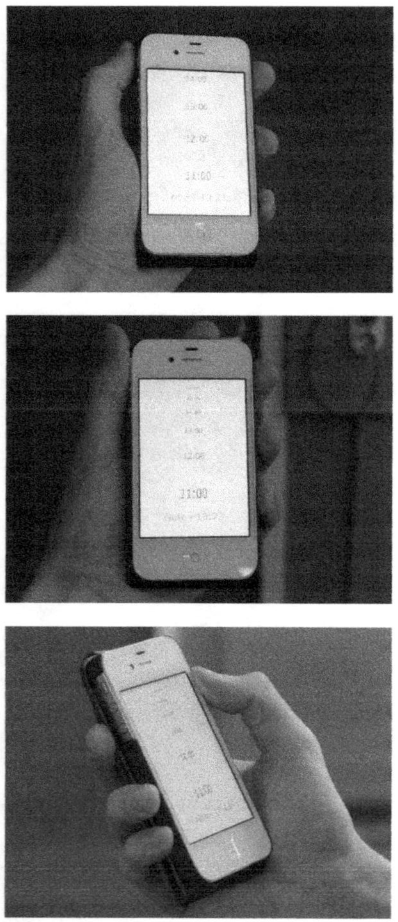

Figure 4. By using the inclination of the calendar, it is possible to look further or closer in time.

and use it might actually be slightly more flexible than utilizing predefined blocks of hours and minutes. Reconsidering hours and minutes (which we here suggest from a phenomenological perspective) has far reaching consequences beyond the calendar. It involves a radical shift in both our thinking and systemic architecture to break with the deeply rooted convention. However, if we want to build systems that cope with our spontaneous bodily needs (e.g., going to dinner when we are hungry, waking up when we are rested, meeting up with others when the circumstances brought us together), it might be more sensible to let our bodies govern time instead of hours and the clock to direct our being.

Planning shared activities

Coming forth to this embodiment and subjectivity in time-directed products will bring along a major obstacle: the need for people (and systems) to meet up (or in other words synchronize). This emergent issue is already thoroughly overcome by the somewhat objectivity-rooted solutions in which the convenience of conventions in time units and time standards are utilized. Standardization enables us in meeting up in time, despite its directive character.

Phenomenology points to intersubjectivity [2] to deal with such problems. However, the philosophy is highly descriptive and does not give apparent directions for designing beyond recommending that the involved parties (people and systems) engage in continuous interaction for meaning to emerge in context.

Our initial take on this is to provide users with a capability to grasp the engagement of the others in order to get a grip on involvement. Measuring (or inquiring) about how the other people or systems are engaged in the activity (focused or absent) will in the least please provide an understanding and thus grounds to behave appropriately. For example, when I would like to meet with you, see you and get that you just had a tough meeting before, it allows me to address you appropriately if at all. From your side, you might be less reluctant to have this interruption from my side knowing that I need just a little bit of your time in a casual manner. In some way, it boils down to building a common ground about time and involvement between the actors and not from a predefined overlaying grid of minutes and hours *per se*.

Stretching the Design

In the following part we anticipate how these two additional consequences of phenomenology could manifest themselves in the earlier given design case of the re-orientation of the layout. In this design, the snooze function was enabled by a push-away-action (i.e., while meetings come closer in both distance and time, they can be pushed away). This shoving could be done gently or farther thus respectively postponing slightly and more. But then how is this going to work if there is another meeting *behind*? And what if these meetings are actually with other people?

Our solution to this emergent complexity is to be found in what we frame as the *locus* and *focus* people have with their meetings. Meetings and other (preparative) appointments come towards the *now*; they come closer but are of flexible nature contrary to a fixed timeframe. The focus of an event is one's required attention on a gradual scale. The locus of an event is its flexibility over time. Meetings can thus have high or low intensities and be more or less strict in when they occur.

Figure 5. A meeting is pushed away, back into the future. By doing so, other meetings are postponed and shortened.

The functionality to shove around meetings opens up that meetings can be slippery, sturdy and in some can be squeezed in (i.e., take less time but increase in intensity). When a meeting is pushed away (fig. 5), the meetings behind can shrink in or bounce the pushed one back. It is than easier to snooze in open space than when you are quite close to sturdy meetings.

In case this is applied with a multiplicity of people attending meetings, the complexity grows but can be overcome by design decisions (i.e., educated choices concerning the prioritizing of meetings). To some extend the locus and focus is our designerly approach to what we earlier posed as the engagement as representation of subjective experience of time. If we then decide to push or shove a meeting, this will occur in one's own flexibility but also in the flexibility of meetings of the others involved. Changing (shrinking, moving or flattening) will not always be possible, but that is what such a system will reflect as well (e.g., if the meeting cannot be moved for someone else it cannot be moved for me either).

Closing remarks

We believe after building primitive prototypes and walkthrough scenarios that by utilizing a focus and locus it might be possible to bypass the use of discretely defined time in terms of hours and minutes. However, for this to be successful it is required for people to establish a different relationship with time. One that demands a stronger bodily engagement yet embedded in ones every day life. Having lunch might not always turn out to happen at 12.00, instead, through pushing and pulling the event around people are enabled to have it when they are actually hungry. In case the pushing and pulling does not establish this, we suggest exploring this 'listening to the body' by actually utilizing identifiers in context such as physiological cues (e.g., measuring 'hunger') and other indicators (e.g., activity recognition in terms of ones ability to engage fully in meetings) that help a calendar understand that the person needs energy.

It is fair to say that the presented design is far from complete and that emerging issues are far from being solved and foreseen when we fully intend to stretch phenomenology in a designerly approach. For instance in the design of the calendar: what about the location of people and thus distance of traveling, the personal relationship people have or the importance of working on certain projects in defining the (inter)subjective locus and focus of events? How is this practically possible to connect all calendars of people? And how are we to cope with calendars that are not open for this flexibility? Do we need hybrids?

What we intended to stretch in this work in progress paper is that phenomenology offers inspiration for design and that it could result in profoundly different ideas that preliminary centralize the uniqueness of people. What we acknowledge is that this requires different ways of thinking and different underlying system architectures to handle the emergent complexity that was covered by solutions that depart from the conventions not the subjectivity. Phenomenology-inspired design might not deliver a good solution to use problems that demand a certain different (perhaps more practical) approach. However, we do believe that phenomenology offers an alternative way of looking at the world, and that the products that centralize the human and its full-embodied skillset are worthwhile exploring.

References

[1] Abram, D. (2010) *Becoming Animal.* New York: Vintage

[2] Dourish, P. (2001). *Where the Action Is. The Foundations of Embodied Interaction.* Boston (MA), USA: MIT Press.

[3] Gibson, J.J. (1986). *The Ecological Approach to Visual Perception.* Hillsdale: Lawrence Erlbaum Associates, Inc. (Original work published 1979)

[4] Heidegger, M. (1963). *Being and Time* (J. Macquarrie and E. Robinson, Trans.). New York: Harper and Row (Original work published in 1927)

[5] Hummels, C.C.M. & Lévy, P.D. (2013) Matter of Transformation: Designing an Alternative Tomorrow Inspired by Phenomenology. *Interactions*, 20(6), 42-49.

[6] Merleau-Ponty, M. (1962). *Phenomenology of Perception* (C. Smith, Trans.). New York, NY: Humanities Press. (Original work published in 1945)

[7] Stienstra, J.T. (2015). Embodying Phenomenology in Interaction Design Research. *Interactions*, 22(1)

[8] Todes, S. (2001). *Body and World.* Cambridge, MA: The MIT Press (Original work published in 1990)

Supporting Empathy Through Embodiment in the Design of Interactive Systems

Jonny Huck
Paul Coulton
David Gullick
Imagination Lancaster, LICA Building
Lancaster University
Lancaster, LA1 4YW.
j.huck2@lancaster.ac.uk
p.coulton@lancaster.ac.uk
d.gullick@lancaster.ac.uk

Phillip Powell
Jennifer Roberts
InstEAD,
Department of Economics,
University of Sheffield,
9 Mappin Street,
Sheffield, S1 4DT.
p.a.powell@sheffield.ac.uk
j.r.roberts@sheffield.ac.uk

Andrew Hudson-Smith
Martin De-Jode
Panagiotis Mavros
CASA, UCL
1st Floor,
90 Tottenham Court Road,
London, W1T 4.
a.hudson-smith@ucl.ac.uk
m.dejode@ucl.ac.uk
p.mavros@ucl.ac.uk

TEI '15, Jan 16-19, 2015, Stanford, CA, USA.
ACM 978-1-4503-3305-4/15/01.
http://dx.doi.org/10.1145/2677199.2687892

Abstract
Whilst empathy is considered an essential component of what it means to be human, it is frequently absent as a design objective when creating modern communication systems. This paper presents an approach to designing *for*, as opposed to *with*, empathy using the example of two design interventions to create embodied rituals reflecting prayers and worries of individuals within a church community. The aim of these interventions is to facilitate conversation and support within the community, thus generating empathy between community members, and inciting prosocial behaviour through embodied cognition.

Author Keywords
Empathy; Design; Digital Empathy; Embodied Actions

ACM Classification Keywords
H.5.m. Miscellaneous

General Terms
Design, Human Factors.

Introduction
Empathy

Empathy defines our ability to understand and share the feelings of another [1]. It is an emotional capacity that has often been overlooked within the design of digital systems [2]. This is problematic, as empathy may be viewed as one of the essential components of the 'human condition', with observation of atypical empathetic responses suggested as indicators of a number of autism spectrum and personality disorders that inhibit an individual's ability to relate to others. If empathy is indeed such an important facet of humanity, we argue that it should be considered in the design of the ever-increasing number of digital communication systems. In the absence of a full understanding of how designers might address this goal, there is a clear need for research that specifically addresses the notion of *designing for empathy* [2].

Whilst there is a rich and varied literature relating to empathy, how it is experienced, whether and how it may be taught, its effect upon attitudes and behaviour, and its application to a wide variety of applied fields of study [3], it has yet to be completely understood. It is probable that the lack of discussion relating to the incorporation of empathy within digital design is caused by the notion that it, along with other emotions, is extremely difficult [3], or even impossible [4, 5] to sense automatically with a computer. The approach taken here, however, is not to attempt to *sense* empathy, but merely to design systems in such a way as to afford empathetic feelings and behaviour within a community.

The positive effects of empathy go far beyond improving attitudes and motivating prosocial behaviour (voluntary behaviour intended to benefit others) [3]. Indeed, it has been found that inducing empathy towards animals and plants can increase pro-environmental behaviour [6]. It follows, therefore, that designing for the promotion of empathy within a community could increase pro-community and prosocial behaviour: improving the coherence and 'spirit' of the community, and thus potentially increasing the happiness and wellbeing of its members.

It should be noted that the concept of *designing for empathy* is completely distinguished from the similarly named field of 'Empathic Design', which is concerned more with *designing with empathy* for a particular user group. There is, in fact, very little in the current design literature relating to the creation of systems for facilitating or encouraging empathetic behaviour between subjects [2].

Rituals and Embodiment

There is a significant strand of the psychological literature that attests to the potency of physical acts and 'rituals', demonstrating the notable and sometimes surprising effects that behaviour can have on the human psyche. The link between mind and body has been explored most profitably in an area that has become known popularly as 'embodied cognition': the concept that certain states of the body modify states of the mind [7]. There are a range of studies that illustrate the positive psychological effects of carrying out particular actions, such as Zhong and Liljenquist [8] and Xu et al. [9], which reported that participants who *physically* washed their hands after recalling an unethical deed experienced significantly reduced negative moral emotions (i.e., shame, guilt etc.).

[1] *Votive candles* are lit in a church, normally (in a Christian Church) before a statue or image of Jesus Christ; Mary, Mother of Christ; or another Saint. The candle is a symbol of a '*prayer intention*' – the purpose for which you will pray, and follows the common Christian symbolism of light representing God.

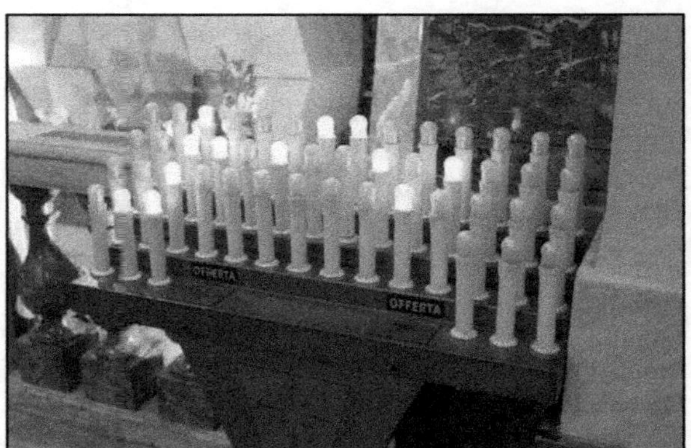

Figure 1. Electrified votive candles in Sicily.

In a separate line of research, Brinol et al. [10] asked participants to write their likes and dislikes relating to their physical bodies on a piece of paper. The researchers found that those individuals who then tore up and discarded this paper relied less upon those thoughts in forming subsequent judgements than those who kept them, and that this effect was enhanced if the retained paper was kept in a safe place (i.e., in a participant's pocket). The effects of such ritualistic actions on our thoughts, feelings and behaviours do not even need to have a logical or causal connection in order to be influential. A series of experiments by Norton and Gino [11] illustrated that engaging in novel physical rituals (designed and assigned by an experimenter) reduced the grief reported after recalling a series of loss events.

The above experiments illustrate the effect of physical actions upon the regulation of emotional states. In another experiment by Brinol et al. [10], the authors found evidence that these effects were stronger when a physical action was performed rather than simply imagined, and Xu et al. [9] reported that physically undertaking an act (washing hands) was more effective than simply watching the act on a video. This therefore suggests that facilitating the (physical) expression of such empathetic concern has the potential to have positive psychological benefits for those involved.

Designing for Empathy

This work has taken place in collaboration with an existing cohesive community: the congregation of St Peter De Beauvoir Town Anglican Church in Hackney, London. A church community was chosen as they already have a number of embodied rituals in place, intended to facilitate members in sharing their prayers and worries in a personal way with God. It is these personal rituals (and their associated artefacts) that will be digitally augmented in order to enable these personal thoughts and feelings to be shared with their community (if they so wish) in the expectation that this will afford the development of empathy. The design of these augmentations has taken place following extensive discussion with the Vicar relating to the usage and potential of each ritual. The pre-existing artefacts associated with the rituals will remain in the church alongside the new augmented versions, so that members of the congregation only have to utilise the augmented systems if they so wish.

Digital Votive Candles

The first system designed for the project relates to the lighting of *votive candles*[1] as a physical ritual symbolising a prayer intention, often relating to a specific person or outcome. This is an act common within many branches of Christianity as well as Hinduism, Buddhism and other religious groups. At St Peter De Beauvoir Town, votive candles are lit within the church itself, and the associated prayer intentions are held privately to the individual. It is thought that this symbolic physical act of lighting a candle reinforces the positive benefits associated with a prayer.

The objective for the augmentation of the votive candles is to maintain the embodied ritual of lighting a candle, but allow the associated prayer intention to be *shared* with the rest of the community, in the hope that this will create a greater level of empathy within the community. A physical artefact will therefore be

Figure 2. The '*4Candles*' digital votive candles.

introduced into the church to fulfil this function. There is already evidence of both the electrification and digitisation of votive candles (e.g. Figure 1 and [12] respectively), but thus far there have been no attempts to extend the impact of these symbolic acts within a community, either through the increased functionality of systems, by the facilitation of communication.

The '*4Candles*' digital votive candles artefact comprises a physical candelabra (containing four digitally enhanced wax candles) with a built-in touch screen interface, as is illustrated in Figure 2. The touch screen runs an application (Figure 3) that can be used by participants to light a candle with their own prayer intention. When idle, the application cycles a display of the previous prayer intentions associated with the candles, along with an animated flickering candle that is intended to draw the attention of passing members of the community.

The prayer on screen changes every 30 seconds, and with each change one of the digital candles is extinguished and re-lit in order to symbolise the original lighting of the candle for that particular prayer intention. In this way, all of the logged prayers will be regularly displayed within the church for their requested period of time, and thus shared with any other members of the church community that are present. Before display, each message requires approval by the Vicar via a simple web interface. In this way, abuse of the system can be avoided, and any inappropriate or offensive messages can be prevented from being displayed upon the screen in the church, which is a highly sensitive location.

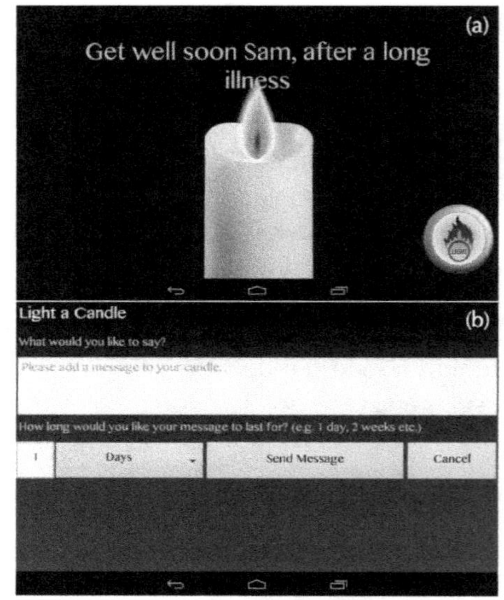

Figure 3. Screenshots of the'*4Candles*' Android application.

The act of extinguishing and re-lighting a candle each time a new prayer intention is displayed also furthers the impression that the system is 'active', as well as reinforcing the notion that a prayer intention *belongs* to a particular candle, as would be the case with a traditional votive candle. Crucially though, the physical extinguishing of the candles contributes to the physicality of the ritual of lighting a candle, which is intended to further the effect of embodied cognition within the act of lighting a candle, promoting the benefits of embodied cognition to the user, as well as helping to ensure that the augmented version is viewed as being comparable in experience to lighting a candle in the traditional manner.

Digital Font

The second system designed to facilitate empathy within the church is that of the font, which is currently used for members of the congregation (normally children) to 'let go' of their fears and worries by the ritual of placing a pebble (representing the worry) into the water and physically letting go of it. Whilst not as commonplace as the votive candles, and indeed not the traditional function of the (baptismal) font in a church[2],

[2] A *baptismal font* is normally used as part of the Christian sacrament of *Baptism* (also known as *Christening* by some Christian denominations), whereby holy water from the font is symbolically poured over the head of the subject (normally a child), as part of their initiation into the church.

this ritual represents a very effective literal representation of 'letting go' of one's worries, and as such will benefit from the positive effects of embodied cognition. As with the prayer intentions associated with the votive candles, however, these worries are currently kept privately to the individual. They are not shared either with the Vicar or other members of the community as part of this ritual, and as such do not promote communication within the community, or any of the benefits that may arise from this.

Once again, the objective of the digital font is therefore to increase engagement with the ritual and facilitate communication within the community, this time of their collective worries, in order to further develop understanding and hopefully empathy between community members. As the current font ritual already represents a classic example of embodied cognition, a non-invasive digital augmentation of the existing font the introduction of a new artefact.

The "Font of Solace" digital font is based around a tablet computer running a custom application that allows the user to 'write' their worry onto the screen using the provided stylus, before 'sending' this worry to the font. When the users then physically touch the water (detected with a *Microsoft Kinect*), the words that they wrote appear in the water (via an overhead projector) before drifting away into the virtual '*ether*'. As with the candles, this hand-written message is also logged to a central server, and requires approval from the Vicar before appearing on a display screen within the church. This display will once again cycle through all of the most recent worries that people have logged, so that they may be shared with the rest of the community, for the purpose of generating empathy.

The use of hand-written text disappearing into the '*ether*' is intended to reinforce the embodiment of the ritual, with the disappearing worry represented in the user's own handwriting making the ritual more 'personal' than it would in an anonymous typeface. Maintaining the requirement for the user to physically touch the water retains the effective physical metaphor of 'letting go' of the worry, as opposed to simply pressing a button, or interacting with a screen.

Conclusion

Whilst very much a 'work in progress' this research is intended to stimulate debate around *designing for empathy*, particularly in a community setting. Two systems have been presented that are designed to allow a congregation to communicate their prayers and worries not only to God, as is currently the case, but also to other members of the community through existing ritual acts. It is intended that these rituals will have a positive effect upon the psyche of users through embodied cognition; and that this communication will enable the community to be more aware of its own members, develop a greater understanding of each other, and afford the development of mutual empathy.

Our approach centred upon the use of an existing cohesive community, and upon the principle of extending the functionality of existing symbolic rituals and their associated artefacts within the church setting. This approach has minimised the required level motivation for community members to use these artefacts, which facilitate rituals with which they are already familiar and may even routinely enact already. Similarly, the selection of a pre-existing community is intended to facilitate conversation, as community members would be expected to feel more able to talk to

Figure 4. The stone baptismal font with projector and Microsoft Kinect mounted above it [INSET].

each other than may be the case with a group of strangers.

Future work on this project will comprise an evaluation of the experience of these systems by members of the church, and the extent to which they were able to afford the development of empathy within the community.

Acknowledgements

The authors would like to thank Julia Porter-Pryce, Vicar of St Peter De Beauvoir Town, for her support and enthusiasm for this project and the EPSRC through grant EP/L003635/1.

References

[1] Oxford Dictionaries: http://www.oxforddictionaries.com/definition/english/empathy. Last accessed 04/08/2014.

[2] Coulton, P., Huck, J., Hudson-Smith, A., Ralph, B., Mavros, P., Roberts, J., & Powell, P. (2014). Designing interactive systems to encourage empathy between users. In *DIS Companion '14 Proceedings of the 2014 companion publication on Designing interactive systems.* (pp. 13-16). New York: ACM. 10.1145/2598784.2602770

[3] Belman, J., & Flanagan, M. (2009). Designing Games to Foster Empathy. *International Journal of Cognitive Technology*, *14*(2), 11.

[4] Gaver, W. (2009). Designing for emotion (among other things). *Philosophical Transactions of the Royal Society B: Biological Sciences, 364*(1535), 3597-3604.

[5] Boehner, K., DePaula, R., Dourish, P., & Sengers, P. (2005, August). Affect: from information to interaction. In *Proceedings of the 4th decennial conference on Critical computing: between sense and sensibility* (pp. 59-68). ACM.

[6] Berenguer, J. (2007). The effect of empathy in proenvironmental attitudes and behaviors. *Environment and Behavior*, *39*(2), 269-283.

[7] Wilson, A. D., & Golonka, S. (2011). Embodied cognition is not what you think it is. *Front Psychol*, *4*: 58

[8] Zhong, C-B., & Liljenquist, K. (2006). Washing away your sins: Threatened morality and physical cleansing. *Science*, *313*, 1451-1452.

[9] Xu, H., Begue, L., & Bushman, B. J. (2014). Washing the guilt away: effects of personal versus vicarious cleansing on guilty feelings and prosocial behaviour. *Front Hum Neurosci*, *8: 97.*

[10] Brinol, P., Gasco, M., Petty, R. E., & Horcajo, J. (2013). Treating thoughts as material objects can increase or decrease their impact on evaluation. *Psychological Science*, *24*, 41-47.

[11] Norton, M. I., & Gino, F. (2014). Rituals alleviate grieving for loved ones, lovers, and lotteries. *Journal of Experimental Psychology: General*, *143*, 266-272.

[12] Light a Candle: http://www.gratefulness.org/candles. Last accessed 04/08/2014.

Situated Apparel: Designing to Reinforce Affective Communication

Ye Tao
Zhejiang University
38 Zheda Ave.
Hangzhou, 310027 China
taoye@zju.edu.cn

Xiaolian Zhang
Zhejiang University
38 Zheda Ave.
Hangzhou, 310027 China
xiaolian@zju.edu.cn

Hongyu Chen
Zhejiang University
38 Zheda Ave.
Hangzhou, 310027 China
hongyu89@foxmail.com

Fangtian Ying
Zhejiang University
38 Zheda Ave.
Hangzhou, 310027 China
yingft@gmail.com

Fei Meng
Zhejiang University
38 Zheda Ave.
Hangzhou, 310027 China
mf31415@gmail.com

Cheng Yao
Zhejiang University
38 Zheda Ave.
Hangzhou, 310027 China
yaoch@zju.edu.cn

TEI '15, Jan 16-19 2015, Stanford, CA, USA
ACM 978-1-4503-3305-4/15/01.
http://dx.doi.org/10.1145/2677199.2687893

Abstract
There is a prosperity in wearable media in data monitoring. Since the apparel can show personal tastes, emotions and attitudes, what if our clothes could express affective information throughout different situations? This paper presents a system for enhancing the experience of situated-base affective communication by information visualization. The paper discusses the leading features in a variety of specific contexts such as the information monitoring, the remote communication and the customization.

Author Keywords
Interactive fashion; wearable media; affective communication; intelligent light

ACM Classification Keywords
H.5.2. Information interfaces and presentation (e.g., HCI): User Interfaces; Interaction styles.

General Terms
Human Factors; Design.

Introduction
At present, wearable media have primarily focused on data collection and its analysis, while light fashion design is mostly shown as an art. Though these are two different research areas, fashion, with its unique

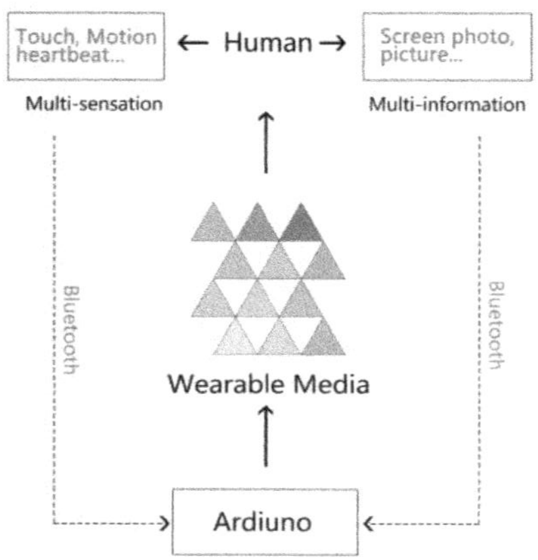

Figure 2. The system setup.

emotional attributes, can be explored in human-computer interaction. We believe that live apparel systems can offer a natural perception and emotional amplification experience by attempting to capture and visualize rich data through the embedded sensor technology.

For the first time, we are able to create a wide variety of enhanced affective communication scenarios by introducing LED-based information I/O system. We explored the following scenarios through three applications: the real-time data visualization for human-object interaction scenarios, the synchronous telematics for human-human interaction scenarios, and the customizing on smart phone for human-environment interaction scenarios.

Related Work

Emotion is constructed as a relational concept, developed within the intersubjective space as an embodied experience [5]. Karrie has done significant work in designing and analyzing sociable and emotional communication within public space scenarios, such as Chit Chat Club [3] and Telemurals [2]. Based on prior studies and social psychology theory, the emotional identity and resonance can be stimulated by cross-infection and interoperability obtained in communication scenarios. This paper will explore the situated communication by fashion medium.

Clothing is a medium for showing personal tastes, emotions, and attitudes. In recent years, wearable designs are increasing to take into consideration the embedded technology, such as, SmartBand, Led fashion, and Awakened Apparel [4]. Being related to our work, Fos [1], a wearable LED display system, has been designed to display dynamic information while the outdoor sport is controlled by smart phone. However, the emotional and the situated communication are not involved.

Design and Implementation

Figure 1. The origami patterns exploration.

In the initial design, the clothes with printed patterns in the front were used, thus the design should coordinate with fashion style instead of patterns as a part of clothes. The origami patterns (Figure 1) were employed to correspond with the effect of led lights echoing form. The reason to choose origami is that have a strong diffuse reflecting power. The user can feel the light from the halo, without looking directly at light. For the others, this is gorgeous e-fashion, not glaring light pollution.

The system (Figure 2) fundamentals consist of two data inputs (the monitoring data from sensors and the data manually entered from mobile terminal), the full-color Led for output, ardiuno for computational processing, and Bluetooth for data transport. C++ is used for the computational processing and the effect output.

The system setup will give many possibilities in human-computer interaction in wearable media area. We explored the following scenarios through three applications to create three affective experiences.

Scenario 1: human-object interaction

SmartBand can be regarded as a way of human-object interaction, which can detect the data of human activity, can simultaneously display them in the mobile terminal and can give some feedback about the wearing process. In the case of SmartBand, this natural trait is reduced by indirection information connection between objects, which would cause obstruction for subjective perceptions.

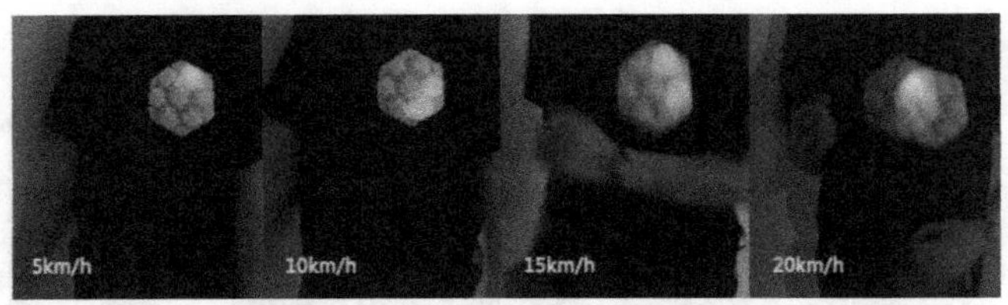

Figure 3. Sport detection is in a natural way to obtain motion information. The vrot of the lighting is according to the motion rate.

We propose a scenario where subjects are in behavioural process with need for direct information display from objects. Situated Apparel was designed to imitate heart rate variation by the light rate of dynamic change, which could achieve emotional self-motivation for subjects.

During jogging situation (Figure 3), it always has trouble to handle smartphone or smartband. With the heartbeat frequency flicker from coat at night, the user can be protected by security alert, and they can further control their own movement from the visual hint intuitively.

Scenario 2: human-human interaction

In contrast to our first scenario, where we are simulating natural human perception during subject behavior, our second application attempts the opposite by allowing the subject to activate the social interaction. Simulating the interaction between the two items can be a catalyst to express emotional communication between subjects.

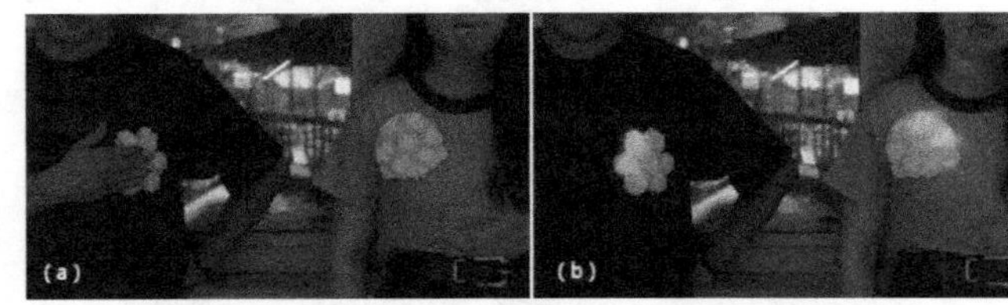

Figure 4. Two connected items, here is Situated Apparel, is used for social interaction. (a) One person touch it to activate the mode, which means "hi", then the light will be auto bright in a rotary way. (b) The receiver got the message by lighting in a same way.

In our case, Situated Apparel, as a bridge, can achieve social affective communication through corresponding lighting pattern and dynamic effects. For instance, in long-distance communication, the tangible light can be triggered remotely to express "I miss you" through dynamic heart effects. Such calm technology makes the action and the feedback an artistic conception.

Scenario 3: human-environment interaction

Our third and final scenario exemplifies the personalized use of immersive environments by associating the visual environment atmosphere with subjects through smartphone. The atmosphere is achieved by analyzing the mass-tone attune of the environment photo.

Situated Apparel can exhibit the contemporary ambience or the memory of the environment tones to achieve the experience of immersive affective communication. For example, memories of a trip are often stored in the photo. When viewing photos, a record at the time of the tone situation can often evoke memories of that time. In line with the photo, the color-changing lighting will make an immersive experience when browsing photos.

Figure 5. The customizing on smart phone can display in desired color atmosphere and dynamic effect. (a) The user can take a photo or select a stored picture. (b) By analyzing the mass-tone attune, the lighting will build an immersive environment.

Conclusion and Future Work

With the overabundant studies focused solely on the function or the aesthetics, we believe that the Situated Apparel system reveals the possibilities in affective communication within wearable interactive technology. Having access to displaying the dynamic information regarding space-time, such as wireless communication, provides us with a compelling framework, further enhancing the situated experience of affective communication.

Future work will be done in the exploration of the integrated wearable form and of the perfection of the functions for user test to further explore the relationship between communication and emotional scenes.

Acknowledgements

We give our sincere thanks to Enmao Liu, Nannan Lu, and Yujia Lu for their contribution to our project. The project is supported by National Key Technology R&D Program (Grant No. 2013BAH59F00) and the Zhejiang Provincial Key Technology R&D Program (Grant No. 2014C31047 & No. 2014R401265).

References

[1] Fos. https://www.kickstarter.com/projects/erogear/fos-a-truly-wearable-bluetooth-led-display-system/creator_bio.

[2] Karahalios, K. and Donath, J. Telemurals: linking remote spaces with social catalysts. In *Proceedings of the SIGCHI conference on Human factors in computing systems*, ACM Press (2004), 615-622.

[3] Karahalios, K. G. and Dobson, K. Chit chat club: bridging virtual and physical space for social interaction. In *Proc.CHI 2005*, ACM Press (2005), 1957-1960.

[4] Perovich, L., Mothersill, P. and Farah, J. B. Awakened apparel: embedded soft actuators for expressive fashion and functional garments. In Proceedings of the 8th International Conference on Tangible, Embedded and Embodied Interaction. ACM Press (2014), 77-80.

[5] Rajan-Rankin, S. Self-identity, embodiment and the development of emotional resilience. *British Journal of Social Work*, (2013), 1-17.

PhonoBlocks: A Tangible System for Supporting Dyslexic Children Learning to Read

Alissa N. Antle
School of Interactive Arts and Technology
Simon Fraser University,
Surrey, B.C., Canada V3T 0A3
aantle@sfu.ca

Emily S. Cramer
School of Interactive Arts and Technology
Simon Fraser University,
Surrey, B.C., Canada V3T 0A3
ecramer@sfu.ca

Min Fan
School of Interactive Arts and Technology
Simon Fraser University,
Surrey, B.C., Canada V3T 0A3
minf@sfu.ca

TEI '15, Jan 16-19 2015, Stanford, CA, USA
ACM 978-1-4503-3305-4/15/01.
http://dx.doi.org/10.1145/2677199.2687897

Abstract
Dyslexia is defined as severe difficulty learning to read. It affects about 10% of the population in English speaking countries. Severe difficulty learning to read is correlated with tremendous emotional, social and economic costs. In this paper, we describe PhonoBlocks, a tangible user interface to a reading system that uses dynamic colour cues embedded in 3D tangible letters to provide additional decoding information and modalities. PhonoBlocks was developed to support children, aged 5-8 years old, who are having difficulty learning to decode English letter-sound pairs. We present the theoretical foundations as rationale for our core design strategies and decisions. We discuss the assumptions in our design rationale and describe how we will validate our system working with a school for dyslexic children.

Keywords
Tangible user interfaces; dyslexia; children; reading; colour cues; tangible computing; Orton-Gillingham.

ACM Classification Keywords
H.5.2. [Information interfaces and presentation]: User Interfaces.K.3.1 [Computers and Education]: Computer Uses in Education-*Computer-assisted instruction*.

Figure 1. As a child makes the word "FADE" the colours of the vowel "a" change based on the sound it makes. The short "a" in "fad" is yellow; the long "a" in "fade" is red.

Introduction

Dyslexia is a specific learning difficulty that affects individuals' language-acquisition skills, such as learning to read and write [3]. Each language has a unique *alphabetic principle*, the rules that relate single and multiple letter symbols with speech sounds. Children with dyslexia have difficulty learning and automating the alphabetic principle, and therefore have difficulty in word decoding and reading [6]. Recent research suggests that tangible user interfaces (TUIs) may have benefits for children's learning, particularly in domains that involve space or physical properties [1, 8]. Letters are spatial representations. There is little research that has explored how TUIs might be designed to support children with learning disabilities to learn to read (for exceptions, see [4,10]). There are no studies that specifically investigate if using dynamic colour cues or tactile qualities of tangible letters improves reading outcomes for dyslexic children.

Theoretical and empirical research about dyslexia has highlighted the important roles of colour and tactile modalities in several perceptual and cognitive processes that may be related to reading. We applied knowledge from these theories to design a tangible reading system called PhonoBlocks. PhonoBlocks uses 3D tangible letters as both input and part of the output of a system designed to help dyslexic children learn the alphabetic principle for English. Specifically the system changes the colour of 3D tangible letters based on the sounds they make in a word, enables children to use letter shape cues by using traceable (with a finger) 3D letters as input and uses physical constraints of the 3D letters' base to support correct orientation of the letters (e.g. p vs. q, b vs. d).

Theory

Colour Cues

The core challenge children with dyslexia have is learning the relationships between letters and sounds [13]. In the English language alphabetic principle letters and sounds are inconsistently matched. A single letter can have more than one sound. Multi-letter units, such as blends ("nk" as in sink), and stable syllables ("tion" as in motion) have consistent sounds but these sounds cannot be determined from the sounds of the individual letters. Learning to read involves learning rules that relate a letter's sound to its context (i.e., its position with respect to other letters within a word). For example, one rule is that a "'c" sounds like "k" before "a" and "o" but a "c" sounds like "s" sound before "e" and "i". Another rule is that the stable syllable "tion" sounds like "shun". English is particularly complex, and dyslexic children have difficulty learning these rules [7]. Explicating these rules improves reading and is a goal of many interventions [6].

We propose that colouring letters by the sound they make in a particular context, such that a letter's colour changes when the context changes its sound, may help dyslexic children more easily learn these rules. As a child changes the context, say by adding a trailing "e" to make "fad" into "fade", colour of the letter "a" could change to reflect the change from a short "a" sound to a long "a" sound (Figure 1). An interactive system enables us to change a letter's colour to reflect the sound it makes in particular context, which may draw attention to the rule. Similarly, letters placed in stable syllables (e.g. "tion") could each adopt the same colour, which could help children group and remember these units. Based on this theory, our first design requirement was that that colour should be used to

Figure 2. Twenty-seven opaque traceable tangible letters.

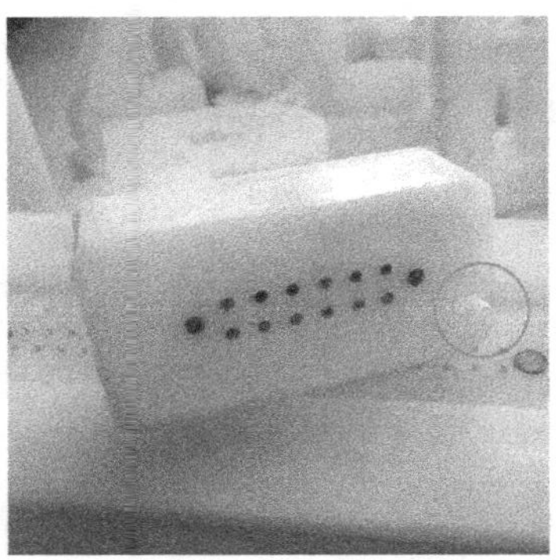

Figure 3. The magnetic notch on each letter and openings in each slot utilizes physical constraints to enforce correct orientation of each letter in its slot.

highlight letter-sound rules for single letters and multi-letter units.

Other challenges dyslexic children have are identifying and discriminating adjacent letters, shifting attention between letters and maintaining previously viewed letters in working memory [6]. Colour cues may also help dyslexic children address these challenges. The atypical letter recognition of dyslexic children seems to be attributed to difficulties they have resolving some letters' differentiating features, such as high-acuity details (r versus i) or reflections (p vs q; b vs d)[6]. By comparison, colours are much easier to discriminate [14], and the colour perception of children with dyslexia is typical or superior [2]. When letters are coloured uniquely, they may be easier to recognize. Compared to 2D letter shape, colours are more memorable, less susceptible to crowding, and make better targets for visual attention [14].

Our secondary design requirement was to use visually distinguishable colours to help children differentiate and remember adjacent and confusable letters.

Tactile Cues
One emerging theory argues that the difficulty that dyslexic children have in identifying similar letters may due to the *mirror generalization* that human brains have evolved over millions of years of evolution to recognize 3D objects [11]. Mirror generalization may help people easily recognize 3D objects in the real life, but it is detrimental for identifying 2D letters, particularly those mirrored ones such as p and q or b and d.

Research in support of Orton-Gillingham (O-G) reading programs has found that teaching children to use their fingers to trace letters may improve reading outcomes by helping them associate letter shapes with distinct motor gestures [3]. Based on this theory we propose that using tactile cues inherent in traceable 3D tangible letters may further improve reading outcomes. 3D letters also enable us to use properties such as texture, colour, and location to convey information that may improve learning the rules for decoding the alphabetic principle.

System Design and Implementation

Learning Goal
The main learning goal was to help dyslexic children, aged 5-8 years old, to improve their understanding of the rules that are part of the alphabetic principle for English, including learning both single and multiple inconsistent letter-sound correspondences.

Design Goals: Colour and Tactile Cues
Our main objective was to create a system that we could use as a research instrument to explore the benefits of adding colour cues and using 3D shaped tangible letters as an interface to a reading system that supports dyslexic children to learn letter-sound correspondences. Based on our requirements, we proposed two groups of design goals: (1) *Colour cues*: colour-code letters by the sound they make in any context for both single and multiple letter groups; display dynamic colours inside 3D letters as well on as display screen (2) *Tactile cues*: design 3D tangible letters so that their size, texture, and shape are easily traceable; design letters so that child can physically (using tactile cues) distinguish the orientation of mirrored or flipped letters.

The PhonoBlocks System
PhonoBlocks is comprised of a touch-screen laptop, an input platform with seven slots, and twenty-seven

tangible Latin (English) letters in upper case (Figure 2). We provide an extra "e" to allow more combinations of vowels. The twenty-seven tangible letters were made with semi-transparent acrylic, with a height of 3 inches, a width of 2.5 inches and a depth of 1.5 inches (as shown in Figure 1). Each letter is fixed on a small acrylic base that enables them to stand and fit into the platform slots. Audio-visual feedback is provided on the digital display including the 2D letter(s) and letter sound(s). At the same time, visual colour feedback appears inside the opaque 3D tangible letter(s) once placed in the input platform's slots.

We are co-designing learning activities with teachers at a school for children with dyslexia, and the actual software associated with learning and practicing the alphabetic principle is completely flexible. Many different activities can be programmed around the core functionality of using the tangible letters. A typical activity might be one in which the system displays a coloured letter-sound pair (e.g. green EA) on the screen. The child is asked to make a word with that combination using the tangible letters (correct answers: EAT, MEAT) and the system provides feedback. Our intention is that children would use PhonoBlocks as an interface to reading software (ours or others') which is related to their curriculum's phonics activities.

Implementation of Colour Cues

Colours were mapped to letters according to their sounds. Consequently, letters adopt different colours according to the context, and different letters adopt similar colours when they sound similar, such as unvoiced 's' (as in sip) and soft 'c' (as in circle). Likewise, when multiple letters create a stable sound unit, such as a digraph ("AE"), blend ("SN") or syllable ("TION"), they adopt the same colour. Otherwise, adjacent letters have different colours. Visually confusable letters are almost never coloured the same.

In order to support colour cues, each letter contains a programmable LED strip. Each letter has a unique arrangement of electronic pogo pins under the bottom of the base which serves as its ID (Figure 3). The input platform contains an Arduino microprocessor that can identify each letter and pass the letter identity and location (slot number) to a custom application running on the laptop written in Processing. When a letter is inserted into a slot, information about the letters' context (e.g. slot number, and which letters are in other slots) is sent to the Processing application. The Processing application then triggers the correct letter sound and sends the correct colour information to the Arduino which then causes that colour to be displayed inside the opaque letter (Figure 1).

Because this is a work in progress, we have not finalized our mappings of colour to sound. Research in cross-modal perception suggests a few promising colour mapping schemas. Wrembel [16] documented *innate* associations between colours and vowels. Watson et al [15] uncovered some evidence that letter shape and frequency affect *synaesthetic* colour-letter associations. Simner et al. suggest that *semantics* may influence colour-sound associations and suggest the use of metaphoric mappings [1, 12]. Our schema may combine elements of innate, synaesthetic and metaphoric approaches, and will be validated by teachers and through a series of small experiments that are part of our ongoing design process.

Implementation of Tactile Cues

The letter size and material was chosen to allow a child to easily grasp, hold, or play with a letter with their hands. The hard edges support tracing. When a child's finger goes over the edge they can immediately feel that their finger has gone over the edge. The features of letter shapes are more salient when children trace 3D letters compared to sandpapers. Children can "feel" the differences between letters by simply grasping them.

We used a physical constraint on manipulation (as described in [9]) to help dyslexic children determine the correct orientation of letters. Each letter has a magnetic, notch on its base (Figure 3, red circle). Each slot has a matching magnetic hole. If the orientation of the letter is correct, the letters' notch fits into the hole and, as additional tactile feedback, the magnets provide a satisfying "click", much like how it feels to close a MacBook. If the letter is not oriented correctly, it does not fit into the slot. The use of this simple physical constraint creates tactile feedback so that a child can easily recognize the correct orientation of each letter without having to visually attend to them.

Discussion

We have outlined our rationale for colour-coding and using tactile cues with tangible letters. In many O-G programs, children often trace coloured letters on sandpaper or posters. Our tangible letters may have three main advantages compared to the traditional O-G approach. First, tangible letters provide an opportunity to leverage the use of physical characteristics of objects (e.g. textures) in learning activities. The multiple cues simultaneously embedded within the object may help children to memorize and understand letter-sound correspondences. In PhonoBlocks, we used the LED strips to create dynamic colours of a letter based on its letter sounds. Although we have not implemented the texture cues, there is a research opportunity to explore the possibilities of other learning materials in future iterations [5]. Second, tangible letters not only enable children to trace letters, but also allow them to physically manipulate letters in the space. The child can group a set of letters together to make up of a letter combination, or practice how to decode a word into a set of subunits. The physical manipulation of concrete letter objects may offload children's cognition or improve their understandings of abstract decoding concepts [1]. Lastly, the tangible letters with physical constraints may enable children to correctly use canonical orientation for letters, particularly for mirrored ones (p,q,d,b). Although we have focused on pronunciation rules and discriminating letters, older children may benefit from a coding scheme that highlighted grammatical or morphological rules; for example, picking out syllables, morphemes, or syntactical structures.

Future Work

Our next steps include user studies to validate the colour mappings and to refine the learning activities. As part of our co-design process, we are currently conducting focus groups with teachers in a school that specializes in working with children with dyslexia. Once complete, we will use PhonoBlocks as a research instrument in a pre-post controlled experiment in the school to investigate if systematic, long term use of our system with the school's learning activities improves reading outcomes for dyslexic children.

Acknowledgements

Thanks for GRAND NEC for funding to pursue this project. Thank you to Jacob B. Freiberg for design and technical support and to Kathleen Akins for her input on our colour coding strategy.

References

[1] Antle, A. N. Research opportunities: Embodied child–computer interaction. *International Journal of Child-Computer Interaction*, 1, 1 (2013), 30-36.

[2] Dautrich, B. R. Visual perceptual differences in the dyslexic reader: Evidence of greater visual peripheral sensitivity to colour and letter stimuli. *Perceptual and Motor Skills*, *76*,3 (1993), 755-764.

[3] Dehaene, S. *Reading in the Brain: The New Science of How We Read*. Penguin, New York, 2009.

[4] Hengeveld, B., Hummels, C., van Balkom, H., Voort, R., & de Moor, J. Wrapping up LinguaBytes, for now. In *Proc. of TEI 2013,* ACM Press (2013), 237-244.

[5] Isgur, J. Establishing letter—sound associations by on object—imaging—projection method. *Journal of Learning Disabilities*, *8*, 6 (1975), 349-353.

[6] Kelly, K & Phillips, S. Theory and Context. In *Teaching Literacy to Learners with Dyslexia: A Multisensory Approach*. SAGE, London, 2011, 7-30.

[7] Landerl, K., Wimmer, H., & Frith, U. The impact of orthographic consistency on dyslexia: A German-English comparison. *Cognition*, *63*, 3 (1997), 315-334.

[8] Marshall, P. Do tangible interfaces enhance learning? In *Proc. of TEI 2007*, ACM Press (2007), 163-170.

[9] Manches, A., O'Malley, C., & Benford, S. Physical manipulation: Evaluating the potential for tangible designs. In *Proc. of TEI 2009,* ACM Press (2009), 77-84.

[10] Pandey, S., & Srivastava, S. Tiblo: A tangible learning aid for children with dyslexia. In *Proc. of DESIRE 2011,* ACM Press (2011), 211-220.

[11] Perea, M., Moret-Tatay, C., & Panadero, V. Suppression of mirror generalization for reversible letters: Evidence from masked priming. *Memory and Language*, 65, 3 (2011), 237-246.

[12] Simner, J., Ward, J., Lanz, M., Jansari, A., Noonan, K., Glover, L., & Oakley, D. A. Nin-random associations of graphemes to colours in synaesthetic and non-synaesthetic populations. *Cognitive Neuropsychology*, 22, 8 (2005), 1069-1085

[13] Stanovich, K. E. Explaining the differences between the dyslexic and the garden-variety poor reader - the phonological-core variable-difference model. *Journal of Learning Disabilities*, *21*, 10 (1988), 590-604.

[14] Stella, X. Y. Feature transitions with saccadic search: Size, colour, and orientation are not alike. In *Advances in Neural Information Processing Systems, (2010),* 2523-2531.

[15] Watson, M. R., Akins, K. A., & Enns, J. T. Second-order mappings in grapheme–color synesthesia. *Psychonomic Bulletin & Review*, 19, 2 (1988), 211-217.

[16] Wrembel, M. On hearing colours—cross-modal associations in vowel perception in a non-synaesthetic population. *Poznań Studies in Contemporary Linguistics*, *45*, 4 (2009), 595-612.

SOFTii: Soft Tangible Interface for Continuous Control of Virtual Objects with Pressure-based Input

Vinh Ngyuen
C-Design Lab
Purdue University
nguye131@purdue.edu

Sang Ho Yoon
C-Design Lab
Purdue University
yoon87@purdue.edu

Karthik Ramani
C-Design Lab
Purdue University
ramani@purdue.edu

Pramod Kumar
C-Design Lab
Purdue University
kumar146@purdue.edu

Ansh Verma
C-Design Lab
Purdue University
verma25@purdue.edu

TEI'15, Jan 16-19 2015, Stanford, CA, USA.
ACM 978-1-4503-3305-4/15/01.
http://dx.doi.org/10.1145/2677199.2687898

Abstract
We present SOFTii, a flexible input system for topography design and continuous control via external force. Our intent is to provide a tactile metaphor for pressure-based surface input. In this study, two prototypes of SOFTii have been fabricated: (a) The first prototype has one pressure surface for topography design with everyday tangible objects, (b) the second prototype, having two force input surfaces, performs as a deformable controller for video games and continuous shape modeling using a SVM algorithm. Both prototypes of SOFTii are constructed by layering Polymethylsiloxane (PDMS), ITO coated PET film, and conductive fabric and foam. The layer configuration allows the capturing of local pressure on the SOFTii surface via distributed electrodes. Here we further discuss the implementation of the device with possible usage scenarios.

Author Keywords
Input Devices, Soft Devices, ITO electrodes, SVM

ACM Classification Keywords
H.5.2. [User Interface (e.g. HCI)]: Graphical user interfaces (GUI); Haptic I/O; Input devices and strategies; Interaction styles; Prototyping.

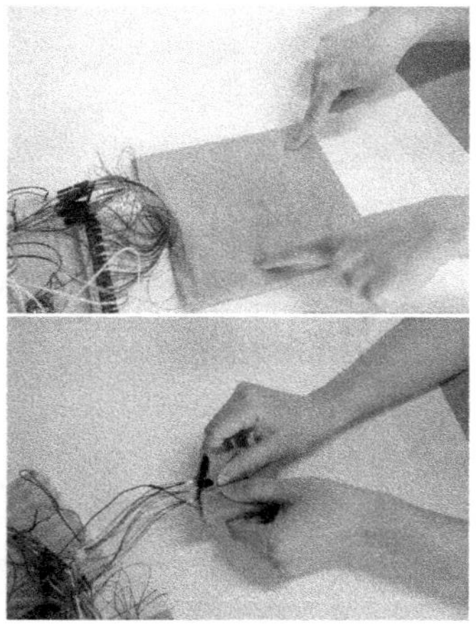

Figure 1: The two prototypes of SOFTII - a pressure sensing pad and a handheld bending device

Introduction and Related Work

In this paper, we attempted to integrate digital design with tangible tools by leveraging soft materials. SOFTii is a robust, flexible input system that provides a pressure-based tactile input metaphor for 3D modeling and game controlling. Our system benefits the advantages of Tangible User Interface (TUI) [3]. It supports quickly adjusting multiple parameters and seeing real-time feedback [9]. The first prototype of SOFTii captures the imprinted coarse shape profile by utilizing the deformable and conductive properties of electrodes distributed on soft materials. This pressure metaphor provides a quick method for topography design. The second prototype utilizes an SVM training model with a magnitude mapping method for the classification and recognition of local bending deformation. The direct pressure-based input and the passive haptic feedback provide a novel tactile experience in continuous shape modeling and game controlling.

Coarse Silhouette Sensing

Some researchers suggested that physical structures can enhance interacting experience between human and computer. One of the most popular techniques for shape sensing is employing a camera to capture the deformable physical shapes, reflecting the computing ideology "What you see is what you get". In particular, the Building Blocks [1] conventionally provides a direct mapping method between the physical shape and virtual geometry data. However, the primitive solid shapes limit the customization feature of the system. Metzget [7] proposes an approach for object detection using conductive foams. This method implies an array of capacitive sensors to detect the object via digital outputs. However, the system is ineffective in measuring the imprinting pressure caused by the physical objects. Our first prototype of SOFTii is inspired by this interpretation for sensing coarse shape silhouette, where the surface itself is a soft deformation-sensitive sensor. A grid of electrodes is utilized to estimate the imprinted pressure on the foam surface.

Soft Tangible Interface

Many unique human-computer interfaces have been proposed with tangible interacting experience. In particular, Pinstripe [4] is a system of textile capacitive touch sensors on clothes. The grid design supports pinching or rolling as input data. However, the touch-based mechanism in Pinstripe is ineffective in comprehending information from force input. Alternatively, PyzoFlex [11] is a pressure sensing device using piezoelectric foil. The array configuration allows surface pressure tracking. Similarly, sandwiching the ITO electrodes in between PDMS was also implemented by Nguyen [8], but was not completely explored. However, using solid materials prevents the system from generating passive haptic feedback and deformability for tangible interaction experience [6].

Shape changing interface

Recently, the shape changing interface has been developing rapidly for their dynamic properties [10]. This opens a different tendency for interactive scheme design, where users can consider physical deformation as a new type of input data. Coelho [2, p. 171] introduces an ideology of utilizing deformable objects for "recording the user's action and applying it in some other place or context". In particular, the inflatable mouse has a similar physical design to a regular computer mouse, but adds new interactive techniques from the ability of detecting the change in its volume [5]. This design inherits some limitations from the *"point & click"* paradigm.

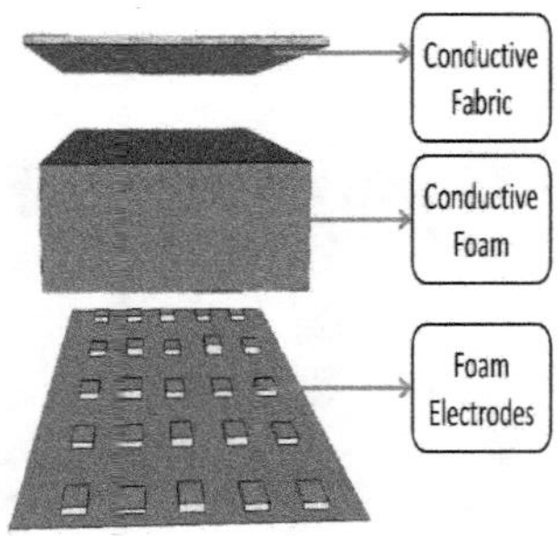

Figure 2: Prototype 1 Layer model

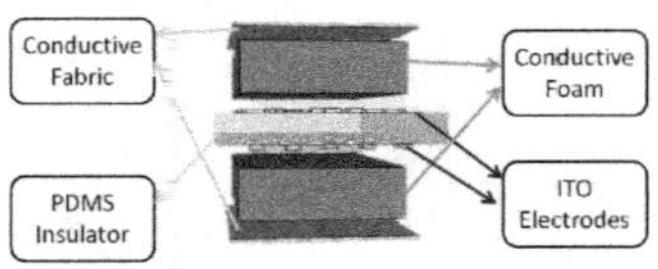

Figure 3: Prototype 2 Layer model

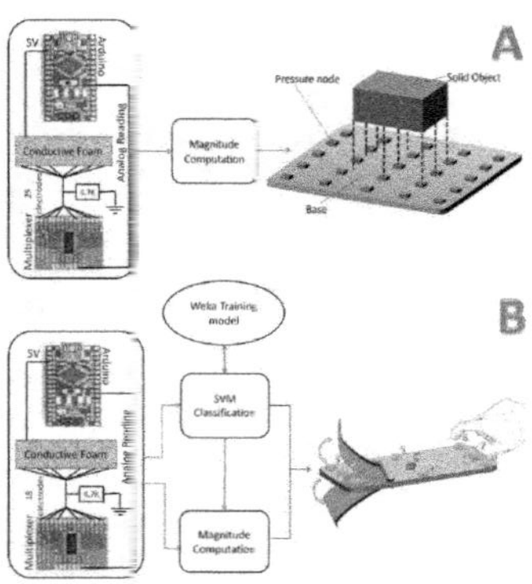

Figure 4: SOFTii - equivalent circuit: A) Prototype 1, B) Prototype 2.

Nevertheless, the volume-sensitive feature provides passive haptic feedback on the hand with air pressure. The second prototype of SOFTii is inspired by shape changing interpretation to provide a pressure-based local bending input metaphor.

SOFTII - System Design

SOFTii utilizes a layer configuration of non-conductive and conductive soft materials. This combination produces a distinct elastic and conductive behavior which can be used to measure shape deformation. The distributed pressures are employed to provide a pressure-based soft input metaphor for 3D topography design and video game applications.

Hardware Prototypes

Two prototypes of SOFTii have been fabricated to perform topography design with coarse silhouette and continuous control with pressure-based deformable input (Figure 1).

Prototype 1 - Coarse Silhouette Sensing
This prototype consists of conductive foam with distributed electrodes underneath one side, while the other is covered by conductive fabric (Figure 2). This configuration allows capturing the imprinted surface deformation. The conductive foam performs as a soft pressure sensor and provides passive haptic feedback simultaneously.

Prototype 2 - Local Bending Sensing
This prototype is constructed by mirroring two conductive foam layers through a PDMS insulator. The device is wrapped around by conductive fabric (Figure 3). The ITO coated PET films offer thin, flexible electrodes which are suitable for the construction of flexible device (0.175mm thick, $50\Omega/in^2$ resistivity). PDMS[1] is selected because of the flexible, soft, and non-conductive properties. The electrode grid supports tracking local pressures on both surfaces. In this study, we hypothesize that users often apply pressure on both sides to bend the prototype. This hypothesis is applied for the training process with the SVM algorithm.

Sensor Evaluation
In both prototypes, the readings are managed by voltage divider via analog multiplexors (CD74HC4067 16-Channel analogous multiplexer), then processed by an Arduino microcontroller[2] (ATmega328, clock speed 16MHz). Therefore, the local pressure resolution is customizable for the purpose. The conductive foam (Open Cell Polyurethane, density $50lb/cuft$, tensile strength 25 psi) provides a flexible, tactile and responsive layer. We hypothesize that connecting a wire directly to the foam is not effective in distributing the voltage across its porous structure. Thus the conductive fabric is used as a voltage distributer (surface resistance: $< 5\Omega/in^2$, thickness 0.45 mm, 78% nylon and 22% elastomer). We perform point pressure tracking test and pressure-based bending test to evaluate the discretely distributed electrodes (Figure 5). The test results indicate that it is visible to capture coarse shape outline with imprinting mechanism. Also, it is possible to identify local deformation (location, direction, and magnitude) using surface distributed pressures.

Computational Model
In this section, we introduce our computational models for the prototypes and their applications.

[1] http://web.mit.edu/6.777/www/matprops/pdms.htm
[2] http://www.arduino.cc

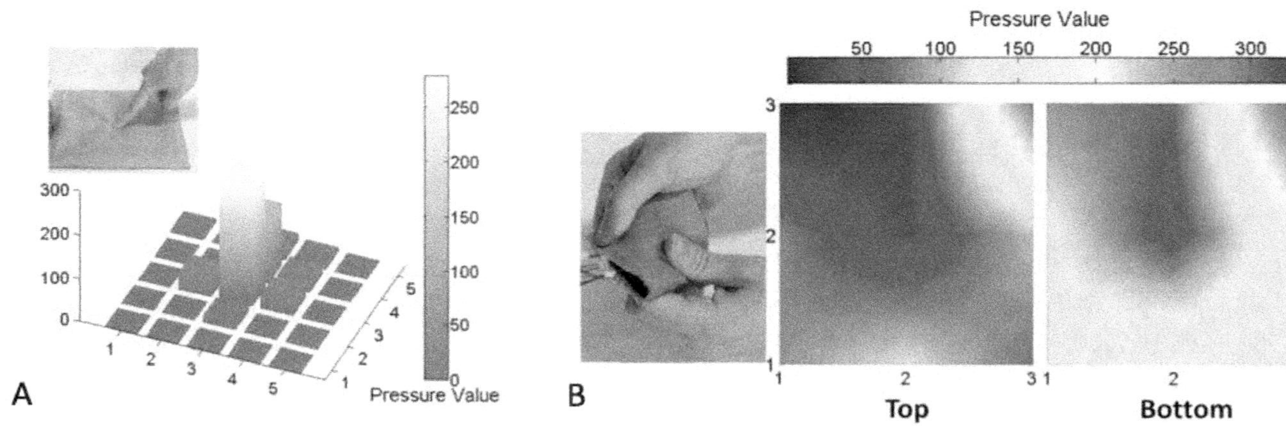

Figure 5: Point pressure experiments on different locations on the surface of SOFTii: A) Pressure observations from pointing finger in the middle part for Prototype 1, B) Pressure-based bending in counter-clockwise direction of top-left corner for Prototype 2.

The First Prototype - Sensor Interpolation
In this setup, the deformation of the conductive foam is recorded with 25 electrodes. These pressure readings are used to derive the coarse shape outline that causes the deformation from the top of the conductive foam. We employ bilinear interpolation to interpolate the sensor values over the active surface. We observed that pressure readings from a sensor diminishes as the point of load is moved away from the sensor. Additionally, loads applied directly on the sensor has negligible affect on the nearby sensors. The interpolated values at each vertex is linearly mapped to the mesh deformation. Moreover, the current setup can run in a single touch tracking mode by estimating the position of touch event. Assuming single-touch input, we calculate the weighted average of all the sensor reading using the following relation:

$$\overline{x} = \frac{\sum_{j=1}^{n}\sum_{i=1}^{m} P_{i,j}x_i}{\sum_{j=1}^{n}\sum_{i=1}^{m} P_{i,j}} \quad \overline{y} = \frac{\sum_{j=1}^{n}\sum_{i=1}^{m} P_{i,j}y_i}{\sum_{j=1}^{n}\sum_{i=1}^{m} P_{i,j}} \tag{1}$$

The Second Prototype - Bending Estimation
The bending magnitude levels are computed using the polynomial regression model:

$$y_j = \sum_{i=0}^{n} a_i x_j^i + \epsilon_j \tag{2}$$

The difference in readings between the upper and the bottom layer represents the local deformation at the

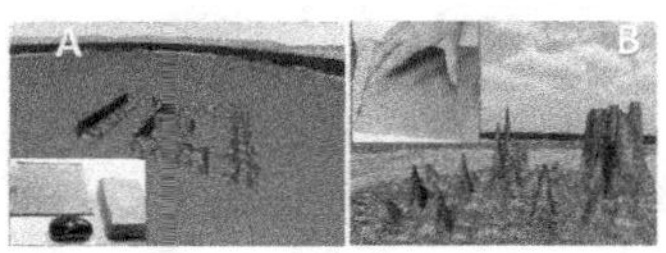

Figure 6: Topography design using everyday objects and hands

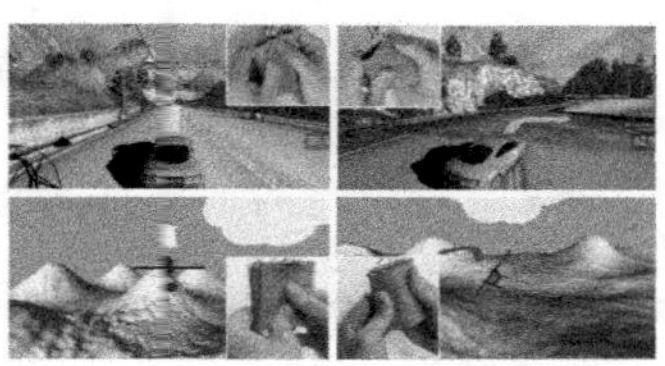

Figure 7: Flexible game controller, based on bendable input: A) Car speed control with direct force input, B) Drifting with flexible force input, C) Airplane altitude control with direct force input, D) Turning with flexible force input.

corresponding node. They are plotted against the magnitude levels to derive the polynomial trend line. A range of 90 degree in each direction is mapped to the bending angles. Thus, an accuracy of 91% is obtained from our polynomial model. *SVM Training:* In this setup, SOFTii is trained with 17 different patterns of local bending states using SVM algorithm via Weka[3] library. These patterns include 8 nodes with 2 bending directions (clockwise and counter-clockwise) for each node, plus a stationary resting position. We obtain a clearly classified training data result by adopting 4 different intensities for each bending state. In this paper, the location and the direction of the bending states are obtained from the patterns of 18 analogous readings.

Interactions

We put effort in utilizing SOFTii as a multimedia input device. The purpose is to provide an intuitive tangible interface between user and computer via force input domain. These interaction methods serve as our proposed ideas for developing application scenarios for Softii.

3D Topography Design with everyday objects

Design Motivation: Here, SOFTii is implemented as a tool for detecting coarse shape silhouette based on the pressure distribution. The system imitates the stamping metaphor to recognize the coarse shape outline. The pressure readings are interpolated. Here SOFTii performs the task using convex objects. The physical objects can be employed directly as the pointer to generate various shapes for the task (Figure 6).

Flexible Game Controller

Traditional personal computer (PC) system games, are currently handled by a combination of key pressing-and-releasing. SOFTii, however, can be customized as a flexible input device for various games. Here, we implement the flexible SOFTii game controller with car racing and flight controlling. The tactility and flexibility of the materials provide pressure-based and deformable input method (Figure 7).

Flexible E-book Reader

Electronic book (e-book) technology is developing rapidly due to its convenience and security. However, the interaction design still has not caught up with the graphical effects. We use the flexible and distributed pressure readings in flipping e-book pages to further improve the tangible experience in e-reading. The direct mapping between the bending angle with the flipping effect allows using SOFTii as a proxy for the pages to be flipped. Two of the bendable corners support manipulating the top most page on each side of an opened e-book (Figure 8).

Local bending recognition

We implement SOFTii as a novel input device to precisely recognize local bending. The ability to distinguish location, direction, and magnitude of local deformation provides a direct interface for shape manipulation. In this paper, the bending magnitude is directly mapped to the virtual deformation to provide precise control using equation 2. The location and direction of the bending is classified and identified by the SVM algorithm (Figure 9).

Future work

In order to obtain a more accurate shape outline with high details, the SOFTii system needs more sensors per unit length. Concurrently, the interpolation model can be further improved with the two-dimensional Gaussian function. Gaussian approach holds the potential to

[3]http://www.cs.waikato.ac.nz/ml/weka/

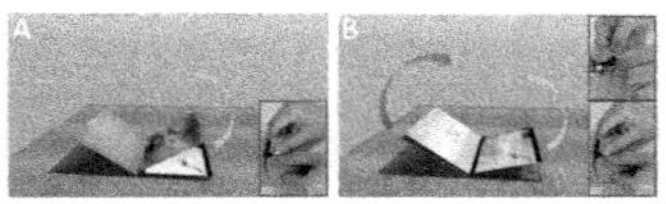

Figure 8: E-book reading by mimicking the page flip motion with bendable input device: A) Turn to next page by bending top right corner in CCW direction, B) Turn to previous or next page by bending top left corner in CW direction or top right corner in CCW direction.

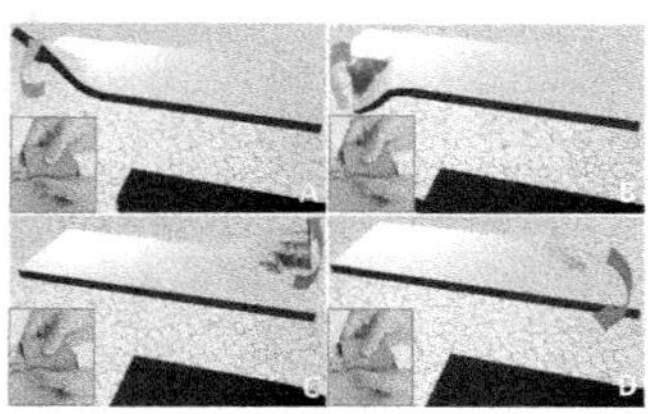

Figure 9: Local bending: A) Left-upper corner in CW direction, B) Left-upper corner in CCW direction, C) Left-upper corner in CCW direction, D) Left-upper corner in CW direction. Magnitude is being controlled by the amount of bending

simulate the "pull effect" of the deformation on the surface with greater accuracy. The flexibility of the system can be ameliorated by reducing the thickness of each layer. In order to improve the sensitivity of SOFTii, some potential materials are waiting to be tested including conductive rubber or conductive PDMS to replace the current conductive foam.

Conclusion

In this study, we introduced SOFTii, a soft interface input device for 3D topography design with everyday objects and continuous control of virtual objects via external force input. Two prototypes of SOFTii have been fabricated with layer configuration. The layer configuration of the soft conductive and non-conductive materials provides a unique tangible interactive experience. The first prototype of SOFTii was able to detect coarse shape silhouette with the imprinted pressure metaphor, where the pressure value is used to generate the height of the topography. The second prototype performed as a deformable input device via external force for video game applications. Additionally, the SVM classifying algorithm assisted in detecting local bending of the device for continuous shape modelling.

References

[1] Anderson, D., Frankel, J. L., Marks, J., Agarwala, A., Beardsley, P., Hodgins, J., Leigh, D., Ryall, K., Sullivan, E., and Yedidia, J. S. Tangible interaction + graphical interpretation: A new approach to 3d modeling.

[2] Coelho, M., and Zigelbaum, J. Shape-changing interfaces. *Personal Ubiquitous Comput.* (2011).

[3] Ishii, H., and Ullmer, B. Tangible bits: Towards seamless interfaces between people, bits and atoms. In *Proceedings of the ACM SIGCHI Conference on Human Factors in Computing Systems* (1997).

[4] Karrer, T., Wittenhagen, M., Lichtschlag, L., Heller, F., and Borchers, J. Pinstripe: eyes-free continuous input on interactive clothing. In *CHI* (2011).

[5] Kim, S., Kim, H., Lee, B., Nam, T.-J., and Lee, W. Inflatable mouse: volume-adjustable mouse with air-pressure-sensitive input and haptic feedback. In *CHI* (2008).

[6] Lee, J. C., Dietz, P. H., Leigh, D., Yerazunis, W. S., and Hudson, S. E. Haptic pen: A tactile feedback stylus for touch screens. In *Proceedings of the 17th Annual ACM Symposium on User Interface Software and Technology* (2004).

[7] Metzger, C., Fleisch, E., Meyer, J., Dansachmueller, M., Graz, I., Kaltenbrunner, M., Keplinger, C., Schwoediauer, R., and Bauer, S. Flexible-foam-based capacitive sensor arrays for object detection at low cost. *Applied Physics Letters* (2008).

[8] Nguyen, V. P., Yoon, S. H., Verma, A., and Ramani, K. Bendid: Flexible interface for localized deformation recognition. In *Proceedings of the 2014 ACM International Joint Conference on Pervasive and Ubiquitous Computing*, UbiComp '14 (2014).

[9] Patten, J., Ishii, H., Hines, J., and Pangaro, G. Sensetable: A wireless object tracking platform for tangible user interfaces. In *Proceedings of the SIGCHI Conference on Human Factors in Computing Systems* (2001).

[10] Poupyrev, I., Nashida, T., and Okabe, M. Actuation and tangible user interfaces: The vaucanson duck, robots, and shape displays. In *Proceedings of the 1st International Conference on Tangible and Embedded Interaction* (2007).

[11] Rendl, C., Greindl, P., Haller, M., Zirkl, M., Stadlober, B., and Hartmann, P. Pyzoflex: Printed piezoelectric pressure sensing foil. In *Proceedings of the 25th Annual ACM Symposium on User Interface Software and Technology* (2012).

People's Emotional Responses to a Plant's Emotional Expression

Jaewon Cho
Human ICT Convergence
Sungkyunkwan University
Korea
ina0914@skku.edu

Sanghoo Park
Human ICT Convergence
Sungkyunkwan University
Korea
jjansuni82@gmail.com

Been Jeon
Human ICT Convergence
Sungkyunkwan University
Korea
Wjsqls1208@skku.edu

Byung-Chull Bae
Interaction Science
Sungkyunkwan University
Korea
byuc@skku.edu

Jun-Dong Cho
Human ICT Convergence
Sungkyunkwan University
Korea
jdcho@skku.edu

TEI '15, Jan 16-19 2015, Stanford, CA, USA
ACM 978-1-4503-3305-4/15/01.
http://dx.doi.org/10.1145/2677199.2687899

Abstract
In this paper we investigate how people emotionally respond to the emotional expression of a plant when external stimuli were given to the plant. For this purpose we built a simple LED emoticon-based device as an emotional proxy for delivering inner states of a plant, assuming the inner states of a plant can be changed depending on either positive or negative external stimuli. Our pilot study suggests that people's attitude on plants can be influenced by observing the emotional expressions of a plant.

Author Keywords
People-plants interaction; Emotion expression of plants; Emoticons

ACM Classification Keywords
H.5.m. Information interfaces and presentation (e.g., HCI): Miscellaneous.

General Terms
Experimentation.

Introduction
The relationship between humans and plants is vital. Plants make positive effects on people in many ways. They provide people with clean oxygen and food as well as making spaces for leisure. Psychologically people

can make themselves feel better and stable with plants [1].

While plants are beneficial to people in various ways as described above, people tend to treat plants with less care compared to dealing with other living things such as animals. It is mainly because plants, unlike animals, cannot express themselves in an explicit way. Suppose plants are able to scream or shed tears when they get hurt. People's attitude to plants will be not exactly the same way that people currently do to plants.

In this paper we are not claiming that plants have emotions. It is beyond the scope of our paper. Our research question is rather about people's emotional responses when they observe a plant's emotional expression in accordance with external stimuli. We hypothesized that people's emotional attachment to a plant would increase when the plant expressed its emotions in real time, though the expression was made simply using emoticons.

Related Work

The interaction between people and plants are two-fold. People observe, nurture, and grow plants. Some people often have a strong empathy with their plants in the process of plant-growing. Plants' impacts on people, meanwhile, are enormous (in a positive manner). As described in the previous section, plants supply us with oxygen, food, life resources, and living environments as well as influencing our sentiments (or feelings) and bodily functions [10]. Indoor plants also contribute to enhancing our pleasantness by alleviating people's tension and anxiety level [2]. More psycho-physiological benefits from plants include visual fatigue alleviation from looking at plants [9], stress reduction [3], and air purification through the absorption and adsorption of harmful gases indoors [11].

Compared to the studies on the positive effects of plants on people, there has been relatively less research on how people affect plants. According to studies, a weak electric current can be measured in plants and it can be changed accordingly to external stimuli [4]. Specifically when negatively physical stimuli such as cutting leaves, hitting with a plastic bar, and touching with a hot object were applied, it was found that the ampere meter was changed rapidly [8].

Just with the studies by [4] and [8] above, we cannot argue that plants have emotions. We may say, however, that plants can respond to external stimuli rather in a way that we hardly recognize. For this reason, our study aims to visualize a plant's responses to external stimuli in such a way that we can easily recognize, that is, in an emotional way using (LED) emoticons. Emoticons have been considered as an effective method of expressing basic emotions such as joy and sorrow [6]. Particularly in Instant Messaging (IM) area, it is known that the use of emoticons can enhance the communication quality [7] and contribute to expressing sympathy [5].

Experimental Study

As a way of investigating the relationship between people and plants, we built a simple emotional proxy for a plant and conducted an experimental pilot study with 11 participants.

Material: A plant's proxy device

As a proxy for delivering the emotional expressions of a plant, we built a simple visualizing device consisting of

The prototype expressing the state and emotion of plant in emoticon and color: (a) Joy (b) Neutral (c) Sadness/Anger.

an Arduino UNO board (main board), 3 Arduino sensors (input devices), and an LED and a buzzer (output devices).

LED, as an output device, was designed to express visually three different states (joy, neutral, sadness/anger). In order to indicate that they are the emotional expressions of a plant, flower-looking petals are added. Joy was represented as a green emoticon of a smiling face. Neutral was coloured in orange with an expressionless face. Sadness/anger was characterized by a red angry face with a buzzer making an alarming sound. [Figure1] shows the prototype of the output expressing the plant's responses to external stimuli in an emotional way.

As input measuring devices we employed three different sensors – temperature, humidity, and sound detection. The temperature sensor was programmed to express three distinct LED states for ranges 20-25℃, was also programmed to express three different LED states for humidity ranging lower than 300, 300-600, and higher than 600. The values for the base temperature and base humidity were accordingly set for a plant to be tested, which can be easily changed in case different plants are employed in the study. The sound sensor was programmed so that the plant can respond with the LED as if it is humming to the sound of music.

In addition to the three input sensors described above, we programmed the Arduino main board to control the LED states by detecting a weak electric current change as a way of simulating a plant's expression to external physical threat. It is basically similar to galvanic skin response-based lie detectors. When a person gets tense, the resistance of the skin is lowered, and a lie detector detects a lie based on the change in the resistance. Inspired by the lie detectors and the fact that plants respond electrically to external stimuli, we connected two pins from the Arduino board to a plant and set the threshold of change in the current flowing between the two. If the current exceeds the threshold value, the LED state is changed. We used this for the change of emoticon as Wizard of Oz approach when the participants exerted physically threatening or damaging actions to our plant.

Figure 1: The prototype as a proxy for the emotional expressions of a plant

Material: A real plant
We employed a plant called 'Pepper Face' (scientific name: Peperomia obtusifolia A.Dietr; See Figure 1) as our study material. The best growing conditions for Pepper Face are between 20 and 25℃ temperature, without direct sunlight, and less watering (only once in 1-2 weeks). In other words, excessive heating and watering are very unfavorable conditions for Pepper Face.

Participants:
In total 11 graduate students (7 males, 4 females; age range between 25 and 32) were recruited as study participants. Among the 11 participants, 9 participants had an experience of growing at least one plant in recent two years and 8 out of the 9 participants had an experience of the death of the plant that they were growing.

Methods and Procedure:
The study was conducted through the survey questionnaires based on each participant's self-report.

Before conducting our study, we first checked the participants' attitudes to plants by showing them pictures of plants in severely bad conditions – such as a badly damaged cactus by people or a dying plant out of water. After watching the four pictures each participant answered how painful he or she felt in 5-point Likert scale (1:Not painful at all; 5: Extremely painful).

Our study consists of four experiments with different external stimuli (three negative stimuli and one positive stimulus). For each experiment two types of survey were conducted. The first survey was done with only explanation and no direct actions applying to the plant (Before). In the second survey participants exerted direct actions on the plant and observed the plant's proxy device expressing the plant's inner states through the LED emoticons. The three negative stimuli include applying physically threatening actions (hitting or tearing out the leaves), applying hot wind to the plant using a hair drier, and watering excessively. Finally we chose playing bright mood music to the plant as a positive stimulus. Before conducting the two surveys, each participant was told that the plant is very sensitive to heat and humidity in a negative way and is fond of listening to music. Figure 2 illustrates applying the four external stimuli to the plant and the plant's responses through its emotional proxy. After the four experiments were done, each participant was asked whether their emotional connection to plants was increased through the experiments.

Figure 2: Conducting Experiments (a) Applying physically threating actions (b) Applying hot wind (c) Watering excessively, and (d) Playing bright-mood music.

Results and Discussion

In the pre-survey on the participants' attitude to the plants with the pictures of damaged or dying plants, the participants answered that they felt painful more than medium (m=3.82; sd=.874). It seems reasonable considering the fact that most of participants (9 out of 11) had an experience of growing plants.

In the four main experiments, participants' average mean ratings over the first three negative stimuli were 3.36 (sd=1.036) after only hearing the explanation

	After only hearing the explanation without watching emoticons	After applying actions with watching emoticons
E1	3.55 (1.036)	4.0 (.775)
E2	3.45 (1.128)	4.18 (.874)
E3	**3.09 (.944)**	**4.36 (.505)**
E4	3.0 (1.095)	4.0 (.894)
Avg	3.27 (1.051)	4.14 (.762)

Table 1. Participants' mean (and standard deviation) of their ratings in the four main experiments, where E1:Applying negative physical stimuli; E2:Applying hot wind as negative stimulus; E3: Excessive watering as negative stimulus; E4: Playing bright-mood music as positive stimulus

without watching the LED emoticon-based proxy device's emotional expression, 4.18 (sd=0.718) after applying direct actions on the plant with watching the change of emoticons. As for the positive stimuli in the fourth experiment (i.e., playing bright-mood music to the plant), the average mean rating was 3.0 (sd=1.095) and 4.0 (sd=.894) respectively. Overall the people's average rating of their emotional connection to the plant was slightly higher with regard to negative stimuli than with regard to positive stimuli, though the difference was not statistically significant.

Performing Fisher's exact test on the collected data suggests that there is a significant difference between the two means in the third experiment (watering excessively to a water-sensitive plant; p=0.0004423). We suspect that the continued negative actions with the first and second experiments may affect the third experiment. There were no statistically significant differences in the other three experiments. Overall the participants' average mean ratings over the four experiments were 3.27 (sd=1.051) before applying actions and 4.14 (sd=.762) after applying actions with the LED emoticon (Refer to Table 1 and Figure 3).

For the question of whether the participant's emotional connection to plants was increased through these experiments, the participants' mean rating was 4.45 (sd=.688) in the 5-point Likert scale (1: Not at all, 3 : Medium, 5 : Extremely).

In general, the participants showed high curiosity and positive responses to our study on the relationship between people and plants. They also suggested that this idea would be useful particularly when growing plants that are sensitive to their surrounding environments such as sunlight, temperature, and water.

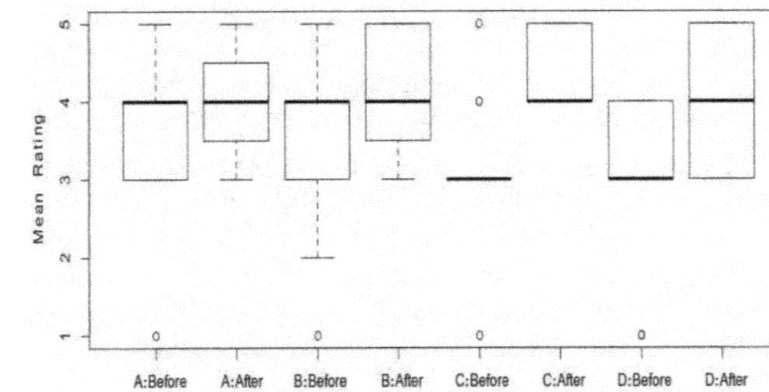

Figure 3: Four experiment results: (A) Applying physical action, (B) Applying hot wind, (C) Watering excessively, and (D) Playing bright-mood music. One only with explanation without direct actions applying to the plant (Before) and the other with direct actions to the plant and observation of the LED emoticon change (After).

Conclusion and Future Work

In this paper we described our effort to investigate the emotional relationship between people and plants. For this purpose we designed and built a simple flower-shaped, LED-based emoticon device using an Arduino board and three sensors (temperature, humidity, and sound detection) as a proxy for emotional expressions of a plant. In our pilot study we let the participants apply four external stimuli (three negative stimuli and one positive stimulus) to a plant and observed their emotional responses through survey questions and discussion.

We believe our research will be beneficial to enhancing our general attitude to plants. Our current research, however, has some limitations. First, we limited the modality of a plant's emotional expression to a simple visual expression through three different types of LED emoticons. Detailed visual expression or inclusion of other modalities (e.g., short text messages) could be more appealing. Interaction through social network systems would be also an interesting research. We leave these as a future work of ours. Second, in our study, we chose four external stimuli to a plant as instantly applying ones. In reality, however, the relationship between a human user and a plant often requires some periods of time, which was not easy to test in a lab environment due to several practical reasons. Moreover, as too many experiments on the same plants could be an abuse to the plants, we had to limit the number of experiments. In our next study we plan to explore the interactive relationship between a human user and a plant over a span of time. Particularly we expect that our system can be beneficial for children to develop their empathic capabilities through the interaction with plants.

Acknowledgement

This research was supported by the Ministry of Trade, Industry and Energy(MOTIE), KOREA, through the Education Support program for Creative and Industrial Convergence (N0000717) and the Brain Korea 21 Plus Program through the National Research Foundation (NRF) funded by the Ministry of Education of Korea (10Z20130000013)

References

[1] Bratman, G,N., Hamilton, J,P., and Daily, G.C. (2012) The Impacts of Nature Experience on Human Cognitive Function and Mental Health. The Year in Ecology and Conservation Biology 1249:118-136.

[2] Bringslimark, T., Hartig, T., and Patil, G.G. (2007) Psychological Benefits of Indoor Plants in Workplaces: Putting Experimental Results into Context. HortScience 45(3):581-587.

[3] Erin, L.W., William, C.W., Virginia, D., and Robert, W. (2011) Healthy Workplaces: The Effects of Nature Contact at Work on Employee Stress and Health. Public Health Reports 126:124-130.

[4] From, M.J., and Lautne, R.S. (2007) Electrical Signals and their Physiological Significance in Plants. Plant, Cell and Environment 30(3):249-257.

[5] Huang, A.H., Yen, D.C., and Zhang, X. (2008) Exploring the Potential Effects of Emoticons. Information & Management 45(7):466-473.

[6] Jakobs, E., Manstead, A.S.R., and Fischer, A.H. (1999) Social Motives and Emotional Feelings as Determinants of Facial Displays: The Case of Smiling. Personality & Social Psychology Bulletin 25(4):424-435.

[7] Luor, T.T., Wu, L.L., Lu, H.P., and Tao, Y.H. (2010) The Effect of Emoticons in Simplex and Complex Task-Oriented Communication: An Empirical Study of Instant Messaging. Computers in Human Behavior 26(5):889-895.

[8] Mousavi, S.A.R., Nguyen, C.T., Farmer, E.E., and Kellenberger, S., (2014) Measuring Surface Potential Changes on Leaves. Nature Protocols 9(8):1997-2004.

[9] Shibata, S., and Suzuki, N. (2004) Effects of an Indoor Plant on Creative Task Performance and Mood. Scandinavian Journal of Psychology 45(5):373-381.

[10] Thomsen, J.D., Andersen, H.K.H.S., and Muller, R. (2011) People-Plant Relationships in an Office Workplace: Perceived Benefits for the Workplace and Employees. HortScience 46(5): 744-752.

[11] Yang, D.S., Svoboda, V.P., Son, K.C., and Stanley, K.J. (2009) Screening Indoor Plants for Volatile Organic Pollutant Removal Efficiency. HortScience 44(5):1377-1381.

Exploring the Application of Interactive Video Projection in Physical Education

Danića Mast
Research Group Healthy Lifestyle in a Supporting Environment
Faculty IT & Design
The Hague University of Applied Sciences
The Hague, The Netherlands
d.mast@hhs.nl

Sanne de Vries
Research Group Healthy Lifestyle in a Supporting Environment
The Hague University of Applied Sciences
The Hague, The Netherlands
s.i.devries@hhs.nl

Jeroen de Krom
Research Group Healthy Lifestyle in a Supporting Environment
Faculty Health, Nutrition & Sport
The Hague University of Applied Sciences
The Hague, The Netherlands
j.dekrom@hhs.nl

TEI'15, January 15–19, 2015, Stanford, California, USA.
ACM 978-1-4503-3305-4/15/01.
http://dx.doi.org/10.1145/2677199.2687901

Abstract
This paper describes explorations into related technology and research regarding the application of interactive video projection within physical education and the gym of the future. We discuss the application of exergaming in physical education, spatial augmented reality as a technology and participatory design with teachers and children as a design method to develop new concepts. Based on our initial findings we propose directions for further research. Further work includes developing new applications based on the wishes, needs and ideas of physical education teachers and children, incorporating opportunities provided by recent technological developments.

Author Keywords
Physical Education, Spatial Augmented Reality, Exergames, Participatory Design, Interactive Video Projection

ACM Classification Keywords
H.5.2 Information Interfaces and Presentation: User Interfaces—evaluation/methodology; interaction styles

H.5.1. Multimedia Information Systems: Artificial, augmented and virtual realities

General Terms

Design, Human Factors

Introduction

At primary schools in the Netherlands, physical education (PE) is used to encourage an active lifestyle by developing fundamental motor skills and practicing different sports. It improves the condition and health of children and enhances team building, cooperation, sportsmanship and fair play. Learning objectives transcend the motor skill level and also include improving attitudes, ethical and social norms and values of children. [11]

Even though interactive technologies have made their way into the physical space in recent years, within physical education the use of technology is still limited and the equipment that is being used in gyms has mainly been unchanged in recent decades.

Recently, video capturing and (projection) screens to provide feedback on previously performed exercises have been introduced to physical education, as well as exergames [3].

The implementation of interactive technologies could provide many opportunities for making physical education more efficient, more motivating and more targeted. More specific, the use of interactive video projection could enhance existing set-ups and provide opportunities for developing new exercises.

In this project we will look into the wishes and ideas of PE teachers, the perception and play of children and the opportunities offered by the space, equipment and technology.

Target groups

Two target groups are important considering physical education: teachers and children. We want to involve both groups in multiple stages within this project to ensure that what we invent, design and develop fits the needs of our target group.

Teachers

Teachers have ample knowledge of didactics and motivational methods, existing exercises and games within physical education. Since teaching PE is their domain, it is important to involve them at moments in this project to gain a good understanding of PE, the problems they encounter and to validate our ideas.

It is important however to choose research methods wisely. Because teachers are experts on teaching PE, they might already have specific ideas on the application of new technologies. This might make it more difficult for them to think out of the box, something we consider important in finding new applications. We think it is important to choose methods that help them to broaden their view as much as possible.

Children

It is just as important to gain good understanding of how students experience PE and the gym as an environment and how we can design taking into account their perception. Children will be using the applications; therefore we need to know what their ideas and preferences are.

Children start physical education in kindergarten, aged 4 years and continue classes till high school, aged 16-18 years. Initially we will focus on physical education in

Figure 1: Equipment being used during a Physical Education class.

Figure 2: Examples of Projection Mapping.

elementary schools since that has so far been the main focus of our research group. Future research might involve adolescents or other target groups.

Space & Sports Equipment

The gym as a space and the sports equipment bring many opportunities for interactive applications but also challenges/constraints that should be investigated.

The gym is an open, versatile space with numerous sports equipment that can be set up in unlimited configurations. An example is shown in figure 1.

Related Technology

We are currently identifying potential technologies that could be applied in the gym of the future. In this chapter we describe technologies we have identified so far, and that we consider interesting to further study regarding their deployment within physical education.

Spatial Augmented Reality

Projection mapping, video mapping or spatial augmented reality (SAR) [13] is an interesting augmented reality technique for using video projection in physical spaces and creates a highly immersive experience [12]. An example can be seen in Figure 2.

A virtual three-dimensional image is projected upon a real three-dimensional surface, wrapping the image around the object [1]. This technique makes versatile, instantly altering appearances of existing surfaces possible [5].

Benefits of this technique are that any object or surface can be turned into anything, creating an augmented reality, adding movement and activity to stationary objects. [7]

There are several practical considerations using SAR. In bright environments, such as a gym, a video projector is needed with a high lumen count; otherwise the projected image will appear too light and unclear.

Another challenge is projecting on larges areas or avoiding shadows. Multiple projectors are required to solve this, causing projection overlap (a brighter area) that has to be eliminated by luminance compensation. [4,5,7]

Furthermore a robust construction is needed for mounting the projector, a slight bump might cause the projection to move or misalign. [4,5,7] We should look into using robust truss systems for mounting a video projector.

Other Input and Output technologies

Besides SAR, a wide range of technologies can be used for sensing objects and people, and for sensing and changing a physical environment [9]. Technologies we are considering are: Sound, Computer Vision, Microcontrollers, Sensors, and Actuators [9]

Related Research

Exergames

Previous research on exergames in physical education is limited but shows physical, social and cognitive benefits [10]. Other benefits include weight loss and less obesity. [3]

Most exergames focus on the goal on getting children physically active, which they seem to do very well by turning exercising into a game and making it more fun to do. [10].

Most research on exergaming focuses on health benefits. In our project it would be interesting to also consider the effects on motor skill development, interplay between children and progress in level of play.

Additionally exergames may offer the possibility that children can exercise much more independently and that PE teachers do not constantly have to monitor the entire class, but can focus on a specific task instead such as coaching individual students. Developing exergames that monitor play and skill levels, and adjust gameplay based on these factors can help doing this.

Cooperative/Participatory Design
Instead of designing applications for users it is interesting to design together with the users in this project. Previous research shows interesting and more versatile outcome when participating with users in creating concepts for technology.

When is comes to designing new technology for children we tend to forget that children are a very specific target group with their own perception. Instead of asking parents or teachers what children might like, we should involve children themselves [2] Children are very creative, intuitive, not limited by social conventions and great at thinking out of the box.

Various research describes methods for involving children in the design process in various roles [2,6]. Important factors to keep in mind are that children have a limited attention span [6], sessions have to be well prepared and participants have become used to their role [2].

Outcomes of design cooperation with children have to be translated into practical concepts, which require empathy and creativity of the researcher.

A familiar environment, preferably within the context of the design problem, works best for creating specific solutions [8]. For our project it might be a good idea to place design sessions with teachers in the gym. By using this location, participants can directly refer to the space and sports equipment.

In general, it might be wise to perform preliminary testing sessions to ensure that the chosen method works for gaining insights [6].

Further Work
This project has started recently and therefore offers many opportunities for further work.

We have started gaining information by conducting informal interviews with PE teachers. We decided on this approach to get a general idea of the challenges and opportunities that were involved and to decide which further steps to take. First outcomes of these interviews are the need for assistive technology to provide support when teaching large groups of children.

Related research shows benefits of exergaming and our informal interviews suggest a need for applications that provide support when teaching. The characteristics of spatial augmented reality promise interesting applications within physical education. We therefore think there is potential for the application of interactive video projection in physical education.

We will continue our research into related techniques and research to form a more solid foundation to build on in the next phases of our project. We will conduct qualitative and quantitative research using methods mentioned in the Related Research chapter involving both teachers and children. Our goal is to get a solid overview of the needs and ideas of both groups and technologies that could be used.

Once we have a clear picture of opportunities and challenges, we will continue with inventing, designing, developing and testing applications.

References

[1] Companje, R., van Dijk, N., Hogenbirk, H., & Mast, D."Globe4D: time-traveling with an interactive four-dimensional globe." Proc. of the 14th annual ACM international conference on Multimedia. ACM, 2006.

[2] Druin, A. (2002). The role of children in the design of new technology. Behaviour and Information Technology, 21(1), 1-25.

[3] Fogel, V. A., Miltenberger, R. G., Graves, R., & Koehler, S. (2010). The effects of exergaming on physical activity among inactive children in a physical education classroom. Journal of applied behavior analysis, 43(4), 591-600.

[4] Lai, A., Soro, A., & Scateni, R. (2010, October). Interactive calibration of a multi-projector system in a video-wall multi-touch environment. In Adjunct proceedings of the 23nd annual ACM symposium on User interface software and technology (pp. 437-438). ACM.

[5] Marner, M. R., Smith, R. T., Porter, S. R., Broecker, M. M., Close, B., & Thomas, B. H. (2011). Large Scale Spatial Augmented Reality for Design and Prototyping (pp. 231-254). Springer New York.

[6] Mast, D., Assessing Children's Experiences with Active and Passive Artificial Companions. Proc. of the 13th Computer-Human Interaction Netherlands Conference, pp 61-73

[7] Mine, M. R., van Baar, J., Grundhöfer, A., Rose, D., & Yang, B. (2012). Projection-Based Augmented Reality in Disney Theme Parks. IEEE Computer,45(7), 32-40.

[8] Muller, Michael J. "Participatory design: the third space in HCI." Human-computer interaction: Development process (2003): 165-185.

[9] Shaer, Orit, and Eva Hornecker. "Tangible user interfaces: past, present, and future directions." Foundations and Trends in Human-Computer Interaction 3.1–2 (2010): 1-137.

[10] Staiano, A. E., & Calvert, S. L. (2011). Exergames for physical education courses: Physical, social, and cognitive benefits. Child development perspectives, 5(2), 93-98.

[11] Stegeman, Harry, ed. Onderwijs in Bewegen. Bohn Stafleu van Loghum, 2008.

[12] Thomas, BH: A survey of visual, mixed, and augmented reality gaming. Comput. Entertain. 10(3), 3:1–3:33 (Dec 2012)

[13] An Experience-Based Chinese Opera Using Live Video Mapping · Xiang-Dan Huang, Byung-Gook Lee, Hyung-Woo Kim, Joon-Jae Lee

Assisting Caregivers of Children with Cerebral Palsy: Towards a Self-Feeding Assessment Spoon

Oren Zuckerman
Media Innovation Lab
School of Communications
IDC Herzliya, Israel
orenz@idc.ac.il

Ayelet Gal-Oz
Media Innovation Lab
School of Communications
IDC Herzliya, Israel
goayelet@idc.ac.il

Ronit Slyper
Media Innovation Lab
School of Communications
IDC Herzliya, Israel
rys@cs.cmu.edu

Tamar Gal
Media Innovation Lab
School of Communications
IDC Herzliya, Israel
tamar.gal@post.idc.ac.il

Tal Keren-Capelovitch
Department of Occupational Therapy
University of Haifa
Haifa, Israel
tlnzvkrn@netvision.net.il

Patrrice L. (Tamar) Weiss
Department of Occupational Therapy
University of Haifa
Haifa, Israel
tamar@research.haifa.ac.il

TEI'15, January 15–19, 2015, Stanford, California, USA.
ACM 978-1-4503-3305-4/15/01.
http://dx.doi.org/10.1145/2677199.2687902.

Abstract
Many children with cerebral palsy (CP) encounter great difficulties mastering self-feeding. We set out to assess the self-feeding skills of young children with CP via a novel instrumented spoon that monitors upper extremity biomechanics involved in eating. We describe the initial stages of an iterative design process, consisting of a focus group with domain experts, and rapid-prototyping. We discuss the physical, assessment and safety requirements for the spoon. In addition, we explain the potential of tangible interfaces to provide professional caregivers with valuable information regarding each child.

Author Keywords
Cerebral palsy; self-feeding; assessment; children; tangible user interface.

ACM Classification Keywords
K.4.2. **[Computers and Society]:** Social Issues - Assistive technologies for persons with disabilities.

General Terms
Design, Human Factors, Measurement.

Introduction

Eating is a complex process with physiological, biomechanical, and behavioral aspects involving the entire body [13]. Typically developing young children gradually shift to higher levels of independent eating, until eventually mastering self-feeding, usually by the age of three years [8, 13, 15]. Disruption in eating may lead to malnutrition, poor growth, developmental delay and loss of general health and well-being [1]. Children with cerebral palsy (CP) often have significant difficulties mastering self-feeding [4, 16]. CP describes a group of developmental disorders of movement and posture leading to activity restriction that is attributed to disturbances occurring in the fetal or infant brain [14]. Motor impairment may be accompanied by a seizure disorder and by disturbances of sensation, cognition, communication and behavior [2].

To date, little data exist concerning the biomechanics of grasping utensils or food and bringing it to the mouth, control over the activity kinematics and kinetics, and issues related to motor planning and learning among children with CP. Tangible user interfaces have the potential to provide such data, thereby making valuable assessment information about each child available to caregivers. Quantitative assessment data will lead to more effective treatment of self-feeding difficulties.

We set out to assess the self-feeding skills of young children with CP via a novel instrumented spoon that monitors several biomechanics variables of the upper extremity involved in self-feeding. The spoon, called SenSpoon, is currently being developed in an iterative and participatory design process, consisting of a focus group with domain experts and rapid-prototyping. In this paper we describe the expert-based design process, present our initial prototype, and discuss avenues for future work.

Related Work

Food-related interactions have been recognized as a challenge for the HCI community, because physical, physiological, cognitive and social factors have to be taken into account [5]. It is particularly challenging to design such interactions for young children, with or without disabilities, due to developmental and safety concerns.

EducaTableware [11] are interactive tableware devices (fork and cup) intended to make eating more enjoyable by emitting sounds when a child eats or drinks. Sensing Fork [9, 10] is a fork-type sensing device, which detects children's eating actions and chosen food items. This device is connected to a smartphone that analyzes sensor data, and provides feedback through a game application. HAPIfork [7] is an electronic fork that tracks eating speed. It vibrates when the user eats too fast, thereby promoting slower and healthier eating. Playful Bottle [3] is an augmented water bottle that uses a smartphone to track water intake. It aims to encourage drinking by using water intake as input for a mobile game. Playful Tray [12] aims to reduce meal completion time with a weight-sensitive tray that tracks children's eating actions. These are then used as input for an interactive game embedded within the tray.

While these systems address various challenges experienced by children while eating and drinking, they have not been adapted to the unique requirements of children with CP and similar developmental disorders. To the best of our knowledge, the only eating-related system designed specifically for children with CP was previously presented by our team [6]. The system, called ExciteTray, is a digital food tray that rewards self-feeding with visual feedback in the form of a colorful light display. It is aimed to motivate young children with CP throughout the gradual process of acquiring independent eating skills.

The SenSpoon extends our previous work by focusing on the needs of professional caregivers, assisting them with assessing the self-feeding skills of children with CP.

System Design Process

SenSpoon is being designed by an interdisciplinary team consisting of HCI researchers, an occupational therapist specializing in CP management, a rehabilitation technology researcher, and an industrial designer. We set out to develop a technology that provides professional caregivers with data concerning the biomechanics of upper extremity involved in eating. Our first step entailed consultation with caregivers who treat children with developmental disabilities in order to learn more about their and the children's needs and requirements.

Participants

Six professional caregivers (3 occupational therapists and 3 physiotherapists) participated in a focus group. Their years of experience range from 18 to 40. All participants regularly assess the skill level of children with disabilities. They were recruited through personal acquaintance with one member of the research team.

Method

Participants were invited to participate in a focus group on assessing self-feeding skills among children with CP, using a novel instrumented spoon. The session lasted approximately two hours. First, participants filled out a questionnaire regarding their professional experience, current use of assistive technologies, and challenges they face when assessing the skill level of children. Second, an industrial designer facilitated a group discussion regarding the physical requirements for the spoon (size, shape and material). Third, an HCI researcher facilitated a group discussion regarding the assessment requirements for the spoon. Lastly, participants were asked to envision what type of output they would like to receive from the spoon, and draw the desired graphical representation of this output. The session was audio recorded with participants' consent. The recordings were later transcribed and independently analyzed by two researchers to identify emerging common themes.

Results and Discussion

Use of assistive technologies: two participants use assistive technologies (e.g., biofeedback, virtual reality); none currently use eating-related assistive technologies.

Challenges for assessing the skill level of children: how to accurately and rapidly map the capabilities of each child in order to devise a treatment plan, how to assess children in real-time during routine daily activities, rather than in a clinical setting.

Potential benefits of technology-based assessment: automated, provides quantitative data, enables customization of treatment plan, engaging and motivating for children.

Potential challenges of technology-based assessment: may be perceived to replace actual therapy or

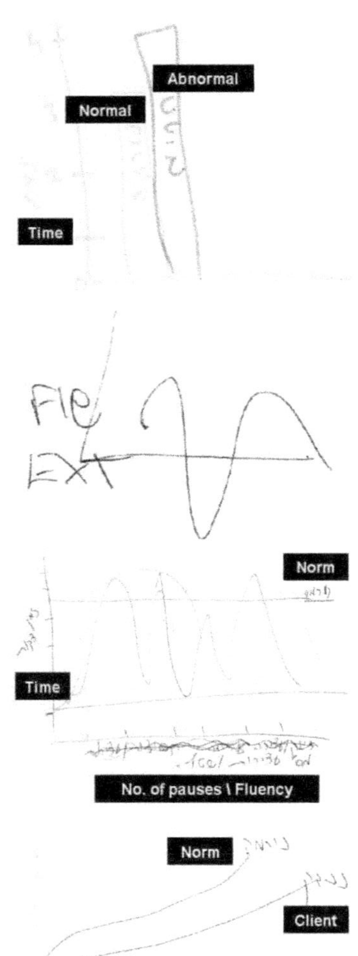

Figure 1. Drawings by caregivers depicting desired output from the spoon. Tags in white font provide translation for non-English text.

interaction with the child, not all caregivers are open to using technology.

Physical requirements for the spoon: must be safe, comfortable to hold, with a size, depth and angle that match the needs of the child. All participants agreed that the spoon should be made out of plastic or silicone, preferably in a neutral color.

Assessment requirements for the spoon: participants would like to monitor the following variables: accuracy, fluency and smoothness of movement, grip force, trajectory from the plate to the mouth, speed of movement, duration of meal, amount of food consumed.

Desired output of the spoon: most participants envisioned the output of the spoon as a series of graphs, comparing various aspects of the child's motor behavior to normative data *("The graph should compare my client to the norm, here's his curve and here's the norm")*. Moreover, the graphs must be simple and easy to comprehend, providing caregivers with a quick overview or snapshot of the child's skill level (*"I need something that is visually simple. I can't waste a lot of time on this, I want to see a screen that immediately displays time and compares fluency"*). See examples of participants' drawings in Figure 1.

Hence, in order to meet the needs of professional caregivers, the optimal design will: (1) utilize several types of sensors to monitor various biomechanical variables during self-feeding, (2) create a plastic or silicone spoon customized to contain all electronic parts, (3) develop an algorithm for integrating and analyzing sensor-based data, and (4) design a graphical user interface for presenting the results of the analysis in a clear and meaningful manner.

Initial Prototype

The SenSpoon uses the IMUduino BTLE board (http://www.femtoduino.com/spex/imuduino-btle) for sensing and communication. This 40x16mm Arduino clone includes a 3-axis gyroscope, 3-axis accelerometer, and 3-axis digital compass. The board also contains a Bluetooth Low Energy chip, which we pair wirelessly with an Android phone to perform data logging. The phone receives the streamed data in realtime, leaving open the possibility of realtime analysis and feedback.

For the initial prototype, a pre-clinical feasibility test, we taped the IMUduino to the handle of an off-the-shelf metal teaspoon, rigging a holder for the five LR44 button cell batteries used to power the board. The assemblage was covered in a plastic sheath for water resistance (see Figure 2). Total weight was 36 grams, no heavier than a stainless steel teaspoon.

Safety Considerations

In order to ensure that the SenSpoon is safe to use, we implemented the following measures: (1) the spoon is battery-operated and does not require high-voltage electricity, (2) all electronics are completely covered, preventing any direct contact between the electronic parts and the child and moist foods, (3) all surface materials are non-toxic, (4) data transmission from the spoon is wireless to prevent tangling of cables while eating. Furthermore, we consulted the head of a bio-medical engineering department at a major medical center. He examined the prototype, and gave written approval that it is safe to use.

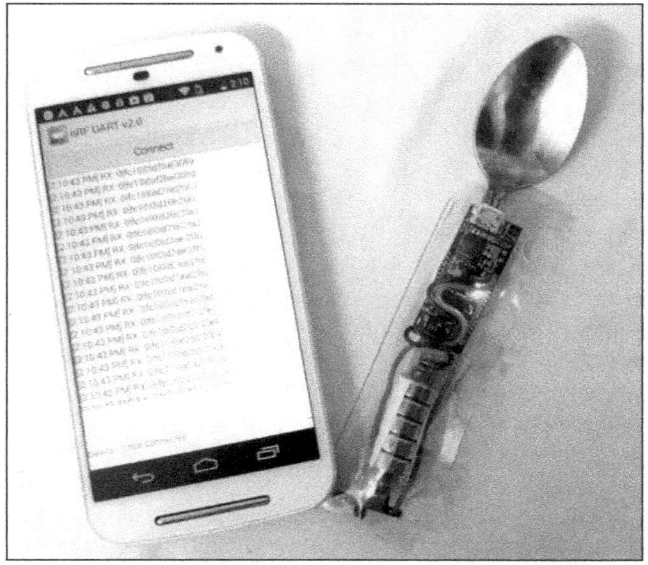

Figure 2. Initial prototype of SenSpoon: a standard spoon augmented with the IMUduino BTLE board to monitor various biomechanical variables during self-feeding. Data is streamed via Bluetooth to a smartphone.

Future Work

We are currently in the process of monitoring self-feeding behaviors of healthy adults using the initial spoon prototype, and developing an algorithm for analyzing sensor-based data. Our next step is the design and creation of a customized plastic or silicone spoon, into which all electronic parts will be incorporated. We will then monitor the self-feeding skills of children with CP as well as typically developing children, in order to establish the discriminant validity of the spoon. As an assessment tool, the spoon should be able to differentiate between children with CP and typically developing children based on upper extremity biomechanical variables. Eventually, the final prototype will be used as an assessment tool for professional caregivers. The final prototype may also assist with treatment for self-feeding difficulties, optimally through integration with other self-feeding assistive technologies, mainly our digital food tray described in [6]. Leveraging tangible interaction for augmenting current clinical practice is expected to benefit both professional caregivers and children with disabilities.

Acknowledgements

We would like to thank Orad Weisberg, Shlomi Azoulai, Yair Uziel, and Shai Yagur for their invaluable assistance with design and prototyping; the physical and occupational therapists who participated in our focus group; and Dr. Yoram Shadmi, director of the Bio-Medical Engineering Department at The Chime Sheba Medical Center for consulting on electrical safety. This research was supported by the I-CORE Program of the Planning and Budgeting Committee and The Israel Science Foundation (grant no. 1716/12).

References

[1] Arverdson, J.C., and Brodsky, L., Eds. *Pediatric swallowing and feeding: Assessment and management*. Singular Publishing Group Inc., San Diego, CA, 1993.

[2] Bax, M., Goldstein, M., Rosenbaum, P., Leviton, A., Paneth, N., Dan, B., Jacobsson, B., and Damiano, D. Proposed definition and classification of cerebral palsy. *Developmental Medicine and Child Neurology 47*, 8 (2005), 571-576.

[3] Chiu, M-C., Chang, S-P., Chang, Y-C., Chu, H-H., Chen, C. C-H., Hsiao, F-H., Ko, J-C. Playful Bottle: A mobile social persuasion system to motivate healthy water intake. In *Proc. UbiComp 2009*, ACM Press (2009), 185-194.

[4] Cokrill, H. Feeding. In E. Bower, Ed. *Finnie's handling the young child with cerebral palsy at home*, 149-164. Butterworth Heinemann Elsevier, UK, 2009.

[5] Comber, R., Ganglbauer, E., Choi, J. H-J., Hoonhout, J., Rogers, Y., O'Hara, K., and Maitland, J. Food and interaction design: Designing for food in everyday life. *Ext. Abstracts CHI 2012*, ACM Press (2012), 2767-2770.

[6] Gal-Oz, A., Weisberg, O., Keren-Capelovitch, T., Uziel, Y., Slyper, R., Weiss, P.L.T., and Zuckerman, O. ExciteTray: Developing an assistive technology to promote self-feeding among young children. In *Proc. IDC 2014*, ACM Press (2014), 297-300.

[7] HAPIfork. http://www.hapi.com/product/hapifork.

[8] Illingworth, R.S. *The Development of the Infant and young child: Abnormal and normal* (7th ed.). Churchill Livingstone, London, UK, 1980.

[9] Kadomura, A., Li, K. C-Y., Chen, A.Y-C., Chu, H-H., Tsukada, K., and Siio, I. Sensing Fork and persuasive game for improving eating behavior. In *Proc. UbiComp 2013 Adjunct*, ACM Press (2013), 71-74.

[10] Kadomura, A., Li, K.C-Y., Chen, A.Y-C., Nakamori, R., Tsukada, K., Siio, I., and Chu, H-H. Sensing Fork: Eating behavior detection utensil and mobile persuasive game. In *Ext. Abstracts CHI 2013*, ACM Press (2013), 1551-1556.

[11] Kadomura, A., Tsukada, K., and Siio, I. EducaTableware: Computer-augmented tableware to enhance the eating experiences. In *Ext. Abstracts CHI 2013*, ACM Press (2013), 3071-3074.

[12] Lo, J-L., Lin, T-Y., Chu, H-H., Chou, H-C., Chen, J-H., Hsu, J. Y-J., and Huang, P. Playful Tray: Adopting ubicomp and persuasive techniques into play-based occupational therapy for reducing poor eating behavior in young children. In *Proc. UbiComp 2007*, Springer Berlin Heidelberg (2007), 38-55.

[13] Morris, S. E., and Klein, M. D. *Pre-feeding skills: A comprehensive resource for feeding development*. Communication Skill Builders, Tucson, AR, 1987.

[14] Rosenbaum, P., Paneth, N., Leviton, A., Goldestein, M., and Bax, M. A report: The definition and classification of cerebral palsy. *Developmental Medicine and Child Neurology 109*, (2007), 8-14.

[15] Sugden, D., and Wade, M. *Typical and atypical motor development*. Mac Keith Press, London, UK, 2013.

[16] Weir, K. A., Bell, K. L., Caristo, F., Ware, R. S., Davies, P. S., Fahey, M., Rawicki, B., and Boyd, R. N. Reported eating ability of young children with cerebral palsy: Is there an association with gross motor function?. *Archives of Physical Medicine and Rehabilitation 94*, 3 (2013), 495-502.

Tangibly Enhancing Haptics

Figure 1: Design evolution

Philip Feldman
UMBC
1000 Hilltop Circle
Baltimore, MD 21250 USA
feld1@umbc.edu

Ravi Kuber
UMBC
1000 Hilltop Circle
Baltimore, MD 21250 USA
rkuber@umbc.edu

TEI 2015, January 15-19, 2015, Stanford, CA, USA
ACM 978-1-4503-3305-4/15/01
http://dx.doi.org/10.1145/2677199.2687903

Abstract
In this paper, we describe the development of a novel, low-cost, compact sensor/actuator that can be integrated with a commercially-available haptic device, such as the Geomagic Touch, to provide additional capability when grasping virtual objects. The focus of this paper is to investigate the impact of modality on a 'picking and placing' task using the prototype. The results of this study suggest that fewer errors were made when grasping objects presented using force-input/vibrotactile output (FV) combined with force-feedback. The multimodal feedback presented via the prototype is thought to offer considerable potential to supporting skilled and semi-skilled workers to perform remote tasks involving fine motor control.

Keywords
Haptic; Tactile; Tangible, Teleoperation; Vibrotactile

ACM Classification Keywords
H.5.2. User Interfaces: Haptic I/O.

Introduction
While teleoperation has most commonly been used to support medical, space and defense initiatives, it can also be applied to tasks where skilled or semi-skilled labor is needed (e.g. remote factory work). This would assist organizations who may experience difficulties recruiting due to their location. Haptic-based

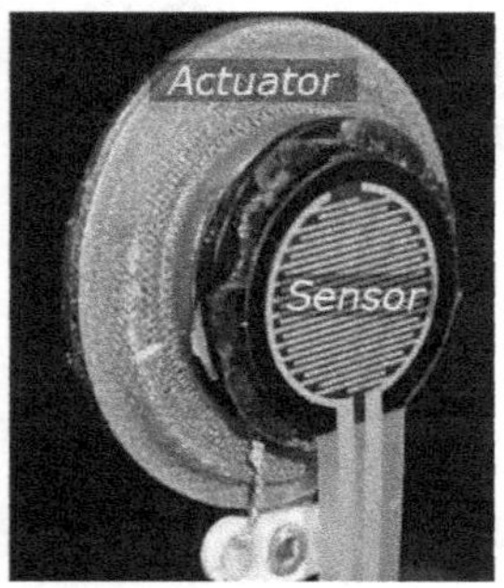

Figure 2: FV Module

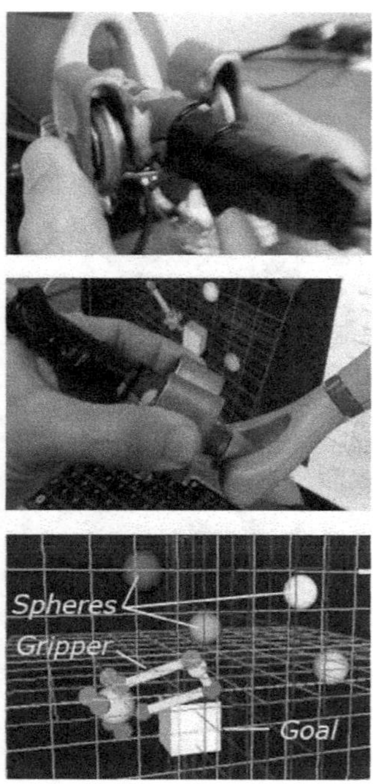

Figure 3: Prototype and Virtual Environment

telepresence could be used for a wide variety of more routine work such as factory and farm labor if the interface could be both low-cost and capable of providing the depth of sensation to support generalized interaction for modestly trained individuals. It is not enough for a user to know that they have collided with an object and push it around. They must be able to grasp an object, apprehend its form and surface characteristics, and then manipulate it quickly and without few or no errors. In short, the interaction must become more natural and tangible.

This paper describes a first step towards determining ways to use touch to support manual tasks, through the development of a low-cost sensor/actuator that measures force and provides vibrotactile feedback (termed: FV). A prototype has been developed, enabling users to perform 'picking and placing' tasks. These types of tasks are often performed within a factory environment. The long term goal of our research is to identify the potential of using such a solution in a telecollaborative context.

Related Work

Force-feedback systems are known to be expensive to purchase. However, lower cost technologies such as the Geomagic Touch (www.geomagic.com) and Novint Falcon (www.novint.com) are available for integration with systems. The user can grasp with the end effector (stylus or ball-like grip) to interact with a virtual or remote surface while feedback is presented to his/her hand.

Extending a low-cost platform, such as the Geomagic Touch, to accommodate more sophisticated interactions such as grasping has been tried several times. Barbagli [1] added four additional channels of force feedback to a three-degree-of-freedom haptic input/output device to support multi-finger, multi-hand exploration and manipulation of virtual objects. Debus et al. [3] developed vibrotactile transducers to provide more tangible sensations to enhance force feedback. However in these cases, additional capability was provided at considerable complexity and expense.

Prototype Designs

Bianchi et al. [2] stated that "research on tangible interaction and digital haptics has rarely intertwined". In our literature search, we found only a few similar examples of FV additions to haptic systems. Stuart et al. [11] examined multimodal (combinations of video, audio and vibrotactile) feedback in conjunction with pressure sensing when applied to handheld devices. They found that selection using auditory and tactile feedback could be as rapid as visual only cues, but not as accurate.

Using the research through design methodology [12], we worked through numerous FV prototypes that would sense force and provide tangible user feedback that could be combined easily with other systems (Figure 1). These efforts produced a simple transducer that had two low-cost components - an acoustic-quality actuator coupled with a resistive force sensor (Figure 2). A pressing force applied by the user can be used to move one axis of the end effector, such as a finger. Contact by the end effector results in reality-based waveforms being sent to the actuator, as suggested by Okamoto et al. [8] and Okamura et al. [9]. This allows the user to develop a sense of what the surface of a remote object feels like.

Table 1: Errors by Condition

Modality	Errors
Visual with Vibrotactile output	19
Visual Only	14
Visual with Force Feedback	7
Visual with Force Feedback & Vibrotactile	3

Table 2: Mean Task Completion Times

Alias	Session 1	Session 2
P01	63.57	57.22
P02	73.03	81.28
P03	55.94	52.38
P05	41.30	30.68
P06	67.56	57.15
P08	42.74	35.88
P10	43.70	31.07
Average	55.41	49.38

The prototype described in this paper was developed to explore the relationship between traditional haptics enhanced by force sensing and vibrotactile feedback. A Geomagic Touch was selected for use in the study. Two FV modules were attached to the device, near the base of the stylus (Figure 3). These modules support a pincer-like gripping action, enabling the user to better grasp a virtual object.

Mounted directly underneath the sensors are vibrotactile actuators that are associated with the sensor. Using a Phidgets interface kit (www.phidgets.com) and the Microsoft XAudio2 API, up to eight sensors and their associated vibrotactile elements can be operated.

Experimental Design and Procedure

'Picking and placing', such as positioning screws in an 'engine block', is a common factory task. Such an activity is relatively straightforward for individuals who exhibit superior levels of manual dexterity and coordination, but can be difficult for automated systems to perform. 'Picking and placing' demands few errors, as these can impact speed and efficiency.

In our study, participants were presented with a 'picking and placing' task where they were asked to interact with a virtual environment to grasp 5 randomly positioned spheres and move each of the spheres into a 'goal'. Contact with each sphere was mapped to a specific vibrotactile frequency with amplitude in proportion to the simulated contact force between the sphere and the gripper element. This was in accordance with Murray et al.'s findings [8]. The left and right gripper interface elements had their own vibrotactile emitters. Force applied to the pressure sensors on the Geomagic Touch (as shown in Figure 2) would cause the grippers to close. Relaxing pressure on the sensors would cause the grippers to open.

The following conditions were examined in our study:

- Visual only
- Visual with force feedback
- Visual with vibrotactile output
- Visual with force feedback and vibrotactile output

Ten participants (2 women, 8 men, aged 21 – 54) were recruited for the exploratory study. All participants were information workers and comfortable with technology. None had prior experience with tactile or haptic systems other than videogame controllers and mobile phones.

Participants were introduced to the prototype, and given as much time as they needed to become comfortable with using the device to grasp virtual objects. The level of vibrotactile amplitude was adjusted during this time to user preference. All participants were instructed to complete the task of placing all spheres in the goal as quickly as possible. In the virtual environment, it was possible to knock the spheres out of range. Any sphere that was not placed in the goal was counted as an error. Time for each task was calculated from the moment that the Start/Next button was pressed to the time that the last sphere was placed in the goal. If the participant was unable to place all the spheres in the goal, the timer was arbitrarily stopped, and the next session begun.

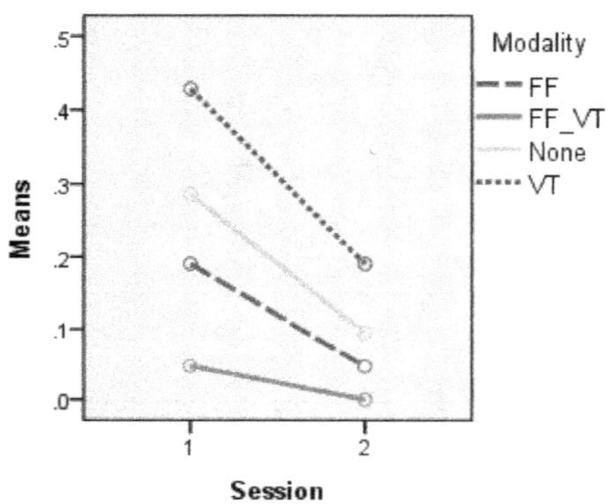

Figure 4: Error Count Means by Session

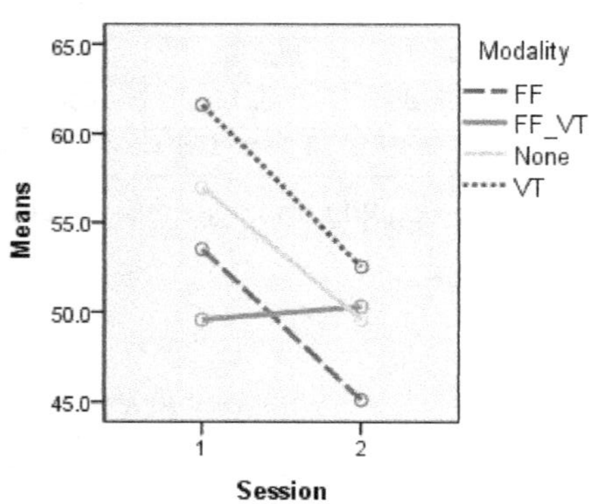

Figure 5: Task Time Means by Session

Errors were calculated per task by subtracting the number of successfully positioned spheres in the goal from the total number of spheres presented in the task.

Results and Discussion

Participants adapted quickly to the interface. Average completion time for all participants was 55.4s per task (SD: 25.0s) for the first session and 49.4s (SD: 22.8s) for the second session. A repeated measures ANOVA was conducted. However, no significant effect could be detected by completion time ($F(1,20)=3.617$, $p=0.072$).

Errors

Seven participants committed a total of 44 errors. These included pushing the sphere beyond the range of the gripper while attempting to grasp it, and placing the sphere in a location where it was occluded by the goal.

The majority of errors occurred in the first session (37 vs. 7) (Table 1). Examining the means plots presented in Figure 4, participants appeared to make fewer errors when the combination of the force-feedback and vibrotactile modalities were used to perform the tasks.

44.1% of errors were made in the visual with vibrotactile output condition. In other studies examining vibrotactile interaction including Debus et al. [3] and Foehrenbach et al. [5], presenting vibrotactile feedback by itself did not appear to provide a significant reduction in errors when performing tasks. On the other hand, findings from our study suggest that fewer errors are made when vibrotactile feedback and force-feedback are presented together, compared to vibrotactile output alone. However, further study would be needed to confirm this.

Task Time

Prior to each session, participants were asked to place the spheres in the goal as quickly and accurately as possible. Completion times are presented in Table 2. Findings have suggested that participants were generally faster in their second session than their first session, and that the times to complete the second task were more consistent.

Looking at the task time means across the sessions in Figure 5, the results were not as clear as with the error count (Figure 4). For session 1, the relationship between the modalities reflected the pattern seen in the error means for the first session. The order in time taken per task was initially the same as the ordering for errors committed. In other words, the vibrotactile modality took the most time (61.6s), and the force feedback plus vibrotactile modality took the least (49.6s). However, when the users performed the tasks the second time, this pattern changed. The force-feedback plus vibrotactile took longer (50.3s vs 49.5s) and the spread of times increased as well (SD: 18.5s vs 28.5s). For all other cases, the average time for the other conditions decreased as training improved. The decrease in performance for the force feedback plus vibrotactile modality was a perplexing result, and may reflect the small sample size. However, Massimino identified a similar effect when he was combining modalities to support users when performing a peg-in-hole task using the E2 Master-Slave manipulator. In this case, the addition of vibrotactile to a force-feedback plus audio configuration increased completion times for the task [6].

Conclusions and Future Work

The goal of this exploratory study was to identify the impact of modality on picking and placing tasks. Findings indicated that there may not be a need for an additional costly force-feedback axis. Rather, a force-sensing/vibrotactile output component mounted to a force feedback base could potentially offer assistance when performing a task. The combination of tangible interaction with force-feedback may provide a low-cost but potentially effective way to enhance simple haptic systems. This study suggests that such a system has the capability to reduce errors made when grasping and releasing, and could possibly be useful for decreasing task time when undertaking a task that requires fine motor skills. Further study would need to be conducted to determine if this is truly the case.

Adding force-sensing components to other devices where the range of "virtual" motion is suitably constrained may be worth pursuing. For example, components can be embedded within in the casing surrounding a smartphone or a videogame controller (e.g. a joystick). As long as the moving base is tracked and used to determine the position and orientation of the gripping "effector", the result may be sufficient. Improvements in the amount and type of vibrotactile information presented may provide a more effective interface (e.g. as observed in the studies by [4] and [10]).

The hardware and software for this study is designed to be extended to support further experiments in low-cost teleoperation. To this end, we intend to configure another Geomagic Touch with the same FV platform and work on connecting it to a manufacturing robot such as Baxter. As such, the next steps will be to develop additional software that supports communication with the target hardware, and the development of software that will support digitizing and virtualizing the work environment so that the operator can operate with responsive haptics without having to account for the types of time lags that are common in teleoperation. Further studies will then focus on developing an effective local human-distant robot interaction with respect to manufacturing-style tasks.

References

[1] Barbagli, F., Salisbury, K., Devengenzo, and R. Enabling multi-finger, multi-hand virtualized grasping. Robotics and Automation, 2003. Proceedings. ICRA'03. IEEE International Conference on. Vol. 1. IEEE, 2003.

[2] Bianchi, A., et al. Haptics for tangible interaction: a vibro-tactile prototype. Proceedings of the fifth international conference on Tangible, embedded, and embodied interaction. ACM, 2011.

[3] Debus, T., et al. Multichannel vibrotactile display for sensory substitution during teleoperation. Proceedings of SPIE–The International Society for Optical Engineering. Vol. 4570. 2001.

[4] DiFilippo, D. and Pai, D. K., Contact interaction with integrated audio and haptics. Proceedings of the International Conference on Auditory Display (ICAD). 2000.

[5] Foehrenbach, S., et al. Natural interaction with hand gestures and tactile feedback for large, high-res displays. Bibliothek der Universität Konstanz, 2008.

[6] Massimino, M., Sensory substitution for force feedback in space teleoperation. Diss. Massachusetts Institute of Technology, 1992.

[7] Murray, A., Klatzky, R., and Khosla, P., Psychophysical characterization and testbed validation of a wearable vibrotactile glove for telemanipulation. Presence: Teleoperators and Virtual Environments 12.2 (2003): 156-182.

[8] Okamoto, S., Wiertlewski, W., and Hayward, V. Anticipatory vibrotactile cueing facilitates grip force adjustment. World Haptics Conference (WHC), 2013. IEEE, 2013

[9] Okamura, A.M., Cutkosky, M.R. and Dennerlein, J.T. Reality-based models for vibration feedback in virtual environments. Mechatronics, IEEE/ASME Transactions on 6.3 (2001): 245-252.

[10] Richmond, J.L. and Pai, D.K., Active measurement of contact sounds. Robotics and Automation, 2000. Proceedings. ICRA'00. IEEE International Conference on. Vol. 3. IEEE, 2000.

[11] Stewart, C., et al. Characteristics of pressure-based input for mobile devices." Proceedings of the SIGCHI Conference on Human Factors in Computing Systems. ACM, 2010.

[12] Zimmerman, J., Forlizzi, J., and Evenson, S. Research through design as a method for interaction design research in HCI. Proceedings of the SIGCHI conference on Human factors in computing systems. ACM, 2007.

Observing Hand Placement and Measurement on Tabletop Using a Depth Camera

Christopher J Martinez
University of New Haven
300 Boston Post Rd
West Haven, CT 06516 USA
cmartinez@newhaven.edu

Katherine Seggerman
University of New Haven
300 Boston Post Rd
West Haven, CT 06516 USA
ksegg1@unh.newhaven.edu

Andy Perez
University of New Haven
300 Boston Post Rd
West Haven, CT 06516 USA
apere6@unh.newhaven.edu

TEI '15, Jan 16-19 2015, Stanford, CA, USA
ACM 978-1-4503-3305-4/15/01.
http://dx.doi.org/10.1145/2677199.2687904

Abstract
Tabletop computing is a new emerging interface that can be realized with low cost using depth sensor cameras such as the Microsoft Kinect. The optimization of the touch interface using depth measurements must take into account the size variations of a diverse population. In this study, we examine a sample population to understand the differences in hand measurements a depth camera would detect on a large tabletop computer. We have broken down the hand into three measurements (the three joints in the hand) that may be of interest to research working in the field. The hand measurements have been taken at different locations on the table to account for changes in the hand position caused by the user stretching their arm.

Author Keywords
Tabletop; hand placement; hand measurement; touch screen; depth camera

ACM Classification Keywords
H.5.2. User Interfaces: Ergonomics

a) 

b) 

Figure 1. Blob detection a) fingertips and b) hand

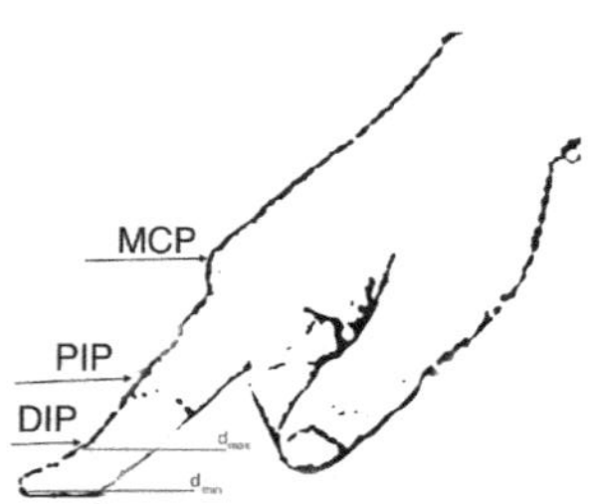

Figure 2. Depth sensor measurement and joint labeling

Introduction

Tabletop computing is a new emerging interface that has been developed to use large screen size that can accommodate multiple users cooperating together. There are many researchers that have examined using a depth camera as the mechanism for detecting touch [1, 2, 4-6, 8]. The most popular configuration for using the depth camera is to have a table that the user stands over, a depth camera is placed overhead aim down on the table to detect if a user places their hand on the tabletop.

Researchers have used the method Wilson describes in [7, 8] as the main method for detecting touch. Wilson examines creating a binary image, black and white color, to detect touch. Every finger touch is represented as a white blob. The creation of the binary image uses the depth camera to locate the distance of an object from the table surface and camera. The interface selects an area (distance) of interest and colors white in the selected area. Figure 1 shows different parts of the hand that can be detected using this method.

The ability to detect touch comes down to finding the proper area of interest for the depth camera. Figure 2 shows how the touch blobs are detected as describe by Wilson. In order for the interface to be accessible by a diverse population a study must be conducted to find out what is the best distance to use find the thickness of a finger (d_{min} and d_{max}) described by Wilson.

In our literature review, there has been little research into how the hand is measured in practice with touch devices. Wilson [8] provides values to use for finger thickness but the values are given as the raw measurement provided by the Kinect and will not extend to other cameras. Murugappan et al. [6] provides data on the size of blob that should be used for detection for good accuracy, 20 mm^2 to 220 mm^2. Kratz et al. in [4] place the depth sensor not above the user but place the camera in the same plane as the finger (finger level). Using the finger level position they examined the area 0 cm (camera location) up to 15 cm in height above the camera. The paper does not discuss why the 15 cm height was chosen. The work in [3] does not utilize a depth camera but hand measurements were used to determine the reach of a thumb on a PDA. The worked showed that distance the thumb had to travel affected the accuracy of the input. We expected to see similar results when using a depth camera.

Based on our literature search we concluded that all depth camera implementations require hand measurement data to filter a touch versus non-touch contact with the surface. All the papers did not have a formal method to determine the hand measurements to detect. In this study, we aim to provide the community with data that takes a sample population and provide measurement data for all three joints on the finger (distal inter-phalangeal (DIP), proximal inter-phalangeal joint (PIP), and metacarpophalangeal (MCP)) that touches the surface. The three joint measurements can be seen in Figure 2.

Sample Population

Our case study was conducted on a college campus that provided a diverse population. The sample population consisted of 35 individuals that span a wide range of attributes that set up a compressive study. The sample of 35 individuals is larger than all of the

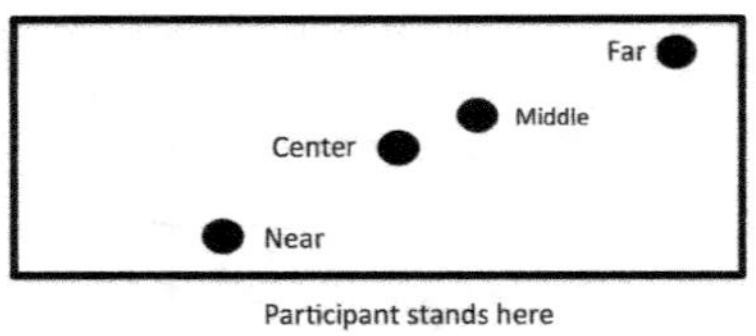

Figure 3 Experiment setup: Table location and hand measurements

previous work. The sample set spanned an age range of 18 to 60, covered 3 different ethnic backgrounds and an individual height range from 5ft to 6ft 4in. The sample was made up of 16 females (46%) and 19 males (54%). All of the male participants were from a technology background of electrical & computer engineering and computer science. Only 5 of the 16 females came from a technology background. All of the participants had experience using a touch screen on a smartphone or tablet but no one had used a tabletop computer before. Since they had not used a tabletop they were not conditioned into using preconceived input patterns.

Experiment Setup

The case study was administrated in the following manner:

1. The tabletop dimensions were width 2 ft, length 4 ft and height 3 ft.
2. The tabletop did not react to touch during testing. A static image of a typical desktop was shown.
3. Icons were placed at specific locations that the participants were asked to touch.
4. Touch locations were (points referred to later in the paper): 1. Center of table (center), 2. Bottom left corner (near), 3. Top right corner (far), and 4. Middle of table 17.25 cm diagonal from center of table (middle).
5. Participants were asked to show gesture to swipe a page in a document back and forward.
6. Participants were asked to show gesture to zoom in on an image.

Figure 3 shows the setup of the touch locations for the experiment.

Experiment measurement

As we performed the experiment asking participants to touch certain locations on the table the hand was measured. Figure 2 shows the hand measurements that we observed with each participant. To make the measurements consistent across everyone's hand the three knuckle joints were chosen. The identification of the joints are: the DIP joint nearest to the finger tip, the PIP or middle joint, and the MCP or largest joint at the top of the hand.

The joint distances were measured in the following manner. As the participant was ask to touch the table a picture was taken from a camera that was leveled with the table. Offline the pictures were examined and the distance from the tabletop to the top of the three joints were calculated. A ruler was place at each of the locations so that we could get an accurate measurement at the point of contact with the table top. The joint distances can be used to create a threshold image from the depth camera as seen in Figure 1.

The DIP joint was measured because the tip of the finger would determine that the user was touching the tabletop. This is the most important measurement for touch detection.

The MCP was measured because in some applications it may be useful to know if the user used their left or right hand to touch the screen. By finding the center point of the MCP blob and the DIP blob we can determine the hand used. A calculation would be needed to determine if the DIP center was left or right

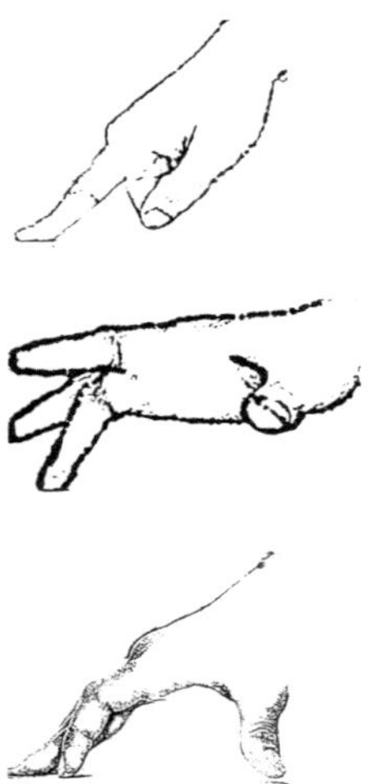

Figure 4. Hand orientations observed: pointing, spread and thumb

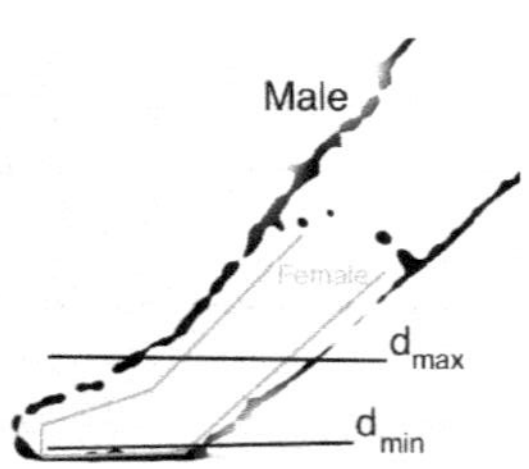

Figure 5. How male measurement covers female range

of the MCP center point. Figure 1 shows blobs detection of the DIP (a) and MCP (b), in this figure the individual spreads out their hand to demonstrate that the threshold is functioning correctly.

The PIP is provided for completeness of our study. There may be need for this measurement in the future so we provided the data.

The information on the participants gesturing for a swipe and zoom were taken by observation and noted as we conducted the study. The gestures were noted to determine if the smartphone gestures would be used on a larger screen.

Observations and measurements

Common hand orientation in touch

We observed that when participants touched the tabletop the hand orientation fell into one of three categories shown in Figure 4. The most common orientation was four fingers under palm (pointer orientation). The pointer orientation works best for the depth camera positioned above the user. Only the pointing finger will be visible by the depth camera with the remaining fingers covered by the top of hand.

The next most frequent hand orientation was spread open hand (spread orientation). The spread orientation was common in female participants, 46% of females used the spread orientation. The spread orientation can lead to errors in the touch detection. If the threshold for blob detection is set too high then multiple fingers will be detected to touch the screen. It is also possible that two or more fingers have no separation leading to one large blob. The large blob will result in the touch being off center from the finger touching the table.

The least common hand orientation was thumb out (thumb orientation), only seen in 2 participants. The thumb orientation would result in an additional touch being detected each time the user presses the tabletop.

The spread orientation and thumb orientation can be handled with additional image processing to remove extra finger touches. In the thumb orientation, the implementation could filter out the thumb. In the spread orientation, one finger would be lower than the other fingers being spread out. The PIP distance can be used. The finger with the lower PIP will be the finger the user desires to be detected. The additional image processing would result in slow processing speed but could be implemented to allow a user to use the tabletop in the most natural manner.

We also examine which finger was used to perform the touch. The index finger was used by 91% of the participants. The remaining 9% used their middle finger. Using a threshold distance to detect a touch, the finger used would have no impact on the accuracy or performance. The use of the right hand was dominant in our study with 77% of the participants using their right hand solely. 21% of the participants used both their left hand and right hand to touch the screen and only 1% used only their left hand.

Swipe and Zoom

The swipe and zoom gestures come from the same touch screen counterparts on smartphones and tablets. With the swipe motion 57% of the participants used multiple fingers on one hand to make a quick

	Total	Male	Female
Near μ	1.75	1.95	1.52
Near σ	0.46	0.48	0.28
Center μ	1.73	1.95	1.47
Center σ	0.43	0.39	0.31
Middle μ	1.69	1.91	1.43
Middle σ	0.39	0.37	0.22
Far μ	1.55	1.77	1.29
Far σ	0.43	0.41	0.26

Table 1. DIP measurements (in cm) mean and standard deviation for different table locations

	Total	Male	Female
Near μ	3.94	4.38	3.46
Near σ	0.74	0.59	0.58
Center μ	3.79	4.10	3.42
Center σ	0.75	0.72	0.61
Middle μ	3.81	4.21	3.34
Middle σ	0.75	0.63	0.62
Far μ	3.62	3.84	3.36
Far σ	0.75	0.71	0.72

Table 2. PIP measurements (in cm) mean and standard deviation for different table locations

swipe/drag motion. The remaining 43% use only one finger to make a quick swipe/drag motion. While the one finger swipe is a natural gesture it is difficult to distinguish from a drag of an object on the screen. The best implementation would be to force all swipes to be multiple fingers.

The zoom gesture defaulted to the pinch motion found on smartphones. The only modification is that half of the participants used two hands to perform the gesture. The other half of participants used the index finger and thumb pinch on one hand. The DIP measures can still be used to determine if a touch has occurred with the thumb. The DIP threshold of the index finger measure will still contain a portion of the thumb.

DIP,PIP and MCP Measurements

The DIP, PIP and MCP measurements were all taken in metric units since the Microsoft Kinect camera presents data in metric units. We present the data for the 4 screen positions (near, center, middle, far) for males, females, and all participants. The measurements are given in Table 1 for DIP, Table 2 for PIP, and Table 3 for MCP.

The measurements show that as one would expect the size of the body between males and females to differ resulting in different hand sizes in all three joints. Our observation shows that it is best to use the mean of males instead of the overall mean in the tabletop application.

The male measurement would become the baseline value used by the detection algorithm. The male mean will cover female's mean plus one standard deviation, so almost all females will be detected. Figure 5 shows an explanation of why to use the male measurements. The males that are outside the mean will still be detected but the size of the blob will be reduced compared to those that are below the mean. If the aggregated mean of both males and females were used we will reduce the percentage of males that would have optimal detection in the system.

The standard deviation increases in size as we move higher up the hand. The increase is due to the angle that the finger is perpendicular to the table. Table 4 shows the angle of the finger for the different table locations. The mean overall all table locations is similar but the high standard deviation shows the wide variation in how people touch the table, from laying down the entire hand on the table to a near 90 degree touch.

The baseline measurement for PIP and MCP should be the male mean plus one standard deviation. No more than one standard deviation should be used so that the PIP and MCP do not overlap regions. In our study using one standard deviation we have no overlapping regions. It is important that we have three regions of the hand so that complex gestures can be examined by the tabletop system. Using this baseline a larger majority of hands would be detected. The individuals that are not detected would be self aware of the touch not being found and adjust the hand position to fit inside the scope of the baseline measurement.

The angle the finger touches the table is affected by the height of the individual, arm length of the individual, and distance the individual stood from the table. We did not ask our participants to allow us to measure height or arm length to avoid being intrusive but these

	Total	Male	Female
Near μ	6.90	7.80	5.99
Near σ	1.50	1.14	1.28
Center μ	6.57	7.25	5.77
Center σ	1.28	0.89	1.21
Middle μ	6.93	7.81	5.89
Middle σ	1.42	0.92	1.19
Far μ	6.75	7.44	5.94
Far σ	1.11	0.78	0.86

Table 3. MCP measurements (in cm) mean and standard deviation for different table locations

	Total	Male	Female
Near μ	51.12	54.06	47.81
Near σ	14.90	15.34	14.14
Center μ	44.94	49.11	40
Center σ	11.82	10.97	11.14
Middle μ	48.86	53.32	43.56
Middle σ	14.01	13.35	13.27
Far μ	45.54	48.21	42.38
Far σ	10.73	10.95	9.88

Table 4. Angle the finger touches the tabletop at different locations

measurements may be examined in the future. We measured the distance the participants stood from the table and found that males average 6.89 cm and standard deviation of 5.45 from the edge of the table and females with an average of 7.79 cm and standard deviation of 6.29. The distance from the table the participant stood ranged from 0 cm (touching the table) to 26 cm. A total of 17% of participants stood 0 cm away and were touching the table. Touching the table could have a problem with the depth camera since there is a chance loose clothing will cover the tabletop. We have experienced problems with t-shirts being detected as touches in our tabletop implementation. We have concluded that if distance from the table is a key issue the system can display a message to the user to adjust where they stand while using the tabletop.

CONCLUSION

A depth camera is a low cost solution to creating a unique tabletop interface. The optimization of the depth camera requires that detection of touches on the table must be detected using a distance from the camera to the table surface and hand. Our case study was conducted to provide quantitative analysis of the human hand over a sample population. Research can use the results in our paper to quickly calculate measurement results that can aid in the development of future tabletop implementation. Our work concludes that the male hand should be used as the baseline sample since the measurements cover the majority of female users. Using an aggregate average from males and females will result in a large number of male hands from registering poorly on the tabletop using the depth camera.

References

[1] Dippon, A., Klinder, G., KinectTouch: Accuracy Test for a Very Low-Cost 2.5D Multitouch Tracking System, Proc. ITS'2011, pp 49 – 52.

[2] Hoggan, E., Nacenta, M., Kristensson, P.O., Williamson, J., Oulasvrta, A. and Lehtio, A. Multi-Touch Pinch Gestures: Performance and Ergonomics, Proc. ITS'13, 2013.

[3] Karlson, A. and Bederson, B. ThumbSpace: Generalized One-Handed Input for Touchscreen-based Mobile Devices, INTERACT 2007, LNCS 4662, Part 1, pp 324-338, 2007.

[4] Kratz, S., Chiu, P. and Back, M. PontPose: Finger Pose Estimation for Touch Input On Mobile Devices using a Depth Sensor, Proc. ITS'13, 2013.

[5] Klompmaker, F., Nebe, K. and Fast, A. dSensingNI: a framework for advanced tangible interaction using a depth camera, Proc of TEI'12, pp 217-224.

[6] Murugappan, S. Vinayk, Elmqvist, N., and Pamani, K. Extended multitouch: recovering touch posture and differentiating users using a depth camera. Proc. UIST'12, pp 487-496.

[7] Wilson, A. TouchLight: an imaging touch screen and display for gesture-based interaction. Proc. ICMI'04. Pp 69-76. 2004.

[8] Wilson, A., Using a Depth Camera as a Touch Sensor, Proc. ITS 2010, pp 69 – 72.

Constructive Play: Designing for Role Play Stories with Interactive Play Objects

Guanyun Wang
Zhejiang University
38 Zheda Ave.
Hangzhou, 310027 China
guanyun@zju.edu.cn

Yunfan Wang
Zhejiang University
38 Zheda Ave.
Hangzhou, 310027 China
castiel.zju@gmail.com

Ye Tao
Zhejiang University
38 Zheda Ave.
Hangzhou, 310027 China
taoye@zju.edu.cn

Cheng Yao
Zhejiang University
38 Zheda Ave.
Hangzhou, 310027 China
yaoch@zju.edu.cn

Enmao Liu
Zhejiang University
38 Zheda Ave.
Hangzhou, 310027 China

Fangtian Ying
Zhejiang University
38 Zheda Ave.
Hangzhou, 310027 China
yingft@gmail.com

TEI '15, Jan 16-19 2015, Stanford, CA, USA
ACM 978-1-4503-3305-4/15/01.
http://dx.doi.org/10.1145/2677199.2687907

Abstract
Objects, whether toys or not, are likely to become the center of children's game, which can trigger children's exploration and imagination, and build the world's environmental and psychological statements by manipulating something, to enhance the autonomy of children and inspire their creativity. This paper, based on scaffolding learning theory, puts forward the learning principle of constructive play suitable for learning in play school, suitable for cognitive behaviors of children aged 5 to 8 years old, and aims to encourage children to think creatively in the course of play, rather than learning knowledge and solve problems. We redesign the images, most commonly used by children RPG storytelling, and embed interactive intelligence, to better help children play games, stimulate their imagination and creativity in storytelling, and encourage them share with their companions and parents.

Author Keywords
Role play stories; interactive objects; constructive play; creativity; design principle.

ACM Classification Keywords
H.5.2. Information interfaces and presentation (e.g., HCI): User Interfaces; Haptic I/O.

General Terms

Human Factors; Design.

Introduction

Children's behaviors in sensorimotor period, for example, interaction with objects, play an important role in cognition composition. Objects, whether toys or not, are likely to become the center of children's game, which can trigger children's exploration and imagination, and build the world's environmental and psychological statements by manipulating something, to enhance the autonomy of children and inspire their creativity. Observation and research show that in formal teaching environments, playing multiple objects aims at learning knowledge and solving problems; in informal environments, however, playing objects is often accompanied by Role Play Games (RPG) storytelling, in which one way input between objects and behaviors generates no feedback and also lacks specific principles to build the course of play, resulting in insignificant actual effect of learning and creation in play.

This paper, based on scaffolding learning theory [5], puts forward the learning principle of constructive play suitable for learning in play school, suitable for cognitive behaviors of children aged 3 to 6 years old, and aims to encourage children to think creatively in the course of play, rather than learning knowledge and solve problems. We redesign the images, most commonly used by children RPG storytelling, and embed interactive intelligence, to better help children play games, stimulate their imagination and creativity in storytelling, and encourage them share with their companions and parents.

Relevant Works

According to Piaget's theory of cognitive constitution, in the sensorimotor stage of cognition, babies can understand the world through sensory information and motor feedback [9], for instance, babies can explore the world by sucking objects, to distinguish objects that "can suck" from that "cannot suck". More neuroimaging studies also show that the sensorimotor behaviors, such as interaction with objects, play an important role in obtaining cognition [4]. Vygotsky (1978) also stressed the importance of the activities and the use of tools in the growth of children [13].

Objects, whether toys or not, are likely to become the center of children's game, which can trigger children's exploration and imagination, and build the world's environmental and psychological statements by manipulating something. For instance, Montessori believes in his educational concept that playing objects can improve autonomy and purposiveness[7]. Meanwhile, as put forward by some scholars, interactive operation can help to stimulate children's creativity [2]. However, designed cases in this aspect are limited and most of them are in formal teaching environment, such as wooden cubes [3], colored rods[6] and Beelight [12], which are for the purpose of knowledge learning and problem solving. In play in informal environment, objects are always different types of toys, including fancy toys such as electronic bricks, Topobo[8], littleBits [1], Cubelets [11] and Blockuits [10], role-playing toys such as robots, and sports toys such as toy cars, etc. In the following sections, this paper defines demand points through field research, put forward assumptions and conduct design.

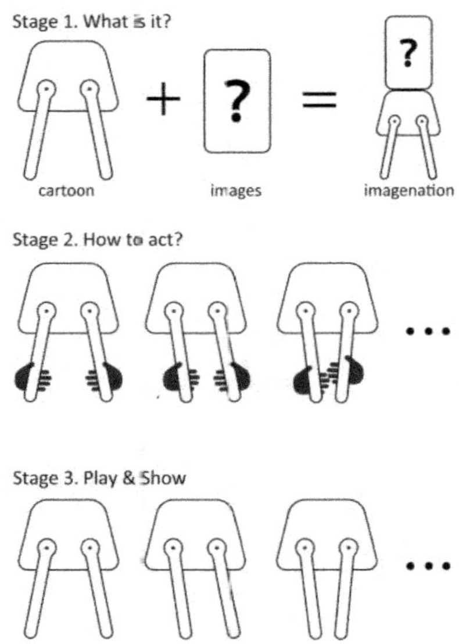

Figure 1. Constructive play for Carnoon

Design Process

We conducted field research on the daily activity arrange of a class-A kindergarten in Hangzhou and found that included in their courses are contents of learning in play, such as storytelling, toy block, role play, outdoor activities, etc. Meanwhile, we interviewed parents of 15 children aged between 5 to 8 years old about playing of their children, finding that almost all the children usually tend to do RPS with toys in their hands at home. This common way of playing is the most natural learning method, but parents haven't paid enough attention to this behavior, resulting in a lack of feedback to the one-way input between objects and behaviors specific principles to build the course of play. As a result, actual effect generated in learning and creation in play is not remarkable. Assuming that children have access to the constructive method in playing in informal environment, can they obtain better capability in cognition and creative thinking by relying on the inner connection type put forward in the scaffolding learning theory?

As mentioned above, RPS is a playing method common in informal environments. This paper, based on the scaffolding learning theory, puts forward the learning principle of constructive play suitable for learning in play school, suitable for cognitive behaviors of children aged 3 to 6 years old, and aims to encourage children to think creatively in the course of play, rather than learning knowledge and solve problems. We put forward the following design principles for constructive play focusing on RPS:

- Allow children to explore freely and lay little stress on the solutions to problems;
- Emphasize creating an environment providing multi-layout of events and opportunities for reflection;
- Create an experience that can be shared to obtain better self-motivation.

According to the above design principles, we redesign the images, most commonly used by children RPG storytelling, and embed interactive intelligence, to better help children play games, stimulate their imagination and creativity in storytelling, and encourage them share with their companions and parents.

Systematic Design

Based on the principle analysis concluded through the above research, we design Cartoon as an image for children to operate games. It aims to:

- Encourage children to imagine freely and assume Cartoon as whatever images they like;
- Create an environment for children to determine events autonomously, encourage their creative thinking, and set and record the movement directions of Cartoon repeatedly to offer opportunities for modification and reflection;
- Encourage children to share plots they design with companions or parents and acquire self-motivation in play.

As Figure 1 indicates, Cartoon owns only abstractive limbs in appearance; therefore what images it represents is totally decided by children. The main body of Cartoon is equipped with hardware, including the main Ardiuno board, rheostat, electric motor and controllable switch, which are able to detect and record track of the movement of limbs, and repeatedly play the recorded data.

The constructive play for Carnoon will broke down into three stages to support the creativity thinking, asking iterative process from "what" to "how".

In the first stage, the children use their imaginations to define what it is. Abstract modeling can motivate them to do so. This is the first step to encourage children to creative think by the freedom of imagination.

The second stage is from the static image into the dynamic behavior. Repeated operation and modify not only conducive to the creation of children's behavior, but also provide an opportunity to reflect on the game.

Knowledge achieved based on the first two phases, the third phase is an interactive behavior to communicate, rather than children's own behavior. This not only provides an opportunity to reflect on the previous behavior of children again, but let them get excited sense of achievement.

Prototype

According to design process and possible scenarios, the prototype structure and functions will be described in this section.

In the design of the prototype of Cartoon (Figure 2), replaceable image paper scraps can be set on the main body to realize the above functions; three functional buttons are set: record, reset and play. When using it, children can easily play fragments they need to record.

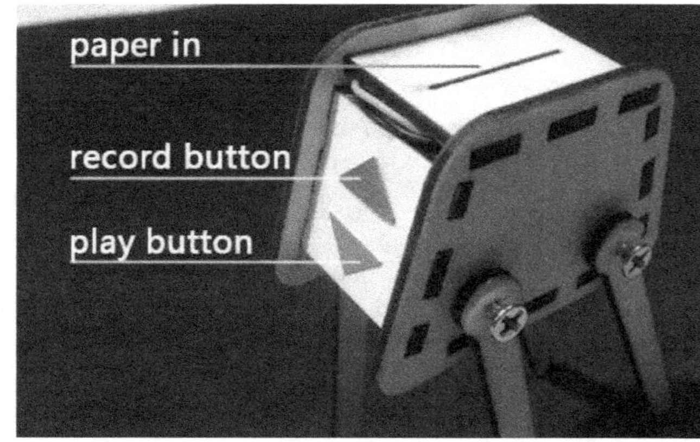

Figure 2. The prototype of Cartoon

The Cartoon body consists of two main parts: Movable limbs and hardware functionality. Movable limbs link to hardware through arbor wheels. The hardware, including the main Ardiuno board, rheostat, electric motor and controllable switch, are able to detect and record track of the movement of each limb, and repeatedly play the recorded data.

Children can operate the limbs as he imagines. Once he has a plan or any ideas, he can record the move track of each limb. Cartoon will repeatedly walk as the recorded data, to cope with children to tell stories.

Usage Scenario

We put forward the constructive play with the purpose of converting using experience from personal creation to social sharing and exerting the educational significance of game playing from the perspective of self-motivation so as to promote creative thinking of children.

Cartoon Serves as the Starting Point to Exert Children's Imagination
We encourage children to get cognition of images through experience, knowledge and impression. As Figure 3 shows, in the test, children paints different images, including true ones from their memories such as humans, animals, and imagined ones such as Ultraman and Optimus Prime.

Figure 3. Child paints different images in user test.

Cartoon Carries Self-compiled and Self-directed Plots
Interaction with children is realized through Cartoon. At the same time when children tell their self-compiled and self-directed plots, Cartoon can record tracks of movements and provide a feedback mechanism for children, helping them better indulge in the playing environment. Repeated modification stimulates children to think frequently (Figure 4).

Figure 4. Child paints different images in user test.

Cartoon Connects the Interaction between Children and Companion
We focus on activities of children following their self-behavior. Cartoon, as a derivative after the children's self-behavior, is the carrier for exchange between them and their companions. Sharing is not only self-motivation for children; at the same time, it can improve the effect of playing and strengthen children's expression ability and self-confidence. That would create a social experience that can be shared to obtain better self-motivation.

Children will play his animated film, while may get evaluated from companions. This communication and interaction will lead to the child's further reflect thinking, and continue to modify animated content. This iterative process of thinking is the basis for creative thinking.

Discussion and Future Work
Through research, design and preliminary user test, we find there are still some problems and limitations with the prototype. At present, when it goes to the second

phase of storytelling, children often forget to press the record button, which affect implementation of follow-up functions.

In the follow-up work, we hope to add some visual digital scenes which can remind recording when helping children create. Also, these scenes can help Cartoon objects better integrate into the environment and acquire a better effect of indulgence in games.

Conclusion

Considering that children can seldom exert the real effect of learning and creation in playing objects, we creatively put forward the constructive play principle, explore the function and form of interactive objects and conduct preliminary tests. The results prove feasibility of the assumption and indicate improvements we need to make. In the future, we are to continue to explore the relationship between operation of interactive objects and self-creation of children. More user tests will help us find out more demand points and better designs.

Acknowledgments

This project was carried out on the workshop organized by Zhejiang University. We thank to children who have participated our design process. The project is supported by National Key Technology R&D Program (Grant No. 2013BAH59F00) and Zhejiang Provincial Key Technology R&D Program (Grant No. 2014C31047 & No. 2014R401264).

References

[1] Bdeir, A. Electronics as material: littleBits. In *Proc. TEI 2009*, ACM Press (2009), 397-400.

[2] Decortis, F., Rubegni, E., Tillon, A. B., & Ackermann, E. Interactive technologies that enhance children's creativity. In *Proc. IDC 2013*, ACM Press (2013) 596-599.

[3] Freer Weiss, D. M. Keeping It Real: The Rationale for Using Manipulatives in the Middle Grades. *Mathematics Teaching in the Middle school 11*, 5(2006), 238-242.

[4] Goswami, U. C. Cognitive development: The learning brain. Psychology Press (2008).

[5] Johansson, M. The work in the classroom for sloyd. *Idskrift 2006*, 153.

[6] Moyer, P. S. Are we having fun yet? How teachers use manipulatives to teach mathematics. *Educational Studies in Mathematics 47*, 2(2001), 175-197.

[7] O'Malley, C. & Stanton-Fraser, D. Literature review in learning with tangible technologies. *Bristol: Nesta FutureLab Series, report 12* (2004).

[8] Parkes, A. J., Raffle, H. S., & Ishii, H. Topobo in the wild: longitudinal evaluations of educators appropriating a tangible interface. *In Proceedings of the SIGCHI Conference on Human Factors in Computing Systems*, ACM Press (2008), 1129-1138.

[9] Piaget, J. The construction of reality in the child (Vol. 82). Routledge (2013).

[10] Prachanronarong, P. Blockuits: innovating building blocks. *In Proc. IDC 2013*, ACM Press (2013), 519-522.

[11] Schweikardt, E. Modular robotics studio. *In Proc. TEI 2011*, ACM Press (2011), 353-356.

[12] Shen, Y., Qiu, Y., Li, K., & Liu, Y. Beelight: helping children discover colors. *In Proc. IDC 2013*, ACM Press (2013), 301-304.

[13] Vygotsky, L.S. Mind in society: The development of higher psychological processes. Cambridge, MA: Harvard University Press (1978).

Time and Design: Seven Sensitivities

Verena Fuchsberger
Christian Doppler Laboratory for "Contextual Interfaces"
ICT&S Center, University of Salzburg, Austria
verena.fuchsberger@sbg.ac.at

Martin Murer
Christian Doppler Laboratory for "Contextual Interfaces"
ICT&S Center, University of Salzburg, Austria
martin.murer@sbg.ac.at

Manfred Tscheligi
Christian Doppler Laboratory for "Contextual Interfaces"
ICT&S Center, University of Salzburg, Austria
manfred.tscheligi@sbg.ac.at

TEI '15, Jan 16-19 2015, Stanford, CA, USA
ACM 978-1-4503-3305-4/15/01.
http://dx.doi.org/10.1145/2677199.2687911

Abstract
In this work in progress, we present a set of seven design sensitivities, which address *time* in interaction design. We exemplarily illustrate how time affects and is affected by tangible, embodied, or embedded artifacts. Thereby, we discuss slow versus fast technology, time as context of use, time as theme, time as content, ephemerality, historicality, and chronology. Those design sensitivities are an initial step towards a framing of the different notions and aspects in regards to time in interaction design.

Author Keywords
Time; Design Space; Interactive Artifacts; Tangible Interaction

ACM Classification Keywords
H.5.m [Information interfaces and presentation (e.g., HCI)]: Miscellaneous.

General Terms
Design, Theory

Introduction
In literature on interaction design, a variety of notions of *time* are described, ranging from ephemeral interfaces [5] to becomingness of materials [3] to designing for temporal events such as Christmas [16] to artistic installations that

turn book pages dependent on the time of day [15]. In this work-in-progress, we aim to sketch a design space of interactive system design that is determined and inspired by notions of time.

Certainly, there is a huge body of knowledge on temporal aspects in several design disciplines. However, for this discussion, we refer to, and aim to contribute to, interactive systems design, as it is, per se, concerned with time. According to Vallgårda [19], form-giving practices not only relate to the physical form and the interaction gestalt, but necessarily include the design of the temporal form of computational things, i.e., its ability to change between states. This trinity of form-giving, and the constant negotiation between the three elements (temporal form, physical form and interaction gestalt) is what Vallgårda considers as the core of interaction design practice. The physical form needs to express the temporal form, which, in turn, must unfold within the limitations of the physical form, both intending to create the interaction gestalt. Temporal expressions are not limited to interactive artifacts, as, e.g., patina or oxidation may affect physical materials as well [19], but, in contrast to interactive artifacts, they are not necessarily a substantial part of the artifact.

In addition to this notion of time, which characterizes every interaction design practice, we present in the following design sensitivities of a "temporal design space". As time is relevant in a vast variety of ways and phases in the design, we draw on the notion of *design sensitivities*. According to Ciolfi [4], design sensitivities aim to suggest relevant issues and inspire creative design by defining spaces for discussion on how interaction design could deal with issues they express, instead of imposing predetermined solutions. Thus, by summarizing relevant issues and notions of time in interaction design as design sensitivities, we aim to contribute to a framing of notions of time, i.e., how time influences interaction design and how interaction design influences time.

Design Sensitivities Regarding Time

Certainly, the sensitivities presented in this paper are not a complete list. Instead, it is an attempt to pay attention to how time can be designed for, used in design, or how it is constraining the design of interactive artifacts. The order of the design sensitivities does not indicate their importance. Instead, they aim to provide a set of reference points, which may be considered separately or in combination for a given design goal. Each of the following subchapters includes a description of the the design sensitivity, complemented with examples and notions from tangible, embodied, or embedded interactions.

Slow versus Fast Technology

Hallnäs and Redström considered time technology as technology expressing the *presence* of time, emphasizing the aesthetics of the materials. They reflected on time by means of slow technology, i.e., technology that stretches time and slows things down. Their examples of slow technology artifacts are not intended to be "used", but part of an environment by adding to its ambience and supporting activities. Odom and colleagues recently introduced the photobox, which is an example for a slow technology. The photobox is a technology for people's homes that prints out randomly selected photos (from the individuals' flickr accounts) at random time intervals. The idea was to slow down the consumption of digital photos and provide pauses for reflection on archived photos [13].

The notion of slow technology contrasts fast technology, which is primarily characterized by efficiency, aiming to take away time. For instance, the Tangible Bots [14] are active, motorized tangibles for interaction with tangible tabletop interfaces, which allowed users to complete movement tasks significantly faster than with passive tangibles [14]. In a CHI workshop in 2004 on "time design", also time as a design feature has been discussed, e.g., response delays, temporal errors, or temporal control [8], indicating issues of fast technology.

An interactive artifact may be sensitive to time in terms of slowness of interaction, i.e., ranging from an emphasis on slow, aesthetic interactions to time-efficient interactions.

Time as Context of Use
Petrelli and colleagues [16] specifically designed Christmas artifacts (e.g., a social Advent calendar that can be shared remotely), trying to augment the experience of a special time of the year. They argue that specificity is essential to convey the feeling of a special occasion, which technology must enable. Another temporal context of use has been described by March et al. [10] by discussing "interaction in the dark", i.e., how designing for interactions at night and the resulting darkness differs from designing for daytime use.

An interactive artifact may be sensitive to the actual time that it is meant to be used in, i.e., times of the day, month, year, or special occasions.

Time as Exclusive Theme
Time can also be the *primary theme* of a technology or an interaction, i.e., the pure purpose of an artifact is to convey time. For instance, Petkov [15] introduced the artwork "A Day in A Life", where he uses an empty book as an intuitive, non-numerical and non-symbolical time display. Thereby, book pages are flipped automatically via an airflow from sunrise to sunset, i.e., from the first page of the book to the last. Bakker and colleagues [1] also designed an artifact that aimed to provide peripheral time awareness for schools, i.e., "CawClock". Among other features, this clock provided tangible tokens, which teachers could use to refer to if pupils did not know how to read the time yet.

An interactive artifact may be sensitive to time as its exclusive theme, i.e., the artifact's purpose is to (visually, tangibly) convey or facilitate reflection on time.

Time as Content
In a variety of interactive artifacts, *timelines* play an essential role, e.g., in interactions with temporal data such as audio and video editing. For instance, Bennett and colleagues [2] presented ChronoTape, an example of a temporal tangible interface. ChronoTape was designed to enable a tangible representation and control of time, which supports and reveals the valuable personal production of family history research as it captures individual annotations in a tangible form. Another form of time as content has been provided by Neustaedter et al. [11], who focused on coordination and awareness through calendars for families. These calendars should structure family activities by notions of days, weeks, months, or years, in which events may be recorded with associated dates or times.

An interactive artifact may be sensitive to temporal data, i.e., it provides ways to interact with topics or content structured along timelines.

Becomingness vs. Ephemerality
Regarding design materials, not only physical materials are affected by time (e.g., patina), but also "smart" materials are subject to temporality. Bergström and colleagues [3] provided the notion of becomingness of materials, i.e.,

things become materials only over time and in the context, either during the design or usage. It is the "transformation of material expression resulting from continuous negotiation with, and within, a given context." [3, p. 158].

In contrast to becomingness of materials, Döring and colleagues [5] presented the concept of ephemeral user interfaces (UIs), i.e., UI elements are intentionally created to last for a limited time only (e.g., water, fire or water bubbles). They argue that humans enjoy ephemeral events (such as ice sculptures), and, thus, transfer this concept to UI design. The limited durability of a – situated – interface is determined by its intrinsic material properties, and the ephemeral materials are assumed to evoke a rich and multisensory experience for the users [5]. In the same vein, Seah et al. [18] presented SensaBubble, a chrono-sensory mid-air display system, which generates scented bubbles that carry information. The temporality of these interfaces is constituted of two forms of persistence, i.e., a projection on the bubbles as visual display until the bubbles burst, and a scent that is released upon bursting. Thereby, they connect tangibility (bursting the bubbles with one's fingers) with ephemerality and multi-sensory experiences [18].

An interactive artifact may be sensitive to time in regards to the temporality of the materials and UIs, ranging from becomingness of materials (becoming materials over time and in the context) to ephemerality of a UI, i.e., how UIs change or vanish over time (lasting for a limited period of time) based on designers', users' or the materials' behavior.

Historicality

Rosner and colleagues [17] introduced an analytic category to theorize materiality, i.e., material traces that reflect skills, use, and time. Material traces of time, for instance, reflect the passage of time and non-human interaction, carrying the "histories" of objects and interaction. The identification of (forward and backward) traces enables to reflect on how time influences a design process to understand better what happens to the materials during the design. Referring to skeuomorphs, Gross et al. [7] traced how holdovers from previous functional material requirements pertain to the design of tangible interactions. They present, among others, an example of an iTypewriter that carries essential characteristics of a mechanical typewriter, both requiring the same interaction, one on paper, the other one on an iPad. The evolution of these skeuomorphs may be style-borrowing (e.g., holdovers in terms of aesthetic qualities), style-mediating (e.g., using similar metaphors for different "materials", such as GUI and TUI) or function-giving (e.g., reapplying functions).

An interactive artifact may be sensitive to preceding time, i.e., incorporating histories of the materials, styles, or functions.

Chronology

Regarding the chronology of time, Lundgren [9] proposed a vocabulary that describes how software can "use" time or sequences of events. Along with a variety of examples, she illustrates different sequential possibilities in form of what she calls *temporal themes*, from live time (now, continuous flow in normal pace, events in sequential order), to real time (continuous flow in normal pace, events in sequential order), sequential events (events in original order, but potentially missing events), disordered events (events in any order, some may be missing), or branched versions (events in any order, some may be missing, alternate sequences). These themes aim to support the analysis, discussion, and design.

An additional notion of chronology may be found in collaborative environments. The distinction between synchronous versus asynchronous interactions is crucial when it comes the purpose of interactions. For instance, Nitsche and Kirschner [12] presented a hybrid interface design for distinct creative practices in real-time 3D filmmaking, aiming to allow real-time collaboration with different practices and control schemas at the same time.

An interactive artifact may be sensitive to how temporal events are arranged, i.e., sequential arrangements of events (chronological order vs. any other ordering principle), or synchronous or asynchronous interactions.

Discussion and Conclusion

All the aforementioned design sensitivities address different dimensions of time, some of them "using" time as a form of material, some considering time a characteristic of the context, etc. Interaction design's practice of working not only with physical, but also with digital material, requires to design not only the physical form but also the temporal form of interactive artifacts. Therefore, time may be understood as a material, which concerns the computation activity itself, its physical representation, or the user's interaction subsequent to the design process.

Having provided a first set of respective design sensitivities, the next steps will be to extend this set and interrelate the sensitivities. For instance, we aim to discuss how they match to models of interaction design practices, e.g., Vallgårda's trinity of forms (temporal form, physical form, and Interaction Gestalt) [19]. Additionally, we aim to reflect on how time not only is related to design practice, but also to usage, drawing on Fuchsberger and colleagues' notion of networks between materials, interaction gestalt, interactive artifacts, designers, and users [6]. All these efforts aim to contribute to a better understanding of how design affects and is affected by temporal aspects, and to increase a respective awareness in the design of interactive artifacts.

Acknowledgements

The financial support by the Austrian Federal Ministry of Science, Research and Economy and the National Foundation for Research, Technology and Development is gratefully acknowledged (Christian Doppler Laboratory for"Contextual Interfaces").

References

[1] Bakker, S., van den Hoven, E., Eggen, B., and Overbeeke, K. Exploring peripheral interaction design for primary school teachers. In *Proceedings of the Sixth International Conference on Tangible, Embedded and Embodied Interaction*, TEI '12, ACM (New York, NY, USA, 2012), 245–252.

[2] Bennett, P., Fraser, M., and Balaam, M. Chronotape: Tangible timelines for family history. In *Proceedings of the Sixth International Conference on Tangible, Embedded and Embodied Interaction*, TEI '12, ACM (New York, NY, USA, 2012), 49–56.

[3] Bergström, J., Clark, B., Frigo, A., Mazé, R., Redström, J., and Vallgårda, A. Becoming materials: material forms and forms of practice. *Digital Creativity 21*, 3 (2010), 155–172.

[4] Ciolfi, L. *Situating" place" in interaction design: enhancing the user experience in interactive environments*. PhD thesis, University of Limerick Limerick, 2004.

[5] Döring, T., Sylvester, A., and Schmidt, A. A design space for ephemeral user interfaces. In *Proc. TEI'13*, ACM (2013), 75–82.

[6] Fuchsberger, V., Murer, M., and Tscheligi, M. Materials, materiality, and media. In *Proceedings of the SIGCHI Conference on Human Factors in Computing Systems*, CHI '13, ACM (New York, NY, USA, 2013), 2853–2862.

[7] Gross, S., Bardzell, J., and Bardzell, S. Skeu the evolution: Skeuomorphs, style, and the material of tangible interactions. In *Proceedings of the 8th International Conference on Tangible, Embedded and Embodied Interaction*, TEI '14, ACM (New York, NY, USA, 2013), 53–60.

[8] Hildebrandt, M., Dix, A., and Meyer, H. A. Time design. In *CHI '04 Extended Abstracts on Human Factors in Computing Systems*, CHI EA '04, ACM (New York, NY, USA, 2004), 1737–1738.

[9] Lundgren, S. Toying with time: Considering temporal themes in interactive artifacts. In *Proceedings of the SIGCHI Conference on Human Factors in Computing Systems*, CHI '13, ACM (New York, NY, USA, 2013), 1639–1648.

[10] March, W., Nafus, D., Swan, L., and Taylor, A. S. Night and darkness: Interaction after dark. In *CHI '08 Extended Abstracts on Human Factors in Computing Systems*, CHI EA '08, ACM (New York, NY, USA, 2008), 3985–3988.

[11] Neustaedter, C., Brush, A. J. B., and Greenberg, S. The calendar is crucial: Coordination and awareness through the family calendar. *ACM Trans. Comput.-Hum. Interact. 16*, 1 (Apr. 2009), 6:1–6:48.

[12] Nitsche, M., and Kirschner, F. Hybrid interface design for distinct creative practices in real-time 3d filmmaking. In *Proceedings of the 7th International Conference on Tangible, Embedded and Embodied Interaction*, TEI '13, ACM (New York, NY, USA, 2013), 303–306.

[13] Odom, W. T., Sellen, A. J., Banks, R., Kirk, D. S., Regan, T., Selby, M., Forlizzi, J. L., and Zimmerman, J. Designing for slowness, anticipation and re-visitation: A long term field study of the photobox. In *Proceedings of the 32Nd Annual ACM Conference on Human Factors in Computing Systems*, CHI '14, ACM (New York, NY, USA, 2014), 1961–1970.

[14] Pedersen, E. W., and Hornbæk, K. Tangible bots: Interaction with active tangibles in tabletop interfaces. In *Proceedings of the SIGCHI Conference on Human Factors in Computing Systems*, CHI '11, ACM (New York, NY, USA, 2011), 2975–2984.

[15] Petkov, I. A day in a life. In *Proceedings of the 8th International Conference on Tangible, Embedded and Embodied Interaction*, TEI '14, ACM (New York, NY, USA, 2013), 325–326.

[16] Petrelli, D., Bowen, S., Dulake, N., and Light, A. Digital christmas: an exploration of festive technology. In *Proceedings of the Designing Interactive Systems Conference*, ACM (2012), 348–357.

[17] Rosner, D. K., Ikemiya, M., Kim, D., and Koch, K. Designing with traces. In *Proceedings of the SIGCHI Conference on Human Factors in Computing Systems*, CHI '13, ACM (New York, NY, USA, 2013), 1649–1658.

[18] Seah, S. A., Martinez Plasencia, D., Bennett, P. D., Karnik, A., Otrocol, V. S., Knibbe, J., Cockburn, A., and Subramanian, S. Sensabubble: A chrono-sensory mid-air display of sight and smell. In *Proceedings of the 32Nd Annual ACM Conference on Human Factors in Computing Systems*, CHI '14, ACM (New York, NY, USA, 2014), 2863–2872.

[19] Vallgårda, A. Giving form to computational things: Developing a practice of interaction design. *Personal Ubiquitous Comput. 18*, 3 (Mar. 2014), 577–592.

Caret Manipulation using Deformable Input in Mobile Devices

Alexander Keith Eady
Carleton University
Ottawa, Ontario
K1S 5B6, Canada
alexeady@cmail.carleton.ca

Audrey Girouard
Carleton University
Ottawa, Ontario
K1S 5B6, Canada
audrey.girouard@carleton.ca

TEI'15, January 15–19, 2015, Stanford, California, USA.
ACM 978-1-4503-3305-4/15/01.
http://dx.doi.org/10.1145/2677199.2687916

Abstract
Caret movement is difficult with touch input because of finger occlusion and the imprecision of interacting with a small display using fingers. We hypothesize that bend might provide a better text manipulation solution. We propose bend gestures to move a single caret or dual carets without requiring hand repositioning. We create a deformable prototype and implement the gestures. We present our bend interactions for caret manipulation and discuss our prototype.

Author Keywords
Deformable User Interface; Flexible Display; Bend Gesture; Caret; Mobile Device

ACM Classification Keywords
H.5.2. Information interfaces and presentation: *User Interfaces – Interaction styles, user-centered design*.

Introduction
Text selection and manipulation can be difficult on mobile devices. These actions require a detailed positioning of the caret on the screen, but thumb and finger occlusion makes this task particularly difficult [7]. Users find it hard to interpret where the caret will be positioned based on the touch event, and misread touches can cause the point of focus to jump or trigger word selection. Researchers and developers have

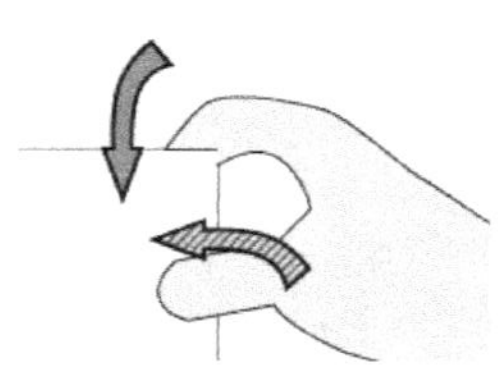

Figure 1. Detectable edges of corner bends (vertical in red, and horizontal in shaded yellow), bi-directionally.

created software solutions such as magnifying tools [7], but they create text occlusion.

We propose that bend gestures offer an opportunity to overcome this weakness of touch interactions for caret manipulation. While Schwesig et al. [6] have found bend interactions not to be suitable for complex tasks such as text entry, Ahmaniemi et al. [1] illustrated that they are best for continuous bipolar parameters, such as the directional movement of a text caret. Bend gestures have the advantage of eliminating finger occlusion on the task. Hence, we believe that they can be useful for micro-interactions such as caret placement by providing precise, occlusion-free, interactions.

In this work in progress, we present our bend interactions techniques for caret and text manipulation, as well as the deformable prototype we designed for single or dual caret manipulation that does not require hand repositioning. We discuss initial observations and future work.

Related Works

Schwesig et al. [6] developed a bendable device called Gummi. They used this prototype to demonstrate that users can quickly discover and learn bend interactions when they apply real-world metaphors to the mapping of gestures. The authors developed two text input systems, one layered and one using a nested grid. Both proved to be ineffective to enter any substantial amount of text.

PaperPhone [4] found that bend interactions are useful in user interface where directionality is involved: directionality links the direction of the bend (up/down) with the action that happens on the display (moving left or right). FlexView [2] corroborated this result. BendFlip [9] demonstrated that bend gestures can replace simple interactions, like button clicks. Finally, Kildal et al. [3] discussed the concept of discrete and continuous gestures applied to deformation gestures. They propose that continuous gestures are suited for the control of the magnitude of a parameter. This was confirmed by a follow up study [1].

Much of the work on deformable user interaction focusses on addressing the shortcomings, imprecision and screen occlusion of touch interactions. However, complex tasks, like text entry, have either been avoided or found inappropriate for deformable interactions. Other than Gummi [6], no other prior work that we could find explored text input or manipulation using deformable input.

Text Manipulation Interaction Techniques

We believe that bend gestures can be useful in text interactions in mobile devices. They can offer interactions techniques similar to the keyboard's directional arrows, to augment text manipulation.

For our text manipulation interaction techniques, we created an intuitive interaction language which makes use of the location, direction, and the edge of the device's corner, as described by Warren et al. [8]. The edge component of our language allows us to manipulate each top corner in four ways, more than the typical corner (Figure 1). This offers the advantage of not having to frequently reposition the hands during text manipulation.

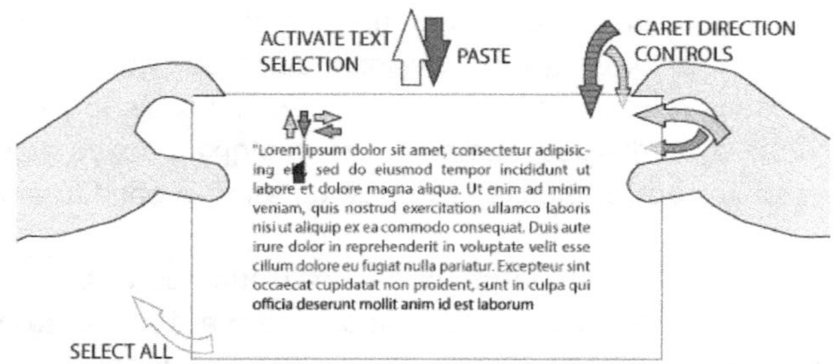

Figure 2. Gestures for single caret control.

Caret Placement: Single Caret

The gestural affordances of the prototype let us control the movement of the text caret through the manipulation of a single upper corner (Figure 2). Bending the right upper corner horizontally upwards moves the caret left and a horizontal downwards bend moves it right (yellow and green respectively in Figure 2). A vertical upwards bend moves the caret downwards, whereas a vertical downwards bend moves the caret up (red/blue). The gestures design follows a push-pull model: an up bend pushes the caret and a down bend pulls the caret. By controlling caret placement from the device's corner, no screen occlusion occurs, allowing unimpaired interaction.

Text Selection: Dual Caret

The true strength of granting caret control through the manipulation of a single corner comes when more complex text manipulation tasks are required. Text selection requires marking a range of text. Delimiting the selected text on a mobile device requires two carets, one starting and one ending, both of which require control. When controlling dual carets (Figure 3), the left upper corner controls the starting caret and the right upper corner controls the end caret. This mapping

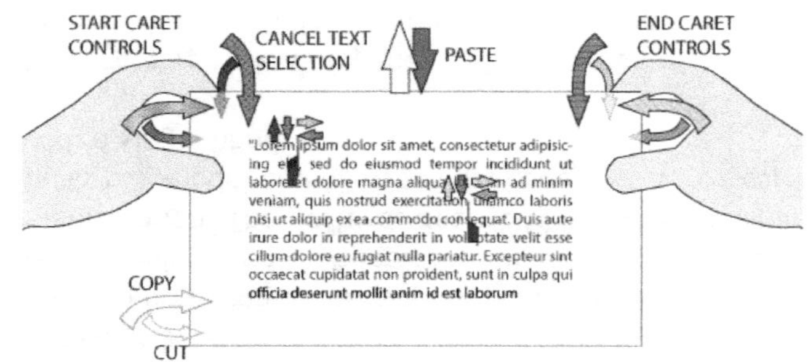

Figure 3. Gestures for dual caret control.

follows the left to right progression of reading in Western languages.

Additional Controls

However, text manipulation requires further functionality; we mapped additional controls to the upper edge of the device and the bottom left corner (Figure 2 and Figure 3). Bending the upper edge requires that both upper corners be activated simultaneously. Bending the edge upwards activates and deactivates text selection. A downwards bend of the same edge allows copied text to be pasted. While text selection is active, an upwards bend of the bottom left corner copies the selected text and a downwards bend cuts it. When text selection is not active, bending the bottom corner selects all the text in the document.

The gesture design allows the caret manipulation to occur without re-gripping. However, other text manipulations (copy, cut, or select all) require the left hand to re-grip. Likewise, transitioning in and out of text selection or pasting text require a coordinated bend of both corners in the same direction. These gestures reduce the likelihood of accidental activation.

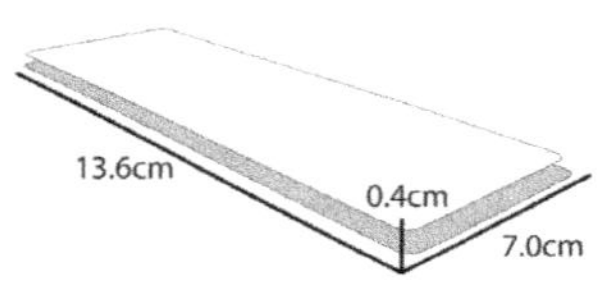

Figure 4. Device dimensions.

Figure 5. Prototype circuit with six bi-directional sensors.

Our Deformable Prototype

We designed our prototype to allow the recording of fine corner deformations. Our prototype involves a fully deformable silicon body with an embedded flexible circuit that incorporates bi-directional bend sensors located in each corner. We followed the design process outlined by Lo and Girouard [5] and modified their fabrication technique.

Our prototype is 13.6 cm x 7.0 cm x 0.4 cm, approximating the size of the average smartphone (Figure 4). We use six bidirectional 1-inch Flexpoint sensors in the device: two sensors are nested in each of the top corners, each parallel to a side, and one sensor in each of the bottom corners (Figure 5).

The flexible circuit was etched into copper clad laminate sheeting, with the circuit marked using a solid ink printer. The bi-directional bend sensors were attached using crimp connectors, with a layer of flexible conductive tape between the circuit and the sensor ensuring an uninterrupted connection even under large deformations of the device. The small connection point created by the crimp connectors allows the entire device to be bent freely in any direction.

We applied a 2mm layer of 60A silicon to the reverse side of the flexible circuit, and another separate 2mm layer of silicon serves to cover the circuit and sensors. The silicon serves as a surface for display, we use a micro projector to cast an image on the prototype to mimic a flexible display.

An 8-pin connector located on the edge of the device allows it to connect to an Arduino Uno, which interprets the sensor data as discrete gestures. The Arduino recognizes any individual sensor activation beyond a certain threshold as a discrete activation. The directionality of the deformation allows each individual sensor to be mapped to two gestures, for a total of 12 gestures. The device also allows deformations that activate multiple sensors, such as bends that affect an entire edge of the device, allowing 14 additional gestures using sensor pairs, for a total of 26. The gestures are used to control the caret in a simple text editor program that allows the basic text manipulations that can be found on mobile devices.

While our current prototype does not include a display, we plan on projecting our user interface on the prototype.

Discussion

Though text entry is better handled by touch than by bend input [6], the ability of deformable interactions address the weaknesses of touch interactions in text manipulation has not been fully explored. In this work in progress, we proposed bend gestures to manipulate the caret in text editors. Our interaction techniques offer no occlusion of the display, minimal hand repositioning, and both intuitive single and dual caret manipulation. The gestures described follow an intuitive push-pull model and allow for the control of a text caret with a single hand.

Our prototype allows for the implementation of deformable interactions as a medium for text manipulation. In addition, there remains room to further expand the interactions explored, with only 14 of a possible 26 single and paired sensor combinations currently mapped to gestures. We are planning a full scale user study using the prototype to evaluate the benefits of text manipulation using bend gestures. We plan on comparing the performance of bend gestures with touch input in single and dual caret manipulation.

One consideration is that current touch applications for mobile devices allow single-handed text entry and manipulation, our current design is formulated around a two-handed interaction with the device. The feasibility of such interactions remains unexplored. The configuration of this device may allow for such inquiry.

Overall, we believe that deformable interactions show promise as a means of overcoming the limitations of touch on mobile devices and can offer a simpler, more intuitive means performing tasks that require precise control.

Acknowledgments

This work was supported and funded by the National Sciences and Engineering Research Council of Canada through a Discovery Grant (402494/2011).

References

1. Ahmaniemi, T., Kildal, J., and Haveri, M. What is a device bend gesture really good for? *Proc. CHI*, (2014), 3503–3512.

2. Burstyn, J., Banerjee, A., and Vertegaal, R. FlexView: An Evaluation of Depth Navigation on Deformable Mobile Devices. *Proc. TEI*, (2012), 193–200.

3. Kildal, J., Paasovaara, S., and Aaltonen, V. Kinetic Device : Designing Interactions with a Deformable Mobile Interface. *Proc. CHI EA*, (2012), 1871–1876.

4. Lahey, B., Girouard, A., Burleson, W., and Vertegaal, R. PaperPhone: Understanding the Use of Bend Gestures in Mobile Devices with Flexible Electronic Paper Displays. *Proc. CHI*, (2011), 1303–1312.

5. Lo, J. and Girouard, A. Fabricating Bendy: Design and Development of Deformable Prototypes. *IEEE Pervasive Special Issue on Fabrication and Printing 13*, 3 (2014), 40–46.

6. Schwesig, C., Poupyrev, I., and Mori, E. Gummi: A Bendable Computer. *Proc. CHI*, (2004), 263–270.

7. Vogel, D. and Baudisch, P. Shift: a technique for operating pen-based interfaces using touch. *Proc. CHI*, (2007), 657–666.

8. Warren, K., Lo, J., Vadgama, V., and Girouard, A. Bending the Rules: Bend Gesture Classification for Flexible Displays. *Proc. CHI*, (2013).

9. Wightman, D., Ginn, T., and Vertegaal, R. BendFlip: Examining Input Techniques for Electronic Book Readers with Flexible Form Factors. *Proc. INTERACT*, (2011), 117–133.

Empathy Objects: Robotic Devices as Conversation Companions

Oren Zuckerman
Media Innovation Lab
School of Communication
IDC Herzliya
P.O.Box 167, Herzliya 46150
ISRAEL
orenz@idc.ac.il

Guy Hoffman
Media Innovation Lab
School of Communication
IDC Herzliya
P.O.Box 167, Herzliya 46150
ISRAEL
hoffman@idc.ac.il

TEI '15, Jan 16-19 2015, Stanford, CA, USA
ACM 978-1-4503-3305-4/15/01.
http://dx.doi.org/10.1145/2677199.2688805

Abstract
We present the notion of Empathy Objects, ambient robotic devices accompanying human-human interaction. Empathy Objects respond to human behavior using physical gestures as nonverbal expressions of their "emotional states". The goal is to increase people's self-awareness to the emotional state of others, leading to behavior change. We demonstrate an Empathy Object prototype, Kip1, a conversation companion designed to promote non-aggressive conversation between people.

Author Keywords
Tangible interfaces; social robots; behavior change; companion devices; ambient devices.

ACM Classification Keywords
H.5.m. Information interfaces and presentation (e.g., HCI): Miscellaneous.

Introduction
When people interact, they are often unaware or only partially aware of the effect their behavior has on others. To address this issue, we propose the notion of *Empathy Objects*: Interactive robotic devices that reflect aspects of the human-human interaction around them, in real-time, through subtle physical gestures.

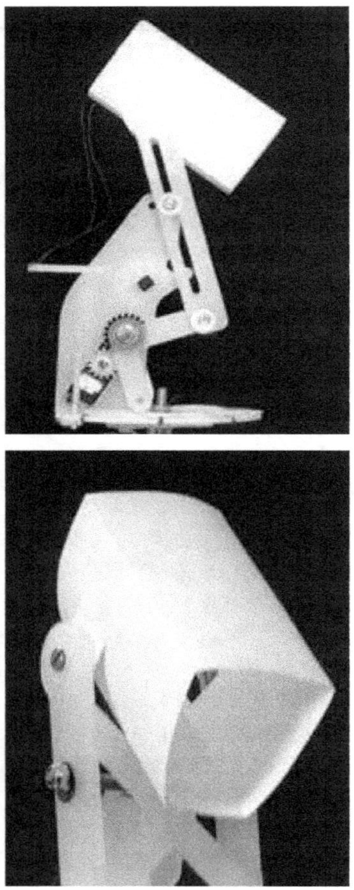

Figure 1. Kip1 our first Empathy Object, shown in a cowering position indicating fear by lowering its "head".

Empathy Objects differ from much of human-computer and human-robot interaction, which is concerned with either the direct interaction between people and technology, or with the technology serving as a communication medium between humans. In contrast, Empathy Objects are designed to peripherally supplement human face-to-face interaction. They are built to subtly influence and enhance it, rather than replace it, mediate it, or distract from it. Empathy Objects thus can also be thought of as a kind of embodied ambient interface for multiple co-located interacting users.

We exemplify our notion of Empathy Objects by presenting the Kip1 prototype. Kip1 is a robotic object listening in on people's conversation. Kip1 was designed to promote calm, non-aggressive conversation between people. The robotic object is designed as a small desktop structure, reminiscent of a lamp (Fig. 1).

When a conversation is taking place near Kip1, it monitors the nonverbal content of the conversation, e.g., speech timing, silences, and loudness. Kip1 tracks the conversation state, and maintains an internal emotional model of its reaction to the conversation. This internal state is then reflected using physical gestures, designed to evoke empathy among the human conversants and hopefully promote a change in their conversation style.

Kip1 exemplifies Shaer and Hornecker's TUI principle of "providing tangible representation to digital information" [18]. The robot's physical gestures are tangible representations of its emotional model, which is the digital information reflecting the conversation happening around the device. Kip1 also follows the Objects for Change [22] principles of implementing established behavior change techniques in the design of a TUI device.

In our first implementation, Kip1 tracks speaking vs. silent segments, and the ongoing and incidental loudness of the conversants. If there is no ongoing conversation, Kip1 is in a calm state, indicated by slow, deep "breathing" gestures. If an ongoing conversation is at a medium or soft level, Kip1 gradually shows curious interest by stretching upwards. If, however, the conversation becomes too loud—interpreted as aggression—Kip1 retracts into a cowering position and indicates fear by shivering and lowering its "head" towards the ground.

Related Work

Kip1 can be thought of simultaneously as an ambient kinetic tangible, a socially expressive robot, and a conversation monitoring interface, and thus relates to these three domains.

Ambient interfaces and kinetic tangibles

Ambient interfaces use visual and auditory cues designed to be processed at the periphery or "background of awareness" [12]. AmbientROOM, for example, is an architectural space displaying data via simulated ripples of water or light patches [12]. In the Water Lamp and Pinwheels projects, subtle changes in light, sound, and movement represent digital information in an ambient way [5]. While AmbientROOM and Water Lamp use projection of light, Pinwheels uses tangible representation, made of folding fiberglass and small motors, mapping digital information to physical motion, thus being a "kinetic tangible". Kip1 continues this tradition, but in addition monitors real-time local information. For a review of "kinetic tangibles" from the early Pinwheels to recent work, see: Ishii *et al.* [13].

Robotic nonverbal expressions of emotional state
Socially interactive robots use both verbal and nonverbal channels in order to express their emotional state. In fact, Fong *et al.* describe the capability to express emotions as one of the indicators of socially interactive robots [7]. In anthropomorphic robots, facial expressions are often used to express emotions, either on a screen [8, 16] or using actuated facial features [1, 4, 15]. Robots that do not have an expressive face or are non-anthropomorphic can use gestures to express emotions [2, 10]. For some robots that have no social articulation at all, such as flying robots, path planning has been used to express emotions [19]. These systems are used either for direct human-robot interaction, or for entertainment robotics. Our work differs as we use the robot's nonverbal expression as an ambient companion to human-human interaction.

Technology mediated conversation
Prior work in technologies that mediate conversation are usually screen based technologies. DiMicco *et al.* used a shared display in a group interaction, showing how much each participant contributed to the conversation [6]. A similar study by Bergstrom and Karahalios used a "conversation clock" screen that visualized the time each participant talked [3]. In contrast, our system does not use screens, but ambient embodied gestures, a tangible modality.

The Kip1 Prototype: System Design

From a technical point of view, Kip1 is a two degree-of-freedom robotic object using a smartphone as its main sensing and computing hardware [9]. A IOIO microcontroller board links the smartphone to two servo motors, driving a number of mechanical linkages designed to express the robot's gestures. In order to maintain the focus of Kip1's users on each other, our design process refrained from using screens as part of the interaction paradigm. Kip1 is similar to some other recent desktop robots that use mobile devices as their sensor and processing platform [9, 14]. Usually the screen shows expressive face-like features and animations, or displays text. We made the design decision to express all feedback through physical gestures alone. This was based on the consideration that to support direct human-human interaction, physical gestures are less distracting than screens. Also, if our aim is a gentle nudge towards behavior change, gestures can play a more subtle role than on-screen information. Finally, as Kip1 is supposed to be in the background, embodied spatial movement is more easily read in peripheral view than on-screen feedback.

The smartphone runs a single application, constantly recording real-time audio and measuring the volume of the audio coming in. It then compares this audio with a baseline room-level and generates a conversation state and resulting emotional model, both in the form of finite state machines. The FSMs are connected to the volume detection subsystem and to each other. The conversation states include SILENCE, STARTED, and ONGOING. The emotional model includes CALM, CURIOUS, and SCARED. The emotional model drives a gesture control system, which triggers gestures, including breathing, stretching, contracting and shivering. This is achieved using a layering of ongoing and one-off parametric motor plans. A full technical description of the robot is detailed in a separate publication.

Usage scenarios

Designing Kip1, we considered various usage scenarios.

Couple's scenario: Couples at home can sometimes get into aggressive communication patterns. Kip1 could be placed in a strategic location around the house, where most of the discussions are taking place. It would constantly monitor ongoing conversations, and when a conversation starts, the "breathing" animation will change to the "curious/interested" gesture, encouraging the couple to talk more to each other. If a conversation is interpreted as "aggressive", Kip1 will retract and shiver, hopefully influencing the couple to change their communication style.

School scenario: In classrooms, both teachers and students are prone to raise their voices, many times unconsciously. Kip1 in a classroom can serve as an objective "referee", reacting to loud voices of both teacher and students, helping both sides increase their awareness to their tone, and setting the ground for mutual responsibility and goal-setting towards a more "volume-controlled" classroom.

Mediation scenario: In mediation sessions, two parties meet in order to resolve a known conflict. Conversation tones and loudness has a strong effect on the other party in such situations, and an escalation may occur at any moment. Kip1 in a mediation session's room can serve as an emotion regulation or "temper regulation" device that objectively maps the temper level in the room, and influences both parties to be more aware to the consequences of their tone.

Future Directions

Kip1 is our first prototype illustrating the Empathy Object concept. Future Empathy Objects will extend current work along these four dimensions:

Interaction and affordance design

Our current implementation of Kip1 is highly focused on one aspect of TUI, providing a tangible representation to digital information, but it does not enable direct physical manipulation. A future version could enable gentle physical manipulation of Kip1 to gradually shift its emotional state (e.g., from scared to calm). This builds on Ishii *et al.*'s idea that "dynamic changes of physical form can be reflected in digital states, and vice versa" [13].

Behavior change research

With respect to Norman's *experiential* and *reflective* modes of cognition [17], we want to evaluate if our affordance design is able to promote a shift towards reflective cognition. Keeping a balance between effective affordances and reflection is not easy, as "inviting affordances and tight mappings tend to discourage reflection" [11].

Reactive materials

Another direction in which we plan to extend our current work is in the reactive properties of Empathy Objects. Inspired by Ishii *et al.*'s Radical Atoms [13] we plan to explore the implementation and integration of combined mechanisms and materials that could affect a stronger emotional reaction among users. We intend to explore materials such as soft textiles, rubber, paper or foams and combining them with new embedded mechanical structures.

Conversation analysis capabilities
In order to pick up on more complex vocalic cues, we are now working to analyze pitch together with loudness to categorize vocal affect. Past work has successfully been able to classify vocal affect in deliberate and spontaneous speech [20, 21]. Combining speech duration patterns with vocal affect could deliver more precise detection of aggressive speaking behavior and thus more expressive feedback.

Future scenarios
Building on the abovementioned extension to our current work, we envision a broader range of human-human situations Empathy Objects can accompany:

Business meeting scenario: A business-focused example is a meeting room discussion. An Empathy Object in a meeting room can listen to the ongoing conversation and track the speakers. The object could subtly cue "stage takers" that they are talking too much, and encourage reserved speakers to speak up.

Teen chat scenario: A group of teen friends meeting at home to socialize. During their chat, an Empathy Object can listen to the conversation and mirror the emotions it recognize. The Empathy Object can help less social people feel more socially accepted by reacting to their participation or mirroring it, promoting a feeling of social bonding.

Additional future scenarios may include interactions between parents and children, dating, negotiations, and more.

Conclusion
We presented the notion of Empathy Objects: a combination of interactive objects and robotic companions aimed to support human-human interaction. We introduced our first Empathy Object prototype, Kip1, a conversation companion designed to promote non-aggressive conversation between people. We presented a future vision of Empathy Objects as part of human-human interaction at home and at work.

Acknowledgements
We would like to thank Shlomi Azoulay, Ofri Omer, Almog Ben-David, and Oran Peretz. This research was supported by the I-CORE Program of the Planning and Budgeting Committee and The ISF grant #1716/12, and by EU FP7 Marie Curie CIG #293733.

References
[1] Bartneck, C. et al. In your face, robot! The influence of a character's embodiment on how users perceive its emotional expressions. *Proc of the Design and Emotion* (2004).

[2] Beck, A. et al. Towards an affect space for robots to display emotional body language. *RO-MAN 2010 - The 19th IEEE International Symposium on Robot and Human Interactive Communication* (2010), 464–469.

[3] Bergstrom, T. and Karahalios, K. Social mirrors as social signals: transforming audio into graphics. *Computer Graphics and Applications, IEEE*. 29, 5 (2009), 22–32.

[4] Breazeal, C. *Designing Sociable Robots*. (2002), MIT Press.

[5] Dahley, A. et al. Water lamp and pinwheels: ambient projection of digital information into

architectural space. *Proc of the ACM SIGG* (1998), 269–270.

[6] DiMicco, J.M. et al. Influencing group participation with a shared display. *Proceedings of the 2004 ACM conference on Computer supported cooperative work* (2004), 614–623.

[7] Fong, T. et al. A survey of socially interactive robots. *Robotics and Autonomous Systems*. 42, 3-4 (Mar. 2003), 143–166.

[8] Gockley, R. et al. Designing robots for long-term social interaction. *2005 IEEE/RSJ International Conference on Intelligent Robots and Systems.(IROS 2005).* (2005), 1338–1343.

[9] Hoffman, G. Dumb Robots, Smart Phones : a Case Study of Music Listening Companionship. *RO-MAN 2012 - The IEEE Int'l Symposium on Robot and Human Interactive Communication* (2012), 358–363.

[10] Hoffman, G. and Weinberg, G. Interactive improvisation with a robotic marimba player. *Autonomous Robots*. 31, 2-3 (Jun. 2011), 133–153.

[11] Hornecker, E. Beyond affordance: tangibles' hybrid nature. *Proceedings of the Sixth International Conference on Tangible, Embedded and Embodied Interaction* (2012), 175–182.

[12] Ishii, H. et al. ambientROOM: integrating ambient media with architectural space. *Proc of the SIGCHI conference on Human factors in computing systems* (1998), 173–174.

[13] Ishii, H. et al. Radical atoms: beyond tangible bits, toward transformable materials. *Interactions*. 19, 1 (2012), 38–51.

[14] Kory, J.M. et al. Robotic learning companions for early language development. *Proceedings of the 15th ACM on International conference on multimodal interaction* (2013), 71–72.

[15] Lutkebohle, I. et al. The bielefeld anthropomorphic robot head "Flobi." *2010 IEEE International Conference on Robotics and Automation* (2010), 3384–3391.

[16] Mizanoor, R. et al. Dynamic Emotion-Based Human-Robot Collaborative Assembly in Manufacturing: The Preliminary Concepts. *hci.cs.wisc.edu*.

[17] Norman, D.A. *Things that make us smart: Defending human attributes in the age of the machine*. (1993), Basic Books.

[18] Shaer, O. and Hornecker, E. Tangible user interfaces: past, present, and future directions. *Foundations and Trends in Human-Computer Interaction*. 3, 1--2 (2010), 1–137.

[19] Sharma, M. et al. Communicating affect via flight path Exploring use of the Laban Effort System for designing affective locomotion paths. *Human-Robot Interaction (HRI), 2013 8th ACM/IEEE International Conference on* (2013), 293–300.

[20] Thomaz, A.L. et al. An embodied computational model of social referencing. *RO-MAN 2005. IEEE International Workshop on Robot and Human Interactive Communication* (2005), 591–598.

[21] Truong, K. et al. Arousal and valence prediction in spontaneous emotional speech: felt versus perceived emotion. (2009), 3–6.

[22] Zuckerman O. Objects for Change: A Case Study of a Tangible User Interface for Behavior Change. In Ext. Abstracts of TEI 2015, ACM Press. (2015). DOI:10.1145/2677199.2687906

EmotiSphere: From Emotion to Music

Galen Chuang
Wellesley College
106 Central Street
Wellesley, MA 02481 USA
gchuang@wellesley.edu

Shelley Wang
Wellesley College
106 Central Street
Wellesley, MA 02481 USA
swang8@wellesley.edu

Sara Burns
Wellesley College
106 Central Street
Wellesley, MA 02481 USA
sburns@wellesley.edu

Orit Shaer
Wellesley College
106 Central Street
Wellesley, MA 02481 USA
oshaer@wellesley.edu

Figure 1. EmotiSphere on its base.

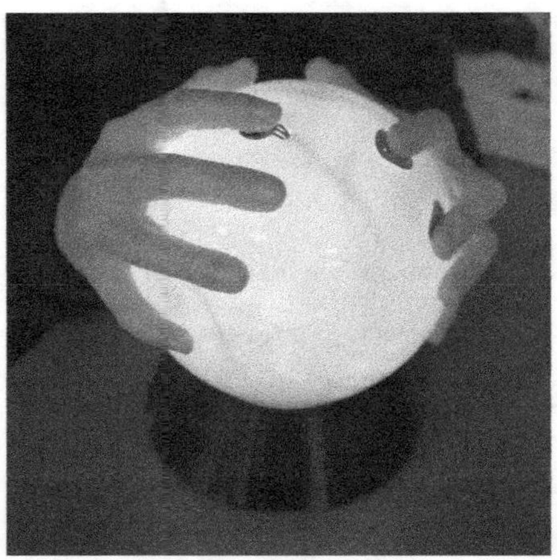

Figure 2. The user places her hands on the sphere so that her fingers rest on the galvanic skin and pulse sensors. Here, the sphere produces green light, indicating the user is relaxed.

TEI '15, Jan 16-19 2015, Stanford, CA, USA
ACM 978-1-4503-3305-4/15/01.
http://dx.doi.org/10.1145/2677199.2688809

Abstract

EmotiSphere is an interactive sensor-based musical instrument that generates music based on a user's current emotional state. Interactions with EmotiSphere draw upon everyday interactions with physical spherical objects, as well as on familiar interactions with music players. EmotiSphere offers a novel way to understand the relationship between emotion and music, and is aimed at people who want to create music and express themselves but do not necessarily possess skills in music composition. We describe the conceptualization and context of EmotiSphere, as well as its technical implementation.

Author Keywords

Tangible interaction; musical instrument; physiological sensors; Arduino

ACM Classification Keywords

H.5.2 [User Interfaces]: Auditory (non-speech) feedback; J.5: [Arts and Humanities]: performing arts; H.5.5: [Sound and Music Computing]: Methodologies and techniques

General Terms

Design, Human Factors, Experimentation

Introduction

Throughout the day, a person experiences a range of ephemeral emotions. Is there a way to utilize the

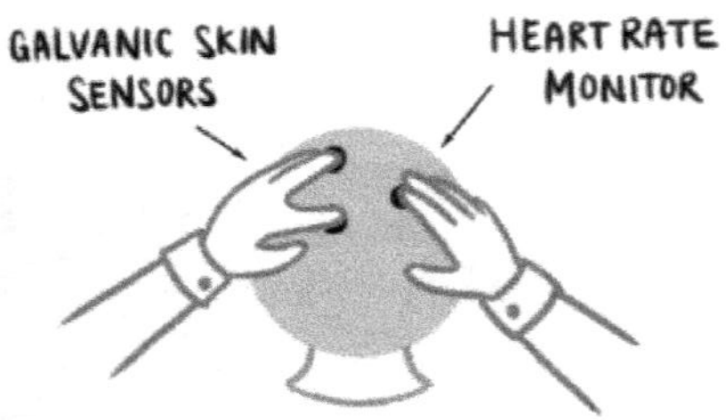

Figure 3. The left hand is placed on two galvanic skin sensors, and the right hand is placed on a pulse sensor.

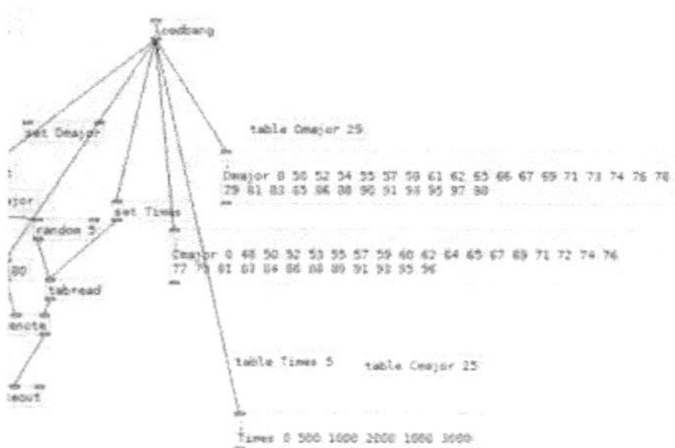

Figure 4. A partial screen shot of Pure Data, the visual programming language used for EmotiSphere's algorithmic music composition.

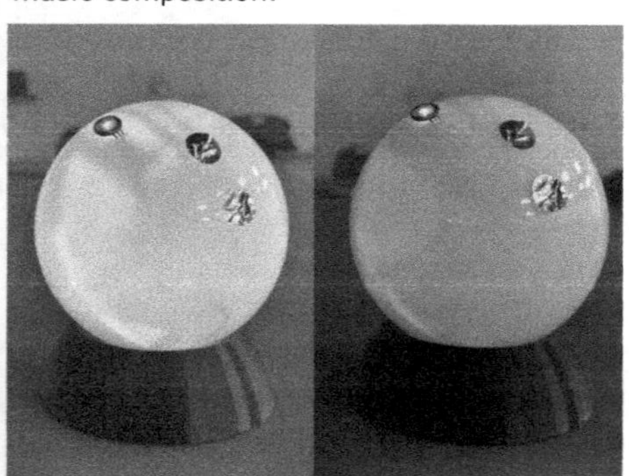

Figure 5. When a relaxed profile is sensed, the sphere glows green. With an angry profile, the sphere glows red.

inherent relationship between music and emotion to create a more tangible translation of emotions felt during the day? EmotiSphere attempts to address this question by translating physiological markers of emotion, gathered through galvanic skin sensors and a pulse sensor, into a composition of sound and light. It can be used in a range of settings, such as at home, at the office, or in a classroom, but is not meant to be portable. Users place their hands on the orb to initiate recording, and can immediately hear the results. Interactions with EmotiSphere draw upon its spherical form, utilizing actions such as shaking, rolling, and rotating.

Related Work

Several projects have examined the relationship between music and emotion, while many others have utilized physiological sensors to measure emotion. Here we describe those most closely related to our work. The "2Hearts" system generates musical compositions from the output of physiological sensors of two people as they interact with one another [6]. "Vocal Vibrations" also utilizes an orb design. When the user holds the Oral Resonant Ball (ORB) and speaks, the ORB reproduces the vibrations created by his or her voice [3]. "ZenTrader" uses a galvanic skin sensor to measure the stress levels of stock traders, and helps prevent them from making risky, emotion-driven decisions [5]. "Inmamusys" is an artificial intelligence system that creates music designed to elicit a certain emotional response [2]. While each of these projects share common elements with EmotiSphere, none of them combine real time computer composition with emotion sensing.

Design and Concept

EmotiSphere allows users to record and store computer-generated music, access previously recorded songs, delete music, navigate in a song database, play and pause songs, and adjust the volume of the music. The orb is connected wirelessly to a computer, where the songs are generated and stored. It rests on a base for stability, and can be removed for certain interactions.

EmotiSphere utilizes its spherical form to guide users through interactions with functionality similar to popular music players. Users activate music generation by placing two fingers of the left hand on the galvanic skin sensors, and one finger of another hand on the pulse sensor, while resting their other fingers naturally on the sphere (Fig. 2, 3). When the user takes his or her hands off the sphere, sensors no longer detect input and recording stops. The song is saved in a database stored in a nearby computer, unless the user deletes the recorded song by immediately shaking the orb (Fig. 6d). To access songs in the database, users can remove the sphere from its base and roll it one full rotation to the left or to the right to navigate between songs (Fig. 6a). The bottom of the sphere is weighted to maintain an upright position after rolling. To play or pause a song, the user can press on the orb in its base (Fig. 6c). To increase or decrease the volume, the user turns the orb clockwise or counterclockwise from above, like a knob (Fig. 6b).

Profiles of emotions are created from skin and pulse sensors, and for each profile a song is generated from an application on the connected computer. Along with a song, LEDs within the sphere will also light up, with color depending on the emotional profile (Fig. 2, 5).

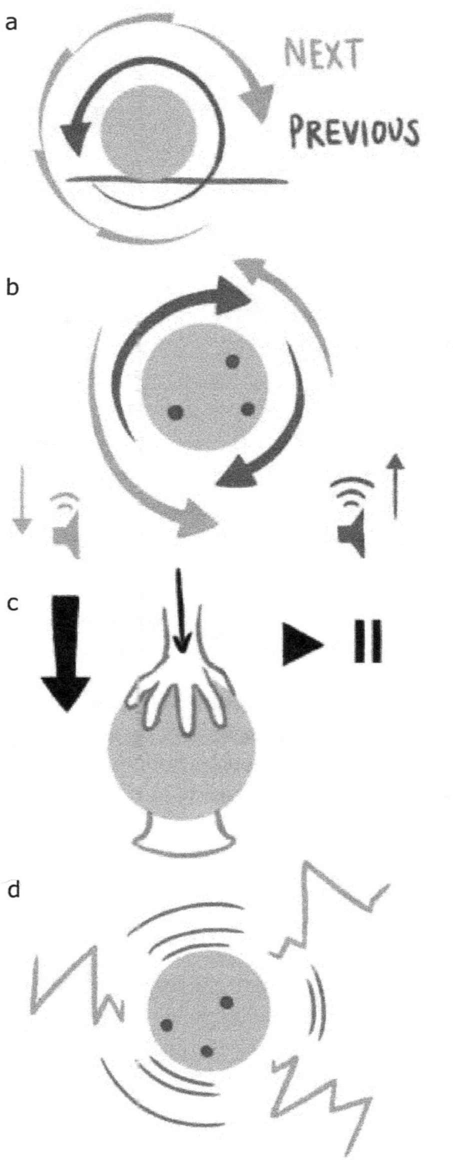

Figure 6. a) Rolling navigates between songs (view from side). **b)** Clockwise rotation increases the volume, while counterclockwise decreases the volume (view from above). **c)** Pushing on the sphere plays and pauses music. **d)** Shaking the sphere deletes the most recent song.

Implementation

EmotiSphere uses Arduino [1] to collect input from galvanic skin sensors and a PulseSensor [8] on the outside of the sphere, as well as a pressure sensor and reed sensors located at the bottom, and an accelerometer. The bottom of the sphere is weighted, and the base contains magnets. Based on the emotional profile of the sensor input, the Arduino also controls RGB LEDs to display different colors associated with different emotions (Fig. 2, 5).

Sensory input is translated into a series of emotional profiles, determined by calculating the change and trend of galvanic skin conductance over ten seconds. According to previous research on physiological signs, frequent fluctuations in skin conductance signify more agitation or arousal and an upward trend of skin conductance indicates relaxation [10]. Combined with heart rate thresholds, skin conductance will be used to generate one of four profiles: relaxed, excited, anxious, or angry. Corresponding LED colors for these profiles are green, yellow, orange, and red, respectively. These colors are chosen in accordance with the findings of a previous study conducted on humans' association of colors to music emotion [7]. Once the emotional profile is determined, the music composition application utilizes the Pure Data [9] programming language to generate a composition utilizing musical parameters such as key, pitch variation, dynamics, and articulation appropriate for the profile. Musical parameters draw upon changing the perceived emotion of computer-generated music [4]. The tempo of the music is mapped to the user's heart rate.

The input from Arduino is sent wirelessly to a connected computer, where the composition program processes it. The resulting composition is played via computer speakers. Interactions with the sphere affect the program running on the computer. For instance, turning the sphere clockwise on the base will increase the volume (Fig. 6b).

Conclusion and Future Work

EmotiSphere is a spherical musical interface that illuminates the relationship between music and the physiological expression of emotion. Interaction is designed to be intuitive to the spherical shape. We plan to improve database interactions, and expand the music production capabilities. The EmotiSphere prototype has been presented in a classroom setting, where it was well accepted. Suggestions included adding the functionality of setting user preferences for algorithmic composition parameters and saving the initial emotional profile reading for successive compositions within a time range, both of which we plan to implement. In the future, we will evaluate EmotiSphere in classroom, office, and home settings.

Acknowledgements

We thank our classmates at Wellesley College for their valuable feedback on EmotiSphere.

References

[1] Arduino http://arduino.cc

[2] Delgado, M., Fajardo W., Molina-Solana, M. Inmamusys: Intelligent multiagent music system. *Expert Systems with Applications* 36.3 (2009): 4574-4580.

[3] Holbrow, C., Jessop, E., Kleinberger, Rébecca. Vocal Vibrations: A Multisensory Experience of the Voice. In *Proc. NIME '14*, 2014.

[4] Livingstone, S., Muhlberger, R., Brown, A., Thompson, W. Changing musical emotion: a computational rule

system for modifying score and performance. *Computer Music Journal* 34.1 (2010): 41-64

[5] Luan Dang, T., Kun Liu, S., Fels, Sidney. ZenTrader, an Emotion-Reactive Interface. In *ICEC 2011*, 2011.

[6] McCaig, G., Fels, S. Playing on Heart-Strings: Experiences with the 2Hearts System. In *Proc. NIME 2002,* 2002.

[7] Palmer, S., Schloss, K., Xu, Z., Prado-Léon, L.R. Music-color associations are mediated by emotion. *PNAS* 110.22 (2013)

[8] PulseSensor http://pulsesensor.myshopify.com

[9] Pure Data http://puredata.info

[10]Villarejo, M. V., Zapirain, B. G., Zorrilla, A. M. A Stress Sensor Based on Galvanic Skin Response (GSR) Controlled by ZigBee. *Sensors* 12.5 (2012): 6075-6101

Touching Notes: A Gesture-Based Game for Teaching Music to Children

Manuela Renzi
DIAG
Sapienza University of Rome
Rome, 00185 Italy
renzi.manuela@hotmail.it

Stavros Vassos
DIAG
Sapienza University of Rome
Rome, 00185 Italy
vassos@dis.uniroma1.it

Tiziana Catarci
DIAG
Sapienza University of Rome
Rome, 00185 Italy
catarci@dis.uniroma1.it

Stephen Kimani
Jomo Kenyatta University
(JKUAT)
Nairobi, 00200 Kenya
stephenkimani@gmail.com

TEI '15, Jan 16-19 2015, Stanford, CA, USA
ACM 978-1-4503-3305-4/15/01.
http://dx.doi.org/10.1145/2677199.2688810

Abstract
In this work we present some findings on how gesture-based interfaces can stimulate and motivate children into learning the basics of music notation. We report on a serious game we developed that relies on a hand detection interface using motion-sensing camera technology. Our initial experiments indicate the accuracy, effectiveness, and user acceptance of the gesture-based interface among children, thereby validating the idea that such interfaces can be used to facilitate the teaching of music concepts.

Author Keywords
Natural User Interface (NUI); Motion-Sensing Interface; Serious Games; Music Learning.

ACM Classification Keywords
H.5.2. Information interfaces and presentation (e.g., HCI): User Interfaces. H.1.2: Models and Principles: User/Machine Systems.

Introduction
Advances in technology are affecting how learning takes place. Modern technological tools are ideally not meant to replace the teacher, but to complement by supporting the teacher and enhancing students' learning experience. Computer and videogames can play an important role by providing attractive and

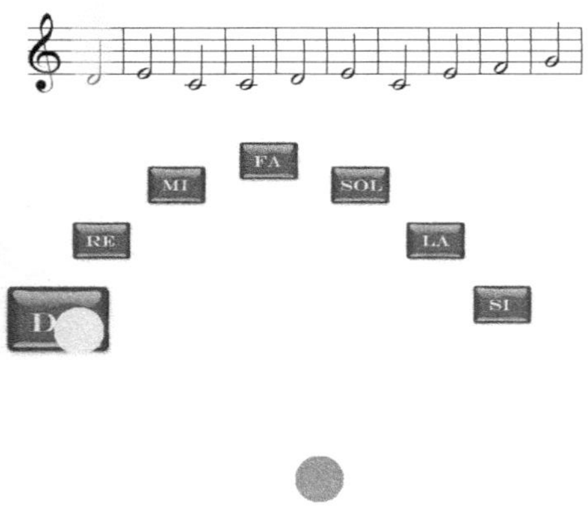

Figure 1. *Touching Notes* "kinect two ovals" interface.

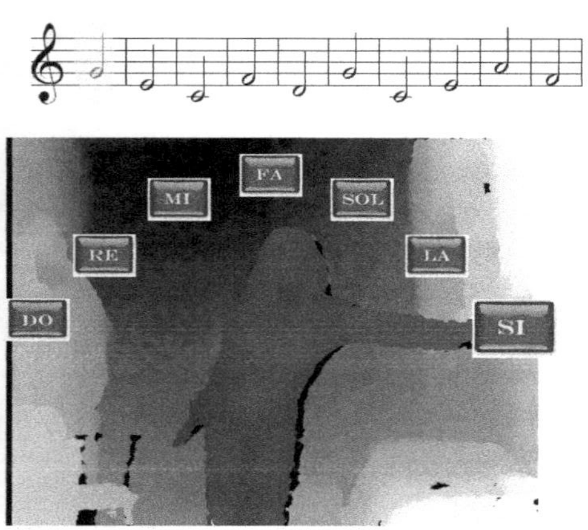

Figure 2. *Touching Notes* "kinect skeleton" interface.

immersive environments through which learning can be easier and more enjoyable for the students. In fact, a critical problem is the low level of engagement of students in traditional teaching methods. With new technological tools though, a playful aspect can be introduced. In this way students can be motivated to experiment, challenge their understanding, and revise their approach in order to improve the outcome of the task they work on. This paper shows a case of how traditional elementary school teaching may be integrated with educational games that make use a motion sensing interface. The aim of this study is to demonstrate how gamification on such interfaces can engage children in the learning of music notation.

Music learning and videogames

The potential of using motion based interaction for learning is grounded on theoretical approaches that recognize the relationship between physical activity and cognitive processes, and are supported by a growing body of evidence from psychology and neurobiology [1]. Embodied cognition theories [2] emphasize the formative role of embodiment (i.e. the way an organism's sensorimotor capacities enable it to successfully interact with the physical environment) in the development of different levels of cognitive skills. Several studies investigate this in the context of videogames such as [3] for full-body games and [4] for games with a motion sensor interface using Kinect.

While learning music, many of the attractive and playful aspects of music are lost until the final stages where one can actually play a musical instrument. With our approach we attempt to offer a more attractive way to learn music notation, which is necessary during the early theoretical stages. There are a lot of practicing aids for music notation such as *ClefTutor,*[1] and a few games such as *Fun with Notes.*[2] Nonetheless there are to the best of our knowledge no games for learning this skill that use a motion-capture interface. Also, there are games with such an interface for simulating *playing instruments* as for example Wii Music,[3] but not for learning music notation; in fact our aim is to combine these aspects in an engaging learning experience.

Touching Notes

Touching Notes has a simple interface. On the top of the screen there is a musical staff with notes that the user has to recognize (Figs. 1 and 2). Below the staff are seven buttons with the names of the notes, and to the right of the boxes there is a block that keeps track of the user's score in terms of notes guessed correctly and incorrectly. The boxes also give user feedback in case of guessed note by performing an animation with an elastic effect. The player has to "touch" the right note in order to advance the sequence. There are two versions of the game, each using a hand detection interface. In the first version, the user sees and controls two colored circles, corresponding to the right hand and left hand respectively (Fig. 1). By motion sensing, hand movements are translated to movement of the colored circles. In the second version, the user sees and controls his/her figure image so as to touch the buttons with his/her hands (Fig. 2).

At any point in the game, the user has to guess the first note on the staff. Whenever a button is touched by means of user's movement, the corresponding note is

[1] http://www.cleftutor.com
[2] https://itunes.apple.com/hk/app/fun-with-notes/id438853364
[3] http://www.wiimusic.com

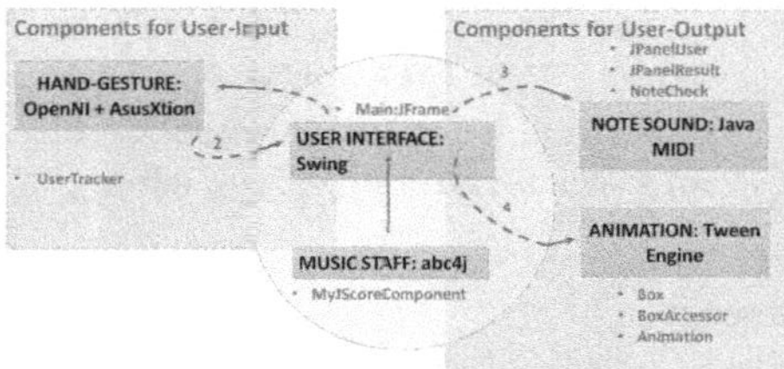

Figure 3. Workflow of events: UI is updated based on motion capture (1-2); when a button is touched appropriate sound and animation is generated (3-4).

	MOUSE	KINECT-TWO OVALS	KINECT-SKELETON
CHILD 1	3.25	6.32	4.33
CHILD 2	2.42	1.92	2.96
CHILD 3	3.68	3.95	3.77
CHILD 4	2.63	2.81	4.12
CHILD 5	2.84	2.90	3.60
CHILD 6	2.50	3.43	3.60

Figure 4. Accuracy comparisons.

	KINECT-SKELETON REPLAY
CHILD 1	4.01
CHILD 2	2.73
CHILD 3	3.57
CHILD 4	3.10
CHILD 5	3.05
CHILD 6	3.60

Figure 5. Kinect skeleton 2nd play.

played by a music synthesizer (Fig. 3). In case the user presses the button with the note that corresponds to the one highlighted on the staff, then the button animates and the score counter of correct guesses increases. Also, the notation on the staff is shifted to the left so that the guessed note disappears and the next note becomes the highlighted one. When the player makes a wrong guess, the staff remains unchanged but the counter of wrong guesses increases.

Evaluation

We started our evaluation by carrying out two experiments to assess the accuracy, effectiveness, and user perceptions pertaining to the *Touching Notes* interface. User interaction data was automatically logged for the two experiments. At the end of both experiments, participants were required to complete a questionnaire in order to determine user perceptions.

Experiment 1: Accuracy

Since this game is a hand-detection interface, it is important to measure the accuracy of this new interface compared with well-known standard interfaces. For now in this particular study, we are comparing with mouse interface given that the mouse interface is relatively universally familiar and common to most users and rather standard. Comparison with other interfaces such as multi-touch will be done in our future studies. The participants were six children from music schools. There were three conditions: *Touching Notes* "kinect two ovals" interface (one with two colored circles), *Touching Notes* "kinect skeleton interface" (one with the user figure image), and mouse interface. The experiment was within-subjects. Each child was assigned a unique order of the conditions. We measured accuracy as the average time it takes to pass from one box to the next having touched the correct notes. Since the children are familiar with music, they don't need to take much time to recognize notes; what we are thus measuring is primarily a measure that has to do with just the nature of the interface (rather than the children's knowledge of music).

RESULTS

There was no significant difference in accuracy between mouse interface with kinect two ovals interface ($F=0.88$, $p=0.36$) as seen in Fig. 4. It however took children more time playing with kinect skeleton interface than it took them with the mouse interface ($F=7.17$, $p=0.02$). Since the mouse interface is rather common, familiar and standard, users may be considered to be already at their best and improved performance even with more practice is highly unlikely. We thus decided to explore further what would happen with a replay of the kinect skeleton interface, and noticed the time taken did reduce (Fig. 5), where the difference is now not significant ($F=2.5$, $p=0.14$).

Experiment 2: Effectiveness

The aim was to investigate the effect of the game interface on participants' learning of music. This was measured by recording the total number of notes that were incorrectly guessed. The participants were twelve children from *non-music schools*. The experiment had two parts. In the first part, children played with each of the three interfaces like in the previous experiment. We assigned every two children a unique order of the three conditions and call FIRST PLAY the first use of any of the three interfaces. In the second part, each child was to recognize notes from the same melody using i) music notation on paper, which we call PAPER, and ii) their favourite interface of the three, which we call

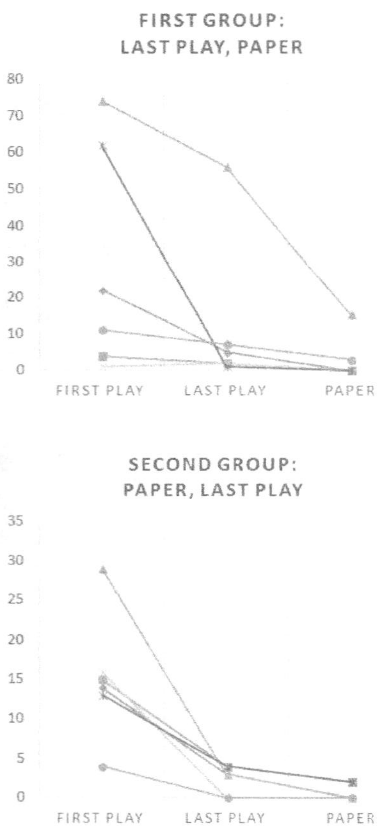

Figure 6. Total incorrect guesses for each participant between FIRST PLAY (first use of any of the three interfaces: mouse, kinect two ovals, and kinect skeleton), LAST PLAY (favourite interface in the second part of the experiment), and PAPER.

LAST PLAY. In this case the children were split into two groups: one started with the favourite interface and then on paper, and the other used the reverse order.

RESULTS

We were interested to find out whether there is an improvement using the *Touching Notes* game between FIRST PLAY and LAST PLAY. We also report on the PAPER use which measures more closely what the children have learned, as it does not allow any feedback for whether the guesses are correct or not. Only one child chose the mouse interface as the favorite interface in LAST PLAY and we chose not to report it as we focus on measuring the outcome with the kinect interfaces. Figures 5,6 show the total incorrect guesses per child in these three stages. In all children LAST PLAY shows an improvement in the level of effectiveness from that of compared to FIRST PLAY. switching between the *Touching Notes* game LAST PLAY and PAPER; the slightly lower number of incorrect guesses for PAPER is due to the fact that no feedback is possible and children don't experiment but take more time to think.

Questionnaire: User Perceptions

The questionnaire covered aspects of user perceptions such as understandability of interface, engagement, fun, etc. The questionnaire was presented to each of the eighteen children in the two experiments. All children understood what the boxes in the *Touching Notes* interface *represent*, and how to *interact* with the interface. All children except one preferred to use the *Touching Notes* interface since it is *more fun* to use and *more attractive* than the mouse interface. Almost all children found the *Touching Notes* kinect interface *intuitive*. Almost all children found the *Touching Notes* interface *engaging*. Seven children gave suggestions e.g. adding time, adding suggestion in case of an incorrect guess, etc.

Conclusions

This paper presented *Touching Notes*, a hand-detection gesture gaming interface that is aimed at facilitating the learning of music concepts. Initial experiments indicate the accuracy, effectiveness, and user acceptance of the interface among children. For most children, physical engagement resulted in a higher level of concentration on the movements that the child wants to perform, leading gradually then to a lower number of incorrect guesses but a higher average time to complete the game. For future work we intend to compare with other common interfaces (e.g. multi-touch), also among children of different age groups.

References

[1] Broaders, S.C., Cook, S.W., Mitchell, Z., and Goldin-Meadow, S. Making children gesture brings out implicit knowledge and leads to learning. *J. Experimental Psychology* 136,4 (2007), 539-550.

[2] Evans, M. 2012. Gestural Interfaces in Learning. *Proc. Society for Information Technology & Teacher Education Int. Conference* (2012), 3337-3340.

[3] Alankus, G., Proffitt, R., Kelleher, C., and Engsberg, J. Stroke Therapy through Motion-Based Games: A Case Study, *ACM SIGACCESS* (2010).

[4] Kandroudi M. and Bratitsis, T. Exploring the Educational Perspectives of XBOX Kinect Based Video Games. *Proc. ECGBL* (2012), 219-227.

Wall Relief: A Health-Oriented Interactive Installation for the Workplace Environment

Halley Profita
Dept. of Computer Science
University of Colorado Boulder
430 UCB, Boulder, CO 80309
halley.profita@colorado.edu

Andy Lim
Microsoft
1 Microsoft Way
Redmond, WA 98052
andylim@exchange.microsoft.com

Donald Brinkman
Microsoft
1 Microsoft Way
Redmond, WA 98052
donaldbr@microsoft.com

Ross Smith
Microsoft
1 Microsoft Way
Redmond, WA 98052
rosss@exchange.microsoft.com

TEI '15, Jan 16-19 2015, Stanford, CA, USA
ACM 978-1-4503-3305-4/15/01.
http://dx.doi.org/10.1145/2677199.2688811

Abstract

Recently, workplace settings are reflecting a shift from traditional work-oriented values to promoting work/life balance and employee well-being. Technology has the ability to contribute to workplace enjoyment through the incorporation of employee activities and health-centric initiatives. Furthermore, tangible computing and interactive media can be used to explore novel interaction methods for positive user-computer experiences. We leverage these concepts to inform the development of a playful and engaging interactive installation aimed at promoting health-oriented experiences in the workplace. In this work, we detail our initial steps and design decisions to address this objective. The result is Wall Relief, a Tai Chi-inspired interactive wall unit developed to create an engaging, ephemeral experience that guides the user through a series of upper-body movements.

Author Keywords

Interactive Installation; Physical Computing; Calming Technologies; Health in the Workplace

ACM Classification Keywords

H.5.m. Information Interfaces and Presentation (e.g., HCI): Miscellaneous; K.4.3 Organizational Impacts

Figure 1. Wall Relief with Kinect.

Introduction

Occupational stress has been shown to have a direct effect on one's emotional, physical, and cognitive health [1, 3]. This can negatively impact one's work (productivity, absenteeism, etc.) and the organization and can spill over into non-work related activities [1]. As the line continues to blur between work and personal domains, additional attention has been given to workplace interventions to offset potential occupational pressures. Such intervention programs include fitness, stress management, and educational initiatives focused on enhancing one's overall well-being, which contribute to positive life-style and behavioral benefits that extend past work into one's personal life [1]. Wall Relief was created to work in tandem with this advantageous organizational ethos by harnessing technology to create a positive interactive experience that can also potentially promote a state of calm.

Over the past few years, technology has often been cited as a potential stressor (e.g., incessant emails, text/call interruptions, etc.) for individuals. However, more recent initiatives have looked at how technology can be used for stress reduction.[1] In line with this area of research, we were interested in how technology could be used to bring soothing and playful experiences into the workplace. We were inspired by the practice of Tai Chi due to its known benefits as a gentle, non-strenuous meditative activity. It incorporates controlled breathing and continuous low-impact movements, which have been shown to alleviate many of the chronic symptoms associated with aging and stress [4]. Tai Chi has been incorporated into other health-centric gaming [5] and artistic expression experiences [2].The goal was to present workers with a playful and engaging interactive experience that could potentially induce a calm and restorative state of mind.

[1]http://calmingtechnology.org/

Interactive Media in the Workplace

An interactive installation will markedly draw attention and elicit user engagement. This element helps invite users in to interact with the device. Given that the workplace is a highly public environment (with varying degrees of appropriate social conduct), we see such an installation as having the most impact in highly visible areas such as a lobby, a community space, or in a meeting room. Locating the device in a lobby could facilitate visitor engagement by providing individuals with a fun, alternative means to waiting. A community space could elicit employee interaction, serving as a conversation starter amongst employees. A meeting room may also serve as an interesting space for such an installation as it may function as an ice breaker or provide a unique interactive experience as meeting-goers wait for all parties to arrive. While a proper user evaluation remains to be done, our objective is to develop interactive media in the workplace that can deliver a positive user experience to promote employee well-being and engagement. Additionally, through the incorporation of Tai Chi elements, we look to explore the notion that an interactive experience can potentially foster a calming takeaway.

Wall Relief

This interactive installation was developed to promote an overall sense of employee well-being and engagement in the workplace. The slow-paced, low-impact upper body movements associated with Tai Chi served as inspiration for the interactive experience of

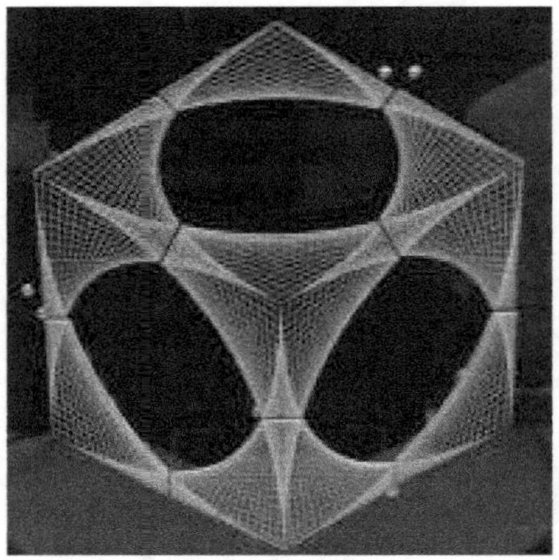

Figure 2. Close-up view of laser engraved design. This design (physical display) is divided into 7 segments (see Figure 3) with each segment forming one united image when in the resting (starting) position. Each segment or panel can articulate independently, moving back and forth, or in a sequence to achieve the appearance of coordinated movement.

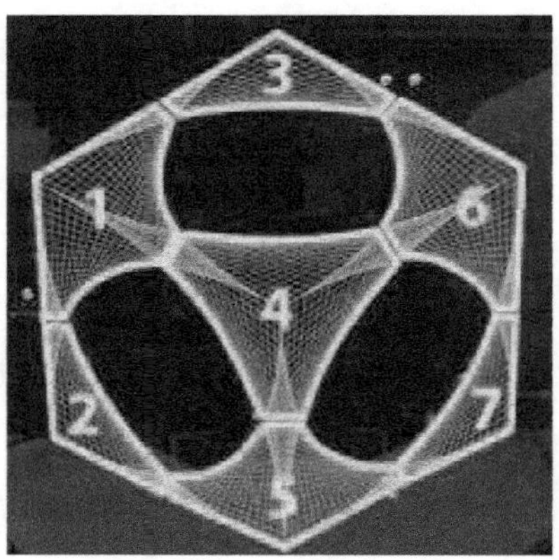

Figure 3. Seven numerically coded segments of Wall Relief. Each panel segment can articulate back and forth (toward/away) from the user.

Wall Relief, with the ultimate intention of these interactive sequences producing an easy to perform, ephemeral, and engaging user experience. Often, the work environment can be associated with marked stressors as employees are preparing for important meetings and product pitches and are working under deadlines. Additionally, individuals acclimating to a new workplace environment (either in an interviewing role or as a new employee with few acquaintances) might experience apprehension in an unfamiliar setting. Wall Relief was designed in an effort to offset these traditional pressures by leveraging technology to introduce playful and interaction-driven experiences in the workplace. User testing still remains to be done to determine if Wall Relief can be used as an effective calming agent in the workplace or, if such an interactive installation is better suited for community spaces aimed at fostering social engagement.

Physical Design

Wall Relief was created using ¼″ black laser cut acrylic and 80/20 10 series aluminum framing for structural support. Wall Relief is a standalone unit designed for a meeting room, common area, or lobby space to encourage interaction and serve as a conversation piece. The image on Wall Relief was achieved via laser raster engraving and white spray paint (see Figure 2). The display is composed of 7 distinct panels (see Figure 3) that can articulate forwards and backwards independently. Each panel is connected to a linear actuator (stepper motor housed in the back compartment), which is used to drive the movement of these wall panels. Panels can be moved in unison or sequentially to create different motion and transition effects. When all panels return to their starting position a unified image is achieved (see Figure 2). Each linear stepper motor was driven by Phidget 1063 controller boards. The linear stepper motors and Phidget controller boards are located behind the image, away from the user's line of sight. The Microsoft Kinect[2] rests atop the display and was used to register user input. The display responds to user input by articulating the individual wall panel segments in the same direction as the user's arm movements.

Design Decisions

While the Wall Relief interaction sequence was loosely based on Tai Chi movements, we do not claim Wall Relief to actually instruct Tai Chi or promote the same health benefits. Tai Chi-inspired movements were chosen due to the known health benefits and stress-relieving properties associated with this martial art [4]. We were inspired by the health benefits of Tai Chi and the potential advantages that this could have in the workplace. Further evaluation is required in order to assess one's user experience with the device and to study any potentially associated stress-relieving or calming effects.

Wall Relief was designed as a standalone centerpiece (as opposed to a wall integrated unit) that could be moved amongst meeting rooms, lobbies, and inter-office neighborhoods. The central image has 7 distinct panels that can actuate independently, permitting for alternating sequencing effects and patterns that can be achieved with reprogramming. When at rest, all 7 panels come together to form a unified image with a standalone aesthetic, thus, giving the device a dual function when not in use. The 3D image was chosen as it creates a mesmerizing optical effect that captivates

[2] http://www.microsoft.com/en-us/kinectforwindows/.

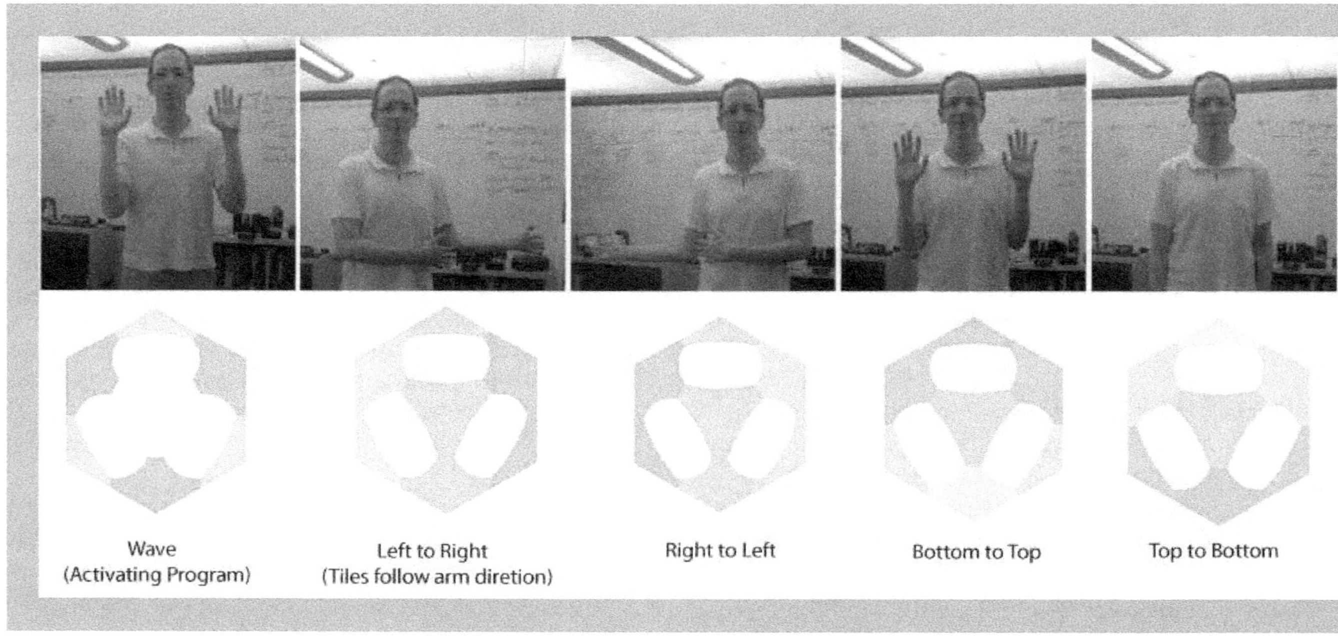

Figure 4. Interaction sequence for Wall Relief. The color intensity shows which panel segments are closer to the user (stronger color) and which panel segments stay at rest (weaker color). The user waves at the device to initiate the program and Wall Relief acknowledges by 'waving' (3 segments articulate forward) back. As the user moves their arms in the appropriate sequence (right, left, up down) Wall Relief will mirror the user's movements by actuating the wall panels to follow one's arms.

users. The theme of 'relief' (stress relief – the ultimate takeaway) is consistent throughout the piece as it is reflected in the installation's name 'Wall Relief'. The appearance of 'relief' etching was adopted to achieve the 3D image – a relief of laser cut lines are highlighted using white spray paint. Wall Relief was designed to be noticeable so that it will garner attention and elicit interest and participation. The Kinect that sits atop of Wall Relief gives users a visual cue that the installation employs interaction. This may help pique one's natural curiosity about the installation and invites the element of discovery amongst participants.

Interactive Experience

Wall Relief uses the Kinect to track and sync a user's movements to the appropriate transitions of the physical display. Wall Relief was designed to assume a standalone aesthetic during non-use, with an articulating back-end when engaged. This articulation is achieved by linear actuators that are attached to each panel segment, which drive each panel toward or away from the user. These panels are programmed to move in a coordinated fashion to follow a user's arm movements. The Wall Relief interaction entails following a sequence of upper-body movements similar (yet modified) to that of Tai Chi (see Figure 4 - both arms move right, then left, then up, then down). The display panels actuate to follow the user's movements and also set a slower, relaxing pace. Thus, when moving one's arms left to right, first the left most panels, 1 and 2 (see Figure 3), move forward then back, followed by the middle-aligned panels, 3, 4, and 5, moving forward and back, and then completed by the right most panels, 6 and 7, moving forward and back. The produced effect is reminiscent of a wave form. If the user doesn't complete the movements in the appropriate sequence, the display will balk and recede to its starting position so that the user can start again and learn the interactive movements used to promote a calming and relaxed state. The ultimate goal is for a user to complete the proper movement sequence three times, resulting in the display producing a celebratory radial dance (each peripheral panel moves forward then back in a clockwise fashion starting at panel 3 and ending at panel 1).

Future Work

As noted in this work, the development of Wall Relief demonstrates our initial efforts to develop an interactive installation for the workplace to promote employee well-being and engagement. Future evaluation of the device is needed *in situ* to assess factors related to user experience, stress relief, and its impact in an organizational setting.

Conclusion

Physical computing and interactive experiences can potentially contribute to health-oriented workplace initiatives focused on employee well-being and community engagement. Wall Relief is one such physical instantiation of how open-source technology can be leveraged to create interactive installations focused on enhancing the workplace environment.

Acknowledgements

This work was funded by Microsoft Research Connections. We would like to thank the Microsoft Research Hardware Lab for their support and guidance in the development of this project.

References and Citations

1. Danna, Karen, & Ricky W. Griffin. "Health and well-being in the workplace: A review and synthesis of the literature." *Journal of Management* 25.3 (1999): 357-384.

2. Jakovich, J. & Beilharz, K. 'Sonic Tai Chi': Auditory Gestures in Reactive Soundspaces (Demo paper and installation) in Pisan, Y. (Ed.) *The Second Australasian Conference on Interactive Entertainment,* Sydney (2005): 243.

3. Lupien, S., McEwen, B., Gunnar, M., & Heim, C. "Effects of stress throughout the lifespan on the brain, behaviour and cognition." *Nature Reviews Neuroscience* 10.6 (2009): 434-445.

4. The Health Benefits of Tai Chi. Harvard Health Publications.http://www.health.harvard.edu/newsletters/Harvard_Womens_Health_Watch/2009/May/The-health-benefits-of-tai-chi.

5. Ubi Soft. "Your Shape: Fitness Evolved – Xbox 360."

Magnetic Files: Exploring Tag Based File Systems Using Embodied Files

David Gullick
Highwire DTC,
Lancaster University, UK
d.gullick@lancaster.ac.uk

Paul Coulton
The LICA Building
Lancaster University, UK
p.coulton@lancaster.ac.uk

Manfred Lau
InfoLab21
Lancaster University, UK
m.lau@lancaster.ac.uk

TEI '15, Jan 16-19 2015, Stanford, CA, USA
ACM 978-1-4503-3305-4/15/01.

http://dx.doi.org/10.1145/2677199.2688812

Abstract

The widespread use of the desktop metaphor during the early adoption of computers has promoted the utilization of files and folders. However many people have use cases that are not well suited to the strict nature of these systems. As a result, alternative file system paradigms are being explored by the research community, and by leading software vendors. Tangible interactions for exploring these alternative file systems have largely been unexplored, despite the many benefits that tangible interfaces could bring to such systems. Those that do explore this area are limited in information bandwidth by the number of feedback channels used to represent this information. Therefore, in this paper we introduce two associated works in progress: one that explores the design of a tag based file system affording tangible interaction; and a second that initiates the consideration of ways that we can increase the information bandwidth of such systems using physically embodied files. We believe this research identifies an important area that tangible interaction designers should explore given the dominance of file systems in computing tasks.

Author Keywords

Embodiment; Tangible; File System; Physical Interaction; Tagged File System; Interface Design;

ACM Classification Keywords

H.5.2 User Interfaces

Figure 1: A closer look at a few of the markers on 'Magnetic Tags'. In our system, 'Magnetic Tags' are detected via individual fudicial markers using an overhead camera. However, many alternative detection methods are possible [9].

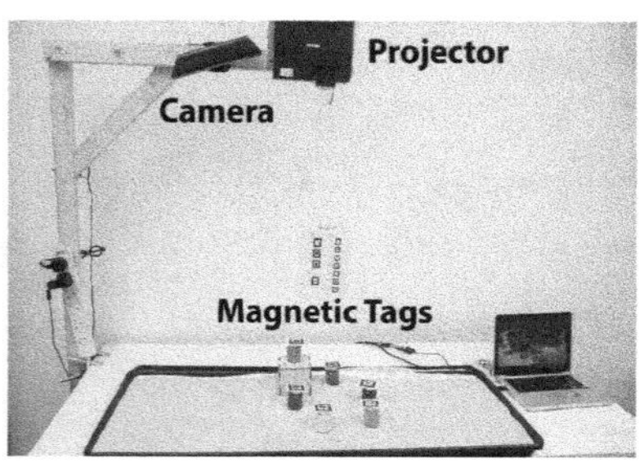

Figure 2: An overview of the 'Magnetic Tags' system. A camera overhead can detect the positioning of 'Magnet Tags' on the workspace. The projector can update the workspace with a dynamic visualization.

Introduction

Traditionally, computers store files in a strictly hierarchical format, with each 'parent' folder containing many associated 'child' files or folders. In addition to a number of low level computing issues, they also have the tendency to *i*) force users to remember the exact location of their files, and *ii*) force users to make difficult decisions about where to place their files [8]. Hierarchical structures are not flexible enough to accommodate content that overlaps two folders that are stored in discrete parts of such a hierarchy. As circumstances change, a hierarchy of files may not reflect the content in a way that is helpful to the user. As a result, many people have abandoned the hierarchy as a search tool, and instead use alternative methods to search and find their files.

This has led to alternative file system paradigms being explored by the research community and leading software vendors [1]. One of these alternatives is the 'tag-based' file system [2, 7]. Put simply, tag based file systems allow the user to keep their files in a large pool, attaching keyword tags to make each file unique. The user can then search this pool by specifying a number of search tags, thus eliminating irrelevant files from their search.

Whilst tangible and embodiment techniques have been applied to interactions with traditional hierarchical file systems [5], very little work has been focused on their application with tag based file systems. In this paper we introduce two projects: the first looking at a novel tangible interaction technique for interacting with these tag based file systems called 'Magnetic Files'; and the second building upon this, to introduce a method for increasing information bandwidth by using embodied files.

Magnetic Files

Magnetic Files is a system comprising of a ceiling mounted projector, a camera and accompanying software that allows a user to visualize their tagged files as pool of information on their workspace. The system setup shown in Figure 2 provides a novel interaction based on the principles of magnetic attraction. The user can then search through their files by interacting with the workspace using 'Magnetic Tags'.

Magnetic Tags

'Magnetic Tags' are physical objects that can be manipulated on the workspace, and are identified by the system using a visual marker (shown in Figure 1). Each 'Magnet' has a single associated tag keyword, and the user has the freedom to combine as many 'Magnetic Tags' as they wish during a search task. When placed, the system detects a 'Magnetic Tag', and each visualized file in the pool responds. Files with a matching tag are attracted towards the 'Magnetic Tag', and those without a matching tag are repelled. In some cases, the strength of the attraction is dependent on the degree to which the 'Magnetic Tag' matches the file tag. For example, while the 'Good Music' tag will attract all rated music, the degree of the attraction is greater for '5 star' music, than it is for '1 star' music.

During typical usage, a user will place multiple 'Magnetic Tags' onto the workspace simultaneously, resulting in localized grouping of files with similar tags. Figure 3 shows an example layout of projected tagged files positioned around a number of 'Magnetic Tags'.

Property	Information
Shape	File Type.
Size	Perceived Importance.
Weight	Word Count or File Size.
Texture	Draft status of file. Rough vs Final.
Rigidity	File type or Word Count.
Temperature	Time since last modified.

Table 1: A table showing some possible physical characteristics (Property) of an embodied file, and what modifying them can mean (Information).

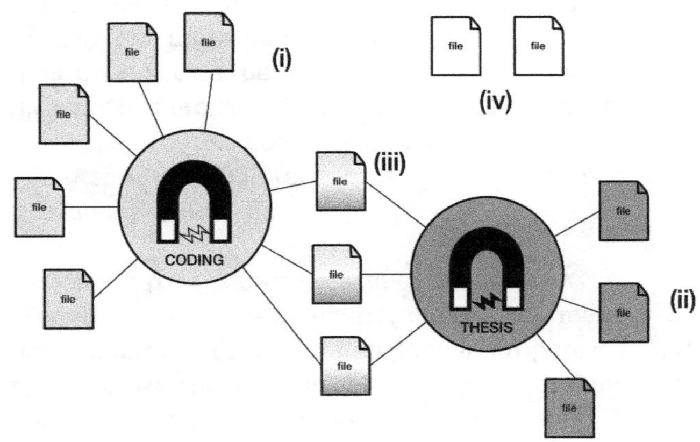

Figure 3: A diagram showing placement of files (squares) when two 'Magnetic Tags' are placed. Shown are; i) files tagged with just 'coding' and not 'thesis, ii) files tagged with just 'thesis' and not 'coding, iii) files tagged with both, and iv) files tagged with neither 'thesis' or 'text file'.

Additional Interactions – 'Absorbing' files

Although primarily a search tool, the 'Magnetic Files' system does offer a number of additional ways to manipulate the files. Some traditional file operations, such as moving a file, are no longer necessary, as files no longer have discrete locations. However, operations such as grouping a set of arbitrary files to perform some group action on this set will still be of use. To facilitate this we have implemented a number of blank magnetic tags. When these blank tags are placed on top of a collection of grouped files, they will 'absorb' this collection of files. The collection of files can then be manipulated as one: for example, they can be dragged to the waste bin area, or the user can choose to store the results of a search in a blank tag for quick access in the future.

Extending the Interactions using Embodied Files

The Magnetic Files project can be used successfully as a tag based file explorer and search tool with only visual feedback. However, the user has to rely entirely upon this feedback to achieve their goal. In order to increase the information bandwidth between system and user, we are investigating the physical embodiment of these tagged files. It has been shown that the physical properties of even small devices can be dynamically adjusted [4, 6]. Using similar techniques, the Embodied Files project aims to communicate information about a file by adjusting its physical properties in a dynamic and responsive way. Table 1 shows a small selection of possible physical characteristics that could be used in order to impart more information to the user.

To investigate this concept, we are creating a number of prototype embodied files, as shown in Figure 4. A combination of wheels (for movement), nichrome wire (for heat), an internal water pump with balloon (for rigidity & shape), and stretched Lycra twisted with a motor (for texture) are controlled via Bluetooth from a nearby computer to indicate various attributes. This will then allow us to link the movement of this embodied file to the Magnetic Files system. In the same way that files projected on to the workspace in the Magnetic Files project would respond to 'Magnetic Tags', the embodied files respond to the 'Magnets Tags' by positioning themselves on the work surface as shown in Figure 5. Furthermore, they will also adjust their physical properties so as to best portray the state of the file that they represent.

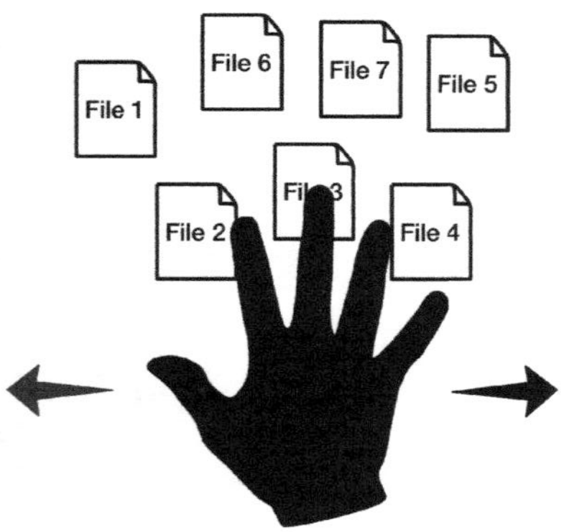

Figure 6: A diagram of the stroke interaction.

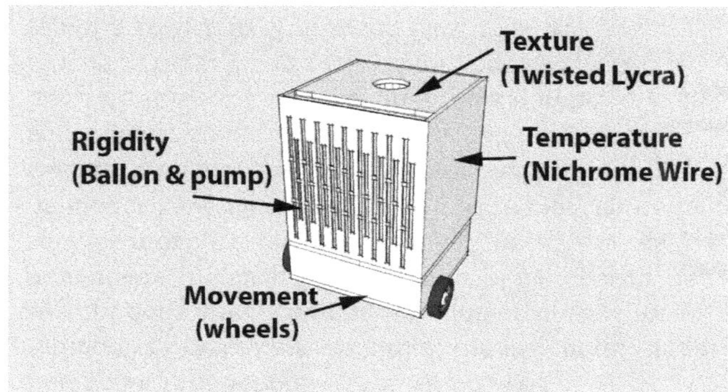

Figure 4: Prototype embodied file. Our prototype measures approximately 20cm tall, although we hope to make them much smaller in the near future.

Future Scenarios

The current prototype demonstrates use of shape, size, temperature and texture to indicate file type and perceived importance in relation to other files. However, we can imagine scenarios in which embodied files can represent multiple additional attributes. In this system we foresee a number of interactions for navigating the files that warrant further study.

Stroking & Squashing

The first of these interactions is stroking. This occurs when the user has positioned a number of embodied files in close proximity, so that they can quickly stroke their hand across the file's surface as shown in Figure 6. From this movement, the user can quickly and effectively determine the texture and temperature of each embodied file. Given our properties in Table 1, where texture represents the draft state of a file, and temperature represents the last modified date of a file, a user can quickly judge which of the files has been recently edited and is in need of more work (the rough, hot file). Similarly, a user can gently squash each file during this stroke to determine the rigidity of the file. From this they can determine more about the state of the file: the file's word count for example.

Collaborative Work

Embodied files can be easily divided between multiple users to help speed up the search process. Users can physically separate groups of files to work on.

Input Techniques

We envisage a number of scenarios where these properties are also used as inputs to the file system, rather than outputs to the user. For example, a user can physically compress a file in order to use a file compression algorithm.

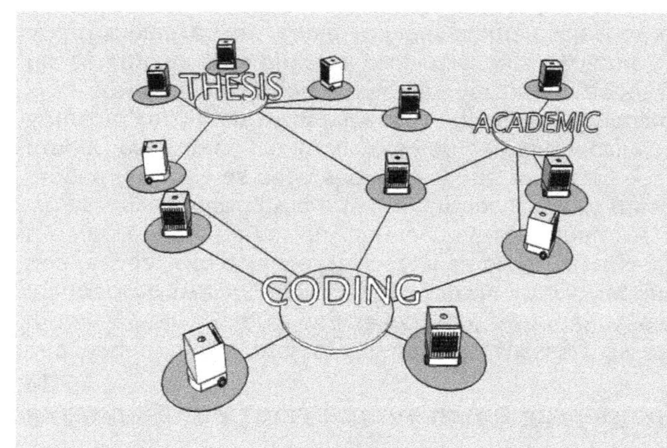

Figure 5: 3D rendering of scenario in which multiple tag base embodied files work together with 'Magnetic Tags'.

Relevance

Tangible systems can usually boast greater accessibility features than their non-tangible counterparts. Using a multi-sensory approach to aid differentiation between files potentially opens up tagged file systems to those that may not otherwise be able to use them.

The design also reflects the changing nature of computing in our daily lives. In many cases the computer location is no longer explicitly defined, and people now have the opportunity to interact with whatever objects are around them [3, 9]. Our interactions with the digital world are evolving, but it seems that our underlying dependence on working with file systems is rooted in an earlier era dominated by the desktop metaphor. The aim of this research is to produce a toolkit that will help fill the identified research gap, and allow such techniques to be explored more widely in varied computing tasks.

Conclusions

As previously discussed, we believe that hierarchical file systems are no longer an apt file storage solution in many scenarios, and that tag based file systems are a promising alternative. However, little work has been done to investigate tangible and embodied interfaces for such file systems, despite the benefits that tangible interfaces could bring to such systems. We believe this research identifies an important area that tangible interaction designers should explore given the dominance of file systems in computer systems, and we have already outlined some exciting interaction scenarios worthy of further research consideration.

References

[1] Agarawala, Anand, and Ravin Balakrishnan. "Keepin'it real: pushing the desktop metaphor with physics, piles and the pen." Proc. of the SIGCHI conference on Human Factors in computing systems. ACM, (2006), 1283-1292

[2] Apple Inc. "OS X tags help you organize your files." *http://support.apple.com/kb/HT5839.* Aug 26, 2014. Web. 01 September (2014).

[3] Hardy, John, et al. "Ubi Displays: A Toolkit for the Rapid Creation of Interactive Projected Displays." The International Symposium on Pervasive Displays. (2013).

[4] Hemmert, Fabian, et al. "Shape-changing mobiles: tapering in two-dimensional deformational displays in mobile phones." CHI'10 Extended Abstracts on Human Factors in Computing Systems. ACM, (2010), 3075-3080

[5] Karypidis, Alexandros, and Spyros Lalis. "The tangible file system." Distributed Computing Systems Workshops, 2003. Proc. 23rd International Conference on. IEEE, (2003), 268-273

[6] Niiyama, Ryuma, Lining Yao, and Hiroshi Ishii. "Weight and volume changing device with liquid metal transfer." Proc. of the 8th International Conference on Tangible, Embedded and Embodied Interaction. ACM, (2014), 49-52

[7] Schenk, Simon, Olaf Görlitz, and Steffen Staab. "TagFS: Bringing semantic metadata to the filesystem." Poster at the 3rd European Semantic Web Conference ESWC, (2006),

[8] Seltzer, Margo I., and Nicholas Murphy. "Hierarchical File Systems Are Dead." HotOS. (2009).

[9] Willis, Karl DD, Takaaki Shiratori, and Moshe Mahler. "HideOut: mobile projector interaction with tangible objects and surfaces." Proc. of the 7th International Conference on Tangible, Embedded and Embodied Interaction. ACM, (2013), 331-338

Social Textiles: Social Affordances and Icebreaking Interactions Through Wearable Social Messaging

Viirj Kan
MIT Media Lab
75 Amherst St.
Cambridge, MA 02142 USA
Viirj@media.mit.edu

Katsuya Fujii
MIT Media Lab
75 Amherst St.
Cambridge, MA 02142 USA
Katsuyaf@media.mit.edu

Judith Amores
MIT Media Lab
75 Amherst St.
Cambridge, MA 02142 USA
Amores@media.mit.edu

Chang Long Zhu Jin
MIT Media Lab
75 Amherst St.
Cambridge, MA 02142 USA
Changzj@media.mit.edu

Pattie Maes
MIT Media Lab
75 Amherst St.
Cambridge, MA 02142 USA
Pattie@media.mit.edu

Hiroshi Ishii
MIT Media Lab
75 Amherst St.
Cambridge, MA 02142 USA
Ishii@media.mit.edu

TEI '15, Jan 16-19 2015, Stanford, CA, USA
ACM 978-1-4503-3305-4/15/01.
http://dx.doi.org/10.1145/2677199.2688816

Abstract

Wearable commodities are able to extend beyond the temporal span of a particular community event, offering omnipresent vehicles for producing icebreaking interaction opportunities. We introduce a novel platform, which generates social affordances to facilitate community organizers in aggregating social interaction among unacquainted, collocated members beyond initial hosted gatherings. To support these efforts, we present functional work-in-progress prototypes for *Social Textiles*, wearable computing textiles which enable social messaging and peripheral social awareness on non-emissive digitally linked shirts. The shirts serve as catalysts for different social depths as they reveal common interests (mediated by community organizers), based on the physical proximity of users. We provide 3 key scenarios, which demonstrate the user experience envisioned with our system. We present a conceptual framework, which shows how different community organizers across domains such as universities, brand communities and digital self-organized communities can benefit from our technology.

Figure 1. Before and after of interaction via skin contact. Information in this instance shows the users' common university.

Keywords
Co-located / Distributed Collaboration; Wearable Computing; Social Media Networking; E-Textiles; Computer-Mediated Communication (CMC)

ACM Classification Keywords
H.5.3 Group and Organization Interfaces; H.5.2 User Interfaces; D.2.2 Design Tools and Techniques

Introduction

Community organizers often employ strategies for generating social interactions such as providing alcohol in social gatherings, team-building activities, solicit disclosure of member information, as well as provide symbolic commodity and merchandise. Objects such as mugs, pens, shirts, badges, notepads and bracelets are symbolic commodities provided through community organizers as they inherit attributes, which translate into social signaling opportunities.

Wearable commodities such as clothing and accessories provide unique opportunities for social advertising as their functions serve as extension to an individual's identity. One prime example of such a wearable commodity is a university's class ring or t- shirt, which identifies an individual as a part of a common representative group carrying shared values of the associated commodity. Because commodities already act as social catalysts [2], they are able to extend beyond the temporal span of a particular social event or occurrence and into extensions of everyday life, offering omnipresent icebreaking interaction opportunities amongst members. Thus, by introducing additional affordances to these commodities while leveraging their existing functionalities as social catalysts, we believe that they can act as effective tools to facilitate social interactions for community organizers. To support these efforts, we present functional work-in-progress prototypes for *Social Textiles*, wearable computing textiles which enable social messaging and peripheral social awareness on non-emissive digitally linked shirts. The shirts serve as social catalysts for different social depths, which reveal common interests between members and exposes varying degrees of private information (figure 1). The disclosure of personal information is mediated by community organizers through defining the shirt's default state and a set of triggered states for which further information will be revealed amongst specific member groups.

Related Work

A number of prior research in computer-mediated communication (CMC) employ methods utilizing wearable commodities as social catalysts. The distinction between our research and existing works is that our development serves to generate social affordances *beyond* initial hosted gatherings, for *community organizers across various domains*.

nTags are active badges that works with personal information submitted into a database. When another wearer of an nTag with similar interests is in close proximity, the name badge shows a percentage that represents the common interests you have with the person you interact with [1]. iBand is a technology-enhanced bracelet that can store, display, and exchange information about you and your relationships. iBand leverages the familiar nature of the handshake, coupled with the qualities of jewelry to act as tangible keepsakes and reminders of relationships [4]. Urbanhermes is a wearable patch that act as a means for social signaling to meet individuals with shared interests. The wearable patch is used to transmit images to strangers with common interests [5].

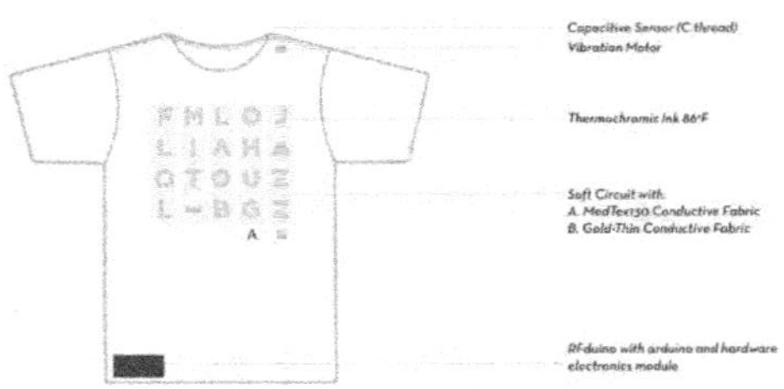

Figure 2. Diagram of shirt components

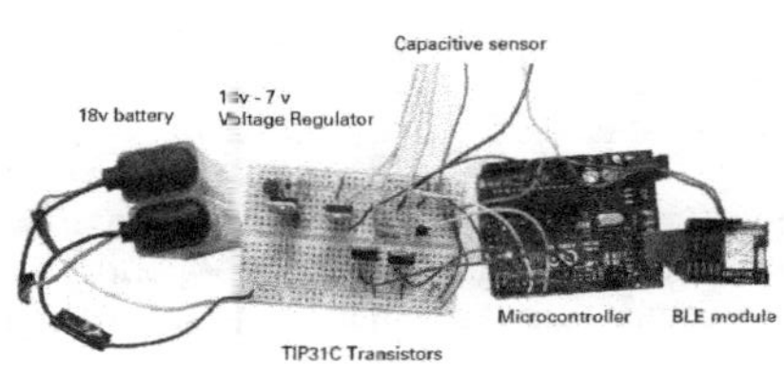

Figure 3. Electronics components with microprocessor, BLE bluetooth module, batteries and supporting electronics circuitry.

Prototype and Technical Design

Our system functions to aggregate social interaction among members beyond the given context of a community organizer's hosted event. It also extends such social affordances every time the shirt is re-worn and serves as an omnipresent social catalyst. As shown in figure 2 and 3, we utilize a series of technologies which communicates with a user's smartphone to detect proximity, deliver haptic feedback, detect human capacitance and activate the thermochromic dyes on the shirt. Here, we describe how the interaction works (see figure 4):

User feels a haptic feedback via a light "tap on the shoulder" as they sense the presence of someone wearing *Social Textiles* within a 12-foot social spatial proximity[1]. We map the metaphor of haptic feedback based on relationship level: acquaintances and friends may ask for attention with a squeeze on the shoulder while unacquainted individuals enact with a soft tap. This brings about an embodied peripheral awareness upon unacquainted users. When users of the same shirt interact through a social greeting with one another via skin contact through a handshake or a high five, wearers of *Social Textiles* gain new 'features' or social information of the interacted parties. This incentivizes and provides social affordances for users to interact with one another, as they are able to see what they have in common, see additional artwork on the shirt design, or discover underlying social information with collocated members.

[1] *Edward Hall's social proxemics diagram highlights the social interaction distances in a physical environment*

Currently we focus on exploring the feasibility of our idea and have built a functional proof-of-concept prototype. The prototype development can be described in two parts: thermochromic soft circuit and electrical hardware. For the soft circuit, we used conductive fabrics (MedTex130 and gold-thin conductive fabric) embedded below a layer thermochromic ink which becomes transparent at 89°F. Thermochromic ink is not dynamic compared to other technologies like LEDs, but is easily replaceable with current printing technology. Also the use of ink and conductive fabrics is suitable for the practicality of maintenance and laundering[6]. The hardware components consist of a microcontroller with a bluetooth low energy module (BLE), vibration motor, a 15V battery and conductive thread as a capacitive sensor sewn on the neck of the shirt. Future work will involve the miniturization and waterproofing of the hardware through a secured waterproof enclosure. The BLE module is used for wireless connection between a user's smartphone and the *Social Textiles* in order to retrieve data among users such as common interests and social proximity which community organizers can utilize to program interaction triggers (demostrated in the scenario & applications section). The capacitive sensor is used to detect skin contact among members to trigger the soft circuit and embedded messages and graphics on the thermochromic shirt.

Towards the development of a fully functional prototype, several technologies are under investigation based on factors such as accessibility, cost, reusability and manufacturing access. For example, E-ink [3], widely known as electronic ink technology for e-readers is under development within the research community as printable inks on fabrics, but is currently not

Figure 4. Interaction scheme shows 1)Haptic feedback: user feels presence of someone wearing the same shirt; 2) Shirt serves as icebreaking interaction; 3) Wearers of the textile gain meaningful interaction as shirt reveals what they have in common other person

accessible. In contrast, LED displays are currently accessible but social and cultural acceptance of emissive displays on wearables is not yet adopted.

Scenario Applications

Here we demonstrate three scenarios where *Social Textiles* are used in different communities:

Brand communities inherit members when individuals self-identify with a particular brand and thus subscribing to the community through purchasing commodities.

John goes to "X brand" clothing store to purchase a *Social Textiles* shirt. He selects a graphic shirt with a single star on it (about the size of a dime). A sign at the store reads "uncover the real design." The next day he wears the new shirt, curious as to when he will in fact discover the shirt's actual design. On the way to lunch, he senses a soft vibration on his left shoulder and it felt a bit like someone just tapped him. He looks around and sees that 7-feet away, is a girl wearing the same shirt as him. She also notices this as they approach one another's direction. John decides to approach her: "Hey we have the same shirt! I'm really curious what this design really looks like. My name is John." They shake hands and the shirt gradually grows from a single star to the constellation Leo.
Within this scenario, the disclosure of personal information between the users (John and Cynthia) is *low*. The *Social Textiles* requires no data of the users' identities to produce the interaction. The design of this particular *Social Textile* motivates individuals to interact by enticing them to uncover the underlying design of the shirt. The common interests and traits between John and Cynthia are left for the two members to discover. Since they both subscribe to purchase shirts from this particular clothing brand, it is likely that they have particular tastes and lifestyle interests in common (represented by the clothing brand). The *Social Textile* does not disclose personal data or guide the social conversation towards any particular subject. Users solicit to gain access to the particular community, based on the brand-mediated design they purchase.

Universities hold school wide orientations in the beginning of each semester to welcome new students. Relationships and collaborations formed across disciplines serve to increase innovation and intellectual capital for the institution.

It is Joie's first week of school at university. During orientation she receives a *Social Textiles* shirt and is instructed to wear it throughout the event. It is difficult to discern exactly what the shirt reads as it is made up of a series of alphabet letters arranged in a grid. While all the shirt designs look similar, Joie observes that depending on which color shirt people were wearing, the arrangements of the letters were slightly different. During lecture at orientation, the dean of student affairs speaks: "It is important to make friends outside your department." In a cheeky expression, the dean continues: "Just to give you a tip for this week, meet as many people as you can with a different color shirt than you - often, new ideas are unlocked through interdisciplinary collaboration ;)." During lunch Joie takes the dean's advice. She walks up to a group of people with different colored shirt designs and introduces herself: "Hey, I'm joie". She reaches in for a handshake with Penny, who is wearing the same color shirt as her. When they shake hands, the group is astounded as they watch all the shirts within the group transform. The text on their shirts "disappear" to reveal that, two of them are EE (Electrical Engineering) majors, one in CS (Computer Science), while Penny and Joie are both in Arch (Architecture).

This scenario highlights how *Social Textiles* can connect interdisciplinary members by revealing different information on the shirts. The disclosure of personal information in this scenario is *medium,* since generic information and semi-personal data is revealed about the users. This information is mediated through the community organizer (in this case, the university) where they facilitate interdepartmental communication between the students. Other potential information can be shown on the same shirts (ie. skillsets; hobbies and club affiliation; or institution name) to aggregate interaction among groups with different traits. In addition to facilitating icebreaking interaction and assembling interdisciplinary teams, the *Social Textiles* can also enable additional affordances for students attending the same university to encounter one another outside of the event (figure 1).

Online communities often self-organize through the digital infrastructure provided by sites like Meetup.com, Twitter.com and Facebook.com. In some situations, digitally organized communities assembled online translate into physical world events and gatherings to form offline support groups or civil activism pursuits. Special interest groups often self-identify and signal to one another publically, through the use of specialty patches, stickers and wearables.

Morgan is an avid fan of underground doom metal music. He does not have any friends who are into this genre, so he often follows particular digital community websites to congregate about his favorite doom metal bands. One day when Morgan went on the website, he found that they released a new *Social Textiles* shirt in the merchandise section of the website. The shirt is minimal and looks like a regular black t-shirt. He decides to order it so he can use it to meet more people that are into doom metal. Morgan finally gets his t-shirt and wears it to work. As he walks into work, he senses the vibration motor. The vibration feels a bit like a squeeze in the arm. He notices that Ben is walking towards him, also wearing a seemingly regular black shirt. The two of them exchange glances as they realize that they are both doom metal fans.

In this scenario, *Social Textiles* connect people with specific niche interests. The disclosure of personal information is *high* since Morgan's interest in doom metal is highly specialized and personal information. The *Social Textiles* shirts can also serve to connect community members with common philosophical beliefs, personalities, emotional statuses and ethics. As illustrated in this scenario, *Social Textiles* has the potential to enable members to bypass superficial or generic interests. It has the capability of connecting people based on specialized personal information through "filtering" individuals, to tune social experiences towards more compatible ones.

Conclusion & Future Work

We believe that our system offers several advantages and distinctions over existing systems. Our contribution towards the development of social affordances through wearable computing textiles extend beyond initial hosted gatherings, and serves as omnipresent social catalysts for community organizers. As illustrated in the scenario applications section, *Social Textiles* can be applied across a variety of domains for connecting communities through icebreaking interactions.

As individual members are a part of multiple communities and are selective in what information they choose to disclose to the public through their fashion, our system is sensitive to users' boundaries for what is considered private versus public. *Social Textiles* leverages the nature of wearable commodities and it's tendencies to reveal different levels of personal information, based on which community group they may have acquired the wearable through. The different community groups highlighted represents the degree of personal information that is disclosed through an individuals' association with them. The level of privacy in *Social Textiles* is maintained by the context and databases already possessed by various community organizers, thus maintaining trust among users of our system.

This paper serves as a conceptual framework for developing social affordances to aggregate interaction among unacquainted, collocated members beyond initial hosted gatherings. Future work will involve fully functional prototypes where we build upon our current proof-of-concept implementations, by incorporating current social media infrastructures and databases. Hardware components are to be miniaturized, waterproofed and integrated into the *Social Textiles* to progress the prototype towards practical, easy-to-maintain, and distributable products. User evaluations to test the effectiveness and depth of social interactions with our technology will be subject of ongoing work. To further facilitate community organizers, user-friendly tools and interfaces for designing, editing and producing *Social Textiles* will be investigated.

Acknowledgements

We thank all our supporting colleagues at the MIT Media Lab, who have provided us the insights and suggestions that enabled us to realize this project.

References

[1] Borovoy, R., Martin, F., & Resnick, M. (1999). Revealing common ground: Augmentation on the edges of interpretive communities. In *Proceedings of the 1999 conference on Computer support for collaborative learning*, 5.

[2] Chew, A., Leclerc, V., Sadi, S., Tang, A., & Ishii, H. (2005). Sparks. In *CHI'05 Extended Abstracts on Human Factors in Computing Systems*, 1276-1279.

[3] Comiskey, B., Albert, J. D., Yoshizawa, H., & Jacobson, J. (1998). An electrophoretic ink for all-printed reflective electronic displays. *Nature*, *394*(6690), 253-255.

[4] Kanis, M., Winters, N., Agamanolis, S., Cullinan, C., & Gavin, A. (2004). iBand: a wearable device for handshake-augmented interpersonal information exchange. In *Adjunct Proceedings of the Sixth International Conference on Ubiquitous Computing.*

[5] Liu, C. M., & Donath, J. S. (2006). Urbanhermes: social signaling with electronic fashion. In *Proceedings of the SIGCHI conference on Human Factors in computing systems*, 885-888.

[6] Zeagler, C., Gilliland, S., Audy, S., & Starner, T. (2013, September). Can I wash it?: the effect of washing conductive materials used in making textile based wearable electronic interfaces. In *Proceedings of the 17th annual international symposium on International symposium on wearable computers*, 143-144.

Note Code – A Tangible Music Programming Puzzle Tool

Vishesh Kumar
Indian Institute of Technology
Guwahati, India
k.vishesh@iitg.ernet.in

Utkarsh Dwivedi
Indian Institute of Technology
Guwahati, India
d.utkarsh@iitg.ernet.in

Tuhina Dargan
Indian Institute of Technology
Guwahati, India
tuhina@iitg.ernet.in

Poorvi Vijay
Indian Institute of Technology
Guwahati, India
poorvi@iitg.ernet.in

Abstract
We present the design of Note Code – a music programming puzzle game designed as a tangible device coupled with a Graphical User Interface (GUI). Tapping patterns and placing boxes in proximity enables programming these 'note-boxes' to store sets of notes, play them back and activate different sub-components or neighboring boxes. This system provides users the opportunity to learn a variety of computational concepts, including functions, function calling and recursion, conditionals, as well as engage in composing music. The GUI adds a dimension of viewing the created programs and interacting with a set of puzzles that help discover the various computational concepts in the pursuit of creating target tunes, and optimizing the program made.

TEI '15, Jan 16-19 2015, Stanford, CA, USA
ACM 978-1-4503-3305-4/15/01.
http://dx.doi.org/10.1145/2677199.2688817

Author Keywords
Computational thinking, puzzle based learning, tangible interaction, tangible music, education

ACM Classification Keywords
H.5.2 - User Interfaces, L.1.2 - Learning Objects.

Introduction
Computational thinking refers to a problem solving technique that uses computer science techniques. Over the past few years, it has gained recognition as a skill not just for computer scientists; but a basic skill required in modern society in domains from art to science and blended into people's daily life, as described by Wing and Papert [1,2]. Computational thinking involves finding patterns, decomposing problems into smaller pieces, and using the provided tools.

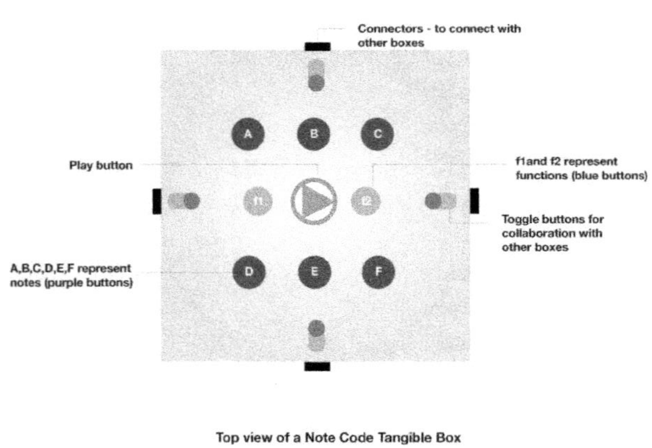

Figure 1. Concept diagram of Note Boxes

There is an incessant construction of tools and systems to make learning programming, or its basic paradigms, simpler for children. Starting with Logo [3], other tools for the same would include AlgoBlock [4], ToonTalk [5], AgentSheets [6], and the largely successful Scratch developed at the MIT Media Lab [7].

Tangible Programming

Piaget and Bruner have showed in the past that it is often more useful to give children concrete examples and objects to enable problem solving, before teaching them the associated symbols. [8,9] This speaks to both, a need for going away from typical syntax, and using more approachable elements (like graphic icons etc.), as well as making tangible tools for the same. McNerney et al reinforce the observation that introduction with syntax is not a suitable way to begin learning to program, especially for primary-middle school aged children [10]. In this spirit, numerous TUIs have been developed to enhance student learning of technology, via technology. Most of these, would be called Resnick's "digital manipulatives" or "programming construction kits" – like 'kinetic recorders' such as Curlybot [11], Topobo [12], or Algorhythm [13]; or helping storytelling by children, such as Telltale [14], and so on.

Tangible music

Numerous tangible music devices have been designed, and prototyped [15], for a variety of purposes. Beginning with the highly popular Reactable, that allows for collaborative music creation by moving tangible markers on a table being followed by sensors – we find BlockJam[16]: a system that involves 'blocks' that store musical pieces, are linked with each others, and are sequentially played by using play blocks. This comes quite close to the tangible aspect of our designed tool as well, though with some crucial differences with respect to stress on the programming paradigms one can interact with. Similar sequencers like Siftables Music Sequencer, based on similar principles, have also been developed.

Music and Computational Thinking

Performamatics [17] is a workshop with a plethora of activities aimed to bridge computational thinking and music, and interest people from both disciplines. Music, and relatedly *sound thinking*, is seen as a ripe avenue to integrate with CT – as both are fertile with patterns, repetition and identification of patters.

Additionally, using computational thinking and programming paradigms allows for an innovative and new approach for music composition, especially in Note Code.

Design and Functionality

Note Code's design and functioning is heavily influenced by concepts of puzzle based learning, since Puzzle-based learning shares many of the pedagogical goals of the emerging paradigm of Computational Thinking [1, 18]; inspired from the drum-bots of Algo.Rhythm, which is conceptually similar to BlockJam and other tangible music systems – recording information in individual blocks, and calling neighboring blocks to play.

Further, the programming concepts we attempted to embed in our interactions and systems, were those of

Figure 2. An initial limited prototype prepared

functional modularity, and conditionals – functions being the only non-intuitive construct for beginners to need to understand and grasp, while being one of the most fundamental concepts in computational thinking – along side control structures like conditions and loops.

To embody these, we built a note-box with buttons for sets of notes, and function buttons to hold recordings of sequences. This ended up being significantly similar to Perlman's Button Box. [19] The differences being recording music, is equal parts 'programming by rehearsal' (not requiring the player to think in terms of abstracted instructions) [19] as well as programming in a language i.e. with relatively abstract instructions, when puzzles (tasks of target tunes required to be created) are worked upon.

To enable activating different blocks from one, we made 'edge calls' so that each of the edges could be executed as a step just like any of the other notes. The ability of receiving edge calls, also provided an avenue for implementing conditionals – such that instructions are conditional on receiving signals on an edge, at that step. The implementation of conditionals on edge signals, and using this as a paradigm of computational thinking to interact with, is a feature that makes Note Code significantly unique compared to the numerous other tangible music systems.

Detailed Working

In our prototype, each note-box had six note buttons (notes A to F), four edge out buttons (call edges 1 to 4), four edge in buttons (if edges 1 to 4) two function buttons, and one play button.

To start recording a function, one of the function buttons would be pressed (F1 or F2), and then a sequence of notes, edge buttons, and function buttons would be pressed – which would be recorded into the initially chosen function. The play button would be pressed to stop a function's recording, and in case no function is being recorded – the play button would 'play' the note-box i.e. call F1.

The edge buttons send a signal to the outgoing connectors on each of the edges. During recording a function, pressing a function button records a function call. Pressing an out edge button calls the edge, and pressing an in edge button records a conditional – if a signal is received on that edge during play, the following instruction will be implemented, otherwise it'll be skipped. For example, following is a set of button presses, and then the corresponding recorded functions as a result of the same:

F1 – note B – note A – call edge 2 – note D – F2 – if edge 1 – F1 – note C – Play

produces the program:

```
f1() {
   B;
   A;
   edge 2;
   D;
   f2();
   if (edge 1) {
      F1(); }
   C; }
```

Each row of instruction takes a beat to 'play', check, or be executed. When another note-box is placed in connection with the edge of an earlier note-box, the corresponding edge calls and conditionals enables the possibility of complex and layered music.

This entire construction has been prototyped by using a microcontroller (Arduino/MaKeyMaKey) inside a hand-sawn plywood box. The microcontroller programming, and coupled GUI, have been made using Processing.

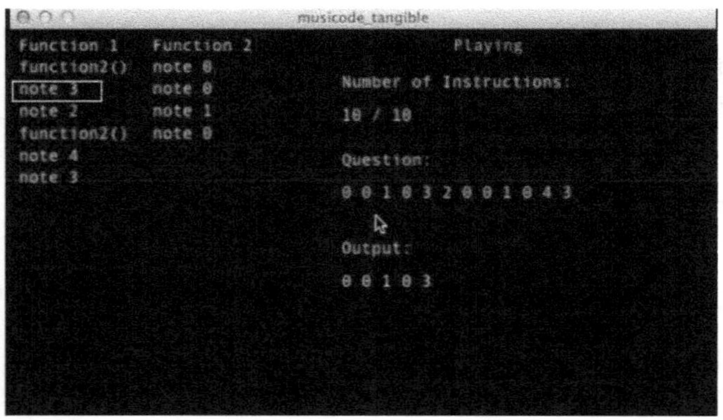

Figure 3. Screenshot of the coupled GUI

Puzzles and GUI

We coupled this system with a GUI (on a connected computer), to help keep track of the contents of the recorded functions. This GUI also had a puzzle component – which would offer the target note sequence, and the minimum number of instructions in which the same should be doable. Our preliminary tests involved seeing how quickly students could grasp the concept of grouping repeated instructions using functions, on a 'puzzle' that involved creating the Happy Birthday tune: " A A B A D C A A B A E D ".

This was preceded and followed by other puzzles to help grasp similar concepts, where the target note sequence was attempted to be melodious as often as possible.

The GUI also helped follow the program flow, by highlighting the instruction being executed at every beat. This helped the players in keeping track of how correctly the program they had made, was behaving.

Discussions and Future Works

We imagine extending the abilities of the described system to make the music composition abilities far richer. It should be possible, to choose different instruments on different boxes, let alone different scales of notes as well. We chose just 6 note buttons for easier implementation, but more – at least 12 notes spanning one octave (per box) would be desirable.

Also, making these note boxes standalone, i.e. not requiring a connected computer, would also help greatly in making this TUI more mobile, and easily playable.

Enriching the GUI for greater ease of appearance and use, and perhaps enhanced functionality with respect to changing boxes' properties (like sound quality, tempo, instrument) would enhance the experience further.

A preliminary testing showed that the ability of creating melodious tunes by solving puzzles, or open endedly exploring on the boxes – to discover either new music, or computational concepts – is highly exciting for both 9th graders as well as college freshmen. We believe that tying seemingly disparate fields like music composition and learning programming exhibits great promise, and further constructs around this should strive to balance simplicity of usage and representation, along side more paradigms like objects, variables, etc.

References

[1] Wing, J.M. Computational thinking and thinking about computing. Philosophical transactions. Series A, Mathematical, physical, and engineering sciences, 366(1881), 3717-25, 2008.

[2] Papert, S. Teaching Children Thinking (AI Memo 247), MIT, Cambridge, MA, 1971.

[3] Papert, S. (1980). Mindstorms: Children, computers, and powerful ideas.

[4] Suzuki H., Kato, H. 1995. Interaction-level support for collaborative learning: AlgoBlock—an open programming language. In The first international conference on Computer support for collaborative learning (CSCL '95), John L. Schnase and Edward L.

Cunnius (Eds.). L. Erlbaum Associates Inc., Hillsdale, NJ, USA, 349-355.

[5] Kahn, K. (1996). ToonTalkTM–An Animated Programming Environment for Children (Vol. 7). (Elsevier, Ed.) Journal of Visual Languages & Computing. Leave & Wegner. (1991). Situated learning: Legitimate peripheral participation. Cambridge University Press.

[6] Repenning, A., Ioannidou, A., & Zola, J. (2000). AgentSheets: End-user programmable simulations. Journal of Artificial Societies and Social Simulation, 3(3)

[7] Resnick et al., M. (2009). Scratch: programming for all. Commun. ACM 52.

[8] Bruner, J. (1966). Theory of Instruction. Cambridge, Mass.: Harvard University Press

[9] Piaget, J. (1973). The child and reality: Problems of genetic psychology.

[10] McNerney, Timothy S. "From turtles to Tangible Programming Bricks: explorations in physical language design." Personal and Ubiquitous Computing 8.5 (2004): 326-337.

[11] Frei, P., & Su, V. (2000). Curlybot: designing a new class of computational toys. In *Proceedings of the SIGCHI conference on Human Factors in Computing Systems* (CHI '00). ACM, New York, NY, USA, 129-136.

[12] Raffle, H. S., Parkes, A. J., & Ishii, H. (2004). Topobo: a constructive assembly system with kinetic memory. Proceedings of the SIGCHI conference on Human factors in computing systems (pp. 647–654).

[13] Peng, H. 2012. Algo.Rhythm: computational thinking through tangible music device. In *Proceedings of the Sixth International Conference on Tangible, Embedded and Embodied Interaction* (TEI '12), Stephen N. Spencer (Ed.). ACM, New York, NY, USA, 401-402.

[14] Ananny, M. (2002). Supporting children's collaborative authoring: practicing written literacy while composing oral texts. Proceedings of the Conference on Computer Support for Collaborative Learning: Foundations for a CSCL Community (pp. 595–596). International Society of the Learning Sciences.

[15] Tangible Music. "URL: http://modin.yuri.at/tangibles." Consultado em 24.04 (2009).

[16] Newton-Dunn, Henry, Nakano, H., Gibson J. "Block jam: a tangible interface for interactive music." Proceedings of the 2003 conference on New interfaces for musical expression. National University of Singapore, 2003.

[17] Jesse M. Heines, Gena R. Greher, and Sarah Kuhn. 2009. Music performamatics: interdisciplinary interaction. *SIGCSE Bull.* 41, 1 (March 2009), 478-482.

[18] Falkner, N., Sooriamurthi, R., Michalewicz, Z. Teaching puzzle-based learning: development of basic concepts. Teaching Mathematics and Computer Science, 2012; 10(1):183-204

[19] McNerney, Timothy S. "From turtles to Tangible Programming Bricks: explorations in physical language design." Personal and Ubiquitous Computing 8.5 (2004): 326-337.

Process Products: Capturing Design Iteration with Digital Fabrication

Tiffany Tseng
MIT Media Lab
75 Amherst St. E14-445C
Cambridge, MA 02139
ttseng@mit.edu

Geoff Tsai
MIT Mechanical Engineering Dept.
77 Massachusetts Ave. 3-446
Cambridge, MA 02139
gtt@mit.edu

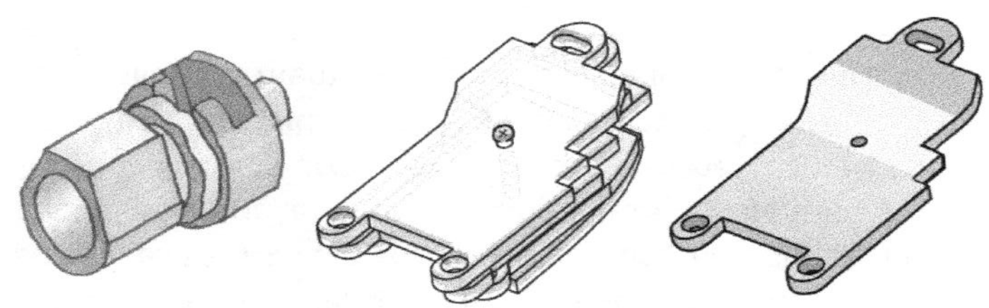

Figure 1: Three examples of proposed *Process Products*: Process Heatmaps, Process Stacks, and Process Textures.

TEI '15, Jan 16-19 2015, Stanford, CA, USA
ACM 978-1-4503-3305-4/15/01.
http://dx.doi.org/10.1145/2677199.2687891

Abstract
This paper introduces the concept of *Process Products*, or digitally fabricated objects embedded with visual representations of design process. The goal of this work is to use automation to capture the iterative process of designing and manufacturing objects using digital fabrication and encapsulate this information directly on the produced objects themselves. Documenting iteration can help designers communicate the evolution of their design, reveal strategies that designers use to create products, and help manufacturers of digital fabrication technologies understand how their tools are used. We propose three potential forms of *Process Products*: Process Heatmaps, Process Stacks, and Process Textures, as a way to spark discussion on capturing and representing iteration in the design of physical objects.

Author Keywords
Digital fabrication; design process; documentation

ACM Classification Keywords
H.5.m. Information interfaces and presentation

Introduction
Digital fabrication has become an increasingly popular process for prototyping and manufacturing designs at a personal scale [1,3]. As digital fabrication technologies

are optimized, the turnaround time for producing prototypes has decreased, enabling designers to quickly iterate on and realize their designs.

Capturing changes across different iterations of a design (and why they occur) can be beneficial both to designers and manufacturers. Documentation of design iterations can help designers communicate the evolution of their design to others and reveal the strategies they use in creating a product, particularly in response to critical or challenging design elements. Additionally, this documentation can provide manufacturers with insights on how their tools are used, allowing them to better focus their tools towards their users' needs.

Digitally fabricated objects are uniquely situated to capture how they were made as the workflow of creating them can generate digital and physical representations of process. Changes to digital design files can be captured using version control tools, and physical manifestations of iteration are created through the fabrication of these design files at various stages in the design process. The digital nature of designing objects for digital fabrication introduces opportunities for passive, automated documentation captured through design software. This is important as the effort required for documentation has been a barrier to designers sharing their work with others [8].

In this paper, we outline opportunities for embedding visual representations of iteration into digitally fabricated objects. While digital tools can offer rich ways to explore process, traditional forms of information visualization often require an external display. Digital fabrication enables new ways to visualize this information directly on the product(s) generated through the fabrication process.
We present three potential manifestations of *Process Products*, or digitally fabricated objects with embedded representations of process, in an effort to spark discussion on capturing and representing iteration in the design process.

Related Work

Existing work has used physical objects as a lens into digital information, often using cameras and other sensors as an intermediary between the physical and digital worlds. Numerous examples of tangible interfaces use the reacTIVision platform, for example, to both tag objects and enable interactions via an external display [4]. In contrast, we propose a series of *Process Products* where there is no external computer or display used to reveal properties of the object — aspects of the design process are represented on the object directly.

In previous work, Rosner and Ryokai developed Spyn, an application for crafters to embed stories into knitted objects [6]. With Spyn, the physical product incorporates yarn embedded with infrared ink, and a cell phone uses computer vision to detect and play back recorded stories left by the designer. Unlike *Process Products* where information is automatically created based on the designer's workflow, these markers must be intentionally woven into the product by the designer.

Similarly, work by Rich combined computer vision with digitally fabricated textures on physical objects to encode information about the object [5]. Like the other examples, the premise of this work was to connect

Design File Properties	Dimensional Changes
	Timeline of changes
Machine Properties	Speed and Power
	Resolution and Orientation
	Job Number
	Time to complete job
Contextual Properties	Material changes
	Design rationale

Table 1: Process properties

physical products with digital information — the user ultimately views the digital information through a computer rather than solely on the object itself.

The proposed work is differentiated from existing work because it represents process directly on designed objects through automated, digital documentation.

Digital Fabrication

Digital fabrication involves translating a digital design file, such as a 3D model or 2D sketch, into a physical product, such as a 3D printed object or laser cut part. Examples of digital fabrication technologies include 3D printers, laser cutters, vinyl cutters, computer numerical control (CNC) routers, and desktop mills. Digital models are created in design software on a computer before being sent to a particular machine for fabrication. When creating a product using these tools, designers define machine and material properties (such as power and speed settings) that specify how the product should be fabricated.

Elements of Digital Fabrication Processes

Designing a product through digital fabrication involves iterating over *design file* properties, *machine* properties, and *contextual* properties (Table 1).

Design file properties include dimensional changes and modifications to the profile of a model. These properties have the potential to be documented automatically in the design software through version control tools. A timeline of changes, such as the date and time changes were made, can also be recorded.

Machine properties are set on the machine itself once the design file is ready to be realized. They include properties such as the speed and power setting for subtractive manufacturing processes (milling and cutting) or resolution and orientation for additive manufacturing processes (3D printing). Additional machine properties include the job number (a proxy for the number of iterations) and the time taken to complete a job.

Contextual properties capture non-digital information, including material changes (such as switching between wood and plastic) and design rationale (why a new iteration is needed). While these properties are not easily measured automatically, they provide the context for interpreting the reasoning behind iterations. One can imagine that the integration of *design file*, *machine*, and *contextual properties* can aid in painting a holistic picture of the digital fabrication process.

Process Products

Below, I describe three examples of workflows for creating *Process Products*. The examples use 3D printing and laser cutting technologies, but principles behind these examples can potentially be applied to other technologies.

Process Heatmaps

A *Process Heatmap* represents changes to digital design files using heatmaps on 3D printed components.

When developing a 3D printed part, designers often makes changes to a 3D model in design software. Changes to the form of a model can arise from factors such as mechanical constraints or aesthetic concerns.

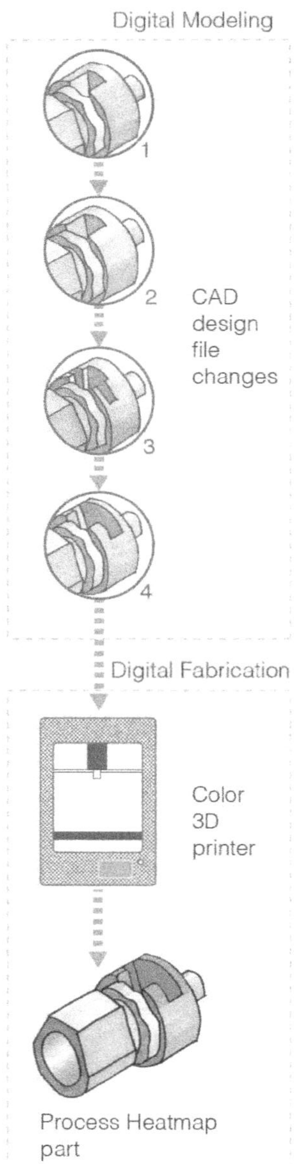

Figure 2: 3D printed *Process Heatmaps*

A physical "difference" of these changes can be represented directly on the 3D printed object using color 3D printing [2,7], where colors can form a heatmap indicating areas of the product that experienced the most iteration (Figure 2). Additionally, the actual profile or shape of any previous iterations of the product could be indicated on the final product using the same methods.

In summary, *Process Heatmaps* represent changes made to a digital design file. Documentation about the evolution of a digital model can be automatically captured in design software. These changes are then physically represented through a colored heatmap on the final 3D printed product

Process Stacks

Process Stacks capture physical differences in the profile of laser-cut test pieces.

Laser cutting is one of the quicker digital fabrication technologies and thus affords fast iteration. Over the course of generating a laser-cut design, the designer continually modifies the digital design file and may create prototypes of each version of a design file. These prototypes, or test pieces, represent physical manifestations of iteration. Physical differences between test pieces can be visually discerned through vertically stacking (Figure 3).

A hole can be dynamically added and cut into the center of each test piece as it is laser cut, allowing a designer to align and stack the test pieces using fasteners. The use of clear material, such as clear plastic, can enable viewers to see additive and subtractive changes to the profile of the laser-cut piece.

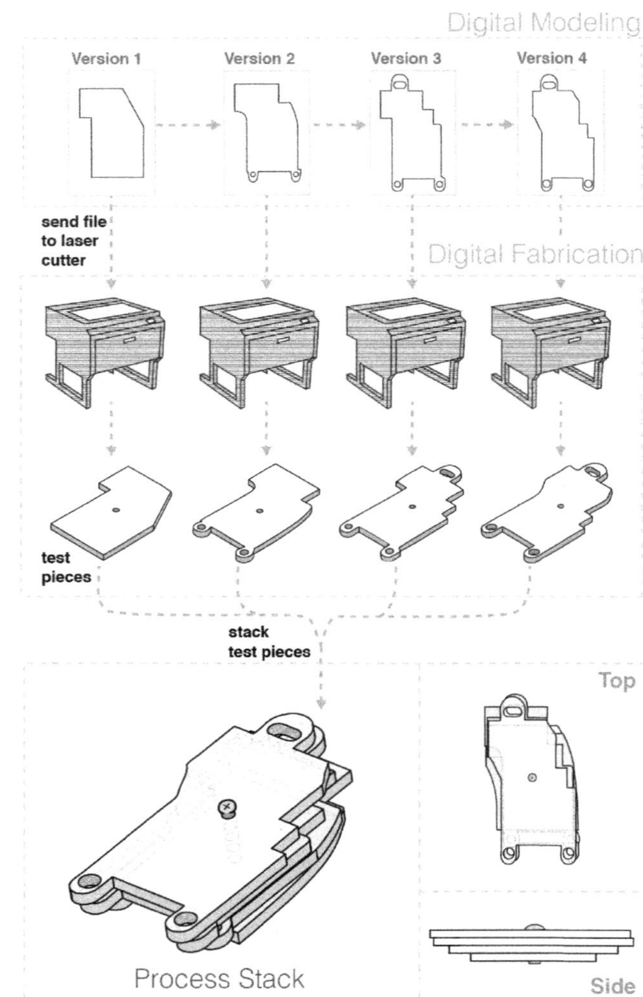

Figure 3. Laser cutting *Process Stacks* workflow

In summary, *Process Stacks* represent changes to a design file over time through the stacking of test pieces. *Process Stacks* enable users to visually understand changes to the profile of the object. Additionally, the height of the stack is an indication of the number of iterations the component experienced before reaching a final design.

Process Textures

The previous two examples focus on changes to the profile of a digital design file, but changes to machine settings can also be represented. *Process Textures* capture changes to speed or power settings required to manufacture a laser-cut component and represent these changes on the surface of the laser-cut object. The textures serve as an indicator of the amount of effort (or number of trials) needed to create the part as well as the nature of the changes made.

Creating a laser-cut component involves adjusting speed and power settings for cutting through a given material. Numerical changes to speed or power settings can be normalized and etched onto the surface of the material, providing both a visual and tactile gradient indicating changes made in the production of the laser cut part (Figure 4). While a simple gradient is shown in Figure 4, one can imagine that more intricate patterns can be utilized.

In summary, *Process Textures* incorporate machine setting changes made to fabricate a given design file. These changes are represented through the surface texture of a component, providing insight into the numerical changes to these settings as well as the number of iterations made over time.

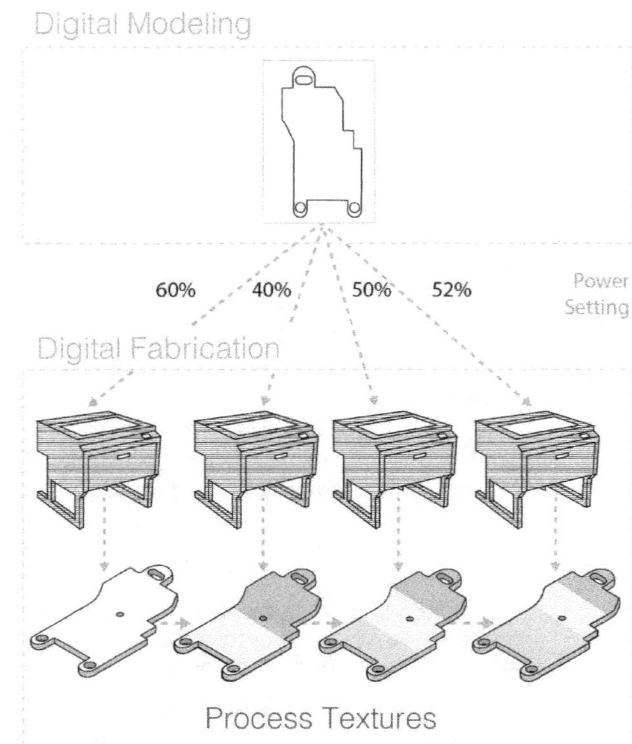

Figure 4. Capturing modifications to machine settings using *Process Textures*

Future Work

To realize *Process Products*, digital design tools need to be developed to capture changes made to design files or machine settings throughout the design process. These version control tools can either be integrated into commonly used design software or as separate extensions.

In this paper, we focus on creating single products. Capturing how assemblies of components change over time is another area for further research.

While *Process Stacks* incorporate test pieces, which traditionally end up as scrap, there are potentially other ways to incorporate scrap material. For example, is there a way to reuse the scrap material with which laser-cut prototypes were cut from?

In the scope of this paper, the concepts proposed focus on capturing *design file* and *machine* properties, but future work can also integrate *contextual properties*, or properties that require input from the designer such as the rationale behind each iteration. This combination can produce even richer forms of process documentation.

Conclusion

This paper introduces the concept of *Process Products* as a means to visually represent iteration in the digital fabrication design process. We propose three manifestations of this concept: Process Heatmaps, Process Stacks, and Process Textures. These examples serve as a way to reveal the iterative design process through digitally automated documentation, capturing how designed objects evolve throughout the digital fabrication workflow. The concepts presented represent a larger research objective of increasing transparency into our design processes in an effort to provide insight into how we design and how the tools we use impact our design process.

Acknowledgments

This work is supported in part by the National Science Foundation Graduate Research Fellowship under Grant No. 1122374.

References

[1] Gershenfeld, N. Fab: The coming revolution on your desktop–from personal computers to personal fabrication. Basic Books, 2008.

[2] Botobjects ProDesk3D Printer. http://www.botobjects.com/our-product

[3] Mota, C. The rise of personal fabrication. *Proceedings of the 8th ACM conference on Creativity and Cognition*. ACM (2011), 279-288.

[4] Reactivision. http://reactivision.sourceforge.net/

[5] Rich, T. Encoding data into physical objects with digitally fabricated textures. Masters Thesis. Massachusetts Institute of Technology, 2013.

[6] Rosner, D.K., and Ryokai, K. Spyn: Augmenting knitting to support storytelling and reflection. *Proceedings of the 10th international conference on Ubiquitous Computing*. ACM (2008), 340-349.

[7] Stratasys Objet Printer. http://www.stratasys.com/3d-printers/design-series/objet500-connex3

[8] Tseng, T., and Resnick M. Product versus process: Representing and appropriating DIY projects online. *Proceedings of the 2014 conference on Designing Interactive Systems*. ACM (2014), 425-428.

Tactile Dialogues: Personalization of Vibrotactile Behavior to Trigger Interpersonal Communication

Kimberly Johanna Schelle
K.J.Schelle@tue.nl
Department of Industrial Design
Eindhoven University of Technology
Eindhoven, the Netherlands

Oscar Tomico
O.Tomico@tue.nl
Department of Industrial Design
Eindhoven University of Technology
Eindhoven, the Netherlands

Carolina Gomez Naranjo
C.Gomez.Naranjo@tue.nl
Department of Industrial Design
Eindhoven University of Technology
Eindhoven, the Netherlands

Stephan Wensveen
S.A.G.Wensveen@tue.nl
Department of Industrial Design
Eindhoven University of Technology
Eindhoven, the Netherlands

Martijn ten Bhömer
M.t.Bhomer@tue.nl
Department of Industrial Design
Eindhoven University of Technology
Eindhoven, the Netherlands

TEI '15, Jan 16-19 2015, Stanford, CA, USA
ACM 978-1-4503-3305-4/15/01.
http://dx.doi.org/10.1145/2677199.2687894

Abstract

This article describes tests that have been conducted with Tactile Dialogues, a textile pillow that can react to touch with vibrotactile stimuli and haptic sensations. Tactile Dialogues is designed to stimulate movement and interpersonal contact for patients in the late stages of dementia, their family members and their caregivers. The most recent prototype of the pillow has been tested during 15 separate visits of family members or caregivers with patients. The aim of these tests is to find out whether personalization of the vibrotactile stimuli is appreciated over a mirroring vibrotactile behavior. We propose a three-scale measurement to help family members and caregivers examine the responses of the patient: muscular relaxation, physical movement and interpersonal contact. Through the semi-structured interviews we identified that family members and caregivers do appreciate the opportunity to personalize the vibrotactile behavior and that the pillow mainly functions as a way to establish communication with the patient.

Author Keywords

Smart textiles; dementia; vibrotactile communication; haptic communication; personalization.

ACM Classification Keywords

H.5.2 [User interfaces]: User centered design

Figure 1 Caregiver and Patient using Tactile Dialogues.

Introduction

Dementia is a common name to describe the different conditions that affect the wellbeing of the human brain and intervene with a patient's ability to read, talk, write and move. The disease, usually associated with old age, affects most of patients' ability to be independent and is a side effect of other diseases of the brain, such as Alzheimer's. The most recurrent symptoms of dementia include memory loss, mood changes, and problems in communications and reasoning [1,8].

Dementia is currently the main cause for elderly entry to residential care, creating more demand for quality facilities [8]. These factors not only weight in the investment on healthcare but also reflect on the conditions of care to dementia patients. In order to allow an active and more independent old age personalized care is necessary but often neglected [8]. Family members can play an important role in this. However when the phase of dementia becomes more severe, visits are becoming more rare, leaving more pressure on professional caregivers. In order to develop more personalized solutions connections between different stakeholders such as service providers, care givers, physiotherapists and family members are required.

Within the Smart Textile Services CRISP project [2] a group of stakeholders is working on "Tactile Dialogues", a smart textile pillow sensible to touch. Smart textiles involve the integration of technology (sensors, computers, actuators) in the textile itself [7]. Tactile Dialogues incorporates vibration motors in different areas that may be activated in different sequences, speed and areas. The product's main goal is to enable a dialogue between a patient with moderate-severe dementia and their family-member, spouse or care giver, by a joint interacting with the product. This provides an activity to overcome the awkward feeling that is often connected to the increasingly alienated relationship. The device provides different vibrotactile stimuli patterns and haptic sensations that combined encourage the patients to move and develop conversations in a more alternative yet bodily way.

In the field of tangible interaction haptic feedback has been used before to elicit inter-personal communication. For example vibrotactile communication was used to develop new language between remote partners [4]. Other authors have showed the value of using vibrotactile feedback in cognitively high-demanding situations, such as in traffic [3]. Vibrotactile feedback offers stimuli which link more directly to bodily capabilities and is therefore an interesting modality for people with dementia.

The interactive possibilities of Tactile Dialogues allow designing personalization of the vibrotactile behavior. This is an aspect worth exploring as this can enable the product to be tailored to particular individual's use characteristics or preferences. In past studies tailoring activities to the capabilities of dementia patients and training families in activity use, resulted in clinically relevant benefits for patients and caregivers, postponed the need for home placement and reduced objective caregiver burden [6]. The current pilot study was set out to examine whether personalization of Tactile Dialogues would lead to a better experience for the patient and family member or caregiver and if so, how personalization should take place.

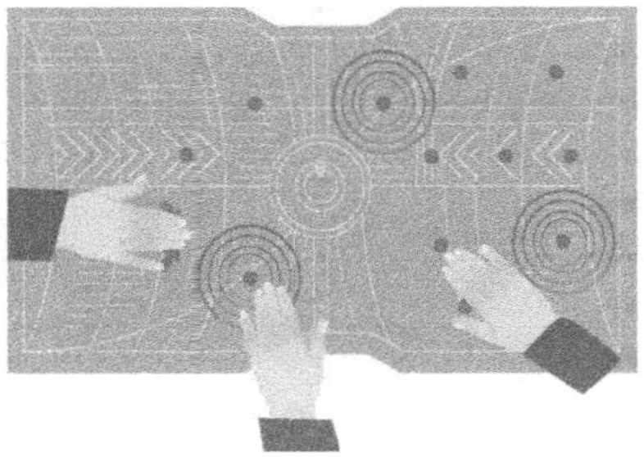

Figure 2 Personalized vibrotactile behavior design for patient 3: 'Search the vibration' game.

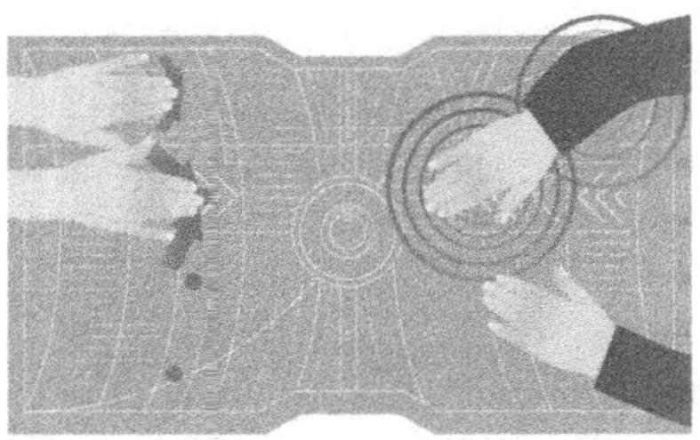

Figure 3 Personalized vibrotactile behavior design for patient 2: Under arm stimulation.

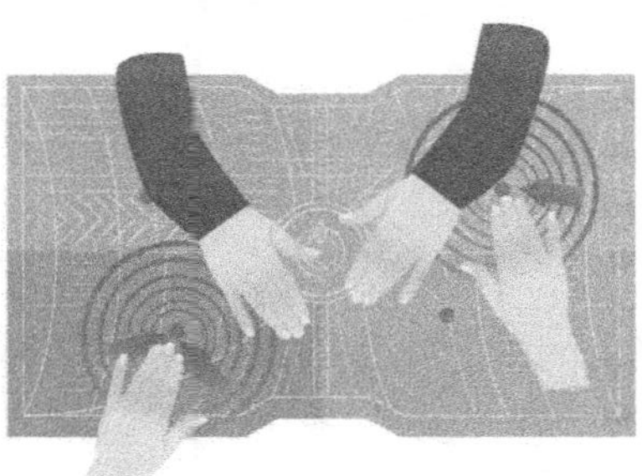

Figure 4 Personalized vibrotactile behavior design for patient 4: Increasing the area of stimulation.

Evaluation of Tactile Dialogues

Tactile Dialogues is designed for patients in the last two stages of dementia, when communication and awareness from part of the patient are extremely limited. The goal of the experiment is to evaluate whether a personalized vibrotactile behavior has a measurable effect in the amount of muscular relaxation, physical movement and interpersonal contact compared to a standard vibrotactile behavior design. The standard vibrotactile behavior was the *mirroring* behavior: touch on one end of the pillow is mirrored with vibrations on the other end. The current study for a personalized vibrotactile behavior with the pillow is conducted during 15 (5x3) sessions. We chose to include three sessions for each pair distributed over different days, as patients with dementia often display a high variety in their awareness of the environment and other symptoms of their condition over different days. After an information evening about Tactile Dialogues three groups of family members and two caregivers signed up to participate for three consecutive session with a patient.

The first pair, a patient (female, age 73) interacted with the pillow together with her daughters (age 48 and age 47). The second pair, the patient (male, age 79) interacted with the pillow with his three daughters (age 51, 48, 45). The third pair, female patient (age 74) interacted with the pillow with her husband (age 77). Except for one session all sessions took place in the presence of a caregiver from the care institution. The fourth and Fifth pair of patients (respectively male, age 78; female age 87) interacted in one session with a family member and caregiver and in follow-up sessions only with a caregiver. The first three pairs gave permission to videotape the sessions.

Session 1

Session one consisted of three phases. First, a short introduction was given about Tactile Dialogues and the *mirroring* vibration pattern. Second, the pair explored the product for approximately 15 minutes. The session ended with a semi-structured interview about the experience with Tactile Dialogues and suggestions for tailoring the vibration pattern to the patient. The first session had two goals: 1) make the pair feel comfortable with using the pillow and 2) explore how the vibration patterns can be tailored to the individual needs of the patient, by discussing ideas of the family members, caregiver and the designers. The co-design of the personalization of Tactile Dialogues took different forms depending on the input of the involved family members and caregivers. Some of them gave concrete suggestions while others were more open to suggestions from the design team. An example of a visualization of a behavior that was created can be found in figure 5. It shows a pattern in which the frequency of the vibration is connected to the amount of pressure that is measured by the input sensor. Other interaction behaviors that were programmed for the different patients can be found in figures 2, 3 and 4. The visualizations were used to communicate the vibration behaviors to the caregivers and family members during the second session.

Session 2

In the second session the pair again used Tactile Dialogues for approximately 15 minutes. The vibration pattern was now personalized and usually consisted of two or three specific behaviors that either the family member or the caregiver could perform. The goal of this session was to make the pair accustomed to using Tactile Dialogues with the personalized settings.

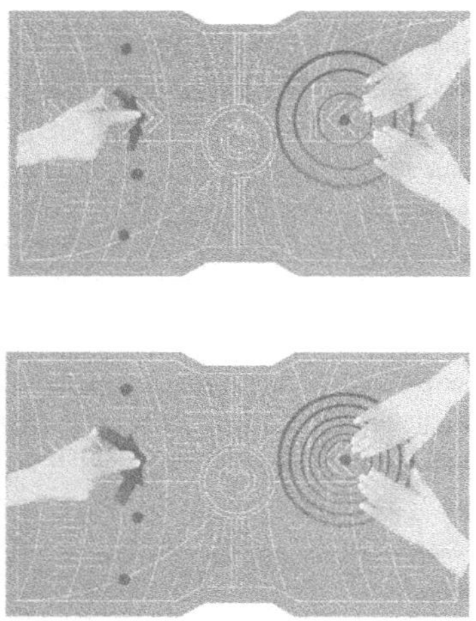

Figure 5 Personalized vibrotactile behavior design for patients 2 and 3 Pressure-Vibration frequency relation.

Categorized responses of the patients; reported by family members & caregiver, 3rd session	
Movement	- Stroking the pillow - Tapping the pillow - Turning body to the co-user
Facial expression	- Raising eyebrows - Smiling / laughing
Relaxation	- Muscle relaxation - Sighing
Contact	- Eye contact - Grabbing hands - (attempt to) Talk
Awareness	- Aware of environment

Table 1. Responses of the patients as reported by family members and caregivers while watching the videos of the third session.

Session 3

In session 3 the pair explored both the *mirroring* and the tailored behaviors. Beforehand a time limit was discussed with the family members and caregivers, to ensure that patients would have enough energy left for exploring the other vibration program after exploring one of them first. This resulted in sessions varying from 5 to 9 minutes per program. In a following semi-structured interview we asked the family members and caregivers about their experience with the product and interaction with the patient over the three sessions. Furthermore, differences in the vibration patterns and their consequences for the pairs were discussed. Furthermore, we asked the family members and caregivers who allowed videotaping to watch the video of the third session and describe and interpret the response of the patient for every minute. We asked them to give a rating on a five point scale for the amount of muscular relaxation, physical movement and interpersonal contact during each minute of the video. Movement and contact were chosen as main outcomes because they were suggested as goals during the design of Tactile Dialogues. Relaxation was added based on observations in session 1 and 2.

Results

The results provide qualitative insights from the semi-structured interviews in session 1 and 3, as well as results from the first attempt to quantify the evaluation of (different settings of) Tactile Dialogues.

During the interview family members and caregivers reported increased relaxation in three out of five patients, increased movement in three out of five patients and increased contact between the patient and co-user, although in very different ways, in four out of five patients. For one patient both the family member and the caregiver reported not to notice any changes in the patient, compared to usual interactions without the pillow. Three groups of family members reported to appreciate the opportunity to actually do a physical activity together with their loved one, instead of just talking or stroking the patient during their usual encounters. None of the family members or caregivers had the feeling that the patients were aware of the mirroring vibration pattern and its opportunities.

In the following sessions we noticed differences between the patients compared to earlier sessions, already without the use of the pillow. For example, patient 5 had trouble waking up in session 2, leading to little interaction with the pillow. Patient 1 was much less aware of her environment during session 2 and 3, while patient 2 was more awake and more aware of his environment in session 3, compared to earlier sessions. After the third session all co-users reported to see value in interacting with Tactile Dialogues, although it was clear that due to the different 'days' that dementia patients experience, the pillow did not cause the same highlights in movement or contact during every session.

None of the family members or caregivers reported a difference in the response of the patient between the *mirroring* and the tailored vibration patterns in the interview. However, all family members felt more comfortable with the tailored pattern and the option to adjust vibration patterns. A daughter of patient 2 described her view on personalizing location and type of vibration as follows: "*I personally liked the second one* [the personalized pattern] *more. It provided more options, e.g. because of the vibration on the area on*

Patient 1	Mirroring FM | CG	Tailored FM | CG
Movement	1.6 | 2.6	2.0 | 2.2
Contact	1.6 | 2.4	2.0 | 2.2
Relaxation	1.4 | 2.4	2.0 | 2.0

Table 2. Average ratings on a 5-point scale for movement, contact and relaxation of patient 1 by the family member(s) (FM) and the caregiver (CG).

Patient 2	Mirroring FM | CG	Tailored FM | CG
Movement	3.0 | 2.4	4.0 | 3.0
Contact	3.8 | 3.0	4.6 | 2.8
Relaxation	2.6 | 2.5	3.8 | 3.4

Table 3. Average ratings on a 5-point scale for movement, contact and relaxation of patient 2 by the family member(s) (FM) and the caregiver (CG).

Patient 3	Mirroring FM | CG	Tailored FM | CG
Movement	3.0 | 3.7	3.0 | 3.8
Contact	3.0 | 5.0	3.0 | 4.7
Relaxation	3.0 | 4.3	3.0 | 4.7

Table 4. Average ratings on a 5-point scale for movement, contact and relaxation of patient 3 by the family member(s) (FM) and the caregiver (CG).

the side of the pillow. That is an area that also counts for him [her father]*, not only his hands, but a larger area. Also the vibration with the short pulsation allows more variation"* (translated from Dutch). Both family members and caregivers felt comfortable enough to be able to try out different vibration patterns with the patient, if a future interface would enable them to do this. Several suggestions on the options that a future interface should provide were given, the most important being able to vary the intensity of the vibration (as the strong change was better received in patients); select the area of vibra tion (because every patient has movement limitations and for this uses the pillow in different positions) and select from up to 4 different vibrating patterns, to mix with location and intensity.

Video analysis
The three groups of family members who gave permission rated the interactions. The ratings are examined only for separate patients and not as a group, because the responses between patients highly varied, a common finding in the condition of dementia [1]. The scales are used as an exploratory quantitative measure of response in the patient and evaluated for differences between family member and caregiver as well as for differences between the vibration programs. The family members recognized a number of responses in the patient (see table 1). Averages from the ratings for the amount of movement, contact and relaxation on every minute of the video are displayed in tables 2, 3 and 4. An analysis of these ratings demonstrated significant correlations between ratings on movement and relaxation for each patient for both the family members and the caregivers (significant ($p < 0.05$) correlations ranging from .474 to .919). An explanation for this can be found in the contractures that patients with dementia in the late stages often experience. In such cases moving their fingers, hands or arms is at the same time relaxation of the contracture. Furthermore, for two out of three patients no significant correlations were found between the ratings of family members and caregivers, indicating that they have a different perspective on the behavior of the patients. This sometimes caused a more in depth conversation about the patient by the family member and caregiver, an outcome that was appreciated by both of them.

Conclusions

This pilot study aimed to explore and evaluate the personalization of Tactile Dialogues for patients with severe dementia. Every vibration pattern triggered different responses depending on the patient's mood in the day of the test, their current stage of dementia and the experience of the family members in talking with the dementia patients. The pillow's goal and result also varied depending on the patient's current needs, in muscular relaxation, contact or movement. These changes in symptoms, needs and goals made it hard to compare the response of the patients to different vibration patterns (*mirroring* and personalized) over time. However, it is clear that Tactile Dialogues does induce a response in the patients. The results obtained further show that caregivers and family members experience the interaction with Tactile Dialogues and the response of the patients in a different way. It is thus clear that future research and design should benefit from both perspectives.

The pillow as seen in the current experiment proved to be a channel that family members and caregivers use as a way to establish communication with the patient.

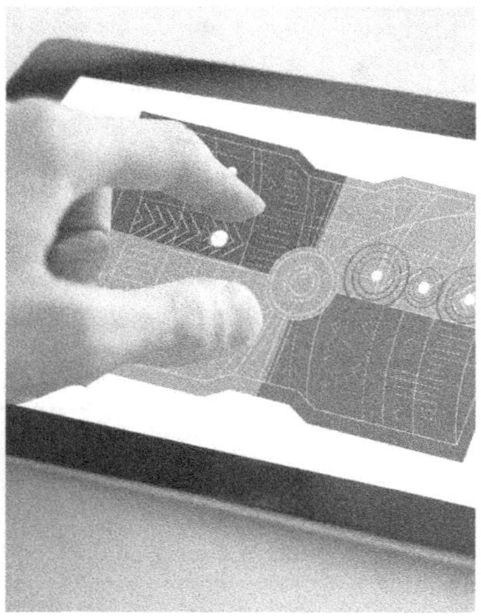

Figure 6 Potential future interface for the personalization of Tactile Dialogues.

The pillow acts initially as a conversation starter and gives the space and inspiration to family member of how to encourage and persuade the patient with dementia to speak and move more. Thus it seems that the value of personalizing the pillow is much more present for the co-user, than the patient itself. Future research could dive deeper in the value for the co-user. As researched by Kramer and Gibson [5] and in the observations of these tests, better results were indeed obtained when the caregiver or family member combined the vibrations patterns with verbal cues and eye contact, something that seemed to be more present when feeling comfortable. Therefore the use of Tactile Dialogues and the personalization of the vibration patterns supported a need of elderly with dementia of constant encouragement and ever changing patterns in stimulation through voice and touch by their family and caregivers.

The current study suggests a future need for family members and caregivers to be able to personalize Tactile Dialogues. A future design must allow caregivers/family members a simple and easy design template as a starting point, as opposed to a blank canvas. Several suggestions are given that can be taken into account for this design. These elements combined give caregivers and family members the opportunity to explore and experience which type of therapy or interactive activity to conduct depending on the patients' mood and physical needs.

Acknowledgements

This work is being carried out as part of the project "Smart Textile Services" sponsored by the Dutch Ministry of Economic Affairs under the CRISP program. We like to thank all the people at De Wever, Orfeas Lyras and Silvin Willemsen.

References

[1] Alzheimer's Society. Dementia 2013 facts infographic. http://alzheimers.org.uk/dementia2013

[2] ten Bhömer, M., Tomico, O., Kleinsmann, M.S., Kuusk, K. & Wensveen, S.A.G. Designing smart textile services through value networks, team mental models and shared ownership. *Proceedings of Serv. Des. '12.* (2012).

[3] Chang, A., Gouldstone, J., Zigelbaum, J., and Hiroshi, I. Pragmatic haptics. In *Proceedings of the 2nd international conference on Tangible and embedded interaction* (TEI '08). ACM Press (2008), 251-254.

[4] Chang, A., O'Modhrain, S., Jacob, R., Gunther, E., and Hiroshi, I. ComTouch: design of a vibrotactile communication device. In: *Proceedings of DIS 2002.* ACM Press (2002), NY.

[5] Kramer, B.J., and Gibson, J.W. The cognitively impaired elderly's response to touch: a naturalistic study. *Journal of Gerontological Social Work,* 18 (1/2), (1991), 175-193.

[6] Kwiseok K., and Cookhwan K. How to design personalization in a context of customer retention. *Journal Electronic Commerce Research and Applications 11, 2* (2012), 101-116.

[7] Schwarz, A., Van Langenhove, L., Guermonprez, P. and Deguillemont, D. A roadmap on smart textiles. *Textile Progress*, 42, 2 (2010), 99–180.

[8] Timlin, G. and Rysenbry, N. *Design for Dementia.* Helen Hamlyn Centre,Royal College of Art, Londen, 2010.

Physical Construction Toys for Rapid Sketching of Tangible User Interfaces

Kristian Gohlke
Bauhaus-Universität Weimar
Geschwister-Scholl-Str. 7, 99423 Weimar
kristian.gohlke@uni-weimar.de

Michael Hlatky
Native Instruments GmbH
Schlesische Str. 29-30, 10997 Berlin
michael.hlatky@native-instruments.de

Bram de Jong
Native Instruments GmbH
Schlesische Str. 29-30, 10997 Berlin
bram.dejong@native-instruments.de

TEI '15, Jan 16-19 2015, Stanford, CA, USA
ACM 978-1-4503-3305-4/15/01.
http://dx.doi.org/10.1145/2677199.2687900

Abstract
Physical construction toys such as *Lego* or similar brick-based systems provide a rich space for tangible interactions. In this paper we explore their potential as a readily available prototyping platform for Tangible User Interfaces. The system enables interaction designers and users to create functional control layouts, tangible experience prototypes, custom interface elements, and grid based interactions from *Lego* bricks. The position, color, orientation and shape of the markerless bricks are tracked using a camera. We have conducted an initial exploration of this design space through an exemplary case study of a tangible interface for music creation: users can construct interactive interface elements such as tangible grids for the arrangement of drum-patterns and different types of continuous controllers for parameter adjustments. The system is currently a work in progress; ongoing efforts are aimed at a more thorough evaluation.

Author Keywords
Tangible Interaction; TUI; Interaction Design; Lego; Prototyping; Music Controllers; HCI; Physical Sketching; Sequencer; Sliding Patterns; Sliding Puzzle.

ACM Classification Keywords
H.5.2. User Interfaces: *Prototyping.* H.5.5 Sound and Music Computing*: Methodologies and techniques.*

Introduction

This paper describes the work-in-progress prototype of a system that enables interaction designers to rapidly create tangible interface layouts and novel interface elements using *Lego* bricks as a readily available construction system. Such experience prototypes [3] can serve as functional interface sketches for rapid evaluation of interface ideas and workflows and can also provide a basis for decision making in user-centered, participatory design processes. We assume that the use of *Lego* as a familiar construction material can increase the user acceptance during the evaluation of early prototypes and might reduce additional overhead for learning [see: 7]. Different *interface widgets* and tangible tokens can be built from *Lego* bricks and placed on a translucent *Lego* baseplate. A camera mounted underneath the baseplate is used to track the bricks. The visual tracking does not require additional visual markers. Currently the *color*, *position*, *orientation*, *size* and *shape* of each object being placed on the baseplate are analyzed. Widgets of the same type and the same color are distinguished by their position. The camera-image is processed in software and displayed on a separate screen that also serves as a back-end for configuring the tangible widgets. The user can assign functionality to each physical interface widget and token by defining active areas through an additional graphical user interface (GUI). The extracted information is mapped to control messages, currently OpenSoundControl (OSC) and MIDI – as our initial case studies are focused on prototyping user interfaces for audio applications. However, the system is prepared to generate other events and messages such as keystrokes, mouse events, HID and serial messages to enable the control of a variety of existing or novel software and hardware.

Related Work

Previous work from members of our research group [2] has explored the use of ubiquitous, readily available household items, such as string, wire, tape, cardboard and similar to identify and conceive ways to create and interact with novel musical instruments.

An audio sequencer that uses a tangible grid and colored tokens has been proposed by Hesse et al. [8]. Their system allows for the creation of drum loops by placing chewing-gum balls on a fixed grid of holes with four rows and sixteen columns, representing one bar of music. The *Tactus* [14] is a musical interface that enables the use of everyday items, such as board game tokens or drawings, to create rhythmic patterns on grids that are tracked by a camera. A marker-based, low-cost approach for evaluation and prototyping of TUIs has been proposed by Costanza et al. [4]. Their system called *d-touch* allows users to work with printable optical markers to create their own tangibles. The *d-touch* system works similar to the *reactivision* framework [10] and has also been demonstrated as a musical interface. An extensive overview of tangible interfaces for music performance and production is available online [11].

The use of *Lego* bricks for creating rhythmic patterns has been demonstrated though a variety of *Lego*-based sequencers that use unmodified bricks such as the *Brickquencer* [23], *BeatBricks* [22], the *SoundMachine* [24] or the *Poco* [25], using *Lego Duplo* bricks. A second category of sequencers uses modified bricks such as the *Lego Sequencer MR2* [1] and similar [21]. The *Stekgreif* [9] is a modular MIDI-controller that allows for the creation of functional music controller layouts from modified *Lego Duplo* bricks with integrated electronics. The recently released *Lego Fusion* [12] consists of a special baseplate that can be tracked visually through an application running on a tablet-computer or smartphone. *Lego* facades with a maximum size of 16x16 bricks can be constructed and imported into an application where they are extruded into virtual 3D-models, serving as content for screen-based mini games. The commercially available *Osmo* [18] uses a tablet-computer with a custom stand and a small mirror attachment that slides over the tablet's built-in camera. The mirror redirects the camera viewing angle in order to detect objects placed on surfaces in front of the device. The objects can be used to interact with a variety of games and other applications. *Palette* [19] is a modular system of physical controllers including a button module, a rotary knob, and a slider that can be freely arranged and connected to a computer through an additional module. Configuration software allows users to create custom controller mappings, to interact with a range of different applications. However, the interactive capabilities are limited by the number of modules available in a given context and new modules cannot be easily created by the user. The *SLAP Widgets* [26] add tactile controls to multi-touch tables. A set of passive, translucent buttons, knobs and sliders can be positioned on an interactive surface and are tracked using markers. Visual feedback is provided by rear projection.

Interface Widgets
Using our system, currently the following interface widgets can be constructed and used for prototyping: *rotary controls*, *linear sliders*, *x/y pads*, *switches* and *grid areas* [see Fig. 1]. *Rotary controls* are constructed from a standard *Lego* brick (e.g. 2x3 brick) that is attached on top of a rotary *Lego* plate (e.g. a 4x4 or 2x2 rotary plate) and then mounted on the translucent baseplate. The overlapping part of the brick can then be tracked using a camera. *Linear sliders* and *x/y pads* are constructed by setting out an area on the baseplate that is delimited by surrounding bricks. One or several *Lego* bricks (e.g. 2x2 brick) that are placed inside the defined area serve as tokens to generate x/y coordinates. Linear sliders are constructed by the same principle but have to be built in such a way that movement is restricted to a single axis. The area of a slider or an x/y pad can also be covered with studless, transparent *Lego* tiles, so that the user can slide tokens across the surface. Alternatively, when no transparent tiles are available, flat colored *Lego* tiles (e.g. 2x2) without studs can also serve as movable tokens, if placed on the surface with their top side facing downwards. Multiple x/y coordinates can be generated simultaneously by using different tokens that are distinguished by color. On/off *switches* are implemented based on the presence or absence of a token (e.g. 2x1 brick) at a user-defined position. The token can either be affixed to the baseplate, or moved into position similar to a small linear slider. Interactive *Grid areas* are essentially rows and columns of multiple switches that can cover larger sections of the interface.

Figure 1. *Right:* examples of widgets, e.g. rotary controls, a grid area, a linear slider, switches, and an x/y pad. *Left:* exemplary collection of the brick types used to construct such widgets.

User Defined Control Layouts

The process of creating control layouts is straightforward. First, the user builds interface widgets based on the examples described above and places them on the interactive surface. A live camera image, shot from underneath the surface is combined with a graphical overlay and displayed on a separate screen that serves as a GUI backend. This backend allows the user to define regions of interest inside the image, declare them as active tracking areas and assign the desired control mappings. Visual feedback is given to indicate whether a physical widget placed on an active area could be recognized or if the widget needs to be modified to improve the tracking. The use of a projector adjacent to the camera would also allow for an integration of a GUI with the interactive surface. However the approach of using a separate screen was sufficient to test our initial assumptions, since the current GUI served solely as a configuration back-end at design time, but is not required when interacting with the tangible widgets.

Image Analysis Engine

In our current setup, a high-definition camera is mounted underneath a translucent *Lego* baseplate measuring 48x48 studs. The image processing is based on the OpenCV [17] library. Perspective correction, using four manually adjustable corner points is applied to the image to remove skewing and compensate for the camera angle. The corrected image is analyzed, using custom algorithms, to deduce the properties of objects being placed on the baseplate. Currently the system is capable of detecting the color, the size, the contours, the orientation and the x/y coordinates of the footprint of objects being placed on the surface. Robust color tracking in HSV color space is achieved through an adaptive color matching algorithm that can be calibrated with a selection of the available brick colors. Additional colors can be defined to distinguish between bricks and the hands of the user. The information derived from the image is then further abstracted and mapped to parameters corresponding to the type of interface widget that the user assigned to a given image area. The underlying data-structure for *linear slider widgets* holds values that correspond to the position of the sliding token within the widget area (i.e. the actual value used to adjust parameters) and the color value of the token. *Rotary control widgets* contain the same information but here the orientation angle corresponds to the parameter value. The data-structure for areas designated as *x/y pads* holds information about the x/y position of each token relative to the widget area, the color value for each token, the number of tokens and their orientation angle. *Switch widgets* contain a binary on/off information (token present or not present) and the color value of the token. *Grid areas* hold the same information as individual switches, but for each cell of the grid. The values of switches and grid areas can be quantized to match the base grid of the *Lego* plate. The individual values for each detected widget are then scaled and mapped to generate the control events and messages as specified by the user.

Case Study: A Tangible Music Controller

We have built a tangible rhythm sequencer [see Fig. 2] as a case study to demonstrate some of the features of a markerless system for sketching TUIs using unmodified *Lego* bricks. The prototypes were built during the *Midihack Stockholm 2014* [15] and the *MusicHackDay Barcelona 2014* [16]. Informal observations were made at these occasions with groups of users (most of them having a background in audio production, music, and/or software development) to identify the potential of our approach as a platform for prototyping TUIs for musical interactions. Our current prototypes can be used create rhythmic drum patterns by arranging colored *Lego*-bricks on a transparent baseplate that is illuminated from below. The case study combines different interface elements. Beyond the user-manipulated physical arrangement of the interface elements, no additional visual feedback is provided.

Figure 2. Case study: a tangible rhythm sequencer with parameter controls. The translucent top surface of the table is covered with different types of widgets. A high definition camera and illumination are mounted underneath.

Variations: Sliding Patterns and Sushi Plates

Inspired by initial observations of people constructing their own physical tools from *Lego* bricks to prepare and share drum patterns, the 48x48 stud baseplate was replaced by eight smaller plates measuring 16x16 studs and an empty area of the same size. Similar to a sliding puzzle toy, the eight plates can be moved on the surface horizontally and vertically [13]. This allows users to shift entire patterns of tokens into the visually tracked area, enabling instant playback and shifting of pre-built drum patterns. The sliding patterns also work in conjunction with regular interface elements by locking individual baseplates to the edge of the surface.

Our system is not restricted to tracking *Lego* bricks. We have demonstrated this through another variation of a tangible music sequencer that uses differently colored sushi plates, running on a sushi conveyor belt as a TUI in an actual live performance setting [20].

Conclusion and Outlook

We presented a work-in-progress system for the rapid creation (*"physical sketching"*) of functional, tangible controller layouts for music production using *Lego* bricks. The controller layouts can be quickly customized and evaluated. Ongoing work is aimed at extending the prototyping capabilities by providing users with more flexibility and customization, to support them in conceiving entirely new interface elements. For example by enabling users to teach the system to detect custom combinations of bricks, similar to a proposed method for optical tracking that replaces pre-printed markers with hand drawn sketches [5]. This approach could be further extended to work with depth cameras similar to the approach described by Gupta et al. [6] to add more volume to the interactive space.

Acknowledgements

The research proposed in this paper is performed in the *GiantSteps* project, which has received funding from the European Community's Seventh Framework Programme FP7/2007-2013 under grant agreement n° 610591.

References

1. Akai, Y. LegoSequencer MR2. yoshiakai.com/2008/Lego%20Sequencer01.html (accessed: July 25th 2014)
2. Andersen, K. Using Props to Explore Design Futures: Making New Instruments. *Proceedings of ACM CHI '14*. ACM Press (2014).
3. Buchenau, M., & Fulton Suri, J. Experience prototyping. *Proc. ACM* DIS *'00*, ACM Press (2000).
4. Costanza, E., et al. Ubicomp to the masses: a large-scale study of two tangible interfaces for download. *Proc. ACM Ubicomp '10.* ACM Press (2014).
5. Costanza, E. & Huang, J. Designable Visual Markers. *Proc. ACM CHI '09*. ACM Press (2009).
6. Gupta, A., et al. DuploTrack: a real-time system for authoring and guiding Duplo block assembly. Proc. UIST '12. ACM Press (2012).
7. Harrison, C., et al. TouchTools: leveraging familiarity and skill with physical tools to augment touch interaction. *Proc. ACM CHI '14*. ACM Press (2014).
8. Hesse, A., & McDiarmid, A. The Bubblegum Sequencer. *Proc. ACM CHI 2008*. ACM Press (2008). www.backin.de/gumball/ (acc.: July 25th 2014)
9. Homann, G., Tzschentke, D., Weidenhaupt, C. & Zentis, P. Stekgreif und an.schlag. *Proc. Mensch & Computer 2008, Berlin.* Logos Verlag.
10. Kaltenbrunner, M., & Bencina, R. reacTIVision: a computer-vision framework for table-based tangible interaction. *Proc. ACM TEI '07*. ACM Press (2007).
11. Kaltenbrunner, M., Tangible Music. modin.yuri.at/tangibles/ (acc.: July 25th 2014).
12. Lego Fusion. www.lego.com/en-us/fusion/ (acc.: July 25th 2014)
13. LegoTechno 2.0 - Sliding Puzzle Sequencer www.youtube.com/watch?v=ei9jyGvRgvs (acc.: November 11th 2014)
14. Mann, Y., Lubow, J., & Freed, A. The Tactus: A Tangible, Rhythmic Grid Interface Using Found-Objects. *Proc. Nime 2009.*
15. MidiHack 2014. www.midihack.com (acc.: July 25th 2014)
16. Music Hack Day Barcelona 2014. new.musichackday.org/2014/barcelona/ (acc: July 25th 2014)
17. OpenCV. www.opencv.org (acc.: July 25th 2014)
18. Osmo. www.playosmo.com (acc: July 25th 2014)
19. Palette. www.palettegear.com (acc.: July 25th 2014)
20. RBMA Presents: Sushi Sequencer (Making Of) www.youtube.com/watch?v=rZFcHIXL7nk (acc.: November 11th 2014)
21. Rosenbaum, E., Lego Sequencer. www.youtube.com/watch?v=eL7FS8KantE (acc.: July 25th 2014)
22. Superquadratic - Beat Bricks. www.vimeo.com/45026119 (acc.: July 25th 2014)
23. The Brickquencer. www.fleg.de/art/brickquencer (acc.: July 25th 2014)
24. The SoundMachine. www.thinkbricks.net/?p=638 (acc.: July 25th 2014).
25. Wagner, T. Poco Sequencer. www.thomaswagner.me/5poco.html (acc.: July 25th 2014)
26. Weiss, M., et al. SLAP widgets: bridging the gap between virtual and physical controls on tabletops. *Proc. ACM CHI '09*. ACM Press (2009).

Objects for Change: A Case Study of a Tangible User Interface for Behavior Change

Oren Zuckerman
Media Innovation Lab
School of Communications
IDC Herzliya
P.O.Box 167, Herzliya 46150
ISRAEL
orenz@idc.ac.il

TEI '15, Jan 16-19 2015, Stanford, CA, USA
ACM 978-1-4503-3305-4/15/01.
http://dx.doi.org/10.1145/2677199.2687906

Abstract
We present Objects for Change (OFC), a set of design considerations based on established behavior change techniques that can serve designers of Tangible User Interfaces (TUI). We highlight empirical findings from behavior change literature, and show how to apply them to inherent TUI properties: (1) visibility and persistency, (2) locality, (3) tangible representation, and (4) affordances. We demonstrate how we applied OFC in the design of a TUI prototype aimed to promote behavior change in planning and organization tasks among youth diagnosed with ADHD.

Author Keywords
Tangible user interfaces; persuasive technologies; behavior change; design guidelines.

ACM Classification Keywords
H.5.2. User Interfaces: Interaction styles, Theory and methods.

Introduction
Our work strives to highlight best practices from the behavior change research community in a way that will aid the TUI community in the design of effective tangible technologies for changing behavior. We review relevant findings from behavior change literature, and

provide a practical set of design considerations for Tangible User Interface (TUI) design. We demonstrate how we utilize these design considerations in the design process of TangiPlan [17], a TUI designed to assist youth diagnosed with Attention Deficit Hyperactivity Disorder (ADHD) in their daily planning and organization tasks.

Related Work

Recent large-scale systematic reviews identified three techniques as particularly effective for achieving behavior change: goal-setting, providing feedback on performance, and self-monitoring [1, 8].

- Goal-setting: Setting a specific goal results in greater effort and performance, compared to not setting a goal or generally urging people to "do their best" [7].
- Providing feedback on performance: This technique involves providing individuals with data about their own behavior or commenting on their behavioral performance, for example identifying a discrepancy between performance and a set goal [9].
- Self-monitoring: This technique refers to keeping a record of a specified behavior to increase awareness of this behavior and the circumstances that precipitate or surround it [2]. Self-monitoring is effective because it encourages the individual to develop a sense of accountability and heightens self-awareness. Even though the accuracy of reporting is often poor, accuracy does not appear to be as important as focusing attention on the behavior [15]. Heightened attention leads the individual to reconsider, and possibly change the monitored behavior [13].

Persuasive technologies are technologies designed to support behavior change in everyday life, and are often based on general behavior change theories and findings. Researchers have been developing frameworks and guidelines to adapt effective behavior change techniques to match computing specificities [12, 13].

The Objects for Change Design Considerations

In this section we apply the key findings from the behavior change literature to TUI design, based on four TUI properties.

Visibility and persistency

Tangible interfaces are physical objects, persistent and visible, and as such become an integrated part of our environment, a constant entity in our daily rituals. They are usually single-purpose, and are constantly visible even when turned off or inactive. Therefore, they can serve as a constant reminder of the task they represent. Prior findings from behavior change literature showed that reminders have positive behavioral outcomes [3]. Usually, reminders are textual in nature. Users must specifically attend to them, which could potentially interrupt ongoing activities. In contrast, TUIs serve as non-textual reminders, constantly present in the visual field. This type of reminders was found to be effective as well [6]. TUI's properties of visibility and persistency should be enhanced by design, leveraging their potential to seamlessly integrate into daily rituals and act as constant reminders of behavior change tasks.

Locality
Tangible objects are associated with a specific physical location, and that location has a certain context, to the task itself and to the user's daily rituals. This could potentially facilitate behavior change, because location has been shown to enhance cognitive processes. Memory is known to be location-dependent, it is easier to recall information in the same location where it was first learned than in a different location [16]. Similarly, learning can be specific to the location in which it occurred [10]. Thus, the object's location can serve a purpose, and may increase relevancy and awareness. Indeed, initial evaluations of location-based persuasive technologies found location to be a valuable addition to the system. For example, Vertoid [18] is a mobile application that investigates the potential of contextualized mobile cues for persuading users to lead a more environmentally-friendly lifestyle. A user study revealed that cues were quite successful when they concerned short, immediate actions performed with objects close to the user. TUI's location-dependent property should be leveraged by designers, creating context and purpose by connecting the TUI location with task location, and promoting short, immediate interactions.

Tangible representation
Persuasive technologies implementing feedback on performance were found to facilitate a desired behavioral change [19]. TUI by definition provides tangible representation to digital information [5]. Thus, TUI can leverage various mediums to provide feedback to users, including physical form, physical movement, light-based visual feedback, and sound, to name a few. TUIs tangible representation could be leveraged to present real-time feedback on performance and progress towards a set goal. The tangible representation could leverage multisensory communication channels, and can help present abstract concepts related to certain behavior change goals in a concrete way.

Affordances
As previously discussed in the review of behavior change literature, self-monitoring is effective because it encourages the individual to develop a sense of accountability and heightens self-awareness [2, 9]. Intuitive TUI affordances could contribute to accountability and self-awareness. However, affordances do not guarantee intuitive interaction. Gaver [4] argues that affordance of an object refers to attributes of both the object and the actor. When affordances are perceptible, they offer a direct link between perception and action. On the other hand, hidden affordances and false affordances lead to mistakes. Gaver emphasizes that affordances are not passively perceived but actively explored.

Affordances are only the first step; leading users towards reflection is the main goal when behavior change is concerned. Reflection leads the individual to reconsider and possibly change behaviors [13]. Norman has differentiated between experiential cognition and reflective cognition [11]. In the experiential cognition mode we perceive and react efficiently and effortlessly, the mode of skilled activity that is conducted fluently without thinking. The reflective mode is a process of comparison and contrast; it requires thought, effort, time, and decision-making. Rogers and Muller [14] introduced the concept of transforms, how a user's experience shifts from perceiving to understanding to reflecting. They suggest two techniques, uncertainty

Figure 1. The TangiPlan prototype consists of a set of objects that represent routine morning tasks, which are spread around the house in locations relevant to a target task. Each object communicates with a central server and offers a visual representation of the time allocated to the corresponding task. Each object also gives real-time feedback of the gradual count-down of time left to complete the task.

and unexpectedness, that can trigger high levels of perception, understanding, and reflection.

TUI affordances could be leveraged to lead users in a gradual way from perception to reflection, in a mixed process of experiential and reflective modes of cognition. Designers must remember that mere usage is not the goal. When behavior change is concerned, the goal is reflection that leads to accountability and self-awareness; which eventually leads to behavior change.

In sum, in order to utilize best practices from behavior change research, we recommend on the following considerations for designers of persuasive TUIs:

1. Leverage TUI's visibility and persistency properties as a constant reminder of the desired change in behavior. Keep the TUI single-purpose and not multi-purpose, design it to be meaningful also when inactive, design it to become an integrated part of daily rituals.

2. Leverage TUI's locality property to enhance context and purpose of the desired change in behavior. Design the TUI to be associated with a daily task that is relevant to the target behavior in order to increase relevancy and awareness. Design the TUI to leverage people's location-dependent memory for easier learning and recall. Take advantage of the TUI integration to daily rituals and design short and immediate interactions that do not require prolong attention or complex cognitive processes.

3. Leverage TUI's property of tangible representation to provide feedback-on-performance and progress towards a goal. Design the TUI to provide real time and meaningful feedback of the goal and the progress towards the goal. Strive to present abstract behavior change concepts in a more concrete and relevant way.

4. Leverage the potential in TUI's affordances. Design effective and sequential affordances, mix experiential and reflective cognition, design transforms that shift a user's experience from perception to reflection. Leverage the effectiveness of self-monitoring and design the TUI to lead users to increased self-awareness and accountability that will hopefully lead to behavior change.

The TangiPlan Prototype Design

TangiPlan [17] is a TUI prototype designed as an assistive technology to help youth with ADHD in planning and organization tasks, specifically during their morning routine (see Figure 1). The design process included interviews with clinicians treating children with ADHD, parents, and children diagnosed with ADHD (see Side Bar on the next page).

OFC design considerations in TangiPlan
Visibility and persistency: TangiPlan objects serve as physical reminders for teen users to perform morning tasks and to keep time in mind. The objects are visible to the user during the morning routine and in various occasions during the day, and become a constant reminder of the desired change in behavior. The objects are single-purpose, each representing one sub-task during the overall morning routine. TangiPlan objects are visible even when not active, constantly reminding the user about the task they represent.

Interview insights from TangiPlan design process

Interviews with clinicians treating children with ADHD [17] revealed a challenge concerning lack of efficiency in maintaining daily routines. The intervention strategies experts offer are: (1) Plan a daily schedule and allocate time for each activity. (2) Separate complicated tasks into smaller ones. (3) Write to-do lists and reminders. (4) Ask for assistance from caregivers. (5) Use a stop-watch to track completion time.

Interviews with parents revealed lack of efficiency in children's ability to follow daily routines, especially in the morning routine.

Interviews with children [17] revealed they tried writing notes but found it tedious, and they tried setting reminders and timers but perceived those smartphone-based techniques as annoying or as a potential distraction due to smartphones multi-purpose nature.

Locality: Each TangiPlan object is placed by the user at a specific location associated with a specific task. Context and purpose are formed by the user's decision where exactly to place the TUI, for example during a paper prototype evaluation a user placed an object representing the "brushing teeth" task near the sink in the bathroom [17]. The specific location and association with the task increases relevancy and awareness. The repetitive process users go through of associating tasks with objects and then with specific locations enhances task-location coupling and leverages location-dependent memory.

Tangible Representation: The abstract concept of time is represented based on an hourglass metaphor, using a vertical column of LED lights that gradually dim off in a sequential process. The user sets the target goal for each task, and the goal is represented using the number of LEDs that are lit in a specific object, before the user activates the object (the "allocated time per task"). Feedback on performance towards the goal is represented after the user activates the object, using the gradual vertical "countdown" of the lights. Real time feedback is provided using LEDs, and the feedback is in context of the task completion process itself (e.g., brushing teeth) but does not require focused attention by the user, peripheral attention is enough to notice the performance level compared with the desired goal.

Affordances: a TangiPlan object is designed with sequential and perceptible affordances [4]. The object's shape is of a truncated square pyramid, directing attention towards the vertical line of LEDs at the front side of the object. The real-time "countdown" of the lights leverages vertical motion as an additional mean to enhance focus on task completion. The design promotes a shift from experiential to reflective mode of cognition using the light's progress towards the goal, as the user has to assess her current rate of progress with the time left to complete a task. A transform is leveraged using the unexpectedness technique [14], when a goal has not been reached the lights are starting to progress upwards as red-colored light instead of the standard downward movement of green-colored light. Self-monitoring is utilized using the real-time feedback on performance and the on-going tracking of one's performance. Accountability is utilized by allowing the user to choose her own tasks and her own goals. Self-awareness is addressed using the overall integration of TangiPlan objects into the daily ritual of morning organization.

Conclusion and Future Work

We presented the Objects for Change design considerations in an effort to aid the TUI community in the design of effective tangible technologies for changing behavior. We showed how we applied those guidelines in the design of the TangiPlan prototype. Further work is needed to evaluate the effectiveness of the OFC design considerations and the TangiPlan prototype as an assistive technology.

Acknowledgements

We would like to thank Ayelet Gal-Oz and the TangiPlan team for their valuable insights regarding this work. This research was supported by the I-CORE Program of the Planning and Budgeting Committee and The Israel Science Foundation (grant no. 1716/12).

References

[1] Ashford, S., Edmunds, J., French, D.P. What is the best way to change self-efficacy to promote lifestyle

and recreational physical activity? A systematic review with meta-analysis. *British Journal of Health Psychology 15,* 2 (2010), 265-288.

[2] Burke, L.E., Conroy, M.B., Sereika, S.M., Elci, O.U., Styn, M.A., Acharya, S.D., Sevick, M.A., Ewing, L.J., and Glanz, K. The effect of electronic self-monitoring on weight loss and dietary intake: A randomized behavioral weight loss. *Obesity 19*, 2 (2011), 338–344.

[3] Fjeldsoe, B.S., Marshall, A.L., and Miller, Y.D. Behavior change interventions delivered by mobile telephone short-message service. *American Journal of Preventive Medicine 36*, 2 (2009), 165-173.

[4] Gaver, W.W. Technology affordances. In *Proc. CHI 1991*, ACM Press (1991), 79-84.

[5] Ishii, H., and Ullmer, B. Tangible bits: Towards seamless interfaces between people, bits, and atoms. In *Proc. CHI 1997*, ACM Press (1997), 234-241.

[6] Koritzky, G., and Yechiam, E. On the value of nonremovable reminders for behavior modification: An application to nail-biting (Onychophagia). *Behavior Modification 35*, 6 (2011), 511-530.

[7] Locke, E.A., and Latham, G.P. Building a practically useful theory of goal setting and task motivation: A 35-year odyssey. *American Psychologist 57*, 9 (2002), 705-717.

[8] Michie, S., Abraham, C., Whittington, C., McAteer, J., and Gupta, S. Effective techniques in healthy eating and physical activity interventions: A meta-regression. *Health Psychology 28*, 6 (2009), 690-701.

[9] Michie, S., Ashford, S., Sniehotta, F.F., Dombrowski, S.U., Bishop, A., and French, D.P. A refined taxonomy of behaviour change techniques to help people change their physical activity and healthy eating behaviours: The CALO-RE taxonomy. *Psychology and Health 26*, 11 (2011), 1-20.

[10] Nadel, L., and Willner, J. Context and conditioning: A place for space. *Physiological Psychology 8*, 2 (1980), 218-228.

[11] Norman, D. *Things that make us smart*. Basic Books, New Work, NY, USA, 1993.

[12] Oinas-Kukkonen, H., and Harjumaa, M. A systematic framework for designing and evaluating persuasive systems. In *Proc. PERSUASIVE 2008*, Springer Berlin Heidelberg (2008), 164-176.

[13] Ploderer, B., Reitberger, W., Oinas-Kukkonen, H., and van Gemert-Pijnen, J. Social interaction and reflection for behaviour change. *Personal and Ubiquitous Computing 18*, 7 (2014), 1667-1676.

[14] Rogers, Y. and Muller, H. A framework for designing sensor-based interactions to promote exploration and reflection in play. *International Journal of Human Computer Studies 64*, 1 (2006), 1-14.

[15] Shay, L.E., Shobert, J.L., Seibert, D., and Thomas, L.E. Adult weight management: Translating research and guidelines into practice. *Journal of the American Academy of Nurse Practitioners 21*, 4 (2009), 197-206.

[16] Smith, S.M., and Vela, E. Environmental context-dependent memory: A review and meta-analysis. *Psychonomic Bulletin & Review 8*, 2 (2001), 203-220.

[17] Weisberg, O., Gal-Oz, A., Berkowitz, R., Weiss, N., Peretz, O., Azoulai, S., Kopelman-Rubin, D., and Zuckerman, O. TangiPlan: Designing an assistive technology to enhance executive functioning among children with ADHD. In *Proc. IDC 2014*, ACM Press (2014), 293-296.

[18] Wozniak, P., and Romanowski, A. Vertoid: Exploring the persuasive potential of location-aware mobile cues. In *Proc. FedCSIS 2013*, IEEE (2013), 1339-1342.

[19] Zuckerman O, and Gal-Oz, A. Deconstructing gamification: Evaluating the effectiveness of continuous measurement, virtual rewards and social comparison for promoting physical activity. *Personal and Ubiquitous Computing 18*, 7 (2014), 1705-1719.

Touch Wire: Interactive Tangible Electricity Game for Kids

Michael Saenz
Texas A&M University
College Station, TX, USA
msaenz015@gmail.com

Joshua Strunk
Texas A&M University
College Station, TX, USA
Joshua.p.strunk@gmail.com

Sharon Lynn Chu
TAMU Embodied Interaction Lab
Texas A&M University
College Station, TX,USA
sharilyn@tamu.edu

Jinsil Hwaryoung Seo
Texas A&M University
College Station, TX, USA
hwaryoung@tamu.edu

TEI 2015, January 15-19, 2015, Stanford, CA, USA
ACM 978-1-4503-3305-4/15/01
http://dx.doi.org/10.1145/2677199.2687912

Abstract
This paper presents Touch Wire, a learning environment for teaching the basics of electricity and electronic design to young children. Touch Wire combines a digital touch screen interface with tangible components to bring the concepts of electronic circuitry to the forefront, while removing the tedium of tasks such as wiring for young children. Grounded in constructivist theories of learning, Touch Wire will overlay information about the underlying electrical mechanics on the tablet interface to scaffold children's learning of electronics. Our demonstrations have given us insight into how to best move forward developing the blended tangible and graphical interfaces of Touch Wire to both enhance the fun experience for children and support their learning of electronic circuitry.

Author Keywords
Tangible interaction; children;learning; electronic circuit; touch interface;tablet

ACM Classification Keywords
H.5.2. User Interfaces: Interaction Styles.

Introduction
With the introduction of physical computing and new 'maker' kits, much work has been done on supporting

children's learning of STEM concepts, like those in electronic circuitry, through the use of tangibles. Similarly, on the consumer market, several electronic kits share the goal of making electronics more approachable and easy to understand. Some focus on the transference of skills later on into more advanced DIY kits that make use of microprocessors, such as the Arduino [1], while others focus on building up a child's abstract understanding of circuits in the form of technical schematics.

A key problem with existing kits is their static nature. Educational kits that aim at teaching electronic circuitry such as Snap Circuits [7] requires a child to be guided by an adult or to use project guides to help her in the construction of circuit-based projects. Few of them take advantage of interactivity to actively guide and scaffold the child's learning process.

In this paper, we propose Touch Wire, an interactive environment that guides children through circuit creation by tapping into the power of both digital and physical representations. Digital representations of an augmented circuitry are presented through an interface on a touch screen, while tangibles are used to represent circuit components that are the focus of learning. A working prototype of Touch Wire has been tested at school events and festivals. Overall, we have received very positive feedback in terms of the potential of the prototype to scaffold the child's learning of electronic circuitry. The rest of this paper provides a brief overview of related works, the design and development approach of Touch Wire, and Preliminary user feedback from public events and fairs.

Related Work

Prior work that provides a tangible interface for the learning of electronic circuitry concepts for children includes *Little Bits. Little Bits* aims to create an easy introduction into electronics through its use of connections and modules [2]. It consists of modules which snap together using magnets. Modules can range from simple LEDs to complex components like timeout modules that allows users to set timers within their circuits. *Little Bits* eliminates the need to worry about many of the simple mistakes that learners can make such as polarity. However the high level of abstraction at which circuit components are presented, with circuitry being hidden inside the module components, makes it inefficient for teaching lower level concepts. *Touch Wire* attempts to maintain the simplicity of use of *Little Bits*, while also injecting enough representational and iconic power into the various interface components to allow children to ease into the learning of low-level concepts of electronic construction.

With regards to educational systems that couple tangibles with digital interfaces, *Flow of Electrons* [3] is an augmented reality tangible workbench that displays information about physical computing components like Arduinos and LEDs on a horizontal surface. The system has been tested with novice users experimenting with how components interconnect in a circuit, but not with children. *Touch Wire* adopts a digital interface similar to *Flow of Electrons*, but shifts the emphasis from tinkering to learning and education. Moreover, the physical components used on the digital surface of *Flow of Electrons* are non-interactive tangibles that are simply the objects the user is learning about, while we infuse interactivity into the tangibles themselves in the form of responsive feedback to reinforce the child's learning.

Figure 2. *Touch Wire* Prototype

Figure 1. *Touch Wire* concept illustration

Design Approach

The design of *Touch Wire* (Figure 1) is grounded in psychological theories of selective attention and constructivist theories of hands-on learning. Our strategy was to focus and guide the child's attention to components that are the subject of learning by materializing these into interactive tangibles, while pushing elements peripheral to the focus components (e.g., wiring) to the background. This allows a child to understand the role of a component of a circuit by analyzing the inputs and outputs of the circuit with and without the component. Once the child has grasped the concepts behind each circuit component, *Touch Wire* adds layers of abstraction to slowly introduce the child to lower level concepts of electricity.

To facilitate this scaffolded approach to learning, the educational goals in *Touch Wire* are integrated within a game framework. The game helps to guide children along a learning path and slowly builds on previous knowledge. For example, in the first level of the game, the child starts out with just a battery and the tangible light component. This helps to introduce the concept of how one would wire a battery to a light. In the next level, we introduce a switch component. The child can still connect the light in the same way as in the previous level, but now the child is encouraged to explore the switch to see how it interacts with the rest of the circuit components.

Touch Wire: System Description

Touch Wire consists of a tablet surface and a set of tangible objects. The digital interface of the tablet surface and the tangible objects work in concert to provide the child with an experience akin to augmented reality [4]. Instead of physical wires connecting the tangibles, virtual wires are represented on the tablet surface. The current prototype of *Touch Wire* (Figure 2) consists of one tangible object and an accompanying Android application. The Currently available tangible object is an LED light. Beginner explorations of electronics with DIY kits typically begin with simple elements like LEDs. The evident switching on and off of a light is also a very effective visual feedback to the user, and thus may also play a motivational role.

On the first game level of the tablet application, the user is presented with graphical icons representing a battery and an LED (the tangible object for level 1). There are '+' and '–' graphical icons representing polarity terminals near both the battery and the LED icons. The child can then drag from a positive terminal to a negative terminal to connect the components with a 'digital wire'. Upon the completion of the circuit, the tangible light, if placed correctly, will light up. We then prompt users to move to level two of the game, which adds a digital switch component. The second game level thus builds on the knowledge from the first, and allows users to play with the switch once the circuit is complete.

Figure 1. Children experiencing *Touchwire*

Implementation
The tablet interface is implemented through Java using the LibGDX [5] game framework. The tangible component's shell was designed using AutoDesk Maya before being 3D printed. The internal workings of the tangible light are determined by an Arduino microprocessor embedded inside of the tangible. The microprocessor connects to an RGB light sensor situated at the bottom of the tangible. An opening in the tangible's shell allows the light sensor to pick up the light intensity from directly underneath the tangible. This allows us to trigger changes in the state of the circuit by displaying bright colors on the tablet screen underneath the tangible. When the tangible is placed on the tablet surface in the appropriate spot, the Arduino reads in the color underneath it and decides if its LED light should be on or off.

Preliminary Observations
The *Touch Wire* prototype has been showcased at local and national STEM-based events, such as the USA Science and Engineering Festival in Washington, DC. Attendees of the events were mainly elementary school students (Figure 3). We have tested slightly modified versions of *Touch* Wire at each event based on our observations of children's interactions with the prototypes. In our first prototype, a child would tap a positive terminal, then a negative to wire two circuit components, with no dragging involved on the touch surface of the tablet. However, we consistently observed that the intuitive reaction of children when presented with the tablet interface was to use a dragging gesture for wiring, instead of tapping. We added the capability of wiring by dragging from one terminal to another in later prototypes of the system.

Children's use of the prototype involving dragging to wire however brought another problem to light. We noticed children would get confused when wires had to cross each other on the screen. A possible solution to this problem would be to allow children to draw free-form wires instead of just connect components in straight lines. Another problem that we have observed is that some children perceive the tangibles to be an intrinsically connected, unmovable part of the digital circuit. Overall, the feedback that we received from parents was very positive. We have received numerous requests from teachers and parents to develop *Touch Wire* for the market as a teaching aid.

Discussion
An important obstacle to introducing young children to building electronic systems is the tedious and sometimes difficult task of wiring. A child can quickly grow frustrated when the wiring between components becomes complex or messy. *Touch Wire* provides an approach to this problem by handling the wiring of components, both digital and tangible, through touch events such as dragging on the tablet.

Many have put forward the benefits of tangibility for learning. Through careful design, we tap into the power of tangibility, but only selectively for focus components of learning, while we compress and represent other non-focus components as graphics in the virtual world.[6] This minimizes the potential for error and simplifies the circuit-building process for the child. This also represents a scaffolded approach whereby more complex features and concerns are hidden until the child has built up enough knowledge, skills and confidence to tackle the more complex challenges. Through control of the digital interface, we are also able to provide scaffolded learning by slowly introducing new and more abstract information into the system environment, such as representing the flow of current through the virtual wires.

Future Work

Motivated by the positive feedback we received with regards to our prototype during our preliminary studies, we are currently working on expanding the range of tangible components that *Touch Wire* can support. The design of *Touch* Wire is flexible enough such that it can easily be adapted for other simple output components. We are also planning to include more interactive tangibles, such as switches and buttons that can send input to the underlying circuit through the use of capacitive tags that can transmit state changes to the screen [8]. We also hope to implement tangible components that do not just sit on the screen but act as representational tools to help teach other concepts of electronics construction. One such tool for example could be a tangible which represents a soldering iron, thus allowing our game to require wires to be "soldered on" to complete connections in later stages.

In terms of the graphical tablet interface, we will also be adding more complex information about significant concepts to learn in electronic circuitry. This includes for instance allowing children to view the current and voltage of the circuits they complete.

Conclusion

Touch Wire is a prototype aimed at teaching electronic circuitry to young children through a scaffolded learning approach. The design contribution of *Touch Wire* is that it optimizes the use of both tangibility and graphical interfaces to support learning in a STEM domain that is increasingly important. Results from preliminary studies of the prototype have shown that *Touch Wire* has great potential to support the development of electronics education for children along with STEM education as a whole. We are pursuing further research into how interactive TUI interfaces mixed with traditional GUI interfaces may prove beneficial in helping children grasp abstract STEM concepts.

References

[1] Arduino. Available from http://www.arduino.cc/

[2] Bdeir A. Electronics as material: LittleBits. Proceedings of TEI '09. ACM Press (2009), 397-400.

[3] Conradi B., Lerch V., Hommer M., Kowalski R., Vletsou I., and Hussmann H. Flow of Electrons: An Augmented Workspace for Learning Physical Computing Experientially. Proc ITS '11. ACM Press (2011), 182-191

[4] Ishii H. Tangible Bits: Beyond Pixels. Proc. TEI'08. ACM Press (2008), xv-xxv.

[5] libGDX. Available from http://libgdx.badlogicgames.com/

[6] Marshall, P. Do tangible interfaces enhance learning?. Proc TEI '07. ACM Press (2007), 163-170

[7] Snap Circuits. Available from http://www.snapcircuits.net/

[8] Yu N., Cheng L., Chan L., Lau S., Hsiao F., Tsai S., Chen M. Y., Huang P., Hsiao I., Tsai D., Hung Y. TUIC: Enabling Tangible Interaction on Capacitive Multi-touch Display. Proc. CHI '11. ACM Press (2011), 2995-3004.

Towards an Anthropomorphic Lamp for Affective Interaction

Leonardo Angelini
University of Applied Sciences and Arts Western Switzerland
Fribourg, Switzerland
leonardo.angelini@hes-so.ch

Maurizio Caon
University of Applied Sciences and Arts Western Switzerland
Fribourg, Switzerland
maurizio.caon@hes-so.ch

Denis Lalanne
University of Fribourg
Fribourg, Switzerland
denis.lalanne@unifr.ch

Omar Abou Khaled
University of Applied Sciences and Arts Western Switzerland
Fribourg, Switzerland
omar.aboukhaled@hes-so.ch

Elena Mugellini
University of Applied Sciences and Arts Western Switzerland
Fribourg, Switzerland
elena.mugellini@hes-so.ch

TEI '15, Jan 16-19 2015, Stanford, CA, USA
ACM 978-1-4503-3305-4/15/01.
http://dx.doi.org/10.1145/2677199.2687914

Abstract
This paper presents the concept of a lamp that allows displaying and collecting user's emotional states. In particular, it displays the emotional information changing colors and facial expressions; in fact, the lamp is characterized by anthropomorphic form and behavior in order to make the interaction more natural and spontaneous. The user can interact with the lamp through tangible gestures typically used in social interactions by humans. Two different scenarios involving the use of the lamp as a companion and for computer-mediated communication are presented.

Author Keywords
Affective computing; computer mediated-communication; life-like object; tangible gestures

ACM Classification Keywords
H.5.m. Information interfaces and presentation (e.g., HCI): Miscellaneous

Introduction
Nowadays, computer-mediated communication is becoming a focal point of our lives; in fact, some psychologists and sociologists claim that the current trend of interpersonal interaction is shifting from the physical to the virtual world [6]. A consequence of the Human-Computer-Human Interaction (HCHI) is that all

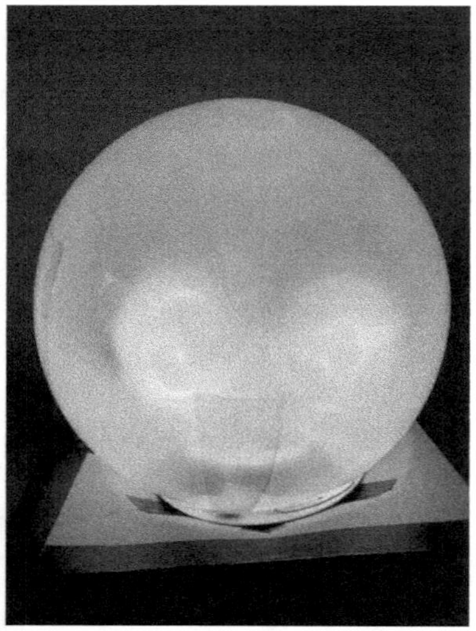

Figure 1. The ADA lamp in the happiness state.

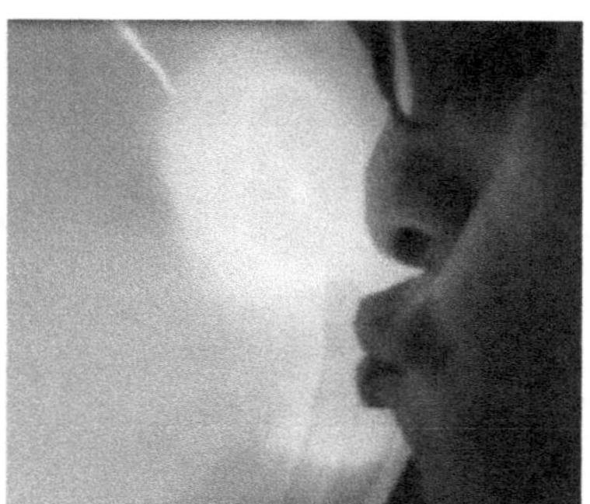

Figure 2. A user kissing the ADA lamp.

the paralanguage of a normal face-to-face communication is missing; for this reason, the computer-mediated communication of emotions is quite complicated. For instance, in instant messaging software and social networks the facial expressions and the prosody of the voice are (inadequately) replaced with emoticons and punctuation. The interpersonal touch, usually provided by contact gestures in a face-to-face interaction, is completely absent in HCHI.

We propose the concept of an anthropomorphic lamp called ADA (Anthropomorphic Display of Affection), which introduces a novel and more natural way for the communication of emotions (see Figure 1). ADA's anthropomorphic features and behavior allows for the exploration of new interaction modalities and facilitates the understanding of shared emotional states. In this paper, we present the concept of the ADA lamp with reference to related works present in the scientific literature. Then, we also show the different steps of the lamp design and development. Finally, we present two different scenarios for the interaction with the lamp: first, as a smart companion and, second, as a means for the distant communication of emotions.

Related work

The "Feather, Scent and Shaker" paper paved the way for the exploration of distant communication of emotions through tangible objects [13]. In this context, the LumiTouch frame was the first object that allowed for an active interaction with touch-gestures on the photo-frame surface and, at the same, time provided a visual feedback in the environment [5]. This form of ambient display exploited the human peripheral vision in order to provide the emotional information communicated by a distant person without interfering with the user's focal attention. The ADA lamp can be used in a similar scenario for intimate mediated interaction and physical telepresence. The benefit provided by using an interface that allows for a richer communication of emotions over a distance was demonstrated in the *cubble* project [9]. In this work, Kowalski et al. used a cube as tangible interface and compared it to a smartphone application for long-distance relationships and they demonstrated that the tangible interface enhanced the user experience and fostered a more frequent interaction leading to emotional closeness. However, Kowalski et al.'s cube did not provide an anthropomorphic affordance for the emotion communication. Moreover, coding emotions as single colors cannot be considered as a universal interface and, in fact, the *cubble* users preferred defining their personal associations between colors and affective states.

An emerging trend in affective computing is the design of life-like tangible objects. In fact, Schmitz conducted a review of the current scientific literature and presented a detailed analysis and some guidelines for the adoption of anthropomorphism and animism as paradigms for object design [12]. Life-like objects should not only have an anthropomorphic or zoomorphic form but should also present a behavior similar to a living being. Schmitz claims that such interactive life-like objects enable building a more intuitive and more durable relationship with the user. In the literature, it is possible to find some examples of zoomorphic companions for the communication of emotions; a popular example is the Nabaztag rabbit, which communicates different kinds of information with ear postures, light and sound [10]. The Hapticat is a companion that behaves like a cat [15]; a very similar

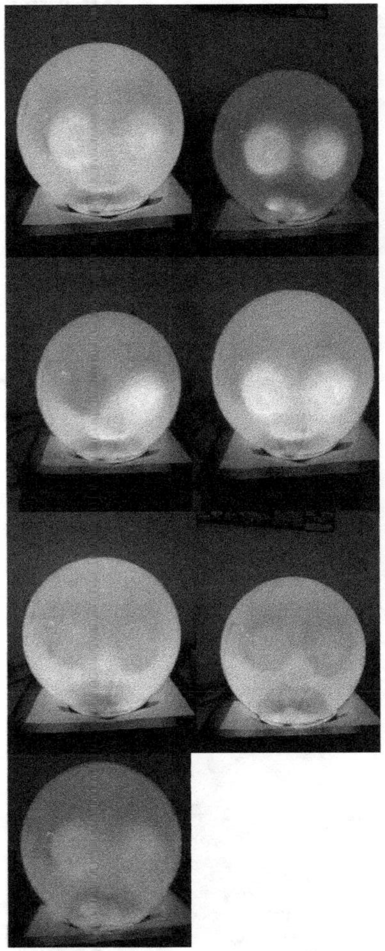

Figure 3. The five emotional states of the ADA lamp: happy, sad, trusty (eye blink) (2x), ecstasy (2x) and angry.

concept has been proposed by Philips for their iCat, which is a robot resembling a cat and able to display emotional information performing human-like facial expressions[14]. Burneleit et al. explored the possibility of making household appliances to behave like animals with the *impatient toaster;* their tests showed that users were emotionally engaged while interacting with this life-like toaster [1]. We chose to give life to a lamp and to characterize it with anthropomorphic features. Similarly to the iCat, ADA is able to mimic human facial expressions in order to communicate emotional states; at the same time, ADA changes color according to the specific emotion in order to provide information via the peripheral visual attention. Moreover, ADA recognizes contact gestures that humans usually use in inter-personal communication. For instance, it is possible to caress, hug or kiss the lamp to make it happy (see Figure 2) and to slap or shake it to make it angry. Beyond the role of companion, the ADA lamp can be used to communicate emotional states to a distant person for affective computer-mediated relationships.

Concept

The concept of the ADA lamp is the result of an interactive experience with systems for the computer-mediated communication of emotions through ambient displays. Indeed, during a live demo at the ACII 2013 conference, Caon et al. conducted an observation study on two different types of ambient displays for emotion sharing, a RGB lamp and a robotic painting [4]. Their analysis, presented in [3], highlighted the difference of emotional engagement during the interaction with the system and the amount of attention that users gave to the different forms of feedback. The robotic painting captured all the users' attention; this robotic painting, called Aphrodite, represents the Venus head from Botticelli's "the Birth of Venus" and is able to mimic human facial expressions to communicate particular emotional states. The lamp, in this work was designed to change colors according to affective information and to be placed in the users' peripheral visual attention; however, although the lamp was placed near to Aphrodite, the users completely ignored it because they were too engaged in interacting with the painting. This observation confirmed Schmitz theory about life-like objects. For this reason, we decided to design a RGB lamp conferring it anthropomorphic features. The current ADA prototype changes color and mimics facial expression to communicate emotional states. The color-emotion mapping has been based on the Plutchick's wheel of emotions [11]. The user can interact with ADA through tangible gestures [8]. The anthropomorphic aspect helps leveraging the affordance for the natural adoption of gesture for interpersonal touch that we use with other living beings. In particular, ADA can recognize the following gestures: caressing, hugging and kissing for positive valence, slapping and shaking for negative valence.

Interaction scenarios

The ADA lamp can be used in multiple contexts. In this paper, we present two particular interaction scenarios: first as a smart companion and then as interface for affective interaction in long distance relationships.

In the first scenario, the anthropomorphic lamp presents personal intelligence and behavior; it reacts to the user's gestures and tries to attract her attention showing unpredictable behaviors. The latter can create a sense of surprise that can sustain the user engagement on the long term [12]. An advanced version of the lamp could adapt its behavior to the

Figure 4. In the top, the cylindrical structure of the LED strip; below, the Arduino Uno with the EasyVR shield and the MPR121 and ADXL345 sensors.

current mood of the user. The companion lamp could be used just for entertainment or to share emotional states on the social networks, of course, in addition to illuminating the surrounding environment.

In the second scenario, the lamp can function as an interface for emotional telepresence and affective computer-mediated communication. In fact, ADA will represent the emotional states of a distant loved person. The emotional state can be shared via private messages on social networks or interacting directly with the lamp. The emotional state of the lamp can also change according to the gesture performed from the distant person on the other lamp: a gesture with positive valence will make the lamp to go to a positive emotional state and vice-versa. In this way, the separated people can naturally interact directly through a couple of ADA lamps without the support of other digital interfaces.

Prototype Development

The first phase of the development was focused on the realization of a lamp with an anthropomorphic form. A commercial spherical table lamp fitted perfectly the purpose of obtaining a form similar to a human head. The light bulb has been replaced with a strip with 60 RGB addressable LEDs disposed on a cylindrical structure. An internal separation with paper structures conveys the lights of specific LEDs for the left and right eyes and for a frown and a smiling mouth. LED colors and intensities are individually controlled through an Arduino Uno board (Figure 4). By selectively lighting up the different zones with different colors, it is possible to choose an arbitrary color for each face region, to hide one of the two mouths or simulate an eye blink. The five different facial expressions are shown in Figure 3.

As a second step, we implemented the recognition of gestures performed on the surface of the ADA lamp through a MPR121 capacitive sensor connected to the Arduino. Six transparent Indium Tin Oxide (ITO) electrodes have been attached all around the lamp surface and connected to the MPR121. Touch gestures such as caressing, hugging and caressing, are recognized through a simple threshold-based algorithm that check the contact on the different zones covered by the electrodes. Slapping and shaking are recognized through an ADXL345 accelerometer connected to the Arduino.

Finally, we implemented the anthropomorphic behavior of the companion lamp with a state diagram. The states in the diagram in Figure 5 represent the 5 different emotional states of the lamp, with their corresponding colors and facial expressions. Transitions to another state can be obtained by performing on the lamp a gesture, a sequence of gestures, or by a period of inactivity, i.e., absence of any gesture. In Figure 5 we show an implementation of the state diagram for the companion scenario of the lamp. In order to improve clarity, we illustrated separately the transition diagram for negative valence gestures and inactivity (on the left) and the transition diagram for positive valence gestures (on the right). Multiple arrows of the same color depict gestures that need to be performed multiple times in order to activate the transition. The transition diagram and the gesture recognition algorithms are executed in a C# application running in a PC. The ADA lamp is connected to the PC through a USB serial connection. The state diagram can be easily customized to obtain different behavior of the lamp. For example, following the examples provided by the provoking article of Buttrick et al. [2], one could imagine that the lamp reacts in a positive manner to gesture with a negative valence and, vice versa, gets angry when the user perform gestures with positive valence. The state diagram can have input also from other stimuli, for example inferring the mood of the user from Twitter or from life-logging devices.

Future work and tests
In order to enrich the interaction modalities of the lamp, we considered the implementation of haptic feedback through a vibration motor and audio feedback through an EasyVR module. Using this module, it is also possible to implement vocal inputs, such as short phrases or vocal sounds.

Two user evaluations are planned. A first large public experience, ideally during a conference demonstration, will be focused on evaluating the reaction of the users in the short term. In particular, we would like to measure the time spent by each user observing the lamp and interacting with it, the number of different gesture discovered by each user and the total number of gesture performed for each type. The users reaction will be compared for the two examples of state diagram illustrated in the previous paragraph. The second experience will be focused on investigating the user interactions with the lamp in a longer time perspective. Also the second interaction scenario will be studied more in depth: Hemmert et al. demonstrated that it is important to carefully design devices for emotional telepresence because they can result awkward or disturbing [7]. For this reason, it is crucial to conduct further research on user acceptance and also studying potential cultural differences in the degrees of acceptance.

Description of gesture – arrow colors mapping.

Figure 5a :

- Black: shaking or slapping
- Blue: inactivity

Figure 5b :

- Yellow: caressing
- Green: hugging
- Red: kissing

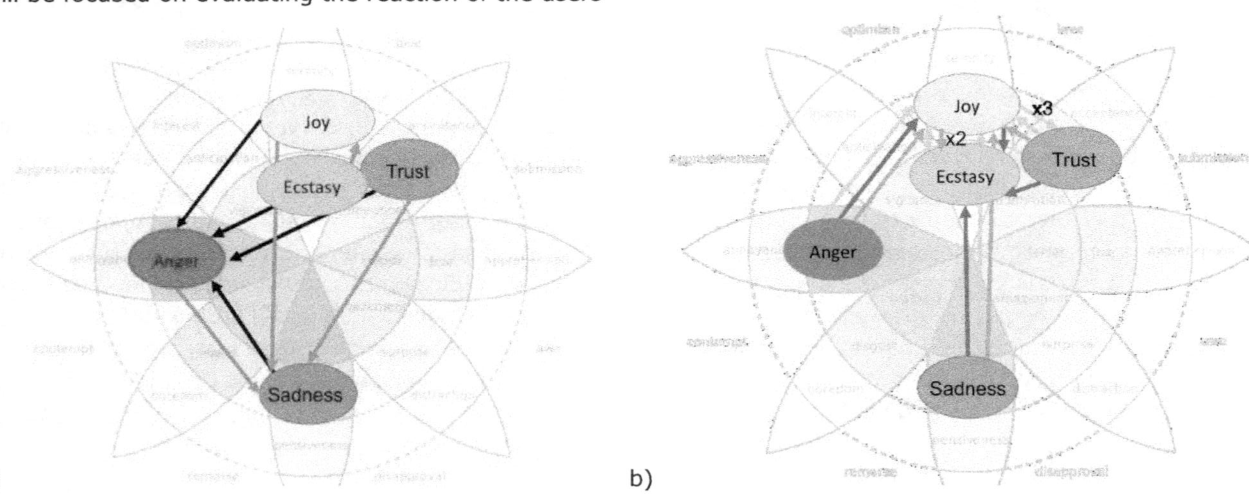

a) b)

Figure 5. a) On the left, the diagram for the negative valence gestures; b) on the right, the diagram for positive valence gestures.

Conclusion

In this paper, we presented the design of an anthropomorphic lamp that is able to display emotional states through colorful facial expressions and to collect user's emotional states expressed through tangible gestures. The special anthropomorphic design is intended to facilitate the interaction with the lamp by leveraging the user ability to recognize facial expressions and to express emotional states through contact gestures that are typically performed with other humans. Two different application scenarios for the ADA lamp have been illustrated and the scenario of a companion lamp has been also implemented in a functional prototype. In this scenario, the lamp is animated through a customizable state diagram where gestures allow the transition between the different lamp internal states. Based on literature, we believe that the anthropomorphic design of the lamp could help keeping high the interest in interacting with the lamp or through the lamp. Of course, this hypothesis needs to be supported with several future user experiments. We propose to conduct one of these experiments during an interactive demonstration at the TEI conference.

References

[1] Burneleit, E., Hemmert, F., & Wettach, R. Living interfaces: the impatient toaster. *In Proc. of TEI'09* (pp. 21-22). ACM.

[2] Buttrick, L., Linehan, C., Kirman, B., and O'Hara, D. Fifty shades of CHI: the perverse and humiliating human-computer relationship. In *CHI EA'14* (pp. 825-834). 2014. ACM.

[3] Caon, M., Angelini, L., Khaled, O. A., Lalanne, D., Yue, Y., and Mugellini, E. Affective Interaction in Smart Environments. *Procedia Computer Science*, *32*, pp. 1016-1021. 2014.

[4] Caon, M., Khaled, O. A., Mugellini, E., Lalanne, D., and Angelini, L. Ubiquitous Interaction for Computer Mediated Communication of Emotions. In *Proc. of ACII'13* (pp. 717-718).

[5] Chang, A., Resner, B., Koerner, B., Wang, X., and Ishii, H. LumiTouch: an emotional communication device. In *CHI'01 EA* (pp. 313-314). 2001. ACM

[6] Clubb, O. L. Human-to-Computer-to-Human Interactions (HCHI) of the communications revolution. *Interactions*, *14*(2), 35-39. (2007).

[7] Hemmert, F., Gollner, U., Löwe, M., Wohlauf, A., & Joost, G. Intimate mobiles: grasping, kissing and whispering as a means of telecommunication in mobile phones. *In Proc. Of MobileHCI 2011 (pp. 21-24)*. ACM.

[8] Hoven, E., Mazalek, A.: Grasping gestures: Gesturing with physical artifacts. *Artificial Intelligence for Engineering Design*, *Analysis and Manufacturing*. 25, 255–271. (2011).

[9] Kowalski, R., Loehmann, S., and Hausen, D. cubble: a multi-device hybrid approach supporting communication in long-distance relationships. In *Proc. of TEI'13*. pp. 201-204. ACM.

[10] Peters, L. Nabaztag wireless communicator. Personal Computer World, 2. 2006.

[11] Plutchik,R. The Nature of Emotions, *American Scientist*, 89(4), 344-350, 2001.

[12] Schmitz, M. Concepts for life-like interactive objects. In *Proc. of TEI'11* (pp. 157-164). ACM.

[13] Strong, R., and Gaver, B. Feather, scent and shaker: supporting simple intimacy. In *Proc.of CSCW'*96. 1996 Vol. 96, No. 96, pp. 29-30.

[14] van Breemen, A., Yan, X., & Meerbeek, B. iCat: an animated user-interface robot with personality. *In Proc. of AAMAS 2005 (pp. 143-144)*. ACM.

[15] Yohanan, S., Chan, M., Hopkins, J., Sun, H., and Maclean, K. Hapticat : Exploration of Affective Touch. *Proc. of ICMI'05*, ACM (2005), 222–229.

Composing Interaction: Exploring Tangible Notation Systems For Design

Bart Hengeveld
Eindhoven University of Technology
Dept. of Industrial Design
Den Dolech 2, 5612 AZ,
Eindhoven, The Netherlands
B.J.Hengeveld@TUe.nl

TEI'15, January 15–19, 2015, Stanford, California, USA.
ACM 978-1-4503-3305-4/15/01.
http://dx.doi.org/10.1145/2677199.2687915

Abstract
In this paper we discuss our recent research into notation systems for interaction design. Inspired by music notation—a standardized yet open system with which a composition (i.e., a musical design) can be communicated—we suspect that similar notation systems can be designed for interaction design. We describe our research approach to this suspicion and describe several outcomes of our research, which all lean heavily on tangibility, manipulability and shareability.

Author Keywords
Tangible interaction; notation systems; embodiment; ambiguity; experience design.

ACM Classification Keywords
H.5.2 User Interfaces

Introduction
Like many other researchers, the authors of this paper find inspiration in music. By this we do not mean being inspired to write a paper while listening to music, but rather the various intricate processes and mechanisms going on in and around music, from the act of composition, to improvised performance (e.g., [2], [3]) and anything in between. The aspect of music that is at the center of this paper is music notation, referring to

any system used to (visually) represent aurally perceived music through the use of (written) symbols. The most widely known and used system in the Western world is of course that based on flagged dots and horizontal lines, organized according to their pitch and temporal quality: notes with a higher pitch are placed on higher lines (even help lines), lower sounding notes on lower lines; notes played simultaneously are stacked on top of each other, while notes played in a sequence are put in a row. However, music notation is not only 'notes and lines', but includes a range of additional symbols to indicate musical aspects ranging from very concrete (e.g., a time signature indicating the number of beats per bar) to more ambiguous. For example, the expression '*crescendo poco a poco*', meaning 'slowly but certainly louder', leaves room for interpretation: from how loud to how loud, how slowly but certainly? It is exactly this mix of definition and openness that we find so intriguing about music notation, especially from the perspective of interaction design. We explain this in the following by comparing the two.

Capturing designed experiences

Let's consider music composers as designers of music. Like any designer they give form to a certain medium with the aim of enabling people to have a specific experience. Where architects give form to spaces, industrial designers to objects and interaction designers to interactions, composers use music. They consider, perhaps more than any of the other aforementioned, the temporal aspects of an experience and try to capture this in a musical design.

Now, where we, interaction designers, mostly use static representations for expressing and transferring and communicating our experience designs (e.g., through sketches, models) before moving into more experienceable and often time-consuming forms of representation (e.g., video demos, prototypes), composers have a very accessible, low-cost tool at hand: music notation. A time-centric system that allows for exactness (for elements in the musical design that the designer considers as fixed), but also leaves room for designed interpretation, as such allowing their 'users' to interpret the design and make it their own.

The question we address in this paper is: if such a notation system works for designers of music, why would it not work for designers of interactive experiences? Can we create a notation system for design that allows us to communicate the essence of our *designed* experience while still allowing the user to create his or her own ritual? And of course, does such a notation system make sense?

In the following sections we illustrate our approach, give an overview of the most relevant findings and discuss the impact of our work on the field of tangible and embodied interaction.

Approach

We have approached this research interest through two, two-week design research workshops at our Department of Industrial Design with 40 first- and second-year graduate students. The setup incorporated the following sequence of steps:

1. *Introduction*. At the kickoff of the workshops we introduced the students to the research interest and exposed them to various notation systems. Among others, we exposed them to traditional music notation but also to other forms of music

notation such as that of John Cage, showing them the composition "Water Walk" on YouTube, plus parts of the notation. In addition we looked at notation systems from various unrelated disciplines, such as Laban Movement Analysis, pace notes used in rally driving and altitude maps for hikers. All systems that combine exactness with interpretation.

2. *Making a video diary of a personal ritual*. After the introduction each student was asked to individually document a personal ritual through an expressive video diary. The default ritual was each student's 'coffee ritual', 'ritual' referring to all aspects involved in how they drink coffee. For example, for one student might the ritual might involve grinding beans and sitting in the sun taking 15 minutes minimum for proper enjoyment, while for another the ritual might be getting up from their desk, taking a ten-second walk to the coffee machine, refilling the tumbler and saying a brief hello to others before heading back. If a student would not be a coffee drinker, a similar ritual could be examined (most often, drinking tea or having breakfast). The purpose of having students capture their ritual in a dairy was to force them to consider (a) which elements beyond functional ones were essential to their ritual and (b) how they could best communicate the ritual as they experience it to people not experiencing it, using the stylistic tricks they know from the movie industry. They were stimulated to be accurate in lighting, viewpoints and editing of their video, and to add a fitting soundtrack to it.

3. *Analyzing the ritual and capturing it in a self-designed notation system*. All individual videos were watched in a plenary session with all students. This allowed for discussing results and rationales, as well as for identifying patterns and anomalies. After the plenary video session each student was asked to make a representation of their ritual using a notation system of their own design. It was stressed that the term "notation system" did not necessarily imply that their design should be paper-based; on the contrary it was stressed that the term notation should be interpreted as broad as they wanted in order to keep options open for other potentially powerful media.

4. *Grouping up and applying step 2 to each other's work*. All students presented their notated rituals and accompanying notation systems, after which they were teamed up in groups of four to compare approaches and results. As one activity to support this, they were asked to apply their own notation system to the rituals of their group mates in order to find strengths, weaknesses, insights and oversights; to see which elements of their notation system were actually generally applicable, and which seemed to apply better to the more idiosyncratic parts of their rituals.

5. *Designing a new notation system and using it to make a design brief for another group.* Based on their findings all student teams were asked to design another notation system. This new one could combine elements from the individual notations systems as designed during Step 2, but could also be completely new if this would make

more sense.
In addition the student teams were asked to use their own team's notation system to set up a design brief for another team. The general topic of each brief was to design a novel picnic experience. Each team could define an original picnic experience (e.g., a winter picnic, a picnic for 100 participants, etcetera) as long as they could somehow transfer this via their brief. The aim of the briefs was not to be defined to the last detail, but rather to explore the limitations of communicability of their notation system.

6. *Exchanging design briefs and designing the experience*. The new notation systems were not plenary discussed. In fact, the only contact between teams was the few minutes necessary for exchanging design briefs. Students thereafter had two days to develop and build the picnic design as they interpreted it from their brief.

7. *Evaluating the results and reporting findings*. At the end of the research case all teams gathered together and tried out each other's designs. Consequently this led to a series of picnic experiences. After each picnic experience the design was discussed, as well as the match between what the 'brief definers' had put in and what the 'brief interpreters' took from it.
All students were asked to report their individual and group findings.

8. *Evaluating the potential of notation systems for interaction design*. Lastly a plenary discussion was organized to compare notation systems and to evaluate their sense or nonsense. The insights from this evaluation are illustrated in the Findings section at the end of the paper.

Each of these steps (apart from step 6) was discussed with all participants in plenary sessions.

Results
The workshop resulted in a large number of notation system designs. Here we outline two of the more promising recurring approaches.

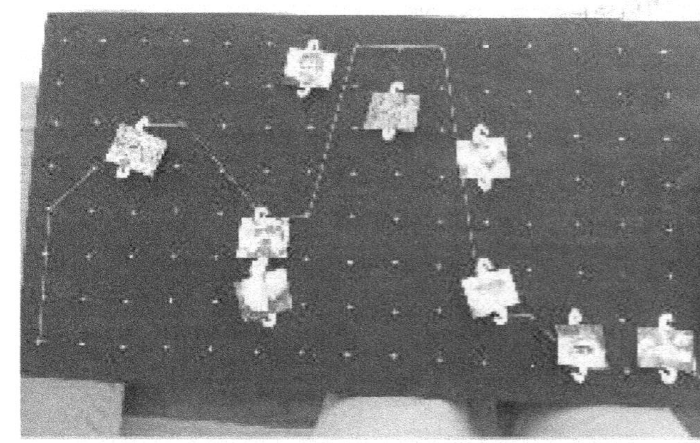

Figure 1: Many designs were based on a pegboard setup, using strings to represent the 'route' of the experience and various labels signifying key moments and their character.

Pegboards
A prominent group of notation system designs (both individually as well as two group designs) is one where the designs are based on a pegboard principle. One such example is shown in Figure 1, designed by Ineke Neutelings. The notation system consists of a pegboard, string and labels that can be hung form the

string or from another label. The string is used to creates a route through the pegs, which can be straight and to-the-point (signifying equally to-the-point interactions) or elaborate and meandering (signifying slower, perhaps richer interactions). Several labels are provided to connect to the string or pegs at pivotal points in the interaction design, to add moodboardy elements. This design was eventually developed into a whiteboard-based variant, using magnetic 'pegs' instead of fixed ones. This enabled easier manipulation of the design during group discussions.

The pegboard variant appeared in many forms but all had in common that (1) they capitalized on visualizing 'the experience as it unfolds', through expressive string-routes and supporting associative materials; and (2) they were freely and frequently manipulated during discussions throughout the design process of the brief.

Hexn

A second approach is one based on modular, tangible token sets. This approach is best illustrated through Hexn, a design by Wout Kregting, Matthijs Willems and Stef Wouters. Hexn is a set of hexagonal discs, some blank, others containing one of 38 icons organized in four categories: Emotions, Senses, Feeling and Context. The discs can be combined in any form or order to create collage-like representations of an experience or experience design. One such example is shown in Figure 2 where a romantic break-up is depicted.

Two aspects that are interesting about Hexn are that (1) contrary to music notation Hexn *fully* relies on ambiguity and personal interpretation (although we should mention that the briefs were very accurately interpreted by all participants), and (2) contrary to other designed notation systems (such as the pegboard ones) Hexn is visually directionless. In almost all other notation system designs experiences were visualized with a clear beginning, ending and reading direction, but Hexn rather presented a single-image experience collage.

Figure 2: A romantic break-up visualized using Hexn, a notation system for creating collage-like, nonlinear representations of experiences.

In their design brief however (Step 5) the designers of the Hexn system chose not to present a static end composition, instead they presented their design brief in the form of a 1:48 minute movie.

Findings

Here we briefly discuss the most significant findings emerging from Step 8.

First of all it is fair to point out that *none* of the participating students indicated that they wanted a notation system for interaction design: they all were quite happy with the visualization and prototyping tools that are currently available. On the other hand, *all* of them pointed out independently that the notation systems they designed were surprisingly valuable tools for communication and discussion, both of a final design as well as during the design process. All students indicated that the systems they designed helped them consider and explain all phases and facets of their experiences/designs better than e.g., sketching. Several reasons were given for this: (1) As most of the designed notation systems were based on tangible components they allowed for easy sharing and equal accessibility to all in the group. This greatly facilitated collaboration, more than when sketching; (2) As a consequence, a shared space for discussion was created. Individual bits of the notation could be picked up or pointed out and as such discussed separately as part of the overall experience design; (3) Due to the manipulability of the tangible notation systems individual parts of the total experience design could be separately discussed and refined and even reordered for a better experience. As such the systems contributed to more explicit awareness of the fact that no experience starts out-of-the-blue: all experiences have a build-up and wrap-up; (4) The fact that many of the notation systems were quite ambiguous made that they stimulated discussions aimed at concretizing.

Conclusion

In this paper we described our ongoing research into potential notation systems for interaction design. Although our preliminary findings do not suggest such a system has yet been successfully found, we can certainly conclude that the systems serve as powerful discussion tools for interactive experiences. Similar insights have recently been published by Buur et. al. [1]. The reasons given are largely in line with the benefits of tangibility and embodiment as described by Shaer and Hornecker [5] and should certainly look familiar to followers of Donald Schön [4]. Although our work is far from complete we believe our research can contribute greatly to the field of interaction design. If only to show that interactive experiences are by definition multimodal and should be explored as such. The work presented in this paper illustrates how this can be done in an accessible and efficient manner.

Acknowledgements

We thank all the students taking part in the course, in particular the designers mentioned in this paper.

References

[1] Buur, J., Caglio, A., & Jensen, L. C. (2014). *Human actions made tangible: analysing the temporal organization of activities*. In Proc DIS 2014 (pp. 1065-1073). ACM.

[2] Hengeveld, B., Frens, J. & Funk, M. (2013). *Investigating How To Design For Systems Through Designing A Group Music Improvisation System*. Proc. IASDR 2013, Tokyo, Japan.

[3] Junggeburth, M., Giacolini, L., Rooij, T. van, Hout, B. van, Hengeveld, B.J., Funk, M. & Frens, J.W. (2013) *Experio: a laser- triggered dance music generator*. Proc. DeSForM 2013. Wuxi, China.

[4] Schön, D. A. (1983) *The reflective practitioner: How professionals think in action*, Basic Books.

[5] Shaer, O., & Hornecker, E. (2010). Tangible user interfaces: past, present, and future directions. *Foundations and Trends in Human-Computer Interaction*, *3*(1–2), 1-137.

Tactile Letters: a Tangible Tabletop with Texture Cues Supporting Alphabetic Learning for Dyslexic Children

Min Fan
School of Interactive Arts and Technology
Simon Fraser University,
Surrey, B.C., Canada V3T 0A3
minf@sfu.ca

Alissa N. Antle
School of Interactive Arts and Technology
Simon Fraser University,
Surrey, B.C., Canada V3T 0A3
aantle@sfu.ca

TEI '15, Jan 16-19 2015, Stanford, CA, USA
ACM 978-1-4503-3305-4/15/01.
http://dx.doi.org/10.1145/2677199.2688806

Abstract
Dyslexic children have great difficulty in learning to read. While research in HCI suggests that tangible user interfaces (TUIs) have the potential to support children learning to read, few studies have explored how to help dyslexic children learn to read. Even fewer studies have specifically investigated the design space of texture cues in TUIs in supporting learning to read. In this paper, we present *Tactile Letters*, a multimodal tangible tabletop with texture cues developed to support English letter-sound correspondence learning for dyslexic children aged 5-6 years old. This prototype is used as a research instrument to investigate the role of texture cues in a multimodal TUI in alphabetic learning. We discuss the current knowledge gap, the theoretical foundations that informed our core design strategy, and the subsequent design decisions we made while developing Tactile Letters.

Keywords
Tangible user interfaces; dyslexia; children; reading; texture cues; material.

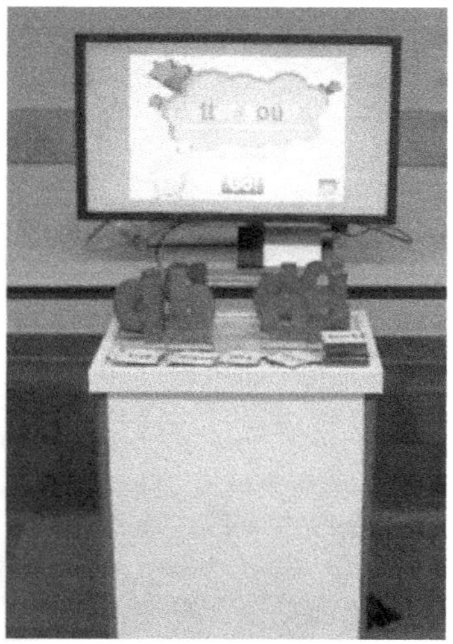

Figure 1. Tactile Letters: a TUI with a display and a set of tangible letters with or without texture cues.

Figure 2. Tangible letters with texture cues.

ACM Classification Keywords

H.5.2. [Information interfaces and presentation]: User Interfaces.K.3.1 [Computers and Education]: Computer Uses in Education-*Computer-assisted instruction*.

Introduction

Dyslexia is a specific learning difficulty that influences learning to read [10]. Children with dyslexia struggle to automate the 'alphabetic principle' (i.e. letter-sound correspondences) and therefore have difficulty in word decoding and reading [4]. Research in HCI suggests that tangible user interfaces (TUIs) have the potential to support learning to read for children [17, 19], but it has seldom explored how to better help dyslexic children learn to read [8,13]. Moreover, we have not seen any studies that specifically investigated the role of texture cues in TUIs in supporting learning to read.

The important role of tracing letters in learning to read for dyslexic children has been highlighted in previous research [2,3,4,10]. In many successful multisensory programs, dyslexic children are encouraged to see letters, hear their sounds, and trace them with their fingers on a textured surface such as sandpaper [4,10], cards [16], digital screens [1] or physical letters made of foam [2,3]. Despite using different surfaces, these tracing activities share one common characteristic. That is, dyslexic children trace all the letters on the ***same*** textured surface in each approach. The new opportunity provided by TUIs is to better leverage the use of ***various*** textures through constantly coupling them with cross-modal digital information (e.g., associating textures with letter sounds) [12]. The association between textures (embedded in letter shapes) and letter sounds may act as affordances to efficiently support dyslexic children learning letter-sound correspondences. We believe it is of great value to explore the design space of texture cues in TUIs designed for alphabetic learning for dyslexic children. Filling this knowledge gap would lead us to a better understanding of how to design TUI learning materials and texture cues to better augment visual/auditory modalities of information representations.

In this paper, a proposed tangible tabletop incorporating two sets of letters (one with texture cues and the other without texture cues) was designed to help dyslexic children aged 5-6 years to learn letter-sound correspondences (Figures 1 and 2). The core design strategy of texture cues is based on the metaphoric mapping strategy used in education [8]. This prototype is a research instrument that allows us to investigate whether a tangible tabletop with texture cues can help dyslexic children learn letter-sound correspondences more effectively than a tabletop without texture cues.

Related Work

Learning to Read in Dyslexic Children

Learning to read is a systematic, complex and difficult process, particularly when learning opaque languages such as English, where the orthographic rules are not entirely consistent [4]. For dyslexic children, the most difficult part in learning to read is understanding letter-sound correspondences [4]. They also have difficulty in identifying mirrored or flipped letters [4]. However, dyslexic children can learn to read well under systematic and multisensory instruction. Multisensory training involves activities that make clear links between multiple senses (e.g., visual, auditory, and tactile) to teach children basic reading, spelling, and writing skills [10]. Many empirical studies have

Figure 3. In level 1, a child placed a tangible letter "b" and three letter cards on the interactive table. Digital images and sounds were triggered.

Figure 4. In level 2, a child placed two tangible letters "oa" on the interactive table. Because "oa" were irregular, the system triggered the visual-audio feedback to indicate they are grouped.

demonstrated that multisensory training has great potential to induce strong reading improvements in dyslexic children [11,16].

The importance role of tracing activities in learning to read for dyslexic children has been highlighted in both education and neuroscience communities [2,3,4,16]. Researchers suggest that tracing the contours of textured letters could help dyslexic children associate each letter with a distinct motor gesture and therefore benefits them in learning mirrored or flipped ***letter shapes,*** such as *b, d, p,* and *q* [4,16]. Some further suggest that tracing physical letters involves more than simply learning letter shapes [2, 3]. Bara and his colleagues presented two studies that specifically investigated how tracing the contour of physical letters could benefit learning the alphabetic principle in kindergarten children. In one study targeting non-dyslexic children with a mean age of 5 years old, the results revealed that improvement in the pseudo-word reading task was greater after visual-haptic training than with visual training alone [2]. Similar results were found in the second study, which focused on children from low socio-economic status families, who usually have reading difficulties [3]. Bara et al. suggest that the multiple cues naturally embedded in the physical letters (e.g., colour, shape, and texture) add values in learning letter-sound correspondences**.** Although the studies did not focus on texture cues, the results showed the potential of using textures together with visual and auditory cues to help dyslexic children effectively learn ***letter-sound correspondences***.

TUIs for Learning to Read for Dyslexic Children

Research in HCI suggests that TUIs have potential to support learning to read for children for three main reasons. First, TUIs incorporate intuitive spatial mappings through consistently coupling digital data with physical artefacts [12]. Literacy is inherently spatial for learners who need to decipher a series of letters in a certain spatial order. Second, by incorporating physical objects, TUIs engage multiple senses (i.e., visual, auditory, and tactile) [12], which is also important in learning to read [10]. Moreover, TUIs promote attention and engage children in playful literacy learning [19].

The implication of TUIs for learning to read for children is considerable [17,19], but it has not been fully explored in the context of dyslexia. Only several works have been found. The *Tiblo* prototype consists of interactive blocks with colour and sound cues designed to help dyslexic children aged 8-12 years old to remember and follow sequence-based instructions (e.g., reading narratives/or words). The evaluation study suggested that children had great interest in playing around multimodalities in TUIs [13]. Hengeveld et al. developed *LinguaBytes*, a tangible interface including a set of digitally augmented dolls, pictogram cards, and puzzle pieces designed for toddlers with disabilities aged 1-4 years old [8]. The researchers concluded that the TUI afforded more natural and accessible interaction for the children.

These studies suggest the potential of designing multimodal TUIs to help dyslexic children learn to read. However, few studies have discussed which specific design feature(s) of TUIs may benefit learning outcomes. The role of texture cue as a design element in learning to read remains unclear. This demonstrates the opportunity to explore design space of tactile modality, particularly texture cues, in supporting literacy education for dyslexic children. The results will

Figure 5. Twenty-four pieces of letter cards

Letter	Object	Material
a	Apple	Shiny smooth paper
b	Balloon	Rubber
d	Dog	Fur
o	Orange	Leather
p	Pillow	Pillow cloth
q	Quilt	Quilt cloth

Table 1. Letter-Material Mapping Strategies (texture cues) based on the OIP method.

contribute to a better understanding of designing learning materials in TUIs [5,7].

Theoretical Foundations

Cross-modal research suggests that human beings naturally associate letters or letter sounds with textures. Research on synesthesia suggests that some synesthetes can see textures on certain letters [6], while studies on sound symbolism suggest that human beings may associate frequency of sounds or phonetic sounds with roughness of textures [14].

The metaphoric approach suggests that human beings are able to associate letters/sounds with certain objects/materials based on what is learnt in everyday life. In education programs, researchers and practitioners often use the Object-Imaging-Projection method (OIP) to teach children letter-sound correspondences [9]. This method associates letters/sounds with particular objects that have forms very similar to the letter shapes and whose beginning sounds are the letter sounds. For example, "a/a/" is often associated with "apple.

In our prototype, we designed the texture cues based on the metaphoric approach because (1) this approach has been applied in the education domain [9]; and (2) we target children and this mapping strategy may provide better contextual information (e.g., word/picture associated with the letter) that helps them to learn to read [1].

Prototype Design and Implementation

Learning Goal

The main learning goal was to help dyslexic children aged 5-6 years old to improve their understanding of the 'alphabetic principle,' including learning both transparent (one-to-one) and opaque letter-sound correspondences. Due to time restrictions, a limited set of eight graphemes was chosen, including four consonants and four vowels. They are b/b/, d/d/, p/p/, q/kw/, a/a/, o/o/, oo/u/, and oa/au/.

Design Goals

Our main objective was to create a system that we could use as a research instrument to explore the learning effects of adding texture cues in a tangible tabletop that enabled dyslexic children to learn letter-sound correspondences. We proposed three specific design goals, as follows: (1) *Systematic learning*: Learning contents should start from simple to complex; (2) *Texture cues*: The system should allow for two conditions of playing: with texture cues or without texture cues; (3) *Affordances*: Affordances should be designed to ensure dyslexic children easily distinguish mirrored or flipped letters.

Overview

In Tactile Letters, dyslexic children can choose an appropriate level and learn about letter sounds by placing 3D tangible letter(s) or letter card(s) on the interactive table. Each tangible letter (sound) is associated with three letter cards with a pseudo-word on each (Figure 5). Visual-audio feedback is provided once children make correct/incorrect associations between 3D tangible letters and letter cards (Figures 3 and 4).

Implementation

The research prototype is comprised a digital display, an interactive table, 24 pieces of letter cards, and two sets of 3D tangible letters (Figures 1,2,5). The

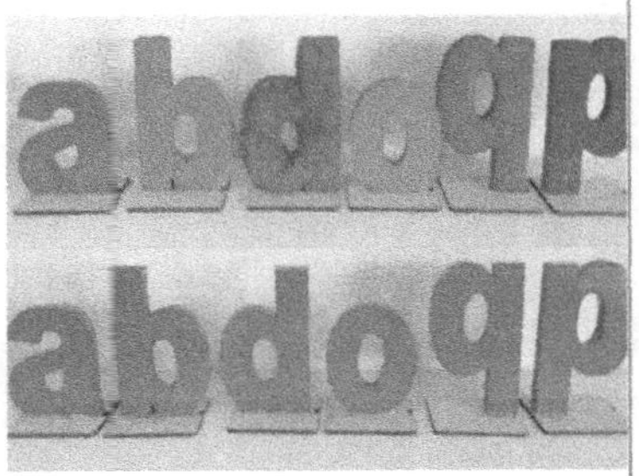

Figure 6. Tangible letters with texture cues (up) and the same set of letters without texture cues (down).

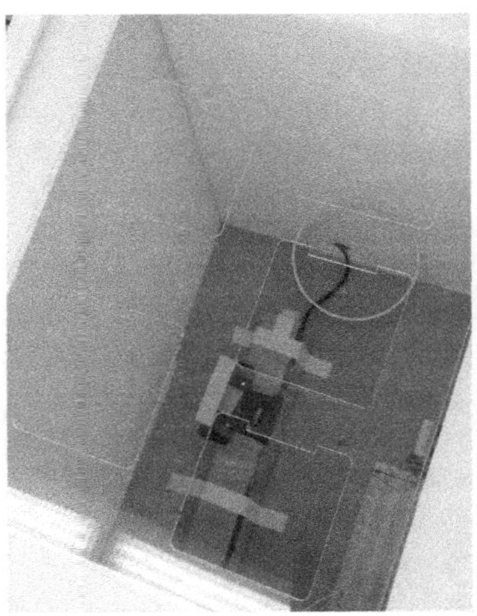

Figure 7. A transparent acrylic frame with constraints

interactive table contains a camera vision system implemented with a reacTIVision engine. Each tangible letter or letter card is identified by the reacTIVision engine, which passes identification and location information to a custom application written in Processing.

Two Levels of Learning Contents
This application includes two levels of learning contents. The first level was designed to support learning of single letter-sound correspondences (e.g., b/b/) while the second level was designed to support learning of opaque letter-sound correspondences. In level-1, when the user places one tangible letter and three letter cards on the interactive table, this action triggers the associated digital contents on the display, including the letter sound(s), the object, and the 2D uppercase and lowercase letters (Figure 3). In level-2, the user can place two letters on the interactive table. When the first letter is placed on the table, the system displays the letter and plays its sound. The user then can place the second letter. If the two adjacent letters do not generate a new sound, the system displays the second letter and plays its sound. If the two adjacent letters generate a new sound (e.g. oo/u/), the system triggers the new sound and displays a red frame to indicate the two letters are grouped. The user then is allowed to place letter cards to practice the new sound (Figure 4).

Texture Cues and Non-texture Cues
There are two sets of 3D tangible letters and each set contains seven letters (*a, o, o, b, d, p, q*). In one set, each letter's wood surface is wrapped with a particular texture. The design of texture cues was based on the OIP method (Table 1). In the second set, all the letters have the same standard texture (wood with sticky paper). In order to control the possible influence of colour, all letters are a single colour – red (Figure 6).

Affordances
In order to allow dyslexic children to know the correct orientation of letters, a transparent acrylic frame with constraints was also designed. When placing the frame on the digital tabletop, the notch on the frame (the red circle in Figure 7) has to match the one on the 3D letter, which results in the correct placement of 3D letters. When children are more familiar with the learning contents, they can remove the frame.

Discussion and Future Work
In this paper, we discuss the knowledge gap, the theoretical foundations, and the design and implementation of our research instrument. The design of texture cues leverages the use of physical characteristics of objects to support learning. Although several works have explored the design space of materials in TUIs [5,7], none of them focused on using texture cues to promote learning. We believe there is an opportunity to investigate the potential of texture cues in learning to read based on research on dyslexia. It is also worth noting that there are various mapping strategies based on different theoretical approaches. Although we have employed the metaphoric strategy, we believe there is potential to explore other approaches in future research.

Our next step is to conduct a small-scale user study to refine the prototype design. Then we will conduct a controlled comparative experiment with this prototype to investigate the role of texture cues of a tangible tabletop in supporting learning to read for dyslexic children.

Acknowledgements

Thanks for Xiaolan Wang and Rui Pan for helping with the prototype and demo video production.

References

[1] Abdullah, M.H.L.,Hisham, S.& Parumo, S. MyLexics: an assistive courseware for Dyslexic children to learn basic Malay language. ACM SIGACCESS *Accessibility and Computing* 95(2009), 3-9.

[2] Bara, F., Gentaz, E., Cole, P., Sprenger-Charolles, L. The visuo-haptic and haptic exploration of letters increases the kindergarten-children's understanding of the alphabetic principle. *Cognitive development*, *19*, 3(2004), 433-449.

[3] Bara, F., Gentaz, E., Cole, P. Haptics in learning to read with children from low socio-economic status families. *British Journal of Developmental Psychology*, *25*, 4(2007), 643-663.

[4] Dehaene, S. (2009). *Reading in the brain: The new science of how we read*. Penguin, New York, 2009.

[5] Djajadiningrat, T., Wensveen, S., Frens, J., & Overbeeke, K. Tangible products: redressing the balance between appearance and action. *Pers, Ubiq. Comput*, *8*, 5(2004), 294-309.

[6] Eagleman, D. M., & Goodale, M. A. (2009). Why color synesthesia involves more than color. *Trends in cognitive sciences*, *13*(7), 288-292.

[7] Jung, H., & Stolterman, E. (2011). Material probe: exploring materiality of digital artifacts. In *Proc.of TEI 2011,*ACM Press (2011), 153-156.

[8] Hengeveld, B. Hummels, C., van Balkom, H.,Voort, R., & de Moor, J. Wrapping up LinguaBytes, for now. In *Proc. of TEI 2013,* ACM Press (2013), 237-244.

[9] Isgur, J. Establishing Letter—Sound Associations by on Object—Imaging—Projection Method. *Journal of Learning Disabilities, 8*, 6(1975), 349-353.

[10] Kelly, K & Phillips, S. *Teaching literacy to learners with dyslexia: A Multisensory Approach*. SAGE, London, 2011.

[11] Oakland, T. et al. An Evaluation of the Dyslexia Training Program A Multisensory Method for Promoting Reading in Students with Reading Disabilities. *Journal of Learning Disabilities*, *31*, 2(1998), 140-147.

[12] O'Malley, C., & Fraser, D.S. *Literature review in learning in tangible technologies.* NESTA futurelab report 12, Bristol, 2004.

[13] Pandey, S., & Srivastava, S. Tiblo: a tangible learning aid for children with dyslexia. In *Proc. of DESIRE 2011*, ACM Press (2011), 211-220.

[14] Peeva, D., Baird, B., Izmirli, O., & Blevins, D. Haptic and sound correlations: Pitch, Loudness and Texture. In *Proc.of IV 2004*, IEEE (2004), 659-664.

[15] Perea, M., Moret-Tatay, C., & Panadero, V. Suppression of mirror generalization for reversible letters: Evidence from masked priming. *Memory and Language*, *65*, 3(2011), 237-246.

[16] Regtvoort, A. G., & van der Leij, A. Early intervention with children of dyslexic parents: Effects of computer-based reading instruction at home on literacy acquisition. *Learning and individual differences*, *17*, 1(2007), 35-53.

[17] Sluis, R. J. W., et al. Read-It: five-to-seven-year-old children learn to read in a tabletop environment. In *Proc. of IDC' 04.* ACM Press (2004), 73-80.

[18] Spector, F., & Maurer, D. The colors of the alphabet: Naturally-biased associations between shape and color. *Journal of Experimental Psychology: Human Perception and Performance*, *37*, 2(2011), 484-495.

[19] Sung, J. Y. et al. Shadow Box: an interactive learning toy for children. In *Proc. of DIGITEL 2007.* IEEE (2007), 206-208.

L-Shift: Encoding and Shifting Material Properties and Functionalities with Phase-shifting Liquid

Sang-won Leigh
MIT Media Lab,
77 Massachusetts Ave.
Cambridge, MA 02139 USA
sangwon@media.mit.edu

Patrick Johan Nicolaas van Hoof
MIT Sloan School of Management,
50 Memorial Dr E52-325
Cambridge, MA 02139 USA
pvanhoof@mit.edu

Krithika Jagannath
Harvard Graduate School of Education
Appian Way,
Cambridge, MA 02138 USA
krithika_jagannath@mail.harvard.edu

Pattie Maes
MIT Media Lab,
77 Massachusetts Ave.
Cambridge, MA 02139 USA
pattie@media.mit.edu

Hiroshi Ishii
MIT Media Lab,
77 Massachusetts Ave.
Cambridge, MA 02139 USA
ishii@media.mit.edu

TEI '15, Jan 16-19 2015, Stanford, CA, USA
ACM 978-1-4503-3305-4/15/01.
http://dx.doi.org/10.1145/2677199.2688807

Abstract
Forces of gravity and the concept of a fixed center of mass severely limit the opportunities for product design and user interaction with those products. In this paper, we present *L-Shift*, a fictional material in which the weight distribution of physical objects is manipulated dynamically. It is a material that shifts its phase between solid and liquid and, therefore, allows for changes in weight distribution and rigidity. This gives designers many more options, as products can be re-shaped, re-balanced and stiffened as needed. Through prototyping with sodium acetate – a material that has properties close to the proposed fictional one – we explore user scenarios and future possibilities. We envision that it is possible to manipulate such physical properties of objects dynamically, which will open up new opportunities for designing interactive and more responsive products.

Author Keywords
Phase-shifting materials; Dynamic mass distribution; Radical atoms

ACM Classification Keywords
H.5.2. Information interfaces and presentation: Prototyping

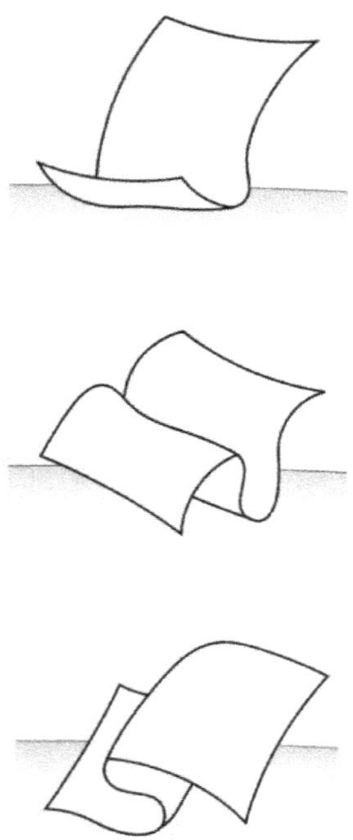

Figure 1. Example configurations of impossible or unstable balance. They cannot balance properly because their shapes induce a torque that makes the structures difficult to stand up.

Introduction

Objects in everyday life typically have fixed shape and use, e.g. furniture. Designers use materials and shapes to position the furniture in a specific way – to give a specific use for it. If we want to use it for different purposes, we might want to shape/position it differently. Furniture or any product that transforms could dynamically adapt to the users' need. However, it is difficult to have such product, mainly because we lack a medium that promises both flexibility and stability in structure. Even though a shape can be altered, fixed mass distribution prevents us from letting the shape to position in certain ways (fig 1).

What if we could mold a sheet of material into different organic and geometrical shapes, and move the center of mass to allow for functional use by rebalancing the object? Not only would such a mechanism enable users to create and use several forms for a single type of furniture such as a chair, but it could also be used to change shape from one type to another. For example, a chair could be turned into a table. Not just any table, a table that has a unique shape that was previously impossible to give any functional use to, because it could not balance itself.

We present a mechanism that enables controlling the shape and weight distribution of objects to render various shapes or balances. This mechanism can be considered "pre-programmed" and enabled (or activated) through manual interaction. As a proof of concept, we developed prototypes to demonstrate how shifting weight: 1) creates shapes that sustains balance in otherwise impossible ways, 2) makes a single shape to balance in several different ways, 3) impacts the sound of a musical instrument by manipulating its resonance properties. In addition, we discuss fixing and releasing the weight distribution and, subsequently, the shape and balance of the object as well. This provides a new perspective on affordances [5], as they can be now altered, released or fixed.

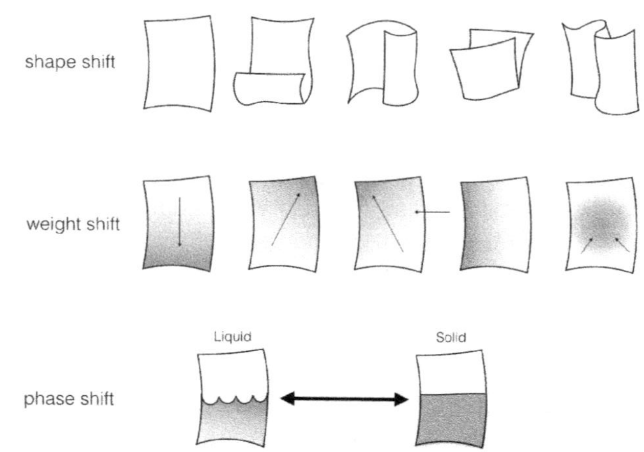

Figure 2. Using a material that can shift between liquid and solid phases, an object can be shaped and balanced differently

Related Work

Tonski [1] demonstrated the balancing of a 170-year old sofa in an "impossible" position. Gajamohan et al. presented balancing robots that can stand up in impossible positions and move themselves [4]. Hemmert et al. [6] demonstrated the use of dynamic weight-shifting on mobile devices by utilizing linear actuators. These works successfully rendered the possibility of using balance and imbalance, within a rigid form factor, as meaningful mediums.

Other related works stem from the area of shape-changing interfaces. Yao et al. [12] used deformable

Figure 3. A shape with uniform weight-distribution cannot get balanced (top), whereas weight-shifting enables it (bottom)

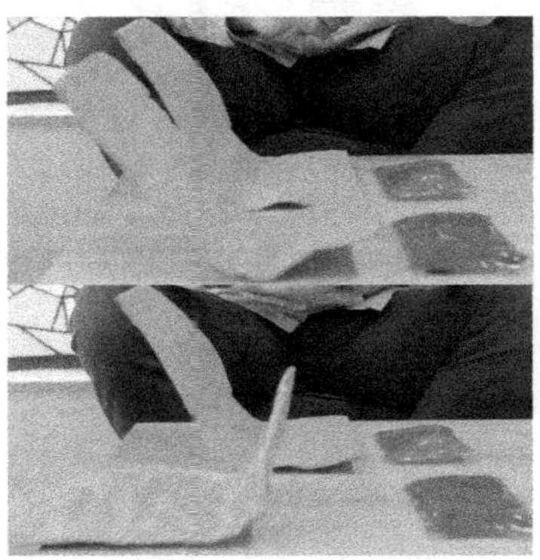

Figure 4. Turning into solid state, the material will fix the weight distribution. Unlike in liquid state (front) where leaning the object changes its balance, the fixed weight distribution will allow an object to come back to the fixed balance automatically. (back)

materials to create shape-changing interfaces, thereby providing different functionalities and/or different types of feedback. Follmer et al. [2] presented a use of a material in which its stiffness can be programmed. The most relevant work to ours would be weight-changing device presented by Niiyama et al. [10]. There also have been many discussions about shape-shifting and related affordances [3, 7, 8, 9, 11].

These works presented novel ways of actuating and deforming objects' physical properties mechanically or pneumatically. However, the manipulation of both the shape and balance is not fully explored yet, thereby limiting the possibility of building free-form structures with different balances.

L-Shift Material

We present *L-Shift* (Liquid-Shift), a fictional material that can shift its shape, weight-distribution, and phase between liquid and solid. *L-shift* lets users create any shape and encode different weight distributions, while teaching the product how to (re-)balance. By transforming the liquid material into a solid state, the shape and balance can be fixed semi-permanently. Although we have not yet prototyped at this stage of the research, the phase-shift could theoretically also be computer-controlled using electrodes. They could be merged into a protocol that allows for changing an object's shape, weight-distribution, and rigidity (liquid or solid). We envision the following steps:

Shape/Weight-shifting

In liquid state the material becomes flexible, so users can easily change the shape and redistribute the weight.

Phase-shifting

By triggering the phase shift from liquid to solid state, users can fix the shape and balance (weight distribution). This allows for the new fixed shape and balance to afford a specific functional use for its users.

Reverse phase-shifting

By adding energy to the material, it can be shifted back to its liquid state - again allowing for reshaping and redistributing of the weight.

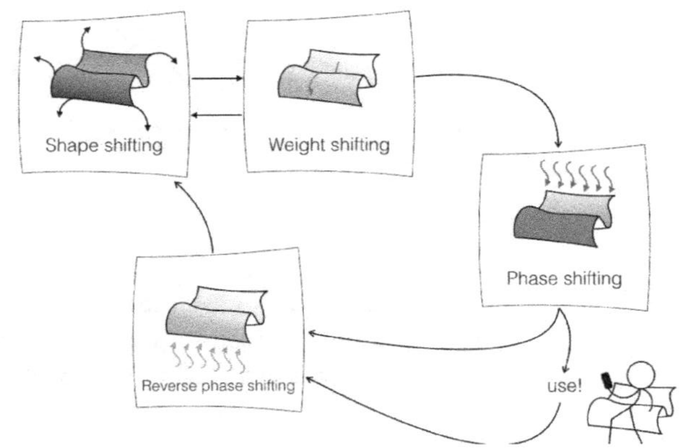

Figure 5. Changing/fixing/releasing shapes and balances.

Prototype

Primarily used in heat pads, sodium acetate is very good at super cooling. It freezes at 54°C, but can stay liquid and stable at a much lower temperature. Clicking/bending a metal disk, however, has the ability to force a few molecules to flip to the solid state, and the rest of the liquid then rushes to solidify as well. This process is called "nucleation", during which the solute molecules in the solvent start to gather into clusters on a nanometer scale. This solid form of sodium acetate can be easily restored to liquid state again by placing it

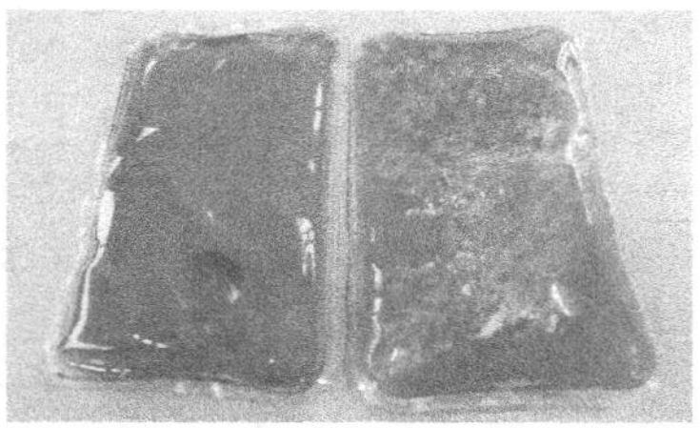

Figure 6. Two different states of sodium acetate at room temperature. Super cooled liquid state (left) and solid state (right).

Figure 7. Inside view of the prototype. Sodium acetate is contained in a plastic bag supported by wireframes.

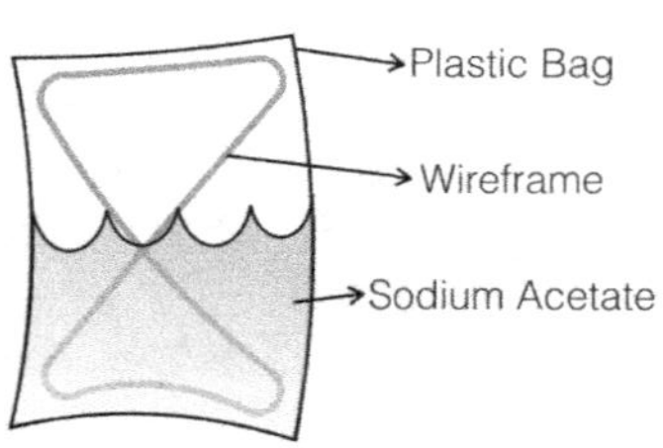

Figure 8. The plastic bag contains sodium acetate, and wireframes are attached to the bag.

in boiling water for fifteen to twenty minutes. This process of shifting between liquid and solid phases can be repeated multiple times.

We used sodium acetate in sealed bags to control the weight of a structure shaped as an envelope made out of thin steel wire. (fig 8) Using the wire envelope, we made different types of furniture such as a chair, sofa and table. These configurations, however, would not balance even on flat surfaces without bags containing the liquid. After adding the bags with sodium acetate, we were able to make various configurations balance by controlling the flow of the liquid. To fix a particular configuration, we crystalized the liquid by bending a small metal disk inside it, thereby inducing agitation.

Encoding and Shifting Affordances

The concept of encoding and shifting material properties presents a new perspective on affordances provided by an object or a tool. They can be changed dynamically, because an object's shape and balance can be shifted – providing different hints for how a user could use it. Also, the affordances can be fixed and released by shifting the material from liquid to solid state and vice versa.

Using balance as affordance

In product design, an object's position and balance determine how users understand its usage. A good example is furniture. Designers use materials and weight to position the furniture in a specific way. However, what if we want to use it for different purposes? If so, we might want to position it differently (or change its shape to a different one). Weight shifting allows objects to rebalance and – as a consequence – change their affordances. Figure 9 describes different examples of changing both shape and weight distribution to alter the functionality of objects.

Figure 9(a). Example of shape/weight-shift for creating different styles of chairs: normal chair (left), to a floor chair via shape-shift (center), to a beach chair via weight-shift (right).

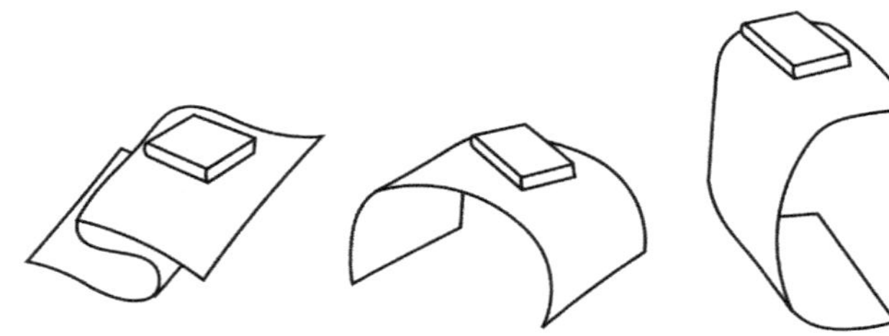

Figure 9(b). Side table (left), to a wide coffee table via shape-shift (center), then to a tall table via rotating 90 degrees (right)).

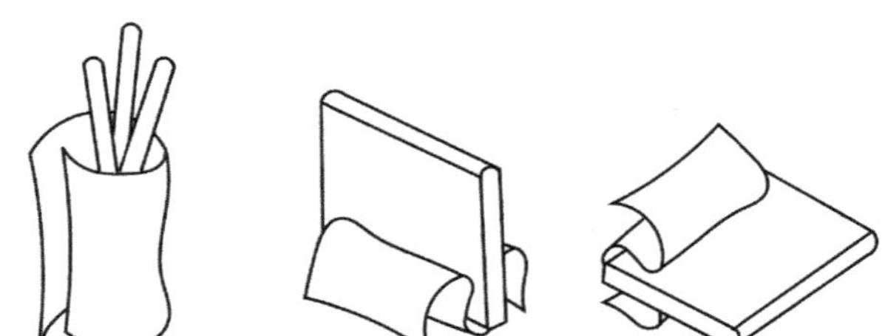

Figure 9(c). Pen holder (left), to a book holder via shape-shift (center), to another book holder that works in a different way via rotating 90 degrees (right).

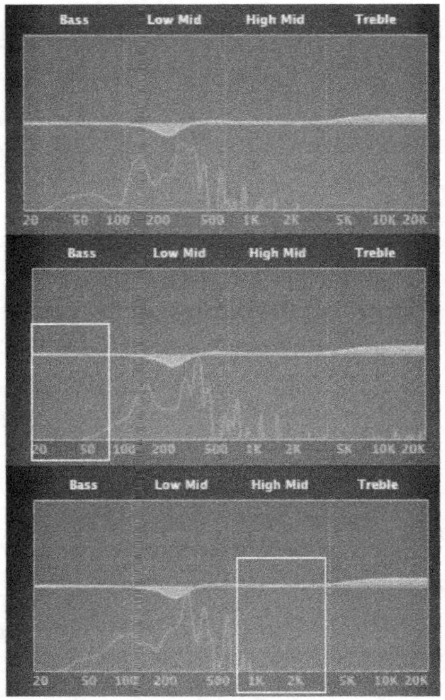

Figure 10. Using the *L-Shift* concept, we explored how weight-change impacts sound.

Figure 11. By attaching water bags and water pumps, the acoustic properties of a guitar body can be changed. This experiment shows new possibilities of building acoustic instruments with *L-Shift* materials.

Malleability of affordance
L-Shift enables fixing and releasing an object's shape, the mass distribution inside and, therefore, its functionality. By fixing the mass distribution users can fix the functionalities provided. By releasing it, users can encode and change the functionality of an object as its shape and balance become malleable. This presents a new possibility of altering the malleability of a product's affordances. By dynamically shifting between fixed and malleable states, a *L-Shift* product allows for a user manipulation of its affordance as needed.

More Applications

Product Design
Designs such as Jacob Tonski's couch [1] have a strong visual appeal and represent powerful metaphors. We think that practical applications of such concepts would be 1) a lamp that can balance itself in a new way or 2) tools such as knives or hammers that can balance themselves to limit injuries by changing their position when falling. If a material itself could control its weight distribution, the balancing capability can be embedded into products without interfering with visual design.

Tangible Interfaces
As its shape and balance can be altered, *L-Shift* can greatly expand the capability of tangible interfaces. The shape of a tangible interface manifests the property of the data it's representing, while its balance can add an additional layer of information about the status of the data. In addition to that, differently posed/balanced tangible tokens would imply different uses of them. For instance, users can temporarily pull a background task into foreground by holding a tangible controller upside-down, in imbalance. However, thanks to gravity, it will come back to its original balance once the user stops holding it, pushing the task back into the background.

Construction
L-Shift could be useful in installing temporary structures for outdoor events for entertainment, or a variety of other purposes. For instance, modular structures made of *L-Shift* materials could be used in the fluid state during design stages to try out different shapes. Then, just prior to the event the material could be triggered to change from a liquid into a solid state in order to fix the structure. After the event is over, the entire structure could be taken apart by triggering the material back into fluid state, thus providing an easy way of re-using materials in temporary construction.

Musical Instrument
Altering the mass distribution inside an object not only changes its balance or rigidity, it also modifies its acoustic resonance characteristics. Acoustic instruments built with *L-Shift* materials would allow for players to alter their instruments' sound characteristics in a fully analog way without using any electronic effects. We also experimented with an acoustic guitar and computer-controlled water pumps to simulate weight-shifting on top of a guitar's body. By altering the weight attached to different parts on the body of the guitar, we demonstrated that the guitar changes its sound characteristics (fig 10, 11).

Limitation and Future Work

We are aware that the prototypes we built are initial explorations of these concepts and, therefore, may have limitations. That said, they demonstrate various new directions for future research. One possibility is to build on existing shape-shifting concepts [12] and build phase-shifting materials in a way that they also make

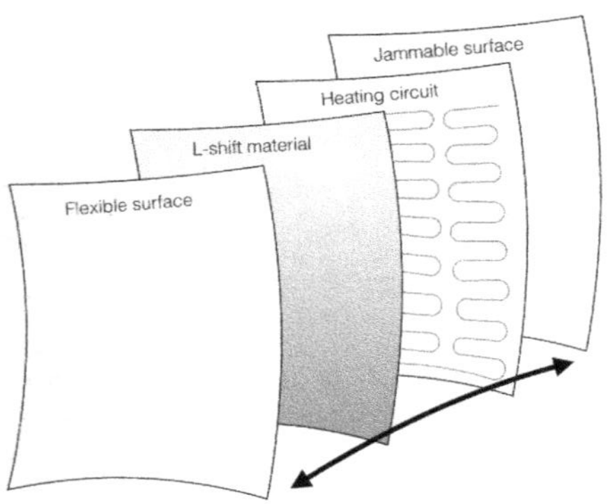

Figure 12. An envisioned implementation of *L-Shift*. Molded layers of phase-shifting material, heating circuitry, and jammable material will allow deforming, balance-shifting, and stiffening of the material.

weight distribution inside objects possible. Another direction is to design products using actuators that could change the center of mass within the product material itself. This would make it possible to build such configurations as illustrated by Jacob Tonski [1] or even construct different shapes on demand in real-time. We also propose exploring a more comprehensive design and engineering of the material that comprises layers of *L-Shift* material, heating circuitry, and jammable material. (fig 12). This will allow the pursuit of a more sophisticated use of weight-shifting/fixing in products.

Conclusion

This paper presents the idea of dynamically controlling the weight distribution of objects to create various shapes, configurations and functions. The concept of dynamic weight-shift suggests a wide array of interesting possibilities and applications. However, more work has to be done before this mechanism can be made available in everyday objects. More meaningful metaphors could also be further explored in order to create new designs and interactions, using dynamic weight control.

References

[1] Tonski, J., *Balance from within*, 2012 http://www.jacobtonski.com/balance-from-within/

[2] Follmer, S., Leithinger, D., Olwal, A., Cheng, N., Ishii, H., Jamming User Interfaces: Programmable Particle Stiffness and Sensing for Malleable and Shape-Changing Devices, *In Proc. UIST '12,* 2012

[3] Follmer, S., Leithinger, D., Olwal, A., Hogge, A., Ishii, H., inFORM: Dynamic Physical Affordances and Constraints through Shape and Object Actuation, *In Proc. UIST '13,* 2013.

[4] Gajamohan, M., Muehlebach, M., Widmer, T., D'Andrea, R., The Cubli: A Reaction Wheel-based 3D Inverted Pendulum, *In Proc. European Control Conference,* pp. 268-274, July 2013

[5] Gibson, J.J., The Ecological Approach to Visual Perception. *New York: Houghton-Mifflin*, 1979

[6] Hemmert, F., Hamann, S., Löwe, M., Zeipelt, J., and Joost, G. Weight-Shifting Mobiles: Two-Dimensional Gravitational Displays in Mobile Phones. *In Proc. CHI '10,* 3087–3091.

[7] Horev, O. 'TALKING TO THE HAND' An exploration into shape shifting objects and morphing interfaces, *Master Thesis,* Interaction Design Institute Ivrea, (2006).

[8] Kim, S., Kim, H., Lee, B., Nam, T.-J., and Lee, W. Inflatable mouse: Volume-adjustable Mouse with Air-pressure-sensitive Input and Haptic Feedback. *In Proc. CHI '08*, 2008, 211-214.

[9] Lakatos, D., Ishii, H., Towards Radical Atoms — Form-giving to transformable materials, *Cognitive Infocommunications (CogInfoCom)*, 2012.

[10] Niiyama, R., Yao, L., and Ishii, H., Weight and volume changing device with liquid metal transfer. *In Proc. TEI '14*.

[11] Togler, J., Hemmert, F., and Wettach, R. Living interfaces: The Thrifty Faucet. *In Proc. TEI '09,* 2009, 43-44.

[12] L. Yao, R. Niiyama, J. Ou, S. Follmer, C. Della Silva, H. Ishii, PneUI: pneumatically actuated soft composite materials for shape changing interfaces, *In Proc. UIST '13,* 2013

Collective Sound Checks

Exploring Intertwined Sonic and Social Affordances of Mobile Web Applications

Norbert Schnell
IRCAM – Centre Pompidou
STMS lab IRCAM-CNRS-UPMC
Paris, France
norbert.schnell@ircam.fr

Sébastien Robaszkiewicz
IRCAM – Centre Pompidou
STMS lab IRCAM-CNRS-UPMC
Paris, France
sebastien.robaszkiewicz@ircam.fr

Frédéric Bevilacqua
IRCAM – Centre Pompidou
STMS lab IRCAM-CNRS-UPMC
Paris, France
frederic.bevilacqua@ircam.fr

Diemo Schwarz
IRCAM – Centre Pompidou
STMS lab IRCAM-CNRS-UPMC
Paris, France
diemo.schwarz@ircam.fr

TEI 2015, January 15–19, 2015, Stanford, California, USA.
ACM 978-1-4503-3305-4/15/01.
http://dx.doi.org/10.1145/2677199.2688808

Abstract

We present the *Collective Sound Checks*, an exploration of user scenarios based on mobile web applications featuring motion-controlled sound that enable groups of people to engage in spontaneous collaborative sound and music performances. These new forms of musical expression strongly shift the focus of design from human-computer interactions towards the emergence of computer mediated interactions between players based on sonic and social affordances of ubiquitous technologies. At this early stage, our work focuses on experimenting with different user scenarios while observing the relationships between different interactions and affordances.

Author Keywords

Sound, music, collaborative, mobile devices, web technologies, HTML 5, sonic interaction, social interaction

ACM Classification Keywords

H.5.2 [Information Interfaces and Presentation]: User Interfaces – Auditory (non-speech) feedback; H.5.3 [Information Interfaces and Presentation]: Group and Organization Interfaces – Collaborative computing; H.5.5 [Information Interfaces and Presentation]: Sound and Music Computing – Systems

Introduction

Recent mobile devices include a full set of features (*e.g.* multimodal sensing, digital processing, audiovisual rendering), which turns them into powerful computing platforms within reach of anyone. Many sectors took advantage of this development and artists have adopted mobile technologies as an opportunity to create new forms of artistic expression [1].

Many works on collaborative music interfaces and multi-user instruments have investigated the design of hardware interfaces and centralized computer music systems [2, 5]. Even if the design of collaborative music making scenarios based on mobile devices inherits many aspects from these approaches, the intrinsic autonomy and ubiquity of mobile technologies demands to profoundly reconsider the emergence of play and collaboration in this context.

Early research on *mobile music* has focused on how to use mobile devices for sensor driven sound and music generation [10, 4]. Commercial applications have turned mobile devices into self-contained musical instruments [11] and augmented reality soundscapes[1]. Further research focused on the phones' mobility and ubiquity to explore setups that involve a larger number of users: Wang's and Essl's *Mobile Phone Orchestras* [12, 7] let the electronic music ensemble members perform for an audience, whereas Lee & Freeman's *echobo* [6] invites the audience to play simplified mobile phone-based instruments that follow a chord progression determined by the artist and broadcast over a local network.

While solo performances, music ensembles, and participative concerts based on mobile technologies usually feature trained performers, mobile devices also conquered sound and multimedia installations in which technology supports the audience's autonomous interactions. Especially in this field, the ubiquity of mobile devices has shifted the focus of design from the users' interactions with technology to the mediation of interactions among users mediated by technology. In this sense, the installation *Schminky*, a networked sound game setup in a café, for example, "was specifically designed to promote social interaction" [9]. The creators of the installation PESI [3] intend to extend mobile music instrument with social interactions mediated by an additional technical setup based on optical tracking.

Our current research project[2] focuses on developing scenarios and mobile web applications for creating sound environments and music performances in various contexts including dedicated events to spontaneous gatherings. While the design of digital music applications is usually articulated with physical (*i.e.* acoustic) properties of devices and spaces, here, social behaviors take an important part in the design of scenarios and applications. In this context of emerging ubiquitous computing, this work-in-progress aims at presenting a first step towards understanding how human–computer interactions may influence — and blend with — social interactions in the field of sound and music.

Scenarios and Application Prototypes

To systematically investigate the interconnections between sonic and social affordances in a flexible setting we created the *Collective Sound Checks*. This series of workshops in collaboration with the *Studio 13/16* at the Centre Pompidou in Paris allows us to explore collective performance scenarios based on mobile web application

[1] http://rjdj.me/

[2] http://cosima.ircam.fr/

prototypes with teenagers. Each workshop lasts 4 hours during which the participants are free to join and to leave the activities at their will. The workshop space is large enough so that the participants equipped with their smartphones can experience the distribution of sound sources over larger distances and gather to multiple smaller groups when necessary (see figure 1). They are free to explore the web applications at their will and have access to all of them from the start. At some point, the workshop leaders might suggest particular rules for playing. A workshop is usually attended by 20 to 50 participants, who stay between 15 and 90 minutes. We held a first series of 3 workshops in May and June 2014 and another series of 4 workshops between October and December. The periods between the workshops allows us to iterate on the applications and refine the scenarios based on the participants' feedback.

Figure 1: A group of participants playing with the *soundscapes* at the Studio 13/16 at the *Centre Pompidou*.

We faced multiple challenges while designing these scenarios. First of all, the aesthetics and social affordances of the proposed applications had to match the age group of the participants. Secondly, given the open organization of the workshops, most of the applications had to instantly catch the attention of the teenagers and allow them to jump in freely. Finally, we wanted to allow the participants to engage with the applications for longer periods within the 4-hour workshops, exploring different possibilities, developing their performance skills, and collaboratively constructing sound environments or musical performances.

Setup and Technologies

The participants were provided with a small hand-held loudspeaker connected via a mini-jack audio cable to a mobile device (see figure 2).

Figure 2: Mobile device connected to a loudspeaker provided to the participants of the Collective Sound Checks.

The hand-held loudspeakers amplify the sound sufficiently so that the sound experiences created by the applications is not too much disturbed by environmental noises and conversations between participants. Nevertheless, all scenarios work with the internal loudspeakers of the mobile devices.

The applications are based on upcoming HTML 5 web standards such as Javascript, Web Audio API, Device Motion, and Web Sockets. The motion sensing relies on the embedded sensors of the mobile devices (*i.e.* accelerometers and gyroscopes). This choice allows for rapid prototyping and for ease of deployment in the workshops, as well as for spontaneous demos and performances in any other context using a local HTTP server and WiFi network. Some of the prototype applications that do not require any synchronization or communication between the mobile devices have been published on the project's web site.[3]

Scenarios

The first web applications we explored in the *Collective Sound Checks* is a set of *soundscapes* turning mobile devices into sound-emitting devices that react to motion. While the participants can use these applications individually to explore different techniques and metaphors, we encourage them to create spontaneous performances and environments of distributed sound sources by walking around in the workshop space or by gathering together and exploring different movements and simple choreographies. Further applications are based on network infrastructures that synchronize the mobile devices or connect them to a common instrument.

Drone. This application reacts to the device rotation and responds with the amplitude and frequency modulation of a set of oscillators generating a bass drone. Strongly shaking the device generates the sound of

[3] http://cosima.ircam.fr/checks

electric discharges. This application started from the idea to collectively create a complex bass drone sound composed of a large number of sources. In the first prototypes, we noticed that a drone sound modulated by the movement dynamics of a device strongly evoked Star Wars *lightsabers*, especially in the context of a workshop for teenagers. We finally let this reference govern the sound and interaction design of the application, so that the initial affordance of the application has been extended by the possibility to simulate lightsaber fights between two or multiple participants.

Birds. This application provides a collection of bird sounds played by jiggling the device. Following the metaphor of twittering, multiple participants can improvise non-verbal conversations answering each other's calls. When participants are distributed over a larger space, it generates a forest-like atmosphere of spatialised bird calls answering each other.

Monks. This application allows players to create a choir of singing voices controlled with simple movements. The users can select a female or a male voice (an extract of a Meredith Monk recording or a Tibetan chant), where the roll angle of the mobile device modifies the pitch and timbre. With this application, participants generate meditative polyphonic sound textures filling up the space. This creates a quiet and reflective atmosphere in which they walk slowly, paying attention to each other.

Rainstick. Following the rainstick metaphor, in this application the player tilts the device from its horizontal position to produce the sound of different grains, liquids or masses pouring or rolling from one side to the other. The player can choose between different sounds such as *water*, *wood*, and *stone*. While the other *soundscapes* are based on direct mappings of motion capture parameters to sound synthesis parameters, this application introduces a physical model — of a mass particle sliding on a tilted surface — that mediates between the performers movements and the evolution of the sound. One way the teenagers use this application is to stand in a circle with the devices pointing to the floor, and to raise one after the other the device to make the sound move around the circle. Hereby, the participants learn to adjust their movements to the behavior of the physical model to make the sound move continuously around the circle.

We Will Rock You: Reloaded. This application invites multiple players to perform Queen's song *We Will Rock You* with a set of simple instruments and to create their own versions of the song.
The first shared goal for a group of participants is usually to recreate the song as they recall it. When the players get familiar with the instruments and with playing together, they usually start to draw away from the original song to create their own improvisations. Since the players have to stay in beat with each other they usually remain close together and keep eye contact like the members of a band. They often organize themselves by forming a strong rhythmic basis with the *drums* part ("stomp-stomp-clap"), while the others improvise with the *voice solo*, the *choirs* or the *guitar riff* parts.

Shaker. In this scenario, the participants are invited to record arbitrary percussive sounds (with their voice, or using props), which they can then perform by shaking their devices. All devices are automatically beat synchronized over the network so that multiple players can easily perform together.
At the *Collective Sound Checks*, the participants record their sounds using a microphone on a stand with a foot

pedal in the middle of the space, which creates further social interactions between the participants. When someone finishes a recording, all participants can load this recording on their device and play with it. That way, the participants can experiment with different sounds and create an ensemble by recording complementary materials.

The Matrix. In this scenario, the players are sitting on a grid (for instance, 3 rows by 4 columns, for a total of 12 people). Their mobile devices form a matrix of screens and loudspeakers that are used to spatialize sound and light. In the current version, *The Matrix* is performed by one player at a time. A representation of the matrix appears on the screen of a player who controls the movement of sound and light across the matrix of smartphones by moving his finger on the mobile screen. He remotely plays on other people's smartphones that emit sound and light modulated by the finger trajectory and speed. After a fixed time, another player takes over the performance. The rules the collective instrument imposes on the players opens a large field of experimentation. We could observe how performers picked up and developed particular playing techniques and sound–movement patterns from previous performers. While some participants could appreciate listening to the current performer playing, others complained about the long time they had to wait for their turn without playing.

Discussion and Conclusion

The Collective Sound Checks allowed us to explore different modes of interaction driven by mobile web applications in a flexible setup. The participants clearly enjoyed playing with the applications and some of them stayed up to 1.5 hours exploring different scenarios. They enthusiastically engaged in discussions on the scenarios and possible evolutions. Many of them asked for accessing the applications online to play outside the workshop.

The development of the applications has been governed by two interwoven perspectives: the motion-sound relationships in the interaction with the mobile devices, and the social interactions between the participants.
The role of digital technology in the scenarios is manifold. First of all, it provides motion–sound relationships that enable the user to individually explore different modes and metaphors of sonic interaction and expression. In each of the presented scenarios, the sound reacts differently to the device's movements. Secondly, the technology mediates the interaction between players in different ways. While in applications like the *soundscapes* and *We Will Rock You: Reloaded*, technology provides complementary elements that afford collective playing, in the case of *The Matrix*, it provides an infrastructure that connects the participants' devices to a common instrument. Each case ultimately induces a very different attention to the collective interaction.
Finally, in some of the scenarios, technology facilitates music playing. All of the applications have been designed to include participants independently of their musical skills. For instance, in the *Shaker* scenario, the application provides a common steady tempo to all players who consequently can focus on other aspects of their performance like varying rhythmic patterns and dynamics. This offers more room for improvisations and leads to interactions between the users that easily combine music performance with dancing.

The presented applications let us explore some initial ideas of how mobile web applications can support spontaneous collective performances. Future developments will seek to explore further spontaneous collaborative behaviors through adequate affordances of the proposed applications. While for now, the incentives and challenges implied by the proposed scenarios focus on sound production and music playing, following up on former projects [8], we would like to introduce extra-musical interactions, rules, and challenges. This could be seen as a gamification of music playing or simply as creating playful performances mixing musical and extra-musical challenges. While we will continue the workshops with teenagers, a generally exigent population of users, we seek to diversify the user groups and cultural contexts within future endeavors. Current ideas include artistic collaborations on participative concerts, as well as concerts without stage in which the audience members provide the infrastructure for diffusing audiovisual elements out of their pockets and are involved as players at the same time.

Acknowledgements

The developments described in this article have been conducted in the context of the *CoSiMa* research project, partially funded by the french National Research Agency (ANR, project ANR-13-CORD-0010). We would like to thank our colleagues Victor Saiz, Benjamin Matuszewski and Samuel Goldszmidt as well as our partners of the Studio 13/16, Orbe, and NoDesign for their valuable contributions to this work.

References

[1] F. Behrendt. From Calling a Cloud to Finding the Missing Track: Artistic Approaches to Mobile Music. NIME '05, Vancouver, Canada, 2005.

[2] T. Blaine and S. Fels. Contexts of Collaborative Musical Experiences. NIME '03, pages 129–134, Singapore, Singapore, 2003.

[3] N. Correia, K. Tahiroğlu, and M. Espada. PESI: Extending Mobile Music Instruments with Social Interaction. TEI '13, Barcelona, Spain, 2013.

[4] G. Essl and M. Rohs. ShaMus – A Sensor-Based Integrated Mobile Phone Instrument. ICMC '07, pages 27–31, Copenhagen, Denmark, 2007.

[5] S. Jordà. Multi-user instruments: Models, examples and promises. NIME '05, pages 23–26, 2005.

[6] S. W. Lee and J. Freeman. *echobo*: A Mobile Music Instrument Designed of Audience to Play. NIME '13, Seoul, Corea, 2013.

[7] J. Oh, J. Herrera, N. Bryan, L. Dahl, and G. Wang. Evolving The Mobile Phone Orchestra. NIME '10, Sydney, Australia, 2010.

[8] N. Rasamimanana, F. Bevilacqua, J. Bloit, N. Schnell, E. Fléty, A. Cera, U. Petrevski, and J.-L. Frechin. The urban musical game: Using sport balls as musical interfaces. In *CHI '12 Extended Abstracts on Human Factors in Computing Systems*, CHI EA '12, pages 1027–1030, New York, NY, USA, 2012. ACM.

[9] J. Reid, R. Hull, T. Melamed, and D. Speakman. Schminky: The Design of a Café-Based Digital Experience. *Personal Ubiquitous Computing*, 7(3-4):197–202, July 2003.

[10] A. Tanaka. Mobile music making. NIME '04, pages 154–156, Singapore, 2004.

[11] G. Wang. Designing Smule's iPhone Ocarina. NIME '09, Pittsburgh, 2009.

[12] G. Wang, G. Essl, and H. Penttinen. MoPho: Do Mobile Phones Dream of Electric Orchestras. ICMC '08, Belfast, UK, 2008.

Costumes as Game Controllers: An Exploration of Wearables to Suit Social Play

Katherine Isbister
NYU Game Innovation Lab
5 Metrotech Center
Brooklyn, NY 11201 USA
Katherine.isbister@nyu.edu

Kaho Abe
NYU Game Innovation Lab
5 Metrotech Center
Brooklyn, NY 11201 USA
kaho@kahoabe.net

TEI '15, Jan 16-19 2015, Stanford, CA, USA
ACM 978-1-4503-3305-4/15/01.
http://dx.doi.org/10.1145/2677199.2688813

Abstract

We present an ongoing project exploring the use of costumes as game controllers. This collaboration between an artist and a researcher involves creating and evaluating a game for two players that uses costumes to drive core mechanics and interactions. We aim to give players a sense of transformation and connection, and to create an engaging spectacle for others. We discuss the design of the game, iterations in its form, and our plans for conducting user research with the finished game.

Author Keywords

Games; Physical Games; Wearables; Costumes; Embodied Interaction.

ACM Classification Keywords

H.5.m. Information interfaces and presentation (e.g., HCI): Miscellaneous.

Introduction

Playing games (whether digital or non-digital) is known to put people into a safe space—a 'magic circle'—that can allow for playful identity transformation and can encourage social connection [1],[2]. This project explores whether and how these effects can be

Figure 1. The popularity of Cosplay and Live action role play (LARP) show that wearing costumes to engage in character-based role play is enjoyable for some.

augmented with the introduction of costumes that function as game controllers. It is part of a larger initiative the authors are part of aimed at strengthening ties between computation/wearables and fashion [3]. The intent is to encourage cross-pollination between these worlds toward more adept and appropriate use of technology in wearables as well as in the larger fashion industry.

The Computational Fashion project supported the artist as a fellow for a year, with the researcher as her partner in a joint project. They proposed to explore the notion of costumes as game controllers, by creating a two-person movement-based, costume-enabled game that would also function as an engaging spectacle. The idea was to generate an object-lesson for thinking differently about the role of fashion/costuming in conceiving of wearable technologies, and also, thinking creatively about the role of wearables in the gaming space.

Project Vision and Values: The Lightning Bug Game

The resulting game-in-progress is part of the overarching body of work of the artist. She has developed several physically-based social games that make use of wearable elements, ranging from gloves and vests, to modified hard hats. In each of her games, physical contact or close proximity between players functions as a game mechanic. Her games also typically create an engaging spectacle for observers. The game also draws upon strong recent work in game research and independent game design practice examining the relationship between sociality and movement-based gaming [4], [5].

With the present game, the artist aimed to leverage the tradition in games of putting players into the role of characters in a story through the vehicle of avatars [6]. In a screen-based game, players control the avatars, create a relationship with them, and experience the game through them. But what happens when players dress up in costumes? Could they start to perform the role of the avatar? And what happens when we then embed technology into the costumes that allow players to navigate and play through the game experience using the costumes? Would that draw players into a more compelling, fully-realized world? Both the artist and the researcher felt that costume-based controllers could help players to engage roles in the game and perform them above and beyond what happens when inhabiting on-screen avatars. We can already see examples of this kind of immersive experience in live-action role playing games and cosplay (see Figure 1). Wearing the costume of a beloved character and acting out relevant narrative scenarios can help to create a rich, fantastical world, removing us from our everyday lives and identities. It's more than just wearing the costumes—it is experiencing the character and the story physically and emotionally.

The working hypothesis for this game in terms of social interaction between players, was that the deeper we fall into the 'magic circle' of the game world, the more opportunities there are for interactions and experiences not only with the technology, but also with each other, that we would otherwise not have in our regular day-to-day lives.

The artist noted that culturally, the act of putting on a costume is often seen as a process of transformation; costumes can signify power that wasn't there before—

think of super heroes and their transformations. She observed the presence of special gestures that often accompanied such transformations in fictional heroes (see Figure 2) and planned to incorporate this into the core mechanics of the game itself.

The artist came up with an initial guiding vision of the play experience, which she calls the lightning bug game. Players represent the last remaining lightning bugs in a world consumed by pollution, and must cooperate with each other in order to fight against a virtual enemy of darkness. Each player has a distinct role—one player shoots and the other collects power—and they both must help each other by holding hands in order to transfer power form one player to the other in order to fight. See Figure 3 for an overview of the components of the game.

Figure 2. 'Henshin' pose of the original Kamen Riders (a Japanese superhero TV series).

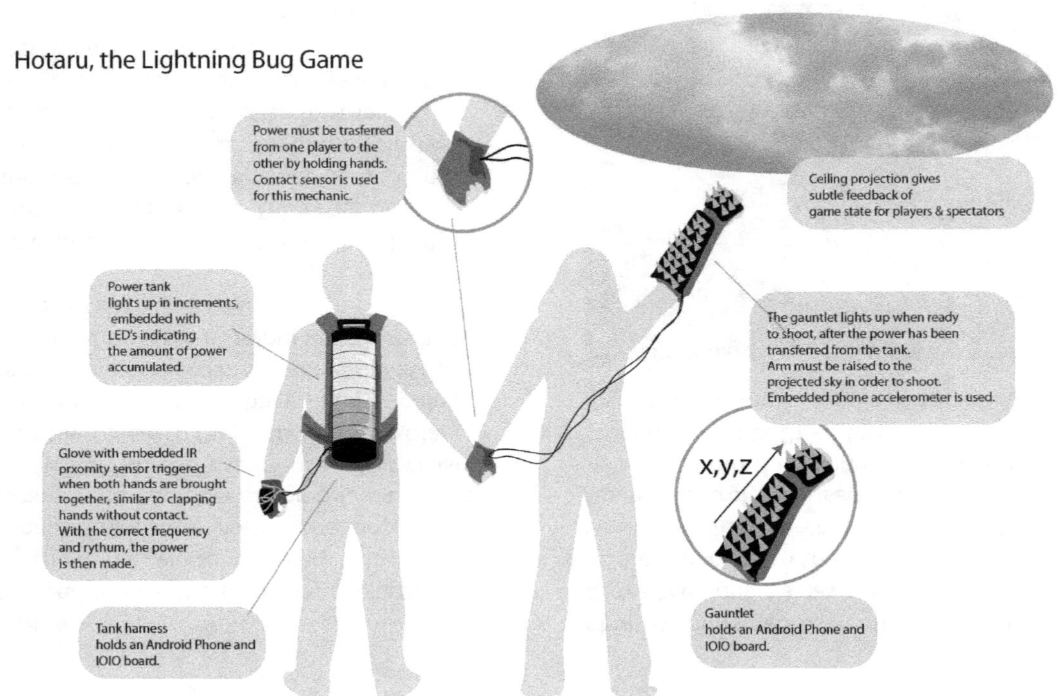

Figure 3. An overview of the components of the Lightning Bug Game.

Figure 4. Playtesting a version of the gauntlet and backpack at a festival in Poland. By Martin Christopher Welker for Invisible Playground
at Playpublik Festival Krakow 2014

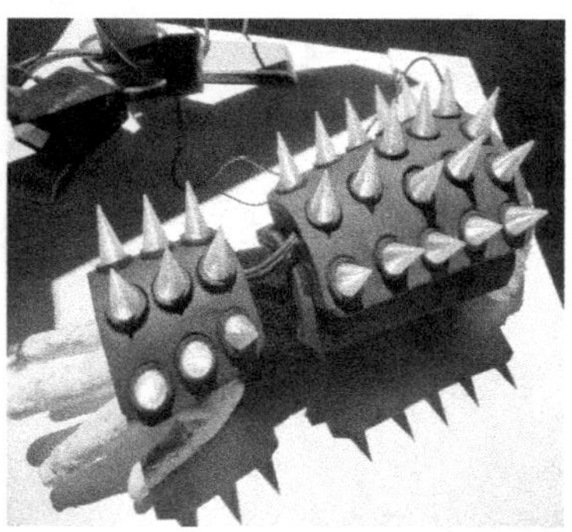

Figure 5. The gauntlet wearable. The projecting spikes flash to indicate energy is available for use in the gameplay. Photographer: Kaho Abe
At Eyebeam Artist Showcase January 2013

Project Process

The artist has driven the aesthetic vision, choices, and development of the game, working closely with the researcher to contextualize the work in the larger frame of relevant research and approaches for evaluating the nature and qualities of the end experience. The artist is in residence in the research lab, and takes part in weekly lab group meetings. There have been ongoing weekly discussions between artist and researcher as the game has evolved through multiple iterations and playtesting sessions (see Figure 4).

One interesting aspect of the collaboration has been mutual reflection on work practice. The artist did extensive material investigations and radically changed the technological underpinnings of the game in ways that would not be typical work practice for the researcher's lab group. This led us to discussions about the role of materials and materiality in design work practice [7], [8], and is something we plan to elucidate more when presenting the finished work and player responses to it. The artist also embeds her practice in a network of game designers who playtest one another's work, and she leverages festivals and other events as ways to workshop her game and improve it. Again, these work practices differ from the researcher's typical lab practice.

Current Progress

After several months of development during the Eyebeam Computation Fashion Fellowship, the artist playtested the prototype with the public at Eyebeam. This initial iteration included cooperative play between the two players, one wearing a gauntlet (see Figure 5) and the other a power pack (see Figure 6). These wearables both had embedded Android-based mobile phones connected to Adafruit mini IOIO boards that drove the light displays. Bluetooth connected the Android phones to the IOIO boards, so that the phone would not drain the battery in the IOIO board. Open Sound Control was used over the dedicated wifi network. Both the main game program on the computer and both Android apps were coded in Processing using Ketai, OSC and PIOIO libraries.

Figure 6. The first iteration of the Lightning Bug game combined the wearable elements with a large half-dome used as a projection surface.

The players were enclosed in a hand-sewn giant projection half dome that extended to 10 feet high and 20 feet wide (see Figure 6). Each player also had a glove on the other hand with a contact patch. The player with the energy backpack had to 'collect' energy

Figure 7. We have been trying out playful methods for evaluation. Here, a player creates a 'Mister Potatohead' illustrating his experience of gameplay, and talks about what it means.

in a pool of light, by rubbing her hands together, then move to the dome and join hands with the player with the gauntlet. While energy remained, the player with the gauntlet could aim a laser beam from the gauntlet at the projection screen to target enemies. Above the play area, suspended from the ceiling was a circular mirror, a projector used for projection mapping, and a web cam used for tracking the laser from the gauntlet. This configuration allows for the projection and the tracking to happen without getting blocked by the players' bodies.

Though the dome created a powerful focal point for spectators, it drew players' attention away from one another and the playful coordination and performance of gestures. It also drew spectators' gaze away from players. Instead of a large projection dome surface, the current version has a smaller, more removed projection on the ceiling for feedback only, giving players as well as spectators information about the game state and progression.

In addition, a glove embedded with a proximity sensor, has been added to the player who holds the tank. A new mechanic has been introduced, where the player must use consistent frequency and rhythm of movement of hands in order to generate power, instead of the prior mechanic of rubbing hands together in a different location under a pool of light. When the player has achieved a consistent frequency of the movement of the hands, the tank which is normally depleting gradually fills up.

When the players then have to immediately hold hands to transfer the power before the tank depletes again. The shooter's gauntlet is then lit up, indicating that the power has been transferred and it is ready to shoot. The laser has been replaced with the use of the embedded accelerometer in the gauntlet. In other words, with the laser removed, there is less emphasis on aiming for the shooter, and more on the tasks, gestures and coordination that the players have to do together in order to play the game.

Finally when the shooting is completed, the players have to repeat the process again in order to fight the virtual enemy. The score is based on how many times the team of players are able to shoot with in the game time limit and then in turn, whether the virtual enemy has been destroyed.

Further development before TEI takes place will include making the look of the projection more relevant to the story and a leader board to encourage pairs to compete with each other. Additional playtesting will ensure effective use of the projection for feedback.

Strategy for Evaluation

Beyond examining playability and enjoyment for players, and spectator comprehension and enjoyment of the game, we have been experimenting with how to evaluate whether we have truly reached the experiential aims for the project—creating a sense of transformation and connectedness, a feeling of immersion in fantasy roles, and an engaging spectacle for those who observe gameplay. We would prefer to make any assessment that we do around the game fit well with the experience of the game itself, so that it is less disruptive for players and spectators. We believe it is possible to design playful and lightweight assessment strategies that can get at our research questions. This will make it more possible to gather rich information about the play experience in settings like game festivals, without disrupting the ambience and flow. As an example, we experimented with asking players to create 'Mister Potatohead' renditions of their experience of the game at a playtest (see Figure 7), and then describe what the figure represented. We got richly textured descriptions of the play experience from this exercise that helped to get at the question of transformation. We are also experimenting with setting up a spectator Twitter hashtag to encourage comments during play, that we can later analyze to better understand the spectator experience. And we plan to set up a photo-booth style series of before and after snapshots of players to see whether their interpersonal physical dynamics (gaze, physical proximity, poses) change after as opposed to before beginning play. Players could access these photos in an online stream, turning the data collection into a souvenir of the experience as well.

Plans for TEI and Beyond

We plan to bring the Lightning Bug Game to TEI for attendees to play, which will also allow us to try out and further refine our evaluation strategies. We are aiming toward a full-scale release and evaluation of the game at IndieCade East (in February 2015 in New York). We believe the game will be an interesting experience for TEI attendees, and could spark discussion about the relationship between costuming, wearable technology, and games.

Acknowledgements

Thanks to Eyebeam Atelier for support of this project through use of a Rockefeller Cultural Innovation Fund grant awarded to them. Thanks to the Game Innovation Lab, and to all those who participated in the creation and playtesting of this game.

References

[1] B. DeKoven, *The well-played game: a player's philosophy*. 2013.

[2] K. S. Tekinbas and E. Zimmerman, *Rules of Play: Game Design Fundamentals*. Cambridge, Mass: The MIT Press, 2003.

[3] "Computational Fashion." (http://fashion.eyebeam.org).

[4] B. Simon, "Wii are Out of Control: Bodies, Game Screens and the Production of Gestural Excess," Social Science Research Network, Rochester, NY, SSRN Scholarly Paper ID 1354043, Mar. 2009.

[5] Wilson, Douglas, "Designing for the Pleasures of Disputation -or- How to make friends by trying to kick them!," submitted to the IT University of Copenhagen, Mar-2012.

[6] K. Isbister and T. Schafer, *Better Game Characters by Design: A Psychological Approach*. Amsterdam ; Boston: CRC Press, 2005.

[7] M. Wiberg, "Methodology for materiality: interaction design research through a material lens," *Pers. Ubiquitous Comput.*, vol. 18, no. 3, pp. 625–636, Mar. 2014.

[8] Y. Fernaeus and P. Sundström, "The Material Move How Materials Matter in Interaction Design Research," in *Proceedings of the Designing Interactive Systems Conference*, New York, NY, USA, 2012, pp. 486–495.

clayodor: Retrieving Scents through the Manipulation of Malleable Material

Cindy Hsin-Liu Kao*
MIT Media Lab
75 Amherst Street
Cambridge, MA 02139
cindykao@media.mit.edu

Ermal Dreshaj*
MIT Media Lab
75 Amherst Street
Cambridge, MA 02139
ermal@media.mit.edu

Judith Amores*
MIT Media Lab
75 Amherst Street
Cambridge, MA 02139
amores@media.mit.edu

Sang-won Leigh*
MIT Media Lab
75 Amherst Street
Cambridge, MA 02139
sangwon@media.mit.edu

Xavier Benavides*
MIT Media Lab
75 Amherst Street
Cambridge, MA 02139
xavib@media.mit.edu

Pattie Maes
MIT Media Lab
75 Amherst Street
Cambridge, MA 02139
pattie@media.mit.edu

Ken Perlin
NYU Media Research Lab
719 Bwy, Rm 1202
NY, NY 10003
perlin@cs.nyu.edu

Hiroshi Ishii
MIT Media Lab
75 Amherst Street
Cambridge, MA 02139
ishii@media.mit.edu

* Indicates equal contribution

TEI'15, Jan 16-19 2015, Stanford, CA, USA
ACM 978-1-4503-3305-4/15/01.
http://dx.doi.org/10.1145/2677199.2688814

Abstract
clayodor (\klei-o-dor\) is a clay-like malleable material that changes smell based on user manipulation of its shape. This work explores the tangibility of shape changing materials to capture smell, an ephemeral and intangible sensory input. We present the design of a proof-of-concept prototype, and discussions on the challenges of navigating smell though form.

Author Keywords
Malleable Interface; Olfaction; Smell

ACM Classification Keywords
H.5.2 Information interfaces and presentation (e.g., HCI): Miscellaneous

General Terms
Design; Human Factors

Introduction
Recent HCI research has moved beyond static and rigid physical interfaces to dynamically controlled materials. For example, research has explored materials with dynamically changing qualities such as shape [5, 7, 17], stiffness [6, 14], weight [12], and optical properties [16]. For the last decade, researchers from CMU and Intel have worked towards the realization of *Claytronics* [1], a future material composed by nanoscale computers in the form of atoms. This will

potentially enable direct and dynamic user manipulations with programmable materials.

Building on top of the possibilities of shape changing interfaces, we envision *clayodor*, a clay-like malleable material that changes smell based on user manipulation of its shape. We explore the tangibility of shaping a malleable material to capture an ephemeral and intangible sensor input: smell. By allowing users to take this material into their hands and physically shape it into various meaningful forms, we are aiming to explore the potential mental model of coupling these forms with smells. Similarly, Obrist et al [13] has also indicated the evocative quality of scent to connect people to memories and past experiences. However, there is no focus on the power for objects to be used as a symbol in the production or recall of smell. Further, we posit that because smell is a distinctively difficult sense to describe, shaping and molding objects has potential to forgo the necessity for users to attempt at providing descriptions of smells for recall. On a poetic note, our work explores how shaping materials into symbolic forms serves as triggers to scents that connect people to past experiences.

In this paper, we present a prototypical implementation of a malleable interface combined with smell-composing device. The prototype is technically interesting, but yet in a preliminary form as its size is big and it has a limited sensing capability. However, we envision *clayodor* to be a material consisting of voxels embedded with tiny pressure sensors and scent-releasing discs. Various deformed shapes would create different pressure distributions and trigger the discs to release corresponding smells. The discussion on limitations of current technology will be presented in later sections.

Related Work

The history of olfactory research can be dated to *Sensorama* [8] in 1962. Ten years ago, the HCI research community started looking into the challenges and possibilities for smell-based technology [9]. One main challenge is the complexity to produce arbitrary smells on demand. Humans have a thousand different olfactory receptors in our nose, each sensing a different chemical bond [10]. Reproducing arbitrary smell would therefore require a thousand-dimension space, which presents significant challenges compared to the 3-dimensional space of vision (RGB). Another challenge is the difficulty of creating as systemic and reproducible classification scheme for smell. As humans refer to smells through ambiguous descriptions, it is difficult to create rigorous categorization for universal reference.

Recent HCI research efforts focus on *user interaction* with smell-based technology, rather than the chemical engineering challenge of reproducing specific scents. To the best of our knowledge, most systems use off the shelf aromas in their prototypes, focusing research effort on interaction design. Brewster et al. [4] developed a smell-based photo-tagging tool (*Olfoto*) to elicit memories though smell. Commercial product *Scentee* [2] lets you associate particular smells with smartphone notifications.

The *Smelling Screen* [11] is a display system that can generate smell distribution on a 2D screen. Ranasinghe et al. [15] explored using smell for digital communication, enabling the sharing of smell over the Internet. By recreating smell though form, *clayodor*

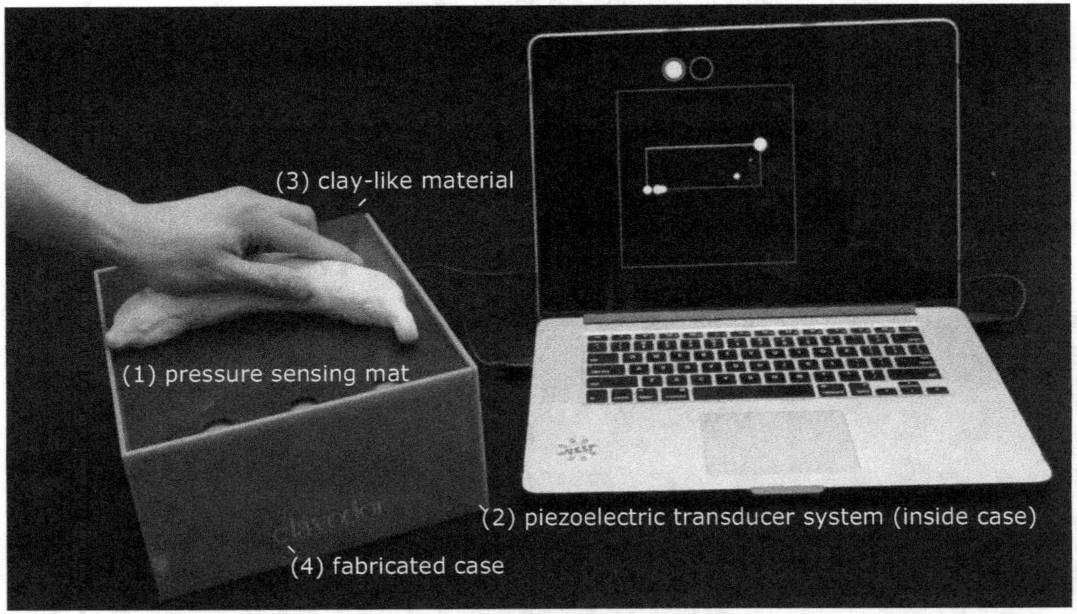

Figure 1. *clayodor* prototype

explores the possibility of form as a user-designated navigator for smell.

Prototype

Due to current technical limitations, e.g., sensor size and sensitivity, we implement the proof-of-concept prototype through external sensing and clay-like material. The current prototype allows us to explore user interactions and elicit insight.

The prototype (Figure 1) consists of (1) a pressure sensing multi-touch mat from *TactonicTechnologies* [3], (2) an Arduino controlled piezoelectric transducer system that generates scent by vaporizing liquid fragrances (3) clay material for user manipulation, and (4) a fabricated case.

Users can form the clay material into different shapes, and place it onto the pressure-sensing mat. The mat is integrated with a machine-learning algorithm that distinguishes between different shapes. Once the shape is detected and recognized, the piezoelectric transducer system triggers the respective scent. The piezoelectric transducer system consists of multiple small discs connected to containers filled with different scented liquids. When a certain signal is received, the corresponding disc starts vibrating at high frequency, turning liquid into vapor.

Application Scenario

Retrieving scents

In this application we enable users to form the shapes of objects according to their mental modals, and retrieve the smell associated with the shapes. Figure 2 presents an application to retrieve fruit scent. To smell the scent of certain fruits, the users can shape the material into the form of the fruit based on their mental modals, and *clayodor* will release the corresponding scent.

Recalling memories

From the study by Obrist *et. al.* [13] on human perceptions towards smell, the strongest quality people saw in smell was its ability to connect them to the past. We explore how *clayodor* recalls past memories by enabling users to reshape objects that are etched into their minds. An example is a user who is recalling the scent of her grandmother's homemade buns. By reshaping *clayodor* to the shape of buns, it starts giving

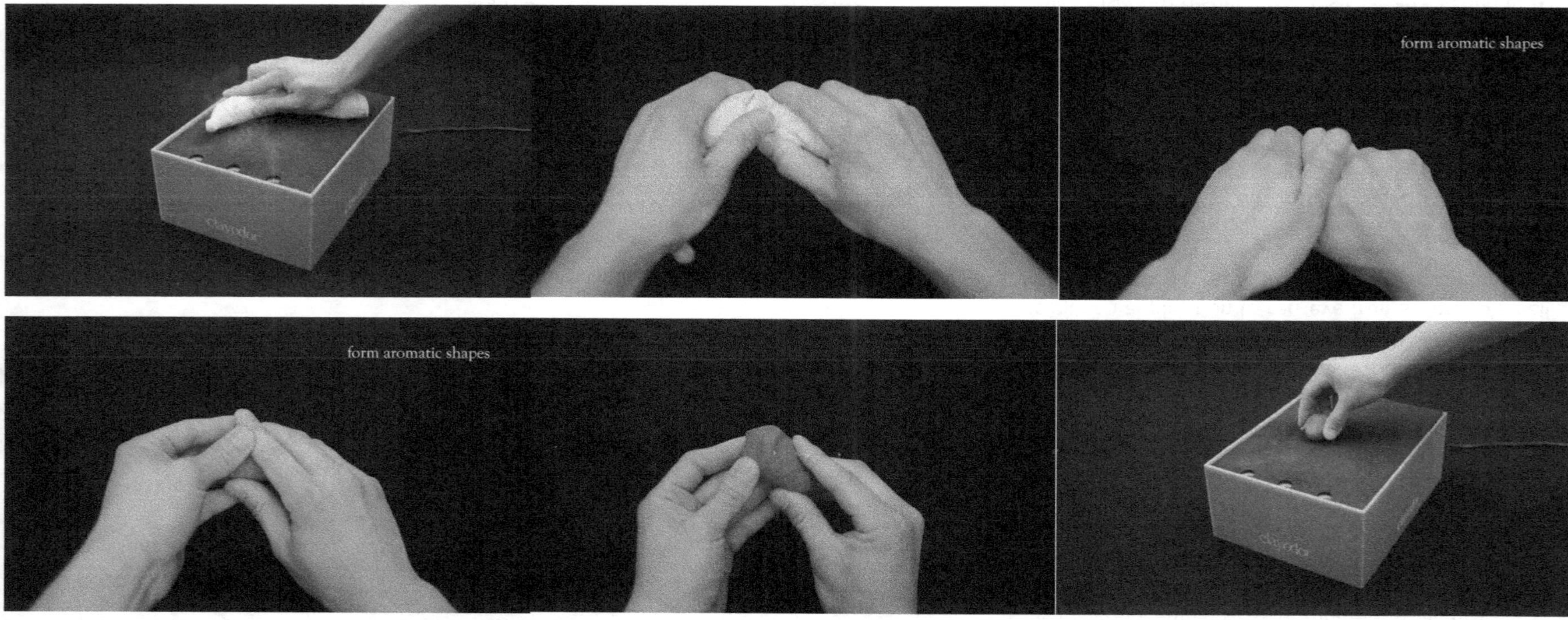

Figure 2. *Shaping clay for retrieving different fruit scents*

off the smell of the buns she misses so much, bringing her back to her childhood memory.

Discussion and Limitation

Retrieving the intangible through the tangible

This work is fundamentally exploring the question of capturing the ephemeral though the tangible. However, this raises the question of whether tangible form is the most intuitive mental link to smell for humans. What about linking a visual image with smell? Or even a color with smell? Or even a sound with smell? Which would be the most intuitive and rich connection to retrieve this ephemeral sense? Or does it vary based on different scenarios? With *clayodor* as a first exploration, we see this as a rich space for future research.

Mapping smell and form

This work raises the question of the feasibility of mapping form with smell. What granularity of recognition would the system need to support? For instance, for the system to distinguish between an orange and a peach, which are both round, the system would need to support recognition of texture and fine details. This would also pose challenge on the user, who would have to shape the subtle differences with their hands. We see the need to articulate a basic design vocabulary to map form and smell.

Conclusion and Future Work

In this paper, we presented a prototypical system that allows retrieving scents through manipulating malleable tangible interface. By fusing pressure sensing and scent-composing technology, we explored the possibility of fine-grained navigation through different smells via tangible interaction. The current prototype is not well integrated, however, we envision that *clayodor* will be a material consisting of voxels comprising tiny pressure sensors and scent-releasing discs because each hardware modules' can be easily reduced to small sizes. The next step towards this vision is to make modular blocks consisting of those hardware modules.

Acknowledgements

We thank the TAs of the Shared Tangible Augmented Reality course: Felix Heibeck, Basheer Tome, Philipp Schoessler, and Xiao Xiao for their feedback and encouragements.

References

[1] Claytronics Project. http://www.cs.cmu.edu/~./claytronics/

[2] Scentee Product. http://www.scentee.com/

[3] Tactonic Technologies. http://www.tactonic.com/

[4] Brewster, S., McGookin, D., Miller, C. Olfoto: designing a smell-based interaction. *Proc. CHI (2006)*, 653–662.

[5] Coelho, M. and Zigelbaum, J., Shape-changing interfaces. *Personal and Ubiquitous Computing Vol.15*, Issue 2, Springer-Verlag London (2010), 161–173.

[6] Follmer, S., Leithinger, D., Olwal, A., Cheng, N., and Ishii, H. Jamming user interfaces: programmable particle stiffness and sensing for malleable and shape-changing devices. *UIST '12*

[7] Sean Follmer, Daniel Leithinger, Alex Olwal, Akimitsu Hogge, and Hiroshi Ishii. inFORM: dynamic physical affordances and constraints through shape and object actuation. *UIST'13.*

[8] M. L. Heilig, Sensorama Simulator, *U.S. Patent 3 050 870*, August 28, 1962.

[9] Kaye, J. "Jofish." Making Scents: aromatic output for HCI. *Interactions 11*, 1 (2004), 48–61.

[10] Lawless, Harry T. Olfactory psychophysics. In Beauchamp & Bartoshuk (eds.), Tasting and Smelling, *Handbook of Perception and Cognition*, 2nd ed., 1997, pp. 125-174

[11] Matsukura, H., Yoneda, T., Ishida, H. Smelling Screen: Development and Evaluation of an Olfactory Display System for Presenting a Virtual Odor Source. *IEEE TVCG 19*, 4 (2013), 606–615.

[12] Ryuma Niiyama, Lining Yao, and Hiroshi Ishii. 2014. Weight and volume changing device with liquid metal transfer. *In Proceedings of the 8th International Conference on Tangible, Embedded and Embodied Interaction (TEI '14).* ACM, New York, NY, USA, 49-52.

[13] Marianna Obrist, Alexandre Tuch, and Kasper Hornbæk. Opportunities for Odor: Experiences with Smell and Implications for Technology, *ACM CHI 2014*

[14] Jifei Ou, Lining Yao, Daniel Tauber, Jürgen Steimle, Ryuma Niiyama, and Hiroshi Ishii. jamSheets: thin interfaces with tunable stiffness enabled by layer jamming. *TEI'14.*

[15] Ranasinghe, N., Karunanayaka, K., Cheok, A.D., Fernando, O.N.N., Nii, H., Gopalakrishnakone, P. Digital taste and smell communication. *Proc. BodyNets* (2011), 78–84.

[16] Willis, K., Brockmeyer, E., Hudson, S., and Poupyrev, I. Printed Optics: 3D Printing of Embedded

Optical Elements for Interactive Devices. *In Proc. UIST 2012*, ACM Press (2012), 589–598

[17] Lining Yao, Ryuma Niiyama, Jifei Ou, Sean Follmer, Clark Della Silva, and Hiroshi Ishii. PneUI: pneumatically actuated soft composite materials for shape changing interfaces. *UIST'13*.

A Study to Empower Children to Design Movable Tactile Pictures for Children with Visual Impairments

Jeeeun Kim
Computer Science
University of Colorado Boulder
430 UCB
Boulder, CO 80309 USA
jeeeun.kim@colorado.edu

Tom Yeh
Computer Science
University of Colorado Boulder
430 UCB
Boulder, CO 80309 USA
tom.yeh@colorado.edu

Hyunjoo Oh
ATLAS
University of Colorado Boulder
430 UCB
Boulder, CO 80309 USA
hyunjoo.oh@colorado.edu

Figure 1. Example 3D printed tactile pictures for children with visual impairments

TEI '15, Jan 16-19 2015, Stanford, CA, USA
ACM 978-1-4503-3305-4/15/01.
http://dx.doi.org/10.1145/2677199.2688815

Abstract
3D Printing has shown a great potential to print tactile picture books, in order to cultivate emergent literacy for children with visual impairments. However, currently available 3D design tools are hard to learn, resulting in children to be excluded from the participatory design of tactile pictures. Also, existing 3D design software lacks of functionality to incorporate mobility and rich textures, which is critical aspect of the effective tactile picture. In this paper, we review our formative studies, presenting a hands-on design process for children to empower their own creativities into 3D tactile pictures design, and to engage them to bring other materials to enhance touch experiences.

Author Keywords
Tactile Movable Pictures; Tangible Design Toolkit; 3D Design; Children; Maker Culture; Participatory Design

ACM Classification Keywords
H.5.m. Information interfaces and presentation

Introduction
3D Printing has been spotlighted as a promising method to publish tactile picture books for developing emergent literacy for children with visual impairments

Figure 2. Students' tactile picture designs with hands-on materials, including LEGO and play-dough. Children enjoyed combining LEGO bricks and crafts materials to integrate textures, mobility into their design.

[9][10]. Figure 1 shows 3D printed tactile picture books. Effective tactile pictures integrate (1) salient shape, (2) mobility, (3) textures, and (4) vivid color for children with residual vision [8][11]. Although 3D printing promises replicability and customizability [5], currently available 3D design tools fail to integrate mobility and rich textures into a 3D printable tactile picture. Also, these tools are not accessible for novice, especially for children who have a prodigious potential to be external design experts. Here we propose a design process with special LEGO kits to empower children to represent mobility of objects into tactile pictures, and incorporate textures and color contrasts.

Design Barriers for Children

Participatory design methodologies have suggested working with children as design partner [3]. Although variety of easy 3D design tools are available, such as SketchUp, and tons of online tutorials and workshops explain how to create 3D models quickly and effectively [13], those 3D design software is still hard for children to learn. Children know the most intuitive and creative ways to interpret 2D visuals into 3D with their unique design perspective, but complicated interactions of 3D software results in steep learning curves [4]. Since designers and children can contribute to design tasks with their own expertise, they need a proper design kit to maximize their creativities [3]. The challenge remains unresolved: *How to empower children engage in the design of tactile pictures with proper design framework and tools?*

Tangible Hands-on Fabrication

Hands-on Fabrication leads children to interact with them, by prompting their intellectual curiosities [2]. With abundant tangibles, children were equipped to participate in design tasks. We came up with ideas to provide movable LEGO fabrication kits for children – to empower their imagination to design 3D tactile pictures tangibly, also to engage them to create a storytelling.

Formative Study: Design Workshops

We conducted three design workshops with 8 to 25 children each (ages 6-16, Figure 3). We first introduced them the idea of 3D printed tactile picture books, and elements of good tactile pictures. Then, we presented several children's books and fostered them to choose one to model. They spent the next 30 minutes to construct models, given LEGO bricks, play-doh, and other traditional craft materials. Figure 2 shows examples of the models built in the three workshops.

Figure 3. Design Workshop for high school students

Our workshops revealed two major findings. First, most children showed interest in building movable structures. For example, Figure 2 shows a boy riding a hot balloon that flies, from *Harold and the Purple Crayon* by Crockett Johnson (top); It also shows an example of the gorilla with two arms moving back and forth tapping its chest, from *From Head to Toe,* by Eric Carle (middle).

The second finding is that children loved integrating LEGO blocks with other crafting materials, such as play-doh and wood sticks. Despite limitations of LEGO bricks

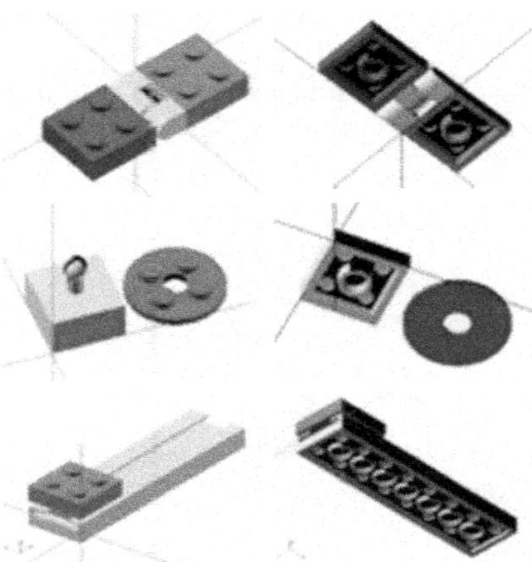

Figure 4. Special LEGO blocks to define interaction types on children's lift-the-flap books hinge, spinner, and track (from top to bottom)

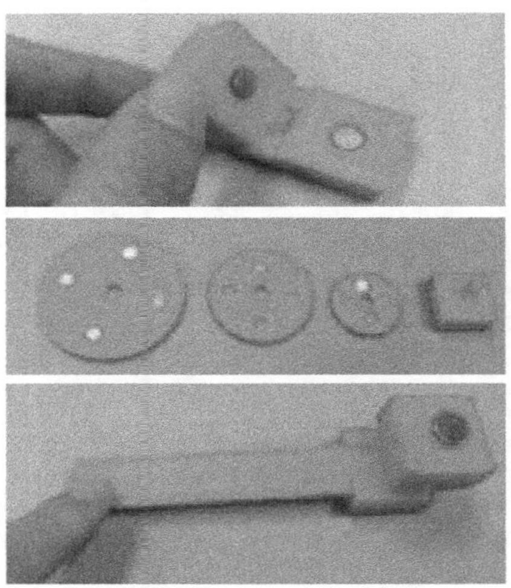

Figure 5. Three different structures of 3D printed blocks: hinge, spinner and track (from top to bottom). We embedded magnets on top, to make other materials attachable.

of attaching other materials than bricks itself, children tried to joint them in their own ways. Figure 2 additionally shows a crocodile from *Animals In Danger* by William McCay (bottom), with LEGO teeth in its mouth. The participant who designed gorilla picture (middle) even asked us to prepare magnets, to embed them into his arm and chest to stick them together.

Movable and Attachable LEGO Bricks

These key findings motivated us to investigate how to widen kinetic movements and textural aspects that children can integrate into prototyping, using the context of original LEGO already has. In this section, we illustrate our ongoing exploration on *movable* and *attachable* LEGO bricks to act as an interface to tactile picture design process. This experiment consists of three layers: generic LEGO bricks, movable LEGO set, and other additional craft materials.

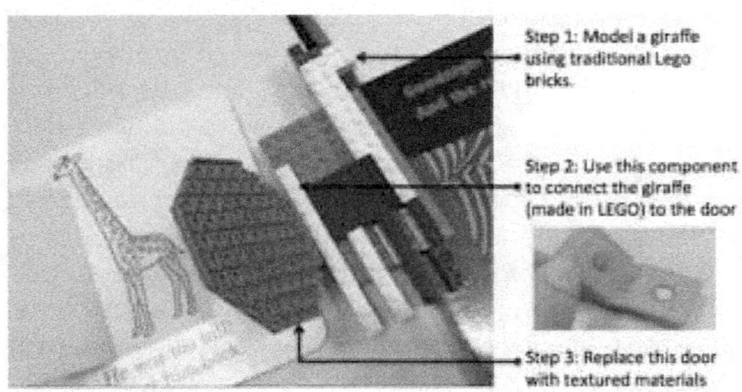

Figure 6. Tactile Picture design process with design kit

We expect children to (1) model basic tactile pictures with traditional LEGO bricks, (2) bring movable LEGOs to embody physical mobility and kinetic movements, and (3) refine their tactile pictures with paper, textural materials by combining them altogether.

1st layer: Generic Lego Brick Base

To bring children as design partners in collaborative design, it is important to give them basic constraints, such as page size. We took the universal LEGO compatible block generator from Thingvierse [13] (No. 178627), because it is parametric. Given width, height, and depth as number, it generates the unified size of picture book page as a design canvas, with given numbers of convex slots on top that makes itself compatible with original LEGO bricks. This base would give children the concept that they are designing tactile "pictures" on a "canvas". The unified size of canvas reduces disadvantages of crowd sourced design, by unifying page resolution, enabling children to assemble original LEGOs as design components at the same time.

2nd layer: Movables

We designed three types of movable LEGO blocks supporting representative motions commonly shown in children's pop-up book: lifting/opening, pulling/pushing, and spinning. These three movements are the most common expressions we found from our preliminary research on 25 children's book, used to incorporate kinetic interactions. Figure 4 shows OpenSCAD design of movable LEGOs, Figure 5 shows 3D printed parts with modified design, to embed magnets. Those blocks can be assembled with both generic LEGO underneath, and additional craft materials above. Figure 6 shows the process how these three components are united to construct one tactile picture. Despite the fact that recently selling LEGO set has its own hinge module, we consider to use this new block since hinge provided by traditional LEGO is not sufficient to cover diverse motions and the degree of mobility that many existing children's book covers.

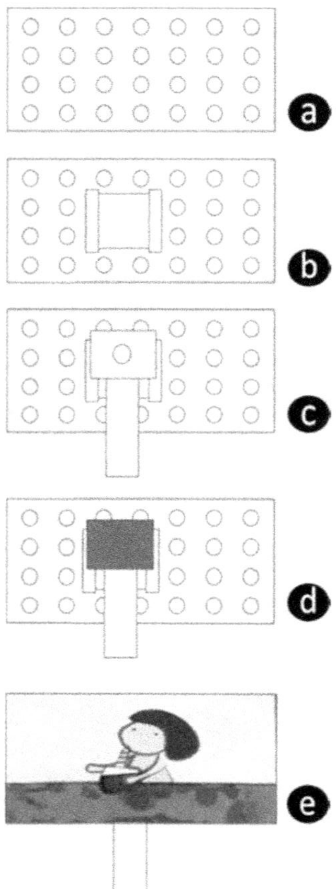

Figure 7. Step by step process assembling original/special LEGO bricks and tactile pictures. On the canvas (a), movable block is fabricated (b) (c), and tactile pictures are added to represent motion (d) and (e).

3rd layer: Tactile Pictures
The top layer of tactile picture is open-ended for integrating any kinds of materials, design, and textures with magnets attached. From our preliminary research, we received a fair amount of informal feedback that soft materials, such as fabric and furry leather should be amalgamated, in order to enrich textures. Limited texture of 3D printing by plastic surface does not successfully reinforce blind children's touch experience. Therefore, we designed a paper drawing cutout that is attached with magnets, which pulls opposite polar embedded on top of the 2nd layer's movable blocks. Through this layer, we aim to widen expressive freedom that children can add other materials in their design process.

A Design Case Study using New LEGO Bricks

Inspired by Lucy Cousins' series of interactive board books, the stories of *Maisy Mouse*, we designed four movable pictures using our blocks. Each page is based on different structures enabling different motions, pulling and pushing, spinning, and lifting. Those three structures accordingly supported different storytelling elements such as jumping a rope, drinking soda, riding a Ferris wheel, etc. Our goal was to explore the potential of using the three blocks we proposed: whether the movable and attachable blocks can enhance the scope of current tactile expressions to deliver storytelling indicating certain motions.

Track
The first brick is the track enclosing a slot and a slider. These blocks supported a scene of the girl drinking juice. It enables users to change the rest amount of juice by sliding down handle of the slider. Blue colored soda is attached to the top of track sliding up and down through a slot. It can be a good example of enabling blind children to experience the concept hardly seeable, and touchable in the real world.

Figure 8. A girl drinks juice is represented by track

Spinner
The second brick is the wheel containing an axe and a spinning disc. As discs are detachable, we fabricated a small disc to show a girl rolls down the hill, and assembled a big disc to show a Ferris wheel at an amusement park. This movable is a good example takes LEGO's benefits, which is ability to be built with different sized bricks on same base. Also, based on picture's elements, different numbers of additional movables are being attached, as shown in Figure 9.

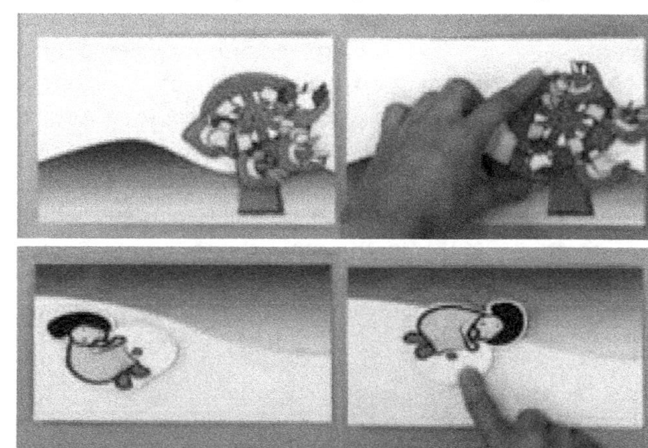

Figure 9. The group of friends riding a Ferris wheel at the fairground (top), and a girl rolling down the hill (bottom).

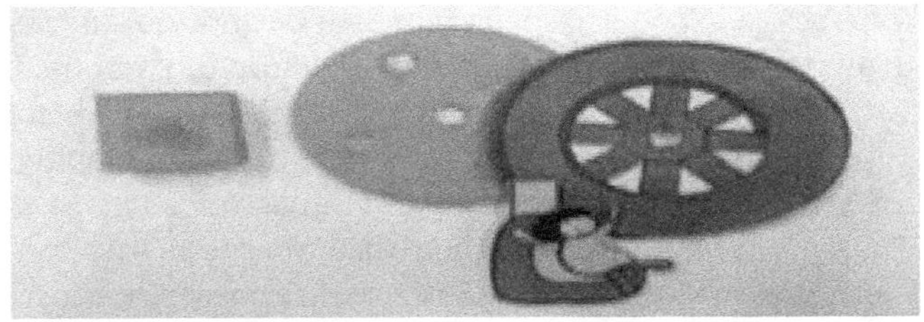

Figure 10. Tactile picture is attached on top of disc, which is replaceable for the wheel, using magnet

Hinge
The last movable block we experimented is a set of hinges. We connected hinges to our character's two hands and tips of rope, so that a girl hop over flapping rope up and down (Figure 11). The hinge is the most versatile movable brick that has been widely used to children's pop-up books we researched. Hinge can be possibly applied to the flag and dowel to make it waves, to the door of a house or a car body to make it opened, to the flower leaves to make it blossom, even to the head of a human or animal to make them nod, etc. From this example we tried to enrich textures using complimentary materials. The paper tactile picture vividly colored is fully equipped with threads, yarn and fabrics, as shown in Figure 10.

Texture of rope, grass and cloth added version of hinge application

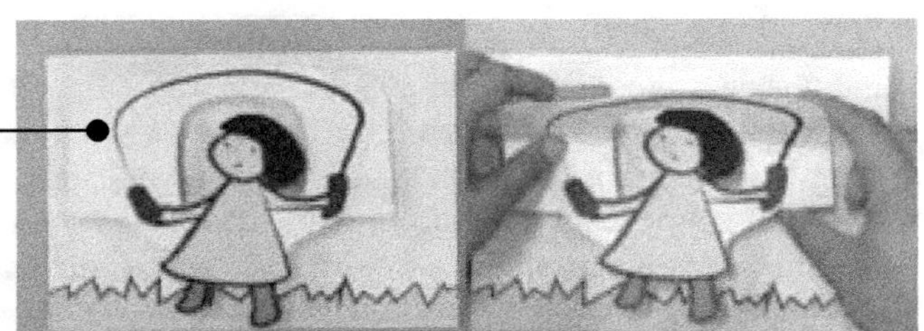

Figure 11. A girl jumping the rope is represented by two hinges attaching to hands and tips of rope to be flappable.

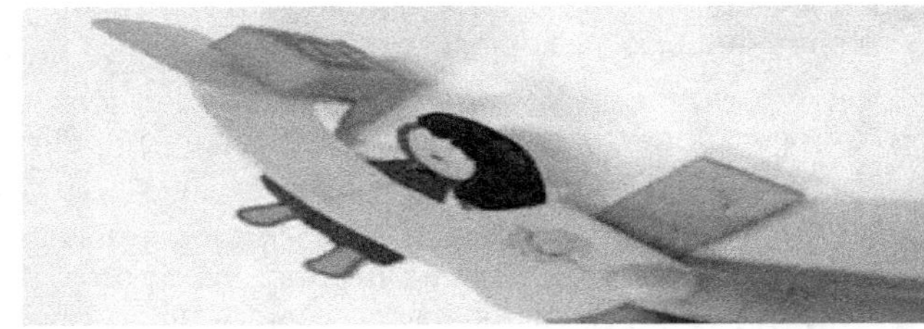

Figure 13. Tactile picture of a girl is attached to set of hinges with magnets

Contribution
Tactile picture design toolkit and tangible design process lowers barriers in 3D design for children. We believe that they do not need to be 3D software experts to participate in the tactile picture design. Our hands-on design toolkit and series of design process empower children to create tactile pictures tangibly – similarly with crafting and DIY activities – as an accessible way of design 3D tactile pictures with kinetic movements.

In addition, our design kit provides a great potential for open-ended applications. Compared to texture-less 3D printed plastic tactile pictures, the kit dispenses wider range of variations with different design technics, not only combining soft material to augment textural experiences, but also consolidating color contrasts.

Future Works
In order to validate the effectiveness of this new design process, we plan to test the design process with target users – sighted children. We will observe how children embody kinetic attributes with movable and attachable new LEGO bricks, and transcribe physical mobility into their tactile picture design. For this target user study, we will provide various textural materials, observing how children put them together to enrich textures.

In this paper, we defined three basic movements. As physical objects have more degrees of freedom of mobility, we will define several more movement types and reflect them to our new LEGO bricks that help children embody mobility in tactile pictures design.

As our ultimate goal is generating replicable, reusable, and customizable digital 3D tactile pictures for parents and teachers of children with visual impairments, we must consider how design results from this process can be digitized and shared with stakeholders, including even librarians. The 3rd layer's open-ended applications are hardly recognized and printed by 3D printer, so we need to investigate method to convert a physical design into 3D-printable digital files. Recently, 3D scanner to find the best match from warehouse [6], and special LEGO block editor [7] were considered. We leave the challenge *How to map each object from layers to 3D printable digital formats?* for the future works.

Acknowledgements

We represent our thanks to Suzette Wright, for giving us specific guide to outline good tactile pictures based up of her long time of devotion on tactile picture books at the American Printing House for the Blind (APH). We also thank awesome children who eagerly showed their interests in our project while participation in the workshops, presenting their great creativity through hands-on design, and thank to Dr. Stacey Ann Forsyth for structuring the entire teen's café program and inviting us to organize workshops. We also appreciate her for introducing inspiring children's books we should try to transcribe into tactile pictures. We also express our thanks to Mark D. Gross, for taking our idea and giving us the first valuable review.

References

[1] Antle, A., Droumeva, M., & Ha, D. Thinking with Hands: An Embodied Approach to the Analysis of Children's Interaction with Computational Objects *CHI'09*

[2] Deung, Y., Antle, A., Neustaedter, C., & Bevans, A. Tango cards: a card-based esign tool for informing the design of tangible learning games *DIS'14*

[3] Druin, A., Cooperative Inquiry: Developing New Technologies for Children with Children *CHI'99*

[4] Follmer, S., Ishii, H. KidCAD: digitally remixing toys through tangible tools *CHI'12*

[5] Kim, J., Stangl, A., Eisenberg, A., & Yeh, T. 3D Printed Tactile Pictures for Children with Visual Impairments. *TEI'14 Works-in-Progress*

[6] Kim, J., Stangl, A., & Yeh, T. Using LEGO to model 3D tactile pictures by sighted children for blind children. *SUI'14*

[7] Mueller, S., Mohr, T., Guenther, K., Brohnhofen, J., & Baudisch, P. faBrickation: fast 3D Printing of Functional objects by integrating construction kit building blocks *CHI'14*

[8] Philippe C., (2009). The Typhlo & Tactus Guide to Children's Book with tactile illustrations, *Les Doigts Qui Revent*

[9] Stangl, A., Kim, J., & Yeh, T. 3D Printed tactile picture books for children with visual impairments: a design Probe. *IDC'14*

[10] Stangl, A., Kim, J., & Yeh, T. Technology to Support Emergent Literacy Skills in Young Children with Visual Impairments. *Extended Abs. CHI'14*

[11] Suzette, W., (2013) Guide to Designing Tactile Illustrations for Children's Books, *American Printing House for the Blind*

[12] Thingiverse http://thingivers.com

[13] Zeleznik, R., Herndon, K., and Hughes, J., SKETCH: an interface for sketching 3D scenes *SIGGRAPH'06*

Olegoru: A Soundscape Composition Tool to Enhance Imaginative Storytelling with Tangible Objects

Chuan-Che (Jeff) Huang*
chuanche@umich.edu

Yu-Jen Lin*
yjlintw@umich.edu

Xinda Zeng*
xinda@umich.edu

Mark W. Newman*
mwnewman@umich.edu

Sile O'Modhrain*
sileo@umich.edu

* University of Michigan
School of Information

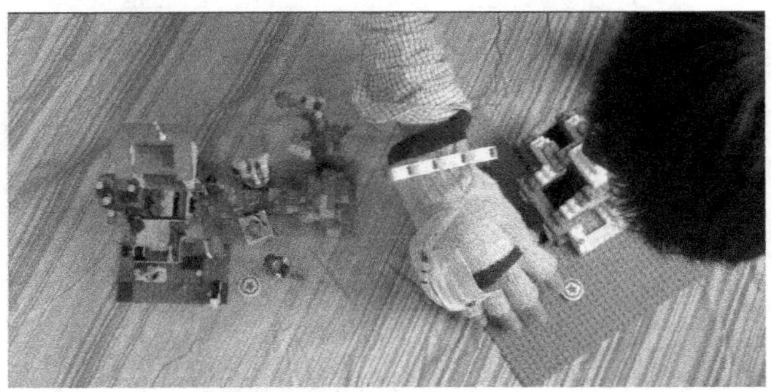

Figure 1: Children could interact with Olegoru via speech, non-verbal voice and gesture to compose sound effects for their stories.

TEI '15, Jan 16-19, 2015, Stanford, CA, USA.
ACM 978-1-4503-3305-4/15/01.
http://dx.doi.org/10.1145/2677199.2687895

Abstract
Learning storytelling is beneficial for children's development. Various tools have been proposed to expand the set of materials children can use to compose their stories. However, most previous research focuses on enhancing the visual aspect of storytelling and underexplores the acoustic elements needed for children's stories. In this paper, Olegoru[1], a sound composition tool in the form of magic gloves and soul stones, is proposed to augment children's storytelling when using physical objects. Children can create contextual and regional sound effects as well as event-based acoustics through speech, non-verbal and gestural interaction, and could potentially enable children to create more immersive story-worlds. To investigate the technical feasibility of such tool, a preliminary prototype was built that accepts a limited number of vocalized sound effects and vocabulary.

Author Keywords
Storytelling; Physical computing; Sound tagging; Soundscape; Children

ACM Classification Keywords
H.5.2 User Interfaces

General Terms
Design; Human Factors

[1] Olegoru is a play on the word "Oregoru", which means music boxes in Japanese, and the word LEGO.

Introduction
Encouraging imaginative storytelling is beneficial for children's development––much research has demonstrated that the everyday social and physical dynamics of interaction with the world can be learned via storytelling, as well as aspects of living such as creativity, communication and motor skills. Therefore, one particular challenge for the Human-Computer Interaction researcher is to design tools that further expand the set of physical and virtual materials available for storytelling, thus allowing children to compose more complex, immersive and realistic stories while at the same time making the interface intuitive.

There are many digital storytelling tools [5, 10] that allow children to create stories with a high degree of freedom and more immersive environments. However, these digital tools distance children from the physical worlds and the physical objects they've already engaged with. They require children to adapt to the limited control afforded by devices such as computer mice and touch-pads for creating their stories and underutilize children's powerful motor and communication skills––their hands and voices. This limitation forces children to spend more time learning the control tools before they can engage in storytelling. In addition, research has demonstrated the potential benefits for children of using tangible materials for learning [3, 4]. For example, physical objects can support collaboration and allow children to manipulate objects in parallel easily.

To better enrich children's storytelling in the physical world, many researchers have developed physical interactive toys that augment the capabilities of physical objects such as [2, 6, 7, 8, 12]. For example, Lego Mindstorm [9] is a set of programmable Lego blocks that enables children to create the behaviors of physical objects. Children can thus make robotic animals that walk and respond to human commands in their stories. Storyrooms and Magic Wand [7], on the other hand, allow children to assign simple if-then rules for computer-augmented soft toys, such as blinking a stuffed star whenever it is touched. Although these tools have enhanced the interactivity of physical worlds, they focus more on augmenting the visual aspect of storytelling. The acoustic aspect, however, is underexplored in these projects. For instance, there is still no easy mechanism for children to compose the sound of the sea, a cannon, sword fighting and storms that are needed for their pirate stories.

Some researchers have explored sound composition tools for children (e.g., SoundBlock & SoundScratch [3]) and there have been a few commercial products available (e.g., LEGO SoundBrick and Sound Lab [15]) that allow children to manipulate sound effects easily using physical objects. However, these products either focus more on instrumental sound effects, or provide a very limited set of short sound effects. They are still far from the complexity of soundscapes such as those discussed by Schafer and Westerkamp [11, 14]. In addition to the introduction of rich natural and historical soundscapes, Schafer argues that the awareness of our sound environment is important as it pervades everything we do. As an outcome of this thinking, a series of curricula were developed by Schafer and others for elementary school children to encourage creation of soundscapes, in addition to more traditional music training. Inspired by Schafer, Westerkamp and the recent development of environmental sound synthesizers [13], we therefore propose Olegoru, an interactive toy that allows children to improvisationally compose various contextual sound and short sound effects using speech, non-verbal voice and gesture. In doing so, we strive to increase the richness and immersiveness of children's imaginative play.

Interaction Concepts
Olegoru contains a fingerless magic glove, and a set of intelligent bricks called "soul stones". Children ages 8-12 can use Olegoru while constructing their LEGO

Figure 2: A soul stone could be placed at a region of a story-world. It allows children to assign sound effects to a specific region (around 30cm.)

Figure 3: A child could attach a soul stone to a LEGO mini-figure and assign a laser shooting sound to it. After that, once the child shakes the mini-figure, the real laser gun sound effects would be played.

stories. They can issue speech and non-verbal commands to the magic glove to create various sound backdrops. In addition, sound effects can be assigned to a specific region or object. We first introduce the then illustrate how they are implemented.

Form Factors of the Design
The design metaphor for our system is a magic glove. The storyteller (in this case the child) wears the magic glove, which has a microphone embedded in it. The glove metaphor is inspired by movies and fantasy stories, such as Frozen, where gloves are used to either hide or augment the magic capabilities of a protagonist. Therefore, for children familiar with such stories, gloves often incorporate a sense of magic and thereby become an object for casting spells; such spells might be accompanied by 'magic words', utterances that are designed to evoke a magical world, complete with a magical soundscape. The advantage of this magic glove design is that children's hands are usually occupied when playing Lego. The glove design allows children to focus their hands on manipulating objects while still being able to compose the soundscape.

Global Soundscape Creation
Using Olegoru, children are able to create the sound backdrop for their stories. This feature allows children to set the general tone of the stories. For example, in a pirate story, the sound backdrop could be the sound of sea waves or the sound of a storm. In Olegoru, Children can compose a global soundscape through casting the spell "Oleg", and then provide a command, such as "give me some wind", or "this is a sea". The keyword "Oleg" activates the speech recognition system, thus allowing the subsequent sentence to be recognized and matched to a specific sound effect.

Regional Soundscape Tagging
Aside from global soundscape creation, Olegoru also supports regional soundscape creation-–contextual sounds that are limited to certain small areas of the play space. For example, in a pirate story, a child might want to create the sound for a treasure island, and separate it out from the sound of the surrounding sea. To enable sound assignment for distinct regions, we designed a kind of intelligent LEGO brick, which we called a soul stone that is embedded with RF-based (e.g, Bluetooth) proximity sensors. A child can first tap a particular soul stone, and issue a speech command to assign a sound effect to a soul stone corresponding to a small region. This regional sound effect will appear when their hand, wearing the magic glove, moves close to the soul stone, and will disappear when the glove moves away.

Imperative and Declarative Commands
Sometimes it is un-natural for children to issue imperative commands such as "I want to hear the sound of wind" while they construct their stories. Children usually just assign a meaning to a LEGO set, "this is a forest", they might say. To incorporate this observation into the design, thus enabling more intuitive sound composition, we allow children to use both imperative and declarative commands for playing with different sound effects. The commands "This is a forest" and "I want to hear the sound of wind", for example, might result in similar sound effects.

Non-verbal Sound Tagging
Olegoru also enables children to tag a sound effect to a specific object using non-verbal voice commands, and allow the activation of the tagged sound by shaking the object. Often, when children are immersed in storytelling, they make various sounds that serve as an imitation of the characters in their imagined scenario. For example, a child might say "Shu" to imitate the sound of laser guns, or "Wuf" to imitate the sound of a dog barking. While we don't want to discourage children from making these sounds themselves, as this is also a means for children to express their creativity; in fact we want to augment this non-verbal aspect to allow for more complex and immersive sound

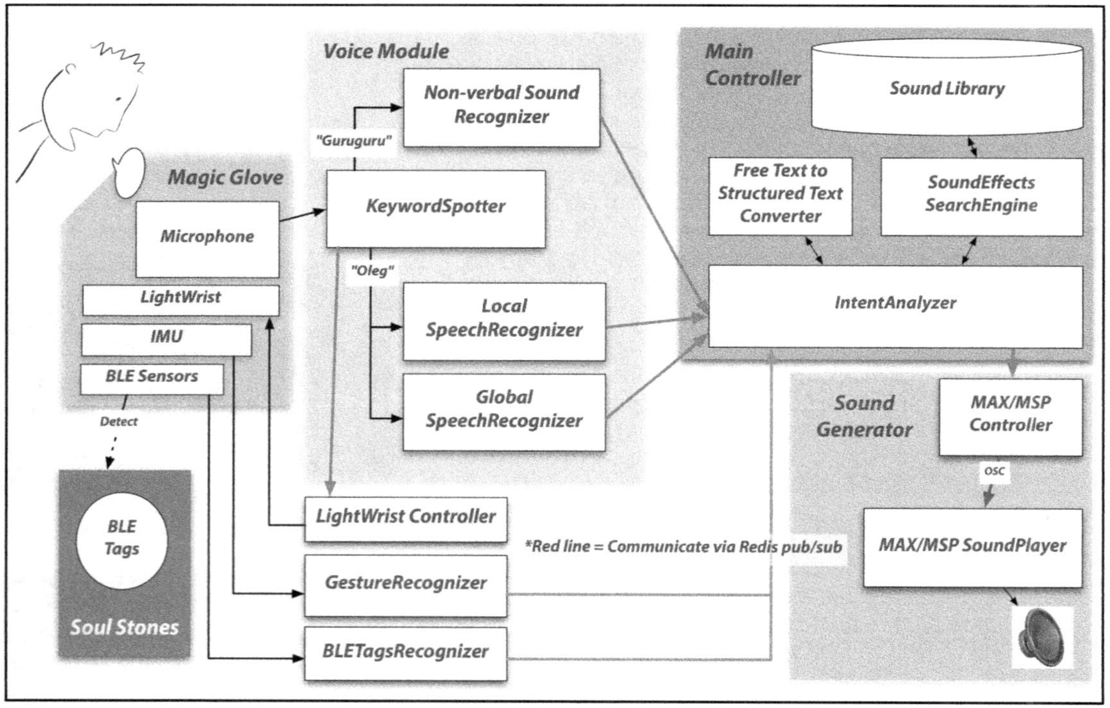

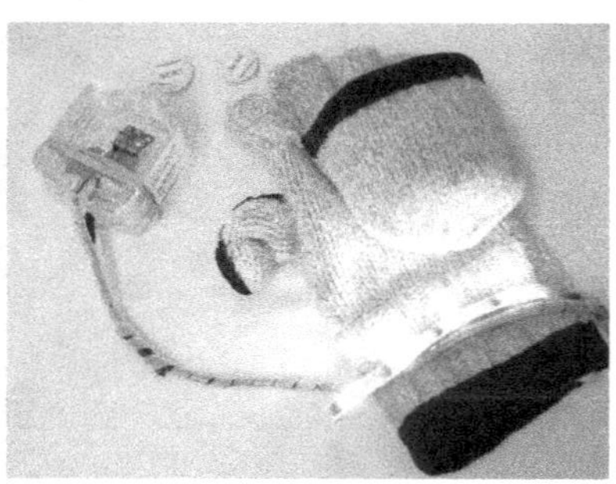

Figure 4 & 5: (Top) System Architecture. (Left) The first magic glove prototype.

composition. We therefore introduce an interaction called non-verbal sound tagging. A child could first tap on a LEGO module that is a soul stone, cast the spell "Guruguru", and then assign a sound effect using non-verbal voice utterances such as "Shu" for a laser gun or "Wuf" for a barking dog. The real sound effects would be attached to this module, and the child could activate the sound by shaking the object.

Preliminary Prototype

To better demonstrate the design concept, we implemented a preliminary prototype that consists of four components, namely: magic glove & soul stones, the voice module, a main controller, and the sound generator (See Figure 4).

Magic Glove & Soul Stones

Magic glove and soul stones are the input interfaces of the system. We embedded several sensors and actuators within the magic glove: a lavaliere microphone, an inertial measurement unit (IMU), an LED strip and a Bluetooth Low Energy sensor. We used RadioShack's 33-3013 Omnidirectional Microphone to capture the audio input. Also, an MPU-6050 IMU module was adopted for gesture detection. A shaking gesture is detected when the value from any axis constantly exceeds a pre-defined threshold over a period of time. We also sewed an LED strip onto the magic glove to provide visual feedback about the state of the magic glove. The LED lights up for a short period of time when either of the keywords "Oleg" or "Guruguru" are detected. This provides an indication of whether the magic glove is listening to the commands. Finally, to allow sound tagging, we instrumented the glove with a Bluetooth Low Energy sensor to track the proximity of soul stones assigned with sound effects. The soul stones are currently implemented using Bluetooth Stick N' Find tags. These soul stones can be either attached to an object or a region. The proximity of a soul stone is inferred via the Received Signal Strength Indication (RSSI) given by Bluetooth. Since RSSI does not provide centimeter-level accuracy, we wrap the BLE sensor with multiple layers of tin foil [1] to limit the range of detection from 10 meters to within 30-50 cm. We then simply set a RSSI threshold to determine if a soul stone is close or not.

Voice Module

The voice module is primarily designed to process audio information. A keyword spotter implemented with the CMU Sphinx [16] is continuously listening to children's utterances. If the keyword "Oleg" is detected, the verbal recognizer will be activated while the non-verbal recognizer will be triggered if "Guruguru" is uttered. We built a non-verbal recognizer using HTK [17]. Several Hidden Markov Models were trained for recognizing our pre-defined non-verbal sounds. For the speech recognizer, we implemented both a local and a global recognizer. The local recognizer is also based on the CMU Sphinx and has a small dictionary that contains mostly words related to sound effects. In addition, a grammar-based language model is used. The global recognizer is based on Google Web Speech API. Using both local and global recognizers allows us to boost the detection accuracy, as the local recognizer performs well for spotting pre-defined sound-related keywords, while the global recognizer is better at inferring out-of-grammar sentences.

Main Controller

The main controller handles the input and output information in order to understand the player's intent and then to instruct the system to take corresponding actions. For speech, we built a natural language processing module with wit.ai [18] to structurize free texts. Specifically, this module resolves a verbal dictation to a pre-defined intent, such as the playing of a sound effect, as well as extracting the sound-related keywords from the dictation. For non-verbal sounds, the keywords of intended sounds are already identified in the recognition process. The main controller then takes such keywords and communicates with a sound effect search engine to retrieve related sound files from a sound effects library. For our initial prototype, a small set of sound effects were extracted from the BBC Sound Effects Library [19] and annotated with textual information related to the context of the sound. The main controller also accounts for gestural events and the proximity of soul stones to allow object sound tagging and sound activation.

Sound Generator

We built a sound generator for the playback of sound effects. Although the preliminary prototype only supports the playback of one sound effect at a time as the decision logic of the main controller is relatively simple, the sound generator, implemented using MAX/MSP can technically layer multiple sound effects together to provide an immersive auditory experience.

Conclusion and Future Work

In this paper, we highlight the opportunities for developing soundscape composition tools to enhance children's imaginative storytelling while playing with physical objects. An interactive toy, Olegoru is introduced to allow children to improvisationally compose various contextual sound effects and event-based acoustics using speech, non-verbal voice and gesture.

In the form of magic glove and soul stones, Olegoru supports four interaction concepts--global and regional soundscape creation, imperative and declarative command recognition, and non-verbal sound tagging. However, our first prototype has some limitations. The local speech recognizer uses phoneme models that were trained using adult's voices, thus it might not currently perform well for children. In addition, the non-verbal recognizer only supports five different sound effects, and the models were also trained on adult's voices. We are interested in using a children's speech corpus to enhance our speech recognition system and to collect more non-verbal utterances for training the non-verbal recognizer. The proximity detection for soul stones needs to be improved as well, as we currently use close-source Stick N' Find tags that have a slow sensor update rate, which results in slower detection and reduced accuracy. We therefore would like to explore other open-source BLE tags that allow the adjustment of the low-level BLE settings to increase the detection accuracy. Finally, we would like to gain knowledge about how children interact with this toy in a user study. We are interested in how our four interaction concepts might increase the complexity of the soundscapes children could create, thus potentially making children's story-worlds more immersive and engaging. In addition, we are curious about how children's knowledge and awareness of their sound environments might be improved through using Olegoru.

Acknowledgements
We thank Emily Provost for providing insights on the implementation of our speech and non-verbal recognizers.

References
[1] Cheung, K.C., Intille, S.S., and Larson, K. An inexpensive bluetooth-based indoor positioning hack. *Proc. UbiComp06 Extended Abstracts*, (2006).

[2] Glos, J.W. and Cassell, J. Rosebud: Technological Toys for Storytelling. *CHI '97 Extended Abstracts on Human Factors in Computing Systems*, ACM (1997), 359–360.

[3] Harrison, J. SoundBlocks and SoundScratch : tangible and virtual digital sound programming and manipulation for children, 2005. http://dspace.mit.edu/handle/1721.1/33885.

[4] Marshall, P. Do Tangible Interfaces Enhance Learning? *Proceedings of the 1st International Conference on Tangible and Embedded Interaction*, ACM (2007), 163–170.

[5] MineCraft. https://minecraft.net.

[6] Montemayor, J., Druin, A., Chipman, G., Farber, A., and Guha, M.L. Sensing, storytelling, and children: Putting users in control. (2003).

[7] Montemayor, J., Druin, A., Chipman, G., Farber, A., and Guha, M.L. Tools for Children to Create Physical Interactive Storyrooms. *Comput. Entertain. 2*, 1 (2004), 12–12.

[8] Montemayor, J., Druin, A., Farber, A., Simms, S., Churaman, W., and D'Amour, A. Physical Programming: Designing Tools for Children to Create Physical Interactive Environments. *Proceedings of the SIGCHI Conference on Human Factors in Computing Systems*, ACM (2002), 299–306.

[9] Resnick, M. Behavior Construction Kits. *Commun. ACM 36*, 7 (1993), 64–71.

[10] Resnick, M., Maloney, J., Monroy-Hernández, A., et al. Scratch: Programming for All. *Commun. ACM 52*, 11 (2009), 60–67.

[11] Schafer, R.M. *The Soundscape.* Destiny Books, Rochester, VT, United States, 1993.

[12] Umaschi, M. Soft Toys with Computer Hearts: Building Personal Storytelling Environments. *CHI '97 Extended Abstracts on Human Factors in Computing Systems*, ACM (1997), 20–21.

[13] Verron, C., Aramaki, M., Kronland-Martinet, R., and Pallone, G. A 3-D Immersive Synthesizer for Environmental Sounds. *IEEE Transactions on Audio, Speech, and Language Processing 18*, 6 (2010), 1550–1561.

[14] Westerkamp, H. Linking soundscape composition and acoustic ecology. *Organised Sound 7*, 01 (2002), 51–56.

[15] Molecule Synth:An Electronic Musical Instrument for Everyone. https://www.kickstarter.com/projects/travisfeldman/molecule-synth.

[16] CMU Sphinx - Speech Recognition Toolkit. http://cmusphinx.sourceforge.net.

[17] HTK. http://htk.eng.cam.ac.uk.

[18] wit.ai. https://wit.ai.

[19] BBC Sound Effects Library. http://www.sound-ideas.com/sound-effects/bbc-1-40-cds-sound-effects-library.html.

Arduino in Museum Exhibition: Lessons Learned When Working with Design Students Inexperienced in Coding

Jennie Schaeffer
Mälardalens högskola, Department of Information Design
Smedjegatan 37
Eskilstuna, Sweden
jennie.schaeffer@mdh.se

Rikard Lindell
Mälardalens högskola, Department of Computer science and Networks
Högskoleplan 1
Västerås, Sweden
rikard.lindell@mdh.se

TEI 2015, January 15-19, 2015, Stanford, CA, USA
ACM *978-1-4503-3305-4/15/01.*
http://dx.doi.org/10.1145/2677199.2687896

Abstract
This work-in-progress paper describes the lessons learned when introducing Arduino and Processing programming into a museum exhibition design course. 20 information design students from Sweden, with no previous knowledge in programming, participated in the course. The students' task was to create five interactive exhibition stations at a museum in five weeks. As an experiment, Arduino and Processing programming was introduced into the course in 2014. The ambition with the experiment was to enlarge the information design students' repertoire and find ways to develop the interactive aspects of the exhibition medium.

The aim of the paper is to identify and discuss challenges and strengths when introducing code as design material in information design education. The findings presented are based on the students' reflection stories.
This work is in progress and we aim in the future to 1) continue the analysis of the material 2) with the findings develop the information design education further and 3) explore the relation between tangible and intangible experience of interactive museum artifacts from a designer's and a museum visitor's perspective. We consider this to be an important matter with branches into the TEI community. We appreciate any feedback on our work.

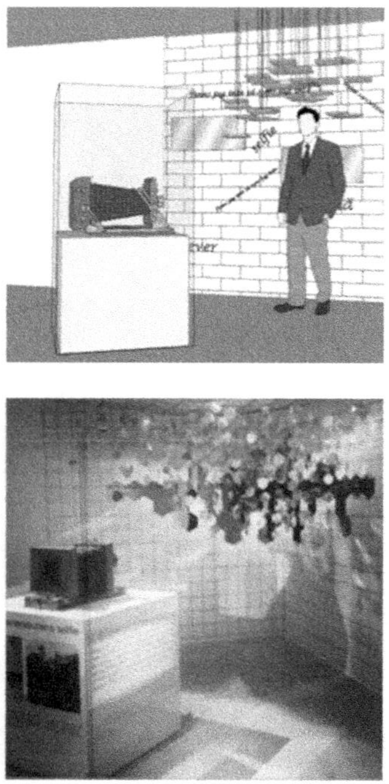

Figure 1: "Self-image"
A sketch (top) and the final design at the museum (bottom) ©Sophia Lindroth, Amellia Franzén and Cecilia Engblom. Photograph J.Schaeffer

Author Keywords
Museum exhibitions; Design Education; Cultural Heritage; Arduino

ACM Classification Keywords
User Interfaces; Design Tools and Techniques

Introduction
In a project called "The stored things come to life", BA-students in an exhibition design course and two design researchers collaborated with a County museum in mid-Sweden. 60.000 objects the storage of the County museum were used as a starting point for a design process. One of the goals for the project was to integrate sensor technologies and audio with text, lights, and the stories with the stored objects in an exhibition.

The course included literature studies and lectures on exhibition design and on interaction, reflection writing, supervision, visits, and lectures by sound artists and researches. In 2014, Arduino and Processing programming was introduced in the course as an experiment to enlarge the students' repertoire. The students had no previous programming experience. For the activity of coding, the course provided two 4 hours introductory workshops and additional 1-2 hours per group supervising-on-demand thereafter. The two introductory workshops for the Arduino were designed to be open and driven by one common denominator of the groups: using a sensor signal to trigger a sound. The students used the Arudino as an I/O device connected to Processing on a computer to enable audio output. As a result of the workshops the students had a boiler-plate system as raw material to tinker with for their proposed designs.

One of the basic assumptions in the paper is that not only programmers can have access to, and work with the material of code. This assumption is a result of our previous studies of programming language code as a design material [8]. Another input were initiatives of using the Arduino microcontroller for inexperienced designers [3], in museum settings [6] and in education [1]. The Arduino have made it possible for designers to work with digital materials and designing digital artifacts without "armies of computer scientists" [9].

The museum domain's awareness of artifacts and the context in which they are presented resonance with the attention to materiality within the TEI community [10]. In addition to the growing research on interactive artifacts in museums [4,5,7], the education for the exhibition designer is an important area for the TEI community that has been less in focus. This paper contributes to focus on the role of the design education for digital artifacts in the museum context.

Aim, Objectives and Research Question
Our long-term objective is to contribute to an update of the Swedish design education, by enlarging the exhibition design students' repertoire. The long-term objective is also to study the effects of "code interventions" on the user experience of the exhibitions, and the effects of treating code as a design material in experience design on different levels of the design process.
The aim of the paper is to identify and discuss challenges and strengths when introducing code as design material in an information design education.

Our approach was inductive. The empirical data consist of the students' reflection stories, observations, films, photographs, and discussions with the students during

"Self-Image"

In the design process, one group wanted to make a camera from the museum collection come to life for the visitor by linking to 'selfies' of yesterday and today.

On the podium an image and text describing one of the first selfies in the world was placed. In front of the camera they created an immersive bathroom environment with mirrors, intended to draw the visitor in front of the camera (see figure 1).

The sound was a multi voiced discussion. Three young women were in a club toilet taking selfies and talking about themselves and how they looked The sound was activated by a sensor placed on the floor that reacted on movement when a visitor entered into the toilet.

Text encouraged the visitors to take their own selfie and upload it to the museum hashtag.

the course. The initial investigation of the data was done with the intention to formulate interesting areas for research and find theoretical approaches relevant to the material.

Combining initial findings and theory, we formulated a research question for this paper:

How do the students express their experience of familiarity and unfamiliarity of the new situation when introducing code as design material in their information design education?

To answer the question, the method was to read the reflection stories and find how the students express their experience of familiarity and unfamiliarity of the new situation. We marked excerpts of the text, discussed them, and compared the different excerpts with each other in order to find out if there were any similarities that could be generated from the particular experiences.

Theory

In accordance with Donald Schön's (1983) discussion of design, we see design as a reflective conversation with the situation. One theoretical key to the approach used (to introduce the digital interactive technology into the course) is the notion of 'repertoire' by Schön [11]. We consider the students as practitioners that have already built up a collection of images, ideas, examples and actions that they can draw upon. Schön saw this as central to reflective thought, and that the repertoire is constantly enlarging on the bases of the unfinished:

> When a practitioner makes sense of a situation he perceives to be unique, he sees it as something already present in his repertoire. To see this site as that one is not to subsume the first under a familiar category or rule. It is, rather, to see the unfamiliar, unique situation as both similar to and different from the familiar one, without at first being able to say similar or different with respect to what. The familiar situation functions as a precedent, or a metaphor, or... an exemplar for the unfamiliar one. [12]

Following the reasoning of Schön [11] the students as practitioners do not have a full understanding of the new situation, but when in action, they bring fragments of both familiarity and unfamiliarity into play. In the reflection stories they begin to verbalize and reflect on familiarity and unfamiliarity in the new situation.
From more recent research, related to design action, the theoretical concept of 'thinkering' is discussed by Fernaeus and Vallgårda in 2014 [2]. The tinkering with materials is an important process in making interactive artifacts and implies negotiations between physical form, temporal from, and the interactive gestalts through bricolage of materials.

Findings of familiarity and unfamiliarity

Below we present the findings of the experience of familiar and the unfamiliar in the design situation reported in the students' reflective stories. One student reacted on the unfamiliarity of the Arduino:

> Around the same time, we were introduced in the Arduino world. There, we were thrown into the programming, wiring and choice of sensors. It was new knowledge and new challenges to master. Here I began to feel that we worked well in the group and was able to cooperate with each other and the whole thing ran on even when we ran into problems. The second day of the Arduino workshop I felt terrible good when we got together a difficult programming and connected a crystal display. Here we began to understand how the codes fit together and how we would connect the various wires to carry the current correctly.

Arduino is here described as a "world". It could imply that in that world there are unknown languages, artifacts and ways to be with the material. The expression of "thrown into the programming", is a way to describe the meeting with the unknown. Based on this student's reflections, things that made it work where the group working together and the feeling of solving tasks successfully. This contributed to a state that the student describes as "began to understand how the codes fit together". This could be interpreted as the expression of understanding and recognizing code *as a material* was a way to connect to the unfamiliarity and recognizing the possibility to understand how code could be fitted together.

Another student recognized the familiarity of immateriality in the unfamiliar situation:

> It made me think about the invisible environment - the atmosphere, which we humans create in a room or in a place. How we can choose and actively work with the atmosphere. I have through my former job as a plant technician visited innumerable office spaces where the invisible environment is as tangible as the physical. [...] Parts of the presentations of the Arduino kit and software program processing was as understandable to me as if they had been held on a Extraterrestrial language. [...] I like to take on new technological challenges. But conducting a technical challenge, fun, one you can still see, touch and understand. Then software processing, no, it felt unattractive and I let another technical talented and interested group member do it. The decision was probably the most favorable for the project but maybe a loss of knowledge for me personally.

The student could find a familiarity with her previous design repertoire, related to "the invisible environment". The student reports the importance of creating atmospheres for spatial experiences. It appears that this familiarity did not help the student, and eventually the student did not participate in the programming. The reflection show that the *immateriality of code* made the technological challenge "unattractive" and that the group setting made it possible to *avoid* to go into interaction with the newly introduced material.
Another student found the coding as an experience described as being in the dark, but was helped through the metaphor of knitting - described as a little a light in the dark (knitting is a mandatory subject in all Swedish undergraduate schools).

> What caught my interest and made me see little light in the dark was when Rikard alleged that programming works much the same way as a knitting description. This interest defaulted with time, and the group became more and more frustrated and not content with the technology and finally we even put ideas down because of technology hassles and incomprehension. We poked along during the workshops with different exercises and programmed and were pleased when we managed to do some exercise. In the workshops on Arduino and programming, I have almost always been a question mark. I have heard the words that had been said but I had no connection to them, or what was said. Fortunately, we had a team member who hung in during the instructions and understood.

"Poke along" indicated that the students were tinkering with the technology to get it working, and when it did, the student describes a feeling of satisfaction. However, the unfamiliarity in this situation made it difficult for this student to use the new knowledge in the project.

One student related to the fact that the sound and the digital interactive aspects of the course did not come to life when visiting sound artists studios and installations in the course; it was just "boring". But at a museum visit there was possibility to understand the new unfamiliar situation from the familiarity with the exhibition context.

> Over the weekend I was at the Technical Museum with the family, where there was a bed that was yawning and snoring. This gave me more a sense of how sound can be used in exhibitions. The bed was appealing and attracted visitors. Many tried to lie down in bed to see if it would happen any more. Unfortunately it did not. It had been possible to use simple sensors that react when someone lay in bed. It had worked to split the audio to yawn, played to attract visitors and snoring when someone tried to go to bed. [...] Sound in information design feels like it should have a clear thought to help the viewer to understand the design. Here lies the importance of information and the ability for the visitor to take part of it.

In the description it seems like the museum context gave an understanding of how the unknown coding could be used when embodied in an exhibition, and that was in similarity with almost all the refection stories. The familiarity with spatial design also seems to make the experience to work with lightning design (a part of the course also new to their repertoire) more unproblematic:

> The light laboration was very interesting and educational, because I never worked with light, it was cool to try hands-on and you learn a lot by getting the try things out instead of just having theory. It's very interesting how the light affects the perception of an object or a person. Previously, I know the using the backlight but had no idea how to use a head light and a lifting light. Light can affect the perception of a room to an incredibly extent which is important for us when designing in the museum. The light can completely change the mood and thus the experience of what we design.

This quotation shows that the student's familiarity with the situation helps to understand the techniques for lighting, and gives ability to reason about detailed concepts of lighting, which were not occurring in the reflections on digital technology.

Reflections/ Lessons learned

The course content is broad and range from a discussion about art versus design, technical aspects of exhibitions, archive excursions, processing programming and practical design work. The students learned enough during the course to present 5 functioning interactive exhibits at a museum, but the repertoire was more enlarged for some students then for others.

The students strived to find examples in their previous repertoire that could serve as an example for the new one, and some seems to support the students ability to enlarge the repertoire and some not. Our findings indicate that it is important to carefully identify *what* in the previous repertoire to connect to. Activated previous experience of immateriality did not help to understand coding whereas previous experience of materiality, of for instance knitting, did. There was a tendency that the things that explained the way code could be touched, felt, and smelled were supportive. One student described code as "unattractive" on the base of its immateriality. The students that recognized the inherent materiality based on familiarity in their previous repertoire, started to understand the relations behind the coding and were able to enter into the coding with more successful results.

The reflection stories show that sometimes the new situation was in a way too different, so the students tended to identify other aspects of the task than the Arduino and Processing coding that were more familiar to them and thus spend time to explore those aspects. Time and effort was instead spent on sketch the whole space, discussing construction and placement of text - a reflection in action. But, for these students the reflection in action for coding, to understand it as a material that could be altered and generate variations that could be tested, did not develop during the course.

We are interested in how to link the unfamiliar to the familiar and recognizing the unfamiliar in the light of the familiar. This is where the learning takes place and the repertoire can be enlarged. The strengths in the course are that the some students enlarged their repertoire. One lesson learned is to introduce the task more clearly in advance and in that do a tighter connection to the familiar of the students' previous repertoire. The challenge is to find ways to relate to their previous repertoire when introducing Arduino, maybe by metaphors or relating to how they think of material in their previous education. Another possibility to try out is to design the course in a way that give the students more time to experiment and test programming and one way could be to in fact reduce the familiar elements in the course the use of light, texts etc. but still relate to them when introducing Arduino.

Future work

The future work is first to continue the analysis of the material. We have for instance left out the theory of social constructivism in this paper. Second, with the findings we aim develop the education further. For instance in information design we will strive to introduce the Arduino and Processing programming more in line with the students current repertoire. Furthermore, we will also seek ways to improve the education in computer science in the basic programming courses. Third, we will explore the relation between tangible and intangible experience of interactive museum artifacts, from the designer's experience of the design process, the designer's intended experience for the museum visitor, the museum visitor's experience of the artifact, and museum visitor's experience as designer.

References

[1] Buechley, L. Eisenberg, M., Catchen, J. and Crockett, A. (2008). "The LilyPad Arduino: using computational textiles to investigate engagement, aesthetics, and diversity in computer science education." *Proc. CHI '08*, pp. 423-432.

[2] Fernaeus, Y. Vallgårda, A. (2014). "Ajna: negotiating forms in the making of a musical cabinet." *Proc. DIS '14*, pp. 915-924.

[3] Gibb, A. (2010) "New Media Art, Design, and the Arduino Microcontroller: A Malleable Tool" Master thesis, Pratt Institue.

[4] Hatala, M., Kalantari, L., Wakkary, R., and Newby, K.(2004) "Ontology and rule based retrieval of sound objects in augmented audio reality system for museum visitors" *Proc. SAC '04*

[5] Hornecker, E., and Stifter, M., (2006) "Learning from interactive museum installations about interaction design for public settings" *Proc. 18th Australia conf. on CHI: Design: Activities, Artefacts and Environments*

[6] Kakarountas, A.; Dragoumanos, S.; Kakarountas, K., "Extending visitor's reality at museums," *Proc. IISA 2014*, pp.196.

[7] Licht, A. (2009). "Sound Art: Origins, development and ambiguities." Organised Sound, 14, pp 3-10.

[8] Lindell, R. (2014) Crafting interaction: "The epistemology of modern programming." Personal and Ubiquitous Computing Volume 18, Issue 3, pp 613-24

[9] Robles, E, Wiberg; M (2011). "From materials to materiality: thinking of computation from within an Icehotel". *ACM Interactions 18*, pp. 32-37.

[10] Rogers, Y. (2011). "Interaction design gone wild: striving for wild theory". *ACM Interactions 18*, pp. 58-62.

[11] Schön, D.A. (1983). The reflective practitioner: how professionals think in action. New York: Basic Books.

[12] Schön, D.A. 1983, p. 138

Tangible Interactive Ambient Display Prototypes to Support Learning Scenarios

Dirk Börner
Valkenburgerweg 177
6419 AT Heerlen
The Netherlands
dirk.boerner@ou.nl

Bernardo Tabuenca
Valkenburgerweg 177
6419 AT Heerlen
The Netherlands
bernardo.tabuenca@ou.nl

Jeroen Storm
Valkenburgerweg 177
6419 AT Heerlen
The Netherlands
jeroen.storm@ou.nl

Sven Happe
MD.H Mediadesign Hochschule
Werdener Straße 4
40227 Düsseldorf, Germany
s.happe@mediadesign-fh.de

Marcus Specht
Valkenburgerweg 177
6419 AT Heerlen
The Netherlands
marcus.specht@ou.nl

TEI '15, Jan 16-19 2015, Stanford, CA, USA
ACM 978-1-4503-3305-4/15/01.
http://dx.doi.org/10.1145/2677199.2687908

Abstract
This paper describes the research and development of tangible interactive ambient display prototypes to support learning scenarios. Therefore a prototypical system design called the *Feedback Cube* is presented. The prototypes combine motion sensors, visual and auditive actuators, as well as wireless communication capabilities in a cubic layout. An initial formative study underpins the prototypes' potential to facilitate interaction and/or indicate feedback. Based on the presented results possible applications scenarios in a learning context are outlined.

Author Keywords
Tangible interaction; prototyping; design; research; development; feedback; sensors; actuators

ACM Classification Keywords
H.5.m. Information interfaces and presentation (e.g., HCI): Miscellaneous.

Introduction
Following similar principles, "*tangible bits*" by Ishii and Ullmer [6] and "*ambient displays*" by Wisneski et al. [10] both paved the way for embodied interaction. Tangible interfaces are considered as more natural and intuitive than traditional types of interfaces [4]. Ambient systems are subtle and non-intrusive means

for interfacing people with peripheral information. With all these characteristics in mind, both concepts offer great potential to support learning scenarios in various ways. Also related research work in this domain supports that. A review on tangibles for learning by O'Malley and Fraser [7] concluded that tangibles bring physical activity and active manipulation to the forefront of learning, i.e. they reduce the learners' cognitive load in order to enable learners to allocate the resources relevant for the task. With similar conclusions Börner et al. [3] reviewed ambient displays for learning and highlighted their potential to support learning implicitly by raising, enhancing, or supporting awareness, changing behavior, giving feedback, providing assistance and guidance, or just by presenting information.

The presented research and development in this paper aims to utilize both embodied interaction principles to support learning scenarios. With the underlying idea to combine both approaches in a flexible and easy-to-use system, the main focus lies on the exploration and formative evaluation of a respective prototypical system design called the *Feedback Cube*.

Prototypical System Design

To study the support of learning scenarios with tangible interfaces and ambient displays, respective prototypes were developed. The design process followed a system design approach, i.e. putting the actual system in the center of the process and arranging a set of components to create the desired design solution [8]. For the envisioned system, the ability to detect motion, provide visual and auditive cues, and communicate wirelessly were considered as most important. Based on these criteria, the components were chosen and assembled. Instead of using another existing system this offered the possibility and flexibility to change and customize the prototypical design at any time.

Hardware Platform

For the prototypical system design a cubic shape was chosen. As solid three-dimensional objects, cubes represent familiar physical structures that can be utilized for tangible manipulation, spatial interaction, or expressive representation as characterized in Hornecker and Buur's framework of tangible interaction [5].

The exterior of the cube prototypes was made from high-density fiberboard and semi-transparent Plexiglas, whereas five sides of the cube are opaque and only the top is semi-transparent. The interior comprises a set of various sensor, actuator, and communication components as well as the necessary hardware to operate them. The cubes have an edge length of 100mm, so that all components fit in, while still ensuring a reasonable size for tangible interaction. The hardware operating the prototypes is based on the open-source electronics platform Arduino[1]. The main components are an Arduino Uno microcontroller board, an Arduino WiFi/Wireless SD shield, and a TinkerKit[2] Sensor shield. The wireless shield enables the microcontroller to connect and communicate wirelessly either via wireless or mesh networks. The integrated micro-SD card slot can be used to read and store files. The sensor shield provides an easy-to-use hub to connect sensor and actuator components directly to the microcontroller. All hardware components can be

1 http://www.arduino.cc
2 http://www.tinkerkit.com

powered either by a built-in rechargeable battery or tethered via the integrated USB interface.

Sensors And Actuators
The hardware platform is enhanced with various sensor and actuator components. The sensors are used to detect changes in the environment, providing input to the prototypical system. The actuators are used to act upon the detected changes, providing a system output.

As sensor components the prototypes include a TinkerKit Accelerometer, Gyroscope, and Hall sensor. The three-axis accelerometer measures acceleration and can be used to detect movement. The two-axis gyroscope measures orientation and can be used to detect movement and rotation. The measured output of the accelerometer and the gyroscope were combined to emulate an inertial measurement unit. This allows more accurate measurement of the prototypes' inclination relative to the ground. Finally the hall sensor measures changes in the surrounding magnetic field, which can be used for instance to calculate the distance to a nearby magnet.

As visual actuator the prototypes include an Adafruit[3] NeoPixel ring mounted below the semi-transparent side of the cube. The ring consists of 16 RGB LEDs that can be individually addressed via their built-in microcontroller. Using the available Arduino library the color and brightness of each LED can be controlled. Furthermore the prototypes include a 12-Watt mini speaker that can be used as auditive actuator.

3 http://www.adafruit.com

System Characteristics

The specified form factor, used hardware platform, and chosen sensor and actuator components enable different possibilities to use the *Feedback Cubes*. In general the prototypes can either facilitate some kind of interaction with users or objects (interaction facilitator), indicate feedback information to users or the immediate surrounding (feedback indicator), or do both at the same time.

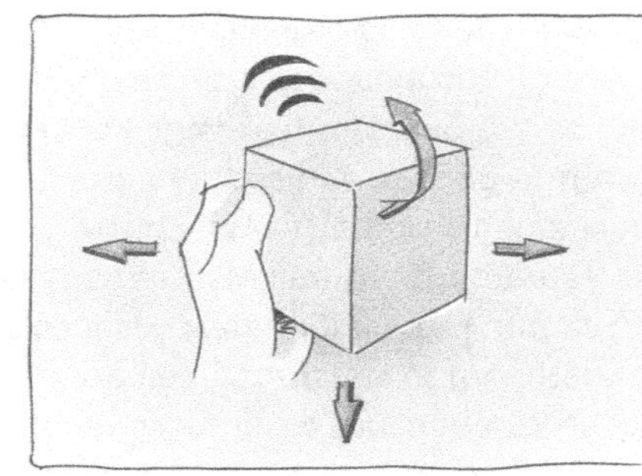

Figure 1. Interaction facilitator concept.

Interaction Facilitator
The interaction facilitator concept as illustrated in Figure 1 is characterized by the prototypes' sensor components. The used accelerometer and gyroscope are able to detect movement on the x-, y-, and z-axis and rotation on the x-, and y-axis (five degrees of freedom). More specifically moving the prototype along the axes, i.e. forward, backward, left, right, up, and down, as well as rotating the prototype along the axes, i.e. rolling and tilting, can be detected. The used hall sensor is able to detect changes in the surrounding magnetic field and thus the presence of magnetic objects, e.g. other prototypes can be detected. Other

means of facilitating interaction are the communication components. The prototypes have built-in serial communication facilities that can be used, e.g. via the available USB-to-serial converter. Furthermore the used WiFi shield enables the prototypes to take client and/or server roles for communication within wireless networks. Alternatively the used wireless shield enables the prototypes to support point-to-point, point-to-multipoint, and peer-to-peer mesh network topologies with other prototypes.

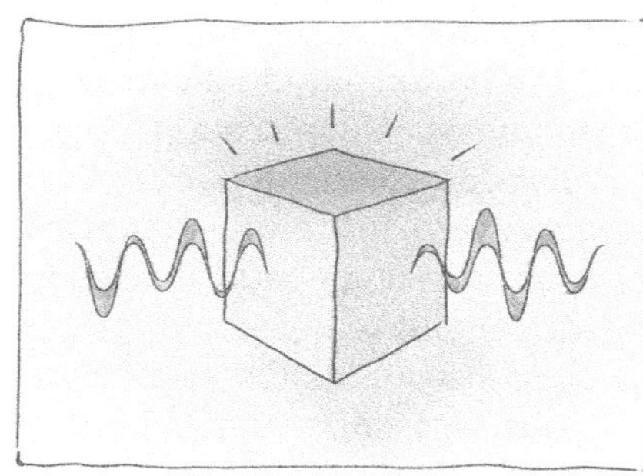

Figure 2. Feedback indicator concept.

Feedback Indicator
The feedback indicator concept as illustrated in Figure 2 is characterized by the prototypes' actuator components. The used LEDs are capable of displaying the full RGB color space with 16777216 colors at 256 brightness levels. All 16 RGB LEDs on the ring can be controlled individually, which allows programming various visual patterns and effects, such as fading, blinking, or color transitions. The used mini speaker can produce sounds in response to the electrical signal input delivered by the microcontroller.
Programmatically manipulating the signal input allows creating various audio patterns and effects, such as playing single tones, complex melodies, or even encoded audio files. When using the integrated storage capabilities, it is also possible to create an accessible music and sound effect library.

Formative Study

To explore usability issues of the *Feedback Cubes* a formative study was conducted with a group of 8 participants. All participants were experts in the field of learning sciences with either a technical or educational background. In a first round, after introducing the general idea and the basic functionality of the prototypes, the characteristics of the interaction facilitator concept were highlighted and each participant had the chance to examine the prototypes and test the respective functionality. The participants were then asked to fill in an all-positive version of the System Usability Scale (SUS) [9], focusing their ratings solely on the interaction facilitator concept. In a second round the procedure was repeated once again for the feedback indicator concept.

The interaction facilitator concept received a mean score of 71.9 (SD = 10.3). The feedback indicator concept received a mean score of 69.1 (SD = 15.8). When comparing both scores to other hardware systems [1], the interaction facilitator concept scored higher than 52.3% of the other systems with a "C" grade at an acceptable level, which can be described as "Good". The feedback indicator concept scored higher than 41.6% of the other systems with a "D" grade at a marginal level, which can be described as "Ok". The results show above average ratings for both concepts with room for further improvements. The interaction facilitator concept scored higher than the feedback indicator concept. The participants stated that the tangible interaction is much more intuitive, while the ambient display principle requires an additional mapping to make sense of the provided information. It can be assumed that this changes once the mapping is clearly defined.

After evaluating the perceived usability of the single concepts, the whole group was asked to capture their general impressions about the prototypes using a modified electronic version of the Product Reaction Cards originally developed by Benedek and Miner [2]. The group was asked to agree on 6 cards with words that described their experience with the prototypes best and comment on their selection. The group agreed on the following selection of words: *engaging*, *straight forward*, *customizable*, *responsive*, *fragile*, and *familiar*. The group commented that the prototypes are *familiar* in a sense that form and function are evident without creating additional obstacles or distraction. However, the prototypes' design was also characterized as *fragile* and several improvements were suggested to make it more robust. Besides that, the prototypes were characterized as *engaging* due to the fact that specific user inter- and reactions are encouraged. The interactive and especially the indicator functions were characterized as *straight forward* and *responsive* with the potential to implement feedback and direct interaction mechanisms. The group also commented that the prototypes are *customizable* in a sense that various individual and collaborative scenarios could be supported.

Discussion And Conclusions

Following the formative study the participants were asked to think about and discuss specific learning scenarios that could be supported. This discussion, the given system characteristics, as well as the formative results, helped to outline the following application scenarios. Based on the introduced interaction facilitator concept the *Feedback Cubes* could for instance support memorization tasks by enabling users to easily relate visual and spatial information. Under the assumption that using the tangible interactive prototypes facilitates retention, the prototypes would augment the task. The users would receive visual instructions for a randomized sequence of moves that they have to repeat with the prototypes. After each correct repetition one more random move could be added to the sequence. In a collaborative group setting the interaction capabilities of the prototypes could also be used to moderate an ongoing discussion session, e.g. if a common agreement is needed at the end of the session. Each opposing party would receive a *Feedback Cube* and could confirm or decline arguments by tilting the prototype left and right. Whenever the parties agree on the same argument the prototypes should be moved closer to each other, reaching the final agreement when both prototypes touch each other.

Other application scenarios based on the feedback indicator concept could support the users' individual or group performance by increasing the awareness on certain indicators. The assumption would be that this increased awareness triggers reflection and eventually provokes users to adapt their behavior accordingly. In this context the ambient display functionality of the prototypes would be used to provide this feedback. In a collaborative setting with several groups, each group could receive one *Feedback Cube* that indicates for instance the (externally measured) general speech volume within the group. Whenever the volume gets too loud (and thus prevents the exchange of arguments in the discussion) the prototype makes the group aware of that through visual or auditive feedback. In a similar manner the prototypes could also be used as personal peripheral displays. For instance in combination with a time/task management application the *Feedback Cube* could indicate the timing or completion of certain tasks. In combination with an activity tracking application the prototype could provide an overview of individual performance parameters or patterns.

In conclusion the presented system design of tangible interactive ambient display prototypes allows utilizing embodied interaction principles to support learning scenarios. A formative study underpinned the prototypes' potential to facilitate interaction and/or indicate feedback. Especially the interactive capabilities were considered as functional and encouraging, while several improvements were suggested. Finally the gathered insights informed application scenarios of the *Feedback Cubes* in a learning context, which will be implemented as proof of concept for further evaluation in a next step.

Acknowledgments

The presented research and development is partly funded by the METALOGUE project. METALOGUE is a Seventh Framework Programme collaborative project funded by the European Commission under grant agreement number: 611073 (http://www.metalogue.eu).

References

[1] Bangor, A., Kortum, P.T. and Miller, J.T. Determining What Individual SUS Scores Mean: Adding an Adjective Rating Scale. *Journal of Usability Studies 4*, 3 (2009), 114-123.

[2] Benedek, J. and Miner T. Measuring Desirability: New methods for evaluating desirability in a usability lab setting. In *Proceedings of Usability Professionals Association 2003*, UXPA (2002), 8-12.

[3] Börner, D., Kalz, M., and Specht, M. Beyond the channel: A literature review on ambient displays for learning. *Computers & Education 60*, 1 (2013), 426–435.

[4] Dourish, P. *Where the action is: the foundations of embodied interaction*. MIT Press, 2001.

[5] Hornecker, E. and Buur, J. Getting a grip on tangible interaction. In *Proceedings of the ACM SIGCHI Conference on Human Factors in Computing Systems (CHI'06)*, ACM Press (2006), 437–446.

[6] Ishii, H. and Ullmer, B. Tangible bits: towards seamless interfaces between people, bits and atoms. In *Proceedings of the ACM SIGCHI Conference on Human Factors in Computing Systems (CHI'97)*, ACM Press (1997), 234-241.

[7] O'Malley, C. and Fraser, D. S. *Literature Review in Learning with Tangible Technologies*. 2004.

[8] Saffer, D. *Designing for Interaction: Creating Innovative Applications and Devices*. New Riders, 2007.

[9] Sauro. J. and Lewis, J. When Designing Usability Questionnaires, Does It Hurt to Be Positive? In *Proceedings of the ACM SIGCHI Conference in Human Factors in Computing Systems (CHI 2011)*, ACM Press (2011), 2215-2224.

[10] Wisneski, C., Ishii, H., Dahley, A., Gorbet, M., Brave, S., Ullmer, B., and Yarin, P. Ambient displays: turning architectural space into an interface between people and digital information. In *Cooperative buildings: Integrating information, organization, and architecture*, Springer (1998), 22–32

"Tangible Lights": In-Air Gestural Control of Home Lighting

Tor Sørensen
Aarhus University
Åbogade 34
8200 Aarhus N
tors@cs.au.dk

Oskar D. Andersen
Aarhus University
Åbogade 34
8200 Aarhus N
oskarand@cs.au.dk

Timothy Merritt
Aarhus School of Architecture
Nørreport 20
8000 Aarhus C
timothy.merritt@aarch.dk

TEI '15, Jan 16-19 2015, Stanford, CA, USA
ACM 978-1-4503-3305-4/15/01.
http://dx.doi.org/10.1145/2677199.2687909

Abstract
While there has been much focus on tangible lighting interfaces embedded in physical objects and smartphones as remote control, there has not been sufficient attention on how the expressivity of bodily movement can be used when designing interactions with light. Therefore, we investigate interaction with lighting technology beyond the smartphone and physical controllers. We examine the usefulness of the in-air gestural interaction style for lighting control. We bring forward "Tangible Lights", which serves as a novel interface for in-air interaction with lighting, drawing on existing knowledge from the tangible world. Tangible Lights has been subject to initial evaluations.

Author Keywords
Interactive lighting; lighting control; in-air gestures; user interfaces; home customization

ACM Classification Keywords
H.5.2. Information interfaces and presentation (e.g., HCI): User Interfaces.

Introduction
Lighting is a key aspect of the design of interior spaces, which serves functional purposes of illuminating tasks, accentuating the objects and materials in the room, and setting the atmosphere experienced by the occupants. More recently, the commercially available, mul-

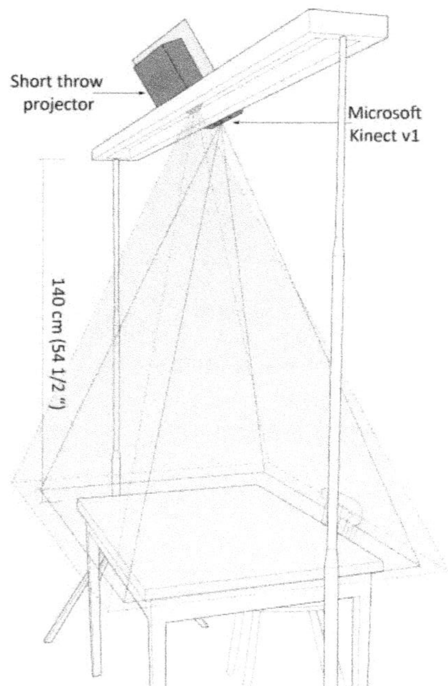

Figure 1. Technical setup

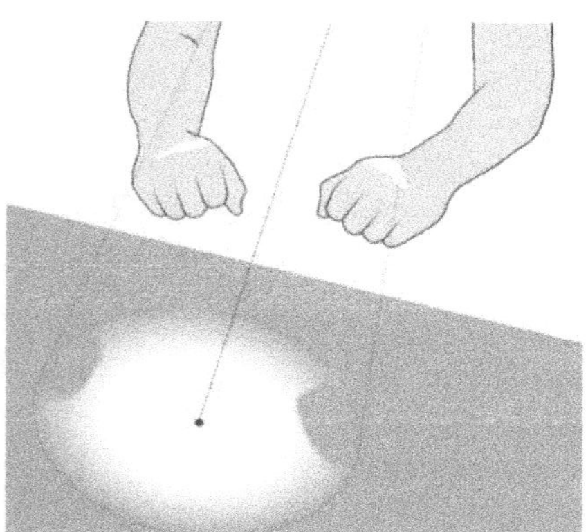

Figure 2. Mapping two hands to a cast light. Light strikes on top of hands and causes shadows

ticolored light emitting diodes (LEDs) have been introduced in the home domain providing new possibilities when using and controlling light. How can technology and interactive lighting enable new customization possibilities of the home and support desirable experiences in daily life? We take a step towards this vision by combining interactive lighting with in-air gestures. As a result we present the "Tangible Lights" platform for in-air gestural lighting control at the dining table. As our work is currently in progress, this paper focuses on the initial aspects of interaction and mapping.

Commercially, we have started to see interconnected smart bulbs for the home, which can be controlled from smartphone apps, e.g. Philips Hue, Samsung Smart Bulb, Stack Alba, and LIFX. We see several practical benefits in utilizing the smartphone as a central platform for interaction, e.g. dynamic interface; 'always' with you; remote access and control without dedicated remote controllers. However, this direction comes with a list of shortcomings: smartphones can be displaced from the user, other residents and guests cannot interact without connecting to the wireless infrastructure, and interacting users are not necessarily situated in the lighting environment they are controlling [7]. Socially, the action of physically switching the lights on/off or adjusting the brightness provides immediate, visible clues to other people in the context.

With the new possibilities of the emerging LED technology come new challenges. In research, this has been recognized by Aliakseyeu et al. [1] who set up a workshop on "Designing Interactive Lighting" at DIS 2012, and by Offermans et al. [8] who explored the initial design space of interactive lighting interfaces, and present important aspects regarding the interaction in a relational model. Researchers have also developed various physical interfaces for lighting control [2, 6, 7, 8].

Focusing on In-Air Gestures

Research has found that interactions relying on bodily movement possess unique interaction qualities in terms of expressivity and supporting the capabilities of the body [4, 5]. In-air gestures as an input style effectively allows for communication of your intentions to other participants through interaction and allows for the possibility of engaging multiple users simultaneously. However, working with in-air gestures also poses challenges, such as the lack of tactile and haptic feedback due to the inherently invisible interface. As with the "live mic" problem in audio, when is the control system listening? Moreover, we find the "segmentation issue", which deals with the temporal length of interactions. When does a gesture start and end? Our work combines the area of interactive light control with the interaction style of in-air gestures. This style of interaction can be seen as radically different from typical smartphone and tangible controllers.

Use Scenario: Dinner with Friends at Home

We created a scenario to illustrate some of the existing practices in the home, which Tangible Lights is envisioned to support. The scenario illustrate the current practice of decorating and setting a table, where considerable effort and thoughts are put into creating the right atmosphere both in terms of ordinary decorations and attention to lighting.

Julia awaits three guests for dinner and starts cooking dinner two hours before. She wants to set the table, and she finds four identical, nice looking plates and cups. She figures she wants to do something extraordinary and brings in colored linen napkins and arranges

Figure 3. Mapping one hand to a cast light. Light strikes on top of the hand and causes a shadow

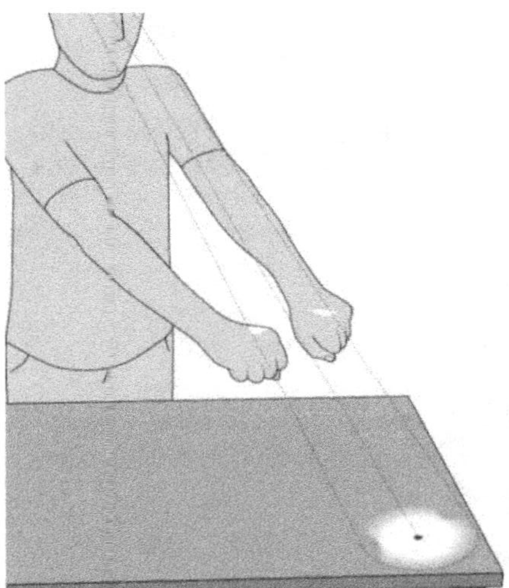

Figure 4. The mapping scheme allows reaching far corners

them evenly on top of the plates. Julia also wants to do something to the lighting to create a sense of coziness. She decides to dim the main light via the dimmer in the wall where it has been set to full brightness due to the darkness outside. Further, she decides to switch on two small lamps near the dark corners of her living room, and brings in two candlelights for the table. As her guests are welcomed they immediately comment on the lovely atmosphere and the detailed table decorations. After the dinner, Julia puts the brightness back up while her guests help her move the dishes to the kitchen. The friends suddenly decide on playing a board game while chit-chatting and having evening coffee. One of the friends notices the now bright lights from above the table, and locates the wall dimmer in order to again fit the relaxed atmosphere.

Tangible Lights

We now present our system called "Tangible Lights" which serves as an interactive lighting platform around the dining table. Tangible Lights enables the user to customize the light setting at the table with precise control through several, individual illuminated regions, which can be manipulated freely in the space above the tabletop. As a result, the position and size of each individual illuminated region can be manipulated through in-air gestures as desired. The name Tangible Lights stems from our intentions of creating an interface where the user feels as if she is holding onto the lights and controlling it at her fingertips. To accommodate this, we seek to draw on her existing knowledge from daily life when grabbing and moving physical objects around. The challenge here is that lights are generally perceived as non-tangible, although they do have an insignificant small physical mass, and the warmth of intense light can be felt on the skin.

Technically, the platform consists of a short-throw projector and a Microsoft Kinect sensor (see Fig. 1). The short-throw projector serves as the light source as it provides an easy and dynamic way to position an arbitrary amount of illuminated regions on the tabletop. The Kinect sensor continuously streams depth maps to the gesture recognition software at 30 frames per second. Our software is an extension of the C# wrapper for the KinectArms project developed for quick mock-ups by Genest et al. [3].

Direct Mapping between Hands and Light

To interact with the lighting in Tangible Lights, we needed a way to map the hands to the cast light. As it is our intention to design for the experience of tangibility of manipulating cast lights, we have sought inspiration in the domain of tangible user interfaces (TUI). We have applied a direct mapping scheme, which refers to the design of interfaces, particularly in the TUI domain, where input and output is tightly coupled in space.

For our design of the direct mapping, a cast light is enabled for interaction when hands interfere the projected light beam. This looks different in the case of one or two hands as seen in Fig. 2-3. As a natural consequence of using one global light source (i.e. the projector), the center of the cast light is occluded by the hand creating a shadow on the tabletop (also seen in Fig. 2-3). This provides two concurrent means of visual feedback for the person interacting to visually make contact with and maneuver a lit region around the table.

As a result of our designed mapping, it is possible to reach far corners of larger tables, since the light cast on the tabletop is positioned with an offset to the interacting hand(s) as seen in Fig. 4.

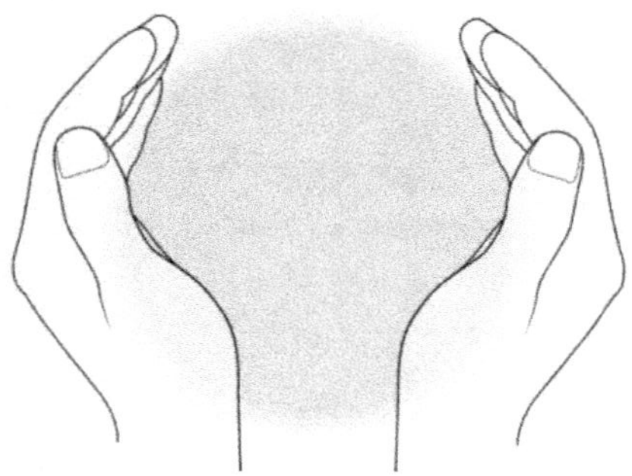

Figure 5. Spawning a new light by holding hands in a vertical position

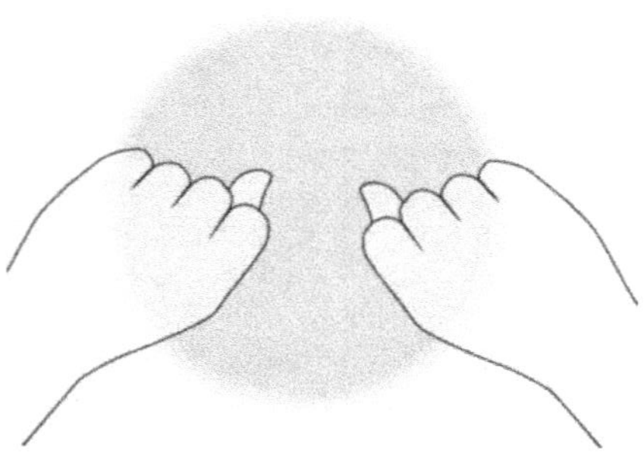

Figure 6. Grabbing a cast light by closing the hands near its perimeter

Figure 7. Moving a cast light by moving the hands

Designing the Interactions

The interactions designed provide a set of interconnected actions for manipulating the light setting. Actions include spawning, selecting, deselecting, moving, scaling, and removing lights. To simplify the interactions, we draw inspiration from known daily life actions such as grabbing, holding onto a plate or cup. We have explored different interaction alternatives requiring both one and two hands, as the number of hands is found to possess different qualities, which will be explained in the following. On-going evaluations have helped shape the interactions to their current form as presented here.

Spawn gesture

It is possible to create a new illuminated region by holding two hands in a vertical position as if holding onto a physical bowl (Fig. 5). This hints that the lights can be physically contained within the circle enclosed by the hands.

Grab and move gestures

A cast light is selected with two hands by "grabbing the light" near its perimeter as if it was a physical steering wheel (Fig. 6). This interaction, of course, yields no physical feedback as when grabbing an actual steering wheel. The grab gesture can also be performed with one hand, as two hands could yield a problem when carrying objects such as dishes, plates and cup. In use, the one-handed grab often allows for quicker positioning than the two-handed grab. The one-handed grab is initiated near the center of the cast light on the table and can be viewed in Fig. 3. Once grabbed, the newly spawned and existing cast lights can be moved according to the position of the hands in a 2D plane above the tabletop (Fig. 7).

Scale gesture

When selected, cast lights can be scaled up and down in size. The user can resize the lights to highlight physical objects on the table, e.g. dishes, cups, plates, plants etc. When interacting with two hands it might seem natural to just move the hands away from each other (Fig. 8), building on experience from the real world. Here, flexible objects such as bags, rubber bands, fabric, etc. can be expanded by grabbing and pulling hands in opposite directions. For scaling with one hand we seek inspiration in the behavior of a flashlight. Moving it closer or further from a surface results in a smaller or larger cast light, respectively (Fig. 11).

Release gesture

In Tangible Lights, releasing (i.e. unselecting) an already grabbed light is implemented as the reverse grab gesture. In other words, when not intending to manipulate a cast light anymore, the person extends her fingers. The final hand posture for two-handed interaction can be seen in Fig. 9.

Remove gesture

Lastly, to remove a cast light completely from the table, the light is pressed (squeezed) together with two hands or reduced in size with one hand moved very close to the table. Essentially, this is the scale gestures being used to make the light continuously smaller until it disappears (Fig. 10).

Initial Evaluation Results

Based on our current lab and contextual evaluations with 21 people, we have categorized our initial findings.

Tangibility of Cast Lights

As our set of gestures is conceptualized based on tangible phenomena, we want to understand how people

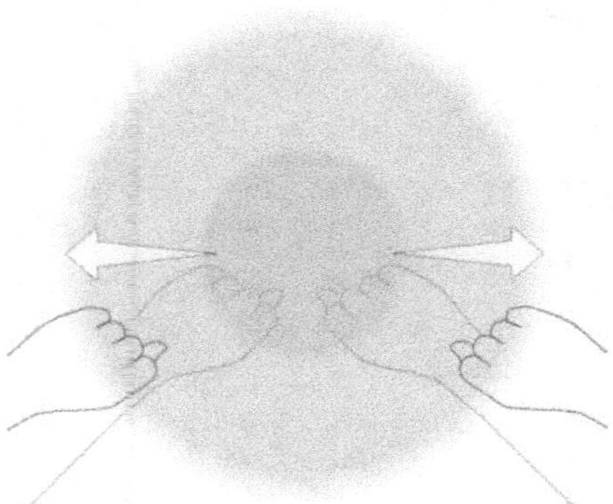

Figure 8. Scaling of a cast light by pulling in both directions

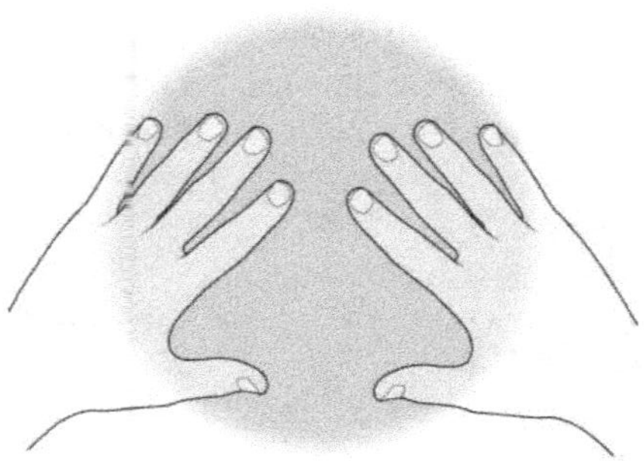

Figure 9. Releasing a grab by extending the fingers (reverse grab gesture)

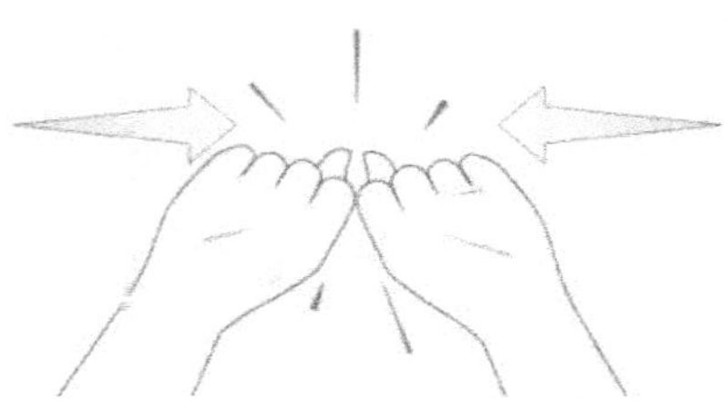

Figure 10. Removing a cast light from the table by squeezing it together

feel when using them, and how they learned and understood the suggested tangible qualities. Thus far, we have mainly had people trying different gesture variations when selecting and have asked them to reflect upon the differences. Our current evaluations suggest that the grab and release gestures are generally an accepted and straightforward way of selecting and deselecting a cast light. As one person explained *"it [grabbing the lights] just came natural to me... I had totally forgotten about last time"*. For him, grabbing was an unconscious action.

Contextual Implications

An important part of our evaluation is to reflect upon the context for which our design is intended. A first impression is that users are able to start highlighting objects on the table as soon as the grabbing concept is explained. During contextual evaluations, one of the house residents stated, *"I can see this being used in practice, now when we do all this other stuff [setting the table with napkins and candles]"*. This category is subject to further contextual evaluations.

Direct Mapping and Alignment

The alignment of hand and cast light was, for many people, an intuitive way of selecting light, and was expressed by one participant, *"it is easy to just move my hand in [above the table] and, like, interfere with the light beam"*. However, when not instructed or demonstrated, we also observed a tendency to reach out directly above the cast light trying to select a light (exemplified with one hand in Fig. 12). Following a quick how-to demonstration, people were able to adapt to our intended mapping. It would be interesting to collect more detailed information on how the two mapping alternatives are understood.

Although we intended to provide a smooth interaction experience, we encountered some technical challenges, which affected the perceived mapping. When observing interaction sessions, the largest technical breakdown occurred when people continuously reached out for a specific cast light, but did not get in contact with it. This was caused by system instabilities of either not recognizing the hand, the gesture, or by the mapping being misaligned in the software. Beyond technical improvements, the question is, how can we help the user to understand the mapping?

Gestures and Functionality

Once shown or told how to select and move lights, people were able to independently explore the scaling functionality by moving the hands apart (or up and down if one hand). Scaling actions were almost always performed during the very first interaction and can arguably be contributed to the system behavior of being reactive to changing distances between hands (or height if one hand).

When interacting, the light is visible on the hands. Once selected, the instantaneous visual feedback of the cast light moving according to hand movement provided an easy way for people to control the light around the table. However, approaching the table, new users do not know that it is possible to reach out for lights with the hands unless the functionality is explained. In the near future we will explore how the use of different feedforward techniques [9] can help to communicate the functionalities and provide suggestions for use. We intend to explore a number of iterations focused on how subtle behavior such as movement and pulsation of cast lights can invite interaction.

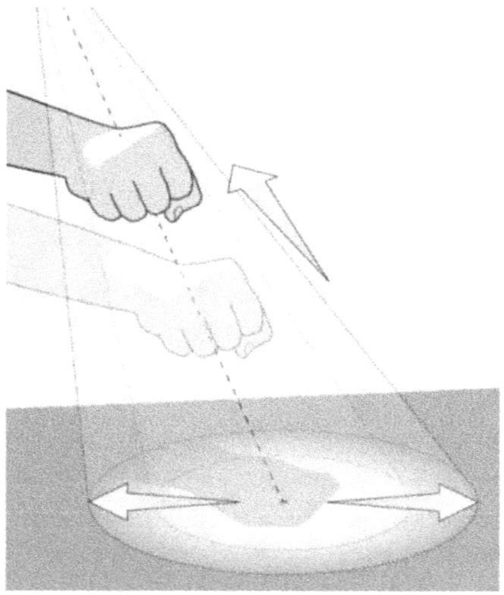

Figure 11. One hand scaling of a cast light by varying the height of the hand

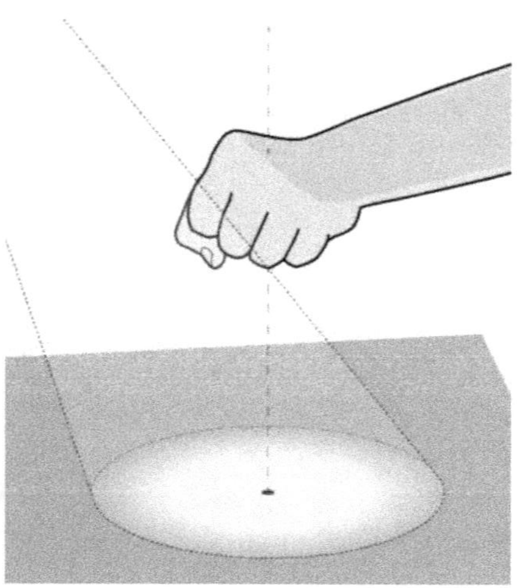

Figure 12. We observed a tendency to grab lights directly above the cast light instead of interfering the light beam

Discussion and Future Work

Tangible Lights requires a relatively high amount of interaction effort. By integrating gestures for color and brightness control, the interaction effort is intensified. In contrast, it is interesting to explore use cases where the user is not likely to put in much effort beyond a focus on satisfying the functional needs, e.g. study or office work, where the lighting need is task-oriented rather than customization.

Tangible Lights is designed as individual, manipulatable spotlights inspired by the tangible interaction paradigm. To keep this effect, it is necessary to perceive the edges of a cast light. As the living environment often uses diffused lighting, we have sought to make each light appear more natural by adjusting the projector by softening the focus adjustment and applying a gradient to the edges of the cast light. As a result, we found a balance between blurring the edges and yet still support the recognition of individual spots.

Through evaluations we have observed several users adding elements of playfulness, such as sliding or "throwing" cast lights around the table or by other means adding some "life" to the lights. We agree that this might allow for delightful experiences. Thus, in the near future we wish to explore how implementing subtle behaviors might add to the interaction experience. Further, we will explore the social dimension of the interface, as current evaluations have already hinted at various opportunities to support interesting and playful experiences.

Lastly, we see a potential in exploring how controlling the lights via gestures at the table can be integrated with the existing home lighting. This includes outlining how gestures performed above the tabletop can affect other areas of the home, which arguably accounts for a large part of setting an atmosphere. Moving the in-air control away from the table and into other areas of the home provides yet another path for further exploration.

References

[1] Aliakseyeu, D., Meerbeek, B., Mason, J., Essen, H.A. van, Offermans, S.A.M., Wiethoff, A.J., Streitz, N., and Lucero, A. Designing interactive lighting. In *Proc. DIS 2012*, ACM Press (2012), 801-802.

[2] Cheng, B., Kim, M., Lin, H., Fung, S., Bush, Z., and Seo, J.H. Tessella: interactive origami light. In *Proc. TEI 2012*, Stephen N. Spencer (Ed.), ACM Press (2012), 317-318.

[3] Genest, A.M., Gutwin, C., Tang, A., Kalyn, M., and Ivkovic, Z. Kinectarms: A toolkit for capturing and displaying arm embodiments in distributed tabletop groupware. In *Proc. CSCW 2013*, ACM Press (2013), 157–166.

[4] Jacob, R.J.K., Girouard, A., Hirshfield, L.M., Horn, M.S., Shaer, O., Solovey, E.T, and Zigelbaum, J. Reality-based interaction: a framework for post-WIMP inter-faces. In *Proc. CHI 2008*, ACM Press (2008), 201-210.

[5] Leithinger, D., Lakatos, D., DeVincenzi, A., Blackshaw, M., and Ishii, H. Direct and gestural interaction with relief: a 2.5D shape display. In *Proc. UIST 2011*, ACM Press (2011), 541-548.

[6] Magielse R. and Offermans, S.A.M. Future Lighting Systems. *Ext. Abstracts CHI 2013*, ACM Press (2013), 2853-2854.

[7] Magielse, R., Hengeveld, B.J., and Frens, J.W. Designing a light controller for a multi-user lighting environment. In *Proc. IASDR 2013*.

[8] Offermans, S.A.M., Essen, H.A. van, Eggen, J.H. User interaction with everyday lighting systems. In *Personal and Ubiquitous Computing*, (2014).

[9] Wensveen, S.A.G., Djajadiningrat, J.P., and Overbeeke, C.J. Interaction frogger: A design framework to couple action and function through feedback and feedforward. In *Proc. DIS 2004*, ACM Press (2004), 177–184.

i.Ge: Exploring New Game Interaction Metaphors with Interactive Projection

Patrick Oswald
University of Applied
Sciences Potsdam
14469 Potsdam, Germany
patrick.oswald@fh-potsdam.de

Reto Wettach
University of Applied
Sciences Potsdam
14469 Potsdam, Germany
wettach@fh-potsdam.de

Jordi Tost
University of Applied
Sciences Potsdam
14469 Potsdam, Germany
jordi.tost.val@fh-potsdam.de

TEI '15, Jan 16-19 2015, Stanford, CA, USA
ACM 978-1-4503-3305-4/15/01.
http://dx.doi.org/10.1145/2677199.2687910

Abstract
Video games are traditionally presented and visualized on a screen (flat, portable, touch sensitive or projected) and are mostly restricted by predefined scenarios and character movements. Although the ways in which we interact with games have improved over recent years, the interaction is still limited to their functions and game presets and still happens inside the screen. In this paper we explore new interaction paradigms using *i.Ge* [4], a video game level editor that allows users to interact with their own environment to create game content with every-day physical objects in real time. At this stage, *i.Ge* explores new ways to interact with the real world by augmenting it with interactive projections, reducing the gap between the real and the digital world in a spatial augmented reality. We also propose other novel naturalistic approaches to create and interact with digital content that involve embodiment and more use of depth.

Author Keywords
Mixed Reality; Spatial Augmented Reality; HCI; Tangible Interaction; Interactive Projection; Game Design

ACM Classification Keywords
H.5.2 Information interfaces and presentation: User Interfaces - Input devices and strategies, Interaction styles; H.5.1 Information interfaces and presentation: Multimedia Information Systems - Artificial, augmented, and virtual realities

Introduction
Traditionally, video games are screen-bound. Although the ways in which people interact with video games have evolved over recent years (Wii-Remote, Kinect, etc.), the digital world we are interacting with is still confined to the screen and limited to predefined scenarios.

We propose to bring the game out of the screen into the user's daily surrounding physical environment by detecting and mixing it with the virtual world she or he is playing in. We do this in order to close the gap between the real and digital world combining both into one single spatial augmented reality and thereby enhancing the interactive gaming experience. Furthermore, we want to encourage and enhance gamers' creativity by making it possible to create level content with almost any physical object - using them directly as level elements or creating augmented virtual content with them.

Finally, our approach tries to inspire entirely new collaborative and challenging multiplayer game concepts and physical-virtual game mechanics. Moreover, we believe that the techniques and observations presented in this paper are relevant not only for the game design field, but also for the exploration of new more naturalistic human-computer interactions.

Related Work
In the field of human-computer interaction, there have been some projects that explored game design and interaction in a spatial augmented reality, some using the real environment as a canvas for the game in a static way or using the projector as interaction tool. *Build Your World and Play In It* [1] uses a pre-built wooden block construction as projection surface and an IR stylus to create digital content, where creating and playing are separated in two independent interaction modes. In this paper we will present solutions that involve digital content creation directly with real world objects.

Twinkle [7] is a gaming interface for interacting with an arbitrary physical flat surface using a handheld projector. The projected character can interact with non-white physical objects in the viewport of the camera attached to the projector. It also uses the objects' color to cause different reactions on the game character when colliding with them. *MotionBeam* [5] explored gesturing with the handheld projector itself, proposing a wide range of interaction possibilities.

Most of these projects perform a flat detection of the real world and use color information to affect digital content or target additional one. *i.Ge* [4] presents a real-time video game level editor using every-day objects to construct a two dimensional playground (level) for a Jump'n'Run game detecting some depth information like hands and color information to target different digital content depending on its color.

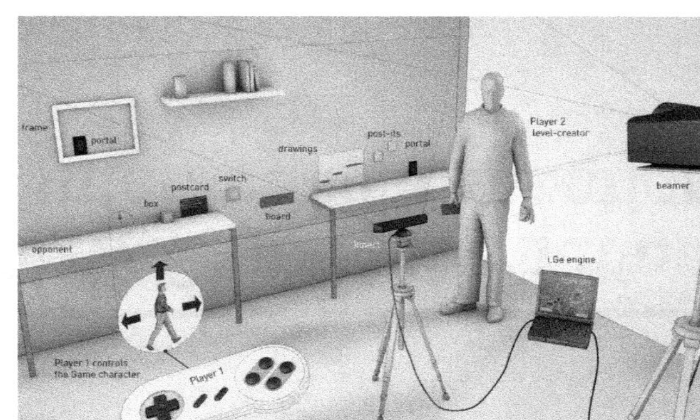

Figure 1. illustrated *i.Ge* Set-up

We see a whole new range of possibilities to develop meaningful and fun interactions and applications that involve a greater use of depth and a more realistic mixture between the real and digital worlds. Some of these unexplored metaphors and possibilities are explained and exemplified in this paper.

i.Ge System Principles

i.Ge is an interactive video game engine that allows users to interact and play with their own environment in real time. As illustrated in Figure 1, all the interaction takes place inside the room, which is turned into the game scenario, mixing it with the virtual game content, mediated through a Microsoft Kinect and a projector. For our demo scenario, we chose a simple Jump'n'Run and an ordinary game pad, both widely known by users and the gaming community, in order to focus the players attention and learning process on the novel interaction paradigms and not on how to play the game.

Spatial Augmented Reality (SAR), the technique of merging the real world with projected images (Figure 2), presents a solution to this problem, not only by taking the game outside of the screen, but also by inspiring novel interaction techniques.

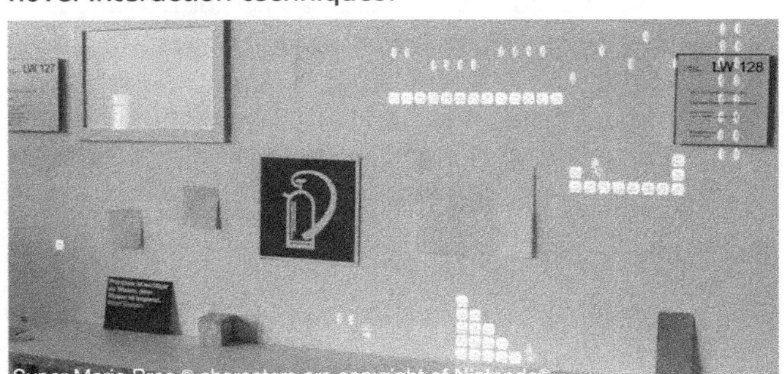

Figure 2. real *i.Ge* scenario

Figure 3. Creating level content with real physical objects

At this stage, *i.Ge* supports interactive level creation with physical objects (Figure 3). Moreover, the game character can also interact with other digital elements like opponents, projectiles or bonus objects. They can be generated by detecting some characteristics of the attached physical objects, for example, their position and color. In our demo, when a new green object (or a sketched one) with a given proportion (height greater than width) is detected, a carnivorous plant is placed above it Figure 4. If there are another tubes in the stage, they will also be detected as teleportation tubes and will teleport our character from one tube to the other, for example to reach the content inside a frame (Figure 2).

Figure 4. Creating mixed content

As seen, game level content can be:

- *Physical:* elements attached to or sketched in the scene and recognized as game content like platforms or obstacles (Figure 3).
- *Digital:* common video game content like items, coins, enemies, moving platforms, projectiles, etc.
- *Mixed:* a digitally augmented physical object or digital content can be created by the placement of a given object depending on its proportion and color (Figure 4).

Spatial Augmented Reality also presents some limitations and thus challenges:

- The dynamic creation and edition of digital content.
- The mixture between the 3D elements of the real world with the 2D flat elements of the digital one.

Implementation

The current set-up includes a Microsoft Kinect (640x480px up to 30 fps) to scan the environment, a common projector, and a game controller. For the stage detection, the software side implements computer vision algorithms using Processing and the OpenCV library [3]. The game level elements are detected using a contour detection algorithm over the RGB channel provided by the Kinect, as long as they are not too small (because of the video source resolution) and rich in contrast. The game engine extracts their bounding boxes (position and size) and applies them physical properties in order to detect collisions between them and the game character or other projected digital content. *i.Ge* also performs a color detection algorithm for each real object in order to assign them different behaviors or generate digital content depending on their color. To avoid game creators from obstructing the viewport and being detected as level elements, we also use the depth camera to ignore their boundaries. Since the performance requirements are increasing with the new detection algorithms, the software side is currently being ported to openFrameworks (C++) for a better performance on real-time detection.

Limitations and Further Work

The dynamic creation and manipulation of digital content is one of the challenges of Spatial Augmented Reality or interactive projection. In the first prototype, our system presented a limitation concerning the use of digital content. Bonus elements (e.g. coins) or enemies were hard-coded and could not be created dynamically when the game started. Further options to create digital content are: color detection, shape recognition and marker detection.

Another challenge is the mixture between the 3D elements of the real world with the flat 2D elements of the digital one in terms of interaction. In the first prototype, our system was doing an almost flat object and scene detection and the game character could only move in the X and Y coordinates. Implementing a greater use of depth and considering the third dimension will open a wider range of interaction possibilities. For example, the user could push the digital character to walk through in front of a real object (for example, a

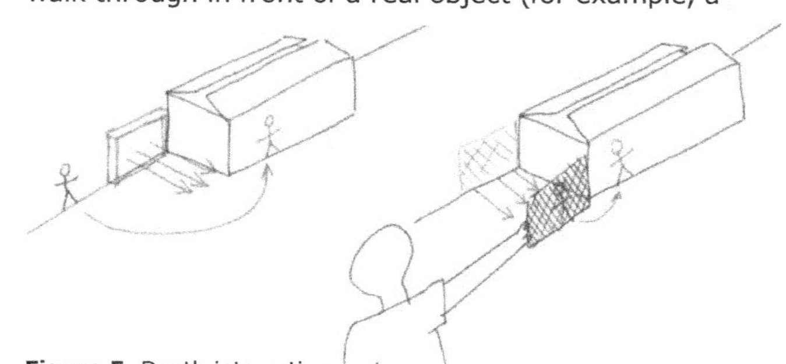

Figure 5. Depth interaction

box), bringing it with the hand or a card to the front (Figure 5). The same concept could be used for another scenario: the character needs to reach an object that changes its position in the Z axis (Figure 6).

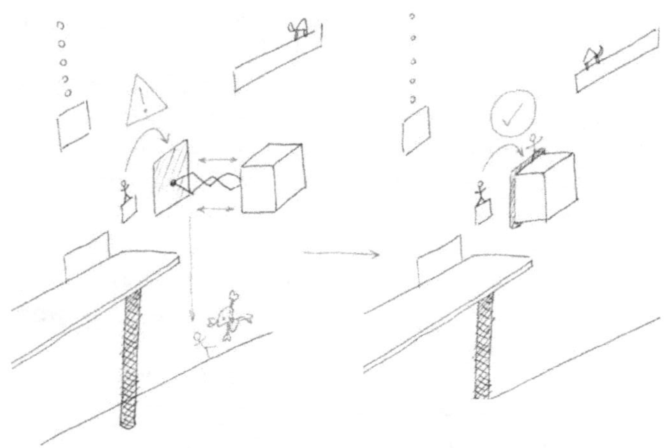

Figure 6. Depth interaction

Another potentially interesting area for further exploration is to increase the use of body interaction. At this stage, *i.Ge* concentrates on the use of the real environment to create game level content and the player uses a game pad for interacting with the level content. Nevertheless, *i.Ge* could also increase the use of body interaction by observing real life interactions to create a more naturalistic gameplay experience (Figure 7 illustrates an example). With it, we want to explore new concepts to extend *i.Ge*, but also to inspire new interaction metaphors for others working in this field.

As future work, we plan to extend *i.Ge* to enable more interaction possibilities and game concepts. To achieve this we plan to a) increase the use of depth to enhance the use of space and provide users more ways to interact with physical objects, b) provide a better and more efficient approach to create, manage and interact with digital content (bonus items, enemies, etc.) and c) empower embodied interaction. In order to achieve this, a couple of technical issues have to be solved: we have to reconsider the ways in which we deal with 3D objects and their perspective to improve calibration and projection mapping, and also the ways in which we deal with light in environments with changing light conditions.

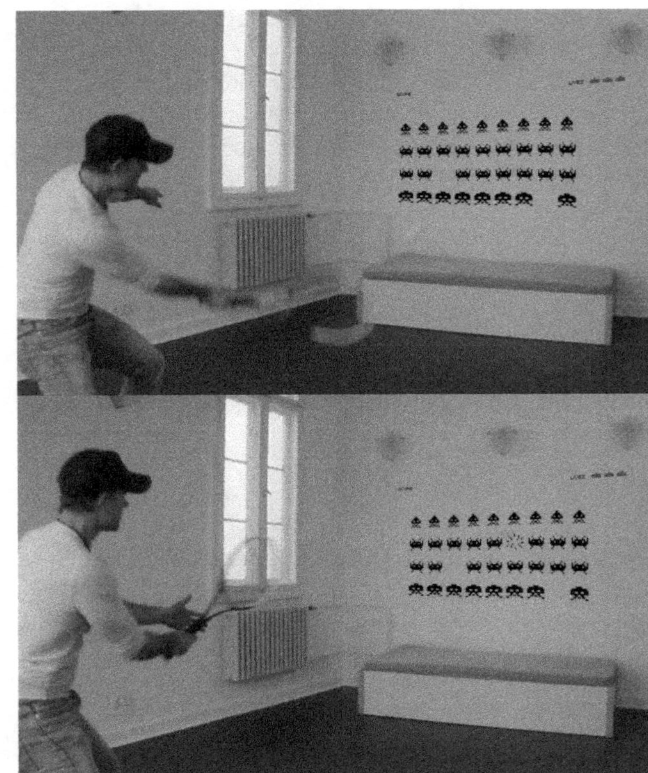

Figure 7. More embodied interaction

Figure 8. Hand-drawn character

Game Design Aspects

In our prototype we took Nintendo's Super Mario Bros. characters (Super Mario Bros.® is a registered trademark of Nintendo®) and an ordinary game pad in order to make the character gameplay as intuitive as possible and to focus players attention and learning process on the novel interaction paradigms.

Nevertheless, we started working on our own character and game designs that are better suited to the problem of merging flat digital content in the three-dimensional real world, in order to deliver a more tense connection between them in a more beneficial and realistic way. A first concept art is shown in Figure 8.

Conclusion

This paper presents novel interaction techniques and concepts in the field of interactive projection and game design, presenting the real world as a video game stage. By placing, moving or removing every-day objects into and from the stage in real time, players can create and play the level simultaneously, opening new possibilities of playing and collaborating.

However, there are challenges that need to be addressed before this system can be presented as an end product. We believe that our ideas described in this paper illustrate novel uses of interactive projection in the daily real environment (Spatial Augmented Reality) and will inspire new concepts, not only in game design, but also in the human-interaction field in general.

Acknowledgements

We would like to thank the students of the Physical Computing course at the University of Applied Sciences Potsdam for their participation in the ideation workshop and helpful feedback.

References

1. Jones, B. R., Sodhi, R., Campbell, R. H., Garnett, G., and Bailey, B. P. Build your world and play in it: Interacting with surface particles on complex objects. In *9th International Symposium on Mixed and Augmented Reality (ISMAR)*, IEEE (2010), 165-174.
2. Jones, B. R., Benko, H., Ofek, E., and Wilson, A. D. IllumiRoom: peripheral projected illusions for interactive experiences. In Proc. *CHI'11*, ACM (2013), 869-878.
3. OpenCV for Processing, by Greg Borenstein. A Processing library for the OpenCV computer vision library. https://github.com/atduskgreg/opencv-processing
4. Oswald, P., Tost, J., and Wettach, R. The Real Augmented Reality: Real-time game editor in a Spatial Augmented Environment. In Proc. ACE'14, ACM (2014)
5. Willis, K. D., Poupyrev, I., and Shiratori, T. Motionbeam: a metaphor for character interaction with handheld projectors. In Proc. *CHI'11*, ACM (2011), 1031-1040.
6. Wilson, A., Benko, H., Izadi, S., and Hilliges, O. Steerable augmented reality with the Beamatron. In Proc. *UIST'12*, ACM (2012), 413-422.
7. Yoshida, T., Hirobe, Y., Nii, H., Kawakami, N., and Tachi, S. Twinkle: Interacting with physical surfaces using handheld projector. In Proc. *Virtual Reality Conference (VR)*, IEEE (2010), 87-90.

Author Index

www.ingramcontent.com/pod-product-compliance
Lightning Source LLC
LaVergne TN
LVHW080107011026
849160LV00013B/1047